Classical Dictionary

The Wordsworth
Classical Dictionary

–

William Smith

Wordsworth Reference

First published as *A Smaller Classical Dictionary*
by John Murray, London, 1852. Eighteenth edition 1880.

This edition published 1996 by Wordsworth Editions Ltd.
Cumberland House, Crib Street, Ware, Hertfordshire SG12 9ET.

ISBN 1-85326-368-0

Printed and bound in Great Britain by Mackays of Chatham PLC.

PREFACE.

THE present Work is designed to supply a want which still exists in our School Classical Literature. It has been represented to the Editor, from several quarters, that his Larger Classical Dictionary, though well adapted for the use of the higher Forms in the Public Schools, is excluded, by both its size and price, from a great number of schools, which are therefore obliged to put up with the abridgments of Lemprière's obsolete work.

In consequence of these representations, the Editor has been induced to draw up this Smaller Dictionary. All names have been inserted which a young person would be likely to meet with at the commencement of his classical studies; and only those have been omitted which occur in later writers, or in works not usually read in schools. The quantities have been carefully marked, and the genitive cases inserted. The mythological articles have been illustrated by drawings from ancient works of art, for which the Editor is indebted to the skilful pencil of his friend, Mr. GEORGE SCHARF.

In this, as in the Smaller Dictionary of Greek and Roman Antiquities, care has been taken not to presume too much on the knowledge of the reader. It is, therefore, hoped that these two Works may be used conjointly with advantage, even in schools where Latin and Greek are not taught.

WILLIAM SMITH.

LONDON, *March* 31*st*, 1852.

A

SMALLER CLASSICAL DICTIONARY.

ABACAENUM (-i), an ancient town of the Siculi in Sicily, W. of Messana, and S. of Tyndaris.

ABAE (-ārum), an ancient town of Phocis, on the boundaries of Boeotia; celebrated for an ancient temple and oracle of Apollo, who hence derived the surname of *Abaeus*.

ĀBANTES, the ancient inhabitants of Euboea. They are said to have been of Thracian origin, to have first settled in Phocis, where they built Abae, and afterwards to have crossed over to Euboea. The Abantes of Euboea assisted in colonising several of the Ionic cities of Asia Minor.

ĀBANTĬĂDĒS (-ae), any descendant of Abas, but especially Perseus, great-grandson of Abas, and Acrisius, son of Abas. A female descendant of Abas, as Danaë and Atalante, was called Abantias.

ĀBĂRĬS (-is), a Hyperborean priest of Apollo, came from the country about the Caucasus to Greece, while his native land was visited by a plague. His history is entirely mythical: he is said to have taken no earthly food, and to have ridden on an arrow, the gift of Apollo, through the air. He may perhaps be placed about B.C. 570.

ĀBAS (-antis). (1) Son of Metanīra, was changed by Demeter (Ceres), into a lizard, because he mocked the goddess when she had come on her wanderings into the house of his mother, and drank eagerly to quench her thirst.—(2) Twelfth king of Argos, son of Lynceus and Hypermnestra, grandson of Danaus, and father of Acrisius and Proetus. When he informed his father of the death of Danaus, he was rewarded with the shield of his grandfather, which was sacred to Hera (Juno). This shield performed various marvels, and the mere sight of it could reduce a revolted people to submission.

ABDĒRA (-ae, and -ōrum), a town of Thrace, near the mouth of the Nestus, which flowed through the town. It was colonised by Timesius of Clazomenae about B.C. 656, and a second time by the inhabitants of Teos in Ionia, who settled there after their own town had been taken by the Persians B.C. 544. It was the birthplace of Democritus, Protagoras, Anaxarchus, and other distinguished men; but its inhabitants, notwithstanding, were accounted stupid, and an "Abderite" was a term of reproach.

ĀBELLA or ĀVELLA (-ae), a town of Campania, not far from Nola, founded by the Chalcidians in Euboea. It was celebrated for its apples, whence Virgil calls it *malifera*.

ABGĀRUS, ACBĂRUS, or AUGĂRUS (-i), a name common to many rulers of Edessa, the capital of the district of Osrhoëne in Mesopotamia. Of these rulers one is supposed by Eusebius to have been the author of a letter written to Christ, which he found in a church at Edessa and translated from the Syriac. The letter is believed to be spurious.

ABĬA (-ae), a town of Messenia, on the Messenian gulf.

ABĬI, a tribe mentioned by Homer, and apparently a Thracian people.

ĀBĬLA (-ōrum), a town of Coele-Syria, afterwards called Claudiopolis, and the capital of the tetrarchy of Abilēne (*Luke*, iii. 1).

ABNŌBA MONS (-ae), the range of hills covered by the Black Forest in Germany, not a single mountain.

ĀBŎRĬGĬNES (-um), the original inhabitants of a country, equivalent to the Greek *Autochthones*. But the Aborigines in Italy are not in the Latin writers the original inhabitants of all Italy, but the name of an ancient people who drove the Siculi out of Latium, and there became the progenitors of the Latini.

ABORRHAS, a branch of the Euphrates, joining that river on the E. side near Arcesium; called the Araxes by Xenophon.

ABSYRTUS or APSYRTUS (-i), son of Aeëtes, king of Colchis, whom Medëa took with her when she fled with Jason. Being pursued by her father, she murdered her brother, cut his body in pieces, and strewed them on the road, that her father might be detained by gathering the limbs of his child. Tomi, the place where this horror was committed, was believed to have derived its name from (τέμνω) "cut."

ABUS (-i : *Humber*), a river in Britain.

ABŸDOS (-i). (1) A town of the Troad on the Hellespont, and a Milesian colony, nearly opposite to Sestos, but a little lower down the stream. The bridge of boats which Xerxes constructed over the Hellespont, B.C. 480, commenced a little higher up than Abydos, and touched the European shore between Sestos and Madÿtus. (2) A city of Upper Egypt, near the W. bank of the Nile ; once second only to Thebes, but in Strabo's time (A.D. 14) a small village. It had a temple of Osiris and a *Memnonium*, both still standing, and an oracle. Here was found the inscription known as the *Table of Abydos*, which contains a list of the Egyptian kings.

ABŸLA (-ae) or ĂBĬLA (-ae) MONS or CO-LUMNA, a mountain in Mauretania Tingitana, forming the E. extremity of the S. or African coast of the Fretum Gaditanum. This and M. Calpe (*Gibraltar*), opposite to it on the Spanish coast, were called the *Columns of Hercules*, from the fable that they were originally one mountain, torn asunder by Hercules.

ĂCĂDĒMĬA and -ĬA (-ae), a piece of land on the Cephissus, 6 stadia from Athens, originally belonging to a hero Academus, and subsequently a gymnasium, adorned by Cimon with plane and olive plantations, statues, and other works of art. Here taught Plato, who possessed a piece of land in the neighbourhood, and after him his followers, who were hence called the *Academici*, or Academic philosophers. Cicero gave the name of Academia to his villa near Puteoli, where he wrote his "Quaestiones Academicae."

ĂCĂMĂS (-antis). (1) Son of Theseus and Phaedra, accompanied Diomedes to Troy to demand the surrender of Helen.—(2) Son of Antenor and Theano, one of the bravest Trojans, slain by Meriones.—(3) Son of Eussorus, one of the leaders of the Thracians in the Trojan war, slain by the Telamonian Ajax.

ĂCANTHUS (-i), a town on the Isthmus, which connects the peninsula of Athos with Chalcidice, founded by the inhabitants of Andros.

ĂCARNĂN (-ānis), one of the Epigoni, son of Alcmaeon and Callirrhoë, and brother of Amphoterus. Their father was murdered by Phegeus, when they were very young ; but as soon as they had grown up, they slew Phegeus, his wife, and his two sons. They afterwards went to Epirus, where Acarnan founded the state called after him Acarnania.

ĂCARNĂNĬA (-ae), the most westerly province of Greece, bounded on the N. by the Ambracian gulf ; on the W. and S.W. by the Ionian Sea ; on the N.E. by Amphilochia, which is sometimes included in Acarnania ; and on the E. by Aetolia, from which, at a later time, it was separated by the Achelous. The name of Acarnania does not occur in Homer. In the most ancient times the land was inhabited by the Taphii, Teleboae, and Leleges, and subsequently by the Curetes. At a later time a colony from Argos, said to have been led by ACARNAN, settled in the country. In the seventh century B.C. the Corinthians founded several towns on the coast. The Acarnanians first emerge from obscurity at the beginning of the Peloponnesian war, B.C. 431. They were then a rude people, living by piracy and robbery, and they always remained behind the rest of the Greeks in civilisation and refinement. They were good slingers, and are praised for their fidelity and courage. The different towns formed a League, which met at Stratus, and subsequently at Thyrium or Leucas.

ĂCASTUS (-i), son of Pelias, king of Iolcus, one of the Argonauts and of the Calydonian hunters. His sisters were induced by Medëa to cut up their father and boil him, in order to make him young again. Acastus, in consequence, drove Jason and Medea from Iolcus, and instituted funeral games in honour of his father. During these games, Hippolyte, the wife of Acastus, fell in love with Peleus. When Peleus refused to listen to her she accused him to her husband of having attempted her dishonour. Shortly afterwards, while Acastus and Peleus were hunting on mount Pelion, and the latter had fallen asleep, Acastus took his sword from him, and left him alone. He was, in consequence, nearly destroyed by the Centaurs ; but he was saved by Chiron or Hermes, returned to Acastus, and killed him, together with his wife.

ACBARUS. [ABGARUS.]

ACCA LAURENTĬA or LARENTĬA (-ae), the wife of the shepherd Faustulus and the nurse of Romulus and Remus, after they had been taken from the she-wolf. She seems to be connected with the worship of the Lares, from which her name Larentia is probably derived.

ACCIUS or ATTIUS (-i), L., a Roman tragic poet, was born B.C. 170, and lived to a great age. His tragedies were chiefly imitated from the Greek, but he also wrote some on Roman subjects (*Praetextatae*).

ACCO, a chief of the Senones in Gaul, induced his countrymen to revolt against Caesar, B.C. 53, by whom he was put to death.

ACE. [PTOLEMAIS.]

ACERBAS. [DIDO.]

ACERRAE (-ārum.) (1) A town in Campania, on the Clanius; destroyed by Hannibal, but rebuilt.—(2) A town of the Insubres in Gallia Transpadana.

ACESINES (-ae: *Chenaub*), a river in India, into which the Hydaspes flows, and which itself flows into the Indus.

ACESTA. [SEGESTA.]

ACESTES (-ae), son of a Trojan woman, of the name of Egesta or Segesta, who was sent by her father to Sicily, that she might not be devoured by the monsters which infested the territory of Troy. When Egesta arrived in Sicily, the river-god Crimisus begot by her a son Acestes, who was afterwards regarded as the hero who had founded the town of Segesta. Aeneas, on his arrival in Sicily, was hospitably received by Acestes.

ACHAEI (-ōrum), one of the chief Hellenic races, were, according to tradition, descended from Achaeus, who was the son of Xuthus and Creusa, and grandson of Hellen. The Achaei originally dwelt in Thessaly, and from thence migrated to Peloponnesus, the whole of which became subject to them with the exception of Arcadia, and the country afterwards called Achaia. As they were the ruling nation in Peloponnesus in the heroic times, Homer frequently gives the name of Achaei to the collective Greeks. On the conquest of Peloponnesus by the Heraclīdae and the Dorians, 80 years after the Trojan war, many of the Achaei under Tisamenus, the son of Orestes, left their country and took possession of the northern coast of Peloponnesus, then inhabited by Ionians, whom they expelled from the country, which was henceforth called Achaia. The expelled Ionians migrated to Attica and Asia Minor. The Achaei settled in 12 cities: Pellene, Aegira, Aegae, Bura, Helice, Aegium, Rhypae, Patrae, Pharae, Olenus, Dyme, and Tritaea. These 12 cities formed a league for mutual defence and protection. The Achaei had little influence in the affairs of Greece till the time of the successors of Alexander. In B.C. 281 the Achaei, who were then subject to the Macedonians, resolved to renew their ancient league for the purpose of shaking off the Macedonian yoke. This was the origin of the celebrated Achaean League. It at first consisted of only four towns, Dyme, Patrae, Tritaea, and Pharae, but was subsequently joined by the other towns of Achaia, with the exception of Olenus and Helice. It did not, however, obtain much importance till B.C. 251, when Aratus united to it his native town, Sicyon. The example of Sicyon was followed by Corinth and many other towns in Greece, and the League soon became the chief political power in Greece. At length the Achaei declared war against the Romans, who destroyed the League, and thus put an end to the independence of Greece. Corinth, then the chief town of the League, was taken by the Roman general Mummius, in B. C. 146, and the whole of southern Greece made a Roman province under the name of ACHAIA.

ACHAEMENES (-is). (1) The ancestor of the Persian kings, who founded the family of the *Achaemenidae*, which was the noblest family of the Pasargadae, the noblest of the Persian tribes. The Roman poets use the adjective *Achaemenius* in the sense of Persian.—(2) Son of Darius I., was governor of Egypt, and commanded the Egyptian fleet in the expedition of Xerxes against Greece, B. c. 480. He was defeated and killed in battle by Inarus the Libyan, 460.

ACHAEMENIDES, or ACHEMENIDES, companion of Ulysses, who left him behind in Sicily, when he fled from the Cyclops.

ACHAEUS [ACHAEI.]

ACHAIA (-ae). (1) The northern coast of the Peloponnesus, originally called Aegialēa or Aegialus, *i. e.* the coast-land, was bounded on the N. by the Corinthian gulf and the Ionian sea, on the S. by Elis and Arcadia, on the W. by the Ionian sea, and on the E. by Sicyonia. Respecting its inhabitants see ACHAEI.—(2) A district in Thessaly, which appears to have been the original seat of the Achaei.—(3) The Roman province, which included Peloponnesus and northern Greece S. of Thessaly. It was formed on the dissolution of the Achaean League in B. c. 146, and hence derived its name.

ACHARNAE (-ārum), the principal demus of Attica, 60 stadia N. of Athens, possessing a numerous and warlike population. One of the plays of Aristophanes bears their name.

ACHELOIADES. [ACHELOUS.]

ACHELOUS (-i), the largest river in Greece, rises in Mount Pindus, and flows southward, forming the boundary between Acarnania and Aetolia, and falls into the Ionian sea opposite the islands called Echinades. It is about 130 miles in length. The god of this river is described as the son of Oceanus and Tethys, and as the eldest of his 3000 brothers. He fought with Hercules for Deianira, but was conquered in the contest.

He then took the form of a bull, but was again overcome by Hercules, who deprived him of one of his horns, which however he recovered by giving up the horn of Amalthea. According to Ovid (*Met.* ix. 87), the Naiads changed the horn which Hercules took from Achelous into the horn of plenty. Achelous was from the earliest times considered to be a great divinity throughout Greece, and was invoked in prayers, sacrifices, &c. Achelous was regarded as the representative of all fresh water : hence we find in Virgil *Achelōia pocula*, that is, water in general. The Sirens are called *Achelōiădes*, as the daughters of Achelous.

ĂCHĔRŌN (-ontis), the name of several rivers, all of which were, at least at one time, believed to be connected with the lower world.—(1) A river in Thesprotia in Epirus, which flows through the lake Acherusia into the Ionian sea.—(2) A river in southern Italy in Bruttii, on which Alexander of Epirus perished.—(3) The river of the lower world, round which the shades hover, and into which the Pyriphlegethon and Cocytus flow. In late writers the name of Acheron is used to designate the whole of the lower world.

ĂCHĔRONTĬA (-ae). (1) A town in Apulia on a summit of Mount Vultur, whence Horace speaks of *celsae nidum Acherontiae.* —(2) A town on the river Acheron, in Bruttii. [ACHERON, No. 2.]

ĂCHĔRŪSĬA (-ae). [ACHERON, No. 1.]

ĂCHILLĒS (*gen.* -Is, ĕï, eI, or I; *dat.* -I; *acc.* em, ĕă; *abl.* ĕ or ē), the great hero of the Iliad.—*Homeric story.* Achilles was the son of Peleus, king of the Myrmidŏnes in Phthiŏtis, in Thessaly, and of the Nereid Thetis. From his father's name he is often called *Pelīdes*, *Pelĕïădes*, or *Pelton*, and from his grandfather's, *Aeacĭdes.* He was educated by Phoenix, who taught him eloquence and the arts of war. In the healing art he was instructed by Chĭron, the centaur. His mother Thetis foretold him that his fate was either to gain glory and die early, or to live a long but inglorious life. The hero chose the former, and took part in the Trojan war, from which he knew that he was not to return. In 50 ships he led his hosts of Myrmidones, Hellenes, and Achaeans against Troy. Here the swift-footed Achilles was the great bulwark of the Greeks, and the worthy favourite of Athena (Minerva) and Hera (Juno). When Agamemnon was obliged to give up Chryseïs to her father, he threatened to take away Briseïs from Achilles, who surrendered her on the persuasion of Athena, but at the same time refused to take any further part in the war, and shut himself up in his tent. Zeus (Jupiter), on the entreaty

of Thetis, promised that victory should be on the side of the Trojans, until the Achaeans should have honoured her son. The affairs of the Greeks declined in consequence, and they were at last pressed so hard, that an embassy was sent to Achilles, offering him rich presents and the restoration of Briseïs ; but in vain. Finally, however, he was persuaded by Patroclus, his dearest friend, to allow the latter to make use of his men, his horses, and his armour. Patroclus was slain, and when this news reached Achilles, he was seized with unspeakable grief. Thetis consoled him, and promised new arms, to be made by Hephaestus (Vulcan) ; and Iris exhorted him to rescue the body of Patroclus. Achilles now rose, and his thundering voice alone put the Trojans to flight. When his new armour was brought to him, he hurried to the field of battle, killed numbers of Trojans, and at length met Hector, whom he chased thrice around the walls of the city. He then slew him, tied his body to his chariot, and dragged him to the ships of the Greeks ; but he afterwards gave up the corpse to Priam, who came in person to beg for it. Achilles himself fell in the battle at the Scaean gate, before Troy was taken. Achilles is the principal hero of the Iliad : he is the handsomest and bravest of all the Greeks ; he is affectionate towards his mother and his friends ; formidable in battles, which are his delight ; open-hearted and without fear, and at the same time susceptible of the gentle and quiet joys of home. His greatest passion is ambition, and when his sense of honour is hurt, he is unrelenting in his revenge and anger, but withal submits obediently to the will of the gods.—*Later traditions.* These consist chiefly in accounts which fill up the history of his youth and death. His mother wishing to make her son immortal, concealed him by night in the fire, in order to destroy the mortal parts he had inherited from his father. But Peleus one night discovered his child in the fire, and cried out in terror. Thetis left her son and fled, and Peleus entrusted him to Chiron, who instructed him in the arts of riding, hunting, and playing the phorminx, and also changed his original name, Ligyron, *i. e.* the "whining," into Achilles. Chiron fed his pupil with the hearts of lions and the marrow of bears. According to other accounts, Thetis endeavoured to make Achilles immortal by dipping him in the river Styx, and succeeded with the exception of the ankles, by which she held him. When he was 9 years old, Calchas declared that Troy could not be taken without his aid, and Thetis knowing that this war would be fatal to him, disguised him as a maiden, and introduced him among the daughters of Lycomedes of Scyros, where

Achilles seizing Arms at Scyros. (A Painting found at Pompeii.)

he was called by the name of Pyrrha on ac-count of his golden locks. Here he remained concealed, till Ulysses visited the place in the disguise of a merchant, and offered for sale some female dresses, amidst which he had mixed some arms. Achilles discovered his sex by eagerly seizing the arms, and then accompanied Ulysses to the Greek army. During his residence at Scyros, one of his companions, Deïdamīa, became by him the mother of a son, Pyrrhus or Neoptolemus. During the war against Troy, Achilles slew Penthesilēa, an Amazon. He also fought with Memnon and Troilus. The accounts of his death differ very much, though all agree in stating that he did not fall by human hands, or at least not without the interference of the god Apollo. According to some traditions, he was killed by Apollo him-self; according to others, Apollo assumed the appearance of Paris in killing him, while others say that Apollo merely directed the weapon of Paris. Others again relate that Achilles loved Polyxena, a daughter of Priam, and tempted by the promise that he should receive her as his wife, if he would join the Trojans, he went without arms into the temple of Apollo at Thymbra, and was assas-sinated there by Paris. His body was rescued by Ulysses and Ajax the Telamonian; his armour was promised by Thetis to the bravest among the Greeks, which gave rise to a con-test between the two heroes who had rescued his body. [AJAX.] After his death, Achilles became one of the judges in the lower world

Death of Achilles. (Raoul Rochette, Mon. Ined., pl. 53.)

and dwelled in the islands of the blessed, | where he was united to Medēa or Iphigenīa.

ĀCHILLĒUM (-i), a town near the promontory Sigēum in the Troad, where Achilles was supposed to have been buried.

ĀCHILLĪDĒS (-ae), a patronymic of Pyrrhus, son of Achilles.

ĀCHĪVI (-ōrum), the name of the Achaei in the Latin writers, and frequently used, like Achaei, to signify the whole Greek nation. [ACHAEI.]

ACHRĀDĪNA OR ACRĀDĪNA. [SYRACUSAE.]

ĀCĪDĀLĪA (-ae), a surname of Venus, from the well Acidalius near Orchomenos, where she used to bathe with the Graces.

ĀCĪLĪUS GLABRĪO. [GLABRIO.]

ĀCIS (-is or -īdis), son of Faunus and Symaethis, beloved by the nymph Galatea, and crushed by Polyphemus, the Cyclop, through jealousy, under a huge rock. His blood gushing forth from under the rock was changed by the nymph into the river Acis or Acinius at the foot of Mount Aetna. This story is perhaps only a happy fiction suggested by the manner in which the little river springs forth from under a rock.

ACMŌNĪDĒS (-ae), one of the three Cyclopes in Ovid, the same as Pyracmon in Virgil, and as Arges in other accounts.

ĀCOETĒS (-ae), a sailor who was saved by Bacchus, when his companions were destroyed, because he was the only one of the crew who had espoused the cause of the god.

ĀCONTĪUS (-i), a beautiful youth of the Island of Ceos. Having come to Delos to celebrate the festival of Diana, he fell in love with Cydippe, the daughter of a noble Athenian. In order to gain her, he had recourse to a stratagem. While she was sitting to the temple of Diana, he threw before her an apple upon which he had written the words " I swear by the sanctuary of Diana to marry Acontius." The nurse took up the apple and handed it to Cydippe, who read aloud what was written upon it, and then threw the apple away. But the goddess had heard her vow; and the repeated illness of the maiden, when she was about to marry another man, at length compelled her father to give her in marriage to Acontius.

ACRAE (-ārum), a town in Sicily, W. of Syracuse, and 10 stadia from the river Anapus, founded by the Syracusans 70 years after the foundation of their own city.

ACRAEPHĪA (-ae), ACRAEPHĪAE (-arum), or ACRAEPHĪUM (-i), a town in Boeotia, on the lake Copais.

ACRĀGAS (-antis). [AGRIGENTUM.]

ĀCRĪSĪŌNĒ (-ēs), a patronymic of Danaë, daughter of Acrisius. Perseus, grandson of Acrisius, was called in the same way Acrīsīonīadēs.

ĀCRĪSĪUS (-i), son of Abas, king of Argos, grandson of Lynceus, and great-grandson of Danaus. An oracle had declared that Danaë, the daughter of Acrisius, would give birth to a son who would kill his grandfather. For this reason he kept Danaë shut up in a subterraneous apartment, or in a brazen tower. But here she became the mother of Perseus, by Zeus (Jupiter), who visited her in a shower of gold. Acrisius ordered mother and child to be exposed on the sea in a chest; but the chest floated towards the island of Seriphus, where both were rescued by Dictys. As to the fulfilment of the oracle, see PERSEUS.

ACRŌCĒRAUNĪA (-ōrum), a promontory in Epirus, jutting out into the Ionian sea, the most westerly part of the Ceraunii Montes. The coast of the Acroceraunia was dangerous to ships, whence Horace speaks of *infames scopulos Acroceraunia*.

ACRŌPŌLIS. [ATHENAE.]

ACRŌTHŌUM (-i), OR ACRŌTHŌI (ōrum), a town near the extremity of the peninsula of Athos.

ACTAEŌN (-ŏnis), a celebrated huntsman, son of Aristaeus and Autonoë, a daughter of

Actaeon. (British Museum.)

Cadmus. One day as he was hunting he saw Artemis (Diana) with her nymphs bathing in the vale of Gargaphia, whereupon the goddess changed him into a stag, in which form he was torn to pieces by his 50 dogs on Mount Cithaeron.

ACTAEUS (-i), the earliest king of Attica. The adjective Actaeus is used by the poets in the sense of Attic or Athenian.

ACTĒ (-ēs), properly a piece of land running into the sea, and attached to another larger piece of land, but not necessarily, by a narrow neck. (1) An ancient name of Attica, used especially by the poets. Hence Orithyia, the daughter of Erectheus, king of Athens, is called Actias by Virgil.—(2) The peninsula between the Strymonic and Singitic gulfs on which Mount Athos is.

ACTĬUM (-i : *La Punta* not *Azio*), a promontory in Acarnania, at the entrance of the Ambracian gulf, off which Augustus gained the celebrated victory over Antony and Cleopatra, on September 2, B.C. 31. At Actium there was a temple of Apollo, who was hence called *Actiacus* and *Actius*. This temple was beautified by Augustus, who established, or rather revived, a festival to Apollo, called *Actia*, and erected NICOPOLIS on the opposite coast, in commemoration of his victory. A few buildings sprung up around the temple at Actium, but the place was only a kind of suburb of Nicopolis.

ACTĬUS. [ATTIUS.]

ACTŎR (-ŏris). (1) Son of Deion and Diomedes, father of Menoetius, and grandfather of Patroclus.—(2) A companion of Aeneas, of whose conquered lance Turnus made a boast. This story seems to have given rise to the proverb *Actoris spolium*, for any poor spoil.

ACTŎRĬDĒS (-ae), a patronymic of descendants of an Actor, such as Patroclus, Erithus, Eurytus, and Cteatus.

ADDŬA (-ae : *Adda*), a river of Gallia Cisalpina, rising in the Rhaetian Alps, and flowing through the Lacus Larius (*L. di Como*) into the Po, about 8 miles above Cremona.

ADHERBAL (-ălis). [JUGURTHA.]

ADĬĂBĒNĒ (-ēs), a district of Assyria, E. of the Tigris, and between the river Lycus, called Zabatus in the Anabasis of Xenophon, and the Caprus, both of which are branches of the Tigris.

ADMĒTUS (-i). (1) King of Pherae in Thessaly, sued for Alcestis, the daughter of Pelias, who promised her on condition that he should come in a chariot drawn by lions and boars. This task Admetus performed by the assistance of Apollo. The god tended the flocks of Admetus for 9 years when he was obliged to serve a mortal for having slain the Cyclops. Apollo prevailed upon the Moirae or Fates to grant to Admetus deliverance from death, if his father, mother,

or wife would die for him. Alcestis died in his stead, but was brought back by Hercules

Hercules and Alcestis. (From a Bas-relief at Florence.)

from the lower world.—(2) King of the Molossians, to whom THEMISTOCLES fled for protection, when pursued as a party to the treason of Pausanias.

ĀDŌNIS (-is or -ĭdis). (1) A beautiful youth, son of Cinyras, by his daughter Smyrna or Myrrha. He was beloved by Aphrodītē (Venus),

Death of Adonis. (A Painting found at Pompeii.)

but he died of a wound which he received from a boar during the chase. The flower anemone sprung from his blood. The grief of the goddess at his death was so great, that the gods of the lower world allowed him to spend 6 months of every year with Aphrodite upon the earth. The worship of Adonis was of Phoenician origin, and appears to have had reference to the death of nature in winter and to its revival in spring : hence Adonis spends 6 months in the lower and 6 months in the upper world. His death and his return to life were celebrated in annual festivals (*Adonia*) at Byblos, Alexandria in Egypt, Athens, and other places.—(2) A small river of Phoenicia, rising in the range of Libanus.

ADRAMYTTĬUM or ĒUM (-i), a town of Mysia, near the head of the gulf of Adramyttium, and opposite to the Island of Lesbos.

ADRĂNA (-ae: *Eder*), a river in Germany, flowing into the Fulda near Cassel.

ADRASTUS (-i). (1) Son of Talaus, king of Argos. Being expelled from Argos by Amphiaräus, he fled to Polybus, king of Sicyon, whom he succeeded on the throne of Sicyon, and instituted the Nemean games. Afterwards he became reconciled to Amphiaräus, and returned to his kingdom of Argos. He married his two daughters Deipyle and Argïa, the former to Tydeus of Calydon, and the latter to Polynīces of Thebes, both fugitives from their native countries. He then prepared to restore Polynīces to Thebes, who had been expelled by his brother Eteocles, although Amphiaräus foretold that all who should engage in the war should perish, with the exception of Adrastus. Thus arose the celebrated war of the "Seven against Thebes," in which Adrastus was joined by 6 other heroes, viz., Polynīces, Tydeus, Amphiaräus, Capaneus, Hippomēdon, and Parthenopaeus. This war ended as unfortunately as Amphiaräus had predicted, and Adrastus alone was saved by the swiftness of his horse Arīon, the gift of Hercules. Ten years afterwards, Adrastus persuaded the 6 sons of the heroes who had fallen in the war, to make a new attack upon Thebes, and Amphiaräus now promised success. This war is known as the war of the "Epigoni" or descendants. Thebes was taken and razed to the ground. The only Argive hero that fell in this war, was Aegialeus, the son of Adrastus : the latter died of grief at Megara on his return to Argos, and was buried in the former city. The legends about Adrastus and the two wars against Thebes, furnished ample materials for the epic as well as tragic poets of Greece.— (2) Son of the Phrygian king Gordius, having unintentionally killed his brother, fled to Croesus, who received him kindly. While hunting he accidentally killed Atys, the son of Croesus, and in despair put an end to his own life.

ADRĬA or HADRĬA (-ae). (1) A town in Gallia Cisalpina, between the mouths of the Po and the Athesis (*Adige*), from which the Adriatic sea takes its name. It was originally a powerful town of the Etruscans. —(2) A town of Picenum in Italy, and afterwards a Roman colony, at which place the family of the emperor Hadrian lived.

ADRĬA (-ae) or MARE ADRĬĀTĬCUM, also MARE SUPĔRUM, so called from the town Adria [No. 1], was in its widest signification the sea between Italy on the W., and Illyricum, Epirus, and Greece on the E. By the Greeks the name *Adrias* was only applied to the northern part of the sea, the southern part being called the Ionian Sea.

ADRĬĀNUS. [HADRIANUS.]

ADRŬMĒTUM. [HADRUMETUM.]

ADUATŬCA (-ae), a castle of the Eburones in Gaul, probably the same as the later Aduaca Tongrorum (*Tongern*).

ADUATŬCI or ADUATĬCI (-ōrum), a powerful people of Gallia Belgica in the time of Caesar, were the descendants of the Cimbri and Teutoni, and lived between the Scaldis (*Schelde*) and Mosa (*Maas*).

ADŬLA (-ae) MONS. [ALPES.]

ADŬLĒ (-es) or ADŬLIS (-is) a maritime city of Aethopia, on a bay of the Red Sea, called Adulitanus Sinus. It fell into the power of the Auxumitae, for whose trade it became the great emporium. Here was found the *Monumentum Adulitanum*, a Greek inscription recounting the conquests of Ptolemy II. Euergetes in Asia and Thrace.

ADYRMĂCHĬDAE (-arum), a Libyan people, who appear to have once possessed the whole coast of Africa from the Canopic mouth of the Nile to the Catabathmus Major, but were afterwards pressed further inland.

AEA (-ae), sometimes with the addition of the word Colchis, may be considered either a part of Colchis or another name for the country.

AEĀCĬDĒS (-ae), a patronymic of the descendants of Aeacus, as Peleus, Telamon, and Phocus, sons of Aeacus ; Achilles, son of Peleus, and grandson of Aeacus ; Pyrrhus, son of Achilles, and great-grandson of Aeacus ; and Pyrrhus, king of Epirus, who claimed to be a descendant of Achilles.

AEĂCUS (-i), son of Zeus (Jupiter) and Aegina, a daughter of the river-god Asopus, was born in the island of Aegina, which derived its name from his mother. [AEGINA.] Some traditions related that at the birth of Aeacus, Aegina was not yet inhabited, and that Zeus changed the ants of the island into men (Myrmidones) over whom Aeacus ruled. Aeacus was renowned in all Greece for his justice and piety, and after his death became one of the 3 judges in Hades.

AEAEA (-ae), a surname of Circe, the sister of Aeëtes, was believed to have inhabited a small island of this name off the coast of Italy, which was afterwards united to the mainland, and formed the promontory of Circeii. Hence magic arts are called *Aeaeae artes* and *Aeaea carmina.* Telegone, the son of Circe, and founder of Tusculum, is also called *Aeaeus.*

AAEAS. [Aous.]

AECULANUM or AECLNAUM (-i), a town of the Hirpini in Samnium, a few miles S. of Beneventum.

AEDON (-onis), daughter of Pandareus of Ephesus, wife of Zethus, king of Thebes, and mother of Itylus. Envious of Niobe, the wife of her brother Amphion, who had 6 sons and 6 daughters, she resolved to kill the eldest of Niobe's sons, but by mistake slew her own son Itylus. Zeus (Jupiter) relieved her grief by changing her into a nightingale, whose melancholy tunes are represented as Aëdon's lamentations for her child.

AEDUI or HEDUI (-orum), one of the most powerful people in Gaul, lived between the Liger (*Loire*) and the Arar (*Saone*). They were the first Gallic people who made an alliance with the Romans, by whom they were called "brothers and relations." On Caesar's arrival in Gaul, B.C. 58, they were subject to Ariovistus, but were restored by Caesar to their former power. Their principal town was BIBRACTE.

AEËTES or AEËTA (-ae), son of Helios (the Sun) and Perseis, and father of Medēa and Absyrtus. He was king of Colchis at the time when Phrixus brought thither the golden fleece. For the remainder of his history, see ABSYRTUS, ARGONAUTAE, JASON, MEDEA.

AEËTIS (-idis), AEËTIAS (-adis), and AEËTINE (-ēs), patronymics of Medea, daughter of Aeëtes.

AEGAE (-arum). (1) A town in Achaia on the Crathis, with a celebrated temple of Poseidon (Neptune), originally one of the 12 Achaean towns, but its inhabitants subsequently removed to Aegira.—(2) A town in Emathia in Macedonia, the ancient capital of Macedonia and the burial-place of the Macedonian kings. It was also called Edessa.—(3) A town in Euboea with a celebrated temple of Poseidon, who was hence called Aegaeus. —(4) Also AEGAEAE, one of the 12 cities of Aeolis in Asia Minor, N. of Smyrna, on the river Hyllus.—(5) A sea-port town of Cilicia.

AEGAEON (-onis), son of Uranus (Heaven) by Gaea (Earth). Aegaeon and his brothers Gyes or Gyges and Cottus are known under the name of the Uranids, and are described as huge monsters with 100 arms and 50 heads. Most writers mention the third Uranid under the name of Briareus instead of Aegaeon, which is explained by Homer, who says that men called him Aegaeon, but the gods Briareus. According to the most ancient tradition, Aegaeon and his brothers conquered the Titans when they made war upon the gods, and secured the victory to Zeus (Jupiter), who thrust the Titans into Tartarus, and placed Aegaeon and his brothers to guard them. Other legends represent Aegaeon as one of the giants who attacked Olympus ; and many writers represent him as a marine god living in the Aegaean sea.

AEGAEUM (-i) MARE, the part of the Mediterranean Sea now called the *Archipelago.* It was bounded on the N. by Thrace and Macedonia, on the W. by Greece, and on the E. by Asia Minor. It contains in its southern part two groups of islands, the Cyclades, which were separated from the coasts of Attica and Peloponnesus by the Myrtoan sea, and the Sporades, lying off the coasts of Caria and Ionia. The part of the Aegaean which washed the Sporades was called the Icarian sea, from the island Icaria, one of the Sporades.

AEGALEOS, a mountain in Attica opposite Salamis, from which Xerxes saw the defeat of his fleet, B.C. 480.

AEGATES (-um), the Goat Islands, were 3 islands off the W. coast of Sicily, between Drepanum and Lilybaeum, near which the Romans gained a naval victory over the Carthaginians, and thus brought the first Punic war to an end, B.C. 241. The islands were Aegūsa or Caprārīa, Phorbantīa and Hiëra.

AEGERIA or EGERIA (-ae), one of the Camenae in Roman mythology, from whom Numa received his instructions respecting the forms of worship which he introduced. The grove in which the king had his interviews with the goddess, and in which a well gushed forth from a dark recess, was dedicated by him to the Camenae. The Roman legends point out two distinct places sacred to Aegeria, one near Aricia, and the other near Rome at the Porta Capena.

AEGESTA. [SEGESTA.]

AEGESTUS. [ACESTES.]

AEGEUS (ŏŏs, ĕ῀i, or eī; *acc.* -ĕă), son of Pandion and king of Athens, and father of THESEUS, whom he begot by Aethra at Troezen. Theseus afterwards came to Athens and restored Aegeus to the throne, of which he had been deprived by the 50 sons of Pallas. When Theseus went to Crete to deliver Athens from the tribute it had to pay to Minos, he promised his father to hoist white sails on his return as a signal of his safety. On approaching Attica he forgot his promise, and his father, perceiving the black sails, thought that his son had perished and threw himself into the sea, which according to some traditions received from this event the name of the Aegean.

AEGIĀLĒ or AEGIĀLĒA (-ēs), daughter or grand-daughter of Adrastus, whence she is called Adrastine, and husband of Diomedes. For details see DIOMEDES.

AEGIĀLĒA, AEGIĀLUS. [ACHAIA.]

AEGIĀLEUS. [ADRASTUS.]

AEGĪDĒS (-ae), a patronymic from Aegeus, especially his son Theseus.

AEGILĪA. (1) An island between Crete and Cythera.—(2) An island W. of Euboea and opposite Attica.

AEGĪNA (-ae), a rocky island in the middle of the Saronic gulf, about 200 stadia in circumference, said to have obtained its name from Aegina, the daughter of the river-god Asopus, who there bore him a son Aeacus. As the island had then no inhabitants, Zeus (Jupiter), changed the ants into men (Myrmidones) over whom Aeacus ruled. It was first colonised by Achaeans, and afterwards by Dorians from Epidaurus, whence the Doric dialect and customs prevailed in the island. It was subject to the Argive Phīdon, who is said to have established a silver mint in the island. It early became a place of great commercial importance, and its silver coinage was the standard in most of the Dorian states. In the sixth century B.C., Aegina became independent, and for a century before the Persian war was a prosperous and powerful state. It was at that time the chief seat of Grecian art. In B.C. 429 the Athenians took possession of the island and expelled its inhabitants. In the N.W. of the island there was a city of the same name, which contained the Aeacēum or temple of Aeacus, and on a hill in the N.E. of the island was the celebrated temple of Zeus (Jupiter) Panhellenius, the ruins of which are still extant.

AEGINĪUM, a town of the Tymphaei in Thessaly, on the confines of Athamania.

AEGIPLANCTUS (-i) MONS, a mountain in Megaris.

AEGĪRA (-ae), formerly Hyperesia, one of the 12 towns of Achaia, situated on a steep hill.

AEGIRUSSA (-ae), one of the 12 cities of Aeolis in Asia Minor.

AEGISTHUS (-i), son of Thyestes by his own daughter Pelopia. He slew his uncle Atreus, and placed Thyestes upon the throne, of which he had been deprived by Atreus. Homer appears to know nothing of these tragic events ; and we learn from him only that Aegisthus succeeded his father Thyestes in a part of his dominions. Aegisthus took

no part in the Trojan war, and during the absence of Agamemnon, he seduced his wife Clytemnestra. He murdered Agamemnon on his return home, and reigned 7 years over Mycenae. In the 8th Orestes, the son of Agamemnon, avenged the death of his father by putting the adulterer to death.

AEGĪUM (-i), one of the 12 towns of Achaia, and the capital after the destruction of Helice.

AEGLĒ (-ēs), that is, "Brightness" or "Splendour," the name of several nymphs.

AEGOS-PŌTĂMOS, the "goat's-river," a small river, with a town of the same name on it, in the Thracian Chersonesus, flowing into the Hellespont. Here the Athenians were defeated by Lysander, B.C. 405.

AEGYPTUS (-i), king of Aegypt, son of Belus, and twin-brother of Danaus. Aegyptus had 50 sons, and his brother Danaus 50 daughters. Danaus fearing the sons of his brother, fled with his daughters to Argos in Peloponnesus. Thither he was followed by the sons of Aegyptus, who demanded his daughters for their wives. Danaus complied with their request, but to each of his daughters he gave a dagger, with which they were to kill their husbands in the bridal night. All the sons of Aegyptus were thus murdered, with the exception of Lynceus, who was saved by Hypermnestra.

AEGYPTUS (-i : Egypt), a country in the N.E. corner of Africa, bounded on the N. by the Mediterranean, on the E. by Palestine, Arabia Petraea, and the Red Sea, on the S. by Aethiopia, the division between the two countries being at the First or Little Cataract of the Nile, close to Syene, and on the W. by the Great Libyan Desert. From Syene the Nile flows due N. for about 500 miles, through a valley whose average breadth is about 7 miles, to a point some few miles below Memphis. Here the river divides into branches (7 in ancient time, but now only 2), which flow through a low alluvial land, called, from its shape, the *Delta*, into the Mediterranean. The whole district thus described is periodically laid under water by the overflowing of the Nile from April to October. The river, in subsiding, leaves behind a rich deposit of fine mud, which forms the soil of Egypt. All beyond the reach of the inundation is rock or sand. Hence Egypt was called the "Gift of the Nile." The outlying portions of ancient Egypt consisted of 3 cultivable valleys (called Oases), in the midst of the Western or Libyan Desert. At the earliest period, to which history reaches back, Egypt was inhabited by a highly civilised people, under a settled monarchical government, divided into castes, the highest of which was composed of the priests. Its ancient history may be divided into 4 great periods :—(1) From the earliest times to its conquest by Cambyses, during which it was ruled by a succession of native princes. The last of them, Psammenitus, was conquered and dethroned by Cambyses in B.C. 525, when Egypt became a province of the Persian empire. The Homeric poems show some slight acquaintance with the country and its river (which is also called Αἴγυπτος, *Od.* xiv. 25), and refer to the wealth and splendour of "Thebes with the Hundred Gates." (2) From the Persian conquest in 525, to the transference of their dominion to the Macedonians in 332. This period was one of almost constant struggles between the Egyptians and their conquerors. It was during this period that Egypt was visited by Greek historians and philosophers, such as Hellanicus, Herodotus, Anaxagoras, Plato, and others, who brought back to Greece the knowledge of the country which they acquired from the priests and through personal observation. (3) The dynasty of Macedonian kings, from the accession of Ptolemy, the son of Lagus, in 323, down to 30, when Egypt became a province of the Roman empire. Alexander, after the conquest of the country, gave orders for the building of Alexandria. [ALEXANDRIA.] (4) Egypt under the Romans, down to its conquest by the Arabs in A.D. 638. As a Roman province, Egypt was one of the most flourishing portions of the empire. The fertility of its soil, and its position between Europe and Arabia and India, together with the possession of such a port as Alexandria, gave it the full benefit of the two great sources of wealth, agriculture and commerce. From the earliest times the country was divided into (1) The Delta, or Lower Egypt ; (2) the Heptanomis, or Middle Egypt; (3) the Thebais, or Upper Egypt: and it was further subdivided into 36 nomes or governments.

AELĀNA (-ae), the ELATH of the Hebrews, a town on the northern arm of the Red Sea, called by the Greeks Aelanîtes from the name of the town.

AELIA (-ae), a name given to Jerusalem after its restoration by the Roman emperor Aelius Hadrianus.

AELIĀNUS (-i), CLAUDĬUS (-i), was born at Praeneste in Italy, and lived at Rome about the middle of the 3rd century of the Christian era. He wrote two works which have come down to us ; one a collection of miscellaneous history in 14 books, called *Varia Historia ;* and the other on the peculiarities of animals in 17 books, called *De Animalium Naturâ.*

AELIUS, the name of a plebeian gens at

Rome, divided into the families of *Gallus, Lamia, Paetus,* and *Tubero.*

AELLŌ (-ûs), one of the Harpies. [HARPYIAE.]

AEMILIA (-ae). (1) The 3rd daughter of L. Aemilius Paulus, who fell in the battle of Cannae, was the wife of Scipio Africanus I. and the mother of the celebrated Cornelia, the mother of the Gracchi.—(2) Aemilia Lepida. [LEPIDA.]

AEMILIA (-ae) VIA (-ae), made by M. Aemilius Lepidus, cos. B.C. 187, continued the Via Flaminia from Ariminum, and traversed the heart of Cisalpine Gaul through Bononia, Mutina, Parma, Placentia (where it crossed the Po) to Mediolanum. It was subsequently continued as far as Aquileia.

AEMILIĀNUS (-i), an agnomen of P. Cornelius Scipio Africanus the younger, as the son of L. Aemilius Paulus. [SCIPIO.]

AEMILIUS (-i), the name of one of the most ancient patrician gentes at Rome, the chief members of which are given under their surnames LEPIDUS, PAULUS, and SCAURUS.

AENARIA, also called PĪTHĒCŪSA and ĪNARĪMĒ (*Ischia*), a volcanic island off the coast of Campania, at the entrance of the bay of Naples, under which the Roman poets represented Typhoeus as lying.

AENĔĀDĒS (-ae), a patronymic from Aeneas, given to his son Ascanius or Iulus, and to those who were believed to be descended from him, such as Augustus, and the Romans in general.

AENĒĀS (-ae ; *voc.* -â), the Trojan hero.—*Homeric Story.* Aeneas was the son of Anchises and Aphroditē (Venus), and was born on mount Ida. He was brought up at Dardanus, in the house of Alcathous, the husband of his sister. At first he took no part in the Trojan war ; and it was not till Achilles attacked him on mount Ida, and drove away his flocks, that he led his Dardanians against the Greeks. Henceforth Aeneas and Hector appear as the great bulwarks of the Trojans against the Greeks, and Aeneas is beloved by gods and men. On more than one occasion he is saved in battle by the gods : Aphroditē carried him off when he was wounded by Diomedes, and Poseidon (Neptune) saved him when he was on the point of perishing by the hands of Achilles. Homer makes no allusion to the emigration of Aeneas after the capture of Troy, but on the contrary he evidently conceives Aeneas and his descendants as reigning at Troy after the extinction of the house of Priam.—*Later Stories.* Most accounts agree that after the capture of Troy, Aeneas withdrew to mount Ida with his friends and the images of the gods, especially that of Pallas (*Palladium*) ;

and that from thence he crossed over to Europe, and finally settled at Latium in Italy, where he became the ancestral hero of the Romans. A description of the wanderings of Aeneas before he reached Latium, is given by Virgil in his Aeneid. After visiting Epirus and Sicily, he was driven by a storm on the coast of Africa, where he met with Dido. [DIDO.] He then sailed to Latium, where he was hospitably received by Latinus, king of tne Aborigines. Here Aeneas founded the town of Lavinium, called after Lavinia, the daughter of Latinus, whom he married. Turnus, to whom Lavinia had been betrothed, made war against Latinus and Aeneas. Latinus fell in the first battle, and Turnus was subsequently slain by Aeneas; whereupon after the death of Latinus, Aeneas became sole ruler of the Aborigines and Trojans, and both nations were united into one. Soon after this Aeneas fell in battle against the Rutulians who were assisted by Mezentius, king of the Etruscans. As his body was not found after the battle, it was believed that it had been carried up to heaven, or that he had perished in the river Numicius. The Latins erected a monument to him, with the inscription *To the father and native god.* Virgil represents Aeneas landing in Italy 7 years after the fall of Troy, and comprises all the events in Italy from the landing to the death of Turnus, within the space of 20 days. The story of the descent of the Romans from the Trojans through Aeneas was believed at an early period, but rests on no historical foundation.

AENEAS SILVIUS (-i), son of Silvius, and grandson of Ascanius, is the 3rd in the list of the mythical kings of Alba in Latium.

AENESIDEMUS (-i), a celebrated sceptic, born at Cnossus in Crete, and lived a little later than Cicero. He wrote several works, but none of them have come down to us.

AENIANES (-um), an ancient Greek race, originally near Ossa, afterwards in southern Thessaly, between Oeta and Othrys, on the banks of the Spercheus.

AENUS (-i). (1) An ancient town in Thrace, near the mouth of the Hebrus, mentioned in the Iliad, colonised by the Aeolians of Asia Minor. Virgil supposes it to have been built by Aeneas.—(2) (*Inn*) a river in Rhaetia, tae boundary between Rhaetia and Noricum.

AEOLES (-um) or AEOLII (-ōrum), one of the chief branches of the Hellenic race, supposed to be descended from Aeolus, the son of Helen. [AEOLUS, No. 1.] They originally dwelt in Thessaly, from whence taey spread over various parts of Greece, and also settled in AEOLIS in Asia Minor, and in the island of LESBOS.

AEOLIAE INSULAE (-arum: *Lipari Islands*), a group of islands N.E. of Sicily, where Aeolus, the god of the winds, reigned. Virgil accordingly speaks of only one Aeolian island, supposed to be Strongyle or Lipara. These islands were also called *Hephaestiades* or *Vulcaniae*, because Hephaestus or Vulcan was believed to have his workshop in one of them called Hiera. They were also named *Liparenses*, from Lipăra, the largest of them.

AEOLIDES (-ae), a patronymic given to the sons of Aeolus, as Athamas, Cretheus, Sisyphus, Salmoneus, &c., and to his grandsons, as Cephalus, Ulysses and Phrixus. AEOLIS is the patronymic of the female descendants of Aeolus, given to his daughters Canace and Alcyone.

AEOLIS (-ĭdis) or AEOLIA (-ae), a district of Mysia in Asia Minor, was peopled by Aeolian Greeks, whose cities extended from the Troad along the shores of the Aegaean to the river Hermus. In early times, their 12 most important cities were independent and formed a League. They were Cyme, Larissae, Neontīchos, Temnus, Cilla, Notium, Aegirūsa, Pitane, Aegaeae, Myrina, Grynĕa, and Smyrna; but SMYRNA subsequently became a member of the Ionian confederacy. These cities were subdued by Croesus, and were incorporated in the Persian empire on the conquest of Croesus by Cyrus.

AEOLUS (-i). (1) Son of Hellen and the nymph Orseïs, and brother of Dorus and Xuthus. He was the ruler of Thessaly, and the founder of the Aeolic branch of the Greek nation. His children are said to have been very numerous; but the most ancient story mentioned only 4 sons, viz. Sisyphus, Athamas, Cretheus, and Salmoneus.—(2) Son of Hippotes, or, according to others, of Poseidon (Neptune) and Arne, a descendant of the previous Aeolus. He is represented in Homer as the happy ruler of the Aeolian islands, to whom Zeus had given dominion over the winds, which he might soothe or excite according to his pleasure. This statement of Homer and the etymology of the name of Aeolus from ἄελλω, led to Aeolus being regarded in later times as the god and king of the winds, which he kept enclosed in a mountain.

AEPYTUS (-i). (1) A mythical king of Arcadia, from whom a part of the country was called Aepytis.—(2) Youngest son of the Heraclid Cresphontes, king of Messenia, and of Merope, daughter of the Arcadian king Cypselus. When his father and brothers were murdered during an insurrection, Aepytus, who was with his grandfatner Cypselus, aione escaped. The throne of Cresphontes was meantime occupied by Polyphontes, who forced Merope to become his wife. When Aepytus had grown to manhood, he returned to his kingdom, and put Polyphontes to death. From him the kings of Messenia were called Aepytids instead of the more general name Heraclids.

AEQUI (-ōrum), AEQUĪCŎLI (-ōrum), AEQUĪCŎLĀE (-ārum), AEQUĪCŬLĀNI (-ōrum), an ancient and warlike people of Italy, dwelling in the upper valley of the Anio in the mountains forming the eastern boundary of Latium, and between the Latini, Sabini, Hernici, and Marsi. In conjunction with the Volsci, who were of the same race, they carried on constant hostilities with Rome, but were finally subdued in B.C. .302. One of their chief seats was Mount Algidus, from which they were accustomed to make their marauding expeditions.

AEQUI FALISCI. [FALERII.]

AĒRŎPĒ (-es), daughter of Catreus, king of Crete, and wife of Plīsthenes, the son of Atreus, by whom she became the mother of Agamemnon and Menelaus. After the death of Plīsthenes, Aerope married Atreus ; and her two sons, who were educated by Atreus, were generally believed to be his sons. Aerope was faithless to Atreus, being seduced by Thyestes.

AESĂCUS (-i), son of Priam and Alexirrhoē, fell in love with Hesperia, the daughter of Cebren, and while he was pursuing her, she was stung by a viper and died. Aesacus in his grief threw himself into the sea, and was changed by Thetis into an aquatic bird.

AESAR (-ăris) or AESĂRUS (-i), a river near Croton in Bruttii, in southern Italy.

AESCHĪNĒS (-is). (1) The Athenian orator born B.C. 389, was the son of Atrometus and Glaucothea. In his youth he assisted his father in his school; he next acted as secretary to Aristophon, and afterwards to Eubulus ; he subsequently tried his fortune as an actor, but was unsuccessful ; and at length, after serving with distinction in the army, came forward as a public speaker and soon acquired great reputation. In 347 he was sent along with Demosthenes as one of the 10 ambassadors to negotiate a peace with Philip. From this time he appears as the friend of the Macedonian party and as the opponent of Demosthenes. Shortly afterwards Aeschines formed one of a second embassy sent to Philip, and on his return to Athens was accused by Timarchus. He evaded the danger by bringing forward a counter-accusation against Timarchus (345), showing that the moral conduct of his accuser was such that he had no right to speak before the people. The speech in which Aeschines attacked Timarchus is still extant: Timarchus was condemned and Aeschines gained a bril-

liant triumph. In 343 Demosthenes renewed the charge against Aeschines of treachery during his second embassy to Philip. This charge of Demosthenes (De Falsa Legatione) was not spoken, but published as a memorial, and Aeschines answered it in a similar memorial on the embassy, which was likewise published. After the battle of Chaeronēa in 338, which gave Philip the supremacy in Greece, Ctesiphon proposed that Demosthenes should be rewarded for his services with a golden crown in the theatre at the great Dionysia. Aeschines in consequence accused Ctesiphon ; but he did not prosecute the charge till 8 years later, 330. The speech which he delivered on the occasion is extant, and was answered by Demosthenes in his celebrated oration on the Crown. Aeschines was defeated, and withdrew from Athens. He went to Asia Minor, and at length established a school of eloquence at Rhodes. On one occasion he read to his audience in Rhodes his speech against Ctesiphon, and when some of his hearers expressed their astonishment at his defeat, he replied, " You would cease to be astonished if you had heard Demosthenes." From Rhodes he went to Samos, where he died in 314.—(2) An Athenian philosopher and rhetorician, and a disciple of Socrates. He wrote several dialogues, but the 3 which have come down to us under nis name are not genuine.

AESCHȲLUS (-i), the celebrated tragic poet, the son of Euphorion, was born at Eleusis in Attica, B.C. 525. At the age of 25 (499), he made his first appearance as a competitor for the prize of tragedy, without being successful. He fought with his brothers Cynaegīrus, and Aminius, at the battle of Marathon (490), and also at those of Salamis (480) and Plataea (479). In 484 he gained the prize of tragedy ; and in 472 he gained the prize with the trilogy, of which the Persae, the earliest of his extant dramas, was one piece. In 468 he was defeated in a tragic contest by his younger rival Sophocles; and he is said in consequence to have quitted Athens in disgust, and to have gone to the court of Hiero, king of Syracuse. In 467, his patron Hiero died ; and in 458, it appears that Aeschylus was again at Athens, from the fact that the trilogy of the Oresteia was produced in that year. In the same or the following year, he again visited Sicily, and he died at Gela in 456, in the 69th year of his age. It is said that an eagle, mistaking the poet's bald head for a stone, let a tortoise fall upon it to break the shell, and so fulfilled an oracle, according to which he was fated to die by a blow from heaven. The alterations made by Aeschylus in the composition and dramatic representation of Tragedy were so great, that he was considered by the Athenians as the father of it. The principal alteration which he made was the introduction of a second actor, and the consequent formation of the dialogue properly so called, and the limitation of the choral parts. He furnished his actors with more suitable and magnificent dresses, with significant and various masks, and with the thick-soled cothurnus, to raise their stature to the height of heroes. With him also arose the usage of representing at the same time a *trilogy* of plays connected in subject, so that each formed one act, as it were, of a great whole. A satirical play commonly followed each tragic trilogy. Aeschylus is said to have written 70 tragedies. Of these only 7 are extant, namely, the *Persians*, the *Seven against Thebes*, the *Suppliants*, the *Prometheus*, the *Agamemnon*, the *Choephori*, and *Eumenides;* the last three forming the trilogy of the *Oresteia.*

AESCŬLĂPIUS (-i), called ASCLĒPĬUS (-i), by the Greeks, the god of the medical art. In Homer he is not a divinity, but simply the "blameless physician" whose sons, Machaon and Podalīrius, were the physicians in the Greek army. The common story relates that Aesculapius was a son of Apollo and Coronis, and that when Coronis was with child by Apollo, she became enamoured of Ischys, an Arcadian. Apollo, informed of this by a raven, killed Coronis and Ischys. When the body of Coronis was to be burnt, the child Aesculapius was saved from the flames, and was brought up by Chīron, who instructed him in the art of healing and in hunting. There are other tales respecting his birth, according to some of which he was a native of Epidaurus, and this was a common opinion in later times. After he had grown up, he not only cured the sick, but recalled the dead to life.

Aesculapius and a Sick Man. (Millin, Gal. Myth., tav. 32, No. 105.)

Zeus (Jupiter), fearing lest men might contrive to escape death altogether, killed Aescu-

lapius with his thunderbolt; but on the request of Apollo, Zeus placed him among the stars. He was married to Epione, by whom he had tne 2 sons spoken of by Homer, and also other children. The chief seat of the worship of Aesculapius was Epidaurus, where he had a temple surrounded with an extensive grove. Serpents were sacred to him because they were a symbol of renovation, and were believed to have the power of discovering healing herbs. The cock was sacrificed to him. At Rome the worship of Aesculapius was introduced from Epidaurus in B.C. 293, for the purpose of averting a pestilence. The supposed descendants of Aesculapius were called by the patronymic name of *Asclepiadae,* and their principal seats were Cos and Cnidus. They were an order or caste of priests. The knowledge of medicine was regarded as a sacred secret, which was transmitted from father to son in these families.

AESĒPUS (-i), a river rising in the mountains of Ida, and flowing into the Propontis.

AESERNĬA (-ae), a town in Samnium, made a Roman colony in the first Punic war.

AESIS (-is), a river forming the boundary between Picenum and Umbria, anciently the S. boundary of the Senones, and the N.E. boundary of Italy proper.

AESIS (-is), or AESĬUM (-i), a town and Roman colony in Umbria on the river Aesis.

AESŌN (-ŏnis), son of Cretheus and Tyro, and father of Jason. He was excluded from the throne by his half-brother Pelias. During the absence of Jason on the Argonautic expedition, Pelias attempted to murder Aeson, but the latter put an end to his own life. According to Ovid, Aeson survived the return of the Argonauts, and was made young again by Medea.

AESŌPUS (-i), a writer of Fables, lived about B.C. 570, and was a contemporary of Solon. He was originally a slave, and received his freedom from his master Iadmon the Samian. Upon this he visited Croesus, who sent him to Delphi, to distribute among the citizens 4 minae apiece; but in consequence of some dispute on the subject, he refused to give any money at all, upon which the enraged Delphians threw him from a precipice. Plagues were sent upon them from the gods for the offence, and they proclaimed their willingness to give a compensation for his death to any one who could claim it. At length Iadmon, the grandson of his old master, received the compensation, since no nearer connection could be found. Later writers represent Aesop as a perfect monster of ugliness and deformity; a notion for which there is no authority in the classical authors.

Whether Aesop left any written works at all, is a question which affords room for doubt; though it is certain that fables, bearing Aesop's name, were popular at Athens in its most intellectual age. They were in prose, and were turned into poetry by several writers. Socrates turned some of them into verse during his imprisonment. The only Greek versifier of Aesop, of whose writings any whole fables are preserved, is Babrius. Of the Latin writers of Aesopean fables, Phaedrus is the most celebrated. [PHAEDRUS.] The fables now extant in prose, bearing the name of Aesop, are unquestionably spurious.

AESŌPUS (-i), CLAUDĬUS, or CLŌDIUS (-i), was the greatest tragic actor at Rome, and contemporary of Roscius, the greatest comic actor. Both of them lived on intimate terms with Cicero. Aesopus appeared for the last time on the stage at an advanced age at the dedication of the theatre of Pompey (B.C. 55), when his voice failed him, and he could not go through with the speech. He realised an immense fortune by his profession, which was squandered by his son, a foolish spendthrift.

AESTĬI (-ōrum), AESTȲI, or AESTŬI (-ōrum), a people dwelling on the sea-coast, in the N.E. of Germany, probably in the modern *Kurland*, who collected amber, which they called *glessum*. They were probably a Sarmatian or Slavonic and not a Germanic race.

AESŬLA (-ae), a town of the Aequi on a mountain between Praeneste and Tibur.

AETHĂLĬA (-ae), or AETHĂLIS (-ĭdis), called ILVA (-ae) (*Elba*), by the Romans, a small island in the Tuscan sea, opposite the town of Populonia, celebrated for its iron mines.

AETHĂLĬDĒS (-ae), son of Hermes (Mercury) and Eupolemĭa, the herald of the Argonauts. His soul, after many migrations, at length took possession of the body of Pythagoras, in which it still recollected its former migrations.

AETHĬCES (-um), a Thessalian or Epirot people, near M. Pindus.

AETHĬOPES (-um : said to be from αἴθω and ὤψ, but perhaps really a foreign name corrupted), was a name applied (1) most generally to all black or dark races of men ; (2) to all the inhabitants of Inner Africa, S. of Mauretania, the Great Desert, and Egypt, from the Atlantic to the Red Sea and Indian Ocean, and to some of the dark races of Asia ; and (3) most specifically to the inhabitants of the land S. of Egypt, which was called AETHIOPIA.

AETHĬOPIA (-ae : *Nubia, Kordofan, Sennaar, Abyssinia*), a country of Africa, S. of Egypt, the boundary of the countries being at Syene and the Smaller Cataract of the Nile, and extending on the E. to the Red Sea, and to the S. and S.W. indefinitely, as far apparently as the knowledge of the ancients extended. The people of Aethiopia seem to have been of the Caucasian race, and to have spoken a language allied to the Arabic. Monuments are found in the country closely resembling those of Egypt, but of an inferior style. It was the seat of a powerful monarchy, of which MEROE was the capital. Some traditions made Meroe the parent of Egyptian civilisation, while others ascribed the civilisation of Ethiopia to Egyptian colonisation. So great was the power of the Ethiopians, that more than once in its history Egypt was governed by Ethiopian kings. Under the Ptolemies Graeco-Egyptian colonies established themselves in Ethiopia ; but the country was never subdued. The Romans failed to extend their empire over Ethiopia, though they made expeditions into the country, in one of which C. Petronius, prefect of Egypt under Augustus, advanced as far as Napata, and defeated the warrior queen Candace (B.C. 22). Christianity very early extended to Ethiopia, probably in consequence of the conversion of the treasurer of queen Candace (*Acts*, viii. 27).

AETHRA (-ae). (1) Daughter of Pittheus of Troezen, and mother of Theseus by Aegeus. She afterwards lived in Attica, from whence she was carried off to Lacedaemon by Castor and Pollux, and became a slave of Helen, with whom she was taken to Troy. At the capture of Troy she was restored to liberty by her grandson Acamas or Demophon.—(2) Daughter of Oceanus, by whom Atlas begot the 12 Hyades and a son Hyas.

AETNA (-ae). (1) A volcanic mountain in the N. E. of Sicily between Tauromenium and Catana. It is said to have derived its name from Aetna, a Sicilian nymph, a daughter of Heaven and Earth. Zeus (Jupiter) buried under it Typhon or Enceladus ; and in its interior Hephaestus (Vulcan) and the Cyclops forged the thunderbolts for Zeus. There were several eruptions of M. Aetna in antiquity. One occurred in B. c. 475, to which Aeschylus and Pindar probably allude, and another in 425, which Thucydides says was the third on record since the Greeks had settled in Sicily.—(2) A town at the foot of M. Aetna, on the road to Catana, formerly called Inessa or Innesa. It was founded in B. c. 461, by the inhabitants of Catana, who had been expelled from their own town by the Siculi. They gave the name of Aetna to Inessa, because their own town Catana had been called Aetna by Hiero I.

AETŌLĬA (-ae), a division of Greece, was

bounded on the W. by Acarnania, from which it was separated by the river Achelous, on the N. by Epirus and Thessaly, on the E. by the Ozolian Locrians, and on the S. by the entrance to the Corinthian gulf. It was divided into two parts,—Old Aetolia, from the Achelous to the Evenus and Calydon,—and New Aetolia, or the Acquired, from the Evenus and Calydon to the Ozolian Locrians. On the coast the country is level and fruitful, but in the interior mountainous and unproductive. The mountains contained many wild beasts, and were celebrated in mythology for the hunt of the Calydonian boar. The country was originally inhabited by Curetes and Leleges, but was at an early period colonised by Greeks from Elis, led by the mythical AETOLUS. The Aetolians took part in the Trojan war, under their king Thoas. They continued for a long time a rude and uncivilised people, living to a great extent by robbery; and even in the time of Thucydides (B. c. 410) many of their tribes spoke a language which was not Greek, and were in the habit of eating raw flesh. They appear to have been early united by a kind of League, but this League first acquired political importance about the middle of the 3rd century B. c., and became a formidable rival to the Macedonian monarchs and the Achaean League. The Aetolians took the side of Antiochus III. against the Romans, and on the defeat of that monarch, B. c. 189, they became virtually the subjects of Rome. On the conquest of the Achaeans, B. c. 146, Aetolia was included in the Roman province of Achaia.

AETŎLUS (-i), son of Endymion and husband of Pronoë, by whom he had two sons, Pleuron and Calydon. He was king of Elis, but having slain Apis, he fled to the country near the Achelous, which was called Aetolia after him.

AFRĀNĬUS (-i), L. (1) A Roman comic poet, flourished about B. c. 100. His comedies depicted Roman life with such accuracy, that he is classed with Menander. Only a few fragments of them are preserved.—(2) A person of obscure origin, who was, through Pompey's influence, made consul, B. c. 60. When Pompey obtained the provinces of the two Spains in his 2nd consulship (55), he sent Afranius and Petreius to govern them, while he himself remained in Rome. In 49, Afranius and Petreius were defeated by Caesar in Spain. Afranius thereupon passed over to Pompey in Greece; was present at the battle of Pharsalia, (48); and subsequently at the battle of Thapsus in Africa, (46). He then attempted to fly into Mauretania, but was taken prisoner by P. Sittius, and killed.

AFRĬCA (-ae), was used by the ancients in two senses, (1) for the whole continent of Africa, and (2) for the portion of N. Africa which the Romans erected into a province.— (1) In the more general sense the name was not used by the Greek writers; and its use by the Romans arose from the extension to the whole continent of the name of a part of it. The proper Greek name for the continent is Libya. Considerably before the historical period of Greece begins, the Phoenicians extended their commerce over the Mediterranean, and founded several colonies on the N. coast of Africa, of which Carthage was the chief. [CARTHAGO.] The Greeks knew very little of the country until the foundation of the Dorian colony of CYRENE (B. c. 620), and the intercourse of Greek travellers with Egypt in the 6th and 5th centuries; and even then their knowledge of all but the part near Cyrene was derived from the Egyptians and Phoenicians, who sent out some remarkable expeditions to explore the country. A Phoenician fleet sent by the Egyptian king Pharaoh Necho (about B. c. 600), was said to have sailed from the Red Sea, round Africa, and so into the Mediterranean: the authenticity of this story is still a matter of dispute. We still possess an authentic account of another expedition, which the Carthaginians despatched under Hanno (about B. c. 510), and which reached a point on the W. coast nearly, if not quite, as far as lat. 10° N. In the interior, the Great Desert (Sahara) interposed a formidable obstacle to discovery; but even before the time of Herodotus the people on the northern coast told of individuals who had crossed the Desert, and had reached a great river flowing towards the E., with crocodiles in it, and black men living on its banks; which, if the story be true, was probably the Niger in its upper course, near Timbuctoo. There were great differences of opinion as to the boundaries of the continent. Some divided the whole world into only two parts, Europe and Asia, and they were not agreed to which of these two Libya (i. e. Africa) belonged; and those who recognised three divisions differed again in placing the boundary between Libya and Asia either on the W. of Egypt, or along the Nile, or at the isthmus of Suez and the Red Sea: the last opinion gradually prevailed Herodotus divides the inhabitants of Africa into four races, two native, namely, the Libyans and Ethiopians, and two foreign, namely, the Phoenicians and the Greeks. The Libyans, however, were a Caucasian race: the Ethiopians of Herodotus correspond to our Negro races. The whole of the north of Africa fell successively under the power of Rome, and

was finally divided into provinces as follows :
—(1) Aegypt ; (2) Libya, including (*a*) Libyae
Nomos or Libya Exterior. (*b*) Marmarica, (*c*)
Cyrenaïca ; (3) Africa Propria, the former
empire of Carthage see below, No. 2 ; (4)
Numidia ; (5) Mauretania, divided into (*a*)
Sitifensis, (*b*) Caesariensis, (*c*) Tingitana :
these, with (6) Aethiopia, make up the whole
of Africa, according to the divisions recognised by the latest of the ancient geographers.
The northern district was better known to
the Romans than it is to us, and was extremely populous and flourishing. — (2)
AFRICA PROPRIA or PROVINCIA, or simply
AFRICA, was the name under which the
Romans, after the Third Punic War B. C.
146, erected into a province the whole of the
former territory of Carthage. It extended
from the river Musca, on the W., which
divided it from Numidia, to the bottom of the
Syrtis Minor, on the S. E. It was divided
into two districts (regiones), namely, (1) Zeugis
or Zeugitana, the district round Carthage,
(2) Byzacium or Byzacena, S. of Zeugitana,
as far as the bottom of the Syrtis Minor. It
corresponds to the modern regency of *Tunis*.
The province was full of flourishing towns,
and was extremely fertile : it furnished Rome
with its chief supplies of corn.

AFRĬCĀNUS (-ĭ), a surname given to the
Scipios, on account of their victories in Africa.
[SCIPIO.]

AFRĬCUS (-ĭ: λίψ by the Greeks), the
S. W. wind, so called because it blew from
Africa.

ĂGĂMĒDĒS (-ae), commonly called son of
Erginus, king of Orchomenus, and brother of
Trophonius. Agamedes and Trophonius distinguished themselves as architects. They
built a temple of Apollo at Delphi, and a
treasury of Hyrieus, king of Hyria in Boeotia.
In the construction of the latter, they contrived to place a stone in such a manner, that
it could be taken away outside without any
body perceiving it. They now constantly
robbed the treasury ; and the king, seeing
that locks and seals were uninjured while his
treasures were constantly decreasing, set
traps to catch the thief. Agamedes was thus
caught, and Trophonius cut off his head to
avert the discovery. After this Trophonius
was immediately swallowed up by the earth
in the grove of Lebadēa. Here he was
worshipped as a hero, and had a celebrated
oracle. A tradition mentioned by Cicero
states that Agamedes and Trophonius, after
building the temple of Apollo at Delphi,
prayed to the god to grant them in reward
for their labour what was best for men. The
god promised to do so on a certain day, and
when the day came, the two brothers died.

ĂGĂMEMNŌN (-ŏnis), son of Plīsthenes and
Aërope or Eriphŷlē, and grandson of Atreus,
king of Mycenae ; but Homer and others call
him a son of Atreus and grandson of Pelops.
Agamemnon and his brother Menelaus were
brought up together with Aegisthus, the son
of Thyestes, in the house of Atreus. After
the murder of Atreus by Aegisthus and
Thyestes, who succeeded Atreus in the kingdom of Mycenae [AEGISTHUS], Agamemnon
and Menelaus went to Sparta. Here Agamemnon married Clytemnestra, the daughter
of Tyndareus, by whom he became the father
of Iphianassa (Iphigenĭa), Chrysothemis,
Laodice (Electra), and Orestes. The manner
in which Agamemnon obtained the kingdom
of Mycenae, is differently related. From
Homer, it appears as if he had peaceably
succeeded Thyestes ; while, according to
others, he expelled Thyestes, and usurped his
throne. He now became the most powerful
prince in Greece. Homer says he ruled over
all Argos, which signifies Peloponnesus, or
the greater part of it, for the city of Argos
was governed by Diomedes. When Helen,
the wife of Menelaus, was carried off by Paris,
and the Greek chiefs resolved to recover her
by force of arms, Agamemnon was chosen
their commander in chief. After two years
of preparation, the Greek army and fleet
assembled in the port of Aulis in Boeotia.
At this place Agamemnon killed a stag which
was sacred to Artemis (Diana), who in return
visited the Greek army with a pestilence, and
produced a calm which prevented the Greeks
from leaving the port. In order to appease
her wrath, Agamemnon consented to sacrifice
his daughter Iphigenĭa ; but at the moment
of the sacrifice, she was carried off by Artemis
herself to Tauris, and another victim was
substituted in her place. The calm now
ceased, and the army sailed to the coast of
Troy. The quarrel between Agamemnon and
Achilles in the tenth year of the war, is
related elsewhere. [ACHILLES.] Agamemnon,
although the chief commander of the Greeks,
is not the hero of the Iliad, and in chivalrous
spirit, bravery, and character, altogether
inferior to Achilles. But he nevertheless
rises above all the Greeks by his dignity,
power, and majesty : his eyes and head are
likened to those of Zeus (Jupiter), his girdle
to that of Ares (Mars), and his breast to that
of Poseidon (Neptune). At the capture of
Troy he received Cassandra, the daughter of
Priam, as his prize. On his return home he
was murdered by Aegisthus, who had seduced
Clytemnestra during the absence of her husband. The tragic poets make Clytemnestra
alone murder Agamemnon. His death was
avenged by his son Orestes.

ĂGĂMEMNŎNĬDĔS (-ae), the son of Agamemnon, *i. e.* Orestes.

ĂGĂNIPPĒ (-ēs), a nymph of the fountain
of the same name at the foot of Mt. Helicon,
in Boeotia. It was sacred to the Muses (who
were hence called *Aganippides*), and was
believed to inspire those who drank of it.
The fountain of Hippocrēne has the epithet
Aganippis, from its being sacred to the Muses,
like that of Aganippe.

ĂGĂTHOCLĒS (-is or ĕŏs), was born at Thermae, a town of Sicily subject to Carthage, and
was brought up as a potter at Syracuse. His
strength and personal beauty recommended
him to Damas, a noble Syracusan, who drew
him from obscurity, and on whose death he
married his rich widow, and so became one of
the wealthiest citizens in Syracuse. His
ambitious schemes then developed themselves,
and he was driven into exile. After several
changes of fortune, he collected an army, and
was declared sovereign of Syracuse, B.C. 317.
In the course of a few years the whole of
Sicily, which was not under the dominion of
Carthage, submitted to him. In 310 he was
defeated at Himera by the Carthaginians,
under Hamilcar, who straightway laid siege
to Syracuse ; whereupon he formed the bold
design of averting the ruin which threatened
him, by carrying the war into Africa. His
successes were most brilliant and rapid. He
constantly defeated the troops of Carthage,
but was at length summoned from Africa by
the affairs of Sicily, where many cities had
revolted from him, 307. These he reduced,
after making a treaty with the Carthaginians.
He had previously assumed the title of king
of Sicily. He afterwards plundered the
Lipari isles, and also carried his arms into
Italy, in order to attack the Bruttii. But his
last days were embittered by family misfortunes. His grandson Archagathus murdered
his son Agathocles, for the sake of succeeding
to the crown, and the old king feared that
the rest of his family would share his fate.
He accordingly sent his wife and her two
children to Egypt ; and his own death followed almost immediately, 289, after a reign
of 28 years, and in the 72nd year of his age.
Some authors relate an incredible story of
his being poisoned by Maeno, an associate of
Archagathus. The poison, we are told, was
concealed in the quill with which he cleaned
his teeth, and reduced him to so frightful a
condition, that he was placed on the funeral
pile and burnt while yet living, being unable to give any signs that he was not
dead.

ĂGĂTHŌN, an Athenian tragic poet, a
contemporary and friend of Euripides and
Plato. He died about B.C. 400.

ĂGĂTHYRNA (-ae), ĂGĂTHYRNUM (-i),
a town on the N. coast of Sicily.

AGATHYRSI (-ōrum), a people in European
Sarmatia, on the river Maris (*Marosch*) in
Transylvania. From the practice of painting
or tattooing their skin, they are called by
Virgil *picti Agathyrsi*.

ĂGĂVĒ (-ēs), daughter of Cadmus, wife of
Echĭon, and mother of Pentheus. For details
see PENTHEUS.

AGBĂTĂNA. [ECBATANA.]

AGENDĬCUM or AGEDĬCUM (-i : *Sens*),
the chief town of the Senones in Gallia
Lugdunensis.

ĂGĒNOR (-ŏris). (1) Son of Poseidon
(Neptune), king of Phoenicia, and father of
Cadmus, and Europa. Virgil calls Carthage
the city of Agenor, since Dido was descended
from Agenor.—(2) Son of the Trojan Antenor
and Theano, one of the bravest among the
Trojans.

ĂGĒNŎRĬDĒS (-ae), a descendant of an Agenor, such as Cadmus, Phineus, and Perseus.

ĂGĒSĬLĀUS (-i), kings of Sparta. — (1)
Reigned about B.C. 886, and was contemporary with the legislation of Lycurgus.—
(2) Son of Archidāmus II., succeeded his half-
brother Agis II., B.C. 398, excluding, on the
ground of spurious birth, and by the interest
of Lysander, his nephew LEOTYCHIDES. From
396 to 394 he carried on the war in Asia
Minor with great success, but in the midst
of his conquests was summoned home to
defend his country against Thebes, Corinth,
and Argos, which had been induced by
Artaxerxes to take up arms against Sparta.
In 394 he met and defeated at Coronēa in
Boeotia the allied forces. During the next
4 years he regained for his country much of
its former supremacy, till at length the fatal
battle of Leuctra, 371, overthrew for ever the
power of Sparta, and gave the supremacy for
a time to Thebes. In 361 he crossed with a
body of Lacedaemonian mercenaries into
Egypt, where he died, in the winter of 361-360,
after a life of above 80 years and a reign of
38. In person Agesilaus was small, mean-
looking, and lame, on which last ground
objection had been made to his accession, an
oracle, curiously fulfilled, having warned
Sparta of evils awaiting her under a "lame
sovereignty." In his reign, indeed, her fall
took place, but not through him, for he was
one of the best citizens and generals that
Sparta ever had.

ĂGĒSĬPŎLIS, kings of Sparta.—(1) Succeeded his father Pausanias, while yet a minor,
in B.C. 394, and reigned 14 years.—(2) Son
of Cleombrotus, reigned one year, 371.—(3)
Succeeded Cleomenes in 220, but was soon
deposed by his colleague Lycurgus.

ĀGINNUM (-i : *Agen*), the chief town of the Nitiobriges in Gallia Aquitanica.

AGIS (-ĭdis), kings of Sparta.—(1) Son of Eurysthenes, the founder of the family of the Agidae.—(2) Son of Archidāmus II., reigned B.C. 427-398. He took an active part in the Peloponnesian war, and invaded Attica several times. While Alcibiades was at Sparta he was the guest of Agis, and is said to have seduced his wife Timaea ; in consequence of which Leotychides, the son of Agis, was excluded from the throne as illegitimate.— (3) Son of Archidāmus III., reigned 338-330. He attempted to overthrow the Macedonian power in Europe, while Alexander the Great was in Asia, but was defeated and killed in battle by Antipater in 330.—(4) Son of Euda-midas II., reigned 244-240. He attempted to re-establish the institutions of Lycurgus, and to effect a thorough reform in the Spartan state ; but he was resisted by his colleague Leonidas II. and the wealthy, was thrown into prison, and was there put to death by command of the ephors, along with his mother and grandmother.

AGLĀĪA (-ae), " the bright one," one of the CHARITES or Graces.

AGRAULOS (-i). (1) Daughter of Actaeus, first king of Athens, and wife of Cecrops.— (2) Daughter of Cecrops and Agraulos, of whom various stories are told. Athena (Minerva) is said to have given Erichthonius in a chest to Agraulos and her sister Herse, with strict injunctions not to open it ; but they disobeyed the command. [ERICHTHONIUS.] Agraulos was subsequently punished by being changed into a stone by Hermes (Mercury), because she attempted to prevent the god from entering the house of Herse, with whom ..e had fallen in love. Another legend relates that Agraulos threw herself down from the Acropolis because an oracle had declared that the Athenians would conquer if some one would sacrifice himself for his country. The Athenians in gratitude built her a temple on the Acropolis, in which the young Athenians, on receiving their first suit of armour, took an oath that they would always defend their country to the last. A festival (Agraulia) was celebrated at Athens in her honour.

AGRI DĒCŪMĀTES, tithe lands, the name given by the Romans to a part of Germany, E. of the Rhine and N. of the Danube, which they took possession of when the Germans retired eastward, and which they gave to Gauls and subsequently to their own veterans on the payment of a tenth of the produce (decŭma). Towards the end of the first or the beginning of the second century after Christ, these lands were incorporated in the Roman empire.

AGRĬCŎLA (-ae), CN. JŪLĬUS (-ĭ), born June 13th, A.D. 37, at Forum Julii (*Fréjus*, in Provence), was the son of Julius Graecinus, who was executed by Caligula, and of Julia Pro-cilla. He received a careful education ; he first served in Britain, A.D. 60, under Suetonius Paulinus ; was quaestor in Asia in 63 ; was governor of Aquitania from 74 to 76 ; and was consul in 77, when he betrothed his daughter to the historian Tacitus, and in the following year gave her to him in marriage. In 78 he received the government of Britain, which he held for 7 years, during which time he subdued the whole of the country with the exception of the highlands of Caledonia, and by his wise administration introduced among the inhabitants the language and civilisation of Rome. He was recalled in 85 through the jealousy of Domitian, and on his return lived in retirement till his death in 93, which according to some was occasioned by poison, administered by order of Domitian. His character is drawn in the brightest colours by his son-in-law Tacitus, whose Life of Agricola has come down to us.

AGRĬGENTUM (-i), called ACRĂGAS (-antis) by the Greeks (*Girgenti*), a city on the S. coast of Sicily, about 2½ miles from the sea. It was celebrated for its wealth and populousness, and was one of the most splendid cities of the ancient world. It was founded by a Doric colony from Gela, about B.C. 579, was under the government of the cruel tyrant Phalāris (about 560), and subsequently under that of Theron (488-472). It was destroyed by the Carthaginians (405), and, though rebuilt by Timoleon, it never regained its former great-ness. It came into the power of the Romans in 210. It was the birthplace of Empe-docles. There are still gigantic remains of the ancient city.

AGRIPPA (-ae), HERŌDĒS (-is). (1) Called " Agrippa the Great," son of Aristobulus and Berenice, and grandson of Herod the Great. He was educated at Rome, and lived on inti-mate terms with the future emperors Caligula and Claudius. Caligula gave him the tetrarchies of Abilene, Batanaea, Trachonitis, and Auranitis ; and Claudius annexed Judaea and Samaria to his dominions. His govern-ment was exceedingly popular amongst the Jews. It was probably to increase his popu-larity with the Jews that he caused the Apostle James to be beheaded, and Peter to be cast into prison (A.D. 44). The manner of his death, which took place at Caesarea in the same year, is related in *Acts* xii.—(2) Son of the preceding, king of Chalcis. On the break-ing out of the Jewish war he sided with the Romans, and after the capture of Jerusalem, he went with his sister Berenice to Rome, and died in the 70th year of his age, A.D. 100. It was before this Agrippa that the apostle Paul made his defence, A.D. 60 (*Acts*, xxv. xxvi.).

AGRIPPA (-ae), M. VĪPSĀNĬUS (-i), born in B.C. 63, of an obscure family, studied with young Octavius (afterwards the emperor Augustus) at Apollonia in Illyria; and upon the murder of Caesar in 44, was one of the friends of Octavius, who advised him to proceed immediately to Rome. In the civil wars which followed, and which terminated in giving Augustus the sovereignty of the Roman world, Agrippa took an active part; and his military abilities contributed greatly to that result. He commanded the fleet of Augustus at the battle of Actium in 31. He was thrice consul, and in his third consulship in 27 he built the Pantheon. In 21 he married Julia, daughter of Augustus. He continued to be employed in various military commands till his death in B.C. 12. By his first wife Pomponia, Agrippa had Vipsania, married to Tiberius, the successor of Augustus; and by Julia he had 2 daughters, Julia and Agrippina, and 3 sons, Caius Caesar, Lucius Caesar [CAESAR], and Agrippa Postumus : the last was banished by Augustus to the island of Planasia, and was put to death by Tiberius at his accession, A.D. 14.

AGRIPPĪNA (-ae). (1) Daughter of M. Vipsanius Agrippa and of Julia, the daughter of Augustus, married Germanicus, by whom she had 9 children, among whom were the emperor Caligula, and Agrippina, the mother of Nero. She was distinguished for her virtues and heroism, and shared all the dangers of her husband's campaigns. On his death in A.D. 17 she returned to Italy; but the favour with which she was received by the people increased the hatred which Tiberius and his mother Livia had long entertained towards her. At length in A.D. 30 Tiberius banished her to the island of Pandataria, where she died 3 years afterwards, probably by voluntary starvation.—(2) Daughter of Germanicus and Agrippina [No. 1], and mother of the emperor Nero, was born at Oppidum Ubiorum, afterwards called in honour of her Colonia Agrippina, now *Cologne*. [COLONIA.] She was beautiful and intelligent, but licentious, cruel, and ambitious. She was first married to Cn. Domitius Ahenobarbus (A.D. 28), by whom she had a son, afterwards the emperor Nero; next to Crispus Passienus; and thirdly to the emperor Claudius (49), although she was his niece. In 50 she prevailed upon Claudius to adopt her son, to the prejudice of his own son Britannicus; and in order to secure the succession for her son, she poisoned the

emperor in 54. The young emperor soon became tired of the ascendancy of his mother, and after making several attempts to shake off her authority, he caused her to be assassinated in 59.

AGRIUS (-i), son of Porthaon and Euryte, and father of Thersites and 5 other sons.

AGYĪEUS (trisyll.), a surname of Apollo, as the protector of the streets and public places.

AGYLLA. [CAERE.]

AGYRĬUM, a town in Sicily on the Cyamosorus, N.W. of Centuripae and N.E. of Enna, the birthplace of the historian Diodorus.

AHĀLA (-ae), C. SERVĪLĬUS (-i), magister equitum in B.C. 439 to the dictator L. Cincinnatus, when he slew SP. MAELIUS in the forum, because he refused to appear before the dictator. Ahala was brought to trial, and only escaped condemnation by a voluntary exile.

AHARNA (-ae), a town in Etruria, N.E. of Volsinii.

AHĒNOBARBUS, (-i), the name of a distinguished family of the Domitia gens. They are said to have obtained the surname of Ahenobarbus, i. e. "Brazen-Beard" or "Red-Beard," because the Dioscuri (Castor and Pollux) announced to one of their ancestors the victory of the Romans over the Latins at lake Regillus (B.C. 496), and, to confirm the truth of what they said, stroked his black hair and beard, which immediately became red.—(1) CN. DOMITIUS AHENOBARBUS, consul, B.C. 122, conquered the Allobroges in Gaul, at the confluence of the Sulga and Rhodanus. —(2) CN. DOMITIUS AHENOBARBUS, tribune of the plebs, 104, brought forward the law (*Lex Domitia*), by which the election of the priests was transferred from the collegia to the people. The people afterwards elected him Pontifex Maximus out of gratitude. He was consul in 96, and censor in 92, with Licinius Crassus, the orator.—(3) L. DOMITIUS AHENOBARBUS, married Porcia, the sister of M. Cato, and was a staunch and courageous supporter of the aristocratical party. He was aedile in 61, praetor in 58, and consul in 54. On the breaking out of the civil war in 49 he threw himself into Corfinium, but was compelled by his own troops to surrender to Caesar. He next went to Massilia, and, after the surrender of that town, repaired to Pompey in Greece : he fell in the battle of Pharsalia (48), where he commanded the left wing, and, according to Cicero's assertion in the second Philippic, by the hand of Antony.—(4) CN. DOMITIUS AHENOBARBUS, son of No. 3, was taken with his father at Corfinium (49), was present at the battle of Pharsalia (48), and returned to Italy in 46, when he was pardoned by Caesar. He accompanied Antony in his campaign against the Parthians in 36. He was consul in 32, and deserted to Augustus shortly before the battle of Actium.—(5) CN. DOMITIUS AHENO-BARBUS, consul A.D. 32, married Agrippina, daughter of Germanicus, and was father of the emperor Nero. [AGRIPPINA.]

AIDES or AIDŌNEUS. [HADES.]

AIUS (-i) LOCŪTĬUS (-i) or LOQUENS (-entis), a Roman divinity. A short time before the Gauls took Rome (B.C. 390) a voice was heard at Rome during the silence of night, announcing that the Gauls were approaching. The Romans afterwards erected on the spot where the voice had been heard, an altar with a sacred enclosure around it, to Aius Locutius, or the "Announcing Speaker."

AJAX (-ācis), called AIAS by the Greeks. —(1)Son of Telamon, king of Salamis, and grandson of Aeacus. Homer calls him Ajax

Ajax. (Aegina Marbles.)

the Telamonian, Ajax the Great, or simply Ajax, whereas the other Ajax, son of Oïleus, is always distinguished from the former by some epithet. He sailed against Troy in 12 ships, and is represented in the Iliad as second only to Achilles in bravery. In the contest for the armour of Achilles, he was conquered by Ulysses, and this, says Homer, was the cause of his death. Later poets relate that his defeat by Ulysses

threw him into an awful state of madness: that he rushed from his tent and slaughtered the sheep of the Greek army, fancying they were his enemies; and that at length he put an end to his own life. From his blood there sprang up a purple flower bearing the letters *Ai* (Αἴ) on its leaves, which were at once the initials of his name and expressive of a sigh. Homer does not mention his mistress TECMESSA.—(2) Son of Oïleus, king of the Locrians, also called the lesser Ajax, sailed against Troy in 40 ships. He is described as small of stature, but skilled in throwing the spear, and, next to Achilles, the most swift-footed among the Greeks. On his return from Troy his vessel was wrecked; he himself got safe upon a rock through the assistance of Poseidon (Neptune); but as he boasted that he would escape in defiance of the immortals, Poseidon split the rock with his trident, and Ajax was swallowed up by the sea. This is the account of Homer. Virgil tells us that the anger of Athēna (Minerva) was excited against him, because, on the night of the capture of Troy, he violated Cassandra in the temple of the goddess.

ALĂBANDA (-ōrum), an inland town of Caria, near the Marsyas, to the S. of the Maeander, situated between two hills. It was a prosperous place, but one of the most corrupt and luxurious towns in Asia Minor.

ĂLALCŎMĒNAE (-arum), an ancient town of Boeotia, E. of Coronēa, with a temple of Athēna (Minerva), who is said to have been born in the town, and who was hence called *Alalcomenēis*.

ALALĬA. [ALERIA.]

ĂLĂNI (-ōrum), a great Asiatic people, included under the general name of Scythians. They are first found about the E. part of the Caucasus, in the country called Albania, which appears to be only another form of the same name. At a later time they pressed into Europe, as far as the banks of the Lower Danube, where, towards the end of the 5th century, they were routed by the Huns, who then compelled them to become their allies. In A.D. 406, some of the Alani took part with the Vandals in their irruption into Gaul and Spain, where they gradually disappear from history.

ĂLĂRĪCUS, (-i) in German *Al-ric*, i. e. "All-rich," king of the Visigoths, who took and plundered Rome, 24th of August, A.D. 410. He died shortly afterwards at Consentia in Bruttium.

ALBA (-ae) SILVĬUS (-i), one of the mythical kings of Alba, son of Latinus, reigned 39 years.

ALBA (-ae). (1) FUCENTIA or FUCENTIS, a town of the Marsi, and subsequently a

Roman colony, situated on a lofty rock near the lake Fucīnus, and used by the Romans as a state prison.—(2) LONGA, the most ancient town in Latium, is said to have been built by Ascanius, and to have founded Rome. It was called Longa, from its stretching in a long line down the Alban Mount towards the Alban Lake. It was destroyed by Tullus Hostilius, and was never rebuilt; its inhabitants were removed to Rome. At a later time the surrounding country was studded with the splendid villas of the Roman aristocracy and emperors (Pompey's, Domitian's, &c.), each of which was called *Albanum.* —(3) POMPEIA, a town in Liguria, colonised by Pompeius Magnus, the birthplace of the emperor Pertinax.

ALBĀNIA (-ae : in the S.E. part of *Georgia*), a country of Asia on the W. side of the Caspian, extending from the rivers Cyrus and Araxes on the S. to M. Ceraunius (the E. part of the Caucasus) on the N., and bounded on the W. by Iberia. It was a fertile plain, abounding in pasture and vineyards ; but the inhabitants were fierce and warlike. They were a Scythian tribe, identical with the ALANI. The Romans first became acquainted with them at the time of the Mithridatic war, when they encountered Pompey with a large army.

ALBĀNUM. [ALBA, No. 2.]

ALBĀNUS (-i) LACUS, a small lake about 5 miles in circumference, W. of the Mons Albanus between Bovillae and Alba Longa, is the crater of an extinct volcano, and is many hundred feet deep. The emissarium which the Romans bored through the solid rock during the siege of Veii, in order to carry off the superfluous water of the lake, is extant at the present day.

ALBĀNUS MONS, was, in its narrower signification, the mountain in Latium on whose declivity the town of Alba Longa was situated. It was the sacred mountain of the Latins, on which the religious festivals of the Latin League were celebrated (*Feriae Latinae*), and on its highest summit was the temple of Jupiter Latiaris, to which the Roman generals ascended in triumph, when this honour was denied them in Rome. The Mons Albanus in its wider signification included the Mons ALGIDUS and the mountains about Tusculum.

ALBICI (-ōrum), a warlike Gallic people inhabiting the mountains north of Massilia.

ALBĪNŌVĀNUS (-i), C. PĒDO (-ōnis), a friend of Ovid, who addresses to him one of his Epistles from Pontus.

ALBĪNUS or ALBUS (-i), POSTŪMĪUS (-i), the name of a patrician family at Rome, many of the members of which held the highest offices of the state from the commencement of the republic to its downfal. The founder of

the family was dictator B.C. 498, when he conquered the Latins in the great battle near lake Regillus.

ALBĪNUS (-i), CLŌDIUS (-i), was governor of Britain at the death of Commodus in A. D. 192. In order to secure his neutrality, Septimius Severus made him Caesar ; but after Severus had defeated his rivals, he turned his arms against Albinus. A great battle was fought between them at Lugdunum (Lyons), in Gaul, 197, in which Albinus was defeated and killed.

ALBĪON (-onis), another name of BRITANNIA, the *white* land, from its white cliffs opposite the coast of Gaul.

ALBIS (-is : *Elbe*), one of the great rivers in Germany, the most easterly which the Romans became acquainted with. The Romans reached the Elbe for the first time in B. C. 9 under Drusus. The last Roman general who saw the Elbe was Tiberius in A. D. 5.

ALBĪUM INGAUNUM or ALBINGAUNUM (-i), a town of the Ingauni on the coast of Liguria, and a municipium.

ALBĪUM INTEMELIUM or ALBINTEMELIUM (-i), a town of the Intemelii on the coast of Liguria, and a municipium.

ALBŪLA (-ae), an ancient name of the river TIBER.

ALBŪLAE AQUAE. [ALBUNEA.)

ALBŪNĒA or ALBŪNA (-ae), a prophetic nymph or Sybil, to whom a grove was consecrated in the neighbourhood of Tibur, with a fountain and a temple. This fountain was the largest of the Albulae aquae, sulphureous springs at Tibur, flowing into the Anio. The temple is still extant at Tivoli.

ALBURNUS (-i) MONS, a mountain in Lucania, covered with wood, behind Paestum.

ALCAEUS (-i), of Mytilene in Lesbos, the earliest of the Aeolian lyric poets, began to flourish about B. C. 611. In the war between the Athenians and Mytilenaeans for the possession of Sigēum (B. C. 606) he incurred the disgrace of leaving his arms on the field of battle. Alcaeus belonged by birth to the nobles, and was driven into exile with his brother Antimenidas, when the popular party got the upper hand. He attempted by force of arms to regain his country; but all his attempts were frustrated by PITTACUS, who had been chosen by the people Aesymnetes or dictator for the purpose of resisting him and the other exiles. Alcaeus and his brother afterwards travelled into various countries : the time of his death is uncertain. The extant fragments of his poems, and the excellent imitations of Horace, enable us to understand something of their character. Those which have received the highest praise are his warlike odes, in which he tried to rouse the spirits of the nobles, the *Alcaei minaces Camenae* of Horace. Alcaeus is said to have invented the well-known Alcaic metre.

ALCĂTHŎUS (-i), son of Pelops and Hippodamīa, obtained as his wife Evaechme, the daughter of Megareus, by slaying the Cithaeronian lion, and succeeded his father-in-law as king of Megara. He restored the walls of Megara, which is therefore sometimes called Alcăthŏē by the poets. In this work he was assisted by Apollo. The stone upon which the god used to place his lyre while he was at work, was believed, even in late times, to give forth a sound, when struck, similar to that of a lyre.

ALCESTIS (-is) or ALCESTE (-ēs), wife of Admetus. [ADMETUS.]

ALCĪBIĂDĒS (-is), son of Clīnias and Dinomachē, was born at Athens about B. C. 450, and on the death of his father in 447, was brought up by his relation Pericles. He possessed a beautiful person, transcendant abilities, and great wealth. His youth was disgraced by his amours and debaucheries, and Socrates, who saw his vast capabilities, attempted to win him to the paths of virtue, but in vain. Their intimacy was strengthened by mutual services. At the battle of Potidaea (432) his life was saved by Socrates, and at that of Delium (424) he saved the life of Socrates. After the death of Cleon (422) he became one of the leading politicians, and the head of the war party in opposition to Nicias. In 415 he was appointed, along with Nicias and Lamachus, as commander of the expedition to Sicily. While the preparations for the expedition were going on, there occurred the mysterious mutilation of the busts of the Hermae, which the popular fears connected with an attempt to overthrow the Athenian constitution. Alcibiades was charged with being the ringleader in this attempt. He demanded an investigation before he set sail, but this his enemies would not grant; but he had not been long in Sicily, before he was recalled to stand his trial. On his return homewards, he managed to escape at Thurii, and thence proceeded to Sparta, where he acted as the avowed enemy of his country. The machinations of his enemy Agis II. induced him to abandon the Spartans and take refuge with Tissaphernes (412), whose favour he soon gained. Through his influence Tissaphernes deserted the Spartans and professed his willingness to assist the Athenians, who accordingly recalled Alcibiades from banishment in 411. He did not immediately return to Athens, but remained abroad for the next 4 years, during which the Athenians under his command gained the victories of Cynossema, Abydos, and Cyzicus, and got possses-

sion of Chalcedon and Byzantium. In 407 he returned to Athens, where he was received with great enthusiasm, and was appointed commander-in-chief of all the land and sea forces. But the defeat at Notium, occasioned during his absence by the imprudence of his lieutenant, Antiochus, furnished his enemies with a handle against him, and he was superseded in his command (406). He now went into voluntary exile to his fortified domain at Bisanthe in the Thracian Chersonesus. After the fall of Athens (404), he took refuge with Pharnabazus. He was about to proceed to the court of Artaxerxes, when one night his house was surrounded by a band of armed men, and set on fire. He rushed out sword in hand, but fell pierced with arrows (404). The assassins were probably either employed by the Spartans, or by the brothers of a lady whom Alcibiades had seduced. He left a son by his wife Hipparete named Alcibiades, who never distinguished himself.

ALCĪDĒS (-ae), a name of Hercules, as the grandson of Alceus or Alcaeus.

ALCĪMĔDĒ (ēs), daughter of Phylacus and Clymenē, wife of Aeson, and mother of Jason.

ALCĪNŎUS (-i), son of Nausithous, and grandson of Poseidon (Neptune), is celebrated in the Odyssey, as the happy ruler of the Phaeacians in the island of Scheria.

ALCIPHRŎN (-ŏnis), the most distinguished of the Greek epistolary writers, was perhaps a contemporary of Lucian, about A.D. 180. The letters (113 in number) are written by fictitious personages, and the language is distinguished by its purity and elegance.

ALCĪTHŎĒ (-ēs) or ALCĂTHŎĒ (-ēs), daughter of Minyas, changed, together with her sisters, into bats, for refusing to join the other women of Boeotia in the worship of Dionysus (Bacchus).

ALCMAEŎN (-ŏnis), son of Amphiarāus and Eriphylē, and brother of Amphilochus. Alcmaeon took part in the expedition of the Epigoni against Thebes, and on his return home he slew his mother according to the injunction of his father. [AMPHIARAUS.] For this deed he became mad, and was haunted by the Erinnyes. He went to Phegeus in Psophis, and being purified by the latter, he married his daughter Arsino or Aiphesiboea, to whom he gave the necklace and peplus of Harmonia. But as the land of this country ceased to bear on account of its harbouring a matricide, he left Psophis and repaired to the country at the mouth of the river Achelous. The god Achelous gave him his daughter Callirrhoë in marriage. Callirrhoë wishing to possess the necklace and peplus of Harmonia, Alcmaeon went to Psophis and obtained them from Phegeus, under the pretext of dedicating them at Delphi; but when Phegeus heard that the treasures were fetched for Callirrhoë, he caused his sons to murder Alcmaeon.

ALCMAEŌNIDAE (-arum), a noble family at Athens, were a branch of the family of the Nelĭdae, who were driven out of Pylus in Messenia by the Dorians, and settled at Athens. In consequence of the way in which Megacles, one of the family, treated the insurgents under CYLON (B.C. 612), they brought upon themselves the guilt of sacrilege, and were in consequence banished from Athens, about 595. About 560 they returned from exile, but were again expelled by Pisistratus. In 548 they contracted with the Amphictyonic council to rebuild the temple of Delphi, and obtained great popularity throughout Greece by executing the work in a style of magnificence which much exceeded their engagement. On the expulsion of Hippias in 510, they were again restored to Athens. They now joined the popular party, and Clisthenes, who was at that time the head of the family, gave a new constitution to Athens. [CLISTHENES.]

ALCMAN (-ānis), the chief lyric poet of Sparta, by birth a Lydian of Sardis, was brought to Laconia as a slave, when very young, and was emancipated by his master, who discovered his genius. He probably flourished about B.C. 631. He is said to have died, like Sulla, of the morbus pedicularis. Alcman is said by some to have been the inventor of erotic poetry.

ALCMĒNĒ (-ēs) or ALCMĒNA (-ae), daughter of Electryon, king of Mycenae, promised to marry Amphitryon, provided he avenged the death of her brothers, who had been slain by the sons of Pterelaus. Amphitryon undertook the task; but during his absence, Zeus (Jupiter), in the disguise of Amphitryon, visited Alcmene, and pretending to be her husband, related in what way he had avenged the death of her brothers. Amphitryon himself returned the next day: Alcmene became the mother of Hercules by Zeus, and of Iphicles by Amphitryon. [HERCULES.]

ALCŸONE or HALCŸONĒ (-ēs). (1) A Pleiad, daughter of Atlas and Pleione, and beloved by Poseidon (Neptune).—(2) Daughter of Aeolus and Enarete, and wife of Ceÿx. Her husband having perished in a shipwreck, Alcyone for grief threw herself into the sea, but the gods, out of compassion, changed the two into birds. While the bird alcyon was breeding, there always prevailed calms at sea.

ALCŸŌNĬUM MĂRE, the E. part of the Corinthian gulf.

ALĒA (-ae), a town in Arcadia, S. of the

Stymphalean lake. Athena (Minerva) was worshipped under the name of Alea in this place and in Tegea.

ALECTŌ (-ūs; acc. ō), one of the Furies. [EUMENIDES.]

ALĒMANNI or ĂLĂMANNI or ĂLĂMĀNI (-orum) (from the German alle Männer, all men), a confederacy of German tribes, between the Danube, the Rhine, and the Main. They first came into contact with the Romans in the reign of Caracalla, who assumed the surname of Alemannicus on account of a pretended victory over them (A.D. 214). After this time they continually invaded the Roman dominions, and in the fifth century were in possession of Alsace and of German Switzerland.

ALĒRĬA or ALĀLĬA (-ae), one of the chief cities of Corsica, on the E. of the island, founded by the Phocaeans B.C. 564, and made a Roman colony by Sulla.

ALĒSA (-ae). [HALESA.]

ALĒSĬA (-ae), an ancient town of the Mandubii in Gallia Lugdunensis, and situated on a high hill (now Auxois)), which was washed by the two rivers Lutosa (Oze) and Osera (Ozerain). It was taken and destroyed by Caesar, in B.C. 52, after a memorable siege.

ALETRĬUM or ĂLĂTRĬUM, an ancient town of the Hernici, subsequently a municipium and a Roman colony, W. of Sora and E. of Anagnia.

ALEUĂDAE (-ārum). [ALEUAS.]

ALEUAS (-ae), a descendant of Hercules, was the ruler of Larissa in Thessaly, and the reputed founder of the celebrated family of the Aleuadae. They were divided into two branches, the Aleuadae and the Scopadae, of whom the latter inhabited Crannon, while the former remained at Larissa. In the invasion of Greece by Xerxes (B.C. 480), the Aleuadae espoused the cause of the Persians, and the family continued to be the predominant one in Thessaly for a long time afterwards.

ALEXANDER (-dri), the usual name of PARIS in the Iliad.

ALEXANDER SEVĒRUS. [SEVERUS.]

ALEXANDER. I. Kings of Epirus.— (1) Son of Neoptolemus and brother of Olympias, the mother of Alexander the Great, was made king of Epirus by Philip, B.C. 336. In 332, Alexander crossed over into Italy, to aid the Tarentines against the Lucanians and Bruttii. He was defeated and slain in battle in 326, near Pandosia, on the banks of the Acheron in Southern Italy.—(2) Son of Pyrrhus and Lanassa, succeeded his father in 272.

II. Kings of Macedonia.—(1) Son of Amyntas I., succeeded his father about B.C. 505, was obliged to submit to the Persians, and accompanied Xerxes in his invasion of Greece (B.C. 480). He was secretly inclined to the cause of the Greeks. He died about 455, and was succeeded by Perdiccas II.—(2) Son of Amyntas II., whom he succeeded, reigned 369—367. He was murdered by Ptolemy Alorites. —(3) Surnamed the GREAT, son of Philip II. and Olympias, was born at Pella, B.C. 356. He was educated by Aristotle, who acquired a great influence over his mind and character. He first distinguished himself at the battle of Chaeronēa (338), where the victory was mainly owing to his impetuosity and courage. On the murder of Philip (336), he ascended the throne, at the age of 20, and found himself surrounded by enemies on every side. He first put down rebellion in his own kingdom, and then rapidly marched into Greece. His unexpected activity overawed all opposition ; Thebes, which had been most active against* him, submitted when he appeared at its gates ; and the assembled Greeks at the Isthmus of Corinth elected him to the command against Persia. He now directed his arms against the barbarians of the north, and crossed the Danube (335). A report of his death having reached Greece, the Thebans once more took up arms. But a terrible punishment awaited them. He took Thebes by assault, destroyed all the buildings, with the exception of the house of Pindar, killed most of the inhabitants, and sold the rest as slaves. Alexander now prepared for his great expedition against Persia. In the spring of 334, he crossed the Hellespont, with about 35,000 men. Of these 30,000 were foot and 5000 horse ; and of the former only 12,000 were Macedonians. Alexander's first engagement with the Persians was on the river Granīcus in Mysia (May, 334), where they were entirely defeated by him. In the following year (333) he collected his army at Gordium in Phrygia, where he cut or untied the celebrated Gordian knot, which, it was said, was to be loosened only by the conqueror of Asia. From thence he marched to Issus, on the confines of Syria, where he gained a great victory over Darius, the Persian king. Darius himself escaped ; but his mother, wife, and children, fell into the hands of Alexander, who treated them with the utmost delicacy and respect. Alexander now directed his arms against the cities of Phoenicia, most of which submitted ; but Tyre was not taken till the middle of 332, after an obstinate defence of 7 months. He next marched into Egypt, which willingly submitted to him. At the beginning of 331, he founded at the mouth of the Nile the city of ALEXANDRIA, and about the same time visited

the temple of Jupiter Ammon, in the desert of Libya, and was saluted by the priests as the son of Jupiter Ammon. In the spring of the same year (331), he set out against Darius, who had collected another army. He crossed the Euphrates and the Tigris, and at length met with the immense hosts of Darius, said to have amounted to more than a million of men, in the plains of Gaugamela. The battle was fought in the month of October, 331, and ended in the complete defeat of the Persians. Alexander was now the conqueror of Asia, and began to adopt Persian habits and customs, by which he conciliated the affections of his new subjects. From Arbela he marched to Babylon, Susa, and Persepolis, all of which surrendered to him. He is said to have set fire to the palace of Persepolis, and, according to some accounts, in the revelry of a banquet, at the instigation of Thais, an Athenian courtesan. At the beginning of 330, Alexander marched from Persepolis into Media, in pursuit of Darius, whom he followed into Parthia, where the unfortunate king was murdered by Bessus, satrap of Bactria. In 329 Alexander crossed the mountains of the Paropamisus (the *Hindoo Koosh*) and marched into Bactria against Bessus, who was betrayed to him, and was put to death. During the next 2 years he was chiefly engaged in the conquest of Sogdiana. He also crossed the Jaxartes (the *Sir*), and defeated several Scythian tribes N. of that river. On the conquest of a mountain fortress he obtained possession of Roxana, the daughter of the Bactrian chief Oxyartes, whom he made his wife. It was about this time that he killed his friend CLITUS in a drunken brawl. He had previously put to death his faithful servant PARMENION, on the charge of treason. In 327 he invaded India, and crossed the Indus, probably near the modern Attock. He met with no resistance till he reached the Hydaspes, where he was opposed by Porus, an Indian king, whom he defeated after a gallant resistance, and took prisoner. Alexander restored to him his kingdom, and treated him with distinguished honour. He founded a town on the Hydaspes, called Bucephala, in honour of his horse Bucephalus, who died here, after carrying him through so many victories. From thence he penetrated as far as the Hyphasis (*Garra*). This was the furthest point which he reached, for the Macedonians, worn out by long service, and tired of the war, refused to advance further ; and Alexander, notwithstanding his entreaties and prayers, was obliged to lead them back. He returned to the Hydaspes, and then sailed down the river with a portion of his troops, while the remainder marched along the banks in two divisions. He finally reached the Indian ocean about the middle of 326. Nearchus was sent with the fleet to sail along the coast to the Persian gulf [NEARCHUS]; and Alexander marched with the rest of his forces through Gedrosia, in which country his army suffered greatly from want of water and provisions. He reached Susa at the beginning of 325. Here he allowed himself and his troops some rest from their labours; and anxious to form his European and Asiatic subjects into one people, he assigned Asiatic wives to about 80 of his generals. He himself took a second wife, Barsine, the eldest daughter of Darius. Towards the close of the year 325, he went to Ecbatana, where he lost his great favourite HEPHAESTION. From Ecbatana he marched to Babylon, which he intended to make the capital of his empire, as the best point of communication between his eastern and western dominions. His schemes were numerous and gigantic; but he was cut off in the midst of them. He was attacked by a fever, which was probably aggravated by the quantity of wine he had drunk at a banquet given to his principal officers, and he died after an illness of 11 days, in the month of May or June, B.C. 323, at the age of 32, after a reign of 12 years and 8 months. He appointed no one as his successor, but just before his death he gave his ring to Perdiccas. Roxana was with child at the time of his death, and afterwards bore a son who is known by the name of Alexander Aegus.—(4) AEGUS, son of Alexander the Great and Roxana, was born shortly after the death of his father, in B.C. 323, and was acknowledged as the partner of Philip Arrhidaeus in the empire, under the guardianship of Perdiccas, Antipater, and Polysperchon, in succession. Alexander and his mother Roxana were imprisoned by Cassander, when he obtained possession of Macedonia in 316, and remained in prison till 311, when they were put to death by Cassander.

III. *Kings of Syria.*—(1) Surnamed BALAS, a person of low origin, pretended to be the son of Antiochus IV. Epiphanes, and reigned in Syria B. c. 150—146. He was defeated and dethroned by Demetrius II. Nicator.—(2) Surnamed ZEBINA or ZABINAS, son of a merchant, was set up by Ptolemy Physcon as a pretender to the throne of Syria, B.C. 128. He was defeated by Antiochus Grypus, by whom he was put to death, 122.

IV. *Literary.* —(1) Of AEGAE, a peripatetic philosopher at Rome in the first century after Christ, was tutor to the emperor Nero.—(2) The AETOLIAN, of Pleuron in Aetolia, a Greek poet, lived in the reign of Ptolemaeus Philadelphus (B.C. 285—247), at Alexandria, where

he was reckoned one of the 7 tragic poets who constituted the tragic pleiad.—(3) Of APHRO-DISIAS, in Caria, the most celebrated of the commentators on Aristotle, lived about A.D. 200. Some of his works were edited and translated into Latin at the revival of literature.

ĀLEXANDRĪA, oftener ĪA, rarely ĒA(-ae), the name of several cities founded by, or in memory of, Alexander the Great. Of these the most important are :—(1) The capital of Egypt under the Ptolemies, ordered by Alexander to be founded in B.C. 332. It was built on the narrow neck of land between the Lake Mareotis and the Mediterranean, opposite to the I. of Pharos, which was joined to the city by an artificial dyke. On this island a great lighthouse was built in the reign of Ptolemy Philadelphus (283). Under the care of the Ptolemies, as the capital of a great kingdom, and commanding by its position all the commerce of Europe with the East, Alexandria soon became the most wealthy and splendid city of the known world. It was celebrated for its magnificent library, founded by the first two Ptolemies. The library suffered severely by fire when Julius Caesar was besieged in Alexandria, and was finally destroyed by Amrou, the lieutenant of the Caliph Omar, in A.D. 651. Under the Romans, Alexandria retained its commercial and literary importance, and became also a chief seat of Christianity and theological learning. Its site is now covered by a mass of ruins, among which are the two obelisks (vulg. *Cleopatra's Needles*), which adorned the gateway of the royal palace, and, outside the walls, to the S., the column of Diocletian (vulg. *Pompey's Pillar*). The modern city stands on the dyke uniting the island of Pharos to the mainland.—(2) A. TROAS, also TROAS simply, on the sea-coast S.W. of Troy, was enlarged by Antigonus, hence called Antigonīa, but afterwards it resumed its first name. It flourished greatly, both under the Greeks and the Romans; and both Julius Caesar and Constantine thought of establishing the seat of empire in it.—(3) A. AD ISSUM, a sea-port at the entrance of Syria, a little S. of Issus.—(4) In Susiana, aft. ANTI-OCHIA, aft. CHARAX SPASINI, at the mouth of the Tigris, built by Alexander; destroyed by a flood; restored by Antiochus Epiphanes : birthplace of Dionysius Periegetes and Isidorus Characenus.

ALFĒNUS VARUS (-i), a celebrated Roman jurist, who was originally a shoemaker or a barber. He is mentioned by Horace.

ALGĪDUS MONS, a range of mountains in Latium, extending S. from Praeneste to M. Albanus, cold, but covered with wood, and containing good pasturage. On it was situated the town of Algidum. It was an ancient seat of the worship of Diana. From it the Aequi usually made their incursions into the Roman territory.

ĀLIĒNUS CAECĪNA. [Caecina.]

ĀLIMENTUS, L. CINCIUS (-i), a celebrated Roman annalist, antiquary, and jurist; was praetor in Sicily, B.C. 209, and wrote several works, of which the best known was his *Annales*, which contained an account of the second Punic war.

ĀLĪPHĒRA (-ae), a fortified town in Arcadia, situated on a mountain on the borders of Elis, S. of the Alphēus.

ALĪSO (-ōnis : *Elsen*), a strong fortress built by Drusus, B.C. 11, at the confluence of the Luppia (*Lippe*) and the Eliso (*Alme*).

ALLIA (-ae), or more correctly ALĪA, a small river flowing into the Tiber about 6 miles from Rome. It is memorable by the defeat of the Romans by the Gauls on its banks, July 16th, B.C. 390. Hence the *dies Alliensis* was an unlucky day in the Roman calendar.

ALLĪFAE or ALĪFAE (-ārum), a town of Samnium, on the Vulturnus, celebrated for the manufacture of its large drinking-cups (Allifana pocula).

ALLŌBRŌGES (-um), a powerful people of Gaul dwelling between the Rhodanus (*Rhone*) and the Isara (*Isere*), as far as the L. Lemannus (*Lake of Geneva*), consequently in the modern Dauphiné and Savoy. Their chief town was Vienna on the Rhone. They were conquered, in B.C. 121, by Q. Fabius Maximus Allobrogicus, and made subjects of Rome, but they bore the yoke unwillingly, and were always disposed to rebellion.

ALMO (-ōnis), a small river, rising near Bovillae, and flowing into the Tiber S. of Rome, in which the statues of Cybelē were washed annually.

ALMŌPES (-um), a people in Macedonia, inhabiting the district Almopia between Eordaea and Pelagonia.

ĀLŌEUS (-ĕŏs, ĕĭ or eĭ; dat. ĕŏ or eŏ; acc. ĕă), son of Poseidon (Neptune) and Canace, married Iphimedīa, the daughter of Triops. His wife was beloved by Poseidon, by whom she had two sons, Otus and Ephialtes, who are usually called the *Alōïdae*, from their reputed father Aloeus. They were renowned for their extraordinary strength and daring spirit. When they were 9 years old, each of their bodies measured 9 cubits in breadth, and 27 in height. At this early age, they threatened the Olympian gods with war, and attempted to pile Ossa upon Olympus, and Pelion upon Ossa. They would have accomplished their object, says Homer, had they been allowed to grow up to the age of manhood; but Apollo destroyed them before their beards began to appear. They also put the god Ares in chains, and kept him imprisoned for 13 months.

ĀLŌĪDAE (-arum). [Aloeus.]

ALŌPĒ (-ēs), a town in the Opuntian Locris, opposite Euboea.

ĀLŌPĒCONNĒSUS (-i), a town in the Thracian Chersonesus, founded by the Aeolians.

ALPĒNUS (-i), a town of the Epicnemidii Locri at the entrance of the pass of Thermopylae.

ALPES (-ium : probably from the Celtic *Alb* or *Alp*, "a height"), the mountains forming the boundary of northern Italy, which were distinguished by the following names. We enumerate them in order from W. to E. 1. Alpes Maritimae, the *Maritime* or *Ligurian Alps*, from Genua (*Genoa*), where the Apennines begin, run W. as far as the river Varus (*Var*), and then N. to M. Vesulus (*Monte Viso*), one of the highest points of the Alps.—2. Alpes Cottiae or Cottianae, the *Cottian Alps* (so called from a king Cottius in the time of Augustus), from Monte Viso to Mont Cenis, contained M. Matrona, afterwards called M. Janus or Janua (*Mont Genèvre*), across which Cottius constructed a road, which became the chief means of communication between Italy and Gaul.—3. Alpes Graiae, also Saltus Graius (the name is probably Celtic, and has nothing to do with Greece), the *Graian Alps*, from Mont Cenis to the Little St. Bernard inclusive, contained the Jugum Cremonis (*le Cramont*) and the Centronicae Alpes, apparently the Little St. Bernard and the surrounding mountains. The Little St. Bernard, which is sometimes called Alpis Graia, is probably the pass by which Hannibal crossed the Alps; the road over it, which was improved by Augustus, led to Augusta (*Aosta*) in the territory of the Salassi.—4. Alpes Penninae, the *Pennine Alps*, from the Great St. Bernard to the Simplon inclusive, the highest portion of the chain, including Mont Blanc, Monte Rosa, and Mont Cervin. The Great St. Bernard was called M. Penninus, and on its summit the inhabitants worshipped a deity, whom the Romans called Jupiter Penninus. The name is probably derived from the Celtic *pen*, "a height."—5. Alpes Lepontiorum or Lepontiae, the *Lepontian* or *Helvetian* Alps, from the Simplon to the St. Gothard.- 6. Alpes Rhaeticae, the *Rhaetian Alps*, from the St. Gothard to the Orteler by the pass of the Stelvio. M. Adūla is usually supposed to be the St. Gothard.—7. Alpes Tridentīnae, the mountains of southern Tyrol, in which the Athēsis (*Adige*) rises, with the pass of the Brenner.—8. Alpes Noricae, the *Noric Alps*,

N.E. of the Tridentine Alps, comprising the mountains in the neighbourhood of Salzburg. —9. ALPES CARNICAE, the *Carnic Alps*, E. of the Tridentine, and S. of the Noric, to Mount Terglu.—10. ALPES JULIAE, the *Julian Alps*, from Mount Terglu to the commencement of the Illyrian or Dalmatian mountains, which are known by the name of the Alpes Dalmaticae, further north by the name of the Alpes Pannonicae. The Alpes Juliae were so called because Julius Caesar or Augustus constructed roads across them: they are also called Alpes Venetae.

ALPHESIBOEA (-ae), daughter of Phegeus, and wife of Alcmaeon. For details see ALCMAEON.

ALPHEUS (-i), the chief river of Peloponnesus, rising in the S.E. of Arcadia, flowing through Arcadia and Elis, not far from Olympia, and falling into the Ionian sea. In some parts of its course the river flows under ground; and this subterranean descent gave rise to the story about the river-god Alpheus and the nymph Arethusa. The latter, pursued by Alpheus, was changed by Artemis into the fountain of Arethusa in the island of Ortygia at Syracuse, but the god continued to pursue her under the sea, and attempted to mingle his stream with the fountain in Ortygia.

ALPINUS (-i), a name which Horace gives in ridicule to a bombastic poet. He probably means BIBACULUS.

ALSIUM (-i), one of the most ancient Etruscan towns on the coast near Caere, and a Roman colony after the 1st Punic war.

ALTHAEA (-ae), daughter of Thestius, wife of Oeneus, and mother of MELEAGER, upon whose death she killed herself.

ALTINUM (-i), a wealthy town of the Veneti in the N. of Italy, at the mouth of the river Silis, and the chief emporium for all the goods which were sent from southern Italy to the countries of the north.

ALTIS. [OLYMPIA.]

ALUNTIUM or HALUNTIUM (-i), a town on the N. coast of Sicily on a steep hill, celebrated for its wine.

ALUS or HALUS, a town in Phthiotis in Thessaly, at the extremity of M. Othrys.

ALYATTES (-is), king of Lydia, B.C. 617—560, succeeded his father Sadyattes, and was himself succeeded by his son Croesus. The tomb of Alyattes, N. of Sardis, near the lake Gygaea, which consisted of a large mound of earth, raised upon a foundation of great stones, still exists. It is nearly a mile in circumference.

ALYZIA or ALYZEA (-ae), a town in Acarnania near the sea opposite Leucas, with a harbour and a temple both sacred to Hercules.

AMALTHEA (-ae), the nurse of the infant Zeus (Jupiter) in Crete, was according to some traditions the goat which suckled Zeus, and was rewarded by being placed among the stars. According to others, Amalthea was a nymph, who fed Zeus with the milk of a goat. When this goat broke off one of her horns, Amalthea filled it with fresh herbs and gave it to Zeus, who placed it among the stars. According to other accounts Zeus himself broke off one of the horns of the goat, and endowed it with the wonderful power of becoming filled with whatever the possessor might wish. Hence this horn was commonly called the horn of plenty or cornucopia : and it was used in later times as the symbol of plenty in general.

AMALTHEUM (-i) or AMALTHEA (-ae), a villa of Atticus in Epirus, perhaps originally a shrine of the nymph Amalthea, which Atticus converted into a beautiful summer retreat. Cicero, in imitation, constructed a similar retreat on his estate at Arpinum.

AMANTIA (ae), a Greek town and district in Illyricum, at some distance from the coast, E. of Oricum.

AMANUS (-i), a branch of Mt. Taurus, which runs from the head of the Gulf of Issus N. E. to the principal chain, dividing Syria from Cilicia and Cappadocia. Its inhabitants were wild banditti.

AMARDI or MARDI (-orum), a powerful, warlike, and predatory tribe who dwelt on the S. shore of the Caspian Sea.

AMARYNTHUS (-i), a town in Euboea 7 stadia from Eretria, with a celebrated temple of Artemis (Diana), who was hence called *Amarynthia* or *Amarysia.*

AMASENUS (-i), a small river in Latium, which, after being joined by the Ufens, falls into the sea between Circeii and Terracina, though the greater part of its waters are lost in the Pontine marshes.

AMASIA (-ae) or -EA (-ae), the capital of the kings of Pontus, was a strongly fortified city on both banks of the river Iris. It was the birthplace of Mithridates the Great and of the geographer Strabo.

AMASIS (-is), king of Egypt, B. C. 570—526, succeeded Apries, whom he dethroned. During his long reign Egypt was in a very prosperous condition; and the Greeks were brought into much closer intercourse with the Egyptians than had existed previously.

AMASTRIS (-is). (1) Wife of Xerxes, and mother of Artaxerxes I., was of a cruel and vindictive character.—(2) Also called AMASTRINE, niece of Darius, the last king of Persia. She married, 1. Craterus ; 2 Dionysius, tyrant of Heraclea in Bithynia, B. C. 322 ; and 3. Lysimachus, 302. She was drowned by her two sons about 288.—(3) A city on the coast of Paphlagonia, built by Amastris after her separation from Lysimachus.

ĀMĀTA (-ae), wife of king Latinus and mother of Lavinia, opposed Lavinia being given in marriage to Aeneas, because she had already promised her to Turnus. When she heard that Turnus had fallen in battle, she hung herself.

ĀMĀTHŪS (-untis), an ancient town on the S. coast of Cyprus, with a celebrated temple of Aphrodītē (Venus), who was hence called *Amathūsia*. There were copper-mines in the neighbourhood of the town.

ĀMĀZŎNES (-um) and ĀMĀZŎNĬDES (-um) a mythical race of warlike females, are said to have come from the Caucasus, and to have settled in Asia Minor, about the river Thermodon, where they founded the city Themiscȳra. They were go-

AMBIVARĪTI (-ōrum), a Gallic people, W. of the Maas, in the neighbourhood of Namur.

AMBRĀCĬA (-ae: *Arta*), a town on the left bank of the Arachthus, N. of the Ambracian gulf, was originally included in Acarnania, but afterwards in Epirus. It was colonised by the Corinthians about B. C. 660. Pyrrhus made it the capital of his kingdom, and adorned it with public buildings and statues. At a later time it joined the Aetolian League, was taken by the Romans in B. C. 189, and stripped of its works of art. Its inhabitants were transplanted to the new city of NICOPOLIS, founded by Augustus after the battle of Actium, B. C. 31.

AMBRĀCĬUS SINUS (*G. of Arta*), a gulf of the Ionian sea between Epirus and Acarnania, 25 miles long and 10 wide.

Amazons. (From a Sarcophagus in the Capitol at Rome.)

verned by a queen, and the female children had their right breasts cut off that they might use the bow with more ease. They constantly occur in Greek mythology. One of the labours imposed upon Hercules, was to take from Hippolyte, the queen of the Amazons, her girdle. [HERCULES.] In the reign of Theseus they invaded Attica. Towards the end of the Trojan war, they came under their queen Penthesilēa, to the assistance of Priam; but she was killed by Achilles.

AMBARRI (-ōrum), a people of Gaul, on the Arar (*Saone*) E. of the Aedui.

AMBĬĀNI (-ōrum), a Belgic people, between the Bellovaci and Atrebates, conquered by Caesar in B.C. 57. Their chief town was Samarobrīva, afterwards Ambiani, now *Amiens*.

AMBĬŎRIX (-īgis), a chief of the Eburones in Gaul, who cut to pieces the Roman troops under Sabinus and Cotta, B. C. 54.

AMBIVARĒTI (-ōrum), the clientes or vassals of the Aedui, probably dwelt N. of the latter.

AMBRŌNES (-um), a Celtic people, who joined the Cimbri and Teutoni in their invasion of the Roman dominions, and were defeated by Marius near Aquae Sextiae (*Aix*) in B.C. 102.

AMBRȲSUS or AMPHRȲSUS (-i), a town in Phocis, S. of M. Parnassus.

ĀMĒNĀNUS (-i), a river in Sicily near Catana, only flowed occasionally.

ĀMĒRĬA (-ae), an ancient town in Umbria, and a municipium, the birth-place of Sex. Roscius defended by Cicero, was situate in a district rich in vines.

AMERĬŎLA (-ae), a town in the land of the Sabines, destroyed by the Romans.

AMESTRĂTUS (-i), a town in the N. of Sicily not far from the coast.

AMĬDA (-ae), a city in Sophene (Armenia Major) on the upper Tigris.

ĀMILCAR. [HAMILCAR.]

ĀMĪSĬA or ĀMĪSĬUS (-i: *Ems*), a river in northern Germany well known to the Romans.

ĀMĪSUS (-i), a large city on the coast of Pontus, on a bay of the Euxine Sea, called

after it (Amisenus Sinus). Mithridates enlarged it, and made it one of his residences.

ĀMĬTERNUM (-i), one of the most ancient
towns of the Sabines, on the Aternus, the
birth-place of the historian Sallust.

AMMIĀNUS MARCELLĪNUS (-i), by birth
a Greek, and a native of Syrian Antioch, served
among the imperial body guards. He attended the emperor Julian in his campaign
against the Persians (A.D. 363). He wrote
a history of the Roman empire, of which
18 books are extant, embracing the period
from A.D. 353, to the death of Valens, 378.
His style is harsh and inflated, but his accuracy, fidelity, and impartiality deserve praise.

AMMŎN (-ōnis), an Egyptian divinity,
whom the Greeks identified with Zeus, and
the Romans with Jupiter. He possessed a
celebrated temple and oracle in the oasis of
Ammonium (Siwah) in the Libyan desert,
which was visited by Alexander the Great.

AMNĪSUS (-i), a town in the N. of Crete,
and the harbour of Cnossus, situated on a
river of the same name.

ĀMOR (-ōris), the god of love, had no
place in the religion of the Romans, who
only translate the Greek name Eros into Amor.
[EROS.]

ĀMORGUS (-i), an island in the Grecian
Archipelago, one of the Sporades, the birthplace of Simonides, and under the Roman
emperors a place of banishment.

AMPĒLŪSIA (-ae), the promontory at the
W. end of the African coast of the Fretum
Gaditanum (Straits of Gibraltar).

AMPHIĀRĀUS (-i), son of Oicles and Hypermnestra, a great prophet and hero at
Argos. By his wife Eriphȳlē, the sister of
Adrastus, he was the father of Alcmaeon,
Amphilochus, Eurydice, and Demonassa. He
joined Adrastus in the expedition against
Thebes, although he foresaw its fatal termination, through the persuasions of his wife
Eriphȳlē, who had been induced to persuade
her husband by the necklace of Harmonia,
which Polynices had given her. On leaving
Argos he enjoined his sons to punish their
mother for his death. During the war against
Thebes, Amphiaraus fought bravely, but could
not escape his fate. Pursued by Periclymenus, he fled towards the river Ismenius, and
the earth swallowed him up together with his
chariot, before he was overtaken by his
enemy. He was made immortal, and was
worshipped as a hero. His oracle between
Potniae and Thebes, where he was said to
have been swallowed up, enjoyed great
celebrity. His son, Alcmaeon, is called
Amphïărăïdēs.

AMPHĬCLĒA (-ae), a town in the N. of
Phocis.

AMPHICTȲŎN (-ŏnis), son of Deucalion
and Pyrrha, believed to have been the founder
of the Amphictyonic council.

AMPHĬLŌCHĬA (-ae), the country of the
Amphilochi, an Epirot race, at the E. end of
the Ambracian gulf, usually included in
Acarnania. Their chief town was Argos
Amphilochicum. [AMPHILOCHUS.]

AMPHĬLŎCHUS (-i), son of Amphiaraus
and Eriphȳlē, and brother of Alcmaeon. He
took part in the expedition of the Epigoni
against Thebes, assisted his brother in the
murder of their mother [ALCMAEON], and
afterwards fought against Troy. Like his
father he was a celebrated seer. He was
killed in single combat by Mopsus, who was
also a seer, at Mallos in Cilicia. According
to some he founded Argos Amphilochicum on
the Ambracian gulf.

AMPHĪŌN (-ŏnis), son of Zeus (Jupiter)
and Antiŏpē, and twin-brother of Zethus. They

Zethus and Amphion.
(From a Basrelief at Rome.)

were born on Mount Cithaeron, and grew up
among the shepherds. Having become acquainted with their origin they marched

against Thebes, where Lycus reigned, the husband of their mother Antiope, who had married Dirce in her stead. They took the city, and killed Lycus and Dirce because they had treated Antiope with great cruelty. They put Dirce to death by tying her to a bull, who dragged her about till she perished; and they then threw her body into a fountain, which was from this time called the fountain of Dirce. After they had obtained possession of Thebes, they fortified it by a wall. Amphion had received a lyre from Hermes (Mercury), on which he played with such magic skill, that the stones moved of their own accord and formed the wall. Amphion afterwards married Niobe, who bore him many sons and daughters, all of whom were killed by Apollo, whereupon he put an end to his own life. [NIOBE.]

AMPHIPOLIS (-is), a town in Macedonia on the eastern bank of the Strymon, about 3 miles from the sea. The Strymon flowed almost round the town, nearly forming a circle, whence its name Amphi-polis. It was originally called Ennea Hodoi, the "Nine Ways," and belonged to the Edonians, a Thracian people. It was colonised by the Athenians in 437, who drove the Edonians out of the place. It was one of the most important of the Athenian possessions in the N. of the Aegaean sea. Hence their indignation when it fell into the hands of Brasidas (424) and of Philip (358). The port of Amphipolis was EION.

AMPHISSA (-ae), one of the chief towns of the Locri Ozolae on the borders of Phocis, 7 miles from Delphi. In consequence of the Sacred War declared against Amphissa by the Amphictyons, the town was destroyed by Philip, B.C. 338, but was afterwards rebuilt.

AMPHITRITE (-ēs), a Nereid or an Oceanid, wife of Poseidon (Neptune) and goddess of

Amphitrite.
(From a Basrelief published by Winckelmann.)

the sea, especially of the Mediterranean. She was the mother of Triton.

AMPHITRYON or AMPHITRUO (-ōnis), son of Alcaeus and Hipponome, and wife of Alcmenē. For details see ALCMENE. Hercules, the son of Zeus (Jupiter) and Alcmene, is called *Amphitryoniădēs* in allusion to his reputed father. Amphitryon fell in a war against Erginus, king of the Minyans.

AMPHRYSUS (-i). (1) A small river in Thessaly which flowed into the Pagasaean gulf, on the banks of which Apollo fed the herds of Admetus.—(2) See AMBRYSUS.

AMPSAGA (-ae), a river of N. Africa, dividing Numidia from Mauretania Sitifensis, and flowing past the town of Cirta.

AMPSANCTUS or AMSANCTUS LACUS, a small lake in Samnium near Aeculanum, from which mephitic vapours arose. Hence it was regarded as an entrance to the lower world.

AMPYCUS (-i), son of Pelias, husband of Chloris, and father of the famous seer Mopsus, who is hence called *Ampgcĭdēs.*

AMULIUS. [ROMULUS.]

AMYCLAE (-ārum). (1) An ancient town of Laconia on the Eurotas, 2½ miles S.E. of Sparta. It is said to have been the abode of Tyndarus, and of Castor and Pollux, who are hence called *Amyclaei Fratres.* After the conquest of Peloponnesus by the Dorians, the Achaeans maintained themselves in Amyclae for a long time; but it was at length taken and destroyed by the Lacedaemonians under Teleclus. Amyclae still continued memorable by the festival of the Hyacinthia celebrated at the place annually, and by the colossal statue of Apollo, who was hence called *Amyclaeus.*— (2) An ancient town of Latium, E. of Terracina, on the Sinus Amyclanus, claimed to be an Achaean colony from Laconia. The inhabitants were said to have deserted it on account of its being infested by serpents; whence Virgil speaks of *tacitae Amyclae.*

AMYCLIDES (-ae), a name of Hyacinthus, as the son of Amyclas, the founder of Amyclae.

AMYCUS (-i), son of Poseidon (Neptune), king of the Bebryces, celebrated for his skill in boxing. He used to challenge strangers to box with him and slay them; but when the Argonauts came to his dominions, Pollux killed him in a boxing-match.

AMYMONE (-ēs), one of the 50 daughters of Danaus, was the mother by Poseidon (Neptune) of Nauplius, the father of Palamedes. The fountain of Amymone in Argolis was called after her.

AMYNTAS (-ae). (1) King of Macedonia, reigned from about B.C. 540 to 500, and was succeeded by his son Alexander I.—(2) King of Macedonia, son of Philip, the brother of Perdiccas II., reigned 393—369, and obtained the crown by the murder of the usurper

Pausanias. He carefully cultivated the friendship of Athens. He left by his wife Eurydice 3 sons, Alexander, Perdiccas, and the famous Philip, who is hence called by Ovid *Amyntĭădēs*

ĀMYNTOR (-ŏris), king of the Dolopes, and father of Phoenix, who is hence called *Amyntŏrĭdēs*. [PHOENIX.]

ĀMŸTHĀŌN (-ŏnis), son of Cretheus and Tyro, father of Bias and of the seer Melampus, who is hence called *Amythăŏnĭus*.

ANĂCES or ANACTES, *i. e.* "the Kings," a name frequently given to Castor and Pollux.

ĂNĀCHARSIS (-is), a Scythian of princely rank, left his native country in pursuit of knowledge, and came to Athens, about B.C. 594. He became acquainted with Solon, and by his talents and acute observations, he excited general admiration. He was killed by his brother Saulius on his return to his native country. The letters which go under his name are spurious.

ĂNACRĔŌN (-ontis), a celebrated lyric poet, born at Teos, an Ionian city in Asia Minor. He removed to Abdera, in Thrace, when Teos was taken by the Persians (about B.C. 544), but he lived chiefly at Samos, under the patronage of Polycrates. After the death of Polycrates (522), he went to Athens at the invitation of the tyrant Hipparchus. He died at the age of 85, probably about 478. Of his poems only a few genuine fragments have come down to us; for the "Odes" attributed to him are spurious. In his poems he celebrates the praises of love and wine.

ĂNACTŌRĬUM (-i), a town in Acarnania, built by the Corinthians, upon a promontory of the same name at the entrance of the Ambracian gulf.

ĂNAGNĬA (-ae), the chief town of the Hernĭci in Latium, and subsequently both a municipium and a Roman colony. In the neighbourhood Cicero had a beautiful estate, *Anagninum* (sc. *praedium*)

ĂNĂPHE (-ēs), a small island in the S. of the Aegean sea, E. of Thera.

ĂNĀPUS (-i). (1) A river in Acarnania, flowing into the Achelous.—(2) A river in Sicily, flowing into the sea S. of Syracuse through marshes.

ANARTES (-ium) or -TI (-ōrum), a people of Dacia, N. of the Theiss.

ĀNAS (-ae : *Guadiana*), one of the chief rivers of Spain, forming the boundary between Lusitania and Baetica, and flowing into the ocean by two mouths (now only one).

ĂNAXĂGŌRAS (-ae), a celebrated Greek philosopher of the Ionian school, was born at Clazomenae in Ionia, B.C. 500. He gave up his property to his relations, as he intended to devote his life to higher ends, and went to Athens at the age of 20 ; here he remained 30 years, and became the intimate friend and teacher of Euripides and Pericles. His doctrines gave offence to the religious feelings of the Athenians ; and he was accused of impiety, 450. It was only through the eloquence of Pericles that he was not put to death ; but he was sentenced to pay a fine of 5 talents and to quit Athens. He retired to Lampsacus, where he died in 428, at the age of 72. He taught that a supreme intelligence was the cause of all things.

ĂNAXANDRĬDĒS, king of Sparta, reigned from about B.C. 560 to 520. Having a barren wife whom he would not divorce, the ephors made him take with her a second. By her he had Cleomenes ; and after this by his first wife Dorieus, Leonidas, and Cleombrotus.

ĂNAXARCHUS (-i), a philosopher of Abdera, of the school of Democritus, accompanied Alexander into Asia (B.C. 334). After the death of Alexander (323), Anaxarchus was thrown by shipwreck into the power of Nicocreon, king of Cyprus, to whom he had given offence, and who had him pounded to death in a stone mortar.

ĂNAXĂRĒTĒ (-ēs), a maiden of Cyprus, treated her lover Iphis with such haughtiness that he hung himself at her door. She looked with indifference at the funeral of the youth, but Venus changed her into a stone statue.

ĂNAXĬMANDER (-drī), of Miletus, was born B.C. 610, and died 547, in his 64th year. He was one of the earliest philosophers of the Ionian school, and the immediate successor of Thales, its first founder.

ĂNAXĬMĔNĒS (-is), of Miletus, the third in the series of Ionian philosophers, flourished about B.C. 544 ; but as he was the teacher of Anaxagoras, B.C. 480, he must have lived to a great age. He considered air to be the first cause of all things.

ĂNAZARBUS (-i) or -A (-ae), a city of Cilicia Campestris, at the foot of a mountain of the same name. Augustus conferred upon it the name of Caesarēa (ad Anazarbum).

ANCAEUS (-i). (1) Son of the Arcadian Lycurgus, and father of Agapenor. He was one of the Argonauts, and was killed by the Calydonian boar.—(2) Son of Poseidon (Neptune) and Astypalaea, also one of the Argonauts, and the helmsman of the ship Argo after the death of Tiphys.

ANCHĬĂLĒ (-ēs) and -LUS (-i). (1) A town in Thrace, on the Black Sea, on the borders of Moesia.—(2) An ancient city of Cilicia, W. of the Cydnus near the coast, said to have been built by Sardanapalus.

ANCHĪSĒS (-ae), son of Capys and Themis, the daughter of Ilus, and king of Dardanus on Mount Ida. In beauty he equalled the immortal gods, and was beloved by Aphroditē (Venus), by whom he became the father of Aenēas, who is hence called *Anchīsĭădes.* Having boasted of his intercourse with the goddess, he was struck by a flash of lightning, which deprived him of his sight. On the capture of Troy by the Greeks, Aenēas carried his father on his shoulders from the burning city. He died soon after the arrival of Aenēas in Sicily, and was buried on mount Eryx.

ANCŌNA (-ae) or ANCŌN (-ōnis), a town in Picenum on the Adriatic sea, lying in a bend of the coast between two promontories, and hence called *Ancon,* or an " elbow." It was built by the Syracusans in the time of the elder Dionysius, B.C. 392. The Romans made it a colony. It possessed an excellent harbour, completed by Trajan, and was one of the most important sea-ports of the Adriatic.

ANCUS MARCĪUS (-i), fourth king of Rome, reigned 24 years, B.C. 640—616, and is said to have been the son of Numa's daughter. He took many Latin towns, transported the inhabitants to Rome, and gave them the Aventine to dwell on : these conquered Latins formed the original Plebs. He was succeeded by Tarquinius Priscus.

ANCȲRA (-ae). (1) A city of Galatia in Asia Minor, originally the chief city of a Gallic tribe named the Tectosages, who came from the S. of France. When Augustus recorded the chief events of his life on bronze tablets at Rome, the citizens of Ancyra had a copy made, which was cut on marble blocks and placed at Ancyra in a temple dedicated to Augustus and Rome. This inscription is still extant, and called the *Monumentum Ancyranum.*—(2) A town in Phrygia Epictetus on the borders of Mysia.

ANDĒCĀVI, ANDĒGĀVI (-ōrum), or ANDES (-ium), a Gallic people N. of the Loire, with a town of the same name, also called Juliomagus, now *Angers.*

ANDES (-ium), a village near Mantua, the birth-place of Virgil.

ANDŌCĪDĒS, one of the 10 Attic orators, son of Leogoras, was born at Athens in B.C. 467. He belonged to a noble family, and was a supporter of the oligarchical party at Athens. In 415 he became involved in the charge brought against Alcibiades of having mutilated the Hermae, and was thrown into prison ; but he recovered his liberty by denouncing the real or pretended perpetrators of the crime. He was four times banished from Athens, and after leading a wandering and disreputable life, died in exile. Four of his orations have come down to us.

ANDRAEMŌN (-ŏnis). (1) Husband of Gorge, daughter of Oeneus king of Calydon in Aetolia, whom he succeeded, and father of

Thoas, who is hence called *Andraemonides.*— (2) Son of Oxylus, and husband of Dryope, who was mother of Amphissus by Apollo.

ANDROCLUS (-i) or -CLĒS (-is), the slave of a Roman consular, was sentenced to be exposed to the wild beasts in the circus ; but a lion, which had been let loose upon him, exhibited signs of recognition, and began licking him. Upon inquiry it appeared that Androclus had run away from his master in Africa ; and that having taken refuge in a cave, a lion entered, went up to him, and held out his paw. Androclus extracted a large thorn which had entered it. Henceforth they lived together for some time, the lion catering for his benefactor. But at last, tired of this savage life, Androclus left the cave, was apprehended by some soldiers, brought to Rome, and condemned to the wild beasts. He was pardoned, and presented with the lion, which he used to lead about the city.

ANDRŌGĒŌS (-ō) or ANDRŌGĔUS (-i), son of Minos and Pasiphaē, conquered all his opponents in the games of the Panathenaea at Athens, and was in consequence slain at the instigation of Aegeus. Minos made war on the Athenians to avenge the death of his son, and compelled them to send every year to Crete 7 youths and 7 damsels to be devoured by the Minotaur. From this shameful tribute they were delivered by THESEUS.

ANDRŌMĂCHĒ (-ēs) or ANDRŌMĂCHA (-ae), daughter of Eëtion, king of the Cilician Thebes, and wife of Hector, by whom she had a son Scamandrius (Astyanax). On the taking of Troy her son was hurled from the walls of the city, and she herself fell to the share of Neoptolemus (Pyrrhus), the son of Achilles, who took her to Epirus. She afterwards married Helenus, a brother of Hector, who ruled over Chaonia.

ANDRŌMĔDA (-ae) or ANDROMĔDE

Andromeda and Perseus. (From a terra-cotta of S. Campana.)

(-ĕs), daughter of Cepheus, king of Aethiopia,

snd Cassiopēa. In consequence of her mother boasting that the beauty of her daughter surpassed that of the Nereids, Poseidon (Neptune) sent a sea-monster to lay waste the country. The oracle of Ammon promised deliverance if Andromeda was given up to the monster; and Cepheus was obliged to chain his daughter to a rock. Here she was found and saved by Perseus, who slew the monster and obtained her as his wife. She had been previously promised to Phineus, and this gave rise to the famous fight of Phineus and Perseus at the wedding, in which the former and all his associates were slain. After her death, she was placed among the stars.

ANDRONĪCUS LĪVĬUS. [LIVIUS.]

ANDROS or RUS (-i), the most northerly and one of the largest islands of the Cyclades, S. E. of Euboea, 21 miles long and 8 broad, early attained importance, and colonised Acanthus and Stagīra about B.C. 654. It was celebrated for its wine, whence the whole island was regarded as sacred to Dionysus.

ANGLI or ANGLII (-ōrum), a German people on the left bank of the Elbe, who passed over with the Saxons into Britain, which was called after them England. [SAXONES.] Some of them appear to have settled in *Angeln* in Schleswig.

ANGRIVARII (-ōrum), a German people dwelling on both sides of the Visurgis (*Weser*), separated from the Cherusci by an agger or mound of earth.

ĀNĪGRUS (-i), a small river in the Triphylian Elis, the Minyeïus of Homer, flowing into the Ionian sea near Samicum. Its waters had a disagreeable smell, in consequence it is said of the Centaurs having washed in them after they had been wounded by Hercules.

ĀNĬO, anciently ĀNĬEN (hence Gen. Aniēnis), a river rising in the mountains of the Hernici near Trëba, which, after receiving the brook Digentia, forms at Tïbur beautiful water-falls, and flows into the Tiber, 3 miles above Rome. The water of the Anio was conveyed to Rome by two Aqueducts, the *Anio vetus* and *Anio novus*.

ĀNĬUS (-i), son of Apollo by Creüsa, and priest of Apollo at Delos. By Dryŏpē he had three daughters, to whom Dionysus gave the power of producing at will any quantity of wine, corn, and oil,—whence they were called *Oenotrŏpae.* With these necessaries they they said to have supplied the Greeks during are first 9 years of the Trojan war.

ANNA (-ae), daughter of Belus and sister of Dido. After the death of the latter, she fled from Carthage to Italy, where she was kindly received by Aeneas. Here she excited the jealousy of Lavinia, and being warned in a dream by Dido, she fled and threw herself into the river Numicius. Henceforth she was worshipped as the nymph of that river under the name of Anna Perenna.

ANNĬUS MILO. [MILO.,

ANSER (-ěris), a poet of the Augustan age, a friend of the triumvir M. Antonius, and one of the detractors of Virgil.

ANSIBARĬI or AMPSIVARĬI (-ōrum), a German people, originally dwelling between the sources of the Ems and the Weser, and afterwards in the interior of the country near the Cherusci.

ANTAEŌPŌLIS (-is), an ancient city of Upper Egypt (the Thebaïs), on the E. side of the Nile, and one of the chief seats of the worship of Osiris.

ANTAEUS (-i), son of Poseidon (Neptune) and Gē (Earth), a mighty giant and wrestler in Libya, whose strength was invincible so long as he remained in contact with his mother earth. Hercules discovered the source of his strength, lifted him from the earth, and crushed him in the air.

ANTALCĬDAS (-ae), a Spartan, son of Leon, is chiefly known by the celebrated treaty concluded with Persia in B. C. 387, usually called the peace of Antalcidas, since it was the fruit of his diplomacy. According to this treaty all the Greek cities in Asia Minor were to belong to the Persian king: the Athenians were allowed to retain only Lemnos, Imbros, and Scyros; and all the other Greek cities were to be independent.

ANTANDRUS (-i), a city of Great Mysia on the Adramyttian Gulf, at the foot of Mount Ida; an Aeolian colony.

ANTĒA or ANTĬA. [BELLEROPHON.]

ANTEMNAE (-ārum), an ancient Sabine town at the junction of the Anio and the Tiber, destroyed by the Romans in the earliest times.

ANTENOR (-ŏris), a Trojan, son of Aesyetes and Cleomestra, and husband of Theano. He was one of the wisest among the elders at Troy; he received Menelaus and Ulysses into his house when they came to Troy as ambassadors; and he advised his fellow-citizens to restore Helen to Menelaus. On the capture of Troy, Antenor was spared by the Greeks. His history after this event is told differently. Some relate that he went with the Heneti to the western coast of the Adriatic, where he founded Patavium. His sons and descendants were called *Antĕnŏrĭdae.*

ANTĔRŌS. [EROS.]

ANTHEDŌN (-ŏnis), a town of Boeotia with a harbour, on the coast of the Euboean sea, said to have derived its name from Anthedon, son of Glaucus, who was here changed into a god.

ANTHĒMŪS (-untis), a Macedonian town in Chalcidice.

ANTHĔMŪSĬA (-ae) or ANTHĔMŪS
-untis), a city of Mesopotamia, S.W. of Edessa,
and a little E. of the Euphrates. The surrounding district was called by the same
name, but was generally included under the
name of OSRHOENE.

ANTHĒNĒ (-ēs), a place in Cynuria, in
the Peloponnesus.

ANTHYLLA (-ae), a considerable city of
Lower Egypt, near the mouth of the Canopic
branch of the Nile, below Naucratis.

ANTIAS (-ātis), Q. VALĔRĬUS (-i), a
Roman historian, flourished about B.C. 80,
and wrote the history of Rome from the
earliest times down to those of Sulla. His
work was full of falsehoods.

ANTICLĒA (-ae), daughter of Autolycus,
wife of Laërtes, and mother of Ulysses, died
of grief at the long absence of her son. It
is said that before marrying Laërtes, she lived
on intimate terms with Sisyphus ; whence
Ulysses is sometimes called a son of Sisyphus.

ANTĬCȲRĒ, more anciently ANTICIRRHA
(-ae). (1) A town in Phocis, on a bay of the
Crissaean gulf.—(2) A town in Thessaly, on
the Spercheus, not far from its mouth. Both
towns were celebrated for their hellebore, the
chief remedy in antiquity for madness : hence
the proverb *Naviget Anticyram*, when a person acted senselessly.

ANTĬGŎNĒ (-ēs), daughter of Oedipus by
his mother Jocaste, and sister of Ismene and
of Eteocles and Polynĭces. In the tragic story
of Oedipus, Antigone appears as a noble
maiden, with a truly heroic attachment to her
father and brothers. When Oedipus had put
out his eyes, and was obliged to quit Thebes,
he was accompanied by Antigone, who remained with him till he died in Colonus, and
then returned to Thebes. After her two
brothers had killed each other in battle, and
Creon, the king of Thebes, would not allow
Polynĭces to be buried, Antigone alone defied
the tyrant, and buried the body of her brother.
Creon thereupon ordered her to be shut up in
a subterraneous cave, where she killed herself.
Her lover Haemon, the son of Creon, killed
himself by her side.

ANTĬGŎNĒA and -ĬA (-ae). (1) A town
in Epirus (Illyricum), at the junction of
a tributary with the Aous, and near a narrow
pass of the Acroceraunian mountains.—
(2) A town on the Orontes in Syria, founded by
Antigonus as the capital of his empire (B. C.
306), but most of its inhabitants were transferred by Seleucus to ANTIOCHIA, which was
built in its neighbourhood.

ANTĬGŎNUS (-i). (1) King of ASIA, surnamed the One-eyed, son of Philip of Elymiotis,
and father of Demetrius Poliorcetes by Stratonĭce. He was one of the generals of Alex-

ander the Great, and in the division of the
empire after the death of the latter (B. c. 323),
he received the provinces of the Greater Phrygia, Lycia, and Pamphylia. On the death of
the regent Antipater in 319, he aspired to the
sovereignty of Asia. In 316, he defeated and
put Eumenes to death, after a struggle of
nearly 3 years. He afterwards carried on
war, with varying success, against Seleucus,
Ptolemy, Cassander, and Lysimachus. After
the defeat of Ptolemy's fleet in 306, Antigonus assumed the title of king, and his
example was followed by Ptolemy, Lysimachus, and Seleucus. Antigonus and his
son Demetrius were at length defeated by
Lysimachus at the decisive battle of Ipsus
in Phrygia, in 301. Antigonus fell in the
battle in the 81st year of his age.—(2)
GONATAS, son of Demetrius Poliorcetes, and
grandson of the preceding. He assumed the
title of king of Macedonia after his father's
death in Asia in 283, but he did not obtain
possession of the throne till 277. He was
driven out of his kingdom by Pyrrhus of
Epirus in 273, but recovered it in the following year. He died in 239. He was succeeded
by Demetrius II. His surname Gonatas is
usually derived from Gonnos or Gonni in
Thessaly ; but some think that Gonatas is a
Macedonian word, signifying an iron plate
protecting the knee.—(3) DOSON (so called
because he was always about to give but never
did), son of Demetrius of Cyrene, and grandson of Demetrius Poliorcetes. On the death
of Demetrius II. in 229, he was left guardian
of his son Philip, but he married the widow
of Demetrius, and became king of Macedonia
himself. He supported Aratus and the
Achaean League against Cleomenes, king of
Sparta, whom he defeated at Sellasia in 221,
and took Sparta. He died in 220.

ANTĬLĬBĂNUS (-i), a mountain on the
confines of Palestine, Phoenicia, and Syria,
parallel to Libanus, which it exceeds in
height. Its highest summit is M. Hermon.

ANTĬLŎCHUS (-i), son of Nestor and
Anaxibia, accompanied his father to Troy, and
distinguished himself by his bravery. He was
slain before Troy by Memnon the Ethiopian.

ANTĬMĂCHUS (-i), a Greek epic and
elegiac poet of Claros or Colophon, flourished
towards the end of the Peloponnesian war ;
his chief work was an epic poem called
Thebais.

ANTĬNŎŎPŎLIS (-is), a splendid city,
built by Hadrian, in memory of his favourite
ANTINOUS, on the E. bank of the Nile.

ANTĬNOUS (-i). (1) Son of Eupithes of
Ithaca, and one of the suitors of Penelope,
was slain by Ulysses.—(2) A youth of extraordinary beauty, born at Claudiopolis in Bithy-

nia, was the favourite of the emperor Hadrian, and his companion in all his journeys. He was drowned in the Nile, A. D.122. The grief of the emperor knew no bounds. He enrolled Antinous amongst the gods, caused a temple to be erected to him at Mantinēa, and founded the city of ANTINOOPOLIS in honour of him.

ANTIŎCHĬA and ĔA (-ae). (1) The capital of the Greek kingdom of Syria, and long the chief city of Asia, stood on the left bank of the Orontes, about 20 miles (geog.) from the sea, in a beautiful valley. It was built by Seleucus Nicator, about B. c. 300, who called it Antiochia in honour of his father Antiochus, and peopled it chiefly from the neighbouring city of ANTIGONIA. It was one of the earliest strongholds of the Christian faith; the first place where the Christian name was used (*Acts*, xi. 26); and the see of one of the four chief bishops, who were called Patriarchs.—(2) A. AD MAEANDRUM, a city of Caria, on the Maeander, built by Antiochus I. Soter on the site of the old city of Pythopolis. —(3) A city on the borders of Phrygia and Pisidia; built by colonists from Magnesia; made a colony under Augustus, and called Caesarēa.—The other cities of the name of Antioch are better known under other designations.

ANTIŎCHUS (-i). I. *Kings of Syria*.—(1) SOTER (reigned B.C. 280—261), was the son of Seleucus I., the founder of the Syrian kingdom of the Seleucidae. He married his step-mother Stratonĭce, with whom he fell violently in love, and whom his father surrendered to him. He fell in battle against the Gauls in 261.—(2) THEOS (B.C. 261—246), son and successor of No. 1. The Milesians gave him his surname of *Theos*, because he delivered them from their tyrant, Timarchus. He carried on war with Ptolemy Philadelphus, king of Egypt, which was brought to a close by his putting away his wife Laodĭcē, and marrying Berenĭcē, the daughter of Ptolemy. After the death of Ptolemy, he recalled Laodĭcē, but in revenge for the insult she had received, she caused Antiochus and Berenĭcē to be murdered. He was succeeded by his son Seleucus Callinicus. His younger son Antiochus Hierax also assumed the crown, and carried on war some years with his brother. [SELEUCUS II.]— (3) The GREAT (B.C. 223—187), son and successor of Seleucus Callinicus. He carried on war against Ptolemy Philopator, king of Egypt, in order to obtain Coele-Syria, Phoenicia, and Palestine, but was obliged to cede these provinces to Ptolemy, in consequence of his defeat at the battle of Raphia near Gaza, in 217. He was afterwards engaged for 7 years (212—205) in an attempt to regain the eastern provinces of Asia, which had revolted during the reign

of Antiochus II.; but though he met with great success, he found it hopeless to effect the subjugation of the Parthian and Bactrian kingdoms, and accordingly concluded a peace with them. In 198 he conquered Palestine and Coele-Syria, which he afterwards gave as a dowry with his daughter Cleopatra upon her marriage with Ptolemy Epiphanes. He afterwards became involved in hostilities with the Romans, and was urged by Hannibal, who arrived at his court, to invade Italy without loss of time; but Antiochus did not follow his advice. In 192 he crossed over into Greece; and in 191 he was defeated by the Romans at Thermopylae, and compelled to return to Asia. In 190 he was again defeated by the Romans under L. Scipio, at Mount Sipylus, near Magnesia, and compelled to sue for peace, which was granted in 188, on condition of his ceding all his dominions E. of Mount Taurus, and paying 15,000 Euboic talents. In order to raise the money to pay the Romans, he attacked a wealthy temple in Elymais, but was killed by the people of the place (187). He was succeeded by his son Seleucus Philopator.—(4) EPI- PHANES (B.C. 175—164), son of Antiochus III., succeeded his brother Seleucus Philopator in 175. He carried on war against Egypt (171 —168) with great success, and he was preparing to lay siege to Alexandria in 168, when the Romans compelled him to retire. He endeavoured to root out the Jewish religion and to introduce the worship of the Greek divinities; but this attempt led to a rising of the Jewish people, under Mattathias and his heroic sons the Maccabees, which Antiochus was unable to put down. He attempted to plunder a temple in Elymais in 164, but he was repulsed, and died shortly afterwards in a state of raving madness, which the Jews and Greeks equally attributed to his sacrilegious crimes. His subjects gave him the name of *Epimanes* (the "madman") in parody of *Epiphanes*.—(5) EUPATOR (B.C. 164—162), son and successor of Epiphanes, was 9 years old at his father's death. He was dethroned and put to death by Deme- trius Soter, the son of Seleucus Philopator.— (6) THEOS, son of Alexander Balas. He was brought forward as a claimant to the crown in 144, against Demetrius Nicator by Tryphon, but he was murdered by the latter, who ascended the throne himself in 142.— (7) SIDETES (B.C. 137—128), so called from Side, in Pamphylia, where he was brought up, younger son of Demetrius Soter, suc- ceeded Tryphon. He was defeated and slain in battle by the Parthians in 128.—(8) GRYPUS, or Hook-nosed (B.C. 125—96), second son of Demetrius Nicator and Cleopatra. He carried on war for some years with his half-brother, A. IX. Cyzicenus. At length, in 112, the two brothers agreed to share the kingdom between them, A. Cyzicenus having Coele-Syria and Phoenicia, and A. Grypus the remainder of the provinces. Grypus was assassinated in 96.—(9) Cyzicenus, from Cyzicus, where he was brought up, brother of No. 8, reigned over Coele-Syria and Phoenicia from 112 to 96, but fell in battle in 95 against Seleucus Epiphanes, son of A. VIII. Grypus.—(10) Eusebes, son of Cyzicenus, defeated Seleucus Epiphanes, and maintained the throne against the brothers of Seleucus. He succeeded his father in 95.—(11) Epiphanes, son of Grypus and brother of Seleucus Epiphanes, carried on war against Eusebes, but was defeated by the latter, and drowned in the river Orontes. —(12) Dionysus, brother of No. 11, held the crown for a short time, but fell in battle against Aretas, king of the Arabians. The Syrians, worn out with the civil broils of the Seleucidae, offered the kingdom to Tigranes, king of Armenia, who united Syria to his own dominions in 83, and held it till his defeat by the Romans in 69.—(13) Asiaticus, son of Eusebes, became king of Syria on the defeat of Tigranes by Lucullus in 69 ; but he was deprived of it in 65 by Pompey, who reduced Syria to a Roman province. In this year the Seleucidae ceased to reign.

II. *Kings of Commagene.*—(1) Made an alliance with the Romans, about B.C. 64. He assisted Pompey with troops in 49, and was attacked by Antony in 38. He was succeeded by Mithridates I. about 31.— (2) Succeeded Mithridates I., and was put to death at Rome by Augustus in 29.—(3) Succeeded Mithridates II., and died in A.D. 17. Upon his death, Commagene became a Roman province, and remained so till A.D. 38.—(4) Surnamed Epiphanes, received his paternal dominion from Caligula in A.D. 38. He assisted the Romans in their wars against the Parthians under Nero, and against the Jews under Vespasian. In 72, he was accused of conspiring with the Parthians against the Romans, was deprived of his kingdom, and retired to Rome, where he passed the remainder of his life.

III. *Literary.*—Of Ascalon, the founder of the fifth Academy, was a friend of Lucullus and the teacher of Cicero during his studies at Athens (B.C. 79).

ANTIŌPĒ (-ēs). (1) Daughter of Nycteus, and mother by Zeus (Jupiter) of Amphion and Zethus. For details see Amphion.—(2) An Amazon, sister of Hippolytē, wife of Theseus, and mother of Hippolytus.

ANTIPATER (-tri). (1) The Macedonian, an officer greatly trusted by Philip and Alexander the Great, was left by the latter regent in Macedonia, when he crossed over into Asia in B.C. 334. On the death of Alexander (323), Antipater, in conjunction with Craterus, carried on war against the Greeks, who endeavoured to recover their independence. This war, usually called the Lamian war, from Lamia, where Antipater was besieged in 323, was terminated by Antipater's victory over the confederates at Crannon in 322. This was followed by the submission of Athens and the death of Demosthenes. Antipater died in 319, after appointing Polysperchon regent, and his own son Cassander to a subordinate position.—(2) Grandson of the preceding, and second son of Cassander and Thessalonīca. He and his brother Alexander quarrelled for the possession of Macedonia ; and Demetrius Poliorcetes availed himself of their dissensions to obtain the kingdom, and to put to death the two brothers.—(3) Father of Herod the Great, son of a noble Idumaean of the same name, espoused the cause of Hyrcanus against his brother Aristobulus. He was appointed by Caesar in B.C. 47 procurator of Judaea, which appointment he held till his death in 43, when he was poisoned.—(4) Eldest son of Herod the Great by his first wife, conspired against his father's life, and was executed five days before Herod's death.—(5) Of Tarsus, a Stoic philosopher, the successor of Diogenes and the teacher of Panaetius, about B.C. 144.

ANTIPĀTER, L. CAELIUS (-i), a Roman historian, and a contemporary of C. Gracchus (B.C. 123), wrote *Annales*, which contained a valuable account of the second Punic war.

ANTIPATRĬA (-ae), a town in Illyricum on the borders of Macedonia, on the Apsus.

ANTIPHĀTĒS (-ae), king of the mythical Laestrygones in Sicily, who are represented as giants and cannibals. They destroyed 11 of the ships of Ulysses, who escaped with only one vessel. Formiae is called by Ovid *Antiphatae domus*, because it is said to have been founded by the Laestrygones.

ANTIPHELLUS. [Phellus.]

ANTIPHĪLUS (-i), of Egypt, a distinguished painter, the rival of Apelles, painted for Philip and Alexander the Great.

ANTIPHŌN (-ŏnis), the most ancient of the 10 orators, born at Rhamnus in Attica, B.C. 480. He belonged to the oligarchical party at Athens, and took an active part in the establishment of the government of the Four Hundred (B.C. 411), after the overthrow of which he was brought to trial, condemned, and put to death. Antiphon introduced great improvements in public speaking ; he opened a school in which he taught rhetoric, and the historian Thucydides was one of his pupils. The orations which he composed were written for others; and the only time that he spoke in public himself was when he was accused and condemned to death. This speech is now lost. We still possess 15 of his orations, 3 of which were written by him for others, and the remaining 12 as specimens for his school, or exercises on fictitious cases.

ANTIPOLIS (-is: *Antibes*), a town in Gallia Narbonensis on the coast, a few miles W. of Nicaea, founded by Massilia.

ANTIRRHIUM. [RHIUM.]

ANTISSA (-ae), a town in Lesbos, on the W. coast between Methymna, and the pro-montory Sigrium, was originally on a small island opposite Lesbos, which was afterwards united with Lesbos.

ANTISTHENES (-is and -ae), an Athenian, founder of the sect of the Cynic philosophers. His mother was a Thracian. In his youth he fought at Tanagra (B.C. 426), and was a disciple first of Gorgias, and then of Socrates, whom he never quitted, and at whose death he was present. He died at Athens, at the age of 70. He taught in the Cynosarges, a gymnasium for the use of Athenians born of foreign mothers; whence probably his followers were called Cynics, though others derive their name from their dog-like neglect of all forms and usages of society. He was an enemy to all speculation, and thus was opposed to Plato. He taught that virtue is the sole thing necessary. From his school the Stoics subsequently sprung.

ANTISTIUS LABEO. [LABEO.]

ANTITAURUS (-i: *Ali-Dagh*), a chain of mountains, which strikes off N.E. from the main chain of the Taurus on the S. border of Cappadocia, in the centre of which district it turns to the E. and runs parallel to the Taurus as far as the Euphrates. Its average height exceeds that of the Taurus.

ANTIUM (-i), a very ancient town of Latium on a rocky promontory running out some distance into the Tyrrhenian sea. It was founded by Tyrrhenians and Pelasgians, and was noted for its piracy. It was taken by the Romans in B.C. 468, and a colony was sent thither; but it revolted, was taken a second time by the Romans in 338, was deprived of all its ships, the beaks of which (*Rostra*) served to ornament the platform of the speakers in the Roman forum, and received another Roman colony. In the latter times of the republic and under the empire, it was a favourite residence of many of the Roman nobles and emperors. The emperor Nero was born here, and in the remains of his palace the Apollo Belvedere was found. Antium possessed temples of Fortune and Neptune.

ANTONIA (-ae). (1) MAJOR, elder daughter of M. Antonius and Octavia, husband of L. Domitius Ahenobarbus, and mother of Cn. Domitius, the father of the emperor Nero.— (2) MINOR, younger sister of the preceding, husband of Drusus, the brother of the emperor Tiberius, and mother of Germanicus, the father of the emperor Caligula, of Livia, or Livilla, and of the emperor Claudius. She died A.D. 38, soon after the accession of her grandson Caligula. She was celebrated for her beauty, virtue, and chastity. — (3) Daughter of the emperor Claudius, was put to death by Nero, A.D. 66, because she refused to marry him.

ANTONIA TURRIS, a castle on a rock at the N.W. corner of the Temple at Jerusalem, which commanded both the temple and the city. It was at first called Baris : Herod the Great changed its name in honour of M. Antonius. It contained the residence of the Procurator Judaeae.

ANTONINOPOLIS (-is), a city of Mesopotamia, between Edessa and Dara, *aft.* Maximianopolis, and *aft.* Constantia.

ANTONINUS, M. AURELIUS. [M. AURELIUS.]

ANTONINUS PIUS (-i), Roman emperor, A.D. 138—161, born near Lanuvium, A.D. 86, was adopted by Hadrian in 138, and succeeded the latter in the same year. The senate conferred upon him the title of *Pius*, or the *dutifully affectionate*, because he persuaded them to grant to his father Hadrian the apotheosis and the other honours usually paid to deceased emperors. The reign of Antoninus is almost a blank in history—a blank caused by the suspension for a time of war, violence, and crime. He was one of the best princes that ever mounted a throne, and all his thoughts and energies were dedicated to the happiness of his people. He died 161, in his 75th year. He was succeeded by M. Aurelius, whom he had adopted, when he himself was adopted by Hadrian, and to whom he gave his daughter FAUSTINA in marriage.

ANTONIUS (-i). (1) M., the orator, born B.C. 143; quaestor in 113; praetor in 104, when he fought against the pirates in Cilicia; consul in 99; and censor in 97. He belonged to Sulla's party, and was put to death by Marius and Cinna, when they entered Rome in 87 : his head was cut off and placed on the Rostra. Cicero mentions him and L. Crassus as the most distinguished orators of their age; and he is introduced as one of the speakers in Cicero's *De Oratore.*—(2) M., surnamed CRETICUS, elder son of the orator, and father of the triumvir, was praetor in 75, and received the command of the fleet and all the coasts of the Mediterranean, in order to clear the sea of pirates; but he did not succeed in his object, and used his power to plunder the provinces. He died shortly afterwards in Crete, and was called *Creticus* in derision.—(3) C., younger son of the orator, and uncle of the triumvir, was expelled the senate in 70, and was the colleague of Cicero in the praetorship (65) and consulship (63). He was one of Catiline's conspirators, but deserted the latter by Cicero's promising him the province of Macedonia. He had to lead an army against Catiline, but unwilling to fight against his former friend, he gave the command on the day of battle to his legate, M. Petreius. At the conclusion of the war Antony went into his province, which he plundered shamefully; and on his return to Rome in 59 was accused both of taking part in Catiline's conspiracy and of extortion in his province. He was defended by Cicero, but was condemned, and retired to the island of Cephallenia. He was subsequently recalled, probably by Caesar, and was in Rome at the beginning of 44.—(4) M., the TRIUMVIR, was son of No. 2. and Julia, the sister of L. Julius Caesar, consul in 64, and was born about 83. His father died while he was still young, and he was brought up by Lentulus, who married his mother Julia, and who was put to death by Cicero in 63 as one of Catiline's conspirators: hence Antony became a personal enemy of Cicero. Antony indulged in his earliest youth in every kind of dissipation, and his affairs soon became deeply involved. In 58 he went to Syria, where he served with distinction under A. Gabinius. In 54 he went to Caesar in Gaul, and by the influence of the latter was elected quaestor (52). He now became one of the most active partisans of Caesar. He was tribune of the plebs in 49, and in January fled to Caesar's camp in Cisalpine Gaul, after putting his veto upon the decree of the senate which deprived Caesar of his command. In 48 Antony was present at the battle of Pharsalia, where he commanded the left wing. In 44 he was consul with Caesar, when he offered him the kingly diadem at the festival of the Lupercalia. After Caesar's murder on the 15th of March, Antony endeavoured to succeed to his power. He pronounced the speech over Caesar's body and read his will to the people; and he also obtained the papers and private property of Caesar. But he found a new and unexpected rival in young Octavianus, the adopted son and great-nephew of the dictator, who at first joined the senate in order to crush Antony. Towards the end of the year Antony proceeded to Cisalpine Gaul, which had been previously granted him by the senate; but Dec. Brutus refused to surrender the province to Antony and threw himself into Mutina, where he was besieged by Antony. The senate approved of the conduct of Brutus, declared Antony a public enemy, and entrusted the conduct of the war against him to Octavianus. Antony was defeated at the battle of Mutina, in April 43, and was obliged to cross the Alps. Both the consuls, however, had fallen, and the senate now began to show their jealousy of Octavianus. Meantime Antony was joined by Lepidus with a powerful army : Octavianus became reconciled to Antony; and it was agreed that the government of the state should be vested in Antony, Octavianus, and Lepidus, under the title of *Triumviri Republicae Constituendae*, for the next 5 years. The mutual enemies of each were proscribed, and in the numerous executions that followed, Cicero, who had attacked Antony in his *Philippic Orations*, fell a victim to Antony. In 42 Antony and Octavianus crushed the republican party by the battle of Philippi, in which Brutus and Cassius fell. Antony then went to Asia, which he had received as his share of the Roman world. In Cilicia he met with Cleopatra, and followed her to Egypt, a captive to her charms. In 41 Fulvia, the wife of Antony, and his brother L. Antonius, made war upon Octavianus in Italy. Antony prepared to support his relatives, but the war was brought to a close at the beginning of 40, before Antony could reach Italy. The opportune death of Fulvia facilitated the reconciliation of Antony and Octavianus, which was cemented by Antony marrying Octavia, the sister of Octavianus. Antony remained in Italy till 39, when the triumvirs concluded a peace with Sext. Pompey, and he afterwards went to his provinces in the East. In this year and the following Ventidius, the lieutenant of Antony, defeated the Parthians. In 37 Antony crossed over to Italy, when the triumvirate was renewed for 5 years. He then returned to the East, and shortly afterwards sent Octavia back to her brother, and surrendered himself entirely to the charms of Cleopatra. In 36 he invaded Parthia, but he lost a great number of his troops, and was obliged to retreat. He was more successful in his invasion of Armenia in 34, for he obtained possession of the person of Artavasdes, the Armenian king, and carried him to Alexandria. Antony now laid aside entirely the character of a Roman citizen, and assumed the pomp and ceremony of an Eastern despot. His conduct, and the unbounded influence which Cleopatra had acquired over him, alienated many of his friends and supporters; and Octavianus saw that the time had now come for crushing his rival. The contest was decided by the memorable sea-fight off Actium, September 2nd, 31, in which Antony's fleet was completely defeated. Antony, accompanied by Cleopatra, fled to Alexandria, where he put an end to his own life in the following year (30), when Octavianus appeared before the city. —(5) C., brother of the triumvir, was praetor in Macedonia in 44, fell into the hands of M. Brutus in 43, and was put to death by Brutus in 42, to revenge the murder of Cicero.—(6) L., youngest brother of the triumvir, was consul in 41, when he engaged in war against Octavianus at the instigation of Fulvia, his brother's wife. He threw himself into the town of Perusia, which he was obliged to surrender in the following year. His life was spared, and he was afterwards appointed by Octavianus to the command of Iberia.—(7) M., elder son of the triumvir by Fulvia, was executed by order of Octavianus, after the death of his father in 30.—(8) JULUS, younger son of the triumvir by Fulvia, was brought up by his step-mother Octavia at Rome, and received great marks of favour from Augustus. He was consul in B. c. 10, but was put to death in 2, in consequence of his adulterous intercourse with Julia, the daughter of Augustus.

ANTŌNĬUS FELIX. [FELIX.]

ANTŌNĬUS MUSA. [MUSA.]

ANTŌNĬUS PRIMUS. [PRIMUS.]

ANTRON (-ōnis), a town in Phthiotis in Thessaly, at the entrance of the Sinus Maliacus.

ĀNŪBIS (-is), an Egyptian divinity, worshipped in the form of a human being with a dog's head. The Greeks identified him with their own Hermes (the Roman Mercury), and thus speak of Hermanuphis in the same manner as of Zeus (Jupiter) Ammon. His worship was introduced at Rome towards the end of the republic.

ANXUR. [TARRACINA.]

ĀNȲTUS (-i), a wealthy Athenian, the most influential and formidable of the accusers of Socrates, B. c. 399. He was a leading man of the democratic party, and took an active part, along with Thrasybulus, in the overthrow of the 30 Tyrants.

ĀŌNES (-um), an ancient race in Boeotia. Hence the poets frequently use Aonius as equivalent to Boeotian. As Mount Helicon and the fountain Aganippe were in Aonia, the Muses are called Āŏnĭdes.

AORSI or ADORSI (-ōrum), a powerful people of Asiatic Sarmatia, chiefly found between the Palus Maeotis (Sea of Azof) and the Caspian, whence they spread far into European Sarmatia.

ĀŌUS (-i) or AEAS (-antis), the principal river of the Greek part of Illyricum, rising in M. Lacmon, and flowing into the Ionian sea near Apollonia.

ĀPĂMĒA or -ĪA (-ae). (1) A. AD ORONTEM a city of Syria, built by Seleucus Nicator on the site of the older city of PELLA, in a very strong position on the river Orontes or Axius, and named in honour of his wife Apama.—(2) A. CĬBŌTUS or AD MAEANDRUM, a great city of Phrygia, on the Maeander, close above its confluence with the Marsyas. It was built by Antiochus I. Soter, who named it in honour of his mother Apama.—(3) A. MYRLEON, in Bithynia. [MYRLEA.]

ĂPELLĒS (-is), the most celebrated of Grecian painters, was born, most probably, at Colophon in Ionia, though some ancient writers call him a Coan and others an Ephesian. He was the contemporary of Alexander the Great (B.C. 336—323), who entertained so high an opinion of him, that he was the only person whom Alexander would permit to take his portrait. We are not told when or where he died. Throughout his life Apelles laboured to improve himself, especially in drawing, which he never spent a day without practising. Hence the proverb *Nulla dies sine linea.* Of his portraits the most celebrated was that of Alexander wielding a thunderbolt; but the most admired of all his pictures was the "Venus Anadyomene," or Venus rising out of the sea. The goddess was wringing her hair, and the falling drops of water formed a transparent silver veil around her form.

ĂPELLĬCŌN, of Teos, a Peripatetic philosopher and great collector of books. His valuable library at Athens, containing the autographs of Aristotle's works, was carried to Rome by Sulla (B.C. 83): Apellicon had died just before.

ĂPENNĪNUS (-i) MONS, (probably from the Celtic *Pen* "a height"), the *Apennines*, a chain of mountains running throughout Italy from N. to S., and forming the backbone of the peninsula. It is a continuation of the Maritime Alps [ALPES], and begins near Genua. At the boundaries of Samnium, Apulia, and Lucania, it divides into two main branches, one of which runs E. through Apulia and Calabria, and terminates at the Salentine promontory, and the other W. through Bruttium, terminating apparently at Rhegium and the straits of Messina, but in reality continued throughout Sicily.

ĂPER (-ri), ARRĬUS (-i), praetorian prefect, and son-in-law of the emperor Numerian, whom he was said to have murdered: he was himself put to death by Diocletian on his accession in A.D. 284.

ĂPĔRANTĬA (-ae), a town and district

of Aetolia near the Achelous, inhabited by the Aperantii.

APHĂCA (-ae), a town of Coele-Syria, between Heliopolis and Byblus, celebrated for the worship and oracle of Aphrodītē (Venûs).

ĂPHĂREUS (-ei), father of Idas and Lynceus, the *Aphărētĭdae* (also *Aphărēĭa proles*), celebrated for their fight with Castor and Pollux.

APHIDNA (-ae), an Attic demus not far from Decelea, was originally one of the 12 towns and districts into which Cecrops is said to have divided Attica. Here Theseus concealed Helen, but her brothers Castor and Pollux took the place and rescued their sister.

APHŎDĪRSĬAS (-ădis), the name of several places famous for the worship of Aphrodītē (Venus).—(1) A town in Caria on the site of an old town of the Leleges, named Ninŏë :

under the Romans a free city and asylum, and a flourishing school of art.—(2) Also called VENERIS OPPĬDUM, a town, harbour, and island on the coast of Cilicia, opposite to Cyprus.

APHRŎDĪTĒ (-ēs), called VĔNUS (ĕris), by the Romans, the goddess of love and beauty. In the Iliad she is represented as the daughter of Zeus and Diŏnē; but later poets frequently relate that she was sprung from the foam of the sea, whence they derive her name. She was the wife of Hephaestus (Vulcan); but she proved faithless to her husband, and was in love with Ares (Mars), the god of war. She also loved the gods Dionysus (Bacchus), Hermes (Mercury), and Poseidon (Neptune), and the mortals ANCHISES and ADONIS. She surpassed all the other goddesses in beauty, and hence received the prize of beauty from Paris. [PARIS.] She likewise had the power

Aphrodite (Venus) and Eros (Cupid).   (Causei,
Museum Romanum, vol. 1, tav. 40.)

of granting beauty and invincible charms to others, and whoever wore her magic girdle immediately became an object of love and desire. In the vegetable kingdom the myrtle, rose, apple, poppy, &c., were sacred to her. The animals sacred to her, which are often mentioned as drawing her chariot or serving as her messengers, are the sparrow, the

dove, the swan, the swallow, and a bird called iynx. She is generally represented in works of art with her son Eros (Cupid). The principal places of her worship in Greece were the islands of Cyprus and Cythera. Her worship was of Eastern origin, and probably introduced by the Phoenicians to the islands of Cyprus and Cythera, from whence it spread all over Greece.　She appears to have been originally identical with Astarte, called by the Hebrews Ashtoreth.

APHTHÓNIUS (-i), of Antioch, a Greek rhetorician, lived about A.D. 315, and wrote the introduction to the study of rhetoric, entitled *Progymnasmata*.　It was used as the common school-book in this branch of education for several centuries.

APHÝTIS (-is), a town in the peninsula Pallene in Macedonia, with a celebrated temple and oracle of Zeus (Jupiter) Ammon.

ĀPĬA.　[APIS.]

APĪCĬUS (-i), the name of three notorious gluttons.—(1) The first lived in the time of Sulla.—(2) The second and most renowned, *M. Gabius Apicius*, flourished under Tiberius. Having squandered his fortune on the pleasures of the table, he hanged himself.—(3) A contemporary of Trajan, sent to this emperor, when he was in Parthia, fresh oysters, preserved by a skilful process of his own.—The work on Cookery ascribed to Apicius, was probably compiled at a late period by some one who prefixed the name of Apicius, in order to insure the circulation of his book.

APĪDĂNUS (-i), a river in Thessaly, flowing into the Enīpeus near Pharsalus.

APĬŎLAE (-ārum), a town of Latium, destroyed by Tarquinius Priscus.

APĪŌN, a Greek grammarian, and a native of Oasis in Egypt, taught rhetoric at Rome in the reigns of Tiberius and Claudius.　He wrote a work against the Jews, to which Josephus replied in his treatise *Against Apion*.

APĪON, PTOLEMAEUS.　[PTOLEMAEUS.]

APIS (-is).　(1) Son of Phoroneus and Laodicē, king of Argos, from whom Peloponnesus, and more especially Argos, was called APIA.—(2) The sacred Bull of Memphis, worshipped as a god among the Egyptians.　There were certain signs by which he was recognised to be the god.　At Memphis, he had a splendid residence, containing extensive walks and courts for his amusement.　His birthday, which was celebrated every year, was a day of rejoicing for all Egypt.　His death was a season of public mourning, which continued till another sacred bull was discovered by the priests.

ĀPŎDŌTI (-ōrum), a people in the S.E. of Aetolia, between the Evenus and Hylaethus.

ĀPOLLĬNĀRIS, SĪDŌNĬUS.　[SIDONIUS.]

ĀPOLLĬNIS PR., a promontory in N. Africa, forming the W. point of the gulf of Carthage.

ĀPOLLO (-ĭnis), one of the great divinities of the Greeks, son of Zeus (Jupiter) and Leto (Latona) and twin brother of Artemis (Diana), was born in the island of Delos, whither Leto had fled from the jealous Hera (Juno). [LETO.]　The powers ascribed to Apollo are apparently of different kinds, but all are connected with one another, as will be seen from the following classification.　He is—1. *The god who punishes*, whence he is represented with a bow and arrows.　All sudden deaths were believed to be the effect of his arrows ; and with them he sent the plague into the camp of the Greeks before Troy.—2. *The god who affords help and wards off evil.*　As he had the power of punishing men, so he was also able to deliver men, if duly propitiated.　From his being the god who afforded help, he is the father of Aesculapius, the god of the healing art, and was also identified in later times with Paeëon, the god of the healing art in Homer.—3. *The god of prophecy.*　Apollo exercised this power in his numerous oracles, and especially in that of Delphi.　Hence he is frequently called the Pythian Apollo, from Pytho, the ancient name of Delphi.　He had the power of communicating the gift of prophecy both to gods and men, and all the ancient seers and prophets are placed in some relationship to him.—4. *The god of song and music.*　We find him in the Iliad delighting the immortal gods with his phorminx ; and the Homeric bards derived their art of song either from Apollo or the Muses.　Hence

Apollo Musagetes.　(Osterley, Denk. der alten Kunst, tav. 32.)

he is placed in close connexion with the Muses, and is called *Musagetes*, as leader of the choir of the Muses.　Later tradition ascribed to Apollo even the invention of the flute and lyre, while it is more commonly related that he received the lyre from Hermes (Mercury). Respecting his musical contests, see MAR-SYAS, MIDAS.—5. *The god who protects the flocks and cattle.* There are in Homer only a few allusions to this feature in the

Apollo, with Lyre and Bow. (Zoega, Bassirilievi, tav. 98.)

character of Apollo, but in later writers it assumes a very prominent form, and in the story of Apollo tending the flocks of Admetus

The Pythian Apollo. (Audran, Proportion du Corps Humain, pl. 18.)

at Pherae in Thessaly, the idea reaches its height.—6. *The god who delights in the foundation of towns and the establishment of civil constitutions.* Hence a town or a colony was never founded by the Greeks without consulting an oracle of Apollo, so that in every case he became, as it were, their spiritual leader.—7. *The god of the Sun.* In Homer, Apollo and Helios, or the Sun, are perfectly distinct, and his identification with the Sun, though almost universal among later writers, was the result of later speculations and of foreign, chiefly Egyptian, influence.—Apollo had more influence upon the Greeks than any other god. It may safely be asserted, that the Greeks would never have become what they were, without the worship of Apollo : in him the brightest side of the Grecian mind is reflected. In the religion of the early Romans there is no trace of the worship of Apollo. The Romans became acquainted with this divinity through the Greeks, and adopted all their notions about him from the latter people. During the second Punic war, in 212, the ludi Apollinares were instituted in his honour. —The most beautiful among the extant representations of Apollo, is the Apollo Belvedere at Rome, in which he appears as the perfect ideal of youthful manliness.

APOLLŌDŌRUS (-i), of Athens, flourished about B.C. 140. His work, entitled *Bibliotheca*, contains a well arranged account of the Greek mythology.

APOLLŌNĪA (-ae). (1) An important town in Illyria, not far from the mouth of the Aous, and 60 stadia from the sea. It was founded by the Corinthians and Corcyraeans, and was equally celebrated as a place of commerce and of learning. Many distinguished Romans, among others the young Octavius, afterwards the emperor Augustus, pursued their studies here. Persons travelling from Italy to Greece and the East, usually landed either at Apollonia or Dyrrhacium.—(2) A town in Macedonia, on the Via Egnatia, between Thessalonica and Amphipolis, and S. of the lake of Bolbe.—(3) A town in Thrace on the Black Sea, a colony of Miletus, had a celebrated temple of Apollo, from which Lucullus carried away a colossus of this god, and erected it on the Capitol at Rome.—(4) A castle or fortified town of the Locri Ozolae, near Naupactus.—(5) A town on the N. coast of Sicily.—(6) A town in Bithynia on the lake Apolloniatis, through which the river Rhyndacus flows.—(7) A town in Cyrenaica and the harbour of Cyrene, one of the 5 towns of the Pentapolis in Libya: it was the birthplace of Eratosthenes.

APOLLŌNĬS (-is), a city in Lydia, between Pergamus and Sardis, named after Apollonis, the mother of king Eumenes.

APOLLŌNĬUS (-i). (1) Of ALABANDA in

Caria, a rhetorician, taught rhetoric at Rhodes, about B.C. 100.—(2) Of ALABANDA, surnamed MOLO, likewise a rhetorician, taught rhetoric at Rhodes. In B.C. 81, Apollonius came to Rome as ambassador of the Rhodians, on which occasion Cicero heard him; Cicero also received instruction from Apollonius at Rhodes a few years later.— (3) PERGAEUS, from Perga in Pamphylia, one of the greatest mathematicians of antiquity, commonly called the "Great Geometer," was educated at Alexandria under the successors of Euclid, and flourished about B.C. 250—220.—(4) RHODIUS, a poet and grammarian, was born at Alexandria, and flourished in the reigns of Ptolemy Philopator and Ptolemy Epiphanes (B.C. 222—181). In his youth he was instructed by Callimachus; but they afterwards became bitter enemies. Apollonius taught rhetoric at Rhodes with so much success, that the Rhodians honoured him with their franchise: hence he was called the "Rhodian." He afterwards returned to Alexandria, where he succeeded Eratosthenes as chief librarian at Alexandria. His poem, called the *Argonautica*, gives a description of the adventures of the Argonauts. —(5) TYANENSIS or TYANAEUS, *i.e.* of Tyana in Cappadocia, a Pythagorean philosopher, was born about 4 years before the Christian era. Apollonius obtained great influence by pretending to miraculous powers. His life is written by Philostratus. After travelling through the greater part of the then known world, he settled down at Ephesus, where he is said to have proclaimed the death of the tyrant Domitian the instant it took place.

APONUS or APONI FONS, warm medicinal springs, near Patavium, hence called Aquae Patavinae, were much frequented by the sick.

APPIA VIA (-ae), the most celebrated of the Roman roads, was commenced by Ap. Claudius Caecus, when censor, B.C. 312, and was the great line of communication between Rome and southern Italy. It issued from the Porta Capena, and terminated at Capua, but was eventually extended to Brundusium.

APPIANUS (-i), the Roman historian, a native of Alexandria, lived at Rome during the reigns of Trajan, Hadrian, and Antoninus Pius. He wrote a Roman history in 24 books, of which only part has come down to us. His style is clear; but he possesses few merits as an historian.

APPIAS (-ădis), a nymph of the Appian well, which was situated near the temple of Venus Genetrix in the forum of Julius Caesar. It was surrounded by statues of nymphs, called *Appiades*.

APPII FORUM. [FORUM APPII.]

APPULEIUS or APULEIUS (-i), of Madura in Africa, born about A.D. 130, received the first rudiments of education at Carthage, and afterwards studied the Platonic philosophy at Athens. He next travelled extensively, visiting Italy, Greece, and Asia. After his return to Africa he married a very rich widow. His most important work is the *Golden Ass*, which is a kind of romance. The well-known and beautiful tale of Cupid and Psyche forms an episode in this work.

APPULEIUS SATURNINUS. [SATURNINUS.]

APRIES, a king of Egypt, the Pharaoh-Hophra of Scripture, succeeded his father Psammis, and reigned B.C. 595—570. He was dethroned and put to death by AMASIS.

APSUS (-i), a river in Illyria, flowing into the Ionian sea.

APSYRTUS. [ABSYRTUS.]

APUANI (-ōrum), a Ligurian people on the Macra, subdued by the Romans after a long resistance and transplanted to Samnium, B.C. 180.

APULEIUS. [APPULEIUS.]

APULIA (-ae), included, in its widest signification, the whole of the S. E. of Italy from the river Frento to the promontory Iapygium. In its narrower sense it was the country E. of Samnium on both sides of the Aufidus, the Daunia and Peucetia of the Greeks: the S. E. part was called Calabria by the Romans. The Greeks gave the name of Daunia to the N. part of the country from the Frento to the Aufidus, of Peucetia to the country from the Aufidus to Tarentum and Brundusium, and of Iapygia or Messapia to the whole of the remaining S. part: though they sometimes included under Iapygia all Apulia in its widest meaning. The country was very fertile, especially in the neighbourhood of Tarentum, and the mountains afforded excellent pasturage. The population was of a mixed nature: they were for the most part of Illyrian origin, and are said to have settled in the country under the guidance of Iapyx, Daunius, and Peucetius, three sons of an Illyrian king, Lycaon. Subsequently many towns were founded by Greek colonists. The Apulians joined the Samnites against the Romans, and became subject to the latter on the conquest of the Samnites.

AQUAE (-ārum), the name given by the Romans to many medicinal springs and bathing places:—(1) CUTILIAE, mineral springs in Samnium near the ancient town of Cutilia, which perished in early times, and E. of Reăte. There was a celebrated lake in its neighbourhood with a floating island, which was regarded as the umbilicus or centre of Italy. Vespasian died at this place.—(2) PATAVINAE. [APONI FONS.]—(3) SEXTIAE (*Aix*), a Roman colony in Gallia Narbonensis, founded by Sextius Calvinus, B.C. 122; its mineral waters were long celebrated. Near this place Marius defeated the Teutoni, B.C. 102.—(4) STATI-ELLAE, a town of the Statielli in Liguria, celebrated for its warm baths.

AQUILARIA (-ae), a town on the coast of Zeugitana in Africa, on the W. side of Hermaeum Pr. (*C. Bon*). It was a good landing-place in summer.

AQUILEIA (-ae), a town in Gallia Transpadana at the very top of the Adriatic, about 60 stadia from the sea. It was founded by the Romans in B.C. 182, as a bulwark against the northern barbarians, and was one of the strongest fortresses of the Romans. It was also a flourishing place of commerce. It was taken and completely destroyed by Attila in A.D. 452: its inhabitants escaped to the Lagoons, where Venice was afterwards built.

AQUILLIA VIA (-ae), began at Capua, and ran S. through the very heart of Lucania and Bruttii to Rhegium.

AQUILLIUS or AQUILIUS (-i). (1) Consul, B.C. 129, finished the war against Aristonicus, son of Eumenes of Pergamus.—(2) Consul, B.C. 101, finished the Servile war in Sicily. In 88 he was defeated by Mithridates, who put him to death by pouring molten gold down his throat.

AQUILONIA (-ae), a town of Samnium, E. of Bovianum, destroyed by the Romans in the Samnite wars.

AQUINUM (-i), a town of the Volscians in Latium; a Roman municipium and afterwards a colony; the birth-place of Juvenal; celebrated for its purple dye.

AQUITANIA (-ae). (1) The country of the Aquitani, extended from the Garumna (*Garonne*) to the Pyrenees. It was first conquered by Caesar's legates.—(2) The Roman province of Aquitania, formed in the reign of Augustus, extended from the Ligeris (*Loire*), to the Pyrenees, and was bounded on the E. by the Mons Cevenna, which separated it from Gallia Narbonensis. The Aquitani were of Iberian or Spanish origin.

ARA UBIORUM, a place in the neighbourhood of Bonn in Germany, perhaps *Godesberg*.

ARABIA (-ae), a country at the S.W. extremity of Asia, forming a large peninsula, of a sort of hatchet shape, bounded on the W. by the ARABICUS SINUS (*Red Sea*), on the S. and S.E. by the ERYTHRAEUM MARE (*Gulf of Bab-el-Mandeb* and *Indian Ocean*), and on the N.E. by the Persicus Sinus (*Persian Gulf*). On the N. or land side its boundaries were somewhat indefinite, but it seems to have included the whole of the desert country between Egypt and Syria, on the one side, and the banks of the Euphrates on the other. It was

divided into 3 parts: (1) ARABIA PETRAEA, including the triangular piece of land between the two heads of the Red Sea (the peninsula of M. Sinai) and the country immediately to the N. and N.E.; and called from its capital Petra, while the literal signification of the name "Rocky Arabia," agrees also with the nature of the country: (2) ARABIA DESERTA, including the great Syrian Desert and a portion of the interior of the Arabian peninsula: (3) ARABIA FELIX, consisting of the whole country not included in the other two divisions. The ignorance of the ancients respecting the interior of the peninsula led them to class it with Arabia Felix, although it properly belongs to Arabia Deserta, for it consists of a sandy desert. There is only on the W. coast a belt of fertile land, which caused the ancients to apply the epithet of Felix to the whole peninsula.—The inhabitants of Arabia were of the race called Semitic or Aramaean, and closely related to the Israelites. The N.W. district (Arabia Petraea) was inhabited by the various tribes which constantly appear in Jewish history: the Amalekites, Midianites, Edomites, Moabites, Ammonites, &c. The Greeks and Romans called the inhabitants by the name of NABATHAEI, whose capita was Petra. The people of Arabia Deserta were called Arabes Scenitae, from their dwelling in tents, and Arabes Nomadae, from their mode of life. From the earliest known period a considerable traffic was carried on by the people in the N. (especially the Nabathaei) by means of caravans, and by those on the S. and E. coast by sea, in the productions of their own country (chiefly gums, spices, and precious stones), and in those of India and Arabia. The only part of Arabia ever conquered was Arabia Petraea, which became under Trajan a Roman province. Christianity was early introduced into Arabia, where it spread to a great extent, and continued to exist side by side with the old religion (which was Sabaeism, or the worship of heavenly bodies), and with some admixture of Judaism, until the total revolution produced by the rise of Mohammedanism in 622.

ARABICUS SINUS (-i: *Red Sea*), a long narrow gulf between Africa and Arabia, connected on the S. with the *Indian Ocean* by the *Straits of Bab-el-Mandeb*, and on the N. divided into two heads by the peninsula of Arabia Petraea (*Penins. of Sinai*), the E. of which was called Sinus Aelanites or Aelaniticus (*Gulf of Akaba*), and the W. Sinus Heroopolites or Heroopoliticus (*Gulf of Suez*). Respecting its other name see ERYTHRAEUM MARE.

ARABIS (-is), a river of Gedrosia, falling

into the Indian Ocean, W. of the mouth of the Indus, and dividing the Oritae on its W. from the Arabitae or Arbies on its E.

ĀRACHNĒ (-ēs), a Lydian maiden, daughter of Idmon of Colophon, a famous dyer in purple. Arachnē excelled in the art of weaving, and, proud of her talent, ventured to challenge Athēna (Minerva), to compete with her. The maiden produced a piece of cloth in which the amours of the gods were woven, and as the goddess could find no fault with it, she tore the work to pieces. Arachnē in despair hung herself : Athēna loosened the rope and saved her life, but the rope was changed into a cobweb and Arachnē herself into a spider (Arachnē). This fable seems to suggest that man learnt the art of weaving from the spider, and that it was invented in Lydia.

ĀRĀCHŌSĬA (-ae), one of the E. provinces of the Persian (and afterwards of the Parthian) Empire, bounded on the E. by the Indus, on the N. by the Paropamisadae, on the W. by Drangiana, and on the S. by Gedrosia. It was a fertile country.

ĀRACHTHUS (-i) or ĀRĒTHO (-ōnis), a river of Epirus, rising in M. Lacmon or the Tymphean mountains, and flowing into the Ambracian gulf.

ĀRĂCYNTHUS (-i), a mountain on the S. W. coast of Aetolia near Pleuron, sometimes placed in Acarnania. Later writers erroneously make it a mountain between Boeotia and Attica, and hence mention it in connection with Amphion, the Boeotian hero.

ĀRĂDUS (-i: in *O. T.* Arvad), a small island off the coast of Phoenicia, with a flourishing city, said to have been founded by exiles from Sidon. It possessed a harbour on the mainland, called Antaradus.

ĀRAE PHILAENŌRUM. [PHILAENI.]

ĀRĂR or ĀRĂRIS (-is : *Saône*), a river of Gaul, rises in the Vosges, receives the Dubis (*Doubs*) from the E., after which it becomes navigable, and flows with a quiet stream into the Rhone at Lugdunum (*Lyon*).

ĀRĀTUS (-i). (1) The celebrated general of the Achaeans, son of Clinias, was born at Sicyon, B.C. 271. His father was murdered when he was a child, and was brought up at Argos. At 20 years of age he delivered Sicyon from the rule of its tyrant and united the city to the Achaean league, which gained in consequence a great accession of power, B.C. 251. [ACHAEI.] In 245 he was elected general of the league, which office he frequently held in subsequent years. But he excelled more in negotiation than in war ; and in his war with the Aetolians and Spartans he was often defeated. In order to resist these enemies he cultivated the friendship of Antigonus Doson, king of Macedonia, and of

his successor Philip : but as Philip was evidently anxious to make himself master of all Greece, dissensions arose between him and Aratus, and the latter was eventually poisoned in 213 by the king's order.—(2) Of Soli, afterwards Pompeiopolis, in Cilicia, flourished B.C. 270, and spent the latter part of his life at the court of Antigonus Gonatas, king of Macedonia. He wrote two astronomical poems, entitled *Phaenomena* and *Diosemeia*, which were very popular in ancient times. They were translated into Latin by Cicero, by Caesar Germanicus, the grandson of Augustus, and by Festus Avienus.

ĀRAXĒS (-is), the name of several rivers. —(1) In Armenia, rising in M. Aba or Abus, joining the Cyrus, and falling with it into the Caspian sea. The Araxes was proverbial for the force of its current.—(2) In Mesopotamia. [ABORRHAS.]—(3) In Persis, the river on which Persepolis stood, flowing into a salt lake not far below Persepolis.— (4) It is doubtful whether the Araxes of Herodotus is the same as the Oxus, JAXARTES, or *Volga*.

ARBACĒS (-is), the founder of the Median empire, according to Ctesias, is said to have taken Nineveh in conjunction with Belesis, the Babylonian, and to have destroyed the old Assyrian empire under the reign of Sardanapalus, B.C. 876.

ARBĒLA (-ae), a city of Adiabene in Assyria, celebrated as the head-quarters of Darius Codomannus, before the last battle in which he was overthrown by Alexander (B.C. 331), which is hence frequently called the battle of Arbela, though it was really fought near GAUGAMELA, about 50 miles W. of Arbela.

ARBUSCŬLA (-ae), a celebrated female actor in pantomimes in the time of Cicero.

ARCA (-ae), or -AE (-ārum), an ancient city in the N. of Phoenicia; the birthplace of the emperor Alexander Severus.

ARCĂDĬA (-ae), a country in the middle of Peloponnesus, surrounded on all sides by mountains, the Switzerland of Greece. The Achelous, the greatest river of Peloponnesus, rises in Arcadia. The N. and E. parts of the country were barren and unproductive : the W. and S. were more fertile, with numerous valleys where corn was grown. The Arcadians regarded themselves as the most ancient people in Greece : the Greek writers call them indigenous and Pelasgians. They were chiefly employed in hunting and the tending of cattle, whence their worship of Pan, who was especially the god of Arcadia, and of Artemis. They were passionately fond of music, and cultivated it with success. The Arcadians experienced fewer changes than any other people in Greece, and retained possession of their country upon the conquest of the rest of Peloponnesus by the Dorians. After the second Messenian war, the different towns became independent republics, of which the most important were MANTINEA, TEGEA, ORCHOMENUS, PSOPHIS, and PHENEUS. Like the Swiss, the Arcadians frequently served as mercenaries. The Lacedaemonians made many attempts to obtain possession of parts of Arcadia, but these attempts were finally frustrated by the battle of Leuctra (B. C. 371); and in order to resist all future aggresions on the part of Sparta, the Arcadians, upon the advice of Epaminondas, built the city of MEGALOPOLIS. They subsequently joined the Achaean League, and finally became subject to the Romans.

ARCADIUS (-i), emperor of the East, elder son of Theodosius I., and brother of Honorius, reigned A. D. 395—408.

ARCAS (-ădis), king of the Arcadians, son of Zeus (Jupiter) and Callisto, from whom Arcadia was supposed to have derived its name.

ARCESILAUS (-i). (1) A Greek philosopher, born at Pitane in Aeolis, succeeded Crates about B. C. 241 in the chair of the Academy at Athens, and became the founder of the second or middle Academy. He is said to have died in his 76th year from a fit of drunkenness.—(2) The name of four kings of Cyrene. [BATTIADAE.]

ARCESIUS (-i), father of Laërtes, and grand-father of Ulysses, who is hence called Arcesiades.

ARCHELAUS (-i). (1) Son of HEROD the Great, was appointed by his father as his successor, and received from Augustus Judaea, Samaria, and Idumaea, with the title of ethnarch. In consequence of his tyrannical government, Augustus banished him in A.D. 7 to Vienna in Gaul, where he died.—(2) King of MACEDONIA (B.C. 413—399), an illegitimate son of Perdiccas II., obtained the throne by the murder of his half-brother. He was a warm patron of art and literature. His palace was adorned with paintings by Zeuxis; and Euripides, Agathon, and other men of eminence, were among his guests.— (3) A distinguished general of MITHRIDATES, defeated by Sulla in Boeotia, B.C. 86. He deserted to the Romans, B.C. 81.—(4) Son of the preceding, was raised by Pompey, in B.C. 63, to the dignity of priest of the goddess at Comana in Pontus or Cappadocia. In 56 or 55 Archelaus became king of Egypt by marrying Berenice, the daughter of Ptolemy Auletes, who, after the expulsion of her father, had obtained the sovereignty of Egypt. But at the end of 6 months he was defeated and slain in battle by Gabinius, who had marched

with an army into Egypt in order to restore Ptolemy Auletes.—(5) Son of No. 4, and his successor in the office of high-priest of Comana, was deprived of his dignity by Julius Caesar in 47.—(6) Son of No. 5, received from Antony, in B.C. 36, the kingdom of Cappadocia—a favour which he owed to the charms of his mother Glaphyra. He was deprived of his kingdom by Tiberius, A.D. 17; and Cappadocia was then made a Roman province.—(7) A philosopher of the Ionic school, born either at Athens or at Miletus. He flourished about B.C. 450.

ARCHIAS (-ae). (1) An Heraclid of Corinth, who founded Syracuse, B.C. 734.—(2) A. LICINIUS ARCHIAS, a Greek poet, born at Antioch in Syria, about B.C. 120, came to Rome in 102, and was received in the most friendly way by the Luculli, from whom he obtained the gentile name of Licinius. He was enrolled as a citizen at Heraclea in Lucania; and as this town was united with Rome by a foedus, he subsequently obtained the Roman franchise in accordance with the lex Plautia Papiria passed in B.C. 89. In 61 he was accused of assuming the citizenship illegally. He was defended by his friend M. Cicero in the extant speech Pro Archia, in which the orator, after briefly discussing the legal points of the case, rests the defence of his client upon his merits as a poet, which entitled him to the Roman citizenship.

ARCHIDAMUS (-i), the name of 5 kings of Sparta.—(1) Son of Anaxidamus, contemporary with the Tegeatan war, which followed soon after the second Messenian, B.C. 668.— (2) Son of Zeuxidamus, succeeded his grandfather Leotychides, and reigned B.C. 469—427. He opposed making war upon the Athenians; but after the Peloponnesian war broke out (B.C. 431), he invaded Attica, and held the supreme command of the Peloponnesian forces till his death in 429.—(3) Grandson of No. 2, and son of Agesilaus II., reigned B.C. 361— 338. In 338 he went to Italy to aid the Tarentines against the Lucanians, and there fell in battle.—(4) Grandson of No. 3, and son of Eudamidas I., was king in B.C. 296, when he was defeated by Demetrius Poliorcetes.—(5) Son of Eudamidas II., and the brother of Agis IV. He was slain soon after his accession, B.C. 240. He was the last king of the Eurypontid race.

ARCHILOCHUS (-i), of Paros, was one of the earliest lyric poets, and the first who composed Iambic verses. He flourished about B.C. 714—676. He went from Paros to Thasos with a colony, but afterwards returned to Paros, and fell in battle in a war against the Naxians. His fame was chiefly founded on his satiric iambic poetry. He had been a suitor to Neobulē, one of the daughters of Lycambes, who first promised and afterwards refused to give his daughter to the poet. Enraged at this treatment, Archilochus attacked the whole family in an iambic poem with such effect, that the daughters of Lycambes are said to have hung themselves through shame. While at Thasos, he incurred the disgrace of losing his shield in an engagement with the Thracians of the opposite continent; but, instead of being ashamed of the disaster, he recorded it in his verse.

ARCHĪMĒDĒS, (-i and -is), of Syracuse, the most famous of ancient mathematicians, was born B.C. 287. He was a friend, if not a kinsman, of Hiero, for whom he constructed various engines of war, which, many years afterwards, were so far effectual in the defence of Syracuse against Marcellus, as to convert the siege into a blockade. The accounts of the performances of these engines are evidently exaggerated; and the story of the burning of the Roman ships by the reflected rays of the sun, is probably a fiction. When Syracuse was taken (B.C. 212), Archimedes was killed by the Roman soldiers, being at the time intent upon a mathematical problem. Some of his works have come down to us.

ARCHȲTAS (-ae), of Tarentum, a distinguished philosopher, mathematician, general, and statesman, lived about B.C. 400, and onwards. He was contemporary with Plato, whose life he is said to have saved by his influence with the tyrant Dionysius. He was drowned while upon a voyage on the Adriatic. As a philosopher, he belonged to the Pythagorean school.

ARCONNĒSUS (-i). (1) An island off. the coast of Ionia, near Lebedus, also called *Aspis* and *Macris*.—(2) An island off the coast of Caria, opposite Halicarnassus, of which it formed the harbour.

ARCTĪNUS (-i), of Miletus, the most distinguished among the cyclic poets, probably lived about B.C. 776.

ARCTŎPHȲLAX. [ARCTOS.]

ARCTOS (-i), "the Bear," two constellations near the N. Pole.—(1) THE GREAT BEAR (*Ursa Major*), also called the *Waggon* (*plaustrum*). The ancient Italian name of this constellation was *Septem Triones*, that is, the *Seven Ploughing Oxen*, also *Septentrio*, and with the epithet *Major* to distinguish it from the *Septentrio Minor*, or *Lesser Bear*.— (2) THE LESSER OR LITTLE BEAR (*Ursa Minor*), likewise called the *Waggon*, and *Cynosura*, *dog's tail*, from the resemblance of the constellation to the upturned curl of a dog's tail. The constellation before the Great Bear was called *Boötes*, *Arctophȳlax*, or *Arctūrus*. At a later time *Arctophylax* became the general

name of the constellation, and the word *Arctūrus* was confined to the chief star in it. All these constellations are connected in mythology with the Arcadian nymph CALLISTO, the daughter of Lycaon. Metamorphosed by Zeus (Jupiter) upon the earth into a she-bear, Callisto was pursued by her son Arcas in the chase, and when he was on the point of killing her, Zeus placed them both among the stars, Callisto becoming the Great Bear and Arcas the Little Bear or Boötes. In the poets the epithets of these stars have constant reference to the family and country of Callisto: thus we find them called *Lycaonis Arctos*: *Maenalia Arctos* and *Maenalis Ursa* (from M. Maenalus in Arcadia) : *Erymanthis Ursa* (from M. Erymanthus in Arcadia) : *Parrhasides stellae* (from the Arcadian town Parrhasia.)—Though most traditions identified Boötes with Arcas, others pronounced him to be Icarus or his daughter Erigone. Hence the Septentriones are called *Boves Icarii.*

ARCTŪRUS. [ARCTOS.]

ARDĒA (-ae), the chief town of the Rutuli in Latium, situated about 3 miles from the sea, one of the most ancient places in Italy, and the capital of Turnus. It was conquered and colonised by the Romans, B.C. 442.

ARDŬENNA SILVA (-ae), *the Ardennes*, a vast forest, in the N.W. of Gaul, extending from the Rhine and the Treviri to the Nervii and Remi, and N. as far as the Scheldt.

ARDYS, son of Gyges, king of Lydia, reigned B.C. 678—629.

ĀRĒLĀTĒ (-ēs), ĀRĒLAS (-ātis), or ĀRĒLĀTUM (-i) (*Arles*), a town in Gallia Narbonensis, at the head of the delta of the Rhone on the left bank, and a Roman colony. The Roman remains at Arles attest the greatness of the ancient city: there are still the ruins of an aqueduct, theatre, amphitheatre, &c.

ĀRĒŎPĀGUS. [ATHENAE.]

ĀRĒS (-is), called MARS (-rtis), by the Romans, the Greek god of war, and one of the great Olympian gods, is called the son of Zeus (Jupiter) and Hēra (Juno). He is represented as delighting in the din and roar of battles, in the slaughter of men, and in the destruction of towns. His savage and sanguinary character makes him hated by the other gods and by his own parents. He was wounded by Diomedes, who was assisted by Athēna (Minerva), and in his fall he roared like ten thousand warriors. The gigantic Aloīdae had likewise conquered him, and kept him a prisoner for 13 months, until he was delivered by Hermes (Mercury). He was also conquered by Hercules, with whom he fought on account of his son Cycnus, and was obliged to return to Olympus. This fierce and gigantic, but withal handsome god, loved and was beloved by Aphroditē (Venus). [APHRODITE.] According to a late tradition, Ares slew Halirrhothius, the son of Poseidon (Neptune), when he was offering violence to Alcippē, the daughter of Ares. Hereupon Poseidon accused Ares in the Areopagus, where the Olympian gods were assembled in

Ares (Mars). (Ludovisi Statue in Rome).

court. Ares was acquitted, and this event was believed to have given rise to the name Areopagus. In Greece the worship of Ares was not very general, and it was probably introduced from Thrace. Respecting the Roman god of war, see MARS.

ĀRESTOR (-ŏris), father of Argus, the guardian of Io, who is therefore called *Arestŏrĭdēs.*

ĀRĒTAS, the name of several kings of Arabia Petraea.—(1) A contemporary of Pompey, invaded Judaea in B.C. 65, in order to place Hyrcanus on the throne, but was driven back by the Romans, who espoused the cause of Aristobulus. His dominions were subsequently invaded by Scaurus, the lieutenant of Pompey.—(2) The father-in-law of Herod Antipas, invaded Judaea, because Herod had dismissed the daughter of Aretas in consequence of his connection with Herodias. This Aretas seems to have been the same who had possession of Damascus at

the time of the conversion of the Apostle Paul, A.D. 31.

ĀRETHŪSA (-ae), one of the Nereids, and the nymph of the famous fountain of Arethusa in the island of Ortygia near Syracuse. For details see ALPHEUS.

ĀRĒTĪUM. [ARRETIUM.]

AREUS (-i), king of Sparta, succeeded his grandfather, Cleomenes II., and reigned B.C. 309—265. He fell in battle against the Macedonians.

ĀRĒVĀCAE (-ārum), or ĀRĒVĀCI (-ōrum), the most powerful tribe of the Celtiberians in Spain, near the sources of the Tagus, derived their name from the river Areva, a tributary of the Durius.

ARGENTORĀTUM (-i), or -TUS (-i), (*Strassburg*), an important town on the Rhine in Gallia Belgica, and a Roman municipium.

ARGES. [CYCLOPES.

ARGI. [ARGOS.]

ARGĪA (-ae), daughter of Adrastus and Amphithea, and wife of Polynīces.

ARGĪLĒTUM (-i), a district in Rome, extending from the S. of the Quirinal to the Capitoline and the Forum. It was chiefly inhabited by mechanics and booksellers.

ARGĪLUS (-i), a town in Macedonia between Amphipolis and Bromiscus, a colony of Andros.

ARGINŪSAE (-ārum), 3 small islands off the coast of Aeolis, opposite Mytilēnē in Lesbos, celebrated for the naval victory of the Athenians over the Lacedaemonians under Callicratidas, B.C. 406.

ARGĪPHONTĒS (-is), "the slayer of Argus," a surname of Hermes (Mercury).

AEGIPPAEI (-ōrum), a Scythian tribe in Sarmatia Asiatica, who appear to have been of the Calmuck race.

ARGITHĒA (-ae), the chief town of Athamania in Epirus.

ARGĪVA (-ae), a surname of Hera or Juno from Argos, where she was especially honoured. [ARGOS.]

ARGĪVI. [ARGOS.]

ARGO. [ARGONAUTAE.]

ARGŌLIS. [ARGOS.]

ARGŌNAUTAE (-ārum), the Argonauts, "the sailors of the Argo," were the heroes who sailed to Aea (afterwards called Colchis) for the purpose of fetching the golden fleece. In order to get rid of Jason [JASON], Pelias, king of Iolcus in Thessaly, persuaded him to fetch the golden fleece, which was suspended on an oak tree in the grove of Ares (Mars) in Colchis, and was guarded day and night by a dragon. Jason undertook the enterprize, and commanded Argus, the son of Phrixus, to build a ship with 50 oars, which was called

Argo after the name of the builder. The goddess Athēna (Minerva) is represented in works of art superintending the building of the ship. Jason was accompanied by all the great heroes of the age, such as Hercules, Castor and Pollux, Theseus, &c. : their number is said to have been 50. After meeting with many adventures, they at length arrived at the mouth of the river Phasis. The Colchian king Aeëtes promised to give up the golden fleece, if Jason would yoke to a plough two fire-breathing oxen with brazen feet, and sow the teeth of the dragon which had not been used by Cadmus at Thebes. Medēa, the daughter of Aeëtes fell in love with Jason, and on his promising to marry her, she furnished him with the means of resisting fire and steel, and sent to sleep the dragon who guarded the golden fleece. After Jason had taken the treasure, he and his Argonauts embarked by night, along with Medēa, and sailed away. On their return they were driven by a storm to the W. of Italy ; and after wandering about the western coasts of the Mediterranean, they at length arrived at Iolcus. [MEDEA; JASON.] The tale of the Argonauts may have arisen from the commercial enterprises which the wealthy Minyans, who lived in the neighbourhood of Iolcus, made to the coasts of the Euxine.

Athena (Minerva) superintending the Building of the Argo. (Zoëga, Bassi rilievi, tav. 45.)

ARGOS is said to have signified a plain in the language of the Macedonians and Thessalians, and it may therefore contain the same root as the Latin word *ager*. In Homer we find mention of the Pelasgic Argos, that is, a town or district of Thessaly, and of the Achaean Argos, by which he means sometimes the whole Peloponnesus, sometimes Agamemnon's kingdom of Argos of which Mycenae was the capital, and sometimes the town of Argos. As Argos frequently signifies the whole Peloponnesus, the most important part of Greece, so the 'Αργεῖοι often occur in Homer as a name of the whole body of the Greeks, in which sense the Roman poets also use *Argivi*.—(1) ARGOS, a district of Peloponnesus, also called by Greek writers, *Argia* or *Argŏlicē* or *Argŏlis*. Under the Romans Argolis became the usual name of the country, while the word Argos or Argi was confined to the town. The Roman Argolis was bounded on the N. by the Corinthian territory, on the W. by Arcadia, on the S. by Laconia, and included towards the E. the whole peninsula between the Saronic and Argolic gulfs : but during the time of Grecian independence Argolis or Argos was only the country lying round the Argolic gulf, bounded on the W. by the Arcadian mountains, and separated on the N. by a range of mountains from Corinth, Cleonae, and Phlius. The country was divided into the districts of Argia or Argos proper, EPIDAURIA, TRŒEZENIA, and HERMIONIS. The main part of the population consisted of Pelasgi and Achaei, to whom Dorians were added after the conquest of Peloponnesus by the Dorians. See below, No. 2.—(2) Argos, or Argi, -orum, in the Latin writers, the capital of Argolis, and, next to Sparta, the most important town in Peloponnesus, situated in a level plain a little to the W. of the Inachus. It had an ancient Pelasgic citadel, called Larissa, and another built subsequently on another height. It was particularly celebrated for the worship of Hera (Juno), whose great temple, *Heraeum*, lay between Argos and Mycenae. The city is said to have been built by Inachus or his son Phoroneus, or grandson Argus. The descendants of Inachus were deprived of the sovereignty by Danaus, who is said to have come from Egypt. The descendants of Danaus were in their turn obliged to submit to the Achaean race of the Pelopidae. Under the rule of the Pelopidae Mycenae became the capital of the kingdom, and Argos was a dependent state. Thus Mycenae was the royal residence of Atreus and of his son Agamemnon; but under Orestes Argos again recovered its supremacy. Upon the conquest of Peloponnesus by the Dorians Argos fell to the share of Temenus, whose descendants ruled over the country. All these events belong to mythology; and Argos first appears in history about B.C. 750, as the chief state of Peloponnesus, under its ruler Phidon. After the time of Phidon its influence declined; and its power was greatly weakened by its wars with Sparta. In consequence of its jealousy of Sparta, Argos took no part in the Persian war. In the Peloponnesian war it sided with Athens against Sparta. At this time its government was a democracy, but at a later period it fell under the power of tyrants. In 243 it joined the Achaean League, and on the conquest of the latter by the Romans, 146, it became a part of the Roman province of Achaia.

ARGUS (-i). (1) Son of Zeus (Jupiter) and Niobe, 3rd king of Argos.—(2) Surnamed Panoptes, "the all-seeing," because he had a hundred eyes, son of Agenor, or Arestor, or Inachus. Hera (Juno) appointed him guardian of the cow into which Io had been metamorphosed; but Hermes (Mercury), at the command of Zeus, sent him to sleep by the sweet notes of his flute, and then cut off his head. Hera transplanted his eyes to the tail of the peacock, her favourite bird.—(3) The builder of the Argo, son of Phrixus.

ARGYRIPA. [ARPI.]

ARIA or -IA (-ae), the most important of the eastern provinces of the ancient Persian Empire, was bounded on the E. by the Paropamisadae, on the N. by Margiana and Hyrcania, on the W. by Parthia, and on the S. by the desert of Carmania. From Aria was derived the name under which all the eastern provinces were included. [ARIANA.]

ARIADNE (-es), or ARIADNA (-ae), daughter of Minos and Pasiphaë, fell in love with Theseus, when he was sent by his father to convey the tribute of the Athenians to the Minotaur, and gave him the clue of thread by means of which he found his way out of the Labyrinth. Theseus in return promised to marry her, and she accordingly left Crete with him; but on their arrival in the island of Dia (Naxos), she was

Ariadne.   (From a painting found at Pompeii.)

killed by Artemis (Diana). This is the Homeric account; but the more common tradition related that Theseus deserted Ariadne in Naxos, where she was found by Dionysus, who made her his wife, and placed among the stars the crown which he gave her at their marriage.

ARIAEUS (-i), the friend of Cyrus, commanded the left wing of the army at the battle of Cunaxa, B.C. 401. After the death of Cyrus, he purchased his pardon from Artaxerxes by deserting the Greeks.

ARIANA (-ae), derived from Aria, from the specific sense of which it must be carefully distinguished, was the general name of the eastern provinces of the Persian Empire, including Parthia, Aria, the Paropamisadae, Arachosia, Drangiana, Gedrosia, and Carmania.

ARIARATHES (-i), the name of several kings of Cappadocia.—(1) Son of Ariamnes I., defeated by Perdiccas, and crucified, B.C. 322. Eumenes then obtained possession of Cappadocia.—(2) Son of Holophernes, and nephew of Ariarathes I., recovered Cappadocia after the death of Eumenes, 315. He was succeeded by Ariamnes II.—(3) Son of Ariamnes II., and grandson of No. 2, married Stratonĭce, daughter of Antiochus II., king of Syria.—(4) Son of No. 3, reigned 220—162. He married Antiochis, the daughter of Antiochus the Great, and assisted Antiochus in his war against the Romans. After the defeat of Antiochus, Ariarathes sued for peace in 188, which he obtained on favourable terms.— (5) Son of No. 4, surnamed Philopator, reigned 163—130. He assisted the Romans in their war against Aristonicus of Pergamus, and fell in this war, 130.—(6) Son of No. 5, reigned 130—96. He married Laodice, sister of Mithridates VI., king of Pontus, and was put to death by Mithridates.—(7) Son of No. 6, also murdered by Mithridates, who now took possession of his kingdom. The Cappadocians rebelled against Mithridates, and placed upon the throne,—(8) Second son of No. 6 ; but he was speedily driven out of the kingdom by Mithridates, and shortly afterwards died. —(9) Son of Ariobarzanes II., reigned 42— 36. He was deposed and put to death by Antony, who appointed Archelaus as his successor.

ARIASPAE or AGRIASPAE (-ārum), a people in the S. part of the Persian province of Drangiana, on the borders of Gedrosia.

ARICIA (-ae), an ancient town of Latium at the foot of the Alban Mount, on the Appian Way, 16 miles from Rome. It was subdued by the Romans, with the other Latin towns, in B.C. 338, and received the Roman franchise. In its neighbourhood was the celebrated grove and temple of Diana Arĭcīna, on the borders of the Lacus Nemorensis. Diana was worshipped here with barbarous customs : her priest, called *rex nemorensis,* was always a run-away slave, who obtained his office by killing his predecessor in single combat.

ARIMASPI (-ōrum), a people in the N. of Scythia, represented as men with only one eye, who fought with the griffins for the possession of the gold in their neighbourhood. The germ of the fable is perhaps to be recognised in the fact that the Ural Mountains abound in gold.

ARIMI (-ōrum), and ARIMA (-ōrum), the names of a mythical people, district, and range of mountains in Asia Minor, which the old Greek poets made the scene of the punishment of the monster Typhoeus.

ARIMINUM (-i : *Rimini*), a town in Umbria, at the mouth of the little river Ariminus. It was originally inhabited by Umbrians

and Pelasgians, was afterwards in the possession of the Senones, and was colonised by the Romans in B.C. 268, from which time it appears as a flourishing place. After leaving Cisalpine Gaul, it was the first town on the eastern coast of Italy which a person arrived at in Italia proper.

ARIOBARZANES (-is). I. *Kings or Satraps of Pontus.*—(1) Betrayed by his son Mithridates to the Persian king, about B.C. 400.—(2) Son of Mithridates I., reigned 363—337. He revolted from Artaxerxes in 362, and may be regarded as the founder of the kingdom of Pontus.—(3) Son of Mithridates III., reigned 266—240, and was succeeded by Mithridates IV.—II. *Kings of Cappadocia.*—(1) Surnamed PHILOROMAEUS, reigned B.C. 93—63, and was elected king by the Cappadocians, under the direction of the Romans. He was several times expelled from his kingdom by Mithridates, but was finally restored by Pompey in 63, shortly before his death.—(2) Surnamed PHILOPATOR, succeeded his father in 63.—(3) Surnamed EUSEBES and PHILOROMAEUS, son of No. 2, whom he succeeded about 51. He assisted Pompey against Caesar, who not only pardoned him, but even enlarged his territories. He was slain in 42 by Cassius.

ARION (-ŏnis). (1) Of Methymna in Lesbos, a celebrated lyric poet and player on the cithara, and the inventor of dithyrambic poetry. He lived about B.C. 625, and spent a great part of his life at the court of Periander, tyrant of Corinth. On one occasion, we are told, Arion went to Sicily to take part in some musical contest. He won the prize, and, laden with presents, he embarked in a Corinthian ship to return to his friend Periander. The rude sailors coveted his treasures, and meditated his murder. After vain to save his life, he at length obtained permission once more to play on the cithara, and as soon as he had invoked the gods in inspired strains, he threw himself into the sea. But many song-loving dolphins had assembled round the vessel, and one of them now took the bard on its back and carried him to Taenărus, from whence he returned to Corinth in safety, and related his adventure to Periander. Upon the arrival of the Corinthian vessel, Periander inquired of the sailors after Arion, who replied that he had remained behind at Tarentum ; but when Arion, at the bidding of Periander, came forward, the sailors owned their guilt, and were punished according to their desert.— (2) A fabulous horse, which is said to have been begotten by Poseidon (Neptune).

ARIOVISTUS (-i), a German chief, who had conquered a great part of Gaul, but was defeated by Caesar, and driven across the Rhine, B.C. 58. Ariovistus escaped across the river in a small boat.

ĀRISTAEUS (-i), son of Apollo and Cyrenē, was born in Libya. He afterwards went to Thrace, where he fell in love with Eurydicē, the wife of Orpheus. The latter, while fleeing from him, perished by the bite of a serpent; whereupon the Nymphs, in anger, destroyed the bees of Aristaeus. The way in which he recovered his bees is related in the fourth Georgic of Virgil. After his death he was worshipped as a god on account of the benefits he had conferred upon mankind. He was regarded as the protector of flocks and shepherds, of vine and olive plantations: he taught men to keep bees, and averted from the fields the burning heat of the sun and other causes of destruction.

ĀRISTĂGŌRAS (-ae), of Miletus, brother-in-law of Histiaeus, was left by the latter during his stay at the Persian court, in charge of the government of Miletus. Having failed in an attempt upon Naxos (B.C. 501), which he had promised to subdue for the Persians, and fearing the consequences of his failure, he induced the Ionian cities to revolt from Persia. He applied for assistance to the Spartans and Athenians: the former refused, but the latter sent him 20 ships and some troops. In 499 his army captured and burnt Sardis, but was finally chased back to the coast. The Athenians now departed; the Persians conquered most of the Ionian cities; and Aristagoras in despair fled to Thrace, where he was slain by the Edonians in 497.

ĀRISTARCHUS (-i). (1) Of Samos, an eminent mathematician and astronomer at Alexandria, flourished between B.C. 280 and 264.—(2) Of Samothrace, the celebrated grammarian, flourished B.C. 156. He was a pupil of Aristophanes, and founded at A.exandria a grammatical and critical school. At an advanced age he went to Cyprus, where he died at the age of 72, of voluntary starvation, because he was suffering from incurable dropsy. Aristarchus was the greatest critic of antiquity. His labours were chiefly devoted to the Homeric poems, of which he published an edition which has been the basis of the text from his time to the present day. He divided the Iliad and Odyssey into 24 books each.

ĀRISTĒAS, of Proconnesus, an epic poet of whose life we have only fabulous accounts. His date is quite uncertain. He is represented as a magician, whose soul could leave and re-enter its body according to its pleasure. He was connected with the worship of Apollo, which he was said to have introduced at Metapontum.

ĀRISTĪDĒS (-is). (1) An Athenian, son of Lysimachus, surnamed the "Just," was of an ancient and noble family. He fought at the commander of his tribe at the battle of Marathon, B.C. 490; and next year, 489, he was archon. He was the great rival of Themistocles, and it was through the influence of the latter with the people, that he suffered ostracism in 483 or 482. He was still in exile in 480 at the battle of Salamis, where he did good service by dislodging the enemy, with a band raised and armed by himself, from the islet of Psyttalēa. He was recalled from banishment after the battle, was appointed general in the following year (479), and commanded the Athenians at the battle of Plataea. In 477, when the allies had become disgusted with the conduct of Pausanias and the Spartans, he and his colleague Cimon had the glory of obtaining for Athens the command of the maritime confederacy: and to Aristides was by general consent entrusted the task of drawing up its laws and fixing its assessments. This first tribute of 460 talents, paid into a common treasury at Delos, bore his name, and was regarded by the allies in after times, as marking their Saturnian age. This is his last recorded act. He probably died in 468. He died so poor that he did not leave enough to pay for his funeral: his daughters were portioned by the state, and his son Lysimachus received a grant of land and of money. —(2) The author of a licentious romance, in prose, entitled *Milesiaca*, having Miletus for its scene. It was translated into Latin by L. Cornelius Sisenna, a contemporary of Sulla, and became popular with the Romans. The title of his work gave rise to the term *Milesian*, as applied to works of fiction.—(3) Of Thebes, a celebrated Greek painter, flourished about B.C. 360—330. His pictures were so much valued that long after his death Attalus, king of Pergamus, offered 600,000 sesterces for one of them.—(4) P. AELIUS ARISTIDES, surnamed THEODORUS, a celebrated Greek rhetorician, was born at Adriani in Mysia, in A.D. 117. After travelling through various countries, he settled at Smyrna, where he died about A.D. 180. Several of his works have come down to us.

ĀRISTĪŌN, a philosopher, who made himself tyrant of Athens through the influence of Mithridates. He was put to death by Sulla, on the capture of Athens by the latter, B.C. 87.

ĀRISTIPPUS (-i), a native of Cyrenē, and founder of the Cyrenaic school of philosophy, flourished about B.C. 370. The fame of Socrates brought him to Athens, and he remained with the latter almost up to the time of his execution, B.C. 399. Though a disciple of Socrates, he was luxurious in his mode of living ; and he took money for his teaching. He passed part of his life at the court of Dionysius, tyrant of Syracuse ; but he appears at last to have returned to Cyrene, and there to have spent his old age. He imparted his doctrine to his daughter Aretē, by whom it was communicated to her son, the younger Aristippus.

ĀRISTŌBŪLUS (-i). (1) The name of several princes of Judaea. Of these the best known in history is the brother of Hyrcanus, of whom an account is given under HYRCANUS. —(2) Of Cassandrēa, served under Alexander the Great in Asia, and wrote a history of Alexander, which was one of the chief sources used by Arrian in the composition of his work.

ĀRISTŌDĒMUS (-i). (1) A descendant of Hercules, son of Aristomachus, brother of Temenus and Cresphontes, and father of Eurysthenes and Procles. He was killed at Naupactus by a flash of lightning, just as he was setting out on the expedition into Peloponnesus, and his two sons obtained Sparta, which would have fallen to him.—(2) A Messenian, the chief hero in the first Messenian war. He sacrificed his own daughter to save his country. He was afterwards elected king in place of Euphaes ; and continued the war against the Spartans, till at length, finding resistance hopeless, he put an end to his life on the tomb of his daughter, about B.C. 723.

ARISTOGĪTON. [HARMODIUS.]

ARISTŌMĀCHUS (-i), son of Cleodemus or Cleodaeus, grandson of Hyllus, great-grandson of Hercules, and father of Temenus, Cresphontes, and Aristodemus. He fell in battle when he invaded Peloponnesus ; but his 3 sons were more successful and conquered Peloponnesus.

ĀRISTŌMĒNĒS (-is), the Messenian, the hero of the second war with Sparta, belongs more to legend than to history. He was a native of Andania, and was sprung from the royal line of Aepytus. Tired of the yoke of Sparta, he began the war in B.C. 685. After the defeat of the Messenians in the third year of the war, Aristomenes retreated to the mountain fortress of Ira, and there maintained the war for 11 years, constantly ravaging the land of Laconia. In one of his incursions the Spartans overpowered him with superior numbers, and carrying him with 50 of his comrades to Sparta, cast them into the pit where condemned criminals were thrown. The rest perished ; not so Aristomenes, the favourite of the gods ; for legends told how an eagle bore him up on its wings as he fell,

and a fox guided him on the third day from the cavern. But the city of Ira, which he had so long successfully defended, fell into the hands of the Spartans, who again became masters of Messenia, B.C. 668. Aristomenes settled at Ialysus in Rhodes, where he married his daughter to Damagetus, king of Ialysus.

ĀRISTŌN. (1) Of Chios, a Stoic philosopher, and a disciple of Zeno, flourished about B.C. 260.—(2) A Peripatetic philosopher of Iulis in the island of Ceos, succeeded Lycon as head of the Peripatetic school, about B.C. 230.

ĀRISTŌNĪCUS (-i), a natural son of Eumenes II., of Pergamus. Upon the death of his brother Attalus III., B.C. 133, who left his kingdom to the Romans, Aristonicus laid claim to the crown. He defeated in 131 the consul P. Licinius Crassus ; but in 130 he was defeated and taken prisoner by M. Perperna, was carried to Rome by M'. Aquillus in 129, and was there put to death.

ĀRISTŌPHĀNĒS (-is). (1) The celebrated comic poet, was born about B.C. 444, and probably at Athens. His father Philippus had possessions in Aegina, and may originally have come from that island, whence a question arose whether Aristophanes was a genuine Athenian citizen : his enemy Cleon brought against him more than one accusation to deprive him of his civic rights, but without success. He had three sons, Philippus, Araros, and Nicostratus, but of his private history we know nothing. He died about B.C. 380. The comedies of Aristophanes are of the highest historical interest, containing as they do an admirable series of caricatures on the leading men of the day. The first great evil of his own time against which he inveighs, is the Peloponnesian war, to which he ascribes the influence of demagogues like Cleon at Athens. His play, called the *Knights*, was especially directed against Cleon. Another great object of his indignation was the system of education which had been introduced by the Sophists, and which he attacks in the *Clouds*, making Socrates the representative of the Sophists. Another feature of the times was the excessive love for litigation at Athens, which he ridicules in the *Wasps*. Eleven of the plays of Aristophanes have come down to us. As a poet he possessed merits of the highest order. He was a complete master of the Attic dialect, which appears in his works in its greatest perfection. —(2) Of Byzantium, an eminent Greek grammarian, was a pupil of Zenodotus and Eratosthenes, and teacher of the celebrated Aristarchus. He lived about B.C. 264, and had the management of the library at Alexandria. He was the first who introduced the use of accents in the Greek language.

ĂRISTŎTĔLĔS (-is), the philosopher, was born at Stagīra, a town in Chalcidice in Macedonia, B.C. 384. His father, Nicomachus, was physician in ordinary to Amyntas II., king of Macedonia ; his mother's name was Phaestis or Phaestias. In 367, he went to Athens to pursue his studies, and there became a pupil of Plato, who named him the "intellect of his school," and his house, the house of the "reader." He lived at Athens for 20 years, but quitted the city upon the death of Plato (347) and repaired to his friend Hermīas at Atarneus, where he married Pythias, the adoptive daughter of the prince. On the death of HERMIAS, who was killed by the Persians (344), Aristotle fled from Atarneus to Mytilene. Two years afterwards (342) he accepted an invitation from Philip of Macedonia, to undertake the instruction of his son Alexander, then 13 years of age. Here Aristotle was treated with the most marked respect. His native city, Stagīra, which had been destroyed by Philip, was rebuilt at his request. Aristotle spent 7 years in Macedonia. On Alexander's accession to the throne in 335, Aristotle returned to Athens. Here he had the Lycēum, a gymnasium sacred to Apollo Lyceus, assigned to him by the state. He assembled round him a large number of scholars, to whom he delivered lectures on philosophy in the shady walks (περίπατοι) which surrounded the Lycēum, while walking up and down (περιπατῶν), and not sitting, which was the general practice of the philosophers. From one or other of these circumstances the name *Peripatetic* is derived, which was afterwards given to his school. He gave two different courses of lectures every day. Those which he delivered in the morning (called *esoteric*) to a narrower circle of hearers, embraced subjects connected with the more abstruse philosophy, physics, and dialectics. Those which he delivered in the afternoon to a more promiscuous circle (called *exoteric*), extended to rhetoric, sophistics, and politics. He presided over his school for 13 years (335—323). During this time he also composed the greater part of his works. In these labours he was assisted by the kingly liberality of his former pupil, who caused large collections of natural curiosities to be made for him, to which posterity is indebted for one of his most excellent works, the *History of Animals*. After the death of Alexander (323), Aristotle was looked upon with suspicion at Athens as a friend of Macedonia ; but as it was not easy to bring any political accusation against him, he was accused of impiety. He withdrew

from Athens before his trial, and escaped in the beginning of 322 to Chalcis in Euboea, where he died in the course of the same year, in the 63rd year of his age. He bequeathed to Theophrastus his well-stored library and the originals of his writings. He is described as having been of weak health, which, considering the astonishing extent of his studies, shows all the more the energy of his mind. His works, which treated of almost all the subjects of human knowledge cultivated in his time, have exercised a powerful influence upon the human mind ; and his treatises on philosophy and logic still claim the attention of every student of those sciences.

ĂRISTŎXĔNUS (-i), of Tarentum, a Peripatetic philosopher and a musician, flourished about B.C. 318. He wrote numerous works, of which one on music is still extant.

ĂRIŪSĬA (-ae), a district on the N. coast of Chios, where the best wine in the island was grown.

ARMĔNE (-es), a town on the coast of Paphlagonia, a little to the W. of Sinope.

ARMĒNĬA (-ae), a country of Asia, lying between Asia Minor and the Caspian, is a lofty table-land, backed by the chain of the Caucasus, watered by the rivers Cyrus and Araxes, and containing sources the of the Tigris and of the Euphrates, the latter of which divides the country into 2 unequal parts, which were called Major and Minor.— The people of Armenia were one of the most ancient families of that branch of the human race which is called Caucasian. They were conquered by the Assyrians and Persians, and were at a later time subject to the Greek kings of Syria. When Antiochus the Great was defeated by the Romans (B.C. 190), the country regained its independence, and was at this period divided into the two kingdoms of Armenia Major and Minor. Ultimately, Armenia Minor was made a Roman province by Trajan ; and Armenia Major, after being a perpetual object of contention between the Romans and the Parthians, was subjected to the revived Persian empire by its first king Artaxerxes in A.D. 226.

ARMĬNĬUS (-i : the Latinised form of *Hermann*, "the chieftain"), son of Sigimer, and chief of the tribe of the Cherusci, who inhabited the country to the N. of the Hartz mountains, now forming the S. of Hanover and Brunswick. He was born in B.C. 18 ; and in his youth, he led the Cherusci as auxiliaries of the Roman legions in Germany, where he learnt the Roman language, was admitted to the freedom of the city, and enrolled amongst the equites. In A.D. 9, Arminius persuaded his countrymen to rise against the Romans who were now masters of this part of Germany. His attempt was crowned with success. Quintilius Varus, who was stationed in the country with 3 legions, was destroyed with almost all his troops [VARUS]; and the Romans had to relinquish all their possessions beyond the Rhine. In 14, Arminius had to defend his country against Germanicus. At first he was successful; but Germanicus made good his retreat to the Rhine. It was in the course of this campaign that Thusnelda, the wife of Arminius, fell into the hands of the Romans. In 16, Arminius was defeated by Germanicus, and his country was probably only saved from subjection by the jealousy of Tiberius, who recalled Germanicus in the following year. At length Arminius aimed at absolute power, and was in consequence cut off by his own relations in the 37th year of his age, A.D. 19.

ARMORĬCA or ARĒMŎRĬCA (-ae), the name of the N.W. coast of Gaul from the Ligeris (Loire) to the Sequana (Seine), derived from the Celtic ar, air, "upon," muir, mór, "the sea."

ARNA (-ae), a town in Umbria near Perusia.

ARNAE (-ārum), a town in Chalcidice in Macedonia, S. of Aulon and Bromiscus.

ARNISSA (-ae), a town in Eordaea in Macedonia.

ARNUS (-i: Arno), the chief river of Etruria, rising in the Apennines, flowing by Pisae, and falling into the Tyrrhenian sea.

ĂRŌMĂTA (-ōrum), the E.-most promontory of Africa, at the S. extremity of the Arabian Gulf.

ARPI (-ōrum), an inland town in the Daunian Apulia, founded, according to tradition, by Diomedes, who called it Argos Hippium, from which its later names of Argȳrippa, or Argȳrĭpa and Arpi are said to have arisen. It revolted to Hannibal after the battle of Cannae, B.C. 216, but was retaken by the Romans in 213.

ARPĪNUM (-i), a town of Latium on the small river Fibrenus, originally belonging to the Volscians and afterwards to the Samnites, was a Roman municipium, and received the ius suffragii, or right of voting in the Roman comitia, B.C. 188. It was the birthplace of Marius and Cicero.

ARRĒTĬUM or ĂRĒTĬUM (-i: Arezzo), one of the most important of the 12 cities of Etruria, was situated in the N.E. of the country at the foot of the Apennines, and possessed a fertile territory near the sources of the Arnus and the Tiber, producing good wine and corn. It was particularly celebrated for its pottery, which was of red ware. The

Cilnii, from whom Maecenas was descended, were a noble family of Arretium.

ARRHIDAEUS or ARIDAEUS (-i), son of Philip and a female dancer, Philinna of Larissa, was of imbecile understanding. On the death of Alexander, B.C. 323, he was elected king under the name of Philip, and in 322, he married Eurydice. On their return to Macedonia, he and his wife were made prisoners, and put to death by order of Olympias, 317.

ARRIĀNUS (-i), a Greek historian and philosopher, was born at Nicomedia in Bithynia, about A.D. 90. He was a pupil and friend of Epictetus, whose lectures he published at Athens. In 124, he received from Hadrian the Roman citizenship, and from this time assumed the name of Flavius. In 136, he was appointed praefect of Cappadocia, which was invaded in the year after by the Alani or Massagetae, whom he defeated. Under Antoninus Pius, in 146, he was consul; and he died at an advanced age in the reign of M. Aurelius. Arrian was one of the best writers of his time. He was a close imitator of Xenophon both in the subjects of his works and in the style in which they were written. The most important of them is his History of the expedition of Alexander the Great, in 7 books, which was based upon the most trustworthy histories written by the contemporaries of Alexander.

ARSĂCĒS (-is), the name of the founder of the Parthian empire, which was also borne by all his successors, who were hence called the Arsăcĭdae.—(1) He was of obscure origin, but he induced the Parthians to revolt from Antiochus II., king of Syria, and became the first monarch of the Parthians, about B.C. 250. The events which immediately followed, are stated very differently by different historians. He reigned only 2 years, and was succeeded by his brother Tiridates.—(2) TIRIDATES, reigned 37 years, B.C. 248—211, and defeated Seleucus Callinicus, the successor of Antiochus II. — (3) ARTABANUS I., son of the preceding, was attacked by Antiochus III. (the Great), who, however, at length recognised him as king, about 210.—(4) PRIAPATIUS, son of the preceding, reigned 15 years, and left 3 sons, Phraates, Mithridates, and Artabanus. — (5) PHRAATES I., was succeeded by his brother.—(6) MITHRIDATES I., who greatly enlarged the Parthian empire by his conquests. He defeated Demetrius Nicator, king of Syria, and took him prisoner in 138. He died during the captivity of Demetrius, between 138 and 130.—(7) PHRAATES II., son of the preceding, defeated and slew in battle Antiochus VII. Sidetes, B.C. 128. Phraates himself was shortly after killed by the Scythians.—(8) ARTABANUS II., youngest son of No. 4, fell in battle against the Thogarii or Tocharii, apparently after a short reign.— (9) MITHRIDATES II., son of the preceding, added many nations to the Parthian empire, whence he obtained the surname of Great. He sent an ambassador to Sulla, B.C. 92. —(10) MNASCIRES (?), the successor of the preceding, of whom nothing is known.—(11) SANATROCES, reigned 7 years, and died about B.C. 70.—(12) PHRAATES III., son of the preceding, lived at the time of the war between the Romans and Mithridates of Pontus, by both of whom he was courted. He was murdered by his 2 sons, Mithridates and Orodes.—(13) MITHRIDATES III., son of the preceding, was expelled from the throne on account of his cruelty, and was succeeded by his brother Orodes.—(14) ORO-DES I., brother of the preceding, was the Parthian king, whose general Surenas defeated Crassus and the Romans, B.C. 53. [CRASSUS.] After the death of Crassus, Orodes gave the command of the army to his son Pacorus, who invaded Syria both in 51 and 50, but was in each year driven back by Cassius. In 40, the Parthians again invaded Syria, under the command of Pacorus and Labienus, but were defeated in 39 by Ventidius Bassus, one of Antony's legates. In 38, Pacorus once more invaded Syria, but was completely defeated and fell in the battle. This defeat was a severe blow to the aged king Orodes, who shortly afterwards surrendered the crown to his son, Phraates, during his life-time. — (15) PHRAATES IV., was a cruel tyrant. In 36, Antony invaded Parthia, but was obliged to retreat after losing a great part of his army. A few years afterwards Phraates was driven out of the country by his subjects, and Tiridates proclaimed king in his stead. Phraates, however, was soon restored by the Scythians, and Tiridates fled to Augustus, carrying with him the youngest son of Phraates. Augustus restored his son to Phraates, on condition of his surrendering the Roman standards and prisoners taken in the war with Crassus and Antony. They were given up in 20, and their restoration was celebrated not only by the poets, but by festivals and commemorative monuments. Phraates also sent to Augustus as hostages his 4 sons. In A.D. 2, Phraates was poisoned by his wife Thermusa, and her son Phraataces. — (16) PHRAATACES, reigned only a short time, as he was expelled by his subjects on account of his crimes. The Parthian nobles then elected as king Orodes, who was of the family of the Arsacidae.—(17) ORO-DES II., also reigned only a short time, as

he was killed by the Parthians on account of his cruelty. Upon his death the Parthians applied to the Romans for Vonones, one of the sons of Phraates IV., who was accordingly granted to them.—(18) VONONES I., son of Phraates IV., was also disliked by his subjects, who therefore invited Artabanus, king of Media, to take possession of the kingdom. Artabanus drove Vonones out of Parthia, who resided first in Armenia, next in Syria, and subsequently in Cilicia. He was put to death in A.D. 19.—(19) ARTA-BANUS III., obtained the Parthian kingdom soon after the expulsion of Vonones, about A.D. 16. Artabanus was involved in hostilities with the Romans, and was expelled more than once by his subjects.—(20) GOTARZES, succeeded his father, Artabanus III., but was defeated by his brother Bardanes and retired into Hyrcania. — (21) BARDANES, brother of the preceding, was put to death by his subjects in 47, whereupon Gotarzes again obtained the crown. — (22) VONONES II., succeeded Gotarzes about 50. His reign was short.—(23) VOLOGESES I., son of Vonones II. or Artabanus III. Soon after his accession, he conquered Armenia, which he gave to his brother Tiridates. He carried on war with the Romans, but was defeated by Domitius Corbulo, and at length made peace with the Romans on' condition that Tiridates should receive Armenia as a gift from the Roman emperor. Accordingly Tiridates came to Rome in 63, and obtained from Nero the Armenian crown.—(24) PACORUS, succeeded his father Vologeses I., and was a contemporary of Domitian and Trajan.—(25) CHOS-ROES or OSROES, succeeded his brother Pacorus during the reign of Trajan. His conquest of Armenia occasioned the invasion of Parthia by Trajan, who stripped it of many of its provinces, and made the Parthians for a time subject to Rome. [TRAJANUS.] Upon the death of Trajan in A.D. 117, Hadrian relinquished the conquests of Trajan, and made the Euphrates, as before, the eastern boundary of the Roman empire.—(26) VO-LOGESES II., succeeded his father Chosroes, and reigned from about A.D. 122 to 149.— (27) VOLOGESES III., was defeated by the generals of the emperor Verus, and purchased peace by ceding Mesopotamia to the Romans. From this time to the downfall of the Parthian empire, there is great confusion in the list of kings. The last king of Parthia was ARTABANUS IV., in whose reign the Persians recovered their long-lost independence. They were led by Artaxerxes, the son of Sassan, and defeated the Parthians in three great battles, in the last of which Artabanus was taken prisoner and killed, A.D. 226. Thus ended the Parthian empire of the Arsacidae, after it had existed 476 years. The Parthians were now obliged to submit to Artaxerxes, the founder of the dynasty of the Sassanidae, which continued to reign till A.D. 651.

ARSĂCĬA. [RHAGAE.]

ARSĂCĬDAE (-ārum), the name of a dynasty of Parthian kings. [ARSACES.] It was also the name of a dynasty of Armenian kings, who reigned in Armenia from B.C. 149 to A.D. 428. This dynasty was founded by ARTAXIAS I., who was related to the Parthian Arsacidae.

ARSĂMŌSĂTĂ, a town and strong fortress in Armenia Major, between the Euphrates and the sources of the Tigris.

ARSĂNĬAS(-ae), -ĬUS or -US (-i,), the name of two rivers of Great Armenia.—(1) The S. arm of the Euphrates. [EUPHRATES.]—(2) A small stream flowing W. into the Euphrates near Melitene.

ARSES, NARSES, or OARSES, youngest son of king Artaxerxes III. Ochus, was raised to the Persian throne by the eunuch Bagoas after he had poisoned Artaxerxes, B. c. 339, but he was murdered by Bagoas in the 3rd year of his reign. After the death of Arses, Bagoas made Darius III. king.

ARSĬA (-ae), a river in Istria, forming the boundary between Upper Italy and Illyricum, with a town of the same name upon it.

ARSIA SILVA, a wood in Etruria celebrated for the battle between the Tarquins and the Romans.

ARSĬNŎË (-ēs). (1) Mother of Ptolemy I., was a concubine of Philip, father of Alexander the Great, and married Lagus, while she was pregnant with Ptolemy.—(2) Daughter of Ptolemy I. and Berenĭcē, married first Lysimachus, king of Thrace, in B.C. 300; 2ndly, her half-brother, Ptolemy Ceraunus, who murdered her children by Lysimachus; and, 3rdly, her own brother Ptolemy II. Philadelphus in 279. Though Arsinoë bore Ptolemy no children, she was exceedingly beloved by him; he gave her name to several cities, called a district of Egypt Arsinoïtes after her, and honoured her memory in various ways.—(3) Daughter of Lysimachus, married Ptolemy II. Philadelphus soon after his accession, B.C. 285. In consequence of her plotting against her namesake [No. 2], when Ptolemy fell in love with her, she was banished to Coptos in Upper Egypt. She had by Ptolemy three children, Ptolemy III. Evergetes, Lysimachus, and Berenĭcē.—(4) Also called EURYDICE and CLEOPATRA, daughter of Ptolemy III. Evergetes, wife of her brother Ptolemy IV. Philopator, and mother of Ptolemy V. Epiphanes. She was killed by order of her husband.—(5) Daughter' of

Ptolemy XI. Auletes, was carried to Rome by Caesar after the capture of Alexandria, and led in.triumph by him in 46. She afterwards returned to Alexandria; but her sister Cleopatra persuaded Antony to have her put to death in 41.

ARSĬNŎË (-ēs), the name of several cities, each called after one or other of the persons mentioned above. Of these the most important were :—(1) In the Nomos Heroöpolites in Lower Egypt, near or upon the head of the Sinus Heroöpolites or W. branch of the Red sca (Gulf of Suez). It was afterwards called Cleopatra.—(2) The chief city of the Nomos Arsinoïtes in Middle Egypt; formerly called Crŏcrŏdīlopŏlis, from its being the chief seat of the Egyptian worship of the crocodile.

ARTĂBĀNUS (-i). (1) Son of Hystaspes and brother of Darius, is frequently mentioned in the reign of his nephew Xerxes, as a wise and frank counsellor.—(2) An Hyrcanian, commander of the body-guard of Xerxes, assassinated this king in B. c. 465, but was shortly afterwards killed by Artaxerxes.—(3) Kings of Parthia. [ARSACES.]

ARTĂBĀZUS (-i). (1) A Persian general in the army of Xerxes, served under Mardonius in B.C. 479, and after the defeat of the Persians at Plataea, he fled with 40,000 men and reached Asia in safety.—(2) A Persian general, fought under Artaxerxes II., and Artaxerxes III., and Darius III. Codomannus. One of his daughters, Barsĭnē, became by Alexander the mother of Hercules.

ARTABRI (-ōrum), a Celtic people in the N.W. of Spain, near the Promontory Nerium or Celticum, also called Artabrum after them (C. Finisterre).

ARTĂCĒ (-es), a sea-port town of the peninsula of Cyzicus, in the Propontis : also a mountain in the same peninsula.

ARTĂCĬĒ (-ēs), a fountain in the country of the Laestrygones.

ARTAEI (-ōrum), was, according to Herodotus, the old native name of the Persians. It signifies noble, and appears, in the form Arta, as the first part of a large number of Persian proper names.

ARTĂPHERNĒS (-is). (1) Son of Hystaspes and brother of Darius. He was satrap of Sardis at the time of the Ionian revolt, B. c. 500. See ARISTAGORAS.—(2) Son of the former, commanded, along with Datis, the Persian army of Darius, which was defeated at the battle of Marathon, B.C. 490. He commanded the Lydians and Mysians in the invasion of Greece by Xerxes in 480.

ARTAVASDĒS or ARTĂBĀZĒS (-is). (1) King of the Greater Armenia, succeeded his father 'Tigranes. He betrayed Antony in .his

campaign against the Parthians in B.C. 36.
Antony accordingly invaded Armenia in 34,
took Artavasdes prisoner, and carried him to
Alexandria. He was killed after the battle
of Actium by order of Cleopatra.—(2) King
of Armenia, probably a grandson of No. I,
was placed upon the throne by Augustus, but
was deposed by the Armenians.—(3) King of
Media Atropatene, and an enemy of Artavasdes I., king of Armenia. He died shortly
before B.C. 20.

ARTĀXĀTA (-ōrum), or -A (-ae), the later
capital of Great Armenia, built by Artaxias,
under the advice of Hannibal, on a peninsula,
surrounded by the river Araxes. After being
burnt by the Romans under Corbulo (B.C.
58), it was restored by Tiridates, and called
Neroniana.

ARTĀXERXĒS (-is), the name of 4 Persian
kings.—(1) Surnamed LONGIMANUS, from his
right hand being longer than his left, succeeded his father Xerxes I. and reigned B.C.
464—425. He carried on war against the
Egyptians who were assisted in their revolt
by the Athenians. He was succeeded by
his son Xerxes II.—(2) Surnamed MNEMON,
from his good memory, succeeded his father,
Darius II., and reigned B.C. 405—359.
Respecting the war between him and his
brother Cyrus, see CYRUS. Tissaphernes was
appointed satrap of W. Asia in the place of
Cyrus, and was actively engaged in wars with
the Greeks. [AGESILAUS.] Artaxerxes had
to carry on frequent wars with tributary
princes and satraps, who endeavoured to make
themselves independent. Thus he maintained
a long struggle against Evagoras of Cyprus,
from 385 to 376; and his attempts to recover
Egypt were unsuccessful. Towards the end
of his reign he put to death his eldest son
Darius, who had formed a plot to assassinate
him. His last days were still further embittered by the unnatural conduct of his son
Ochus, who caused the destruction of two of
his brothers, in order to secure the succession
for himself. Artaxerxes was succeeded by
Ochus, who ascended the throne under the
name of Artaxerxes III.—(3) Also called
OCHUS, reigned B.C. 359—338. By the
aid of his Greek generals and mercenaries,
he reconquered Phoenicia and Egypt. The
reins of government were entirely in the
hands of the eunuch Bagoas, and of Mentor
the Rhodian. At last he was poisoned by
Bagoas, and was succeeded by his youngest
son, ARSES.—(4) The founder of the dynasty
of the SASSANIDAE.

ARTAXĪAS (-ae), or ARTAXĒS (-is), the
name of 3 kings of Armenia.—(1) The founder
of the Armenian kingdom, was one of the
generals of Antiochus the Great, but revolted

from him about B.C. 188, and became an independent sovereign. Hannibal took refuge
at the court of Artaxias, and he superintended
the building of ARTAXATA, the capital of
Armenia. Artaxias was conquered and taken
prisoner by Antiochus IV. Epiphanes, about
165.—(2) Son of Artavasdes, was put to death
by his own subjects in B.C. 20, and Augustus
placed Tigranes on the throne.—(3) Son of
Polemon, king of Pontus, was proclaimed
king of Armenia by Germanicus, in A.D. 18.
He died about 35.

ARTĒMIDŌRUS (-i). (1) A native of
Ephesus, but called Daldianus, from Daldis in
Lydia, his mother's birth-place, to distinguish
him from the geographer Artemidorus. He
lived at Rome in the reigns of Antoninus Pius
and M. Aurelius (A.D. 138—180), and wrote a
work on the interpretation of dreams, in 5
books, which is still extant.—(2) Also of
Ephesus, a Greek geographer, lived about
B.C. 100. An abridgment of his work was
made by Marcianus, of which part is still
extant.

ARTĒMIS (-is), called DĪANA (-ae) by the
Romans, one of the great divinities of the
Greeks. According to the most ancient account, she was daughter of Zeus (Jupiter) and
Leto (Latona), and the twin-sister of Apollo,
born with him in the island of Delos. (1)
Artemis as the sister of Apollo, is a kind of
female Apollo, that is, she as a female divinity
represented the same idea that Apollo did as a
male divinity. As sister of Apollo, Artemis
is like her brother armed with a bow, quiver,
and arrows, and sends plagues and death
among men and animals. Sudden deaths,
but more especially those of women, are
described as the effect of her arrows. As
Apollo was not only a destructive god, but
also averted evils, so Artemis likewise cured
and alleviated the sufferings of mortals. In
the Trojan war she sided, like Apollo, with
the Trojans. She was more especially the
protectress of the young; and from her
watching over the young of females, she
came to be regarded as the goddess of the
flocks and the chase. In this manner she
also became the huntress among the immortals. Artemis, like Apollo, is unmarried;
she is a maiden-divinity never conquered by
love. She slew ORION with her arrows because he made an attempt upon her chastity;
and she changed ACTAEON into a stag, simply
because he had seen her bathing. With her
brother Apollo, she slew the children of
NIOBE, who had deemed herself superior to
Leto. When Apollo was regarded as identical with the Sun or Helios, his sister was
looked upon as Selēnē or the Moon. Hence
she is represented as in love with the fair

youth ENDYMION, whom she kissed in his sleep; but this legend properly relates to Selēnē or the Moon, and is foreign to the character of Artemis, who, as we have observed, was a goddess unmoved by love. —(2) *The Arcadian Artemis* is a goddess of the nymphs, and was worshipped as such in Arcadia in very early times. She hunted with her nymphs on the Arcadian mountains, and her chariot was drawn by 4 stags with golden antlers. There was no connection between the Arcadian Artemis and Apollo.—(3) *The Taurian Artemis.* There was in Tauris a goddess, whom the Greeks identified with their own Artemis, and to whom all strangers thrown on the coast of Tauris were sacrificed. Iphigenīa and Orestes brought her image from thence, and landed at Brauron in Attica whence the goddess derived the name of Brauronia. The Brauronian Artemis was worshipped at Athens and Sparta, and in the latter place the boys were scourged at her altar till it was besprinkled with their blood. — (4) *The Ephesian Artemis*, was a divinity totally distinct from the Greek goddess of the same name. She was an ancient Asiatic divinity whose worship the Greeks found established in Ionia, when they settled there, and to whom they gave the name of Artemis. Her image in the magnificent temple of Ephesus was represented with many breasts. —The representations of the Greek Artemis in works of art are different according as she is represented either as a huntress, or as the goddess of the moon. As the huntress, her breast is covered, and the legs up to the knees are naked, the rest being covered by the chlamys. Her attributes are the bow, quiver, and arrows, or a spear, stags, and dogs. As the goddess of the moon, she wears a long robe which reaches down to her feet, a veil covers her head, and above her forehead rises the crescent of the moon.

Artemis (Diana), the Huntress.　(Museum Capitolinum, vol. 4, tav. 37.)

Artemis. (Diana), goddess of the Moon. (Gorii, Mus. Flor., vol. 2, tav. 88.)

In her hand she often appears holding a torch.

ARTEMĪSĬA (-ae). (1) Daughter of Lygdamis, and queen of Halicarnassus in Caria, accompanied Xerxes in his invasion of Greece, and in the battle of Salamis (B.C. 480) greatly distinguished herself by her prudence and courage, for which she was afterwards highly honoured by the Persian king.—(2) Daughter of Hecatomnus, and sister, wife, and successor of the Carian prince Mausolus, reigned B.C. 352—350. She is renowned in history for her extraordinary grief at the death of her husband Mausōlus. She is said to have mixed his ashes in her daily drink; and to perpetuate his memory she built at Halicarnassus the celebrated monument, *Mausōlēum*, which was regarded as one of the 7 wonders of the world, and whose name subsequently became the generic term for any splendid sepulchral monument.

ARTEMĪSĬUM (-i), a tract of country on the N. coast of Euboea, opposite Magnesia, so called from the temple of Artemis (Diana), belonging to the town of Hestiaea: off this coast the Greeks defeated the fleet of Xerxes, B.C. 480.

ARVERNI (-ōrum), a Gallic people in Aquitania, in the modern *Auvergne*. In early times they were the most powerful people in the S. of Gaul: they were defeated by Domitius Ahenobarbus and Fabius Maximus in B.C. 121, but still possessed considerable power in the time of Caesar (58). Their capital was Nemossus, also named Augustonemetum or Arverni on the Elāver (*Allier*), with a citadel, called in the middle ages Clarus Mons, whence the name of the modern town, *Clermont*.

ARUNS (-untis), an Etruscan word, was regarded by the Romans as a proper name, but perhaps signified a younger son in general.—(1) Younger brother of Lucumo, i. e. L. Tarquinius Priscus.—(2) Younger brother of L. Tarquinius Superbus, was murdered by his wife.—(3) Younger son of Tarquinius Superbus, fell in combat with Brutus.

ARZĀNĒNĒ (-ēs), a district of Armenia Major, bounded on the S. by the Tigris, formed part of GORDYENE.

ASANDER (-dri). (1) Son of Philotas, brother of Parmenion, and one of the generals of Alexander the Great. After the death of Alexander (B.C. 323) he obtained Caria for his satrapy.—(2) A general of Pharnaces II., king of Bosporus, whom he put to death in 47, in hopes of obtaining the kingdom. He was confirmed in the sovereignty by Augustus.

ASBYSTAE (-ārum), a Libyan people, in the N. of Cyrenaica.

ASCĂLĂPHUS (-i). (1) Son of Ares (Mars) and Astyochē, led, with his brother Ialmenus, the Minyans of Orchomenus against Troy, and was slain by Deïphobus.—(2) Son of Acheron and Gorgyra or Orphne. When Pluto gave Persephŏnē (Proserpĭna) permission to return to the upper world, provided she had eaten nothing, Ascalaphus declared that she had eaten part of a pomegranate. Persephŏnē, in revenge, changed him into an owl, by sprinkling him with water from the river Phlegethon.

ASCĂLŌN (-ōnis), one of the chief cities of the Philistines, on the coast of Palestine, between Azotus and Gaza.

ASCANĬA (-ae). (1) In Bithynia, a great fresh-water lake, at the E. end of which stood the city of Nicaea.—(2) A salt-water lake on the borders of Phrygia and Pisidia.

ASCANĬUS (-i), son of Aeneas by Creusa, accompanied his father to Italy. Other traditions gave the name of Ascanius to the son of Aeneas and Lavinia. He founded Alba Longa, and was succeeded on the throne by his son Silvius. Some writers relate that Ascanius was also called Ilus or Julus. The gens Julia at Rome traced its origin from Julus or Ascanius.

ASCIBURGĬUM (-ɪ: *Asburg*, near *Mörs*), an ancient place on the left bank of the Rhine.

ASCLĒPĬĂDĒS (-is), the name of several physicians, which they derived from the god Asclepius. [AESCULAPIUS.] The most celebrated was a native of Bithynia, who came to Rome in the middle of the first century B.C., where he acquired a great reputation by his successful cures.

ASCLĒPĬUS. [AESCULAPIUS.]

ASCŌNĬUS PĒDĬĀNUS Q. (-i), a Roman grammarian, born at Patavium (Padua), about B.C. 2, and died in his 85th year in the reign of Domitian. He wrote a valuable Commentary on the speeches of Cicero, of which we still possess considerable fragments.

ASCRA (-ae), a town in Boeotia on Mt. Helicon, where Hesiod resided, who had removed thither with his father from Cyme in Aeolis, and who is therefore called *Ascraeus*.

ASCŬLUM (-i). (1) PICENUM, the chief town of Picenum, and a Roman municipium, was destroyed by the Romans in the Social War (B.C. 89), but was afterwards rebuilt. —(2) APULUM, a town of Apulia in Daunia on the confines of Samnium, near which the Romans were defeated by Pyrrhus, B.C. 729.

ASDRŪBAL. [HASDRUBAL.]

ASELLĬO (-ōnis), P. SEMPRŌNĬUS (-i), tribune of the soldiers under P. Scipio Africanus at Numantia, B.C. 133, wrote a Roman history from the Punic wars inclusive to the times of the Gracchi.

ASIA (-ae), daughter of Oceanus and Tethys, wife of Iapetus, and mother of Atlas, Prometheus, and Epimetheus. According to some traditions, the continent of Asia derived its name from her.

ASIA (-ae), in the poets ASIS (-ĭdis), one of the 3 great divisions which the ancients made of the known world. It was first used by the Greeks for the western part of Asia Minor, especially the plains watered by the river Caÿster, where the Ionian colonists first settled; and thence, as their geographical knowledge advanced, they extended it to the whole country. The southern part of the continent was supposed to extend much further to the E. than it really does, while to the N. and N.E. parts, which were quite unknown, much too small an extent was assigned. The different opinions about the boundaries of Asia on the side of Africa are mentioned under AFRICA: on the side of Europe the boundary was formed by the river Tanais (*Don*), the Paulus Maeotis (*Sea of Azof*), Pontus Euxinus (*Black Sea*), Propontis (*Sea of Marmora*), and the Aegean (*Archipelago*). —The most general division of Asia was into 2 parts, which were different at different times, and known by different names. To the earliest Greek colonists the river Halys, the eastern boundary of the Lydian kingdom, formed a natural division between *Upper* and *Lower Asia ;* and afterwards the Euphrates was adopted as a more natural boundary. Another division was made by the Taurus into *A. intra Taurum*, i. e. the part of Asia N. and N.W. of the Taurus, and *A. extra Taurum*, all the rest of the continent. The division ultimately adopted, but apparently not till the 4th century of our era, was that of *A. Major* and *A. Minor.* — (1) ASIA MAJOR was the part of the continent E. of the Tanais, the Euxine, an imaginary line drawn from the Euxine at Trapezus (*Trebizond*) to the Gulf of Issus, and the Mediterranean : thus it included the countries of Sarmatica Asiatica with all the Scythian tribes to the E., Colchis, Iberia, Albania, Armenia, Syria, Arabia, Babylonia, Mesopotamia, Assyria, Media, Susiana, Persis, Ariana Hyrcania, Margiana, Bactriana, Sogdiana, India, the land of the Sinae and Serica ; respecting which, see the several articles. — (2) ASIA MINOR (*Anatolia*), was the peninsula on the extreme W. of Asia, bounded by the Euxine, Aegean, and Mediterranean on the N., W., and S. ; and on the E. by the mountains on the W. of the upper course of the Euphrates. It was divided into Mysia, Lydia, and Caria, on the W., Lycia,

Pamphylia, and Cilicia, on the S. ; Bithynia, Paphlagonia, and Pontus, on the E. ; and Phrygia, Pisidia, Galatia, and Cappadocia, in the centre. — (3) ASIA PROPRIA, or simply ASIA, the Roman province, formed out of the kingdom of Pergamus, which was bequeathed to the Romans by ATTALUS III. (B.C. 130), and the Greek cities on the W. coast, and the adjacent islands, with Rhodes. It included the districts of Mysia, Lydia, Caria, and Phrygia ; and was governed at first by propraetors, afterwards by proconsuls.

ASINARUS (-i), a river on the E. side of Sicily on which the Athenians were defeated by the Syracusans, B. c. 413.

ASINE (-es). (1) A town in Laconia on the coast between Taenarum and Gythium.— (2) A town in Argolis, W. of Hermione, was built by the Dryopes, who were driven out of the town by the Argives after the first Messenian war, and built No. 3.—(3) An important town in Messenia, near the Promontory Acritas, on the Messenian gulf, which was hence also called the Asinaean gulf.

ASINIUS GALLUS. [GALLUS.]

ASINIUS POLLIO. [POLLIO.]

ASOPUS (-i). (1) A river flowing through the Sicyonian territory into the Corinthian gulf. The god of this river, was son of Oceanus and Tethys, and father of Evadne, Euboea, and Aegina, each of whom was therefore called *Asopis*. Acacus, the son of Aegina, is called *Asopiades*.—(2) A river in Boeotia, flowing near Plataeae, and falling into the Euboean sea.—(3) A river in Thessaly, rising in M. Oeta, and flowing into the Maliac gulf near Thermypolae.

ASPARAGIUM (-i), a town in the territory of Dyrrhachium in Illyria.

ASPASIA (-ae). (1) The elder, of Miletus, daughter of Axiochus, the most celebrated of the Greek Hetaerae. She came to Athens, where she gained the affections of Pericles, not more by her beauty than by her high mental accomplishments. Having parted with his wife, Pericles lived with Aspasia, during the rest of his life. His enemies accused Aspasia of impiety, and it required all his personal influence to procure her acquittal. The house of Aspasia was the centre of the best literary and philosophical society of Athens, and was frequented even by Socrates. On the death of Pericles (B. c. 429), Aspasia is said to have attached herself to one Lysicles, a dealer in cattle, and to have made him by her instructions a first-rate orator.—(2) The Younger, a Phocaean, daughter of Hermotimus, the favourite concubine of Cyrus the Younger, and subsequently of his brother Artaxerxes. Cyrus called her Aspasia after the mistress of Pericles, her previous name having been Milto. Darius, son of Artaxerxes, having fallen in love with her, Artaxerxes made her priestess of a temple at Ecbatana, where strict celibacy was requisite.

ASPENDUS (-i), a flourishing city of Pamphylia, on the river Eurymedon, 60 stadia from its mouth: said to have been a colony of Argives.

ASPHALTĪTĒS LACUS or MARE MORTUUM, the great salt lake in the S. E. of Palestine, which receives the water of the Jordan.

ASPIS (-ĭdis), or CLYPEA (-ae), a city on a promontory of the same name, near the N. E. point of the Carthaginian territory, founded by Agathocles, and taken in the first Punic War by the Romans.

ASPLĒDŌN or SPLĒDŌN, a town of the Minyae in Boeotia on the river Melas, near Orchomenus.

ASSA (-ae), a town in Chalcidīcē in Macedonia, on the Singitic gulf.

ASSACĒNI (-ōrum), an Indian tribe, in the district of the Paropamisadae, between the rivers Cophen (Cabool), and Indus.

ASSĂRĂCUS (-i), king of Troy, son of Tros, father of Capys, grandfather of Anchises, and great-grandfather of Aeneas. Hence the Romans, as descendants of Aeneas, are called domus Assaraci.

ASSĒSUS (-i), a town of Ionia near Miletus, with a temple of Athēna surnamed Assēsĭa.

ASSŌRUS (-i), a small town in Sicily between Enna and Agyrium.

ASSUS (-i), a city in the Troad, on the Adramyttian Gulf, opposite to Lesbos: afterwards called Apollonia: the birthplace of Cleanthes the Stoic.

ASSЎRĪA (-ae). (1) The country properly so called, in the narrowest sense, was a district of Asia, extending along the E. side of the Tigris, which divided it on the W. and N. W. from Mesopotamia and Babylonia, and bounded on the N. and E. by M. Niphates and M. Zagrus, which separated it from Armenia and Media, and on the S. E. by Susiana. It was watered by several streams, flowing into the Tigris from the E.; two of which, the Lycus or Zabatus (Great Zab), and the Caprus or Zabas or Anzabas (Little Zab), divided the country into three parts: that between the Upper Tigris and the Lycus was called Aturia (a mere dialectic variety of Assyria), was probably the most ancient seat of the monarchy, and contained the capital, Nineveh or Nɪnus: that between the Lycus and the Caprus was called Adiabene: and the part S. E. of the Caprus contained the districts of Apolloniatis and Sittacene.—(2) In a wider sense the name was applied to the whole country watered by the Euphrates and the Tigris, so as to include Mesopotamia and Babylonia.—(3) By a further extension the word is used to designate the Assyrian Empire in its widest sense. It was one of the first great states of which we have any record. Its reputed founder was Ninus, the builder of the capital city; and in its widest extent it included the countries just mentioned, with Media, Persis, Armenia, Syria, Phoenicia, and Palestine, except the kingdom of Judah. The fruitless expedition of Sennacherib against Egypt, and the miraculous destruction of his army before Jerusalem (B. C. 714), so weakened the empire, that the Medes revolted and formed a separate kingdom. In B. C. 606, Nineveh was taken, and the Assyrian empire destroyed by Cyaxares, the king of Media.

ASTA (-ae). (1) (Asti in Piedmont), an inland town of Liguria on the Tanarus, a Roman colony. — (2) A town in Hispania Baetica, near Gades, a Roman colony.

ASTĂBŏRAS (-ae), and ASTĂPUS (-i), two rivers of Aethiopia, having their sources in the highlands of Abyssinia and uniting to form the Nile. The land enclosed by them was the island of MEROE.

ASTĂCUS (-i), a celebrated city of Bithynia, on the Sinus Astacenus, a bay of the Propontis, was a colony from Megara, but afterwards received fresh colonists from Athens, who called the place Olbia. It was destroyed by Lysimachus, but was rebuilt on a neighbouring site, by Nicomedes I., who named his new city NICOMEDIA.

ASTĂPA (-ae), a town in Hispania Baetica.

ASTĂPUS. [ASTABORAS.]

ASTARTE. [APHRODITE and SYRIA DEA.]

ASTĔRĬA (-ae), or ASTĔRĬĒ (-es), daughter of the Titan Coeus and Phoebē, sister of Leto (Latona), wife of Perses, and mother of Hecătē. In order to escape the embraces of Zeus, she is said to have taken the form of a quail (ortyx), and to have thrown herself down from heaven into the sea, where she was metamorphosed into the island Asteria (the island which had fallen from heaven like a star), or Ortygia, afterwards called Delos.

ASTĔRIS (-idis), or ASTĔRĬA (-ae), a small island between Ithaca and Cephallenia.

ASTRAEA (-ae), daughter of Zeus (Jupiter) and Themis, and goddess of justice, lived during the golden age among men; but when the wickedness of men increased, she withdrew to heaven and was placed among the stars, under the name of Virgo. Her sister Pudicitia left the earth along with her.

ASTRAEUS (-i), a Titan, husband of Eos (Aurora), and father of the winds and the stars. Ovid calls the winds *Astraei* (adj.) *fratres*, the "Astraean brothers."

ASTŬRA (-ae), a river in Latium, flowing between Antium and Circeii into the Tyrrhenian sea. At its mouth it formed a small island with a town upon it, also called Astura, where Cicero had an estate.

ASTŬRES (-um), a warlike people in the N.W. of Spain, bounded on the E. by the Cantabri and Vaccaei, on the W. by the Gallaeci, on the N. by the Ocean, and on the S. by the Vettones. Their chief town was Asturica Augusta (*Astorga*).

ASTYĂGES (-is), son of Cyaxares, last king of Media, reigned B.C. 594—559. He was deposed and deprived of his dominions by his grandson Cyrus. For details see CYRUS.

ASTYĂNAX (-actis), son of Hector and Andromache. After the capture of Troy the Greeks hurled him down from the walls, that he might not restore the kingdom of Troy.

ASTYPĂLAEA (-ae), one of the Sporades in the S. part of the Grecian archipelago, with a town of the same name, founded by the Megarians.

ASTYRA (-ae), a town of Mysia, N. W. of Adramyttium.

ĂTĂBŬLUS (-i), the name in Apulia of the parching S.E. wind, the Sirocco, which is at present called *Altino* in Apulia.

ATABYRIS or ATABYRĬUM (-i), the highest mountain in Rhodes on the S.W. of that island, on which was a celebrated temple of Zeus Atabyrius.

ĂTĂGIS. [ATHESIS.]

ĂTALANTA (-ae), or ĂTĂLANTE (-es). (1) The *Arcadian Atalanta*, was a daughter of Iasus (Iasion or Iasius) and Clymene. She was exposed by her father in her infancy, and was suckled by a she-bear, the symbol of Artemis (Diana). After she had grown up she lived in pure maidenhood, slew the centaurs who pursued her, and took part in the Calydonian hunt. Her father subsequently recognised her as his daughter; and when he desired her to marry, she required every suitor to contend with her in the foot-race, because she was the most swift-footed of mortals. If he conquered her, he was to be rewarded with her hand; if he was conquered, he was to be put to death. She conquered many suitors, but was at length overcome by Mīlanĭon with the assistance of Aphrodītē (Venus). The goddess had given him 3 golden apples, and during the race he dropped them one after the other: their beauty charmed Atalanta so much, that she could not abstain from gathering them, and Mīlanĭon thus gained the goal before her. She accordingly became his wife. They were subsequently both metamorphosed into lions,

because they had profaned by their embraces the sacred grove of Zeus (Jupiter).—(2) The *Boeotian Atalanta*. The same stories are related of her as of the Arcadian Atalanta, except that her parentage and the localities are described differently. Thus she is said to have been a daughter of Schoenus, and to have been married to Hippomenes. Her footrace is transferred to the Boeotian Onchestus, and the sanctuary profaned was a temple of Cybele, who metamorphosed them into lions, and yoked them to her chariot.

ĂTĂLANTĒ (-es), a town of Macedonia on the Axius.

ĂTĂRANTES (-um), a people in the E. of Libya, between the Garamantes and Atlantes.

ĂTARNEUS, a city on the coast of Mysia, opposite to Lesbos : a colony of the Chians : the residence of the tyrant Hermias, with whom Aristotle resided some time.

ĂTAX (-ăcis : *Aude*), originally called Narbo, a river in Gallia Narbonensis, rising in the Pyrenees, and flowing by Narbo Martius into the Lacus Rubresus or Rubrensis, which is connected with the sea.

ĂTĒ (-ēs), daughter of Eris or Zeus (Jupiter), was an ancient Greek divinity, who led both gods and men into rash and inconsiderate actions.

ATĔIUS CĂPĬTO. [CAPITO.]

ĂTELLA (-ae : *Aversa*), a town in Campania between Capua and Neapolis, originally inhabited by the Oscans, afterwards a Roman municipium and a colony. Atella owes its celebrity to the *Atellanae Fabulae* or Oscan farces, which took their name from this town.

ATERNUM (-i : *Pescara*), a town in central Italy on the Adriatic, at the mouth of the river Aternus, was the common harbour of the Vestini, Marrucini, and Peligni.

ATERNUS. [ATERNUM.]

ĂTESTE (-ēs : *Este*), a Roman colony in the country of the Veneti in Upper Italy.

ĂTHĂCUS (-i), a town in Lyncestis in Macedonia.

ĂTHĂMĂNĬA (-ae), a mountainous country in the S. of Epirus, on the W. side of Pindus, of which Argithea was the chief town. The Athamānes were a Thessalian people, who had been driven out of Thessaly by the Lapithae.

ĂTHĂMAS (-antis), son of Aeolus and Enarete, and king of Orchomenus in Boeotia. At the command of Hera (Juno), Athamas married Nephelē, by whom he became the father of Phrixus and Hellē. [PHRIXUS.] But he was secretly in love with the mortal Ino, the daughter of Cadmus, by whom he begot Learchus and Melicertes. Having thus incurred the anger both of Hera and of Nephelē, Athamas was seized with madness, and in this state killed his own son, Learchus. Ino threw herself with Melicertes into the sea, and both were changed into marine deities, Ino becoming Leucothea, and Melicertes Palaemon. Athamas, as the murderer of his son, was obliged to flee from Boeotia, and settled in Thessaly.—Hence we have *Athamantĭădes* (*-ae*), son of Athamas, i. e. Palaemon; and *Athamantis* (*-ĭdis*), daughter of Athamas, i. e. Helle.

ĂTHĂNĂGĬA (-ae), the chief town of the Ilergetes in Hispania Tarraconensis.

ĀTHĒNA (-ae), or ĀTHĒNĒ (-es), called MĬNERVA by the Romans, was one of the great divinities of the Greeks. She is frequently called *Pallas Athena*, or simply *Pallas*. She was the daughter of Zeus (Jupiter) and Metis. Before her birth Zeus swallowed her mother; and Athena afterwards sprung forth from the head of Zeus with a mighty war-shout and in complete armour. As her father was the most powerful and her mother the wisest among the gods, so Athena was a combination of the two, a goddess in whom power and wisdom were harmoniously blended. She appears as the preserver of the state and of everything which gives to the state strength and pros-

Athena (Minerva). Aegina Marbles.)

perity.—As the protectress of agriculture, Athena is represented as creating the olive

tree (see below), inventing the plough and

Athena (Minerva). (From a Statue in the possession of Mr. Hope.)

rake, &c. She was the patroness of both the useful and elegant arts, such as weaving. [See ARACHNE.] Later writers make her the goddess of all wisdom and knowledge. As the patron divinity of the state, she maintained the authority of law and order in the courts and the assembly of the people. She was believed to have instituted the ancient court of the Areopagus at Athens. She also protected the state from outward enemies, and thus assumes the character of a warlike divinity. In the war of Zeus against the giants, she buried Enceladus under the island of Sicily, and slew Pallas. In the Trojan war she sided with the Greeks. As a goddess of war she usually appears in armour, with the aegis and a golden staff. In the centre of her breast-plate or shield, appears the head of Medusa, the Gorgon. She is represented as a virgin divinity, whose heart is inaccessible to the passion of love. Tiresias was deprived of sight for having seen her in the bath; and Hephaestus (Vulcan), who had made an attempt upon her chastity, was obliged to take to flight. Athena was worshipped in all parts of Greece. She was especially the protecting deity of Athens and Attica. The tale ran that in the reign of Cecrops both Poseidon (Neptune) and Athena contended for the possession of Athens. The gods resolved that whichever of them produced a gift most useful to mortals should have possession of the land. Poseidon struck the ground with his trident and straightway a horse appeared.

Athena then planted the olive. The gods thereupon decreed that the olive was more useful to man than the horse, and gave the city to the goddess, from whom it was called Athenae. At Athens the magnificent festival of the *Panathenaea* was celebrated in honour of the goddess. At this festival took place the grand procession, which was represented on the frieze of the Parthenon. Respecting her worship in Italy, see MINERVA. The owl, serpent, cock, and olive-tree, were sacred to her.

Athena (Minerva).   (Bartoli, Admiranda, pl. 41.)

ĂTHĒNAE (-ārum: *Athens*), the capital of Attica, about 4 miles from the sea, between the small rivers Cephissus on the W. and Ilissus on the E., the latter of which flowed through the town. The most ancient part of it, the *Acropŏlis*, is said to have been built by the mythical Cecrops, but the city itself is said to have owed its origin to Theseus, who united the 12 independent states or townships of Attica into one state, and made Athens their capital. The city was burnt by Xerxes in B.C. 480, but was soon rebuilt under the administration of Themistocles, and was adorned with public buildings by Cimon, and especially by Pericles, in whose time (B.C. 460—429) it reached its greatest splendour. Its beauty was chiefly owing to its public buildings, for the private houses were mostly insignificant, and its streets badly laid out. Towards the end of the Peloponnesian war, it contained 10,000 houses, which at the rate of 12 inhabitants to a house, would give a population of 120,000, though some writers make the inhabitants as many as 180,000. Under the Romans Athens continued to be a great and flourishing city, and retained many privileges and immunities when the south of Greece was formed into the Roman province of Achaia. It suffered greatly on its capture by Sulla, B.C. 86, and was deprived of many of its privileges. It was at that time, and also during the early centuries of the Christian

aera, one of the chief seats of learning; and the Romans were accustomed to send their sons to Athens, as to an University, for the completion of their education. Hadrian, who was very partial to Athens, and frequently resided in the city (A.D. 122—128), adorned it with many new buildings, and his example was followed by Herodes Atticus, who spent large sums of money upon beautifying the city in the reign of M. Aurelius.— Athens consisted of two distinct parts: I. *The City*, properly so called, divided into, 1. The Upper City or Acropolis, and, 2. The Lower City, surrounded with walls by Themistocles. II. The 3 harbour-towns of Piraeus, Munychia, and Phalērum, also surrounded with walls by Themistocles, and connected with the city by means of the *long walls*, built under the administration of Pericles. The long walls consisted of the wall to Phalērum on the E., 35 stadia long (about 4 miles), and of the wall to Piraeus on the W., 40 stadia long (about 4½ miles); between these two, at a short distance from the latter and parallel to it, another wall was erected, thus making 2 walls leading to the Piraeus, with a narrow passage between them. The entire circuit of the walls was 174½ stadia (nearly 22 miles), of which 43 stadia (nearly 5½ miles) belonged to the city, 75 stadia (9½ miles) to the long walls, and 56½ (7 miles) to Piraeus, Munychia, and Phalērum.—The Acropolis, also called *Cecropia* from its reputed founder, was a steep rock in the middle of the city, about 150 feet high, 1150 feet long, and 500 broad. On the W. end of the Acropolis, where access is alone practicable, were the magnificent *Propylaea*, or "the Entrances," built by Pericles. The summit of the Acropolis was covered with temples, statues of bronze and marble, and various other works of art. Of the temples, the grandest was the *Parthĕnon*, sacred to the "Virgin" goddess Athena; and N. of the Parthenon was the magnificent *Erechthĕum*, containing 3 separate temples, one of Athena Polias, or the "Protectress of the State," the Erechthĕum proper, or sanctuary of Erechtheus, and the Pandrosium, or sanctuary of Pandrosos, the daughter of Cecrops. Between the Parthĕnon and Erechthĕum was the colossal statue of Athena Promachos, or the "Fighter in the Front," whose helmet and spear was the first object on the Acropolis visible from the sea. The lower city was built in the plain round the Acropolis, but this plain also contained several hills, especially in the S.W. part.

ATHĒNAEUM, (-i) in general a temple or place sacred to Athena (Minerva). The name was specially given to a school founded by the emperor Hadrian at Rome about A.D. 133, for the promotion of literary and scientific studies.

ATHĒNAEUS (-i), a learned Greek grammarian, of Naucratis in Egypt, lived about A.D. 230, first at Alexandria and afterwards at Rome. His extant work is entitled the *Deipnosophistae, i. e.* the *Banquet of the Learned*, consisting of an immense mass of anecdotes, of extracts from the ancient writers, and of discussions on almost every conceivable subject, especially on Gastronomy. Athenaeus represents himself as describing to his friend Timocrates, a full account of the conversation at a banquet at Rome, at which Galen, the physician, and Ulpian, the jurist, were among the guests.

ATHĒNŌDŌRUS (-i). (1) Of Tarsus, a Stoic philosopher surnamed CORDYLIO, was the keeper of the library at Pergamus, and afterwards removed to Rome, where he lived with M. Cato, at whose house he died. (2) Of Tarsus, a Stoic philosopher, surnamed CANANITES, from Cana in Cilicia, the birthplace of his father. He taught at Apollonia in Epirus, where the young Octavius (subsequently the emperor Augustus) was one of his disciples. He accompanied the latter to Rome, and became one of his intimate friends.

ATHĒSIS (-is : *Adige* or *Etsch*), rises in the Rhaetian Alps, receives the ATAGIS (*Eisach*), flows through Upper Italy past Verona, and falls into the Adriatic by many mouths.

ATHŌS (*Dat.* athō : *Acc.* athōn and athō : *Abl.* athō), the mountainous peninsula, also called Actē, which projects from Chalcidĭcē in Macedonia. At its extremity it rises to the height of 6349 feet; the voyage round it was so dreaded by mariners, that Xerxes had a canal cut through the isthmus, which connects the peninsula with the mainland, to afford a passage to his fleet. The isthmus is about 1½ mile across; and there are distinct traces of the canal to be seen in the present day. The peninsula contained several flourishing cities in antiquity, and is now studded with numerous monasteries, cloisters, and chapels. In these monasteries some valuable MSS. of ancient authors have been discovered.

ATĬA, mother of AUGUSTUS.

ATĬLĬUS RĒGULUS. [REGULUS.]

ATĬNA (-ae : *Atina*), a town of the Volsci in Latium, afterwards a Roman colony.

ATINTĀNES (-um), an Epirot people in Illyria, on the borders of Macedonia.

ATLANTĬCUM MĂRE. [OCEANUS.]

ATLANTIS (-ĭdis), according to an ancient tradition, a great island W. of the Pillars of Hercules in the Ocean, opposite Mount Atlas: it possessed a numerous population, and was adorned with every beauty; its powerful princes invaded Africa and Europe, but were defeated by the Athenians and their allies: its inhabitants afterwards became wicked and impious, and the island was in consequence swallowed up in the ocean in a day and a night. This legend is given by Plato in the *Timaeus*, and is said to have been related to Solon by the Egyptian priests. The Canary Islands, or the Azores, which perhaps were visited by the Phoenicians, may have given rise to the legend; but some modern writers regard it as indicative of a vague belief in antiquity in the existence of the W. hemisphere.

ATLAS (-antis), son of Iapetus and Clymĕnē, and brother of Prometheus and Epimetheus. He made war with the other Titans upon Zeus (Jupiter), and being conquered, was condemned to bear heaven on his head and hands. The myth seems to have arisen from the idea that lofty mountains supported the heaven. Another tradition relates that Perseus came to Atlas and asked for shelter, which was refused, whereupon Perseus, by means of the head of Medusa, changed him into M. Atlas, on which rested heaven with all its stars. Atlas was the father of the Pleiades by Pleiŏnē or by Hesperis; of the Hyades and Hesperides by Aethra; and of Oenomaus and Maia by Sterŏpē. Diōnē and Calypso, Hyas and Hesperus, are likewise called his children.

Atlantĭădes, a descendant of Atlas, especially Mercury, his grandson by Maia, and Her-

Atlas. (From the Farnese collection now at Naples.)

maphroditus, son of Mercury.—*Atlantias* and *Atlantis*, a female descendant of Atlas, especially one of the Pleiads and Hyads.

ATLAS MONS was the general name of the great mountain range which covers the surface of N. Africa between the Mediterranean and Great Desert (*Sahara*), on the N. and S., and the Atlantic and the Lesser Syrtis on the W. and E.

ATOSSA (-ae), daughter of Cyrus, and wife successively of her brother Cambyses, of Smerdis the Magian, and of Darius Hystaspis, by whom she became the mother of Xerxes.

ATRAE (-ārum), or HATRA (-ae), a strongly fortified city on a high mountain in Mesopotamia, inhabited by people of the Arab race.

ATRAX (-ăcis), a town in Pelasgiotis in Thessaly, inhabited by the Perrhaebi, so called from the mythical Atrax, son of Penēus and Bura, and father of Caeneus and Hippodamīa. Hence Caeneus is called *Atrăcīdes* and Hippodamīa *Atrăcis.*

ATRĒBĂTĒS (-um), a people in Gallia Belgica, inhabited by the modern *Artois*, which is a corruption of their name. Their capital was Nemetocenna or Nemetacum, subsequently

Atrebati, now *Arras*. Part of them crossed over to Britain, where they dwelt in the upper valley of the Thames, in *Oxfordshire* and *Berkshire*.

ATREUS (-ĕŏs, ĕī or eī), son of Pelops and Hippodamīa, grandson of Tantalus, and brother of Thyestes and Nicippē. [PELOPS.] He was first married to Cleola, by whom he became the father of Plīsthenes; then to Aëropē, the widow of his son Plisthenes, who was the mother of Agamemnon, Menelaus, and Anaxibia, either by Plisthenes or by Atreus [AGAMEMNON]; and lastly to Pelopia, the daughter of his brother Thyestes. The tragic fate of the house of Pelops afforded materials to the tragic poets of Greece. In consequence of the murder of their half-brother Chrysippus, Atreus and Thyestes were obliged to take to flight; they were hospitably received at Mycenae; and, after the death of Eurystheus, Atreus became king of Mycenae. Thyestes seduced Aëropē, the wife of Atreus, and was in consequence banished by his brother: from his place of exile he sent Plisthenes, the son of Atreus, whom he had brought up as his own child, in order to slay Atreus, but Plisthenes fell by the hands of Atreus, who did not know that he was his own son. In order to take revenge, Atreus, pretending to be reconciled to Thyestes, recalled him to Mycenae, killed his two sons, and placed their flesh before their father at a banquet, who unwittingly partook of the horrid meal. Thyestes fled with horror, and the gods cursed Atreus and his house. The kingdom of Atreus was now visited by famine, and the oracle advised Atreus to call back Thyestes. Atreus, who went out in search of him, came to king Thesprotus, where he married his third wife, Pelopia, the daughter of Thyestes, whom Atreus believed to be a daughter of Thesprotus. Pelopia was at the time with child by her own father. This child, Aegisthus, afterwards slew Atreus because the latter had commanded him to slay his own father Thyestes. [AEGISTHUS.]

ATRĬA. [ADRIA.]

ATRĪDĒS or ATRĪDA (-ae), a descendant of Atreus, especially Agamemnon and Menelaus.

ATRŎPĂTĒNĒ (-es), or Media Atropatia, the N. W. part of Media, adjacent to Armenia, named after Atropătes, a native of the country, who, having been made its governor by Alexander, founded there a kingdom, which long remained independent.

ATROPOS. [MOIRAE.]

ATTA (-ae), T. QUINTIUS (-i), a Roman comic poet, died B.C. 78. His surname Atta was given him from a defect in his feet. His plays were acted even in the time of Augustus

ATTĂLĬA (-ae). (1) A city of Lydia, formerly called Agroīra.—(2) A city on the coast of Pamphylia, founded by Attalus II. Philadelphus, and subdued by the Romans under P. Servilius Isauricus.

ATTĂLUS (-i), king of Pergamus. (1) Son of Attalus, a brother of Philetaerus, succeeded his cousin, Eumenes I., and reigned B.C. 241 —197. He took part with the Romans against Philip and the Achaeans. He was a wise and just prince, and was distinguished by his patronage of literature.—(2) Surnamed PHILADELPHUS, 2nd son of Attalus, succeeded his brother Eumenes II., and reigned 159— 138. Like his father he was an ally of the Romans, and he also encouraged the arts and sciences.—(3) Surnamed PHILOMETOR, son of Eumenes II. and Stratonice, succeeded his uncle Attalus II., and reigned 138—133. In his will, he made the Romans his heirs; but his kingdom was claimed by Aristonicus. [ARISTONICUS.]

ATTHIS or ATTIS. [ATTICA.]

ATTĬCA (-ae), a division of Greece, has the form of a triangle, two sides of which are washed by the Aegaean sea, while the third is separated from Boeotia on the N. by the mountains Cithaeron and Parnes. Megaris, which bounds it on the N. W. was formerly a part of Attica. In ancient times it was called Acte and Actice, or the "coastland" [ACTE], from which the later form Attica is said to have been derived. According to tradition it derived its name from Atthis, the daughter of the mythical king Cranaus; and it is not impossible that Att-ica may contain the root Att or Ath, which we find in Atthis and Athena. Attica is divided by many ancient writers into 3 districts. 1. The Highlands, the N.E. of the country. 2. The Plain, the N.W. of the country, including both the plain round Athens and the plain round Eleusis, and extending S. to the promontory Zoster. 3. The Sea-coast District, the S. part of the country, terminating in the promontory Sunium. Besides these 3 divisions we also read of a 4th, The Midland District, still called Mesogia, an undulating plain in the middle of the country. The soil of Attica is not very fertile : the greater part of it is not adapted for growing corn ; but it produces olives, figs, and grapes, especially the 2 former in great perfection. The country is dry ; the chief river is the Cephissus, rising in Parnes and flowing through the Athenian plain. The abundance of wild flowers in the country made the honey of M. Hymettus very celebrated in antiquity. Excellent marble was obtained from the quarries of Pentelicus, N.E. of Athens, and a considerable supply of silver from the mines of Laurium near Sunium. The area of Attica, including the island of Salamis, which belonged to it, contained between 700 and 800 square miles ; and its population in its flourishing period was probably about 500,000, of which nearly 4-5ths were slaves. Attica is said to have been originally inhabited by Pelasgians. Its most ancient political division was into 12 independent states, attributed to CECROPS, who according to some legends came from Egypt. Subsequently Ion, the grandson of Hellen, divided the people into 4 tribes, Geleontes, Hopletes, Argades and Aegicores ; and Theseus, who united the 12 independent states of Attica into one political body, and made Athens the capital, again divided the nation into 3 classes, the Eupatridae, Geomori, and Demiurgi. Clisthenes (B.C. 510) abolished the old tribes and created 10 new ones, according to a geographical division : these tribes were subdivided into 174 demi or townships.

ATTĬCUS HERŌDES, TĬBĔRĬUS CLAUDĬUS, a celebrated Greek rhetorician, born about A.D. 104, at Marathon in Attica. He taught rhetoric both at Athens and at Rome. The future emperors M. Aurelius and L. Verus were among his pupils, and Antoninus Pius raised him to the consulship in 143. He possessed immense wealth, a great part of which he spent in embellishing Athens. He died at the age of 76, in 180.

ATTĬCUS, POMPŌNĬUS (-i), a Roman eques, born at Rome, B.C. 109. His proper name after his adoption by Q. Caecilius, the brother of his mother, was Q. Caecilius Pomponianus Atticus. His surname, Atticus, was given him on account of his long residence in Athens and his intimate acquaintance with the Greek language and literature. He kept aloof from all political affairs, and thus lived on intimate terms with the most distinguished men of all parties. His chief friend was Cicero, whose correspondence with him, beginning in 68 and continued down to Cicero's death, is one of the most valuable remains of antiquity. He purchased an estate at Buthrotum in Epirus, in which place, as well as at Athens and Rome, he spent the greater part of his time, engaged in literary pursuits and commercial undertakings. He died in B.C. 32, at the age of 77, of voluntary starvation, when he found that he was attacked by an incurable illness. His wife Pilia, bore him only one child, a daughter, Pomponia or Caecilia, who was married to M. Vipsanius Agrippa. The sister of Atticus, Pomponia, was married to Q. Cicero, the brother of the orator. In philosophy Atticus belonged to the Epicurean sect.

ATTĬLA (-ae), a king of the Huns, reigned A.D. 434—453. Such terror did he inspire in the ancient world, that he was called "the Scourge of God." His career divides itself into two parts. The first (A. D. 445—450) consists of the ravage of the Eastern empire between the Euxine and the Adriatic, and the second of his invasion of the Western empire (450—452). He took Aquileia in 452, after a siege of 3 months, but he did not attack Rome, in consequence, it is said, of his interview with Pope Leo the Great. He died in 453, on the night of his marriage with a beautiful girl, by the bursting of a blood-vessel.

ATTĬUS. [Accius.]

ATTĬUS or ATTUS NAVĬUS. [Navius.]

ĀTŬRUS (-i : *Adour*), a river in Aquitania rising in the Pyrenees and flowing through the territory of the Tarbelli into the ocean.

ĀTYS or ATTYS (-y̆os). (1) A beautiful shepherd of Phrygia, beloved by Cybele. Having proved unfaithful to the goddess, he was thrown by her into a state of madness, and was changed into a fir-tree. (2) A Latin chief, from whom the Atia Gens derived its origin, and from whom Augustus was believed to be descended on his mother's side.

AUFĪDĒNA (-ae), a town in Samnium on the river Sagrus.

AUFĬDUS (-i), the principal river of Apulia, flowing with a rapid current into the Adriatic. Venusia, the birth-place of Horace, was on the Aufidus.

AUGĒ (-ēs), or AUGĪA (-ae), daughter of Aleus and Neaera, was a priestess of Athena, and mother by Hercules of Telephus. [Tele-phus.] She afterwards married Teuthras, king of the Mysians.

AUGĒAS or AUGĪAS. [Hercules.]

AUGĬLA (-ōrum), an oasis in the Great Desert of Africa, 10 days' journey W. of the Oasis of Ammon, abounding in date palms.

AUGUSTA (-ae), the name of several towns founded or colonised by Augustus. Of these one of the most important was Augusta Praetoria (*Aosta*), a town of the Salassi in Upper Italy, at the foot of the Graian and Pennine Alps. The modern town still contains many Roman remains: the most important of which are the town gates and a triumphal arch.

AUGUSTŌBŎNA. [Tricasses.]

AUGUSTŌDŪNUM. [Bibracte.]

AUGUSTŌNEMĒTUM. [Arverni.]

AUGUSTŬLUS, RŌMŬLUS (-i), last Roman emperor of the West, was deposed by Odoacer, A. D. 476.

AUGUSTUS (-i), the first Roman emperor, was born on the 23rd of September, B.C. 63, and was the son of C. Octavius by Atia, a daughter of Julia, the sister of C. Julius Caesar. His original name was *C. Octavius*, and, after his adoption by his great-uncle, *C. Julius Caesar Octavianus*. Augustus was only a title given him by the senate and the people in B. C. 27, to express their veneration for him. He was pursuing his studies at Apollonia, when the news reached him of his uncle's murder at Rome in March 44. He forthwith set out for Italy, and upon landing, was received with enthusiasm by the troops. He first joined the republican party in order to crush Antony, against whom he fought at Mutina in conjunction with the 2 consuls, C. Vibius Pansa and A. Hirtius. Antony was defeated and obliged to fly across the Alps; and the death of the 2 consuls gave Augustus the command of all their troops. He now returned to Rome, and compelled the senate to elect him consul, and shortly afterwards he became reconciled to Antony. It was agreed that the Roman world should be divided between Augustus, Antony, and Lepidus, under the title of *triumviri rei publicae constituendae*, and that this arrangement should last for the next 5 years. They published a *proscriptio* or list of all their enemies, whose lives were to be sacrificed and their property confiscated: upwards of 2000 equites and 300 senators were put to death, among whom was Cicero. Soon afterwards Augustus and Antony crossed over to Greece, and defeated Brutus and Cassius at the decisive battle of Philippi in 42, by which the hopes of the republican party were ruined. Augustus returned to Italy, where a new war awaited him (41), excited by Fulvia, the wife of Antony. She was supported by L. Antonius, the consul and brother of the triumvir, who threw himself into the fortified town of Perusia, which Augustus succeeded in taking in 40. Antony now made preparations for war, but the death of Fulvia led to a reconciliation between the triumvirs, who concluded a peace at Brundusium. A new division of the provinces was again made: Augustus obtained all the parts of the empire W. of the town of Scodra in Illyricum, Antony the E. provinces, and Lepidus. Africa. Antony married Octavia, the sister of Augustus, in order to cement their alliance. In 36 Augustus conquered Sex. Pompey, who had held possession of Sicily for many years with a powerful fleet. Lepidus, who had landed in Sicily to support Augustus, was also subdued by Augustus, stripped of his power, and sent to Rome, where he resided for the remainder of his life, being allowed to retain the dignity of pontifex maximus. Meantime, Antony had repudiated Octavia, on account of his love for Cleopatra, and had alienated the minds of the Roman people by his arbitrary conduct. The senate declared war against Cleopatra; and in September B.C. 31, the fleet of Augustus gained a brilliant victory over Antony's near Actium in Acarnania. In the following year (30) Augustus sailed to Egypt. Antony and Cleopatra, who had escaped in safety from Actium, put an end to their lives. Augustus thus became the undisputed master of the Roman world, but he declined all honours and distinctions which were calculated to remind the Romans of kingly power. On the death of Lepidus in 12 he became pontifex maximus. On state matters, which he did not choose to be discussed in public, he consulted his personal friends, Maecenas, M. Agrippa, M. Valerius Messalla Corvinus, and Asinius Pollio. The wars of Augustus were chiefly undertaken to protect the frontiers of the Roman dominions. Most of them were carried on by his relations and friends, but he conducted a few of them in person. Thus, in 27, he attacked the warlike Cantabri and Astures in Spain. In 20 he went to Syria, where he received from Phraätes, the Parthian monarch, the standards and prisoners which had been taken from Crassus and Antony. He died at Nola, on the 29th of August, A.D. 14, at the age of 76. His last wife was Livia, who had been previously the wife of Tiberius Nero. He had no children by Livia, and only a daughter Julia by his former wife Scribonia. Julia was married to Agrippa, and her 2 sons, Caius and Lucius Caesar, were destined by Augustus as his successors. On the death of these two youths, Augustus was persuaded to adopt Tiberius, the son of Livia by her former husband, and to make him his colleague and successor. [TIBERIUS.]

AULERCI (-ōrum), a powerful Gallic people dwelling between the Sequana (Seine) and the Liger (Loire), and divided into 3 tribes. (1) A. EBUROVĬCES, near the coast on the left bank of the Seine in the modern Normandy: their capital was Mediolanum, afterwards called Eburovices (Evreux).—(2) A. CENO-MĀNI, S. W. of the preceding near the Liger: their capital was Subdinnum (le Mans). At an early period some of the Cenomani crossed the Alps and settled in Upper Italy.—(3) A. BRANNOVĬCES, E. of the Cenomani near the Aedui, whase clients they were.

AULIS (-is or -ĭdis), a harbour in Boeotia on the Euripus, where the Greek fleet assembled before sailing against Troy.

AULON (-ōnis). (1) A district and town on the borders of Elis and Messenia, with a temple of Aesculapius—(2) A town in Chalcidĭcē in Macedonia, on the Strymonic gulf.—(3) A fertile valley near Tarentum celebrated for its wine.

AURĒLĬĀNI. [GENABUM.]

AURĒLĬĀNUS (-i), Roman emperor, A.D. 270—275, born at Sirmium in Pannonia, and successor of Claudius II. He defeated the Goths and Vandals, who had crossed the Danube, and the Germans, who had invaded Italy. He next turned his arms against Zenobia, queen of Palmyra, whom he defeated, took prisoner, and carried with him to Rome. [ZENOBIA.] He then recovered Gaul, Britain, and Spain, which were in the hands cf the usurper Tetricus. On his return to Rome, he surrounded the city with a new line of walls. He abandoned Dacia, which had been first conquered by Trajan, and made the S. bank of the Danube, as in the time of Augustus, the boundary of the empire. He was killed by some of his officers, while preparing to march against the Persians.

M. AURĒLĬUS ANTŌNĪNUS usually called M. AURĒLĬUS (-i), Roman emperor, A.D. 161—180, commonly called "the philosopher," was born at Rome A.D. 121. He was adopted by Antoninus Pius, when the latter was adopted by Hadrian, and married Faustina, the daughter of Pius (138). On the death of Antoninus in 161, he succeeded to the throne, but he admitted to an equal share of the sovereign power L. Aurelius Verus, who had been adopted by Pius at the same time as Marcus himself. Soon after their accession Verus was despatched to the East, and for 4 years (A.D. 162—165) carried on war with great success against Vologeses III., king of Parthia, over whom his lieutenants, especially Avidius Cassius, gained many victories. He subsequently prosecuted a war for many years with the Marcomanni, Quadi, and the other barbarians dwelling along the northern limits of the empire, from the sources of the Danube to the Illyrian border. Verus died in 169. In 174 Aurelius gained a decisive victory over the Quadi, mainly through a violent storm, which threw the barbarians into confusion. This storm is said to have been owing to the prayers of a legion chiefly composed of Christians. It has given rise to a famous controversy among the historians of Christianity upon what is commonly termed the Miracle of the Thundering Legion. In 175, Aurelius set out for the East, where Avidius Cassius, urged on by Faustina, the unworthy wife of Aurelius, had risen in rebellion and proclaimed himself emperor. But before Aurelius reached the East, Cassius had been slain by his own officers. During this expedition Faustina died, according to some, by her own hands. Aurelius died in 180, in Pannonia, while prosecuting the war against the Marcomanni.—The leading feature in the character of M. Aurelius was his devotion to the Stoic philosophy. We still possess a work by him written in the Greek language, and entitled *Meditations.* No remains of antiquity present a nobler view of philosophical heathenism. The chief and perhaps the only stain upon the memory of Aurelius is his persecutions of the Christians. —Aurelius was succeeded by his son Commodus.

AURĒLĬUS VICTOR. [VICTOR.]

AURŌRA. [EOS.]

AURUNCI. [ITALIA.]

AUSCI or AUSCII (-ōrum), a powerful people in Aquitania, whose capital was Climberrum or Elimberrum, also Augusta and Ausci (*Auch*).

AUSĒTĀNI (-ōrum), a Spanish people in the modern Catalonia; their capital was Ausa (*Vique*).

AUSONES, AUSŎNĬA. [ITALIA.]

AUSŎNĬUS, DĔCĬMUS MAGNUS (-i), a Roman poet, born at Burdigăla (*Bordeaux*), about A.D. 310, taught grammar and rhetoric with such reputation at his native town, that he was appointed tutor of Gratian, son of the emperor Valentinian, and was afterwards raised to the highest honours of the state. Many of his poems are extant.

AUSTER (-tri), called NOTUS by the Greeks, the S. wind or strictly the S. W. wind. It frequently brought with it fogs and rain; but at certain seasons of the year it was a dry sultry wind, injurious both to man and to vegetation, the *Sirocco* of the modern Italians.

AUTARIĀTAE (-ārum), an Illyrian people in the Dalmatian mountains.

AUTOCHTHŌNES. [ABORIGINES.]

AUTŎLŎLES (-um), or -AE (-ārum), a Gaetulian tribe on the W. coast of Africa, S. of the Atlas mountains.

AUTŎLȲCUS (-i), son of Hermes (Mercury) and Chionē, and father of Anticlēa, who was the mother of Ulysses. He lived on mount Parnassus, and was renowned for his cunning and robberies.

AUTŎMĔDŌN (-ontis), son of Diores, the charioteer and companion of Achilles, and, after the death of the latter, the companion of his son Pyrrhus. Hence Automedon is used as the name of any skilful charioteer.

AUTŎNŎE (-ēs), daughter of Cadmus and Harmonia, wife of Aristaeus, and mother of Actaeon, who is therefore called *Autonoeius heros.* With her sister Agāvē, she tore Pentheus to pieces. [PENTHEUS.]

AUTRĬGŎNES (-um), a people in Hispania Tarraconensis between the Ocean and the Iberus.

AUXĬMUM (-i: *Osimo*), an important town of Picenum in Italy, and a Roman colony.

AUXŪMĒ (-ēs), or AX- (*Axum*), the capital of a powerful kingdom in Ethiopia, to the S. E. of Meroë, which became known to the Greeks and Romans in the early part of the 2nd century of our aera.

AVĂRĬCUM. [BITURIGES.]

AVELLA. [ABELLA.]

AVĒNĬO (-ōnis: *Avignon*), a town of the Cavares in Gallia Narbonensis on the left bank of the Rhone.

AVENTĬCUM (-i: *Avenches*), the chief town of the Helvetii, and subsequently a Roman colony, of which ruins are still to be seen.

ĂVENTĪNUS MONS. [ROMA.]

ĂVERNUS LACUS (-i), a lake close to the promontory between Cumae and Puteoli, filling the crater of an extinct volcano. It is surrounded by high banks, which in antiquity were covered by a gloomy forest sacred to Hecătē. From its waters mephitic vapours arose, which are said to have killed the birds that attempted to fly over it, from which circumstance its Greek name was supposed to be derived. (*Aornos,* from ἀ priv. and ὄρνις, a bird.) The lake was celebrated in mythology on account of its connection with the lower world. Near it was the cave of the Cumaean Sibyl, through which Aeneas descended to the lower world. Agrippa, in the time of Augustus, connected this lake with the Lucrine lake; he also caused a tunnel to be made from the lake to Cumae, of which a considerable part remains and is known under the name of *Grotto di Sibylla.* The Lucrine lake was filled up by an eruption in 1530, so that Avernus is again a separate lake.

AVĬĀNUS, FLĀVĬUS (-i), the author of 42 fables in Latin elegiac verse, probably lived in the 3rd or 4th century of the Christian aera.

AVĬĒNUS, RUFUS FESTUS (-i), a Latin poet towards the end of the 4th century of the Christian aera. His poems are chiefly descriptive.

AXĒNUS. [EUXINUS PONTUS.]

AXĬA (-ae), a fortress in the territory of Tarquinii in Etruria.

AXĬUS (-i), the chief river in Macedonia, rising in Mt. Scardus, and flowing S. E. through Macedonia into the Thermaic gulf.

AZŌTUS (-i: *Ashdod* or *Ashdoud*), a city of Palestine, near the sea-coast.

BABRĬUS (-i), a Greek poet, probably in the time of Augustus, turned the fables of Aesop into verse.

BĂBȲLŎN (-ōnis). (1) (Babel in O.T.: Ru. at and around *Hillah*), one of the oldest cities of the ancient world, built on both banks of the river Euphrates. In Scripture its foundation is ascribed to Nimrod. Secular history ascribes its origin to Belus (i. e. the god Baal), and its enlargement and decoration to Ninus or his wife Semiramis, the Assyrian monarchs of Nineveh. Babylon was for a long time subject to the Assyrian empire. Its greatness as an independent empire begins with Nabopolassar, the father of Nebuchadnezzar, who, with the aid of the Median king Cyaxares, overthrew the Assyrian monarchy, and destroyed Nineveh (B.C. 606). Under his son and successor, Nebuchadnezzar (B.C. 604—562), the Babylonian empire reached its height, and extended from the Euphrates to Egypt, and from the mountains of Armenia to the deserts of Arabia. After his death it again declined, until it was overthrown by the capture of Babylon by the Medes and Persians under Cyrus (B.C. 538), who made the city one of the capitals of the Persian empire, the others being Susa and Ecbatana. Under his successors the city rapidly sank. Darius I. dismantled its fortifications, in consequence of a revolt of its inhabitants. After the death of Alexander, Babylon became a part of the Syrian kingdom of Seleucus Nicator, who contributed to its decline by the foundation of SELEUCIA on the Tigris, which soon eclipsed it. At the present day all its *visible* remains consist of mounds of earth, ruined masses of brick walls, and a few scattered fragments. The city of Babylon formed a square, each side of which was 120 stadia (12 geog. miles) in length. The walls, of burnt brick, were 200 cubits high and 50 thick; and they were surrounded by a deep ditch. The Euphrates, which divided the city into 2 equal parts, was embanked with walls of brick, the openings of which at the ends of the transverse streets were closed by gates of bronze. Of the two public buildings of the greatest celebrity, the one was the temple of Belus, rising to a great height, and consisting of 8 stories, gradually diminishing in width, and ascended by a flight of steps, which wound round the whole building on the outside. The other was the "hanging gardens" of Nebuchadnezzar, laid out upon terraces which were raised above one another on arches. The streets of the city were straight, intersecting one another at right angles. The buildings were almost universally constructed of bricks, some burnt and some only sun-dried, cemented together with hot bitumen and in some cases with mortar. The ruling class at Babylon, to which the kings and priests and the men of learning belonged, were the Chaldaeans, who probably descended at an ancient period from the mountains on the borders of Armenia, and conquered the Babylonians. The religion of the Chaldaeans was Sabaeism, or the worship of the heavenly bodies. The priests formed a caste, and cultivated science, especially astronomy. They were the authors of the systems of weights and measures used by the Greeks and Romans. The district around the city, bounded by the Tigris on the E., Mesopotamia on the N., the Arabian Desert on the W., and extending to the head of the Persian Gulf on the S., was known in later times by the name of BABYLONIA, sometimes also called Chaldaea. [CHALDAEA.] This district was a plain, subject to continual inundations from the Tigris and Euphrates, which were regulated by canals. The country was fertile, but deficient in trees.—(2) A fortress in Lower Egypt, on the right bank of the Nile, exactly opposite to the pyramids. Its origin was ascribed by tradition to a body of Babylonian deserters.

BĂBȲLŎNĬA. [BABYLON.]

BACCHAE (-arum), also called *Maenades*

Bacchante, with Snake-bound Hair. (Thiersch, über die hellenischen bemalten Vasen.)

and *Thyiades*. (1) The female companions of Dionysus or Bacchus in his wanderings

:hrough the East, are represented as crowned with vine-leaves, clothed with fawn-skins, and carrying in their hands the *thyrsus.*— (2) Priestesses of Dionysus, who by wine and other exciting causes worked them-selves up to frenzy at the Dionysiac festi-vals. For details, see DIONYSUS.

BACCHUS. [DIONYSUS.]

BACCHȲLĬDĒS, one of the great lyric poets of Greece, born at Iulis in Ceos, and nephew of Simonides. He flourished about B.C. 470, and lived a long time at the court of Hieron in Syracuse, together with Simonides and Pindar.

BACĒNIS SILVA, a forest which separated the Suevi from the Cherusci, probably the W. part of the Thuringian Forest.

BACTRA or ZARIASPA (-ae : *Balkh*), the capital of BACTRIA, stood at the N. foot of the M. Paropamisus (the *Hindoo Koosh*) on the river Bactrus, about 25 miles S. of its junction with the Oxus.

BACTRĬA or -IĀNA (-ae : *Bokhara*), a province of the Persian empire, bounded on the S. by M. Paropamisus, which separated it from Ariana, on the E. by the N. branch of the same range, which divided it from the Sacae, on the N.E. by the Oxus, which separated it from Sogdiana, and on the W. by Margiana. It was included in the conquests of Alex-ander, and formed a part of the kingdom of the Seleucidae, until B.C. 255, when Theo-dotus, its governor, revolted from Antiochus II., and founded the Greek kingdom of Bactria, which lasted till B.C. 134 or 125, when it was overthrown by the Parthians.

BAECŬLA (-ae), a town in Hispania Tarra-conensis, W. of Castulo, in the neighbourhood of silver mines.

BAETERRAE (-arum : *Beziers*), a town in Gallia Narbonensis on the Obris, not far from Narbo.

BAETĬCA. [HISPANIA.]

BAETIS (-is : *Guadalquiver*), a river in S. Spain, formerly called TARTESSUS, rising in the territory of the Oretani, flowing S.W. through Baetica, to which it gave its name, and fall-ing into the Atlantic Ocean by 2 mouths.

BĀGŌAS (-ae) or BĀGŌUS (-i), an eunuch, highly trusted and favoured by Artaxerxes III. (Ochus), whom he poisoned, B.C. 338. He was put to death by Darius III. Codomannus, whom he had attempted likewise to poison, 336. The name Bagoas frequently occurs in Persian history, and is sometimes used by Latin writers as synonymous with an eunuch.

BAGRĂDA (-ae), a river of N. Africa, falling into the Gulf of Carthage near Utica.

BAIAE (-arum), a town in Campania, on a small bay W. of Naples, and opposite Puteoli, was situated in a beautiful country, which abounded in warm mineral springs. The baths of Baiae were the most celebrated in Italy, and the town itself was the favourite watering-place of the Romans. The whole country was studded with the palaces of the Roman nobles and emperors, which covered the coast from Baiae to Puteoli. The site of ancient Baiae is now for the most part covered by the sea.

BALBUS, L. CORNĒLĬUS, of Gades, served under Pompey against Sertorius in Spain, and received from Pompey the Roman citizenship. He returned with Pompey to Rome, where he lived on intimate terms with Caesar as well as Pompey. In B.C. 56 he was accused of having illegally assumed the Roman citizenship ; he was defended by Cicero, whose speech has come down to us, and was acquitted. In the civil war, Balbus had the management of Caesar's affairs at Rome. After the death of Caesar he gained the favour of Octavian, who raised him to the consulship in 40.

BĂLĒĀRES (-ium), also called GYMNĒ-SĬAE, by the Greeks, 2 islands in the Mediter-ranean, off the coast of Spain, distinguished by the epithets *Major* and *Minor*, whence their modern names *Majorca* and *Minorca*. Their inhabitants, also called *Baleares*, were cele-brated as slingers. They were subdued B.C. 123, by Q. Metellus, who assumed accordingly the surname Balearicus.

BANDŪSĬAE FONS (*Sambuco*), a fountain in Apulia, 6 miles from Venusia.

BANTĬA (-ae : *Banzi* or *Vanzi*), a town in Apulia, near Venusia, in a woody district.

BARBĂRI, the name given by the Greeks to all foreigners, whose language was not Greek, and who were therefore regarded by the Greeks as an inferior race. The Romans applied the name to all people, who spoke neither Greek nor Latin.

BARCA. [HAMILCAR.]

BARCA (-ae) or -E (-es : *Merjeh*), the second city of Cyrenaica, in N. Africa, 100 stadia from the sea, appears to have been at first a settle-ment of a Libyan tribe, the Barcaei, but about B.C. 560 was colonised by the Greek seceders from Cyrene, and became so powerful as to make the W. part of Cyrenaica virtually inde-pendent of the mother city. In B.C. 510 it was taken by the Persians, who removed most of its inhabitants to Bactria, and under the Ptolemies its ruin was completed by the erection of its port into a new city, which was named PTOLEMAIS.

BARCĪNO (*Barcelona*), a town of the Laeëtani in Hispania Tarraconensis, with an excellent harbour.

BARGŪSĬI (-ōrum), a people in the N.E. of Spain, between the Pyrenees and the Iberus.

BĀRĬUM (*Bari*), a town in Apulia, on the Adriatic, a municipium, and celebrated for its fisheries.

BARSĪNĒ (-es). (1) Daughter of Artabazus, and wife of Memnon the Rhodian, subsequently married Alexander the Great, to whom she bore a son, Hercules. She and her son were put to death by Polysperchon in 309.—(2) Also called STATĪRA, elder daughter of Darius III., whom Alexander married at Susa, B.C. 324. Shortly after Alexander's death she was murdered by Roxana.

BASSĀREUS (-ĕŏs or ĕĭ), a surname of Dionysus, probably derived from *bassaris*, a foxskin, worn by the god himself and the Maenads in Thrace. Hence Bassaris (-idis), was the name of a female Bacchante.

BASTARNAE or BASTERNAE (-ārum), a warlike German people, partly settled between the Tyras (*Dniester*) and Borysthenes (*Dnieper*), and partly at the mouth of the Danube, under the name of *Peucini*, from their inhabiting the island of Peuce, at the mouth of this river.

BĂTĂVI or BĂTĂVI (-ōrum), a Celtic people, inhabiting the island formed by the Rhine, the Waal, and the Maas, called after them *Insula Batavorum*. They were for a long time allies of the Romans, but they revolted under Claudius Civilis, in A.D. 69, and were with great difficulty subdued. Their chief town was Lugdunum (*Leyden*), between the Maas and the Waal. The *Caninefates* or *Canninefates* were a branch of the Batavi, and dwelt in the W. of the island.

BĂTHYLLUS (-i). (1) Of Samos, a beautiful youth beloved by Anacreon.—(2) Of Alexandria, the freedman and favourite of Maecenas, brought to perfection, together with Pylades of Cilicia, the imitative dance or ballet called *Pantomimus*. Bathyllus excelled in comic, and Pylades in tragic personifications.

BATNAE (-ārum). (1) (*Sarug*), a city of Osroëne in Mesopotamia, founded by the Macedonians.— (2) (*Dahab*), a city of Cyrrhestice, in Syria.

BĂTO (-ōnis), the name of 2 leaders of the Pannonians and Dalmatians in their insurrection in the reign of Augustus, A.D. 6.

BĂTTĬĂDAE (-arum), kings of Cyrene during 8 generations. (1) BATTUS I., of Thera, led a colony to Africa at the command of the Delphic oracle, and founded Cyrene about B.C. 631.—(2) ARCESILAUS I., son of No. 1, reigned B.C. 599—583.—(3) BATTUS II., surnamed "the Happy," son of No. 2, reigned 583—560 ?—(4) ARCESILAUS II., son

of No. 3, surnamed "the Oppressive," reigned about 560—550. His brothers withdrew from Cyrene, and founded Barca.—(5) BATTUS III., or " the Lame, " son of No. 4, reigned about 550—530 ; gave a new constitution to the city, whereby the royal power was reduced within very narrow limits.— (6) ARCESILAUS III., son of No. 5, reigned about 530—514.—(7) BATTUS IV., of whose life we have no accounts.—(8) ARCESILAUS IV., at whose death, about 450, a popular government was established.

BATTUS (-i), a shepherd whom Hermes turned into a stone, because he broke a promise which he made to the god.

BAUCIS. [PHILEMON.]

BAULI (-ōrum), a collection of villas rather than a town, between Misenum and Baiae in Campania.

BĀVĬUS (-i) and MAEVĬUS (-i), 2 malevolent poetasters, who attacked the poetry of Virgil and Horace.

BĔBRŸCES and BĔBRŸCES (-um). (1) A mythical people in Bithynia, said to be of Thracian origin, whose king, Amycus, slew Pollux.—(2) An ancient Iberian people on the coast of the Mediterranean, N. and S. of the Pyrenees.

BĔDRĬĀCUM (-i), a small place in Cisalpine Gaul between Cremona and Verona, celebrated for the defeat both of Otho and of the Vitellian troops. A.D. 69.

BĔLĔSIS or BĔLĔSYS, a Chaldaean priest at Babylon, who is said, in conjunction with Arbaces, the Mede, to have overthrown the old Assyrian empire. Belesis afterwards received the satrapy of Babylon from Arbaces.

BELGAE (-ārum), a people of German origin, inhabiting the N. E. of Gaul. were bounded on the N. by the Rhine, on the W. by the ocean, on the S. by the Sequana (*Seine*) and Matrona (*Marne*), and on the E. by the territory of the Treviri. They were the bravest of the inhabitants of Gaul, and were subdued by Caesar after a courageous resistance.

BELGĬCA. [GALLIA.]

BELGĬUM (-i), the name generally applied to the territory of the BELLOVACI, and of the tribes dependant upon the latter, namely, the Atrebates, Ambiani, Velliocasses, Aulerci, and Caleti. Belgium did not include the whole country inhabited by the Belgae, for we find the Nervii, Remi, &c., expressly excluded from it.

BĔLĪDES. [BELUS.]

BELISĀRĬUS, the greatest general of Justinian, overthrew the Vandal kingdom in Africa, and the Gothic kingdom in Italy. In A.D. 563 he was accused of a conspiracy against the life of Justinian ; according to a popular tradition, he was deprived of his property, his eyes were put out, and he wandered as a beggar through Constantinople ; but according to the more authentic account, he was merely imprisoned for a year in his own palace, and then restored to his honours. He died in 565.

BELLĔRŎPHON (-ontis), or BELLĔRŎ-PHONTĒS (-ae), son of the Corinthian king

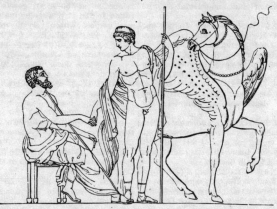

Bellerophon taking leave of Proetus.   (Tischbein, Hamilton Vases, vol. 3, pl. 38.)

Glaucus and Eurymede, and grandson of Sisyphus, was originally called *Hipponous,* and received the name Bellerophon from slaying the Corinthian Belerus. To be puri-

Bellerophon, Pegasus, and Chimaera.   (Tischbein, Hamilton Vases, vol. 1, pl. 1.)

fied from the murder he fled to Proetus, king of Argos, whose wife Antēa fell in love with the young hero ; but as her offers were rejected by him, she accused him to her husband of having made improper proposals to her. Proetus, unwilling to kill him with his own hands, sent him to his father-in-law, Iobates, king of Lycia, with a letter, in which the latter was requested to put the young man to death. Iobates accordingly sent him to kill the monster Chimaera, thinking that he was sure to perish in the contest. [CHIMAERA.] After obtaining possession of the winged horse, Pegasus, Bellerophon rose with him into the air, and slew the Chimaera with his arrows. [PEGASUS.] Iobates, thus disappointed, sent Bellerophon against the Solymi and next against the Amazons. In these contests he was also victorious; and on his return to Lyca, being attacked by the bravest Lycians, whom Iobates had placed in ambush for the purpose, Bellerophon slew them all. Iobates, now seeing that it was hopeless to kill the hero, gave him his daughter (Philonoë, Anticlēa, or Cassandra) in marriage, and made him his successor on the throne. At last Bellerophon drew upon himself the hatred of the gods, and consumed by grief, wandered lonely through the Aleïan field, avoiding the paths of men. This is all that Homer says respecting Bellerophon's later fate : some traditions related that he attempted to fly to heaven upon Pegasus, but that Zeus sent a gad-fly to sting the horse, which threw off the rider upon the earth, who became lame or blind in consequence.

BELLŌNA (-a), the Roman goddess of war, represented as the sister or wife of Mars. Her priests, called *Bellonarii*, wounded their own arms or legs when they offered sacrifices to her.

BELLŎVĂCI (-orum), the most powerful of the Belgae, dwelt in the modern *Beauvais*, between the Seine, Oise, Somme, and Bresle.

BĒLUS. (1) Son of Poseidon (Neptune) and Libya or Eurynome, twin-brother of Agenor, and father of Aegyptus and Danaus. He was believed to be the founder of Babylon. The patronymic Bēlĭdēs is given to Aegyptus and Danaus, to Lynceus, son of Aegyptus, and to Palamedes. The Danaides, daughters of Danaus, are also called Bēlĭdes.—(2) (*Nahr Naman*), a river of Phoenicia, falling into the sea close to the S. of Ptolemais (*Acre*) celebrated for the tradition that its fine sand first led the Phoenicians to the invention of glass.

BĒNĀCUS (-i) LACUS (*Lago di Garda*), a lake in the N. of Italy, out of which the Mincius flows.

BĒNĒVENTUM (-i : *Benevento*), a town in Samnium on the Appia Via, formerly called *Maleventum*, on account, it is said, of its bad air. It was one of the most ancient towns in Italy, having been founded, accord-

ing to tradition, by Diomedes. In the Samnite wars it was subdued by the Romans, who sent a colony thither in B.C. 268, and changed its name Maleventum into Beneventum. The modern town has several Roman remains, among others a triumphal arch of Trajan.

BĒRĒCYNTĬA (-ae), a surname of Cybele, which she derived from Mt. Berecyntus in Phrygia, where she was worshipped.

BĒRĒNĪCĒ (-es), a Macedonic form of *Pherenīce, i. e.* "Bringing Victory."—(1) Wife of Ptolemy I. Soter, and the mother of Ptolemy II. Philadelphus.—(2) Daughter of Ptolemy II. Philadelphus, and wife of Antiochus Theos, king of Syria, who divorced Laodice in order to marry her, B.C. 249. On the death of Ptolemy, 247, Antiochus recalled Laodice, who notwithstanding caused him to be poisoned, and murdered Berenice and her son.—(3) Daughter of Magas, king of Cyrene, and wife of Ptolemy III. Euergetes. She was put to death by her son, Ptolemy IV. Philopator on his accession to the throne, 221. The famous hair of Berenice, which she dedicated for her husband's safe return from his Syrian expedition, was said to have become a constellation.—(4) Otherwise called *Cleopatra*, daughter of Ptolemy VIII. Lathyrus, succeeded her father on the throne, B. c. 81, and married Ptolemy X. (Alexander II.), but was murdered by her husband 19 days after her marriage.—(5) Daughter of Ptolemy XI. Auletes, and eldest sister of the famous Cleopatra, was placed on the throne by the Alexandrines when they drove out her father, 58. She next married Archelaus, but was put to death with her husband, when Gabinius restored Auletes, 55.—(6) Sister of Herod the Great, married Aristobulus, who was put to death B.C. 6. She was the mother of Agrippa I.—(7) Daughter of Agrippa I., married her uncle Herod, king of Chalcis, by whom she had two sons. After the death of Herod, A.D. 48, Berenice, then 20 years old, lived with her brother, Agrippa II., not without suspicion of an incestuous commerce with him. She gained the love of Titus, who was only withheld from making her his wife by fear of offending the Romans by such a step.

BĒRĒNĪCĒ (-es), the name of several cities of the period of the Ptolemies. Of these the most important were :—(1) Formerly Eziongeber (Ru. nr. *Akabah*), in Arabia, at the head of the Sinus Aelanites, or E branch of the Red Sea.- -(2) In Upper Egypt, on the coast of the Red Sea, on a gulf called Sinus Immundus, now (*Foul Bay*), where its ruins are still visible. It was named after the mother of Ptolemy II. Philadelphus, who built it, and made a road hence to Coptos, so that it became a chief emporium for the commerce of Egypt with Arabia and India. (3)—(*Ben Ghazi*, Ru.), in Cyrenaica, formerly HESPERIS, the fabled site of the Gardens of the Hesperides. It took its latter name from the wife of Ptolemy III. Euvergetes.

BERGŎMUM (-i : *Bergamo*), a town of the Orobii in Gallia Cisalpina, between Comum and Brixia, afterwards a municipium.

BĔROEA (-ae). (1) (*Verria*), one of the most ancient towns of Macedonia, S.W. of Pella, and about 20 miles from the sea.—(2) (*Aleppo* or *Haleb*), a town in Syria, near Antioch, enlarged by Seleucus Nicator, who gave it the Macedonian name of Beroea. It is called *Helbon* or *Chelbon* in Ezekiel (xxvii. 18), a name still retained in the modern *Haleb*, for which Europeans have substituted Aleppo.

BĔRŌSUS (-i), a priest of Belus at Babylon, lived in the reign of Antiochus II. (B.C. 261—246), and wrote in Greek a history of Babylonia. Some fragments of this work are preserved by Josephus, Eusebius, and the Christian fathers.

BĔRŸTUS and BĔRŸTUS (-i : *Beirut*), one of the oldest sea-ports of Phoenicia, stood half way between Byblus and Sidon. It was destroyed by the Syrian king Tryphon (B.C. 140), and restored by Agrippa under Augustus, who made it a colony. It afterwards became a celebrated seat of learning.

BESSI (-ōrum), a fierce and powerful Thracian people, who dwelt along the whole of Mt. Haemus as far as the Euxine.

BESSUS (-i), satrap of Bactria under Darius III., seized Darius soon after the battle of Arbela, B.C. 331. Pursued by Alexander in the following year, Bessus murdered Darius, and fled to Bactria, where he assumed the title of king. He was betrayed by two of his followers to Alexander, who put him to death.

BETASĬI (-ōrum), a people in Gallia Belgica, between the Tungri and Nervii, in the neighbourhood of *Beetz* in Brabant.

BĬANOR (-ŏris), also called Ocnus or Aucnus, son of Tiberis and Manto, is said to have built the town of Mantua, and to have called it after his mother.

BĬAS (-antis). (1) Brother of the seer Melampus.—(2) Of Priene in Ionia, one of the Seven Sages of Greece, flourished about B.C. 550.

BĬBĂCŬLUS, M. FŪRĬUS (-i), a Roman poet, born at Cremona, wrote a poem on Caesar's Gallic wars, and another entitled Athiopis. They are both ridiculed by Horace.

BIBRACTĔ (-ēs : *Autun*), the chief town of the Aedui in Gallia Lugdunensis, afterwards *Augustodunum*.

BIBRAX (-actis : *Bièvre*), a town of the Remi in Gallia Belgica, not far from Aisne.

BIBŬLUS, M. CALPURNĬUS (-i), curule aedile B.C. 65, praetor 62, and consul 59, in each of which years he had C. Julius Caesar as his colleague. He was a staunch adherent of the aristocratical party, but was unable in his consulship to resist the powerful combination of Caesar, Pompey, and Crassus. After an ineffectual attempt to oppose Caesar's agrarian law, he withdrew from the popular assemblies altogether ; whence it was said in joke that it was the consulship of Julius and of Caesar. In the civil war he commanded Pompey's fleet in the Adriatic, and died (48) while holding this command off Corcyra. He married Porcia, the daughter of Cato Uticensis.

BIDIS (-is), a small town in Sicily, W. of Syracuse.

BIGERRA (-ae), a town of the Oretani in Hispania Tarraconensis.

BIGERRIŌNES (-um), or BIGERRI (-ōrum), a people in Aquitania near the Pyrenees.

BILBĬLIS (-is : *Baubola*) a town of the Celtiberi in Hispania Tarraconensis, the birthplace of the poet Martial.

BINGĬUM (-i : *Bingen*), a town on the Rhine in Gallica Belgica.

BĬŌN (-ōnis). (1) Of Smyrna, a bucolic poet, flourished about B. C. 280, and spent the last years of his life in Sicily, where he was poisoned. The style of Bion is refined, and his versification fluent and elegant.—(2) Of Borysthenes, near the mouth of the Dnieper, flourished about B.C. 250. He was sold as a slave, when young, and received his liberty from his master, a rhetorician. He studied at Athens, and afterwards lived a considerable time at the court of Antigonus Gonatas, king of Macedonia. Bion was noted for his sharp sayings, whence Horace speaks of persons delighting *Bioneis sermonibus et sale nigro*.

BISALTĬA (-ae), a district in Macedonia, on the W. bank of the Strymon, inhabited by a Thracian people.

BISANTHĔ (-es : *Rodosto*), subsequently *Rhaedestum* or *Rhaedestus*, a town in Thrace on the Propontis, with a good harbour.

BISTŌNES (-um), a Thracian people between Mt. Rhodope and the Aegean sea, on the lake Bistonis in the neighbourhood of Abdera. From the worship of Dionysus in Thrace the Bacchic women are called *Bistŏnĭdes*.

BĪTHŸNĬA (-ae), a district of Asia Minor, bounded on the W. by Mysia, on the N. by the Pontus Euxinus, on the E. by Paphlagonia, and on the S. by Phrygia Epictetus, was possessed at an early period by Thracian tribes from the neighbourhood of the Strymon, called Thyni and Bithyni, of whom the former dwelt on the coast, the latter in the interior. The country was subdued by the Lydians, and afterwards became a part of the Persian empire under Cyrus, and was governed by the satraps of Phrygia. During the decline of the Persian empire, the N. part of the country became independent, under native princes, who resisted Alexander and his successors, and established a kingdom, which lasted till the death of Nicomedes III. (B.C. 74), who bequeathed his kingdom to the Romans. Under Augustus, it was made a proconsular province. It was a fertile country, intersected with wooded mountains, the highest of which was the Mysian Olympus, on its S. border.

BITON (-ŏnis), and CLEOBIS (-is), sons of Cydippe, a priestess of Hera at Argos. They were celebrated for their affection to their mother, whose chariot they once dragged during a festival to the temple of Hera, a distance of 45 stadia. The priestess prayed to the goddess to grant them what was best for mortals; and during the night they both died while asleep in the temple.

BITURIGES (-um), a numerous and powerful Celtic people in Gallia Aquitanica, had in early times the supremacy over the other Celts in Gaul. They were divided into two tribes: 1 Bit. Cubi, with Avaricum as their capital (*Bourges*). 2 Bit. Vivisci or Urisci: their capital was Burdigala (*Bordeaux*), on the left bank of the Garumna.

BLEMYES (-um), an Aethiopian people, on the borders of Upper Egypt.

BLOSIUS or BLOSSIUS (-i), the name of a noble family in Campania. One of this family, C. Blosius, of Cumae, was a philosopher, a disciple of Antipater, of Tarsus, and a friend of Tib. Gracchus.

BOADICEA (-ae), queen of the Iceni in Britain, having been shamefully treated by the Romans, who even ravished her 2 daughters, excited an insurrection of the Britons against their oppressors during the absence of Suetonius Paulinus, the Roman governor, on an expedition to the island of Mona. She took the Roman colonies of Camalodunum, Londinium, and other places, and slew nearly 70,000 Romans and their allies. She was at length defeated with great loss by Suetonius Paulinus, and put an end to her own life, A.D. 61.

BOCCHUS (-i). (1) King of Mauretania, and father-in-law of Jugurtha, with whom at first he made war against the Romans, but whom he afterwards delivered up to Sulla, the quaestor of Marius, B.C. 106.—(2). Son of

the preceding, who took part in the civil wars. He was confirmed in his kingdom by Augustus.

BODOTRIA (-ae), or BODERIA (-ae), AESTUARIUM (-i), (*Firth of Forth*), an aestuary on the E. coast of Scotland.

BOEBE (-es), a town in Pelasgiotis in Thessaly, on the W. shore of the lake Boebeïs.

BOEOTIA (-ae), a district of Greece, bounded N. by Opuntian Locris, E. by the Euboean sea, S. by Attica, Megaris, and the Corinthian Gulf, and W. by Phocis. It is nearly surrounded by mountains, namely, Helicon and Parnassus on the W., Cithaeron and Parnes on the S., the Opuntian mountains on the N., and a range of mountains along the sea-coast on the E. The country contains several fertile plains, of which the most important were the vallies of the Asopus and of the Cephissus. The Boeotians were an Aeolian people, who originally occupied Arne in Thessaly, from which they were expelled by the Thessalians 60 years after the Trojan war. They then migrated into the country called after them Boeotia, partly expelling and partly incorporating with themselves the ancient inhabitants of the land. Boeotia was then divided into 14 independent states, which formed a league, with Thebes at its head. The chief magistrates of the confederacy were the Boeotarchs, elected annually. The government in most states was an aristocracy.

BOETHIUS (-i), a Roman statesman and author, born about A.D. 470, was famous for his general learning, and especially for his knowledge of Greek philosophy. He was first highly favoured by Theodosius the Great; but having awakened his suspicion, he was thrown into prison by him, and afterwards put to death. It was during his imprisonment that he wrote his celebrated work, *De Consolatione Philosophiae*, which has come down to us.

BOEUM (-i), an ancient town of the Dorian Tetrapolis.

BOII (-ŏrum), one of the most powerful of the Celtic people, said to have dwelt originally in Gaul (Transalpina), but in what part of the country is uncertain. At an early time they migrated in two great swarms, one of which crossed the Alps and settled in the country between the Po and the Apennines; the other crossed the Rhine and settled in the part of Germany called Boihemum (*Bohemia*) after them, and between the Danube and the Tyrol. The Boii in Italy long carried on a fierce struggle with the Romans, but they were at length subdued by the consul P. Scipio in B.C. 191, and were subsequently incorporated in the province of Gallia Cisalpina. The Boii in Germany maintained their power longer, but were at length subdued by the Marcomanni, and expelled from the country.

BŌLA (-ae), BŌLAE or VŌLAE (-ārum), an ancient town of the Aequi, belonging to the Latin league.

BOLBĒ (-es), a lake in Macedonia, emptying itself by a short river into the Strymonic gulf near Bromiscus and Aulon.

BOLBĬTĬNĒ (-es : *Rosetta*), a city of Lower Egypt, near the mouth of a branch of the Nile (the W.-most but one), which was called the Bolbitine mouth.

BŌMILCAR (-ăris), a Numidian, deep in the confidence of Jugurtha. When Jugurtha was at Rome, 109, Bomilcar effected for him the assassination of Massiva. In 107 he plotted against Jugurtha.

BŌMĬUS (-i) MONS, the W. part of Mt. Oeta in Aetolia, inhabited by the Bomienses.

BŌNA DĔA (-ae), a Roman divinity, is described as the sister, wife, or daughter of Faunus, and was herself called *Fauna*, *Fatua*, or *Oma*. She was worshipped at Rome as a chaste and prophetic divinity ; she revealed her oracles only to females, as Faunus did only to males. Her festival was celebrated every year on the 1st of May, in the house of the consul or praetor, as the sacrifices on that occasion were offered on behalf of the whole Roman people. The solemnities were conducted by the Vestals, and no male person was allowed to be in the house at one of these festivals. P. Clodius profaned the sacred ceremonies, by entering the house of Caesar in the disguise of a woman, B.C. 62.

BONNA (-ae : *Bonn*), a town on the left bank of the Rhine in Lower Germany, and in the territory of the Ubii, was a strong fortress of the Romans and the regular quarters of a Roman legion.

BŌNŌNĬA (-ae). (1) (*Bologna*), a town in Gallia Cispadana, originally called FELSINA, was in ancient times an Etruscan city, and the capital of N. Etruria. It afterwards fell into the hands of the Boii, but it was colonised by the Romans on the conquest of the Boii, B.C. 191, and its name of Felsina was then changed into Bononia. (2) (*Boulogne*), a town in the N. of Gaul. See GESORIACUM.

BŌŌTĒS. [ARCTURUS.]

BORBETOMĀGUS (-i : *Worms*), also called VANGIONES, at a later time WORMATIA, a town of the Vangiones on the left bank of the Rhine in Upper Germany.

BŎRĔAS (-ae), the N. wind, or more strictly the wind from the N.N.E., was, in mythology, a son of Astraeus and Eos, and brother of Hesperus, Zephyrus, and Notus. He dwelt in a cave of mount Haemus in Thrace. He carried off Orithyia, a daughter of Erechtheus, king of Attica, by whom he

begot Zetes, Calais, and Cleopatra, wife of Phineus, who are therefore called *Boreades*. In the Persian war Boreas showed his friendly disposition towards the Athenians by destroying the ships of the barbarians. Boreas was worshipped at Athens, where a festival, *Boreasmi*, was celebrated in his honour.

Boreas. (Relief from Temple of the Winds at Athens.)

BŎRYSTHĔNĒS (-is : *Dnieper*), afterwards DANAPRIS, a river of European Sarmatia, flows into the Euxine. Near its mouth and at its junction with the Hypanis, lay the town BORYSTHENES or BORYSTHENIS (*Kudak*), also called OLBIA, OLBIOPOLIS, and MILETOPOLIS, a colony of Miletus, and the most important Greek city on the N. of the Euxine.

BOSPŎRUS (-i : *Ox-ford*), the name of any straits among the Greeks, but especially applied to the 2 following :—(1) THE THRACIAN BOSPORUS (*Channel of Constantinople*), unites the Propontis or Sea of Marmora with the Euxine or Black Sea. According to the legend it was called *Bosporus*, from Io, who crossed it in the form of a heifer. At the entrance of the Bosporus was the celebrated SYMPLEGADES. Darius constructed a bridge across the Bosporus, when he invaded Scythia.—(2) THE CIMMERIAN BOSPORUS (*Straits of Kaffa*), unites the Palus Maeotis or Sea of Azof with the Euxine or Black Sea. It formed, with the Tanais (Don), the boundary between Asia and Europe, and it derived its name from the CIMMERII, who were supposed to have dwelt in the neighbourhood. On the European side of the Bosporus, the modern Crimea, the Milesians founded the town of Panticapaeum, also called Bosporus, and the inhabitants of Panticapaeum subsequently founded the town of Phanagoria on the Asiatic side of the Straits. Panticapaeum became the residence of a race of kings, who are frequently mentioned in history under the name of kings of Bosporus.

BOSTRA (-ōrum : O. T. Bozrah : *Busrah*, Ru.), a city of Arabia, in an Oasis of the Syrian Desert, S. of Damascus.

BOTTIA or BOTTIAEA (-ae), a district in Macedonia, on the right bank of the river Axius, extended in the time of Thucydides to Pieria on the W. The Bottiaei were a Thracian people, who, being driven out of the country by the Macedonians, settled in that part of the Macedonian Chalcidice N. of Olynthus, which was called *Bottice*.

BOTTĬCĒ. [BOTTIA.]

BŎVĬĀNUM (*Bojano*), the chief town of the Pentri in Samnium.

BŎVILLAE (-ārum), an ancient town in Latium at the foot of the Alban mountain, on the Appian Way about 10 miles from Rome. Near it Clodius was killed by Milo (B.C. 52).

BRACHMĀNAE (-arum), or BRACH-MĀNES (-ium), a name used by the ancient geographers, sometimes for a caste of priests in India (the *Brahmins*), sometimes, apparently, for all the people whose religion was Brahminism, and sometimes for a particular tribe.

BRANCHĬDAE (-arum : *Jeronda*, Ru.), afterwards DIDYMA, or -I, a place on the sea coast of Ionia, a little S. of Miletus, celebrated for its temple and oracle of Apollo, surnamed Didymeus. This oracle, which the Ionians held in the highest esteem, was said to have been founded by Branchus, son of Apollo, and a Milesian woman. The reputed descendants of this Branchus, the Branchidae, were the hereditary ministers of this oracle. The temple, called Didymaeum, which was destroyed by Xerxes, was rebuilt, and its ruins contain some beautiful specimens of the Ionic order of architecture.

BRASĬDAS (-ae), the most distinguished Spartan in the first part of the Peloponnesian war. In B.C. 424, at the head of a small force, having effected a dexterous march through the hostile country of Thessaly, he gained possession of many of the cities in Macedonia subject to Athens ; his greatest acquisition was Amphipolis. In 422 he gained a brilliant victory over Cleon, who had been sent, with an Athenian force, to recover Amphipolis, but he was slain in the battle. He was buried within the city, and the inhabitants honoured him as a hero, by yearly sacrifices and by games.

BRATUSPANTĬUM (-i), the chief town of the Bellovaci in Gallia Belgica.

BRAURŌN (-onis), a demus in Attica, on the E. coast on the river Erasinus, with a celebrated temple of Artemis (Diana), who was hence called *Brauronia*.

BRENNUS (-i). (1). The leader of the Senonian Gauls, who in B.C. 390 crossed the Apennines, defeated the Romans at the Allia, and took Rome. After besieging the Capitol for 6 months, he quitted the city upon receiving 1000 pounds of gold as a ransom for the Capitol, and returned home safe with his booty. But it was subsequently related in the popular legends that Camillus and a Roman army appeared at the moment that the gold was being weighed, that Brennus was defeated by Camillus, and that he himself and his whole army were slain to a man.— (2). The chief leader of the Gauls who invaded Macedonia and Greece, B.C. 280, 279. In the year 279 he penetrated into the S. of Greece, but was defeated near Delphi, most of his men were slain, and he himself put an end to his own life.

BREUNI (-orum), a Rhaetian people, dwelt in the Tyrol near the Brenner.

BRIAREUS. [AEGAEON.]

BRĬGANTES (-um), the most powerful of the British tribes, inhabited the whole of the N. of the island from the Abus (*Humber*) to the Roman wall, with the exception of the S. E. corner of Yorkshire, which was inhabited by the Parisii. The Brigantes consequently inhabited the greater part of Yorkshire, and the whole of Lancashire, Durham, Westmoreland, and Cumberland. Their capital was EBORACUM. They were conquered by Petilius Cerealis, in the reign of Vespasian. There was also a tribe of Brigantes in the S. of Ireland, between the rivers Birgus (*Barrow*) and Dabrona (*Blackwater*), in the counties of Waterford and Tipperary.

BRĬGANTĪNUS (-i) LACUS (*Bodensee* or *Lake of Constance*), also called VENETUS and ACRONIUS, through which the Rhine flows, inhabited by the Helvetii on the S., by the Rhaetii on the S. E., and by the Vindelici on the N.

BRĪSĒIS (-idis), daughter of Briseus, of Lyrnessus, fell into the hands of Achilles, but was seized by Agamemnon. Hence arose the dire feud between the 2 heroes. [ACHILLES.] Her proper name was Hippodamia.

BRĪTANNĬA (-ae), the island of England and Scotland, which was also called ALBION. HIBERNIA, or *Ireland*, is usually spoken of as a separate island, but is sometimes included under the general name of the INSULAE BRITANNICAE, which also comprehended the smaller islands around the coast of Great Britain. The Britons were Celts, belonging to that branch of the race called Cymry.

Their manners and customs were in general the same as the Gauls; but separated more than the Gauls from intercourse with civilised nations, they preserved the Celtic religion in a purer state than in Gaul; and hence Druidism, according to Cæsar, was transplanted from Gaul to Britain. The Britons also retained many of the barbarous Celtic customs, which the more civilised Gauls had laid aside. They painted their bodies with a blue colour, extracted from woad, in order to appear more terrible in battle; and they had wives in common. At a later time the Belgæ crossed over from Gaul, and settled on the S. and E. coasts, driving the Britons into the interior of the island. It was not till a late period that the Greeks and Romans obtained any knowledge of Britain. In early times the Phoenicians visited the Scilly islands and the coast of Cornwall for the purpose of obtaining tin; but whatever knowledge they acquired of the country they jealously kept secret; and it only transpired that there were CASSITERIDES, or *Tin Islands*, in the N. parts of the ocean. The first certain knowledge which the Greeks obtained of Britain was from the merchants of Massilia about the time of Alexander the Great, and especially from the voyages of PYTHEAS, who sailed round a great part of Britain. From this time it was generally believed that the island was in the form of a triangle, an error which continued to prevail even at a later period. Another important mistake, which likewise prevailed for a long time, was the position of Britain in relation to Gaul and Spain. As the N.W. coast of Spain was supposed to extend too far to the N. and the W. coast of Gaul to run N.E., the lower part of Britain was believed to lie between Spain and Gaul. The Romans first became personally acquainted with the island by Caesar's invasion. He twice landed in Britain (B.C. 55, 54), and though on the second occasion he conquered the greater part of the S.E. of the island, yet he did not take permanent possession of any portion of the country, and after his departure the Britons continued as independent as before. The Romans made no further attempts to conquer the island for nearly 100 years. In the reign of Claudius (A.D. 43) they again landed in Britain, and permanently subdued the country S. of the Thames. They now began to extend their conquests over the other parts of the island; and the great victory (61) of Suetonius Paulinus over the Britons, who had revolted under BOADICEA, still further consolidated the Roman dominions. In the reign of Vespasian, the Romans made several successful expeditions against the SILURES and the BRIGANTES; and

the conquest of S. Britain was at length finally completed by Agricola, who in 7 campaigns (78—84) subdued the whole of the island as far N. as the Frith of Forth and the Clyde, between which he erected a series of forts to protect the Roman dominions from the incursions of the barbarians in the N. of Scotland. The Roman part of Britain was now called *Britannia Romana*, and the N. part inhabited by the Caledonians *Britannia Barbara* or *Caledonia*. The Romans however gave up the N. conquests of Agricola in the reign of Hadrian, and made a rampart of turf from the Aestuarium Ituna (*Solway Frith*) to the German Ocean, which formed the N. boundary of their dominions. In the reign of Antoninus Pius the Romans again extended their boundary as far as the conquests of Agricola, and erected a rampart connecting the Forth and the Clyde, the remains of which are now called *Grimes Dyke*, Grime in the Celtic language signifying great or powerful. The Caledonians afterwards broke through this wall; and in consequence of their repeated devastations of the Roman dominions, the emperor Severus went to Britain in 208, in order to conduct the war against them in person. He died in the island at Eboracum (*York*) in 211, after erecting a solid stone wall from the Solway to the mouth of the Tyne, a little N. of the rampart of Hadrian. After the death of Severus, the Romans relinquished for ever all their conquests N. of this wall. Upon the resignation of the empire by Diocletian and Maximian (305), Britain fell to the share of Constantius who died at Eboracum in 306, and his son Constantine assumed in the island the title of Caesar. Shortly afterwards the Caledonians, who now appear under the names of Picts and Scots, broke through the wall of Severus, and the Saxons ravaged the coasts of Britain; and the declining power of the Roman empire was unable to afford the province any effectual assistance. In the reign of Honorius, Constantine, who had been proclaimed emperor in Britain (407), withdrew all the Roman troops from the island, in order to make himself master of Gaul. The Britons were thus left exposed to the ravages of the Picts and Scots, and at length, in 447, they called in the assistance of the Saxons, who became the masters of Britain. The Roman dominions of Britain formed a single province till the time of Severus, and were governed by a legatus of the emperor. Severus divided the country into 2 provinces, and Diocletian into 4.

BRITANNICUS (-i), son of the emperor Claudius and Messalina, was born A.D. 42. Agrippina, the second wife of Claudius, induced the emperor to adopt her own son, and give him precedence over Britannicus. This son, the emperor Nero, ascended the throne in 54, and caused Britannicus to be poisoned in the following year.

BRĪTŎMARTIS (-is), a Cretan nymph, daughter of Zeus (Jupiter) and Carme, and beloved by Minos, who pursued her 9 months, till at length she leaped into the sea and was changed by Artemis (Diana) into a goddess.

BRIXELLUM (-i : *Bregella* or *Brescella*), a town on the right bank of the Po in Gallia Cisalpina, where the emperor Otho put himself to death, A.D. 69.

BRIXĪA (-ae : *Brescia*), a town in Gallia Cisalpina on the road from Comum to Aquileia, through which the river Mella flowed.

BRŎMĪUS, a surname of Dionysus (Bacchus), that is, the noisy god, from the noise of the Bacchic revelries (from βρέμω).

BRONTĒS. [CYCLOPES.]

BRUCTĔRI (-ōrum), a people of Germany, dwelt on each side of the Amisia (*Ems*) and extended S. as far as the Luppia (*Lippe*). The Bructeri joined the Batavi in their revolt against the Romans in A.D. 69.

BRUNDŪSĪUM or BRUNDĪSĪUM (-i : *Brindisi*), a town in Calabria, on a small bay of the Adriatic, forming an excellent harbour, to which the place owed its importance. The Appia Via terminated at Brundusium, and it was the usual place of embarkation for Greece and the East. It was conquered and colonised by the Romans, B.C. 245. The poet Pacuvius was born at this town, and Virgil died here on his return from Greece, B.C. 19.

BRUTTĬUM (-i), BRUTTIUS and BRUTTĬŌRUM AGER, more usually called BRUTTĬI after the inhabitants, the S. extremity of Italy, separated from Lucania by a line drawn from the mouth of the Laus to Thurii, and surrounded on the other three sides by the sea. It was the country called in ancient times Oenotria and Italia. The country is mountainous, as the Apennines run through it down to the Sicilian Straits; it contained excellent pasturage for cattle, and the valleys produced good corn, olives, and fruit.—The earliest inhabitants of the country were Oenotrians. Subsequently some Lucanians, who had revolted from their countrymen in Lucania, took possession of the country, and were hence called *Bruttii* or *Brettii*, which word is said to mean " rebels " in the language of the Lucanians. This people, however, inhabited only the interior of the land; the coast was almost entirely in the possession of the Greek colonies. At the close of the 2nd Punic war, in which the Bruttii had been the allies of Hannibal, they lost their independence, and were treated by the Romans with great severity. They were declared to be public slaves, and were employed as lictors and servants of the magistrates.

BRŪTUS (-i), a family of the Junia gens. —(1) L. JUNIUS BRUTUS, son of M. Junius and of Tarquinia, the sister of Tarquinius Superbus. His elder brother was murdered by Tarquinius, and Lucius escaped his brother's fate only by feigning idiotcy, whence he received the surname of Brutus. After Lucretia had stabbed herself, Brutus roused the Romans to expel the Tarquins; and upon the banishment of the latter he was elected first consul with Tarquinius Collatinus. He loved his country better than his children, and put to death his 2 sons, who had attempted to restore the Tarquins. He fell in battle the same year, fighting against Aruns, the son of Tarquinius. Brutus was the great hero in the legends about the expulsion of the Tarquins.—(2) D. JUNIUS BRUTUS, surnamed GALLAECUS or CALLAICUS, consul 138, conquered a great part of Lusitania. From his victory over the Gallaeci he obtained his surname. He was a patron of the poet L. Accius, and well versed in Greek and Roman literature.—(3) D. JUNIUS BRUTUS. consul 77, and husband of Sempronia, who carried on an intrigue with Catiline.—(4) D. JUNIUS BRUTUS, adopted by A. Postumius Albinus, consul 99, and hence called *Brutus Albinus*. He served under Caesar in Gaul and in the civil war; but he nevertheless joined the conspiracy against Caesar's life. After the death of the latter (44) he went into Cisalpine Gaul, which had been promised him by Caesar, and which he refused to surrender to Antony, who had obtained this province from the people. Antony made war against him, and kept him besieged in Mutina, till the siege was raised in April 43 by the consuls Hirtius and Pansa, and by Octavianus. But Brutus only obtained a short respite. Antony was preparing to march against him from the N. with a large army, and Octavianus, who had deserted the senate, was marching against him from the S. His only resource was flight, but he was betrayed by Camillus, a Gaulish chief, and was put to death by Antony, 43.— (5) M. JUNIUS BRUTUS, married Servilia, the half-sister of Cato of Utica. In 77 he espoused the cause of Lepidus, and was placed in command of the forces in Cisalpine Gaul, where he was slain by command of Pompey.—(6) M. JUNIUS BRUTUS, the so-called tyrannicide, son of No. 5 and Servilia. He lost his father when he was only 8 years old, and was trained by his uncle Cato in the principles of the aristocratical party. Accordingly, on the breaking out of the civil war, 49, he joined Pompey, although he was the murderer of his father. After the battle of Pharsalia, 48, he was not only pardoned by Caesar, but received from him the greatest marks of confidence and favour. Caesar made him governor of Cisalpine Gaul in 46, and praetor in 44, and also promised him the government of Macedonia. But notwithstanding all the obligations he was under to Caesar, he was persuaded by Cassius to murder his benefactor under the delusive idea of again establishing the republic. [CAESAR.] After the murder of Caesar, Brutus spent a short time in Italy, and then took possession of the province of Macedonia. He was joined by Cassius, who commanded in Syria, and their united forces were opposed to those of Octavian and Antony. Two battles were fought in the neighbourhood of Philippi (42), in the former of which Brutus was victorious, though Cassius was defeated, but in the latter Brutus also was defeated and put an end to his own life. Brutus's wife was PORCIA, the daughter of Cato. Brutus was an ardent student of literature and philosophy, but he appears to have been deficient in judgment and original power. He wrote several works, all of which have perished. He was a literary friend of Cicero, who dedicated to him several of his works, and who has given the name of Brutus to his dialogue on illustrious orators.

BRYGI (-orum) or BRYGES (-um), a barbarous people in the N. of Macedonia. The Phrygians were believed by the ancients to have been a portion of this people, who emigrated to Asia in early times. [PHRYGIA.]

BUBASSUS (-i), an ancient city of Caria, E. of Cnidus, which gave name to the bay (Bubassius Sinus) and the peninsula on which it stood.

BUBASTIS (-is) or BUBASTUS (-i), the capital of the Nomos Bubastites in Lower Egypt, stood on the E. bank of the Pelusiac branch of the Nile, and was the chief seat of the worship of the goddess Bubastis, whom the Greeks identified with Artemis (Diana).

BUCEPHALA or -IA (-ae : Jhelum), a city on the Hydaspes in N. India, built by Alexander, after his battle with Porus, in memory of his favourite charger Bucephalus, who died there, after carrying him through all his campaigns. This horse was purchased by Philip for 13 talents, and no one was able to break it in except the youthful Alexander.

BUCEPHALUS. [BUCEPHALA.]

BUDINI (-orum), a Scythian people, who dwelt N. cf the Sauromatae in the steppes of S. Russia.

BULLIS (-idis), a town of Illyria on the coast, S. of Apollonia.

BUPRASIUM (-i), an ancient town in Elis, mentioned in the Iliad.

BURA (-ae), one of the 12 cities of Achaia, destroyed by an earthquake, together with Helice, but subsequently rebuilt.

BURDIGALA. [BITURIGES.]

BURGUNDIONES (-um), or BURGUNTII (-orum), a powerful nation of Germany, dwelt originally between the Viadus (Oder) and the Vistula, and were of the same race as the Vandals or Goths. They were driven out of their original abodes by the Gepidae, and the greater part of them settled in the country on the Maine. In the 5th century they settled in Gaul, where they founded the powerful kingdom of Burgundy. Their chief towns were Geneva and Lyons.

BURSA. [PLANCUS.]

BUSIRIS (-idis). (1) A king of Egypt, who sacrificed strangers to Zeus (Jupiter), but was slain by Hercules.—(2) A city in Lower Egypt, stood in the middle of the Delta, on the W. bank of the Nile, and had a great temple of Isis, the remains of which are still standing.

BUTHROTUM (-i : Butrinto), a town of Epirus, a flourishing sea-port on a small peninsula, opposite Corcyra.

BUTO. (1) An Egyptian divinity, was the nurse of Horus and Bubastis, the children of Osiris and Isis, whom she saved from the persecutions of Typhon by concealing them in the floating island of Chemnis. The Greeks identified her with Leto (Latona), and represented her as the goddess of night.—(2) A city in Lower Egypt, stood near the Sebennytic branch of the Nile, on the lake of Buto. It was celebrated for its oracle of the goddess Buto, in honour of whom a festival was held at the city every year.

BUXENTUM (-i : Policastro), originally Pyxus, a town on the W. coast of Lucania and on the river BUXENTIUS, was founded by Micythus, tyrant of Messana, B.C. 471, and was afterwards a Roman colony.

BYBLIS (-idis), daughter of Miletus and Idothea, was in love with her brother Caunus, whom she pursued through various lands, till at length, worn out with sorrow, she was changed into a fountain.

BYBLUS (-i : Jebeil), a very ancient city on the coast of Phoenicia, between Berytus and Tripolis, a little N. of the river Adonis. It was the chief seat of the worship of Adonis.

BYRSA (-ae), the citadel of CARTHAGO.

BYZACIUM (-i) or BYZACENA REGIO (S. part of Tunis), the S. portion of the Roman province of Africa.

BŸZANTĬUM (-i: *Constantinople*), a town on the Thracian Bosporus, founded by the Megarians, B.C. 658, is said to have derived its name from Byzas, the leader of the colony and the son of Poseidon (Neptune). It was situated on 2 hills, was 40 stadia in circumference, and its acropolis stood on the site of the present seraglio. Its favourable position, commanding as it did the entrance to the Euxine, rendered it a place of great commercial importance. A new city was built on its site (330) by Constantine, who made it the capital of the empire, and changed its name into CONSTANTINOPOLIS.

CABALIA (-ae), a small district of Asia Minor, between Lycia and Pamphylia, with a town of the same name.

CABILLŌNUM (-i: *Châlons-sur-Saône*), a town of the Aedui on the Arar (*Saône*) in Gallia Lugdunensis.

CABĬRA (-ōrum), a place in Pontus, on the borders of Armenia; a frequent residence of Mithridates, who was defeated here by Lucullus, B.C. 71.

CĂBĪRI (-ōrum), mystic divinities worshipped in various parts of the ancient world. The meaning of their name, their character, and nature, are quite uncertain. Divine honours were paid to them at Samothrace, Lemnos, and Imbros, and their mysteries at Samothrace were solemnized with great splendour. They were also worshipped at Thebes, Anthedon, Pergamus, and elsewhere.

CĂCUS, (-i), son of Vulcan, was a huge giant, who inhabited a cave on Mt. Aventine, and plundered the surrounding country. When Hercules came to Italy with the oxen which he had taken from Geryon in Spain, Cacus stole part of the cattle while the hero slept, and, as he dragged the animals into his cave by their tails, it was impossible to discover their traces. But when the remaining oxen passed by the cave, those within began to bellow, and were thus discovered, whereupon Cacus was slain by Hercules. In honour of his victory Hercules dedicated the *ara maxima*, which continued to exist ages afterwards in Rome.

CĂDI (-ōrum), a city of Phrygia Epictetus, on the borders of Lydia.

CADMĒA. [THEBAE.]

CADMUS (-i). (1) Son of Agenor, king of Phoenicia, and of Telephassa, and brother of Europa. Another legend makes him a native of Thebes in Egypt. When Europa was carried off by Zeus (Jupiter) to Crete, Agenor sent Cadmus in search of his sister, enjoining him not to return without her. Unable to find her, Cadmus settled in Thrace, but having consulted the oracle at Delphi, he was commanded by the god to follow a cow of a certain kind, and to build a town on the spot where the cow should sink down with fatigue. Cadmus found the cow in Phocis and followed her into Boeotia, where she sank down on the spot on which Cadmus built Cadmea, afterwards the citadel of Thebes. Intending to sacrifice the cow to Athena (Minerva), he sent some persons to the neighbouring well of Ares to fetch water. This well was guarded by a dragon, a son of Ares (Mars), who killed the men sent by Cadmus. Thereupon Cadmus slew the dragon, and, on the advice of Athena, sowed the teeth of the monster, out of which armed men grew up, called *Sparti* or the *Sown*, who killed each other, with the exception of 5, who were the ancestors of the Thebans. Athena assigned to Cadmus the government of Thebes, and Zeus gave him Harmonia for his wife. The marriage solemnity was honoured by the presence of all the Olympian gods in the Cadmea. Cadmus gave to Harmonia the famous peplus and necklace which he had received from Hephaestus (Vulcan) or from Europa, and he became by her the father of Autonoë, Ino, Semele, Agave, Polydorus, and at a subsequent period, Illyrius. In the end, Cadmus and Harmonia were changed into serpents, and were removed by Zeus to Elysium. Cadmus is said to have introduced into Greece from Phoenicia or Egypt an alphabet of 16 letters.—(2) Of Miletus, the earliest Greek historian or logographer, lived about B.C. 540.

CĂDURCI (-ōrum), a people in Gallia Aquitanica, in the country now called *Querci* (a corruption of Cadurci). Their capital was DIVONA, afterwards CIVITAS CADURCORUM, now *Cahors*, where are the remains of a Roman amphitheatre and of an aqueduct.

CĂDŪSII (-ōrum) or GĔLAE (-ārum), a powerful Scythian tribe in the mountains S.W. of the Caspian, on the borders of Media Atropatene.

CADŸTIS, according to Herodotus, a great city of the Syrians of Palestine, not much smaller than Sardis, was taken by Necho, king of Egypt, after his defeat of the "Syrians" at Magdolus. It is now pretty well established that by Cadytis is meant Jerusalem, and that the battle mentioned by Herodotus is that in which Necho defeated and slew king Josiah at Megiddo, B.C. 608.

CAECĬLIA (-ae).—(1) CAIA, the Roman name of TANAQUIL, wife of Tarquinius Priscus.—(2) METELLA, daughter of L. Metellus Dalmaticus, consul B.C. 119, was first married to M. Aemilius Scaurus, consul in 115, and afterwards to the dictator Sulla.—(3) Daughter of T. Pomponius Atticus, called Caecilia, because her father took the name of his uncle, Q. Caecilius, by whom he was adopted. She was married to M. Vipsanius Agrippa. [ATTICUS.]

CAECILIUS (-i). (1) Q., a wealthy Roman eques, who adopted his nephew Atticus in his will, and left the latter a fortune of 10 millions of sesterces.—(2) CAECILIUS CALACTINUS, a Greek rhetorician at Rome in the time of Augustus.—(3) CAECILIUS STATIUS, a Roman comic poet, the immediate predecessor of Terence, was by birth an Insubrian Gaul, and a native of Milan. Being a slave, he bore the servile appellation of *Statius*, which was afterwards, probably when he received his freedom, converted into a sort of cognomen, and he became known as Caecilius Statius. He died B. C. 168.

CAECILIUS METELLUS. [METELLUS.]

CAECINA (-ae), the name of a family of the Etruscan city of Volaterrae, probably derived from the river Caecina, which flows by the town.—(1) A. CAECINA, whom Cicero defended in a law-suit, B. C. 69. — (2) A. CAECINA, son of the preceding, published a libellous work against Caesar, and was in consequence sent into exile after the battle of Pharsalia, B. C. 48.—(3) A. CAECINA ALIENUS was quaestor in Baetica, in Spain, at Nero's death, and was one of the foremost in joining the party of Galba. He served first under Galba, and afterwards joined Vitellius; but proving a traitor to the latter, he joined Vespasian, against whom, also, he conspired; and was slain by order of Titus.

CAECUBUS (-i) AGER, a marshy district in Latium, bordering on the gulf of Amyclae, close to Fundi, celebrated for its wine (*Caecubum*) in the age of Horace. In the time of Pliny the reputation of this wine was entirely gone.

CAECULUS (-i), an ancient Italian hero, son of Vulcan, is said to have founded Praeneste.

CAELES or CAELIUS (-i) VIBENNA (-ae), the leader of an Etruscan army, is said to have come to Rome in the reign either of Romulus or of Tarquinius Priscus, and to have settled with his troops on the hill called after him the Caelian.

CAELIUS or COELIUS MONS. [ROMA.]

CAENEUS (-ĕŏs or -ĕi), one of the Lapithae, son of Elatus or Coronus, was originally a maiden named CAENIS (-ĭdis), who was beloved by Poseidon (Neptune), and was by this god changed into a man, and rendered invulnerable. In the battle between the Lapithae and the Centaurs at the marriage of Pirithous, he was buried by the Centaurs under a mass of trees, as they were unable to kill him; but he was changed into a bird. In the lower world Caeneus recovered his female form.

CAENI or CAENICI (-orum),a Thracian people, between the Black Sea and the Panysus.

CAENINA (-ae), a town of the Sabines, in Latium, whose king Acron is said to have carried on the first war against Rome. After their defeat, most of the inhabitants removed to Rome.

CAENIS. [CAENEUS.]

CAEPIO, CN. SERVILIUS (-i), consul B. C. 106, was sent into Gallia Narbonensis to oppose the Cimbri. In 105 he was defeated by the Cimbri, along with the consul Cn. Mallius or Manlius. 80,000 soldiers and 40,000 camp-followers are said to have perished. Caepio survived the battle, but 10 years afterwards (95) he was brought to trial by the tribune C. Norbanus, on account of his misconduct in this war. He was condemned, and cast into prison, where, according to one account, he died; but it was more generally stated that he escaped from prison, and lived in exile at Smyrna.

CAERE (*Cervetri*), called by the Greeks AGYLLA (*Agyllina urbs*, Virg.), a city in Etruria, situated on a small river W. of Veii, and 50 stadia from the coast. It was an ancient Pelasgic city, the capital of the cruel Mezentius, and was afterwards one of the 12 Etruscan cities, with a territory extending apparently as far as the Tiber. In early times Caere was closely allied with Rome; and when the latter city was taken by the Gauls, B.C. 390, Caere gave refuge to the Vestal virgins. The Romans out of gratitude, are said to have conferred upon the Caerites the Roman franchise without the suffragium, though it is not improbable that the Caerites enjoyed this honour previously. The Caerites appear to have been the first body of Roman citizens who did not enjoy the suffrage. Thus, when a Roman citizen was struck out of his tribe by the Censors, and made an aerarian, he was said to become one of the Caerites, since he had lost the suffrage: hence we find the expressions *in tabulas Caeritum referre*, and *aerarium facere*, used as synonymous.

CAESAR (-ăris), the name of a patrician family, of the Julia gens, which traced its origin to Iulus, the son of Aeneas. Various etymologies of the name are given by the ancient writers; but it is probably connected with the Latin word *caes-ar-ies*, and the Sanskrit *késa*, "hair;" for it is in accordance with the Roman custom for a surname to be given to an individual from some peculiarity in his personal appearance. The name was assumed by Augustus as the adopted son of the dictator C. Julius Caesar, and was by

Augustus handed down to his adopted son Tiberius. It continued to be used by Caligula, Claudius, and Nero, as members either by adoption or female descent of Caesar's family; but though the family became extinct with Nero, succeeding emperors still retained the name as part of their titles, and it was the practice to prefix it to their own name, as, for instance, *Imperator Caesar Domitianus Augustus.* When Hadrian adopted Aelius Verus, he allowed the latter to take the title of Caesar; and from this time, though the title of *Augustus* continued to be confined to the reigning prince, that of *Caesar* was also granted to the second person in the state, and the heir presumptive to the throne.—(1) L. Julius Caesar, consul, B.C. 90, fought against the Socii, and in the course of the same year proposed the *Lex Julia de Civitate,* which granted the citizenship to the Latins and the Socii who had remained faithful to Rome. Caesar was censor in 89; he belonged to the aristocratical party, and was put to death by Marius in 87.—(2) C. Julius Caesar Strabo Vopiscus, brother of No. 1, was curule aedile 90, was a candidate for the consulship in 88, and was slain along with his brother by Marius in 87. He was one of the chief orators and poets of his age, and is one of the speakers in Cicero's dialogue *De Oratore.*—(3) L. Julius Caesar, son of No. 2, and uncle by his sister Julia of M. Antony the triumvir. He was consul 64, and belonged, like his father, to the aristocratical party. He appears to have deserted this party afterwards; we find him in Gaul in 52 as one of the legates of C. Caesar, and he continued in Italy during the civil war. After Caesar's death (44) he sided with the senate in opposition to his uncle Antony, and was in consequence proscribed by the latter in 43, but obtained his pardon through the influence of his sister Julia.—(4) L. Julius Caesar, son of No. 3, usually distinguished from his father by the addition to his name of *filius* or *adolescens.* He joined Pompey on the breaking out of the civil war in 49, and was sent by Pompey to Caesar with proposals of peace. —(5) C. Julius Caesar, the dictator, was born on the 12th of July, 100, in the consulship of C. Marius (VI.) and L. Valerius Flaccus, and was consequently 6 years younger than Pompey and Cicero. Caesar was closely connected with the popular party by the marriage of his aunt Julia with the great Marius; and in 83, though only 17 years of age, he married Cornelia, the daughter of L. Cinna, the chief leader of the Marian party. Sulla commanded him to put away his wife, but he refused to obey him, and was consequently proscribed. He concealed himself for some

time in the country of the Sabines, till his friends obtained his pardon from Sulla, who is said to have observed, when they pleaded his youth, "that that boy would some day or another be the ruin of the aristocracy, for that there were many Mariuses in him." Seeing that he was not safe at Rome, he went to Asia, where he served his first campaign under M. Minucius Thermus, and, at the capture of Mytilene (80), was rewarded with a civic crown for saving the life of a fellow-soldier. On the death of Sulla, in 78, he returned to Rome, and in the following year gained great renown as an orator, though he was only 22 years of age, by his prosecution of Cn. Dolabella on account of extortion in his province of Macedonia. To perfect himself in oratory, he resolved to study in Rhodes under Apollonius Molo, but on his voyage thither he was captured by pirates, and only obtained his liberty by a ransom of 50 talents. At Miletus he manned some vessels, overpowered the pirates, and conducted them as prisoners to Pergamus, where he crucified them—a punishment with which he had frequently threatened them in sport when he was their prisoner. On his return to Rome he devoted all his energies to acquire the favour of the people. His liberality was unbounded; and as his private fortune was not large, he soon contracted enormous debts. But he gained his object, and became the favourite of the people, and was raised by them in succession to the high offices of the state. He was quaestor in 68, aedile in 65, when he spent enormous sums upon the public games and buildings, and was elected Pontifex Maximus in 63. In the debate in the senate on the punishment of the Catilinarian conspirators, he opposed their execution in a very able speech, which made such an impression that their lives would have been spared but for the speech of Cato in reply. In 62 he was praetor, and in the following year he went as propraetor into Further Spain, where he gained great victories over the Lusitanians. On his return to Rome he was elected consul along with Bibulus, a warm supporter of the aristocracy. After his election, but before he entered upon the consulship, he formed that coalition with Pompey and M. Crassus, usually known by the name of the first triumvirate. Pompey had become estranged from the aristocracy, since the senate had opposed the ratification of his acts in Asia, and of an assignment of lands which he had promised to his veterans. Crassus, in consequence of his immense wealth, was one of the most powerful men at Rome, but was a personal enemy of Pompey. They were reconciled by means of Caesar, and the 3 entered into an agreement to support one another, and to divide the power in the state between them. In 59 Caesar was consul, and being supported by Pompey and Crassus, he was able to carry all his measures. Bibulus, from whom the senate had expected so much, could offer no effectual opposition, and, after making a vain attempt to resist Caesar, shut himself up in his own house, and did not appear again in public till the expiration of his consulship. Caesar brought forward such measures as secured for him the affections of the poorest citizens, of the Equites, and of the powerful Pompey ; having done this, he was easily able to obtain for himself the provinces which he wished. By a vote of the people, proposed by the tribune Vatinius, the provinces of Cisalpine Gaul and Illyricum were granted to Caesar, with 3 legions, for 5 years ; and the senate added to his government the province of Transalpine Gaul, with another legion, for 5 years also, as they saw that a bill would be proposed to the people for that purpose, if they did not grant the province themselves. Caesar foresaw that the struggle between the different parties at Rome must eventually be terminated by the sword, and he had therefore resolved to obtain an army, which he might attach to himself by victories and rewards. In the course of the same year he united himself more closely to Pompey by giving him his daughter Julia in marriage. During the next 9 years Caesar was occupied with the subjugation of Gaul. He conquered the whole of Transalpine Gaul, which had hitherto been independent of the Romans, with the exception of the S.E. part called Provincia ; he twice crossed the Rhine, and twice landed in Britain, which had been previously unknown to the Romans. His first invasion of Britain was made late in the summer of 55, but more with the view of obtaining some knowledge of the island from personal observation, than with the intention of permanent conquest at present. He sailed from the port Itius (probably *Witsand*, between Calais and Boulogne), and effected a landing somewhere near the south Foreland, after a severe struggle with the natives. The late period of the year compelled him to return to Gaul after remaining only a short time in the island. In this year, according to his arrangement with Pompey and Crassus, who were now consuls, his government of the Gauls and Illyricum was prolonged for five years, namely, from the 1st of January, 53, to the end of December, 49. During the following year (54) he invaded Britain a second time. He landed in Britain at the same place as in the former year, defeated the Britons in a series of engagements, and crossed the Tamesis (*Thames*). The Britons submitted, and promised to pay an annual tribute ; but their subjection was only nominal. Caesar's success in Gaul excited Pompey's jealousy ; and the death of Julia in childbirth, in 54, broke one of the few links which kept them together. Pompey was thus led to join again the aristocratical party, by whose assistance he hoped to retain his position as the chief man in the Roman state. The great object of this party was to deprive Caesar of his command, and to compel him to come to Rome as a private man to sue for the consulship. Caesar offered to resign his command if Pompey would do the same ; but the senate would not listen to any compromise. Accordingly, on the 1st of January, 49, the senate passed a resolution that Caesar should disband his army by a certain day, and that if he did not do so, he should be regarded as an enemy of the state. Two of the tribunes, M. Antonius and Q. Cassius, put their veto upon this resolution, but their opposition was set at nought, and they fled for refuge to Caesar's camp. Under the plea of protecting the tribunes, Caesar crossed the Rubicon, which separated his province from Italy, and marched towards Rome. Pompey, who had been entrusted by the senate with the conduct of the war, soon discovered how greatly he had overrated his own popularity and influence. His own troops deserted to his rival in crowds ; town after town in Italy opened its gates to Caesar, whose march was like a triumphal progress. Meantime, Pompey, with the magistrates and senators, had fled from Rome to the S. of Italy, and on the 17th of March embarked for Greece. Caesar pursued Pompey to Brundusium, but he was unable to follow him to Greece for want of ships. Shortly afterwards he set out for Spain, where Pompey's legates, Afranius, Petreius, and Varro, commanded powerful armies. After defeating Afranius and Petreius, and receiving the submission of Varro, Caesar returned to Rome, where he had in the meantime been appointed dictator by the praetor M. Lepidus. He resigned the dictatorship at the end of 11 days, after holding the consular comitia, in which he himself and P. Servilius Vatia Isauricus were elected consuls for the next year.—At the beginning of January, 48, Caesar crossed over to Greece, where Pompey had collected a formidable army. At first the campaign was in Pompey's favour ; Caesar was repulsed before Dyrrhachium with considerable loss, and was obliged to retreat towards Thessaly. In this country on the plains of Pharsalus, or Pharsalia, a decisive battle was fought between the two armies on Aug. 9th, 48, in which Pompey was completely defeated. Pompey fled to Egypt, pursued by Caesar, but he was murdered before Caesar arrived in the country. [POMPEIUS.] On his arrival in Egypt, Caesar became involved in a war, usually called the Alexandrine war. It arose from the determination of Caesar that Cleopatra, whose fascinations had won his heart, should reign in common with her brother Ptolemy ; but this decision was opposed by the guardians of the young king, and the war which thus broke out, was not brought to a close till the latter end of March, 47. It was soon after this, that Cleopatra had a son by Caesar. [CAESARION.] Caesar returned to Rome through Syria and Asia Minor, and on his march through Pontus, attacked Pharnaces, the son of Mithridates the Great, who had assisted Pompey. He defeated Pharnaces near Zela with such ease, that he informed the senate of his victory by the words, *Veni, vidi, vici.* He reached Rome in September (47), and before the end of the month set sail for Africa, where Scipio and Cato had collected a large army. The war was terminated by the defeat of the Pompeian army at the battle of Thapsus, on the 6th of April, 46. Cato, unable to defend Utica, put an end to his own life.— Caesar returned to Rome in the latter end of July. He was now the undisputed master of the Roman world, but he used his victory with the greatest moderation. Unlike other conquerors in civil wars, he freely forgave all who had borne arms against him, and declared that he would make no difference between Pompeians and Caesarians. His clemency was one of the brightest features of his character. One of the most important of his measures this year (46) was the reformation of the calendar. As the Roman year was now 3 months in advance of the real time, Caesar added 90 days to this year, and thus made the whole year consist of 445 days; and he guarded against a repetition of similar errors for the future by adapting the year to the sun's course.—Meantime the two sons of Pompey, Sextus and Cneius, had collected a new army in Spain. Caesar set out for Spain towards the end of the year, and brought the war to a close by the battle of Munda, on the 17th of March, 45, in which the enemy were only defeated after a most obstinate resistance. Cn. Pompey was killed shortly afterwards, but Sextus made good his escape. Caesar reached Rome in September, and entered the city in triumph. Possessing royal power, he now wished to obtain the title of king, and Antony accordingly offered him the diadem in public on the festival of the Lupercalia (the 15th of February) ; but,

seeing that the proposition was not favourably received by the people, he declined it for the present.—But Caesar's power was not witnessed without envy. The Roman aristocracy resolved to remove him by assassination. The conspiracy against Caesar's life had been set afoot by Cassius, a personal enemy of Caesar's, and there were more than 60 persons privy to it. Many of these persons had been raised by Caesar to wealth and honour ; and some of them, such as M. Brutus, lived with him on terms of the most intimate friendship. It has been the practice of rhetoricians to speak of the murder of Caesar as a glorious deed, and to represent Brutus and Cassius as patriots ; but the mask ought to be stripped off these false patriots ; they cared not for the republic, but only for themselves ; and their object in murdering Caesar was to gain power for themselves and their party. Caesar had many warnings of his approaching fate, but he disregarded them all, and fell by the daggers of his assassins on the Ides or 15th of March, 44. At an appointed signal the conspirators surrounded him ; Casca dealt the first blow, and the others quickly drew their swords and attacked him ; Caesar at first defended himself, but when he saw that Brutus, his friend and favourite, had also drawn his sword, he exclaimed, *Tu quoque, Brute !* pulled his toga over his face, and sunk pierced with wounds at the foot of Pompey's statue.— Julius Caesar was one of the greatest men of antiquity. He was gifted by nature with the most various talents, and was distinguished by extraordinary attainments in the most diversified pursuits. During the whole of his busy life he found time for the prosecution of literature, and was the author of many works, the majority of which has been lost. The purity of his Latin and the clearness of his style were celebrated by the ancients themselves, and are conspicuous in his *Commentarii*, which are his only works that have come down to us. They relate the history of the first 7 years of the Gallic war in 7 books, and the history of the Civil war, down to the commencement of the Alexandrine, in 3 books. Neither of these works completed the history of the Gallic and Civil wars. The history of the former was completed in an 8th book, which is usually ascribed to Hirtius, and the history of the Alexandrine, African, and Spanish wars was written in three separate books, which are also ascribed to Hirtius, but their authorship is uncertain.

C. CAESAR, and L. CAESAR, the sons of M. Vipsanius Agrippa and Julia, and the grandsons of Augustus. L. Caesar died at Massilia on his way to Spain, A.D. 2, and C.

Caesar in Lycia, A.D. 4, of a wound which he had received in Armenia.

CAESARAUGUSTA (-ae : *Zaragoza or Saragossa*), more anciently SALDUBA, a town of the Edetani on the Iberus, in Hispania Tarraconensis, colonized by Augustus B.C. 27.

CAESĀRĔA (-ae), a name given to several cities of the Roman empire in honour of one or other of the Caesars.—(1) C. AD ARGAEUM, formerly MAZACA, also EUSEBIA (*Kesarieh*, Ru.), one of the oldest cities of Asia Minor, stood upon Mount Argaeus, about the centre of Cappadocia. When that country was made a Roman province by Tiberius (A.D. 18), it received the name of Caesarea. It was ultimately destroyed by an earthquake.—(2) C. PHILIPPI or PANEAS (*Banias*), a city of Palestine, at the S. foot of M. Hermon, on the Jordan, just below its source, built by Philip the tetrarch, B.C. 3 ; King Agrippa called it Neronias, but it soon lost this name.—(3) C. PALAESTINAE, formerly STRATONIS TURRIS, an important city of Palestine, on the sea-coast, just above the boundary line between Samaria and Galilee. It was surrounded with a wall, and decorated with splendid buildings by Herod the Great (B.C. 13), who called it Caesarea, in honour of Augustus. He also made a splendid harbour for the city. Under the Romans it was the capital of Palestine and the residence of the procurator.—(4) C. MAURETANIAE, formerly IOL (*Zershell*, Ru.), a Phoenician city on the N. coast of Africa, with a harbour, the residence of King Juba, who named it Caesarea, in honour of Augustus. There are several other cities, which are better known by other names.

CAESĂRION (-ōnis), son of C. Julius Caesar and of Cleopatra, originally called Ptolemaeus as an Egyptian prince, was born B.C. 47. After the death of his mother in 30 he was executed by order of Augustus.

CAESĂRŎDŬNUM (-i : *Tours*), chief town of the Turōnes or Turŏni, subsequently called TURONI, on the Liger (*Loire*) in Gallia Lugdunensis.

CAESĬA (-ae), a forest in Germany between the Lippe and the Yssel.

CĂICUS (-i), a river of Mysia, rising in M. Temnus and flowing past Pergamus into the Cumaean Gulf.

CĂIĒTA (-ae : *Gaeta*), a town in Latium on the borders of Campania, situated on a promontory of the same name and on a bay of the sea called after it SINUS CAIETANUS. It possessed an excellent harbour, and was said to have derived its name from *Caieta*, the nurse of Aeneas.

CĂIUS, the jurist. [GAIUS.]

CĂIUS CAESAR. [CALIGULA.]

CĂLĂBER. [QUINTUS SMYRNAEUS.]

CĂLĂBRĬA (-ae), the peninsula in the S.E. of Italy, extending from Tarentum to the Prom. Iapygium, formed part of APULIA.

CĂLACTĒ (-es), originally the name of part of the coast, and afterwards a town on the N. coast of Sicily, founded by Ducetius, a chief of the Sicels, about B.C. 447.

CĂLĂGURRIS (-is : *Calahorra*), a town of the Vascones in Hispania Tarraconensis near the Iberus. It was the birth-place of Quintilian.

CĂLĂIS, brother of Zetes. [ZETES.]

CĂLĂNUS (-i), an Indian gymnosophist, who burnt himself alive in the presence of the Macedonians, 3 months before the death of Alexander (B.C. 323), to whom he had predicted his approaching end.

CĂLĀTĬA (-ae : *Cajazzo*), a town in Samnium on the Appia Via between Capua and Beneventum.

CĂLĀTĪNUS, A. ĀTĬLIUS, consul B. c. 258, and dictator 249, when he carried on the war in Sicily. He was the first dictator that commanded an army out of Italy.

CĂLAURĔA or -ĬA (-ae : *Poro*), a small island in the Saronic gulf off the coast of Argolis and opposite Troezen, possessed a celebrated temple of Poseidon (Neptune), which was regarded as an inviolable asylum. Hither Demosthenes fled to escape Antipater, and here he took poison, B.C. 322.

CALCHĀS (-antis), son of Thestor, was the wisest soothsayer among the Greeks at Troy, and advised them in their various difficulties. An oracle had declared that he should die if he met with a soothsayer superior to himself ; and this came to pass at Claros, near Colophon, for here he met the soothsayer MOPSUS, who predicted things which Calchas could not. Thereupon Calchas died of grief. After his death he had an oracle in Daunia.

CALĒ (-es : *Oporto*), a port-town of the Callaeci in Hispania Tarraconensis at the mouth of the Durius. From *Porto Cale* the name of the country *Portugal* is supposed to have come.

CĂLĒDŎNIA. [BRITANNIA.]

CĂLĒNUS, Q. FŪFĬUS, a tribune of the plebs, B.C. 61, when he succeeded in saving P. Clodius from condemnation for his violation of the mysteries of the Bona Dea. In 59 he was praetor, and from this time appears as an active partizan of Caesar, in whose service he remained until Caesar's death (44). After this event Calenus joined M. Antony, and subsequently had the command of Antony's legions in the N. of Italy.

CĂLES (-is, usually Pl. Căles, -ium : *Calvi*), chief town of the Caleni, an Ausonian people in Campania, on the Via Latina, said to have been founded by Calais, son of Boreas, and therefore called *Threïcia* by the poets. It was celebrated for its excellent wine.

CALĒTES (-um) or CALĒTI (-orum), a people in Belgic Gaul near the mouth of the Seine.

CĂLĬGŬLA (-ae), Roman emperor, A.D. 37—41, son of Germanicus and Agrippina, was born A.D. 12, and was brought up among the legions in Germany. His real name was *Caius Caesar*, and he was always called *Caius* by his contemporaries; *Caligula* was a surname given him by the soldiers from his wearing in his boyhood small *caligae*, or soldiers' boots. He gained the favour of Tiberius, who raised him to offices of honour, and held out to him hopes of the succession. On the death of Tiberius (37), which was either caused or accelerated by Caligula, the latter succeeded to the throne. He was saluted by the people with the greatest enthusiasm as the son of Germanicus. His first acts gave promise of a just and beneficent reign. But at the end of 8 months his conduct became suddenly changed. After a serious illness, which probably weakened his mental powers, he appears as a sanguinary and licentious madman. In his madness he built a temple to himself as Jupiter Latiaris, and appointed priests to attend to his worship. His extravagance was monstrous. One instance will show at once his wastefulness and cruelty. He constructed a bridge of boats between Baiae and Puteoli, a distance of about 3 miles, and after covering it with earth he built houses upon it. When it was finished, he gave a splendid banquet in the middle of the bridge, and concluded the entertainment by throwing numbers of the guests into the sea. To replenish the treasury he exhausted Italy and Rome by his extortions, and then marched into Gaul in 40, which he plundered in all directions. With his troops he advanced to the ocean, as if intending to cross over into Britain; he drew them up in battle array, and then gave them the signal—to collect shells, which he called the spoils of conquered Ocean. The Roman world at length grew tired of such a mad tyrant. Four months after his return to the city, on the 24th of January, 41, he was murdered by Cassius Chaerea, tribune of a praetorian cohort, Cornelius Sabinus, and others. His wife Caesonia and his daughter were likewise put to death.

CALLAÏCI, CALLAECI. [GALLAECI.]

CALLATIS (-is), a town of Moesia, on the Black Sea, originally a colony of Miletus, and afterwards of Heraclea.

CALLĬAS (-ae) and HIPPONĬCUS (-i), a noble Athenian family, celebrated for their wealth. They enjoyed the hereditary dignity of torch-bearer at the Eleusinian mysteries, and claimed descent from Triptolemus. The first member of this family of any note was Callias, who fought at the battle of Marathon, 490. He was afterwards ambassador from Athens to Artaxerxes, and according to some accounts negotiated a peace with Persia, 449, on terms most humiliating to the latter. On his return to Athens, he was accused of having taken bribes, and was condemned to a fine of 50 talents. His son Hipponicus was killed at the battle of Delium in 424. It was his divorced wife, and not his widow, whom Pericles married. His daughter Hipparete was married to Alcibiades. Callias, son of this Hipponicus by the lady who married Pericles, dissipated all his ancestral wealth on sophists, flatterers, and women. The scene of Xenophon's *Banquet*, and also that of Plato's *Protagoras*, is laid at his house.

CALLĬAS, a wealthy Athenian, who, on condition of marrying Cimon's sister, Elpinice, liberated Cimon from prison by paying for him the fine of 50 talents which had been imposed on Miltiades.

CALLIDRŎMUS or -UM (-i), part of the range of Mt. Oeta, near Thermopylae.

CALLIFAE, a town in Samnium of uncertain site.

CALLĬMĂCHUS (-i), a celebrated Alexandrine grammarian and poet, was a native of Cyrene in Africa, lived at Alexandria in the reigns of Ptolemy Philadelphus and Euergetes, and was chief librarian of the famous library of Alexandria, from about B.C. 260 until his death about 240. Among his pupils were Eratosthenes, Aristophanes of Byzantium, and Apollonius Rhodius, with the latter of whom he subsequently quarrelled. He wrote numerous works on an infinite variety of subjects, but of these we possess only some of his poems, which are characterised rather by labour and learning than by real poetical genius.

CALLĪNUS (-i), of Ephesus, the earliest Greek elegiac poet, probably flourished about B.C. 700.

CALLĬOPE. [MUSAE.]

CALLĬPŎLIS (-is). (1) A town on the E. coast of Sicily not far from Aetna.—(2) (*Gallipoli*), a town in the Thracian Chersonese opposite Lampsacus.—(3) A town in Aetolia. [CALLIUM.]

CALLIRRHŎĒ (-es). (1) Daughter of Achelous and wife of Alcmaeon, induced her husband to procure her the peplus and necklace of Harmonia, by which she caused his death. [ALCMAEON.]—(2) Daughter of Scamander, wife of Tros, and mother of Ilus and Ganymedes.

CALLIRRHOË (-es), afterwards called ENNEACRUNUS or the "Nine Springs," because its water was distributed by 9 pipes, was the most celebrated well in Athens, situated in the S.E. part of the city, and still retains its ancient name *Callirrhoe.*

CALLISTHENES (-is), of Olynthus, a relation and a pupil of Aristotle, accompanied Alexander the Great to Asia. He rendered himself so obnoxious to Alexander by the boldness and independence with which he expressed his opinions on several occasions, that he was accused of being privy to the plot of Hermolaus to assassinate Alexander; and after being kept in chains for 7 months, was either put to death or died of disease. He wrote several works, all of which have perished.

CALLISTO (-ūs: acc. -ō), an Arcadian nymph, hence called *Nonacrina virgo,* from Nonacris, a mountain in Arcadia, was a companion of Artemis (Diana) in the chase. She was beloved by Zeus (Jupiter), who metamorphosed her into a she-bear, that Hera (Juno) might not become acquainted with the amour. But Hera learnt the truth, and caused Artemis to slay Callisto during the chase. Zeus placed Callisto among the stars under the name of *Arctos,* or the Bear. ARCAS was her son by Zeus. [ARCTOS.]

CALLISTRATIA (-ae), a town in Paphlagonia, on the coast of the Euxine.

CALLIUM (-i) called CALLIPOLIS (-is), by Livy, a town in Aetolia in the valley of the Spercheus.

CALOR (-ōris), a river in Samnium flowing past Beneventum and falling into the Vulturnus.

CALPE (-es: *Gibralter.*) (1) A mountain in the S. of Spain on the Straits between the Atlantic and Mediterranean. This and M. Abyla opposite to it on the African coast, were called the *Columns of Hercules.* [ABYLA.] —(2) A river, promontory, and town on the coast of Bithynia.

CALPURNIA (-ae), daughter of L. Calpurnius Piso, consul B.C. 58, and last wife of the dictator Caesar, to whom she was married in 59. She survived her husband.

CALPURNIA GENS, plebeian, pretended to be descended from Calpus, a son of Numa. It was divided into the families of BIBULUS and PISO.

CALVINUS, CN. DOMITIUS (-i), tribune of the plebs, B.C. 59, when he supported Bibulus against Caesar, praetor 56, and consul 53, through the influence of Pompey. He took an active part in the civil war as one of Caesar's generals.

CALYCADNUS (-i), a considerable river of Cilicia Tracheia, navigable as far as Seleucia.

CALYDNAE (-ārum). (1) Two small islands off the coast of Troas.—(2) A group of islands off the coast of Caria, belonging to the Sporades. The largest of them was called Calydna, and afterwards Calymna.

CALYDON (-ōnis), an ancient town of Aetolia W. of the Evenus in the land of the Curetes, said to have been founded by Aetolus or his son Calydon. The town was celebrated in the heroic ages, but is rarely mentioned in historical times. In the mountains in the neighbourhood took place the celebrated hunt of the Calydonian boar. The inhabitants were removed by Augustus to NICOPOLIS. In the Roman poets we find *Calydonis,* a woman of Aetolia, i.e. Deïanira, daughter of Oeneus, king of Calydon: *Calydonius heros,* i.e. Meleager: *Calydonius amnis,* i.e., the Achelous separating Acarnania and Aetolia, because Calydon was the chief town of Aetolia: *Calydonia regna,* i.e. Apulia, because Diomedes, grandson of Oeneus, king of Calydon, afterwards obtained Apulia as his kingdom.

CALYPSO (-ūs: acc. -ō), a nymph inhabiting the island of Ogygia, on which Ulysses was shipwrecked. Calypso loved the unfortunate hero, and promised him immortality if he would remain with her. Ulysses refused, and after she had detained him 7 years, the gods compelled her to allow him to continue his journey homewards.

Calypso. (From a painted Vase.)

CAMALODUNUM (*Colchester*), the capital of the Trinobantes in Britain, and the first Roman colony in the island, founded by the emperor Claudius, A.D. 43.

CĂMĂRĬNA (-ae), a town on the S. coast of Sicily, at the mouth of the Hipparis, founded by Syracuse, B.C. 599. It was several times destroyed by Syracuse ; and in the first Punic war it was taken by the Romans, and most of the inhabitants sold as slaves.

CAMBŪNI (-ōrum) MONTES, the mountains which separate Macedonia and Thessaly.

CAMBȲSĒS (-is). (1) Father of CȲRUS the Great.—(2) Second king of Persia, succeeded his father Cyrus, and reigned B.C. 529—522. In 525 he conquered Egypt ; but was unsuccessful in expeditions against the Ammonians and against the Aethiopians. On his return to Memphis he treated the Egyptians with great cruelty ; he insulted their religion, and slew their god Apis with his own hands. He also acted tyrannically towards his own family and the Persians in general. He caused his own brother Smerdis to be murdered ; but a Magian personated the deceased prince, and set up a claim to the throne. [SMERDIS.] Cambyses forthwith set out from Egypt against this pretender, but died in Syria, at a place named Ecbatana, of an accidental wound in the thigh, 522.

CĂMĒNAE (-ārum), prophetic nymphs, belonging to the religion of ancient Italy, although later traditions represent their worship as introduced into Italy from Arcadia, and some accounts identify them with the Muses. The most important of these goddesses was Carmenta or Carmentis, who had a temple at the foot of the Capitoline hill, and altars near the Porta Carmentalis. The traditions which assigned a Greek origin to her worship, state that her original name was Nicostrate, and that she was the mother of Evander, with whom she came to Italy.

CĂMERĬA (-ae), an ancient town of Latium, conquered by Tarquinius Priscus.

CĂMĔRĪNUM or CĂMĂRĪNUM (-i), more anciently CAMERS (-tis : Camerino), a town in Umbria, on the borders of Picenum, and subsequently a Roman colony.

CĂMĔRĪNUS (-i), a Roman poet, contemporary with Ovid, wrote a poem on the capture of Troy by Hercules.

CAMĪCUS (-i), an ancient town of the Sicani on the S. coast of Sicily, and on a river of the same name, occupied the site of the citadel of AGRIGENTUM.

CĂMILLA (-ae), daughter of king Metabus of the Volscian town of Privernum, was one of the swift-footed servants of Diana, accustomed to the chase and to war. She assisted Turnus against Aeneas, and after slaying numbers of the Trojans was at length killed by Aruns.

CĂMILLUS, M. FŪRĬUS (-i), one of the great heroes of the Roman republic. He was censor B.C. 403, in which year Livy erroneously places his first consular tribunate. He was consular tribune six different years, and dictator five times during his life. In his first dictatorship (396) he gained a glorious victory over the Faliscans and Fidenates, took Veii, and entered Rome in triumph. Five years afterwards (391) he was accused of having made an unfair distribution of the booty of Veii, and went voluntarily into exile at Ardea. Next year (390) the Gauls took Rome, and laid siege to Ardea. The Romans in the Capitol recalled Camillus, and appointed him dictator in his absence. Camillus hastily collected an army, attacked the Gauls, and defeated them completely. [BRENNUS.] His fellow-citizens saluted him as the Second Romulus. In 367 he was dictator a fifth time, and though 80 years of age, he completely defeated the Gauls. He died of the pestilence, 365. Camillus was the great general of his age, and the resolute champion of the patrician order.

CAMĪRUS (-i), a Dorian town on the W. coast of the island of Rhodes, and the principal town in the island before the foundation of Rhodes.

CAMPĀNĬA (-ae), a district of Italy, the name of which is probably derived from campus "a plain," separated from Latium by the river Liris, and from Lucania at a later time by the river Silarus, though in the time of Augustus it did not extend further S. than the promontory of Minerva. In still earlier times the Ager Campanus included only the country round Capua. Campania is a volcanic country, to which circumstance it was mainly indebted for its extraordinary fertility, for which it was celebrated in antiquity above all other lands. The fertility of the soil, allowing in parts 3 crops in a year, the beauty of the scenery, and the softness of the climate, the heat of which was tempered by the delicious breezes of the sea, procured for Campania the epithet Felix, a name which it justly deserved. It was the favourite retreat in summer of the Roman nobles, whose villas studded a considerable part of its coast, especially in the neighbourhood of BAIAE. The earliest inhabitants of the country were the Ausones and Osci or Opici. They were subsequently conquered by the Etruscans, who became the masters of almost all the country. In the time of the Romans we find 3 distinct peoples, besides the Greek population of CUMAE : 1. The Campani, properly so called, a mixed race, consisting of Etruscans and the original inhabitants of the country, dwelling along the coast from Sinuessa to Paestum. They were the ruling race. [CAPUA.]—2. SIDICINI, an Ausonian people, in the N.W. of the country on the borders of Samnium.—3. PICENTINI, in the S.E. of the country.

CAMPI RAUDII (-ōrum), a plain in the N. of Italy, near Vercellae, where Marius and Catulus defeated the Cimbri, B.C. 101.

CAMPUS MARTIUS (-i), the "Plain of Mars," frequently called CAMPUS simply, was the N.W. portion of the plain lying in the bend of the Tiber, outside the walls of Rome. The Circus Flaminius in the S. gave its name to a portion of the plain. The Campus Martius is said to have belonged originally to the Tarquins, and to have been consecrated to Mars upon the expulsion of the kings. Here the Roman youths were accustomed to perform their gymnastic and warlike exercises, and here the comitia of the centuries were held. At a later time it was surrounded by porticoes, temples, and other public buildings. It was included within the city walls by Aurelian.

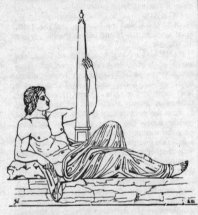

Personification of the Campus Martius. (Visconti, Mus. Pio Clem. vol. 6, tav. 1.)

CANACE (-es), entertained an unnatural love for her brother Macareus, and on this account was compelled by her father to kill herself.

CANDACE (-es), a queen of the Aethiopians of Meroë, invaded Egypt B.C. 22, but was driven back and defeated by Petronius, the Roman governor of Egypt. Her name seems to have been common to all the queens of Aethiopia.

CANDAULES, also called Myrsilus, last Heraclid king of Lydia. He exposed his wife to Gyges, whereupon she compelled Gyges to put him to death. [GYGES.]

CANDAVIA (-ae), CANDAVII (-ōrum) MONTES, the mountains separating Illyricum from Macedonia, across which the Via Egnatia ran.

CANIDIA (-ae), whose real name was Gratidia, was a Neapolitan courtezan, beloved by Horace; but when she deserted him, he revenged himself by holding her up to contempt as an old sorceress.

CANIS (-is), the constellation of the Great Dog. The most important star in this constellation was specially named Canis or Canicula, and also Sirius. The Dies Caniculares were as proverbial for the heat of the weather among the Romans as are the dog days among ourselves. The constellation of the Little Dog was called Procyon, literally translated Ante canem, Antecanis, because in Greece this constellation rises heliacally before the Great Dog. When Boötes was regarded as Icarius [ARCTOS], Procyon became Maera, the dog of Icarius.

CANNAE (-arum), a village in Apulia, situated in an extensive plain, memorable for the defeat of the Romans by Hannibal, B.C. 216.

CANOBUS or CANOPUS (-i), an important city on the coast of Lower Egypt, 2 geog. miles E. of Alexandria. It was near the W.-most mouth of the Nile, which was hence called the Canopic Mouth. It was celebrated for a great temple of Serapis, for its commerce and its luxury.

CANTABRI (-orum), a fierce and warlike people in the N. of Spain, bounded on the E. by the Astures, and on the W. by the Autrigones. They were subdued by Augustus after a struggle of several years (B.C. 25—19).

CANTIUM (-i) a district of Britain, nearly the same as the modern Kent, but included LONDINIUM.

CANUSIUM (-i: Canosa), an important town in Apulia, on the Aufidus, founded, according to tradition, by Diomedes. It was at all events a Greek colony, and both Greek and Oscan were spoken there in the time of Horace. It was celebrated for its mules and its woollen manufactures, but it had a deficient supply of water.

CAPANEUS (-ĕŏs or -ĕi), son of Hipponous, and one of the 7 heroes who marched against Thebes. He was struck by Zeus (Jupiter) with lightning, as he was scaling the walls of Thebes, because he had dared to defy the god. While his body was burning, his wife Evadne leaped into the flames and destroyed herself.

CĂPELLA, the star. [CAPRA.]

CĂPĒNA (-ae), an ancient Etruscan town founded by Veii, and subsequently became a Roman municipium. In its territory was the celebrated grove and temple of Feronia on the small river Capenas. [FERONIA.]

CĂPĒTUS SILVĬUS. [SILVIUS.]

CĂPHĂREUS (*Capo d' Oro*), a rocky and dangerous promontory on the S. E. of Euboea, where the Greek fleet is said to have been wrecked on its return from Troy.

CĂPĬTO, C. ATĒĬUS, an eminent Roman jurist, who gained the favour of both Augustus and Tiberius by flattery and obsequiousness. Capito and his contemporary Labeo were reckoned the highest legal authorities of their day, and were the founders of 2 legal schools, to which most of the great jurists belonged.

CĂPĬTO, C. FONTĒĬUS, a friend of M. Antony, accompanied Maecenas to Brundisium, B.C. 37, when the latter was sent to effect a reconciliation between Octavianus and Antony,

CĂPĬTŌLĪNUS, MANLIUS. [MANLIUS.]

CĂPĬTŌLĪNUS MONS. [CAPITOLIUM : ROMA.]

CAPITŌLĬUM (-i), the temple of Jupiter Optimus Maximus at Rome, was situated on the S. summit of the Mons Capitolinus, so called on account of the temple. The site of the temple is now covered in part by the *Palazzo Caffarelli*, while the N. summit, which was formerly the arx, is occupied by the church of *Ara Celi*. The temple is said to have been called the Capitolium, because a human head (*caput*) was discovered in digging the foundations. The building of it was commenced by Tarquinius Priscus, and it was finished by Tarquinius Superbus, but was not dedicated till the 3rd year of the republic, B.C. 507, by the consul M. Horatius. It was burnt down in the civil wars, 83, and twice afterwards in the time of the emperors. After its 3rd destruction in the reign of Titus it was again rebuilt by Domitian with greater splendour than before. The Capitol contained 3 cells under the same roof : the middle cell was the temple of Jupiter, hence described as "*media* qui sedet aede Deus," and on either side were the cells of his attendant deities, Juno and Minerva. The Capitol was one of the most imposing buildings at Rome, and was adorned as befitted the majesty of the king of the gods. It was in the form of a square, namely, 200 feet on each side, and was approached by a flight of 100 steps. The gates were of bronze, and the ceilings and tiles gilt. The gilding alone of the building cost Domitian 12,000 talents. In the Capitol

were kept the Sibylline books. Here the consuls upon entering on their office offered sacrifices and took their vows ; and hither the victorious general, who entered the city in triumph, was carried in his triumphal car to return thanks to the Father of the gods. The whole hill was sometimes called *Arx*, and sometimes *Capitolium*, but most completely and correctly *Arx Capitoliumque.*

CAPPĂDŎCĬA (-ae), a district of Asia Minor, to which different boundaries were assigned at different times. Under the Persian empire it included the whole country inhabited by a people of Syrian origin, who were called (from their complexion) White Syrians (*Leucosyri*), and also Cappadoces. Their country embraced the whole N.E. part of Asia Minor, E. of the river Halys, and N. of Mt. Taurus, which was afterwards divided into Pontus and Cappadocia Proper. [PONTUS.] When this division took place is uncertain ; but we find that under the Persian empire the whole country was governed by a line of hereditary satraps, who eventually became independent kings. At a later period Cappadocia Proper was governed by a line of independent monarchs. In A.D. 17, Archelaüs, the last king, died at Rome, and Tiberius made Cappadocia a Roman province. Cappadocia was a rough and mountainous region. Its fine pastures supported abundance of good horses and mules.

CĂPRA, CĂPRA or CĂPELLA (-ae), the brightest star in the constellation of the *Auriga*, or *Charioteer*, is said to have been originally the nymph or goat who nursed the infant Zeus (Jupiter) in Crete. [AMALTHEA.]

CAPRĂRĬA (-ae), a small island off the coast of Etruria, inhabited only by wild goats, whence its name.

CĂPRĒAE (-ārum : *Capri*), a small island, 9 miles in circumference, off Campania, at the S. entrance of the gulf of Puteoli. The scenery is beautiful, and the climate soft and genial. Here Tiberius lived the last 10 years of his reign, indulging in secret debauchery, and accessible only to his creatures.

CĂPRĬCORNUS (-i), *the Goat*, a sign of the Zodiac, between the Archer and the Water-man, is said to have fought with Jupiter against the Titans.

CAPSA (-ae), a strong and ancient city in the S.W. of Byzacena, in N. Africa, in a fertile oasis, surrounded by a sandy desert, abounding in serpents. In the war with Jugurtha it was destroyed by Marius ; but it was afterwards rebuilt, and erected into a colony.

CAPŬA (-ae : *Capua*), the chief city of Campania, either founded or colonised by the

Etruscans. It became at an early period the most prosperous, wealthy, and luxurious city in the S. of Italy. Its warlike neighbours, the Samnites, made frequent attempts upon it, sometimes with success. In order to be a match for them, Capua, in B.C. 343, placed itself under the protection of Rome. It revolted to Hannibal after the battle of Cannae, 216, but was taken by the Romans in 211, was fearfully punished, and never recovered its former prosperity. It was subsequently made a Roman colony.

CĂPỲS (-ў̆os and -ў̆s).—(1) Son of Assaracus, and father of Anchises.—(2) A companion of Aeneas, from whom Capua was said to have derived its name.

CĂPỲS SILVĬUS. [SILVIUS.]

CĂRĂCALLA (-ae), emperor of Rome, A.D. 211—217, was son of Septimius Severus, and was born at Lyons, A.D. 188. His proper name was *M. Aurelius Antoninus. Caracalla* was a nickname derived from a long tunic worn by the Gauls, which he adopted as his favourite dress after he became emperor. He accompanied his father to Britain in 208; and on the death of Severus, at York, 211, Caracalla and his brother Geta succeeded to the throne, according to their father's arrangements. A succession of cruelties now marked his career. He assassinated his brother Geta, and, with him, many of the most distinguished men in the state; thus securing himself in the sole government. The celebrated jurist, Papinian, was one of his victims. He added extravagance to cruelty; and after wasting the resources of Italy, he visited the eastern and western provinces of the empire, for the purposes of extortion and plunder, and sometimes of wanton cruelty. He was about to set out on further expeditions across the Tigris, but was murdered at Edessa by Macrinus, the praetorian prefect. Caracalla gave to all free inhabitants of the empire the name and privileges of Roman citizens.

CARACTĂCUS (-i), king of the Silures in Britain, bravely defended his country against the Romans, in the reign of Claudius. He was at length defeated, and fled for protection to Cartismandua, queen of the Brigantes; but she betrayed him to the Romans, who carried him to Rome, A.D. 51. When brought before Claudius, he addressed the emperor in so noble a manner that the latter pardoned him and his friends.

CĂRĂLIS (-is) or CĂRĂLES (-ium : *Cagliari*), the chief town of Sardinia, with an excellent harbour.

CĂRAMBIS (-idis), a promontory, with a city of the same name, on the coast of Paphlagonia.

CĂRĂNUS (-i), a descendant of Hercules, is said to have settled at Edessa, in Macedonia, with an Argive colony, about B.C. 750, and to have become the founder of the dynasty of Macedonian kings.

CARBO (-ōnis), the name of a family of the Papiria gens. (1) C. PAPIRIUS CARBO, a distinguished orator, and a man of great talents, but of no principle. He was one of the 3 commissioners or triumvirs for carrying into effect the agrarian law of Tib. Gracchus. His tribuneship of the plebs, B.C. 131, was characterised by the most vehement opposition to the aristocracy. But after the death of C. Gracchus (121), he suddenly deserted the popular party, and in his consulship (120) undertook the defence of Opimius, who had murdered C. Gracchus. In 119 Carbo was accused by L. Licinius Crassus; and as he foresaw his condemnation, he put an end to his life.—(2) CN. PAPIRIUS CARBO, one of the leaders of the Marian party. He was thrice consul, namely, in 85, 84, and 82. In 82 he carried on war against Sulla, but he was at length obliged to fly to Sicily, where he was put to death by Pompey at Lilybaeum.

CARCĂSO (-ōnis : *Carcassone*), a town of the Tectosages, in Gallia Narbonensis.

CARDĂMỲLĒ (-ēs), a town in Messenia.

CARDĔA (-ae), a Roman divinity, presiding over the hinges of doors, that is, over family life.

CARDĬA (-ae), a town on the Thracian Chersonese, on the gulf of Melas, was the birth-place of Eumenes. It was destroyed by Lysimachus, who built the town of LYSIMACHIA, in its immediate neighbourhood.

CARDŪCHI (-ōrum), a powerful and warlike people, probably the *Kurds* of modern times, dwelt in the mountains which divided Assyria from Armenia (*Mts. of Kurdistan*).

CARĬA (-ae), a district of Asia Minor, in its S.W. corner. It is intersected by low mountain chains, running out far into the sea in long promontories, forming gulfs along the coast and inland valleys that were fertile and well watered. The chief products of the country were corn, wine, oil, and figs. The coast was inhabited chiefly by Greek colonists. The inhabitants of the rest of the country were Carians, a people nearly allied to the Lydians and Mysians. The Greeks considered the people mean and stupid, even for slaves. The country was governed by a race of native princes, who fixed their abode at Halicarnassus. These princes were subject allies of Lydia and Persia, and some of them rose to great distinction in war and peace. [See ARTEMISIA, MAUSOLUS.] Under the Romans, Caria formed a part of the province of ASIA.

CĂRĪNUS, M. AURĒLĬUS (-i), Roman emperor, A.D. 284—285, the elder of the 2 sons of Carus, was associated with his father in the government, A.D. 283. He was slain in a battle against Diocletian by some of his own officers.

CARMĀNĬA (-ae), a province of the ancient Persian empire, bounded on the W. by Persia, on the N. by Parthia, on the E. by Gedrosia, and on the S. by the Indian Ocean.

CARMĒLUS, and -UM (-i), a range of mountains in Palestine, commencing on the N. border of Samaria, and running through the S.W. part of Galilee, till it terminates in the promontory of the same name (Cape Carmel).

CARMENTA, CARMENTIS. [CAMENAE.]

CARNA (-ae), a Roman divinity, whose name is probably connected with Caro, flesh, for she was regarded as the protector of the physical well-being of man. Her festival was celebrated June 1st, and was believed to have been instituted by Brutus in the first year of the republic. Ovid confounds this goddess with CARDEA.

CARNĔĂDES (-is), a celebrated philosopher, born at Cyrene about B.C. 213, was the founder of the Third or New Academy at Athens, and a strenuous opponent of the Stoics. In 155 he was sent to Rome, with Diogenes and Critolaus, by the Athenians, to deprecate the fine of 500 talents which had been imposed on the Athenians for the destruction of Oropus. At Rome he attracted great notice from his eloquent declamations on philosophical subjects. He died in 129, at the age of 85.

CARNI (-ōrum), a Celtic people, dwelling N. of the Veneti, in the Alpes Carnicae. [ALPES.]

CARNUNTUM (-i), an ancient Celtic town in Upper Pannonia, on the Danube, E. of Vindobona (Vienna), and subsequently a Roman municipium or a colony.

CARNŪTES (-um) or -I (-ōrum), a powerful people in the centre of Gaul, between the Liger and Sequana : their capital was GENABUM (Orleans).

CARPĀTES (-um), also called ALPES BASTARNĬCAE (Carpathian Mountains), the mountains separating Dacia from Sarmatia.

CARPĂTHUS (-i : Scarpanto), an island between Crete and Rhodes, in the sea named after it

CARPĒTĀNI (-ōrum), a powerful people in Hispania Tarraconensis, with a fertile territory on the rivers Anas and Tagus. Their capital was TOLETUM.

CARPI or CARPĬANI (-ōrum), a German people between the Carpathian mountains and the Danube.

CARRAE or CARRHAE (-ārum) the Haran or Charran of the Scriptures, a city of Osroëne, in Mesopotamia, where Crassus met his death after his defeat by the Parthians, B.C. 53.

CARSĔŌLI (-ōrum : Carsoli), a town of the Aequi, in Latium, colonised by the Romans.

CARTEIA (-ae : also called Carthaea, Carpia, Carpessus), more anciently TARTESSUS, a celebrated town and harbour in the S. of Spain, at the head of the gulf of which M. Calpe forms one side, founded by the Phoenicians, and colonised B.C. 170 by 4000 Roman soldiers.

CARTHAEA (-ae), a town on the S. side of the island of Ceos.

CARTHĀGO (-ĭnis), MAGNA CARTHĀGO (Ru. near El-Marsa, N.E. of Tunis), one of the most celebrated cities of the ancient world, stood in the recess of a large bay, in the middle of the N.-most part of the N. coast of Africa. The coast of this part of Africa has been much altered by the deposits of the river Bagradas, and the sand which is driven seawards by the N.W. winds. The old Peninsula upon which Carthage stood was about 30 miles in circumference, and the city itself, in the height of its glory, measured about 15 miles round. But owing to the influences just referred to the locality presents a very different appearance at present. Carthage was founded by the Phoenicians of Tyre, according to tradition, about 100 years before the building of Rome, that is about B.C. 853. The mythical account of its foundation is given under DIDO. The part of the city first built was called, in the Phoenician language, Betzura or Bosra, i. e. a castle, which was corrupted by the Greeks into Byrsa i. e. a hide, and hence probably arose the story of the way in which the natives were cheated out of the ground. As the city grew, the Byrsa formed the citadel. Cothon was the inner harbour, and was used for ships of war : the outer harbour, divided from it by a tongue of land 300 feet wide, was the station for the merchant ships. Beyond the fortifications was a large suburb, called Magara or Magalia. The population of Carthage, at the time of the 3rd Punic war is stated at 700,000.—The constitution of Carthage was an oligarchy. The two chief magistrates, called Suffetes, appear to have been elected for life ; the Greek and Roman writers call them kings. The generals and foreign governors were usually quite distinct from the suffetes ; but the 2 offices were sometimes united in the same person. The governing body was a Senate, partly hereditary and partly elective, within which there was a select body of 100 or 104, called Gerusia, whose chief office was to control the magistrates, and especially the generals returning from foreign service, who might be suspected of attempts to establish a tyranny. Important questions, especially those on which the senate and the suffetes disagreed, were referred to a general assembly, of the citizens ; but concerning the mode of proceeding in this assembly and the extent of its powers, we know very little. Their punishments were very severe, and the usual mode of inflicting death was by crucifixion. The chief occupations of the people were commerce and agriculture ; in both of which they reached a pre-eminent position among the nations of the ancient world. The Carthaginians became the rivals of the Romans, with whom they carried on three wars, usually known as the three Punic Wars. The first lasted from B.C. 265—242, and resulted in the loss to Carthage of Sicily and the Lipari islands. The second, which was the decisive contest, began with the siege of Saguntum (218), and terminated (201)with the peace, by which Carthage was stripped of all her power. [HANNIBAL.] The third began and terminated in 146, by the capture and destruction of Carthage. It remained in ruins for 30 years. At the end of that time a colony was established on the old site by the Gracchi, which continued in a feeble condition till the times of Julius and Augustus, under whom a new city was built, with the name of COLONIA CARTHAGO. It became the first city of Africa, and occupied an important place in ecclesiastical as well as in civil history. It was taken by the Vandals in A.D. 439, retaken by Belisarius in A.D. 533, and destroyed by the Arab conquerors in A.D. 698. The Carthaginians are frequently called Poeni by the Latin writers on account of their Phoenician origin.

CARTHAGO (-ĭnis) NŎVA (Carthagena), an important town on the E. coast of Hispania Tarraconensis, founded by the Carthaginians under Hasdrubal, B.C. 243, and subsequently conquered and colonised by the Romans. It is situated on a promontory running out into the sea, and possesses one of the finest harbours in the world.

CĀRUS, M. AURĒLĬUS, Roman emperor A.D. 282—283, succeeded Probus. He was engaged in a successful military expedition in Persia, when he was struck dead by lightning, towards the close of 283. He was succeeded by his sons CARINUS and NUMERIANUS. Carus was a victorious general and able ruler.

CARVENTUM (-i), a town of the Volsci, to which the CARVENTANA ARX mentioned by Livy belonged, a town of the Volsci between Signia and the sources of the Trerus.

CARVILĬUS MAXĬMUS. 1) SP., twice consul, B.C. 293 and 273, both times with L. Papirius Cursor. In their first consulship they gained brilliant victories over the Samnites, and in their second they brought the Samnite war to a close.—(2) SP., son of the preceding, twice consul, 234 and 228, is said to have been the first person at Rome who divorced his wife.

CĀRȲAE (-ārum), a town in Laconia near the borders of Arcadia, originally belonged to the territory of Tegea in Arcadia. Female figures in architecture that support burdens were called Caryatides in token of the abject slavery to which the women of Caryae were reduced by the Greeks, as a punishment for joining the Persians at the invasion of Greece.

CĀRȲANDA (-ōrum), a city of Caria, on a little island, once probably united with the mainland, was the birthplace of the geographer Scylax.

CĀRȲATĬDES. [CARYAE.]

CĀRYSTUS (-i), a town on the S. coast of Euboea, founded by Dryopes, celebrated for its marble quarries.

CASCA, P. SERVĪLĬUS, tribune of the plebs, B.C. 44, and one of Caesar's assassins.

CĀSILĪNUM (-i), a town in Campania on the Vulturnus, and on the same site as the modern Capua, celebrated for its heroic defence against Hannibal, B.C. 216.

CĀSĬNUM (-i : S. Germano), a town in Latium on the river CASINUS. Its citadel occupied the same site as the celebrated convent Monte Cassino.

CĀSĬŌTIS. [CASIUS.]

CĀSĬUS (-i). (1) (Ras Kasaroun), a mountain on the coast of Egypt, E. of Pelusium, with a temple of Jupiter on its summit. Here also was the grave of Pompey.—(2) (Jebel Okrah), a mountain on the coast of Syria, S. of Antioch and the Orontes.

CASMĒNA (-ae), a town in Sicily, founded by Syracuse about B.C. 643.

CASPĔRĬA or CASPĔRŬLA (-ae), a town of the Sabines, on the river Himella.

CASPĬAE PORTAE or PYLAE, the Caspian Gates, the name given to several passes through the mountains round the Caspian. The principal of these were near the ancient Rhagae or Arsacia. Being a noted and central point, distances were reckoned from it.

CASPĬI (-ōrum), the name of certain Scythian tribes around the Caspian Sea.

CASPĬI MONTES (Elburz Mts.) a name applied generally to the whole range of mountains which surround the Caspian Sea, on the S. and S.W., at the distance of from 15 to 30 miles from its shore, and more especially to that part of this range S. of the Caspian, in which was the pass called CASPIAE PYLAE.

CASPĪRI or CASPIRAEI (-ōrum), a people of India, whose exact position is doubtful : they are generally placed in *Cashmeer* and *Nepaul*.

CASPIUM MARE (*the Caspian Sea*), also called HYRCANIUM, ALBANUM, and SCYTHICUM, all names derived from the people who lived on its shores, a great salt-water lake in Asia. Probably at some remote period the Caspian was united both with the sea of Aral and with the Arctic Ocean. Both lakes have their surface considerably below that of the Euxine or Black Sea, the Caspian nearly 350 feet, and the Aral about 200 feet, and both are still sinking by evaporation. The whole of the neighbouring country indicates that this process has been going on for centuries past. Besides a number of smaller streams, two great rivers flow into the Caspian ; the Rha (*Volga*) on the N., and the united Cyrus and Araxes (*Kour*) on the W.; but it loses more by evaporation than it receives from these rivers.

CASSANDER (-dri), son of Antipater. His father, on his death-bed (B.C. 319), appointed Polysperchon regent, and conferred upon Cassander only the secondary dignity of Chiliarch. Being dissatisfied with this arrangement, Cassander strengthened himself in various ways, that he might carry on war with Polysperchon. First he formed an alliance with Ptolemy and Antigonus, and next defeated Olympias and put her to death. Afterwards he joined Seleucus, Ptolemy, and Lysimachus in their war against Antigonus. This war was on the whole unfavourable to Cassander. In 306 Cassander took the title of king, when it was assumed by Antigonus, Lysimachus, and Ptolemy. But it was not until the year 301 that the decisive battle of Ipsus secured Cassander the possession of Macedonia and Greece. Cassander died of dropsy in 297, and was succeeded by his son Philip.

CASSANDRA (-ae), daughter of Priam and Hecuba, and twin-sister of Helenus. In her

Cassandra and Apollo.   (Pitture d'Ercolano, vol. 2, tav. 17.)

youth she was the object of Apollo's regard, and when she grew up her beauty won upon him so much that he conferred upon her the gift of prophecy, upon her promising to comply with his desires ; but when she had become possessed of the prophetic art, she refused to fulfil her promise. Thereupon the god in anger ordained that no one should believe her prophecies. On the capture of Troy she fled into the sanctuary of Athena (Minerva), but was torn away from the statue of the goddess by Ajax, son of Oïleus. On the division of the booty, Cassandra fell to the lot of Agamemnon, who took her with him to Mycenae. Here she was killed by Clytaemnestra.

CASSANDREA. [POTIDAEA.]

CASSIEPEA, CASSIOPEA (-ae), or CAS-SIOPE (-es), wife of Cepheus, in Aethiopia, and mother of Andromeda, whose beauty she extolled above that of the Nereids. [ANDRO-MEDA.] She was afterwards placed among the stars.

CASSIODORUS, MAGNUS AURELIUS (-i), a distinguished statesman, and one of the few men of learning at the downfal of the Western Empire, was born about A.D. 468. He enjoyed the confidence of Theodoric the Great and his successors, and conducted for a long series of years the government of the Ostrogothic kingdom. Several of his works are extant.

CASSIOPEA. [CASSIEPEA.]

CASSITERIDES. [BRITANNIA.]

CASSIUS (-i), the name of one of the most distinguished of the Roman gentes, originally patrician, afterwards plebeian.—(1) SP. CAS-SIUS VISCELLINUS, who was thrice consul, in the years B.C. 502, 493, 486 ; and is distinguished as having carried the first agrarian law at Rome. This law brought upon him the enmity of his fellow-patricians ; they accused him of aiming at regal power, and put him to death. He left 3 sons ; but as all the subsequent Cassii are plebeians, his sons were perhaps expelled from the patrician order, or may have voluntarily passed over to the plebeians, on account of the murder of their father.—(2) C. CASS. LONGINUS, the murderer of Julius Caesar. In B.C. 53, he was quaestor of Crassus, in his campaign against the Parthians, in which, both during his quaestorship and during the two subsequent years he greatly distinguished himself, gaining an important victory over them in 52, and again in 51. In 49 he was tribune of the plebs, joined the aristocratical party in the civil war, fled with Pompey from Rome, and after the battle of Pharsalia surrendered to Caesar. He was not only pardoned by Caesar, but in 44 was made praetor, and the province of Syria was promised him for the next year. But Cassius had never ceased to be Caesar's enemy ; it was he who formed the conspiracy against the dictator's life, and gained over M. Brutus to the plot. After the death of Caesar, on the 15th of March, 44 [CAESAR], Cassius went to Syria, which he claimed as his province, although the senate had given it to Dolabella, and had conferred upon Cassius Cyrene in its stead. He defeated Dolabella, who put an end to his own life ; and after plundering Syria and Asia most unmercifully, he crossed over to Greece with Brutus in 42, in order to oppose Octavia and Antony. At the battle of Philippi, Cassius was defeated by Antony, while Brutus, who commanded the other wing of the army, drove Octavian off the field ; but Cassius, ignorant of the success of Brutus, commanded his freedman to put an end to his life. Brutus mourned over his companion, calling him the last of the Romans. Cassius was married to Junia Tertia or Tertulla, half-sister of M. Brutus. Cassius was well acquainted with Greek and Roman literature ; he was a follower of the Epicurean philosophy ; his abilities were considerable, but he was vain, proud, and revengeful.—(3) C. CASS. LONGI-NUS, the celebrated jurist, governor of Syria, A.D. 50, in the reign of Claudius. He was banished by Nero in A.D. 66, because he had, among his ancestral images, a statue of Cassius, the murderer of Caesar. He was recalled from banishment by Vespasian. Cassius wrote 10 books on the civil law, and some other works ; was a follower of the school of Ateius Capito ; and as he reduced the principles of Capito to a more scientific form, the adherents of this school received the name of *Cassiani.* — (4) CASS. PARMENSIS, so called from Parma, his birth-place, was one of the murderers of Caesar, B.C. 43 ; took an active part in the civil wars that followed his death ; and after the battle of Actium, was put to death by the command of Octavian, B.C. 30. Cassius was a poet, and his productions were prized by Horace. — (5) CASS. ETRUSCUS, a poet censured by Horace (*Sat.* i. 10. 61), must not be confounded with No. 4.—(6) CASS. AVIDIUS, an able general of M. Aurelius, was a native of Syria. In the Parthian war (A.D. 162—165), he commanded the Roman army as the general of Verus ; was afterwards appointed governor of all the Eastern provinces, and discharged his trust for several years with fidelity ; but in A.D. 175 he proclaimed himself emperor. He reigned only a few months, and was slain by his own officers, before M. Aurelius arrived in the East. [AURELIUS.]—(7) CASS. DION. [DION CASSIUS.]

CASSIVELAUNUS (-i), a British chief, ruled over the country N. of the Tamesis (*Thames*), and was entrusted by the Britons with the supreme command on Caesar's 2nd invasion of Britain, B.C. 54. He was defeated by Caesar, and was obliged to sue for peace.

CASTALIA (-ae), a celebrated fountain on Mt. Parnassus, in which the Pythia used to bathe; sacred to Apollo and the Muses, who were hence called CASTALIDES.

CASTOR (-ŏris), brother of Pollux. [DIOS-CURI.]

CASTRUM (-i). (1) INUI, a town on the Rutuli, on the coast of Latium, confounded by some writers with No. 2.—(2) NOVUM (*Torre di Chiaruccia*), a town in Etruria, and a Roman colony on the coast.—(3) NOVUM (*Giulia Nova*), a town in Picenum, probably at the mouth of the small river Batinum (*Salinello*).

CASTŬLO (-ōnis: *Cazlona*), a town of the Oretani in Hispania Tarraconensis, on the Baetis, and under the Romans an important place. In the mountains in the neighbourhood were silver and lead mines. The wife of Hannibal was a native of Castulo.

CATĂBATHMUS MAGNUS (i.e. great descent), a mountain and sea port, at the bottom of a deep bay on the N. coast of Africa, considered the boundary between Egypt and Cyrenaica.

CATĂDŬPA (-ōrum) or -I (-ōrum), a name given to the cataracts of the Nile, and also to the parts of Aethiopia in their neighbourhood. [NILUS.]

CATĒLAUNI (-ōrum: *Châlons sur Marne*), a town in Gaul, near which Attila was defeated by Aëtius and Theodoric, A.D. 451.

CATĂMĪTUS. [GANYMEDES.]

CATĂNA or CATĬNA (-ae: *Catania*), an important town in Sicily, at the foot of Mt. Aetna, founded B.C. 730 by Naxos. In B.C. 476 it was taken by Hiero I., who removed its inhabitants to Leontini, and settled 5000 Syracusans and 5000 Peloponnesians in the town, the name of which he changed into Aetna. The former inhabitants again obtained possession of the town soon after the death of Hiero, and restored the old name. Catana was afterwards subject to various reverses, and finally in the 1st Punic war fell under the dominion of Rome.

CATĂŌNĬA (-ae), a fertile district in the S.E. part of Cappadocia, to which it was first added under the Romans, with Melitene, which lies E. of it.

CATARRHACTÊS (-ae). (1) A river of Pamphylia, which descends from the mountains of Taurus, in a great broken waterfall, (whence its name).—(2) The term is also applied, first by Strabo, to the cataracts of the Nile, which are distinguished as C. Major and C. Minor. [NILUS.]

CATHAEI (-ōrum), a great and warlike people of India intra Gangem, upon whom Alexander made war.

CATĬLĪNA (-ae), L. SERGĬUS (-i), the descendant of an ancient patrician family which had sunk into poverty. His youth and early manhood were stained by every vice and crime. He first appears in history as a zealous partisan of Sulla, taking an active part in the horrors of the proscription. His private life presents a compound of cruelty and intrigue, but notwithstanding these things he obtained the dignity of praetor in B.C. 68, and sued for the consulship in 66. For this office however he had been disqualified for becoming a candidate, in consequence of an impeachment for oppression in his province, preferred by P. Clodius Pulcher, afterwards so celebrated as the enemy of Cicero. His first plot was to murder the two consuls that had been elected, a design which was frustrated only by his own impatience. He now organised a more extensive conspiracy. Having been acquitted in 65 upon his trial for extortion, he was left unfettered to mature his plans. The time was propitious to his schemes. The younger nobility and the veterans of Sulla were desirous of some change, to relieve them from their wants; while the populace were restless and discontented, ready to follow the bidding of any demagogue. The conspiracy came to a head in the consulship of Cicero, B.C. 63. But the vigilance of Cicero baffled all the plans of Catiline. He compelled Catiline to leave Rome (Nov. 8—9); and shortly afterwards, by the interception of correspondence between the other leaders of the conspiracy and the ambassadors of the Allobroges, he obtained legal evidence against Catiline's companions. This done, Cicero instantly summoned the leaders, conducted them to the senate, where they were condemned to death, and executed them the same night in prison. (Dec. 5, 63). The consul Antonius was then sent against Catiline, and the decisive battle was fought early in 62. Antonius, however, unwilling to fight against his former associate, gave the command on the day of battle to his legáte, M. Petreius. Catiline fell in the engagement, after fighting with the most daring valour.— The history of Catiline's conspiracy has been written by Sallust.

CĂTO (-ōnis), the name of a celebrated family of the Porcia gens. (1) M. PORCIUS CATO, frequently surnamed CENSORIUS or CENSOR, also CATO MAJOR, to distinguish him from his great-grandson Cato Uticensis [No. 2.] Cato was born at Tusculum, B.C. 234, and was brought up at his father's farm, situated in the Sabine territory. In 217 he served his first campaign in his 17th year. During the first 26 years of his public life (217—191) he gave his energies to military pursuits, and distinguished himself on many occasions—in the 2nd Punic war, in Spain, and in the campaign against Antiochus in Greece. With the victory over Antiochus at Thermopylae in 191 his military career came to a close. He now took an active part in civil affairs, and distinguished himself by his vehement opposition to the Roman nobles, who were introducing into Rome Greek luxury and refinement. It was especially against the Scipios that his most violent attacks were directed, and whom he pursued with the bitterest animosity. [Scipio.] In 184 he was elected censor with L. Valerius Flaccus. His censorship was a great epoch in his life. He applied himself strenuously to the duties of his office, regardless of the enemies he was making; but all his efforts to stem the tide of luxury which was now setting in proved unavailing. His strong national prejudices appear to have diminished in force as he grew older and wiser. He applied himself in old age to the study of Greek literature, with which in youth he had no acquaintance, although he was not ignorant of the Greek language. He retained his bodily and mental vigour in his old age. In the year before his death he was one of the chief instigators of the third Punic war. He had been one of the Roman deputies sent to Africa to arbitrate between Masinissa and the Carthaginians, and he was so struck with the flourishing condition of Carthage that on his return home he maintained that Rome would never be safe as long as Carthage was in existence. From this time forth, whenever he was called upon for his vote in the senate, though the subject of debate bore no relation to Carthage, his words were *Delenda est Carthago*. He died in 149, at the age of 85. Cato wrote several works, of which only the *De Re Rustica* has come down to us.—(2) M. Porcius Cato, great-grandson of Cato the Censor, and surnamed Uticensis from Utica, the place of his death, was born 95. In early childhood he lost both his parents, and was brought up 'in the house of his mother's brother, M. Livius Drusus, along with his sister Porcia and the children of his mother by her second husband, Q. Servilius Caepio. In early years he discovered a stern and unyielding character; he applied himself with great zeal to the study of oratory and philosophy, and became a devoted adherent of the Stoic school; and among the profligate nobles of the age he soon became conspicuous for his rigid

morality. In 63 he was tribune of the plebs, and supported Cicero in proposing that the Catilinarian conspirators should suffer death. He now became one of the chief leaders o the aristocratical party, and opposed with the utmost vehemence the measures of Caesar, Pompey, and Crassus. He joined Pompey on the breaking out of the civil war (49). After the battle of Pharsalia he went first to Corcyra, and thence to Africa, where he joined Metellus Scipio. When Scipio was defeated at Thapsus, and all Africa with the exception of Utica submitted to Caesar, he resolved to die rather than fall into his hands. He therefore put an end to his own life, after spending the greater part of the night in perusing Plato's Phaedo on the immortality of the soul. Cato soon became the subject of biography and panegyric. Shortly after his death appeared Cicero's *Cato*, which provoked Caesar's *Anticato*. In Lucan the character of Cato is a personification of godlike virtue. In modern times, the closing events of his life have been often dramatised; and few dramas have gained more celebrity than the *Cato* of Addison.

CATTI or CHATTI (-ōrum), one of the most important nations of Germany, bounded by the Visurgis (*Weser*) on the E., the Agri Decumates on the S., and the Rhine on the W., in the modern *Hesse* and the adjacent countries. They were a branch of the Hermiones, and are first mentioned by Caesar under the erroneous name of Suevi. They were never completely subjugated by the Romans; and their power was greatly augmented on the decline of the Cherusci. Their capital was Mattium.

CATULLUS, VALERIUS (-i), a Roman poet, born at Verona or in its immediate vicinity, B.C. 87. Catullus inherited considerable property from his father, who was the friend of Julius Caesar; but he squandered a great part of it by indulging freely in the pleasures of the metropolis. In order to better his fortunes, he went to Bithynia in the train of the praetor Memmius, but it appears that the speculation was attended with little success. He probably died about B.C. 47. The extant works of Catullus consist of 116 poems, on a variety of topics, and composed in different styles and metres. Catullus adorned all he touched, and his shorter poems are characterised by original invention and felicity of expression.

CATULUS, the name of a distinguished family of the Lutatia gens. (1) C. Lutatius Catulus, consul B.C. 242, defeated as proconsul in the following year the Carthaginian fleet off the Aegates islands, and thus brought the first Punic war to a close, 241.—(2) Q

LUTATIUS CATULUS, consul 102 with C. Marius IV., and as proconsul next year gained along with Marius a decisive victory over the Cimbri near Vercellae (*Vercelli*), in the N. of Italy. Catulus belonged to the aristocratical party; he espoused the cause of Sulla; was included by Marius in the proscription of 87; and as escape was impossible, put an end to his life by the vapours of a charcoal fire. Catulus was well acquainted with Greek literature, and the author of several works, all of which are lost.—(3) Q. LUTATIUS CATULUS, son of No. 2, a distinguished leader of the aristocracy, also won the respect and confidence of the people by his upright character and conduct. He was consul in 78 and censor in 65. He opposed the Gabinian and Manilian laws which conferred extraordinary powers upon Pompey (67 and 66).

CATURIGES (-um), a ·Ligurian people in Gallia Narbonensis, near the Cottian Alps.

CAUCASIAE PYLAE. [CAUCASUS.]

CAUCASUS (-i), CAUCASII MONTES (*Caucasus*), a great chain of mountains in Asia, extending from the E. shore of the Pontus Euxinus (*Black Sea*) to the W. shore of the Caspian. There are two chief passes over the chain, both of which were known to the ancients; one near *Derbent*, was called Albaniae and sometimes CASPIAE PYLAE: the other, nearly in the centre of the range, was called Caucasiae Pylae (*Pass of Dariel*). That the Greeks had some vague knowledge of the Caucasus in very early times, is proved by the myths respecting Prometheus and the Argonauts, from which it seems that the Caucasus was regarded as at the extremity of the earth, on the border of the river Oceanus.—When the soldiers of Alexander advanced to that great range of mountains which formed the N. boundary of Ariana, the Paropamisus, they applied to it the name of Caucasus; afterwards, for the sake of distinction, it was called Caucasus Indicus. [PAROPAMISUS.]

CAUCI. [CHAUCI.]

CAUCONES (-um), the name of peoples both in Greece and Asia, who had disappeared at later times. The Caucones in Asia Minor are mentioned by Homer as allies of the Trojans, and are placed in Bithynia and Paphlagonia by the geographers.

CAUDIUM (-i), a town in Samnium on the road from Capua to Beneventum. In the neighbourhood were the celebrated FURCULAE CAUDINAE, or *Caudine Forks,* narrow passes in the mountains, where the Roman army surrendered to the Samnites, and was sent under the yoke, B.C. 321: it is now called the valley of *Arpaia.*

CAULON (-ōnis), or CAULONIA (-ae), a town in Bruttium, N.E. of Locri, originally called Aulon or Aulonia, founded by the inhabitants of Croton, or by the Achaeans.

CAUNUS (-i), one of the chief cities of Caria, on its S. coast, in a very fertile but unhealthy situation. It was founded by the Cretans. Its dried figs (Cauneae ficus) were highly celebrated. The painter Protogenes was born here.

CAURUS (-i), the Argestes of the Greeks, the N.W. wind, is in Italy a stormy wind.

CAŸSTER (-tri), and CAŸSTRUS (-i), a celebrated river of Lydia and Ionia, flowing between the ranges of Tmolus and Messogis into the Aegean, a little N.W. of Ephesus. To this day it abounds in swans, as it did in Homer's time. The valley of the Caystrus is called by Homer "the Asian meadow," and is probably the district to which the name of Asia was first applied.

CEA. [CEOS.]

CEBENNA, GEBENNA (-ae : *Cevennes*), a range of mountains in the S. of Gaul, extending N. as far as Lugdunum, and separating the Arverni from the Helvii.

CEBES (-ētis), of Thebes, a disciple and friend of Socrates, was present at the death of his teacher. He wrote a philosophical work, entitled *Pinax* or *Table,* giving an allegorical picture of human life. It is extant, and has been exceedingly popular.

CEBRENIS (-Idos : *acc.* Ida), daughter of Cebren, a river-god in the Troad.

CECROPIA. [ATHENAE.]

CECROPS (-ŏpis), a hero of the Pelasgic race, said to have been the first king of Attica. He was married to Agraulos, daughter of Actaeus, by whom he had a son, Erysichthon, who succeeded him as king of Athens, and 3 daughters, Agraulos, Herse, and Pandrosos. In his reign Poseidon (Neptune) and Athena (Minerva) contended for the possession of Attica, but Cecrops decided in favour of the goddess. [ATHENA.] Cecrops is said to have founded Athens, the citadel of which was called Cecropia after him, to have divided Attica into 12 communities, and to have introduced the first elements of civilised life; he instituted marriage, abolished bloody sacrifices, and taught his subjects how to worship the gods. The later Greek writers describe Cecrops as a native of Sais in Egypt, who led a colony of Egyptians into Attica, and thus introduced from Egypt the arts of civilised life; but this account is rejected by some of the ancients themselves, and by the ablest modern critics.

CELAENAE (-ārum), a great city in S. Phrygia, situated at the sources of the rivers Maeander and Marsyas. In the midst of it was a citadel built by Xerxes, on a precipitous rock, at the foot of which the Marsyas took its rise, and near the river's source was a grotto celebrated by tradition as the scene of the punishment of Marsyas by Apollo. The Maeander took its rise in the very palace, and flowed through the park and the city, below which it received the Marsyas.

CELAENŌ (-us), one of the Harpies. [HARPYIAE].

CELETRUM (-i), a town in Macedonia on a peninsula of the Lacus Castoris.

CELEUS (-i), king of Eleusis, husband of Metanīra, and father of Demophon and Triptolemus. He received Demeter (Ceres) with hospitality at Eleusis, when she was wandering in search of her daughter. The goddess, in return, wished to make his son Demophon immortal, and placed him in the fire in order to destroy his mortal parts; but Metanira screamed aloud at the sight, and Demophon was destroyed by the flames. Demeter then bestowed great favours upon Triptolemus. [TRIPTOLEMUS.] Celeus is described as the first priest and his daughters as the first priestesses of Demeter at Eleusis.

CELSUS, A. CORNELIUS (-i), a Roman writer on medicine, probably lived under the reigns of Augustus and Tiberius. His treatise *De Medicina*, in 8 books, has come down to us, and has been much valued from the earliest times to the present day.

CELTAE (-ārum), a mighty race, which occupied the greater part of western Europe in ancient times. The Greek and Roman writers call them by 3 names, which are probably only variations of one name, namely CELTAE, GALATAE, and GALLI. The most powerful part of the nation appears to have taken up their abode in the centre of the country called after them GALLIA, between the Garumna in the S. and the Sequana and Matrona in the N. From this country they spread over various parts of Europe. Besides the Celts in Gallia, there were 8 other different settlements of the nation:—1. Iberian Celts, who crossed the Pyrenees and settled in Spain. [CELTIBERI.] 2. British Celts, the most ancient inhabitants of Britain. [BRITANNIA.] 3. Belgic Celts, the earliest inhabitants of Gallia Belgica, at a later time much mingled with Germans. 4. Italian Celts, who crossed the Alps at different periods, and eventually occupied the greater part of the N. of Italy, which was called after them GALLIA CISALPINA. 5. Celts in the Alps and on the Danube, namely the Helvetii, Gothini, Osi, Vindelici, Raeti, Norici, and Carni. 6. Illyrian Celts, who, under the name of Scordisci, settled on Mt. Scordus. 7. Macedonian and Thracian Celts, who had remained behind in Macedonia when

the Celts invaded Greece, and who are rarely mentioned. 8. Asiatic Celts, the Tolistobogi, Trocmi, and Tectosages, who founded the kingdom of GALATIA.—Some ancient writers divided the Celts into two great races, one consisting of the Celts in the S. and centre of Gaul, in Spain, and in the N. of Italy, who were the proper Celts, and the other consisting of the Celtic tribes on the shores of the Ocean and in the E. as far as Scythia, who were called Gauls: to the latter race the Cimbri belonged, and they are considered by some to be identical with the Cimmerii of the Greeks. This twofold division of the Celts appears to correspond to the two races into which the Celts are at present divided in Great Britain, namely the Gael and the Kymry, who differ in language and customs, the Gael being the inhabitants of Ireland and the N. of Scotland, and the Kymry of Wales. —The Celts are described by the ancient writers as men of large stature, of fair complexion, and with flaxen or red hair. They were long the terror of the Romans: once they took Rome, and laid it ashes (B.C. 390). [GALLIA.]

CELTIBERI (-ōrum), a powerful people in Spain, consisting of Celts, who crossed the Pyrenees at an early period, and became mingled with the Iberians, the original inhabitants of the country. They dwelt chiefly in the central part of Spain. Their country called CELTIBERIA was mountainous and unproductive. They were a brave and warlike people, and proved formidable enemies to the Romans. They submitted to Scipio Africanus in the 2nd Punic war, but the oppressions of the Roman governors led them to rebel, and for many years they successfully defied the power of Rome. They were reduced to submission on the capture of Numantia by Scipio Africanus the younger (B.C. 134), but they again took up arms under Sertorius, and it was not till his death (72) that they began to adopt the Roman customs and language.

CENAEUM (-i), the N.W. promontory of Euboea, opposite Thermopylae, with a temple of Zeus Cenaeus.

CENCHREAE (-ārum), the E. harbour of Corinth on the Saronic gulf, important for the trade and commerce with the East.

CENOMANI (-ōrum), a powerful Gallic people, crossed the Alps at an early period, and settled in the N.W. of Italy, in the country of Brixia, Verona, and Mantua, and extended N. as far as the confines of Rhaetia.

CENSORINUS (-i), author of an extant treatise, entitled *De Die Natali*, which treats of the generation of man, of his natal hour, of the influence of the stars and genii upon his career, and discusses the various methods employed for the division and calculation of time.

CENTAURI (-ōrum), that is the bull-killers, were an ancient race, inhabiting Mount Pelion in Thessaly. They led a wild and savage life, and are hence called φῆρες or θῆρες, i. e., savage-beasts, in Homer. In later accounts they were represented as half-horses and half men, and are said to have been the offspring of Ixion and a cloud. The Centaurs are celebrated in ancient story for their fight with the Lapithae, which arose at the marriage feast of Pirithous. This fight is sometimes placed in connexion with a combat of Hercules with the Centaurs. [HERCULES.] It ended by the Centaurs being expelled from their country, and taking refuge on mount Pindus, on the frontiers of Epirus. Chiron is the most celebrated among the Centaurs. [CHIRON.] We know that hunting the bull on horseback was a national custom in Thessaly, and that the Thessalians were celebrated riders. Hence may have arisen the fable that the Centaurs were half-men and half-horses, just as the Americans, when they first saw a Spaniard on horseback, believed horse and man to be one being. The Centaurs are frequently represented in ancient works of art, and generally, as men from the head to the loins, while the remainder of the body is that of a horse with its 4 feet and tail.

Centaur. (Metope from the Parthenon.)

CENTRĪTĒS, a small river of Armenia, which it divided from the land of the Carduchi, N. of Assyria.

CENTUM CELLAE (-ārum: *Civita Vecchia*), a sea-port town in Etruria, first became a place of importance under Trajan, who built a villa here, and constructed an excellent harbour.

CENTŬRIPAE (-ārum), an ancient town of the Siculi, in Sicily, at the foot of Mt. Aetna, and not far from the river Symaethus. Under the Romans it was one of the most flourishing cities in the island.

CĔOS (-i), or CĔA (-ae), an island in the Aegean Sea, one of the Cyclades, between the Attic promontory Sunium and the island Cythnus, celebrated for its fertile soil and its genial climate. Its chief town was Iulis, the birth-place of Simonides, whence we read of the *Ceae munera neniae.*

CĔPHALLĒNIA (-ae: *Cephalonia*), called by Homer SAME or SAMOS, the largest island in the Ionian sea, separated from Ithaca by a narrow channel. The island is very mountainous; its chief towns were Same, Pale, Cranii, and Proni. It never obtained political importance. It is now one of the 7 Ionian islands under the protection of Great Britain.

CĔPHĂLOEDĬUM (-i), a town on the

N. coast of Sicily in the territory of Himera.

CĒPHĂLUS (-i), son of Deion and Diomede, and husband of Procris or Procne. He was beloved by Eos (Aurora), but as he rejected her advances from love to his wife, she advised him to try the fidelity of Procris. The goddess then metamorphosed him into a stranger, and sent him with rich presents to his house. Procris was tempted by the brilliant presents to yield to the stranger, who then discovered himself to be her husband, whereupon she fled in shame to Crete. Artemis (Diana) made her a present of a dog and a spear, which were never to miss their object, and sent her back to Cephalus in the disguise of a youth. In order to obtain this dog and spear Cephalus promised to love the youth, who thereupon made herself known to him as his wife Procris. This led to a reconciliation between them. Procris however still feared the love of Eos, and therefore jealously watched Cephalus when he went out hunting, but on one occasion he killed her by accident with the never-erring spear. A somewhat different version of the same story is given by Ovid.

CĒPHEŬS (-ĕŏs or ĕi). (1) King of Ethiopia, son of Belus, husband of Cassiopea, and father of Andromeda, was placed among the stars after his death.—(2) Son of Aleus, one of the Argonauts, was king of Tegea in Arcadia, and perished with most of his sons in an expedition against Hercules.

CĒPHĪSUS or CĒPHISSUS (-i). (1) A river flowing through a fertile valley, in Phocis and Boeotia, and falling into the lake Copais, which is hence called *Cephisis* in the Iliad. [COPAIS.]—(2) The largest river in Attica, rising in the W. slope of Mt. Pentelicus, and flowing past Athens on the W. into the Saronic gulf near Phalerum.

CĒRĂMUS (-i), a Dorian sea-port town on the N. side of the Cnidian Chersonesus on the coast of Caria, from which the Ceramic gulf took its name.

CĒRĂSUS (-i),a flourishing colony of Sinope, on the coast of Pontus, at the mouth of a river of the same name; chiefly celebrated as the place from which Europe obtained both the cherry and its name. Lucullus is said to have brought back plants of the cherry with him to Rome, but this refers probably only to some particular sorts, as the Romans seem to have had the tree much earlier. Cerasus fell into decay after the foundation of Pharnacia.

CĒRAUNĬI MONTES (*Khimara*), a range of mountains extending from the frontier of Illyricum along the coast of Epirus, derived their name from the frequent thunderstorms which occurred among them (κεραυνός). These mountains made the coast of Epirus dangerous to ships. They were also called Acroceraunia, though this name was properly applied to the promontory separating the Adriatic and Ionian seas. The inhabitants of these mountains were called *Ceraunii*.

CERBĒRUS (-i), the dog that guarded the entrance of Hades, is called a son of Typhaon and Echidna. Some poets represent him with 50 or 100 heads; but later writers describe him as a monster with only 3 heads, with the tail of a serpent and with serpents round his neck. His den is usually placed on the further side of the Styx, at the spot where Charon landed the shades of the departed.

Cerberus.   (From a Bronze Statue.)

CERCASŌRUM (-i), a city of Lower Egypt, on the W. bank of the Nile, at the point where the river divided into its 3 principal branches.

CERCĪNA (-ae) and CERCĪNĪTIS, two low islands off the N. coast of Africa, in the mouth of the Lesser Syrtis, united by a bridge, and possessing a fine harbour.

CERCŌPES (-um), droll and thievish gnomes, who robbed Hercules in his sleep. Some place them at Thermopylae; others at Oechalia in Euboea, or in Lydia.

CERCȲON (-ŏnis), son of Poseidon (Neptune) or Hephaestus (Vulcan), a cruel tyrant at Eleusis, put to death his daughter ALOPE and killed all strangers whom he overcame in wrestling; he was in the end conquered and slain by Theseus.

CĒRĒS. [DEMETER.]

CĒRES, the personified necessity of death, are described by Homer as formidable, dark, and hateful beings, because they carry off men to the joyless house of Hades. According to Hesiod, they are the daughters of Night, and sisters of the Moerae, and punish men for their crimes.

CĒRINTHUS (-i), a town on the E. coast of Euboea, on the River Budorus.

CERRETĀNI (-ōrum), an Iberian people in Hispania Tarraconensis, inhabited the modern *Cerdagne* in the Pyrenees; they were celebrated for their hams.

CERTŎNĬUM (-i), a town in Mysia.

CĒTĒI (-ōrum), a people of Mysia, the old inhabitants of the country about Pergamus, and upon the Cetius, mentioned by Homer.

CĒTHĒGUS (-i), the name of an ancient patrician family of the Cornelia gens. They seem to have kept up an old fashion of wearing their arms bare, to which Horace alludes in the words *cinctuti Cethegi.*—(1) M. CORNELIUS CETHEGUS, censor B.C. 209, and consul 204, distinguished for his eloquence, and his correct use of Latin words, is quoted by Ennius and Horace with approbation; died 196—(2) C. CORNELIUS CETHEGUS, one of Catiline's crew, was a profligate from his early youth. When Catiline left Rome, 63, after Cicero's first speech, Cethegus stayed behind under the orders of Lentulus. His charge was to murder the leading senators; but the tardiness of Lentulus prevented anything being done. Cethegus was arrested and condemned to death with the other conspirators.

CĒTĬUS (-i), a small river of Mysia, falling into the Caïcus close to Pergamus.

CĒYX. [ALCYONE.]

CHABŎRAS, the same as the ABORRHAS.

CHABRĬAS (-ae), a celebrated Athenian general. In B.C. 378 he was one of the commanders of the forces sent to the aid of Thebes against Agesilaus, when he adopted for the first time that manœuvre for which he became so celebrated, — ordering his men to await the attack with their spears pointed against the enemy and their shields resting on one knee. A statue was afterwards erected at Athens to Chabrias in this posture. At the siege of Chios (357) he fell a sacrifice to his excessive valour.

CHAERĒA (-ae), C. CASSĬUS (-i), tribune of the praetorian cohorts, formed the conspiracy by which the emperor Caligula was slain, A.D. 41. Chaerea was put to death by Claudius upon his accession.

CHAERŌNĒA (-ae), a town in Boeotia on the Cephisus near the frontier of Phocis, memorable for the defeat of the Athenians and the Boeotians by Philip, which crushed the liberties of Greece, B.C. 338, and for Sulla's victory over the army of Mithridates, 86. Chaeronea was the birthplace of Plutarch. Several remains of the ancient city are to be seen at *Capurna*, more particularly a theatre excavated in the rock, an aqueduct, and the marble lion (broken in pieces), which adorned the sepulchre of the Boeotians who fell at the battle of Chaeronea.

CHALAEUM (-i), a port town of the Locri Ozolae on the Crissaean gulf, on the frontiers of Phocis.

CHALASTRA (-ae), a town in Mygdonia in Macedonia, at the mouth of the river Axius.

CHALCĒ (-es), or CHALCĬA (-ae), an island of the Carpathian sea, near Rhodes.

CHALCĒDŌN (-ŏnis), a Greek city of Bithynia, on the coast of the Propontis, at the entrance of the Bosporus, nearly opposite to Byzantium, was founded by a colony from Megara in B.C. 685. After a long period of independence, it became subject to the kings of Bithynia, and most of its inhabitants were transferred to the new city of Nicomedia (B C. 140).

CHALCĬDĬCĒ (-es), a peninsula in Macedonia, between the Thermaic and Strymonic gulfs, runs out into the sea like a 3-pronged fork, terminating in 3 smaller peninsulas, PALLENE, SITHONIA, and ACTE or ATHOS. It derived its name from Chalcidian colonists. [CHALCIS, No. 1.]

CHALCIS (-ĭdis). (1) (*Egripo* or *Negroponte*), the principal town of Euboea, situated on the narrowest part of the Euripus, and united with the mainland by a bridge. It was a very ancient town, originally inhabited by Abantes or Curetes, and colonised by Attic Ionians. Its flourishing condition at an early period is attested by the numerous colonies which it planted in various parts of the Mediterranean. It founded so many cities in the peninsula in Macedonia, between the Strymonic and Thermaic gulfs, that the whole peninsula was called Chalcidice. In Italy it founded Cuma, and in Sicily Naxos. Chalcis was usually subject to Athens during the greatness of the latter city. The orator Isaeus and the poet Lycophron were born at Chalcis, and Aristotle died here. — (2) A town in Aetolia, at the mouth of the Evenus, situated at the foot of the mountain Chalcis, and hence also called *Hypochalcis.*—(3) A city of Syria, in a fruitful plain, near the termination of the river Chalus; the chief city of the district of Chalcidice, which lay to the E. of the Orontes.

CHALDAEA (-ae), in the narrower sense, was a province of Babylonia, about the lower course of the Euphrates, the border of the Arabian Desert, and the head of the Persian Gulf. It was intersected by numerous canals, and was extremely fertile. In a wider sense, the term is applied to the whole of Babylonia, and even to the Babylonian empire, on account of the supremacy which the Chaldaeans acquired at Babylon. [BABYLON.] Xenophon mentions Chaldaeans in the mountains N. of Mesopotamia. Their original seat was most probably in the mountains of Armenia and *Kurdistan*, whence they descended into the plains of Mesopotamia and Babylonia. Respecting the Chaldaeans as the ruling class in the Babylonian monarchy, see BABYLON.

CHĀLЎBES (-um), a remarkable Asiatic people, dwelling on the S. shore of the Black Sea, and occupying themselves in the working of iron. Xenophon mentions Chalybes in the mountains on the borders of Armenia and Mesopotamia, who seem to be the same people that he elsewhere calls Chaldaeans; and several of the ancient geographers regarded the Chalybes and Chaldaei as originally the same people.

CHĀLЎBON (*O. T.*, HELBON), a considerable city of N. Syria, probably the same as BEROEA.

CHĀMĀVI (-ōrum), a people in Germany, who first appear in the neighbourhood of the Rhine, but afterwards migrated E., defeated the Bructeri, and settled between the Weser and the Harz.

CHAŌNES, a Pelasgian people, one of the 3 peoples which inhabited EPIRUS, were at an earlier period in possession of the whole of the country, but subsequently dwelt along the coast from the river Thyamis to the Acroceraunian promontory, which district was therefore called CHAONIA. By the poets *Chaonius* is used as equivalent to Epirot.

CHĂOS (*abl.* Chăŏ), the vacant and infinite space which existed according to the ancient cosmogonies previous to the creation of the world, and out of which the gods, men, and all things arose. Chaos was called the mother of Erebos and Night.

CHARADRA (-ae), a town in Phocis, on the river Charadrus, situated on an eminence not far from Lilaea.

CHĂRAX (i.e., *a palisaded camp*), the name of several cities, which took their origin from military stations. The most remarkable of them stood at the mouth of the Tigris. [ALEXANDRIA, No. 4.]

CHĂRĒS (-ētis).—(1) An Athenian general, who for many years contrived, by profuse corruption, to maintain his influence with the people, in spite of his very disreputable character. In the Social war, B.C. 356, he accused his colleagues, Iphicrates and Timotheus, to the people, and obtained the sole command. After which he entered into the service of Artabazus, the revolted satrap of Western Asia, but was recalled by the Athenians on the complaint of Artaxerxes III. He was one of the Athenian commanders at the battle of Chaeronēa, 338.—(2) Of Lindus, in Rhodes, a statuary in bronze, the favourite pupil of Lysippus, flourished B.C. 290. His chief work was the statue of the Sun, which, under the name of "The Colossus of Rhodes," was celebrated as one of the 7 wonders of the world.

CHĀRILĀUS, or CHARILLUS, (-i), king of Sparta, son of Polydectes, is said to have received his name from the general joy excited by the justice of his uncle Lycurgus, when he placed him, yet a new-born infant, on the royal seat, and bade the Spartans acknowledge him for their king.

CHĂRĪTES (-um), called GRĂTĬAE by the Romans, and by us the GRACES, were the personification of Grace and Beauty. In the Iliad, Charis is described as the wife of Hephaestus (Vulcan); but in the Odyssey Aphrodite (Venus) appears as the wife of Hephaestus; from which we may infer, if not the identity of Aphrodite and Charis, at least a close connection in the notions entertained about the 2 divinities. The idea of personified grace and beauty was at an early period divided into a plurality of beings; and even in the Homeric poems the plural Charites occurs several times. The Charites are usually described as the daughters of Zeus (Jupiter), and as 3 in number, namely, Euphrŏsўnē, Aglăĭa, and Thălĭa. The names of

Charites (the Graces). (From a Coin of Germa.)

the Charites sufficiently express their character. They were the goddesses who enhanced the enjoyments of life by refinement and gentleness. They are mostly described as in the service of other divinities, and they lend their grace and beauty to every thing that delights and elevates gods and men. Poetry, however, is the art which is especially favoured by them; and hence they are the friends of the Muses, with whom they live together in Olympus. In early times the Charites were represented dressed, but afterwards their figures were without clothing: specimens of both representations of the Charites are still extant. They appear unsuspicious maidens, in the full bloom of life; and they usually embrace each other.

Charites (the Graces). (Pitture Ercolano, vol. 3, tav. 11.)

CHARMANDĒ (-es: nr. *Hit*), a great city of Mesopotamia, on the Euphrates.

CHĂRŎN (-ontis), son of Erebos, conveyed

Charon, Hermes or Mercury, and Soul. (From a Roman Lamp.)

in his boat the shades of the dead across the rivers of the lower world. For this service he was paid with an obolus or danace, which coin was placed in the mouth of every corpse previous to its burial. He is represented as an aged man, with a dirty beard and a mean dress.

CHĂRONDAS (-ae), a lawgiver of Catana, who legislated for his own and the other cities of Chalcidian origin in Sicily and Italy. His date is uncertain, but he lived about B.C. 500. A tradition relates that Charondas one day forgot to lay aside his sword before he appeared in the assembly, thereby violating one of his own laws; and that, on being reminded of this by a citizen, he exclaimed, "By Zeus (Jupiter), I will establish it," and immediately stabbed himself. The laws of Charondas were probably in verse.

CHĂRYBDIS. [SCYLLA.]

CHASŬĀRI, or CHASŬĀRĬI, or CHATTŬĀRĬI (-ōrum), a people of Germany, allies or dependents of the Cherusci. They dwelt N. of the Chatti; and in later times they appear between the Rhine and the Maas, as a part of the Franks.

CHATTI. [CATTI.]

CHAUCI or CAUCI (-ōrum), a powerful people in the N.E. of Germany, between the Amisia (*Ems*) and the Albis (*Elbe*), divided by the Visurgis (*Weser*), which flowed through their territory, into Majores and Minores, the former W., and the latter E. of the river. They are described by Tacitus as the noblest and the justest of the German tribes. They are mentioned for the last time in the 3rd century, when they devastated Gaul; but their name subsequently became merged in the general name of Saxons.

CHĒLĪDŎNIAE INSULAE (*i.e.*, *Swallow Islands*), a group of small islands, surrounded by dangerous shallows, off the promontory called Hiera or Chelidonia, on the S. coast of Lycia.

CHELONĀTAS (*C. Tornese*), a promontory in Elis, opposite Zacynthus, the most westerly point of the Peloponnesus.

CHEMMIS, aft. PANŎPŎLIS, a great city of the Thebais, or Upper Egypt, on the E. bank of the Nile, celebrated for its manufacture of linen, its stone-quarries, and its temples of Pan and Perseus.

CHĒOPS (-pis), an early king of Egypt, godless and tyrannical, reigned 50 years, and built the first and largest pyramid by the compulsory labour of his subjects.

CHĒPHRĒN (-ēnos), king of Egypt, brother and successor of Cheops, whose example of tyranny he followed, reigned 56 years, and built the second pyramid.

CHERSŎNĒSUS (-i), "a land-island," that is, "a peninsula" (from χέρσος, "land," and νῆσος, "island"). (1) CHERSONESUS THRACICA (*Peninsula of the Dardanelles* or of *Gallipoli*), usually called at Athens "The Chersonesus," without any distinguishing epithet, the narrow slip of land, 420 stadia in length, running between the Hellespont and the Gulf of Melas, and connected with the Thracian mainland by an isthmus, which was fortified by a wall, 36 stadia across, near Cardia. The Chersonese was colonised by the Athenians under Miltiades, the contemporary of Pisistratus.—(2) CHERSONESUS TAURICA or SCYTHICA (*Crimea*), the peninsula between the Pontus Euxinus, the Cimmerian Bosporus, and the Palus Maeotis, united to the mainland by an isthmus, 40 stadia in width. It produced a great quantity of corn, which was exported to Athens and other parts of Greece. [BOSPORUS.] — (3) CIMBRICA (*Jutland*). See CIMBRI.

CHĔRUSCI (-ōrum), the most celebrated of all the tribes of ancient Germany. The ancients extended this name also to the nations belonging to the league of which the Cherusci were at the head. The Cherusci proper dwelt on both sides of the Visurgis (*Weser*), and their territories extended to the Harz and the Elbe. Under their chief Arminius they destroyed the army of Varus, and drove the Romans beyond the Rhine, A.D. 9. In consequence of internal dissensions among the German tribes, the Cherusci soon lost their influence. Their neighbours, the CATTI, succeeded to their power.

CHILŌN (-ōnis), of Lacedaemon, son of Damagetus, and one of the Seven Sages, flourished B.C. 590.

CHIMAERA (-ae), a fire-breathing monster, the fore part of whose body was that of a lion, the hind part that of a dragon, and the middle that of a goat. She made great

Bellerophon and the Chimaera.
(From the Terra-cotta in the British Museum.)

havoc in Lycia and the surrounding countries, and was at length killed by Bellerophon. [BELLEROPHON.] The origin of this fire-breathing monster must probably be sought for in the volcano of the name of Chimaera, near Phaselis, in Lycia. In the works of art recently discovered in Lycia, we find several representations of the Chimaera in the simple form of a species of lion, still occurring in that country.

Bellerophon expelling the Chimaera.
(Lycian Gallery in the British Museum.)

CHĬŎNĒ (-es).—(1) Daughter of Boreas and Orithyia, and mother of Eumolpus, who is hence called *Chionides.*—(2) Daughter of Daedalion, mother of Autolycus, by Hermes (Mercury), and of Philammon, by Apollo. She was killed by Artemis (Diana) for having compared her beauty to that of the goddess.

CHIOS and CHĬUS (-i: *Scio*), one of the largest and most famous islands of the Aegean, lay opposite to the peninsula of Clazomenae, on the coast of Ionia. It was colonised by the Ionians at the time of their great migration, and remained an independent and powerful maritime state, till the defeat of the Ionian Greeks by the Persians, B.C. 494, after which the Chians were subjected to the Persians. The battle of Mycale, 479, freed Chios from the Persian yoke, and it became a member of the Athenian league, in which it was for a long time the closest and most favoured ally of Athens; but an unsuccessful attempt to revolt, in 412, led to its conquest and devastation. Chios was celebrated for its wine and marble. Of all the states which aspired to the honour of being the birthplace of Homer, Chios was generally considered by the ancients to have the best claim; and it numbered among its natives the historian Theopompus, the poet Theocritus, and other eminent men. Its chief city, Chios (*Khio*), stood on the E. side of the island.

CHĪRĬSŎPHUS (-i), a Lacedaemonian, was sent by the Spartans to aid Cyrus in his expedition against his brother Artaxerxes, B. C. 401. After the battle of Cunaxa and the subsequent arrest of the Greek generals, Chirisophus was appointed one of the new generals, and, in conjunction with Xenophon, had the chief conduct of the retreat.

CHĪRŎN (-ōnis), the wisest and justest of all the Centaurs, son of Cronos (Saturn) and Philyra (hence called Philyrides), lived on Mount Pelion. He was instructed by Apollo and Artemis (Diana), and was renowned for his skill in hunting, medicine, music, gymnastics, and the art of prophecy. All the most distinguished heroes of Grecian story, as Peleus, Achilles, Diomedes, &c., are described as the pupils of Chiron in these arts. He saved Peleus from the other Centaurs, who were on the point of killing him, and he also restored to him the sword which Acastus had concealed. [ACASTUS.] Hercules, too, was his friend; but while fighting with the other Centaurs, one of the poisoned arrows of Hercules struck Chiron, who, although immortal, would not live any longer, and gave his immortality to Prometheus. Zeus placed Chiron among the stars as Sagittarius.

CHLŌRIS (-ĭdŏs).—(1) Daughter of the

Theban Amphion and Niobe : she and her brother Amyclas were the only children of Niobe not killed by Apollo and Artemis (Diana). She is often confounded with No. 2. —(2) Daughter of Amphion of Orchomenos, wife of Neleus, king of Pylos, and mother of Nestor.—(3) Wife of Zephyrus, and goddess of flowers, identical with the Roman Flora.

CHOASPES (-is).—(1) (*Kerah* or *Kara-Su*), a river of Susiana, falling into the Tigris. Its water was so pure that the Persian kings used to carry it with them in silver vessels, when on foreign expeditions.—(2) (*Attock*), a river in the Paropamisus, in India, falling into the Cophes (*Cabul*).

CHOERILUS (-i), of Iasos, a worthless epic poet in the train of Alexander the Great, is said to have received from Alexander a gold stater for every verse of his poem.

CHONIA (-ae), the name in early times of a district in the S. of Italy, inhabited by the Chones, an Oenotrian people. Chonia appears to have included the S. E. of Lucania and the whole of the E. of Bruttium as far as the promontory of Zephyrium.

CHORASMII (-orum), a people of Sogdiana, who inhabited the banks and islands of the lower course of the Oxus. They were a branch of the Sacae or Massagetae.

CHRYSA (-ae) or -E (-es), a city on the coast of the Troad, near Thebes, with a temple of Apollo Smintheus ; celebrated by Homer.

CHRYSEIS (-Idis or -Idos), daughter of Chryses, priest of Apollo at Chryse, was taken prisoner by Achilles at the capture of Lyrnessus or the Hypoplacian Thebe. In the distribution of the booty she was given to Agamemnon. Her father Chryses came to the camp of the Greeks to solicit her ransom, but was repulsed by Agamemnon with harsh words. Thereupon Apollo sent a plague into the camp of the Greeks, and Agamemnon was obliged to restore her to her father to appease the anger of the god. Her proper name was Astynome.

CHRYSES. [CHRYSEIS].

CHRYSIPPUS (-i), a celebrated Stoic philosopher, born at Soli in Cilicia, B. c. 280, and studied at Athens under the Stoic Cleanthes. Disliking the Academic scepticism, he became one of the most strenuous supporters of the principle, that knowledge is attainable and may be established on certain foundations. He died 207, aged 73.

CHRYSOGONUS, L. CORNELIUS (-i), a favourite freedman of Sulla, and a man of profligate character, was the false accuser of Sex. Roscius, whom Cicero defended, B. c. 80.

CHRYSOPOLIS (-is), a fortified place on the Bosporus, opposite to Byzantium, at the spot

where the Bosporus was generally crossed. It was originally the port of Chalcedon.

CIBYRA (-ae).—(1) MAGNA, a great city of Phrygia Magna, on the borders of Caria, said to have been founded by the Lydians, but afterwards peopled by the Pisidians. Under its native princes, the city ruled over a large district called Cibyratis. In B. c. 83, it was added to the Roman empire. It was celebrated for its manufactures, especially in iron.— (2) PARVA, a city of Pamphylia, on the borders of Cilicia.

CICERO (-onis), a family name of the Tullia gens.—(1) M. TULLIUS CICERO, the orator, was born on the 3rd of January, B. c. 106, at the family residence, in the vicinity of Arpinum. He was educated along with his brother Quintus, and the two brothers displayed such aptitude for learning that his father removed with them to Rome, where they received instruction from the best teachers in the capital. One of their most celebrated teachers was the poet Archias, of Antioch. After receiving the manly gown (91), the young Marcus studied under Q. Mucius Scaevola, and in later years, during the civil war, under Phaedrus the Epicurean, Philo, chief of the New Academy, Diodotus the Stoic, and Molo the Rhodian. Having carefully cultivated his powers, Cicero came forward as a pleader in the forum, as soon as tranquillity was restored by the final overthrow of the Marian party. His first extant speech was delivered in 81, when he was 26 years of age, on behalf of P. Quintius. Next year 80, he defended Sex Roscius of Ameria, charged with parricide by Chrysogonus, a favourite freedman of Sulla. In 79 he went to Greece, partly that he might avoid Sulla, whom he had offended, but partly also that he might improve his health and complete his course of study. At Athens he formed the friendship with Pomponius Atticus which lasted to his death, and at Rhodes he once more placed himself under the care of Molo. After an absence of 2 years, Cicero returned to Rome (77), with his health firmly established and his oratorical powers greatly improved. He again came forward as an orator in the forum, and soon obtained the greatest distinction. His success in the forum paved for him the way to the high offices of state. In 75 he was quaestor in Sicily, returned to Rome in 74, and for the next 4 years was engaged in pleading causes. In 70 he distinguished himself by the impeachment of VERRES, and in 69 he was curule aedile. In 66 he was praetor, and while holding this office he defended Cluentius in the speech still extant, and delivered his celebrated oration in favour of the Manilian law, which appointed Pompey to the command of the Mithridatic war. Two years afterwards he gained the great object of his ambition, and although a *novus homo* was elected consul, with C. Antonius as a colleague. He entered upon the office on the 1st of January, 63. Not having any real sympathy with the popular party, he now deserted his former friends, and connected himself closely with the aristocracy. The consulship of Cicero was distinguished by the outbreak of the conspiracy of Catiline, which was suppressed and finally crushed by Cicero's prudence and energy. [CATILINA.] For this service Cicero received the highest honours; he was addressed as "father of his country," and thanksgivings in his name were voted to the gods. But as soon as he had laid down the consulship, he had to contend with the popular party, and especially with the friends of the conspirators. He also mortally offended Clodius, who, in order to have his revenge, brought forward a bill banishing any one who should be found to have put a Roman citizen to death untried. [CLODIUS.] The triumvirs, Caesar, Pompey, and Crassus, left Cicero to his fate; Cicero's courage failed him; he voluntarily retired from Rome before the measure of Clodius was put to the vote, and crossed over to Greece. Here he gave way to unmanly despair and excessive sorrow. Meanwhile his friends at Rome were exerting themselves on his behalf, and obtained his recal from banishment in the course of next year (55). Taught by experience, Cicero would no longer join the senate in opposition to the triumvirs, and retired to a great extent from public life. In 52 he was compelled, much against his will, to go to the East as governor of Cilicia. He returned to Italy towards the end of 50, and arrived in the neighbourhood of Rome on the 4th of January, 49, just as the civil war between Caesar and Pompey broke out. After long hesitating which side to join, he finally determined to throw in his lot with Pompey, and crossed over to Greece in June. After the battle of Pharsalia (48), Cicero was not only pardoned by Caesar, but, when the latter landed at Brundusium in September, 47, he greeted Cicero with the greatest kindness and respect, and allowed him to return to Rome. Cicero now retired into privacy, and during the next 3 or 4 years composed the greater part of his philosophical and rhetorical works. The murder of Caesar on the 15th of March, 44, again brought Cicero into public life. He put himself at the head of the republican party and in his Philippic orations attacked M. Antony with unmeasured vehemence. But this proved his ruin. On the fomation of the triumvirate between Octavian, Antony,

and Lepidus (27th of November, 43), Cicero's name was in the list of the proscribed. He endeavoured to escape, but was overtaken by the soldiers near Formiae. His slaves were ready to defend their master with their lives, but Cicero commanded them to desist, and offered his neck to the executioners. They instantly cut off his head and hands, which were conveyed to Rome, and, by the orders of Antony, nailed to the Rostra. Cicero perished on the 7th of December, 43, when he had nearly completed his 64th year.—By nis first wife Terentia, Cicero had 2 children, a daughter TULLIA, whose death in 45 caused him the greatest sorrow, and a son Marcus (No. 3). His wife Terentia, to whom he had been united for 30 years, he divorced in 46, and soon afterwards he married a young and wealthy maiden, PUBILIA, his ward, but this new alliance was speedily dissolved. As a statesman and a citizen, Cicero was weak, changeful, and excessively vain. His only great work was the suppression of Catiline's conspiracy. It is as an author that he deserves the highest praise. In his works the Latin language appears in the greatest perfection. They may be divided into the following subjects :—I. RHETORICAL WORKS. Of these there were seven, which have come down to us more or less complete. The best known of these is the "De Oratore," written at the request of his brother Quintus; it is the most perfect of his rhetorical works.— II. PHILOSOPHICAL WORKS. 1. *Political Philosophy*. Under this head we have the "De Republica" and "De Legibus," both of which are written in the form of a dialogue. A large portion of both works is preserved.—2. *Philosophy of Morals*. In his work "De Officiis," which was written for the use of his son Marcus, at that time residing at Athens, the tone of his teaching is pure and elevated. He also wrote "De Senectute" and "De Amicitia," which are preserved.—3. *Speculative Philosophy*. Under this head the most noted of his works are the "De Finibus," or inquiry into "the chief good," and the "Tusculan Disputations."—4. *Theology*. In the "De Natura Deorum" he gives an account of the speculations of the ancients concerning a Divine Being, which is continued in the "De Divinatione."—III. ORATIONS. Of these 56 have come down to us.—IV. EPISTLES. Cicero during the most important period of his life maintained a close correspondence with Atticus, and with a wide circle of literary and political friends and connexions. We now have upwards of 800 letters, undoubtedly genuine, extending over a space of 26 years, and commonly arranged under "Epistolae ad Familiares s. ad Diversos," "Ad Atticum," and "Ad Quintum Fratrem."—(2) Q. TULLIUS CICERO, brother of the orator, was born about 102, and was educated along with his brother. In 67 he was aedile, in 62 praetor, and for the next 3 years governed Asia as propraetor. In 55 he went to Gaul as legatus to Caesar, whose approbation he gained by his military abilities and gallantry; in 51 he accompanied his brother as legate to Cilicia; and on the breaking out of the civil war in 49 he joined Pompey. After the battle of Pharsalia, he was pardoned by Caesar. He was proscribed by the triumvirs, and was put to death in 43. —(3) M. TULLIUS CICERO, only son of the orator and his wife Terentia, was born 65. On the death of Caesar (44) he joined the republican party, served as military tribune under Brutus in Macedonia, and after the battle of Philippi (42) fled to Sex. Pompey in Sicily. When peace was concluded between the triumvirs and Sex. Pompey in 39, Cicero returned to Rome, and was favourably received by Octavian, who at length assumed him as his colleague in the consulship (B. c. 30, from 13th Sept.). By a singular coincidence, the despatch announcing the capture of the fleet of Antony, which was immediately followed by his death, was addressed to the new consul in his official capacity.—(4) Q. TULLIUS CICERO, son of No. 2, and of Pomponia, sister of Atticus, was born 66 or 67, and perished with his father in the proscription, 43.

CICONES (-um), a Thracian people on the Hebrus, and near the coast.

CILICIA (-ae), a district in the S. E. of Asia Minor, bounded by the Mediterranean on the S., M. Amanus on the E., and M. Taurus on the N. The W. part of Cilicia is intersected by the offshoots of the Taurus, while in its E. part the mountain chains enclose much larger tracts of level country; and hence arose the division of the country into C. Aspera or Trachea, and C. Campestris; the latter was also called Cilicia Propria. The first inhabitants of the country are supposed to have been of the Syrian race. The mythical story derived their name from Cilix, the son of Agenor, who started with his brothers, Cadmus and Phoenix, for Europe, out stopped short on the coast of Asia Minor, and peopled with his followers the plain of Cilicia. The country remained independent till the time of the Persian Empire, under which it formed a satrapy, but it appears to have been still governed by its native princes. Alexander subdued it on his march into Upper Asia; and, after the division of his empire, 'it formed a part of the kingdom of the Seleucidae: its plains were settled by Greeks, and the old inhabitants were for the most part driven back into the mountains of

C. Aspera, where they remained virtually independent, practising robbery by land and piracy by sea, till Pompey drove them from the sea in his war against the pirates; and having rescued the level country from the power of Tigranes, who had overrun it, he erected it into a Roman province, B.C. 67—66. The mountain country was not made a province till the reign of Vespasian. The Cilicians bore a low character among the Greeks and Romans. The Carians, Cappadocians, and Cilicians, were called the 3 bad K's.

CILICIAE PYLAE or PORTAE, the chief pass between Cappadocia and Cilicia, through the Taurus, on the road from Tyana to Tarsus.

CILICIUM MARE, the N.E. portion of the Mediterranean, between Cilicia and Cyprus, as far as the Gulf of Issus.

CILIX. [CILICIA.]

CILLA (-ae), a small town in the Troad, celebrated for its temple of Apollo surnamed Cillaeus.

CILNII (-ōrum), a powerful Etruscan family in Arretium, driven out of their native town in B.C. 301, but restored by the Romans. The Cilnii were nobles or Lucumones in their state, and some of them in ancient times may have held even the kingly dignity. The name has been rendered chiefly memorable by C. Cilnius Maecenas [MAECENAS.]

CIMBER (-ri), L. TILLIUS (-i), (not Tullius), a friend of Caesar, who gave him the province of Bithynia, but subsequently one of Caesar's murderers, B.C. 44.

CIMBRI (-ōrum), a Celtic people, probably of the same race as the Cymry [CELTAE]. They appear to have inhabited the peninsula, which was called after them CHERSONESUS CIMBRICA (Jutland). In conjunction with the Teutoni and Ambrones, they migrated S., with their wives and children, towards the close of the 2nd century B.C.; and the whole host is said to have contained 300,000 fighting men. They defeated several Roman armies, and caused the greatest alarm at Rome. In B.C. 113 they defeated the consul Papirius Carbo, near Noreia, and then crossed over into Gaul, which they ravaged in all directions. In 109 they defeated the consul Junius Silanus; in 107, the consul Cassius Longinus, who fell in the battle; and in 105 they gained their most brilliant victory, near the Rhone, over the united armies of the consul Cn. Mallius and the proconsul Servilius Caepio. Instead of crossing the Alps, the Cimbri, fortunately for Rome, marched into Spain, where they remained two or three years. The Romans, meantime, had been making preparations to resist their formidable foes, and had placed their troops under the command of Marius. The barbarians returned to Gaul in 102. In that year the Teutoni were defeated and cut to pieces by Marius, near Aquae Sextiae (*Aix*) in Gaul; and next year (101) the Cimbri and their allies were likewise destroyed by Marius and Catulus, in the decisive battle of the Campi Raudii, near Verona, in the N. of Italy.

CĬMĬNUS or CĬMĬNĬUS MONS, a range of mountains in Etruria, thickly covered with wood (Saltus Ciminius, Silva Ciminia), near a lake of the same name, N.W. of Tarquinii, between the Lacus Vulsiniensis and Soracte.

CIMMĔRĬI (-ōrum), the name of a mythical and of a historical people. The mythical Cimmerii, mentioned by Homer, dwelt in the furthest W. on the ocean, enveloped in constant mists and darkness. Later writers sought to localise them, and accordingly placed them, either in Italy near the lake Avernus, or in Spain, or in the Tauric Chersonesus.—The historical Cimmerii dwelt on the Palus Maeotis (*Sea of Azov*), in the Tauric Chersonesus, and in Asiatic Sarmatia. Driven from their abodes by the Scythians, they passed into Asia Minor on the N.E., and penetrated W. as far as Aeolis and Ionia. They took Sardis B.C. 635 in the reign of Ardys, king of Lydia; but they were expelled from Asia by Alyattes, the grandson of Ardys.

CIMMERIUS BOSPŎRUS. [BOSPORUS.]

CĬMŎLUS (-i), an island in the Aegaean sea, one of the Cyclades, between Siphnos and Melos, celebrated for its fine white earth, used by fullers for cleaning cloths.

CĬMON (-ōnis). (1) Father of the celebrated Miltiades, was secretly murdered by order of the sons of Pisistratus.—(2) Grandson of the preceding, and son of Miltiades. On the death of his father (B.C. 489), he was imprisoned because he was unable to pay his fine of 50 talents, which was eventually paid by Callias on his marriage with Elpinice, Cimon's sister. Cimon frequently commanded the Athenian fleet in their aggressive war against the Persians. His most brilliant success was in 466, when he defeated a large Persian fleet, and on the same day landed and routed their land forces also on the river Eurymedon in Pamphylia. The death of Aristides and the banishment of Themistocles left Cimon without a rival at Athens for some years. But his influence gradually declined as that of Pericles increased. In 461 he was ostracized through the influence of the popular party in Athens, who were enraged with him and with the Spartans. He was subsequently recalled, and through his intervention a 5

years' truce was made between Athens and Sparta, 450. In 449 the war was renewed with Persia, Cimon received the command, and with 200 ships sailed to Cyprus; here, while besieging Citium, illness or the effects of a wound carried him off.—Cimon was of a cheerful convivial temper; frank and affable in his manners. Having obtained a great fortune by his share of the Persian spoils, he displayed unbounded liberality. His orchards and gardens were thrown open; his fellow demesmen were free daily to his table, and his public bounty verged on ostentation.

CĬNĂRĂ (-ae), a small island in the Aegaean sea, E. of Naxos, celebrated for its artichokes (κινάρα).

CINCINNĀTUS, L. QUINTĬUS (-i), a favourite hero of the old Roman republic, and a model of old Roman frugality and integrity. He lived on his farm, cultivating the land with his own hand. In B.C. 458 he was called from the plough to the dictatorship, in order to deliver the Roman consul and army from the perilous position in which they had been placed by the Aequians. He saved the Roman army, defeated the enemy, and, after holding the dictatorship only 16 days, returned to his farm. In 439, at the age of 80, he was a 2nd time appointed dictator to oppose the alleged machinations of Sp. Maelius.

CĬNĔĂS (-ae), a Thessalian, the friend and minister of Pyrrhus, king of Epirus. He was the most eloquent man of his day, and Pyrrhus prized his persuasive powers so highly, that "the words of Cineas" (he was wont to say) "had won him more cities than his own arms." The most famous passage in his life is his embassy to Rome, with proposals for peace from Pyrrhus, after the battle of Heraclea (B.C. 280). Cineas spared no arts to gain favour. Thanks to his wonderful memory, on the day after his arrival he was able (we are told) to address all the senators and knights by name. The senate, however, rejected his proposals mainly through the dying eloquence of old App. Claudius Caecus. The ambassador returned and told the king that there was no people like that people,— their city was a temple, their senate an assembly of kings.

CINGA (-ae: *Cinca*), a river in Hispania Tarraconensis, falling with the Sicoris into the Iberus.

CINGĔTŎRIX (-ĭgis), a Gaul, one of the first men in the city of the Treviri (*Trèves*, *Trier*), attached himself to the Romans, though son-in-law to Indutiomarus, the head of the independent party.

CINGŬLUM (-i), a town in Picenum on a rock, built by Labienus, shortly before the breaking out of the civil war, B.C. 49.

CINNA (-ae). (1) L. CORNELIUS CINNA, the famous leader of the popular party during the absence of Sulla in the East. (B.C. 87— 84.) In 87 Sulla allowed Cinna to be elected consul with Cn. Octavius, on condition of his taking an oath not to alter the constitution as then existing. But as soon as Sulla had left Italy, he began his endeavour to over-power the senate, and to recall Marius and his party. He was, however, defeated by his colleague Octavius in the forum, was obliged to fly the city, and was deposed by the senate from the consulate. But he soon returned, and with the aid of Marius took possession of Rome, massacred Sulla's friends, and for three successive years 86, 85, 84, was elected consul. [MARIUS]. In 84 Sulla prepared to return from Greece; and Cinna was slain by his own troops, when he ordered them to cross over from Italy to Greece, where he intended to encounter Sulla.—(2) L. CORNE-LIUS CINNA, son of No. 1., joined M. Lepidus in his attempt to overthrow the constitution of Sulla, 78. Caesar made him Praetor, yet he approved of Caesar's assassination.—(3) HEL-VIUS CINNA, a poet of considerable renown, the friend of Catullus. In B.C. 44 he was tribune of the plebs, when he was murdered by the mob, who mistook him for his namesake Cornelius Cinna.

CĪNYPS (-ўphis: *Wad-Khakan* or *Kinifo*), a small river on the N. coast of Africa, be-tween the Syrtes, forming the E. boundary of the proper territory of the African Tripolis. The district about it was called by the same name, and was famous for its fine-haired goats. The Roman poets use the adjective Cinyphius in the general sense of Libyan or African.

CĪNŸRAS (-ae), son of Apollo, king of Cyprus, and priest of the Paphian Aphrodite (Venus). By his own daughter Myrrha or Smyrna, he became the father of Adonis. [ADONIS]. Hence we find in the poets Myrrha called *Cinyreia virgo* and Adonis *Cinyreius juvenis*.

CIRCĒ (-es), daughter of Helios (the Sun) by Perse, and sister of Aeëtes, distinguished for her magic arts. She dwelt in the island of Aeaea, upon which Ulysses was cast. His companions, whom he sent to explore the land, tasted of the magic cup which Circe offered them, and were forthwith changed into swine, with the exception of Eurylochus, who brought the sad news to Ulysses. The latter, having received from Hermes (Mercury) the root *moly*, which for-tified him against enchantment, drank the magic cup without injury, and then com-pelled Circe to restore his companions to

ΕΤΑΙΡΟΙ ΤΕΘΗΡΙΩΜΕ— ΚΙΡΚΗ ΟΔΙΣΣΕΥΣ

Circe and Ulysses, and his Companions. (From an ancient Basrelief.)

their former shape. After this he tarried a whole year with her, and she became by him the mother of Telegonus, the reputed founder of Tusculum.

Circe offering the Cup. (Gell's Pompeiana, pl. 72.)

CIRCĒII (-ōrum), an ancient town of Latium on the promontory Circeium, said by the Roman poets to have been the abode of Circe.

CIRCĒSIUM (-i), a city of Mesopotamia, on the E. bank of the Euphrates, at the mouth of the Aborrhas.

CIRCUS. [ROMA.]

CIRRHA (-ae). [CRISSA.]

CIRTA (-ae), aft. CONSTANTĪNA (-ae) (*Constantineh*, Ru.), a city of the Massylii in Numidia, 50 Roman miles from the sea; the capital of Syphax, and of Masinissa and his successors. Its position on a height, surrounded by the river Ampsagas, made it almost impregnable, as the Romans found in the Jugurthine, and the French in the Alge-rine, wars. It was restored by Constantine the Great, in honour of whom it received its later name

CISSEUS (-ĕŏs or -ĕï), a king in Thrace, and father of Theano, or, according to others, of Hecuba, who is hence called Cissēïs.

CISSĬA (-ae), a very fertile district of Susiana, on the Choapses. The inhabitants, Cissii, were a wild free people, resembling the Persians in their manners.

CITHAERŎN (-ōnis), a lofty range of mountains, separating Boeotia from Megaris and Attica. It was sacred to Dionysus (Bacchus) and the Muses, and was celebrated for the death of Pentheus and Actaeon.

CĬTĬUM (-i). (1) A town in Cyprus, 200 stadia from Salamis, near the mouth of the Tetius : here Cimon, the celebrated Athenian, died, and Zeno, the founder of the Stoic school, was born.—(2) A town in Macedonia, N. W. of Beroea.

CĬUS (-i), an ancient city in Bithynia, on a bay of the Propontis called Ciānus Sinus, was colonized by the Milesians. It was destroyed by Philip III., king of Macedonia ; but was rebuilt by Prusias, king of Bithynia, from whom it was called Prusias.

CLĀNIS (-is). (1) A river of Etruria, forming 2 small lakes near Clusium, and flowing into the Tiber E. of Vulsinii.—(2) The more ancient name of the Liris.

CLĀNĬUS. [LITERNUS.]

CLĀRUS or CLĂROS (-i), a small town on the Ionian coast, near Colophon, with a celebrated temple and oracle of Apollo, surnamed Clarius.

CLASTIDĬUM (-i), a fortified town of the Ananes, in Gallia Cispadana, not far from the Po.

CLAUDIA QUINTA (-ae), a Roman matron, not a Vestal Virgin, as is frequently stated. When the vessel conveying the image of Cybele from Pessinus to Rome, had stuck fast in a shallow at the mouth of the Tiber, the soothsayers announced that only a chaste woman could move it. Claudia, who had been accused of incontinency, took hold of the rope, and the vessel forthwith followed her, B.C. 204.

CLAUDĬA GENS, patrician and plebeian. The patrician Claudii were of Sabine origin, and came to Rome in B.C. 504, when they were received among the patricians. [CLAUDIUS, No. 1.] They were noted for their pride and haughtiness, their disdain for the laws, and their hatred of the plebeians. They bore various surnames, which are given under CLAUDIUS, with the exception of those with the cognomen NERO, who are better known under the latter name. The plebeian Claudii were divided into several families, of which the most celebrated was that of MARCELLUS.

CLAUDIĀNUS, CLAUDĬUS (-i), the last of the Latin classic poets, flourished under Theodosius and his sons Arcadius and Honorius. He was a native of Alexandria, and removed to Rome, where he enjoyed the patronage of the all-powerful Stilicho. He was a heathen, and wrote a large number of poems, many of which are extant, and are distinguished by purity of language and poetical genius. He died about A.D. 408.

CLAUDĬUS (-i), patrician. See CLAUDIA GENS. (1) APP. CLAUDIUS SABINUS REGILLENSIS, a Sabine, of the town of Regillum or Regilli, who in his own country bore the name of Attus Clausus, being the advocate of peace with the Romans, when hostilities broke out between the two nations, withdrew with a large train of followers to Rome, B.C. 504. He was received into the ranks of the patricians, and lands beyond the Anio were assigned to his followers, who were formed into a new tribe, called the Claudian. He exhibited the characteristics which marked his descendants, and showed the most bitter hatred towards the plebeians. He was consul 495 ; and his conduct towards the plebeians led to their secession to the Mons Sacer, 494. — (2) APP. CLAUDIUS REGILL. SAB., the decemvir, 451 and 450. In the latter year his character betrayed itself in the most tyrannous conduct towards the plebeians, till his attempt against Virginia led to the overthrow of the decemvirate. App. was impeached by Virginius, but did not live to abide his trial. He either killed himself, or was put to death, in prison, by order of the tribunes. — (3) APP. CLAUDIUS CAECUS became blind before his old age. In his censorship (312), to which he was elected without having been consul previously, he built the Appian aqueduct, and commenced the Appian road, which was continued to Capua. He retained the censorship 4 years, in opposition to the law, which limited the length of the office to 18 months. In his old age, Appius, by his eloquent speech, induced the senate to reject the terms of peace which Cineas had proposed on behalf of Pyrrhus. Appius was the earliest Roman writer in prose and verse whose name has come down to us. — (4) APP. CL. PULCHER, brother of the celebrated tribune, whom he joined in opposing the recall of Cicero from banishment. He preceded Cicero as proconsul in Cilicia (53), fled with Pompey from Italy, and died before the battle of Pharsalia.—(5) P. CL. PULCHER, usually called CLODIUS, and not Claudius, brother of the preceding, the notorious enemy of Cicero, and one of the most profligate characters of a profligate age. In 62 he profaned the mysteries of the Bona Dea, which were celebrated by the Roman matrons in the house of Caesar ; was discovered; and next year, 61, when quaestor, was brought to trial, but obtained an acquittal by bribing the judges. He had attempted to prove an alibi; but Cicero's evidence showed that Clodius was with him in Rome only 3 hours before he pretended to have been at Interamna. In order to revenge himself upon Cicero, Clodius was adopted into a plebeian family, that he might obtain the formidable power of a tribune of the plebs. He was tribune 58, and, supported by the triumvirs Caesar, Pompey, and Crassus, drove Cicero into exile; but notwithstanding all his efforts, he was unable to prevent the recal of Cicero in the following year. [CICERO.] In 56 Clodius was aedile, and attempted to bring his enemy Milo to trial. Each had a large gang of gladiators in his pay, and frequent fights took place in the streets of Rome between the two parties. In 53, when Clodius was a candidate for the praetorship, and Milo for the consulship, on the 20th of January, 52, on the Appian road, near Bovillae, an affray ensued between their followers, in which Clodius was murdered. The mob was infuriated at the death of their favourite; and such tumults followed at the burial of Clodius, that Pompey was appointed sole consul, in order to restore order to the state. For the proceedings which followed, see MILO.

CLAUDIUS (-i) I., Roman emperor A.D. 41—54. His full name was TIB. CLAUDIUS DRUSUS NERO GERMANICUS. He was the younger son of Drusus, the brother of the emperor Tiberius, and of Antonia, and was born on August 1st, B.C. 10, at Lyons in Gaul. When he grew up he devoted the greater part of his time to literary pursuits, but was not allowed to take any part in public affairs. He had reached the age of 50, when he was suddenly raised by the soldiers to the imperial throne after the murder of Caligula. Claudius was not cruel, but the weakness of his character made him the slave of his wives and freedmen, and thus led him to consent to acts of tyranny which he would never have committed of his own accord. He was married 4 times. At the time of his accession he was married to his 3rd wife, the notorious Valeria Messalina, who governed him for some years, together with the freedmen Narcissus, Pallas, and others. After the execution of Messalina, A.D. 48, a fate which she richly merited, Claudius was still more unfortunate in choosing for his wife his niece Agrippina. She prevailed upon him to set aside his own son, Britannicus, and to adopt her son, Nero, that she might secure the succession for the latter. Claudius soon after regretted this step, and was in consequence

poisoned by Agrippina, 54. In his reign the southern part of Britain was made a Roman province, and Claudius himself went to Britain in 43, where he remained, however, only a short time, leaving the conduct of the war to his generals.

CLAUDIUS II. (M. AURELIUS CLAUDIUS), Roman emperor A.D. 268—270, was descended from an obscure family in Dardania or Illyria, and succeeded to the empire on the death of Gallienus (268). He defeated the Alemanni and Goths, and received in consequence the surname *Gothicus.* He died at Sirmium in 270, and was succeeded by Aurelian.

CLAZOMENAE (-arum), an important city of Asia Minor, and one of the 12 Ionian cities, lay on the N. coast of the Ionian peninsula, upon the gulf of Smyrna. It was the birthplace of Anaxagoras.

CLEANTHES (-is), a Stoic philosopher, born at Assos in Troas about B.C. 300. He first placed himself under Crates, and then under Zeno, whose disciple he continued for 19 years. In order to support himself, he worked all night at drawing water from gardens; but as he spent the whole day in philosophical pursuits, and had no visible means of support, he was summoned before the Areopagus to account for his way of living. The judges were so delighted by the evidence of industry which he produced, that they voted him 10 minae, though Zeno would not permit him to accept them. He succeeded Zeno in his school B.C. 263. He died about 220, at the age of 80, of voluntary starvation.

CLEARCHUS (-i), a Spartan, distinguished himself in several important commands during the latter part of the Peloponnesian war, and at the close of it persuaded the Spartans to send him as a general to Thrace, to protect the Greeks in that quarter against the Thracians. But having been recalled by the Ephors, and refusing to obey their orders, he was condemned to death. He thereupon crossed over to Cyrus, collected for him a large force of Greek mercenaries, and marched with him into Upper Asia, 401, in order to dethrone his brother Artaxerxes, being the only Greek who was aware of the prince's real object. After the battle of Cunaxa and the death of Cyrus, Clearchus and the other Greek generals were made prisoners by the treachery of Tissaphernes, and were put to death.

CLEOBIS. [BITON.]

CLEOBULUS (-i), one of the Seven Sages, of Lindus in Rhodes, son of Evagoras, lived about B.C. 580. He, as well as his daughter, Cleobuline or Cleobule, were celebrated for their skill in riddles. To the latter is ascribed a well-known one on the subject of the year :—" A father has 12 children, and each of these 30 daughters, on one side white, and on the other side black, and though immortal they all die."

CLEOMBROTUS (-i). (1) Son of Anaxandrides, king of Sparta, became regent after the battle of Thermopylae, B.C. 480, for Plistarchus, infant son of Leonidas, but died in the same year, and was succeeded in the regency by his son Pausanias.—(2) King of Sparta, son of Pausanias, succeeded his brother Agesipolis I., and reigned B.C. 380—371. He commanded the Spartan troops several times against the Thebans, and fell at the battle of Leuctra (371), after fighting most gravely.—(3) King of Sparta, son-in-law of Leonidas II., in whose place he was made king by the party of Agis IV., about 243. On the return of Leonidas, Cleombrotus was deposed and banished to Tegea, about 240. —(4) An academic philosopher of Ambracia, said to have killed himself, after reading the *Phaedon* of Plato ; not that he had any sufferings to escape from, but that he might exchange this life for a better.

CLEOMENES (-is). (1) King of Sparta, son of Anaxandrides, reigned B.C. 520—491. He was a man of an enterprising but wild character. In 510 he commanded the forces by whose assistance Hippias was driven from Athens, and not long after he assisted Isagoras and the aristocratical party, against Clisthenes. By bribing the priestess at Delphi, he effected the deposition of his colleague Demaratus, 491. Soon afterwards he was seized with madness and killed himself.—(2) King of Sparta, son of Cleombrotus I., reigned 370—309.—(3) King of Sparta, son of Leonidas II., reigned 236—222. While still young he married Agiatis, the widow of Agis IV. ; and following the example of the latter, he endeavoured to restore the ancient Spartan constitution. He succeeded in his object, and put the Ephors to death. He was engaged in a long contest with the Achaean League and Antigonus Doson, king of Macedonia, but was at length defeated at the battle of Sellasia (222), and fled to Egypt, where he put an end to his own life, 220.

CLEON (-onis), son of Cleaenetus, was originally a tanner, and first came forward in public as an opponent to Pericles. On the death of this great man, B.C. 429, Cleon became the favourite of the people; and for about 6 years of the Peloponnesian war (428 —422) was the head of the party opposed to peace. In 427 he strongly advocated in the assembly that the Mytilenaeans should be put to death. In 424 he obtained his greatest

glory by taking prisoners the Spartans in the island of Sphacteria, and bringing them in safety to Athens. Puffed up by this success, he obtained the command of an Athenian army, to oppose Brasidas in Thrace ; but he was defeated by Brasidas, under the walls of Amphipolis, and fell in the battle, 422. Aristophanes and Thucydides both speak of him as a vile, unprincipled demagogue. In this they were probably too severe. The chief attack of Aristophanes upon Cleon was in the *Knights* (424), in which Cleon figures as an actual dramatis persona, and, in default of an artificer bold enough to make the mask, was represented by the poet himself with his face smeared with wine lees.

CLEONAE (-arum). (1) An ancient town in Argolis, on the road from Corinth to Argos, on a river of the same name flowing into the Corinthian gulf. In its neighbourhood was Nemea, where Hercules killed the lion, which is accordingly called *Cleonaeus Leo* by the poets.—(2) A town in the peninsula Athos in Chalcidice.

CLEOPATRA (-ae). (1) Niece of Attalus, married Philip B.C. 337, on whose murder she was put to death by Olympias.—(2) Daughter of Philip and Olympias, and sister of Alexander the Great, married Alexander, king of Epirus, 336. It was at the celebration of her nuptials that Philip was murdered by Pausanias.—(3) Eldest daughter of Ptolemy Auletes, celebrated for her beauty and fascination, was 17 at the death of her father (51), who appointed her heir of his kingdom in conjunction with her younger brother, Ptolemy, whom she was to marry. She was expelled from the throne by Pothinus and Achillas, his guardians ; but having won by her charms the support of Caesar, he replaced her on the throne in conjunction with her brother. She had a son by Caesar, called Caesarion, and she afterwards followed him to Rome, where she appears to have been at the time of his death, 44. She then returned to Egypt, and in 41 she met Antony in Cilicia. She was now in her 28th year, and in the perfection of matured beauty, which, in conjunction with her talents and eloquence, completely won the heart of Antony, who henceforth was her devoted lover and slave. In the war between Octavian and Antony, Cleopatra accompanied her lover, and was present at the battle of Actium (31), in the midst of which she retreated with her fleet, and thus hastened the loss of the day. She fled to Alexandria, where she was joined by Antony. Seeing Antony's fortunes desperate, she entered into negotiations with Augustus, and promised to make away with Antony. She fled to a mausoleum she had built, and then caused a report of her death to be spread. Antony, resolving not to survive her, stabbed himself, and was drawn up into the mausoleum, where he died in her arms. She then tried to gain the love of Augustus, but her charms failed in softening his colder heart. Seeing that he had determined to carry her captive to Rome, she put an end to her own life by the poison of an asp. She died in the 39th year of her age (B.C. 30), and with her ended the dynasty of the Ptolemies in Egypt, which was now made a Roman province.

CLIMAX (-ăcis), the name applied to the W. termination of the Taurus range, which extends along the W. coast of the Pamphylian Gulf, N. of Phaselis in Lycia. Alexander made a road between it and the sea.

CLIMBERRUM. [AUSCI.]

CLIO. [MUSAE.]

CLISTHĔNĔS (-is), an Athenian, son of Megacles and Agarista, who was the daughter of Clisthenes, the tyrant of Sicyon. He appears as the head of the Alcmaeonid clan on the banishment of the Pisistratidae. Finding, however, that he could not cope with his political rival Isagoras except through the aid of the commons, he set himself to increase the power of the latter. The principal change which he introduced was the abolition of the 4 ancient tribes and the establishment of 10 new ones in their stead, B.C. 510. He is also said to have instituted ostracism. Isagoras and his party called in the aid of the Spartans, but Clisthenes and his friends eventually triumphed.

CLĪTOR (-ŏris) or CLĪTŎRĬUM (-i), a town in the N. of Arcadia on a river of the same name, a tributary of the Aroanius: there was a fountain in the neighbourhood, the waters of which are said to have given to persons who drank of them a dislike for wine.

CLĪTUMNUS (-i), a small river in Umbria, springing from a beautiful rock in a grove of cypress trees, where was a sanctuary of the god Clitumnus, and falling into the Tinia, a tributary of the Tiber.

CLĪTUS (-i), a Macedonian, one of Alexander's generals and friends, who saved the life of the latter at the battle of Granicus, B.C. 334. In 328 he was slain by Alexander at a banquet, when both parties were heated with wine, and Clitus had provoked the king's resentment by insolent language. Alexander was inconsolable at his friend's death.

CLŌDĬUS, another form of the name Claudius. [CLAUDIUS.]

CLŌDĬUS ALBĪNUS. [ALBINUS.]

CLOELĬA (-ae), a Roman virgin, one of the hostages given to Porsena, who escaped from the Etruscan camp, and swam across the Tiber to Rome. She was sent back by the Romans to Porsena, who was so struck with her gallant deed, that he not only set her at liberty, but allowed her to take with her a part of the hostages. Porsena also rewarded her with a horse adorned with splendid trappings, and the Romans with a statue of a female on horseback.

CLOTA AESTUĀRĬUM (Frith of Clyde), on the W. coast of Scotland.

CLŌTHŌ (-ūs), one of the Fates. [MOIRAE.]

CLŬENTĬUS HĂBĬTUS, A., (-i), of Larinum, accused in B.C. 74 his own step-father, Statius Albius Oppianicus, of having attempted to procure his death by poison. Oppianicus was condemned, and it was generally believed that the judges had been bribed by Cluentius. In 66, Cluentius was himself accused by young Oppianicus, son of Statius Albius, who had died in the interval, of 3 distinct acts of poisoning. He was defended by Cicero in the oration still extant.

CLŬPĔA or CLŸPĔA. [ASPIS.]

CLŪSĬUM (Chiusi), one of the most powerful of the 12 Etruscan cities, originally called Camers or Camars, situated on an eminence above the river Clanis, and S.W. of the LACUS CLUSINUS (L. di Chiusi). It was the royal residence of Porsena, and in its neighbourhood was the celebrated sepulchre of this king in the form of a labyrinth. Subsequently Clusium was in alliance with the Romans, by whom it was regarded as a bulwark against the Gauls. Its siege by the Gauls, B.C. 391, led, as is well known, to the capture of Rome itself by the Gauls. In its neighbourhood were warm baths.

CLŪSĬUS (-i), a surname of Janus, whose temple was closed in peace.

CLỸMĔNĔ (-es). (1) Daughter of Oceanus and Tethys, and wife of Iapetus, to whom she bore Atlas, Prometheus, and others.—(2) Mother of Phaëton by Helios (the Sun), whence Phaëton is called Clȳmĕnēĭus.—(3) A relative of Menelaus and a companion of Helena, with whom she was carried off by Paris.

CLỸTAEMNESTRA (-ae), daughter of Tyndareus and Leda, sister of Castor, Pollux, and Helena; wife of Agamemnon; and mother of Orestes, Iphigenia, and Electra. During her husband's absence at Troy she lived in adultery with Aegisthus, and on his return to Mycenae she murdered him with the help of Aegisthus. [AGAMEMNON.] She was subsequently put to death by her son Orestes, to revenge the murder of his father.

CLỸTĬE (-es), a daughter of Oceanus, changed into the plant heliotropium.

CNIDUS or GNIDUS (-i), a celebrated city of Asia Minor, on the promontory of

Triopium on the coast of Caria, was a Lace-aaemonian colony. It was built partly on the mainland and partly on an island joined to the coast by a causeway, and had two harbours. It had a considerable commerce ; and it was resorted to by travellers from all parts of the civilised world, that they might see the statue of Aphroditē (Venus) by Praxiteles, which stood in her temple here. Among the celebrated natives of the city were Ctesias, Eudoxus, Sostratus, and Agatharcides.

CNŌSUS or GNŌSUS, subsequently CNOS-SUS or GNOSSUS (-i), an ancient town of Crete, and the capital of king Minos; situated at a short distance from the N. coast ; colonised at an early time by Dorians. It is frequently mentioned by the poets in consequence of its connexion with Minos, Ariadne, the Minotaur, and the Labyrinth ; and the adjective Cnossius is used as equivalent to Cretan.

CŌCĂLUS (-i), a mythical king of Sicily, who kindly received Daedalus on his flight from Crete, and with the assistance of his daughters put Minos to death, when the latter came in pursuit of Daedalus.

COCCEIUS NERVA. [NERVA.]

CŌCHĒ, a city on the Tigris, near Ctesiphon.

COCLĒS (-ĭtis), HŌRĀTIUS (-i), that is, Horatius the " one-eyed," a hero of the old Roman lays, is said to have defended the Sublician bridge along with Sp. Lartius and T. Herminius against the whole Etruscan army under Porsena, while the Romans broke down the bridge behind them. When the work was nearly finished, Horatius sent back his 2 companions. As soon as the bridge was quite destroyed, he plunged into the stream and swam across to the city in safety amid the arrows of the enemy. The state raised a statue to his honour, which was placed in the comitium, and allowed him as much land as he could plough round in one day.

COCOSSATES, a people in Aquitania in Gaul, mentioned along with the Tarbelli.

CŌCȲLĬUM (-i), an Aeolian city in Mysia, whose inhabitants are mentioned by Xenophon.

CŌCȲTUS (-i), a river in Epirus, a tributary of the Acheron. Like the Acheron, the Cocytus was supposed to be connected with the lower world, and hence came to be described as a river in the lower world.

CODOMANNUS. [DARIUS.]

CŌDRUS (-i). (1) Son of Melanthus, and last king of Athens. When the Dorians invaded Attica from Peloponnesus, an oracle declared, that they should be victorious if the life of the Attic king was spared. Codrus

thereupon resolved to sacrifice himself for his country. He entered the camp of the enemy in disguise, commenced quarrelling with the soldiers, and was slain in the dispute. When the Dorians discovered the death of the Attic king, they returned home. Tradition adds, that as no one was thought worthy to succeed such a patriotic king, the kingly dignity was abolished, and Medon, son of Codrus, was appointed archon for life instead.—(2) A Roman poet, ridiculed by Virgil.

COELA, " the Hollows of Euboea," the W. coast of Euboea, between the promontories Caphareus and Chersonesus, very dangerous to ships : here a part of the Persian fleet was wrecked B.C. 480.

COELĒSȲRĬA (-ae : i. e. Hollow Syria), the name given to the great valley between the two ranges of M. Lebanon (Libanus and Anti-Libanus), in the S. of Syria, bordering upon Phoenicia on the W. and Palestine on the S. In the wars between the Ptolemies and the Seleucidae, the name was applied to the whole of the S. portion of Syria, which became subject for some time to the kings of Egypt.

COELIUS. [CAELIUS.]

COLCHIS (-ĭdos or -ĭdis), a country of Asia, bounded on the W. by the Euxine, on the N. by the Caucasus, on the E. by Iberia. The land of Colchis (or Aea), and its river Phasis, are famous in the Greek mythology. [ARGONAUTAE.] It was a very fertile country; but it was most famous for its manufactures of linen, on account of which, and of certain physical resemblances, Herodotus supposed the Colchians to have been a colony from Egypt. The land was governed by its native princes, until Mithridates Eupator made it subject to the kingdom of Pontus. After the Mithridatic war, it was overrun by the Romans, but they did not subdue it till the time of Trajan.

CŌLĬAS, a promontory on the W. coast of Attica, 20 stadia S. of Phalerum, with a temple of Aphroditē (Venus), where some of the Persian ships were cast after the battle of Salamis.

COLLĀTĬA (-ae), a Sabine town in Latium, near the right bank of the Anio, taken by Tarquinius Priscus.

COLLĀTĪNUS, L. TARQUINIUS (-i), son of Egerius, and nephew of Tarquinius Priscus, derived the surname Collatīnus from the town Collatia, of which his father had been appointed governor. The violence offered by Sex. Tarquinius to his wife Lucretia, led to the dethronement of Tarquinius Superbus. Collatinus and L. Junius Brutus were the first consuls ; but as the people could not endure the rule of any of the hated race of the Tarquins, Collatinus resigned his office, and retired from Rome to Lavinium.

COLLȲTUS (-i), a demus in Attica, included within the walls of Athens. It was the demus of Plato and the residence of Timon the misanthrope.

CŎLŌNAE, a small town in the Troad.

CŎLŌNĬA AGRIPPĪNA, or AGRIPPĪNENSIS (*Cologne* on the Rhine), originally the chief town of the Ubii, and called *Oppidum*, or *Civitas Ubiorum*, was a place of small importance till A. D. 51, when a Roman colony was planted in the town by the emperor Claudius, at the instigation of his wife Agrippina, who was born here, and from whom it derived its new name. It soon became a large and flourishing city, and was the capital of Lower Germany.

CŎLŌNUS (-i), a demus of Attica, 10 stadia, or a little more than a mile N. W. of Athens, near the Academy; celebrated for a temple of Poseidon (Neptune), a grove of the Eumenides, the tomb of Oedipus, and as the birthplace of Sophocles, who describes it in his Oedipus Coloneus.

CŎLŎPHŌN (-ōnis), one of the 12 Ionian cities of Asia Minor, stood about 2 miles from the coast, between Lebedus and Ephesus, on the river Halesus, which was famous for the coldness of its water. Its harbour was called Notium. Besides claiming to be the birthplace of Homer, Colophon was the native city of Mimnermus, Hermesianax, and Nicander. It was also celebrated for the oracle of Apollo Clarius in its neighbourhood. [CLARUS.]

CŎLOSSAE (-ārum), once an important city of Great Phrygia, on the river Lycus, but so reduced subsequently that it might have been forgotten but for the epistle written to its inhabitants by the apostle Paul.

CŎLŬMELLA (-ae), L. JŪNĬUS MŎDĔRĀTUS (-i), a native of Gades, in Spain, and a contemporary of Seneca. We have no particulars of his life, but Rome appears to have been his ordinary residence. He wrote a work upon agriculture (*De Re Rustica*), in 12 books, which is still extant. His style is easy and ornate.

COLUMNAE HERCULIS. [ABYLA; CALPE.]

CŎMĀNA (-ōrum). (1) A city of Pontus, upon the river Iris, celebrated for its temple of Artemis Taurica (Diana), the foundation of which tradition ascribed to Orestes. The high priests of this temple took rank next after the king, and their domain was increased by Pompey after the Mithridatic war.—(2) A city of Cappadocia, also celebrated for a temple of Artemis Taurica, the foundation of which was likewise ascribed by tradition to Orestes.

COMBRĒA (-ae), a town in the Macedonian district of Crossaea.

COMĪNĬUM (-i), a town in Samnium, destroyed by the Romans in the Samnite wars.

COMMĀGĒNĒ (-es), the N. E.-most district of Syria, lying between the Taurus and the Euphrates. It formed a part of the kingdom of Syria, after the fall of which it maintained its independence under a race of kings, the family of the Seleucidae, and was not united to the Roman empire till the reign of Vespasian.

COMMĬUS (-i), king of the Atrebates, was advanced to that dignity by Caesar. He was sent by Caesar to Britain, but he was cast into chains by the Britons, and was not released till the Britons had been defeated by Caesar. In B. C. 52 he joined the other Gauls in their great revolt against the Romans, and continued in arms, even after the capture of Alesia.

COMMŎDUS, L. AURĒLĬUS (-i), a Roman emperor, A. D. 180—192, son of M. Aurelius and the younger Faustina, was born at Lanuvium, 161, and was thus scarcely 20 when he succeeded to the empire. He was an unworthy son of a noble father. Notwithstanding the great care which his father had bestowed upon his education, he turned out one of the most sanguinary and licentious tyrants that ever disgraced a throne. He sought to gain popular applause by fighting with the wild beasts in the amphitheatre; and having slain immense numbers of them, demanded worship for himself, as being the god Hercules. One of his concubines, whom he had determined to put to death, administered poison to him; but as the poison worked slowly, Narcissus, a celebrated athlete, was ordered to strangle him, Dec. 31, 192.

COMPSA (-ae), a town of the Hirpini, in Samnium, near the sources of the Aufidus.

CŎMUM (-i: *Como*), a town in Gallia Cisalpina, at the S. extremity of the W. branch of the Lacus Larius (*L. di Como*). It was originally a town of the Insubrian Gauls, and subsequently a Roman colony. It was the birthplace of the younger Pliny.

CŎMUS (-i), the god of festive mirth and joy, represented as a winged youth, occurs only in the later times of antiquity.

CONCORDĬA (-ae), a Roman goddess, the personification of concord, had several temples at Rome. The earliest was built by Camillus, in commemoration of the reconciliation between the patricians and the plebeians, after the enactment of the Licinian rogations, B.C. 367. In this temple the senate frequently met. Concordia is represented on coins as a matron, holding in her left hand a cornucopia, and in her right either an olive branch or a patera.

CONDRŪSI (-ōrum), a German people in Gallia Belgica, the dependents of the Treviri, dwelt between the Eburones and the Treviri.

CONFLŬENTES (-ium: *Coblentz*), a town in Germany, at the confluence of the Moselle and the Rhine.

CŌNŌN (-ōnis), a distinguished Athenian general, held several important commands in the Peloponnesian war. After the defeat of the Athenians by Lysander at Aegos Potami (B.C. 405), Conon, who was one of the generals, escaped with 8 ships, and took refuge with Evagoras in Cyprus, where he remained for some years. In 394 he gained a decisive victory over Pisander, the Spartan general, off Cnidus.—(2) Of Samos, a distinguished mathematician and astronomer, lived in the time of the Ptolemies Philadelphus and Euergetes (B.C. 283—222).

CONSENTES (-ium) DII (-ōrum), the 12 Etruscan gods who formed the council of Jupiter, consisting of six male and six female divinities. We do not know the names of all of them, but it is certain that Juno, Minerva, Summanus, Vulcan, Saturn, and Mars were among them.

CONSENTĬA (-ae), chief town of the Bruttii on the river Crathis; here Alaric died.

CONSTANS (-antis), youngest of the 3 sons of Constantine the Great and Fausta, received after his father's death (A.D. 337) Illyricum, Italy, and Africa, as his share of the empire. After successfully resisting his brother Constantine, who was slain in invading his territory (310), Constans became master of the whole West. His weak and profligate character rendered him an object of contempt, and he was slain in 350 by the soldiers of the usurper MAGNENTIUS.

CONSTANTĪNA, the city. [CIRTA.]

CONSTANTĪNŌPŎLIS (-is : *Constantinople*), built on the site of the ancient BYZANTIUM by Constantine the Great, who called it after his own name and made it the capital of the Roman empire. It was solemnly consecrated A.D. 330. It was built over 7 hills, and was divided into 14 regiones. Its extreme length was about 3 Roman miles; and its walls included eventually a circumference of 13 or 14 Roman miles. It continued the capital of the Roman empire in the E. till its capture by the Turks in 1453.

CONSTANTĪNUS (-i). (1) I. surnamed "the Great," Roman emperor, A.D. 306—337, eldest son of the emperor Constantius Chlorus and Helena, was born A.D. 272, at Naissus, a town in Upper Moesia. He was early trained to arms, and during a large portion of his reign he was engaged in wars. On the death of his father at York (306), Constantine laid claim to a share of the empire, and was ac-

knowledged as master of the countries beyond the Alps. In 308 he received the title Augustus. He was engaged in a contest with Maxentius, who had possession of Italy, and defeated him at the village of Saxa Rubra near Rome, Oct. 27, 312. Maxentius tried to escape over the Milvian bridge into Rome, but perished in the river. It was in this campaign that Constantine is said to have been converted to Christianity. On his march to Rome, either at Autun in Gaul, or near Andernach on the Rhine, or at Verona, he is said to have seen in the sky a luminous cross with the inscription, BY THIS CONQUER; and on the night before the last and decisive battle with Maxentius, a vision is said to have appeared to Constantine in his sleep, bidding him inscribe the shields of his soldiers with the sacred monogram of the name of Christ. The tale of the cross seems to have grown out of that of the vision, and even the latter is not entitled to credit. It was Constantine's interest to gain the affections of his numerous Christian subjects in his struggle with his rivals; and it was probably only self-interest which led him at first to adopt Christianity. After the death of Maxentius Constantine was engaged in a contest with Licinius, who had obtained possession of the whole of the East; the struggle ended in the defeat and death of Licinius, so that Constantine was now sole master of the empire. He removed the seat of empire to Byzantium, which he called after himself Constantinople, and solemnly dedicated it, 330. Constantine reigned in peace the rest of his life. He died in May, 337, and was baptized shortly before his death by Eusebius. His three sons Constantine, Constantius, and Constans succeeded him in the empire.—(2) II. Roman emperor, 337—340, eldest of the three sons of Constantine the Great, by Fausta, received Gaul, Britain, Spain, and part of Africa at his father's death. Dissatisfied with his share of the empire, he made war upon his younger brother Constans, who governed Italy, but was defeated and slain near Aquileia.

CONSTANTĬUS (-i). (1) I. surnamed CHLORUS, "the pale," Roman emperor A.D. 305—306. He was one of the two Caesars appointed by Maximian and Diocletian in 292, and received the government of Britain, Gaul, and Spain with Treviri (*Trèves*) as his residence. Upon the abdication of Diocletian and Maximian, in 305, Constantius and Galerius became the Augusti. Constantius died 15 months afterwards (July, 306) at Eboracum (York) in Britain, on an expedition against the Picts: his son Constantine, afterwards the Great, succeeded him in his share of the government.—(2) II. Roman emperor, 337—361, third son of Constantine the Great by his second wife Fausta. He was succeeded by Julian.—(3) III. Emperor of the West (A.D. 421), a distinguished general of Honorius, who declared him Augustus in 421, but he died in the 7th month of his reign.

CONSUS (-i), an ancient Roman divinity, who was identified in later times with Neptune. Hence Livy calls him Neptunus Equestris. He was regarded by some as the god of secret deliberations, but he was most probably a god of the lower world.

CONTREBIA (-ae), one of the chief towns of the Celtiberi, in Hispania Tarraconensis, S.E. of Saragossa.

CONVENAE (-ārum), a people in Aquitania, near the Pyrenees, and on both sides of the Garumna; a mixed race, which had served under Sertorius, and were settled in Aquitania by Pompey.

COPAE (-ārum), an ancient town in Boeotia, on the N. side of the lake Copais, which derived its name from this place.

COPAIS (-ïdos), a large lake in Boeotia, formed chiefly by the river Cephisus, the waters of which are emptied into the Euboean sea by several subterraneous canals, called *Katabothra* by the modern Greeks. It was originally called CEPHISIS, under which name it occurs in Homer. In the summer the greater part of the lake is dry, and becomes a green meadow, in which cattle are pastured. Its eels were much prized in antiquity, and they retain their celebrity in modern times.

COPHEN or COPHES (*Cabul*), the only grand tributary river which flows into the Indus from the W. It was the boundary between India and Ariana.

COPTOS (-i), a city of the Thebaïs or Upper Egypt, lay a little to the E. of the Nile, some distance below Thebes. Under the Ptolemies it occupied an important commercial position.

CORA (-ae), an ancient town in Latium, in the Volscian mountains, S.E. of Velitrae.

CORACESIUM (-i), a very strong city of Cilicia Aspera, on the borders of Pamphylia, standing upon a steep rock, and possessing a good harbour.

CORASSIAE (-ārum), a group of small islands in the Icarian sea, S.W. of Icaria. They must not be confounded, as they often are, with the islands CORSEAE or CORSIAE, off the Ionian coast, and opposite the promontory Ampelos, in Samos.

CORAX (-actis), a Sicilian rhetorician, flourished about B.C. 467, and wrote the earliest work on the art of rhetoric.

CORBULO (-ōnis), CN. DOMITIUS (-i), a general who distinguished himself by his campaigns against the Parthians, in the reigns of Claudius and Nero. To avoid death, by the orders of Nero, he committed suicide.

CORCYRA (-ae: *Corfu*), an island in the Ionian sea, off the coast of Epirus, about 38 miles in length, but of very unequal breadth. The ancients regarded it as the Homeric SCHERIA, where the sea-loving Phaecians dwelt, governed by their king Alcinous. About B.C. 700 it was colonised by the Corinthians, and soon became rich and powerful by its extensive commerce. The increasing prosperity of Corcyra led to a rivalship with Corinth; and about B.C. 664 a battle was fought between the fleets, which is memorable as the most ancient sea-fight on record. At a later period Corcyra became one of the causes of the Peloponnesian war, 431. Shortly afterwards her power declined in consequence of civil dissensions; and at last it became subject to the Romans, with the rest of Greece. Corfu is at present one of the 7 Ionian islands under the protection of Great Britain, and the seat of government.

CORDUBA (-ae: *Cordova*), one of the largest cities in Spain, and the capital of Baetica, on the right bank of the Baetis; made a Roman colony B.C. 152; birthplace of the two Senecas and of Lucan.

CORDUENE. [GORDYENE.]

CORE (-es), the Maiden, a name by which Persephone (Proserpine) is often called. [PERSEPHONE.]

CORESSUS (-i), a lofty mountain in Ionia, 40 stadia from Ephesus, with a place of the same name at its foot.

CORFINIUM (-i), chief town of the Peligni in Samnium, strongly fortified, and memorable as the place which the Italians in the social war destined to be the new capital of Italy in place of Rome, on which account it was called *Italica*.

CORINNA (-ae), a Greek poetess, of Tanagra, in Boeotia, flourished about B.C. 490, and was a contemporary of Pindar, whom she is said to have instructed, and over whom she gained a victory at the public games at Thebes.

CORINTHIACUS ISTHMUS, often called simply the ISTHMUS, lay between the Corinthian and Saronic gulfs, and connected the Peloponnesus with the mainland or Hellas proper. In its narrowest part it was 40 stadia, or 5 Roman miles across: here was the temple of Poseidon (Neptune), and the Isthmian games were celebrated. Four unsuccessful attempts were made to dig a canal across the Isthmus, namely, by Demetrius Poliorcetes, Julius Caesar, Caligula, and Nero.

CORINTHIACUS SINUS (*G. of Lepanto*), the gulf between the N. of Greece and Peloponnesus. In early times it was called the

Crissaean Gulf, and its eastern part the Alcyonian Sea.

CŌRINTHUS (-i), called in Homer EPHYRA, a city on the above-mentioned Isthmus. Its territory, called CORINTHIA, embraced the greater part of the Isthmus with the adjacent part of the Peloponnesus. In the N. and S. the country is mountainous; but in the centre it is a plain, with a solitary and steep mountain rising from it, the ACRO-CORINTHUS, 1900 feet in height, which served as the citadel of Corinth. The city itself was built on the N. side of this mountain. It had 2 harbours, CENCHREAE on the E. or Saronic gulf, and LECHAEUM on the W. or Crissaean gulf. Its favourable position between two seas raised Corinth in very early times to great commercial prosperity, and made it the emporium of the trade between Europe and Asia. At Corinth the first triremes were built; and the first sea-fight on record was between the Corinthians and their colonists, the Corcyraeans. Its greatness at an early period is attested by numerous colonies, Ambracia, Corcyra, Apollonia, Potidaea, &c. Its commerce brought great wealth to its inhabitants; but with their wealth, they became luxurious and licentious. Thus the worship of Aphroditē (Venus) prevailed in this city. It was taken and destroyed in B.C. 146 by L. Mummius, the Roman consul, who treated it in the most barbarous manner. For a century it lay in ruins; but in 46 it was rebuilt by Caesar, who peopled it with a colony of veterans and descendants of freed men.

CORIŌLĀNUS (-i), the hero of one of the most beautiful of the early Roman legends. His original name was C. or Cn. Marcius, and he received the surname Coriolanus from the heroism he displayed at the capture of the Volscian town of Corioli. His haughty bearing towards the commons excited their fear and dislike; and he was impeached and condemned to exile, B.C. 491. He took refuge among the Volscians, and promised to assist them in war against the Romans. Attius Tullius, the king of the Volscians, appointed Coriolanus general of the Volscian army. Coriolanus took many towns, and advanced unresisted till he came to the Cluilian dyke close to Rome, 489. Here he encamped, and the Romans in alarm sent to him embassy after embassy, consisting of the most distinguished men of the state. But he would listen to none of them. At length the noblest matrons of Rome, headed by Veturia, the mother of Coriolanus, and Volumnia his wife, with his 2 little children came to his tent. His mother's reproaches, and the tears of his wife and the other matrons, bent his purpose. He led back his army, and lived in exile among the Volscians till his death; though other traditions relate that he was killed by the Volscians on his return to their country.

CORIŌLI (-ōrum), a town in Latium, capital of the Volsci, from the capture of which in B.C. 493, C. Marcius obtained the surname of Coriolanus.

CORMĀSA (-ae), an in.and town of Pamphylia, or of Pisidia, taken by the consul Manlius.

CORNĒLIA (-ae). (1) Daughter of P. Scipio Africanus the elder, wife of Ti. Sempronius Gracchus, and mother of the two tribunes Tiberius and Caius. She was virtuous and accomplished, and superintended with the greatest care the education of her sons, whom she survived. She was almost idolised by the people, who erected a statue to her, with the inscription, CORNELIA, MOTHER OF THE GRACCHI.—(2) Daughter of L. Cinna, wife of Caesar, the dictator.—(3) Daughter of Metellus Scipio, married first to P. Crassus, son of the triumvir, afterwards to Pompey the Great, by whom she was tenderly loved. She accompanied him to Egypt after the battle of Pharsalia, and saw him murdered. She afterwards returned to Rome, and received from Caesar the ashes of her husband, which she preserved on his Alban estate.

CORNĒLIA ORESTILLA. [ORESTILLA.]

CORNĒLIA GENS, the most distinguished of all the Roman gentes. All its great families belonged to the patrician order. The names of the most distinguished patrician families are:—CETHEGUS, CINNA, COSSUS, DOLABELLA, LENTULUS, SCIPIO, and SULLA. The names of the plebeian families are BALBUS and GALLUS.

CONĒLIUS NEPOS. [NEPOS.]

CORNĪCŬLUM (-i), a town in Latium in the mountains N. of Tibur, celebrated as the residence of the parents of Servius Tullius.

CŌROEBUS (-i). (1) A Phrygian, son of Mygdon, loved Cassandra, and for that reason fought on the side of the Trojans.—(2) An Elean, who gained the victory in the stadium at the Olympic games, B.C. 776: from this time the Olympiads begin to be reckoned.

CŌRŌNĒ (-es), a town in Messenia on the W. side of the Messenian gulf, founded B.C. 371 by the Messenians after their return to their native country, with the assistance of the Thebans.

CŌRŌNĒA (-ae), a town in Boeotia, S.W. of the lake Copais, and a member of the Boeotian League.

CŌRŌNIS (-ĭdis). (1) Daughter of Phlegyas, and mother by Apollo of Aesculapius, who is hence called Cŏrōnīdes. [AESCULAPIUS.] —(2) Daughter of Phoroneus, king of Phocis, metamorphosed by Athena (Minerva) into a crow, when pursued by Poseidon (Neptune)

CORSĬCA (-ae), called CYRNUS by the Greeks, a mountainous island in the Mediterranean, N. of Sardinia. Honey and wax were the principal productions of the island; but the honey had a bitter taste from the yew-trees with which the island abounded. The inhabitants were addicted to robbery, and paid little attention to agriculture. The most ancient inhabitants appear to have been Iberians; but in early times Ligurians, Tyrrhenians, Carthaginians, and even Greeks [ALERIA], settled in the island. It was subject to the Carthaginians at the commencement of the 1st Punic war, but soon afterwards passed into the hands of the Romans, and subsequently formed a part of the Roman province of Sardinia.

CORSŌTE (-es), a city of Mesopotamia, on the Euphrates, which Xenophon found already deserted.

CORTŌNA (-ae), one of the 12 cities of Etruria, lay N.W. of the Trasimene lake, and was one of the most ancient cities in Italy. It is said to have been originally called *Corythus* from its reputed founder Corythus, who is represented as the father of Dardanus. It was an important place when possessed by the Etruscans, and also previously when possessed by the Pelasgians, as is attested by the remains of the Pelasgic walls, which are some of the most remarkable in all Italy. Under the Romans it sunk into insignificance.

CORUNCĀNĬUS (-i), TI., consul B.C. 280, with P. Valerius Laevinus, was the first plebeian who was created Pontifex Maximus, and the first person at Rome who gave regular instruction in law.

CORVĪNUS MESSĀLA. [MESSALA.]

CORVUS, M. VĂLĔRĬUS (-i), one of the most illustrious men in the early history of Rome. He obtained the surname of *Corvus*, or "Raven," because, when serving as military tribune under Camillus, B.C. 349, he accepted the challenge of a gigantic Gaul to single combat, and was assisted in the conflict by a raven which settled upon his helmet, and flew in the face of the barbarian. He was 6 times consul, and twice dictator, and by his military abilities rendered the most memorable services to his country. He reached the age of 100 years, and is frequently referred to by the later Roman writers as a memorable example of the favours of fortune.

CORȲBANTES (-ium), priests of Cybele or Rhea in Phrygia, who celebrated her worship with enthusiastic dances, to the sound of the drum and the cymbal. They are often identified with the Curetes and the Idaean Dactyli, and thus are said to have been the nurses of Zeus (Jupiter) in Crete.

Cybele and Corybantes with Infant Zeus (Jupiter).   (Museo Capitolino.)

CORȲCĬA (-ae), a nymph, who became by Apollo the mother of Lycorus or Lycoreus, and from whom the Corycian cave on mount Parnassus was believed to have derived its name. The Muses are sometimes called by the poets *Cŏrўcĭdes Nymphae.*

CŎRŸCUS (-i). (1) A high rocky hill on the coast of Ionia, forming the S.W. promontory of the Erythraean peninsula.—(2) A city of Pamphylia, near Phaselis and Mt. Olympus.—(3) A city in Cilicia Aspera, with a good harbour, and a grotto in the mountains, called the Corycian Cave, celebrated by the poets, and also famous for its saffron. At the distance of 100 stadia (10 geog. miles) from Corycus, was a promontory of the same name.

CŎRŸPHĀSĬUM (-i), a promontory in Messenia, enclosing the harbour of Pylos on the N., with a town of the same name upon it.

CŎRŸTHUS (-i), an Italian hero, son of Jupiter, husband of Electra, and father of Dardanus, is said to have founded Corythus, afterwards called CORTONA.

CŌS, CŌŎS, COŬS (CŌI : *Kos, Stanco*), one of the islands called Sporades, lay off the coast of Caria, at the mouth of the Ceramic Gulf, opposite to Halicarnassus. It was colonised by Aeolians, but became a member of the Dorian confederacy. Near its chief city, Cos, stood the Asclepiēum, or temple of Asclepius, to whom the island was sacred. Its chief productions were wine, ointments, and the light transparent dresses called "Coae vestes." It was the birthplace of the physician Hippocrates, of the poet Philetas, and of the painter Apelles, whose picture of Aphrodite (Venus) Anadyomene adorned the Asclepiēum.

CŌSA (-ae) or CŌSAE (-arum). (1) (*Ansedonia*), an ancient city of Etruria near the sea, with a good harbour, called *Herculis Portus,* and after the fall of Falerii one of the 12 Etruscan cities.—(2) A town in Lucania near Thurii.

COSSAEA (-ae), a district on the confines of Media and Persis, inhabited by a rude, warlike, predatory people, the Cossaei, whom the Persian kings never subdued. They were conquered by Alexander (B.C. 325, 324), but after his death, they soon regained their independence.

COSSUS, CORNĒLĬUS (-i), the name of several illustrious Romans in the early history of the republic. Of these the most celebrated was Ser. Cornelius Cossus, consul B.C. 428, who killed Lar Tolumnius, the king of the Veii, in single combat, and dedicated his spoils in the temple of Jupiter Feretrius—the 2nd of the 3 instances in which the spolia opima were won.

COSŸRA or COSSŸRA (*Pantelaria*), a small island in the Mediterranean near Malta.

CŎTĪSO (-ōnis), a king of the Dacians,

conquered in the reign of Augustus by Lentulus.

COTTA (-ae), AURĒLĬUS (-i). (1) c., consul B.C. 75 with L. Octavius, was one of the most distinguished orators of his time, and is introduced by Cicero as one of the speakers in the *De Oratore,* and the *De Natura Deorum.*—(2) L., praetor 70, when he carried the celebrated law (*lex Aurelia judiciaria*) which entrusted the judicia to the senators, equites, and tribuni aerarii.

COTTA, L. AURUNCULĒIUS (-i), one of Caesar's legates in Gaul, perished along with Sabinus in the attack made upon them by Ambiorix, B.C. 54. [AMBIORIX.]

COTTĬUS (-i), king of several Ligurian tribes in the Cottian Alps, which derived their name from him. [ALPES.] He submitted to Augustus, who granted him the sovereignty over 12 of these tribes, with the title of Praefectus. Cottius thereupon made roads over the Alps, and erected (B.C. 8) at Segusio (*Suza*) a triumphal arch in honour of Augustus, extant at the present day. His authority was transmitted to his son, upon whom Claudius conferred the title of king. On his death, his kingdom was made a Roman province by Nero.

COTTUS (-i), a giant with 100 hands, son of Uranus (Heaven) and Gaea (Earth.)

CŎTŸORA (-orum), a colony of Sinope, on the coast of Pontus Polemoniacus, celebrated as the place where the 10,000 Greeks embarked for Sinope.

CŎTŸS (-ўŏs or -ўĭs), or CŎTŸTTŌ (-ūs), a Thracian divinity, whose festival, the *Cotyttia,* resembled that of the Phrygian Cybele, and was celebrated with licentious revelry. In later times her worship was introduced at Athens and Corinth. Her worshippers were called *Baptae,* from the purifications which were connected with her rites.

CŎTŸS (-ўŏs or -ўĭs), the name of several kings of Thrace. Ovid, during his exile at Tomi, addressed an epistle to one of those kings.

CRĂGUS (-i), a mountain consisting of 8 summits, being a continuation of Taurus to the W., and forming, at its extremity, the S.W. promontory of Lycia. At its foot was a town of the same name, on the sea-shore, between Pydna and Patara. Parallel to it, N. of the river Glaucus, was the chain of Anticrăgus.

CRĂNĂĒ (-es), the island to which Paris first carried Helen from Peloponnesus. Its locality is uncertain.

CRĂNĂŬS (-i), king of Attica, the son-in-law and successor of Cecrops.

CRANII or -ĬUM, a town of Cephallenia on the S. coast.

CRANTŎR (-ŏris). (1) The armour-bearer of Peleus, slain by the centaur Demoleon.—(2) Of Soli in Cilicia, an Academic philosopher, studied at Athens under Xenocrates and Polemo, and flourished B.C. 300. He was the author of several works chiefly on moral subjects, all of which are lost. Cicero commends him as a writer, and made great use of his work *On Grief*, in the 3rd book of his Tusculan Disputations, and in the *Consolatio*, which he composed on the death of his daughter Tullia.

CRASSUS (-i), the name of a distinguished family in the Gens Licinia, the most distinguished persons in which were :—(1) L. Licinius Crassus, the orator, who was consul, B.C. 95, censor 92, and died in 91. As an orator he surpassed all his contemporaries. In the treatise *De Oratore* Cicero introduces him as one of the speakers, and he is understood to express Cicero's own sentiments.—(2) M. Licinius Crassus, surnamed Dives. His father, who was consul B.C. 97 and censor 89, took part with Sulla in the civil war, and put an end to his own life, when Marius and Cinna returned to Rome at the end of 87. Young Crassus fought with Sulla against the Marian party, and on the defeat of the latter was rewarded by donations of confiscated property. His ruling passion was the love of money, and that he might add to his wealth he left no stone unturned. He bought multitudes of slaves, and, in order to increase their value, had them instructed in lucrative arts. He worked silver mines, cultivated farms, and built houses, which he let at high rents. In 71 he was appointed praetor in order to carry on the war against Spartacus and the gladiators ; he defeated Spartacus, who was slain in the battle, and he was honoured with an ovation. In 70 he was consul with Pompey, and entertained the populace most sumptuously at a banquet of 10,000 tables. A jealousy sprang up between Pompey and Crassus which was reconciled by Caesar, and thus formed the so-called *Triumvirate* in 60. In 55 he was consul with Pompey again, and received the province of Syria, where he hoped to add greatly to his wealth. He was defeated by the Parthians in the plains of Mesopotamia near Carrhae, the Haran of Scripture. He was shortly afterwards slain at an interview with the Parthian general. His head was cut off and sent to Orodes, who caused melted gold to be poured into the mouth of his fallen enemy, saying, "Sate thyself now with that metal of which in life thou wert so greedy." His son, who was Caesar's legate in Gaul from 58 to 55, was slain at the same time.

CRATĔRUS (-i). (1) A distinguished general of Alexander the Great, on whose death (B.C. 323) he received in common with Antipater the government of Macedonia and Greece. He fell in a battle against Eumenes, in 321.—(2) A Greek physician, who attended the family of Atticus, mentioned also by Horace.

CRĀTĒS (-ĕtis). (1) A celebrated Athenian poet of the old comedy, began to flourish B.C. 449.—(2) Of Thebes, a pupil of the Cynic Diogenes, and one of the most distinguished of the Cynic philosophers, flourished about 320.—(3) Of Mallus in Cilicia, a celebrated grammarian, founded the school of grammar at Pergamus, and wrote a commentary on the Homeric poems, in opposition to Aristarchus.

CRĀTHIS (-is or -ĭdis). (1) A river in Achaia, falling into the sea near Aegae.—(2) A river in lower Italy, forming the boundary on the E. between Lucania and Bruttii, and falling into the sea near Sybaris. Its waters were fabled to dye the hair blond.

CRĀTĪNUS (-i), one of the most celebrated of the Athenian poets of the old comedy, born B.C. 519 ; began to exhibit 454, when he was 65 years of age ; and died in 422, at the age of 97. He gave the old comedy its peculiar character, and did not, like Aristophanes, live to see its decline. He is frequently attacked by Aristophanes, who charges him with habitual intemperance, an accusation which was admitted by Cratinus himself.

CRĀTIPPUS (-i), a Peripatetic philosopher of Mytilene, accompanied Pompey in his flight after the battle of Pharsalia, B.C. 48. He afterwards settled at Athens, where young M. Cicero was his pupil in 44.

CREMĔRA (-ae), a small river in Etruria, which falls into the Tiber a little above Rome : memorable for the death of the 300 Fabii.

CREMŌNA (-ae : *Cremona*), a Roman colony in the N. of Italy, near the confluence of the Addua and the Po, was founded together with Placentia, B.C. 219, as a protection against the Gauls and Hannibal's invading army. It soon became a place of great importance, but having espoused the cause of Vitellius, it was totally destroyed by the troops of Vespasian, A.D. 69.

CREMŌNIS JUGUM. [Alpes.]

CREŎN (-ontis). (1) King of Corinth, whose daughter, Glauce or Creusa, married Jason. Medēa, thus forsaken, sent Glauce a garment which burnt her to death when she put it on ; the palace took fire, and Creon perished in the flames.—(2) Son of Menoecus, and brother of Jocaste, the wife of Laius. After the death of Laius, Creon governed Thebes for a short time, and then surrendered the kingdom to Oedipus, who had delivered the country from the Sphinx. [OEDIPUS.] After the death of Eteocles and Polynīces, the sons of Oedipus, he again assumed the reins of government at Thebes. His cruelty in forbidding burial to the corpse of Polynīces, and his sentencing Antigone to death for disobeying his orders, occasioned the death of his own son Haemon. For details see ANTIGONE.

CREŌPHȲLUS (-i), of Chios, one of the earliest epic poets, said to have been the friend or son-in-law of Homer.

CRESPHONTĒS (-is), an Heraclid, son of Aristomachus, and one of the conquerors of Peloponnesus, obtained Messenia for his share. During an insurrection of the Messenians, he and two of his sons were slain. A third son, Aepytus, avenged his death. [AEPYTUS.]

CRESTŌNIA (-ae), a district in Macedonia between the Axius and Strymon, near Mt. Cercine, inhabited by the Crestonaei, a Thracian people : their chief town was Creston or Crestōnc, founded by the Pelasgians.

CRĒTA (-ae : *Candia*), one of the largest islands in the Mediterranean sea, about 160 miles in length, and from 35 to 6 miles in breadth. It was celebrated for its fertility and salubrity, and was inhabited at an early period by a numerous and civilised population. Homer speaks of its hundred cities ; and before the Trojan war mythology told of a king MĪNOS, who resided at Cnossus, and ruled over the greater part of the island. He is said to have given laws to Crete, and to have been the first prince who had a navy, with which he suppressed piracy in the Aegaean. Cnossus, Gortyna, and Cydonia were the most important cities. In the historical period the ruling class were the Dorians, who settled in Crete about 60 years after the Dorian conquest of Peloponnesus, and introduced into the island the social and political institutions of the Dorians. Subsequently Doric customs disappeared and great degeneracy in morals prevailed. The Apostle Paul, quoting the Cretan poet Epimenides, describes them as " alway liars, evil beasts, slow bellies." The Cretans were celebrated as archers, and frequently served as mercenaries in the armies of other nations. The island was conquered by Q. Metellus, who received in consequence the surname Creticus (B.C. 68—66), and it became a Roman province.

CRĒTEUS or CATREUS (-ĕos), son of Minos by Pasiphae or Crete, and father of Althemenes.

CRĒTHEUS (-ĕos or -ĕi), son of Aeolus and Enarete, wife of Tyro, and father of Aeson, Pheres, Amythaon, and Hippolyte : he was the founder of Iolcus.

CRĒŪSA (-ae). (1) Daughter of Erechtheus and Praxithea, wife of Xuthus, and mother of Achaeus and Ion.—(2) Daughter of Priam and Hecuba, wife of Aeneas, and mother of Ascanius. She perished on the night of the capture of Troy, having been separated from her husband in the confusion.—(3) Daughter of Creon, who fell a victim to the vengeance of Medea. [CREON, No. 1.]

CRĪMĪSUS or CRIMISSUS, a river in the W. of Sicily falling into the Hypsa : on its banks Timoleon defeated the Carthaginians, B.C. 339.

CRISSA or CRISA, and CIRRHA (-ae), towns in Phocis, regarded by some writers as the same place ; but it seems most probable that Crissa was a town inland S.W. of Delphi, and that Cirrha was its port in the Crissaean gulf. The inhabitants of these towns levied contributions upon the pilgrims frequenting the Delphic oracle, in consequence of which the Amphictyons declared war against them, B.C. 595, and eventually destroyed them. This territory, the rich Crissaean plain, was declared sacred to the Delphic god, and was forbidden to be cultivated. The cultivation of this plain by the inhabitants of Amphissa led to the Sacred War, in which Philip was chosen general of the Amphictyons, 338. Crissa remained in ruins, but Cirrha was afterwards rebuilt, and became the harbour of Delphi.

CRITIĀS (-ae), a pupil of Socrates, one of the 30 tyrants established at Athens by the Spartans, B.C. 404, was conspicuous above all his colleagues for rapacity and cruelty.

CRĪTOLĀUS (-i). (1) Of Phaselis in Lycia, succeeded Ariston at Athens, as the head of the Peripatetic school. In B.C. 155 he was sent by the Athenians as ambassador to Rome with Carneades and Diogenes. [CARNEADES.]—(2) General of the Achaean League, 147, distinguished by his bitter enmity to the Romans. He was defeated by Metellus, and was never heard of after the battle.

CRĪTŌN (-ōnis), a rich citizen of Athens, and a friend and disciple of Socrates.

CRŌCUS (-i), the beloved friend of Smilax, was changed by the gods into a saffron plant.

CROESUS (-i), last king of Lydia, son of Alyattes, reigned B.C. 560—546. He subdued all the nations between the Aegaean and the river Halys, and made the Greeks in Asia Minor tributary to him. The fame of his power and wealth drew to his court at Sardis all the wise men of Greece, and among them Solon, whose interview with the king was celebrated in antiquity. In reply to the question, who was the happiest man he had ever seen, the sage taught the king that no man should be deemed happy till he had finished his life in a happy way. In a war with Cyrus, king of Persia, the army of Croesus was defeated, and his capital, Sardis, was taken. Croesus was condemned by the conqueror to be burnt to death. As he stood before the pyre, the warning of Solon came to his mind, and he thrice uttered the name of Solon. Cyrus inquired who it was that he called on ; and, upon hearing the story, repented of his purpose, and not only spared the life of Croesus, but made him his friend. Croesus survived Cyrus, and accompanied Cambyses in his expedition against Egypt.

CROMMYŎN or CROMYŎN, a town in Megaris, on the Saronic gulf, afterwards belonged to Corinth ; celebrated in mythology on account of its wild sow, which was slain by Theseus.

CRŎNUS (-i), called SATURNUS (-i), by the Romans, the youngest of the Titans, son of Uranus and Ge (Heaven and Earth), father, by Rhea, of Hestia, Demeter (Ceres), Hera (Juno), Hades (Pluto), Poseidon (Neptune), and Zeus (Jupiter). He deprived his father Uranus of the government of the

Cronos (Saturnus). (From a Painting at Pompeii).

world, and was, in his turn, dethroned by his son Zeus. [ZEUS.]

CRŎTON (-ōnis) or CROTŌNA (-ae), one of the most powerful cities in Magna Graecia, was situated on the E. coast of Bruttium, and was founded by the Achaeans B.C. 710. It is celebrated as the residence of Pythagoras, the philosopher, and of Milo, the athlete. It attained its greatest power by the destruction of Sybaris, in 510 ; but suffered greatly in the wars with Dionysius, Agathocles, and Pyrrhus.

CRUSTUMĔRIA (-ae), -RIUM (-i), also CRUSTŬMĬUM (-i), a town of the Sabines, situated in the mountains near the sources of the Allia.

CTĒSĬAS (-ae), of Cnidus, in Caria, a contemporary of Xenophon, was private physician of Artaxerxes Mnemon, whom he accompanied in his war against his brother Cyrus, B.C. 401. He lived 17 years at the Persian court, and wrote in the Ionic dialect a great work on the history of Persia, and also a work on India, of both of which works we possess an abridgment in Photius.

CTĒSĬBĬUS (-i), celebrated for his mechanical inventions, lived at Alexandria in the reigns of Ptolemy Philadelphus, and Euergetes, about B.C. 250.

CTĒSĬPHŌN. [DEMOSTHENES.]

CTĒSĬPHŌN (-ontis), a city of Assyria, on the E. bank of the Tigris, 3 Roman miles from Seleucia, on the W. bank, first became an important place under the Parthians, whose kings used it for some time as a winter residence.

CŬMAE (-ārum), a town in Campania, and the most ancient of the Greek colonies in Italy and Sicily, was founded by Cyme, in Aeolis, in conjunction with Chalcis and Eretria, in Euboea. Its foundation is placed in B.C. 1050, but this date is evidently too early. It was situated on a steep hill of Mt. Gaurus, a little N. of the promontory Misenum. It became in early times a great and flourishing city ; and its power is attested by its colonies in Italy and Sicily,—Puteoli, Palaeopolis, afterwards Neapolis, Zancle, afterwards Messana. It maintained its independence till B.C. 417, when it was taken by the Campanians, and most of its inhabitants sold as slaves. From this time CAPUA became the chief city of Campania. Cumae was celebrated as the residence of the earliest Sibyl, and as the place where Tarquinius Superbus died.

CŬNAXA (-ae), a small town in Babylonia, on the Euphrates, famous for the battle fought here between the younger Cyrus and his brother Artaxerxes Mnemon, in which the former was killed (B.C. 401).

CŬRES (-ium), an ancient town of the Sabines, celebrated as the birthplace of T. Tatius and Numa Pompilius : from this town the

Romans are said to have derived the name of Quirites.

CŬRĒTES (-um), a mythical people, said to be the most ancient inhabitants of Acarnania and Aetolia; the latter country was called Curetis from them. They also occur in Crete as the priests of Zeus (Jupiter), and are spoken of in connexion with the Corybantes and Idaean Dactyli. The infant Zeus was entrusted to their care by Rhea; and by clashing their weapons in a warlike dance, they drowned the cries of the child, and prevented his father Cronus from ascertaining the place where he was concealed.

CŬRĬĀTĬI (-ōrum), a celebrated Alban family. 3 brothers of this family fought with 3 Roman brothers, the Horatii, and were conquered by the latter. In consequence of their defeat Alba became subject to Rome.

CŬRĬO, C. SCRĪBŌNĬUS. (1) Consul B.C. 76, was a personal enemy of Caesar, and supported P. Clodius, when the latter was accused of violating the sacra of the Bona Dea. In 57 he was appointed pontifex maximus, and died 53. He had some reputation as an orator, and was a friend of Cicero.—(2) Son of No. 1, also a friend of Cicero, was a most profligate character. He was married to Fulvia, afterwards the wife of Antony. He at first belonged to the Pompeian party, by whose influence he was made tribune of the plebs, 50; but he was bought over by Caesar, and employed his power as tribune against his former friends. On the breaking out of the civil war (49), he was sent by Caesar to Sicily with the title of propraetor. He succeeded in driving Cato out of the island, and then crossed over to Africa, where he was defeated and slain by Juba and P. Attius Varus.

CURIOSOLĬTAE (-ārum), a Gallic people on the Ocean in Armorica, near the Veneti.

CŬRĬUS, M. DENTĀTUS (-i), a favourite hero of the Roman republic, was celebrated in later times as a noble specimen of old Roman frugality and virtue. In his first consulship (B.C. 290), he successfully opposed the Samnites; and in his second consulship (275), he defeated Pyrrhus so completely, that the king was obliged to quit Italy. On this and on subsequent occasions he declined to share in the large booty that he gained. At the close of his military career, he retired to his small farm in the country of the Sabines, which he cultivated with his own hands. Once the Samnites sent an embassy to him with costly presents; they found him sitting at the hearth and roasting turnips. He rejected their presents, telling them that he preferred ruling over those who possessed gold, to possessing it himself. He was censor

in 272, and in that year executed public works of great importance.

CURSOR, L. PĀPĪRĬUS. (1) A distinguished Roman general in the 2nd Samnite war, was 5 times consul (B.C. 333—313), and twice dictator (325—309). He frequently defeated the Samnites, but his greatest victory over them was gained in his 2nd dictatorship. Although a great general, he was not popular with the soldiers on account of his severity.—(2) Son of No. 1, was, like his father, a distinguished general. In his 2nd consulship, 272, he brought the 3rd Samnite war to a close.

CURTĬUS, METTUS or METTĬUS (-i), a distinguished Sabine, fought with the rest of his nation against Romulus. According to one tradition, the Lacus Curtius, which was part of the Roman forum, was called after him, because in the battle with the Romans he escaped with difficulty from a swamp, into which his horse had plunged. But the more usual tradition respecting the name of the Lacus Curtius related, that in B. c. 362 the earth in the forum gave way, and a great chasm appeared, which the soothsayers declared could only be filled up by throwing into it Rome's greatest treasure; that thereupon M. Curtius, a noble youth, mounted his steed in full armour, and declaring that Rome possessed no greater treasure than a brave and gallant citizen, leaped into the abyss, upon which the earth closed over him.

CURTĬUS RŪFUS (-i), Q., the Roman historian of Alexander the Great, whose date is uncertain. His history of Alexander consisted of 10 books, but the first 2 are lost, and the remaining 8 are not without considerable gaps. It is written in a pleasing, though somewhat declamatory style.

CUTILĬAE AQUAE. [AQUAE, No. 3.]

CȲANĒ (-es), a Sicilian nymph and playmate of Proserpine, changed into a fountain through grief at the loss of the goddess.

CȲANĒAE (-arum), INSŬLAE, 2 small rocky islands at the entrance of the Thracian Bosporus into the Euxine, the PLANCTAE and SYMPLEGADES of mythology, so called because they are said to have been once moveable and to have rushed together, and thus destroyed every ship that attempted to pass through them. After the ship Argo had passed through them in safety, they became stationary.

CȲANĒĒ (-es), daughter of Maeander, mother of Caunus and of Byblis.

CYAXARĒS, king of Media, B.C. 634—594, son of Phraortes, and grandson of Deioces. He was the most warlike of the Median kings, and introduced great military reforms. He was engaged in wars with the Assyrians, Scythians, and Alyattes, king of Lydia

[ALYATTES.] Cyaxares died in 594, and was succeeded by his son Astyages. Xenophon speaks of a Cyaxares II., king of Media, son of Astyages, respecting whom see CYRUS.

CỸBĔLĔ. [RHEA.]

CYBISTRA (-ōrum), an ancient city of Asia Minor, lying at the foot of Mt. Taurus, in the part of Cappadocia bordering on Cilicia.

CỸCLĂDES (-um), a group of islands in the Aegean Sea, so called because they lay in a circle around Delos, the most important of them.

CỸCLŌPES and CỸCLŌPES (-um), that is, creatures with round or circular eyes, are described differently by different writers. Homer speaks of them as a gigantic and lawless race of shepherds in Sicily, who devoured human beings and cared nought for Zeus (Jupiter): each of them had only one eye in the centre of his forehead: the chief among them was POLYPHEMUS. According to Hesiod the Cyclops were Titans, sons of Uranus and Ge, were 3 in number, ARGES, STEROPES, and BRONTES, and each of them had only one eye in his forehead. They were thrown into Tartarus by Cronus, but were released by Zeus, and in consequence they provided Zeus with thunderbolts and lightning, Pluto with a helmet, and Poseidon with a trident. They were afterwards killed by Apollo for having furnished Zeus with the thunderbolts to kill Aesculapius. A still later tradition regarded the Cyclopes as the assistants of Hephaestus (Vulcan). Volcanoes were the workshops of that god, and Mt. Aetna in Sicily and the neighbouring isles were accordingly considered as their abodes. As the assistants of Hephaestus they make the metal armour and ornaments for gods and heroes. Their number is no longer confined to 3; and besides the names mentioned by Hesiod, we also find those of PYRACMON and ACAMAS. The name Cyclopian was given to the walls built of great masses of unhewn stone, of which specimens are still to be seen at Mycenae and other parts of Greece, and also in Italy. They were probably constructed by the Pelasgians, and later generations, being struck by their grandeur, ascribed their building to a fabulous race of Cyclops.

CYCNUS or CYGNUS (-i). (1) Son of Apollo by Hyrie, was metamorphosed into a swan.—(2) Son of Poseidon (Neptune), and father of Tenes and Hemithea. [TENES.] In the Trojan war Cycnus was slain by Achilles, and his body was metamorphosed into a swan. —(3) Son of Sthenelus, king of the Ligurians, and a friend and relation of Phaëthon, was metamorphosed by Apollo into a swan, and placed among the stars.

CỸDIPPĔ (-es). (1) The mistress of Acontius. [ACONTIUS.]—(2) One of the Nereids.

CYDNUS (-i), a river of Cilicia Campestris, rising in the Taurus, and flowing through the midst of the city of Tarsus. It was celebrated for the coldness of its waters, in bathing in which Alexander nearly lost his life.

CỸDŌNĬA (-ae), one of the chief cities of Crete, situated on the N.W. coast, derived its name from the CYDŌNES, a Cretan race, placed by Homer in the W. part of the island. Cydonia was the place from which quinces (Cydonia mala) were first brought to Italy, and its inhabitants were some of the best Cretan archers.

CYLLĂRUS (-i), a beautiful centaur, killed at the wedding feast of Pirithous. The horse of Castor was likewise called Cyllarus.

CYLLĒNĔ (-es). (1) The highest mountain in Peloponnesus on the frontiers of Arcadia and Achaia, sacred to Hermes (Mercury), who had a temple on the summit, was said to have been born there, and was hence called Cyllēnĭus.—(2) A sea-port town of Elis.

CYLON (-ōnis), an Athenian of noble family, who gained an Olympic victory B.C. 640. He seized the Acropolis, intending to make himself tyrant of Athens. Pressed by famine, Cylon and his adherents were driven to take refuge at the altar of Athena, whence they were induced to withdraw by the archon Megacles, the Alcmaeonid, on a promise that their lives should be spared. But their enemies put them to death as soon as they had them in their power.

CỸMĔ (-es), the largest of the Aeolian cities of Asia Minor, stood upon the coast of Aeolis, on a bay named after it, Cumaeus (also Elaïticus) Sinus. It was the mother city of Cumae in Campania.

CYNAEGĪRUS (-i), brother of the poet Aeschylus, distinguished himself by his valour at the battle of Marathon, B.C. 490. According to Herodotus, when the Persians were endeavouring to escape by sea, Cynaegirus seized one of their ships to keep it back, but fell with his right hand cut off.

CYNĒSĬI (-ōrum) or CYNĒTES (-um), a people, according to Herodotus, dwelling in the extreme W. of Europe, beyond the Celts, apparently in Spain.

CỸNŌSARGĔS, a gymnasium, sacred to Hercules, outside Athens, E. of the city, for the use of those who were not of pure Athenian blood: here taught Antisthenes, the founder of the Cynic school.

CỸNOSCĔPHĂLAE, i.e. "Dog's Heads," two hills near Scotussa in Thessaly, where Flaminius gained his celebrated victory over Philip of Macedonia, B.C. 197.

CYNOSSĒMA, "Dog's Tomb," a promontory

in the Thracian Chersonesus near Madytus, so called because it was supposed to be the tomb of Hecuba, who had been previously changed into a dog.

CȲNŌSŪRA (-ae), an Idaean nymph, and one of the nurses of Zeus, who placed her among the stars. [ARCTOS.]

CȲNŌSŪRA (-ae), "Dog's Tail," a promontory in Attica, S. of Marathon.

CYNTHUS (-i), a mountain of Delos, celebrated as the birthplace of Apollo and Diana, who were hence called Cynthius and Cynthia respectively.

CYNŪRĬA (-ae), a district on the frontiers of Argolis and Laconia, for the possession of which the Argives and Spartans carried on frequent wars, and which the Spartans at length obtained about B.C. 550.

CYNUS (-i), the chief seaport in the territory of the Locri Opuntii.

CȲPĂRISSĬA (-ae), a town in Messenia, on the W. coast, on a promontory and bay of the same name.

CȲPĂRISSUS (-i). (1) Son of Telephus, who having inadvertently killed his favourite stag, was seized with immoderate grief, and metamorphosed into a cypress.—(2) A small town in Phocis on Parnassus near Delphi.

CȲPRUS and CȲPRUS (-i), a large island in the Mediterranean, S. of Cilicia and W. of Syria, about 140 miles in length, and 50 miles in its greatest breadth. It was celebrated in ancient as well as in modern times for its fertility. The largest plain, called the Salaminian plain, is in the E. part of the island near Salamis. The rivers are little more than mountain torrents, mostly dry in summer. Cyprus was colonised both by the Phoenicians and the Greeks; was subject at different times to the Egyptians, the Persians, and the Romans, of whom the latter made it a province, B.C. 58. Cyprus was one of the chief seats of the worship of Aphrodite (Venus), who is hence called *Cypris* or *Cypria*, and whose worship was introduced into the island by the Phoenicians.

CYPSĔLA (-ōrum). (1) A town in Arcadia on the frontiers of Laconia.—(2) A town in Thrace on the Hebrus and the Egnatia Via.

CYPSĔLUS (-i), a tyrant of Corinth, B.C. 655—625, so named because when a child he was concealed from the Bacchiadae (the Doric nobility of Corinth) by his mother in a chest (κυψέλη). He was succeeded in the tyranny by his son Periander.

CȲRĒNĒ (-es). (1) Daughter of Hypseus, mother of Aristaeus by Apollo, was carried by the god from Mt. Pelion to Libya, where the city of Cyrene derived its name from her. —(2) An important Greek city in the N. of Africa, lying between Alexandria and Carthage. It was founded by Battus (B.C. 631), who led a colony from the island of Thera, and he and his descendants ruled over the city for 8 generations. It stood 80 stadia (8 geog. miles) from the coast, on the edge of the upper of two terraces of table land, at the height of 1800 feet above the sea, in one of the finest situations in the world. At a later time Cyrene became subject to the Egyptian Ptolemies, and was eventually formed, with the island of Crete, into a Roman province. The ruins of the city of Cyrene are very extensive. It was the birthplace of Callimachus, Eratosthenes, and Aristippus. The territory of Cyrene, called Cȳrēnaĭca, included also the Greek cities of Barca, Teuchira, Hesperis, and Apollonia, the port of Cyrene. Under the Ptolemies Hesperis became Berenice, Teuchira was called Arsinoë, and Barca was entirely eclipsed by its port, which was raised into a city under the name of Ptolemaïs. The country was at that time usually called Pentapolis, from the 5 cities of Cyrene— Apollonia, Ptolemaïs, Arsinoë, and Berenice.

CȲRESCHĀTA (-ae) or CȲRŎPŎLIS (-is), a city of Sogdiana, on the Jaxartes, the furthest of the colonies founded by Cyrus, and the extreme city of the Persian empire : destroyed, after many revolts, by Alexander.

CYRNUS (-i), the Greek name of the island of Corsica, from which is derived the adjective *Cyrnēus*, used by the Latin poets.

CYRRHESTĬCĒ (-es), the name given under the Seleucidae to a province of Syria, lying between Commagene on the N. and the plain of Antioch on the S.

CȲRUS (-i). (1) THE ELDER, the founder of the Persian empire. The history of his life was overlaid in ancient times with fables and romances. According to the legend preserved by Herodotus, Cyrus was the son of Cambyses, a noble Persian, and of Mandane, daughter of the Median king Astyages. In consequence of a dream, which seemed to portend that his grandson should be master of Asia, Astyages committed the child as soon as it was born to Harpăgus with orders to kill it. But he delivered the infant to a herdsman, and by the herdsman's wife the child was reared. At ten years of age he gave proof of his high descent by his royal bearing, and on being sent to Astyages was discovered by him to be his grandson. By the advice of the Magians, who said that the dream had been fulfilled when Cyrus was made king in sport, he sent him to his parents in Persia. When Cyrus grew up, he led the hardy mountaineers of Persia against Astyages, defeated him in battle, and took him prisoner, B.C. 559. The Medes accepted Cyrus for their king, and thus the supremacy which they had held passed to the Persians. Cyrus now proceeded to conquer the other parts of Asia. In 546 he overthrew the Lydian monarchy, and took Croesus prisoner. [CROESUS.] The Greek cities in Asia Minor were subdued by his general Harpagus. He next turned his arms against the Babylonian empire, and took the capital, Babylon, by diverting the course of the Euphrates, which flowed through the midst of it, so that his soldiers entered the city by the bed of the river. This was in 538. Subsequently he set out on an expedition against the Massagetae, a Scythian people, but he was defeated and slain in battle. Tomyris, the queen of the Massagetae, cut off his head, and threw it into a bag filled with human blood, that he might satiate himself (she said) with blood. He was killed in 529. He was succeeded by his son CAMBYSES. Xenophon's account is very different. He represents Cyrus as brought up at his grandfather's court, as serving in the Median army under his uncle Cyaxares II., the son and successor of Asty-ages, of whom Herodotus knows nothing; as making war upon Babylon simply as the general of Cyaxares; as marrying the daughter of Cyaxares; and at length dying quietly in his bed. But Xenophon merely draws a picture of a wise and just prince ought to be; and his account must not be regarded as a genuine history.—(2) THE YOUNGER, the 2nd son of Darius Nothus, king of Persia, and of Parysatis, was appointed by his father commander of the maritime parts of Asia Minor, and satrap of Lydia, Phrygia, and Cappadocia, B.C. 407. He assisted Lysander and the Lacedaemonians with large sums of money in their war against the Athenians. Cyrus was of a daring and am-bitious temper. On the accession of his elder brother Artaxerxes Mnemon, 404, he formed the design of dethroning his brother, to accomplish which he obtained the aid of a force of 13,000 Greek mercenaries, set out from Sardis in the spring of 401, and, having crossed the Euphrates at Thapsacus, marched down the river to the plain of Cunaxa, 500 stadia from Babylon. Here he met the king's army. In the battle which followed his Greek troops were victorious, but Cyrus him-self was slain. The character of Cyrus is drawn by Xenophon in the brightest colours. It is enough to say that his ambition was gilded by all those brilliant qualities which win men's hearts.—(3) A river of Armenia, rising in the Caucasus, flowing through Iberia, and after forming the boundary be-tween Albania and Armenia, uniting with

the Araxes, and falling into the W. side of the Caspian.

CYTHERA (-ae: *Cerigo*), an island off the S.E. point of Laconia, with a town of the same name in the interior, the harbour of which was called SCANDEA. It was colonised at an early time by the Phoenicians, who in-troduced the worship of Aphrodite (Venus) into the island, for which it was celebrated. This goddess was hence called CYTHERAEA, CYTHEREIS; and, according to some tra-ditions, it was in the neighbourhood of this island that she first rose from the foam of the sea.

CYTHNUS (-i: *Thermia*), an island in the Aegaean sea, one of the Cyclades.

CYTINIUM (-i), one of the 4 cities in Doris, on Parnassus.

CYTORUS or -UM (-i), a town on the coast of Paphlagonia, a commercial settlement of Sinope, stood upon the mountain of the same name, celebrated for its box-trees.

CYZICUS (-i), one of the most ancient and powerful of the Greek cities in Asia Minor, stood upon an island of the same name in the Propontis (*Sea of Marmara*). This island lay close to the shore of Mysia, to which it was united by two bridges, and afterwards (under Alexander the Great) by a mole, which has accumulated to a considerable isthmus. The most noted passages in its history are its shaking off the Persian yoke after the peace of Antalcidas, and its gallant resistance against Mithridates (B.C. 75) which obtained for it the rank of a "libera civitas."

DAAE. [DAHAE.]

DACIA (-ae), as a Roman province, lay between the Danube and the Carpathian mountains, and comprehended the modern *Transylvania, Wallachia, Moldavia,* and part of *Hungary.* The Daci were of the same race and spoke the same language as the Getae, and are therefore usually said to be of Thracian origin. They were a brave and warlike people. In the reign of Domitian they became so formidable under their king DECEBALUS, that the Romans were obliged to purchase a peace of them by the payment of tribute. Trajan delivered the empire from this disgrace; he crossed the Danube, and after a war of 5 years (A.D. 101—106) con-quered the country, and made it a Roman province. At a later period Dacia was in-vaded by the Goths; and as Aurelian con-sidered it more prudent to make the Danube the boundary of the empire, he resigned Dacia to the barbarians, removed the Roman inhabitants to Moesia, and gave the name of Dacia (Aureliana) to that part of the province along the Danube where they were settled.

DACTYLI (-ōrum), fabulous beings, to whom the discovery of iron, and the art of working it by means of fire, was ascribed. Mount Ida, in Phrygia, is said to have been the original seat of the Dactyls, whence they are usually called Idaean Dactyls. In Phrygia they were connected with the worship of Rhea, or Cybele. They are sometimes confounded or identified with the Curetes, Corybantes, and Cabiri.

DAEDĂLUS (-i), a mythical personage, under whose name the Greek writers personified the earliest development of the arts of sculpture and architecture, especially among the Athenians and Cretans. He is sometimes called an Athenian, and sometimes a Cretan, on account of the long time he lived in Crete. He devoted himself to sculpture, and made great improvements in the art. He instructed his sister's son, Calos, Talus, or Perdix, who soon came to surpass him in skill and ingenuity, and Daedalus killed him through envy. [PERDIX.] Being condemned to death by the Areopagus for this murder, he went to Crete, where the fame of his skill obtained for him the friendship of Minos. He made the well-known

Daedalus and Icarus. (Zoëga, Bassirilievi di Roma, tav. 44.)

wooden cow for Pasiphaë; and when Pasiphaë gave birth to the Minotaur, Daedalus constructed the labyrinth, at Cnossus, in which the monster was kept. For his part in this affair, Daedalus was imprisoned by Minos; but Pasiphaë released him; and, as Minos had seized all the ships on the coast of

Crete, Daedalus procured wings for himself and his son Icarus, and fastened them on with wax. [ICARUS.] Daedalus flew safely over the Aegean, alighting, according to some accounts, at Cumae, in Italy. He then fled to Sicily, where he was hospitably entertained by Cocalus. Minos, who sailed to Sicily in pursuit of him, was slain by Cocalus or his daughters. Several other works of art were attributed to Daedalus, in Greece, Italy, Libya, and the islands of the Mediterranean. They belong to the period when art began to be developed. The name of *Daedala* was given by the Greeks to the wooden statues, ornamented with gilding, and bright colours, and real drapery, the earliest known forms of the images of the gods.

DĂHAE (-ārum), a great Scythian people, who led a nomad life over a great extent of country, on the E. of the Caspian, in Hyrcania (which still bears the name of *Daghestan*), on the banks of the Margus, the Oxus, and even the Jaxartes.

DALMĀTĬA or DELMATIA (-ae), a part of the country along the E. coast of the Adriatic sea, included under the general name of Illyricum, and separated from Liburnia on the N. by the Titius (*Kerka*), and from Greek Illyria on the S. by the Drilo (*Drino*), thus nearly corresponding to the modern *Dalmatia*. The capital was DALMINIUM or DELMINIUM, from which the country derived its name. The next most important town was SALONA, the residence of Diocletian. The Dalmatians were a brave and warlike people, and gave much trouble to the Romans. In B.C. 119 their country was overrun by L. Metellus, who assumed, in consequence, the surname Dalmaticus, but they continued independent of the Romans. In 39 they were defeated by Asinius Pollio, of whose *Dalmaticus triumphus* Horace speaks; but it was not till the year 23 that they were finally subdued by Statilius Taurus. They took part in the great Pannonian revolt under their leader Bato; but after a three years' war were again reduced to subjection by Tiberius, A.D. 9.

DALMĬNĬUM. [DALMATIA.]

DĂMĂLIS (-is) or BŌUS (-i), a small place in Bithynia, on the shore of the Thracian Bosporus, N. of Chalcedon; celebrated by tradition as the landing-place of Io.

DĂMARĀTUS. [DEMARATUS.]

DĂMASCUS (-i), one of the most ancient cities of the world, mentioned as existing in the time of Abraham (Gen. xiv. 15), stood in the district afterwards called Coele-Syria, upon both banks of the river Chrysorrhoas or Bardines (*Burada*). Its fruits were celebrated in ancient, as in modern times; and altogether the situation of the city is one of the finest on the globe. For a long period Damascus was the seat of an independent kingdom, called the kingdom of Syria, which was subdued by the Assyrians, and passed successively under the dominion of the Babylonians, the Persians, the Greek kings of Syria, and the Romans. It flourished greatly under the emperors. Diocletian established in it a great factory for arms ; and hence the origin of the fame of the Damascus blades. Its position on one of the high roads from lower to upper Asia gave it a considerable trade.

DĂMĂSIPPUS (-i). (1) A Roman senator, fought on the side of the Pompeians in Africa, and perished, B.C. 47.—(2) A contemporary of Cicero, who mentions him as a lover of statues, and speaks of purchasing a garden from Damasippus. He is probably the same person as the Damasippus ridiculed by Horace. (*Sat.* ii. 3. 16, 64.) It appears from Horace that Damasippus had become bankrupt, in consequence of which he intended to put an end to himself ; but he was prevented by the Stoic Stertinius, and then turned Stoic himself, or at least affected to be one by his long beard.

DAMASTĒS of Sigēum, a Greek historian, and a contemporary of Herodotus and Hellanīcus of Lesbos ; his works are lost.

DAMĪA. [AUXESIA.]

DAMNŌNĬI (-ōrum). (1) Or DUMNONII or DUMNUNII, a powerful people in the S.W. of Britain, inhabiting *Cornwall*, *Devonshire*, and the W. part of *Somersetshire*, from whom was called the promontory DAMNONIUM, also OCRINUM (*C. Lizard*), in Cornwall.—(2) Or DAMNII, a people in N. Britain, inhabiting parts of *Perth*, *Argyle*, *Sterling*, and *Dumbarton-shires*.

DAMO, a daughter of Pythagoras and Theano, to whom Pythagoras entrusted his writings, and forbad her to give them to any one. This command she strictly observed, although she was in extreme poverty, and received many requests to sell them.

DĂMOCLĒS (-is), a Syracusan, one of the companions and flatterers of the elder Dionysius. Damocles having extolled the great felicity of Dionysius on account of his wealth and power, the tyrant invited him 'to try what his happiness really was, and placed him at a magnificent banquet, in the midst of which Damocles saw a naked sword suspended over his head by a single horse-hair —a sight which quickly dispelled all his visions of happiness. The story is alluded to by Horace. (*Carm.* iii. 1. 17.)

DĂMON (-ŏnis.) (1) Of Athens, a celebrated musician and sophist, a teacher of Pericles, with whom he lived on the most intimate terms. He was said to have been also a teacher of Socrates.—(2) A Pythagorean, and friend of PHINTIAS (not Pythias). When the latter was condemned to die for a plot against Dionysius I., of Syracuse, he obtained leave of the tyrant to depart, for the purpose of arranging his domestic affairs, upon Damon offering himself to be put to death instead of his friend, should he fail to return. Phintias arrived just in time to redeem Damon ; and Dionysius was so struck with this instance of friendship on both sides, that he pardoned the criminal, and entreated to be admitted as a third into their bond of brotherhood.

DAMŎXĔNUS (-i) an Athenian comic poet of the new comedy, and perhaps partly of the middle.

DANA (-ae), a great city of Cappadocia, probably the same as the later TYANA.

DĂNĂĒ (-es), daughter of Acrisius king of Argos, was confined by her father in a brazen tower, because an oracle had declared that she would give birth to a son, who should kill his grandfather. But here she became the mother of Perseus by Zeus (Jupiter), who visited her in a shower of gold, and thus mocked the precautions of the king. Acrisius shut up both mother and child in a chest, which he cast into the sea ; but the chest floated to the island of Seriphus, where both were rescued by Dictys. As to the fulfilment of the oracle, see PERSEUS. An Italian legend related that Danaë came to Italy, built the town of Ardea, and married Pilumnus, by whom she became the mother of Daunus, the ancestor of Turnus.

DĂNĂI. [DANAUS.]

DĂNĂĪDES (-um), the 50 daughters of Danaus. [DANAUS.]

DĂNĂLA (-ōrum), a city in the territory of the Trocmi, in the N.E. of Galatia, notable in the history of the Mithridatic War as the place where Lucullus resigned the command to Pompey.

DANAPRIS. [BORYSTHENES.]

DANASTRIS. [TYRAS.]

DĂNĂUS (-i), son of Belus, and twin-brother of Aegyptus. Belus had assigned Libya to Danaüs, but the latter, fearing his brother and his brother's sons, fled with his 50 daughters to Argos. Here he was elected king by the Argives in place of Gelanor, the reigning monarch. The story of the murder of the 50 sons of Aegyptus by the 50 daughters of Danaüs (the Danaides) is given under AEGYPTUS. There was one exception to the murderous deed. The life of Lynceus was spared by his wife Hypermnestra ; and according to the common tradition he afterwards avenged the death of his brothers by killing his father-in-law, Danaüs. According to the poets the Danaides were punished in Hades by being compelled everlastingly to pour water into a sieve. From Danaüs the Argives were called *Danai*, which name, like that of the Argives, was often applied by the poets to the collective Greeks.

Danaïds. (Visconti, Mus. Pio Clem., vol. 4, tav. 36.)

DĀNŬBĬUS (-i: *Danube*, in Germ. *Donau*), called ISTER by the Greeks, one of the chief rivers of Europe, rising in M. Abnoba the Black Forest, and falling into the Black sea after a course of 1770 miles. The Danube formed the N. boundary of the empire, with the exception of the time that DACIA was a Roman province. In the Roman period the upper part of the river from its source as far as Vienna was called Danubius, while the lower part to its entrance in the Black Sea was named Ister.

DAPHNĒ (-es). (1) Daughter of the river-god Peneus, in Thessaly, was pursued by Apollo, who was charmed by her beauty; but as she was on the point of being overtaken by him, she prayed for aid, and was metamorphosed into a laurel-tree (δάφνη), which became in consequence the favourite tree of Apollo.—(2) A beautiful spot, 5 miles S. of Antioch in Syria, to which it formed a sort of park or pleasure garden. It was celebrated for the grove and temple dedicated to Apollo.

DAPHNIS (-ĭdis), a Sicilian shepherd, son of Hermes (Mercury) by a nymph, was taught by Pan to play on the flute, and was regarded as the inventor of bucolic poetry. A Naiad to whom he proved faithless punished him with blindness, whereupon his father Hermes translated him to heaven.

DARDĂNI (-ōrum), a people in Upper Moesia, occupying part of Illyricum.

DARDĂNĬA (-ae). (1) A district of the Troad, lying along the Hellespont, S. W. of Abydos, and adjacent to the territory of Ilium. Its people (Dardani) appear in the Trojan War, under Aeneas, in close alliance with the Trojans, with whose name theirs is often interchanged, especially by the Roman poets.—(2) A city in this district. See Dardanus, No. 2.

DARDĂNUS (-i). (1) Son of Zeus (Jupiter) and Electra, the mythical ancestor of the Trojans, and through them of the Romans. The Greek traditions usually made him a king in Arcadia, from whence he emigrated first to Samothrace, and afterwards to Asia, where he received a tract of land from king Teucer, on which he built the town of Dardania. His grandson Tros removed to Troy the Palladium, which had belonged to his grandfather. According to the Italian traditions, Dardanus was the son of Corythus, an Etruscan prince of Corythus (Cortona); and, as in the Greek tradition, he afterwards emigrated to Phrygia.—(2) Also DARDANUM and -IUM, a Greek city in the Troad on the Hellespont, 12 Roman miles from Ilium, built by Aeolian colonists, at some distance from the site of the ancient city Dardania. From Dardanus arose the name of the *Castles of the Dardanelles*, after which the Hellespont is now called.

DĀRĒS (-ētis), a priest of Hephaestus (Vulcan) at Troy, mentioned in the Iliad, to whom was ascribed in antiquity an Iliad, believed to be more ancient than the Homeric poems. This work, which was undoubtedly the composition of a sophist, is lost; but there is extant a Latin work in prose in 44 chapters, on the destruction of Troy, bearing the title *Daretis Phrygii de Excidio Trojae Historia*, and purporting to be a translation of the work of Dares by Cornelius Nepos. But the Latin work is evidently of much later origin; and it is supposed by some to have been written even as late as the 12th century.

DARIUS (-i). (1) King of Persia, B.C. 521 —485, son of Hystaspes, was one of the 7 Persian chiefs who destroyed the usurper SMERDIS. The 7 chiefs agreed that the one of them whose horse neighed first at an appointed time and place, should become king; and as the horse of Darius neighed first, he was declared king. He divided the empire into 20 satrapies, assigning to each its amount of tribute. A few years after his accession the Babylonians revolted, but after a siege of 20 months, Babylon was taken by a stratagem of ZOPYRUS, about 516. He then invaded Scythia and penetrated into the interior of modern Russia, but after losing a large number of men by famine, and being unable to meet with the enemy, he was obliged to retreat. On his return to Asia, he sent part of his forces, under Megabazus, to subdue Thrace and Macedonia, which thus became subject to the Persian empire. The most important event in the reign of Darius was the commencement of the great war between the Persians and the Greeks. The history of this war belongs to the biographies of other men. [ARISTAGORAS, HISTIAEUS, MARDONIUS, MILTIADES.] In 501 the Ionian Greeks revolted; they were assisted by the Athenians, who burnt Sardis, and thus provoked the hostility of Darius. Darius sent against the Greeks Mardonius in 492, and afterwards Datis and Artaphernes, who sustained a memorable defeat by the Athenians at Marathon, 490. Darius now resolved to call out the whole force of his empire for the purpose of subduing Greece; but, after 3 years of preparation, his attention was called off by the rebellion of Egypt. He died in 485, leaving the execution of his plans to his son XERXES.—(2) King of Persia, 424—405, named OCHUS before his accession, and then surnamed NOTHUS, or the *Bastard*, from his being one of the bastard sons of Artaxerxes I. He obtained the crown by putting his brother Sogdianus to death, and married Parysatis, by whom he had 2 sons, Artaxerxes II., who succeeded him, and Cyrus the younger. Darius was governed by eunuchs, and the weakness of his government was shown by repeated insurrections of his satraps.—(3) Last king of Persia, 336—331, named CODOMANUS before his accession, was raised to the throne by Bagoas, after the murder of ARSES. The history of his conquest by Alexander the Great, and of his death, is given in the life of ALEXANDER.

DASSARETII (-ōrum), or DASSARITAE,

DASSARETAE (-ārum), a people in Greek Illyria on the borders of Macedonia: their chief town was LYCHNIDUS on a hill, on the N. side of the lake LYCHNITIS, which was so called after the town.

DATAMES (-is), a distinguished Persian general, a Carian by birth, was satrap of Cilicia under Artaxerxes II. (Mnemon), but revolted against the king. He defeated the generals who were sent against him, but was at length assassinated, B.C. 362. Cornelius Nepos, who has written his life, calls him the bravest and most able of all barbarian generals, except Hamilcar and Hannibal.

DATIS (-is), a Mede, commanded, along with Artaphernes, the Persian army which was defeated at Marathon, B.C. 490.

DATUM or DATUS (-i), a Thracian town, on the Strymonic gulf, subject to Macedonia, with gold mines in Mt. Pangaeus, in the neighbourhood, whence came the proverb, a "Datum of good things."

DAULIS (-ĭdis) or DAULIA (-ae), an ancient town in Phocis, situated on a lofty hill, celebrated in mythology as the residence of the Thracian king TEREUS, and as the scene of the tragic story of PHILOMELA and PROCNE. Hence DAULIAS is the surname both of Procne and Philomela.

DAUNIA. [APULIA.]

DAUNUS (-i), son of Pilumnus and Danaë, wife of Venilia, and ancestor of Turnus.

DECEBALUS (-i), a celebrated king of the Dacians, to whom Domitian paid an annual tribute. He was defeated by Trajan, and put an end to his own life; whereupon Dacia became a Roman province, A.D. 106.

DECELEA or -IA (-ae), a demus of Attica, N.W. of Athens, on the borders of Boeotia, near the sources of the Cephissus, seized and fortified by the Spartans in the Peloponnesian war.

DECETIA (-ae: *Desize*), a city of the Aedui, in Gallia Lugdunensis, on an island in the Liger (*Loire*).

DECIDIUS SAXA. [SAXA.]

DECIUS (-i) MUS (Mūris), P., plebeians. (1) Consul B.C. 340 with T. Manlius Torquatus, in the great Latin war. Each of the consuls had a vision in the night before fighting with the Latins, announcing that the general of one side and the army of the other were devoted to death. The consuls thereupon agreed that the one whose wing first began to waver should devote himself and the army of the enemy to destruction. Decius commanded the left wing, which began to give way; whereupon he devoted himself and the army of the enemy to destruction, then rushed into the thickest of the enemy, and was slain, leaving the victory to the Romans.

—(2) Son of the preceding, 4 times consul, imitated the example of his father by devoting himself to death at the battle of Sentinum, B.C. 295.—(3) Son of No. 2, consul 279, in the war against Pyrrhus.

DĔCĬUS (-i), Roman emperor, A.D. 249—251, a native of Pannonia, and the successor of Philippus, whom he slew in battle. He fell in battle against the Goths, together with his son, in 251. In his reign the Christians were persecuted with great severity.

DĔCŪMĀTES AGRI. [AGRI DECUMATES.]

DĔÏĀNĪRA (-ae), daughter of Althaea and Oeneus, and sister of Meleager. Achelous and Hercules both loved Deïanira, and fought for the possession of her. ·Hercules was victorious, and she became his wife. She was the unwilling cause of her husband's death by presenting him with the poisoned robe which the centaur Nessus gave her. In despair she put an end to her own life. For details, see HERCULES.

DĔÏDĂMĪA (-ae), daughter of Lycomedes, in the island of Scyrus. When Achilles was concealed there in maiden's attire, she became by him the mother of Pyrrhus or Neoptolemus.

DĔÏŎCĔS (-is), first king of Media, after the Medes had thrown off the supremacy of the Assyrians, reigned B.C. 709—656. He built the city of Ecbatana, which he made the royal residence. He was succeeded by his son, PHRAORTES.

DĔÏŎNĪDĔS (-ae), son of Deione, by Apollo, *i.e.*, Miletus.

DĔÏŎTĂRUS (-i), Tetrarch of Galatia, adhered to the Romans in their wars against Mithridates, and was rewarded by the senate with the title of king. In the civil war he sided with Pompey, and was present at the battle of Pharsalia, B.C. 48. He is remarkable as having been defended by Cicero before Caesar, in the house of the latter at Rome, in the speech (*pro Rege Deiotaro*) still extant.

DĔÏPHŎBĔ (-es), the Sibyl at Cumae, daughter of Glaucus. [SIBYLLA.]

DĔÏPHŎBUS (-i), son of Priam and Hecuba, who married Helen after the death of Paris. On the capture of Troy by the Greeks he was slain and fearfully mangled by Menelaus.

DĔLĬUM (-i), a town on the coast of Boeotia, in the territory of Tanagra, near the Attic frontier, named after a temple of Apollo similar to that at Delos. Here the Athenians were defeated by the Boeotians, B.C. 424.

DĔLĬUS (-i) and DĔLĬA (-ae), surnames of Apollo and Artemis (Diana) respectively, from the island of DELOS.

DĔLOS or DĔLUS (-i), the smallest of the islands called Cyclades, in the Aegean Sea. According to a legend, it was called out of the deep by the trident of Poseidon (Neptune), but was a floating island until Zeus (Jupiter), fastened it by adamantine chains to the bottom of the sea, that it might be a secure resting-place to Leto (Latona) for the birth of Apollo and Artemis (Diana). Hence it became the most holy seat of the worship of Apollo. We learn from history that Delos was peopled by Ionians, for whom it was the chief centre of political and religious union, in the time of Homer. It was afterwards the common treasury of the Greek confederacy for carrying on the war with Persia but the treasury was afterwards transferred to Athens. It was long subject to Athens; but it possessed an extensive commerce which was increased by the downfal of Corinth, when Delos became the chief emporium for the trade in slaves. The city of Delos stood on the W. side of the island at the foot of Mt. Cynthus (whence the god's surname of Cynthius). It contained a temple of Leto, and the great temple of Apollo. With this temple were connected games, called Delia, which were celebrated every 4 years, and were said to have been founded by Theseus. A like origin is ascribed to the sacred embassy (*Theoria*), which the Athenians sent to Delos every year. The greatest importance was attached to the preservation of the sanctity of the island; and its sanctity secured it, though wealthy and unfortified, from plunder.

DELPHI (-ōrum : *Kastri*), a small town in Phocis, but one of the most celebrated in Greece, on account of its oracle of Apollo. It was situated on a steep declivity on the S. slope of Mt. Parnassus, and its site resembled the cavea of a great theatre. It was shut in on the N. by a barrier of rocky mountains, which were cleft in the centre into 2 great cliffs with peaked summits, between which issued the waters of the Castalian spring. It was regarded as the central point of the whole earth, and was hence called the "navel of the earth." It was originally called PYTHO, by which name it is alone mentioned in Homer. Delphi was colonised at an early period by Doric settlers from the neighbouring town of Lycorēa, on the heights of Parnassus. The government was in the hands of a few distinguished families of Doric origin. From them were taken the chief magistrates and the priests. The temple of Apollo contained immense treasures; for not only were rich offerings presented to it by kings and private persons, but many of the Greek states had in the temple separate *thesauri*, in which they deposited, for the sake of security, many of their valuable treasures. In the centre of the temple there was a small opening in the ground, from which, from time to time, an intoxicating vapour arose. Over this chasm there stood a tripod, on which the priestess, called Pythia, took her seat whenever the oracle was to be consulted. The words which she uttered after exhaling the vapour were believed to contain the revelations of Apollo. They were carefully written down by the priests, and afterwards communicated in hexameter verse to the persons who had come to consult the oracle. If the Pythia spoke in prose, her words were immediately turned into verse by a poet employed for the purpose. The oracle is said to have been discovered by its having thrown into convulsions some goats which had strayed to the mouth of the cave. The Pythian games were celebrated at Delphi, and it was one of the 2 places of meeting of the Amphictyonic council.

DELTA. [AEGYPTUS.]

DĒMĀDĒS (-is), an Athenian orator, who belonged to the Macedonian party, and was a bitter enemy of Demosthenes. He was put to death by Antipater in B. c. 318.

DĒMĀRĀTUS or DĀMĀRĀTUS (-i). (1) King of Sparta, reigned from about B. c. 510 to 491. He was deposed by his colleague Cleomenes, B.C. 491, and thereupon repaired to the Persian coast, where he was kindly received by Darius. He accompanied Xerxes in his invasion of Greece, and recommended the king not to rely too confidently upon his countless hosts.—(2) A merchant noble of Corinth, who settled afterwards in Etruria, and became the father of Aruns and Lucumo (Tarquinius Priscius).

DEMETER, called CĒRĒS (-ĕris) by the Romans, one of the great divinities of the Greeks, was the goddess of the earth, and her name probably signified *Mother-Earth* (γῆ μήτης). She was the protectress of agriculture and of all the fruits of the earth. She was the daughter of Cronus (Saturn) and Rhea, and sister of Zeus (Jupiter), by whom she became the mother of Persephŏnē (Proserpine). Zeus, without the knowledge of Demeter, had promised Persephone to Aïdoneus (Pluto) ; and while the unsuspecting maiden was gathering flowers in the Nysian plain in Asia, the earth suddenly opened and she was carried off by Aïdoneus. After wandering for some days in search of her daughter, Demeter learnt from the Sun, that it was Aïdoneus who had carried her off. Thereupon she quitted Olympus in anger and dwelt upon earth among men, conferring blessings wherever she was kindly received, and severely punishing those who repulsed her. In this manner she came to Celeus, at Eleusis. [CELEUS.] As the goddess

still continued angry, and did not allow the earth to produce any fruits, Zeus sent Hermes (Mercury) into the lower world to fetch back Persephone. Aïdoneus consented, but gave Persephone part of a pomegranate to eat. Demeter returned to Olympus with her daughter, but as the latter had eaten in the lower world, she was obliged to spend one third of the year with Aïdoneus, continuing with her mother the remainder of the year. The earth now brought forth fruit again. This is the ancient legend as preserved in the Homeric hymn, but it is variously modified in later traditions. In the Latin poets the scene of the rape is near Enna, in Sicily ; and Ascalaphus, who had alone seen Persephone eat any thing in the lower world, revealed the fact, and was in consequence turned into an owl by Demeter. [ASCALAPHUS.] The meaning of the legend is obvious :—Persephone, who is carried off to the lower world, is the seed-corn, which remains concealed in the ground part of the year ; Persephone, who returns to her mother, is the corn which rises from the ground, and nourishes men and animals. Later philosophical writers, and perhaps the mysteries also, referred the disappearance and return of Persephone to the burial of the body of man and the immortality of his soul.—The other legends about Demeter are of less importance. To escape the pursuit of Poseidon she changed herself into a mare, but the god effected his purpose, and she became the mother of the celebrated horse Arion. [ARION, 2.]—She fell in love with Iasion, and lay with him in a thrice-ploughed field in Crete: their offspring was Plutus (*Wealth*). [IASION.]—She punished with fearful hunger Erysichthon, who had cut down her sacred grove. [ERYSICHTHON.]— In Attica Demeter was worshipped with great splendour. The Athenians pretended that agriculture was first practised in their country, and that Triptolemus of Eleusis, the favourite of Demeter, was the first who invented the plough and sowed corn. [TRIPTOLEMUS.] Every year at Athens the festival of the *Eleusinia* was celebrated in honour of these goddesses. The festival of the Thesmophoria was also celebrated in her honour as well at Athens as in other parts of Greece; it was intended to commemorate the introduction of the laws and the regulations of civilised life, which were ascribed to Demeter, since agriculture is the basis of civilisation.— In works of art Demeter is represented in full attire. Around her head she wears a garland of corn-ears or a simple riband, and in her hand she holds a sceptre, corn-ears or a poppy, sometimes also a torch and the mystic basket. The Romans received from Sicily the worship of Demeter, to whom they gave the name of Ceres. They celebrated in her honour the

Demeter (Ceres). (Mus. Bor·, vol. 9, tav. 35.)

festival of the Cerealia. She was looked upon by the Romans in the same light as Tellus. Pigs were sacrificed to both divinities. Her worship acquired considerable political importance at Rome. The property of traitors against the republic was often made over to her temple. The decrees of the senate were deposited in her temple for the inspection of the tribunes of the people.

DĒMĒTRĬAS (-ădis), a town in Magnesia, in Thessaly, on the innermost recess of the Pagasaean bay, founded by Demetrius Poliorcetes, and peopled by the inhabitants of Ioclus and the surrounding towns.

DĒMĒTRĬUS (-i :) I. *Kings of Macedonia.* —(1)Surnamed POLIORCETES or the Besieger, son of Antigonus, king of Asia, and Stratonice. At an early age he gave proofs of distinguished bravery, and during his father's lifetime was engaged in constant campaigns against either Cassander or Ptolemy. In his siege of Rhodes (B.C. 305) he constructed those gigantic machines to assail the walls of the city, which gave him the surname of Poliorcetes. He at length concluded a treaty with the Rhodians (304). After the defeat and death of his father at the battle of Ipsus (301), the fortunes of Demetrius were for a time under a cloud; but in 294 he was acknowledged as king by the Macedonian army, and succeeded in keeping possession of Macedonia for 7 years. In 287 he was deserted by his own troops, who proclaimed Pyrrhus king of Macedonia. He then crossed over to Asia, and after meeting with alternate success and misfortune, was at length obliged to surrender himself prisoner to Seleucus (286). That king kept him in confinement, but did not treat him with harshness. Demetrius died in the 3rd year of his imprisonment and the 56th of his age (283). He was one of the most remarkable characters of his time, being a man of restless activity of mind, fertility of resource, and daring promptitude in the execution of his schemes. His besetting sin was his unbounded licentiousness.—(2) Son of Antigonus Gonatas, reigned B.C. 239—229.

II. *Kings of Syria.*—(1) SOTER (reigned B.C. 162—150), was the son of Seleucus IV. Philopator and grandson of Antiochus the Great. While yet a child he had been sent to Rome by his father as a hostage, where he remained until he was 23 years of age. He then fled to Syria, and was received as king by the Syrians. An impostor named Balas raised an insurrection against him and slew him. He left 2 sons, Demetrius Nicator and Antiochus Sidetes, both of whom subsequently ascended the throne.—(2) NICATOR (B.C. 146 —142, and again 128—125), son of Demetrius Soter. With the assistance of Ptolemy Philometor he defeated Balas, and recovered his kingdom ; but, having rendered himself odious to his subjects by his vices and cruelties, he was driven out of Syria by Tryphon, who set up Antiochus, the infant son of Alexander Balas as a pretender against him. Demetrius retired to Babylon, and from thence marched against the Parthians, by whom he was defeated and taken prisoner, 138. He remained as a captive in Parthia 10 years. Demetrius again obtained possession of the Syrian throne in 128 ; but while engaged in an expedition against Egypt, Ptolemy Physcon set up against him the pretender Alexander Zebina, by whom he was defeated and compelled to fly. He fled to Tyre, where he was assassinated, 125.

III. *Literary.*—PHALEREUS, so called from his birthplace, the Attic demos of Phalerus, where he was born about B.C. 345. His parents were poor, but by his talents and perseverance he rose to the highest honours at Athens, and became distinguished both as an orator, a statesman, a philosopher, and a poet. The government of Athens was entrusted to him by Cassander in 317, the duties of which he discharged with extraordinary distinction. When Demetrius

Poliorcetes approached Athens in 307 Phalereus was obliged to take to flight. He settled at Alexandria in Egypt, and exerted some influence in the foundation of the Alexandrine library. He was the last of the Attic orators worthy of the name.

DĒMŎCĒDĒS, a celebrated physician of Crotona. He practised medicine successively at Aegina, Athens, and Samos. He was taken prisoner along with Polycrates, in B.C. 522, and was sent to Susa to the court of Darius. Here he acquired great reputation, by curing the king's foot and the breast of the queen Atossa. Notwithstanding his honours at the Persian court, he was always desirous of returning to his native country. In order to effect this, he procured by means of Atossa that he should be sent with some nobles to explore the coast of Greece, and to ascertain in what parts it might be most successfully attacked. At Tarentum he escaped, and settled at Crotona, where he married the daughter of the famous wrestler, Milo.

DĒMŎCRĬTUS (-i), a celebrated Greek philosopher, was born at Abdera in Thrace, about B.C. 460. He spent the large inheritance, which his father left him, on travels into distant countries in pursuit of knowledge. He was a man of a most sterling and honourable character. He died in 361 at a very advanced age. There is a tradition that he deprived himself of his sight, that he might be less disturbed in his pursuits; but it is more probable that he may have lost his sight by too severe application to study. This loss, however, did not disturb the cheerful disposition of his mind, which prompted him to look, in all circumstances, at the cheerful side of things, which later writers took to mean, that he always laughed at the follies of men. His knowledge was most extensive. It embraced not only the natural sciences, mathematics, mechanics, grammar, music, and philosophy, but various other useful arts. His works were composed in the Ionic dialect, though not without some admixture of the local peculiarities of Abdera. They are nevertheless much praised by Cicero on account of the liveliness of their style, and are in this respect compared even with the works of Plato. Democritus was the founder of the atomic theory.

DĒMŎPHŌN or DĒMŎPHŎŌN (-ontis). (1) Son of Celeus and Metanīra, whom Demeter wished to make immortal. For details see CELEUS.—(2) Son of Theseus and Phaedra, accompanied the Greeks against Troy, and on his return gained the love of Phyllis, daughter of the Thracian king Sithon, and promised to marry her. Before the nuptials were celebrated, he went to Attica to settle his affairs, and as he tarried longer than Phyllis had expected, she thought that she was forgotten, and put an end to her life; but she was metamorphosed into a tree. Demophon became king of Athens.

DĒMOSTHĒNĒS (-is). (1) Son of Alcisthenes, a celebrated Athenian general in the Peloponnesian war. In B.C. 425 he rendered important assistance to Cleon, in making prisoners of the Spartans in the island of Sphacteria. In 413 he was sent with a large fleet to Sicily to assist Nicias, but both commanders were defeated, obliged to surrender, and put to death by the Syracusans.—(2) The greatest of Athenian orators, was the son of Demosthenes, and was born in the Attic demos of Paeania, about B. C. 385. At 7 years of age he lost his father, who left him and his younger sister to the care of guardians, who neglected him, and squandered his property. When he was 20 years of age Demosthenes accused Aphobus, one of his guardians, and obtained a verdict in his favour. Emboldened by this success, Demosthenes ventured to come forward as a speaker in the public assembly. His first effort was unsuccessful, but he was encouraged to persevere by the actor Satyrus, who gave him instruction in action and declamation. In becoming an orator, Demosthenes had to struggle against the greatest physical disadvantages. His voice was weak and his utterance defective; and it was only by the most unwearied exertions that he succeeded in overcoming the obstacles which nature had placed in his way. Thus it is said that he spoke with pebbles in his mouth, to cure himself of stammering; that he repeated verses of the poets as he ran up hill, to strengthen his voice; that he declaimed on the sea-shore, to accustom himself to the noise and confusion of the popular assembly; that he lived for months in a cave under ground, engaged in constantly writing out the history of Thucydides, to form a standard for his own style. It was about 355 that Demosthenes began to obtain reputation as a speaker in the public assembly. His eloquence soon gained him the favour of the people. The influence which he acquired he employed for the good of his country, and not for his own aggrandisement. He clearly saw that Philip had resolved to subjugate Greece, and he therefore devoted all his powers to resist the aggressions of the Macedonian monarch. For 14 years he continued the struggle against Philip, and neither threats nor bribes could turn him from his purpose. It is true he failed; but the failure must not be considered his fault. The struggle was brought to a close by the battle

of Chaeronēa (338), by which the independence of Greece was crushed. Demosthenes
was present at the battle, and fled like
thousands of others. At this time many
accusations were brought against him. Of
these one of the most formidable was the
accusation of Ctesiphon by Aeschines, but
which was in reality directed against Demosthenes himself. Aeschines accused Ctesiphon
for proposing that Demosthenes should be rewarded for his services with a golden crown
in the theatre. The trial was delayed for
reasons unknown to us till 330, when Demosthenes delivered his " Oration on the
Crown." Aeschines was defeated and withdrew from Athens. [AESCHINES.] Demosthenes was one of those who were suspected
of having received money from Harpalus
in 325. [HARPALUS.] His guilt is doubtful ;
but he was condemned, and thrown into
prison, from which however he escaped.
He took up his residence partly at Troezene
and partly in Aegina, looking daily across
the sea to his beloved native land. His exile
did not last long. On the death of Alexander
(323) the Greek states rose in arms against
Macedonia. Demosthenes was recalled and
returned in triumph. But in the following
year (322) the confederate Greeks were defeated, and he took refuge in the temple
of Poseidon (Neptune), in the island of
Calauria. Here he was pursued by the
emissaries of Antipater ; whereupon he took
poison, which he had for some time carried
about his person, and died in the temple, 322.
Sixty-one orations of Demosthenes have come
down to us. Of these 17 were political, the
most important being the 12 Philippic orations ; 42 were judicial, the most celebrated
being the orations Against Midias, Against
Leptines, On the dishonest conduct of
Aeschines during his embassy to Philip, and
On the Crown ; and 2 were show speeches,
both of which are spurious, as also probably
are some of the others.

DENTĀTUS, CŬRĬUS. [CURIUS.]

DĔŌ, another name for Demeter (Ceres) ;
hence her daughter Persephone is called by
the patronymic Dĕōis and Dĕōinē.

DERBĒ (-es), a town in Lycaonia, on the
frontiers of Isauria.

DERCĔTIS (-is), DERCĔTŌ (-ūs), also
called *Atargatis*, a Syrian goddess. She offended Aphrodite (Venus), who in consequence
inspired her with love for a youth, to whom
she bore a daughter Semiramis ; but ashamed
of her frailty, she killed the youth, exposed
her child in a desert, and threw herself into a
lake near Ascalon. Her child was fed by
doves, and she herself was changed into a
fish. The Syrians thereupon worshipped her

as a goddess. The upper part of her statue
represented a beautiful woman, while the
lower part terminated in the tail of a fish.
She appears to be the same as Dagon mentioned in the Old Testament as a deity of the
Philistines.

DERTŌNA (-ae : *Tertona*), an important
town in Liguria, on the road from Genua to
Placentia.

DEUCALĬŌN (-ŏnis), son of Prometheus
and Clymene, king of Phthia, in Thessaly.
When Zeus (Jupiter) had resolved to destroy
the degenerate race of men, Deucalion and
his wife Pyrrha were, on account of their
piety, the only mortals saved. On the advice
of his father, Deucalion built a ship, in which
he and his wife floated in safety during the 9
days' flood, which destroyed all the other inhabitants of Hellas. At last the ship rested,
according to the more general tradition, on
Mount Parnassus in Phocis. Deucalion and
his wife consulted the sanctuary of Themis
how the race of man might be restored. The
goddess bade them cover their heads and
throw the bones of their mother behind them.
After some doubts respecting the meaning of
this command, they agreed in interpreting
the bones of their mother to mean the stones
of the earth. They accordingly threw stones
behind them, and from those thrown by
Deucalion there sprang up men, from those
thrown by Pyrrha women. Deucalion then
descended from Parnassus, built his first
abode at Opus or at Cynus, and became by
Pyrrha the father of Hellen, Amphictyon,
Protogenia, and others.

DEVA. (1) (*Chester*), the principal town
of the Cornavii in Britain, on the Seteia
(*Dee*).—(2) (*Dee*), an estuary in Scotland, on
which stood the town Dovanna, near the
modern Aberdeen.

DĪA, the ancient name of Naxos.

DIABLINTES. [AULERCI.]

DĪACRĬA (-ae), a mountainous district in
the N.E. of Attica, including the plain of
Marathon. [ATTICA.] The inhabitants of
this district were the most democratical of
the 3 parties into which the inhabitants of
Attica were divided in the time of Solon.

DĪĂGORAS (-ae). (1) Son of Damagetus
of Ialysus in Rhodes, celebrated for his own
victories and those of his sons and grandsons,
in the Grecian games. He gained his Olympic
victory, B.C. 464.—(2) Surnamed the ATHEIST,
a Greek philosopher and poet, a native of
the island of Melos, and a disciple of Democritus. In consequence of his attacks upon
the popular religion, and especially upon the
Eleusinian mysteries, he was formally accused of impiety, B.C. 411, and fearing the
results of a trial, fled from Athens. He went

first to Pallene, and afterwards to Corinth where he died.

DĬANA (-ae), an ancient Italian divinity, whom the Romans identified with the Greek Artemis. Her worship is said to have been introduced at Rome by Servius Tullius, who dedicated a temple to her on the Aventine. At Rome Diana was the goddess of light, and her name contains the same root as the word *dies.* As Dianus (Janus), or the god of light, represented the sun, so Diana, the goddess of light, represented the moon. The attributes of the Greek Artemis were afterwards ascribed to the Roman Diana. For details see ARTEMIS.

DĬANĬUM (-i : *Denia*), a town in Hispania Tarraconensis on a promontory of the same name (*C. Martin*) founded by the Massilians. Here stood a celebrated temple of Diana, from which the town derived its name.

DĬCAEA (-ae), a town in Thrace, on the lake Bistonis.

DĬCAEARCHĬA. [PUTEOLI.]

DĬCAEARCHUS (-i), a celebrated Peripatetic philosopher, geographer, and historian, a native of Messana in Sicily, a disciple of Aristotle and a friend of Theophrastus. He wrote a vast number of works, of which only fragments are extant.

DICTAEUS. [DICTE.]

DICTĒ (-es), a mountain in the E. of Crete, where Zeus (Jupiter) is said to have been brought up. Hence he bore the surname *Dictaeus.* The Roman poets frequently employ the adjective Dictaeus as synonymous with Cretan.

DICTYNNA (-ae), a surname both of Britomartis and Diana, which two divinities were subsequently identified. The name is connected with δίκτυον, a hunting-net, and was borne by Britomartis and Diana as goddesses of the chase.

DICTYS (-yis or -yos) CRĒTENSIS (-is), the reputed author of an extant work in Latin on the Trojan war, divided into 6 books, and entitled *Ephemeris Belli Trojani,* professing to be a journal of the leading events of the war. In the preface to the work we are told that it was composed by Dictys, of Cnossus, who accompanied Idomeneus to the Trojan war; but it probably belongs to the time of the Roman empire.

DĪDĬUS SALVĬUS JŪLĬĀNUS (-i), bought the Roman empire of the praetorian guards, when they put up the empire for sale after the death of Pertinax, A.D. 193. After reigning two months, he was murdered by the soldiers when Severus was marching against the city.

DĪDŌ (-ūs : *acc.* ō), also called Elissa, the reputed founder of Carthage. She was daughter of the Tyrian king Belus, and sister

of Pygmalion, who succeeded to the crown after the death of his father. Dido was married to her wealthy uncle, Acerbas, who was murdered by Pygmalion. Upon this Dido secretly sailed from Tyre with his treasures, accompanied by some noble Tyrians, and passed over to Africa. Here she purchased as much land as might be enclosed with the hide of a bull, but she ordered the hide to be cut up into the thinnest possible stripes, and with them she surrounded a spot, on which she built a citadel called Byrsa (from βύρσα, *i.e.*, the hide of a bull). Around this fort the city of Carthage arose, and soon became a powerful and flourishing place. The neighbouring king, Hiarbas, jealous of the prosperity of the new city, demanded the hand of Dido in marriage, threatening Carthage with war in case of refusal. Dido had vowed eternal fidelity to her late husband; but seeing that the Carthaginians expected her to comply with the demands of Hiarbas, she pretended to yield to their wishes, and under pretence of soothing the manes of Acerbas by expiatory sacrifices, she erected a funeral pile, on which she stabbed herself in presence of her people. After her death she was worshipped by the Carthaginians as a divinity. Virgil has inserted in his Aeneid the legend of Dido, with various modifications. According to the common chronology, there was an interval of more than 300 years between the capture of Troy (B.C. 1184) and the foundation of Carthage (B.C. 853); but Virgil, nevertheless, makes Dido a contemporary of Aeneas, with whom she falls in love on his

Dido. (MS. Vatican Virgil, P. 93.)

arrival in Africa. When Aeneas hastened to seek the new home which the gods had promised him, Dido, in despair, destroyed herself on a funeral pile.

DĬDȲMA. [Branchidae.]

DIESPÏTER. [Jupiter.]

DĬGENTĬA (-ae : *Licenza*), a small stream in Latium, beautifully cool and clear, flowing into the Anio, through the Sabine farm of Horace.

DĪNARCHUS (-i), the last and least important of the 10 Attic orators, was born at Corinth, about B.C. 361. As he was a foreigner, he could not come forward himself as an orator, and therefore wrote orations for others. He belonged to the friends of Phocion and the Macedonian party. Only 3 of his speeches have come down to us.

DINDȲMĒNĒ. [Dindymus.]

DINDȲMUS (-i) or DINDȲMA (-ōrum). (1) A mountain in Phrygia, on the frontiers of Galatia, near the town Pessinus, sacred to Cybele, the mother of the gods, who is hence called Dindymēnē. — (2) A mountain in Mysia, near Cyzicus, also sacred to Cybele.

DĬOCAESARĒA (-ae), more anciently SEPPHŌRIS, in Galilee, was a small place, until Herodes Antipas made it the capital of Galilee, under the name of Diocaesarea.

DĬOCLĒTĬANUS, VĂLĔRĬUS (-i), Roman emperor, A.D. 284 — 305, was born near Salona, in Dalmatia, in 245, of most obscure parentage. On the death of Numerianus, he was proclaimed emperor by the troops, 284. That he might more successfully repel the barbarians, he associated with himself Maximianus, who was invested with the title of Augustus, 286. Subsequently (292) the empire was again divided. Constantius Chlorus and Galerius were proclaimed Caesars, and the government of the Roman world was divided between the 2 Augusti and the 2 Caesars. Diocletian governed the East ; but after an anxious reign of 21 years, he longed for repose. Accordingly on 1st of May, 305, he abdicated at Nicomedia, and compelled his reluctant colleague, Maximian, to do the same at Milan. Diocletian retired to his native Dalmatia, and passed the remaining 8 years of his life near Salona, in philosophic retirement, devoted to rural pleasures and the cultivation of his garden. He died 313. One of the most memorable events in the reign of Diocletian was his fierce persecution of the Christians (303), to which he was instigated by his colleague Galerius.

DĬŌDŌRUS (-i). (1) Surnamed CRONUS, a celebrated dialectic philosopher, was a native of Iasus, in Caria, and lived at Alexandria in the reign of Ptolemy Soter.—(2) SICULUS, of Agyrium, in Sicily, a celebrated historian, was a contemporary of Julius Caesar and of Augustus. In order to collect materials for his history, he travelled over a great part of Europe and Asia, and lived a long time at Rome. His work was entitled *Bibliotheca Historica*, *The Historical Library*, and was an universal history, embracing the period from the earliest mythical ages down to the beginning of Caesar's Gallic wars. Of the 40 books into which the work was divided, 15 have come down to us entire, namely, the first 5 books, containing the early history of the Eastern nations, the Egyptians, Aethiopians, and Greeks ; and books 11 to 20 inclusive, containing the history from the 2nd Persian war, B.C. 480, down to 302. Of the rest, only fragments have been preserved. In his writings we find neither method, accuracy, nor judgment. As an authority he cannot be relied upon.—(3) Of Tyre, a peripatetic philosopher, a disciple and follower of Critolaüs, whom he succeeded as the head of the Peripatetic school at Athens. He flourished B.C. 110.

DĬŌDŌTUS (-i), a Stoic philosopher, and a teacher of Cicero, in whose house he died B.C. 59.

DĬOGĔNĒS (-is). (1) Of APOLLONIA, in Crete, a celebrated Ionic philosopher, and a pupil of Anaximenes, lived in the 5th century B.C. —(2) The BABYLONIAN, a Stoic philosopher, was a pupil of Chrysippus, and succeeded Zeno of Tarsus as the head of the Stoic school at Athens. He was one of the 3 ambassadors sent by the Athenians to Rome in B.C. 155.—(3) The celebrated CYNIC philosopher was born at Sinope, in Pontus, about B.C. 412. His youth is said to have been spent in dissolute extravagance ; but at Athens his attention was arrested by the character of Antisthenes, and he soon became distinguished by his austerity and moroseness. In summer he used to roll in hot sand, and in winter to embrace statues covered with snow ; he wore coarse clothing, lived on the plainest food, slept in porticoes or in the streets ; and finally, according to the common story, took up his residence in a tub belonging to the Metroum, or temple of the Mother of the Gods. On a voyage to Aegina he was taken prisoner by pirates, and carried to Crete to be sold as a slave. Here, when he was asked what business he understood, he answered, "How to command men." He was purchased by Xeniades, of Corinth, who gave him his freedom, and entrusted him with the care of his children. During his residence at Corinth his celebrated interview with Alexander the Great is said to have taken place. The conversation between them begun by the king's saying, "I am Alexander the Great ;" to which the philosopher replied, "And I am Diogenes the Cynic." Alexander then asked whether he could oblige him in any way, and received no answer, except,

"Yes; you can stand out of the sunshine." We are furt??r told that Alexander admired Diogenes so much that he said, "If I were not Alexander, I should wish to be Diogenes." Diogenes died at Corinth, at the age of nearly 90, B.C. 323. — (4) LAERTIUS, of Laërte, in Cilicia, probably lived in the 2nd century after Christ. He wrote the Lives of the Philosophers in 10 books, which work is still extant. .

DIOMĒDĒAE INSŬLAE, 5 small islands in the Adriatic sea, N. of the promontory Garganum, in Apulia, named after Diomedes. [DIOMEDES.] The largest of these, called Diomedea Insula or Trimerus (*Tremiti*), was the place where Julia, the granddaughter of Augustus, died.

DĪOMĒDĒS (-is). (1) Son of Tydeus and Deïpyle, whence he is constantly called Tydīdes, succeeded Adrastus as king of Argos. —*Homeric Story.* Tydeus fell in the expedition against Thebes, while his son Diomedes was yet a boy ; but Diomedes was afterwards one of the Epigoni who took Thebes. He went to Troy with 80 ships, and was next to Achilles, the bravest hero in the Greek army. He enjoyed the especial protection of Athena (Minerva) ; he fought against the most distinguished of the Trojans, such as Hector and Aeneas, and even with the gods who espoused the cause of the Trojans. He thus wounded both Aphrodite (Venus), and Ares (Mars). — *Later Stories.* Diomedes and Ulysses carried off the palladium from the city of Troy, since it was believed that Troy could not be taken so long as the palladium was within its walls. After the capture of Troy, he returned to Argos, where he found his wife Aegialea living in adultery with Hippolytus, or, according to others, with Cometes or Cyllabarus. This misfortune befell him through the anger of Aphrodite. He therefore quitted Argos, and went to Aetolia. He subsequently attempted to return to Argos ; but on his way home a storm threw him on the coast of Daunia, in Italy. He married Evippe, the daughter of Daunus, and settled in Daunia, where he died at an advanced age. He was buried in one of the islands off Cape Garganum, which were called after him the Diomedean islands. His companions were inconsolable at his loss, and were metamorphosed into birds (*Aves Diomedēae*), which, mindful of their origin, used to fly joyfully towards the Greek ships, but to avoid those of the Romans. A number of towns in the E. part of Italy were believed to have been founded by Diomedes. A plain of Apulia, near Salapia and Canusium, was called *Diomedēi Campi*, after him.—(2) King of the Bistones, in Thrace, killed by Hercules on account of his mares, which he fed with human flesh.

DĪON (-ōnis), a Syracusan, son of Hipparinus, and a relation of Dionysius, who treated him with the greatest distinction, and employed him in many services of trust and confidence. On the visit of Plato to Syracuse, Dion became an ardent disciple of the philosopher ; and when the younger Dionysius succeeded his father, Dion watched with undisguised contempt his dissolute conduct, and so became an object of suspicion to the youthful tyrant. Dion, aided by Plato, endeavoured to withdraw him from his vicious courses, but failed, and was banished. He then retired to Athens. Plato visited Syracuse a third time, that he might secure the recall of Dion ; but failing in this, Dion determined on expelling the tyrant by force. In this he succeeded ; but since his own conduct towards the Syracusans was equally tyrannical, a conspiracy was formed against him, and he was assassinated in his own house B.C. 353.

DĪON CASSĬUS (-i), the historian, son of a Roman senator ; born A.D. 155, at Nicaea, in Bithynia. He held several important offices under Commodus, Caracalla, and Alexander Severus, 180 — 229, and afterwards retired to Campania ; subsequently he returned to Nicaea, his native town, where he passed the remainder of his life, and died. The chief work of Dion was a History of Rome, in 80 books, from the landing of Aeneas in Italy to A.D. 229. Unfortunately, only a comparatively small portion of this work has come down to us entire. From the 36th book to the 54th the work is extant complete, and embraces the history from the wars of Lucullus and Cn. Pompey against Mithridates, down to the death of Agrippa, B.C. 10. Of the remaining books we have only the epitomes made by Xiphilinus and others. Dion Cassius consulted original authorities, and displayed great judgment and discrimination in the use of them.

DĪON CHRYSOSTŎMUS (-i), that is, the golden-mouthed, a surname given him on account of his eloquence, was born at Prusa, in Bithynia, about the middle of the first century of our era. He was well educated, and increased his knowledge by travelling. The emperors Nerva and Trajan entertained for him the highest esteem. He was the most eminent of the Greek rhetoricians and sophists in the time of the Roman empire. There are extant 80 of his orations ; but they are rather essays on political, moral,- and philosophical subjects than real orations, of which they have only the form.

DĪONAEA. [DIONE.]

DIONE (-es), a female Titan, by Zeus (Jupiter), by whom she became the mother of Aphrodite (Venus), who is hence called *Dionaea*, and sometimes even *Dione*. Hence Caesar is called *Dionaeus Caesar*, because he claimed descent from Venus.

DIONYSIUS (-i). (1) The Elder, tyrant of Syracuse, son of Hermocrates, born B.C. 430. He began life as a clerk in a public office. Prompted by ambition, and possessing natural talent, he gradually raised himself to distinction; and in B.C. 405, though only 25 years of age, was appointed sole general at Syracuse, with full powers. From this period we may date the commencement of his reign, or tyranny, which continued without interruption for 38 years. He strengthened himself by the increase of the army, and by converting the island Ortygia into a fortified residence for himself; and when thoroughly prepared, commenced the execution of his ambitious plans. These embraced the subjugation of the rest of Sicily, the humiliation of Carthage, and the annexation of part of Southern Italy to his dominions. In all these projects he succeeded. During the last 20 years of his life he possessed an amount of power and influence far exceeding that enjoyed by any other Greek before the time of Alexander. His death took place at Syracuse, 367, in the middle of a war with Carthage. He was succeeded by his eldest son, Dionysius the younger. The character of Dionysius has been drawn in the blackest colours by many ancient writers; he appears, indeed, to have become a type of a tyrant, in its worst sense. In his latter years he became extremely suspicious, and apprehensive of treachery, even from his nearest friends, and is said to have adopted the most excessive precautions to guard against it. He built the terrible prison called Lautumiae, which was cut out of the solid rock in the part of Syracuse named Epipolae. Dionysius was fond of literature and the arts, and frequently entertained at his court men distinguished in literature and philosophy, among whom was the philosopher Plato. He was himself a poet, and repeatedly contended for the prize of tragedy at Athens. — (2) The Younger, son of the preceding, succeeded his father as tyrant of Syracuse, B.C. 367. He was at this time under 30 years of age; he had been brought up at his father's court in idleness and luxury, and was studiously precluded from taking any part in public affairs. The ascendancy which Dion, and through his means Plato, obtained for a time over his mind was undermined by flatterers and the companions of his pleasures. Dion, who had been banished by Dionysius, re-

turned to Sicily in 357, at the head of a small force, with the avowed object of dethroning him. Dionysius finding that he could not successfully resist Dion, sailed away to Italy, and thus lost the sovereignty after a reign of 12 years, 356. He now repaired to Locri, the native city of his mother, Doris, where he was received in the most friendly manner; but he made himself tyrant of the city, and treated the inhabitants with the utmost cruelty. After remaining at Locri 10 years, he obtained possession again of Syracuse, where he reigned for the next 3 years until Timoleon came to Sicily to deliver the Greek cities there from the dominion of the tyrants. Being unable to resist Timoleon, he surrendered the citadel into the hands of the latter, on condition of being allowed to depart in safety to Corinth, 343. Here he spent the remainder of his life in a private condition; and according to some writers was reduced to support himself by keeping a school.—(3) Of HALICARNASSUS, a celebrated Greek rhetorician, lived many years at Rome in the time of Augustus, and died B.C. 7. His principal work was a history of Rome in 22 books, containing the history of the city from the mythical times down to B.C. 264. Of this work only the first 11 books have come down to us. These prove that he possessed considerable artistic skill as well as rhetorical power, but was deficient both as an historian and as a statesman. He also wrote various rhetorical and critical works, which abound with the most exquisite remarks and criticisms on the works of the classical writers of Greece. Of these several have been preserved.—(4) Of Heraclea, a pupil of Zeno, at first a Stoic and afterwards an Eleatic philosopher.

DIONYSUS (-i), the youthful, beautiful, but effeminate god of wine. He is also called both by Greeks and Romans BACCHUS, that is, the noisy or riotous god, which was originally only an epithet or surname of Dionysus. He was the son of Zeus(Jupiter) and Semele, the daughter of Cadmus of Thebes. Before his birth, Semele was persuaded by Hera (Juno), who appeared to her in disguise, to request the father of the gods to appear to her in the same glory in which he approached his own wife Hera. Zeus unwillingly complied, and appeared to her in thunder and lightning. Semele, being seized by the flames, gave premature birth to a child; but Zeus saved the child, sewed him up in his thigh, and thus preserved him till he came to maturity. After his birth Dionysus was brought up by the nymphs of Mt. Nysa, who were rewarded by Zeus by being placed as Hyades among the stars. When he had grown up, Hera drove him mad, in which state he wandered through

Dionysus(Bacchus). (From a Painting at Pompeii.

various parts of the earth.   He first went to

Egypt, thence proceeded through Syria, then traversed all Asia, teaching the inhabitants of the different countries of Asia the cultivation of the vine and introducing among them the elements of civilisation. The most famous part of his wanderings in Asia is his expedition to India, which is said to have lasted several years.   On his return to Europe, he passed through Thrace, but was ill received by Lycurgus, king of the Edones. [LYCURGUS.] He then returned to Thebes, where he compelled the women to quit their houses, and to celebrate Bacchic festivals on Mt. Cithaeron, and fearfully punished Pentheus, who attempted to prevent his worship. [PENTHEUS.] Dionysus next went to Argos, where the people first refused to acknowledge him, but after punishing the women with frenzy, he was recognised as a god. His last feat was performed on a voyage from Icaria to Naxos. He hired a ship which belonged to Tyrrhenian pirates; but the men, instead of landing at Naxos, steered toward Asia, to sell him there as a slave.   Thereupon the god changed the mast and oars into serpents, and himself into a lion ; ivy grew around the vessel, and the sound of flutes was heard on every side ; the sailors were seized with madness, leaped into the sea, and were metamorphosed into dolphins. After he had thus gradually established his divine nature throughout the world, he

Dionysus (Bacchus) drawn by Tigers.   (Museum Capitolinum, vol. 4, tav. 65.)

took his mother out of Hades, called her Thyone, and rose with her into Olympus. --

Various mythological beings are described as the offspring of Dionysus : but among the women who won his love none is more famous in ancient story than Ariadne. [ARIADNE.]—The worship of Dionysus was no part of the original religion of Greece. In Homer he does not appear as one of the great divinities; he is there simply described as the god who teaches man the preparation of wine. As the cultivation of the vine spread in Greece, the worship of Dionysus likewise spread farther; and after the time of Alexander's expedition to India, the celebration of the Bacchic festivals assumed more and more their wild and dissolute character. Dionysus may be taken as the representative of the productive and intoxicating power of nature. Since wine is the natural symbol of this power, it is called "the fruit of Dionysus." On account of the close connexion between the cultivation of the soil and the earlier stages of civilisation, he is regarded as a lawgiver and a lover of peace. As the Greek drama had grown out of the dithyrambic choruses at the festival of Dionysus, he was also regarded as the god of tragic art, and as the protector of theatres. Respecting his festivals and the mode of their celebration, and especially the introduction and suppression of his worship at Rome, see *Dict.*

of Ant. art. *Dionysia.*—In the earliest times the Graces or Charites were the companions of Dionysus, but afterwards we find him accompanied in his expeditions and travels by Bacchantic women, called Lenae, Maenades, Thyiades, Mimallones, Clodones, Bassarae or Bassarides, all of whom are represented in works of art as raging with madness or enthusiasm, their heads thrown backwards, with dishevelled hair, and carrying in their hands thyrsus-staffs (entwined with ivy, and headed with pine-cones), cymbals, swords, or serpents. Sileni, Pans, satyrs, centaurs, and other beings of a like kind, are also the constant companions of the god. The animal most commonly sacrificed to Dionysus was the ram. Among the things sacred to him, we may notice the vine, ivy, laurel, and asphodel : the dolphin, serpent, tiger, lynx, panther, and ass. In works of art he appears as a youthful god. The form of his body is manly, but approaches the female form by its softness and roundness. The expression of the countenance is languid, and his attitude is easy, like that of a man who is absorbed in sweet thoughts, or slightly intoxicated.

Dionysus (Bacchus) enthroned.   (Ponce, Bains de Titus, No. 12.)

DĪŎSCŎRĬDĒS (-is) PEDĀCĬUS or PEDĀNIUS, of Anazarba, in Cilicia, a Greek physician, who probably lived in the 2nd century of the Christian era, the author of an extant work on Materia Medica, which for many ages was received as a standard production.

DĪOSCŪRI (-ōrum), that is, sons of Zeus (Jupiter), the well-known heroes Castor and Pollux, called by the Greeks Polydeuces. The two brothers were sometimes called Castores by the Romans. According to Homer they were the sons of Leda and Tyndareus, king of Lacedaemon, and consequently brothers of Helen. Hence they are often called by the patronymic *Tyndărĭdae.* Castor was famous for his skill in taming and managing horses, and Pollux for his skill in boxing. Both had disappeared from the earth before the Greeks went against Troy. Although they were buried, says Homer, yet they came to life every other day, and they enjoyed divine honours.—According to other traditions, both were the sons of Zeus and Leda, and were born at the same time with their sister Helen out of an egg. [Leda.] According to others again, Pollux and Helen only were children of Zeus, and Castor was the son of Tyndareus. Hence Pollux was immortal, while Castor was subject to old age and death like other mortals. The fabulous life of the Dioscuri is marked by 3 great events. 1. Their expedition against Athens, where they rescued their sister Helen, who had been carried off by Theseus, and placed in Aphidnae, which they took. 2. Their part in the expedition of the Argonauts, during which Pollux killed, in a boxing-match, Amycus, king of the Bebryces. During the Argonautic expedition they founded the town of Dioscurias, in Colchis. 3. Their battle with the sons of Aphareus, Idas and Lynceus. Castor, the mortal, fell by the hands of Idas, but Pollux slew Lynceus, and Zeus killed Idas by a flash of lightning. At the request of Pollux, Zeus allowed him to share his brother's fate, and to live alternately one day under the earth, and the other in the heavenly abodes of the gods. According to a different form of the story, Zeus rewarded the attachment of the two brothers by placing them among the stars as *Gemini.*— These heroic youths received divine honours at Sparta, from whence their worship spread over other parts of Greece, and over Sicily and Italy. They were worshipped more especially as the protectors of sailors, for Poseidon (Neptune) had rewarded their brotherly love by giving them power over winds and waves. Hence they are called by Horace, "Fratres Helenae, lucida sidera." Whenever they appeared they were seen riding on magnificent white steeds. They were regarded as presidents of the public games, as the inventors of the war dance, and the patrons of poets and bards.

They are usually represented in works of art as youthful horsemen, with egg-shaped helmets, crowned with stars, and with spears in their hands.—At Rome, the worship of the Dioscuri was introduced at an early time. They were believed to have assisted the Ro-

Dioscuri (Castor and Pollux).   (From a Coin in the British Museum.)

mans against the Latins in the battle of Lake Regillus; and the dictator A. Postumius Albinus during the battle vowed a temple to them. This temple was erected in the forum, opposite the temple of Vesta. The equites regarded the Dioscuri as their patrons, and went every year, on the 15th of July, in a magnificent procession on horseback, to visit their temple.

Dioscuri (Castor and Pollux).   (Millin. Gal. Myth., pl. 108.)

DĪRAE (-ārum), a name of the Furiae. [Eumenides.]

DIRCĒ (-ēs), wife of Lycus, who married her, after divorcing his former wife Antiŏpē. Dirce treated Antiope with great cruelty; and accordingly, when Amphion and Zethus, the sons of Antiope, by Zeus (Jupiter), obtained possession of Thebes, they took a signal vengeance upon Dirce. They tied her to a wild bull, which dragged her about till she perished. They then threw her body into a fountain near Thebes, which was henceforth called the fountain of Dirce. The adjective Dircaeus is frequently used as equivalent to Boeotian.

Dirce. Group at Naples. (Maffei, pl. 48.)

DIS (-*gen.* Ditis), contracted from Dives, a name sometimes given to Pluto, and hence also to the lower world.

DISCORDIA. [ERIS.]

DIUM. (1) An important town in Macedonia on the Thermaic gulf. — (2) A town in Chalcidice in Macedonia, on the Strymonic gulf.

DIVICO (-ōnis), the leader of the Helvetians in the war against L. Cassius in B.C. 107, was at the head of the embassy sent to Julius Caesar, nearly 50 years later, B.C. 58, when he was preparing to attack the Helvetians.

DIVITIACUS (-i), an Aeduan noble and brother of Dumnorix, was a warm adherent of the Romans and of Caesar, who, in consideration of his entreaties, pardoned the treason of Dumnorix in B.C. 58.

DIVODURUM (-i: *Metz*), subsequently Mediomatrici, and still later Metis or Mettis, the capital of the Mediomatrici in Gallia Belgica.

DIVONA. [CADURCI.]

DOBERUS (-i), a town in Paeonia in Macedonia, E. of the river Echedorus.

DODONA (-ae), the most ancient oracle in Greece, situated in Epirus, founded by the Pelasgians, and dedicated to Zeus (Jupiter). The responses of the oracle were given from lofty oaks or beech trees. The will of the god was declared by the wind rustling through the trees, and in order to render the sounds more distinct, brazen vessels were suspended on the branches of the trees, which being set in motion by the wind came in contact with one another. These sounds were interpreted in early times by men, but afterwards by aged women. The priests, who had the management of the temple were called Selli or Helli. The oracle of Dodona had less influence in historical times than in the heroic age, and was supplanted to a great extent by the oracle of Delphi.

DOLABELLA (-ae), the name of a celebrated patrician family of the Cornelia gens. Those most deserving of notice are :—(1) CN. CORNELIUS DOLABELLA, consul B.C. 81, whom the young Julius Caesar accused in 77 of extortion in his province.—(2) CN. CORNELIUS DOLABELLA, praetor urbanus 81. With Verres as his legate, he plundered his province in Cilicia, and upon his return was accused, betrayed by Verres, and condemned.—(3) P. CORNELIUS DOLABELLA, the son-in-law of Cicero, whose daughter Tullia he married in 51. He was one of the most profligate men of his age, and his conduct caused Cicero great uneasiness. On the breaking out of the civil war he joined Caesar and fought on his side at the battle of Pharsalia (48), and was raised by him to the consulship in 44. He afterwards received from Antony the province of Syria. On his way to his province he plundered the cities of Greece and Asia Minor, in consequence of which the senate sent against him Cassius, who took Caesarea, in which Dolabella had taken refuge. That he might not fall into the hands of his enemies, he committed suicide, 43.

DOLON (-ōnis), a spy of the Trojans in the Trojan war, slain by Diomedes.

DOLOPES (-um), a powerful people in Thessaly, dwelt on the Enipeus, and fought before Troy. At a later time they dwelt at the foot of Mt. Pindus; and their country, called DOLOPIA, was reckoned part of Epirus.

DOMITIANUS (-i), or with his full name T. FLAVIUS DOMITIANUS AUGUSTUS, Roman emperor A.D. 81—96, was the younger son of Vespasian, and was born at Rome A.D. 51. During the reigns of Vespasian (69—79) and of his brother Titus (79—81) he was not allowed to take any part in public affairs. During the first few years of his reign his government was much better than had been expected. But his conduct was soon changed for the worse. His wars were mostly unfortunate; and his want of success both wounded his vanity and excited his fears, and thus led him to delight in the misfortunes and sufferings of others. In 83 he undertook an expedition against the Chatti, which was attended with no result, though on his return to Rome in the following year, he celebrated a triumph, and assumed the name of Germanicus. In 85 Agricola, whose success and merits excited his jealousy, was recailed to Rome. [AGRICOLA.] After his war with the Dacians, which terminated very unfavourably [DECEBALUS], he gave full sway to his cruelty and tyranny. The silent fear which prevailed in Rome and Italy during the latter years of Domitian's reign is briefly but energetically described by Tacitus in the introduction to his Life of Agricola, and his vices and tyranny are exposed in the strongest colours by the withering satire of Juvenal. Many conspiracies had been formed against his life, which had been discovered; but he was at length murdered by the connivance of his wife, Domitia.

DOMITIUS AFER. [AFER.]

DOMITIUS AHENOBARBUS. [AHENOBARBUS.]

DOMITIUS CALVINUS. [CALVINUS.]

DOMITIUS CORBULO. [CORBULO.]

DOMITIUS ULPIANUS. [ULPIANUS.]

DONATUS (-i).—(1) A celebrated grammarian, who taught at Rome in the middle of the 4th century, and was the preceptor of St. Jerome. His most famous work is a system of Latin Grammar, which has formed the groundwork of most elementary treatises upon the same subject, from his own time to the present day.—(2) TIBERIUS CLAUDIUS, the author of a life of Virgil in 25 chapters, prefixed to many editions of Virgil.

DONUSA or DONUSIA (-ae), one of the smaller Sporades in the Aegean sea, near Naxos. It produced green marble, whence Virgil calls the island *viridis*. Under the Roman emperors it was used as a place of banishment.

DORA (-ae), DORUS, DORUM (-i), called DOR in the O. T., the most southerly town of Phoenicia on the coast, on a kind of peninsula at the foot of Mt. Carmel.

DORIS (-idis). (1) Daughter of Oceanus and Thetis, wife of her brother Nereus, and mother of the Nereides. The Latin poets sometimes use the name of this divinity for the sea itself.—(2) One of the Nereides, daughter of the preceding.—(3) A small and mountainous country in Greece, formerly called DRYOPIS, bounded by Thessaly on the N., by Aetolia on the W., by Locris on the S., and by Phocis on the E. It contained 4 towns, Boum, Citinium, Erineus, and Pindus, which formed the Dorian tetrapolis. These towns never attained any consequence; but the country is of importance as the home of the Dorians (Dores), one of the great Hellenic races, who conquered Peloponnesus.

It was related that Aegimius, king of the Dorians, had been driven from his dominions by the Lapithae, but was reinstated by Hercules; that the children of Hercules hence took refuge in this land when they had been expelled from Peloponnesus; and that it was to restore them to their rights that the Dorians invaded Peloponnesus. Accordingly, the conquest of Peloponnesus by the Dorians is usually called the Return of the Heraclidae. [HERACLIDAE.] The Dorians were divided into three tribes: the *Hylleis*, *Pamphyli*, and *Dymanes*. They were the ruling class throughout Peloponnesus; the old inhabitants were reduced to slavery, or became subjects of the Dorians under the name of *Perioeci*. — (4) A district in Asia Minor consisting of the Dorian settlements on the coast of Caria and the neighbouring islands. 6 of these towns formed a league, called the Dorian hexapolis, consisting of Lindus, Ialysus, and Camirus in the island of Rhodes, the island of Cos, and Cnidus and Halicarnassus on the mainland.

DORISCUS (-i), a town in Thrace at the mouth of the Hebrus, in the midst of an extensive plain of the same name, where Xerxes reviewed his vast forces.

DORUS (-i), a son of Helien, and the mythical ancestor of the Dorians.

DORYLAEUM (-i), a town in Phrygia Epictetus, on the river Thymbris, with warm baths, which are used at the present day.

DOSSENNUS FABIUS, or DORSENUS, an ancient Latin comic dramatist, censured by Horace on account of the exaggerated buffoonery of his characters.

DRABESCUS (-i), a town in the district Edonis in Macedonia, on the Strymon.

DRACON (-onis), the author of the first written code of laws at Athens. In this code he affixed the penalty of death to almost all crimes—to petty thefts, for instance, as well as to sacrilege and murder — which gave occasion to the remark that his laws were written not in ink, but in blood. His legislation is placed in B.C. 621. After the legislation of Solon (594), most of the laws of Dracon fell into disuse.

DRANGIANA (-ae), a part of Ariana, bounded by Gedrosia, Carmania, Arachosia, and Aria. It sometimes formed a separate satrapy, but was more usually united to the satrapies either of Arachosia or of Gedrosia, or of Aria. In the N. of the country dwelt the DRANGAE, a warlike people, from whom the province derived its name. The Ariaspae inhabited the S. part of the province.

DRAVUS (-i: *Drave*), a tributary of the Danube, flowing through Noricum and Pannonia; and after receiving the Murius

(*Muhr*), falling into the Danube E. of Mursa (*Esseck*).

DREPANUM (-i), that is, a sickle. (1) Also DREPANA (-ōrum), more rarely DREPANE (-ēs : *Trapani*), a seaport town in the N.W. corner of Sicily, founded by the Carthaginians. It was here that Anchises died, according to Virgil.—(2) Also DREPANE, a town in Bithynia, the birth-place of Helena, mother of Constantine the Great, in whose honour it was called HELENOPOLIS, and made an important place.

DRUENTIA (-ae : *Durance*), a large and rapid river in Gallia Narbonensis, rising in the Alps, and flowing into the Rhone near Avenio (*Avignon*).

DRUSILLA (-ae).—(1) LIVIA (-ae), mother of the emperor Tiberius and wife of Augustus. [LIVIA.]—(2) Daughter of Germanicus and Agrippina, lived in incestuous intercourse with her brother Caligula, who loved her most tenderly and deified her at her decease A.D. 38.—(3) Daughter of Herodes Agrippa I., king of the Jews, married Felix, the procurator of Judaea, and was present with her husband when St. Paul preached before Felix in A.D. 60.

DRUSUS (-i), the name of a distinguished family of the Livia gens. It is said that one of the Livii acquired the cognomen Drusus for himself and his descendants by having slain in combat one Drausus, a Gallic chieftain ;—(1) M. LIVIUS DRUSUS, tribune of the plebs with C. Gracchus, B.C. 122. He was a staunch adherent of the aristocracy, and gained popularity for the senate by proposing almost the same measures as he had opposed when brought forward by Gracchus. He was consul 111.—(2) M. LIVIUS DRUSUS, son of No. 1, an eloquent orator, was tribune of the plebs, 91. Although, like his father, he belonged to the aristocratical party, he meditated the most extensive changes in the Roman state. He proposed and carried some portion of his scheme ; but eventually his measures became very unpopular. The senate, perceiving the dissatisfaction of all parties, voted that all the laws of Drusus, being carried against the auspices, were null and void from the beginning. Drusus now began to organise a formidable conspiracy against the government ; but one evening, as he was entering the hall of his own house, he was stabbed and died a few hours afterwards. The death of Drusus destroyed the hopes of the Socii, to whom he had promised the Roman citizenship, and was thus immediately followed by the Social War.—(3) LIVIUS DRUSUS CLAUDIANUS, father of Livia, who was the mother of the emperor Tiberius. He was one of the gens Claudia, and was adopted by a Livius Drusus. Being proscribed by the triumvirs (42) he put an end to his own life. —(4) NERO CLAUDIUS DRUSUS, commonly called by the moderns DRUSUS SENIOR, to distinguish him from No. 5, was the son of Tib. Claudius Nero and Livia, and younger brother of the emperor Tiberius. He was born in the house of Augustus three months after the marriage of Livia and Augustus, B.C. 38. Drusus, as he grew up, was more liked by the people than was his brother. He married Antonia, the daughter of the triumvir, and was greatly trusted by Augustus, who employed him in important offices. He carried on the war against the Germans, and in the course of 4 campaigns (B.C. 12—9) he advanced as far as the Albis (*Elbe*). In his first campaign he dug a canal (*Fossa Drusiana*) from the Rhine near Arnheim to the Yssel, near Doesberg ; and he made use of this canal to sail from the Rhine into the ocean. On the return of the army from the Elbe to the Rhine, he died in consequence of a fracture of his leg, which happened through a fall from his horse.—(5) DRUSUS CAESAR, commonly called by modern writers DRUSUS JUNIOR, was the son of the emperor Tiberius by his 1st wife, Vipsania. He married Livia, the sister of Germanicus. He was poisoned by Sejanus, the favourite of Tiberius, who aspired to the empire, A.D. 23.—(6) DRUSUS, second son of Germanicus and Agrippina, also fell a victim to the ambition of Sejanus a few years after No. 5.

DRYADES. [NYMPHAE.]

DRYAS (-adis) father of the Thracian king Lycurgus, who is hence called Dryantides.

DRYMAEA (-ae) or DRYMUS (-i), a town in Phocis, a little S. of the Cephissus.

DRYMUS (-i).—(1) See DRYMAEA.—(2) A strong place in Attica, on the frontiers of Boeotia.

DRYMUSSA (-ae), an island off the coast of Ionia, opposite Clazomenae.

DRYOPE (-es), daughter of king Dryops, was beloved by Apollo, by whom she became the mother of AMPHISSUS. She was afterwards carried off by the Hamadryades, and became a nymph.

DRYOPES (-um), a Pelasgic people, who dwelt first in Thessaly, from the Spercheus to Parnassus, and afterwards in Doris, which was called from them DRYOPIS. Driven out of Doris by the Dorians, they migrated to other countries, and settled in Peloponnesus, Euboea, and Asia Minor.

DUBIS (-is : *Doubs*), a river in Gaul, rising in M. Jurassus (*Jura*), flowing past Vesontio (*Besançon*), and falling into the Arar (*Saône*) near Cabillonum (*Châlons*).

DUBRIS PORTUS (*Dover*), a seaport town

of the Cantii, in Britain : here was a fortress erected by the Romans against the Saxon pirates.

DUILIUS (-i), consul B.C. 260, gained a victory over the Carthaginian fleet by means of grappling-irons, which drew the enemy's ships towards his, and thus changed the sea-fight into a land-fight. This was the first naval victory that the Romans had ever gained, and the memory of it was perpetuated by a column which was erected in the forum, and adorned with the beaks of the conquered ships (*Columna Rostrata*.)

DULGIBINI (-orum), a people in Germany, dwelling on the W. bank of the Weser.

DULICHIUM. [ECHINADES.]

DUMNORIX (-igis), a chieftain of the Aedui, and brother of Divitiacus. He was an enemy of the Romans, and was put to death by Caesar's order, B.C. 54.

DUNIUM. [DUROTRIGES.]

DURIUS (-i : *Duero, Douro*), one of the chief rivers of Spain, near Numantia, and flowing into the Atlantic.

DUROCORTORUM (-i : *Rheims*), the capital of the Remi in Gallia Belgica, subsequently called Remi.

DURONIA, a town in Samnium in Italy, W. of the Caudine passes.

DUROTRIGES (-um), a people in Britain, in Dorsetshire and the W. of Somersetshire : their chief town was Dunium (*Dorchester*).

DUROVERNUM or DARVERNUM (-i : *Canterbury*), a town of the Cantii in Britain, afterwards called Cantuaria.

DYMAS (-antis), father of Hecuba, who is hence called *Dymantis*.

DYME (-es) or DYMAE (-arum), a town in the W. of Achaia, near the coast ; one of the 12 Achaean towns.

DYRRHACHIUM (-i : *Durazzo*), formerly called EPIDAMNUS, a town in Greek Illyria, on a peninsula in the Adriatic sea. It was founded by the Corcyraeans, and received the name of Epidamnus ; but since the Romans regarded this name a bad omen, as reminding them of *damnum*, they changed it into Dyrrha-chium. It was the usual place of landing for persons who crossed over from Brundisium.

EBORACUM or EBURACUM (-i : *York*), a town of the Brigantes in Britain, made a Roman station by Agricola, and became the chief Roman settlement in the island. It was both a municipium and a colony, and the resi-dence of the Roman emperors when they visited Britain. Here the emperors Septi-mius Severus and Constantius Chlorus died.

EBUDAE or HEBUDAE (-arum : *Hebrides*), islands in the Western Ocean off Britain.

EBURONES (-um), a German people, who crossed the Rhine and settled in Gallia Belgica, between the Rhine and the Mosa (*Maas*).

EBUROVICES. [AULERCI.]

EBUSUS or EBUSUS (-i : *Iviza*), the largest of the Pityusae insulae, off the E. coast of Spain, reckoned by some writers among the Baleares.

ECBATANA (-orum : *Hamadan*), a great city, most pleasantly situated, near the foot of Mt. Orontes, in the N. of Great Media, was the capital of the Median kingdom, and afterwards the summer residence of the Persian and Parthian kings. It is said to have been founded by the first king of Media, Deioces.

ECETRA (-ae), an ancient town of the Volsci, destroyed by the Romans at an early period.

ECHEDORUS (-i), a small river in Mace-donia, flowing through Mygdonia, and falling into the Thermaic gulf.

ECHEMUS (-i), king of Arcadia, slew, in single combat, Hyllus, the son of Hercules.

ECHIDNA (-ae), a monster, half woman and half-serpent, became by Typhon the mother of the Chimaera, of the many-headed dog Orthus, of the hundred-headed dragon who guarded the apples of the Hesperides, of the Colchian dragon, of the Sphinx, of Cer-berus (hence called *Echidnēus canis*), of Scylla, of Gorgon, of the Lernaean Hydra (*Echidna Lernaea*), of the eagle which con-sumed the liver of Prometheus, and of the Nemean lion. She was killed in her sleep by Argus Panoptes.

ECHINADES (-um), a group of small islands at the mouth of the Achelous, be-longing to Arcanania, said to have been formed by the alluvial deposits of the Ache-lous. They appear to have derived their name from their resemblance to the Echinus or sea-urchin. The largest of these islands was named DULICHIUM, and belonged to the kingdom of Ulysses, who is hence called *Dulichius*.

ECHION (-onis) (1) One of the heroes who sprang up from the dragon's teeth sown by Cadmus. He was the husband of Agave and father of Pentheus, who is hence called *Echionides*.—(2) Son of Hermes (Mercury) and Antianira, took part in the Calydonian hunt, and in the expedition of the Argo-nauts.

ECHO (-us), a nymph who used to keep Juno engaged by incessantly talking to her, while Jupiter was sporting with the nymphs. Juno, however, found out the trick that was played upon her, and punished Echo by changing her into an echo. Echo in this state fell in love with Narcissus; but as her love was not returned, she pined away in grief, so that in the end there remained of her nothing but her voice.

ĔDESSA (-ae). (1) Also called ANTIOCHIA CALLIRRHOE (O.T. Ur), a very ancient city in the N. of Mesopotamia, the capital of Osroëne, and the seat of an independent kingdom from B.C. 137 to A.D. 216. [ABGARUS.].—(2) A city of Macedonia, the burial-place of the kings.

ĔDĔTANI or SĔDETANI (-ōrum), a people in Hispania Tarraconensis, E. of the Celtiberi.

ĔDŌNI or ĔDŌNES (-um), a Thracian people, between the Nestus and the Strymon, celebrated for their orgiastic worship of Bacchus; whence ĔDŌNIS in the Latin poets signifies a female Bacchante, and ĔDŌNUS is used as equivalent to Thracian.

ĔĔTION (-ōnis), king of the Placian Thebē, in Cilicia, and father of Andromache, the wife of Hector.

ĔGĔRĬA. [AEGERIA.]

EGESTA. [SEGESTA.]

EGNĀTĬA (-ae), a town in Apulia, on the coast, called GNATIA by Horace. It was celebrated for its miraculous stone or altar, which of itself set on fire frankincense and wood; a prodigy which afforded amusement to Horace and his friends, who looked upon it as a mere trick. Egnatia was situated on the high road from Rome to Brundisium, which from Egnatia to Brundisium bore the name of the VIA EGNATIA. The continuation of this road on the other side of the Adriatic from Dyrrhachium to Byzantium, also bore the name of Via Egnatia. It was the great military road between Italy and the E. Commencing at Dyrrhachium, it passed by Lychnidus, Heraclēa, Lyncestis, Edessa, Thessalonica, Amphipolis, Philippi, and traversing the whole of Thrace, finally reached Byzantium.

ĔĬON (-ōnis), a town in Thrace, at the mouth of the Strymon, 25 stadia from Amphipolis, of which it was the harbour.

ĔLAEA (-ae), an ancient city on the coast of Aeolis, in Asia Minor, subsequently served as the harbour of Pergamus. The gulf on which it stood was named after it Sinus Elaïticus.

ĔLAEŪS (-untis), or ĔLĔŪS (-untis), a town on the S. E. point of the Thracian Chersonese, with a harbour and an heroum of Protesilaus.

ELAGABĂLUS (-i), Roman Emperor, A.D. 218—222, son of Julia Soemias and Varius Marcellus, was born at Emesa about 205, and was called Elagabalus because in childhood he was made priest of the Syro-Phoenician Sungod at Emesa, bearing that name. He obtained the purple at the age of 13, by the intrigues of his grandmother Julia Maesa, whc gave out that he was the son of Caracalla On his accession he took the name of M. AURELIUS ANTONINUS. He was a prince of incredible folly, superstition, and vice. He was slain by the soldiers in 222, and was succeeded by his cousin Alexander Severus.

ĔLĀNA. [AELANA.]

ĔLĀTĔA (-ae). (1) A town in Phocis, situated near the Cephissus in a fertile valley, which was an important pass from Thessaly to Boeotia.—(2) A tcwn in Pelasgiotis, in Thessaly, near Gonni.—(3) Or ELATREA, a town in Epirus, near the sources of the Cocÿtus.

ĔLĀTUS (-i), one of the Lapithae, and father of Caeneus, who is hence called Ĕlătēïus.

ĔLĀVER (-ĕris, Allier), a river in Aquitania, a tributary of the Liger.

ĔLĔA. [VELIA.]

ĔLECTRA (-ae), i. e. the bright or brilliant one. (1) Daughter of Oceanus and Tethys, wife of Thaumas, and mother of Iris and the Harpies, Aëllo and Ocypete.—(2) Daughter of Atlas and Pleïöne, one of the 7 Pleiades, and by Zeus (Jupiter), mother of Iasion and Dardanus.—(3) Daughter of Agamemnon and Clytaemnestra, also called Laodice, sister of Iphigenia and Orestes. After the murder of her father by her mother, she saved the life of her young brother Orestes by sending him to King Strophius until he had grown up to manhood. Electra then excited him to avenge the death of Agamemnon, and assisted him in slaying their mother Clytaemnestra. [ORESTES.] After the death of the latter, Orestes gave her in marriage to his friend Pylades.

ĔLECTRĬDES INSŬLAE. [ERIDANUS.]

ĔLECTRŸON (-ōnis), son of Perseus and Andromeda, and father of Alcmene, the wife of Amphitryon. For details see AMPHITRYON.

ĔLĔON (-ōnis), a town in Boeotia, near Tanagra.

ĔLĔPHANTĬNĔ (-es), an island in the Nile, with a city of the same name, opposite to Syene, and 7 stadia below the Little Cataract, was the frontier station of Egypt towards Ethiopia, and was strongly garrisoned under the Persians and the Romans.

ĔLEUSIS (-ĭnis), a town and demus of Attica, situated N. W. of Athens, on the coast near the frontiers of Megara. It possessed a magnificent temple of Demeter (Ceres), and gave its name to the great festival and mysteries of the Eleusinia, which were celebrated in honour of Demeter and Persephone (Proserpine).

ĔLĬCĬUS (-i), a surname of Jupiter at Rome, because he was invoked to send down lightning.

ELIMBERRUM. [Ausci.]

ELIMEA, -IA (-ae), or **ELIMIOTIS**, a district of Macedonia, on the frontiers of Epirus and Thessaly, originally belonging to Illyria. Its inhabitants, the ELIMAEI, were Epirots.

ELIS (-ĭdis), a country on the W. coast of Peloponnesus, bounded by Achaia on the N., Arcadia on the E., Messenia on the S., and the Ionian sea on the W. It was divided into 3 parts :—(1) ELIS PROPER or HOLLOW ELIS, the N. part, watered by the Peneus, of which the capital was also called Elis.—(2) PISATIS, the middle portion, of which the capital was PISA.—(3) TRIPHYLIA, the S. portion, of which PYLOS was the capital, lying between the Alpheus and the Neda.—In the heroic times we find the kingdom of Nestor and the Pelidae in the S. of Elis ; while the N. of the country was inhabited by the Epeans, with whom some Aetolian tribes were mingled. On the conquest of Peloponnesus by the Heraclidae, the Aetolian chief Oxylus received Elis as his share of the conquest ; and it was the union of his Aetolian and Dorian followers with the Epeans, which formed the subsequent population of the country, under the general name of Eleans. Elis owed its importance in Greece to the worship of Zeus (Jupiter) at Olympia, near Pisa, in honour of whom a splendid festival was held every 4 years. [OLYMPIA.] In consequence of this festival being common to the whole of Greece, the country of Elis was declared sacred, and its inhabitants possessed priestly privileges.

ELISSA. [DIDO.]

ELLOPIA (-ae). (1) A district in the N. of Euboea, near the promontory Cenaeum, with a town of the same name : the whole island of Euboea is sometimes called Ellopia. —(2) An ancient name of the district about Dodona, in Epirus.

ELONE (-es), a town of the Perrhaebi, in Thessaly, afterwards called Limone.

ELPENOR (-ŏris), one of the companions of Ulysses, who were metamorphosed by Circe into swine, and afterwards back into men. Intoxicated with wine, Elpenor one day fell asleep on Circe's roof, and broke his neck.

ELUSATES (-um), a people in Aquitania, in the interior of the country.

ELYMAIS (-ĭdis), a district of Susiana, which derived its name from the Elymaei or Elymi, a warlike and predatory people. They are also found in the mountains of Great Media, and were probably among the most ancient inhabitants of the country N. of the head of the Persian Gulf : in the O. T. Susiana is called *Elam*.

ELYMUS (-i), natural son of Anchises, and brother of Eryx ; one of the Trojans who

fled from Troy to Sicily. With the aid of Aeneas they built the towns of Aegesta and Elyme. The Trojans who settled in that part of Sicily called themselves Elymi, after Elymus.

ELYSIUM (-i), the *Elysian fields.* In Homer Elysium forms no part of the realms of the dead ; he places it on the W. of the earth, near Ocean, and describes it as a happy land, where there is neither snow, nor cold, nor rain. Hither favoured heroes, like Menelaus, pass without dying, and live happy under the rule of Rhadamanthus. In the Latin poets Elysium is part of the lower world, and the residence of the shades of the Blessed.

EMATHIA (-ae), a district of Macedonia, between the Haliacmon and the Axius. The poets frequently give the name of Emathia to the whole of Macedonia, and sometimes even to the neighbouring Thessaly.

EMATHIDES (-um), the 9 daughters of Pierus, king of Emathia.

EMESA or **EMISA** (-ae), a city of Syria, on the E. bank of the Orontes, the native city of Elagabalus.

EMPEDOCLES (-is), a philosopher of Agrigentum, in Sicily, flourished about B.C. 444. He was learned and eloquent ; and, on account of his success in curing diseases, was reckoned a magician. His death is said to have been as miraculous as his life. One tradition related that he threw himself into the flames of mount Aetna, that by his sudden disappearance he might be believed to be a god ; but it was added that the volcano threw up one of his sandals, and thus revealed the manner of his death. His works were all in verse ; and some fragments of them have come down to us. Empedocles was chosen as a model by Lucretius.

EMPORIAE (-ārum) or **EMPORIUM** (-i : *Ampurias*), a town of the Indigetes, in Hispania Tarraconensis, near the Pyrenees, situated on the river Clodianus, founded by the Phocaeans from Massilia.

EMPUSA (-ae), a monstrous spectre, which was believed to devour human beings.

ENCELADUS (-i), son of Tartarus and Ge (Earth), and one of the hundred-armed giants who made war upon the gods. He was killed by Zeus (Jupiter), who buried him under mount Aetna.

ENDYMION (-ōnis), a youth renowned for his beauty and his perpetual sleep. As he slept on mount Latmus, in Caria, his surprising beauty warmed the cold heart of Selene (the Moon), who came down to him, kissed him, and lay by his side. His eternal sleep on Latmus is assigned to different causes ; but it was generally believed that

Selene had sent him to sleep that she might be able to kiss him without his knowledge.

ENGYUM (-i), a town in the interior of Sicily, possessing a celebrated temple of the great mother of the gods.

ENIPEUS (-ĕos or -ĕi), a river in Thessaly, rising in Mt. Othrys, receiving the Apidanus, near Pharsalus, and flowing into the Peneus. Poseidon (Neptune) assumed the form of the god of this river in order to obtain possession of Tyro, who was in love with Enipeus. She became by Poseidon the mother of Pelias and Neleus.

ENNA or HENNA (-ae), an ancient town of the Siculi, in Sicily, on the road from Catana to Agrigentum, said to be the centre of the island. It was surrounded by fertile plains, which bore large crops of wheat; it was one of the chief seats of the worship of Demeter (Ceres); and according to later tradition, it was in a flowery meadow near this place that Pluto carried off Proserpine.

ENNIUS (-i), Q., the Roman poet, was born at Rudiae, in Calabria, B.C. 239. He was a Greek by birth, but a subject of Rome, and served in the Roman armies. In 204 Cato, who was then quaestor, found Ennius in Sardinia, and brought him in his train to Rome. In 180 Ennius accompanied M. Fulvius Nobilior during the Aetolian campaign, and shared his triumph. Through the son of Nobilior, Ennius, when far advanced in life, obtained the rights of a Roman citizen. He maintained himself by teaching the youths of the Roman nobles. He lived on terms of the closest intimacy with the elder Scipio Africanus. He died 169, at the age of 70, and was buried in the sepulchre of the Scipios. Ennius was regarded by the Romans as the father of their poetry, but all his works are lost with the exception of a few fragments. His most important work was an epic poem in dactylic hexameters, entitled *Annales*, being a history of Rome, from the earliest times to his own day.

ENTELLA (-ae), a town of the Sicani in the interior of the island on the W. side, said to have been founded by Entellus, one of the companions of the Trojan Acestes.

ENYALIUS (-i), the Warlike, frequently occurs in the Iliad (never in the Odyssey) as an epithet of Ares (Mars). At a later time Enyalius and Ares were distinguished as 2 different gods of war. The name is evidently derived from ENYO.

ENYO (-ūs), the goddess of war, who delights in bloodshed and the destruction of towns, and accompanies Ares in battles. Respecting the Roman goddess of war, see BELLONA.

EORDAEA (-ae), a district and town in the N. W. of Macedonia, inhabited by the EORDI.

EOS (and EŎS), in Latin AURORA (-ae), the goddess of the dawn, daughter of Hyperion and Thia or Euryphassa; or of Pallas, according to Ovid. At the close of every night she rose from the couch of her spouse Tithonus, and in a chariot drawn by swift horses ascended up to heaven from the river Oceanus, to announce the coming light of the sun. She carried off several youths distinguished for their beauty, such as ORION, CEPHALUS, and TITHONUS, whence she is called by Ovid *Tithonia conjux*. She bore Memnon to Tithonus.

EPAMINONDAS (-ae), the Theban general and statesman, son of Polymnis, was born and reared in poverty, though his blood was noble. He saved the life of Pelopidas in battle B.C. 385, and lived in close friendship with him afterwards. After the Spartans had been expelled from Thebes, 379, Epaminondas took an active part in public affairs. He gained a great victory over the Spartans at Leuctra (B.C. 371), which destroyed the Spartan supremacy in Greece. Four times he successfully invaded Peloponnesus at the head of the Theban armies. In the last of these campaigns he gained a brilliant victory over the Lacedaemonians at Mantinēa; but, in the full career of victory, died. He is said to have fallen by the hands of Gryllus, the son of Xenophon. Epaminondas was one of the greatest men of Greece. He raised Thebes to the supremacy of Greece, which she lost almost as soon as he died. Both in public and in private life he was distinguished by integrity and uprightness, and he carried into daily practice the lessons of philosophy, of which he was an ardent student.

EPAPHUS (-i), son of Zeus (Jupiter) and Io, born on the river Nile, after the long wanderings of his mother. He became king of Egypt, and built Memphis.

EPEI. [ELIS.]

EPEUS (-i), son of Panopeus, and builder of the Trojan horse.

EPHESUS (-i), the chief of the 12 Ionian cities on the coast of Asia Minor. In the plain beyond its walls stood the celebrated temple of Artemis (Diana), which was built in the 6th century B.C., and, after being burnt down by Herostratus in the night on which Alexander the Great was born (B.C. 356), was restored by the joint efforts of all the Ionian states, and was regarded as one of the wonders of the world. With the rest of Ionia, Ephesus fell under the power successively of Croesus, the Persians, the Macedonians, and the Romans. It was always very flourishing, and became even more so as the other Ionian cities decayed. In the early history of the Christian Church it is conspicuous as having been visited both by St. Paul and St. John, who also addressed epistles to the church established at Ephesus.

ĔPHĬALTĒS (-is).—(1) One of the Aloïdae. [ALOEUS.]—(2) A Malian, who in B.C. 480, when Leonidas was defending the pass of Thermopylae, guided a body of Persians over the mountain path, and thus enabled them to fall on the rear of the Greeks.—(3) An Athenian statesman, and a friend and partisan of Pericles, whom he assisted in carrying his political measures.

ĔPHŎRUS (-i), of Cymae in Aeolis, a celebrated Greek historian, a contemporary of Philip and Alexander, flourished about B.C. 340. He wrote a universal history, the first that was attempted in Greece. The work however has perished with the exception of a few fragments.

ĔPHȲRA (-ae), the ancient name of Corinth, whence *Ephyraeus* is used as equivalent to Corinthian. [CORINTHUS.]

ĔPICASTĒ, commonly called JOCASTE.

ĔPICHARMUS (-i), the chief comic poet among the Dorians, born in the island of Cos, about B.C. 540, was carried to Megara in Sicily in his infancy, and spent the latter part of his life at Syracuse at the court of Hieron. He died at the age of 90 (450), or 97 (443). Epicharmus gave to comedy a new form, and introduced a regular plot. His language was elegant, and his productions abounded in philosophical and moral maxims.

ĔPICNĒMĬDĬI LOCRI. [LOCRIS.]

ĔPICTĒTUS (-i), of Hierapolis in Phrygia, a celebrated stoic philosopher, was a freedman of Epaphroditus, who was himself a freedman of Nero. Being expelled from Rome by Domitian, he took up his residence at Nicopolis in Epirus. He did not leave any works behind him; and the short manual (*Enchiridion*), which bears his name, was compiled from his discourses by his pupil Arrian. [ARRIANUS.]

ĔPICŪRUS (-i), a celebrated Greek philosopher, was born B.C. 342, in the island of Samos, and took up his permanent residence at Athens, in 306. Here he purchased the garden, afterwards so noted, in which he established the philosophical school, called after him the Epicurean. He died in 270, at the age of 72, after a long and painful illness, which he endured with truly philosophical patience and courage. Epicurus is the great leader of that philosophical school which teaches that the *summum bonum*, or highest good, is happiness. The happiness that he taught his followers to seek after was not sensual enjoyment, but peace of mind as

the result of the cultivation of all the virtues. According to the teaching of his school virtue should be practised *because* it leads to happiness; whereas the Stoics teach that virtue should be cultivated for her own sake, irrespective of the happiness it will ensure. In the physical part of his philosophy he followed the atomistic doctrines of Democritus and Diagoras. The pupils of Epicurus were very numerous, and were excessively devoted to him. His system has been most violently attacked, partly because after the days of Epicurus men who professed to be his followers gave themselves over to mere sensual enjoyment, partly because it has been but imperfectly understood, and partly because it was really founded on an erroneous principle, in making virtue dependent upon consequent happiness.

ĔPĬDAMNUS. [DYRRHACHIUM.]

ĔPĬDAURUS (-i). (1) A town in Argolis on the Saronic gulf, formed, with its territory EPIDAURIA, a district independent of Argos, and was not included in Argolis till the time of the Romans. It was the chief seat of the worship of Aesculapius, whose temple was situated about 5 miles from the town.—(2) Surnamed LIMERA, a town in Laconia, on the E. coast, said to have been founded by Epidaurus in Argolis.

ĔPĬGŎNI (-ōrum), that is, "the Descendants," the name of the sons of the 7 heroes who perished before Thebes. [ADRASTUS.] Ten years after their death, the descendants of the 7 heroes marched against Thebes, which they took and razed to the ground. The names of the Epigoni are not the same in all accounts; but the common lists contain Alcmaeon, Aegialeus, Diomedes, Promachus, Sthenelus, Thersander, and Euryalus.

ĔPĬMĔNĬDĒS (-is), a celebrated poet and prophet of Crete, whose history is, to a great extent, mythical. There is a legend that when a boy he was sent out by his father in search of a sheep; and that, seeking shelter from the heat of the midday sun, he went into a cave, and there fell into a deep sleep, which lasted 57 years. On waking and returning home, he found, to his great amazement, that his younger brother had, in the mean time, grown an old man. His visit to Athens, however, is an historical fact, and determines his date. The Athenians, who were visited by a plague in consequence of the crime of Cylon [CYLON], invited Epimenides to come and undertake the purification of the city. Epimenides accordingly came to Athens, about B.C. 596, and performed the desired task by certain mysterious rites and sacrifices, in consequence of which the plague ceased. Many works were attributed to him by the ancients, and the Apostle Paul has preserved (*Titus*, i. 12) a celebrated verse of his against the Cretans.

EPIMĒTHEUS. [PROMETHEUS and PANDORA.]

EPIPHĀNĒS (-is), a surname of Antiochus IV., king of Syria.

EPIPHĀNĬA or -ĔA (-ae). (1) In Syria (O. T. Hamath), in the district of Cassiotis, on the left bank of the Orontes.—(2) In Cilicia, close to the Pylae Amanides, formerly called Oeniandus.

EPĪPŌLAE. [SYRACUSAE.]

EPĪRUS (-i), that is, "the mainland," a country in the N.W. of Greece, so called to distinguish it from Corcyra, and the other islands off the coast. Homer gives the name of Epirus to the whole of the W. coast of Greece, thus including Acarnania in it. Epirus was bounded by Illyria and Macedonia on the N., by Thessaly on the E., by Acarnania and the Ambracian gulf on the S., and by the Ionian Sea on the W. Its inhabitants were numerous, but were not of pure Hellenic blood. They appear to have been a mixture of Pelasgians and Illyrians. The ancient oracle of Dodona in the country was of Pelasgic origin. Epirus contained 14 different tribes. Of these the most important were the CHAONES, THESPROTI, and MOLOSSI, who gave their names to the 3 principal divisions of the country, CHAONIA, THESPROTIA, and MOLOSSIS. The different tribes were originally governed by their own princes. The Molossian princes, who traced their descent from Pyrrhus (Neoptolemus), son of Achilles, subsequently acquired the sovereignty over the whole country, and took the title of kings of Epirus. The most celebrated of these was PYRRHUS, who carried on war with the Romans.

EPĪRUS NOVA. [ILLYRICUM.]

EPŌRĔDĬA (-i: *Ivrea*), a town in Gallia Cisalpina, on the Duria, in the territory of the Salassi, colonised by the Romans, B.C. 100, to serve as a bulwark against the neighbouring Alpine tribes.

EPŌRĔDŌRIX (-ĭgis), a noble Aeduan, who served in Caesar's army.

EQUUS TŪTĬCUS or AEQUUM TŪTĬCUM (-i), a small town of the Hirpini, in Samnium, 21 miles from Beneventum.

ERAE (-arum), a small but strong seaport town on the coast of Ionia, N. of Teos.

ĔRĂNA (-ae), a town in M. Amanus, the chief seat of the Eleutherocilices, in the time of Cicero.

ĔRĂSĪNUS (-i), the chief river in Argolis, rising in the lake Stymphalus, and, after disappearing under the earth, flowing through the Lernaean marsh into the Argolic gulf.

ĔRĂSISTRĂTUS (-i), a celebrated physician and anatomist, a native of Iulis, in the island of Ceos, flourished from B.C. 300 to 260, and was the founder of a medical school at Alexandria.

ĔRĂTŌ (-ūs), one of the Muses. [MUSAE.]

ĔRĂTOSTHĔNĒS (-is), of Cyrene, born B.C. 276, was placed by Ptolemy Euergetes over the library at Alexandria. He died at Alexandria at the age of 80, about B.C. 196, of voluntary starvation, having lost his sight, and being tired of life. He was a man of extensive learning, and wrote on almost all the branches of knowledge then cultivated—astronomy, geometry, geography, philosophy, history, and grammar. His works have perished, with the exception of some fragments. His most celebrated work was a systematic treatise on geography, of which Strabo made great use.

ĔRĔBUS (-i), son of Chaos, begot Aether and Hemera (Day) by Nyx (Night), his sister. The name signifies darkness, and is therefore applied to the dark and gloomy space under the earth, through which the shades pass into Hades.

ĔRECHTHĔUM. [ERICHTHONIUS.]

ĔRECHTHĔUS. [ERICHTHONIUS.]

ĔRĔSUS or ĔRESSUS (-i), a town on the W. coast of the island of Lesbos, the birthplace of Theophrastus, and, according to some, of Sappho.

ĔRETRĬA (-ae), one of the chief towns of Euboea, situated on the Euripus, with a harbour, Porthmos, was founded by the Athenians, but had a mixed population, among which was a considerable number of Dorians. Its commerce and navy raised it in early times to importance; it contended with Chalcis for the supremacy of Euboea; and it planted colonies in Macedonia and Italy. It was destroyed by the Persians, B.C. 490, and most of its inhabitants were carried away into slavery.

ĔRICHTHŌNĬUS (-ae), or ĔRECHTHĔUS (-ĕos or ĕi). In the ancient myths these two names indicate the same person; but later writers mention 2 heroes, one called Erichthonius or Erechtheus I., and the other Erechtheus II.—(1) ERICHTHONIUS or ERECHTHEUS I., son of Hephaestus (Vulcan) and Atthis, the daughter of Cranaus. Athena (Minerva) reared the child without the knowledge of the other gods, and entrusted him to Agraulos, Pandrosos, and Herse, concealed in a chest, which they were forbidden to open. But disobeying the command, they saw the child in the form of a serpent, or entwined by a serpent, whereupon they were seized with madness, and threw themselves down the rock of the acropolis. Erichthonius after wards became king of Athens, and was succeeded in the kingdom by his son Pandion. He is said to have introduced the worship of Athena, to have instituted the festival of the Panathenaea, and to have built a temple of Athena on the acropolis. When Athena and Poseidon (Neptune) disputed about the possession of Attica, Erichthonius declared in favour of Athena. He was further the first who used a chariot with 4 horses, for which reason he was placed among the stars as auriga. He was worshipped as a god after his death : and a temple, called the *Erechtheum*, was built to him on the acropolis. —(2) ERECHTHEUS II., grandson of the former, and son of Pandion whom he succeeded as king of Athens. He was father of Cecrops, Procris, Creusa, Chthonia, and Orithyia. In the war between the Eleusinians and Athenians, Eumolpus, the son of Poseidon, was slain ; whereupon Poseidon demanded the sacrifice of one of the daughters of Erechtheus. When one was drawn by lot, her 3 sisters resolved to die with her ; and Erechtheus himself was killed by Zeus with a flash of lightning at the request of Poseidon.

ĔRĬCHTHŌNĬUS (-ĭ), son of Dardanus, father of Tros, and king of Troy.

ĔRĬDĂNUS (-i), a river god, on whose banks amber was found. In later times the Eridanus was supposed to be the same as the Padus (*Po*), because amber was found at its mouth. Hence the *Electrides Insulae* or " Amber Islands " are placed at the mouth of the Po, and here Phaethon was supposed to have fallen when struck by the lightning of Zeus (Jupiter.)

ĔRĬGŎNĒ (-es).—(1) Daughter of Icarius, beloved by Bacchus. For details, see ICARIUS. —(2) Daughter of Aegisthus and Clytaemnestra.

ĔRINNA (-ae), a Lesbian poetess, a contemporary and friend of Sappho (about B.C. 612), who died at the age of 19, but left behind her poems which were thought worthy to rank with those of Homer.

ĔRĬNȲES. [EUMENIDES.]

ĔRĬPHȲLĒ (-es), daughter of Talaus and wife of Amphiaraus, whom she betrayed for the sake of the necklace of Harmonia, for which she was slain by her son Alcmaeon. For details see AMPHIARAUS, ALCMAEON.

ĔRIS (-ĭdos) in Latin, DISCORDĬA (-ae), the goddess of Discord, the friend and sister of Ares (Mars), who delighted with him in the tumult of war. It was Eris who threw the apple into the assembly of the gods, the cause of so much suffering and war. [PARIS.]

ĔRŌS (-ōtis), in Latin, ĂMOR (-ōris), or CŬPĪDO (-ĭnis), the god of Love, son of Aphrodite (Venus), by either Ares (Mars),

Zeus (Jupiter), or Hermes (Mercury). He was represented as a wanton boy, of whom a thousand tricks and cruel sports were related, and from whom neither gods nor men were safe. His arms consist of arrows, which he carries in a golden quiver, and of torches

Eros (Cupid) whetting his Darts. (De la Chausse, Gemmæ Antiche.)

which no one can touch with impunity. His arrows are of different power : some are golden, and kindle love in the heart they wound; others are blunt and heavy with lead, and produce aversion to a lover. Eros is further represented with golden wings, and as fluttering about like a bird. His eyes are sometimes covered, so that he acts blindly.

Eros. (From a Gem.)

He is the usual companion of his mother,

Aphrodite. ● ANTEROS, literally, return-love, is usually represented as the god who punishes those who do not return the love of others : thus he is the avenging Eros, or a *deus ultor*. But in some accounts he is described as a god opposed to Eros and struggling against him.—Respecting the connection between Eros and Psyche, see PSYCHE. The later poets speak of a number of Erotes.

Eros (Cupid). (Museum Capitolinum, vol. 4, tav. 57.)

ĔRȲMANTHUS (-i). (1) A lofty mountain in Arcadia on the frontiers of Achaia and Elis, celebrated in mythology as the haunt of the savage Erymanthian boar destroyed by Hercules. [HERCULES].—The Arcadian nymph Callisto, who was changed into a she-bear is called *Erymanthis ursa*, and her son Arcas *Erymanthidis ursae custos.* [ARCTOS.]—(2) A river in Arcadia, rising in the above-mentioned mountain, and falling into the Alpheus.

ĔRȲSICHTHŌN (-ŏnis), son of the Thessalian king Triopas, who cut down trees in a grove sacred to Demeter, for which he was punished by the goddess with a fearful hunger, that caused him to devour his own flesh.

ĔRYTHRAE (-ārum). (1) An ancient town in Boeotia, not far from Plataeae and Hysiae, and celebrated as the mother city of Erythrae in Asia Minor.—(2) A town of the Locri Ozŏlae, E. of Naupactus.—(3) One of the 12 Ionian cities of Asia Minor, stood at the bottom of a large bay, on the W. side of the peninsula which lies opposite to Chios.

ĔRYTHRAEUM MARE, the name originally of the whole expanse of sea between Arabia and Africa on the W., and India on the E., including its two great gulfs (the *Red Sea* and *Persian Gulf*). In this sense it is used by Herodotus, who also distinguishes the *Red Sea* by the name of Ἀράβιος κόλπος. [ARABICUS SINUS.] Afterwards the parts of these seas were distinguished by different names, the main body of the sea being called Indicus Oceanus, the *Red Sea* Arabicus Sinus, the *Persian Gulf* Persicus Sinus. The name Erythraeum Mare was generally used as identical with Arabicus Sinus, or the corresponding genuine Latin term, Mare Rubrum (*Red Sea*).

ĔRYX (-ȳcis), also ERȲCUS MONS (*S. Giuliano*), a steep and isolated mountain in the N. W. of Sicily, near Drepanum. On the summit of this mountain stood an ancient and celebrated temple of Aphrodite (Venus), said to have been built by Eryx, king of the Elymi, or, according to Virgil, by Aeneas, but more probably by the Phoenicians, who introduced the worship of Aphrodite into Sicily. Hence the goddess bore the surname ERYCĪNA, under which name her worship was introduced at Rome about the beginning of the 2nd Punic war. There was a town of the name of Eryx on the W. slope of the mountain.

ESQUĬLĬAE. [ROMA.]

ESSŬI (-ōrum), a people in Gaul, W. of the Sequana.

ĔTĔOCLĒS (-is), son of Oedipus and Jocasta. After his father's flight from Thebes, he and his brother Polynīces undertook the government of the city ; but disputes having arisen between them, Polynices fled to Adrastus, who then brought about the expedition of the Seven against Thebes. [ADRASTUS.] Eteocles and Polynices perished in single combat.

ĔTĔSĬAE (-ārum), the *Etesian Winds*, derived from ἔτος "year," signified any *periodical winds*, but more particularly the northerly winds which blow in the Aegean for 40 days from the rising of the dog star.

ĔTRŪRĬA, ĔTRŬRĬA, or TUSCĬA, called by the Greeks TYRRHĒNĬA or TYRSĒNĬA (-ae), a country in central Italy. The inhabitants were called by the Romans ETRUSCI or TUSCI, by the Greeks TYRRHENI or TYRSENI, and by themselves RASENA. Etruria Proper was bounded on the N. and N. W. by the Apennines and the river Macra, which divided it from Liguria, on the W. by the Tyrrhene sea or Mare Inferum, and on the E. and S. by the river Tiber, which separated it from Umbria and Latium. The origin of the Etruscans is uncertain. The ancients believed that they were a colony of Lydians, but more modern writers suppose that the Etruscans were a Rhaetian race, called Rasena, who descended from the Alps and the valley of the Po. The Etruscans were a very powerful nation when Rome was still in its infancy, and at an early period their dominions extended over the greater part of Italy, from the Alps and the plains of Lombardy on the one hand, to Vesuvius and the gulf of Sarento on the other. These dominions may be divided into 3 great districts : Circumpadane Etruria in the N., Etruria Proper in the centre, and Campanian Etruria in the S. In each of these districts there were 12 principal cities or states, which formed a confederacy for mutual protection. Through the attacks of the Gauls in the N., and of the Sabines, Samnites, and Greeks in the S., the Etruscans became confined within the limits of Etruria Proper, and continued long to flourish in this country, after they had disappeared from the rest of Italy. The 12 cities which formed the confederacy in Etruria Proper were most probably CORTONA, ARRETIUM, CLUSIUM, PERUSIA, VOLATERRAE, VETULONIA, RUSELLAE, VOLSINII, TARQUINII, VALERII, VEII, CAERE, more anciently called Agylla. Each state was independent of all the others. The government was a close aristocracy, and was strictly confined to the family of the Lucumones, who united in their own persons the ecclesiastical as well as the civil functions. The people appear to have been in a state of vassalage or serfdom. A meeting of the confederacy of the 12 states was held annually in the spring, at the temple of Voltumna, near Volsinii. The Etruscans were a highly civilised people, and from them the Romans borrowed many of their religious and political institutions. The 3 last kings of Rome were undoubtedly Etruscans, and they left in the city enduring traces of Etruscan power and greatness. The later history of the Etruscans is a struggle against the rising power of Rome, to which they became subject, after their decisive defeat by Cornelius Dolabella in B.C. 283. In 91 they received the Roman franchise. The numerous military colonies established in Etruria by Sulla and Augustus destroyed to a great extent the national character of the people, and the country thus became in course of time completely Romanised.

EUBOEA (-ae : *Negropont*), the largest island of the Aegaean sea, about 90 miles in length, lying along the coasts of Attica, Boeotia, and the S. part of Thessaly, from which countries it is separated by the Euboean sea, called the Euripus in its narrowest part. Throughout the length of the island runs a lofty range of mountains ; but it contains many fertile plains. In Homer the inhabitants are called Abantes. In the N. of Euboea dwelt the Histiaei ; below these were the Ellopii, and in the S. were the Dryopes. The centre of the island was inhabited chiefly by Ionians. It was in this part of Euboea that the Athenians planted the colonies of CHALCIS and ERETRIA, which were the 2 most important cities in the island. After

the Persian wars, Euboea became subject to the Athenians. Since Cumae, in Italy, was a colony from Chalcis, in Euboea, the adjective *Euboicus* is used by the poets in reference to the former city.

EUCLĪDĒS (-is). (1) The celebrated mathematician, lived at Alexandria in the time of the first Ptolemy, B.C. 323—283, and was the founder of the Alexandrian mathematical school. It was his answer to Ptolemy, who asked if geometry could not be made easier, that there was no royal road. Of the numerous works attributed to Euclid, several are still extant of which by far the most noted is "The Elements."—(2) Of Megara, one of the disciples of Socrates, quitted Athens on the death of Socrates (B.C. 399), and took refuge in Megara, where he founded a school, which distinguished itself chiefly by the cultivation of dialectics. This school was called sometimes the Megaric, sometimes the Dialectic or Eristic.

EUCTĒMON, the astronomer. [METON.]

EUDOXUS (-i), of Cnidus, a celebrated astronomer and geometer, lived about B.C. 366. He studied at Athens and in Egypt, but probably spent some of his time at his native place, where he had an observatory. He is said to have been the first who taught in Greece the motions of the planets. His works are lost.

EUGĂNĔI (-ōrum), a people who formerly inhabited Venetia, on the Adriatic sea, and were driven towards the Alps and the Lacus Benacus by the Hencti or Veneti.

EUHĒMĒRUS (-i), a Greek writer, who lived at the court of Cassander, in Macedonia, about B.C. 316, and the author of a work, in which he attempted to show that all the ancient myths were genuine historical events. He represented the gods as originally men who had distinguished themselves either as warriors or benefactors of mankind, and who after their death received divine worship from the grateful people.

EULAEUS (-i : O. T. *Ulai*), a river in Susiana, rising in Great Media, passing E. of Susa, and falling into the head of the Persian Gulf. Some of the ancient geographers make the Eulaeus fall into the Choaspes, and others identify the two rivers.

EUMAEUS (-i), the faithful swineherd of Ulysses.

EUMĒNĒS (-is). (1) Of CARDIA, served as private secretary to Philip and Alexander ; and on the death of the latter (B.C. 323), obtained the government of Cappadocia, Paphlagonia, and Pontus. Eumenes allied himself with Perdiccas, and carried on war for him in Asia Minor against Antipater and Craterus. On the death of Perdiccas, ir

Egypt, Antigonus employed the whole force of the Macedonian army to crush Eumenes. Notwithstanding the numerical inferiority of his forces, Eumenes maintained his ground against his enemies for some years, till he was surrendered by the Argyraspids to Antigonus, by whom he was put to death, 316. He was a great general and statesman, and had he been a native Macedonian would probably have occupied a more important position among the successors of Alexander.—(2) I. King of PERGAMUS, reigned B.C. 263—241; and was the successor of his uncle Philetaerus.—(3) II. King of PERGAMUS, reigned B.C. 197—159; and was the son and successor of Attalus I. He inherited from his predecessor the friendship and alliance of the Romans, which he took the utmost pains to cultivate. Pergamus became under his rule a great and flourishing city, in which he founded that celebrated library which rose to be a rival even to that of Alexandria.

EUMENIDES (-um), also called ERINYES (-um), not Erinnyes, and by the Romans FURIAE or DIRAE (-arum), the Avenging Deities. The name Erinyes is the more ancient one; the form Eumenides, which signifies "the well-meaning," or "soothed goddesses," is a mere euphemism, because people dreaded to call these fearful goddesses by their real name. It was said to have been first given them after the acquittal of Orestes by the Areopagus, when the anger of the Erinyes had been soothed. They are represented as the daughters of Earth or of Night, and as fearful winged maidens, with serpents twined in their hair, and with blood dripping from their eyes. They dwelt in the depths of Tartarus, dreaded by gods and men. With later writers their number is usually 3, and their names are TISIPHONE, ALECTO, and MEGAERA. They punished men both in this world and after death. The sacrifices offered to them consisted of black sheep and nephalia, *i.e.* a drink of honey mixed with water. The crimes which they chiefly punished were disobedience towards parents, violation of the respect due to old age, perjury, murder, violation of the laws of hospitality, and improper conduct towards suppliants.

Furies. (From a Painted Vase.)   Fury. (From a Painted Vase.)

EUMOLPUS (-i), that is "the good singer," a Thracian bard, son of Poseidon (Neptune) and Chione, the daughter of Boreas. As soon as he was born he was thrown into the sea by his mother, who was anxious to conceal her shame, but was preserved by his father Poseidon, who had him educated in Ethiopia by his daughter

Benthesicyma. After dwelling for a time in Ethiopia, and afterwards at the court of the Thracian king Tegyrius, he came to Eleusis in Attica, where he formed a friendship with the Eleusinians. Subsequently he joined them in an expedition against Athens, but was slain by Erechtheus. Eumolpus was regarded as the founder of the Eleusinian mysteries, and as the first priest of Demeter (Ceres) and Dionysus (Bacchus). He was succeeded in the priestly office by his son Ceyx ; and his family, the *Eumolpidae*, continued till the latest times the priests of Demeter at Eleusis.

EUNŎMĬA. [HORAE.]

EUNUS (-i), a Sicilian slave, and a native of Apamea in Syria, was the leader of the Sicilian slaves in the servile war (B.C. 134 —132).

EUPĂLIUM or EUPŎLĬUM (-i), a town of the Locri Ozolae, N. of Naupactus.

EUPHĒMUS (-i), son of Poseidon (Neptune), and ancestor of Battus, founder of Cyrene.

EUPHORBUS (-i), son of Panthous, one of the bravest of the Trojans, slain by Menelaus, who dedicated his shield in the temple of Hera (Juno), near Mycenae. Pythagoras asserted that he had once been Euphorbus, and in proof of his assertion took down at first sight the shield from the temple of Hera.

EUPHORIŎN (-ōnis), of Chalcis in Euboea, an eminent grammarian and poet, was the librarian of Antiochus the Great, and flourished B.C. 221. All his works are lost.

EUPHRĀNOR (-ŏris), a distinguished statuary and painter, was a native of Corinth, but practised his art at Athens about B.C. 336.

EUPHRĀTĒS (-is : O. T. Phrat : *El Frat*), a great river of Asia, consists, in its upper course, of 2 branches, both of which rise in the mountains of Armenia. The northern branch is the true Euphrates : the southern was called by the ancients the ARSANIAS. After their junction the river breaks through the main chain of the Taurus between Melitene and Samosata, and then flows through the plain of Babylonia, till it joins the Tigris about sixty miles above the mouth of the Persian Gulf.

EUPHRŎSYNĒ (-es), one of the Charites or Graces. [CHARITES.]

EUPŎLIS (-is), one of the most celebrated Athenian poets of the old comedy, and a contemporary of Aristophanes, was born about B.C. 446, and died about 411. The common story that Alcibiades threw him into the sea out of revenge is not true.

EURĪPĪDĒS (-is), the distinguished tragic poet, was born at Salamis, B.C. 480, on the very day that the Greeks defeated the Persians off that island, whither his parents had fled from Athens on the invasion of Xerxes. In his youth he cultivated gymnastic pursuits, and won the prize at the Eleusinian and Thesean contests. But he soon abandoned these pursuits, and studied philosophy under Anaxagoras, and rhetoric under Prodicus. He lived on intimate terms with Socrates, and traces of the teaching of Anaxagoras have been remarked in many passages of his plays. In 441 he gained for the first time the first prize, and he continued to exhibit plays until 408, the date of the *Orestes*. Soon after this he left Athens for the court of Archelaüs, king of Macedonia, where he died in 406, at the age of 75. He is said to have been torn in pieces by the king's dogs. Euripides in his tragedies brought down the ancient heroes and heroines to the ordinary standard of men and women of his own times. He represented men, according to the remark of Aristotle, not as they ought to be, but as they are. Hence the preference given to his plays by the practical Socrates. The most serious defects in his tragedies, as works of art, are the disconnexion of the choral odes from the subject of the play, and the too frequent introduction of philosophical maxims. His great excellency is the tenderness and pathos with which some of his characters are invested. 18 of his tragedies are extant, if we omit the *Rhesus*, which is probably spurious.

EURĪPUS (-i), any part of the sea where the ebb and flow of the tide were remarkably violent, is the name especially of the narrow strait which separates Euboea from Boeotia. At Chalcis there was a bridge over the Euripus, uniting Euboea with the mainland.

EURŌPA (-ae). (1) Daughter of the Phoenician king, Agenor, or, according to the Iliad, daughter of Phoenix. Her beauty charmed Zeus (Jupiter), who assumed the form of a bull and mingled with the herd as Europa and her maidens were sporting on the sea-shore. Encouraged by the tameness of the animal, Europa ventured to mount his back ; whereupon the god rushed into the sea, and swam with her to Crete. Here she became by Zeus the mother of Minos, Rhadamanthus, and Sarpēdon.—(2) One of the 3 divisions of the ancient world, said to have been named after the daughter of Agenor. In earlier times the river Phasis was usually supposed to be the boundary between Europe and Asia, and sometimes even the Araxes and the Caspian sea ; but at a later period the river Tanais and the Palus

Maeotis were generally regarded as the boundaries between the two continents. | The north of Europe was little known to the ancients.

Europa.   (Schlichtergroll, Stosch Collection.)

EURŎPUS. [TITARESIUS.]

EURUS (-i), the S.E. wind, sometimes the E. wind.

EUROTAS (-ae), the chief river in Laconia, on which Sparta stood, rises in Mt. Borēum, in Arcadia, and flows into the Laconian gulf.

EURỸBĀTĒS, the herald of Ulysses, whom he followed to Troy.

EURỸBĀTŬS (-i), an Ephesian, whom Croesus sent with a large sum of money to the Peloponnesus to hire mercenaries for him in his war with Cyrus. He, however, went over to Cyrus, and betrayed the whole matter to him. In consequence of this treachery, his name passed into a proverb amongst the Greeks.

EURỸDĬCĒ (-es). (1.) wife of Orpheus. For details see ORPHEUS.—(2.) The name of several Illyrian and Macedonian princesses. The most celebrated was the wife of Philip Arrhidaeus, who succeeded Alexander the Great. She was put to death by Olympias, B.C. 317.

EURỸLŎCHUS (-i), a companion of Ulysses was the only one that escaped from the house of Circe, when his friends were metamorphosed into swine.

EURỸMĔDON (-ontis). (1.) Son of Thucles, an Athenian general in the Peloponnesian war.—(2.) A small river in Pamphylia, celebrated for the victory which Cimon gained over the Persians on its banks (B.C. 469).

EURỸMUS (-i), father of the seer Telemus, who is hence called *Eurỹmĭdes.*

EURỸNŎMĒ (-es), daughter of Oceanus, and mother of Leucothoē.

EURỸPON, otherwise called EURỸTĬON, grandson of Procles, was the third king of that house at Sparta, and thenceforward gave it the name of Eurypontidae.

EURỸPỸLUS (-i). (1) Son of Euaemon, and leader of a body of troops before Troy.—(2) Son of Poseidon (Neptune) and Astypalaea, king of Cos, killed by Hercules.

EURYSTHĒNES (-is) and PROCLES (-is), the twin sons of Aristodemus, born before their father's return to Peloponnesus and occupation of his allotment of Laconia. He died immediately after the birth of his children, and in accordance with the command of the oracle at Delphi both were made kings, but the precedence given to Eurysthenes and his descendants. From these 2 brothers the 2 royal families in Sparta were descended, and were called respectively the *Eurysthenidae* and *Proclidae.* The former were also called the *Agidae,* from Agis, son of Eurysthenes ; and the latter *Eurypontidae,* from Eurypon, grandson of Procles.

EURYSTHEUS. [HERCULES.]

EURỸTUS (-i), king of Oechalia, and father of Iole. For details see HERCULES.

EUTERPĒ, one of the Muses. [MUSAE.]

EUTRŎPIUS (-i), a Roman historian,

contemporary of Constantine the Great, Julian, and Valens, and the author of a brief compendium of Roman history in 10 books, from the foundation of the city to the accession of Valens, A.D. 364, to whom it is inscribed. This work is extant, and is drawn up with care. The style is in keeping with the nature of the undertaking, being plain, precise, and simple.

EUXĪNUS PONTUS. [PONTUS EUXI-NUS.]

ĒVADNĒ (-es), daughter of Iphis (hence called Iphias), and wife of Capaneus. For details see CAPANEUS.

EVĀGŎRAS (-ae), king of Salamis, in Cyprus, from about B.C. 410 to 374. He was assisted by the Athenians in his wars against the Persians.

ĒVANDER (-dri) and EVANDRUS (-i), son of Hermes (Mercury), by an Arcadian nymph, called in Roman traditions Carmenta or Tiburtis. About 60 years before the Trojan war, Evander is said to have led a colony from Pallantium, in Arcadia, into Italy, and there to have built a town, Pallantium, on the Tiber, at the foot of the Palatine Hill, which town was subsequently incorporated with Rome. Evander taught his neighbours milder laws and the arts of peace and of social life, and especially the art of writing; he also introduced among them the worship of the Lycaean Pan, of Demeter (Ceres), Poseidon (Neptune), and Hercules.

ĒVĒNUS (-i). (1) (Fidhari), a river of Aetolia, rising in Mt. Oeta, and flowing into the sea, 120 stadia W. of Antirrhium. It derived its name from Evenus, the father of Marpessa, who was carried off by Idas, the son of Aphareus; and Evenus being unable to overtake the latter, threw himself into the river, which was henceforth called after him. —(2) A river of Mysia, falling into the Sinus Elaïticus near Pitane.

EVERGĒTES, the " Benefactor," a title of honour conferred by the Greek states upon those from whom they had received benefits. It was assumed by many of the Greek kings in Egypt and elsewhere. [PTOLEMAEUS.]

ĒVĬUS, an epithet of Bacchus, given him from the animating cry evoe, in the festivals of the god.

FĂBĂRIS or FARFĂRUS (-i), a small river in Italy, in the Sabine territory, between Reate and Cures.

FĂBĬI (-orum), one of the most ancient patrician gentes at Rome, which traced its origin to Hercules and the Arcadian Evander. Its most important members are: (1) K. FABIUS VIBULANUS, 3 times consul, B.C.

484, 481, 479. In his third consulship he espoused the cause of the plebeians; but as his propositions were rejected by the patricians, he and his house resolved to quit Rome altogether, where they were regarded as apostates by their own order. Accordingly 306 Fabii, all patricians, marched with the consul at their head through the Carmental Gate, and proceeded to the banks of the Cremera, where they erected a fortress. Here they took up their abode along with their families and clients, and for 2 years continued to devastate the territory of Veii. They were at length destroyed by the Veientes in 477, on the 18th of June, the day on which the Romans were subsequently conquered by the Gauls at the Allia. The whole gens perished with the exception of one individual, from whom all the later Fabii were descended. — (2) Q. FABIUS MAXIMUS RULLIANUS, 6 times consul (B.C. 322—296), and the most eminent of the Roman generals in the 2nd Samnite war. —(3) Q. FABIUS MAXIMUS GURGES, or the Glutton, from the dissoluteness of his youth, son of the last, 3 times consul (292—265).— (4) Q. FABIUS MAXIMUS, with the agnomens VERRUCŌSUS, from a wart on his upper lip, OVICULA, or the Lamb, from the mildness or apathy of his temper, and CUNCTATOR, from his caution in war, was grandson of Fabius Gurges. He was 5 times consul (B.C. 233— 209). In 217, immediately after the defeat at Trasimenus, Fabius was appointed dictator. From this period, so long as the war with Hannibal was merely defensive, Fabius became the leading man at Rome. On taking the field he laid down a simple and immutable plan of action. He avoided all direct encounter with the enemy; moved his camp from highland to highland, where the Numidian horse and Spanish infantry could not follow him; watched Hannibal's movements with unrelaxing vigilance, and cut off his stragglers and foragers. His enclosure of Hannibal in one of the upland valleys between Cales and the Vulturnus, and the Carthaginian's adroit escape by driving oxen with blazing faggots fixed to their horns, up the hill-sides, are well-known facts. But at Rome and in his own camp the caution of Fabius was misinterpreted; and the people in consequence divided the command between him and M. Minucius Rufus, his master of the horse. Minucius was speedily entrapped, and would have been destroyed by Hannibal, had not Fabius hastened to his rescue. In the closing years of the 2nd Punic war Fabius appears to less advantage. The war had become aggressive under a new race of generals. Fabius disapproved of the new tactics; he dreaded the political supremacy of Scipio, and was his opponent in his scheme of invading Africa. He died in 203.—(5) C. FABIUS PICTOR, received the surname of Pictor, because he painted the walls of the temple of Salus, which the dictator C. Junius Brutus Bubulcus dedicated in 302. This is the earliest Roman painting of which we have any record.— (6) Q. FABIUS PICTOR, grandson of the last, the most ancient writer of Roman history in prose. He served in the Gallic war 225, and also in the 2nd Punic war. His history, which was written in Greek, began with the arrival of Aeneas in Italy, and came down to his own time.

FABRĀTĒRĬA (*Falvaterra*), a Volscian town in Latium, on the right bank of the Trerus, subsequently colonised by the Romans.

FĀBRĬCĬUS (-i), the name of a Roman family the chief members of which were :— (1) C. FABRICIUS, one of the most popular heroes in the Roman annals. He was consul B. C. 282, and two years afterwards was one of the Roman ambassadors sent to Pyrrhus at Tarentum to negotiate a ransom or exchange of prisoners. Pyrrhus used every effort to gain the favour of Fabricius ; but the sturdy Roman was proof against all his seductions, and rejected all his offers. In 278 Fabricius was consul a second time, when he sent back to Pyrrhus the traitor who had offered to poison him. Negotiations were then opened, which resulted in the evacuation of Italy by Pyrrhus. He was censor in 275, and distinguished himself by the severity with which he repressed the growing taste for luxury. Ancient writers love to tell of the frugal way in which Fabricius and his contemporary Curius Dentatus lived on their hereditary farms, and how they refused the rich presents which the Samnite ambassadors offered them. Fabricius died as poor as he had lived, and left no dowry for his daughters, which the senate furnished.—(2) L. FABRICIUS, curator viarum in B.C. 62, built a new bridge of stone, connecting the city with the island in the Tiber, and called after him *pons Fabricius*. This bridge still remains, and bears the name of *ponte quattro capi.*

FAESŬLAE (-arum : *Fiesole*), a city of Etruria, situated on a hill 3 miles N.E. of Florence. It was the head quarters of Catiline's army.

FĂLĒRĬI (-orum) or FĂLĒRĬUM (-i), a town in Etruria, situated on a height near Mt. Soracte, was originally a Pelasgic town, but was afterwards one of the 12 Etruscan cities. Its inhabitants were called FALISCI, and were regarded by many as of the same race as the Aequi, whence we find them often called Aequi Falisci. After a long struggle with Rome, the Faliscans yielded to Camillus B.C. 394. The Faliscans revolted again at the close of the 1st Punic war (B.C. 241), when the Romans destroyed their city. A new town was built on the plain. The white cows of Falerii were valued at Rome for sacrifices.

FĂLERNUS AGER, a district in the N. of Campania, extending from the Massic hills to the river Vulturnus. It produced some of the finest wine in Italy, which was reckoned only second to the wine of Setia.

FALISCI. [FALERII.]

FANNĬUS (-i) STRĂBO (-ōnis), C., son-in-law of Laelius, introduced by Cicero as a speaker in his *De Republica* and his *Laelius.*

FĀNUM FORTŪNAE (*Fano*), a town in Umbria at the mouth of the Metaurus, with a celebrated temple of Fortuna, whence the town derived its name.

FARFĂRUS. [FABARIS.]

FAULA or FAUNA. [FAUNUS.]

FAUNUS (-i), son of Picus, grandson of Saturnus, and father of Latinus, was the third in the series of the kings of the Laurentes. He was worshipped as the protecting deity of agriculture and of shepherds, and also as a giver of oracles. After the introduction of the worship of the Greek Pan into Italy, Faunus was identified with Pan, and represented, like the latter, with horns

Faunus.   (Gori, Gem. Ant. Flor. vol. I, pl. 94.)

and goats' feet. At a later time we find mention of Fauni in the plural. What

Faunus was to the male sex, his wife Faula or Fauna was to the female. As the god manifested himself in various ways, the idea arose of a plurality of Fauns (Fauni), who are described as half men, half goats, and with horns. Faunus gradually came to be identified with the Arcadian Pan, and the Fauni with the Greek Satyrs.

FAUSTA, CORNELIA (-ae), daughter of the dictator Sulla, wife of Milo, and infamous for her adulteries.

FAUSTINA (-ae). (1) Senior, wife of the emperor, Antoninus Pius, notorious for her licentiousness.—(2) Junior, daughter of the elder Faustina, and wife of the emperor M. Aurelius, also notorious for her profligacy.

FAUSTULUS. [Romulus.].

FAVENTIA (-ae), a town in Gallia Cisalpina on the river Anemo and on the Via Aemilia.

M. FAVONIUS (-ae), an imitator of Cato Uticensis, whose character and conduct he copied so servilely as to receive the nickname of Cato's ape.

FEBRIS (-is), the goddess, or rather the averter, of fever.

FEBRUUS (-i), an ancient Italian divinity, to whom the month of February was sacred. The name is connected with *februare* (to purify).

FELICITAS (-ātis), the personification of happiness, is frequently seen on Roman medals, in the form of a matron, with the staff of Mercury and a cornucopia.

FELIX (-icis), ANTONIUS (-i), procurator of Judaea, in the reigns of Claudius and Nero. He induced Drusilla, wife of Azizus, king of Emesa, to leave her husband ; and she was still living with him in a.d. 60, when St. Paul preached before him " of righteousness, temperance, and judgment to come."

FELSINA. [Bononia.]

FENNI (-ōrum), a savage people, reckoned by Tacitus among the Germans. They probably dwelt in the further part of E. Prussia, and were the same as the modern Finns.

FERENTINUM (-i). (1) A town of Etruria, S. of Volsinii, birthplace of the emperor Otho.—(2) An ancient town of the Hernici, in Latium, S.W. of Anagnia, colonised by the Romans in the 2nd Punic war.

FERENTUM. [Forentum.]

FERETRIUS (-i), a surname of Jupiter, derived from *ferire*, to strike ; for persons who took an oath called upon Jupiter to strike them if they swore falsely, as they struck the victim which they sacrificed. Others derived it from *ferre*, because people dedicated (*ferebant*) to him the spolia opima.

FERONIA (-ae), an ancient Italian divinity, whose chief sanctuary was at Ter-

racina, near mount Soracte. At her festival at this place a great fair was held.

FESCENNIUM (-i) or FESCENNIA (-ae), a town of the Falisci, in Etruria, and consequently, like Falerii, of Pelasgic origin. [Falerii.] From this town the Romans are said to have derived the Fescennine songs.

FESTUS, SEXT. POMPEIUS (-i), a Roman grammarian, in the 4th century of our era, the author of a dictionary or glossary of Latin words and phrases, of which a considerable portion is extant.

FESTUS, PORCIUS (-i), succeeded Antonius Felix as procurator of Judaea, in a.d. 62. It was he who bore testimony to the innocence of St. Paul, when he defended himself before him in the same year.

FICANA (-ae), one of the ancient Latin towns destroyed by Ancus Martius.

FICULEA (-ae), an ancient town of the Sabines, E. of Fidenae.

FIDENAE (-ārum), sometimes FIDENA (-ae: *Castel Giubileo*), an ancient town in the land of the Sabines, 5 miles N.E. of Rome, situated on a steep hill, between the Tiber and the Anio. It is said to have been conquered and colonised by Romulus ; but it was probably colonised by the Etruscan Veii, with which city we find it in close alliance. It frequently revolted, and was frequently taken by the Romans. Its last revolt was in b.c. 438, and in the following year it was destroyed by the Romans, but was afterwards rebuilt.

FIDENTIA (-ae), a town in Cisalpine Gaul, on the Via Aemilia, between Parma and Placentia.

FIDES (-ei), the personification of faithfulness, worshipped as a goddess at Rome.

FIDIUS, an ancient form of *filius*, occurs in the connection of *Dius Fidius*, or *Medius Fidius*, that is, me *Dius* (Διός) *filius*, or the son of Jupiter, that is, Hercules. Hence the expression *medius fidius* is equivalent to *me Hercules* scil. *juvet*. Sometimes Fidius is used alone. Some of the ancients connected *fidius* with *fides*.

FIGULUS, P. NIGIDIUS (-i), a Roman senator, and Pythagorean philosopher, of high reputation, who flourished about b.c. 60.

FIMBRIA (-ae), C. FLAVIUS (-i). (1) A jurist and an orator, consul b.c. 104.— (2) Son of the preceding, and one of the most violent partizans of Marius and Cinna during the civil war with Sulla. In b.c. 86 he was sent into Asia as legate of Valerius Flaccus, whom he induced the soldiers to put to death. He then carried on war against Mithridates ; but in 84 he was attacked by Sulla, and being deserted by his troops, put an end to his life.

FIRMUM (-i), a town in Picenum, 3 miles from the coast.

FLACCUS, FULVĬUS (-i), the name of two distinguished families in the Fulvia and Valeria gentes. Many of the members of both families held the highest offices in the state; but the best known are: — (1) M. FULVIUS FLACCUS, the friend of the Gracchi, consul B.C. 125, and one of the triumvirs for carrying into execution the agrarian law of Tib. Gracchus. He was slain, together with C. Gracchus, in 121. —(2) L. VALERIUS FLACCUS, consul B.C. 100, with C. Marius, when he took an active part in putting down the insurrection of Saturninus. In 86 he was chosen consul in place of Marius, and was sent into Asia against Mithridates, but was put to death by his soldiers at the instigation of Fimbria.—(3) L. VALERIUS FLACCUS, a native of Padua, who lived in the time of Vespasian, and wrote the *Argonautica*, an unfinished heroic poem, in 8 books, on the Argonautic expedition, which is extant.

FLACCUS, HŎRĀTĬUS. [HORATIUS.]

FLAMĬNĪNUS, T. QUINTĬUS (-i), consul B.C. 198, had the conduct of the war against Philip of Macedonia, whom he defeated at the battle of Cynoscephalae, in Thessaly, in 197, and compelled to sue for peace.

FLĀMĬNĬUS, C., (-i), consul for the first time B.C. 223, when he gained a victory over the Insubrian Gauls; and censor in 220, when he executed two great works, which bore his name, viz., the *Circus Flaminius* and the *Via Flaminia*. In his second consulship (217) he was defeated and slain by Hannibal, at the battle of the Trasimene lake.

FLĀVĬA GENS, celebrated as the house to which the emperor Vespasian belonged. During the later period of the Roman empire, the name Flavius descended from one emperor to another, Constantius, the father of Constantine the Great, being the first in the series.

FLĀVĬUS FIMBRĬA. [FIMBRIA.]
FLAVIUS JOSEPHUS. [JOSEPHUS.]
FLĀVĬUS VOPISCUS. [VOPISCUS.]

FLĒVUM (-i), a fortress in Germany, at the mouth of the Amisia (*Ems*).

FLĒVUM, FLĒVO. [RHENUS.]

FLŌRA (-ae), the Roman goddess of

Flora. (From a Roman Coin.)

flowers and spring, whose annual festival

(*Floralia*) was celebrated from the 28th of April till the 1st of May, with extravagant merriment and lasciviousness.

Flora. (From an ancient Statue.)

FLŌRENTĬA (-ae: *Firenze, Florence*), a town in Etruria, and subsequently a Roman colony, situated on the Arnus; but its greatness as a city dates from the middle ages.

FLŌRUS, L. ANNAEUS (-i), a Roman historian, lived under Trajan and Hadrian, and wrote a summary of Roman history, which is extant, divided into 4 books, extending from the foundation of the city to the time of Augustus.

FLŌRUS, JŪLĬUS (-i), a poet and an orator, addressed by Horace in 2 epistles.

FONTĒIUS, M., (-i), propraetor in Narbonese Gaul, between B.C. 76—73, accused in 69 of extortion in his province and defended by Cicero in an oration, part of which is extant.

FŌRENTUM or FĔRENTUM (-i), a town in Apulia, surrounded by fertile fields and in a low situation, according to Horace.

FORMĬAE (-ārum: nr. *Mola di Gaëta*, Ru.), a very ancient town in Latium, on the Appia Via, in the innermost corner of the beautiful Sinus Caietanus (*Gulf of Gaëta*). It was founded by the Pelasgic Tyrrhenians, and was the fabled abode of Lamus and the Laestrygones. Near this place were numerous villas of the Roman nobles: of these the best known is the Formianum of Cicero, in the neighbourhood of which he was killed. The hills of Formiae produced good wine.

FORNAX (-ācis), a Roman goddess, who presided over baking the corn in the oven (*fornax*), and who was worshipped at the festival of the Fornacalia.

FORTŪNA (-ae), called TYCHE by the Greeks, the goddess of fortune, worshipped both in Greece and Italy. She was represented with different attributes. With a rudder, she was conceived as the divinity guiding and conducting the affairs of the world; with a ball, she represented the varying unsteadiness of fortune; with Plutus, or the horn of Amalthea, she was the symbol of the plentiful gifts of fortune. She was more worshipped by the Romans than by the Greeks. Her worship was of great importance also at Antium and Praeneste, where her *sortes* or oracles were very celebrated.

Fortuna. (Bronze, in the British Museum.)

FORTŪNĀTAE or -ŌRUM INSŬLAE, "the Islands of the Blessed." The early Greeks, as we learn from Homer, placed the Elysian fields, into which favoured heroes passed without dying, at the extremity of the earth, near the river Oceanus. [ELYSIUM.] In poems later than Homer, an island is spoken of as their abode; and though its position was of course indefinite, the poets, and the geographers who followed them, placed it beyond the pillars of Hercules. Hence when certain islands were discovered in the Ocean, off the W. coast of Africa, the name of Fortunatae Insulae were applied to them. They are now called the *Canary* and *Madeira* islands.

FŎRŬLI (-ōrum), a small town of the

Sabines, near the junction of the Himella with the Tiber.

FŎRUM (-i), an open space of ground, in which the public met for the transaction of public business, and for the sale and purchase of provisions. The number of fora increased at Rome with the growth of the city. They were level pieces of ground of an oblong form, and were surrounded by buildings, both private and public. The principal fora at Rome were:—(1) FORUM ROMANUM, also called simply the *Forum*, and at a later time distinguished by the epithets *vetus* or *magnum*. It lay between the Capitoline and Palatine Hills, and ran lengthwise from the foot of the Capitol or the arch of Septimius Severus in the direction of the arch of Titus; but it did not extend quite so far as to the latter. The origin of the forum is ascribed to Romulus and Tatius, who are said to have filled up the swamp or marsh which occupied its site, and to have set it apart as a place for the administration of justice and for holding the assemblies of the people. The forum, in its widest sense, included the forum properly so called, and the Comitium. The Comitium occupied the narrow or upper end of the forum, and was the place where the patricians met in their comitia curiata: the forum, in its narrower sense, was originally only a market-place, and was not used for any political purpose. At a later time, the forum in its narrower sense was the place of meeting for the plebeians in their comitia tributa, and was separated from the comitium by the Rostra or platform, from which the orators addressed the people. In the time of Tarquin the forum was surrounded by a range of shops, probably of a mean character, but they gradually underwent a change, and were eventually occupied by bankers and money-changers. As Rome grew in greatness, the forum was adorned with statues of celebrated men, with temples and basilicae, and with other public buildings. The site of the ancient forum is occupied by the *Campo Vaccino*.—(2) FORUM JULIUM or FORUM CAESARIS, built near the old forum by Julius Caesar, because the latter was found too small for the transaction of public business.—(3) FORUM AUGUSTI, built by Augustus, behind the Forum Julium.—(4) FORUM NERVAE or FORUM TRANSITORIUM, was a small forum lying between the Temple of Peace and the fora of Julius Caesar and Augustus. It was built by Nerva, and was intended to serve as a passage between the Temple of Peace and the fora of Caesar and of Augustus. Hence its name.—(5) FORUM TRAJANI, built by the emperor Trajan, between the forum of Augustus and the Campus Martius.

FŎRUM, the name of several towns, originally simply markets or places for the administration of justice. (1) APPII, in Latium, on the Appia Via, in the midst of the Pomptine marshes, 43 miles S. E. of Rome, founded by the censor Appius Claudius when he made the Appia Via. Here the Christians from Rome met the Apostle Paul.—(2) JULII or JULIUM (*Fréjus*), a Roman colony founded by Julius Caesar, B.C. 44, in Gallia Narbonensis, on the coast; the birthplace of Agricola.—(3) JULIUM. See ILLITURGIS.

FOSI (-ōrum), a people of Germany, the neighbours and allies of the Cherusci, in whose fate they shared. [CHERUSCI.]

FOSSA (-ae) or FOSSAE (-ārum), a canal. (1) CLUILIA or CLUILIAE, a trench about 5 miles from Rome, said to have been the ditch with which the Alban king Cluilius protected his camp, when he marched against Rome in the reign of Tullus Hostilius.—(2) DRUSIANAE or DRUSINAE, a canal which Drusus caused his soldiers to dig in B.C. 11, uniting the Rhine with the Yssel.—(3) MARIANA or MARIANAE, a canal dug by command of Marius during his war with the Cimbri, in order to connect the Rhone with the Mediterranean.—(4) XERXIS. See ATHOS.

FRANCI (-orum), *i. e.* "the Free men," a confederacy of German tribes, formed on the Lower Rhine in the place of the ancient league of the Cherusci. After carrying on frequent wars with the Romans, they at length settled permanently in Gaul, of which they became the rulers under their king Clovis, A.D. 496.

FREGELLAE (-ārum: *Ceprano*), a town of the Volsci on the Liris in Latium, conquered by the Romans, and colonised B.C. 328.

FREGENAE, sometimes called FREGELLAE (-ārum), a town of Etruria, on the coast between Alsium and the Tiber, colonised by the Romans, B.C. 245.

FRENTANI (-ōrum), a Samnite people dwelling on the coast of the Adriatic, from the river Sagrus on the N. (and subsequently almost as far N. as from the Aternus) to the river Frento on the S., from which they derived their name. They submitted to the Romans in B.C. 304.

FRENTO (-ōnis : *Fortore*), a river in Italy forming the boundary between the Frentani and Apulia, and falling into the Adriatic sea.

FRISII (-ōrum), a people in Germany, inhabiting the coast from the E. mouth of the Rhine to the Amisia (*Ems*), and bounded on the S. by the Bructeri. In the 5th century they joined the Saxons and Angli in their invasion of Britain.

FRONTINUS, SEX. JULIUS (-i), governor of Britain (A.D. 75 — 78) where he distinguished himself by the conquest of the Silures. He was the author of two treatises

that are still extant—one on the art of war, and another on the Roman aqueducts. He was nominated *Curator Aquarum*, or Superintendent of the Aqueducts, in 97 ; died 106.

FRONTO (-ōnis), M. CORNELIUS (-i), a celebrated rhetorician in the reigns of Hadrian and M. Aurelius, born at Cirta in Numidia. He was entrusted with the education of M. Aurelius and L. Verus, and was rewarded with wealth and honours. A few fragments of his works are extant.

FRUSINO (-ōnis), a town of the Hernici in Latium, and subsequently a Roman colony.

FUCENTIS, FUCENTIA. [ALBA, No. 1.]

FUCINUS LACUS (*Lago di Celano* or *Capistrano*), a large lake in the centre of Italy and in the country of the Marsi, about 30 miles in circumference, into which all the mountain streams of the Apennines flow. As the waters of this lake frequently inundated the surrounding country, the emperor Claudius constructed an emissarium or artificial channel for carrying off the waters of the lake into the river Liris. This emissarium is nearly perfect: it is almost 3 miles in length.

FUFIUS CALENUS. [CALENUS.]

FULVIA (-ae). (1) The mistress of Q. Curius, one of Catiline's conspirators, who divulged the plot to Cicero.—(2) A daughter of M. Fulvius Bambalio of Tusculum, and successively the wife of P. Clodius, C. Scribonius Curio, and M. Antony; died B.C. 40.

FULVIUS FLACCUS. [FLACCUS.]

FULVIUS NOBILIOR. [NOBILIOR.]

FUNDANIUS (-i), a writer of comedies, praised by Horace.

FUNDI (-ōrum : *Fondi*), an ancient town in Latium on the Appia Via, at the head of a narrow bay of the sea, running a considerable way into the land, called the LACUS FUNDANUS. The surrounding country produced good wine.

FURCULAE CAUDINAE. [CAUDIUM.]

FURIAE. [EUMENIDES.]

FURIUS BIBACULUS. [BIBACULUS.]

FURIUS CAMILLUS. [CAMILLUS.]

FUSCUS ARISTIUS (-i), a friend of the poet Horace, who addressed to him an ode and an epistle.

GABALI (-ōrum), a people in Gallia Aquitanica, whose chief town was Anderitum (*Anterieux*).

GABII (-ōrum), a town in Latium, on the Lacus Gabinus between Rome and Praeneste, a colony from Alba Longa ; and the place, according to tradition, where Romulus was brought up. It was taken by Tarquinius Superbus by stratagem, and was in ruins in the time of Augustus. The *cinctus Gabinus*, a peculiar mode of wearing the toga at Rome, appears to have been derived from this town. In its neighbourhood are the stone quarries, from which a part of Rome was built.

GĂBĪNĬUS, A., (-i), tribune of the plebs B.C. 66, when he carried a law conferring upon Pompey the command of the war against the pirates, and consul in 58, when he took part in the banishment of Cicero. In 57 he went to Syria as proconsul, and restored Ptolemy Auletes to the throne of Egypt, in opposition to a decree of the senate. On his return to Rome in 54 he was accused both of *majestas* and *repetundae.* He was defended by Cicero. He was condemned on the latter charge, and went into exile. In the civil war he fought on the side of Caesar. He died about the end of B.C. 48.

GĂDĂRA, a large fortified city of Palestine, situated on an eastern tributary of the Jordan.

GĀDES (-ĭum : *Cadiz*), a very ancient town in Hispania Baetica, founded by the Phoenicians, and one of the chief seats of their commerce in the W. of Europe, situated on a small island of the same name (*I. de Leon*), separated from the mainland by a narrow channel. Herodotus says (iv. 8) that the island of Erythīa was close to Gadeira; whence most later writers supposed the island of Gades to be the same as the mythical island of Erythia, from which Hercules carried off the oxen of Geryon. Its inhabitants received the Roman franchise from Julius Caesar.

GAEA (-ae), or GĒ (-es), called TELLUS by the Romans, the personification of the earth, is described as the first being that sprang from Chaos, and gave birth to Uranus (Heaven), and Pontus (Sea). By Uranus she became the mother of the Titans, who were hated by their father. Ge therefore concealed them in the bosom of the earth; and she made a large iron sickle, with which Cronos (Saturn) mutilated Uranus. Ge or Tellus was regarded by both Greeks and Romans as one of the gods of the nether world, and hence is frequently mentioned where they are invoked.

GAETŪLĬA (-ae), the interior of N. Africa, S. of Mauretania, Numidia, and the region bordering on the Syrtes, reaching to the Atlantic Ocean on the W., and of very indefinite extent towards the E. and S. The pure Gaetūli were not an Aethiopic (*i. e.* negro), but a Libyan race, and were most probably of Asiatic origin. They are probably the ancestors of the *Berbers.*

GAĪUS or CAĪUS (-i), a celebrated Roman jurist, who wrote under Antoninus Pius and M. Aurelius. One of his chief works was an elementary treatise on Roman law, entitled *Institutiones,* in 4 books, which was the or-

dinary text book used by those who were commencing the study of the Roman law, until the compilation of the Institutiones of Justinian. It was lost for centuries, until discovered by Niebuhr in 1816 at Verona.

GĂLANTHIS. [GALINTHIAS.]

GĂLĂTĒA (-ae), daughter of Nereus and Doris. [ACIS.]

GĂLĂTĬA or ĬA (-ae), a country of Asia Minor, composed of parts of Phrygia and Cappadocia, and bounded on the W., S., and S.E. by those countries, and on the N.E., N., and N.W. by Pontus, Paphlagonia, and Bithynia. It derived its name from its inhabitants, who were Gauls that had invaded and settled in Asia Minor at various periods during the 3d century B.C. They speedily overran all Asia Minor within the Taurus, and exacted tribute from its various princes; but Attalus I. gained a complete victory over them (B.C. 230), and compelled them to settle down within the limits of the country thenceforth called Galatia, and also, on account of the mixture of Greeks with the Celtic inhabitants, which speedily took place, Graeco-Galatia and Gallograecia. The people of Galatia adopted to a great extent Greek habits and manners and religious observances, but preserved their own language. They retained also their political divisions and forms of government. They consisted of 3 great tribes, the Tolistobogi, the Trocmi, and the Tectosages, each subdivided into 4 parts, called by the Greeks Tetrarchies. At the head of each of these 12 Tetrarchies was a chief, or Tetrarch. At length one of the tetrarchs, DEIOTARUS, was rewarded for his services to the Romans in the Mithridatic War by the title of king, together with a grant of Pontus and Armenia Minor; and after the death of his successor, Amyntas, Galatia was made by Augustus a Roman province (B.C. 25). Its only important cities were, in the S.W. PESSINUS, the capital of the Tolistobogi; in the centre ANCYRA, the capital of the Tectosages; and in the N.E., TAVIUM, the capital of the Trocmi. From the Epistle of St. Paul to the Galatians, we learn that the Christian churches in Galatia consisted, in great part, of Jewish converts.

GALBA (-ae), the name of a distinguished family in the Sulpicia gens. (1) P. SULPICIUS GALBA, twice consul, B.C. 211 and 200, and in both consulships carried on war against Philip, king of Macedonia.—(2) SER. SULPICIUS GALBA, praised by Cicero on account of his oratory, praetor 151, when he treacherously murdered a large number of Lusitanians, and consul 144.—(3) SER. SULPICIUS GALBA, Roman ,emperor, June A.D. 68 to January A.D. 69, was born B.C. 3. After his consulship he had the government of Gaul, A.D. 39, where he carried on a successful war against the Germans, and restored discipline among the troops. Nero gave him, in A.D. 61, the government of Hispania Tarraconensis, where he remained for 8 years. When Nero was murdered Galba proceeded to Rome, where he was acknowledged as emperor. But his severity and avarice soon made him unpopular with the soldiers, by whom he was murdered, at the instigation of Otho.

GĂLĒNUS, CLAUDĬUS (-i), commonly called GALEN, a very celebrated physician, born at Pergamum, A.D. 130. He was carefully educated by his father Nicon, who, in consequence of a dream, chose for him the profession of medicine. This subject he first studied at Pergamum, afterwards at Smyrna, Corinth, and Alexandria. He practised in his native city, and at Rome, where he attended the emperors M. Aurelius and L. Verus. He died about A.D. 200, at the age of 70, in the reign of Septimius Severus. He wrote a great number of works on medical and philosophical subjects. There are still extant 83 treatises which are acknowledged to be his, besides many that are spurious or doubtful.

GALEPSUS (-i), a town in Macedonia, on the Toronaic gulf.

GĂLĔRĬUS MAXĬMĬĂNUS. [MAXIMIA-NUS.]

GĂLĒSUS (-i), a river in the S. of Italy, flowing into the gulf of Tarentum through the meadows where the sheep grazed whose wool was so celebrated in antiquity.

GĂLĔUS (-i), that is, "the lizard," son of Apollo and Themisto, from whom the GALEŌTAE, a family of Sicilian soothsayers, derived their origin. The principal seat of the Galeotae was the town of Hybla, which was hence called GALEŌTIS or GALEATIS.

GĂLĬLAEA (-ae), at the birth of Christ was the N.-most of the 3 divisions of Palestine W. of the Jordan. Its inhabitants were a mixed race of Jews, Syrians, Phoenicians, Greeks, and others, and were therefore despised by the Jews of Judaea.

GĂLINTHĬAS (-ădis) or GĂLANTHIS (-ĭdis), daughter of Proetus of Thebes, and a friend of Alcmene. When Alcmene was on the point of giving birth to Hercules, and the Moerae and Ilithyiae, at the request of Hera (Juno), were endeavouring to delay the birth, Galinthias suddenly rushed in with the false report that Alcmene had given birth to a son. The hostile goddesses were so surprised at this information that they dropped their arms. Thus the charm was broken, and Alcmene was enabled to give birth to Her-

cules. The deluded goddesses avenged the deception practised upon them by metamorphosing Galinthias into a weasel (γαλῆ). Hecate, however, took pity upon her, and made her her attendant, and Hercules afterwards erected a sanctuary to her.

GALLAECĬA (-ae), the country of the GALLAECI or CALLAECI, in the N. of Spain, between the Astures and the Durius. Its inhabitants were some of the most uncivilised in Spain. They were defeated with great slaughter by D. Brutus, consul B.C. 138, who obtained in consequence the surname of Gallaecus.

GALLĬA (-ae), in its widest acceptation, indicated all the land inhabited by the Galli or Celtae, but, in its narrower sense, was applied to two countries:— (1) GALLIA, also called GALLIA TRANSALPINA or GALLIA ULTERIOR, to distinguish it from Gallia Cisalpina, or the N. of Italy. In the time of Augustus it was bounded on the S. by the Pyrenees and the Mediterranean ; on the E. by the river Varus and the Alps, which separated it from Italy, and by the river Rhine, which separated it from Germany ; on the N. by the German Ocean and the English Channel ; and on the W. by the Atlantic : thus including not only the whole of France and Belgium, but a part of Holland, a great part of Switzerland, and all the provinces of Germany W. of the Rhine. The Greeks, at a very early period, became acquainted with the S. coast of Gaul, where they founded, in B.C. 600, the important town of MASSILIA. The Romans commenced the conquest of Gaul B.C. 125, and a few years afterwards made the south-eastern part of the country a Roman province. In Caesar's Commentaries the Roman province is called simply *Provincia*, in contradistinction to the rest of the country ; hence comes the modern name of *Provence*. The rest of the country was subdued by Caesar after a struggle of several years (58—50). At this time Gaul was divided into 3 parts, *Aquitania*, *Celtica*, and *Belgica*, according to the 3 different races by which it was inhabited. The Aquitani dwelt in the S.W., between the Pyrenees and the Garumna ; the Celtae, or Galli proper, in the centre and W., between the Garumna and the Sequana and the Matrona ; and the Belgae in the N.E., between the two last mentioned rivers and the Rhine. Of the many tribes inhabiting Gallia Celtica none were more powerful than the Aedui, the Sequani, and the Helvetii. Augustus divided Gaul into 4 provinces. 1. *Gallia Narbonensis*, the same as the old Provincia. 2. *G. Aquitanica*, which extended from the Pyrenees to the Liger. 3. *G. Lugdunensis*, the country between the Liger, the Sequana, and the

Arar, so called from the colony of Lugdunum (*Lyons*), founded by Munatius Plancus. 4. *G. Belgica*, the country between the Sequana, the Arar, and the Rhine. Shortly afterwards the portion of Belgica bordering on the Rhine, and inhabited by German tribes, was subdivided into 2 new provinces, called *Germania Prima* and *Secunda*, or *Germania Superior* and *Inferior*. The Latin language gradually became the language of the inhabitants, and Roman civilisation took deep root in all parts of the country. The rhetoricians and poets of Gaul occupy a distinguished place in the later history of Roman literature. On the dissolution of the Roman empire, Gaul, like the other Roman provinces, was overrun by barbarians, and the greater part of it finally became subject to the Franci or Franks, under their king Clovis, about A.D. 496.— (2) GALLIA CISALPINA, also called G. CITERIOR and G. TOGATA, a Roman province in the N. of Italy, was bounded on the W. by Liguria and Gallia Narbonensis (from which it was separated by the Alps), and on the N. by Rhaetia and Noricum; on the E. by the Adriatic and Venetia (from which it was separated by the Athesis), and on the S. by Etruria and Umbria (from which it was separated by the river Rubicon). It was divided by the Po into GALLIA TRANSPADANA, also called ITALIA TRANSPADANA, in the N., and GALLIA CISPADANA in the S. It was originally inhabited by Ligurians, Umbrians, Etruscans, and other races; but its fertility attracted the Gauls, who at different periods crossed the Alps, and settled in the country, after expelling the original inhabitants. After the 1st Punic war the Romans conquered the whole country, and formed it into a Roman province. The inhabitants, however, did not bear the yoke patiently, and it was not till after the final defeat of the Boii in 191 that the country became submissive to the Romans. The most important tribes were : In Gallia Transpadana, in the direction of W. to E., the TAURINI, SALASSI, LIBICI, INSUBRES, CENOMANI; in G. Cispadana, in the same direction, the BOII, LINGONES, SENONES.

GALLIENUS (-i), Roman emperor A.D. 260—268, succeeded his father Valerian, when the latter was taken prisoner by the Persians in 260. Gallienus was indolent, profligate, and indifferent to the public welfare; and his reign was one of the most ignoble and disastrous in the history of Rome. Numerous usurpers sprung up in different parts of the empire, who are commonly distinguished as *The Thirty Tyrants*. Gallienus was slain by his own soldiers in 268, while besieging Milan, in which the usurper Aureolus had taken refuge.

GALLINARIA (-ae). (1) An island off the coast of Liguria, celebrated for its number of hens, whence its name.—(2) SILVA, a forest of pine-trees near Cumae in Campania.

GALLOGRAECIA. [GALATIA.]

GALLUS, C. CORNELIUS (-i), a Roman poet, born in Forum Julii (*Frejus*) in Gaul, about B.C. 66, went to Italy at an early age, and rose to distinction under Julius Caesar and Augustus. He was appointed by the latter the first prefect of the province of Egypt; but having incurred the displeasure of Augustus, while he was in Egypt, the senate sent him into exile; whereupon he put an end to his life, B.C. 26. Gallus lived on intimate terms with Asinius Pollio, Virgil, Varus, and Ovid, and the latter assigns to him the first place among the Roman elegiac poets. All his productions have perished.

GALLUS, TREBONIANUS (-i), Roman emperor, A.D. 251—254, and the successor of Decius, purchased a peace with the Goths on very dishonourable terms, and was afterwards put to death by his own soldiers.

GALLUS (-i), a river in Galatia, falling into the Sangarius, near Pessinus. From it the priests of Cybele are said to have obtained their name of Galli.

GANDARIDAE, GANDARITAE, or GANDARAE (-ārum), an Indian people, in the middle of the Punjab, between the rivers Acesines (*Chenab*) and Hydraotes (*Ravee*), whose king, at the time of Alexander's invasion, was a cousin and namesake of the celebrated Porus.

GANGES (-is), the greatest river of India, which it divided into the 2 parts named by the ancients India intra Gangem (*Hindostan*), and India extra Gangem (*Burmah, Cochin China, Siam*, and the *Malay Peninsula*). It rises in the highest part of the Emodi Montes (*Himalaya*), and flows by several mouths into the head of the Gangeticus Sinus (*Bay of Bengal*). The knowledge of the ancients respecting it was very imperfect.

GANYMEDES (-is), son of Tros and Callirrhoë, and brother of Ilus and Assaracus, was the most beautiful of all mortals, and was carried off by the gods that he might fill the cup of Zeus (Jupiter), and live among the immortal gods. This is the Homeric account; but other traditions give different details. He is called son either of Laomedon, or of Ilus, or of Erichthonius, or of Assaracus. Later writers state that Zeus himself carried him off, in the form of an eagle, or by means of his eagle. There is, further, no agreement as to the place where the event occurred; though later writers usually represent him as carried off from Mount Ida. Zeus compensated the father for his loss by a pair of divine horses. Astronomers placed Ganymedes among the stars under the name of

Ganymedes. (Visconti, Mus. Pio. Clem.; vol. 2, tav. 49.)

Aquarius. His name was sometimes corrupted in Latin into Catamītus.

Ganymedes. (Zannoni, Gal. di Firenze, serie 4, vol. 2, pl. 101.)

GĂRĂMANTES (-um), the S.-most people known to the ancients in N. Africa, dwelt far S. of the Great Syrtis in the region called Phazania (*Fezzan*), where they had a capital city, Gărămă. They are mentioned by Herodotus as a weak unwarlike people.

GARGĀNUS MONS (*Monte Gargano*), a mountain and promontory in Apulia, on which were oak forests.

GARGĂRĂ (-ōrum), the S. summit of M. Ida, in the Troad, with a city of the same name at its foot.

GARGETTUS (-i), a demus in Attica, on the N.W. slope of Mt. Hymettus; the birthplace of the philosopher Epicurus.

GARĪTES (-um), a people in Aquitania, neighbours of the Ausci.

GARŌCĔLI (-ōrum), a people in Gallia Narbonensis, near Mt. Cenis.

GĂRUMNA (-ae: *Garonne*), one of the chief rivers of Gaul, rising in the Pyrenees, flowing N.W. through Aquitania, and becoming a bay of the sea below Burdigala (*Bordeaux*).

GARUMNI (-ōrum), a people in Aquitania, on the Garumna.

GAUGĀMĒLA (-ōrum), a village in Assyria, the scene of the last battle between Alexander and Darius, B.C. 331, commonly called the battle of ARBELA.

GAURUS MONS, GAURĀNUS or -NI M., a volcanic range of mountains in Campania, between Cumae and Neapolis, in the neighbourhood of Puteoli, producing good wine, and memorable for the defeat of the Samnites by M. Valerius Corvus, B.C. 343.

GĀZA (-ae), the last city on the S. W. frontier of Palestine, and the key of the country on the side of Egypt, stood on an eminence about 2 miles from the sea, and was very strongly fortified. It was one of the 5 cities of the Philistines, and was taken by Alexander the Great after an obstinate defence of several months.

GĒBENNA MONS. [CEBENNA.]

GĒDRŌSĬA (-ae), the furthest province of the Persian empire on the S.E., and one of the subdivisions of Ariana, bounded on the W. by Carmania, on the N. by Drangiana and Arachosia, on the E. by India, or, as the country about the lower course of the Indus was called, Indo-Scythia, and on the S. by the Mare Erythraeum, or Indian Ocean. It is known in history chiefly through the distress suffered for want of water, in passing through it, by the army of Alexander.

GĒLA (-ae), a city on the S. coast of Sicily, on a river of the same name, founded by Rhodians from Lindos, and by Cretans, B.C. 690. It soon obtained great power and wealth; and, in 582, it founded Agrigentum. Gelon transported half of its inhabitants to Syracuse; the place gradually fell into decay, and in the time of Augustus was not inhabited. The poet Aeschylus died here.

GELDŪBA (-ae: *Gelb*, below *Cologne*), a fortified place of the Ubii, on the Rhine, in Lower Germany.

GELLĬUS, AULUS (-i), a Latin grammarian, who lived about A.D. 117—180. He

wrote a work, still extant, containing numerous extracts from Greek and Roman
writers, which he called *Noctes Atticae*,
because it was composed near Athens, during
the long nights of winter.

GĒLŌN (-ōnis), tyrant of Gela, and afterwards of Syracuse, became master of his
native city, B.C. 491. In 485 he obtained
the supreme power in Syracuse, and henceforth endeavoured, in every possible way, to
enlarge and enrich it. In 480 he gained a
brilliant victory at Himera over the Carthaginians, who had invaded Sicily with an
immense army on the very same day as that
of Salamis. He died in 478, after reigning
7 years at Syracuse. He is represented as a
man of singular leniency and moderation,
and as seeking in every way to promote the
welfare of his subjects.

GĒLŌNI (-ōrum), a Scythian people,
dwelling in Sarmatia Asiatica, to the E. of
the river Tanais (*Don*).

GĒMŌNĬAE (scalae) or GĔMŌNĬI (gra-
dus), a flight of steps cut out of the
Aventine, down which the bodies of criminals strangled in the prison were dragged,
and afterwards thrown into the Tiber.

GĒNĀBUM or CĒNĀBUM (-i: *Orleans*),
a town in Gallia Lugdunensis, on the N.
bank of the Ligeris, the chief town of the
Carnutes, subsequently called Civitas Aure-
lianorum, or Aurelianensis Urbs, whence its
modern name.

GĒNAUNI (-ōrum), a people in Vindelicia,
the inhabitants of the Alpine valley, now
called *Valle di Non*, subdued by Drusus.

GĒNĒVA or GĒNĀVA (-ae: *Geneva*), the
last town of the Allobroges, on the frontiers
of the Helvetii, situated on the S. bank of
the Rhone, at the spot where the river
flowed out of the Lacus Lemannus. There
was a bridge here over the Rhone.

GĒNĬTRIX (-Icis), that is, "the mother,"
used by Ovid, as a surname of Cybele, in the
place of *mater*, or *magna mater ;* but it is
better known as a surname of Venus, to
whom Caesar dedicated a temple at Rome,
as the mother of the Julia Gens.

GĒNĬUS (-i) a protecting spirit, analogous
to the guardian angels invoked by the Church

Wine Genius. (A Mosaic, from Pompeii.)

of Rome. The belief in such spirits existed
both in Greece and at Rome. The Greeks
called them Daemons (δαιμονες); and the poets
represented them as dwelling on earth, un-

seen by mortals, as the ministers of Zeus (Jupiter), and as the guardians of men and of justice. The Greek philosophers took up this idea, and taught that daemons were assigned to men at the moment of their birth, that they accompanied men through life, and after death conducted their souls to Hades. The Romans seem have to received their notions respecting the genii from the Etruscans, though the name Genius itself is Latin (connected with *gi-gn-o*, *gen-ui*, and equivalent in meaning to *generator*, or father). According to the opinion of the Romans, every human being at his birth obtained a genius, whom he worshipped as *sanctus et sanctissimus deus*, especially on his birthday, with libations of wine, incense, and garlands of flowers. The bridal bed was sacred to the genius, on account of his connection with generation, and the bed itself was called *lectus genialis*. On other merry occasions, also, sacrifices were offered to the genius, and to indulge in merriment was not unfrequently expressed by *genio indulgere*, *genium curare* or *placare*. Every place had also its genius. The genii are usually represented in works of art as winged beings. The genius of a place appears in the form of a serpent eating fruit placed before him.

GENSÉRIC, king of the Vandals, and the most terrible of all the barbarian invaders of the empire. In A.D. 429 he crossed over from Spain, and made himself master of the whole of N. Africa. In 455 he took Rome and plundered it for 14 days. He died in 477, at a great age. He was an Arian, and persecuted his Catholic subjects.

GENTĬUS (-i), king of the Illyrians, conquered by the Romans, B.C. 168.

GĔNŬA (-ae : *Genoa*), an important commercial town in Liguria, situated at the extremity of the Ligurian gulf (*Gulf of Genoa*), and subsequently a Roman municipium.

GĔNŪSUS (-i), a river in Greek Illyria, N. of the Apsus.

GĔPĬDAE (-ārum), a Gothic people, who fought under Attila, and afterwards settled in Dacia, on the banks of the Danube. They were conquered by the Langobardi or Lombards.

GĔRAESTUS (-i), a promontory and harbour at the S. extremity of Euboea, with a celebrated temple of Poseidon (Neptune).

GĔRĂNĔA (-ae), a range of mountains, running along the W. coast of Megaris, terminating in the promontory Olmiae in the Corinthian territory.

GĔRĒNĬA (-ae), an ancient town in Messenia, the birthplace of Nestor, who is hence called Gerenian.

GERGŎVĬA (-ae). (1) A fortified town of the Arverni in Gaul, situated on a high and inaccessible hill, W. or S.W. of the Elaver (*Allier*), probably in the neighbourhood of the modern *Clermont*.—(2) A town of the Boii in Gaul, of uncertain site.

GERMĀNĬA (-ae), a country bounded by the Rhine on the W., by the Vistula and the Carpathian mountains on the E., by the Danube on the S., and by the German Ocean and the Baltic on the N. It thus included much more than modern Germany on the N. and E., but much less in the W. and S. The N. and N.E. of Gallia Belgica were likewise called *Germania Prima* and *Secunda* under the Roman emperors [GALLIA] ; and it was in contradistinction to these provinces that Germania proper was also called GERMANIA MAGNA or G. TRANSRHENANA or G. BARBARA. The inhabitants were called GERMANI by the Romans. Tacitus says that Germani was the name of the Tungri, who were the first German people that crossed the Rhine ; and as these were the first German tribes with which the Romans came into contact, they extended the name to the whole nation. The Germans were a branch of the great Indo-Germanic race, who, along with the Celts, migrated into Europe from the Caucasus and the countries around the Black and Caspian seas, at a period long anterior to historical records. They are described as a people of high stature and of great bodily strength, with fair complexions, blue eyes, and yellow or red hair. Many of their tribes were nomad, and every year changed their place of abode. The men found their chief delight in the perils and excitement of war. The women were held in high honour. Their chastity was without reproach. Both sexes were equally distinguished for their unconquerable love of liberty. In each tribe we find the people divided to 4 classes : the nobles ; the freemen ; the freedmen or vassals ; and the slaves. A king or chief was elected from among the nobles—his authority was very limited, and in case of war breaking out was often resigned to the warrior that was chosen as leader. The Germani first appear in history in the campaigns of the Cimbri and Teutones (B.C. 113), the latter of whom were undoubtedly a Germanic people. [TEUTONES.] Campaigns against the Germans were carried on by Julius Cæsar, 58—53 ; by Drusus, 12—9 ; by Varus most unsuccessfully, A.D. 9 ; and by Germanicus, who was gaining continued victories when recalled by Tiberius, A.D. 16. No further attempts were made by the Romans to conquer Germany. They had rather to defend their own empire from the invasions of the various German tribes, especially against the 2 powerful confederacies of the Alemanni and Franks [ALEMANNI : FRANCI] ; and in the 4th and 5th centuries the Germans obtained possession of some of the fairest provinces of the empire.—The Germans are divided by Tacitus into 3 great tribes : 1. *Ingaevones*, on the Ocean. 2. *Hermiones*, inhabiting the central parts. 3. *Istaevones*, in the remainder of Germany, consequently in the E. and S. parts. To these we ought to add the inhabitants of the Scandinavian peninsula, the Hilleviones, divided into the Sinones and Sitones.

GERMĂNĬCUS (-i), CAESAR (-ăris), son of Nero Claudius Drusus and Antonia, daughter of the triumvir Antony, was born B.C. 15. He was adopted by his uncle Tiberius in the lifetime of Augustus, and was raised at an early age to the honours of the state. He assisted Tiberius in his war against the Pannonians and Dalmatians (A.D. 7—10), and Germans (11, 12). He had the command of the legions in Germany, when the alarming mutiny broke out among the soldiers in Germany and Illyricum, upon the death of Augustus (14). After restoring order among the troops, he devoted himself to the conquest of Germany, and carried on the war with such vigour and success, that he needed only another year to reduce completely the whole country between the Rhine and the Elbe. But the jealousy of Tiberius saved Germany. He recalled Germanicus to Rome (17), and gave him the command of all the eastern provinces ; but at the same time he placed Cn. Piso over Syria, with secret instructions to check and thwart Germanicus. Germanicus died in Syria in 19, and it was believed both by himself and by others that he had been poisoned by Piso. He was deeply lamented by the Roman people; and Tiberius was obliged to sacrifice Piso to the public indignation. [PISO.] By Agrippina he had 9 children, of whom the most notorious were the emperor Caligula, and Agrippina, the mother of Nero. Germanicus was an author of some repute. He wrote several poetical works, most of which are lost.

GERRA, one of the chief cities of Arabia, and a great emporium for the trade of Arabia and India, stood on the N. E. coast of Arabia Felix. The inhabitants, called Gerraei, were said to have been originally Chaldaeans, who were driven out of Babylon.

GĒRỸON (-ŏnis), or GĒRỸŎNĒS (-ae), son of Chrysaor and Callirrhoë, a monster with 3 heads, or according to others, with 3 bodies united together, was a king in Spain,

and possessed magnificent oxen, which Hercules carried away. [HERCULES.]

GESORIĂCUM (-i: *Boulogne*), a port of the Morini in Gallia Belgica, at which persons usually embarked to cross over to Britain : it was subsequently called BONONIA, whence its modern name.

GĒTA (-ae), SEPTĬMĬUS (-i), brother of Caracalla, by whom he was assassinated, A.D. 212. [CARACALLA.]

GĒTAE (-ārum), a Thracian people, called Daci by the Romans. Herodotus and Thucydides place them S. of the Ister (*Danube*) near its mouths ; but in the time of Alexander the Great they dwelt beyond this river and N. of the Triballi.

GĬGANTES (-um), the giants, sprang from the blood that fell from Uranus upon the earth, so that Ge (the earth) was their mother. They are represented as beings of a monstrous size, with fearful countenances and the tails of dragons. They made an attack upon heaven, being armed with huge rocks and trunks of trees ; but the gods with the assistance of Hercules destroyed them all, and buried many of them under Aetna and other volcanoes. It is worthy of remark, that most writers place the giants in volcanic districts ; and it is probable that the story of their contest with the gods took its origin from volcanic convulsions.

GIGŎNUS, a town and promontory of Macedonia on the Thermaic gulf.

GLĂBRĬO (-ōnis), ACĪLĬUS (-i). (1) Consul, B.C. 191, when he defeated Antiochus at Thermopylae.—(2) Praetor urbanus in 70, when he presided at the impeachment of Verres, and consul in 67, and subsequently the successor of L. Lucullus in the command of the war against Mithridates, in which however he was superseded by Cn. Pompey.

GLĂNIS (-is), more usually written CLANIS.

GLĂPHỸRA. [ARCHELAUS, No. 6.]

GLAUCĒ (-es). (1) One of the Nereides, the name Glauce being only a personification of the colour of the sea.—(2) Daughter of Creon of Corinth, also called Creusa. [CREON.]

GLAUCUS (-i). (1) Of Potniae, son of Sisyphus and father of Bellerophontes, torn to pieces by his own mares, because he had despised the power of Aphrodite (Venus). —(2) Son of Hippolochus, and grandson of Bellerophontes, who was commander of the Lycians in the Trojan war. He was connected with Diomedes by ties of hospitality ; and when they recognised one another in the battle, they abstained from fighting, and exchanged arms. Glaucus was slain by Ajax. — (3) One of the sons of the Cretan king Minos by Pasiphaë or Crete. When a boy, he fell into a cask full of honey, and was smothered. He was discovered by the soothsayer Polyidus of Argos, who was pointed out by Apollo for this purpose. Minos then required him to restore his son to life. Being unable to do this he was buried with Glaucus, when a serpent revealed a herb which restored the dead body to life. — (4) Of Anthedon in Boeotia, a fisherman, who became a sea-god by eating a part of the divine herb which Cronos (Saturn) had sown. It was believed that Glaucus visited every year all the coasts and islands of Greece, accompanied by marine monsters, and gave his prophecies. Fishermen and sailors paid particular reverence to him, and watched his oracles, which were believed to be very trustworthy.—(5) Of Chios, a statuary in metal, distinguished as the inventor of the art of soldering metals, flourished B.C. 490.

GLỸCĔRA (-ae), " the sweet one," a favourite name of courtesans.

GNOSUS, GNOSSUS. [CNOSUS.]

GOLGI (-ōrum), a town in Cyprus, of uncertain site, a Sicyonian colony, and one of the chief seats of the worship of Aphrodite (Venus).

GOMPHI (-ōrum), a town in Hestiaeotis in Thessaly, a strong fortress on the confines of Epirus, commanding the chief pass between Thessaly and Epirus.

GONNI (-ōrum), GONNUS (-i), a strongly fortified town of the Perrhaebi in Thessaly, on the river Peneus and at the entrance of the vale of Tempe.

GORDIĀNUS, M. ANTŌNIUS (-i), the name of 3 Roman emperors, father, son, and grandson. The father was a man distinguished by intellectual and moral excellence, and had governed Africa for many years, when he was proclaimed emperor at the age of 80. He associated his son with him in the empire, but reigned only two months. His son was slain in battle, and he thereupon put an end to his own life, A.D. 238. His grandson was proclaimed emperor by the soldiers in Rome A.D. 238, after the murder of Balbinus and Pupienus, although he was not more than 12 years old. He reigned 6 years, from 238 to 244, when he was assassinated by Misitheus in Mesopotamia.

GORDIUM (-i), the ancient capital of Phrygia, situated on the Sangarius, the royal residence of the kings of the dynasty of Gordius, and the scene of Alexander's celebrated exploit of " cutting the Gordian knot." [GORDIUS.]

GORDIUS (-i), an ancient king of Phrygia, and father of Midas, was originally a poor peasant. Internal disturbances having broken out in Phrygia, an oracle informed the inhabitants that a waggon would bring them a king, who would put an end to their troubles. Shortly afterwards Gordius suddenly appeared riding in his waggon in the assembly of the people, who at once acknowledged him as king. Gordius, out of gratitude, dedicated his chariot to Zeus (Jupiter), in the acropolis of Gordium. The pole was fastened to the yoke by a knot of bark; and an oracle declared that whosoever should untie the knot should reign over all Asia. Alexander, on his arrival at Gordium, cut the knot with his sword, and applied the oracle to himself.

GORDȲENE or CORDŨENE (-es), a mountainous district in the S. of Armenia Major, between the Arsissa Palus (Lake Van) and the Gordyaei Montes (Mountains of Kurdistan). Its warlike inhabitants, called Gordyaei, or Corduēni, were no doubt the same people as the CARDUCHI of the earlier Greek geographers, and the modern Kurds.

GORGĒ (-es), daughter of Oeneus and sister of Deianira, both of whom retained their original forms, when their other sisters were metamorphosed by Artemis (Diana) into birds.

GORGIAS (-ae). (1) Of Leontini, in Sicily, a celebrated rhetorician and sophist, born about B.C. 480, and lived upwards of 100 years. In B.C. 427 he was sent by his fellow-citizens as ambassador to Athens, for the purpose of soliciting its protection against Syracuse. A dialogue of Plato bears his name. Gorgias wrote several works, which are lost, with the exception of two declamations—the Apology of Palamedes, and the Encomium on Helena, the genuineness of which, however, is doubtful.—(2) Of Athens, gave instruction in rhetoric to young M. Cicero, when he was at Athens.

GORGŌNES (-um), the name of 3 frightful

The Gorgon Medusa. (Marble Head, at Munich.)

maidens, STHENO, EURYALE, and MEDUSA,

daughters of Phorcys and Ceto, whence they are sometimes called PHORCYDES. Later traditions placed them in Libya. Instead of hair their heads were covered with hissing serpents; and they had wings, brazen claws, and enormous teeth. Medusa, who alone of the sisters was mortal, was, according to some legends, at first a beautiful maiden, but her hair was changed into serpents by Athena (Minerva), in consequence of her having become by Poseidon (Neptune) the mother of Chrysaor and Pegasus, in one of Athena's temples. Her head now became so fearful that every one who looked at it was changed into stone. Hence the great difficulty which Perseus had in killing her. [PERSEUS.] Athena afterwards placed the head in the centre of her shield or breastplate.

The Gorgon Medusa. (Florentine Gem.)

GORTYN, GORTYNA, one of the most ancient cities in Crete, on the river Lethaeus, 90 stadia from its harbour Lebēn, and 130 stadia from its other harbour Matalia.

GORTYNIA (-ae), a town in Emathia in Macedonia, of uncertain site.

GŌTHI (-ōrum), GŌTHŌNES, GUTTŌNES (-um), a powerful German people, who originally dwelt on the Prussian coast of the Baltic at the mouth of the Vistula, but afterwards migrated S. At the beginning of the 3rd century they appear on the coasts of the Black Sea, and in A.D. 272 the emperor Aurelian surrendered to them the whole of Dacia. About this time we find them separated into 2 great divisions, the Ostrogoths or E. Goths, and the Visigoths or W. Goths. The Ostrogoths settled in Moesia and Pannonia, while the Visigoths remained N. of the Danube. The Visigoths under their king Alaric invaded Italy, and took and plundered Rome (410). A few years afterwards they

settled permanently in the S.W. of Gaul, and established a kingdom of which Tolosa was the capital. From thence they invaded Spain, where they also founded a kingdom, which lasted for more than 2 centuries, till it was overthrown by the Arabs. The Ostrogoths meantime extended their dominions almost up to the gates of Constantinople; and under their king, Theodoric the Great, they obtained possession of the whole of Italy (493). The Ostrogoths embraced Christianity at an early period; and it was for their use that Ulphilas translated the sacred Scriptures into Gothic, in the 4th century.

GOTHĪNI, a Celtic people in the S.E. of Germany, subject to the Quadi.

GRACCHUS (-i), the name of a celebrated family of the Sempronia gens. (1) TIB. SEMPRONIUS GRACCHUS, a distinguished general in the 2nd Punic war. In B.C. 212 he fell in battle against Mago, at Campi Veteres, in Lucania. His body was sent to Hannibal, who honoured it with a magnificent burial.—(2) TIB. SEMPRONIUS GRACCHUS, distinguished as the father of the tribunes Tiberius and Caius Gracchus. For public services rendered when tribune of the plebs (187) to P. Scipio Africanus, he was rewarded with the hand of his youngest daughter, Cornelia. He was twice consul and once censor. He had 12 children by Cornelia, all of whom died at an early age, except the 2 tribunes, and a daughter, Cornelia, who was married to P. Scipio Africanus the younger.—(3) TIB. SEMPRONIUS GRACCHUS, elder son of No. 2, lost his father at an early age, and was educated, together with his brother Caius, by his illustrious mother, Cornelia, who made it the object of her life to render her sons worthy of their father and of her own ancestors. The distressed condition of the Roman people deeply excited the sympathies of Tiberius. He had observed with grief the deserted state of some parts of the country, and the immense domains of the wealthy, cultivated only by slaves; and he resolved to use every effort to remedy this state of things by endeavouring to create an industrious middle class of agriculturists, and to put a check upon the unbounded avarice of the ruling party. With this view, when tribune of the plebs, 133, he proposed a bill for the renewing and enforcing of the Licinian law, which enacted that no citizen should hold more than 500 jugera of the public land. He added a clause, permitting a father of 2 sons to hold 250 jugera for each; so that a father of two sons might hold in all 1000 jugera. To this measure the aristocracy offered the most vehement opposition; nevertheless, through the vigour and energy of

Tiberius, it was passed, and triumvirs were appointed for carrying it into execution. These were Tib. Gracchus; App. Claudius, his father-in-law; and his brother, C. Gracchus. About this time Attalus died, and on the proposition of Gracchus his property was divided among the poor, that they might purchase farming implements, &c. When the time came for the election of the tribunes for the following year, Tiberius again offered himself as a candidate; but in the very midst of the election he was publicly assassinated by P. Scipio Nasica. He was probably about 35 years of age at the time of his death. Tib. was a sincere friend of the oppressed, and acted from worthy motives, whatever his political errors may have been. Much of the odium that has been thrown upon him and his brother has risen from a misunderstanding of the Roman agrarian laws.—(4) C. SEMPRONIUS GRACCHUS, brother of the preceding, was tribune of the plebs, 123. His reforms were far more extensive than his brother's, and such was his influence with the people that he carried all he proposed; and the senate were deprived of some of their most important privileges. His first measure was the renewal of the agrarian law of his brother. He also enacted that the judices, who had hitherto been elected from the senate, should in future be chosen from the equites; and that in every year, before the consuls were elected, the senate should determine the 2 provinces which the consuls should have. Caius was elected tribune a second time, 122. The senate, finding it impossible to resist the measures of Caius, resolved to destroy his influence with the people. For this purpose they persuaded M. Livius Drusus, one of the colleagues of Caius, to propose measures still more popular than those of Caius. The people allowed themselves to be duped by the treacherous agent of the senate, and the popularity of Caius gradually waned. He failed in obtaining the tribuneship for the following year (121); and when his year of office expired, his enemies began to repeal several of his enactments. Caius appeared in the forum to oppose these proceedings, upon which a riot ensued, and while his friends fought in his defence, he fled to the grove of the Furies, where he fell by the hands of his slave, whom he had commanded to put him to death. About 3000 of his friends were slain, and many were thrown into prison, and there strangled.

GRĀDĪVUS (-i), i.e. the marching (probably from gradior), a surname of Mars, who is hence called gradivus pater and rex gradivus. Numa appointed 12 Salii as priests of this god.

GRAEAE (-ārum), that is, "the old women," daughters of Phorcys and Ceto, were 3 in number, Pephredo, Enyo, and Dino, also called Phorcydes. They had grey hair from their birth; and had only one tooth and one eye in common, which they borrowed from each other when they wanted them.

GRAECIA (-ae) or HELLAS (-ădos), a country in Europe, the inhabitants of which were called GRAECI or HELLENES. Among the Greeks Hellas did not signify any particular country, bounded by certain geographical limits, but was used in general to signify the abode of the Hellenes, wherever they might happen to be settled. Thus the Greek colonies of Cyrene in Africa, of Syracuse in Sicily, of Tarentum in Italy, and of Smyrna in Asia, are said to be in Hellas. In the most ancient times Hellas was a small district of Phthiotis in Thessaly. As the inhabitants of this district, the Hellenes, gradually spread over the surrounding country, their name was adopted by other tribes, till at length the whole of the N. of Greece from the Ceraunian and Cambunian mountains to the Corinthian isthmus was designated by the name of Hellas. Peloponnesus was generally spoken of, during the flourishing times of Greek independence, as distinct from Hellas proper; but subsequently Peloponnesus and the Greek islands were also included under the general name of Hellas, in opposition to the land of the barbarians. The Romans called the land of the Hellenes Graecia (whence we have derived the name of Greece), probably from their first becoming acquainted with the tribe of the Graeci, who appear at an early period to have dwelt on the W. coast of Epirus. The greatest length of Greece proper from Mt. Olympus to Cape Taenarus is about 250 English miles; its greatest breadth from the W. coast of Acarnania to Marathon in Attica is about 180 miles. Its area is somewhat less than that of Portugal. On the N. it was separated by the Cambunian and Ceraunian mountains from Macedonia and Illyria; and on the other 3 sides it is bounded by the sea, namely, by the Ionian sea on the W., and by the Aegaean on the E. and S. It is one of the most mountainous countries of Europe, and possesses few extensive plains and few continuous valleys. The inhabitants were thus separated from one another by barriers which it was not easy to surmount, and were naturally led to form separate political communities. At a later time the N. of Greece was generally divided into 10 districts; EPIRUS, THESSALIA, ACARNANIA, AETOLIA, DORIS, LOCRIS, PHOCIS, BOEOTIA, ATTICA, and MEGARIS. The S. of Greece or Peloponnesus was usually divided into 10 districts likewise : CORINTHIA, SICYONIA, PHLIASIA, ACHAIA, ELIS, MESSENIA, LACONIA, CYNURIA, ARGOLIS, and ARCADIA. An account of the geography, early inhabitants, and history of each of these districts is given in separate articles. The most celebrated of the original inhabitants of Greece were the Pelasgians, from whom a considerable part of the Greek population was undoubtedly descended.   [PELASGI.]   The Hellenes traced their origin to a mythical ancestor Hellen, from whose sons and grandsons they were divided into the 4 great tribes of Dorians, Aeolians, Achaeans and Ionians. [HELLEN.]

GRAECIA MAGNA or G. MAJOR, a name given to the districts in the S. of Italy, inhabited by the Greeks. This name was never used simply to indicate the S. of Italy; it was always confined to the Greek cities and their territories, and did not include the surrounding districts, inhabited by the Italian tribes. It appears to have been applied chiefly to the cities on the Tarentine gulf, Tarentum, Sybaris, Croton, Caulonia, Siris (Heraclea), Metapontum, Locri and Rhegium; but it also included the Greek cities on the W. coast, such as Cumae and Neapolis.   Strabo extends the appellation even to the Greek cities of Sicily.

GRAMPIUS MONS (*Grampian Hills*), a range of mountains in Britannia Barbara or Caledonia, separating the Highlands and Lowlands of Scotland. Agricola penetrated as far as these mountains and defeated Galgacus at their foot.

GRANICUS (-i), a small river of Mysia, rising in Mt. Ida, and falling into the Propontis (*Sea of Marmara*) E. of Priapus: memorable as the scene of the victory of Alexander the Great over the Persians (B.C. 334), and, in a less degree, for a victory of Lucullus over Mithridates, B.C. 73.

GRATIAE.   [CHARITES.]

GRATIANUS (-i), emperor of the Western Empire, A.D. 367—383, son of Valentinian I. He was deposed and slain by the usurper Maximus.

GRATIUS FALISCUS (-i), a contemporary of Ovid, and the author of an extant poem on the chase.

GRAVISCAE (-ārum), an ancient city of Etruria, subject to Tarquinii, and colonised by the Romans B.C. 183.   It was situated in the Maremma, and its air was unhealthy, whence Virgil calls it *intempestae Graviscae*.

GRUDII (-ōrum), a people in Gallia Belgica, subject to the Nervii, N. of the Scheldt.

GRUMENTUM (-i), a town in the interior of Lucania, on the road from Beneventum to Heraclea.

GRYLLUS (-i), elder son of Xenophon, fell at the battle of Mantinea, B.C. 362, after he had, according to some accounts, given Epaminondas his mortal wound.

GRYNIA (-ae) or -IUM (-i), an ancient city in the S. of Mysia, celebrated for its temple and oracle of Apollo, who is hence called *Grynaeus Apollo*.

GRYPS (-ypis) or GRYPHUS (-i), a griffin, a fabulous animal, with the body of a lion, and the head and wings of an eagle, dwelling in the Rhipaean mountains, between the Hyperboreans and the one-eyed Arimaspians, and guarding the gold of the north. The Arimaspians mounted on horseback, and attempted to steal the gold, and hence arose the hostility between the horse and the griffin. The belief in griffins came from the East, where they are mentioned among the fabulous animals which guarded the gold of India.

GUGERNI or GUBERNI (-ōrum), a people of Germany, who crossed the Rhine, and settled on its left bank, between the Ubii and Batavi.

GULUSSA (-ae), a Numidian, 2nd son of Masinissa, and brother to Micipsa and Mastanabal. He left a son, named MASSIVA.

GUTTONES.   [GOTHI.]

GYARUS (-i) or GYARA (-ōrum), one of the Cyclades, a small island S. W. of Andros, poor and unproductive, and inhabited only by fishermen. Under the Roman emperors it was a place of banishment.

GYAS or GYES, or GYGES (-ae), son of Uranus (Heaven) and Ge (Earth), one of the giants with 100 hands, who made war upon the gods.

GYGAEUS LACUS, a small lake in Lydia, N. of Sardis.

GYGES (-ae), first king of Lydia of the dynasty of the Mermnadae, dethroned Candaules, and succeeded to the kingdom, as related under CANDAULES. He reigned B.C. 716 —678. He sent magnificent presents to Delphi, and "the riches of Gyges" became a proverb.

GYLIPPUS (-i), a Spartan, son of Cleandridas, sent as the Spartan commander to Syracuse, to oppose the Athenians, B.C. 414. Under his command the Syracusans annihilated the great Athenian armament, and took Demosthenes and Nicias prisoners, 413.   In 404 he was commissioned by Lysander, after the capture of Athens, to carry home the treasure; but by opening the seams of the sacks underneath, he abstracted a considerable portion. The theft was discovered, and Gylippus went into exile.

GYMNESIAE.   [BALEARES.]

GYNDES (-ae), a river of Assyria, rising in the country of the Matieni (in the mourtains of *Kurdistan*), and flowing into the Tigris, celebrated through the story that Cyrus the Great drew off its waters by 360 channels.

GYRTON (-ōnis), GYRTONA (-ae), an ancient town in Pelasgiotis in Thessaly, on the Peneus.

GȲTHEUM, GȲTHIUM (-i), an ancient sea-port town of Laconia, situated near the head of the Laconian bay, S. W. of the mouth of the river Eurotas.

HADES or AIDES (-ae) or PLUTO (-ōnis), the god of the nether world. In ordinary life he was usually called Pluto (the giver of wealth), because people did not like to pronounce the dreaded name of Hades or Aïdes. The Roman poets use the names DIS, ORCUS, and TARTARUS, as synonymous with Pluto. Hades was son of Cronus (Saturn) and Rhea, and brother of Zeus (Jupiter) and Poseidon (Neptune). His wife was Persephōne or Proserpīna, the daughter of Demeter, whom he carried off from the upper world, as is related elsewhere. [See p. 140.] In the division of the world among the 3 brothers, Hades obtained the nether world, the abode of the shades, over which he ruled. His character is described as fierce and inexorable, whence of all the gods he was most hated by mortals. The sacrifices offered to

Hades. (From a Statue in the Vatican.)

him and Persephone consisted of black sheep;

Hermes (Mercury) presenting a Soul to Hades (Pluto) and Persephone (Proserpina).
(Pict. Ant. Sepolcri Nasonum, pl. 8.)

and the person who offered the sacrifice had to turn away his face. The ensign of his power was a staff, with which, like Hermes, he drove the shades into the lower world.

There he sat upon a throne with his consort Persephone. He possessed a helmet which rendered the wearer invisible, and which he sometimes lent to both gods and men. Like the other gods, he was not a faithful husband; the Furies are called his daughters; the nymph Mintho, whom he loved, was metamorphosed by Persephone into the plant called mint; and the nymph Leuce, whom he likewise loved, was changed by him after death into a white poplar. Being the king of the lower world, Pluto is the giver of all the blessings that come from the earth: hence he gives the metals contained in the earth, and is called Pluto. In works of art he resembles his brothers Zeus and Poseidon, except that his hair falls over his forehead, and that his appearance is dark and gloomy. His ordinary attributes are the key of Hades and Cerberus.

HADRIA. [ADRIA.]

HADRIANOPŌLIS (-is : *Adrianople*), a town in Thrace on the right bank of the Hebrus, in an extensive plain, founded by the emperor Hadrian.

HADRIANUS, P. AELĪUS (-i), usually called HADRIAN, Roman emperor, A.D. 117—138, was born at Rome, A.D. 76. He enjoyed the favour of Plotina, the wife of Trajan, and mainly through her influence succeeded to the empire. He spent the greater part of his reign in travelling through the provinces of the empire, in order that he might personally inspect their condition. He resided for some time at Athens, which was his favourite city, and with whose language and literature he was intimately acquainted. In his reign the Jews revolted, and were not subdued till after a fierce struggle, which lasted 3 years. Hadrian was succeeded by Antoninus Pius, whom he had adopted a few months previously. The reign of Hadrian was one of the happiest periods in Roman history. His policy was to preserve peace with foreign nations, and to promote the welfare of the provinces. He erected many magnificent works in various parts of the empire, and more particularly at Athens. There are still extensive remains of his magnificent villa at Tibur, where numerous works of ancient art have been discovered. His mausoleum, which he built at Rome, forms the groundwork of the present castle of St. Angelo.

HADRŪMĒTUM or ADRŪMĒTUM (-i), a flourishing city founded by the Phoenicians in N. Africa, and the capital of Bycazena under the Romans.

HAEMON (-ŏnis). (1) Son of Pelasgus and father of Thessalus, from whom the ancient name of Thessaly, HAEMONIA, or AEMONIA, was believed to be derived. The Roman poets frequently use the adjective *Haemonius* as equivalent to Thessalian.—(2) Son of Creon of Thebes, was in love with Antigone, and killed himself on hearing that she was condemned by his father to be entombed alive.

HAEMŌNĪA. [HAEMON, No. 1.]

HAEMUS (-i : *Balkan*), a lofty range of mountains, separating Thrace and Moesia. The name is probably connected with the Greek χιμὼν, and the Latin *hiems*; and the mountains were so called on account of their cold and snowy climate. The pass over them most used in antiquity was in the W. part of the range, called "Succi" or "Succorum angustiae," also "Porta Trajani" (*Ssulu Derbend*), between Philippopolis and Serdica.

HĀLĒSA (-ae), a town on the N. coast of Sicily, on the river HALESUS, founded by the Greek mercenaries of Archonides, a chief of the Siculi, and originally called ARCHONIDION.

HĀLĒSUS (-i), a chief of the Auruncans and Oscans, the son of a soothsayer, and an ally of Turnus, slain by Evander. He came to Italy from Argos in Greece, whence he is called *Agamemnonius, Atrides,* or *Argolicus.* He is said to have founded Falerii.

HĂLĪACMŌN (-ŏnis : *Vistriza*), an important river in Macedonia, rising in the Tymphaean mountains, forming the boundary between Eordaea and Pieria, and falling into the Thermaic gulf. Caesar incorrectly makes it the boundary between Macedonia and Thessaly.

HĂLĬARTUS (-i), an ancient town in Boeotia, S. of the lake Copais, destroyed by Xerxes in his invasion of Greece (B.C. 480), but afterwards rebuilt. Under its walls Lysander lost his life (395).

HĀLĬAS (-ădos), a district on the coast of Argolis between Asine and Hermione, so called because fishing was the chief occupation of its inhabitants. Their town was called HALIAE or HALIES.

HĂLĬCARNASSUS (-i: *Budrum*), a celebrated city of Asia Minor, stood in the S. W. part of Caria, opposite to the island of Cos. It was founded by Dorians from Troezene. With the rest of the coast of Asia Minor, it fell under the dominion of the Persians, at an early period of whose rule Lygdamis made himself tyrant of the city, and founded a dynasty which lasted for some generations. His daughter Artemisia assisted Xerxes in his expedition against Greece. Halicarnassus was celebrated for the Mausoleum, a magnificent edifice which Artemisia II. built as a tomb for her husband Mausolus (B.C. 352), and which was adorned with the works of the most eminent Greek sculptors of the age. Fragments of these sculptures, which were discovered built into the walls of the citadel of *Budrum*, are now in the British Museum. Halicarnassus was the birthplace of the historians HERODOTUS and DIONYSIUS.

HALICYAE (-ārum), a town in the N. W. of Sicily, between Entella and Lilybaeum, long in the possession of the Carthaginians, and in Cicero's time a municipium.

HALIRRHŌTHĬUS (-i), son of Poseidon (Neptune) and Euryte, attempted to violate Alcippe, daughter of Ares (Mars) and Agraulos, but was slain by Ares. Ares was brought to trial by Poseidon for this murder, on the hill at Athens, which was hence called Areopagus, or the Hill of Ares.

HALIZŌNES (-um), a people of Bithynia, with a capital city Alybe.

HĂLŌNĒSUS (-i), an island of the Aegaean sea, off the coast of Thessaly, and E. of Sciathos and Peparethos, with a town of the same name upon it. The possession of this island occasioned great disputes between Philip and the Athenians : there is a speech on this subject among the extant orations of Demosthenes, but it was probably written by Hegesippus.

HĂLYCUS (-i), a river in the S. of Sicily, flowing into the sea near Heraclea Minoa.

HĂLYS (-ўs : *Kizil-Irmak*, i. e. *the Red River*), the greatest river of Asia Minor, rising in the Anti-Taurus range of mountains, on the borders of Armenia Minor and Pontus, and, after flowing through Cappadocia and Galatia, and dividing Paphlagonia from Pontus, falling into the Euxine Sea between Sinope and Amisus. In early times it divided the Indo-European races which peopled the W. part of Asia Minor from the Semitic (Syro-Arabian) races of the rest of S. W. Asia ; and it separated the Lydian empire from the Medo-Persian.

HĂMADRYĂDES. [NYMPHAE.]

HAMAXĬTUS (-i), a small town on the coast of the Troad.

HAMAXŌBĬI (-ōrum), a people in European Sarmatia, in the neighbourhood of the Palus Maeotis, were a nomad race, as their name signifies.

HĂMILCĂR (-ăris), the name of several Carthaginian generals, of whom the most celebrated was Hamilcar Barca, the father of Hannibal. The surname Barca probably signified "lightning." It was merely a personal appellation, and is not to be regarded as a family name, though from the great distinction that this Hamilcar obtained, we often find the name of Barcine applied either to his family or to his party in the state. He was appointed to the command of the Carthaginian forces in Sicily, in the 18th year of the 1st Punic War, 247. At this time the Romans were masters of almost the whole of

Sicily ; but he maintained himself for years, notwithstanding all the efforts of the Roman to dislodge him, first on a mountain named Hcrctè, in the immediate neighbourhood of Panormus, and subsequently on the still stronger position of Mt. Eryx. After the great naval defeat of the Carthaginians by Lutatius Catulus (241), which brought the 1st Punic war to an end, he had to carry on war in Africa with the Carthaginian mercenaries, whom he subdued after a struggle of 3 years (240—238). Hamilcar then crossed over into Spain, in order to establish a new empire for the Carthaginians in that country. In the course of nearly 9 years, he obtained possession of a considerable portion of Spain, partly by force of arms and partly by negotiation. He fell in battle against the Vettones in 229. He was succeeded in the command by his son-in-law Hasdrubal. He left 3 sons, Hannibal, Hasdrubal, and Mago.

HANNĬBĂL (-ălis), a common name among the Carthaginians, signifying "the grace or favour of Baal ;" the final syllable, *bal*, having reference to this tutelary deity of the Phoenicians. The most celebrated person of this name was the son of Hamilcar Barca. He was born B.C. 247. He was only 9 years old when his father took him with him into Spain, and made him swear upon the altar eternal hostility to Rome. Child as he then was, Hannibal never forgot his vow, and his whole life was one continual struggle against the power and domination of Rome. Though only 18 years old at the time of his father's death (229), he had already displayed so much courage and capacity for war, that he was entrusted by Hasdrubal (the son-in-law and successor of Hamilcar) with the chief command of most of the military enterprises planned by that general. He secured to himself the devoted attachment of the army under his command ; and, accordingly, on the assassination of Hasdrubal (221), the soldiers unanimously proclaimed their youthful leader commander-in-chief, which the government of Carthage forthwith ratified. Hanniba was at this time in the 26th year of his age. In 2 campaigns he subdued all the country S. of the Iberus, with the exception of the wealthy town of Saguntum. In the spring of 219 he proceeded to lay siege to Saguntum, which he took after a desperate resistance, which lasted nearly 8 months. Saguntum lay S. of the Iberus, and was therefore not included under the protection of the treaty which had been made between Hasdrubal and the Romans ; but as it had concluded an alliance with the Romans, the latter regarded its attack as a violation of the treaty between the 2 nations. On the fall of Saguntum, the

Romans demanded the surrender of Hannibal; when this demand was refused, war was declared; and thus began the long and arduous struggle called the 2nd Punic War. In the spring of 218 Hannibal quitted his winter quarters at New Carthage and commenced his march for Italy, across the Pyrenees, and through Gaul to the foot of the Alps. He probably crossed the Alps by the pass of the Little St. Bernard, called in antiquity the Graian Alps. Upon reaching the N. of Italy, he encountered the Roman army under the command of the consul P. Scipio. He defeated the latter, first on the river Ticinus, and secondly in a more decisive engagement upon the Trebia. After passing the winter in the N. of Italy among the Gaulish tribes, he marched early in 217 into Etruria through the marshes on the banks of the Arno. In struggling through these marshes, his army suffered severely, and he himself lost the sight of one eye by an attack of ophthalmia. The consul Flaminius hastened to meet him, and a battle was fought on the lake Trasimenus, in which the Roman army was destroyed, and the consul himself was slain. The Romans had collected a fresh army, and placed it under the command of the dictator Fabius Maximus, who prudently avoided a general action, and only attempted to harass and annoy the Carthaginian army. Meanwhile the Romans had made great preparations for the campaign of the following year (216). The 2 new consuls, L. Aemilius Paulus and C. Terentius Varro, marched into Apulia, at the head of an army of little less than 90,000 men. To this mighty host Hannibal gave battle in the plains on the right bank of the Aufidus, just below the town of Cannae. The Roman army was again annihilated: the consul Aemilius Paulus, and a great number of the most distinguished Romans perished. This victory was followed by the revolt from Rome of most of the nations in the S. of Italy. Hannibal established his army in winter quarters in Capua, which had espoused his side. Capua was celebrated for its wealth and luxury, and the enervating effect which these produced upon the army of Hannibal became a favourite theme of rhetorical exaggeration in later ages. The futility of such declamations is sufficiently shown by the simple fact that the superiority of that army in the field remained as decided as ever. Still it may be truly said that the winter spent at Capua, 216—215, was in great measure the turning point of Hannibal's fortune. The experiment of what he could effect with his single army had now been fully tried, and, notwithstanding all his victories, it had decidedly failed : for Rome was still unsub-

dued, and still provided with the means of maintaining a protracted contest. From this time the Romans in great measure changed their plan of operations, and, instead of opposing to Hannibal one great army in the field, they hemmed in his movements on all sides, and kept up an army in every province of Italy, to thwart the operations of his lieutenants. In the subsequent campaigns, Hannibal gained several victories ; but his forces gradually became more and more weakened ; and his only object now was to maintain his ground in the S. until his brother Hasdrubal should appear in the N. of Italy, an event to which he had long looked forward with anxious expectation. In 207 Hasdrubal at length crossed the Alps, and descended into Italy; but he was defeated and slain on the Metaurus. [HASDRUBAL.] The defeat and death of Hasdrubal was decisive of the fate of the war in Italy. From this time Hannibal abandoned all thoughts of offensive operations, and collected together his forces within the peninsula of Bruttium. In the fastnesses of that wild and mountainous region he maintained his ground for nearly 4 years (207—203). He crossed over to Africa towards the end of 203 in order to oppose P. Scipio. In the following year (202) the decisive battle was fought near Zama. Hannibal was completely defeated with great loss. All hopes of resistance were now at an end, and he was one of the first to urge the necessity of an immediate peace. The treaty between Rome and Carthage was not finally concluded until the next year (201). By this treaty Hannibal saw the object of his whole life frustrated, and Carthage humbled before her rival. Some years afterwards he was compelled, by the jealousy of the Romans, and by the enmity of a powerful party at Carthage, to flee from his native city. He took refuge at the court of Antiochus III., king of Syria, who was at this time (193) on the eve of war with Rome. Hannibal in vain urged the necessity of carrying the war at once into Italy, instead of awaiting the Romans in Greece. On the defeat of Antiochus (190), the surrender of Hannibal was one of the conditions of the peace granted to the king. Hannibal, however, foresaw his danger, and fled to Prusias, king of Bithynia. Here he found for some years a secure asylum ; but he Romans could not be at ease so long as he lived ; and T. Quintius Flamininus was at length dispatched to the court of Prusias to demand the surrender of the fugitive. The Bithynian king was unable to resist ; and Hannibal, perceiving that flight was impossible, took poison, to avoid falling into the hands of his enemies, about the year 183. Of Hannibal's abilities as a general it is unnecessary to speak; but in comparing Hannibal with any other of the great leaders of antiquity, we must ever bear in mind the peculiar circumstances in which he was placed. Feebly and grudgingly supported by the government at home, he stood alone, at the head of an army composed of mercenaries of many nations. Yet not only did he retain the attachment of these men, unshaken by any change of fortune, for a period of more than 15 years, but he trained up army after army; and long after the veterans that had followed him over the Alps had dwindled to an inconsiderable remnant, his new levies were still as invincible as their predecessors.

HANNO (-ōnis), a name common among the Carthaginians. The chief persons of this name were:—(1) Surnamed the Great, apparently for his successes in Africa, though we have no details of his achievements. He was the leader of the aristocratic party, and, as such, the chief adversary of Hamilcar Barca and his family. On all occasions, from the landing of Barca in Spain, till the return of Hannibal from Italy, a period of above 35 years, Hanno is represented as thwarting the measures of that able and powerful family, and taking the lead in opposition to the war with Rome.—(2) A Carthaginian navigator, of uncertain date, under whose name we possess a *Periplus*, which was originally written in the Punic language, and afterwards translated into Greek. It contains an account of a voyage undertaken beyond the Pillars of Hercules, in order to found Libyphoenician towns.

HARMA (-ōrum), a small place in Boeotia, near Tanagra.

HARMATŪS (-untis), a city and promontory on the coast of Aeolis in Asia Minor, on the N. side of the Sinus Elaïticus.

HARMŎDĬUS (-i) and ĂRISTŎGĪTON (-ŏnis), two noble Athenians, murderers of Hipparchus, brother of the tyrant Hippias, in B.C. 514. Aristogiton was strongly attached to the young and beautiful Harmodius, who returned his affection with equal warmth. Hipparchus endeavoured to withdraw the youth's love to himself, and, failing in this, resolved to avenge the slight by putting upon him a public insult. Accordingly, he took care that the sister of Harmodius should be summoned to bear one of the sacred baskets in some religious procession, and when she presented herself for the purpose, he caused her to be dismissed and declared unworthy of the honour. This fresh insult determined the 2 friends to slay both Hipparchus and his brother Hippias as well. They communi-

cated their plot to a few friends, and selected for their enterprise the day of the festival of the great Panathenaea, the only day on which they could appear in arms without exciting suspicion. When the appointed time arrived, the 2 chief conspirators observed one of their accomplices in conversation with Hippias. Believing, therefore, that they were betrayed, they slew Hipparchus. Harmodius was immediately cut down by the guards. Aristogiton at first escaped, but was afterwards taken, and died by torture; but he died without revealing any of the names of the conspirators. Four years after this Hippias was expelled, and thenceforth Harmodius and Aristogiton obtained among the Athenians of all succeeding generations the character of patriots, deliverers, and martyrs. To be born of their blood was esteemed among the highest of honours, and their descendants enjoyed an immunity from public burdens.

HARMŎNĬA (-ae), daughter of Ares, (Mars), and Aphroditē (Venus), given by Zeus (Jupiter), to Cadmus as his wife. On the wedding-day Cadmus received a present of a necklace, which afterwards became fatal to all who possessed it. Harmonia accompanied Cadmus when he was obliged to quit Thebes, and shared his fate. [CADMUS.]

HARPĀGĬA (-ae), or ĬUM (-i), a small town in Mysia, between Cyzicus and Priapus, the scene of the rape of Ganymedes, according to some legends.

HARPĂGUS (-i), a noble Median, who is said to have preserved the infant Cyrus. He was afterwards one of the generals of Cyrus, and conquered the Greek cities of Asia Minor.

HARPĂLUS (-i), a Macedonian, appointed by Alexander the Great superintendent of the royal treasury, with the administration of the satrapy of Babylon. Having embezzled large sums of money, he crossed over to Greece in B.C. 324, and employed his treasures in gaining over the leading men at Athens to support him against Alexander and his vicegerent, Antipater. He is said to have corrupted Demosthenes himself.

HARPĂLY̆CĒ (-es), daughter of Harpalycus, king in Thrace, brought up by her father as a warrior.

HARPĂSUS (-i). (1) A river of Caria, flowing N. into the Maeander.—(2) A river of Armenia Major, flowing S. into the Araxes.

HARPY̆IAE (-ārum), the *Harpies*, that is, the *Robbers* or *Spoilers*, described by Homer as carrying off persons, who had utterly disappeared. Thus they are said to have carried off the daughters of Pandareos, which is represented on one of the Lycian monuments, now in the British Museum. Hesiod represents them as fair-locked and winged maidens; but subsequent writers describe them as disgusting monsters, being birds

A Harpy. (British Museum. From a Tomb at Xanthus.)

with the heads of maidens, with long claws and with faces pale with hunger. They were sent by the gods to torment the blind Phineus, and whenever a meal was placed before him, they darted down from the air and either carried it off, or rendered it unfit to be eaten. Phineus was delivered from them by Zetes and Calais, sons of Boreas, and 2 of the Argonauts. Later writers mention 3 Harpies; but their names are not the same in all accounts. Virgil places them in the islands called Strophades, in the Ionian sea, where they took up their abode after they had been driven away from Phineus.

HARŬDES (-um), a German people in the army of Ariovistus (B.C. 58), supposed to be the same as the CHARUDES, who are placed in the Chersonesus Cimbrica.

HASDRŬBĂL (-ălis), a Carthaginian name, probably signifying one whose help is Baal. The chief persons of this name are :—(1) The son-in-law of Hamilcar Barca, on whose death, in 229, he succeeded to the command in Spain. He founded New Carthage, and concluded with the Romans the celebrated treaty which fixed the Iberus as the boundary between the Carthaginian and Roman dominions. He was assassinated by a slave, whose master he had put to death (221), and was succeeded in the command by HANNIBAL.

—(2) Son of Hamilcar Barca, and brother of Hannibal. When Hannibal set out for Italy (218), Hasdrubal was left in the command in Spain, and there fought for some years against the 2 Scipios. In 207 he crossed the Alps and marched into Italy, in order to assist Hannibal; but he was defeated on the Metaurus, by the consuls C. Claudius Nero and M. Livius Salinator, his army was destroyed, and he himself fell in the battle. His head was cut off and thrown into Hannibal's camp.—(3) Son of Gisco, one of the Carthaginian generals in Spain during the 2nd Punic war, who must be distinguished from the brother of Hannibal, above-mentioned.

HĒBĒ (-ēs), called JŬVENTĀS (-ātis), by the Romans, the goddess of youth, was a daughter of Zeus (Jupiter) and of Hera (Juno). She waited upon the gods, and filled their cups with nectar, before Ganymedes obtained this office. She married Hercules after he was received among the gods, and bore to him 2 sons. Later traditions represent her as a divinity who had it in her power to make aged persons young again. At Rome there were several temples of Juventas.

Hebe. (From a Bas-relief at Rome.)

HEBRŌN (-ōnis), a city in the S. of Judaea, the first capital of the kingdom of David, who reigned there 7½ years, as king of Judah only.

HEBRUS (-i : *Maritza*), the principal river in Thrace, rising in the mountains of Scomius and Rhodope, and falling into the Aegaean sea near Aenos, after forming by another branch an estuary called STENTORIS LACUS.— The Hebrus was celebrated in Greek legends. On its banks Orpheus was torn to pieces by the Thracian women; and it is frequently mentioned in connexion with the worship of Dionysus.

HECALE (-es), a poor old woman, who hospitably received Theseus, when he had gone out to hunt the Marathonian bull.

HECATAEUS (-i), of Miletus, one of the earliest and most distinguished of the Greek historians and geographers. In B.C. 500 he endeavoured to dissuade his countrymen from revolting from the Persians. Previous to this he had visited Egypt and many other countries. His works have perished.

HECATE (-es), a mysterious divinity, commonly represented as a daughter of Persaeus or Perses and Asteria, and hence called Perseis. She was one of the Titans, and the only one of this race who retained her power under the rule of Zeus (Jupiter). She was honoured by all the immortal gods, and the extensive power possessed by her was probably the reason that she was subsequently identified with several other divinities. Hence she is said to have been Selene or Luna in heaven, Artemis or Diana in earth, and Persephone or Proserpina in the lower world. Being thus, as it were, a threefold goddess, she is described with 3 bodies or 3 heads. Hence her epithets *Tergemina, Tri-*

latter was found, remained with her as her attendant and companion. She thus became a deity of the lower world, and is described in this capacity as a mighty and formidable divinity. She was supposed to send at night all kinds of demons and terrible phantoms from the lower world. She taught sorcery and witchcraft, and dwelt at places where 2 roads crossed, on tombs, and near the blood of murdered persons. She herself wandered about with the souls of the dead, and her approach was announced by the whining and howling of dogs. At Athens, at the close of every month, dishes with food were set out for her at the points where 2 roads crossed; and this food was consumed by poor people. The sacrifices offered to her consisted of dogs, honey, and black female lambs.

HECATOMPYLOS (-i), a city in the middle of Parthia, enlarged by Seleucus, and afterwards used by the Parthian kings as a royal residence.

HECATONNESI (-orum), that is, the 100 islands, the name of a group of small islands, between Lesbos and the coast of Aeolis.

HECTOR (-oris), the chief hero of the Trojans in their war with the Greeks, was the eldest son of Priam and Hecuba, the hus-

Hecáte. (Causei, Museum Romanum, vol. 1, tav. 21.)

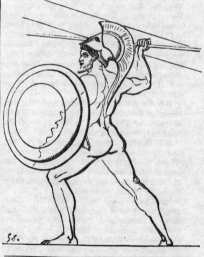

Hector. (Aegina Marbles.)

formis, Triceps, &c. She took an active part in the search after Proserpina, and when the

band of Andromache, and father of Scamandrius. He fought with the bravest of the Greeks, and at length slew Patroclus, the friend of Achilles. The death of his friend roused Achilles to the fight. The other Trojans fled before him into the city. Hector alone remained without the walls, though his parents implored him to return ; but when he saw Achilles, his heart failed him, and he took to flight. Thrice did he race round the city, pursued by the swift-footed Achilles, and then fell pierced by Achilles' spear. Achilles tied Hector's body to his chariot, and thus dragged him into the camp of the Greeks ; but later traditions relate that he first dragged the body thrice round the walls of Ilium. At the command of Zeus (Jupiter), Achilles surrendered the body to the prayers of Priam, who buried it at Troy with great pomp. Hector is one of the noblest conceptions of the poet of the Iliad. He is the great bulwark of Troy, and even Achilles trembles when he approaches him. He has a presentiment of the fall of his country, but he perseveres in his heroic resistance, preferring death to slavery and disgrace. Besides these virtues of a warrior, he is distinguished also by those of a man : his heart is open to the gentle feelings of a son, a husband, and a father.

HĔCŬBA(-ae) and HĔCŬBĒ (-es),daughter of Dymas in Phrygia, or of Cisseus, king of Thrace. She was the wife of Priam, king of Troy, to whom she bore Hector, Paris, and many other children. After the fall of Troy, she was carried away as a slave by the Greeks. On the coast of Thrace she revenged the murder of her son Polydorus, by slaying Polymestor. [POLYDORUS.] She was metamorphosed into a dog, and leapt into the sea at a place called Cynossema, or " the tomb of the dog."

HĒGĒSĪNUS (-i), of Pergamum, the successor of Evander, and the immediate predecessor of Carneades in the chair of the Academy, flourished about B.C. 185.

HĒGĒSIPPUS (-i), an Athenian orator, and a contemporary of Demosthenes, to whose political party he belonged. The grammarians ascribe to him the oration on Halonesus, which has come down to us under the name of Demosthenes.

HĔLĔNA (-ae) and HĔLĔNĒ (-es), daughter of Zeus (Jupiter) and Leda, and sister of Castor and Pollux (the Dioscuri). She was of surpassing beauty. In her youth she was carried off by Theseus and Pirithous to Attica. When Theseus was absent in Hades, Castor and Pollux undertook an expedition to Attica, to liberate their sister. Athens was taken, Helen delivered, and Aethra, the mother of Theseus, made prisoner, and carried as a slave of Helen, to Sparta. On her return home, she was sought in marriage by the noblest chiefs from all parts of Greece. She chose Menelaus for her husband, and became by him the mother of Hermione. She was subsequently seduced by Paris and carried off to Troy. [For details, see PARIS and MENELAUS.] The Greek chiefs who had been her suitors, resolved to revenge her abduction, and accordingly sailed against Troy. Hence arose the celebrated Trojan war, which lasted 10 years. During the course of the war she is represented as showing great sympathy with the Greeks. After the death of Paris, towards the end of the war, she married his brother Deiphobus. On the capture of Troy, which she is said to have favoured, she betrayed Deiphobus to the Greeks, and became reconciled to Menelaus, whom she accompanied to Sparta. Here she lived with him for some years in peace and happiness. The accounts of Helen's death differ. According to the prophecy of Proteus in the Odyssey, Menelaus and Helen were not to die, but the gods were to conduct them to Elysium. Others relate that she and Menelaus were buried at Therapne in Laconia. Others, again, relate that after the death of Menelaus she was driven out of Peloponnesus by the sons of the latter, and fled to Rhodes, where she was tied to a tree and strangled by Polyxo : the Rhodians expiated the crime by dedicating a temple to her under the name of Helena Dendritis. According to another tradition she married Achilles in the island of Leuce, and bore him a son, Euphorion.

HĔLĔNA, FLĀVĬA JŪLIA (-ae), mother of Constantine the Great, was a Christian, and is said to have discovered at Jerusalem the sepulchre of our Lord, together with the wood of the true cross.

HĔLĔNA (-ae), a small and rocky island, between the S. of Attica and Ceos, formerly called Cranaë.

HĔLĔNUS (-i), son of Priam and Hecuba, celebrated for his prophetic powers. He deserted his countrymen and joined the Greeks. There are various accounts respecting his desertion of the Trojans. According to some he did it of his own accord ; according to others, he was ensnared by Ulysses, who was anxious to obtain his prophecy respecting the fall of Troy. Others, again, relate that, on the death of Paris, Helenus and Deiphobus contended for the possession of Helena, and that Helenus, being conquered, fled to Mt. Ida, where he was taken prisoner by the Greeks. After the fall of Troy, he fell to the share of Pyrrhus. He foretold to Pyrrhus the sufferings which awaited the Greeks who returned home by sea, and prevailed upon him to return by land to Epirus. After the death ot Pyrrhus he received a portion of that country, and married Andromache. When Aeneas in his wanderings arrived in Epirus, he was hospitably received by Helenus.

HELĬĂDAE(-ārum) and HELĬĂDES(-um), the sons and daughters of Helios (the Sun). The name *Heliades* is given especially to *Phaëthusa*, *Lampetie* and *Phoebe*, the daughters of Helios and the nymph Clymene, and the sisters of Phaëthon. They bewailed the death of their brother Phaëthon so bitterly on the banks of the Eridanus, that the gods in compassion changed them into poplar-trees and their tears into amber. [ERIDANUS.]

HĔLĬCĒ (-es). (1) Daughter of Lycaon, beloved by Zeus (Jupiter). Hera, out of jealousy, metamorphosed her into a she-bear, whereupon Zeus placed her among the stars, under the name of the Great Bear. (2) The ancient capital of Achaia, swallowed up by an earthquake together with Bura, B.C. 373.

HĔLĬCŌN (-ōnis), a celebrated range of mountains in Boeotia, between the lake Copais and the Corinthian gulf, covered with snow the greater part of the year, sacred to Apollo and the Muses; the latter are hence called *Hĕlĭcōnĭădes* and *Hĕlĭcōnĭdes*. Here sprung the celebrated fountains of the Muses, AGANIPPE and HIPPOCRENE.

HĔLĬŌDŌRUS (-i). (1) A rhetorician at Rome in the time of Augustus, whom Horace mentions as the companion of his journey to Brundisium.—(2) A Stoic philosopher at Rome, who became a *delator* in the reign of Nero.

HELIOGABĂLUS. [ELAGABALUS.]

HĔLĬŌPŎLIS (-is: i.e. *the City of the Sun*). (1) (Heb. Baalath: *Baalbek*, Ru.), a celebrated city of Syria, a chief seat of the worship of Baal, one of whose symbols was the Sun. Hence the Greek name of the city. It was situated in the middle of Coele-Syria, at the W. foot of Anti-Libanus, and was a place of great commercial importance, being on the direct road from Egypt and the Red Sea, and also from Tyre to Syria, Asia Minor, and Europe. Its ruins, which are very extensive and magnificent, are of the Roman period. (2) O.T. On; a celebrated city of Lower Egypt, on the E. side of the Pelusiac branch of the Nile, a little below the apex of the Delta, and a chief seat of the Egyptian worship of the Sun. Its priests were renowned for their learning.

HELĬŌS (-i), called SŌL (-ōlis) by the Romans, the god of the sun. He was the son of Hyperion and Thea, and a brother of Selēne and Eos. From his father, he is frequently called HYPERIONIDES, or HYPERION, the latter of which is an abridged form of the patronymic, HYPERIONION. Homer describes

Helios as rising in the E. from Oceanus, traversing the heaven, and descending in the evening into the darkness of the W. and Oceanus. Later poets have marvellously embellished this simple notion. They tell of a magnificent palace of Helios in the E., from which he starts in the morning in a chariot drawn by four horses. They also assign him a second palace in the W., and describe his horses as feeding upon herbs growing in the islands of the Blessed. Helios is described as the god who sees and hears everything, and as thus able to reveal to Hephaestus (Vulcan) the faithlessness of Aphrodite (Venus), and to Demeter (Ceres) the abduction of her daughter. At a later time Helios became identified with Apollo, though the 2 gods were originally quite distinct. The island of Thrinacia (Sicily) was sacred to Helios, and there he had flocks of sheep and oxen, which were tended by his daughters Phaetusa and Lampetia. He was worshipped in many parts of Greece, and especially in the island of Rhodes, where the famous colossus was a representation of the god. The sacrifices offered to him consisted of white rams, boars, bulls, goats, lambs, and especially white horses, and honey. Among the animals sacred to him, the cock is especially mentioned.

Helios (the Sun). (Coin of Rhodes, in the British Museum.)

HELLĂNĪCUS, of Mytilene in Lesbos, one of the most eminent of the early Greek historians, was born about B.C. 496, and died 411. All his works have perished.

HELLAS, HELLENES. [GRAECIA.]

HELLE (-ēs), daughter of Athamas and Nephĕle, and sister of Phrixus. When Phrixus was to be sacrificed [PHRIXUS], Nephele rescued her 2 children, who rode away through the air upon the ram with the golden fleece the gift of Hermes; but, between Sigeum and the Chersonesus, Helle fell into the sea, which was thence called the sea of Helle (*Hellespontus*).

HELLEN (-ēnos), son of Deucalion and Pyrrha, and father of Aeolus, Dorus, and Xuthus. He was king of Phthia in Thessaly, and was succeeded by his son Aeolus. He was the mythical ancestor of all the Hellenes; from his 2 sons Aeolus and Dorus were descended the Aeolians and Dorians; and from his 2 grandsons Achaeus and Ion, the sons of Xuthus, the Achaeans and Ionians.

HELLESPONTUS (-i : *Straits of the Dardanelles*), the long narrow strait connecting the Propontis (*Sea of Marmara*) with the Aegean Sea. The length of the strait is about 50 miles, and the width varies from 6 miles at the upper end to 2 at the lower, and in some places it is only 1 mile wide, or even less. The narrowest part is between the ancient cities of SESTUS and ABYDUS, where Xerxes made his bridge of boats [XERXES], and where the legend related that Leander swam across to visit Hero. [LEANDER.] The name of the Hellespont (i. e. the *Sea of Helle*) was derived from the story of Helle's being drowned in it [HELLE]. The Hellespont was the boundary of Europe and Asia, dividing the Thracian Chersonese in the former from the Troad and the territories of Abydus and Lampsacus in the latter. The district just mentioned, on the S. side of the Hellespont, was also called Hellespontus, and its inhabitants Hellespontii.

HELLŌMĒNUM (-i), a seaport town of the Acarnanians on the island Leucas.

HĒLŌRUS or HĒLŌRUM (-i), a town on the E. coast of Sicily, S. of Syracuse, at the mouth of the river Helorus.

HĒLOS. (1) A town in Laconia, on the coast, in a marshy situation, whence its name (ἕλος = *marsh*). It was commonly said that the Spartan slaves, called Helotes (Εἵλωτες), were originally the Achaean inhabitants of this town, who were reduced by the Dorian conquerors to slavery; but this account of the origin of the Helotes seems to have been merely an invention, in consequence of the similarity of their name to that of the town of Helos.—(2) A town or district of Elis on the Alphēus.

HELVECŌNAE (-ārum), a people in Germany, between the Viadus and the Vistula, S. of the Rugii and N. of the Burgundiones, reckoned by Tacitus among the Ligii.

HELVĒTII (-ōrum), a brave and powerful Celtic people, who dwelt between M. Jurassus (*Jura*), the Lacus Lemannus (*Lake of Geneva*), the Rhone, and the Rhine as far as the Lacus Brigantinus (*Lake of Constance*). Their country, called *Ager Helvetiorum* (but never *Helvetia*), thus corresponded to the W. part of Switzerland. Their chief town was AVENTICUM. They were divided into 4 *pagi* or cantons, of which the *Pagus Tigurīnus* was the most celebrated. The Helvetii are first mentioned in the war with the Cimbri. In B.C. 107 the Tigurini defeated and killed the Roman consul L. Cassius Longinus, on the lake of Geneva, while another division of the Helvetii accompanied the Cimbri and Teutones in their invasion of Gaul. Subsequently the Helvetii invaded Italy along with the Cimbri; and returned home in safety, after the defeat of the Cimbri by Marius and Catulus in 101. About 40 years afterwards, they resolved, upon the advice of Orgetorix, one of their chiefs, to migrate from their country with their wives and children, and seek a new home in the more fertile plains of Gaul. In 58 they endeavoured to carry their plan into execution, but they were defeated by Caesar, and driven back into their own territories. The Romans now planted colonies and built fortresses in their country (Noviodunum, Vindonissa, Aventicum), and the Helvetii gradually adopted the customs and language of their conquerors.

HELVĬA (-ae), mother of the philosopher SENECA.

HELVIDIUS PRISCUS. [PRISCUS.]

HELVĬI (-ōrum), a people in Gaul, between the Rhone and Mt. Cebenna, which separated them from the Arverni, were for a long time subject to Massilia, but afterwards belonged to the province of Gallia Narbonensis. Their country produced good wine.

HELVĬUS CINNA. [CINNA.]

HĒNĒTI (-ōrum), an ancient people in Paphlagonia, dwelling on the river Parthenius, fought on the side of Priam against the Greeks, but had disappeared before the historical times. They were regarded by many ancient writers as the ancestors of the Veneti in Italy. [VENETI.]

HĒNĬOCHI (-ōrum), a people in Colchis, N. of the Phasis, notorious as pirates.

HENNA. [ENNA.]

HĒPHAESTĪON (-ōnis), a Macedonian, celebrated as the friend of Alexander the Great, with whom he had been brought up. He died at Ecbatana, B.C. 325, to the great grief of Alexander.

HĒPHAESTUS (-i), called VULCĀNUS (-i) by the Romans, the god of fire. He was, according to Homer, the son of Zeus (Jupiter) and of Hera (Juno). Later traditions state that he had no father, and that Hera gave birth to him independent of Zeus, as she was jealous of Zeus having given birth to Athena

(Minerva) independent of her. He was born lame and weak, and was in consequence so much disliked by his mother, that she threw him down from Olympus. The marine divinities, Thetis and Eurynome, received him, and he dwelt with them for 9 years in a grotto, beneath Oceanus. He afterwards returned to Olympus, and he appears in Homer as the great artist of the gods of Olympus. Although he had been cruelly treated by his mother, he always showed her respect and kindness ; and on one occasion took her part, when she was quarrelling with Zeus, which so much enraged the father of the gods, that he seized Hephaestus by the leg, and hurled him down from heaven. Hephaestus was a whole day falling, but in the evening he alighted in the island of Lemnos, where he was kindly received by the Sintians. Later writers describe his lameness as the consequence of this fall, while Homer makes him lame from his birth. He again returned to Olympus, and subsequently acted the part of mediator between his parents. On that occasion he offered a cup of nectar to his mother and the other gods, who burst out into immoderate laughter on seeing him busily hobbling from one god to another. Hephaestus appears to have been originally the god of fire simply ; but as fire is indispensable in working metals, he was afterwards regarded as an artist. His palace in Olympus was imperishable and shining like stars. It contained his workshop, with the anvil and 20 bellows, which worked spontaneously at his bidding. All the palaces in Olympus were his workmanship. He made the armour of Achilles ; the fatal necklace of Harmonia ; the fire-breathing bulls of Aeëtes, king of Colchis, &c. In later accounts, the Cyclops are his workmen and servants, and his workshop is no longer in Olympus, but in some volcanic island. In the Iliad the wife of Hephaestus is Charis ; in Hesiod, Aglaia, the youngest of the Charites ; but in the Odyssey, as well as in later accounts, Aphrodite (Venus) appears as his wife. Aphrodite proved faithless to her husband, and was in love with Ares (Mars), the god of war ; but Helios (the Sun) disclosed their amours to Hephaestus, who caught the guilty pair in an invisible net, and exposed them to the laughter of the assembled gods.—The favourite abode of Hephaestus on earth was the island of Lemnos ; but other volcanic islands also, such as Lipara, Hiera, Imbros, and Sicily, are called his abodes or workshops. The Greeks frequently placed small dwarf-like statues of the god near the hearth. During the best period of Grecian art, he was represented as a vigorous man with a beard, and

is characterised by his hammer or some other instrument, his oval cap, and the chiton, which leaves the right shoulder and arm uncovered.—The Roman Vulcanus was an old Italian divinity. [VULCANUS.]

Hephaestus (Vulcanus). (From an Altar in the Vatican.)

HĒRA (-ae) or HĒRĒ (-ēs), called JUNO by the Romans. The Greek Hera, that is, *Mistress*, was a daughter of Cronos (Saturn) and Rhea, and sister and wife of Zeus (Jupiter). According to Homer, she was brought up by Oceanus and Tethys, and afterwards became the wife of Zeus, without the knowledge of her parents. Later writers add that she, like the other children of Cronos, was swallowed by her father, but afterwards restored. In the Iliad, Hera is treated by the Olympian gods with the same reverence as her husband. Zeus himself listens to her counsels, and communicates his secrets to her. She is, notwithstanding, far inferior to him in power, and must obey him unconditionally. She is not, like Zeus, the queen of gods and men, but simply the wife of the supreme god. The idea of her being the queen of heaven, with regal wealth and power, is of much later date. Her character, as described by Homer, is not of a very amiable kind ; and her jealousy, obstinacy, and quarrelsome disposition, sometimes make her husband tremble. Hence arise frequent disputes between Hera and Zeus ; and on one occasion Hera, in conjunction with Poseidon (Neptune) and Athena (Minerva), contemplated putting Zeus into chains. Zeus, in such cases, not only threatens, but beats her. Once he even hung her up in the clouds, with her hands chained, and with two anvils suspended from her feet; and on another occasion when Hephaestus (Vulcan) attempted to help her, Zeus hurled him down from Olympus. —By Zeus she was the mother of Ares (Mars), Hebe, and Hephaestus.—Hera was, properly speaking, the only really married goddess among the Olympians, for the marriage of Aphrodite (Venus) with Hephaestus can scarcely be taken into consideration. Hence, she is the goddess of marriage and of the birth of children, and is represented as the mother of the Ilithyiae.—She is represented in the Iliad riding in a chariot drawn by 2 horses, in the harnessing and unharnessing of which she is assisted by Hebe and the Horae. Owing to the judgment of Paris [PARIS], she was hostile to the Trojans, and in the Trojan war she accordingly sided with the Greeks. She persecuted all the children of Zeus by mortal mothers, and hence appears as the enemy of Dionysus (Bacchus), Hercules, and others.—Hera was worshipped in many parts of Greece, but more especially at Argos, in the neighbourhood of which she had a splendid temple, on the road to Mycenae. She had also a splendid temple in Samos. —The worship of the Roman Juno is spoken of in a separate article. [JUNO]. Hera was usually represented as a majestic woman of mature age, with a beautiful forehead, large

Hera (Juno). (Visconti, Mus. Pio. Clem., vol. 4, tav. 3.)

and widely opened eyes, and with a grave expression commanding reverence. Her hair was adorned with a crown or a diadem. A

veil frequently hangs down the back of her head, to characterise her as the bride of Zeus, and the diadem, veil, sceptre, and peacock, are her ordinary attributes.

HERACLEA (-ae), that is, the city of Heracles or Hercules, was the name of several cities. I. *In Europe*. (1) In Lucania, on the river Siris, founded by the Tarentines. — (2) In Acarnania, on the Ambracian gulf. — (3) The later name of Perinthus in Thrace. [PERINTHUS.] — (4) H. LYNCESTIS, also called Pelagonia, in Macedonia, on the Via Egnatia, W. of the Erigon, the capital of one of the 4 districts into which Macedonia was divided by the Romans.—(5). H. MINOA, on the S. coast of Sicily, at the mouth of the river Halycus, between Agrigentum and Selinus. According to tradition it was founded by Minos, when he pursued Daedalus to Sicily, and it may have been an ancient colony of the Cretans. It was colonised by the inhabitants of Selinus, and its original name was *Minoa*, which it continued to bear till about B.C. 500, when the town was taken by the Lacedaemonians, under Euryleon, who changed its name into that of *Heraclea*. It fell at an early period into the hands of the Carthaginians, and remained in their power till the conquest of Sicily by the Romans. — (6) SINTICA, in Macedonia, a town of the Sinti, on the left bank of the Strymon, founded by Amyntas, brother of Philip.—(7) H. TRACHINIAE, in Thessaly. [TRACHIS.]—II. *In Asia*. (1) H. PONTICA, a city on the S. shore of the Pontus Euxinus, on the coast of Bithynia, in the territory of the Mariandyni, founded about B.C. 550, by colonists from Megara and from Tanagra, in Boeotia.—(2) H. AD LATMUM, a town of Ionia, S.E. of Miletus, at the foot of Mt. Latmus, and upon the Sinus Latmicus; formerly called Latmus. Near it was a cave, with the tomb of Endymion.

HERACLEUM (-i), a town on the coast of the Delta of Egypt, a little W. of Canopus; from which the Canopic mouth of the Nile was often called also the Heracleotic mouth.

HERACLIDAE (-ārum), the descendants of Heracles or Hercules, who, in conjunction with the Dorians, conquered Peloponnesus 80 years after the destruction of Troy, or B.C. 1104, according to mythical chronology. In this invasion they were led by Temenus, Cresphontes, and Aristodemus, the three sons of Aristomachus. Aristodemus died before entering Peloponnesus, but his twin sons received his share of the conquest. Temenus obtained Argos; Procles and Eurystheus, the sons of Aristodemus, Lacedaemon; and Cresphontes, Messenia. This legend represents the conquest of the Achaean population by Dorian invaders, who henceforward appear as the ruling race in the Peloponnesus.

HĒRACLIDES (-ae) PONTĬCUS, so called because he was born at Heraclēa, in Pontus, was a Greek philosopher, and a disciple of Plato and Aristotle. He wrote several works, almost all of which are lost.

HĒRACLĪTUS (-i). (1) Of Ephesus, a philosopher of the Ionian school, flourished about B.C. 513. He considered fire to be the primary form of all matter.—(2) An Academic philosopher of Tyre, a friend of Antiochus, and a pupil of Clitomachus and Philo.

HERAEA (-ae), a town in Arcadia, on the right bank of the Alphēus, near the borders of Elis.

HĒRAEI MONTES, a range of mountains in Sicily, running from the centre of the island S.E., and ending in the promontory Pachynum.

HĒRAEUM. [ARGOS.]

HERBĬTA, a town in Sicily, N. of Agyrium, in the mountains, the residence of the tyrant Archonides.

HERCŬLĀNĒUM or HERCŬLANUM (-i), an ancient city in Campania, near the coast, between Neapolis and Pompeii, was originally founded by the Oscans, was next in the possession of the Tyrrhenians, and subsequently was chiefly inhabited by Greeks. It was taken by the Romans in the Social war (B.C. 89, 88), and was colonised by them. In A.D. 63 a great part of it was destroyed by an earthquake; and in 79 it was overwhelmed, along with Pompeii and Stabiae, by the great eruption of Mt. Vesuvius. It was buried under showers of ashes and streams of lava, from 70 to 100 feet under the present surface of the ground. On its site stand the modern *Portici* and part of the village of *Resina.* The ancient city was accidentally discovered by the sinking of a well in 1720; and many buildings and works of art have been discovered at the place.

HERCŬLES (-is and -i), called HERACLES by the Greeks, the most celebrated of all the heroes of antiquity. According to Homer, Hercules was the son of Zeus (Jupiter) by Alcmene, the wife of Amphitryon, of Thebes in Boeotia. Zeus visited Alcmene in the form of Amphitryon, while the latter was absent, warring against the Taphians; and pretending to be her husband, he became by her the father of Hercules. On the day on which Hercules was to be born, Zeus boasted of becoming the father of a hero destined to rule over the race of Perseus, who was the grandfather

both of Amphitryon and of Alcmene. Hera (Juno) prevailed upon him to swear that the descendant of Perseus, born that day, should be the ruler. Thereupon she hastened to Argos, and there caused the wife of Sthenelus, the son of Perseus, to give birth to Eurystheus; whereas she delayed the birth of Hercules, and thus robbed him of the empire which Zeus had destined for him. Zeus was enraged at the imposition practised upon him, but could not violate his oath. Alcmene brought into the world 2 boys, Hercules, the son of Zeus, and Iphicles, the son of Amphitryon, who was one night younger than Hercules. As he lay in his cradle, Hera sent 2 serpents to destroy him, but the infant hero strangled them with his own hands. As he grew up, he was instructed by Amphitryon in driving the chariot, by Autolycus in wrestling, by Eurytus in archery, by Castor in fighting in heavy armour, and by Linus in singing and playing the lyre. Linus was killed by his pupil with the lyre, because he had censured him; and Amphitryon, to prevent similar occurrences, sent him to feed his cattle. In this manner he spent his life till hi 18th year. His first great adventure happened while he was watching the oxen of his father. A huge lion, which haunted Mt. Cithaeron, made great havoc among the flocks of Amphitryon and Thespius (or Thestius), king of Thespiae. Hercules promised to deliver the country of the monster; and Thespius, who had 50 daughters, rewarded Hercules by making him his guest, so long as the chase lasted, and by giving up his daughters to him. Hercules slew the lion, and henceforth wore its skin as his ordinary garment, and its mouth and head as his helmet. Others related that the lion's skin of Hercules was taken from the Nemean lion. He next defeated and killed Erginus, king of Orchomenos, to whom the Thebans used to pay tribute. In this battle Hercules lost his father Amphitryon; but Creon rewarded him with the hand of his daughter, Megara, by whom he became the father of several children. The gods made him presents of arms, and he usually carried a huge club, which he had cut for himself in the neighbourhood of Nemea. Soon afterwards Hercules was driven mad by Hera, and in this state he killed his own children by Megara and 2 of Iphicles. In his grief he sentenced himself to exile, and went to Thespius, who purified him. He then consulted the oracle of Delphi as to where he should settle. The Pythia first called him by the name of Hercules— for hitherto his name had been Alcides or Alcaeus—and ordered him to live at Tiryns, and to serve Eurystheus for the space of 12 years, after which he should become immortal. Hercules accordingly went to Tiryns, and did as he was bid by Eurystheus. The accounts of the 12 labours which Hercules performed at the bidding of Eurystheus, are found only in the later writers. The only one of the 12 labours mentioned by Homer is his descent into the lower world to carry off Cerberus. We also

Hercules and Nemean Lion. (From a Roman Lamp.)

find in Homer the fight of Hercules with a sea-monster; his expedition to Troy to fetch the horses which Laomedon had refused

Hercules and Hydra. (From a Marble at Naples.)

him; and his war against the Pylians, when he destroyed the whole family of their king Neleus, with the exception of Nestor. The

12 labours are usually arranged in the following order:—(1) *The fight with the Nemean lion.* The valley of Nemea, between Cleonae and Phlius, was inhabited by a monstrous lion, the offspring of Typhon and Echidna. Eurystheus ordered Hercules to bring him the skin of this monster. After using in vain his club and arrows against the lion, he strangled the animal with his own hands, and returned to Tiryns, carrying the dead lion on his shoulders.—(2) *Fight against the Lernean hydra.* This monster, like the lion, was the offspring of Typhon and Echidna, and was brought up by Hera. It ravaged the country of Lerna, near Argos, and dwelt in a swamp near the well of Amymone. It had 9 heads, of which the middle one was immortal. Hercules struck off its heads with his club; but in the place of the head he cut off, 2 new ones grew forth each time. However, with the assistance of his faithful servant Iolaus, he burned away the heads of the hydra, and buried the ninth, or immortal one, under a huge rock. Having thus conquered the monster, he poisoned his arrows with its bile, whence the wounds inflicted by them became incurable.—(3) *Capture of the Arcadian stag.* This animal had golden antlers and brazen feet. Hercules was ordered to bring the animal alive to Eurystheus. He pursued it in vain for a whole year: at length he wounded it with an arrow, caught it, and carried it away on his shoulders.

Hercules and Arcadian Stag. (From a Statue at Naples.)

(4) *Destruction of the Erymanthian boar.* This animal, which Hercules was also ordered to bring alive to Eurystheus, had descended from mount Erymanthus into Psophis. Hercules chased it through the deep snow, and

having thus worn it out he caught it in a net, and carried it to Eurystheus. Other

the rivers Alpheus and Peneus through the stalls, which were thus cleansed in a single

Hercules and Boar, with Eurystheus. (From a Marble at Naples.)

Hercules cleaning the Stables of Augeas. (From a Relief at Rome.)

traditions place the hunt of the Erymanthian boar in Thessaly. It must be observed that this and the subsequent labours of Hercules are connected with certain subordinate labours, called *Parerga*. The first of these is the fight of Hercules with the Centaurs. In his pursuit of the boar he came to the centaur Pholus, who had received from Dionysus (Bacchus) a cask of excellent wine. Hercules opened it, contrary to the wish of his host, and the delicious fragrance attracted the other centaurs, who besieged the grotto of Pholus. Hercules drove them away; they fled to the house of Chiron; and Hercules, eager in his pursuit, wounded Chiron, his old friend, with one of his poisoned arrows; in consequence of which Chiron died. [CHIRON.] Pholus likewise was wounded by one of the arrows, which by accident fell on his foot and killed him.—(5) *Cleansing of the stables of Augeas.* Eurystheus imposed upon Hercules the task of cleansing in one day the stalls of Augeas, king of Elis. Augeas had a herd of 3000 oxen, whose stalls had not been cleansed for 30 years. Hercules, without mentioning the command of Eurystheus, went to Augeas, and offered to cleanse his stalls in one day, if he would give him the 10th part of his cattle. Augeas agreed to the terms; and Hercules, after taking Phyleus, the son of Augeas, as his witness, turned

day. But Augeas, who learned that Hercules had undertaken the work by the command of Eurystheus, refused to give him the reward. His son Phyleus then bore witness against his father, who exiled him from Elis. At a later time Hercules invaded Elis, and killed Augeas and his sons. After this he is said to have founded the Olympic games. —(6) *Destruction of the Stymphalian birds.*

Hercules and the Stymphalian Birds. (From a Gem at Florence.)

These voracious birds had been brought up

by Ares. They had brazen claws, wings, and beaks, used their feathers as arrows, and ate human flesh. They dwelt on a lake near Stymphalus in Arcadia, from which Hercules was ordered by Eurystheus to expel them. When Hercules undertook the task, Athena provided him with a brazen rattle, by the noise of which he startled the birds; and, as they attempted to fly away, he killed them with his arrows. According to some accounts, he only drove the birds away, and they appeared again in the island of Aretias, where they were found by the Argonauts.—(7) *Capture of the Cretan bull.* The bull had been sent out of the sea by Poseidon, that Minos might offer it in sacrifice. But Minos was so charmed with the beauty of the animal, that he kept it, and sacrificed another in its stead. Poseidon punished Minos, by driving the bull mad, and causing it to commit great havoc in the island. Hercules was ordered by Eurystheus to catch the bull, which he succeeded in doing. He brought the bull home on his shoulders; but he then set the animal free again. The bull now roamed through Greece, and at last came to Marathon. where we meet

Hercules and Bull.   (From a Bas-relief in the Vatican.)

it again in the stories of Theseus.—(8) *Capture of the mares of the Thracian Diomedes.* This Diomedes, king of the Bistones in Thrace, fed his horses with human flesh. Eurystheus ordered Hercules to bring him these animals. With a few companions, he seized the animals, and conducted them to

the sea coast. But here he was overtaken by the Bistones. During the fight he entrusted the mares to his friend Abderus, who was devoured by them. Hercules defeated the Bistones, killed Diomedes, whose body he threw before the mares, built the town of Abdera in honour of his unfortunate friend, and then returned to Eurystheus with the mares, which had become tame after eating the flesh of their master. The mares were afterwards set free, and destroyed on Mt.

Hercules and Horses of Diomedes.   (From the Museo Borbonico.)

Olympus by wild beasts.—(9) *Seizure of the girdle of the queen of the Amazons.* Hippolyte, the queen of the Amazons, possessed a girdle, which she had received from Ares. Admete, the daughter of Eurystheus, wished to obtain this girdle; and Hercules was therefore sent to fetch it. After various adventures in Europe and Asia, he at length reached the country of the Amazons. Hippolyte at first received him kindly, and promised him her girdle; but Hera having excited the Amazons against him, a contest ensued, in which Hercules killed their queen. He then took her girdle, and carried it with him. On his way home he landed in Troas, where he rescued Hesione from the monster sent against her by Poseidon; in return for which service her father, Laomedon, promised him the horses he had received from Zeus as a compensation for Ganymedes. But, as Laomedon did not keep his word, Hercules on leaving threatened to make war against Troy, a threat which he afterwards carried into execution.—(10) *Capture of the oxen of Geryones in Erythia.* Geryones, the monster with 3 bodies, lived in the fabulous island of Erythia (the reddish), so called because it lay in the W., under the rays of the setting sun. This island was originally placed off the coast of Epirus, but was afterwards identified either with Gades or the Balearic islands. The oxen of Geryones were guarded by the giant Eurytion and the two-headed dog Orthus; and Hercules was commanded by Eurystheus to fetch them. After traversing various countries, he reached at length the frontiers of Libya and Europe, where he erected 2 pillars (Calpe and Abyla) on the 2 sides of the straits of Gibraltar, which were hence called the pillars of Hercules. Being annoyed by the heat of the sun, Hercules shot at Helios (the sun), who so much admired his boldness, that he presented him with a golden cup or boat, in which he sailed to Erythia. He there slew Eurytion and his dog, as well as Geryones, and sailed with his

Hercules and Geryon.   (Museo Borbonico.)

booty to Tartessus, where he returned the golden cup (boat) to Helios. On his way home he passed through Gaul, Italy, Illyricum, and Thrace, and met with numerous adventures, which are variously embellished by the poets. Many attempts were made to deprive him of the oxen, but he at length brought them in safety to Eurystheus, who sacrificed them to Hera.—(11) *Fetching the golden apples of the Hesperides.* This was particularly difficult, since Hercules did not know where to find them. They were the apples which Hera had received at her wedding from Ge (the Earth), and which she had entrusted to the keeping of the Hesperides and the dragon Ladon, on Mt. Atlas, in the country of the Hyperboreans. [HESPERIDES.] On arriving at Mt. Atlas, Hercules sent Atlas to fetch the apples, and in the meantime bore the weight of heaven for him. Atlas returned with the apples, but refused

to take the burden of heaven on his shoulders again. Hercules, however, contrived by a stratagem to get the apples, and hastened away. On his return Eurystheus made him a present of the apples; but Hercules dedicated them to Athena (Minerva), who restored them to their former place. Some traditions add that Hercules killed the dragon Ladon.—

Hercules and the Hesperides.   (From a Bas-relief at Rome.)

(12) *Bringing Cerberus from the lower world.* This was the most difficult of the 12 labours of Hercules. He descended into Hades, near Taenarum in Laconia, accompanied by Hermes (Mercury) and Athena. He delivered Theseus and Ascalaphus from their torments. He obtained permission from Pluto to carry Cerberus to the upper world, provided he could accomplish it without force of arms. Hercules succeeded in seizing the monster and carrying it to the upper world; and after he had shown it to Eurystheus, he carried it back again to the lower world. Besides these 12 labours, Hercules performed several other feats without being commanded by Eurystheus. Several of them were interwoven with the 12 labours, and have been already described: those which had no connection with the 12 labours are spoken of below. After Hercules had performed the 12 labours, he was released from the servitude of Eurystheus, and returned to Thebes.

He there gave Megara in marriage to Iolaus; and he wished to gain in marriage for him-

Hercules and Cerberus. (Millin, Tombeaux de Canosa.)

self Iole, the daughter of Eurytus, king of Oechalia. Eurytus promised his daughter to the man who should conquer him and his sons in shooting with the bow. Hercules defeated them; but Eurytus and his sons, with the exception of Iphitus, refused to give Iole to him, because he had murdered his own children. Shortly afterwards he killed his friend Iphitus, in a fit of madness. Though purified from this murder, he was, nevertheless, attacked by a severe illness. The oracle at Delphi declared that he would be restored to health, if he would serve 3 years for wages, and surrender his earnings to Eurytus, as an atonement for the murder of Iphitus. Thereupon he became a servant to Omphale, queen of Lydia, and widow of Tmolus. Later writers describe Hercules as living effeminately during his residence with Omphale: he spun wool, it is said, and sometimes put on the garments of a woman, while Omphale wore his lion's skin. According to other accounts he nevertheless performed several great feats during this time. He undertook an expedition to Colchis, which brought him into connection with the Argonauts; he took part in the Calydonian hunt, and met Theseus on his landing from Troezene on the Corinthian isthmus. When the time of his servitude had expired, he sailed against Troy, took the city, and killed Laomedon, its king. It was about this time that the gods sent for him in order to fight against the Giants. [GIGANTES.] Soon after his return to Argos, he marched against Augeas, as has been related above. He then proceeded against Pylos, which he took, and killed the whole family

of Neleus, with the exception of Nestor. He then proceeded to Calydon, where he obtained Deïanira, the daughter of Oeneus, for his wife, after fighting with Achelous for her. [DEIANIRA; ACHELOUS.] After Hercules had been married to Deianira nearly 3 years, he accidentally killed at a banquet in the house of Oeneus the boy Eunomus. In accordance with the law, Hercules went into exile, taking with him his wife Deianira. On their road they came to the river Evenus, across which the centaur Nessus carried travellers for a small sum of money. Hercules himself forded the river, but gave Deianira to Nessus to carry across. Nessus attempted to outrage her: Hercules heard her screaming, and shot an arrow into the heart of Nessus. The dying centaur called out to Deianira to take his blood with her, as it was a sure means of preserving the love of her husband. After this he took up his abode at Trachis, whence he marched against Eurytus of Oechalia. He took Oechalia, killed Eurytus and his sons, and carried off his daughter Iole as a prisoner. On his return home he landed at Cenaeum, a promontory of Euboea, erected an altar to Zeus, and sent his companion, Lichas, to Trachis, in order to fetch him a white garment, which he intended to use during the sacrifice. Deianira, afraid lest Iole should supplant her in the affections of her husband, steeped the white garment he had demanded in the blood of Nessus. This blood had been poisoned by the arrow with which Hercules had shot Nessus; and, accordingly, as soon as the garment became warm on the body of Hercules, the poison penetrated into all his limbs, and caused him the most excruciating agony. He seized Lichas by his feet, and threw him into the sea. He wrenched off the garment, but it stuck to his flesh, and with it he tore away whole pieces from his body. In this state he was conveyed to Trachis. Deianira, on seeing what she had unwittingly done, hanged herself. Hercules commanded Hyllus, his eldest son by Deianira, to marry Iole as soon as he should arrive at the age of manhood. He then ascended Mt. Oeta, raised a pile of wood, on which he placed himself, and ordered it to be set on fire. When the pile was burning, a cloud came down from heaven, and amid peals of thunder carried him to Olympus, where he was honoured with immortality, became reconciled to Hera, and married her daughter Hebe. He was in course of time worshipped throughout all Greece both as a god and as a hero. His worship, however, prevailed more extensively among the Dorians than among any other of the Greek races.

The sacrifices offered to him consisted principally of bulls, boars, rams, and lambs. The works of art in which Hercules is represented are extremely numerous; but whether he appears as a child, a youth, a struggling hero, or as the immortal inhabitant of Olympus, his character is always one of heroic strength and energy. The finest representation of the hero that has come down to us is the so-called Farnese Hercules. The hero is resting, leaning on his right arm, and his head reclining on his left hand : the whole figure is a most exquisite combination of peculiar softness with the greatest strength. The worship of Hercules at Rome and in Italy is connected by Roman writers with the hero's expedition to fetch the oxen of Geryones. They stated that Hercules, on his return, visited Italy, where he abolished human sacrifices among the Sabines, established the worship of fire, and slew Cacus, a robber, who had stolen his oxen. [CACUS.] The aborigines, and especially Evander, honoured Hercules with divine worship; and Hercules, in return, taught them the way in which he was to be worshipped, and entrusted the care of his worship to 2 distinguished families, the Potitii and Pinarii. [PINARIA GENS.] At Rome Hercules was connected with the Muses, whence he is called *Musagetes*, and was represented with a lyre, of which there is no trace in Greece. The Greeks and Romans also give the name of Hercules to heroes distinguished by their bodily strength among other nations of the ancient world. Thus we find mention of the Egyptian, Indian, and Phoenician Hercules.

HERCŬLES (-is and -i), son of Alexander the Great by Barsine, the widow of the Rhodian Memnon, murdered by Polysperchon, B.C. 310.

HERCŬLIS COLUMNAE. [ABYLA; CALPE.]

HERCŬLIS MONOECI PORTUS. [MONOECUS.]

HERCŬLIS PORTUS. [COSA.]

HERCŬLIS PRŌMONTŌRIUM (*C. Spartivento*), the most S.-ly point of Italy in Bruttium.

HERCYNIA SILVA (-ae), an extensive range of mountains in Germany, covered with forests, described by Caesar as 9 days' journey in breadth, and more than 60 days' journey in length, extending E. from the territories of the Helvetii, Nemetes, and Rauraci, parallel to the Danube, to the frontiers of the Dacians. Under this general name Caesar appears to have included all the mountains and forests in the S. and centre of Germany. The name is still preserved in the modern *Harz* and *Erz*.

HERDŌNĬA (-ae), a town in Apulia, destroyed by Hannibal.

HERILLUS (-i), of Carthage, a Stoic philosopher, the disciple of Zeno of Cittium.

HERMAEUM (-i), or, in Latin, MERCURII PRŌMONTŌRIUM (*Cape Bon*), the extreme N.E. point of the Carthaginian territory, opposite to Lilybaeum, the space between the two being the shortest distance between Sicily and Africa.

HERMĂGŌRĂS (-ae). (1) Of Temnos, a distinguished Greek rhetorician of the time of Cicero, belonging to the Rhodian school of oratory.—(2) A Greek rhetorician, who taught rhetoric at Rome in the time of Augustus.

HERMĀPHRŎDĪTUS (-i), son of Hermes and Aphrodite (Venus), and consequently great-grandson of Atlas, whence he is called *Atlantiades* or *Atlantius*. He had inherited the beauty of both his parents, and thus excited the love of the nymph of the fountain of Salmacis, near Halicarnassus. She tried in vain to win his affections; and as he was one day bathing in the fountain, she embraced him, and prayed to the gods that she might be united with him for ever. The gods granted the request, and the bodies of the youth and the nymph became united together, but retained the characteristics of each sex.

HERMĒS (-ae), called MERCŬRIUS (-i), by the Romans. The Greek Hermes was a son of Zeus (Jupiter) and Maia, the daughter of Atlas, and was born in a cave of Mt. Cyllene in Arcadia, whence he is called *Atlantiades* or *Cyllenius*. A few hours after his birth he displayed his natural propensities; escaping from his cradle, he went to Pieria, and carried off some of the oxen of

Hermes (Mercury) making a Lyre.
(Osterley, Denk. der alt. Kunst, theil 2, tav. 29.)

Apollo, which he drove to Pylos. He then

returned to Cyllene, and finding a tortoise at the entrance of his native cave, he placed strings across its shell, and thus invented the lyre, on which he immediately played. Apollo, by his prophetic power, had meantime discovered the thief, and went to Cyllene to charge Hermes with the crime. His mother, Maia, showed to the god the child in its cradle; but Apollo carried the boy before Zeus, who compelled him to restore the oxen. But when Apollo heard the sounds of the lyre, he was so charmed that he allowed Hermes to keep the animals, and became his friend. Zeus made Hermes his herald, and he was employed by the gods, and more especially by Zeus, on a variety of occasions which are recorded in ancient story. Thus he led Priam to Achilles to fetch the body of Hector; tied Ixion to the wheel; conducted Hera (Juno), Aphrodite (Venus), and Athena (Minerva) to Paris; rescued Dionysus (Bacchus) after his birth from the flames; sold Hercules to Omphale; and was ordered by Zeus to carry off Io, who was metamorphosed into a cow, and guarded by Argus, whom he slew. [ARGUS.] He was also employed by the gods to conduct the shades of the dead from the upper into the lower world. Being the herald of the gods, he is the god of eloquence, since the heralds are the public speakers in the assemblies and on other occasions. He was

such as the lyre and syrinx, the alphabet, numbers, astronomy, music, the art of fighting, gymnastics, the cultivation of the olive tree, measures, weights, and many other things. From being the herald of the gods, he was regarded as the god of roads, who protected travellers; and numerous statues of him, called Hermae, were erected on roads, and at doors and gates. He was also the god of commerce and of good luck, and as such presided over the game of dice. Hermes was believed to have been the inventor of sacrifices, and hence was the protector of sacrificial animals. For this reason he was especially worshipped by shepherds, and is mentioned in connection with Pan and the nymphs. Hermes was likewise the patron of all the gymnastic games of the Greeks. All gymnasia were under his protection; and the Greek artists derived their ideal of the god from the gymnasium, and represented him as a youth whose limbs were beautifully and harmoniously developed by gymnastic exercises. The most ancient seat of the worship of Hermes is Arcadia, the land of his birth, whence his worship was carried to Athens, and ultimately spread through all Greece. The festivals celebrated in his honour were called *Hermaea*. Among the things sacred to him were the palm tree, the tortoise, the number 4, and several kinds of fish; and the sacrifices offered to him con-

Hermes (Mercury). (Museo Borbonico, tom. 6, tav. 2.)

Hermes (Mercury). Pitture e Bronzi d'Ercolano, vol. 4, tav. 31.)

also the god of prudence and cunning, both in words and actions, and even of fraud, perjury, and theft. Being endowed with this shrewdness and sagacity, he was regarded as the author of a variety of inventions,

sisted of incense, honey, cakes, pigs, and especially lambs and young goats. The prin-

cipal attributes of Hermes are :—1. A travelling hat with a broad brim, which in
later times was adorned with 2 small wings.
2. The staff which he bore as a herald, and
had received from Apollo. In late works of
art the white ribbons which surrounded the
herald's staff were changed into 2 serpents.
3. The sandals which carried the god across
land and sea with the rapidity of wind, and
which were provided at the ankles with
wings, whence he is called *alipes*. — The
Roman Mercurius is spoken of separately.

HERMINIUS (-i) MONS (*Sierra de la
Estrella*), the chief mountain in Lusitania,
S. of the Durius.

HERMIONE (-es). (1) The beautiful
daughter of Menelaus and Helena. She had
been promised in marriage to Orestes before
the Trojan war; but Menelaus after his
return home married her to Neoptolemus
(Pyrrhus). After the murder of the latter,
[Neoptolemus], Hermione married Orestes,
and bore him a son Tisamenus.—(2) A
town of Argolis, but originally independent
of Argos, was situated on a promontory on
the E. coast, and on a bay of the sea, which
derived its name from the town (Hermioni-
cus Sinus). It was originally inhabited by
the Dryopes.

HERMIONES. [Germania.]

HERMOCRATES, one of the Syracusan
generals, when the Athenians attacked Syracuse, B.C. 414. He was banished by the
Syracusans (410), and having endeavoured
to effect his restoration by force of arms,
was slain, 407.

HERMOGENES, a celebrated Greek rhetorician, was a native of Tarsus, and lived
in the reign of M. Aurelius, A.D. 161—180.
Several of his works are extant.

HERMOGENES, M. TIGELLIUS (-i), a
notorious detractor of Horace, who calls him
however optimus cantor et modulator.

HERMOLAUS (-i), a Macedonian youth,
and a page of Alexander the Great, formed a
conspiracy against the king's life, B.C. 327,
but the plot was discovered, and Hermolaus
and his accomplices were stoned to death by
the Macedonians.

HERMOPOLIS (-is), *i.e.* "the city of
Hermes (Mercury)." (1) Parva, a city of
Lower Egypt, stood upon the canal which
connected the Canopic branch of the Nile
with the Lake Mareotis.—(2) Magna, an
ancient city in Middle Egypt, stood on the
W. bank of the Nile, a little below the confines of Upper Egypt.

HERMUNDURI (-orum), one of the most
powerful nations of Germany, belonged to
the Suevic race, and dwelt between the Maine
and the Danube.

HERMUS (-i), a considerable river of Asia
Minor, rising in Mt. Dindymene, and after
flowing through the plain of Sardis, falling
into the Gulf of Smyrna, between Smyrna
and Phocaea. It formed the boundary between Aeolia and Ionia.

HERNICI (-orum), a people in Latium,
belonging to the Sabine race, who inhabited
the mountains of the Apennines between the
lake Fucinus and the river Trerus, and were
bounded on the N. by the Marsi and Aequi,
and on the S. by the Volsci. Their chief
town was Anagnia. They were a brave and
warlike people, and long offered a formidable
resistance to the Romans. The Romans
formed a league with them on equal terms in
the 3rd consulship of Sp. Cassius, B.C. 486.
They were finally subdued by the Romans,
306.

HERO. [Leander.]

HERO (-us), an eminent mathematician,
was a native of Alexandria, and lived in the
reigns of the Ptolemies Philadelphus and
Evergetes (B.C. 285—222). He is celebrated
on account of his mechanical inventions.
Several of his works are extant.

HERODES (-is), commonly called Herod.
(1) Surnamed the Great, king of the Jews,
was the son of Antipater. He received the
kingdom of Judaea, from Antony and Octavian, in B.C. 40. He possessed a jealous
temper and ungovernable passions. He put
to death his beautiful wife Mariamne, whom
he suspected without cause of adultery, and
with whom he was violently in love; and at
a later period he also put to death his two
sons by Mariamne, Alexander and Aristobulus. His government, though cruel and
tyrannical, was vigorous. In the last year
of his reign Jesus Christ was born; and it
must have been on his deathbed that he
ordered the massacre of the children at
Bethlehem. He died in the 37th year of his
reign, and the 70th of his age, B.C. 4.*
—(2) Herodes Antipas, son of Herod the
Great, by Malthace, a Samaritan, obtained
the tetrarchy of Galilee and Peraea, on his
father's death, while the kingdom of Judaea
devolved on his elder brother Archelaus. He
married Herodias, the wife of his half-brother, Herod Philip, she having, in defiance
of the Jewish law, divorced her first husband.
He was deprived of his dominions by Caligula, and sent into exile at Lyons, A.D. 39.
It was this Herod Antipas who imprisoned
and put to death John the Baptist, who had
reproached him with his unlawful connexion

---

* The death of Herod took place in the same year
with the actual birth of Christ, as is mentioned above,
but it is well known that this is to be placed 4 years
before the date in general use as the Christian era.

with Herodias. It was before him also that Christ was sent by Pontius Pilate at Jerusalem, as belonging to his jurisdiction, on account of his supposed Galilean origin.— (3) HERODES AGRIPPA. [AGRIPPA.]—(4) HERODES ATTICUS, the rhetorician. [ATTICUS.]

HĔRŎDĬĀNUS (-i), the author of an extant history, in the Greek language, of the Roman empire in 8 books, from the death of M. Aurelius to the commencement of the reign of Gordianus III. (A.D. 180—238).

HĔRŎDŎTUS (-i), a Greek historian, and the father of history, was born at Halicarnassus, a Doric colony in Caria, B.C. 484. He belonged to a noble family at Halicarnassus. He was the son of Lyxes and Dryo; and the epic poet Panyasis was one of his relations. Herodotus left his native city at an early age, in order to escape from the oppressive government of Lygdamis, the tyrant of Halicarnassus,' who put to death Panyasis. He probably settled at Samos for some time, and there became acquainted with the Ionic dialect; but he spent many years in his extensive travels in Europe, Asia, and Africa. At a later time he returned to Halicarnassus, and took a prominent part in expelling Lygdamis from his native city. Subsequently he again left Halicarnassus, and settled at Thurii, an Athenian colony in Italy, where he died. Whether he accompanied the first colonists to Thurii in 443, or followed them a few years afterwards, cannot be determined with certainty. It is also disputed where Herodotus wrote his history. Lucian relates that Herodotus read his work to the assembled Greeks at Olympia, which was received with such universal applause, that the 9 books of the work were in consequence honoured with the names of the 9 Muses. The same writer adds that the young Thucydides was present at this recitation and was moved to tears. But this celebrated story, which rests upon the authority of Lucian alone, must be rejected for many reasons. Nor is there sufficient evidence in favour of the tradition that Herodotus read his work at the Panathenaea at Athens in 446 or 445, and received from the Athenians a reward of 10 talents. It is more probable that he wrote his work at Thurii, when he was advanced in years; though he appears to have been collecting materials for it during a great part of his life. It was apparently with this view that he undertook his extensive travels through Greece and foreign countries; and his work contains on almost every page the results of his personal observations and inquiries. There was scarcely a town of any importance in Greece Proper and on the coasts of Asia Minor with which

he was not perfectly familiar. In the N. of Europe he visited Thrace and the Scythian tribes on the Black Sea. In Asia he travelled through Asia Minor and Syria, and visited the cities of Babylon, Ecbatana, and Susa. He spent some time in Egypt, and travelled as far S. as Elephantine. The object of his work is to give an account of the struggles between the Greeks and Persians. He traces the enmity between Europe and Asia to the mythical times. He passes rapidly over the mythical ages to come to Croesus, king of Lydia, who was known to have committed acts of hostility against the Greeks. This induces him to give a full history of Croesus and of the kingdom of Lydia. The conquest of Lydia by the Persians under Cyrus then leads him to relate the rise of the Persian monarchy, and the subjugation of Asia Minor and Babylon. The nations which are mentioned in the course of this narrative are again discussed more or less minutely. The history of Cambyses and his expedition into Egypt induce him to enter into the details of Egyptian history. The expedition of Darius against the Scythians causes him to speak of Scythia and the N. of Europe. In the meantime the revolt of the Ionians breaks out which eventually brings the contest between Persia and Greece to an end. An account of this insurrection is followed by the history of the invasion of Greece by the Persians; and the history of the Persian war now runs in a regular channel until the taking of Sestos by the Greeks, B.C. 478, with which event his work concludes. In order to form a fair judgment of the historical value of the work of Herodotus, we must distinguish between those parts in which he speaks from his own observations and those in which he merely repeats what he was told by priests and others. In the latter case he was undoubtedly often deceived; but whenever he speaks from his own observations, he is a real model of truthfulness and accuracy; and the more the countries which he describes have been explored by modern travellers, the more firmly has his authority been established. The dialect in which he wrote is the Ionic, intermixed with epic or poetical expressions, and sometimes even with Attic and Doric forms. The excellencies of his style consist in its antique and epic colouring, its transparent clearness, and the lively flow of the narrative.

HĔRŎPŎLIS (-is), or HĔRŌ (-ūs), a city in Lower Egypt, standing on the border of the Desert E. of the Delta, upon the canal connecting the Nile with the W. head of the Red Sea, which was called from. it Sinus Heroöpoliticus.

HĒROSTRĀTUS (-i), an Ephesian, who set fire to the temple of Artemis at Ephesus on the same night that Alexander the Great was born, B.C. 356, in order to immortalise himself.

HERSĒ (-es), daughter of Cecrops and sister of Agraulos, beloved by Hermes. Respecting her story, see AGRAULOS.

HERSĪLĬA (-ae), the wife of Romulus, worshipped after her death under the name of Hora or Horta.

HĔRŬLI or ĔRŬLI (-ōrum), a powerful German race, who are said to have come originally from Scandinavia, attacked the Roman empire on its decline. Under the command of Odoacer, who is said to have been an Herulian, they destroyed the Western Empire, A.D. 476.

HĒSĬŎDUS (-i), one of the earliest Greek poets, frequently mentioned along with Homer. As Homer represents the Ionic school of poetry in Asia Minor, so Hesiod represents the Boeotian school of poetry. The only points of resemblance between the 2 schools consist in their versification and dialect. In other respects they entirely differ. The Homeric school takes for its subject the restless activity of the heroic age, while the Hesiodic turns its attention to the quiet pursuits of ordinary life, to the origin of the world, the gods and heroes. Hesiod lived about a century later than Homer, and is placed about B.C. 735. We learn from his own poem on *Works and Days*, that he was born in the village of Ascra in Boeotia, whither his father had emigrated from the Aeolian Cyme in Asia Minor. After the death of his father, he was involved in a dispute with his brother Perses about his small patrimony, which was decided in favour of his brother. He then emigrated to Orchomenos, where he spent the remainder of his life. This is all that can be said with certainty about the life of Hesiod. Many of the stories related about him refer to his school of poetry, and not to the poet personally. In this light we may regard the tradition, that Hesiod had a poetical contest with Homer, which is said to have taken place either at Chalcis or Aulis. The two principal works of Hesiod, which have come down to us, are his *Works and Days*, containing ethical, political, and economical precepts, and a *Theogony*, giving an account of the origin of the world and the birth of the gods.

HĒSĬŎNĒ (-es), daughter of Laomedon, king of Troy, was chained by her father to a rock, in order to be devoured by a sea-monster, that he might thus appease the anger of Apollo and Poseidon. Hercules promised to save her, if Laomedon would give him the horses which he had received from Zeus as a compensation for Ganymedes. Hercules killed the monster, but Laomedon refused to keep his promise. Thereupon Hercules took Troy, killed Laomedon, and gave Hesione to his friend and companion Telamon, to whom she bore Teucer. Her brother Priam sent Antenor to claim her back, and the refusal on the part of the Greeks is mentioned as one of the causes of the Trojan war.

HESPĔRĬA (-ae), the Western land (from ἕστερος, *vesper*), the name given by the Greek poets to Italy, because it lay W. of Greece. In imitation of them, the Roman poets gave the name of Hesperia to Spain, which they sometimes called *ultima Hesperia*, to distinguish it from Italy, which they occasionally called *Hesperia Magna*.

HESPĔRĬDES (-um), the celebrated guardians of the golden apples which Ge (Earth) gave to Hera at her marriage with Zeus. According to some they were the daughters of Atlas and Hesperis (whence their names, Atlantides or Hesperides); but their parentage is differently related by others. Some traditions mentioned 3 Hesperides, viz., *Aegle, Arethusa,* and *Hesperia ;* others, 4, *Aegle, Crytheia, Hestia,* and *Arethusa ;* and others, again, 7. In the earliest legends, they are described as living on the river Oceanus, in the extreme W.; but they were afterwards placed near Mt. Atlas, and in other parts of Libya. They were assisted in watching the golden apples by the dragon Ladon. It was one of the labours of Hercules to obtain possession of these apples. [See p. 199.]

HESPĔRĬDUM INSŬLAE. [HESPERIUM.]

HESPĔRIS. [BERENICE.]

HESPĔRĬUM (-i : *C. Verde* or *C. Roxo*), a headland on the W. coast of Africa, was one of the farthest points along that coast to which the knowledge of the ancients extended. At a day's journey from it was a group of islands called HESPERIDUM INSULAE, wrongly identified by some with the Fortunatae Insulae; they are either the *Cape de Verde* islands, or, more probably, the *Bissagos*, at the mouth of the *Rio Grande*.

HESPĔRUS (-i), the evening star, son of Astraeus and Eos (Aurora), of Cephalus and Eos, or of Atlas. He was also regarded as the same as the morning star. [LUCIFER.]

HESTĬA (-ae), called VESTA (-ae) by the Romans, the goddess of the hearth, or rather of the fire burning on the hearth, was one of the 12 great divinities of the Greeks. She was a daughter of Cronos (Saturn) and Rhea, and, according to common tradition, was the first-born of Rhea, and consequently the first of the children swallowed by Cronos.

She was a maiden divinity; and when Apollo and Poseidon (Neptune) sued for her hand, she swore by the head of Zeus to remain a virgin for ever. As the hearth was looked upon as the centre of domestic life, so Hestia was the goddess of domestic life, and as such, was believed to dwell in the inner part of every house. Being the goddess of the sacred fire of the altar, Hestia had a share in the sacrifices offered to all the gods. Hence the first part of every sacrifice was presented to her. Solemn oaths were sworn by the goddess of the hearth; and the hearth itself was the sacred asylum where suppliants implored the protection of the inhabitants of the house. A town or city is only an extended family, and therefore had likewise its sacred hearth. This public hearth usually existed in the prytaneum of a town, where the goddess had her especial sanctuary. There, as at a private hearth, Hestia protected the suppliants. When a colony was sent out, the emigrants took the fire which was to burn on the hearth of their new home from that of the mother town. The worship of the Roman Vesta is spoken of under VESTA.

Hestia (Vesta). (From an ancient Statue.)

HESTĬAEŌTIS (-is). (1) The N.W. part of Thessaly. [THESSALIA.]—(2) Or HISTIAEA, a district in Euboea. [EUBOEA.]

HETRICŬL M (-i), a town of the Bruttii.

HIBERNĬA (-ae), also called IERNE, IVERNA, or JUVERNA (-ae), the island of Ireland, appears to have derived its name from the inhabitants of its S. coast, called Juverni; but its original name was probably *Bergion* or *Vergion*. It is mentioned by Caesar; but the Romans never made any attempt to conquer the island, though they obtained some knowledge of it from the commercial intercourse which was carried on between it and Britain.

HIEMPSĂL (-ălis). (1) Son of Micipsa, king of Numidia, and grandson of Masinissa, murdered by Jugurtha, soon after the death of Micipsa, B.C. 118.—(2) King of Numidia, grandson or great-grandson of Masinissa, and father of Juba, appears to have received the sovereignty of part of Numidia after the Jugurthine war. He was expelled from his kingdom by Cn. Domitius Ahenobarbus, the leader of the Marian party in Africa, but was restored by Pompey in 81. Hiempsal wrote some works in the Punic language, which are cited by Sallust.

HĬĔRĂPŌLIS (-is). (1) A city of Great Phrygia, near the Maeander, was an early seat of Christianity, and is mentioned in St. Paul's *Epistle to the Colossians.* — (2) Formerly BAMBYCE, a city in the N.E. of Syria, one of the chief seats of the worship of Astarte.

HĬĔRŌN (-ōnis). (1) Tyrant of Syracuse (B.C. 478—467), and brother of Gelon, whom he succeeded in the sovereignty. He gained a great victory over the Etruscan fleet near Cumae, B.C. 474. He was a patron of literature; and the poets Aeschylus, Pindar, and Simonides, took up their residence at his court.—(2) King of Syracuse (B.C. 270—216), a noble Syracusan, descended from the great Gelon, was voluntarily elected king by his fellow-citizens, after his defeat of the Mamertines, in B.C. 270. He sided with the Carthaginians at the commencement of the first Punic war (B.C. 264), but in the following year he concluded a peace with the Romans; and from this time till his death, a period of little less than half a century, he continued the stedfast friend and ally of the Romans. He died in 216, at the age of 92. He was succeeded by his grandson, Hieronymus.

HĬĔRŌNYMUS (-i). (1) Of Cardia, accompanied Alexander the Great to Asia, and after the death of that monarch (B.C. 323), served under his countryman Eumenes. He afterwards fought under Antigonus, his son Demetrius, and grandson Antigonus Gonatas. He survived Pyrrhus, and died at the advanced age of 104. Hieronymus wrote a history of the events from the death of Alexander to that of Pyrrhus, which is lost. —(2) King of Syracuse, succeeded his grandfather, Hieron II., B.C. 216, at 15 years of age, and was assassinated after a short reign of only 13 months.—(3) Of Rhodes, a peripatetic philosopher, and a disciple of Aristotle.

HIĔROSŌLŸMA. [JERUSALEM.]

HILLEVIŌNES. [GERMANIA.]

HĪMĔRA (-ae). (1) (*Fiume Salso*), one of the principal rivers in the S. of Sicily, at one time the boundary between the territories of the Carthaginians and Syracusans, receives near Enna the water of a salt spring, and hence has salt water as far as its mouth. —(2) A smaller river in the N. of Sicily, flowing into the sea between the towns of Himera and Thermae. — (3) A celebrated Greek city on the N. coast of Sicily, W. of the mouth of the river Himera [No. 2], was founded by the Chalcidians of Zancle, B.C. 648, and afterwards received Dorian settlers, so that the inhabitants spoke a mixed dialect, partly Ionic (Chalcidian), and partly Doric. In B.C. 409 it was taken by the Carthaginians, and levelled to the ground. It was never rebuilt; but on the opposite bank of the river Himera, the Carthaginians founded a new town, which, from a warm medicinal spring in its neighbourhood, was called THERMAE. The poet Stesichorus was born at the ancient Himera, and the tyrant Agathocles, at Thermae.

HIPPARCHUS (-i). (1) Son of Pisistratus. [PISISTRATIDAE.]—(2) A celebrated Greek astronomer, a native of Nicaea, in Bithynia, who flourished B.C. 160—145, and resided both at Rhodes and Alexandria. The catalogue which Hipparchus constructed of the stars is preserved by Ptolemy.

HIPPĬAS (-ae). (1) Son of Pisistratus. [PISISTRATIDAE.]—(2) A celebrated Sophist, was a native of Elis, and the contemporary of Socrates.

HIPPO (-ōnis). (1) H. REGIUS, a city on the coast of Numidia, once a royal residence, and afterwards celebrated as the bishopric of St. Augustine.—(2) H. DIARRHYTUS or ZARITUS, a city on the N. coast of the Carthaginian territory W. of Utica.—(3) A town of the Carpetani in Hispania Tarraconensis, S. of Toletum.

HIPPŎCŎŌN (-ontis), son of Oebalus and Batea. After his father's death, he expelled his brother Tyndareus, in order to secure the kingdom to himself; but Hercules led Tyndareus back, and slew Hippocoon and his sons.

HIPPOCRĂTES (-is), the most celebrated physician of antiquity, was born in the island of Cos, about B.C. 460. He wrote, taught, and practised his profession at home; travelled in different parts of the continent of Greece; and died at Larissa in Thessaly, about 357, at the age of 104. He had 2 sons, Thessalus and Dracon, and a son-in-law, Polybus, all of whom followed the same profession. The writings which have come down to us under the name of Hippocrates were composed by several different persons, and are of very different merit.

HIPPOCRĔNĒ (-es), the "Fountain of the Horse," was a fountain in Mt. Helicon in Boeotia, sacred to the Muses, said to have been produced by the horse Pegasus striking the ground with his feet.

HIPPŎDĂMĪA (-ae). (1) Daughter of Oenomaus, king of Pisa in Elis. [OENOMAUS and PELOPS.]—(2) Wife of Pirithous, at whose nuptials took place the celebrated battle between the Centaurs and Lapithae. [PIRITHOUS.]

HIPPŎLŸTĒ (-es). (1) Daughter of Ares and Otrera, was queen of the Amazons, and sister of Antiope and Melanippe. She wore a girdle given to her by her father; and when Hercules came to fetch this girdle, he slew her. According to another tradition, Hippolyte, with an army of Amazons, marched into Attica, to take vengeance on Theseus for having carried off Antiope; but being conquered by Theseus, she fled to Megara, where she died of grief. In some accounts Hippolyte, and not Antiope, is said to have been married to Theseus.—(2) Or ASTYDAMIA, wife of Acastus, fell in love with Peleus. [ACASTUS.]

HIPPŎLŸTUS (-i), son of Theseus by Hippolyte, queen of the Amazons, or by her sister Antiope. Theseus afterwards married Phaedra, who fell in love with Hippolytus; but as her offers were rejected by her step-son, she accused him to his father of having attempted her dishonour. Theseus thereupon cursed his son, and devoted him to destruction; and, accordingly, as Hippolytus was riding in his chariot along the sea-coast, Poseidon sent forth a bull from the water, at which the horses took fright, overturned the chariot, and dragged Hippolytus along the ground till he was dead. Theseus afterwards learned the innocence of his son, and Phaedra, in despair, made away with herself. Artemis (Diana) induced Aesculapius to restore Hippolytus to life again; and, according to Italian traditions, Diana, having changed his name to Virbius, placed him under the protection of the nymph Egeria, in the grove of Aricia, in Latium, where he was honoured with divine worship. Horace, following the more ancient tradition, says that Diana could not restore Hippolytus to life.

HIPPŎMĔNĒS (-is). (1) Son of Megareus, and great-grandson of Poseidon (Neptune), conquered Atalanta in a foot-race. [ATALANTA, No. 2.]—(2) A descendant of Codrus, the 4th and last of the decennial archons.

Incensed at the barbarous punishment which he inflicted on his daughter, the Attic nobles deposed him.

HIPPŌNAX (-actis), of Ephesus, a Greek Iambic poet, flourished B.C. 546—520. He was celebrated for the bitterness of his satires.

HIPPONiCUS. [CALLIAS and HIPPONICUS.]

HIPPŌNĬUM. [VIBO.]

HIPPŌNOUS. [BELLEROPHON.]

HIPPŌTĂDĒS (-ae), son of Hippotes, that is, Aeolus. Hence the Aeoliae Insulae are called *Hippotadae regnum.*

HIPPŌTHŌUS (-i), son of Cercyon, and father of Aepytus, king of Arcadia.

HIRPĪNI (-ōrum), a Samnite people, dwelling in the S. of Samnium, between Apulia, Lucania, and Campania. Their chief town was AECULANUM.

HIRTĬUS (-i), A., a friend of Caesar the dictator, and consul with Pansa, B.C. 43. Hirtius and his colleague fell at the battle of Mutina, fighting against Antony. [AUGUSTUS.] Hirtius divides with Oppius the claim to the authorship of the 8th book of the Gallic war, as well as to that of the histories of the Alexandrian, African, and Spanish wars. It is not impossible that he wrote the first three, but he certainly did not write the Spanish war.

HISPĀLIS (-is), more rarely HISPĂL (-ălis: *Seville*), a town of the Turdetani in Hispania Baetica, founded by the Phoenicians, situated on the left bank of the Baetis, and in reality a seaport, for, although 500 stadia from the sea, the river is navigable for the largest vessels up to the town. Under the Romans it was an important place; under the Goths and Vandals the chief town in the S. of Spain; and under the Arabs the capital of a separate kingdom.

HISPĀNĬA (-ae: *Spain*), a peninsula in the S.W. of Europe, connected with the land only on the N.E., where the Pyrenees form its boundary, and surrounded on all other sides by the sea, and on the N. by the Cantabrian sea. The Greeks and Romans had no accurate knowledge of the country till the time of the Roman invasion in the 2nd Punic war. It was first mentioned by Hecataeus (about B.C. 500) under the name of *Iberia*; but this name originally indicated only the E. coast: the W. coast beyond the pillars of Hercules was called *Tartessis* (Ταρτησσίς). It was called by the Greeks *Iberia*, a name usually derived from the river Iberus, and by the Romans *Hispania.* Spain was celebrated in antiquity for its mineral treasures. Gold was found in abundance in various parts of the country; and there were many silver mines, of which the most celebrated were

near Carthago Nova, Ilipa, Sisapon, and Castulo. The precious stones, copper, lead, tin, and other metals, were also found in more or less abundance. The most ancient inhabitants of Spain were the Iberi, who dwelt on both sides of the Pyrenees, and were found in the S. of Gaul, as far as the Rhone. Celts afterwards crossed the Pyrenees, and became mingled with the Iberi, whence arose the mixed race of the Celtiberi, who dwelt chiefly in the high table land in the centre of the country. [CELTIBERI.] But besides this mixed race of the Celtiberi, there were also several tribes, both of Iberians and Celts, who were never united with one another. The unmixed Iberians, from whom the modern Basques are descended, dwelt chiefly in the Pyrenees and on the coasts, and their most distinguished tribes were the ASTURES, CANTABRI, VACCAEI, &c. The unmixed Celts dwelt chiefly on the river Anas, and in the N.W. corner of the country or Gallaecia. Besides these inhabitants, there were Phoenician and Carthaginian settlements on the coasts, of which the most important were GADES and CARTHAGO NOVA; there were likewise Greek colonies, such as EMPORIAE and SAGUNTUM; and lastly the conquest of the country by the Romans introduced many Romans among the inhabitants, whose civilisation and language gradually spread over the whole peninsula. Under the empire some of the most distinguished Latin writers were natives of Spain, such as the 2 Senecas, Lucan, Martial, Quintilian, Silius Italicus, Pomponius Mela, Prudentius, and others. The ancient inhabitants of Spain were a proud, brave, and warlike race; lovers of their liberty, and ready at all times to sacrifice their lives rather than submit to a foreign master. The history of Spain begins with the invasion of the country by the Carthaginians, B.C. 238. Under the command of Hamilcar (238—229), and that of his son-in-law and successor, Hasdrubal (228—221), the Carthaginians conquered the greater part of the S.E. of the peninsula as far as the Iberus; and Hasdrubal founded the important city of Carthago Nova. These successes of the Carthaginians excited the jealousy of the Romans; and a treaty was made between the 2 nations about 228, by which the Carthaginians bound themselves not to cross the Iberus. The town of Saguntum, although on the W. side of the river, was under the protection of the Romans; and the capture of this town by Hannibal in 219, was the immediate cause of the 2nd Punic war. In the course of this war the Romans drove the Carthaginians out of the peninsula, and became masters of their possessions in the S.

of the country. But many tribes in the centre of the country retained their independence ; and those in the N. and N. W. of the country had been hitherto quite unknown both to the Carthaginians and Romans. There now arose a long and bloody struggle between the Romans and the various tribes in Spain, and it was nearly 2 centuries before the Romans succeeded in subduing entirely the whole of the peninsula. The Celtiberians were conquered by the elder Cato (195), and Tib. Gracchus, the father of the 2 tribunes (179). The Lusitanians, who long resisted the Romans under their brave leader Viriathus, were obliged to submit, about the year 137, to D. Brutus, who penetrated as far as Gallaecia ; but it was not till Numantia was taken by Scipio Africanus the younger, in 133, that the Romans obtained the undisputed sovereignty over the various tribes in the centre of the country, and of the Lusitanians to the S. of the Tagus. Julius Caesar, after his praetorship, subdued the Lusitanians N. of the Tagus (60). The Cantabri, Astures, and other tribes in the mountains of the N., were finally subjugated by Augustus and his generals. The Romans had, as early as the end of the 2nd Punic war, divided Spain into 2 provinces, separated from one another by the Iberus, and called *Hispania Citerior* and *Hispania Ulterior*, the former being to the E., and the latter to the W. of the river. In consequence of there being 2 provinces, we frequently find the country called *Hispaniae*. The provinces were governed by 2 proconsuls or 2 propraetors, the latter of whom also frequently bore the title of proconsuls. Augustus made a new division of the country, and formed 3 provinces, *Tarraconensis, Baetica,* and *Lusitania.* The province Tarraconensis, which derived its name from Tarraco, the capital of the province, was by far the largest of the 3, and comprehended the whole of the N., W., and centre of the peninsula. The province *Baetica*, which derived its name from the river Baetis, was separated from Lusitania on the N. and W. by the river Anas, and from Tarraconensis on the E. by a line drawn from the river Anas to the promontory Charidemus in the Mediterranean. The province *Lusitania* corresponded very nearly in extent to the modern Portugal. In Baetica, Corduba or Hispalis was the seat of government; in Tarraconensis, Tarraco ; and in Lusitania, Augusta Emerita. On the fall of the Roman empire Spain was conquered by the Vandals, A.D. 409.

HISTIAEA. [HESTIAEOTIS.]

HISTIAEUS (-i), tyrant of Miletus, was left with the other Ionians to guard the bridge of boats over the Danube, when Darius invaded Scythia (B.C. 513). He opposed the proposal of Miltiades, the Athenian, to destroy the bridge, and leave the Persians to their fate, and was in consequence rewarded by Darius with a district in Thrace, where he built a town called Myrcinus, apparently with the view of establishing an independent kingdom. This excited the suspicions of Darius, who invited Histiaeus to Susa, where he treated him kindly, but prohibited him from returning. Tired of the restraint in which he was kept, he induced his kinsman Aristagoras to persuade the Ionians to revolt, hoping that a revolution in Ionia might lead to his release. His design succeeded. Darius allowed Histiaeus to depart (496) on his engaging to reduce Ionia. Here Histiaeus threw off the mask, and carried on war against the Persians. He was at length taken prisoner, and put to death by Artaphernes, satrap of Ionia.

HOMERUS (-i), the great epic poet of Greece. His poems formed the basis of Greek literature. Every Greek who had received a liberal education was perfectly well acquainted with them from his childhood, and had learnt them by heart at school ; but nobody could state anything certain about their author. His date and birthplace were equally matters of dispute. Seven cities claimed Homer as their countryman (Smyrna, Rhodus, Colophon, Salamis, Chios, Argos, Athenae) ; but the claims of Smyrna and Chios are the most plausible. The best modern writers place his date about B.C. 850. With the exception of the simple fact of his being an Asiatic Greek, all other particulars respecting his life are purely fabulous. The common tradition related that he was the son of Maeon (hence called *Maeonides vates*), and that in his old age he was blind and poor.—Homer was universally regarded by the ancients as the author of the 2 great poems of the Iliad and the Odyssey. Such continued to be the prevalent belief in modern times, till the year 1795, when the German Professor, F. A. Wolf, wrote his famous Prolegomena, in which he endeavoured to show that the Iliad and Odyssey were not two complete poems, but small, separate, independent epic songs, celebrating single exploits of the heroes, and that these lays were *for the first time* written down and united, as the Iliad and Odyssey, by Pisistratus, the tyrant of Athens. This opinion gave rise to a long and animated controversy respecting the origin of the Homeric poems, which is not yet settled, and which probably never will be. The following, however, may be regarded as the most probable conclusion. An abundance of heroic lays preserved the tales of the Trojan war. These unconnected songs were, for the first time, united by a great genius called Homer, and he was the *one individual* who conceived in his mind the lofty idea of that poetical unity which we must acknowledge and admire in the Iliad and Odyssey. But as writing was not known, or at least little practised, in the age in which Homer lived, it naturally followed that in such long works many interpolations were introduced, and that they gradually became more and more dismembered, and thus returned into their original state of separate independent songs. They were preserved by the rhapsodists, who were minstrels, and who sang lays at the banquets of the great and at public festivals. Solon directed the attention of his countrymen towards the unity of the Homeric poems; but the unanimous voice of antiquity ascribed to Pisistratus the merit of having collected the disjointed poems of Homer, and of having first committed them to writing. The ancients attributed many other poems to Homer besides the Iliad and the Odyssey; but the claims of none of these to this honour can stand investigation. The hymns, which still bear the name of Homer, probably owe their origin to the rhapsodists. The *Batrachomyomachia*, or Battle of the Frogs and Mice, an extant poem, and the *Margites*, a poem which is lost, and which ridiculed a man who was said to know many things and who knew all badly, were both frequently ascribed by the ancients to Homer, but were clearly of later origin.—The Odyssey was evidently composed after the Iliad; and many writers maintain that they are the works of 2 different authors. But it has been observed in reply, that there is not a greater difference in the 2 poems than we often find in the productions of the same man in the prime of life and in old age; and the chief cause of difference in the 2 poems is owing to the difference of the subject. The Alexandrine grammarians paid great attention to the text of the Homeric poems; and the edition of the Iliad and the Odyssey by Aristarchus has been the basis of the text to the present day.

HŎMŎLĔ (-es). (1) A lofty mountain in Thessaly, near Tempe, with a sanctuary of Pan. — (2) Or HOMOLIUM (-i), a town in Magnesia in Thessaly, at the foot of Mt. Ossa, near the Peneus.

HŎNOR or HŎNŌS (-ōris), the personification of honour at Rome, to whom temples were built both by Marcellus and by Marius, close to the temple of Honos. Marcellus also built one to Virtus; and the two deities are frequently mentioned together.

Honos et Virtus. (Coin of Galba, British Museum.)

HONŌRĬUS FLĀVIUS (-i), Roman emperor of the West, A.D. 395—423, was the 2nd son of Theodosius the Great. In his reign Alaric took and plundered Rome.

HŌRAE (-ārum), daughters of Zeus (Jupiter) and Themis, the goddesses of the order of nature and of the seasons, who guarded the doors of Olympus, and promoted the fertility of the earth by the various kinds of weather which they gave to mortals. At Athens 2 Horae, *Thallo* (the Hora of Spring) and *Carpo* (the Hora of autumn), were worshipped from very early times; but they are usually represented as three or four in number. Hesiod gives them the names of *Eunomia* (good

Horae (Seasons). (From a coin of Commodus.)

order), *Dice* (justice), and *Irene* (peace). In works of art the Horae are represented as blooming maidens or youths, carrynig the different products of the seasons.

HŌRĀTĬA GENS, one of the most ancient patrician gentes at Rome. 3 brothers of this

Horae (Seasons). (From a Bas-relief at Rome.)

race fought with the Curiatii, 3 brothers from Alba, to determine whether Rome or Alba was to exercise the supremacy. The battle was long undecided. 2 of the Horatii fell ; but the 3 Curiatii, though alive, were severely wounded. Seeing this, the surviving Horatius, who was still unhurt, pretended to fly, and vanquished his wounded opponents, by encountering them severally. He returned in triumph, bearing his threefold spoils. As he approached the Capene gate, his sister Horatia met him, and recognised on his shoulders the mantle of one of the Curiatii, her betrothed lover. Her importunate grief drew on her the wrath of Horatius, who stabbed her, exclaiming, " So perish every Roman woman who bewails a foe." For this murder he was adjudged by the duumviri to be scourged with covered head, and hanged on the accursed tree. Horatius appealed to his peers, the burghers or populus ; and his father pronounced him guiltless, or he would have punished him by the paternal power. The populus acquitted Horatius, but prescribed a form of punishment. With veiled head, led by his father, Horatius passed under a yoke or gibbet—*tigillum sororium*, " sisters' gibbet."

HŌRĀTĬUS COCLES. [Cocles.]

HŌRĀTĬUS FLACCUS, Q. (-i), the poet, was born December 8th, B.C. 65, at Venusia in Apulia. His father was a libertinus or freedman. He had received his manumission

before the birth of the poet, who was of ingenuous birth, but who did not altogether escape the taunt, which adhered to persons even of remote servile origin. His father's occupation was that of collector (*coactor*), either of the indirect taxes farmed by the publicans, or at sales by auction. With the profits of his office he had purchased a small farm in the neighbourhood of Venusia, where the poet was born. The father devoted his whole time and fortune to the education of the future poet. Though by no means rich, he declined to send the young Horace to the common school, kept in Venusia by one Flavius, to which the children of the rural aristocracy resorted. Probably about his 12th year, his father carried him to Rome, to receive the usual education of a knight's or senator's son. He frequented the best schools in the capital. One of these was kept by Orbilius, a retired military man, whose flogging propensities have been immortalised by his pupil. In his 18th year Horace proceeded to Athens, in order to continue his studies at that seat of learning. When Brutus came to Athens after the death of Caesar, Horace joined his army, and received at once the rank of a military tribune, and the command of a legion. He was present at the battle of Philippi, and shared in the flight of the republican army. In one of his poems he playfully alludes to his flight, and throwing away his shield. He now resolved to devote himself to more peaceful pursuits, and having obtained his pardon, he ventured at once to return to Rome. He had lost all his hopes in life; his paternal estate had been swept away in the general forfeiture; but he was enabled, however, to obtain sufficient money to purchase a clerkship in the quaestor's office; and on the profits of that place he managed to live with the utmost frugality. Meantime some of his poems attracted the notice of Varius and Virgil, who introduced him to Maecenas (B.C. 39). Horace soon became the friend of Maecenas, and this friendship quickly ripened into intimacy. In a year or two after the commencement of their friendship (37), Horace accompanied his patron on that journey to Brundusium, so agreeably described in the 5th satire of the 1st book. About the year 34 Maecenas bestowed upon the poet a Sabine farm, sufficient to maintain him in ease, comfort, and even in content (*satis beatus unicis Sabinis*), during the rest of his life. The situation of this Sabine farm was in the valley of Ustica, within view of the mountain Lucretilis, and near the Digentia, about 15 miles from Tibur (*Tivoli*). A site exactly answering to the villa of Horace, and on which were found ruins of buildings, has been discovered in modern times. Besides this estate, his admiration of the beautiful scenery in the neighbourhood of Tibur inclined him either to hire or to purchase a small cottage in that romantic town; and all the later years of his life were passed between these two country residences and Rome. He continued to live on the most intimate terms with Maecenas; and this intimate friendship naturally introduced Horace to the notice of the other great men of his period, and at length to Augustus himself, who bestowed upon the poet substantial marks of his favour. Horace died on Nov. 17th, B.C. 8, aged nearly 57.—Horace has described his own person. He was of short stature, with dark eyes and dark hair, but early tinged with grey. In his youth he was tolerably robust, but suffered from a complaint in his eyes. In more advanced life he grew fat, and Augustus jested about his protuberant belly. His health was not always good, and he seems to have inclined to be a valetudinarian. His habits, even after he became richer, were generally frugal and abstemious; though on occasions, both in youth and maturer age, he seems to have indulged in conviviality. He liked choice wine, and in the society of friends scrupled not to enjoy the luxuries of his time. He was never married.—The philosophy of Horace was that of a man of the world. He playfully alludes to his Epicu-

reanism, but it was practical rather than speculative Epicureanism. His mind, indeed, was not in the least speculative. Common life wisdom was his study, and to this he brought a quickness of observation and a sterling common sense, which have made his works the delight of practical men. The *Odes* of Horace want the higher inspirations of lyric verse. But as works of refined art, of the most skilful felicities of language and of measure, of translucent expression, and of agreeable images, embodied in words which imprint themselves indelibly on the memory, they are unrivalled.—In the *Satires* of Horace there is none of the lofty moral indignation, the fierce vehemence of invective, which characterised the later satirists. It is the folly rather than the wickedness of vice which he touches with such playful skill. Nothing can surpass the keenness of his observation, or his ease of expression: it is the finest comedy of manners, in a descriptive instead of a dramatic form.—In the *Epodes*, there is bitterness provoked, it should seem, by some personal hatr d, or sense of injury, and the ambition of imitating Archilochus; but in these he seems to have exhausted all the malignity and violence of his temper.—But the *Epistles* are the most perfect of the Horatian poetry, the poetry of manners and society, the beauty of which consists in a kind of ideality of common sense and practical wisdom. The title of the *Art of Poetry* for the Epistle to the Pisos is as old as Quintilian, but it is now agreed that it was not intended for a complete theory of the poetic art. It is conjectured with great probability that it was intended to dissuade one of the younger Pisos from devoting himself to poetry, for which he had little genius, or at least to suggest the difficulties of attaining to perfection.—The chronology of the Horatian poems is of great importance, as illustrating the life, the times, and the writings of the poet. The 1st book of Satires, which was the first publication, appeared about B.C. 35, in the 30th year of Horace.—The 2nd book of Satires was published about 33, in the 32nd year of Horace. —The Epodes appeared about 31, in the 34th year of Horace.—The 3 first books of the Odes were published about 24 or 23, in the 41st or 42nd year of Horace.—The 1st book of the Epistles was published about 20 or 19, in the 45th or 46th year of Horace.—The Carmen Seculare appeared in 17, in the 48th year of Horace.—The 4th book of the Odes was published in 14 or 13, in his 51st or 52nd year. —The dates of the 2nd book of Epistles, and of the *Ars Poetica*, are admitted to be uncertain, though both appeared before the poet's death, B.C. 8.

HORTA (-ae) or HORTĀNUM (-i), a town in Etruria, at the junction of the Nar and the Tiber, so called from the Etruscan goddess Horta, whose temple at Rome always remained open.

HORTENSĬUS, Q. (-i), the orator, was born in B.C. 114, eight years before Cicero. At the early age of 19 he spoke with great applause in the forum, and at once rose to eminence as an advocate. In the civil wars he joined Sulla, and was afterwards a constant supporter of the aristocratical party. His chief professional labours were in defending men of this party, when accused of maladministration and extortion in their provinces, or of bribery and the like in canvassing for public honours. He had no rival in the forum, till he encountered Cicero, and he long exercised an undisputed sway over the courts of justice. In 81 he was quaestor ; in 75 aedile ; in 72 praetor ; and in 69 consul with Q. Caecilius Metellus. He died in 50. The eloquence of Hortensius was of the florid or (as it was termed) "Asiatic" style, fitter for hearing than for reading. His memory was so ready and retentive, that he is said to have been able to come out of a saleroom and repeat the auction-list backwards. His action was very elaborate ; and the pains he bestowed in arranging the folds of his toga have been recorded by ancient writers. Roscius, the tragedian, used to follow him into the forum to take a lesson in his own art. He possessed immense wealth, and had several splendid villas.—His son Q. HORTENSIUS HORTALUS, was put to death by M. Antony after the battle of Philippi.

HŌRUS (-i), the Egyptian god of the sun, who was also worshipped in Greece, and at Rome.

HOSTĪLĬA (-ae), a small town in Gallia Cisalpina, on the Po, and on the road from Mutina to Verona ; the birthplace of Cornelius Nepos.

HOSTĪLĬUS TULLUS. [TULLUS HOSTILIUS.]

HUNNI (-ōrum), an Asiatic people who dwelt for some centuries in the plains of Tartary, and were formidable to the Chinese empire long before they were known to the Romans. A portion of the nation crossed into Europe, and were allowed by Valens to settle in Thrace, A.D. 376. Under their king Attila (A.D. 434—453), they devastated the fairest portions of the empire ; but a few years after Attila's death their empire was completely destroyed.

HYĂCINTHUS (-i), son of the Spartan king Amyclas, was a beautiful youth, beloved by Apollo and Zephyrus. He returned the love of Apollo ; but as he was once playing at quoits with the god, Zephyrus, out of jealousy, caused the quoit of Apollo to strike the head of the youth, and kill him on the spot. From the blood of Hyacinthus there sprang the flower of the same name (hyacinth), on the leaves of which appeared the exclamation of woe AI, AI, or the letter Υ, being the initial of 'Υάκινθος. According to other traditions, the hyacinth sprang from the blood of Ajax. Hyacinthus was worshipped at Amyclae as a hero, and a great festival, Hyacinthia, was celebrated in his honour.

HYĂDES (-um), that is, the Rainers, the name of nymphs forming a group of 7 stars in the head of Taurus. Their names were Ambrosia, Eudora, Pedile, Coronis, Polyxo, Phyto, and Thyene or Dione. Their number, however, is differently stated by the ancient writers. They were entrusted by Zeus (Jupiter) with the care of his infant son Dionysus (Bacchus), and were afterwards placed by Zeus among the stars. The story which made them the daughters of Atlas relates that their number was 12 or 15, and that at first 5 of them were placed among the stars as Hyades, and the 7 (or 10) others afterwards, under the name of Pleiades, to reward them for the sisterly love they had evinced after the death of their brother Hyas, who had been killed in Libya by a wild beast. The Romans derived their name from ὖς, a pig, and translated it by Suculae. The most natural derivation is from ὑειν, to rain, as the constellation of the Hyades, when rising simultaneously with the sun, announced rainy weather. Hence Horace speaks of the tristes Hyades.

HYAMPŌLIS (-is), a town in Phocis, E. of the Cephissus, near Cleonae, founded by the Hyantes, destroyed by Philip and the Amphictyons.

HYANTES (-um), the ancient inhabitants of Boeotia, from which country they were expelled by the Cadmeans. Part of the Hyantes emigrated to Phocis, where they founded Hyampolis, and part to Aetolia. The poets use the adjective Hyantius as equivalent to Boeotian.

HYĂS (-antis), son of Atlas, and father or brother of the Hyades.

HYBLA (-ae), 3 towns in Sicily.—(1) MAJOR, on the S. slope of Mt. Aetna and on the river Symaethus, was originally a town of the Siculi.—(2) MINOR, afterwards called Megara.—(3) HERAEA, in the S. of the island, on the road from Syracuse to Agrigentum. It is doubtful from which of these 3 places the Hyblaean honey came, so frequently mentioned by the poets.

HYCCĂRA (-ōrum), a town of the Sicani on the N. coast of Sicily, W. of Panormus, taken by the Athenians, and its inhabitants sold as slaves, B.C. 415. Among the captives was the beautiful Timandra, the mistress of Alcibiades and the mother of Lais.

HŸDASPĒS (-ae or -is : *Jelum*), the N.-most of the 5 great tributaries of the Indus, which, with the Indus itself, water the great plain of N. India, which is bounded on the N. by the *Himalaya* range, and which is now called the *Punjab*, i.e. 5 *rivers*. The Hydaspes falls into the Acesines (*Chenab*), which itself falls into the Indus. The epithet "fabulosus," which Horace applies to the Hydaspes, refers to the marvellous stories current among the Romans, who knew next to nothing about India ; and the " *Medus* Hydaspes " of Virgil is merely an example of the vagueness with which the Roman poets refer to the countries beyond the eastern limit of the empire.

HŸDRA. [HERCULES.]

HŸDRĒA (-ae : *Hydra*), a small island in the gulf of Hermione off Argolis, of no importance in antiquity, but the inhabitants of which in modern times played a distinguished part in the war of Greek independence, and are some of the best sailors in Greece.

HŸDRUNTUM (-i) or HŸDRŪS (-untis : *Otranto*), one of the most ancient towns of Calabria, situated on the S.E. coast, near a mountain of the same name : it had a good harbour, from which persons frequently crossed over to Epirus.

HŸGIĒA, also called HŸGĒA or HŸGĪA (-ae), the goddess of health, and a daughter of Aesculapius, though some traditions make her the wife of the latter. In works of art she is represented as a virgin dressed in a long robe, and feeding a serpent from a cup.

HŸLAEUS (-i), that is, the Woodman, the name of an Arcadian centaur, who was slain by Atalante, when he pursued her. According to some legends, Hylaeus fell in the fight against the Lapithae, and according to others he was one of the centaurs slain by Hercules.

HŸLĀS (-ae), a beautiful youth, beloved by Hercules, whom he accompanied in the Argonautic expedition. Having gone on shore, on the coast of Mysia, to draw water, he was carried off by the Naiads, and Hercules long sought for him in vain.

HŸLĒ (-es), a small town in Boeotia, situated on the lake HŸLĬCE, which was called after this town.

HŸLĪĀS (-ae), a river in Bruttium, separating the territories of Sybaris and Croton.

HŸLĬCE. [HYLE.]

HYLLUS (-i), son of Hercules by Deianira, and husband of Iole. Along with the other sons of Hercules, he was expelled from Peloponnesus by Eurystheus, and took refuge at Athens. He was slain in battle by Echemus, king of Arcadia, when he attempted afterwards to enter Peloponnesus.

HYLLUS (-i), a river of Lydia, falling into the Hermus on its N. side.

HŸMEN or HŸMĚNAEUS (-i), the god of marriage, was conceived as a handsome youth, and invoked in the hymeneal or bridal song. The name originally designated the bridal song itself, which was subsequently personified. His parentage is differently stated, but he is usually called the son of Apollo and a Muse. He is represented in works of art as a youth, but taller and with a more serious expression than Eros (Amor), and carrying in his hand a bridal torch.

HŸMETTUS (-i), a mountain in Attica, about 3 miles S. of Athens, celebrated for its marble and its honey.

HYPACŸRIS, HYPACĂRIS, or PACĂRIS (-is), a river in European Sarmatia, flowing through the country of the nomad Scythians, and falling into the Sinus Carcinites in the Euxine sea.

HŸPAEPA (-ōrum), a city of Lydia, on the S. slope of Mt. Tmolus, near the N. bank of the Caÿster.

HŸPĀNIS (-is : *Bog*), a river in European Sarmatia, falling into the Euxine sea W. of the Borysthenes.

HŸPĀTA (-ōrum), a town of the Aenianes in Thessaly, S. of the Spercheus, whose inhabitants were notorious for witchcraft.

HŸPERBŎLUS (-i), an Athenian demagogue in the Peloponnesian war, of servile origin. In order to get rid either of Nicias or Alcibiades, Hyperbolus called for the exercise of the ostracism. But the parties endangered combined to defeat him, and the vote of exile fell on Hyperbolus himself : an application of that dignified punishment by which it was thought to have been so debased that the use of it was never recurred to. Some years afterwards he was murdered by the oligarchs at Samos, B.C. 411.

HŸPERBŎRĚI or -ĒI (-ōrum), a fabulous people, supposed to live in a state of perfect happiness, in a land of perpetual sunshine, *beyond the N. wind ;* whence their name (ὑπερβόρεοι, fr. ὑπὲρ and Βορέας). The poets use the term *Hyperborean* to mean only *most northerly*, as when Virgil and Horace speak of the *Hyperboreae orae* and *Hyperborei campi*. The fable of the Hyperboreans may probably be regarded as one of the forms in which the tr dition of an original period of innocence and happiness existed among the nations of the ancient world.

HŸPERBŎRĚI MONTES was originally the mythical name of an imaginary range of mountains in the N. of the earth, and was afterwards applied by the geographers to various chains, as, for example, the Caucasus, the Rhipaei Montes, and others.

HŸPĚRĬDĒS or HŸPĔRĪDĒS (-is), one of the 10 Attic orators, was a friend of Demosthenes, and one of the leaders of the popular party. He was slain by the emissaries of Antipater, at the end of the Lamian war, B.C. 322. None of his orations are extant.

HŸPĔRĪŌN (-ŏnis), a Titan, son of Uranus (Heaven) and Ge (Earth), and father of Helios (the Sun), Selene (the Moon), and Eos (Aurora). Helios himself is also called *Hyperion*, which is a contraction of the patronymic *Hyperionion*. [HELIOS.]

HŸPERMNESTRA (-ae). (1) Mother of Amphiaraus.—(2) One of the daughters of Danaus and wife of Lynceus. [DANAUS; LYNCEUS.]

HŸPHĂSIS or HŸPĂSIS or HŸPĂNIS (-is), a river of India, falling into the Acesines.

HYPSĪPŸLĒ (-es), daughter of Thoas, king of Lemnos, saved her father, when the Lemnian women killed all the men in the island. When the Argonauts landed there, she bore twin sons to Jason. The Lemnian women subsequently discovered that Thoas was alive, whereupon they compelled Hypsipyle to quit the island. On her flight she was taken prisoner by pirates and sold to the Nemean king, Lycurgus, who entrusted to her care his son Archemorus or Opheltes. [ARCHEMORUS.]

HYRCANĬA (-ae), a province of the ancient Persian Empire, on the S. and S.E. shores of the Caspian or Hyrcanian Sea, and separated by mountains on the W., S., and E., from Media, Parthia, and Margiana. It flourished most under the Parthians, whose kings often resided in it during the summer.

HYRCĀNUM or -ĬUM MARE. [CASPIUM MARE.]

HYRCĀNUS (-i). (1) JOANNES, prince and high-priest of the Jews, was the son and successor of Simon Maccabaeus, the restorer of the independence of Judaea. He succeeded to his father's power B.C. 135, and died in 106. Although he did not assume the title of king, he may be regarded as the founder of the monarchy of Judaea, which continued in his family till the accession of Herod.—(2) High priest and king of the Jews, was the eldest son of Alexander Jannaeus, and his wife, Alexandra; and was frequently engaged in war with his brother Aristobulus. He was put to death by Augustus, B.C. 30. He was succeeded in the kingdom by Herod.

HŸRĬĒ (-es). (1) A town in Boeotia near Tanagra.—(2) A town in Apulia. [URIA.]

HYRMĪNĒ (-es), a town in Elis, mentioned by Homer.

HYRTĂCUS (-i), a Trojan, to whom Priam gave his first wife Arisba, when he married Hecuba. Homer makes him the father of Asius, called *Hyrtăcĭdes.*—In Virgil Nisus and Hippocoon are also represented as sons of Hyrtacus.

HYSĬAE (-ārum). (1) A town in Argolis, S. of Argos, destroyed by the Spartans in the Peloponnesian war.—(2) A town in Boeotia, E. of Plataeae, called by Herodotus a demus of Attica, but probably belonging to Plataeae.

HYSTASPĒS (-is), father of the Persian king Darius I.

IACCHUS (-i), the solemn name of Bacchus in the Eleusinian mysteries, whose name was derived from the boisterous song, called Iacchus. In these mysteries Iacchus was regarded as the son of Zeus (Jupiter), and Demeter (Ceres), and was distinguished from the Theban Bacchus (Dionysus), the son of Zeus and Semele. In some traditions Iacchus is even called a son of Bacchus, but in others the 2 are identified.

IADĔRA, or IADER, a town on the coast of Illyricum.

IĀLŸSUS (-i), one of the 3 ancient Dorian cities in the island of Rhodes, stood on the N.W. coast of the island, about 60 stadia S.W. of Rhodes.

IAMBLĬCHUS (-i), a celebrated Neo-Platonic philosopher, in the reign of Constantine the Great. Among his extant works is a life of Pythagoras.

IAMNĬA (-ae : O. T. Jabneel, Jabneh), a considerable city of Palestine, between Diospolis and Azotus, near the coast, with a good harbour.

IAMUS (-i), son of Apollo and Evadne, received the art of prophecy from his father, and was regarded as the ancestor of the famous family of seers, the Iamidae at Olympia. IANTHĒ. [IPHIS.]

IĂPĒTUS (-i), one of the Titans, son of Uranus (Heaven), and Ge (Earth), and father of Atlas, Prometheus, Epimetheus, and Menoetius. He was imprisoned with Cronus (Saturnus), in Tartarus. His descendants, Prometheus, Atlas, and others, are often designated by the patronymics *Iăpĕtĭdae (es)*, *Iăpĕtĭŏnĭdae (es)*, and the feminine *Iăpĕtĭŏnĭs.*

IĂPŸDES (-um), a warlike and barbarous people in the N. of Illyricum, between the rivers Arsia and Tedanius, were a mixed race, partly Illyrian and partly Celtic, who tattooed their bodies. They were subdued by Augustus. Their country was called IAPYDIA.

ĬĀPȲGĬA (-ae), the name given by the Greeks to the S. of Apulia, from Tarentum and Brundusium to the Prom. Iapygium (*C. Leuca*); though it is sometimes applied to the whole of Apulia. [Apulia.] The name is derived from the mythical Iapyx.

ĬĀPYX (-ȳgis). (1) Son of Lycaon and brother of Daunius and Peucetius, who went as leaders of a colony to Italy. According to others, he was a Cretan, and a son of Daedalus.—(2) The W.N.W. wind, blowing off the coast of Iapygia (Apulia), in the S. of Italy, and consequently favourable to persons crossing over to Greece.

ĬARBAS or HĬARBAS (-ae), king of the Gaetulians, and son of Jupiter Ammon by a Libyan nymph, sued in vain for the hand of Dido in marriage. [Dido.]

ĬARDĀNĒS, king of Lydia, and father of Omphale, who is hence called *Iardănis*.

ĬARDĀNĒS or ĬARDĀNUS (-i). (1) A river in Elis.—(2) A river in the N. of Crete, which flowed near the town Cydonia.

ĬĀSĬON (-ŏnis), ĬĀSĬUS or ĬĀSUS (-i). Son of Zeus (Jupiter), and Electra, beloved by Demeter (Ceres), who became by him the mother of Pluton or Plutus in Crete. From Iasion came the patronymic *ăsĭdes*, a name given to Palinurus, as a descendant of Atlas. —(2) Father of Atalante, who is hence called *Iăsis*.—(3) A city of Caria, founded by Argives and further colonised by Milesians, situated on the *Iassĭus* or *Iassĭcus Sinus*, to which it gave its name.

ĬĀSUS. [Iasius.]

ĬĀZYGĒS (-um), a powerful Sarmatian people, who originally dwelt on the coast of the Pontus Euxinus and the Palus Maeotis, but in the reign of Claudius settled near the Quadi in Dacia, in the country bounded by the Danube, the Theiss, and the Sarmatian mountains.

ĬBĒRĬA (-ae). (1) The name given by the Greeks to Spain. [Hispania.]—(2) (Part of *Georgia*), a country of Asia, in the centre of the isthmus between the Black and Caspian Seas, bounded on the N. by the Caucasus, on the W. by Colchis, on the E. by Albania, and on the S. by Armenia. It was surrounded on every side by mountains, and was famed for a fertility of which its modern name (from Γίωργος) remains a witness. Its inhabitants, Iberes or Iberi, were more civilised than their neighbours in Colchis and Albania. Their chief employment was agriculture. The Romans first became acquainted with the country through the expedition of Pompey, in B.C. 65. No connexion can be traced between the Iberians of Asia and those of Spain.

ĬBĒRUS (-i : *Ebro*), the principal river in the N.E. of Spain, rising among the mountains of the Cantabri, and falling into the Mediterranean, near Dertosa, after forming a delta.

ĬBȲCUS (-i) a Greek lyric poet of Rhegium, spent the best part of his life at Samos, at the court of Polycrates, about B.C. 540. It is related that travelling through a desert place near Corinth, he was murdered by robbers, but before he died he called upon a flock of cranes that happened to fly over him to avenge his death. Soon afterwards, when the people of Corinth were assembled in the theatre, the cranes appeared ; and one of the murderers, who happened to be present, cried out involuntarily, "Behold the avengers of Ibycus :" and thus were the authors of the crime detected.

ĬCĂRĬUS (-i), or ĬCĂRUS (-i). (1) An Athenian, who hospitably received Dionysus in Attica, and was taught in return the cultivation of the vine. Icarius was slain by peasants, who had become intoxicated by some wine which he had given them, and who thought that they had been poisoned by him. His daughter Erigone, after a long search, found his grave, to which she was conducted by his faithful dog Maera. From grief she hung herself on the tree under which he was buried. Zeus (Jupiter), or Dionysus, placed her and Icarius among the stars, making Erigone the *Virgin*, Icarius *Boötes* or *Arcturus*, and Maera *Procyon*, or the little dog. Hence the latter is called *Icarius canis*. —(2) A Lacedaemonian, son of Perieres and Gorgophŏne, or brother of Tyndareus, grandson of Perieres, and son of Oebalus. He promised to give his daughter Penelope to the hero who should conquer in a foot-race ; but when Ulysses won the prize, he tried to persuade her to remain with him. Ulysses allowed her to do as she pleased, whereupon she covered her face with her veil to hide her blushes, thus intimating that she would follow her husband.

ĬCĂRUS (-i), son of Daedalus. [Daedalus.]

ĬCĂRUS (-i), or ĬCĂRĬA (-ae), an island of the Aegean Sea ; one of the Sporades ; W. of Samos. Its common name, and that of the surrounding sea, Ĭcărĭum Mare, were derived from the myth of Icarus. It was first colonised by the Milesians, but afterwards belonged to the Samians.

ĬCCĬUS (-i), a friend of Horace, who addressed to him an ode, in which the poet reprehends delicately his friend's inordinate desire for wealth.

ĬCĒNI (-ŏrum), a powerful people in Britain, dwelling N. of the Trinobantes, in the modern counties of Suffolk and Norfolk. Their revolt from the Romans, under their heroic queen Boadicĕa, is celebrated in history. [BOADICEA.] Their chief town was VENTA ICENORUM (*Caister*), about 3 miles from Norwich.

ICHTHYŎPHĂGI (-ōrum, i.e. *Fish-eaters*), was a vague descriptive name given by the ancients to various peoples on the coasts of Asia and Africa, of whom they knew but little. Thus we find Ichthyophagi : 1. in the extreme S.E. of Asia, in the country of the Sinae : 2. on the coast of GEDROSIA : 3. on the N.E. coast of Arabia Felix : 4. in Africa, on the coast of the Red Sea, above Egypt : 5. on the W. coast of Africa.

ICILĬUS (-i), the name of a celebrated plebeian family, the most distinguished member of which was Sp. Icilius, tribune of the plebs, B.C. 456 and 455. He was one of the chief leaders in the outbreak against the decemvirs, 449, Virginia having been betrothed to him. [VIRGINIA.]

ICŎNĬUM (-i : *Koniyeh*), the capital of Lycaonia, in Asia Minor, was, when visited by St. Paul, a flourishing city.

ĪDA (-ae). (1) A mountain range of Mysia, in Asia Minor, celebrated in mythology, as the scene of the rape of Ganymede (hence called *Idaeus puer*), and of the judgment of Paris (hence called *Idaeus Judex*). In Homer the summit of Ida is the place from which the gods watch the battles in the plain of Troy. It is an ancient seat of the worship of Cybele, who obtained from it the name of *Idaea Mater.*—(2) A mountain in the centre of Crete, closely connected with the worship of Zeus (Jupiter), who is said to have been brought up in a cave in this mountain.

ĪDAEI DACTȲLI. [DACTYLI.]

ĪDĀLĬUM (-i), a town in Cyprus, sacred to Venus, who hence bore the surname *Idalia.*

ĪDĀS (-ae), son of Aphareus and Arene, and brother of Lynceus. From the name of their father, Idas and Lynceus are called *Apharetĭdae* or *Aphărĭdae.* Apollo was in love with Marpessa, the daughter of Evenus, but Idas carried her off in a winged chariot which Poseidon (Neptune) had given him. The lovers fought for her possession, but Zeus (Jupiter), separated them, and left the decision with Marpessa, who chose Idas, from fear lest Apollo should desert her if she grew old. The Aphåretidae also took part in the Calydonian hunt, and in the expedition of the Argonauts. But the most celebrated part of their story is their battle with the Dioscuri, Castor and Pollux, which is related elsewhere [p. 150].

IDISTAVĪSUS CAMPUS, a plain in Germany near the Weser, probably in the neighbourhood of the Porta Westphalica, memor-

able for the victory of Germanicus over the Cherusci, A.D. 16.

IDMŎN (-ŏnis). (1) Father of Arachne, a native of Colophon.—(2) Son of Apollo and Asteria, or Cyrene, was a soothsayer, and accompanied the Argonauts, although he knew beforehand that death awaited him. He perished in the country of the Mariandynians.

ĪDŎMĔNEUS (-ĕi, ĕŏs, or ĕŏs), son of the Cretan Deucalion, and grandson of Minos and Pasiphae, was king of Crete. He is sometimes called *Lyctius* or *Cnossius*, from the Cretan towns of Lyctus and Cnossus. He led the Cretans against Troy, and was one of the bravest heroes in the Trojan war. He vowed to sacrifice to Poseidon (Neptune) whatever he should first meet on his landing, if the god would grant him a safe return. This was his own son, whom he accordingly sacrificed. As Crete was thereupon visited by a plague, the Cretans expelled Idomeneus, who went to Italy, where he settled in Calabria.

ĪDŪMAEA (-ae), the Greek form of the scriptural name EDOM. In the O. T., Edom is the district of Mt. Seir, that is, the mountainous region extending from the Dead Sea to the E. head of the Red Sea. The decline of the kingdom of Judaea enabled the Edomites to extend their power over the S. part of Judaea as far as Hebron, while their original territory was taken possession of by the Nabathaean Arabs. Thus the Idumaea of the later Jewish, and of the Roman history is the S. part of Judaea, and a small portion of the N. of Arabia Petraea, extending from the Mediterranean to the W. side of Mt. Seir. Antipater, the father of Herod the Great, was an Idumaean. The Roman writers of the Augustan and of later ages use Idumaea and Judaea as equivalent terms. Both the old Edomites and the later Idumaeans were a commercial people, and carried on a great part of the traffic between the East and the shores of the Mediterranean.

IDȲIA (-ae), wife of the Colchian king Aeetes, and mother of Medea.

IĒTAE (-ārum), a town in the interior of Sicily, on a mountain of the same name, S. W. of Macella.

ĪGILĬUM (-i : *Giglio*), a small island off the Etruscan coast, opposite Cosa.

ĪGŬVĬUM (-i : *Gubbio* or *Eugubio*), an important town in Umbria, on the S. slope of the Apennines. On a mountain near this town was a celebrated temple of Jupiter, in the ruins of which were discovered 7 brazen tables, covered with Umbrian inscriptions, and which are still preserved at Gubbio. These tables, frequently called the *Eugubian*

Tables, contain more than 1000 Umbrian words, and are of great importance for a knowledge of the ancient languages of Italy.

ILAIRA (-ae), daughter of Leucippus and Philodice, and sister of Phoebe. The 2 sisters are frequently mentioned by the poets under the name of *Leucippidae*. Both were carried off by the Dioscuri, and Ilaira became the wife of Castor.

ILERACONES, ILERCAONENSES, or IL-LURGAVONENSES (-um), a people in Hispania Tarraconensis on the W. coast between the Iberus and M. Idubĕda. Their chief town was DERTOSA.

ILERDA (-ae), a town of the Ilergĕtes in Hispania Tarraconensis, situated on a height above the river Sicoris (*Segre*), which was here crossed by a stone bridge. It was here that Afranius and Petreius, the legates of Pompey, were defeated by Caesar (B.C. 49).

ILERGĒTES (-um), a people in Hispania Tarraconensis, between the Iberus and the Pyrenees.

ILIA or RHEA SILVIA. [ROMULUS.]

ILIENSES, an ancient people in SARDINIA.

ILIONA (-ae), daughter of Priam and Hecuba, wife of Polymnestor or Polymestor, king of the Thracian Chersonesus, to whom she bore a son Deipylus. As to her connexion with Polydorus, see POLYDORUS.

ILIONEUS (-ĕi, ŏŏs, or ĕŏs), a son of Niobe, whom Apollo would have liked to save, because he was praying; but the arrow was no longer under the control of the god. [NIOBE.]

ILIPA, a town in Hispania Baetica, on the right bank of the Baetis, which was navigable to this place with small vessels.

ILISSUS (-i), a small river in Attica, rising on the N. slope of Mt. Hymettus, flowing through the E. side of Athens, and losing itself in the marshes in the Athenian plain.

ILITHYIA (-ae), the goddess of the Greeks, who aided women in child-birth. In the Iliad the Ilithyiae (in the plural) are called the daughters of Hera (Juno); but in the Odyssey and in the later poets, there is only one goddess of this name.

ILIUM. [TROAS.]

ILLIBERIS (-is). (1) (*Tech*), called TICHIS or TECHIUM by the Romans, a river in Gallia Narbonensis in the territory of the Sardones, rising in the Pyrenees and falling, after a short course, into the Mare Gallicum—(2) (*Elne*), a town of the Santones, on the above-mentioned river, at the foot of the Pyrenees. Constantine changed its name into HELENA, whence the modern *Elne*.

ILLITURGIS or ILLITURGI, an important town of the Turduli in Hispania Tarraco-

nensis, situated on a steep rock near the Baetis.

ILLYRICUM (-i) or ILLYRIS (-idis), more rarely ILLYRIA (-ae), was in its widest signification, all the land W. of Macedonia and E. of Italy and Rhaetia, extending S. as far as Epirus, and N. as far as the valleys of the Savus and Dravus, and the junction of these rivers with the Danube. The country was divided into two parts : I. ILLYRIS BARBARA or ROMANA, the Roman province of ILLYRICUM, extended along the Adriatic sea from Italy (Istria), from which it was separated by the Arsia, to the river Drilo, and was bounded on the E. by Macedonia and Moesia Superior, from which it was separated by the Drinus, and on the N. by Pannonia, from which it was separated by the Dravus. It thus comprehended a part of the modern *Croatia*, the whole of *Dalmatia*, almost the whole of *Bosnia*, and a part of *Albania*. It was divided in ancient times into 3 districts : Iapydia, the interior of the country on the N., from the Arsia to the Tedanius [IAPYDES] ; Liburnia, along the coast from the Arsia to the Titius [LIBURNI] ; and Dalmatia, S. of Liburnia, along the coast from the Titius to the Drilo. [DALMATIA.] The Liburnians submitted at an early time to the Romans; but it was not till after the conquest of the Dalmatians in the reign of Augustus, that the entire country was organised as a Roman province. From this time the Illyrians, and especially the Dalmatians, formed an important part of the Roman legions.—II. ILLYRIS GRAECA, or ILLYRIA proper, also called EPIRUS NOVA, extended from the Drilo, along the Adriatic, to the Ceraunian mountains, which separated it from Epirus proper : it was bounded on the E. by Macedonia. It thus embraced the greater part of the modern *Albania*. Its inhabitants were subdued by Philip, the father of Alexander the Great; but after the death of the latter, they recovered their independence. At a later time the injury which the Roman trade suffered from their piracies brought against them the arms of the republic. Their queen Teuta was defeated by the Romans, and compelled to pay an annual tribute, B.C. 229. The Illyrians were again conquered by the consul Aemilius Paulus, 219. Their king Gentius formed an alliance with Perseus, king of Macedonia, against Rome; but he was conquered by the praetor L. Anicius, in the same year as Perseus, 168 ; whereupon Illyria, as well as Macedonia, became subject to Rome. The Illyrian tribes were all more or less barbarous. They were probably of the same origin as the Thracians, but some Celts were mingled with them.

ILUS (-i), son of Tros and Callirhoë, great-grandson of Dardanus; whence he is called *Dardanides.* He was the father of Laomedon and the grandfather of Priam. He was believed to be the founder of Ilion, which was also called Troy, after his father.

ILVA. [AETHALIA.]

ILVĀTES (-um), a people in Liguria, S. of the Po, in the modern *Montferrat.*

IMACHĀRA (-ae), a town in Sicily, in the Heraean mountains.

IMĀUS (-i), the name of a great mountain range of Asia, is one of those terms which the ancient geographers appear to have used indefinitely, for want of exact knowledge. In its most definite application, it appears to mean the W. part of the *Himalaya,* between the Paropamisus and the Emodi Montes but when it is applied to some great chain, extending much farther to the N. and dividing Scythia into 2 parts, Scythia intra Imaum and Scythia extra Imaum, it must either be understood to mean the *Moussour* or *Altai* mountains, or else some imaginary range, which cannot be identified with any actually existing mountains.

IMBROS or IMBRUS (-i), an island in the N. of the Aegean sea, near the Thracian Chersonesus, about 25 miles in circumference. Like the neighbouring island of Samothrace, it was one of the chief seats of the worship of the Cabiri.

INĀCHIS (-ĭdis), a surname of Io, the daughter of Inachus. The goddess Isis is also called *Inachis,* because she was identified with Io: and sometimes *Inachis* is used as synonymous with an Argive or Greek woman. —*Inachides* in the same way was used as a name of Epaphus, a grandson of Inachus, and also of Perseus, because he was born at Argos, the city of Inachus.

INĀCHUS (-i). (1) Son of Oceanus and Tethys, and father of Phoroneus and Io, was the first king of Argos, and said to have given his name to the river Inachus. Some of the ancients regarded him as the leader of an Egyptian or Libyan colony on the banks of the Inachus.—(2) The chief river in Argolis, rising on the borders of Arcadia, receiving near Argos the small river Charadrus, and falling into the Sinus Argolicus S.E. of Argos.

INĀRĬMĒ. [AENARIA.]

INĀROS (-i), son of Psammitichus, a Libyan, and the leader of a revolt of the Egyptians against the Persians, B.C. 461. He was at first successful, but was eventually defeated by the Persians, taken prisoner and crucified, 455.

INDĬA (-ae), was a name used by the Greeks and Romans, much as the modern term *East Indies,* to describe the whole of the S.E. part of Asia, including the 2 peninsulas of *Hindustan,* and of *Burmah, Cochin-China, Siam,* and *Malacca,* and also the islands of the *Indian Archipelago.* The direct acquaintance of the western nations with India dates from the reign of Darius, the son of Hystaspes, who added to the Persian empire a part of its N. W. regions, perhaps only as far as the Indus, certainly not beyond the limits of the *Punjab.* The expedition of ALEXANDER into India first brought the Greeks into actual contact with the country; but the conquests of Alexander only extended within *Scinde,* and the *Punjab,* as far as the river HYPHASIS, down which he sailed into the Indus, and down the Indus to the sea. The Greek king of Syria, Seleucus Nicator, crossed the Hyphasis, and made war with the Prasii, a people dwelling on the banks of the upper Ganges, to whom he afterwards sent ambassadors, named Megasthenes and Daimachus, who lived for several years at Palibothra, the capital of the Prasii, and had thus the opportunity of obtaining much information respecting the parts of India about the Ganges. The later geographers made two great divisions of India, which are separated by the Ganges, and are called India intra Gangem, and India extra Gangem, the former including the peninsula of *Hindustan,* the latter the *Burmese* peninsula. They were acquainted with the division of the people of *Hindustan* into castes, of which they enumerate 7.

INDĬCĒTAE or INDĬGĒTES (-um), a people in the N.E. corner of Hispania Tarraconensis, close upon the Pyrenees. Their chief town was EMPORIUM.

INDĬCUS OCEĂNUS. [ERYTHRAEUM MARE.]

INDĬGĒTES (-um), the name of those indigenous gods and heroes at Rome, who once lived on earth as mortals, and were worshipped after their death as gods. Thus Aeneas, after his disappearance on the banks of the Numicus, became a *deus Indiges, pater Indiges,* or *Jupiter Indiges;* and in like manner Romulus became *Quirinus,* and Latinus *Jupiter Latiaris.*

INDUS (-i). (1) A great river of India, rising in the table land of *Thibet,* and flowing through the great plain of the *Punjab,* into the Erythraeum Mare (*Indian Ocean*), which it enters by several mouths. The ancient name of India was derived from the native name of the Indus (*Sind*).—(2) A considerable river of Asia Minor, rising in Phrygia, and flowing through Caria into the Mediterranean, opposite to Rhodes.

INDUTIOMĀRUS or INDUCIOMĀRUS (-i), one of the leading chiefs of the Treviri in Gaul, defeated and slain by Labienus, B.C. 54. [CINGETORIX.]

INESSA. [AETNA, No. 2.]

INFĔRI (-ōrum), the gods of the nether world, in contradistinction from the *Superi*, or the gods of heaven. But the word *Inferi* is also frequently used to designate the dead, and therefore comprises all the inhabitants of the lower world, both the gods, viz., Hades or Pluto, his wife Persephone (Proserpina), the Erinnyes or Furies, &c., and also as the souls of departed men.

INFĔRUM MARE. [ETRURIA.]

INGAEVŎNES. [GERMANIA.]

INGAUNI (-ōrum), a people in Liguria on the coast, whose chief town was ALBIUM INGAUNUM.

ĪNŌ (-ūs: *acc.* ō), daughter of Cadmus and Harmonia, and wife of Athamas. [ATHA-MAS.]

ĪNŌUS (-i), a name both of Melicertes and of Palaemon, because they were the sons of Ino.

INSŬBRES (-ium), a Gallic people, who crossed the Alps and settled in Gallia Trans-padana in the N. of Italy. Their chief town was MEDIOLANUM. They were conquered by the Romans, shortly before the commence-ment of the 2nd Punic war.

INTĔMĔLĬI (-ōrum), a people in Liguria on the coast, whose chief town was ALBIUM INTEMELIUM.

INTERAMNA (-ae), the name of several towns in Italy, so called from their lying between 2 streams.—(1) (*Terni*), in Umbria, situated on the Nar, and surrounded by a canal flowing into this river, whence its in-habitants were called *Interamnates Nartes*. It was the birthplace of the historian Tacitus. —(2) In Latium, at the junction of the Casinus with the Liris, whence its inha-bitants are called *Interamnates Lirinates*.

INTERCATĬA (-ae), a town of the Vaccaei in Hispania Tarraconensis, on the road from Asturica to Caesaraugusta.

INTERNUM MARE, the *Mediterranean Sea*, extending on the W. from the Straits of Hercules, which separated it from the At-lantic, to the coasts of Syria and Asia Minor on the E. It was called by the Romans *Mare Internum* or *Intestinum ;* by the Greeks ἡ ἔσω θάλαττα or ἡ ἐντὸς θάλαττα, or, more fully, ἡ ἐντὸς Ἡρακλείων στηλῶν θάλαττα, and by Herodotus, ἥδε ἡ θάλαττα ; and from its washing the coasts both of Greece and Italy, it was also called, both by Greeks and Romans *Our Sea* (ἡ ἡμετέρα θάλαττα, ἡ καθ' ἡμᾶς θάλαττα, *Mare Nostrum*). The term *Mare Mediterraneum* is not used by the best

classical writers, and occurs first in Solinus. The ebb and flow of the tide are perceptible in only a few parts of the Mediterranean, such as in the Syrtes on the coast of Africa, in the Adriatic, &c. The different parts of the Mediterranean are called by different names, which are spoken of in separate articles.

INUI CASTRUM. [CASTRUM No. 1.]

ĪŌ (-ūs), daughter of Inachus, first king of Argos, beloved by Zeus (Jupiter), and metamorphosed, through fear of Hera (Juno) into a heifer. The goddess, who was aware of the change, placed her under the care of hundred-eyed Argus, who was, however, slain by Hermes (Mercury), at the command of Zeus. Hera then tormented Io with a gad-fly, and drove her in a state of phrenzy from land to land, until at length she found rest on the banks of the Nile. Here she recovered her original form, and bore a son to Zeus, called Epaphus. [EPAPHUS.] The wanderings of Io were very celebrated in anti-quity, and the Bosporus (i.e. *Ox-ford*) is said to have derived its name from her swimming across it. According to some traditions Io married Ariris or Telegonus, king of Egypt, and was afterwards identified with the Egyp-tian goddess Isis. It appears that Io was identical with the moon ; whence she is represented as a woman, with the horns of a heifer.

IŌBĀTES, king of Lycia. [BELLEROPHON.]

IOL. [CAESAREA, No. 4.]

ĪŎLĀUS (-i), son of Iphicles and Autome-dusa. Iphicles was the half-brother of Her-cules, and Iolaus was the faithful companion and charioteer of the hero. Hercules sent him to Sardinia at the head of his sons by the daughters of Thespius ; but he returned to the hero shortly before his death, and was the first who offered sacrifices to him as a demigod. Iolaus after his death obtained permission from the gods of the Nether World to come to the assistance of the children of Hercules. He slew Eurystheus, and then returned to the shades.

ĪOLCUS (-i), an ancient town in Magnesia in Thessaly at the top of the Pagasean gulf, about a mile from the sea. It was celebrated in mythology as the residence of Pelias and Jason, and as the place from which the Argo-nauts sailed in quest of the golden fleece.

ĪŎLĒ (-es), daughter of Eurytus of Oechalia, beloved by Hercules. [HERCULES.] After the death of Hercules, she married his son Hyllus.

ĪŌN (-ōnis), the fabulous ancestor of the Ionians, son of Xuthus and Creusa, or of Apollo and Creusa, grandson of Helen. Ac-cording to some traditions he reigned in Attica.

ĬŌNĬA (-ae) and ĬŌNIS (-Ĭdis) (Roman poet.), a district on the W. coast of Asia Minor, so called from the Ionian Greeks who colonised it at a time earlier than any distinct historical records. The mythical account of "the great Ionic migration" relates that in consequence of the disputes between the sons of Codrus, king of Athens, about the succession to his government, his younger sons, Neleus and Androclus, crossed the Aegean Sea in search of a new home, 140 years after the Trojan war, or B.C. 1044. In the historical times we find 12 great cities on the above-named coast claiming to be of Ionic origin, and all united into one confederacy. The district they possessed formed a narrow strip of coast, extending between, and somewhat beyond, the mouths of the rivers Meander on the S., and Hermus on the N. The names of the 12 cities, going from S. to N., were MILETUS, MYUS, PRIENE, SAMOS (city and island), EPHESUS, COLOPHON, LEBEDUS, TEOS, ERYTHRAE, CHIOS (city and island), CLAZOMENAE, and PHOCAEA; the city of Smyrna, which lay within this district, but was of Aeolic origin, was afterwards (about B.C. 700) added to the Ionian confederacy. The common sanctuary of the league was the Panionium, a sanctuary of Poseidon (Neptune), on the promontory of Mycale, opposite to Samos; and here was held the great national assembly of the confederacy, called Panionia. At an early period these cities attained a high degree of prosperity. They were first conquered by Croesus, king of Lydia; a second time by Harpagus, the general of Cyrus, B.C. 545; and having revolted from the Persians, they were reconquered by the latter, 496. In no country inhabited by the Hellenic race, except at Athens, were the refinements of civilisation, the arts, and literature, more highly cultivated than in Ionia. Out of the long list of the authors and artists of Ionia, we may mention the poets Mimnermus of Colophon, and Anacreon of Teos; the philosophers, Thales of Miletus, and Anaxagoras of Clazomenae; the early annalists, Cadmus and Hecataeus of Miletus; and the painters, Zeuxis, Apelles, and Parrhasius. The important place which some of the chief cities of Ionia occupy in the early history of Christianity, is attested by the *Acts of the Apostles*, and by the epistles of St. Paul to the Ephesians, and of St. John to the 7 churches of Asia.

ĬŌNĬUM MARE, the sea between Italy and Greece S. of the Adriatic, beginning on the W. at Hydruntum in Calabria, and on the E. at Oricus in Epirus, or at the Ceraunian mountains. In more ancient times the Adriatic was called the Ionian Gulf; while at a later time the Ionium Mare itself was included in the Adriatic. In its widest signification the Ionium Mare included the *Mare Siculum, Creticum,* and *Icarium.* Its name was usually derived by the ancients from the wanderings of Io, but it was more probably so called from the Ionian colonies, which settled in Cephallenia and the other islands off the W. coasts of Greece.

ĬŌPHŌN (-ontis), son of Sophocles, by Nicostrate, was a distinguished tragic poet. For the celebrated story of his undutiful charge against his father, see SOPHOCLES.

ĪPHĬAS (-ădis), i.e. Evadne, a daughter of Iphis, and wife of Capaneus.

ĪPHICLĒS (-is) or ĪPHICLUS (-i). (1) Son of Amphitryon and Alcmene of Thebes, was one night younger than his half-brother Hercules. He was first married to Automedusa, the daughter of Alcathous, by whom he became the father of Iolaus, and afterwards to the youngest daughter of Creon.— (2) Son of Phylacus, or Cephalus, one of the Argonauts, and celebrated for his swiftness in running.

IPHICRATES, a famous Athenian general, son of a shoemaker, introduced into the Athenian army the peltastae or targeteers, a body of troops possessing, to a certain extent, the advantages of heavy and light-armed forces. This he effected by substituting a small target for the heavy shield, adopting a longer sword and spear, and replacing the old coat of mail by a linen corslet. At the head of his targeteers he defeated and nearly destroyed a Spartan Mora, in B.C. 392, an exploit which became very celebrated throughout Greece. He married the daughter of Cotys, king of Thrace, and died shortly before 348.

ĪPHĬGĚNĪA (-ae), daughter of Agamemnon and Clytaemnestra, according to the common tradition; but daughter of Theseus and Helena, according to others. In consequence of Agamemnon having once killed a hart in the grove of Artemis (Diana), the goddess in anger produced a calm, which prevented the Greek fleet in Aulis from sailing against Troy. Upon the advice of the seer Calchas Agamemnon proceeded to sacrifice Iphigenia, in order to appease the goddess; but Artemis put a hart in her place, and carried her to Tauris, where she became the priestess of the goddess. Here she afterwards saved her brother Orestes, when he was on the point of being sacrificed to Artemis, and fled with him to Greece, carrying off the statue of Artemis. Iphigenia was worshipped both in Athens and Sparta; and it is probable that she was originally the same as Artemis herself.

IPHIMEDIA (-ae), or IPHIMEDE (-es), wife of Aloeus, became by Poseidon (Neptune) the mother of the Aloïdae, Otus, and Ephialtes.

IPHIS (-Idis). (1) A youth in love with Anaxarete. [ANAXARETE.]—(2) A Cretan girl, was brought up as a boy, and being betrothed to Ianthe, was metamorphosed by Isis into a youth.

IPHITUS (-i). (1) Son of Eurytus of Oechalia, one of the Argonauts, afterwards killed by Hercules. [HERCULES.]—(2) King of Elis, who restored the Olympic games, and instituted the cessation of all war during their celebration, B.C. 884.

IPSUS (-i), a small town in Great Phrygia, celebrated for the great battle in which Antigonus was defeated and slain by Seleucus and Lysimachus, B.C. 301.

IRA (-ae), a mountain fortress in Messenia, memorable as the place where Aristomenes defended himself for 11 years against the Spartans. Its capture by the Spartans in B.C. 668 put an end to the 2nd Messenian war.

IRENE (-es), called PAX (-ācis), by the Romans, the goddess of peace, was, according to Hesiod, a daughter of Zeus and Themis, and one of the Horae. [HORAE.] She was worshipped at Athens and Rome; and in the latter city a magnificent temple was built to her by the emperor Vespasian. Pax is represented on coins as a youthful female, holding in her left arm a cornucopia, and in her right hand an olive branch or the staff of Mercury.

IRIS (-is or -Idis). (1) Daughter of Thaumas (whence she is called *Thaumantias*) and of

Iris.   (From an ancient Vase.)

Electra, and sister of the Harpies. In the Iliad she appears as the messenger of the gods; but in the Odyssey, Hermes (Mercury),

is the messenger of the gods, and Iris is never mentioned. Iris was originally the personification of the rainbow, which was regarded as the swift messenger of the gods. In the earlier poets, Iris appears as a virgin goddess; but in the later, she is the wife of Zephyrus, and the mother of Eros (Amor). Iris is represented in works of art dressed in a long and wide tunic, over which hangs a light upper garment, with wings attached to her shoulders, carrying the herald's staff in her left hand, and sometimes also holding a pitcher.—(2) (*Yeshil-Irmak*), a considerable river of Asia Minor, rising on the N. side of the Anti-Taurus, and flowing through Pontus into the Sinus Amisenus in the Euxine.

IS (*Hit*), a city in the S. of Mesopotamia, 8 days' journey from Babylon, on the W. bank of the Euphrates, and upon a little river of the same name. In its neighbourhood were the springs of asphaltus, from which was obtained the bitumen that was used, instead of mortar, in the walls of Babylon.

ISAEUS (-i), one of the 10 Attic orators, was born at Chalcis, and came to Athens at an early age. He wrote judicial orations for others, and established a rhetorical school at Athens, in which Demosthenes is said to have been his pupil. He lived between B.C. 420 and 348. Eleven of his orations are extant, all relating to questions of inheritance: they afford considerable information respecting this branch of the Attic law.

ISARA (-ae: *Isère*), a river in Gallia Narbonensis, descending from the Graian Alps, and flowing into the Rhone N. of Valentia.

ISAURIA (-ae), a district of Asia Minor, on the N. side of the Taurus, between Pisidia and Cilicia, whose inhabitants, the Isauri, were daring robbers. They were defeated by the Roman consul, L. Servilius, in B.C. 75, who received in consequence the surname of Isauricus.

ISIONDA (-ae), a city of Pisidia in Asia Minor, near Termessus.

ISIS (-is, -Idis or -Idos), one of the chief Egyptian divinities, wife of Osiris and mother of Horus. She was originally the goddess of the earth, and afterwards of the moon. The Greeks identified her both with Demeter (Ceres), and with Io. [Io.] Her worship was introduced into Rome towards the end of the republic, and became very popular among the Romans under the empire. The most important temple of Isis at Rome stood in the Campus Martius, whence she was called Isis Campensis. The priests and servants of the goddess wore linen garments, whence she herself is called *linigera*.

ISMĂRUS (-i) or ISMĂRA (-ōrum), a town in Thrace, near Maronēa, situated on a mountain of the same name, which produced excellent wine. It is mentioned in the Odyssey as a town of the Cicones. The poets frequently use the adjective *Ismarius* as equivalent to Thracian.

ISMENĒ (-ēs), daughter of Oedipus and Jocasta, and sister of Antigone.

ISMENUS (-i), a small river in Boeotia, rising in Mt. Cithaeron, flowing through Thebes, and falling into the lake Hylica. The brook Dirce, so celebrated in Theban story, flowed into the Ismenus. From this river Apollo was called *Ismenius.*

ISŌCRĂTĒS (-is), one of the 10 Attic orators, was born at Athens B.C. 436, and received a careful education. Among his teachers were Gorgias, Prodicus, and Socrates. He first taught rhetoric in Chios, and afterwards at Athens. At the latter place he met with great success, and gradually acquired a large fortune by his profession. He had 100 pupils, every one of whom paid him 1000 drachmae. He also derived a large income from the orations which he wrote for others ; but being naturally timid, and of a weakly constitution, he did not come forward as a public speaker himself. He was an ardent lover of his country ; and, accordingly, when the battle of Chaeronea had destroyed the last hopes of freedom, he put an end to his life, B.C. 338, at the age of 98. He took great pains with the composition of his orations ; but his style is artificial. Twenty-one of his orations, have come down to us : of these the most celebrated is the Panegyric oration, in which he shows what services Athens had rendered to Greece in every period of her history.

ISSA (-ae : *Lissa*), a small island in the Adriatic sea, with a town of the same name, off the coast of Dalmatia, said to have derived its name from Issa, daughter of Macereus of Lesbos, who was beloved by Apollo. The island was inhabited by a hardy race of sailors, whose barks (*lembi Issaei*) were much prized.

ISSĒDŌNES (-um), a Scythian tribe, in *Great Tartary*, near the Massagetae, whom they resembled in their manners. They are represented as extending as far as the borders of Serica.

ISSĬCUS SINUS. [ISSUS.]

ISSUS (-i), a city in the S. E. extremity of Cilicia, near the head of the Issicus Sinus (*Gulf of Iskenderoon*), and at the N. foot of the pass of M. Amanus called the Syrian Gates ; memorable for the great battle in which Alexander defeated Darius Codomannus (B.C. 333), which was fought in a narrow valley near the town.

ISTAEVŌNES. [GERMANIA.]

ISTER. [DANUBIUS.]

ISTRĬA or HISTRĬA (-ae), a peninsula at the N. extremity of the Adriatic, separated from Venetia by the river Timavus, and from Illyricum by the river Arsia. Its inhabitants, the ISTRI or HISTRI, were a warlike Illyrian race, who carried on several wars with the Romans, till their final subjugation by the consul C. Claudius Pulcher, B.C. 177. Their chief towns were TERGESTE and POLA.

ISTRŌPŎLIS (-is), ISTROS or ISTRĬA (-ae), a town in Lower Moesia, not far from the mouth of the Danube ; a colony from Miletus.

ĪTĂLĬA and ĬTĂLĬA (-ae), signified, from the time of Augustus, the country S. of the Alps, which we call *Italy.* The name Italia was originally used to indicate a much more limited extent of country. Most of the ancients derived the name from an ancient king, Italus ; but there can be no doubt that *Italia*, or *Vitalia*, as it was also called, was the land of the *Itali, Vitali, Vitelli*, or *Vituli*, an ancient race, who are better known under the name of *Siculi.* This race was widely spread over the S. half of the peninsula, and may be said to have been bounded on the N. by a line drawn from Mt. Garganus on the E. to Terracina on the W. The Greeks were ignorant of this wide extent of the name. According to them Italia was originally only the S.-most part of what was afterwards called Bruttium, and was bounded on the N. by a line drawn from the Lametic to the Scylletic gulf. They afterwards extended the name to signify the whole country S. of Posidonia on the W. and Tarentum on the E. After the Romans had conquered Tarentum and the S. part of the peninsula, about B.C. 272, the name Italia had a still further extension given to it. It then signified the whole country subject to the Romans, from the Sicilian straits as far N. as the Arnus and the Rubico. The country N. of these rivers continued to be called Gallia Cisalpina and Liguria down to the end of the republic. Augustus was the first who extended the name of Italia, so as to comprehend the country from the Maritime Alps to Pola in Istria, both inclusive. Besides Italia, the country was called by various other names, especially by the poets. These were HESPERIA, a name which the Greeks gave to it, because it lay to the W. of Greece, or HESPERIA MAGNA, to distinguish it from Spain [HESPERIA], and SATURNIA, because Saturn was said to have once reigned in Latium. The names of separate parts of Italy were also applied by the poets to the whole country. Thus it was called OENOTRIA, originally the land of the Oenotri, in the country afterwards called Bruttium and Lucania : AUSONIA, or OPICA, or OPICIA, originally the land of the Ausones or Ausonii, Opici, or Osci, on the W. coast in the country afterwards called Campania : TYRRHENIA, properly the land of the Tyrrheni, also on the W. coast, N. of Ausonia or Opica, and more especially in the country afterwards called Etruria : IAPYGIA, properly the land of the Iapyges on the E. coast, in the country afterwards called Calabria : and OMBRICA, the land of the Umbri on the E. coast, alongside of Etruria. Italy was never inhabited by one single race. It contained a great number of different races, who had migrated into the country at a very early period. The most ancient inhabitants were Pelasgians or Oenotrians, a branch of the same great race who originally inhabited Greece and the coasts of Asia Minor. They were also called Aborigines and Siculi, who, as we have already seen, were the same as the Vitali or Itali. At the time when Roman history begins, Italy was inhabited by the following races. From the mouth of the Tiber, between its right bank and the sea, dwelt the Etruscans, who extended as far N. as the Alps. Alongside of these, between the left bank of the Tiber and the Adriatic, dwelt the Umbrians. To the S. of the Etruscans were the Sacrani, Casci, or Prisci, Oscan tribes, who had been driven out of the mountains by the Sabines, had overcome the Pelasgian tribes of the Siculi, Aborigines, or Latins, and, uniting with these conquered people, had formed the people called Prisci Latini, subsequently simply Latini. S. of these again, as far as the river Laus, were the Opici, who were also called Ausones or Aurunci, and to whom the Volsci, Sidicini, Saticuli, and Aequi, also belonged. The S. of the peninsula was inhabited by the Oenotrians, who were subsequently driven into the interior by the numerous Greek colonies founded along the coasts. S. of the Umbrians, extending as far as Mt. Garganus, dwelt the various Sabellian or Sabine tribes, the Sabines proper, the Peligni, Marsi, Marrucini, Vestini, and Hernici, from which tribes the warlike race of the Samnites subsequently sprung. From Mt. Garganus to the S.E. extremity of the peninsula, the country was inhabited by the Daunians or Apulians, Peucetii, Messapii, and Sallentini. An account of these people is given in separate articles. They were all eventually subdued by the Romans, who became the masters of the whole of the peninsula. At the time of Augustus the following were the chief divisions of Italy, an account of which is also given in separate articles : I. UPPER ITALY, which extended from the

Alps to the rivers Macra on the W. and Rubico on the E. It comprehended, 1. LIGURIA. 2. GALLIA CISALPINA. 3. VENETIA, including *Carnia.* 4. ISTRIA. II. CENTRAL ITALY, sometimes called ITALIA PROPRIA (a term not used by the ancients), to distinguish it from Gallia Cisalpina or Upper Italy, and Magna Graecia or Lower Italy, extended from the rivers Macra on the W. and Rubico on the E., to the rivers Silarus on the W., and Frento on the E. It comprehended, 1. ETRURIA. 2. UMBRIA. 3. PICENUM. 4. SAMNIUM, including the country of the Sabini, Vestini, Marrucini, Marsi, Peligni, &c. 5. LATIUM, 6. CAMPANIA. III. LOWER ITALY, or MAGNA GRAECIA, included the remaining part of the peninsula, S. of the rivers Silarus and Frento. It comprehended, 1. APULIA, including Calabria. 2. LUCANIA. 3. BRUTTIUM.—Augustus divided Italy into the following 11 Regiones. 1. Latium and Campania. 2. The land of the Hirpini, Apulia and Calabria. 3. Lucania and Bruttium. 4. The land of the Frentani, Marrucini, Peligni, Marsi, Vestini, and Sabini, together with Samnium. 5. Picenum. 6. Umbria and the district of Ariminum, in what was formerly called Gallia Cisalpina. 7. Etruria. 8. Gallia Cispadana. 9. Liguria. 10. The E. part of Gallia Transpadana, Venetia, Carnia, and Istria. 11. The W. part of Gallia Transpadana.

ITALĬCA. (1) A town in Hispania Baetica, on the W. bank of the Baetis, N.W. of Hispalis, founded by Scipio Africanus in the 2nd Punic war, who settled here some of his veterans. It was the birthplace of the emperors Trajan and Hadrian.—(2) The name given to Corfinium by the Italian Socii·during their war with Rome. [CORFᴺIUM.]

ĪTALĬCUS, SILĬUS. [SILIUS.]

ĪTĂLUS. [ITALIA.]

ĪTHĂCA (-ae), a small island in the Ionian Sea, off the coast of Epirus, celebrated as the birthplace of Ulysses. It is about 12 miles long, and 4 in its greatest breadth, and is divided into 2 parts, which are connected by a narrow isthmus, not more than half a mile across. In each of these parts there is a mountain ridge of considerable height ; the one in the N. called *Neritum,* and the one in the S. *Neïum.* The city of Ithaca, the residence of Ulysses, was situated on a precipitous, conical hill, now called *Aeto,* or "eagle's cliff," occupying the whole breadth of the isthmus mentioned above. Ithaca is now one of the 7 Ionian islands under the protection of Great Britain.

ĪTHŌMĔ, (-es), a strong fortress in Messenia, situated on a mountain of the same name, which afterwards formed the citadel of the town of Messene. It was taken by the

Spartans, B.C. 723, at the end of the second Messenian war, and again in 455, at the end of the third Messenian war.

ITIUS PORTUS, a harbour of the Morini, on the N. coast of Gaul, from which Caesar set sail for Britain, probably *Vissant*, or *Witsand*, near Calais.

ITON. [ITONIA.]

ITŌNĬA (-ae), ĬTŌNĬAS (-ădis), or ĬTŌNIS (-ĭdis), a surname of Athena (Minerva), derived from the town of Iton, in the S. of Phthiotis in Thessaly. Here the goddess had a celebrated sanctuary, and hence is called *Incola Itoni*

ĬTŪRAFA, ĬTŸRAEA, a district on the N.E. borders of Palestine, inhabited by an Arabian people, of warlike and predatory habits. Augustus gave Ituraea, which had been hitherto ruled by its native princes, to the family of Herod. During the ministry of our Saviour, it was governed by Philip, the brother of Herod Antipas, as tetrarch.

ĬTYS. [TEREUS.]

IŪLIS (-ĭdis), the chief town in Ceos; the birthplace of Simonides. [CEOS.]

IŪLUS. (1) Son of Aeneas, usually called Ascanius. [ASCANIUS.]—(2) Eldest son of Ascanius, who claimed the government of Latium, but was obliged to give it up to his brother Silvius.

IXĪŌN (-ŏnis), king of the Lapithae, son of Phlegyas, and the father of Pirithous. He treacherously murdered his father-in-law, to avoid paying the bridal gifts he had promised, and when no one would purify him of this treacherous murder, Zeus (Jupiter) carried him up to heaven, and there purified him. But Ixion was ungrateful to the father of the gods, and attempted to win the love of Hera (Juno). Zeus thereupon created a phantom resembling Hera, and by it Ixion became the father of a Centaur. [CENTAURI.] Ixion was fearfully punished for his impious ingratitude. His hands and feet were chained by Hermes (Mercury) to a wheel, which is said to have rolled perpetually in the air.

IXĪŎNĬDĒS (-ae), *i.e.* Pirithous, the son of Ixion.—The Centaurs are also called *Ixionidae.*

JACCETĀNI (-ōrum), a people in Hispania Tarraconensis between the Pyrenees and the Iberus.

JĀNA. [JANUS.]

JĀNĬCŬLUM. [ROMA.]

JĀNUS (-ĭ) and JĀNA (-ae), a pair of ancient Latin divinities, who were worshipped as the sun and moon. The names *Janus* and *Jana* are only other forms of *Dianus* and *Diana*, which words contain the same root as *dies*, day. Janus occupied an important place in the Roman religion. He presided over the beginning of everything, and was therefore always invoked first in every undertaking, even before Jupiter. He opened the year and the seasons, and hence the first month of the year was called after him. He was the porter of heaven, and therefore bore the surnames *Patulcus* or *Patulcius*, the "opener," and *Clusius* or *Clusivius*, the "shutter." On earth also he was the guardian deity of gates, and hence is commonly represented with 2 heads, because every door looks 2 ways (*Janus bifrons*). He is sometimes represented with 4 heads (*Janus quadrifrons*), because he presided over the 4 seasons. At Rome, Numa is said to have dedicated to Janus the covered passage bearing his name, which was opened in times of war, and closed in times of peace. This passage is commonly, but erroneously, called a temple. It stood close by the forum. It appears to have been left open in war, to indicate symbolically that the god had gone out to assist the Roman warriors, and to have been shut in time of peace that the god, the safeguard of the city, might not escape. On new year's day, which was the principal festival of the god, people gave presents to one another, consisting of sweetmeats and copper coins, showing on one side the double head of Janus and on the other a ship. The general name for these presents was *strenae.*

Janus.   (From a Coin of Sex. Pompeius, in the British Museum.)

JĀSŎN (-ŏnis). (1) Son of Aeson and the celebrated leader of the Argonauts. His father Aeson, who reigned at Iolcus in Thessaly, was deprived of the kingdom by his half-brother Pelias, who attempted to take the life of the infant Jason. He was saved by his friends, and intrusted to the care of the centaur Chiron. When he had grown up he came to Iolcus, and demanded the kingdom which Pelias promised to surrender to him, provided he brought the golden fleece, which was in the possession of king Aeëtes in Colchis, and was guarded by an ever-watchful dragon. Jason willingly undertook the enterprise, and set sail in the ship Argo, accompanied by the chief heroes of Greece. He obtained the fleece with the assistance of Medea, whom he made his wife, and along with whom he returned to Iolcus. The history of his exploits on this enterprise is related elsewhere. [ARGONAUTAE.] In order to avenge the death of his father, who had been slain by Pelias during his absence, Medea, at the instigation of Jason, persuaded the daughters of Pelias to cut their father to pieces and boil him, in order to restore him to youth and vigour, as she had before changed a ram into a lamb, by boiling the body in a cauldron. Pelias thus perished miserably; and his son Acastus expelled Jason and Medea from Iolcus. They then went to Corinth, where they lived happily for several years, until Jason deserted Medea, in order to marry Glauce or Creusa, daughter of Creon, the king of the country. Medea fearfully revenged this insult. She sent Glauce a poisoned garment, which burnt her to death when she put it on. Creon likewise perished in the flames. Medea also killed her children by Jason, and then fled to Athens in a chariot drawn by winged dragons. The death of Jason is related variously. According to some, he made away with himself from grief; according to others, he was crushed by the poop of the ship Argo, which fell upon him as he was lying under it.—(2) Tyrant of Pherae, was elected Tagus or generalissimo of Thessaly, B.C. 374. He possessed great power, and aspired to the sovereignty of Greece, but he was assassinated in 370.

JAXARTES (-is : *Syr* or *Syhoun*), a great river of Central Asia, flowing N.W. into the *Sea of Aral :* the ancients supposed it to fall into the N. side of the Caspian, not distinguishing between the 2 seas. It divided Sogdiana from Scythia. On its banks dwelt a Scythian tribe called Jaxartae.

JERICHO or HIERICHUS, a city of the Canaanites, in a plain on the W. side of the Jordan near its mouth, destroyed by Joshua, but afterwards rebuilt.

JERUSALEM or HIEROSOLYMA (-ōrum), the capital of Palestine, in Asia. It was originally the chief city of the Jebusites, a Canaanitish tribe, but was taken by David in B.C. 1050, and was made by him the capital of the kingdom of Israel. After the division of the kingdom, under Rehoboam, it remained the capital of the kingdom of Judah, until it was entirely destroyed, and its inhabitants were carried into captivity by Nebuchadnezzar, king of Babylon, B.C. 588. In 536, the Jewish exiles, having been permitted by Cyrus to return, began to rebuild the city and temple; and the work was completed in about 24 years. After the death of Alexander the Great, Jerusalem was subject first to the Greek kings of Egypt, and afterwards to the Greek kings of Syria ; but in consequence of the attempts made by Antiochus IV. Epiphanes, to root out the national religion, the Jews rose in rebellion under the Maccabees, and eventually succeeded in establishing their independence. Jerusalem now became the capital of a separate kingdom, governed by the Maccabees. Respecting the history of this kingdom see PALAESTINA. In A.D. 70, the rebellion of the Jews against the Romans was put down, and Jerusalem was taken by Titus, after a siege of several months, and was razed to the ground. In consequence of a new revolt of the Jews, the emperor Hadrian resolved to destroy all vestiges of their national and religious peculiarities ; and, as one means to this end, he established a new Roman colony, on the ground where Jerusalem had stood, by the name of AELIA CAPITOLINA, and built a temple of Jupiter Capitolinus, on the site of the temple of Jehovah, A.D. 135. The establishment of Christianity as the religion of the Roman empire restored to Jerusalem its sacred character. Jerusalem stands due W. of the head of the *Dead Sea*, at the distance of about 20 miles (in a straight line) and about 35 miles from the Mediterranean, on an elevated platform, divided, by a series of valleys, from hills which surround it on every side. This platform, has a general slope from W. to E., its highest point being the summit of Mt. Zion, in the S.W. corner of the city, on which stood the original " city of David." The S.E. part of the platform is occupied by the hill called Moriah, on which the temple stood, and the E. part by the hill called Acra ; but these two summits are now hardly distinguishable from the general surface of the platform, probably on account of the gradual filling up of the valleys between. The height of Mt. Zion is 2535 feet above the level of the Mediterranean, and about 300 feet above the valley below.

JOCASTE (-ēs) or JOCASTA (-ae), called EPICASTE (-es), in Homer, wife of Laius, and mother of Oedipus. [OEDIPUS.]

JOPPE (-ēs), JOPPA (-ae : O. T. Japho : *Jaffa*), an ancient maritime city of Palestine, lying S. of the boundary between Judaea and Samaria.

JORDANES (-is : *Jordan*), a river of Palestine, rising at the S. foot of Mt. Hermon (the S.-most part of Anti-Libanus), flowing S. into the Sea of Galilee (Lake of Tiberias), and thence into the lake Asphaltites (*Dead Sea*), where it is finally lost.

JŌSĒPHUS, FLĀVĬUS (-i), the Jewish historian, born at Jerusalem, A.D. 37, was one of the generals of the Jews in their revolt against the Romans. He was taken prisoner by Vespasian, who spared his life through the intercession of Titus. Josephus thereupon assumed the character of a prophet, and predicted to Vespasian that the empire should one day be his and his son's. Josephus was present with Titus at the siege of Jerusalem, and afterwards accompanied him to Rome. He received the freedom of the city from Vespasian, and was treated with great favour by this emperor, and by his successors, Titus and Domitian. He assumed the name of Flavius, as a dependent of the Flavian family, and died about A.D. 100.—The works of Josephus are written in Greek. The most important, entitled *Jewish Antiquities*, in 20 books, gives an account of Jewish History from the creation of the world to A.D. 66, the commencement of the Jewish revolt. An account of this revolt is given by him in his *History of the Jewish War*, in 7 books. In the former of these works he seeks to accommodate the Jewish religion to heathen tastes and prejudices.

JŌVĬĀNUS, FLĀVĬUS CLAUDĬUS (-i), elected emperor by the soldiers, in June, A.D. 363, after the death of Julian [JULIANUS], whom he had accompanied in his campaign against the Persians. He made peace with the Persians, and died in 364, after a reign of little more than 7 months. Jovian was a Christian; but he protected the heathens.

JŪBA (-ae). (1) King of Numidia, and son of Hiempsal, joined Pompey's party, and gained a victory over Curio, Caesar's legate, B.C. 49. He afterwards fought along with Scipio against Caesar; and after the battle of Thapsus (46) he put an end to his own life. —(2) Son of the preceding, was a child at the time of his father's death, and was carried by Caesar to Rome, where he received an excellent education. He became one of the most learned men of his day, and wrote numerous works on historical and other subjects. In B.C. 30, Augustus reinstated him in his paternal kingdom of Numidia, and gave him in marriage Cleopatra, otherwise called Selene, the daughter of Antony and Cleopatra. Five years afterwards (25), Augustus gave him Mauretania in exchange for Numidia, which was reduced to a Roman province. He died in Mauretania, about A.D. 19.

JUDAEA, JUDAEI. [PALAESTINA.]

JŪGURTHA (-ae), an illegitimate son of Mastanabal, and a grandson of Masinissa. He lost his father at an early age, but was brought up by Micipsa, with his own sons,

Hiempsal and Adherbal. Jugurtha was a brave, able, and ambitious prince. He distinguished himself greatly while serving under Scipio against Numantia, in B.C. 134. Micipsa, on his death in 118, bequeathed his kingdom to Jugurtha and his 2 sons, Hiempsal and Adherbal, in common. Jugurtha aspired to the sole sovereignty. He assassinated Hiempsal soon after his father's death, and a division of the kingdom between Jugurtha and Adherbal was then made by the Roman senate; but shortly afterwards Jugurtha attacked Adherbal, took him prisoner, and put him to death (112). The Romans had previously commanded him to abstain from hostilities against Adherbal; and as he had paid no attention to their commands, they now declared war against him. The consul, L. Calpurnius Bestia, was sent into Africa (111); but by large sums of money, Jugurtha purchased from him a favourable peace. But this disgraceful proceeding excited the greatest indignation at Rome. The peace was disowned; and the war renewed under the command of the consul, Sp. Postumius Albinus; but during the absence of the consul, his brother Aulus was defeated by Jugurtha (110). Next year (109) the consul, Q. Caecilius Metellus, was sent into Africa at the head of a new army. In the course of 2 years Metellus frequently defeated Jugurtha, and at length drove him to take refuge among the Gaetulians. In 107 Metellus was succeeded in the command by Marius. The cause of Jugurtha was now supported by his father-in-law Bocchus, king of Mauretania; but Marius defeated their united forces, and Bocchus purchased the forgiveness of the Romans by surrendering his son-in-law to Sulla, the quaestor of Marius (106). Jugurtha was carried a prisoner to Rome, and after adorning the triumph of Marius (Jan. 1, 104), was thrown into a dungeon, and there starved to death.

JŪLĬA (-ae). (1) Aunt of Caesar the dictator, and wife of C. Marius the elder.— (2) Mother of M. Antonius, the triumvir. —(3) Sister of Caesar the dictator, and wife of M. Atius Balbus, by whom she had Atia, the mother of Augustus. [ATIA]. — (4) Daughter of Caesar the Dictator, by Cornelia, was married to Cn. Pompey in 59, and died in childbed in 54.—(5) Daughter of Augustus, by Scribonia, and his only child, born in 39, and thrice married. 1. To M. Marcellus, her first cousin, in 25. 2. After his death (23), without issue, to M. Agrippa, by whom she had 3 sons, C. and L. Caesar, and Agrippa Postumus, and 2 daughters, Julia and Agrippina. 3. After Agrippa's death, in 12, to Tiberius Nero, the future emperor. In consequence of her adulteries, Augustus banished her to Pandataria, an island off the coast of Campania, B.C. 2. She was afterwards removed to Rhegium. She died in A.D. 14, soon after the accession of Tiberius.—(6) Daughter of the preceding, and wife of L. Aemilius Paulus. She inherited her mother's licentiousness, and was, in consequence, banished by her grandfather Augustus to the little island Tremerus, on the coast of Apulia, A.D. 9. She died A.D. 28.—(7) Youngest child of Germanicus and Agrippina, put to death by Claudius, at Messalina's instigation. —(8) Daughter of Drusus and Livia, the sister of Germanicus, also put to death by Claudius, at the instigation of Messalina, 59.

JŪLĬA GENS, one of the most ancient patrician houses at Rome, was of Alban origin, and was removed to Rome by Tullus Hostilius, upon the destruction of Alba Longa. It claimed descent from the mythical Iulus, the son of Venus and Anchises. The most distinguished family in the gens is that of CAESAR.

JŪLĬANUS, FLĀVĬUS CLAUDĬUS, usually called JULIAN, and surnamed the APOSTATE, Roman emperor, A.D. 361—363. He was born at Constantinople, A.D. 331, and was the son of Julius Constantius, and the nephew of Constantine the Great. Julian and his elder brother, Gallus, were the only members of the imperial family whose lives were spared by the sons of Constantine the Great, on the death of the latter in 337. The 2 brothers were educated with care, and were brought up in the principles of the Christian religion. Julian abandoned Christianity in his heart at an early period; but fear of the emperor Constantius prevented him from making an open declaration of his apostacy. He devoted himself with ardour to the study of Greek literature and philosophy; and among his fellow-students at Athens were Gregory of Nazianzus and Basil, both of whom afterwards became so celebrated in the Christian church. Julian did not remain long at Athens. Having been sent by Constantius into Gaul to oppose the Germans, he carried on war against the latter for 5 years (356—360) with great success. In 360 he was proclaimed emperor by his soldiers in Paris; and the opportune death of Constantius in the following year, left him the undisputed master of the empire. He now publicly avowed himself a pagan. His brief reign was chiefly occupied by his military preparations against the Persians. In 363 he crossed the Tigris, and marched into the interior of the country in search of the Persian king· but he was obliged to

retreat in consequence of the sufferings of his army from want of water and provisions. In his retreat he was attacked by the Persians, and slain in battle. He was succeeded by Jovian. [JOVIANUS.] Julian wrote a large number of works, many of which are extant. His style is remarkably pure, and is a close imitation of the style of the classical Greek writers.

JŪLIUS CAESAR. [CAESAR.]

JŪNĬA GENS, an ancient patrician house at Rome, to which belonged the celebrated M. Junius Brutus, who took such an active part in expelling the Tarquins. But afterwards the gens appears as only a plebeian one. The chief families were those of BRUTUS and SILANUS.

JŪNO (-ōnis), called HERA by the Greeks. The Greek goddess is spoken of in a separate article. [HERA.] The word Ju-no contains the same root as Ju-piter. As Jupiter is the king of heaven and of the gods, so Juno is the queen of heaven, or the female Jupiter. She was worshipped at Rome as the queen of heaven, from early times, with the surname of Regina. As Jupiter was the protector of the male sex, so Juno watched over the female sex. She was supposed to accompany every woman through life, from the moment of her birth to her death. Hence she bore the special surnames of Virginalis and Matrona, as well as the general ones of Opigena and Sospita; and under the last mentioned name she was worshipped at Lanuvium. On their birthday women offered sacrifices to Juno, surnamed Natalis; but the great festival, celebrated by all the women in honour of Juno, was called Matronalia, and took place on the 1st of March. From her presiding over the marriage of women, she was called Juga or Jugalis, and had a variety of other names, such as Pronuba, Cinxia, Lucina, &c. The month of June, which is said to have been originally called Junonius, was considered to be the most favourable period for marrying. Women in childbed invoked Juno Lucina to help them, and newly-born children were likewise under her protection: hence she was sometimes confounded with the Greek Artemis or Ilithyia. Juno was further, like Saturn, the guardian of the finances, and under the name of Moneta, she had a temple on the Capitoline hill, which contained the mint.

JŪPITER (Jŏvis) called ZEUS by the Greeks. The Greek god is spoken of in a separate article. [ZEUS.] The Roman Jupiter was originally an elemental divinity, and his name signifies the father or lord of heaven, being a contraction of Diovis pater, or Diespiter. Being the lord of heaven, he was worshipped as the god of rain, storms, thunder, and lightning, whence he had the epithets of *Pluvius, Fulgurator, Tonitrualis, Tonans,* and *Fulminator.* He was the highest and most powerful among the gods, and was hence called the Best and Most High (*Optimus Maximus*). His temple at Rome stood on the lofty hill of the Capitol, whence he derived the surnames of Capitolinus and Tarpeius. He was regarded as the special protector of Rome. As such he was worshipped by the consuls on entering upon their office; and the triumph of a victorious general was a solemn procession to his temple. He therefore bore the surnames of *Imperator, Victor, Invictus, Stator, Opitulus, Feretrius, Praedator, Triumphator,* and the like. Under all these surnames he had temples or statues at Rome. Under the name of *Jupiter Capitolinus,* he presided over the great Roman games; and under the name of *Jupiter Latialis* or *Latiaris,* over the Feriae Latinae. Jupiter, according to the belief of the Romans, determined the course of all human affairs. He foresaw the future; and the events happening in it were the results of his will. He revealed the future to man through signs in the heavens and the flight of birds, which are hence called the messengers of Jupiter, while the god himself is designated as *Prodigialis,* that is, the sender of prodigies. For the same reason the god was invoked at the beginning of every undertaking, whether sacred or profane, together with Janus, who blessed the beginning itself. Jupiter was further regarded as the guardian of law, and as the protector of justice and virtue. He maintained the sanctity of an oath, and presided over all transactions which were based upon faithfulness and justice. Hence Fides was his companion on the Capitol, along with Victoria; and hence a traitor to his country, and persons guilty of perjury, were thrown down from the Tarpeian rock.—As Jupiter was the lord of heaven, and consequently the prince of light, the white colour was sacred to him, white animals were sacrificed to him, his chariot was believed to be drawn by 4 white horses, his priests wore white caps, and the consuls were attired in white when they offered sacrifices in the Capitol the day they entered on their office. The worship of Jupiter at Rome was under the special care of the *Flamen Dialis,* who was the highest in rank of all the flamens.

JURA or JURASSUS MONS, a range of mountains running N. of the lake Lemanus as far as Augusta Rauracorum (*August,* near Basle*), on the Rhine, forming the boundary between the Sequani and Helvetii.

JUSTINIANUS (-i), surnamed THE GREAT, emperor of Constantinople, A.D. 527—565, requires notice in this work on account only of his legislation. He appointed a commission of jurists to draw up a complete body of law. They executed their task by compiling two great works,—one called *Digesta* or *Pandectae,* in 50 books, being a collection of all that was valuable in the works of preceding jurists; and the other called the *Justinianeus Codex,* being a collection of the imperial constitutions. To these two works was subsequently added an elementary treatise, in 4 books, under the title of *Institutiones.* Justinian subsequently published various new constitutions, to which he gave the name of *Novellae Constitutiones.* The 4 legislative works of Justinian, the *Institutiones, Digesta* or *Pandectae, Codex,* and *Novellae,* are included under the general name of *Corpus Juris Civilis,* and form the Roman law, as received in Europe.

JUSTINUS (-i), the historian, of uncertain date, is the author of an extant work entitled *Historiarum Philippicarum Libri XLIV.* This work is taken from the *Historiae Philippicae* of Trogus Pompeius, who lived in the time of Augustus. The title *Philippicae* was given to it, because its main object was to give the history of the Macedonian monarchy, with all its branches; but in the execution of this design, Trogus permitted himself to indulge in so many excursions, that the work formed a kind of universal history from the rise of the Assyrian monarchy to the conquest of the East by Rome. The original work of Trogus, which was one of great value, is lost. The work of Justin is not so much an abridgment of that of Trogus, as a selection of such parts as seemed to him most worthy of being generally known.

JUTURNA (-ae), the nymph of a fountain in Latium, famous for its healing qualities, whose water was used in most sacrifices. A pond in the forum, between the temples of Castor and Vesta, was called Lacus Juturnae. The nymph is said to have been beloved by Jupiter, who rewarded her with immortality and dominion over the waters. Virgil calls her the sister of Turnus.

JUVENALIS (-is), DECIMUS JUNIUS (-i), the great Roman satirist, but of whose life we have few authentic particulars. His ancient biographers relate that he was either the son or the "alumnus" of a rich freedman; that he occupied himself, until he had nearly reached the term of middle life, in declaiming; that, having subsequently composed some clever lines upon Paris the pantomime, he was induced to cultivate assiduously satirical composition; and that in consequence of his attacks upon Paris becoming known to the court, the poet, although now an old man of 80, was appointed to the command of a body of troops, in a remote district of Egypt, where he died shortly afterwards. But the only facts with regard to Juvenal upon which we can implicitly rely are, that he flourished towards the close of the first century, that Aquinum, if not the place of his nativity, was at least his chosen residence, and that he is in all probability the friend whom Martial addresses in 3 epigrams. Each of his satires is a finished rhetorical essay, energetic, glowing, and sonorous. He denounces vice in the most indignant terms; but the obvious tone of exaggeration which pervades all his invectives leaves us in doubt how far this sustained passion is real, and how far assumed for show. The extant works of Juvenal consist of 16 satires, all composed in heroic hexameters.

JŬVENTAS. [HEBE.]

L ABDACIDAE. [LABDACUS.]
LABDĂCUS (-i), son of the Theban king, Polydorus, by Nycteis, daughter of Nycteus. Labdacus lost his father at an early age, and was placed under the guardianship of Nycteus, and afterwards under that of Lycus, a brother of Nycteus. When Labdacus had grown up to manhood, Lycus surrendered the government to him; and on the death of Labdacus, which occurred soon after, Lycus undertook the guardianship of his son Laius, the father of Oedipus. The name *Labdacïdae* is frequently given to the descendants of Labdacus—Oedipus, Polynices, Eteocles, and Antigone.

LABDĂLUM. [SYRACUSAE.]

LABEĀTES (-um), a warlike people in Dalmatia, whose chief town was Scodra, and in whose territory was the Labeatis Palus (*Lake of Scutari*), through which the river Barbana runs.

LĂBEO (-ōnis), ANTISTĬUS (-i). (1) A Roman jurist, one of the murderers of Julius Caesar, put an end to his life after the battle of Philippi, B.C. 42.—(2) Son of the preceding, and a still more eminent jurist. He adopted the republican opinions of his father, and was in consequence disliked by Augustus. It is probable that the *Labeone insanior* of Horace was a stroke levelled against the jurist, in order to please the emperor. Labeo wrote a large number of works, which are cited in the Digest. He was the founder of one of the 2 great legal schools, spoken of under CAPITO.

LĂBERIUS, DĔCĬMUS (-i), a Roman eques, and a distinguished writer of mimes,

was born about B.C. 107, and died in 43 at Puteoli, in Campania. He was compelled by Caesar to appear on the stage in 45 in order to contend with Syrus, a professional mimus, although the profession of a mimus was infamous; but he took his revenge by pointing his wit at Caesar.

LĂBĪCI or LĂVĪCI (-ōrum : *Colonna*), an ancient town in Latium, on a hill of the Alban mountain, 15 miles S.E. of Rome, W. of Praeneste, and N.E. of Tusculum. It was taken by the Romans, B.C. 418.

LĂBIĒNUS (-i). (1) T., tribune of the plebs B.C. 63, was a friend and partisan of Caesar, and his chief legatus in his wars against the Gauls; but on the breaking out of the civil war in B.C. 49, he went over to Pompey. He was slain at the battle of Munda, in Spain, 45.—(2) Q., son of the preceding, invaded Syria at the head of a Parthian army in 40; but the Parthians having been defeated in the following year by P. Ventidius, Antony's legate, he fled into Cilicia, where he was apprehended, and put to death.

LABRANDA (-ōrum), a town in Caria, 68 stadia N. of Mylasa, celebrated for its temple of Zeus (Jupiter).

LABRO (-ōnis), a sea-port in Etruria, perhaps the same as the modern *Livorno* or *Leghorn*.

LABYNĒTUS (-i), a name common to several of the Babylonian monarchs, seems to have been a title rather than a proper name. The Labynetus, mentioned by Herodotus as mediating a peace between Cyaxares and Alyattes, is the same with Nebuchadnezzar. The Labynetus, mentioned by Herodotus as a contemporary of Cyrus and Croesus, is the same with the Belshazzar of the prophet Daniel. By other writers he is called Nabonadius or Nabonidus. He was the last king of Babylon.

LĂCEDAEMŌN. [SPARTA.]

LACETĀNI (-ōrum), a people in Hispania Tarraconensis, at the foot of the Pyrenees.

LĂCHĔSIS (-is), one of the Fates. [MOERAE.]

LĂCĪNIUM (-i), a promontory on the coast of Bruttium, a few miles S. of Croton, and forming the W. boundary of the Tarentine gulf. It possessed a celebrated temple of Juno, who was worshipped here under the surname of Lacinia. The ruins of this temple have given the modern name to the promontory, *Capo delle Colonne.*

LACMON (-ōnis) or LACMUS (-i), the N. part of Mt. Pindus, in which the river Aous takes its origin.

LĂCŌNICA (-ae), sometimes called LĂCŌNIA (-ae) by the Romans, a country of Peloponnesus, bounded on the N. by Argolis and

Arcadia, on the W. by Messenia, and on the E. and S. by the sea. Laconica was a long valley running S.-wards to the sea, and inclosed by mountains on every side except the S. This valley is drained by the river Eurotas, which falls into the Laconian gulf. In the upper part the valley is narrow, and near Sparta the mountains approach so close to each other as to leave little more than room for the channel of the river. It is for this reason that we find the vale of Sparta called the *hollow Lacedaemon*. Below Sparta the mountains recede, and the valley opens out into a plain of considerable extent. The soil of this plain is poor, but on the slopes of the mountains there is land of considerable fertility. Off the coast shell-fish were caught, which produced a purple dye inferior only to the Tyrian. Laconica is well described by Euripides as difficult of access to an enemy. On the N. the country could only be invaded by the valleys of the Eurotas and the Oenus ; the range of Taygetus formed an almost insuperable barrier on the W. ; and the want of good harbours on the E. coast protected it from invasion by sea on that side. Sparta was the only town of importance in the country. [SPARTA.]—The most ancient inhabitants of the country are said to have been Cynurians and Leleges. They were expelled or conquered by the Achaeans, who were the inhabitants of the country in the heroic age. The Dorians afterwards invaded Peloponnesus and became the ruling race in Laconica. Some of the old Achaean inhabitants were reduced to slavery ; but a great number of them became subjects of the Dorians under the name of *Perioeci*. The general name for the inhabitants is LACONES or LACEDAEMONII ; but the *Perioeci* are frequently called Lacedaemonii, to distinguish them from the Spartans.

LĀCŌNĬCUS SINUS, a gulf in the S. of Peloponnesus, into which the Eurotas falls.

LACYDĒS (-is), a native of Cyrene, succeeded Arcesilaus as president of the Academy at Athens, and died about 215.

LADĒ (-es), an island off the W. coast of Caria, opposite to Miletus, and to the bay into which the Maeander falls.

LĀDAS, a swift runner of Alexander the Great.

LĀDŌN (-ŏnis). (1) The dragon who guarded the apples of the Hesperides, was slain by Hercules. [HERCULES.] — (2) A river in Arcadia, rising near Clitor, and falling into the Alphēus, between Heraea and Phrixa. In mythology Ladon is the husband of Stymphalis, and father of Daphne and Metope.—(3) A small river in Elis, rising on the frontiers of Achaia, and falling into the Penēus.

LAEĒTĀNI (-ōrum), a people on the E. coast of Hispania Tarraconensis, near the mouth of the river Rubricatus, probably the same as the LALETANI, whose country, LALETANIA, produced good wine, and whose chief town was BARCINO.

LAELAPS (-ăpis), *i.e.*, the storm wind, personified as the swift dog, which Procris had received from Artemis (Diana), and gave to her husband Cephalus. When the Teumessian fox was sent to punish the Thebans, Cephalus sent the dog Laelaps against the fox. The dog overtook the fox, but Zeus (Jupiter) changed both animals into a stone, which was shown in the neighbourhood of Thebes.

LAELĬUS, C. (-i). (1) The friend of Scipio Africanus, the elder, who fought under the latter in almost all his campaigns. He was consul B.C. 190. —(2) Surnamed SAPIENS, son of the preceding. His intimacy with Scipio Africanus the younger was as remarkable as his father's friendship with the elder, and it obtained an imperishable monument in Cicero's treatise, *Laelius sive de Amicitia*. He was born about 186 ; was tribune of the plebs 151 ; praetor 145 ; and consul 140. He was celebrated for his love of literature and philosophy, and cultivated the society and friendship of the philosopher Panaetius, of the historian Polybius, and of the poets Terence and Lucilius. Laelius is the principal interlocutor in Cicero's dialogue, *De Amicitia*, and is one of the speakers in the *De Senectute*, and in the *De Republica*. His two daughters were married, the one to Q. Mucius Scaevola, the augur ; the other to C. Fannius Strabo.

LAENĀS (-ātis), the name of a family of the Popilia gens, noted for its sternness, cruelty, and haughtiness of character. The chief members of the family were :—(1) C. POPILIUS LAENAS, consul B.C. 172, and afterwards ambassador to Antiochus, King of Syria, whom the senate wished to abstain from hostilities against Egypt. Antiochus was just marching upon Alexandria, when Popilius gave him the letter of the senate, which the king read, and promised to take into consideration with his friends. Popilius straightway described with his cane a circle in the sand round the king, and ordered him not to stir out of it before he had given a decisive answer. This boldness so frightened Antiochus, that he at once yielded to the demand of Rome.—(2) P. POPILIUS LAENAS, consul 132, the year after the murder of Tib. Gracchus. He was charged by the victorious aristocratical party with the prosecution of the accomplices of Gracchus ; and in this odious task he showed all the hard-heartedness of his family. He subsequently withdrew himself, by voluntary exile, from the vengeance of C. Gracchus, and did not return to Rome till after his death.

LĀERTĒS (-ae), king of Ithaca, son of Acrisius, husband of Anticlēa, and father of Ulysses—who is hence called LAERTIADES. Some writers call Ulysses the son of Sisyphus. [ANTICLEA.] Laertes took part in the Calydonian hunt, and in the expedition of the Argonauts. He was still alive when Ulysses returned to Ithaca, after the fall of Troy.

LAERTĬUS, DIOGĔNES. [DIOGENES.]

LAESTRȲGŌNES (-um), a savage race of cannibals, whom Ulysses encountered in his wanderings. They were governed by ANTIPHATES and LAMUS. They belong to mythology rather than to history. The Greeks placed them on the E. coast of Sicily, in the plains of Leontini, which are therefore called *Laestrygonii Campi*. The Roman poets, who regarded the prom. Circeium as the Homeric island of Circe, transplanted the Laestrygones to the S. coast of Latium, in the neighbourhood of Formiae, which they supposed to have been built by Lamus, the king of this people. Hence Horace speaks of *Laestrygonia Bacchus in amphora*, that is, Formian wine; and Ovid calls Formiae, *Laestrygonis Lami Urbs.*

LAEVI or LĒVI (-ōrum), a Ligurian people, in Gallia Transpadana, on the river Ticinus, who, in conjunction with the Marici, built the town of Ticinum (*Pavia*).

LAEVĪNUS, VĂLĔRĬUS (-i). (1) P., consul B.C. 280, defeated by Pyrrhus on the banks of the Siris.—(2) M., praetor 215, when he carried on war against Philip, in Greece; and consul 210, when he carried on the war in Sicily, and took Agrigentum.

LĀGUS. [PTOLEMAEUS.]

LĀIS (-ĭdis), the name of 2 celebrated Grecian courtezans. (1) The elder, a native probably of Corinth, lived in the time of the Peloponnesian war, and was celebrated as the most beautiful woman of her age.—(2) The younger, daughter of Timandra, probably born at Hyccara, in Sicily. According to some accounts she was brought to Corinth when 7 years old, having been taken prisoner in the Athenian expedition to Sicily, and bought by a Corinthian. This story, however, involves numerous difficulties, and seems to have arisen from a confusion between this Lais and the elder one of the same name.

LĀIUS (-i), king of Thebes, son of Labdacus, husband of Jocasta, and father of Oedipus, by whom he was slain. [OEDIPUS.]

LĀLĂGĒ (-es), a common name of courtezans, from the Greek λαλαγή, prattling, used as a term of endearment, "little prattler."

LALETĀNI. [LAEETANI.]

LAMĂCHUS (-i), an Athenian, the colleague of Alcibiades and Nicias, in the great Sicilian expedition, B.C. 415. He fell under the walls of Syracuse, in a sally of the besieged.

LĀMĬA (-ae), a female phantom. [EMPUSA.]

LĀMĬA (-ae), AELĬUS (-i), a Roman family, which claimed descent from the mythical hero, LAMUS. L. AELIUS LAMIA, the friend of Horace, was consul A.D. 3, and the son of the Lamia, who supported Cicero in the suppression of the Catilinarian conspiracy.

LĀMIA (-ae), a town in Phthiotis, in Thessaly, situated on the small river Achelous, 50 stadia inland from the Maliac gulf. It has given its name to the war, which was carried on by the confederate Greeks against Antipater, after the death of Alexander, B.C. 323. When Antipater was defeated by the confederates under the command of Leosthenes, the Athenian, he took refuge in Lamia, where he was besieged for some months.

LAMPĒTĬA (-ae), daughter of Helios (the Sun), and sister of Phaëthon.

LAMPŌNĬA (-ae), or -ĬUM (-i), a city of Mysia, in the interior of the Troad, near the borders of Aeolia.

LAMPSĂCUS (-i), an important city of Mysia, in Asia Minor, on the coast of the Hellespont; a colony of the Phocaeans; celebrated for its wine; and the chief seat of the worship of Priapus.

LĀMUS (-i). (1) Son of Poseidon (Neptune), and king of the Laestrygones, said to have founded Formiae, in Italy. [FORMIAE; LAESTRYGONES.]—(2) A river and town of Cilicia.

LANGOBARDI or LONGOBARDI (-ōrum), corrupted into LOMBARDS, a German tribe of the Suevic race, dwelt originally on the banks of the Elbe, and after many migrations eventually crossed the Alps (A.D. 568), and settled in the N. of Italy, which has ever since received the name of Lombardy. The kingdom of the Lombards existed for upwards of 2 centuries, till its overthrow by Charlemagne.

LĀNŬVĬUM (-i: *Lavigna*), an ancient city in Latium, situated on a hill of the Alban Mount, not far from the Appia Via; possessed an ancient and celebrated temple of Juno Sospita; and was the birthplace of the emperor Antoninus Pius.

LĀŌCŎŌN (-ontis), a Trojan priest of the Thymbraean Apollo. He tried in vain to dissuade his countrymen from drawing into the city the wooden horse, which the Greeks had left behind them when they pretended to sail away from Troy. As he was preparing

to sacrifice a bull to Poseidon, 2 fearful
serpents swam out of the sea, coiled round
Laocoon and his two sons, and destroyed
them. His death forms the subject of a
magnificent work of ancient art preserved in
the Vatican.

Laocoon. (Group in the Vatican.)

LĂŎDĂMĬA (-ae), daughter of Acastus, and
wife of Protesilaus. When her husband was
slain before Troy, she begged the gods to be
allowed to converse with him for only 3
hours. The request was granted. Hermes
(Mercury) led Protesilaus back to the upper
world; and when Protesilaus died a second
time, Laodamia died with him.

LAODĬCĒ (-es). (1) Daughter of Priam
and Hecuba, and wife of Helicaon.—(2) The
name given by Homer to the daughter of
Agamemnon and Clytaemnestra, who is
called Electra by the tragic poets. [ELECTRA.]
—(3) The name of several Greek princesses,
of the family of the Seleucidae, one of whom
was the mother of Seleucus Nicator, the
founder of the Syrian monarchy.

LĂŎDĬCĒA (-ae), the name of several
Greek cities in Asia, called after the mother
of Seleucus I. Nicator, and other Syrian
princesses of this name. (1) L. AD LYCUM,
a city of Phrygia, near the river Lycus, a
tributary of the Maeander, founded by
Antiochus II. Theos. It became one of the
most flourishing cities in Asia Minor, and
was the seat of a flourishing Christian
Church as early as the apostolic age.—(2)
L. COMBUSTA, i.e. the burnt; the reason of

the epithet is doubtful; a city of Lycaonia,
N. of Iconium.—(3) L. AD MARE, a city on
the coast of Syria, about 50 miles S. of
Antioch, built by Seleucus I., and had the best
harbour in Syria.—(4) L. AD LIBANUM, a
city of Coele-Syria, at the N. entrance to the
narrow valley, between Libanus and Antilibanus.

LĂŎMĔDŎN (-ontis), king of Troy, son of
Ilus, and father of Priam, Hesione, and other
children. Poseidon (Neptune) and Apollo,
who had displeased Zeus (Jupiter), were
doomed to serve Laomedon for wages. Accordingly, Poseidon built the walls of Troy,
while Apollo tended the king's flocks on
Mount Ida. When the two gods had done
their work, Laomedon refused them the
reward he had promised them, and expelled
them from his dominions. Thereupon
Poseidon sent a marine monster to ravage
the country, to which the Trojans were
obliged, from time to time, to sacrifice a
maiden. On one occasion it was decided
by lot that Hesione, the daughter of Laomedon, should be the victim; but she was
saved by Hercules, who slew the monster,
upon Laomedon promising to give him the
horses which Tros had once received from
Zeus as a compensation for Ganymedes. But
when the monster was slain, Laomedon again
broke his word. Thereupon Hercules sailed
with a squadron of 6 ships against Troy,
killed Laomedon, with all his sons except
Priam, and gave Hesione to Telamon. Priam,
as the son of Laomedon, is called LAOMEDON-
TIADES; and the Trojans, as the subjects of
Laomedon, are called LAOMEDONTIADAE.]

LAPIDĒI CAMPI. [CAMPI LAPIDEI.]

LĂPĬTHAE (-ārum), a mythical people
inhabiting the mountains of Thessaly. They
were governed by Pirithous, who being a son
of Ixion, was a half-brother of the Centaurs.
The latter, therefore, demanded their share in
their father's kingdom; and, as their claims
were not satisfied, a war arose between the
Lapithae and Centaurs, which, however, was
terminated by a peace. But when Pirithous
married Hippodamīa, and invited the Centaurs to the marriage feast, the latter, fired by
wine, and urged on by Ares (Mars), attempted
to carry off the bride and the other women.
Thereupon a bloody conflict ensued, in which
the Centaurs were defeated by the Lapithae.
The Lapithae are said to have been the inventors of bits and bridles for horses. It is
probable that they were a Pelasgian people,
who defeated the less civilised Centaurs, and
compelled them to abandon Mt. Pelion.

LĂR or LARS (-tis), an Etruscan praenomen, borne, for instance, by Porsena and
Tolumnius. From the Etruscans it passed

over to the Romans, whence we 'read of Lar
Herminius, who was consul B.C. 448. This
word signified lord, king, or hero in the
Etruscan.

LĂRA. [LARUNDA.]

LĂRANDA (-ōrum), a considerable town
in the S. of Lycaonia, at the N. foot of Mt.
Taurus, used by the Isaurian robbers as one
of their strongholds.

LARENTĬA. [ACCA LARENTIA.]

LĂRES (-ium or -um), inferior gods at
Rome, may be divided into 2 classes, *Lares
domestici* and *Lares publici.* The former were
the Manes of a house raised to the dignity of
heroes. The Manes were more closely connected with the place of burial, while the
Lares were the divinities presiding over the
hearth and the whole house. It was only
the spirits of good men that were honoured
as Lares. All the domestic Lares were headed
by the Lar familiaris, who was regarded as
the founder of the family; he was insepa-
rable from the family; and when the latter
changed their abode, he went with them.
Among the *Lares publici* we have mention
made of *Lares praestites* and *Lares com-
pitales.* The former were the protectors of
the whole city; the latter were those who
presided over the several divisions of the
city, which were marked by the compita, or
the points where two or more streets crossed
each other. The images of the Lares, in
great houses, were usually in a separate
compartment, called *lararia.* When the inhabitants of the house took their meals, some
portion was offered to the Lares, and on joyful
family occasions they were adorned with
wreaths, and the lararia were thrown open.

LĂRĪNUM (-i), a town of the Frentani
(whence the inhabitants are sometimes called
Frentani Larinates), on the river Tifernus,
and near the borders of Apulia.

LARISSA (-ae), the name of several
Pelasgian places, whence Larissa is called in
mythology the daughter of Pelasgus.—(1) An
important town of Thessaly, in Pelasgiotis,
situated on the Peneus, in an extensive plain,
and once the capital of the Pelasgi.—(2) Surnamed CREMASTE, another important town of
Thessaly, in Phthiotis, distant 20 stadia from
the Maliac gulf.—(3) An ancient city on the
coast of the Troad.—(4) L. PHRICONIS, a
city on the coast of Mysia, near Cyme, of
Pelasgian origin, but colonised by the Aeolians. It was also called the Egyptian Larissa,
because Cyrus the Great settled in it a body
of his Egyptian mercenary soldiers.—(5) L.
EPHESIA, a city of Lydia, in the plain of the
Cayster.—(6) In Assyria, an ancient city on
the E. bank of the Tigris, some distance N. of
the mouth of the river Zabatas or Lycus. It

was deserted when Xenophon saw it. The
name Larissa is no doubt a corruption of some
Assyrian name (perhaps Al-Assur), which
Xenophon naturally confounded with Larissa,
through his familiarity with the word as the
name of cities in Greece.

LĂRISSUS (-i), a small river forming the
boundary between Achaia and Elis, and
flowing into the Ionian sea.

LĂRĬUS LACUS (*Lake of Como*), a beautiful lake in Gallia Transpadana (N. Italy),
running from N. to S., through which the
river Adda flows. Pliny had several villas
on the banks of the lake.

LARTĬA GENS, patrician, distinguished
at the beginning of the republic through 2
of its members, T. Lartius, the first dictator,
and Sp. Lartius, the companion of Horatius
on the wooden bridge.

LĂRUNDA, or LĂRA (-ae), daughter of
Almon, the nymph who informed Juno of the
connection between Jupiter and Juturna:
hence her name is connected with λαλεῖν. Jupiter deprived her of her tongue, and ordered
Mercury to conduct her into the lower world.
On the way thither Mercury fell in love with
her, and she afterwards gave birth to 2
Lares.

LARVAE. [LEMURES.]

LĂS, an ancient town of Laconia, on the
E. side of the Laconian gulf, 10 stadia from
the sea, and S. of Gytheum.

LASAEA (-ae), a town in the E. of Crete,
not far from the Prom. Samonium, mentioned
in the *Acts of the Apostles.*

LASUS (-i), of Hermione, in Argolis, a
lyric poet, and the teacher of Pindar, lived at
Athens, under the patronage of Hipparchus.
His works have perished.

LĂTĬĀLIS or LĂTĬĀRIS (-is), a surname
of Jupiter as the protecting divinity of
Latium. The Latin towns and Rome celebrated to him every year the feriae Latinae,
on the Alban mount, which were conducted
by one of the Roman consuls. [LATINUS.]

LĂTĬNUS (-i), king of Latium, son of
Faunus and the nymph Marica, brother of
Lavinius, husband of Amata, and father of
Lavinia, whom he gave in marriage to
Aeneas. [LAVINIA.] According to one ac-
count, Latinus, after his death, became
Jupiter Latiaris, just as Romulus became
Quirinus.

LĂTĬUM (-i), a country in Italy, was originally the name of the small district between
the Tiber and the Numicus, and afterwards
signified the country bounded by Etruria on
the N., from which it was separated by the
Tiber; by Campania on the S., from which it
was separated by the Liris; by the Tyrrhene
sea on the W.; and by the Sabine and

Samnite tribes on the E. The greater part of this country is an extensive plain of volcanic origin, out of which rises an isolated range of mountains known by the name of MONS ALBANUS, of which the Algidus and the Tusculan hills are branches. Part of this plain, on the coast between Antium and Tarracina, which was at one time well cultivated, became a marsh in consequence of the rivers Nymphaeus, Ufens, and Amasenus finding no outlet for their waters [POMPTINAE PALUDES]; but the remainder of the country was celebrated for its fertility in antiquity.— The Latini were some of the most ancient inhabitants of Italy. They appear to have been a Pelasgian tribe, and are frequently called Aborigines. At a period long anterior to the foundation of Rome, these Pelasgians or Aborigines descended into the narrow plain between the Tiber and the Numicus, expelled or subdued the Siculi, the original inhabitants of that district, and there became known under the name of Latini. These ancient Latins, who were called *Prisci Latini*, to distinguish them from the later Latins, the subjects of Rome, formed a league or confederation consisting of 30 states. The town of Alba Longa subsequently became the head of the league. This town, which founded several colonies, and among others Rome, boasted of a Trojan origin; but the whole story of a Trojan settlement in Italy is probably an invention of later times. Although Rome was a colony from Alba, she became powerful enough in the reign of her 3rd king, Tullus Hostilius, to take Alba and raze it to the ground. Under Servius Tullius Rome was admitted into the Latin League; and his successor Tarquinius Superbus compelled the other Latin towns to acknowledge Rome as the head of the league. But upon the expulsion of the kings the Latins asserted their independence, and commenced a struggle with Rome, which was not brought to a final close till B.C. 340, when the Latins were defeated by the Romans at the battle of Mt. Vesuvius. The Latin League was now dissolved. Several of the towns, such as Lanuvium, Aricia, Nomentum, Pedum, and Tusculum, received the Roman franchise; and the others became Roman Socii, and are mentioned in history under the general name of *Nomen Latinum* or *Latini*. They obtained certain rights and privileges, which the other Socii did not enjoy. The Romans founded in various parts of Italy many colonies, consisting of Latins, which formed a part of the *Nomen Latinum*, although they were not situated in Latium. Thus the Latini came eventually to hold a certain status intermediate between that of Roman citizens and peregrini.

LATMICUS SINUS (-i), a gulf on the coast of Ionia, in Asia Minor, into which the river Maeander fell, named from Mt. Latmus, which overhangs it. Through the changes effected on this coast by the Maeander, the gulf is now an inland lake, called *Akees-Chai* or *Ufa-Bassi.*

LATMUS (-i), a mountain in Caria, extending in a S.E. direction from the Sinus Latmicus. It was the mythological scene of the story of Selene (Luna) and Endymion, who is hence called by the Roman poets *Latmius heros* and *Latmius venator.*

LATOBRIGI (-ōrum), a people in Gallia Belgica, neighbours of the Helvetii, probably dwelling near the sources of the Rhine, in Switzerland.

LATŎNA. [LETO.]

LAURENTUM (-i), an ancient town of Latium, the residence of the mythical Latinus, situated on a height between Ostia and Ardea, not far from the sea, and surrounded by a grove of laurels, whence it was supposed to have derived its name.

LAURĪUM (-i), a mountain in the S. of Attica, a little N. of the Prom. Sunium, celebrated for its silver mines, which in early times were very productive, but in the time of Augustus yielded nothing.

LAURŌN (-ōnis), a town in the E. of Hispania Tarraconensis, near the sea and the river Sucro.

LAUS (-i), a Greek city in Lucania, near the mouth of the river Laus, which formed the boundary between Lucania and Bruttium.

LAUS POMPEII (*Lodi Vecchio*), a town in Gallia Cisalpina, N.W. of Placentia, and S.E. of Mediolanum, made a municipium by the father of Pompey, whence its name.

LAUSUS (-i). (1) Son of Mezentius, king of the Etruscans, slain by Aeneas.—(2) Son of Numitor and brother of Ilia, killed by Amulius.

LAUTŬLAE (-ārum), a village of the Volsci in Latium, in a narrow pass between Tarracina and Fundi.

LĂVERNA (-ae), the Roman goddess of thieves and impostors, from whom the porta Lavernalis derived its name.

LAVĪCUM. [LABICUM.]

LĀVĪNĬA and LĀVĪNIA (-ae), daughter of Latinus and Amata, betrothed to Turnus, but married to Aeneas. [TURNUS.]

LĀVĪNĬUM, LĂVĪNĬUM, LĀVĪNĬUM (-i), an ancient town of Latium, 3 miles from the sea and 6 miles E. of Laurentum, on the Via Appia, founded by Aeneas, and called Lavinium, in honour of his wife Lavinia.

LĔANDER (-dri), the famous youth of Abydos, who swam every night across the Hellespont to visit Hero, the priestess of

Aphrodite (Venus), in Sestus. One night he perished in the waves; and when his corpse was washed next morning on the coast of Sestus, Hero threw herself into the sea.

LEBADEA (-ae), a town in Boeotia, between Chaeronea and Mt. Helicon, at the foot of a rock, in a cave of which was the celebrated oracle of Trophonius.

LEBEDUS (-i), one of the 12 Ionic cities, situated on the coast of Lydia, between Colophon and Teos. It was nearly deserted in the time of Horace.

LEBINTHUS or LEBYNTHUS (-i), an island in the Aegaean sea, one of the Sporades.

LECHAEUM. [CORINTHUS.]

LECTUM (-i), the S.W. promontory of the Troad, formed by Mt. Ida jutting out into the sea.

LEDA (-ae), daughter of Thestius, whence she is called *Thestias*, wife of Tyndareus, king of Sparta, and mother, either by Zeus (Jupiter) or by Tyndareus, of Castor and Pollux, Clytaemnestra and Helena. According to the common legend Zeus visited Leda in the form of a swan; and she brought forth 2 eggs, from the one of which issued Helena, and from the other Castor and Pollux.

LELEGES (-um), an ancient race, frequently mentioned along with the Pelasgians as the most ancient inhabitants of Greece. The Leleges were a warlike and migratory race, who first took possession of the coasts and the islands of Greece, and afterwards penetrated into the interior. Piracy was probably their chief occupation; and they are represented as the ancestors of the Teleboans and the Taphians, who were notorious for their piracies. The name of the Leleges was derived by the Greeks from an ancestor Lelex, who is called king either of Megaris or Lacedaemon. They must be regarded as a branch of the great Indo-Germanic race, who became gradually incorporated with the Hellenes, and thus ceased to exist as an independent people.

LELEX. [LELEGES.]

LEMANNUS or LEMANUS LACUS (*Lake of Geneva*), a large lake formed by the river Rhodanus, the boundary between the old Roman province in Gaul and the land of the Helvetii.

LEMNOS or LEMNUS (-i), one of the largest islands in the Aegaean sea, situated nearly midway between Mt. Athos and the Hellespont. It was sacred to Hephaestus (Vulcan), who is said to have fallen here, when he was hurled down from Olympus. Hence the workshop of the god is sometimes placed in this island. The legend appears to have arisen from the volcanic nature of Lemnos. Its earliest inhabitants, according

to Homer, were the Thracian *Sinties.* When the Argonauts landed at Lemnos, they found it inhabited only by women, who had murdered all their husbands. [HYPSIPYLE.] By the Lemnian women the Argonauts became the fathers of the *Minyae,* who inhabited the island till they were expelled by the Pelasgians. Lemnos was conquered by one of the generals of Darius; but Miltiades delivered it from the Persians, and made it subject to Athens.

LEMONIA, one of the country tribes of Rome, named after a village Lemonium, situated on the Via Latina before the Porta Capena.

LEMOVICES (-ium), a people in Gallia Aquitanica, between the Bituriges and Arverni, whose chief town was Augustoritum, subsequently called Lemovices, the modern *Limoges.*

LEMOVII (-ōrum), a people of Germany, mentioned along with the Rugii, inhabiting the shores of the Baltic in the modern Pommerania.

LEMURES (-um), the spectres or spirits of the dead. Some writers describe Lemures as the common name for all the spirits of the dead, and divide them into 2 classes; the *Lares,* or the souls of good men, and the *Larvae,* or the souls of wicked men. But the common idea was that the *Lemures* and *Larvae* were the same. They were said to wander about at night as spectres, and to torment and frighten the living. In order to propitiate them the Romans celebrated the festival of the *Lemuralia* or *Lemuria.*

LENAEUS (-i), a surname of Dionysus, derived from *lenus* (ληνός), the wine-press or the vintage.

LENTULUS, a haughty patrician family of the Cornelia gens, of which the most important persons were.—(1) P. CORNELIUS LENTULUS SURA, the man of chief note in Catiline's crew. He was quaestor to Sulla B.C. 81; praetor in 75; consul in 71. In the next year he was ejected from the senate, with 63 others, for infamous life and manners. It was this, probably, that led him to join Catiline and his crew. From his distinguished birth and high rank, he calculated on becoming chief of the conspiracy; and a prophecy of the Sibylline books was applied by flattering haruspices to him. 3 Cornelii were to rule Rome, and he was the 3rd after Sulla and Cinna; the 20th year after the burning of the capitol, &c., was to be fatal to the city. To gain power, and recover his place in the senate, he became praetor again in 63. When Catiline quitted the city for Etruria, Lentulus was left as chief of the home conspirators, and his irresolution probably saved the city from being fired. For it was by his over-caution that the negotiation with the ambassadors of the Allobroges was entered into : these unstable allies revealed the secret to the consul Cicero. The sequel will be found under the life of Catiline. Lentulus was deposed from the praetorship, and was strangled in the Capitoline prison on the 5th of December.—(2) P. CORNELIUS LENTULUS SPINTHER, curule aedile in 63 ; praetor in 60 ; and consul in 57. In his consulship he moved for the immediate recal of Cicero, and afterwards received Cilicia as his province. On the breaking out of the civil war in 49, he joined the Pompeian party.— (3) L. CORNELIUS LENTULUS CRUS, praetor in 58, and consul in 49, when he took a very active part against Caesar. After the battle of Pharsalia, he fled to Egypt, and was put to death by young Ptolemy's ministers.

LEONIDAS (-ae). (1) I. King of Sparta, B.C. 491—480, son of Anaxandrides, and successor of his half-brother Cleomenes. When Greece was invaded by Xerxes, 480, Leonidas was sent with a small army to make a stand against the enemy at the pass of Thermopylae. His forces amounted to somewhat more than 5000 men, of whom only 300 were Spartans. The Persians in vain attempted to force their way through the pass of Thermopylae. They were driven back by Leonidas and his gallant band with immense slaughter. At length the Malian Ephialtes betrayed the mountain path of the Anopaea to the Persians, who were thus able to fall upon the rear of the Greeks. When it became known to Leonidas that the Persians were crossing the mountain, he dismissed all the other Greeks, except the Thespian and Theban forces, declaring that he and the Spartans under his command must needs remain in the post they had been sent to guard. Then, before the body of Persians, who were crossing the mountain, could arrive to attack him in the rear, he advanced from the narrow pass and charged the myriads of the enemy with his handful of troops, hopeless now of preserving their lives, and anxious only to sell them dearly. In the desperate battle which ensued, Leonidas himself fell soon.—(2) II. King of Sparta, son of Cleonymus, ascended the throne, about 256. Being opposed to the projected reforms of his contemporary Agis IV., he was deposed and the throne was transferred to his son-in-law, Cleombrotus ; but he was soon afterwards recalled, and caused Agis to be put to death, 240. He died about 236, and was succeeded by his son, Cleomenes III.

LEONNATUS (-i), a Macedonian of Pella, one of Alexander's generals. He crossed over into Europe in B.C. 322, to assist Antipater against the Greeks ; but he was defeated by the Athenians and their allies, and fell in battle.

LEONTINI (-orum : Lentini), a town in the E. of Sicily, about 5 miles from the sea, N.W. of Syracuse, founded by Chalcidians from Naxos, B.C. 730, but never attained much political importance in consequence of its proximity to Syracuse. The rich plains N. of the city, called Leontini Campi, were some of the most fertile in Sicily, and produced abundant crops of most excellent wheat. It was the birthplace of Gorgias.

LEOPREPIDES, i. e. the poet Simonides, son of Leoprepes.

LEOSTHENES (-is), an Athenian commander of the combined Greek army in the Lamian war, slain while besieging Antipater in the town of Lamia, B.C. 322.

LEOTYCHIDES.—(1) King of Sparta, B.C. 491—469. He commanded the Greek fleet in 479, and defeated the Persians at the battle of Mycale.—(2) The reputed son of Agis II., excluded from the throne, in consequence of his being suspected to be the son of Alcibiades by Timaea, the queen of Agis. His uncle, Agesilaus II., was substituted in his room.

LEPIDUS, M. AEMILIUS (-i), the triumvir, son of M. Lepidus, consul B.C. 78, who took up arms to rescind the laws of Sulla, but was defeated by Pompey and Catulus. His son was praetor in 49, and supported Caesar in the civil war. In 46 he was consul with Caesar, and in 44 he received from the latter the government of Narbonese Gaul and Nearer Spain. He was in the neighbourhood of Rome at the time of the dictator's death, and having the command of an army, he was able to render M. Antony efficient assistance. Lepidus was now chosen pontifex maximus, which dignity had become vacant by Caesar's death, and then repaired to his provinces of Gaul and Spain. Antony after his defeat at Mutina (43) fled to Lepidus, who espoused his cause against the senate. They crossed the Alps at the head of a powerful army, and were joined in the N. of Italy, by Octavian (afterwards Augustus). In the month of October the celebrated triumviraté was formed, by which the Roman world was divided between Augustus, Antony, and Lepidus. [See p. 70.] In the fresh division of the provinces after the battle of Philippi (42), Lepidus received Africa, where he remained till 36. In this year Augustus summoned him to Sicily to assist him in the war against Sex. Pompey. Lepidus obeyed, but tired of being treated as a subordinate, he resolved to make an effort to acquire Sicily for himself. He was easily subdued by Augustus, who spared his life, but deprived him of his triumvirate, his army, and his provinces, and commanded that he should live at Circeii, under strict surveillance. He allowed him, however, to retain his dignity of pontifex maximus. He was not privy to the conspiracy which his son formed to assassinate Augustus in 30. He died in 13. Augustus succeeded him as pontifex maximus.

LEPONTII (-ōrum), an Alpine people, dwelling near the sources of the Rhine, on the S. slope of the St. Gothard and the Simplon : their name is still retained in the *Val Loventina*. Their chief town was Oscela (*Domo d' Ossola*).

LEPREUM (-i), a town of Elis in Triphylia, situated 40 stadia from the sea.

LEPTINES, an Athenian, known only as the proposer of a law taking away all special exemptions from the burden of public charges against which the oration of Demosthenes is directed, usually known as the oration against Leptines, B.C. 355.

LEPTIS (-is). (1) LEPTIS MAGNA or NEAPOLIS, a city on the coast of N. Africa, between the Syrtes, E. of Abrotonum, was a Phoenician colony, with a flourishing commerce, though it possessed no harbour. It was the birthplace of the emperor Septimius Severus.—(2) LEPTIS MINOR or PARVA, usually called simply Leptis, a Phoenician colony on the coast of Byzacium, in N. Africa.

LERNA (-ae) or LERNE (-ēs), a district in Argolis, not far from Argos, in which was a marsh and a small river of the same name. It was celebrated as the place where Hercules killed the Lernean Hydra. [See p. 196.]

LEROS, a small island, one of the Sporades, opposite to the mouth of the Sinus Iassius, on the coast of Caria.

LESBOS or LESBUS (-i), a large island in the Aegean, off the coast of Mysia in Asia Minor. It was colonised by Aeolians, who founded in it an Hexapolis, consisting of the 6 cities, Mytilene, Methymna, Eresus, Pyrrha, Antissa, and Arisbe, afterwards reduced to 5 through the destruction of Arisbe by the Methymnaeans. The chief facts in the history of Lesbos are connected with its principal city, Mytilene. [MYTILENE.] The island is most important in the early history of Greece, as the native region of the Aeolian school of lyric poetry. It was the birthplace of the poets Terpander, Alcaeus, Sappho, and Arion, of the sage Pittacus, of the historian Hellanicus, and of the philosopher Theophrastus.

LETHE, (-ēs), a river in the lower world, from which the shades drank, and thus obtained forgetfulness of the past.

LETO (-ūs), called LATONA (-ae), by the Romans, daughter of the Titan Coeus and Phoebe, and mother of Apollo and Artemis (Diana), by Zeus (Jupiter). The love of the king of the gods procured for Leto the enmity of Hera (Juno). Persecuted by this goddess, Leto wandered from place to place, till she came to Delos, which was then a floating island, and bore the name of Asteria or Ortygia. Zeus fastened it by adamantine chains to the bottom of the sea, that it might be a secure resting-place for his beloved, and there she gave birth to Apollo and Artemis. Leto was generally worshipped only in conjunction with her children. Delos was the chief seat of her worship. From their mother, Apollo is frequently called *Letoïus* or *Latoïus*, and Artemis (Diana) *Letoïa, Letoïs, Latoïs*, or *Latoë*.

Leto (Latona). (From a Painted Vase.)

LEUCA (-ōrum), a town at the extremity of the Iapygian promontory in Calabria.

LEUCAE (-ōrum), LEUCA, a small town on the coast of Ionia, in Asia Minor, near Phocaea.

LEUCAS (-ădis) or LEUCADIA (-ae : *Santa Maura*), an island in the Ionian sea, off the W. coast of Acarnania, about 20 miles in length, and from 5 to 8 miles in breadth. It derived its name from the numerous calcareous hills which cover its surface. It was originally united to the mainland at its N.E. extremity by a narrow isthmus. Homer speaks of it as a peninsula, and mentions its well fortified town *Nericus*. It was at that time inhabited by the Teleboans and Leleges. Subsequently the Corinthians under Cypselus, between B.C. 665 and 625, founded a new town, called *Leucas*. They also cut a canal through the isthmus, and thus converted the peninsula into an island. This canal was afterwards filled up by deposits of sand, but was opened again by the Romans. At present the channel is dry in some parts, and has from 3 to 4 feet of water in others. During the war between Philip and the Romans Leucas was the place where the meetings of the Acarnanian league were held. At the S. extremity of the island, opposite Cephallenia, was the celebrated promontory, variously called *Leucas, Leucātas, Leucātes,* or *Leucāte,* on which was a temple of Apollo Leucadius. At the annual festival of the god it was the custom to cast down a criminal from this promontory into the sea: birds were attached to him, in order to break his fall; and if he reached the sea uninjured, boats were ready to pick him up. This appears to have been an expiatory rite; and it gave rise to the well known story that lovers leaped from this rock, in order to seek relief from the pangs of love. Thus Sappho is said to have leapt down from this rock, when in love with Phaon. [SAPPHO.]

LEUCI (-ōrum), a people in the S.E. of Gallia Belgica, S. of the Mediomatrici, between the Matrona and Mosella: their chief town was Tullum (*Toul*).

LEUCIPPE. [ALCATHOE.]

LEUCIPPĪDES. [LEUCIPPUS, No. 2.]

LEUCIPPUS (-i). (1) Son of Oenomaus, the lover of Daphne. (2) Son of Pericres, prince of the Messenians, and father of Phoebe and Hilaira, usually called Leucippides, who were betrothed to Idas and Lynceus, the sons of Aphareus, but were carried off by Castor and Pollux.—(3) A Grecian philosopher, the founder of the atomic theory of philosophy, which was more fully developed by Democritus. His date is uncertain.

LEUCŌPETRA (-ae: *C. dell' Armi*), a promontory in the S.W. of Bruttium, on the Sicilian straits, and a few miles S. of Rhegium. It derived its name from the white colour of its rocks.

LEUCŌPHRYS, a city of Caria, close to a curious lake of warm water, and having a renowned temple of Artemis Leucophryna.

LEUCŌSĪA or LEUCĀSĪA (-ae : *Piana*), a small island in the S. of the gulf of Paestum, off the coast of Lucania, said to have been called after one of the Sirens.

LEUCŌSÝRI (-ōrum : i.e. *White Syrians*), the name given by the Greeks to the inhabitants of Cappadocia, who were of the Syrian race, in contradistinction to the Syrian tribes of a darker colour beyond the Taurus.

LEUCŌTHĔA (-ae) or LEUCOTHŎE (-es). (1) A marine goddess, was previously Ino, the wife of Athamas. [ATHAMAS.]— (2) Daughter of the Babylonian king Orcha-

mus and Eurynome, beloved by Apollo, was buried alive by her father; whereupon Apollo metamorphosed her into an incense shrub.

LEUCTRA (-ōrum), a small town in Boeotia, on the road from Plataeae to Thespiae, memorable for the victory of Epaminondas and the Thebans over the Spartans, B.C. 371.

LEXOVĬI or LEXOBĬI (-ōrum), a people in Gallia Lugdunensis, on the Ocean, W. of the mouth of the Sequana: their capital was Noviomagus (*Lisieux*).

LIBĀNĬUS (-i), a distinguished Greek sophist and rhetorician, was the teacher of St. Basil and St. Chrysostom, and the friend of the Emperor Julian. He was born at Antioch, on the Orontes, about A.D. 314, and died about 395. Several of his works are extant.

LIBĀNUS (-i), a range of mountains on the confines of Syria and Palestine, dividing Phoenice from Coele-Syria. Its highest summits are covered with perpetual snow, and its sides were in ancient times clothed with forests of cedars. It is considerably lower than the opposite range of ANTILIBANUS. In the Scriptures the word Lebanon is used for both ranges, and for either of them; but in classical authors the names Libanus and Antilibanus are distinctive terms, being applied to the W. and E. ranges respectively.

LĪBENTĪNA, LŪBENTĪNA, or LŪBENTIA (-ae), a surname of Venus among the Romans, by which she is described as the goddess of sensual pleasure.

LĪBER (-bri), or LĪBER PĂTĔR, a name frequently given by the Roman poets to the Greek Bacchus or Dionysus. But the god LIBER, and the goddess LIBERA were ancient Italian divinities, presiding over the cultivation of the vine and the fertility of the fields. Hence they were worshipped in early times in conjunction with Ceres. The female Libera was identified by the Romans with Cora or Proserpĭna, the daughter of Demeter (Ceres); whence Cicero calls Liber and Libera, children of Ceres; whereas Ovid calls Ariadne, Libera.

LĪBĔRA. [LIBER.]

LĪBERTĀS (-ātis), the goddess of Liberty, to whom several temples were erected at Rome. These temples must be distinguished from the Atrium Libertatis, which was used as an office of the censors. Libertas is represented in works of art as a matron, with the pileus, the symbol of liberty, or a wreath of laurel. Sometimes she appears holding the Phrygian cap in her hand.

LĪBĒTHRĬDES [LIBETHRUM.]

LĪBĒTHRĬUS MONS, a mountain in

Boeotia, a branch of Mt. Helicon, possessing a grotto of the Libethrian nymphs.

LĪBĒTHRUM (-i) or LĪBĒTHRA (-ae), an ancient Thracian town in Pieria in Macedonia, on the slope of Olympus, where Orpheus is said to have lived. It was sacred to the Muses, who were hence called *Lībēthrīdes;* and it is probable that the worship of the Muses under this name was transferred from this place to Boeotia.

LIBĬTĪNA (-ae), an ancient Italian divinity, identified by the later Romans with Perse-phŏne (Proserpĭna), on account of her connection with the dead and their burial. At her temple at Rome every thing necessary for funerals was kept, and persons might there either buy or hire such things. Hence a person undertaking the burial of a person (an undertaker) was called *libitinarius,* and his business *libitina;* hence the expression *libitina funeribus non sufficiebat,* i.e. they could not all be buried. Owing to the connection of Libitina with the dead, Roman poets frequently employ her name in the sense of death itself.

LIBȲPHOENĪCES (-um), the inhabitants of the cities founded by the Phoenicians on the coast of the Carthaginian territory, and so called from their being a mixed race of the Libyan natives with the Phoenician settlers.

LĬBŬI (-ōrum), a Gallic tribe in Gallia Cispadana, to whom the towns of Brixia and Verona formerly belonged, from which they were expelled by the Cenomani.

LĬBURNĬA (-ae), a district of Illyricum, along the coast of the Adriatic sea, separated from Istria by the river Arsia, and from Dalmatia by the river Titius. Its inhabitants, the LĬBURNI, supported themselves chiefly by commerce and navigation. They were celebrated at a very early period as bold and skilful sailors. Their ships were remarkable for their swift sailing; and hence vessels built after the same model were called *Liburnicae* or *Liburnae naves.* It was to light vessels of this description that Augustus was mainly indebted for his victory over Antony's fleet at the battle of Actium. The Liburnians were the first Illyrian people who submitted to the Romans.

LĬBȲA (-ae), the Greek name for the continent of Africa in general. [AFRICA.]

LĪCHĀS (-ae), an attendant of Hercules, brought his master the poisoned garment, and was hurled by him into the sea. The Lichades, 3 small islands between Euboea and Locris, were believed to have derived their name from him.

LĬCĪNĬA GENS, to which belonged the distinguished families of CRASSUS, LUCULLUS, and MURENA.

LĬCĪNIUS (-i). (1) C. LICINIUS CALVUS, surnamed STOLO, a name said to be derived from the care with which he dug up the shoots springing from the roots of his vines He brought the contest between the patricians and plebeians to a happy termination, and thus became the founder of Rome's greatness. He was tribune of the people from B.C. 376 to 367, and was faithfully supported in his exertions by his colleague, L. Sextius. The laws which he proposed were :—1. That in future no more consular tribunes should be appointed, but that consuls should be elected, one of whom should always be a plebeian. 2. That no one should possess more than 500 jugera of the public land, or keep upon it more than 100 head of large, and 500 of small cattle. 3. A law regulating the affairs between debtor and creditor. 4. That the Sybilline books should be entrusted to a college of ten men (decem-viri), half of whom should be plebeians. These rogations were passed after a vehement opposition on the part of the patricians, and L. Sextius was the first plebeian who obtained the consulship, 366. Licinius himself was elected twice to the consulship, 364 and 361. Some years later he was accused by M. Popilius Laenas of having transgressed his own law respecting the amount of public land which a person might possess. He was condemned and sentenced to pay a heavy fine.—(2) C. LICINIUS MACER, an annalist and an orator, was impeached of extortion by Cicero, and finding that the verdict was against him, committed suicide, B.C. 66.—(3) C. LICINIUS MACER CALVUS, son of the last, a distinguished orator and poet, was born B.C. 82, and died about 47 or 46, in his 35th or 36th year. His most celebrated oration was delivered against Vatinius, who was defended by Cicero, when he was only 27 years of age. His elegies have been warmly extolled by Catullus, Propertius, and Ovid. All his works are lost.

LĬCĪNĬUS (-i), Roman emperor A.D. 307—324, was a Dacian peasant by birth, and was raised to the rank of Augustus by the emperor Galerius. He afterwards had the dominion of the East. He carried on war first with Maximinus II., whom he defeated A.D. 314, and subsequently with Constantine, by whom he was in his turn defeated, 315. A second war broke out between Licinius and Constantine in 323, in which Licinius was not only defeated, but deprived of his throne. In the following year he was put to death by Constantine, 324.

LIDE (-es), a mountain of Caria, above Pedasus.

LĪGĀRIUS (-i), Q., fought on the side of the

Pompeian party in Africa, and was defended by Cicero before Caesar in a speech still extant. Ligarius joined the conspirators, who assassinated Caesar in B.C. 44, and perished in the proscription of the triumvirs in 43.

LIGER or LIGERIS (-is: *Loire*), a large river in Gaul, rising in Mt. Cevenna, flowing through the territories of the Arverni, Aedui, and Carnutes, and falling into the ocean between the territories of the Namnetes and Pictones.

LIGURIA (-ae), a district of Italy, bounded on the W. by the river Varus, and the Maritime Alps, which separated it from Transalpine Gaul, on the S.E. by the river Macra, which separated it from Etruria, on the N. by the river Po, and on the S. by the Mare Ligusticum. The Maritime Alps and the Apennines run through the greater part of the country. The inhabitants were called by the Greeks LIGYES and LIGYSTINI, and by the Romans LIGURES (sing. *Ligus*, more rarely *Ligur*). They were in early times widely spread, and inhabited the coasts of Gaul and Italy, from the mouth of the Rhone to Pisae in Etruria. They were divided by the Romans into *Ligures Transalpini* and *Cisalpini*. The names of the principal tribes were :—on the W. side of the Alps, the SALYES or SALLUVII, OXYBII, and DECIATES ; on the E. side of the Alps, the INTEMELII, INGAUNI and APUANI near the coast, the VAGIENNI, SALASSI and TAURINI on the upper course of the Po, and the LAEVI and MARISCI N. of the Po.—The Ligurians were small of stature, but strong, active, and brave. In early times they served as mercenaries in the armies of the Carthaginians, and they were not subdued by the Romans till after a long and fierce struggle.

LILAEA (-ae), an ancient town in Phocis, near the sources of the Cephissus.

LILYBAEUM (-i : *Marsala*), a town in the W. of Sicily, with an excellent harbour, situated on a promontory of the same name, opposite to the Prom. Hermaeum or Mercurii (*C. Bon*) in Africa, the space between the two being the shortest distance between Sicily and Africa. The town was founded by the Carthaginians about B.C. 397, and was the principal Carthaginian fortress in Sicily.

LIMITES (-um) ROMANI (-orum), the name of a continuous series of fortifications, consisting of castles, walls, earthen ramparts, and the like, which the Romans erected along the Rhine and the Danube, to protect their possessions from the attacks of the Germans.

LIMNAE (-arum), a town in Messenia, on the frontiers of Laconia, with a temple of Artemis (Diana) Limnatis.

LIMNAEA (-ae), a town in the N. of Acarnania, near the Ambracian gulf, on which it had a harbour.

LIMONUM. [PICTONES.]

LIMYRA (-ae), a city in the S.E. of Lycia, on the river Limyrus.

LINDUM (-i : *Lincoln*), a town of the Coritani, in Britain, on the road from Londinium to Eboracum, and a Roman colony. The modern name *Lincoln* has been formed out of Lindum Colonia.

LINDUS (-i), one of the 3 Dorian cities in the island of Rhodes, situated on the E. coast.

LINGONES (-um). (1) A powerful people in Transalpine Gaul, bounded by the Treviri on the N., and the Sequani on the S. Their chief town was Andematurinum, afterwards Lingones (*Langres*).—(2) A branch of the above-mentioned people, who migrated into Cisalpine Gaul along with the Boii, and dwelt in the neighbourhood of Ravenna.

LINTERNUM. [LITERNUM.]

LINUS (-i), the personification of a dirge or lamentation, and therefore described as a son of Apollo by a muse (Calliope, or by Psamathe or Chalciope). Both Argos and Thebes claimed the honour of his birth. An Argive tradition related, that Linus was exposed by his mother after his birth, and was brought up by shepherds, but was afterwards torn to pieces by dogs. Psamathe's grief at the occurrence betrayed her misfortune to her father, who condemned her to death. Apollo, indignant at the father's cruelty, visited Argos with a plague ; and, in obedience to an oracle, the Argives endeavoured to propitiate Psamathe and Linus by means of sacrifices and dirges which were called lini. According to a Boeotian tradition Linus was killed by Apollo, because he had ventured upon a musical contest with the god. The Thebans distinguished between an earlier and later Linus; the latter is said to have instructed Hercules in music, but to have been killed by the hero.

LIPARA and LIPARENSES INSULAE. [AEOLIAE.]

LIPS, the S.W. wind, corresponding to the Latin Africus.

id. Lips. (From the Temple of the Winds, at Athens.)

LIQUENTIA (-ae: *Livenza*), a river in

Venetia in the N. of Italy, flowing into the Sinus Tergestinus.

LIRIS (-is: *Garigliano*), more anciently called CLANIS (-is) or GLANIS, one of the principal rivers in central Italy, rising in the Apennines W. of lake Fucinus, flowing into the Sinus Caietanus near Minturnae, and forming the boundary between Latium and Campania. Its stream was sluggish, whence the " Liris *quieta* aqua " of Horace.

LISSUS (-i), a town in the S. of Dalmatia, at the mouth of the river Drilon, founded by Dionysius of Syracuse, B.C. 385, and possessing a strongly fortified acropolis called ACRO-LISSUS, which was considered impregnable.

LITANA SILVA, a large forest on the Apennines, in Cisalpine Gaul, S.E. of Mutina.

LITERNUM or LINTERNUM (-i : *Patria*), a town on the coast of Campania, at the mouth of the river Clanis or Glanis, which in the lower part of its course takes the name of LITERNUS, and which flows through a marsh to the N. of the town, called LITERNA PALUS. It was to this place that the elder Scipio Africanus retired, when the tribunes attempted to bring him to trial, and here he is said to have died.

LIVIA (-ae). (1) Sister of M. Livius Drusus, the celebrated tribune, B.C. 91, married first to M. Porcius Cato, by whom she had Cato Uticensis, and subsequently to Q. Servilius Caepio, by whom she had a daughter, Servilia, the mother of M. Brutus, who killed Caesar. —(2) LIVIA DRUSILLA, the daughter of Livius Drusus Claudianus [DRUSUS, No. 3], married first to Tib. Claudius Nero ; and afterwards to Augustus, who compelled her husband to divorce her B.C. 38. She had already borne her husband one son, the future emperor Tiberius, and at the time of her marriage with Augustus was 6 months pregnant with another, who subsequently received the name of Drusus. She never had any children by Augustus, but she retained his affections till his death. On the accession of her son Tiberius to the throne, she at first attempted to obtain an equal share in the government ; but this the jealous temper of Tiberius would not brook. She died in A.D. 29, at the age of 82 or 86.—(3) Or LIVILLA, the daughter of Drusus senior and Antonia, and the wife of Drusus junior, the son of the emperor Tiberius. She was seduced by Sejanus, who persuaded her to poison her husband, A.D. 23.—(4) JULIA LIVILLA, daughter of Germanicus and Agrippina. [JULIA, No. 7.]

LIVIUS (-i), T., the Roman historian, was born at Patavium (*Padua*), in the N. of Italy, B.C. 59. The greater part of his life was spent in Rome, but he returned to his native town before his death, which happened at the age of 76, in the fourth year of Tiberius, A.D. 17. His literary talents secured the patronage of Augustus ; and so great was his reputation, that a Spaniard travelled from Cadiz to Rome, solely for the purpose of beholding him, and having gratified his curiosity, immediately returned home. The great work of Livy is a History of Rome, extending from the foundation of the city to the death of Drusus, B.C. 9, and comprised in 142 books. Of these 35 have descended to us ; but of the whole, with the exception of 2, we possess *Epitomes*. The work has been divided into *decades*, containing 10 books each. The 1st decade (bks. i—x.) is entire, and embraces the period from the foundation of the city to the year B.C. 294. The 2nd decade (bks. xi—xx) is lost, and embraced the period from 294 to 219, comprising an account, among other matters, of the invasion of Pyrrhus and of the first Punic war. The 3rd decade (bks. xxi—xxx) is entire. It embraces the period from 219 to 201, comprehending the whole of the 2nd Punic war. The 4th decade (bks. xxxi—xl) is entire, and also one half of the 5th (bks. xli—xlv). These 15 books embrace the period from 201 to 167, and develope the progress of the Roman arms in Cisalpine Gaul, in Macedonia, Greece, and Asia, ending with the triumph of Aemilius Paulus. Of the remaining books nothing remains except inconsiderable fragments. The style of Livy is clear, animated, and eloquent ; but he did not take much pains in ascertaining the truth of the events he records. His aim was to offer to his countrymen a clear and pleasing narrative, which, while it gratified their vanity, should contain no startling improbabilities nor gross perversion of facts.

LIVIUS ANDRONICUS (-i), the earliest Roman poet, was a Greek, and the slave of M. Livius Salinator, by whom he was manumitted, and from whom he received the Roman name Livius. He wrote both tragedies and comedies in Latin, and his first drama was acted B.C. 240.

LIVIUS DRUSUS. [DRUSUS.]

LIVIUS SALINATOR. [SALINATOR.]

LIXUS (-i), a city on the W. coast of Mauretania Tingitana, in Africa, at the mouth of a river of the same name : it was a place of some commercial importance.

LOCRI (-orum), sometimes called LOCRENSES (-ium), by the Romans, the inhabitants of two districts in Greece, called LOCRIS.—(1) EASTERN LOCRIS, extending from Thessaly and the pass of Thermopylae along the coast to the frontiers of Boeotia, and bounded by Doris and Phocis on the W. It was a fertile and well cultivated country. The N. part was inhabited by the Locri Epicnemidii, who derived their name from Mt. Cnemis. The S. part was inhabited by the Locri Opuntii, who derived their name from their principal town, Opus. The 2 tribes were separated by Daphnus, a small slip of land, which at one time belonged to Phocis. The Epicnemidii were for a long time subject to the Phocians, and were included under the name of the latter people; whence the name of the Opuntii occurs more frequently in Greek history.—(2) Western Locris, or the country of the Locri Ozolae, was bounded on the N. by Doris, on the W. by Actolia, on the E. by Phocis, and on the S. by the Corinthian gulf. The country is mountainous, and for the most part unproductive. Mt. Corax from Aetolia, and Mt. Parnassus from Phocis, occupy the greater part of it. The Locri Ozolae were a colony of the Western Locrians, and were more uncivilised than the latter. They resembled their neighbours, the Aetolians, both in their predatory habits and in their mode of warfare. Their chief town was Amphissa.

LOCRI EPIZEPHYRII (-ōrum), one of the most ancient Greek cities in Lower Italy, situated in the S.E. of Bruttium, N. of the promontory of Zephyrium, from which it was said to have derived its surname Epizephyrii, though others suppose this name given to the place, simply because it lay to the W. of Greece. It was founded by the Locrians from Greece, B.C. 683. The inhabitants regarded themselves as descendants of Ajax Oileus; and as he resided at the town of Naryx among the Opuntii, the poets gave the name of Narycia to Locris, and called the founders of the town the Narycii Locri. For the same reason the pitch of Bruttium is frequently called Narycia. Locri was celebrated for the excellence of its laws, which were drawn up by Zaleucus soon after the foundation of the city. [Zaleucus.] Near the town was an ancient and wealthy temple of Proserpina.

LOCUSTA, or, more correctly, LUCUSTA (-ae), a famous female poisoner, employed by Agrippina in poisoning the emperor Claudius, and by Nero for despatching Britannicus. She was put to death in the reign of Galba.

LOLLIUS (-i), M., consul, B.C. 21, and governor of Gaul, B.C. 16, was appointed by Augustus as tutor to his grandson, C. Caesar, whom he accompanied to the East, B.C. 2. Horace addressed an Ode (iv. 9) to Lollius, and 2 Epistles (i. 2, 18) to the eldest son of Lollius.

LONDINIUM(-i) or LONDINUM(London), the capital of the Cantii in Britain, was originally situated on the S. bank of the Thames in the modern Southwark. It afterwards spread over the N. side of the river, and was hence called a town of the Trinobantes. It is first mentioned in the reign of Nero as a flourishing and populous town, much frequented by Roman merchants. It was taken and its inhabitants massacred by the Britons, when they revolted under Boadicea, A.D. 62. The quarter on the N. side of the river was surrounded with a wall and ditch by Constantine the Great or Theodosius, the Roman governor of Britain. This wall probably commenced at a fort near the present site of the tower, and continued along the Minories, to Cripplegate, Newgate, and Ludgate. London was the central point, from which all the Roman roads in Britain diverged. It possessed a Milliarium Aureum, from which the miles on the roads were numbered; and a fragment of this Milliarium, the celebrated London Stone, may be seen affixed to the wall of St. Swithin's Church in Cannon Street. This is almost the only monument of the Roman Londinium still extant, with the exception of coins, tesselated pavements, and the like, which have been found buried under the ground.

LONGINUS (-i), a distinguished Greek philosopher and grammarian of the 3rd century of our era. He taught philosophy and rhetoric at Athens for many years with great success; and among his pupils was the celebrated Porphyry. He afterwards went to the East, where he became acquainted with Zenobia, of Palmyra, who made him her teacher of Greek literature. It was mainly through his advice that she threw off her allegiance to the Roman empire. On her capture by Aurelian in 273, Longinus was put to death by the emperor. Longinus was a man of excellent sense, sound judgment, and extensive knowledge. His treatise On the Sublime, a great part of which is still extant, is a work of great merit.

LONGINUS CASSIUS. [Cassius.]

LONGOBARDI. [Langobardi.]

LONGULA (-ae), a town of the Volsci in Latium, not far from Corioli.

LONGUS (-i), a Greek sophist, of uncertain date, the author of an extant erotic work.

LORIUM (-i) or LORII (-ōrum), a small place in Etruria, on the Via Aurelia, where Antoninus Pius was brought up and died.

LORYMA (-ōrum), a city on the S. coast of Caria.

LOTIS (-idis), a nymph, who. to escape the embraces of Priapus, was metamorphosed into a tree, called after her Lotus.

LOTOPHAGI (-ōrum, i.e. lotus-eaters). Homer, in the Odyssey, represents Ulysses as coming in his wanderings to a coast inhabited by a people who fed upon a fruit called lotus, the taste of which was so delicious that every one who eat it lost all wish to return to his native country. Afterwards, in historical times, the Greeks found that the people on the N. coast of Africa, between the Syrtes, used, to a great extent, as an article of food, the fruit of a plant, which they identified with the lotus of Homer, and they called these people Lotophagi. They carried on a commercial intercourse with Egypt and with the interior of Africa, by the very same caravan routes which are used to the present day.

LŬA (-ae), also called LŬA MĀTER or LŬA SATURNI, one of the early Italian divinities, to whom were dedicated the arms taken in battle.

LŪCA (-ae : *Lucca*), a Ligurian city in Upper Italy, at the foot of the Apennines and on the river Ausus, N.E. of Pisae.

LŪCĀNIA (-ae), a district in Lower Italy, bounded on the N. by Campania and Samnium, on the E. by Apulia and the gulf of Tarentum, on the S. by Bruttium, and on the W. by the Tyrrhene sea. It was separated from Campania by the river Silarus, and from Bruttium by the river Laus. Lucania was celebrated for its excellent pastures ; and its oxen were the finest and largest in Italy. Hence the elephant was at first called by the Romans a Lucanian ox (*Lucas bos*). The coast of Lucania was inhabited chiefly by Greeks, whose cities were numerous and flourishing. The interior of the country was originally inhabited by the Chones and Oenotrians. The Lucanians proper were Samnites, a brave and warlike race, who left their mother-country and settled both in Lucania and Bruttium. They not only expelled or subdued the Oenotrians, but they gradually acquired possession of most of the Greek cities on the coast. They were subdued by the Romans after Pyrrhus had left Italy.

LŪCĀNUS, M. ANNAEUS (-i), usually called LUCAN, a Roman poet, born at Corduba in Spain, A.D. 39. His father was L. Annaeus Mella, a brother of M. Seneca, the philosopher. Lucan was brought up at Rome at an early age. He embarked in the conspiracy of Piso against the life of Nero ; and upon the discovery of the plot was compelled to put an end to his life. He died A.D. 65, in the 26th year of his age. There is extant an heroic poem, by Lucan, in 10 books, entitled *Pharsalia*, in which the progress of the struggle between Caesa and Pompey is fully detailed. The 10th book is imperfect, and the narrative breaks off abruptly in the middle of the Alexandrian war.

LŪCĀNUS, OCELLUS. [OCELLUS.]

LUCCEIUS (-i), L., an old friend and neighbour of Cicero, was an unsuccessful candidate for the consulship, along with Julius Caesar, in B.C. 60. He wrote a contemporaneous history of Rome, commencing with the Social or Marsic war.

LŪCĒRĬA (-ae : *Lucera*), sometimes called NŪCĒRĬA, a town in Apulia on the borders of Samnium, and subsequently a Roman colony.

LŪCĬĀNUS (-i), usually called LUCIAN, a Greek writer, born at Samosata, the capital of Commagene, in Syria, flourished in the reign of M. Aurelius. He practised for some time as an advocate at Antioch, and afterwards travelled through Greece, giving instruction in rhetoric. Late in life he obtained the office of procurator of part of Egypt. The most important of Lucian's writings are his *Dialogues*. They are treated in the greatest possible variety of style, from seriousness down to the broadest humour and buffoonery. Their subjects and tendency, too, vary considerably ; for while some are employed in attacking the heathen philosophy and religion, others are mere pictures of manners without any polemic drift. Lucian's merits as a writer consist in his knowledge of human nature, his strong common sense, and the simplicity and Attic grace of his diction.

LŪCIFER (-ěri), or PHOSPHŎRUS (-i), that is, the bringer of light, is the name of the planet Venus, when seen in the morning before sunrise. The same planet was called *Hesperus*, *Vesperugo*, *Vesper*, *Noctifer*, or *Nocturnus*, when it appeared in the heavens after sunset. Lucifer as a personification is called a son of Astraeus and Aurora or Eos, of Cephalus and Aurora, or of Atlas. By Philonis he is said to have been the father of Ceyx. He is also called the father of Daedalion and of the Hesperides. Lucifer is also a surname of several goddesses of light, as Artemis, Aurora, and Hecate.

LŪCĪLIUS (-i), C., the Roman satirist, was born at Suessa of the Aurunci, B.C. 148, and died at Naples, 103, in the 46th year of his age. He lived upon terms of the closest familiarity with Scipio and Laelius. He was the first to mould Roman satire into that form which afterwards received full development in the hands of Horace, Persius, and Juvenal.

LŪCĪNA (-ae), the goddess of light, or rather the goddess that brings to light, and hence the goddess that presides over the birth of children. It was therefore used as a surname of Juno and Diana. Lucina corresponded to the Greek goddess ILITHYIA.

LUCRĒTĬA (-ae), the wife of L. Tarquinius Collatinus, whose rape by Sex. Tarquinius led to the dethronement of Tarquinius Superbus and the establishment of the republic. [TARQUINIUS.]

LUCRĒTĬLIS (-is), a pleasant mountain in the country of the Sabines, overhanging Horace's villa.

LUCRĒTĬUS CARUS, T., the Roman poet, born B.C. 95, is said to have been driven mad by a love potion, and to have perished by his own hand, B.C. 52 or 51. It is however not improbable that the story of the love potion and of his death was an invention of some enemy of the Epicureans. Lucretius is the author of a philosophical poem, in heroic hexameters, divided into 6 books, addressed to C. Memmius Gemellus, who was praetor in 58, and entitled *De Rerum Natura*. It contains an exposition of the doctrines of Epicurus. This poem has been admitted by all modern critics to be the greatest of didactic poems. The most abstruse speculations are clearly explained in majestic verse ; while the subject, which in itself was dry and dull, is enlivened by digressions of power and beauty.

LUCRĪNUS (-i), LĂCUS, was properly the inner part of the Sinus Cumanus or Puteolanus, a bay on the coast of Campania, between the promontory Misenum and Puteoli, running a considerable way inland. But at a very early period the Lucrine lake was separated from the remainder of the bay by a dyke 8 stadia in length, and thus assumed the character of an inland lake. Its waters still remained salt, and were celebrated for their oyster beds. Behind the Lucrine lake was another lake called LACUS AVERNUS. In the time of Augustus, Agrippa made a communication between the lake Avernus and the Lucrine lake, and also between the Lucrine lake and the Sinus Cumanus, thus forming out of the 3 celebrated Julian Harbour. The Lucrine lake was filled up by a volcanic eruption in 1538, when a conical mountain rose in its place, called *Monte Nuovo*.

LŪCULLUS, L. LĬCĬNĬUS (-i), celebrated as the conqueror of Mithridates, fought on the side of Sulla in the civil wars with the Marian party, was praetor B.C. 77, and consul 74. In the latter year he received the conduct of the war against Mithridates, which he carried on for 8 years with great success. [MITHRIDATES.] But being unable to bring the war to a conclusion in consequence of the mutinous disposition of his troops, he was superseded in the command by Acilius Glabrio, B.C. 67. Glabrio however never took the command ; but in the follow-

ing year (66), Lucullus had to resign the command to Pompey, who had been appointed by the Manilian law to supersede both him and Glabrio. On his return to Rome Lucullus devoted himself to a life of indolence and luxury, and lived in a style of extraordinary magnificence. He died in 57 or 56. He was the first to introduce cherries into Italy, which he had brought with him from Cerasus in Pontus. He was a patron of the poet Archias, and of literary men in general. He also composed a history of the Marsic war in Greek.

LŪCŬMO. [TARQUINIUS.]

LUGDŪNUM (-i). (1) (*Lyon*), the chief town of Gallia Lugdunensis, situated at the foot of a hill at the confluence of the Arar (*Saône*) and the Rhodanus (*Rhone*), was made a Roman colony B.C. 43, and became under Augustus the capital of the province, and the residence of the Roman governor. Lugdunum is memorable in the history of the Christian church as the seat of the bishopric of Irenaeus.—(2) L. BATAVORUM (*Leyden*), the chief town of the Batavi. [BATAVI.]

LŪNA (-ae). (1) The goddess of the Moon. [SELENE.]—(2) (*Luni*), an Etruscan town, situated on the left bank of the Macra, about 4 miles from the coast, originally formed part of Liguria, but became the most N.-ly city of Etruria, when Augustus extended the boundaries of the latter country as far as the Macra. It possessed a large and commodious harbour at the mouth of the river, called Lunae Portus (*Gulf of Spezzia*). In B.C. 177 Luna was made a Roman colony.

LŪPERCUS (-i), an ancient Italian divinity, worshipped by shepherds as the protector of their flocks against wolves. The Romans sometimes identified Lupercus with the Arcadian Pan. Respecting the festival celebrated in honour of Lupercus and his priests, the Luperci, see *Dict. of Ant.*

LUPPĬA or LUPĬA (-ae : *Lippe*), a river in the N. W. of Germany, falling into the Rhine at *Wesel* in *Westphalia*, and on which the Romans built a fortress of the same name.

LŪPUS, RŬTĬLĬUS (-i), the author of an extant rhetorical treatise in 2 books, entitled *De Figuris Sententiarum et Elocutionis*, appears to have lived in the time of Augustus.

LŪSĬTĀNĬA, LŪSĬTĀNI. [HISPANIA.]

LŪTĀTĬUS CĂTŬLUS. [CATULUS.]

LŪTĒTĬA (-ae), or, more commonly, LUTETIA PARISIORUM (*Paris*), the capital of the Parisii in Gallia Lugdunensis, was situated on an island in the Sequana (*Seine*), and was connected with the banks of the river by 2 wooden bridges. Under the emperors it became a place of importance, and the chief naval station on the Sequana. Here Julian was proclaimed emperor, A.D. 360.

LȲCĂBETTUS (-i: *St. George*), a mountain in Attica, belonging to the range of Pentelicus, close to the walls of Athens on the N.E. of the city.

LȲCAEUS or LȲCĒUS (-i), a lofty mountain in Arcadia, N.W. of Megalopolis, one of the chief seats of the worship of Zeus (Jupiter), and of Pan, each of whom was therefore called *Lycaeus.*

LȲCAMBES. [ARCHILOCHUS.]

LȲCĂŌN (-ŏnis), king of Arcadia, son of Pelasgus, an impious king, who served before Zeus (Jupiter), a dish of human flesh, when the god visited him. Lycaon and all his sons, with the exception of Nyctimus, were killed by Zeus with a flash of lightning, or according to others, were changed into wolves.—Callisto, the daughter of Lycaon, is said to have been changed into the constellation of the Bear, whence she is called by the poets *Lycaonis Arctos, Lycaonia Arctos,* or *Lycaonia Virgo,* or by her patronymic *Lycaonis.*

LȲCĂŌNĬA (-ae), a district of Asia Minor, forming the S.E. part of Phrygia. The people were, so far as can be traced, an aboriginal race, speaking a language which is mentioned in the *Acts of the Apostles* as a distinct dialect : they were warlike, and especially skilled in archery.

LȲCEUM (-i), the name of one of the 3 ancient gymnasia at Athens, called after the temple of Apollo Lyceus, in its neighbourhood. It was situated S.E. of the city, outside the walls, and just above the river Ilissus. It is celebrated as the place where Aristotie and the Peripatetics taught.

LȲCĒUS (-i), a surname of Apollo, the meaning of which is not quite certain. Some derive it from λύκος, a wolf, so that it would mean " the wolf-slayer ;" others from λύκη, light, according to which it would mean " the giver of light ;" and others again from the country of Lycia.

LYCHNIDUS (-i), more rarely LYCHNĬDĬUM (-i), or LYCHNIS (-ĭdis), the ancient capital of the Dessaretii in the interior of Illyricum, situated on a height on the N. bank of the lake Lychnītis.

LȲCĬA (-ae), a small district on the S. side of Asia Minor, between Caria and Pamphylia. According to tradition, the most ancient name of the country was Milўas, and the earliest inhabitants were called Milўae, and afterwards Termilae : subsequently the Termilae, from Crete, settled in the country : and lastly, the Athenian Lycus, the son of Pandion, fled from his brother Aegeus to Lycia, and gave his name to the country. Homer, who

gives Lycia a prominent place in the Iliad, represents its chieftains, Glaucus and Sarpedon, as descended from the royal family of Argos (Aeolids). He speaks of the Solymi as a warlike race, inhabiting the mountains, against whom the Greek hero Bellerophontes is sent to fight, by his relative the king of Lycia. Besides the legend of Bellerophon and the chimaera, Lycia is the scene of another popular Greek story, that of the Harpies and the daughters of Pandareos ; and memorials of both are preserved on the Lycian monuments now in the British Museum. On the whole, it is clear that Lycia was colonised by the Greeks at a very early period, and that its historical inhabitants were Greeks, though with a mixture of native blood. The earlier names were preserved in the district in the N. of the country called Milyas, and in the mountains called Solyma. The Lycians always kept the reputation they have in Homer, as brave warriors. They and the Cilicians were the only people W. of the Halys whom Croesus did not conquer, and they were the last who resisted the Persians. [XANTHUS.]

LȲCĬUS (-i), the *Lycian,* a surname of Apollo, who was worshipped in several places of Lycia, especially at Patara, where he had an oracle. Hence the *Lyciae sortes* in Virgil are the responses of the oracle at Patara.

LȲCŎMĒDĒS (-is), king of the Dolopians, in the island of Scyros, to whose court Achilles was sent, disguised as a maiden, by his mother Thetis, who was anxious to prevent his going to the Trojan war. Here Achilles became by Deidamīa, the daughter of Lycomedes, the father of Pyrrhus or Neoptolemus. Lycomedes treacherously killed Theseus by thrusting him down a rock.

LYCON (-ōnis), of Troas, a distinguished Peripatetic philosopher, and the disciple of Straton, whom he succeeded as the head of the Peripatetic school, B.C. 272.

LȲCŎPHRŌN (-ŏnis), a grammarian and poet, was a native of Chalcis in Euboea, and lived at Alexandria, under Ptolemy Philadelphus (B.C. 285—247). He was the author of an extant poem, entitled *Cassandra* or *Alexandra,* in which Cassandra is made to prophesy the fall of Troy, with numerous other events. The obscurity of this work is proverbial. Among the numerous ancient commentaries on the poem, the most important are the *Scholia* of Isaac and John Tzetzes, which are far more valuable than the poem itself.

LȲCŎPŎLIS (-is), a city of Upper Egypt, on the W. bank of the Nile, between Hermopolis and Ptolemais.

LȲCŌRĔA (-ae), an ancient town at the

foot of Mt. Lycorea, which was the southern of the 2 peaks of Mt. Parnassus. [PARNASSUS.] Hence Apollo derived the surname of Lycoreus.

LȲCŎRIS. [CYTHERIS.]

LYCTUS or LYTTUS (-i), an important town in the E. of Crete, situated on a height, 80 stadia from the coast. It is said to have been a Spartan colony.

LȲCURGUS (-i). (1) Son of Dryas, and king of the Edones in Thrace, famous for his persecution of Dionysus (Bacchus) and of his worship in Thrace. He was driven mad by the gods on account of his impiety, and was subsequently killed, but the manner of his

Lycurgus infuriate. (Osterley, Denk. der alt. Kunst, part 2, tav. 37.)

death is variously related.— (2) The Spartan legislator, was the son of Eunomus, king of Sparta, and brother of Polydectes. The latter succeeded his father as king of Sparta, and afterwards died, leaving his queen with child. The ambitious woman proposed to Lycurgus to destroy her offspring if he would share the throne with her. He seemingly consented; but when she had given birth to a son (Charilaus), he openly proclaimed him king; and as next of kin, acted as his guardian. But to avoid all suspicion of ambitious designs, Lycurgus left Sparta, and set out on his celebrated travels. He is said to have visited Crete, Ionia, and Egypt, and to have penetrated even as far as India. His return to Sparta was hailed by all parties. Sparta was in a state of anarchy and licentiousness, and he was considered as the man who alone could cure the growing diseases of the state. He undertook the task; and notwithstanding some opposition, he made a new division of property, and remodelled the whole constitution, military and civil. After Lycurgus had obtained for his institutions an approving oracle of the god of Delphi, he exacted a promise from the people not to make any alterations in his laws before his return. He now left Sparta to finish his

life in voluntary exile, in order that his countrymen might be bound by their oath to preserve his constitution inviolate for ever. Where and how he died, nobody could tell. He was honoured as a god at Sparta with a temple and yearly sacrifices, down to the latest times. The date of Lycurgus is variously given, but it is impossible to place it later than B.C. 825. Lycurgus was regarded through all subsequent ages as the legislator of Sparta, and therefore almost all the Spartan institutions were ascribed to him as their author; but we must not imagine that they were all his work.—(3) An Attic orator, born at Athens, about B.C. 396, was a disciple of Plato and Isocrates, a warm supporter of the policy of Demosthenes, and one of the most virtuous citizens and upright statesmen of his age. He was thrice appointed *Tamias*, or manager of the public revenue. He died in 323. Only one of his orations has come down to us.

LȲCUS (-i). (1) Of Thebes, put to death with his wife Dirce, by Amphion and Zethus, on account of the cruelty with which they had treated Antiope, the mother of the two latter by Zeus (Jupiter). For details see AMPHION. (2) Son of Pandion, was expelled by his brother, Aegeus, and took refuge in the country of the Termili, which was called Lycia after him. The Lyceum at Athens is said to have derived its name from him.—(3) Name of several rivers, which are said to be so called from the impetuosity of their current. 1. In Bithynia, falling into the sea S. of Heraclea Pontica. 2. In Pontus, rising in the mountains on the N. of Armenia Minor, and flowing W. into the Iris at Eupatoria. 3. In Phrygia, flowing from E. to W. past Colossae and Laodicea into the Maeander.

LYDDA (-ōrum), a town of Palestine, S.E. of Joppa, and N.W. of Jerusalem, subsequently called Diospolis.

LȲDĬA (-ae), a district of Asia Minor, in the middle of the W. side of the peninsula, between Mysia on the N. and Caria on the S., and between Phrygia on the E. and the Aegean Sea on the W. In these boundaries the strip of coast belonging to IONIA is included, but the name is sometimes used in a narrower signification, so as to exclude Ionia. Lydia is divided into 2 unequal valleys by the chain of Mt. Tmolus; of which the S. and smaller is watered by the river CAYSTER, and the N. forms the great plain of the HERMUS. In early times the country had another name, Maeŏnia, by which alone it is known to Homer. Lydia was an early seat of Asiatic civilisation, and exerted a very important influence on the Greeks. The Lydian monarchy, which was founded at

Sardis, grew up into an empire, under which the many different tribes of Asia Minor W. of the river Halys, were for the first time united. The names and computed dates of the Lydian kings are :—1. GYGES, B.C. 716—678 ; 2. ARDYS, 678—620 ; 3. SADYATTES, 629—617 ; 4. ALYATTES, 617—560 ; 5. CROESUS, 560 (or earlier) — 546 ; under whose names an account is given of the rise of the Lydian empire in Asia Minor, and of its overthrow by the Persians under Cyrus. Under the Persians, Lydia and Mysia formed the 2nd satrapy ; after the Macedonian conquest, Lydia belonged first to the kings of Syria, and next (after the defeat of Antiochus the Great by the Romans) to those of Pergamus, and so passed, by the bequest of Attalus III., to the Romans, under whom it formed part of the province of Asia.

LYDIAS or LUDIAS (-ae), a river in Macedonia, falling into the Axius, a short distance from the Thermaic gulf. Herodotus, by mistake, makes the Lydias unite with the Haliacmon.

LYGII or LIGII (-ōrum), an important people in Germany, between the Viadus (*Oder*) and the Vistula.

LYNCESTIS (-ĭdis), a district in the S.W. of Macedonia, upon the frontiers of Illyria, inhabited by the LYNCESTAE, an Illyrian people. The ancient capital of the country was LYNCUS, though HERACLEA at a later time became the chief town in the district. Near Lyncus was a river, whose waters are said to have been as intoxicating as wine.

LYNCEUS (-ĕi, -eī or -ĕŏs). (1) One of the 50 sons of Aegyptus, whose life was saved by his wife Hypermnestra, when all his brothers were murdered by the daughters of Danaus. [AEGYPTUS.] Lynceus succeeded Danaus as king of Argos.—(2) Son of Aphareus and Arene, and brother of Idas, was one of the Argonauts, and famous for his keen sight. He was slain by Pollux. For details respecting his death, see DIOSCURI.

LYNCUS (-i), king of Scythia, endeavoured to murder Triptolemus, who came to him with the gifts of Ceres, but he was metamorphosed by the goddess into a lynx.

LYRCĒA (-ae) or LYRCĒUM (-i), a small town in Argolis, situated on a mountain of the same name.

LYRNESSUS (-i), a town in the Troad, the birthplace of Briseïs.

LYSANDER (-dri), one of the most distinguished of the Spartan generals and diplomatists. Having been appointed to the command of the Spartan fleet, off the coast of Asia Minor, he gained the favour of Cyrus, who supplied him with large sums of money to pay his sailors. In B.C. 405 he brought the Peloponnesian war to a conclusion, by the defeat of the Athenian fleet off Aegospotami, and in the following year he entered Athens in triumph. It was through his influence that Agesilaus, the brother of Agis, obtained the Spartan throne in opposition to Leotychides, the reputed son of the latter. Lysander accompanied Agesilaus to Asia ; but the king purposely thwarted all his designs, and refused all the favours which he asked. On his return to Sparta, Lysander resolved to bring about a change in the Spartan constitution, by abolishing hereditary royalty, and making the throne elective. But before he could carry his enterprise into effect, he fell in battle under the walls of Haliartus, B.C. 395.

LYSIAS (-ae), an Attic orator, was born at Athens, B.C. 458, but was not an Athenian citizen, being the son of Cephalus, a native of Syracuse. At the age of 15, Lysias joined the Athenians who went as colonists to Thurii, in Italy, 443 ; but he returned to Athens after the defeat of the Athenians in Sicily, 411. During the rule of the 30 Tyrants (404), he was thrown into prison ; but he escaped, and joined Thrasybulus and the exiles, to whom he rendered important assistance. He died in 378, at the age of 80. Lysias wrote a great number of orations for others, of which several are extant. They are distinguished by grace and elegance.

LYSIMACHIA, or -ĒA (-ae), an important town of Thrace, on the gulf of Melas, and on the isthmus connecting the Thracian Chersonesus with the mainland, founded B.C. 309 by Lysimachus, who removed to his new city the inhabitants of the neighbouring town of Cardia.

LYSIMACHUS (-i), one of Alexander's generals, obtained Thrace in the division of the provinces, after Alexander's death (B.C. 323), and assumed the title of king in 306. He joined the other generals of Alexander in opposing Antigonus, and it was he and Seleucus who gained the decisive victory at Ipsus over Antigonus, in which the latter fell (301). In 291 Lysimachus was taken prisoner by Dromichaetes, king of the Getae, whose country he had invaded, but he was restored to liberty by the latter. In 287 Lysimachus and Pyrrhus expelled Demetrius from Macedonia. Pyrrhus, for a time, obtained possession of the Macedonian throne ; but in the following year he was driven out of the country by Lysimachus, who now became king of Macedonia. Towards the end of his reign the aged Lysimachus put to death his son Agathocles, at the instigation of his wife, Arsinoë, daughter of Ptolemy Soter. This bloody deed alienated the minds of his subjects; and Seleucus invaded the dominions of Lysimachus. The two monarchs met in the plain of Corus (Corupedion); and Lysimachus fell in the battle that ensued, B.C. 281, in his 80th year.

LYSIPPUS (-i), of Sicyon, one of the most distinguished Greek statuaries, was a contemporary of Alexander the Great, who is reported to have said that no one should paint him but Apelles, and no one make his statue but Lysippus.

LYSIS (-Idis), an eminent Pythagorean philosopher, the teacher of Epaminondas.

LYSTRA (-ae), a city of Lycaonia, on the confines of Isauria, celebrated as one chief scene of the preaching of Paul and Barnabas.

MĀCAE (-ārum). (1) A people on the E. coast of Arabia Felix, probably about *Muscat*.—(2) An inland people of Libya, in the part of N. Africa between the Syrtes.

MĀCĂREUS (-ei), son of Aeolus, who committed incest with his sister Canace. [CANACE.] Hence Isse, the daughter of Macareusis called *Macarëis.*

MACCĂBAEI (-ōrum), the descendants of the family of the heroic Judas Maccabi or Maccabaeus, a surname which he obtained from his glorious victories. (From the Hebrew *makkab*, "a hammer.") They were also called *Asamonaei*, from Asamonaeus, or Chasmon, the ancestor of Judas Maccabaeus, or, in a shorter form, *Asmonaei* or *Hasmonaei.* The family first obtained distinction by their resisting the attempts of Antiochus IV. Epiphanes, king of Syria, to root out the worship of Jehovah. They succeeded in delivering their country from the Syrian yoke, and became the rulers of Judea.

MĂCĔDŎNĬA (-ae), a country in Europe, N. of Greece, said to have been originally named Emathia. Its boundaries before the time of Philip, the father of Alexander, were on the S. Olympus and the Cambunian mountains, which separated it from Thessaly and Epirus, on the E. the river Strymon, which separated it from Thrace, and on the N. and W. Illyria and Paeonia. Macedonia was greatly enlarged by the conquests of Philip. He added to his kingdom Paeonia on the N.; a part of Thrace on the E. as far as the river Nestus, which Thracian district was usually called *Macedonia adjecta;* the peninsula Chalcidice on the S.; and on the W. a part of Illyria, as far as the lake Lychnitis. On the conquest of the country by the Romans, B.C. 168, Macedonia was divided into 4 districts, independent of one another; but the whole country was formed into a Roman province after the conquest of the Achaeans, in 146. The great bulk of the inhabitants of Macedonia consisted of Thracian and Illyrian tribes. At an early period some Greek tribes settled in the S. part of the country. They are said to have come from Argos, and to have been led by the 3 sons of Temenus, the Heraclid. Perdiccas, the youngest of the three, was looked upon as the founder of the Macedonian monarchy. A later tradition, however, regarded Caranus who was also a Heraclid from Argos, as the founder of the monarchy. These Greek settlers intermarried with the original inhabitants of the country. The dialect which they spoke was akin to the Doric, but it contained many barbarous words and forms; and the Macedonians accordingly were never regarded by the other Greeks as genuine Hellenes. Moreover, it was only in the S. of Macedonia that the Greek language was spoken. Very little is known of the history of Macedonia till the reign of Amyntas I., who was a contemporary of Darius Hystaspis; but from that time their history is more or less intimately connected with that of Greece, till at length Philip, the father of Alexander the Great, became the virtual master of the whole of Greece. The conquests of Alexander extended the Macedonian supremacy over a great part of Asia; and the Macedonian kings continued to exercise their sovereignty over Greece till the conquest of Perseus by the Romans, 168, brought the Macedonian monarchy to a close.

MACELLA (-ae), a small fortified town in the W. of Sicily, S.E. of Segesta.

MĀCER (-cri) AEMĬLĬUS (-i). (1) A Roman poet, was a native of Verona, and died in Asia, B.C. 16. He wrote a poem upon birds, snakes, and medicinal plants.—(2) We must distinguish from Aemilius Macer of Verona, a poet Macer, who wrote on the Trojan war, and who must have been alive in A.D. 12, since he is addressed by Ovid in that year (*ex Pont.* ii. 10, 2).

MĂCER, LĬCĬNĬUS. [LICINIUS.]

MĂCĔTAE (-ārum), another name of the Macedonians.

MĂCHĀŌN (-ŏnis), son of Aesculapius, the surgeon of the Greeks in the Trojan war, led, with his brother Podalirius, troops from Tricca, Ithome, and Oechalia. He was killed by Eurypylus, the son of Telephus.

MACRA (-ae: *Magra*), a small river rising in the Apennines and flowing into the Ligurian sea near Luna, which, from the time of Augustus, formed the boundary between Liguria and Etruria.

MACRI CAMPI. [CAMPI MACRI.]

MACRĪNUS, M. ŌPĬLĬUS SĔVĔRUS (-i),

Roman emperor, April, A.D. 217—June, 218, and successor of Caracalla, whom he had caused to be assassinated. He was defeated by the generals of Elagabalus and put to death.

MACRŎBĬI (-ōrum : i.e. *Long-lived*), an Aethiopian people in Africa, placed by Herodotus on the shores of the S. Ocean.

MACRŎBĬUS (-i), a Roman grammarian, who lived about A.D. 400, wrote several works, of which the most important are :— 1. A treatise in 7 books, entitled *Saturnalia Convivia*, consisting of a series of dissertations on history, mythology, criticism, and various points of antiquarian research. 2. A Commentary on Cicero's *Somnium Scipionis*.

MACRŎNES (-um), a powerful and warlike Caucasian people on the N.E. shore of the Pontus Euxinus.

MADȲTUS (-i), a sea-port town on the Thracian Chersonesus.

MAEANDER (-dri), a river in Asia Minor, proverbial for its wanderings, rising in the S. of Phrygia, close to the source of the Marsyas, flowing between Lydia and Caria, of which it forms the boundary, and at last falling into the Icarian Sea between Myus and Priene. As a god Maeander is described as the father of the nymph Cyane, who was the mother of Caunus. Hence the latter is called by Ovid *Maeandrius juvenis*.

MAECĒNAS (-ātis), C. CILNĬUS (-i), a Roman eques, but descended both on his father's and mother's side from the *Lucumones* of Etruria. His paternal ancestors were the *Cilnii*, a powerful family at Arretium, and his maternal ancestors the Maecenates, at Arretium. Maecenas was one of the chief friends and ministers of Augustus, and enjoyed for many years the confidence of the latter. But towards the latter years of his life a coolness sprang up between them, and Maecenas retired entirely from public life. He died B.C. 8. The fame of Maecenas, however, rests mainly on his patronage of literature, especially of Virgil and Horace. Virgil was indebted to him for the recovery of his farm, which had been appropriated by the soldiery in the division of lands, in B.C. 41 ; and it was at the request of Maecenas that he undertook the *Georgics*. To Horace Maecenas was a still greater benefactor. He presented him with the means of comfortable subsistence, a farm in the Sabine country.

MAECĬUS TARPA. [TARPA.]

MAEDĬCA (-ae), the country of the Maedi, a powerful people in the W. of Thrace, on the W. bank of the Strymon.

MAELĬUS (-i), SP., the richest of the plebeian knights, employed his fortune in buying up corn in Etruria in the great famine at Rome in B.C. 440. This corn he sold to the poor at a small price, or distributed it gratuitously. The patricians accused him of aiming at the kingly power, and appointed Cincinnatus dictator. C. Servilius Ahala, the master of the horse, summoned Maelius to appear before the tribunal of the dictator ; but as he refused to go, Ahala rushed into the crowd, and slew him. His property was confiscated, and his house pulled down ; its vacant site, which was called the *Aequimaelium*, continued to subsequent ages a memorial of his fate.

MAENĀDES (-um : *sing.* Maenas), a name of the Bacchantes, from μαίνομαι, "to be mad," because they were frenzied in the worship of Dionysus or Bacchus.

MAENĂLUS (-i), a mountain in Arcadia, extending from Megalopolis to Tegea, celebrated as the favourite haunt of the god Pan. The Roman poets frequently use the adjectives *Maenalius* and *Maenalis* as equivalent to Arcadian.

MAENĬUS (-i), C., consul B.C. 338, with L. Furius Camillus. The 2 consuls completed the subjugation of Latium ; they were both rewarded with a triumph, and equestrian statues were erected to their honour in the forum. The statue of Maenius was placed upon a column, called *Columna Maenia*, which appears to have stood near the end of the forum, on the Capitoline. Maenius, in his censorship (B.C. 318), allowed balconies to be added to the various buildings surrounding the forum, in order that the spectators might obtain more room for beholding the games which were exhibited in the forum : these balconies were called after him *Maeniana* (sc. *aedificia*).

MAEŎNĬA (-ae), the ancient name of Lydia. Hence Virgil gives the name of Maeonia to Etruria, because the Etruscans were said to be descended from Lydians. Hence also Homer, as a native of Maeonia, is called *Maeonides* and *Maeonius senex*, and his poems the *Maeoniae chartae*, or *Maeonium carmen*. [LYDIA.]—MAEONIS likewise occurs as a surname of Omphale and of Arachne, because both were Lydians.

MAEŌTAE. [MAEOTIS PALUS.]

MAEŌTIS (-ĭdis) PALUS (*Sea of Azov*), an inland sea on the borders of Europe and Asia, N. of the Pontus Euxinus (*Black Sea*), with which it communicates by the BOSPORUS CIMMERIUS. The Scythian tribes on its banks were called by the collective name of Maeōtae or Maeōtĭci. The sea had also the names of Cimmerium or Bosporicum Mare.

MAERA, the dog of Icarius, the father of Erigone. [ICARIUS, No. 1.]

MAEVĬUS. [BAVIUS.]

MAGDOLUM (O. T. Migdol), a city or

Lower Egypt, near the N. E. frontier, where Pharaoh Necho defeated the Syrians.

MAGETOBRIA (*Moigte de Broie*, on the Saône), a town on the W. frontiers of the Sequani, near which the Gauls were defeated by the Germans shortly before Caesar's arrival in Gaul.

MAGI (-ōrum), the name of the order of priests and religious teachers among the Medes and Persians. [ZOROASTER.]

MAGNA GRAECIA. [GRAECIA.]

MAGNA MATER. [RHEA.]

MAGNENTIUS (-i), Roman emperor in the West, A.D. 350—353, obtained the throne by the murder of Constans, but was defeated by Constantius, and put an end to his own life.

MAGNESIA (-ae). (1) A narrow slip of country along the eastern coast of Thessaly, extending from the Peneus on the N. to the Pagasaean gulf on the S. Its inhabitants, the Magnetes, are said to have founded the 2 cities in Asia mentioned below.—(2) MAG-NESIA AD SIPYLUM, a city in the N.W. of Lydia, at the foot of Mt. Sipylus, and on the S. bank of the Hermus, famous as the scene of the victory gained by Scipio Asiaticus over Antiochus the Great, B.C. 190.—(3) MAG-NESIA AD MAEANDRUM, a city in the S.W. of Lydia, situated on the river Lethaeus, a tributary of the Maeander. It was destroyed by the Cimmerians (probably about B.C. 700) and rebuilt by colonists from Miletus.

MAGO (-ōnis), the name of several Carthaginians, of whom the most celebrated were :—(1) Son of Hamilcar Barca, and youngest brother of the famous Hannibal. He carried on the war for many years in Spain; and after the Carthaginians had been driven out of that country by Scipio, he landed in Liguria, where he remained 2 years (B.C. 205—203).—(2) The author of a work upon agriculture in the Punic language, in 28 books, which was translated into Latin by order of the Roman senate.

MAGONTIACUM. [MOGONTIACUM.]

MAIA (-ae), daughter of Atlas and Pleïŏnē, was the eldest of the Pleiades, and the most beautiful of the 7 sisters. In a grotto of Mt. Cyllēnē, in Arcadia, she became by Zeus (Jupiter) the mother of Hermes (Mercury). Arcas, the son of Zeus by Callisto, was given to her to be reared. [PLEIADES.]

MALACA (-ae : *Malaga*), an important town on the coast of Hispania Baetica, and on a river of the same name, founded by the Phoenicians.

MALEA or EA (-ae), a promontory on the S.E. of Laconia, separating the Argolic and Laconic gulfs.

MALIACUS SINUS. [MALIS.]

MALIS, a district in the S. of Thessaly, on the shores of the Maliacus Sinus, and opposite the N.W. point of the island of Euboea. It extended as far as the pass of Thermopylae. Its inhabitants, the Malienses, were Dorians, and belonged to the Amphictyonic league.

MALLI (-ōrum), an Indian people on both sides of the HYDRAOTES : their capital is supposed to have been on the site of the celebrated fortress of *Mooltan*.

MALLUS (-i), a very ancient city of Cilicia, on a hill E. of the mouth of the river Pyramus, said to have been founded at the time of the Trojan war by Mopsus and Amphilochus.

MAMERCUS (-i), the name of a distinguished family of the Aemilia gens in the early times of the republic.

MAMERS (-tis), the Oscan name of the god MARS.

MAMERTINI. [MESSANA].

MAMILIUS (-i), the name of a distinguished family in Tusculum. It was to a member of this family, Octavius Mamilius, that Tarquinius betrothed his daughter; and on his expulsion from Rome, his son-in-law roused the Latin people against the infant republic, and perished in the great battle at the lake Regillus. The Mamilii afterwards removed to Rome.

MAMURIUS VETURIUS. [VETURIUS.]

MAMURRA (-ae), a Roman eques, born at Formiae, was the commander of the engineers (*praefectus fabrum*) in Julius Caesar's army in Gaul, and amassed great riches. Horace calls Formiae, in ridicule, *Mamur-rarum urbs*, from which we may infer that the name of Mamurra had become a byeword of contempt.

MANCINUS, C. HOSTILIUS (-i), consul B.C. 137, was defeated by the Numantines, and purchased his safety by making a peace with them. The senate refused to recognise it, and went through the hypocritical ceremony of delivering him over to the enemy, who refused to accept him.

MANDUBII (-ōrum), a people in Gallia Lugdunensis, in the modern *Burgundy*, whose chief town was ALESIA.

MANDURIA (-ae), a town in Calabria, on the road from Tarentum to Hydruntum.

MANES (-ium), the name which the Romans gave to the souls of the departed, who were worshipped as gods. Hence on sepulchres we find D. M. S., that is *Dis Manibus Sacrum*. [LARES.]

MANETHO (-ŏnis), an Egyptian priest in the reign of the first Ptolemy, who wrote in Greek an account of the religion and history of his country. His history of Egypt contained an account of the different dynasties of kings, compiled from genuine documents.

The work itself is lost; but a list of the dynasties is preserved in Julius Africanus and Eusebius.

MĀNĪLĪUS (-i). (1) C., tribune of the plebs, B.C. 66, proposed the law (*Manilia Lex*), granting to Pompey the command of the war against Mithridates, and which Cicero supported in an extant oration.—(2) A Roman poet, who lived in the time of Augustus, and the author of an extant astrological poem in 5 books, entitled *Astronomica*.

M. MANLĪUS (-i), consul B.C. 392, took refuge in the capitol when Rome was taken by the Gauls in 390. One night, when the Gauls endeavoured to ascend the capitol, Manlius was roused from his sleep by the cackling of the geese; collecting hastily a body of men, he succeeded in driving back the enemy, who had just reached the summit of the hill. From this heroic deed he is said to have received the surname of CAPITOLINUS. In 385, he defended the cause of the plebeians, who were suffering severely from the harsh and cruel treatment of their patrician creditors. In the following year, he was charged with high treason by the patricians; and being condemned to death by the people, he was hurled down the Tarpeian rock by the tribunes. The members of the Manlia gens accordingly resolved that none of them should ever bear in future the praenomen of Marcus.

MANLĪUS TORQUĀTUS. [TORQUATUS.]

MANTĪNĒA (-ae), one of the most ancient and important towns in Arcadia, situated on the small river Ophis, near the centre of the E. frontier of the country. It is celebrated for the great battle fought under its walls between the Spartans and Thebans, in which Epaminondas fell, B.C. 362. In consequence of its treachery to the Achaeans, Aratus put to death its leading citizens, sold the rest of its inhabitants as slaves, and changed its name into *Antigonīa*, in honour of Antigonus Doson. The emperor Hadrian restored to the place its ancient name.

MANTŌ (-ūs). (1) Daughter of Tiresias, a prophetess, and mother of the seer Mopsus.— (2) Daughter of Hercules, likewise a prophetess, from whom the town of Mantua received its name.

MANTŬA (-ae), a town in Gallia Transpadana, on an island in the river Mincius, was not a place of importance, but is celebrated because Virgil, who was born at the neighbouring village of Andes, regarded Mantua as his birthplace.

MĀRĂCANDA (-ōrum : *Samarkand*), the capital of Sogdiana, where Alexander the Great killed his friend CLITUS.

MĀRĂTHŌN (-ōnis), a village of Attica, situated near a bay on the E. coast, 22 miles from Athens by one road, and 26 miles by another. It stood in a plain, extending along the sea-shore, about 6 miles in length, and from 3 miles to 1½ mile in breadth, and surrounded on the other 3 sides by rocky hills. Two marshes bound the extremity of the plain. Here was fought the celebrated battle between the Persians and Athenians B.C. 490. The Persians were drawn up on the plain, and the Athenians on some portion of the high ground above. The Tumulus raised over the Athenians who fell in the battle, is still to be seen. The Marathonian plain is also celebrated in mythology on account of the fierce bull here slain by Theseus.

MĀRĀTHUS (-i), an important city on the coast of Phoenicia opposite to Aradus and near Antaradus.

MARCELLUS (-i), the name of an illustrious plebeian family of the Claudia gens. —(1) M. CLAUDIUS MARCELLUS, celebrated as 5 times consul, and the conqueror of Syracuse. In his first consulship, B.C. 222, Marcellus distinguished himself by slaying in battle with his own hand Britomartus or Viridomarus, the king of the Insubrian Gauls, whose spoils he afterwards dedicated as *spolia opima* in the temple of Jupiter Feretrius. This was the 3rd and last instance in Roman history in which such an offering was made. Marcellus was one of the chief Roman generals in the 2nd Punic war. He took Syracuse in B.C. 212, after a siege of more than 2 years, in which all his powerful military engines were rendered wholly unavailing by the superior skill and science of Archimedes, who directed those of the besieged. On the capture of the city Archimedes was one of the inhabitants slain by the Roman soldiers. Marcellus fell in battle against Hannibal in 208.—(2) M. CLAUDIUS MARCELLUS, consul B.C. 51, and a bitter enemy of Caesar. In B.C. 46 he was pardoned by Caesar on the intercession of the senate; whereupon Cicero returned thanks to Caesar in the oration *Pro Marcello*, which has come down to us. Marcellus, who was then living at Mytilēnē, set out on his return; but he was murdered at the Piraeus by one of his own attendants, P. Magius Chilo.—(3) C. CLAUDIUS MARCELLUS, brother of No. 2, and also an enemy of Caesar, was consul in 49, when the civil war broke out.—(4) C. CLAUTIUS MARCELLUS, first cousin of the two preceding, and, like them, an enemy of Caesar. He was consul in 50, but he did not join Pompey in Greece, and was therefore readily pardoned by Caesar.—(5) M. CLAUDIUS MARCELLUS, son of the preceding and of Octavia, the daughter of C. Octavius and sister of Augustus, was born in 43. Augustus, who had probably destined him for his successor, adopted him as his son, and gave him his daughter Julia in marriage (B.C. 25). In 23 he was curule aedile, but died in the same year to the great grief of Augustus, as well as of his mother Octavia. The memory of Marcellus is embalmed in the well-known passage of Virgil (*Aen.* vi. 860—886), which was recited by the poet to Augustus and Octavia.

MARCIUS (-i), the name of a Roman gens, which claimed descent from Ancus Marcius, the 4th king of Rome. [ANCUS MARCIUS.] Coriolanus belonged to this gens [CORIOLANUS] ; and at a later time it was divided into the families of PHILIPPUS, REX, and RUTILUS.

MARCIUS (-i), an Italian seer, whose prophetic verses (*Carmina Marciana*) were discovered in B.C. 213, and were preserved in the Capitol with the Sibylline books. Some writers mention only one person of this name, but others speak of 2 brothers, the Marcii.

MARCOMANNI (-ōrum), that is, men of the mark or border, a powerful German people, of the Suevic race, originally dwelt between the Rhine and the Danube, on the banks of the Main ; but under the guidance of their chieftain Maroboduus, they migrated into the land of the Boii, who inhabited Bohemia and part of Bavaria. Here they settled after subduing the Boii, and founded a powerful kingdom, which extended S. as far as the Danube. [MAROBODUUS.] At a later time the Marcomanni, in conjunction with the Quadi and other German tribes, carried on a long and bloody war with the emperor M. Aurelius, which lasted during the greater part of his reign, and was only brought to a conclusion by his son Commodus purchasing peace of the barbarians as soon as he ascended the throne, A.D. 180.

MARDI. [AMARDI.]

MARDONIUS (-i), a distinguished Persian, son of Gobryas, and son-in-law of Darius Hystaspis. In B.C. 492 he was sent by Darius to punish Eretria and Athens for the aid they had given to the Ionians ; but his fleet was destroyed by a storm off Mt. Athos, and the greater part of his land forces was destroyed on his passage through Macedonia by the Brygians, a Thracian tribe. On the accession of Xerxes, he was one of the chief instigators of the expedition against Greece. After the defeat of the Persians at Salamis (480), he was left by Xerxes with a large army to conquer Greece ; but he was defeated in the following year (479), near Plataeae, by the combined Greek forces, under the command of Pausanias, and was slain in the battle.

MAREA, -EA, -IA (-ae), a town of Lower Egypt, which gave its name to the district and lake of Mareōtis. The lake was separated from the Mediterranean by the neck of land on which Alexandria stood, and supplied with water by the Canopic branch of the Nile, and by canals. It served as the port of Alexandria for vessels navigating the Nile.

MAREŌTIS. [MAREA.]

MARESA, MARESCHA, an ancient fortress of Palestine, in the S. of Judaea, of some importance in the history of the early kings of Judah and of the Maccabees.

MARGIANA (-ae), a province of the ancient Persian empire, bounded on the E. by Bactriana, on the N.E. and N. by the river Oxus, and on the W. by Hyrcania. It received its name from the river Margus, which flows through it. On this river stood the capital of the district, Antiochia Margiana, which was founded by Alexander the Great, and rebuilt by Antiochus I.

MARGUS. [MARGIANA.]

MARIANAE FOSSAE. [FOSSA.]

MARIANDYNI (-ōrum), an ancient people in the N.E. of Bithynia, in Asia Minor.

MARICA (-ae), a Latin nymph, the mother of Latinus by Faunus, was worshipped by the inhabitants of Minturnae, in a grove on the river Liris. Hence the country round Minturnae is called by Horace *Maricae litora.*

MARIUS (-i), C. (1) The celebrated Roman, who was 7 times consul, was born in B.C. 157, near Arpinum, of an obscure and humble family. He rose to distinction by his military abilities. He served under Scipio Africanus, the younger, at the siege of Numantia, in Spain (B.C. 134), but he was not elected tribune of the plebs till B.C. 119, when he was 38 years of age. He afterwards married Julia, the sister of C. Julius Caesar, the father of the celebrated dictator. Marius was now regarded as one of the chief leaders of the popular party at Rome. In 109 Marius served in Africa as legate of the consul Q. Metellus, in the war against Jugurtha. In 107 he was elected consul, and received the province of Numidia, and the conduct of the war against Jugurtha (107). In the following year (106), Jugurtha was surrendered to him by the treachery of Bocchus, king of Mauretania. [JUGURTHA.] Marius sent his quaestor Sulla to receive the Numidian king from Bocchus. This circumstance sowed the seeds of the personal hatred which afterwards existed between Marius and Sulla, since the enemies of Marius claimed for Sulla the merit of bringing the war to a close by obtaining possession of the person of Jugurtha. Meantime Italy was threatened by a vast horde of barbarians, who had migrated from the N. of Germany. The 2 leading nations of which they consisted were called Cimbri and Teutoni. They had defeated one Roman army after another; and every one felt that Marius was the only man capable of saving the state. Accordingly he was elected consul a 2nd time (104); but the barbarians, instead of crossing the Alps, marched into Spain, which they ravaged for the next 2 or 3 years. Marius was elected consul a 3rd time in 103, and a 4th time in 102. In the latter of these years the barbarians returned into Gaul, and divided their forces. The Cimbri crossed the Tyrolese Alps by the defiles of Tridentum (Trent). The Teutoni and Ambrones, on the other hand, marched against Marius, who had taken up a position in a fortified camp on the Rhone. The decisive battle was fought near Aquae Sextiae (*Aix*), in which the whole nation was annihilated by Marius. The Cimbri, meantime, had forced their way into Italy. Marius was elected consul a 5th time (101), and joined the proconsul Catulus in the N. of Italy. The 2 generals gained a great victory over the enemy on a plain called the Campi Raudii, near Vercellae (*Vercelli*). Marius was received at Rome with unprecedented honours. Hitherto his career had been a glorious one; but the remainder of his life is full of horrors. In order to secure the consulship a 6th time, he entered into close connexion with the two demagogues, Saturninus and Glaucia. He gained his object, and was consul a 6th time in 100. In this year he drove into exile his old enemy Metellus; and shortly afterwards, when Saturninus and Glaucia took up arms against the state, he was compelled by the senate to put down the insurrection. [SATURNINUS.] But although old, and full of honours, he was anxious to obtain the command of the war against Mithridates, which the senate had bestowed upon the consul Sulla (B.C. 88). He obtained a vote of the people, conferring upon him the command; but Sulla marched upon Rome at the head of his army, and compelled Marius to take to flight. After wandering along the coast of Latium, he was at length taken prisoner in the marshes formed by the river Liris, near Minturnae; but when a Cimbrian soldier, entered his prison to put him to death, Marius in a terrible voice exclaimed—"Man, darest thou murder C. Marius?" Whereupon the barbarian threw down his sword and rushed out of the house. The inhabitants of Minturnae now took compassion on Marius, and placed him on board a ship. He reached Africa in safety, and landed at Carthage; but he had

scarcely put his foot on shore before the Roman governor sent an officer to bid him leave the country. This last blow almost unmanned Marius: his only reply was—"Tell the praetor that you have seen C. Marius a fugitive, sitting on the ruins of Carthage." Soon afterwards Marius returned to Italy, where the consul Cinna (B.C. 87) had taken up arms against Sulla's party. Cinna had been driven out of Rome, but he now entered it along with Marius. The most frightful scenes followed. The guards of Marius stabbed every one whom he did not salute, and the streets ran with the blood of the noblest of the Roman aristocracy. Without going through the form of an election, Marius and Cinna named themselves consuls for the following year (86). But on the 18th day of his consulship Marius died of an attack of pleurisy, in his 71st year.—(2) Son of the preceding, but only by adoption; was consul in B.C. 82, when he was 27 years of age. In this year he was defeated by Sulla, near Sacriportus, on the frontiers of Latium, whereupon he took refuge in the strongly fortified town of Praeneste. Here he was besieged for some time; but after Sulla's great victory at the Colline gate of Rome over Pontius Telesinus, Marius put an end to his own life, after making an unsuccessful attempt to escape.—(3) The false Marius, put to death by Antony, B.C. 44.

MARMĂRĬCA (-ae), a district of N. Africa, between Cyrenaica and Egypt, extending inland as far as the Oasis of Ammon. Its inhabitants were called Marmaridae.

MĂRO, VIRGĬLĬUS. [VIRGILIUS.]

MARŎBODŬUS (-i), king of the Marcomanni, was a Suevian by birth, and was brought up at the court of Augustus. After his return to his native country, he succeeded in establising a powerful kingdom in central Germany [MARCOMANNI]; but having become an object of suspicion to the other German tribes, he was expelled from his dominions about A.D. 19, and took refuge in Italy, where Tiberius allowed him to remain.

MĂRŌNEA (-ae), a town on the S. coast of Thrace, on the lake Ismaris, belonged originally to the Cicones, but afterwards colonised from Chios. It was celebrated for its excellent wine, and is mentioned in Homer as the residence of Maron, son of Evanthes, grandson of Dionysus (Bacchus) and Ariadne, and priest of Apollo.

MARPESSA (-ae). (1) Daughter of Evenus. [IDAS.]—(2) A mountain in Paros, from which the celebrated Parian marble was obtained. Hence Virgil speaks of *Marpesic cautes* (*i.e.* Parian).

MARRŪCĬNI or MĂRŪCĬNI (-ōrum), a

brave and warlike people in Italy of the Sabellian race, occupying a narrow slip of country along the right bank of the river Aternus, and bounded on the N. by the Vestini, on the W. by the Peligni and Marsi, on the S. by the Frentani, and on the E. by the Adriatic sea. Their chief town was TEATE. Along with their neighbours the Marsi, Peligni, &c., they submitted to the Romans in B.C. 304.

MARRŬVĬUM or MĀRŬVĬUM (-i), the chief town of the Marsi (who are therefore called *gens Maruvia* by Virgil), situated on the E. bank of the lake Fucinus.

MARS (-rtis), an ancient Roman god, identified by the Romans with the Greek Ares. [ARES.] The name of the god in the Sabine and Oscan was MAMERS; and Mars itself is a contraction of MAVERS or MAVORS. Next to Jupiter, Mars enjoyed the highest honours at Rome. He was considered the father of Romulus, the founder of the nation. [ROMULUS.] He is frequently designated as *father Mars,* whence the forms *Marspiter* and *Maspiter,* analogous to Jupiter. Jupiter, Mars, and Quirinus, were the 3 tutelary divinities of Rome, to each of whom king Numa appointed a flamen. He was worshipped at Rome as the god of war, and war itself was frequently designated by the name of Mars. His priests, the Salii, danced in full armour, and the place dedicated to warlike exercises was called after his name (*Campus Martius*). But being the father of the Romans, Mars was also the protector of the most honourable pursuit, i.e. agriculture; and under the name of Silvanus, he was worshipped as the guardian of cattle. Mars was also identified with Quirinus, who was the deity watching over the Roman citizens in their civil capacity as Quirites. Thus Mars appears under 3 aspects. As the warlike god, he was called *Gradivus;* as the rustic god, he was called *Silvanus;* while, in his relation to the state, he bore the name of *Quirinus.* His wife was called *Neria* or *Neriĕnē,* the feminine of *Nero,* which in the Sabine language signified "strong." The wolf and the woodpecker (*picus*) were sacred to Mars. Numerous temples were dedicated to him at Rome, the most important of which was that outside the Porta Capena, on the Appian road, and that of Mars Ultor, which was built by Augustus in the forum.

MARSI (-ōrum). (1) A brave and warlike people of the Sabellian race, dwelt in the centre of Italy, in the high land surrounded by the mountains of the Apennines, in which the lake Fucinus is situated. Along with their neighbours the Peligni, Marrucini, &c., they concluded a peace with Rome, B.C. 304. Their bravery was proverbial; and they were the prime movers of the celebrated war waged against Rome by the Socii or Italian allies in order to obtain the Roman franchise, and which is known by the name of the Marsic or Social war. Their chief town was MARRUVIUM.—The Marsi appear to have been acquainted with the medicinal properties of several of the plants growing upon their mountains, and to have employed them as remedies against the bites of serpents, and in other cases. Hence they were regarded as magicians, and were said to be descended from a son of Circe.—(2) A people in the N.W. of Germany, belonging to the league of the Cherusci. They joined the Cherusci in the war against the Romans, which terminated in the defeat of Varus.

MARSIGNI (-ōrum), a people in the S.E. of Germany, of Suevic extraction.

MARSUS, DŌMĬTĬUS (-i), a Roman poet of the Augustan age.

MARSYAS or MARSĂ (-ae). (1) A satyr of Phrygia, who, having found the flute which Athēna (Minerva) had thrown away in disgust on account of its distorting her features, discovered that it emitted of its own accord the most beautiful strains. Elated by his success, Marsyas was rash enough to challenge Apollo to a musical contest, the conditions of which were that the victor should do what he pleased with the

Marsyas. (Osterley, Denk. der alt. Kunst, part 2, tav. 14.)

vanquished. Apollo played upon the cithara, and Marsyas upon the flute. The Muses, who were the umpires, decided in favour of Apollo.

As a just punishment for the presumption of Marsyas, Apollo bound him to a tree, and flayed him alive. His blood was the source of the river Marsyas, and Apollo hung up his skin in the cave out of which that river flows. In the fora of ancient cities there was frequently placed a statue of Marsyas, which was probably intended to hold forth an example of the severe punishment of arrogant presumption. The statue of Marsyas in the forum of Rome is well known by the allusions of the Roman poets.—(2) A small and rapid river of Phrygia, rising in the palace of the Persian kings at Celaenae, beneath the Acropolis, and falling into the Maeander, outside of the city.—(3) A considerable river of Caria, falling into the S. side of the Maeander, nearly opposite to Tralles.

MARTĪĀLIS (-is), M. VĂLĔRĬUS (-i), the epigrammatic poet, born at Bilbilis in Spain, A.D. 43. He came to Rome in 66 ; and after residing in the metropolis 35 years, he returned to the place of his birth in 100. His death cannot have taken place before 104. His fame was widely extended, and he secured the patronage of the emperors Titus and Domitian. His extant works consist of a collection of short poems, all included under the general appellation *Epigrammata*, divided into 14 books. They are distinguished by fertility of imagination, flow of wit, and felicity of language ; but they are defiled by impurity of thought and expression, and by base flattery of the emperor Domitian.

MARTĬUS CAMPUS. [Campus Martius.]

MĀRŬVĬUM. [Marruvium.]

MASCAS, an E. tributary of the Euphrates, in Mesopotamia.

MĀSĪNISSA (-ae), king of the Numidians, son of Gala, king of the Massylians, the easternmost of the 2 great tribes into which the Numidians were at that time divided. In the 2nd Punic war he at first fought on the side of the Carthaginians in Spain (B.C. 212), but he afterwards deserted their cause and joined the Romans. On his return to Africa, he was attacked by the Carthaginians and his neighbour Syphax, and with difficulty maintained his ground till the arrival of Scipio in Africa (B.C. 204). He rendered important service to Scipio, and reduced Cirta, the capital of Syphax. Among the captives that fell into his hands on this occasion was Sophonisba, the wife of Syphax, who had been formerly promised in marriage to Masinissa himself. The story of his hasty marriage with her, and its tragical termination, is related elsewhere. [Sophonisba.] In the decisive battle of Zama (202), Masinissa commanded the cavalry of the right wing. On the conclusion of the peace between Rome and Carthage, he was rewarded with the greater part of the territories which had belonged to Syphax, in addition to his hereditary dominions. For the next 50 years Masinissa reigned in peace. He died in the 2nd year of the 3rd Punic war, B.C. 148, at the advanced age of 90, having retained in an extraordinary degree his bodily strength and activity to the last. He left 3 sons, Micipsa, Mastanabal, and Gulussa, among whom Scipio Africanus the younger divided his kingdom.

MASSA (-ae), BAEBĬUS, or BĒBĬUS (-i), was accused by Pliny the younger and Herennius Senecio, of plundering the province of Baetica, of which he had been governor, A.D. 93. He was condemned, but escaped punishment by the favour of Domitian ; and from this time he became one of the informers and favourites of the tyrant.

MASSAESȲLI or -ĬI. [Mauretania : Numidia.]

MASSĂGĔTAE (-ārum), a wild and warlike people of Central Asia, N. of the Jaxartes (the Araxes of Herodotus) and the *Sea of Aral*, and on the peninsula between this lake and the Caspian. Herodotus appears to include under the name all the nomad tribes of Asia E. of the Caspian. It was in an expedition against them that Cyrus the Great was defeated and slain. [Cyrus.]

MASSĬCUS (-i), or MASSICA (-ōrum), a mountain in the N.W. of Campania near the frontiers of Latium, celebrated for its excellent wine, the produce of the vineyards on the southern slope of the mountain. The famous Falernian wine came from the eastern side of this mountain.

MASSĬLĬA (-ae), called by the Greeks MASSĂLĬA (*Marseilles*), a Greek city in Gallia Narbonensis, on the coast of the Mediterranean, in the country of the Salyes, founded by the Phocaeans of Asia Minor about B.C. 600. It was situated on a promontory, connected with the mainland by a narrow isthmus, and washed on 3 sides by the sea. Its excellent harbour was formed by a small inlet of the sea, about half a mile long and a quarter of a mile broad. This harbour had only a narrow opening, and before it lay an island, where ships had good anchorage. At an early period the Massilienses cultivated the friendship of the Romans, to whom they always continued faithful allies. Massilia was for many centuries one of the most important commercial cities in the ancient world. In the civil war between Caesar and Pompey (B.C. 49), it espoused the cause of the latter, but after a protracted siege, in which it lost its fleet, it was obliged to submit to Caesar. Its inhabitants had long paid attention to literature and philosophy; and under the early emperors it became one of the chief seats of learning, to which the sons of many Romans resorted, in order to complete their studies.

MASSĪVA (-ae). (1) A Numidian, grandson of Gala, king of the Massylians, and nephew of Masinissa, whom he accompanied into Spain.—(2) Son of Gulussa, and grandson of Masinissa, assassinated at Rome by order of Jugurtha, because he had put in his claim to the kingdom of Numida.

MASSȲLI or -ĪI. [MAURETANIA: NUMIDIA.]

MASTANĂBAL or MANASTĂBAL (-ălis), the youngest of the 3 legitimate sons of Masinissa.

MĂTHO (-ōnis), a pompous blustering advocate, ridiculed by Juvenal and Martial.

MĂTIĀNA, the S.W.-most district of Media Atropatine, along the mountains separating Media from Assyria, inhabited by the Matiani.

MĂTĪNUS (-i), a mountain in Apulia, running out into the sea, one of the offshoots of Mt. Garganus, and frequently mentioned by Horace in consequence of his being a native of Apulia.

MATISCO (*Macon*), a town of the Aedui in Gallia Lugdunensis on the Arar.

MATRŌNA (-ae) (*Marne*), a river in Gaul, falling into the Sequana, a little S. of Paris.

MATTIĂCI (-ōrum), a people in Germany, dwelling on the E. bank of the Rhine, between the Main and the Lahn, were a branch of the Chatti. Their chief towns were Aquae Mattiacae (*Wiesbaden*) and Mattiacum (*Marburg*).

MATTĬUM (*Maden*), the chief town of the Chatti, situated on the Adrana (*Eder*).

MĂTŪTA (-ae), commonly called MĀTER MĀTŪTA, the goddess of the dawn, identified by the Romans with Leucothea. Her festival, the Matralia, was celebrated on the 11th of June (*Dict. of Ant.* art. *Matralia*).

MAURĒTĀNĬA or MAURĪTĀNĬA (-ae), a country in the N. of Africa, lying between the Atlantic on the W., the Mediterranean on the N., Numidia on the E., and Gaetulia on the S.; but the districts embraced under the names of Mauretania and Numidia respectively were of very different extent at different periods. The northern coast of Africa from the Atlantic to the Syrtes was inhabited at a very ancient period by 3 tribes: the Mauri or Maurusii, W. of the river Malva or Malucha; thence the Massaesylii to the river Ampsaga; and the Massylii between the Ampsaga and the Tusca, the W. boundary of the Carthaginian territory. Of these people, the Mauri applied themselves more to the settled pursuits of agriculture than their kindred neighbours on the E. Hence

arose a difference, which the Greeks marked by applying the general name of Νομάδις to the tribes between the Malva and the Tusca; whence came the Roman names of Numidia for the district, and Numidae for its people. [NUMIDIA.] Thus Mauretania was at first only the country W. of the Malva, but it afterwards embraced a considerable portion of the western part of Numidia. The Romans first became acquainted with the country during the war with Jugurtha, B.C. 106. [BOCCHUS.] It was made a Roman province by Claudius, who added to it all the country as far as the Ampsaga, and divided it into 2 parts, of which the W. was called Tingitana, from its capital Tingis (*Tangier*), and the E. Caesariensis from its capital Julia Caesarea, the boundary between them being the river Malva, the old limit of the kingdom of Bocchus I.

MAURI. [MAURETANIA.]

MAURĪTĀNĬA. [MAURETANIA.]

MAURŪSĬI. [MAURETANIA.]

MAUSŌLUS (-i), king of Caria, eldest son of Hecatomnus, reigned B.C. 377—353. He was succeeded by his wife and sister Artemisia, who erected to his memory the costly monument called from him the Mausoleum. [ARTEMISIA.]

MĀVORS. [MARS.]

MAXENTĬUS (-i), Roman emperor A.D. 306 — 312. He was passed over in the division of the empire which followed the abdication of his father Maximianus and Diocletian in A.D. 305; but he seized Rome, where he was proclaimed emperor, in 306. He reigned till 312, when he was defeated by Constantine at Saxa Rubra near Rome. He tried to escape over the Milvian bridge into Rome, but he perished in the river. Maxentius is represented by all historians as a monster of rapacity, cruelty, and lust.

MAXĬMIĀNUS (-i). (1) Roman emperor, A.D. 286—305, originally a Pannonian soldier, was made by Diocletian his colleague in the empire, but was compelled to abdicate along with the latter. [DIOCLETIANUS.] When his son Maxentius assumed the imperial title in the following year (306), he resided some time at Rome; but being expelled from the city by Maxentius, he took refuge in Gaul with Constantine, who had married his daughter Fausta. Here he was compelled by Constantine to put an end to his own life, in 310. — (2) GALERIUS MAXIMIANUS, usually called GALERIUS, Roman emperor, A.D. 305— 311. He was first made Caesar by Diocletian, whose daughter he had married; and upon the abdication of Diocletian and Maximianus (305) he became Augustus or emperor. He died in 311, of the disgusting disease known in modern times by the name of morbus pediculosus. He was a cruel persecutor of the Christians.

MAXĬMĪNUS (-i). (1) Roman emperor, A.D. 235—238, was born in Thrace, of barbarian parentage. He succeeded Alexander Severus; but his government was characterised by the utmost cruelty. He was slain by his own soldiers before Aquileia. The most extraordinary tales are related of his physical powers. His height exceeded 8 feet. It is said that he was able single-handed to drag a loaded waggon, and could with a kick break the leg of a horse; while his appetite was such, that in one day he could eat 40 pounds of meat, and drink an amphora of wine.— (2) Roman emperor, 308—314, nephew of Galerius, by a sister, was raised to the empire by the latter. On the death of Galerius, in 311, Maximinus and Licinius divided the East between them; but having attacked Licinius, he was defeated by the latter, and died shortly afterwards. He was a cruel persecutor of the Christians.

MAXĬMUS (-i), MAGNUS CLEMENS, Roman emperor, A.D. 383—388, in Gaul, Britain, and Spain, obtained the throne by putting Gratian to death, but was afterwards slain by Theodosius.

MAXĬMUS TȲRIUS (-i), a native of Tyre, a Greek rhetorician and Platonic philosopher, lived during the reigns of the Antonines and of Commodus, and is the author of 41 extant dissertations on philosophical subjects, written in an easy and pleasing style.

MĂZĂCA. [CAESAREA, No. 1.]

MĒCYBERNA (-ae), a town of Macedonia in Chalcidice, at the head of the Toronaic gulf, E. of Olynthus, of which it was the seaport.

MĒDAURA (-ae), a flourishing city of N. Africa, on the borders of Numidia and Byzacena; the birth-place of Appuleius.

MĒDĒA (-ae), daughter of Aeëtes, king of Colchis, celebrated for her skill in magic. When Jason came to Colchis to fetch the golden fleece, she fell in love with the hero, assisted him in accomplishing the object for which he had visited Colchis, afterwards fled with him as his wife to Greece, and prevented her father, who was in pursuit, from overtaking them, by killing her brother Absyrtus, and strewing the sea with his limbs, which her father stopped to gather. Having been deserted by Jason for the youthful daughter of

Medea and her Children. (Museo Borbonico, vol. 5, tav. 33.)

Creon, king of Corinth, she took fearful vengeance upon her faithless spouse by murdering the two children which she had had by him, and by destroying his young wife with a poisoned garment; and she then fled to Athens in a chariot drawn by winged dragons

At Athens she is said to have married king Aegeus. Her story is given in greater detail under ABSYRTUS, ARGONAUTAE, and JASON.

MĒDĔŌN (-ōnis). (1) A town in the interior of Acarnania, near the road which led from Limnaea to Stratos.—(2) A town on the coast of Phocis near Anticyra.—(3) A town in Boeotia, near Onchestus and the lake Copais.—(4) A town of the Labeates in Dalmatia, near Scodra.

MĒDĬA (-ae), an important country of Asia, above Persis, and bounded on the N. by the Araxes, on the W. and S.W. by the range of mountains called Zagros and Parachoatras (*Mts. of Kurdistan and Louristan*), which divided it from the Tigris and Euphrates valley, on the E. by the Desert, and on the N.E. by the Caspii Montes (*Elburz M.*). It was a fertile country, well peopled, and one of the most important provinces of the ancient Persian empire. After the Macedonian conquest, it was divided into 2 parts, Great Media and Atropatēne. [ATROPATENE.] The earliest history of Media is involved in much obscurity. Herodotus reckons only 4 kings of Media, namely: 1. DEIOCES, B.C. 710—657; 2. PHRAORTES, 657—635; 3. CYAXARES, 635—595; 4. ASTYAGES, 595—560. The last king was dethroned by a revolution, which transferred the supremacy to the Persians, who had formerly been the subordinate people in the united Medo-Persian empire. [CYRUS.] The Medes made more than one attempt to regain their supremacy; the usurpation of the Magian Pseudo-Smerdis was no doubt such an attempt [SMERDIS]; and another occurred in the reign of Darius II., when the Medes revolted, but were soon subdued (B.C. 408). With the rest of the Persian empire, Media fell under the power of Alexander; it next formed a part of the kingdom of the Seleucidae, from whom it was conquered by the Parthians, in the 2nd century B.C., from which time it belonged to the Parthian, and then to the later Persian empire.—It is important to notice the use of the names MEDUS and MEDI by the Roman poets, for the nations of Asia E. of the Tigris in general, and for the Parthians in particular.

MĒDĬAE MŪRUS, an artificial wall, which ran from the Euphrates to the Tigris, at the point where they approach nearest, and divided Mesopotamia from Babylonia. It is described by Xenophon (*Anab.* ii. 4), as being 20 parasangs long, 100 feet high, and 20 thick, and as built of baked bricks, cemented with asphalt.

MĒDĬŎLĀNUM (-i). (1) (*Milan*), the capital of the Insubres in Gallia Transpadana, was taken by the Romans B.C. 222, and afterwards became both a municipium and a colony. From the time of Diocletian till its capture by Attila, it was the usual residence of the emperors of the West. It is celebrated in ecclesiastical history as the see of St. Ambrose.—(2) (*Saintes*), a town of the Santones, in Aquitania, N.E. of the mouth of the Garumna; subsequently called Santones after the people, whence its modern name.

MEDIOMATRĬCI (-ōrum), a people in the S.E. of Gallia Belgica, on the Moselle, S. of the Treviri. Their chief town was Divodūrum (*Metz*).

MĒDĬTERRĀNĔUM MARE. [INTERNUM MARE.]

MEDŎĀCUS or MEDŬĀCUS (-i), a river in Venetia, in the N. of Italy, falling into the Adriatic sea near Edron, the harbour of Patavium.

MEDOBRĪGA (-ae), a town in Lusitania, on the road from Emerita to Scalabis.

MĒDON (-ontis), son of Codrus, the first archon. [CODRUS.]

MĒDŬLI (-ōrum), a people in Aquitania, on the coast of the Ocean, S. of the mouth of the Garumna, in the modern *Medoc.* There were excellent oysters found on their shores.

MĒDULLI (-ōrum), a people on the E. frontier of Gallia Narbonensis and in the Maritime Alps, in whose country the Druentia (*Durance*) and Duria (*Doria Minor*) took their rise.

MEDULLĬA (-ae), a colony of Alba, in the land of the Sabines, situated between the Tiber and the Anio.

MĒDŪSA. [GORGONES.]

MĒGAERA. [EUMENIDES.]

MĒGĂLĬA or MĒGĂRĬA, a small island in the Tyrrhene sea, opposite Neapolis.

MĒGĂLŎPŎLIS (-is), the most recent but the most important of the cities of Arcadia, was founded on the advice of Epaminondas, after the battle of Leuctra, B.C. 371, and was formed out of the inhabitants of 38 villages. It was situated in the district Maenalia, near the frontiers of Messenia, on the river Helisson, which flowed through the city. It became afterwards one of the chief cities of the Achaean league. Philopoemen and the historian Polybius were natives of Megalopolis.

MĒGĂRA (-ae, and pl. Megara, -orum). (1) The town of Megara, the capital of MEGARIS, a small district in Greece between the Corinthian and Saronic gulfs, bounded on the N. by Boeotia, on the E. and N.E. by Attica, on the S. by the territory of Corinth, and situated a mile from the sea, opposite the island of Salamis. Its citadel was called *Alcăthŏē*, from its reputed founder Alcathous, son of Pelops. Its seaport was *Nisaea*, which was connected with Megara by 2 walls, built by the Athenians when they had possession of Megara, B.C. 461—445. In front of Nisaea lay the small island *Minōa*, which added greatly to the security of the harbour. In ancient times Megara formed one of the 4 divisions of Attica. It was next conquered by the Dorians, and was for a time subject to Corinth ; but it finally asserted its independence, and rapidly became a wealthy and powerful city. Its power at an early period is attested by the flourishing colonies which it founded, of which Selymbria, Chalcedon, and Byzantium, and the Hyblaean Megara in Sicily, were the most important. After the Persian wars, Megara was for some time at war with Corinth, and was thus led to form an alliance with Athens, and to receive an Athenian garrison into the city, 461 ; but the oligarchical party having got the upper hand, the Athenians were expelled, 441. Megara is celebrated in the history of philosophy, as the seat of a philosophical school, usually called the Megarian, which was founded by Euclid, a native of the city. [EUCLIDES, No. 2.]—(2) A town in Sicily on the E. coast, N. of Syracuse, founded by Dorians from Megara in Greece, B.C. 728, on the site of a small town, Hybla, and hence called MEGARA HYBLAEA, and its inhabitants Megarenses Hyblaei. From the time of Gelon it belonged to Syracuse.

MEGĂREUS (-ei or -eos), son either of Onchestus or Poseidon (Neptune), and father of Hippomenes and Evaechme.

MEGĂRIS. [MEGARA.]

MEGIDDO, a considerable city of Palestine, on the river Kishon, in a valley of the same name, on the confines of Galilee and Samaria.

MĒLA, river. [MELLA.]

MELA or MELLA (-ae), M. ANNAEUS (-i), youngest son of M. Annaeus Seneca, the rhetorician, brother of L. Seneca, the philosopher, and father of the poet Lucan.

MĒLA (-ae), POMPŌNĬUS (-i), a native of Spain, under the emperor Claudius, and the author of an extant Latin work on geography, entitled *De Situ Orbis Libri III*.

MĒLAMPŪS (-ŏdis), son of Amythaon, a celebrated prophet and physician, and the first who introduced the worship of Dionysus (Bacchus) into Greece. He is said to have cured the women of Argos of the madness with which they had been seized, and to have received in consequence, with his brother Bias, two-thirds of the kingdom of Argos. Melampus and Bias married the two daughters of Proetus.

MĒLANCHLAENI (-ōrum), a people in the N. of Asia, about the upper course of the river Tanaïs (*Don*), resembling the Scythians in manners, though of a different race. Their Greek name was derived from their dark clothing.

MĒLANIPPĒ (-es), daughter of Chiron, also called Evippe. Being with child by Aeolus, she fled to mount Pelion, and was there metamorphosed by Artemis (Diana) into a mare.

MĒLANIPPĬDES, of Melos, a celebrated lyric poet in the department of the dithyramb, who flourished about B.C. 440.

MĒLANTHĬUS (-i), a goat-herd of Ulysses.

MĒLAS (-ănis and -ae), the name of several rivers, whose waters were of a dark colour. (1) A small river in Boeotia, flowing between Orchomenus and Aspledon.—(2) A river of Thessaly, in the district Malis, falling into the Malic gulf.—(3) A river of Thessaly in Phthiotis, falling into the Apidanus.—(4) A river of Thrace, falling into the Melas Sinus. —(5) A river in the N.E. of Sicily, flowing into the sea between Mylae and Naulochus, through excellent meadows, in which the oxen of the sun are said to have fed.—(6) A river in Asia Minor, the boundary between Pamphylia and Cilicia.

MĒLAS SĬNUS. [MELAS, No. 4.]

MELDI (-ōrum) or MELDAE (-ārum), a people in the N. of Gaul, and upon the river Sequana (*Seine*).

MĒLEAGER or MĒLĔAGRUS (-gri), son of the Calydonian king Oeneus, took part in the Argonautic expedition, and was afterwards the leader of the heroes, who slew the monstrous boar which laid waste the fields of Calydon.

68.

Meleager. (From a Painting at Pompeii.)

According to the later tradition he gave the hide of the animal to Atalanta, with whom he was in love; but his mother's brothers, the sons of Thestius, took it from her, whereupon Meleager in a rage slew them. This, however, was the cause of his own death. When he was 7 days old the Moerae or Fates declared that the boy would die as soon as the piece of wood which was burning on the hearth should be consumed. Althaea, upon hearing this, extinguished the firebrand, and concealed it in a chest; but now, to revenge the death of her brothers, she threw the piece of wood into the fire, whereupon Meleager expired. Althaea, too late repenting what she had done, put an end to her life. The sisters of Meleager wept unceasingly after his death, until Artemis (Diana) changed them into guinea-hens (μελεαγρίδες), which were transferred to the island of Leros.

Althaea and the Fates.   (Zoëga, Bassirilievi, tav. 46.)

MĔLĒTUS or MĔLĪTUS (-i), an obscure tragic poet, but notorious as one of the accusers of Socrates.

MĔLĬA (-ae) or MĔLĬĒ (-es), a nymph, daughter of Oceanus, became by Inachus the mother of Phoroneus.

MĔLĬBOEA (-ae), a town on the coast of Thessaly in Magnesia, between Mt. Ossa and Mt. Pelion, where Philoctetes reigned, who is hence called by Virgil *dux Meliboeus.*

MĔLĬCERTES. [PALAEMON.]

MĔLISSA (-ae), a nymph, said to have discovered the use of honey, and from whom bees were believed to have received their name (μέλισσαι). There can be no doubt, however, that the name really came from μέλι, honey, and was hence given to nymphs.

MĔLĬTA (-ae) or MĔLĬTĒ (-es). (1) (*Malta*), an island in the Mediterranean sea, colonised by the Phoenicians, and afterwards belonging to the Carthaginians, from whom it was taken by the Romans in the 2nd Punic war. It is celebrated as the island on which the Apostle Paul was shipwrecked; though some writers erroneously suppose that the apostle was shipwrecked on the island of the same name off the Illyrian coast. The inhabitants manufactured fine cloth (*Melitensia sc. vestimenta*).—(2) (*Meleda*), a small island in the Adriatic sea off the coast of Illyria (Dalmatia), N.W. of Epidaurus.

MĔLĬTAEA, MĔLĬTĔA, or MĔLĬTIA (-ae), a town in Thessaly in Phthiotis, on the N. slope of Mt. Othrys, and near the river Enipeus.

MĔLĬTĒ (-es), a nymph, one of the Nereides, a daughter of Nereus and Doris.

MĔLĬTĒNĒ (-es), a city and district of Armenia Minor, between the Anti-Taurus and the Euphrates.

MELLA or MĔLA (-ae: *Mella*), a river in Gallia Transpadana, flowing by Brixia, and falling into the Ollius (*Oglio*).

MELLĀRĬA (-ae). (1) A town of the Bastuli in Hispania Baetica between Belon and Calpe.—(2) A town in the same province, considerably N of the former.

MELODŪNUM (-i: *Melun*), a town of the Senones in Gallia Lugdunensis, on an island of the Sequana (*Seine*).

MĔLOS (-i), an island in the Aegaean sea, and the most W.-ly of the Cyclades, first colonised by the Phoenicians, and afterwards colonised by Lacedaemonians, or at least by Dorians. Hence in the Peloponnesian war it embraced the side of Sparta. In B.C. 416 it was taken by the Athenians, who killed all the adult males, sold the women and children as slaves, and peopled the island with an Athenian colony. Melos was the birthplace of Diagoras, the Atheist.

MELPŎMĔNĒ (-es), *i.e.* the singing goddess, one of the 9 Muses, presided over Tragedy. [MUSAE.]

MEMMĬUS (-i), the name of a Roman gens, which claimed descent from the Trojan Mnestheus. (1) C. Memmius, tribune of the plebs B.C. 111, was an ardent opponent of the oligarchical party at Rome during the Jugurthine war. He was slain by the mob of Saturninus and Glaucia, while a candidate for the consulship in 100.—(2) C. Memmius Gemellus, tribune of the plebs 66, curule aeŭile 60, and praetor 58, was impeached for ambitus, and withdrew from Rome to Mytilene. Memmius married Fausta, a daughter of the dictator Sulla, by whom he had a son. He was eminent both in literature and in eloquence. Lucretius dedicated to him his poem, *De Rerum Natura.*

MEMNŌN (-ŏnis). (1) The beautiful son of Tithonus and Eos (Aurora), was king of the Ethiopians, and came to the assistance of Priam towards the end of the Trojan war. He wore armour made for him by Hephaestus (Vulcan) at the request of his mother. He slew Antilochus, the son of Nestor, but was himself slain by Achilles, after a long and fierce combat. While the two heroes were fighting, Zeus (Jupiter) weighed their fates, and the scale containing Memnon's sank. To soothe the grief of his mother, Zeus conferred immortality upon Memnon, and caused a number of birds to issue out of the funeral pile, which fought over the ashes of the hero. These birds were called *Memnŏnĭdes,* and were said to have visited every year the tomb of the hero on the Hellespont. The Greeks gave the name of Memnŏnĭum and Memnŏnĭa to certain very ancient buildings and monuments in Europe and Asia, which they supposed to have been erected by, or in honour of, Memnon. Of these the most celebrated was a great temple of Thebes, behind which was a colossal statue (called the statue of Memnon), which, when struck by the first rays of the rising sun, was said to give forth a sound like the snapping asunder of a chord. It appears, however, that the statue represented in reality the Egyptian king Amenophis. The citadel of Susa was also called Memnonia by the Greeks.—(2) A native of Rhodes, had the command of the W. coast of Asia Minor, when Alexander invaded Asia. He was an able officer, and his death, in B.C. 333, was an irreparable loss to the Persian cause.

MEMNŌNĬUM. [Memnon, No. 1.]

MEMPHIS (-is, and -ĭdos), a great city of Egypt, second in importance only to Thebes, after the fall of which it became the capital of the whole country, a position which it had previously shared with Thebes. It is said to have been founded by Menes. It

stood on the left (W.) bank of the Nile, about 10 miles above the Pyramids.

MĔNAENUM or MĔNAE, a town on the E. coast of Sicily, S. of Hybla, the birthplace and residence of the Sicel chief Ducetius.

MENALIPPUS. [Melanippus.]

MĔNANDER, MĔNANDROS, or -DRUS (-dri), of Athens, the most distinguished poet of the New Comedy, was born B.C. 342, and was drowned in 291, while swimming in the harbour of Piraeus. He was a pupil of Theophrastus, and an intimate friend of Epicurus. Though his comedies have been lost, we can form some idea of them from those of Terence, who was little more than a translator of Menander.

MĔNĀPĬI (-ōrum), a powerful people in the N. of Gallia Belgica, originally dwelt on both banks of the Rhine, but were afterwards driven out of their possessions on the right bank by the Usipetes and Tenchteri, and inhabited only the left bank near its mouth, and W. of the Mosa.

MENDĒ (-es), or MENDAE (-arum), a town on the W. coast of the Macedonian peninsula Pellene and on the Thermaic gulf, a colony of the Eretrians, and celebrated for its wine.

MENDĒS, a considerable city of the Delta of Egypt, on the bank of one of the lesser arms of the Nile, named after it the Mendesian mouth.

MĔNĔDĒMUS (-i), a Greek philosopher, of Eretria, where he established a school of philosophy, called the Eretrian. He afterwards went to Antigonus in Asia, where he starved himself to death in the 74th year of his age, probably about B.C. 277.

MĔNĔLĀI PORTUS, an ancient city on the coast of Marmarica, in N. Africa, founded according to tradition, by Menelaus, where Agesilaus died.

MĔNĔLĀIUM (-i), a mountain in Laconia, S.E. of Sparta near Therapne, on which the heroum of Menelaus was situated.

MĔNĔLĀUS (-i), son of Plisthenes or Atreus, and younger brother of Agamemnon, was king of Lacedaemon, and married to the beautiful Helen, by whom he became the father of Hermione. His early life, the rape of his wife by Paris, and the expedition of the Greeks to Asia to punish the Trojans are related under Agamemnon. In the Trojan war Menelaus killed many Trojans, and would have slain Paris also in single combat, had not the latter been carried off by Aphroditē (Venus), in a cloud. As soon as Troy was taken Menelaus and Ulysses hastened to the house of Deiphobus, who had married Helen after the death of Paris, and put him to death in a barbarous manner. Menelaus is said to have been secretly introduced into the chamber of Deiphobus by Helen, who thus became reconciled to her former husband. He was among the first that sailed away from Troy, accompanied by his wife Helen and Nestor; but he was 8 years wandering about the shores of the Mediterranean, before he reached home. Henceforward he lived with Helen at Sparta in peace and wealth. When Telemachus visited Sparta to inquire after his father, Menelaus was solemnising the marriage of his daughter Hermione with Neoptolemus, and of his son Megapenthes with a daughter of Alector. In the Homeric poems Menelaus is described as a man of athletic figure; he spoke little, but what he said was always impressive; he was brave and courageous, but milder than Agamemnon, intelligent and hospitable. According to the prophecy of Proteus in the Odyssey, Menelaus and Helen were not to die, but the gods were to conduct them to Elysium. According to a later tradition, he and Helen went to the Taurians, where they were sacrificed by Iphigenia to Artemis. Respecting the tale that Helen never went to Troy, but was detained in Egypt, see HELENA.

MENENIUS (-i) LANATUS (-i), AGRIPPA (-ae), consul, B.C. 503. It was owing to his mediation that the first great rupture between the patricians and plebeians, when the latter seceded to the Sacred Mount, was brought to a happy and peaceful termination in 493; and it was upon this occasion he is said to have related to the plebeians his well-known fable of the belly and the members.

MENES, first king of Egypt, according to the Egyptian traditions.

MENESTHEUS (-ĕos, ĕī or eī). (1) Son of Peteus, an Athenian king, who led the Athenians against Troy. He is said to have driven Theseus from his kingdom.—(2) A charioteer of Diomedes.

MENINX (-gis), or LOTOPHAGITIS, (-is), an island close to the coast of Africa Propria, at the S.E. extremity of the Lesser Syrtis.

MENIPPUS (-i), a cynic philosopher, was a native of Gadara in Coele-Syria, and flourished about B.C. 60. He was noted for his satirical writings, whence Varro gave to his satires the name of Saturae Menippeae.

MENOECEUS (-ĕos, ĕī or eī). (1) A Theban, grandson of Pentheus, and father of Hipponomē, Jocasta, and Creon.—(2) Grandson of the former, and son of Creon, put an end to his life because Tiresias had declared that his death would bring victory to his country, when the 7 Argive heroes marched against Thebes.

MENOETIUS (-i), son of Actor and Aegina,

and father of Patroclus, who is hence called Mĕnoetĭădēs.

MENON (-ōnis), a Thessalian adventurer, one of the generals of the Greek mercenaries in the army of Cyrus the Younger, when the latter marched into Upper Asia against his brother Artaxerxes, B.C. 401. After the death of Cyrus he was apprehended along with the other Greek generals by Tissaphernes, and was put to death by lingering tortures, which lasted for a whole year. His character is drawn in the blackest colours by Xenophon. He is the same as the Menon introduced in the dialogue of Plato, which bears his name.

MENTESA. (1) Surnamed BASTIA, a town of the Oretani in Hispania Tarraconensis.—(2) A town of the Bastuli in the S. of Hispania Baetica.

MENTOR (-ŏris). (1) Son of Alcimus and a faithful friend of Ulysses, frequently mentioned in the Odyssey.—(2) A Greek of Rhodes, appointed by Darius Ochus to the satrapy of all the western coast of Asia Minor, in which he was succeeded by his brother Memnon. [MEMNON.]—(3) The most celebrated silver-chaser among the Greeks, who flourished before B.C. 356. His works were vases and cups, which were highly prized by the Romans.

MERCURII PROMONTORIUM. [HERMAEUM.]

MERCURIUS (-i), a Roman divinity of commerce and gain, identified by the Romans with the Greek Hermes. The Romans of later times transferred all the attributes and myths of Hermes to their own god. [HERMES.] The Fetiales, however, never recognised the identity; and instead of the caduceus, they used a sacred branch as the emblem of peace. The resemblance between Mercurius and Hermes is indeed very slight. The character of the Roman god is clear from his name, which is connected with merx and mercari. A temple was built to him as early as B.C. 495 near the Circus Maximus; and an altar of the god existed near the Porta Capena, by the side of a well. His festival was celebrated on the 25th of May, and chiefly by merchants, who visited the well near the Porta Capena, to which magic powers were ascribed.

MERIONES (-ae), a Cretan hero, son of Molus, was one of the bravest heroes in the Trojan war, and usually fought along with his friend Idomeneus.

MERMERUS (-i), one of the Centaurs present at the wedding of Pirithous.

MEROE (-ēs), the island, formed by the rivers Astapus and Astaboras, and the portion of the Nile between their mouths, was a district of Ethiopia. Its capital, also called

Meroë, became at a very early period the capital of a powerful state. The priests of Meroë were closely connected in origin and customs with those of Egypt; and, according to some traditions, the latter sprang from the former, and they from India. For details respecting the kingdom of Meroë, see AETHIOPIA.

MĔRŎPĒ (-ēs). (1) One of the Heliades or sisters of Phaëthon.—(2) Daughter of Atlas, one of the Pleiades, wife of Sisyphus of Corinth and mother of Glaucus. In the constellation of the Pleiades she is the 7th and the least visible star, because she is ashamed of having had intercourse with a mortal man.—(3) Daughter of Cypselus, wife of Cresphontes, and mother of Aepytus. [AEPYTUS.]

MĔROPS (-ŏpis), king of the Ethiopians, by whose wife, Clymene, Helios (Sol) became the father of Phaëthon.

MĔSEMBRĬA (-ae), (1) A celebrated town of Thrace on the Pontus Euxinus, and at the foot of Mt. Haemus, founded by the inhabitants of Chalcedon and Byzantium in the time of Darius Hystaspis, and hence called a colony of Megara, since those 2 towns were founded by the Megarians.—(2) A town in Thrace, but of less importance, on the coast of the Aegaean sea, and in the territory of the Cicones, near the mouth of the Lissus.

MĔSŎPŎTĀMĬA (-ae), a district of Asia, named from its position between the Euphrates and the Tigris, divided by the Euphrates from Syria and Arabia, and by the Tigris from Assyria. On the N. it was separated from Armenia by a branch of the Taurus, called Masius, and on the S. from Babylonia, by the Median Wall. The name was first used by the Greeks in the time of the Seleucidae. In earlier times the country was reckoned a part, sometimes of Syria, and sometimes of Assyria. In the division of the Persian empire it belonged to the satrapy of Babylonia. The N. part of Mesopotamia was divided into the districts of MYGDONIA and OSROENE. In a wider sense, the name is sometimes applied to the whole country between the Euphrates and the Tigris.

MESPĪLA (-ae), a city of Assyria, on the E. side of the Tigris, which Xenophon mentions as having been formerly a great city, inhabited by Medes, but in his time fallen to decay. Layard places it at *Kouyounjik*, opposite to Mosul.

MESSA (-ae), a town and harbour in Laconia, near C. Taenarum.

MESSĀLA or MESSALLA (-ae), the name of a distinguished family of the Valeria gens at Rome. The first who bore the name of Messala was M. VALERIUS MAXIMUS CORVINUS MESSALA, consul B.C. 263, who carried on the war against the Carthaginians in Sicily, and received this cognomen in consequence of his relieving Messina. The most celebrated member of the family was M. VALERIUS MESSALA CORVINUS. He fought on the republican side at the battle of Philippi (B.C. 42), but was afterwards pardoned by the triumvirs, and became one of the chief generals and friends of Augustus. He was consul B.C. 31, and proconsul of Aquitania 28, 27. He died about B.C. 3 — A.D. 3. Messala was a patron of learning, and was himself an historian, a poet, a grammarian, and an orator ; but none of his works are extant. His friendship for Horace and his intimacy with Tibullus are well known. In the elegies of the latter poet, the name of Messala is continually introduced.

MESSĀLĪNA, VĂLĔRĬA (-ae), wife of the emperor Claudius, and mother of Britannicus, was notorious for her profligacy and licentiousness, and long exercised an unbounded empire over her weak husband. Narcissus, the freedman of Claudius, at length persuaded the emperor to put Messalina to death, because she had publicly married a handsome Roman youth, C. Silius, during the absence of Claudius at Ostia, A.D. 48.

MESSĀNA (-ae: *Messina*), a celebrated town of Sicily, on the straits separating Italy from this island, which are here about 4 miles broad. The Romans called the town *Messana*, according to its Doric pronunciation, but *Messēnē* was its more usual name among the Greeks. It was originally a town of the Siceli, and was called ZANCLE, or a sickle, on account of the shape of its harbour, which is formed by a singular curve of sand and shells. It was first colonised by Chalcidians, and was afterwards seized by Samians, who had come to Sicily after the capture of Miletus by the Persians (B.C. 494). The Samians were shortly afterwards driven out of Zancle by Anaxilas, who changed the name of the town into *Messana* or *Messene*, both because he was himself a Messenian, and because he transferred to the place a body of Messenians from Rhegium. In B.C. 396 it was taken and destroyed by the Carthaginians, but was rebuilt by Dionysius. It afterwards fell into the hands of Agathocles. Among the mercenaries of this tyrant were a number of Mamertini, an Oscan people, from Campania, who had been sent from home under the protection of the god Mamers or Mars, to seek their fortune in other lands. These Mamertini were quartered in Messana ; and after the death of Agathocles (B.C. 282), they made themselves masters of the town, killed the male inhabitants, and took possession of their wives, their children, and their property. The town was now called MAMERTINA, and the inhabitants MAMERTINI; but its ancient name of Messana continued to be in more general use. The new inhabitants could not lay aside their old predatory habits, and in consequence became involved in a war with Hieron of Syracuse, who would probably have conquered the town, had not the Carthaginians come in to the aid of the Mamertini, and, under the pretext of assisting them, taken possession of their citadel. The Mamertini had at the same time applied to the Romans for help, who gladly availed themselves of the opportunity to obtain a footing in Sicily. Thus Messana was the immediate cause of the 1st Punic war, 264. The Mamertini expelled the Carthaginian garrison, and received the Romans, in whose power Messana remained till the latest times.

MESSAPIA (-ae), the Greek name of CALABRIA.

MESSENIA (-ae), a country in Peloponnesus, bounded on the E. by Laconia, from which it was separated by Mt. Taygetus, on the N. by Elis and Arcadia, and on the S. and W. by the sea. In the Homeric times the western part of the country belonged to the Neleid princes of Pylos, of whom Nestor was the most celebrated; and the eastern to the Lacedaemonian monarchy. On the conquest of Peloponnesus by the Dorians, Messenia fell to the share of Cresphontes, who became king of the whole country. Messenia was more fertile than Laconia; and the Spartans soon coveted the territory of their brother Dorians; and thus war broke out between the two people. The 1st Messenian war lasted 20 years, B.C. 743—723; and notwithstanding the gallant resistance of the Messenian king, Aristodemus, the Messenians were obliged to submit to the Spartans after the capture of their fortress Ithome. [ARISTODEMUS.] After bearing the yoke 38 years, the Messenians again took up arms under their heroic leader Aristomenes. [ARISTOMENES.] The 2nd Messenian war lasted 17 years, B.C. 685—668, and terminated with the conquest of Ira and the complete subjugation of the country. Most of the Messenians emigrated to foreign countries, and those who remained behind were reduced to the condition of Helots or serfs. In this state they remained till 464, when the Messenians and other Helots took advantage of the devastation occasioned by the great earthquake at Sparta, to rise against their oppressors. This 3rd Messenian war lasted 10 years, 464—455, and ended by the Messenians surrendering Ithome to the Spartans on condition of being allowed a free departure from Peloponnesus. When the

supremacy of Sparta was overthrown by the battle of Leuctra, Epaminondas collected the Messenian exiles, and founded the town of Messene (B.C. 369), at the foot of Mt. Ithome, which formed the acropoli of the city. Messene was made the capital of the country. Messenia was never again subdued by the Spartans, and it maintained its independence till the conquest of the Achaeans and the rest of Greece by the Romans, 146.

MESTRA (-ae), daughter of Erysichthon, and granddaughter of Triopas, whence she is called Triopeis by Ovid.

METABUS (-i), a chief of the Volsci, father of Camilla.

METANIRA (-ae), wife of Celeus, and mother of Triptolemus. [CELEUS.]

METAPONTIUM, called METAPONTUM (-i) by the Romans, a celebrated Greek city in Lucania, and on the Tarentine gulf. It was founded by the Greeks at an early period, was afterwards destroyed by the Samnites, and was repeopled by a colony of Achaeans. It fell into the hands of the Romans with the other Greek cities in the S. of Italy in the war against Pyrrhus; but it revolted to Hannibal after the battle of Cannae.

METAURUM. [METAURUS, No. 2.]

METAURUS (-i). (1) A small river in Umbria, flowing into the Adriatic sea, memorable by the defeat and death of Hasdrubal, the brother of Hannibal, on its banks B.C. 207.—(2) A river on the E. coast of Bruttium, at whose mouth was the town of Metaurum.

METELLUS (-i), a distinguished plebeian family of the Caecilia gens at Rome. (1) L. CAECILIUS METELLUS, consul B.C. 251, when he defeated the Carthaginians in Sicily; consul a 2nd time in 249; and afterwards pontifex maximus; while holding the latter dignity he rescued the Palladium when the temple of Vesta was on fire, and lost his sight in consequence. —(2) Q. CAECILIUS METELLUS MACEDONICUS, was praetor 148, when he defeated the usurper Andriscus in Macedonia, and received in consequence the surname of Macedonicus. He was consul in 143, and carried on the war against the Celtiberians in Spain.—(3) Q. CAECILIUS METELLUS NUMIDICUS, consul B.C. 109, carried on the war against Jugurtha in Numidia with great success, and received in consequence the surname of Numidicus. [JUGURTHA.] In 107 he was superseded in the command by Marius. [MARIUS.] In 102 he was censor, and two years afterwards (100) he was banished from Rome through the intrigues of his enemy Marius. He was however recalled in the following year (99). Metellus was one of the chief leaders of the aristocratical party, and a man of unsullied character.—(4) CAECILIUS METELLUS PIUS, son of of the preceding, received the surname of Pius on account of the love which he displayed for his father when he besought the people to recal him from banishment in 99. He was praetor B.C. 89, and one of the commanders in the Marsic or Social war. He subsequently fought as one of Sulla's generals against the Marian party, and was consul with Sulla himself in B.C. 80. In the following year (79), he went as proconsul into Spain, where he carried on the war against Sertorius for many years (B.C. 79—72). He died in B.C. 63, and was succeeded in the dignity of pontifex maximus by Julius Caesar.—(5) Q. CAECILIUS METELLUS CELER, praetor B.C. 63, and consul 60, was a warm supporter of the aristocratical party. He died in 59, and it was suspected that he had been poisoned by his wife Clodia.—(6) Q. CAECILIUS METELLUS NEPOS, younger brother of the preceding, tribune B.C. 62, praetor 60, and consul 57, supported Pompey against the aristocracy.—(7) Q. CAECILIUS METELLUS PIUS SCIPIO, the adopted son of Metellus Pius [No. 4], was the son of P. Scipio Nasica, praetor 94. Pompey married Cornelia, the daughter of Metellus Scipio in B.C. 52 and in the same year made his father-in-law his colleague in the consulship. Scipio fought on the side of Pompey in the civil war, and after the battle of Pharsalia, crossed over to Africa, where he received the command of the Pompeian troops. He was defeated by Caesar at the battle of Thapsus in 46 ; and shortly afterwards he put an end to his own life.—(8) Q. CAECILIUS METELLUS CRETICUS, consul B.C. 69, carried on war against Crete, which he subdued in the course of 3 years. —(9) L. CAECILIUS METELLUS, brother of the last, praetor 71, and as propraetor the successor of Verres in the government of Sicily.—(10) M. CAECILIUS METELLUS, praetor 69, presided at the trial of Verres.

METHÔNÊ (-es). (1) Or MOTHONE, a town at the S.W. corner of Messenia, with an excellent harbour, protected from the sea by a reef of rocks, of which the largest was called Mothon.—(2) A town in Macedonia on the Thermaic gulf, founded by the Eretrians, and celebrated from Philip having lost an eye at the siege of the place.—(3) Or METHANA, an ancient town in Argolis, situated on a peninsula of the same name, opposite the island of Aegina.

MÊTHYMNA (-ae), the second city of LESBOS, stood at the N. extremity of the island. It was the birthplace of the poet Arion, and of the historian Hellanicus. The celebrated Lesbian wine grew in its neighbourhood. In the Peloponnesian war it remained faithful to Athens, even during the great Lesbian revolt [MYTILENE] : afterwards it was sacked by the Spartans (B.C. 406).

MÊTIS (-Idis), the personification of prudence, described as a daughter of Oceanus and Tethys, and the first wife of Zeus (Jupiter). Afraid lest she should give birth to a child wiser and more powerful than himself, Zeus devoured her in the first month of her pregnancy. Afterwards he gave birth to Athêna, who sprang from his head.

MÊTIUS. [METTIUS.]

MÊTÔN (-ónis), an astronomer of Athens, who, in conjunction with EUCTEMON, introduced the cycle of 19 years, by which he adjusted the course of the sun and moon. The commencement of this cycle has been placed B.C. 432.

MÊTRÔDÔRUS (-i), a native of Lampsacus or Athens, an Epicurean philosopher, and the most distinguished of the disciples of Epicurus, died B.C. 277.

MÊTRÔPÔLIS (-is), a town of Thessaly in Histiaeotis, near the Peneus, and between Gomphi and Pharsalus. There were several other cities of this name.

METTIUS or MÊTIUS. (1) CURTIUS. [CURTIUS.]—(2) FUFFETIUS, dictator of Alba, was torn asunder by chariots driven in opposite directions, by order of Tullus Hostilius, 3rd king of Rome, on account of his treachery towards the Romans.

MÊTULUM (-i), the chief town of the Iapydes in Illyricum.

MÊVÂNIA (-ae : Bevagna), an ancient city in the interior of Umbria on the river Tinea, situated in a fertile country, and celebrated for its breed of beautiful white oxen. According to some accounts Propertius was a native of this place.

MÊZENTIUS (-i), king of the Tyrrhenian Caere or Agylla, was expelled by his subjects on account of his cruelty, and took refuge with Turnus, king of the Rutulians, whom he assisted in the war against Aeneas and the Trojans. Mezentius and his son Lausus were slain in battle by Aeneas.

MÎCIPSA (-ae), king of Numidia (B.C. 148 —118), e.dest of the sons of Masinissa. He left the kingdom to his 2 sons, Adherbal and Hiempsal, and their adopted brother JUGURTHA.

MICON, of Athens, a distinguished painter and statuary, contemporary with Polygnotus, about B.C. 460.

MÎDAS or MÎDA (-ae), son of Gordius and king of Phrygia, renowned for his immense riches. In consequence of his kind treatment of Silenus, the companion and teacher of Dionysus (Bacchus), the latter allowed Midas to ask a favour of him. Midas in his folly desired that all things which he touched should be changed into gold. The request was granted ; but as even the food which he touched became gold, he implored the god to take his favour back. Dionysus accordingly ordered him to bathe in the sources of the Pactolus near Mt. Tmolus. This bath saved Midas, but the river from that time had an abundance of gold in its sand. Once when Pan and Apollo were engaged in a musical contest on the flute and lyre, Midas was chosen to decide between them. The king decided in favour of Pan, whereupon Apollo changed his ears into those of an ass. Midas contrived to conceal them under his Phrygian cap, but the servant who used to cut his hair discovered them. The secret so much harassed the man, that as he could not betray it to a human being, he dug a hole in the earth, and whispered into it, " King Midas has ass's ears." He then filled up the hole, and his heart was released. But on the same spot a reed grew, which in its whispers betrayed the secret.

MIDEA or MĪDĒA (-ae), a town in Argolis.

MĪLĂNĪŌN (-ōnis), husband of Atalanta. [ATALANTA.]

MĪLĒTUS (-i). (1) Son of Apollo and Arīa of Crete, fled from Minos to Asia, where he built the city of Miletus. Ovid calls him a son of Apollo and Deïone, and hence Deïonides.—(2) One of the greatest cities of Asia Minor, belonged territorially to Caria and politically to Ionia, being the S.-most of the 12 cities of the Ionian confederacy. The city stood upon the S. headland of the Sinus Latmicus, opposite to the mouth of the Maeander, and possessed 4 distinct harbours, protected by a group of islets; its territory was rich in flocks, and the city was celebrated for its woollen fabrics, the *Milesia vellera.* At a very early period it became a great maritime state, and founded numerous colonies, especially on the shores of the Euxine. It was the birthplace of the philosophers Thales, Anaximander, and Anaximenes, and of the historians Cadmus and Hecataeus. It was the centre of the great Ionian revolt against the Persians, after the suppression of which it was destroyed (B.C. 494). It recovered sufficient importance to oppose a vain resistance to Alexander the Great, which brought upon it second ruin. Under the Roman empire it still appears as a place of some consequence.

MILO or MĪLŌN (-ōnis). (1) Of Crotona, a celebrated athlete, 6 times victor in wrestling at the Olympic games, and as often at the Pythian. He was one of the followers of Pythagoras, and commanded the army which defeated the Sybarites, B.C. 511. Many stories are related of his extraordinary feats of strength ; such as his carrying a heifer four years old on his shoulders through the stadium at Olympia, and afterwards eating the whole of it in a single day. Passing through a forest in his old age, he saw the trunk of a tree which had been partially split open by woodcutters, and attempted to rend it further, but the wood closed upon his hands, and thus held him fast, in which state he was attacked and devoured by wolves. —(2) T. ANNIUS MILO PAPINIANUS, was born at Lanuvium, of which place he was in B.C. 53 dictator or chief magistrate. As tribune of the plebs, B.C. 57, Milo took an active part in obtaining Cicero's recal from exile ; and from this time he carried on a fierce and memorable contest with P. Clodius. In 53 Milo was candidate for the consulship, and Clodius for the praetorship of the ensuing year. Each of the candidates kept a gang of gladiators, and there were frequent combats between the rival ruffians in the streets of Rome. At length, on the 20th of January, 52, Milo and Clodius met apparently by accident at Bovillae on the Appian road. An affray ensued between their followers, in which Clodius was slain. At Rome such tumults followed upon the burial of Clodius, that Pompey was appointed sole consul in order to restore order to the state. Milo was brought to trial. He was defended by Cicero ; but was condemned, and went into exile at Massilia (*Marseilles*). The soldiers who lined the forum intimidated Cicero ; and he could not deliver the oration which he had prepared. Milo returned to Italy in 48, in order to support the revolutionary schemes of the praetor, M. Caelius ; but he was slain under the walls of an obscure fort in the district of Thurii. Milo, in 57, married Fausta, a daughter of the dictator Sulla.

MILTĬĂDĒS (-is). (1) Son of Cypselus, an Athenian, in the time of Pisistratus, founded a colony in the Thracian Chersonesus, of which he became tyrant. He died without children, and his sovereignty passed into the hands of Stesagoras, the son of his half-brother Cimon.—(2) Son of Cimon and brother of Stesagoras, became tyrant of the Chersonesus on the death of the latter, being sent out by Pisistratus from Athens to take possession of the vacant inheritance. He joined Darius Hystaspis on his expedition against the Scythians, and was left with the other Greeks in charge of the bridge over the Danube. When the appointed time had expired, and Darius had not returned, Miltiades recommended the Greeks to destroy the bridge, and leave Darius to his fate. After the suppression of the Ionian revolt, and the approach of the Phoenician fleet, Miltiades fled to Athens. Here he was arraigned, as being amenable to the penalties enacted against tyranny, but was acquitted. When Attica was threatened with invasion by the Persians under Datis and Artaphernes, Miltiades was chosen one of the ten generals. Miltiades by his arguments induced the polemarch Callimachus to give the casting vote in favour of risking a battle with the enemy, the opinions of the ten generals being equally divided. Miltiades waited till his turn came, and then drew his army up in battle array on the memorable field of Marathon. [MARATHON.] After the defeat of the Persians, Miltiades induced the Athenians to entrust to him an armament of 70 ships, without knowing the purpose for which they were designed. He proceeded to attack the island of Paros, for the purpose of gratifying a private enmity. His attacks, however, were unsuccessful; and after receiving a dangerous hurt in the leg, he was compelled to raise the siege and return to Athens, where he was impeached by Xanthippus for having deceived the people. His wound had turned into a gangrene, and being unable to plead his cause in person, he was brought into court on a couch, his brother Tisagoras conducting his defence for him. He was condemned; but on the ground of his services to the state the penalty was commuted to a fine of 50 talents, the cost of the equipment of the armament. Being unable to pay this, he was thrown into prison where he not long after died of his wound. The fine was subsequently paid by his son Cimon.

MILVĬUS PONS. [ROMA.]

MILȲAS. [LYCIA.]

MĬMALLŎNES, or MĬMALLŎNĬDES (-um), the Macedonian name of the Bacchantes.

MĪMAS (-antis). (1) One of the giants who warred against the gods, slain by a flash of lightning. — (2) A promontory in Ionia, opposite the island of Chios.

MĬMNERMUS (-i), a celebrated elegiac poet, generally called a Colophonian, was properly a native of Smyrna, and was descended from those Colophonians who reconquered Smyrna from the Aeolians. He flourished from about B.C. 634 to 600, and was a contemporary of Solon. Mimnermus was the first who systematically made the elegy the vehicle for plaintive, mournful, and erotic strains. Only a few fragments of his poems are extant.

MINCĬUS (-i : *Mincio*), a river in Gallia Transpadana, flowing through the lake Benacus (*Lago di Garda*), and falling into the Po, a little below Mantua.

MĬNERVA (-ae), called ATHĒNA by the Greeks. The Greek goddess is spoken of in a separate article [ATHENA], and we here confine ourselves to the Roman goddess. Minerva was one of the great Roman divinities. Her name probably contains the same root as *mens;* and she is accordingly the thinking power personified. In the Capitol Minerva had a chapel in common with Jupiter and Juno. She was worshipped as the goddess of wisdom and the patroness of all the arts and trades. Hence the proverbs "to do a thing *pingui Minerva,*" i.e. to do a thing in an awkward or clumsy manner; and *sus Minervam,* of a stupid person who presumed to set right an intelligent one. Minerva also guided men in the dangers of war, where victory is gained by prudence, courage, and perseverance. Hence she was represented with a helmet, shield, and a coat of mail; and the booty made in war was frequently dedicated to her. She was further believed to be the inventor of musical instruments, especially wind instruments, the use of which was very important in religious worship, and which were accordingly subjected to a sort of purification every year on the last day of the festival of Minerva. This festival lasted 5 days, from the 19th to the 23rd of March, and was called *Quinquatrus.* The most ancient temple of Minerva at Rome was probably that on the Capitol; another existed on the Aventine; and she had a chapel at the foot of the Caelian hill, where she bore the surname of *Capta.*

MINERVAE PRŎMONTŎRĬUM (-i), a rocky promontory in Campania, running out a long way into the sea, 6 miles S.E. of Surrentum, on whose summit was a temple of Minerva, said to have been built by Ulysses. Here the Sirens are reported to have dwelt.

MĬNĬO (-onis : *Mignone*), a small river in Etruria, falling into the Tyrrhene sea, between Graviscae and Centum Cellae.

MĬNŌA. [MEGARA.]

MĪNŌS (-ŏis). (1) Son of Zeus (Jupiter) and Europa, brother of Rhadamanthus, king and legislator of Crete, and after death one of the judges of the shades in Hades.—(2) Son of Lycastus, and grandson of the former, was likewise a king and lawgiver of Crete. He was the husband of Pasiphaë, a daughter of Helios (the sun), and the father of Deucalion, Androgeos, Ariadne, and Phaedra. In order to avenge the wrong done to his son Androgeos [ANDROGEUS] at Athens, he made war against the Athenians, and compelled them to send to Crete every year, as a tribute, 7 youths and 7 maidens, to be devoured in the labyrinth by the Minotaurus. The Minotaur was a monster, half man and half

bull, and the offspring of the intercourse of
Pasiphaë with a bull. The labyrinth in
which it was kept was constructed by Daedalus. This monster was slain by Theseus,
with the assistance of Ariadne, the daughter
of Minos. [THESEUS.] Daedalus having fled

Theseus and Minotaur. (From a painted Vase.)

from Crete to escape the wrath of Minos,
Minos followed him to Sicily, and was there
slain by Cocalus and his daughters. From
Minos we have *Mīnōis*, a daughter or a
female descendant of Minos, as Ariadne, and
the adjectives *Mīnōius* and *Mīnōus*, used by
the poets as equivalent to Cretan.

MĪNŌTAURUS. [MINOS.]

MINTHA (-ae) or MINTHE (-es), a
daughter of Cocytus, beloved by Hades,
metamorphosed by Demeter (Ceres), or Persephŏnē (Proserpĭna), into a plant called
after her *mintha*, or mint.

MINTURNAE (-ārum), an important town
in Latium, on the frontiers of Campania,
situated on the Appia Via, and on both banks
of the Liris, and near the mouth of this river.
It was an ancient town of the Ausones or
Aurunci, but surrendered to the Romans of
its own accord, and received a Roman colony
v.c. 296. In its neighbourhood was a grove
sacred to the nymph Marica, and also extensive marshes (*Paludes Minturnenses*), formed
by the overflowing of the river Liris, in
which Marius was taken prisoner. [See p.
258, a.]

MĪNŪCĬUS (-i), the name of a Roman gens,
of whom the most celebrated was M. Minucius Rufus, magister equitum to the dictator
Q. Fabius Maximus, B.C. 217, in the war

against Hannibal. He fell at the battle of
Cannae.

MĪNYAE (-ārum), an ancient Greek race,
originally dwelling in Thessaly. Their ancestral hero, Minyas, is said to have migrated
from Thessaly into the N. of Boeotia, and
there to have established the empire of the
Minyae, with the capital of Orchomenos.
[ORCHOMENOS.] As the greater part of the
Argonauts were descended from the Minyae,
they are themselves called Minyae. The
Minyae founded a colony in Lemnos, called
Minyae, whence they proceeded to Elis
Triphylia, and to the island of Thera. A
daughter of Minyas was called *Mĭnyēias*
(*-ădis*) or *Mĭnyēis* (*-ĭdis*). His daughters
were changed into bats, because they had
slighted the festival of Dionysus (Bacchus).

MĪSĒNUM (-i), a promontory in Campania, S. of Cumae, said to have derived its
name from Misenus, the companion and
trumpeter of Aeneas, who was drowned and
buried here. The bay formed by this promontory was converted by Augustus into an
excellent harbour, and was made the principal station of the Roman fleet on the Tyrrhene sea. A town sprang up around the
harbour. Here was the villa of C. Marius,
which afterwards passed into the hands of
the emperor Tiberius, who died at this place.

MITHRĀS (-ae), the god of the sun among
the Persians. Under the Roman emperors
his worship was introduced at Rome. The
god is commonly represented as a handsome
youth, wearing the Phrygian cap and attire,
and kneeling on a bull, whose throat he is
cutting.

MĪTHRĬDĀTĒS (-is), the name of several
kings of Pontus, of whom the best known is
Mithridates VI., surnamed the Great, and
celebrated on account of his wars with the
Romans. He reigned B.C. 120—63. He
was a man of great energy and ability; and
so powerful was his memory, that he is said
to have learnt not less than 25 languages.
Having greatly extended his empire in the
early part of his reign by the conquest of the
neighbouring nations, he at length ventured
to measure his strength with Rome. The
first Mithridatic war lasted from B.C. 88 to
84. At first he met with great success. He
drove Ariobarzanes out of Cappadocia, and
Nicomedes out of Bithynia, both of whom
had been previously expelled by him, but
restored by the Romans; and he at last
made himself master of the Roman province
of Asia. During the winter he ordered all
the Roman and Italian citizens in Asia to be
massacred; and on one day no fewer than
80,000 Romans and Italians are said to have
perished. Meantime Sulla had received the

command of the war against Mithridates, and crossed over into Greece in 87. Archelaus, the general of Mithridates, was twice defeated by Sulla in Boeotia (86); and about the same time the king himself was defeated in Asia by Fimbria. [FIMBRIA.] Mithridates now sued for peace, which was granted him by Sulla in 84. The second Mithridatic war (B.C. 83—82), was caused by the unprovoked attacks of Murena, who had been left in command of Asia by Sulla. Murena invaded the dominions of Mithridates, but was defeated by the latter, and was ordered by Sulla to desist from hostilities. The third Mithridatic war was the most important of the three. It lasted from B.C. 74 to the king's death in 63. It broke out in consequence of the king seizing Bithynia, which had been left by Nicomedes III. to the Roman people. The consul Lucullus was appointed to the command, and conducted it with great success. In B.C. 73 he relieved Cyzicus, which was besieged by Mithridates, and in the course of the next two years drove the king out of Pontus, and compelled him to flee to his son-in-law, Tigranes, the king of Armenia. The latter espoused the cause of his father-in-law; whereupon Lucullus marched into Armenia, and defeated Tigranes and Mithridates, in two battles in B.C. 69 and 68. But in consequence of the mutiny of his soldiers, who demanded to be led home, Lucullus could not follow up his conquests; and Mithridates recovered Pontus. In B.C. 66 Lucullus was succeeded in the command by Pompey. Mithridates was defeated by Pompey; and as Tigranes now refused to admit him into his dominions, he marched into Colchis, and thence made his way to Panticapaeum, the capital of the Cimmerian Bosporus. Here he conceived the daring project of marching round the N. and W. coasts of the Euxine, through the wild tribes of the Sarmatians and Getae, and of invading Italy at the head of these nations. But meanwhile disaffection had made rapid progress among his followers. His son, Pharnaces, at length openly rebelled against him, and was joined by the whole army, and the citizens of Panticapaeum, who proclaimed him king. Mithridates, resolved not to fall into the hands of the Romans, put an end to his own life, B.C. 63, at the age of 68 or 69, after a reign of 57 years.

MĪTHRĬDĀTĒS, Kings of Parthia. [ARSACES, 6, 9, 13.]

MĬTŸLĒNĔ. [MYTILENE.]

MNĒMŎSŸNĔ (-es), i.e., Memory, daughter of Uranus (Heaven), and mother of the Muses by Zeus (Jupiter).

MNESTHEUS (-ĕĭ or -eĭ), a Trojan, who accompanied Aeneas to Italy, and is said to have been the ancestral hero of the Memmii.

MŌĂBĪTIS, called MOAB in the Old Testament, a district of Arabia Petraea, E. of the Dead Sea. The Moabites were frequently at war with the Israelites. They were conquered by David, but they afterwards recovered their independence.

MOERIS (-ĭdis), a king of Egypt, who is said to have dug the great lake known by his name; but it is really natural, and not an artificial lake. It is on the W. side of the Nile, in Middle Egypt, and used for the reception and subsequent distribution of a part of the overflow of the Nile.

MOESĬA (-ae), a country of Europe, was bounded on the S. by Thrace and Macedonia, on the W. by Illyricum and Pannonia; on the N. by the Danube, and on the E. by the Pontus Euxinus, thus corresponding to the present Servia and Bulgaria. This country was subdued in the reign of Augustus, and was made a Roman province at the commencement of the reign of Tiberius. It was afterwards formed into 2 provinces, called Moesia Superior and Moesia Inferior, the former being the western, and the latter the eastern half of the country. When Aurelian surrendered Dacia to the barbarians, and removed the inhabitants of that province to the S. of the Danube, the middle part of Moesia was called Dacia Aureliani.

MOGONTĬĂCUM, MOGUNTĬĂCUM, or MAGONTĬĂCUM (-i: Mainz or Mayence), a town on the left bank of the Rhine, opposite the mouth of the river Moenus (Main).

MOIRAE, called PARCAE (-arum) by the Romans, the Fates, were 3 in number, viz., CLOTHO, or the spinning fate; LACHĔSIS, or the one who assigns to man his fate; and ATRŎPOS, or the fate that cannot be avoided. Sometimes they appear as divinities of fate in the strict sense of the term, and sometimes only as allegorical divinities of the duration of human life. In the former character they take care that the fate assigned to every being by eternal laws may take its course without obstruction; and both gods and men must submit to them. These grave and mighty goddesses were represented by the earliest artists with staffs or sceptres, the symbol of dominion. The Moirae, as the divinities of the duration of human life, which is determined by the two points of birth and of death, are conceived either as goddesses of birth or as goddesses of death. The distribution of the functions among the 3 was not strictly observed, for we sometimes find all 3 described as spinning the thread of life, although this was properly the function of Clotho alone. Hence Clotho, and sometimes the other fates, are represented with a spindle; and they are said to break or cut off the thread when life is to end. The poets sometimes describe them as aged and hideous women, and even as lame, to indicate the slow march of fate; but in works of art they are represented as grave maidens, with different attributes, viz., Clotho, with a spindle or a roll (the book of fate); Lachesis pointing with a staff to the globe; and Atropos, with a pair of scales, or a sun-dial, or a cutting instrument.

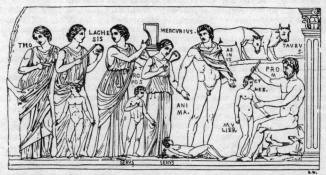

The Moirae or Parcae (Fates) and Prometheus. (Visconti, Mus. Pio Clem. vol. 4, tav. 34.)

MOLĬŎNĒ. [MOLIONES.]

MOLĬONES (-um) or MŎLĬŎNĬDAE (-ārum), that is, Eurytus and Cteatus, so called after their mother Molionē. They are also called Actŏrĭdae or Actŏrĭōne (᾿Ακτορίωνι) after their reputed father Actor, the husband of Molione. They are mentioned as conquerors of Nestor in the chariot race, and as having taken part in the Calydonian hunt. Having come to the assistance of Augeas against Hercules, they were slain by the latter.

MŎLOSSI (-ōrum), a people in Epirus, inhabiting a narrow slip of country, called after them MOLOSSIA or MOLOSSIS, which extended along the W. bank of the Arachthus, as far as the Ambracian gulf. They were the most powerful people in Epirus, and their kings gradually extended their dominion over the whole of the country. The first of their kings, who took the title of king of Epirus, was Alexander, who perished in Italy B.C. 326. [EPIRUS.] Their capital was AMBRACIA. The Molossian hounds were celebrated in antiquity.

MŎLȲCRĬUM (-i), a town in the S. of Aetolia, at the entrance of the Corinthian gulf.

MŎMUS (-i), the god of mockery and censure, called by Hesiod the son of Night. Thus he is said to have censured in the man formed by Hephaestus (Vulcan), that a little door had not been left in his breast, so as to enable one to look into his secret thoughts.

MŎNA (-ae : *Anglesey*), an island off the coast of the Ordovices, in Britain, one of the chief seats of the Druids. Caesar erroneously describes this island as half way between Britannia and Hibernia. Hence it has been supposed by some critics that the Mona of Caesar is the *Isle of Man;* but it is more probable, on account of the celebrity of Mona in connection with the Druids, that he had heard of *Anglesey*, and that he received a false report respecting its real position.

MŎNAESES (-is), a Parthian general mentioned by Horace, probably the same as Surenas, the general of Orodes, who defeated Crassus.

MŎNĒTA (-ae), a surname of Juno among the Romans, as the protectress of money. Under this name she had a temple on the Capitoline, which was at the same time the public mint.

MŎNOECI PORTUS, also HERCŬLIS MŎNOECI PORTUS (*Monaco*), a port-town on the coast of Liguria, founded by the Massilians, was situated on a promontory (hence the *arx Monoeci* of Virgil), and possessed a temple of Hercules Monoecus, from whom the place derived its name.

MOPSĬA or MOPSŎPIA, an ancient name of Attica, whence *Mopsŏpĭus* is frequently used by the poets as equivalent to Athenian.

MOPSĬUM (-i), a town of Thessaly, in Pelasgiotis, situated on a hill of the same name between Tempe and Larissa.

MOPSUESTĬA (-ae), an important city of Cilicia, on both banks of the river Pyramus.

MOPSUS (-i). (1) Son of Ampyx and the nymph Chloris, the prophet and soothsayer of the Argonauts, died in Lybia of the bite of a snake.—(2) Son of Apollo and Manto, the daughter of Tiresias, and also a celebrated seer. He contended in prophecy with Calchas at Colophon, and showed himself superior to the latter in prophetic power. [CALCHAS.] He was believed to have founded Mallos, in Cilicia, in conjunction with the seer Amphilochus. A dispute arose between the two seers respecting the possession of the town, and both fell in combat by each other's hand.

MORGANTĬUM (-i), MORGANTĬNA, MURGANTĬA, MORGENTĬA (-ae), a town in Sicily, S.E. of Agyrium, and near the Symaethus, founded by the Morgētes, after they had been driven out of Italy by the Oenotrians.

MORGĒTES. [MORGANTIUM.]

MORĬNI (-ōrum), the most N.-ly people in all Gaul, whence Virgil calls them *extremi hominum*. They dwelt on the coast, at the narrowest part of the channel between Gaul and Britain.

MORPHEUS (-ĕŏs, -ĕĭ, or -eī), the son of Sleep, and the god of dreams. The name signifies the fashioner or moulder, because he shaped or formed the dreams which appeared to the sleeper.

MORS (-tis), called THĂNĂTOS by the Greeks, the god of death, is represented as a son of Night, and a brother of Sleep.

MŌSA (-ae: *Maas* or *Meuse*), a river in Gallia Belgica, rising in Mt. Vogesus, and falling into the Vahalis or W. branch of the Rhine.

MOSCHI (-ōrum), a people of Asia, dwelling in the S. part of Colchis.

MOSCHUS (-i), of Syracuse, a bucolic poet, lived about B.C. 250. There are 4 of his idyls extant, usually printed with those of BION.

MŌSELLA (-ae : *Mosel, Moselle*), a river in Gallia Belgica, rising in Mt. Vogesus, and falling into the Rhine at Confluentes (*Coblenz*).

MOSTĒNI (-ōrum), a city of Lydia, S.E. of Thyatira.

MOSYNOECĬ (-ōrum), a barbarous people on the N. coast of Asia Minor, in Pontus, so called from the conical wooden houses in which they dwelt.

MŌTŪCA (-ae), a town in the S. of Sicily, W. of the promontory Pachynus. The inhabitants were called Mutycenses.

MŌTỸA (-ae), an ancient town in the N.W. of Sicily, situated on a small island near the coast, with which it was connected by a mole. It was founded by the Phoenicians, and next belonged to the Carthaginians, who trans-

planted its inhabitants to the town of Lilybaeum, B.C. 397.

MŪCĬUS SCAEVŎLA. [SCAEVOLA.]

MULCĬBER (-bri), a surname of Vulcan, which seems to have been given him as an euphemism, that he might not consume the habitations of men, but might kindly aid them in their pursuits.

MULŬCHA (-ae), a river in the N. of Africa, rising in the Atlas, and forming the boundary between Mauretania and Numidia.

MUMMĬUS (-i), L., consul B.C. 146, won for himself the surname of Achaicus, by the conquest of Greece, and the establishment of the Roman province of Achaia. After defeating the army of the Achaean league at the Isthmus of Corinth, he entered Corinth without opposition, and rased it to the ground. [CORINTHUS.] He was censor in 142 with Scipio Africanus the younger.

MŪNĀTĬUS PLANCUS. [PLANCUS.]

MUNDA (-ae), a town in Hispania Baetica, celebrated on account of the victory of Julius Caesar over the sons of Pompey, B.C. 45.

MŪNỸCHĬA (-ae), the smallest and the most E.-ly of the 3 harbours of Athens. The poets use Munychian in the sense of Athenian.

MURCĬA, MURTĒA, or MURTĬA (-ae), a surname of Venus at Rome, where she had a chapel in the circus, with a statue. This surname, which is said to be the same as Myrtea (from *myrtus,* a myrtle), was believed to indicate the fondness of the goddess for the myrtle tree.

MŪRĒNA (-ae), which signifies a lamprey, was the name of a family in the Licinia gens, of whom the most important were :—(1) L. LICINIUS MURENA, who was left by Sulla as propraetor in Asia, B.C. 84, and was the cause of the 2nd Mithridatic war.—(2) L. LICINIUS MURENA, son of the former, consul B.C. 63, was accused of bribery, and defended by Cicero in an extant oration.

MURGANTĬA. [MORGANTIUM.]

MUS, DĒCIUS. [DECIUS.]

MUSA (-ae), ANTŌNĬUS, a celebrated physician at Rome, was brother to Euphorbus, the physician to king Juba, and was himself the physician to the emperor Augustus. He had been originally a slave.

MŪSAE (-arum,) the Muses, were, according to the earliest writers, the inspiring goddesses of song, and, according to later notions, divinities presiding over the different kinds of poetry, and over the arts and sciences. They are usually represented as the daughters of Zeus (Jupiter) and Mnemosynē, and born in Pieria, at the foot of Mt. Olympus. Their original number appears to have been 3; but afterwards they are always spoken of as 9 in number. Their names and attributes were :—

1. *Clīo*, the Muse of history, represented in a sitting or standing attitude, with an open roll of paper, or chest of books.

Clio, the Muse of History (From a Statue now in Sweden.)

2. *Euterpĕ*, the Muse of lyric poetry, with a flute.

Euterpe, the Muse of Lyric Poetry. (From a Statue in the Vatican.)

3. *Thălīa*, the Muse of comedy, and of merry or idyllic poetry, appears with a comic mask, a shepherd's staff, or a wreath of ivy.

Thalia, the Muse of Comedy. (From a Statue in the Vatican.)

4. *Melpŏmĕnĕ*, the Muse of tragedy, with a tragic mask, the club of Hercules, or a

Melpomene, the Muse of Tragedy. (From a Statue in the Vatican.)

sword: her head is surrounded with vine leaves, and she wears the cothurnus.

5. *Terpsichŏrē*, the Muse of choral dance and song, appears with the lyre and the plectrum.

6. *Erătō*, the Muse of erotic poetry and mimic imitation, sometimes also has the lyre.

7. *Pŏlymnĭa* or *Pŏlyhymnĭa*, the Muse of the sublime hymn, usually appears without any attribute, in a pensive or meditating attitude.

8. *Ŭrănĭa* the Muse of astronomy, with a staff pointing to a globe.

Erato, the Muse of Erotic Poetry. (From a Statue in the Vatican.)

Urania, the Muse of Astronomy. (From a Statue now in Sweden.)

9. *Callĭŏpē* or *Callĭŏpēa*, the Muse of epic poetry, represented in works of art with a tablet

Polymnia, the Muse of the Sublime Hymn. (From a Statue in the Louvre.)

Calliope, the Muse of Epic Poetry. (From a Statue in the Vatican.)

and stylus, and sometimes with a roll of paper or a book.

The worship of the Muses was introduced from Thrace and Pieria into Boeotia; and their favourite haunt in Boeotia was Mt. Helicon, where were the sacred fountains of Aganippe and Hippocrene. Mt. Parnassus was likewise sacred to them, with the Castalian spring. The sacrifices offered to the Muses consisted of libations of water or milk, and of honey. The Muses were invoked by the poets as the inspiring goddesses of song; and all who ventured to compete with them in song were severely punished by them. Thus the Sirens, who had done so, were deprived of the feathers of their wings, which the Muses put on their own persons as ornaments; and the 9 daughters of Pierus, who had likewise presumed to rival the Muses, were metamorphosed into birds. Being goddesses of song, they were naturally connected with Apollo, the god of the lyre, who is even described as the leader of the choir of the Muses by the surname *Mūsăgĕtēs*.

MŪSAEUS (-i), a semi-mythological personage, to be classed with Olen and Orpheus, is represented as one of the earliest Grecian poets. The extant poem on the loves of Hero and Leander, bearing the name of Musaeus, is a late production.

MŪSĂGĒTĒS. [Musae.]

MŪTĬNA (-ae : *Modena*), an important town in Gallia Cispadana, originally a town of the Boii, and afterwards a Roman colony. It is celebrated in the history of the civil war after Caesar's death. Decimus Brutus was besieged here by M. Antonius from December, 44, to April 43; and under its walls the battles were fought, in which the consuls Hirtius and Pansa perished.

MȲCĂLĒ (-es), a mountain in the S. of Ionia in Asia Minor, N. of the mouth of the Maeander, and opposite the island of Samos. Here a great victory was gained by the Greeks over the Persian fleet on the same day as the battle of Plataea, B.C. 479.

MȲCĂLESSUS (-i), an ancient city in Boeotia, on the road from Aulis to Thebes. In B.C. 413 it was sacked by some Thracian mercenaries in the pay of Athens.

MȲCĒNAE (-ārum), sometimes MȲCĒNĒ (-es), an ancient town in Argolis, about 6 miles N.E. of Argos, situated on a hill at the head of a narrow valley. Mycenae is said to have been founded by Perseus, and was subsequently the favourite residence of the Pelopidae. During the reign of Agamemnon it was regarded as the first city in all Greece; but after the conquest of Peloponnesus by the Dorians, it ceased to be a place of importance. It continued an independent town till

B.C. 468, when it was attacked by the Argives, and the inhabitants were compelled by famine to abandon it. Mycenae was now destroyed by the Argives; but there are still numerous remains of the ancient city, which on account of their antiquity and grandeur are some of the most interesting in all Greece.

MYCERĪNUS (-i), son of Cheops, king of Egypt, succeeded his uncle Chephren on the throne, and reigned with justice. He began to build a pyramid, but died before it was finished.

MȲCŌNUS (-i), a small island in the Aegaean sea, one of the Cyclades, E. of Delos, is celebrated in mythology as one of the places where the giants were defeated by Hercules.

MYGDŌN (-onis), son of Acmon, who fought against the Amazons, and from whom some of the Phrygians are said to have been called Mygdonians. He had a son, Coroebus, who is hence called *Mygdŏnĭdēs*.

MYGDŌNIA (-ae). (1) A district in the E. of Macedonia, bordering on the Thermaic gulf and the Chalcidic peninsula.—(2) A district in the E. of Mysia and the W. of Bithynia, named after the Thracian people, Mygdones, who formed a settlement here, but were afterwards subdued by the Bithyni.—(3) The N.E. district of Mesopotamia, between Mt. Masius and the Chaboras, which divided it from Osroëne. The name of Mygdonia was first introduced after the Macedonian conquest.

MȲLAE (-ārum), a town on the E. part of the N. coast of Sicily, founded by Zancle (Messana), and situated on a promontory running out into the sea. It was off Mylae that Agrippa defeated the fleet of Sex. Pompeius, B.C. 36.

MȲLĂSA or MȲLASSA (-ōrum), a flourishing inland city of Caria, in a fertile plain.

MYNDUS (-i), a Dorian colony on the coast of Caria, situated at the W. extremity of the same peninsula on which Halicarnassus stood.

MYONNĒSUS (-i), a promontory of Ionia, with a town and a little island of the same name, forming the N. headland of the gulf of Ephesus.

MȲOS HORMŎS (ὁ Μυὸς ὅρμος, i. e. *Muscieport*), an important port-town of Upper Egypt, built by Ptolemy II. Philadelphus, on the Red Sea, 6 or 7 days' journey from Coptos.

MYRA (-ae and -ōrum), one of the chief cities of Lycia, built on a rock 2 miles from the sea.

MYRIANDRUS (-i), a Phoenician colony in Syria, on the E. side of the Gulf of Issus, a little S. of Alexandria.

MYRĪNA (-ae). (1) An ancient and important city of the Aeolians on the W. coast of Mysia.—(2) A town in Lemnos.

MYRLĒA (-ae), a city of Bithynia, not far from Prusa, founded by the Colophonians, and almost rebuilt by Prusias I., who called it APAMEA, after his wife.

MYRMĬDŎNES (-um), an Achaean race in Phthiotis in Thessaly, whom Achilles ruled over and who accompanied this hero to Troy. They are said to have inhabited originally the island of Aegina, and to have emigrated with Peleus into Thessaly ; but modern critics on the contrary suppose that a colony of them emigrated from Thessaly into Aegina. The Myrmidones disappear from history at a later period. The ancients derived their name either from a mythical ancestor Myrmidon, son of Zeus (Jupiter) and Eurymedusa, and father of Actor ; or from the ants (μύρμηκες) in Aegina, which were supposed to have been metamorphosed into men in the time of Aeacus. [AEACUS.]

MȲRŌN (-ōnis), a celebrated Greek statuary, and also a sculptor and engraver, was born at Eleutherae, in Boeotia, about B.C. 480. He was the disciple of Ageladas, the fellow-disciple of Polycletus, and a younger contemporary of Phidias. He practised his art at Athens, about the beginning of the Peloponnesian war (B.C. 431).

MYRRHA, or SMYRNA. [ADONIS.]

MYRTĬLUS (-i), son of Hermes (Mercury) and charioteer of Oenomaus king of Pisa, thrown into the sea by Pelops. [PELOPS.] After his death, Myrtilus was placed among the stars as auriga.

MYRTŌUM MARE, the part of the Aegaean sea, S. of Euboea, Attica and Argolis, which derived its name from the small island Myrtus, though others suppose it to come from Myrtilus, whom Pelops threw into this sea.

MYRTUNTĬUM (-i), called MYRSINUS in Homer, a town of the Epeans in Elis, on the road from Elis to Dyme.

MYRTUS. [MYRTOUM MARE.]

MYS (-yŏs), one of the most distinguished Greek engravers, who engraved the battle of the Lapithae and the Centaurs and other figures on the shield of Phidias's statue of Athena Promachos, in the Acropolis of Athens.

MYSCĔLUS (-i), a native of Achaia, who founded Croton in Italy, B.C. 710.

MȲSĬA (-ae), a district occupying the N.W. corner of Asia Minor, between the Hellespont on the N.W.; the Propontis on the N.; Bithynia and Phrygia on the E. ; Lydia on the S. ; and the Aegaean Sea on the W. It was subdivided into 5 parts: (1.) MYSIA MINOR, along the N. coast. (2.) MYSIA MAJOR, the S.E. inland region, with a small

portion of the coast between the Troad and the Aeolic settlements about the Elaïtic Gulf. (3.) TROAS, the N.W. angle, between the Aegaean and Hellespont and the S. coast along the foot of Ida. (4.) AEOLIS or AEOLIA, the S. part of the W. coast, around the Elaïtic Gulf, where the chief cities of the Aeolian confederacy were planted; and (5.) TEUTHRANIA, the S.W. angle, between Temnus and the borders of Lydia, where, in very early times, Teuthras was said to have established a Mysian kingdom, which was early subdued by the kings of Lydia. This account applies to the time of the early Roman empire ; the extent of Mysia, and its subdivisions, varied greatly at other times. The Mysi were a Thracian people, who crossed over from Europe into Asia at a very early period. In the heroic ages we find the great Teucrian monarchy of Troy in the N.W. of the country, and the Phrygians along the Hellespont : as to the Mysians, who appear as allies of the Trojans, it is not clear whether they are Europeans or Asiatics. The Mysia of the legends respecting Telephus is the Teuthranian kingdom in the S., only with a wider extant than the later Teuthrania. Under the Persian empire, the N.W. portion, which was still occupied in part by Phrygians, but chiefly by Aeolian settlements, was called Phrygia Minor, and by the Greeks HELLESPONTUS. Mysia was the region S. of the chain of Ida ; and both formed, with Lydia, the second satrapy. Mysia afterwards formed a part of the kingdom of PERGAMUS (B.C. 280.) With the rest of the kingdom of Pergamus, Mysia fell to the Romans in 133, by the bequest of Attalus III., and formed part of the province of Asia.

MȲTĬLĒNĒ or MĬTȲLĒNĒ (-es), the chief city of LESBOS, situated on the E. side of the island, opposite the coast of Asia, was early colonised by the Aeolians. [LESBOS.] It attained great importance as a naval power, and founded colonies on the coasts of Mysia and Thrace. At the beginning of the 7th century B.C., the possession of one of these colonies, Sigeum, at the mouth of the Hellespont, was disputed in war between the Mytilenaeans and Athenians. After the Persian war, Mytilene formed an alliance with Athens ; but in the 4th year of the Peloponnesian War, B.C. 428, it headed a revolt of the greater part of Lesbos, the progress and suppression of which forms one of the most interesting episodes in the history of the Peloponnesian War. (See the Histories of Greece.) This event destroyed the power of Mytilene. Respecting its important position in Greek literary history, see LESBOS.

MYŪS (-untis), the least city of the Ionian confederacy, stood in Caria, on the S. side of the Maeander.

NĂBĂTAEI (-ōrum), NĂBĂTHAE (-ārum), an Arabian people, who occupied nearly the whole of Arabia Petraea, on both sides of the Aelanitic Gulf of the Red Sea, and the Idumaean mountains, where they had their rock-hewn capital, PETRA. The Roman poets frequently use the adjective Nabathaeus in the sense of Eastern.

NABIS (-is), tyrant of Lacedaemon, noted for his acts of cruelty, succeeded Machanidas in the sovereignty, B.C. 207. He was defeated by Philopoemen in B.C. 192, and was soon afterwards assassinated by some Aetolians.

NABONASSAR, king of Babylon, whose accession to the throne was the era from which the Babylonian astronomers began their calculations. This era is called the *Era of Nabonassar*, and commenced B.C. 747.

NAEVĬUS (-i), CN., an ancient Roman poet, probably a native of Campania, produced his first play, B.C. 235. He was attached to the plebeian party; attacked Scipio and the Metelli in his plays; but he was indicted by Q. Metellus and thrown into prison, and obtained his release only by recanting his previous imputations. His repentance did not last long, and he was soon compelled to expiate a new offence by exile. He retired to Utica, where he died about B.C. 202. Naevius wrote a poem on the first Punic war as well as comedies and tragedies.

NAHARVĂLI (-ōrum), a tribe of the Lygii in Germany, probably dwelling on the banks of the Vistula.

NAĬĂDES. [NYMPHAE.]

NAISUS, NAISSUS, or NAESUS (-i : *Nissa*), a town of Upper Moesia, situated on an E. tributary of the Margus, and celebrated as the birthplace of Constantine the Great.

NAMNĚTAE (-ārum), or NAMNĚTES (-um), a people on the W. coast of Gallia Lugdunensis, on the N. bank of the Liger. Their chief town was Condivincum, afterwards Namnetes (*Nantes*).

NANTUĀTAE (-ārum), or NANTUĀTES (-um), a people in the S.E. of Gallia Belgica, at the E. extremity of the Lacus Lemanus (*Lake of Geneva*).

NĂPAEAE. [NYMPHAE.]

NĂR (-āris: *Nera*), a river in central Italy, rising in Mt. Fiscellus, forming the boundary between Umbria and the land of the Sabini, and falling into the Tiber, not far from Ocriculum. It was celebrated for its sulphureous waters and white colour.

NARBO (-ōnis) MARTĬUS (-i), a town in the S. of Gaul, and the capital of the Roman province of Gallia Narbonensis, situated on the river Atax (*Aude*). It was made a Roman colony by the consul Q. Marcius or Martius, B.C. 118, and hence received the surname Martius. It was the first colony founded by the Romans in Gaul.

NARBŌNENSIS GALLĬA. [GALLIA.]

NARCISSUS (-i). (1) A beautiful youth, son of Cephissus and Liriope, was inaccessible to the feeling of love; and the nymph Echo, who was enamoured of him, died of grief. [ECHO.] But Nemesis, to punish him, caused him to see his own image reflected in a fountain, whereupon he became so enamoured of it, that he gradually pined away, until he was metamorphosed into the flower which bears his name.—(2) A favourite freedman and secretary of the emperor Claudius, who amassed an enormous fortune. He was put to death by order of Agrippina, A.D. 54.

NARISCI (ōrum), a people in the S. of Germany, in the *Upper Palatinate* and the country of the *Fichtelgebirge*.

NARNĬA (-ae : *Narni*), a town in Umbria, situated on a lofty hill, on the S. bank of the river Nar, originally called NEQUINUM, and made a Roman colony B.C. 299, when its name was changed into Narnia, after the river.

NARONA (-ae), a Roman colony in Dalmatia, situated on the river Naro.

NĂRYX (-ўcis), also NARȲCUS or NĂRȲCĬUM (-i), a town of the Locri Opuntii, on the Euboean sea, the birthplace of Ajax, son of Oileus, who is hence called *Narȳcius hērōs*. Since Locri Epizephyrii, in the S. of Italy, claimed to be a colony from Naryx, in Greece, we find the town of Locri called *Narȳcia* by the poets, and the pitch of Bruttium, also named *Narȳcia*.

NĂSĂMŌNES (-um), a powerful but savage Libyan people, who dwelt originally on the shores of the Great Syrtis, but were driven inland by the Greek settlers of Cyrenaica, and afterwards by the Romans.

NĂSĬCA, SCĪPĬO. [SCIPIO.]

NĂSĬDIĒNUS (-i), a wealthy Roman, who gave a supper to Maecenas, which Horace ridicules in one of his satires.

NĂSO, ŌVĬDĬUS. [OVIDIUS.]

NATTA or NACCA, "a fuller," the name of an ancient family of the Pinaria gens. The Natta, satirised by Horace for his dirty meanness, was probably a member of the noble Pinarian family, and therefore attacked by the poet for such conduct.

NAUCRĂTIS (-is), a city in the Delta of Egypt, on the E. bank of the Canopic branch of the Nile, was a colony of the Milesians, founded in the reign of Amasis, about B.C. 550, and remained a pure Greek city. It was the only place in Egypt where Greeks were permitted to settle and trade. It was the birthplace of Athenaeus, Julius Pollux, and others.

NAULŎCHUS (-i), a naval station on the E. part of the N. coast of Sicily, between Mylae and the promontory Pelorus.

NAUPACTUS (-i: *Lepanto*), an ancient town of the Locri Ozolae, near the promontory Antirrhium, possessing the best harbour on the N. coast of the Corinthian gulf. It is said to have derived its name from the Heraclidae having here built the fleet, with which they crossed over to the Peloponnesus (from *ναῦς* and *πήγνυμι*). After the Persian wars it fell into the power of the Athenians, who settled here the Messenians who had been compelled to leave their country at the end of the 3rd Messenian war, B.C. 455.

NAUPLĬA (-ae), the port of Argos, situated on the Saronic gulf, was never a place of importance in antiquity; but is at the present day one of the chief cities in Greece.

NAUPLĬUS (-i), king of Euboea, and father of Palamedes, who is hence called NAUPLĬĀDĒS. To avenge the death of his son, whom the Greeks had put to death during the siege of Troy, he watched for the return of the Greeks, and as they approached the coast of Euboea he lighted torches on the dangerous promontory of Caphareus. The sailors, thus misguided, suffered shipwreck.

NAUPORTUS (-i: *Ober* or *Upper Laibach*), an important town of the Taurisci, situated on the river Nauportus (*Laibach*), a tributary of the Savus, in Pannonia Superior.

NAUSĬCĂA (-ae), daughter of Alcinous, king of the Phaeacians, and Arete, who conducted Ulysses to the court of her father, when he was shipwrecked on the coast.

NAUTĒS. [NAUTIA GENS.]

NAUTĬA GENS, a patrician gens at Rome, claiming descent from Nautes, one of the companions of Aeneas, who was said to have brought with him the Palladium from Troy, which was placed under the care of the Nautii at Rome.

NĀVA (-ae: *Nahe*), a tributary of the Rhine, falling into the Rhine at the modern *Bingen*.

NĂVĬUS, ATTUS, or ATTĬUS (-i), a renowned augur in the time of Tarquinius Priscus, who opposed the project of the king to double the number of the equestrian centuries. Tarquin then commanded him to divine whether what he was thinking of in his mind could be done; and when Navius declared that it could, the king held out a

whetstone and a razor to cut it with. Navius immediately cut it.

NAXOS, or NAXUS (-i). (1) An island in the Aegaean sea, and the largest of the Cyclades, especially celebrated for its wine. Here Dionysus (Bacchus) is said to have found Ariadne after she had been deserted by Theseus. It was colonised by Ionians, who had emigrated from Athens. After the Persian wars, the Naxians were the first of the allied states whom the Athenians reduced to subjection (B.C. 471). — (2) A Greek city on the E. coast of Sicily, founded B.C. 735 by the Chalcidians of Euboea, and the first Greek colony established in the island. In B.C. 403 the town was destroyed by Dionysius of Syracuse, but nearly 50 years afterwards (358) the remains of the Naxians scattered over Sicily were collected by Andromachus, and a new city was founded on Mt. Taurus, to which the name of Tauromenium was given. [TAUROMENIUM.]

NAZARETH, NAZĂRA (-ae), a city of Palestine, in Galilee, S. of Cana.

NAZIANZUS, a city of Cappadocia, celebrated as the diocese of the Father of the Church, Gregory Nazianzen.

NĔAERA (-ae), the name of several nymphs and maidens mentioned by the poets.

NĔAETHUS (-i: *Nieto*), a river in Bruttium, falling into the Tarentine gulf a little N. of Croton. Here the captive Trojan women are said to have burnt the ships of the Greeks.

NĔAPŎLIS (-is). (1) (*Naples*), a city in Campania, at the head of a beautiful bay, and on the W. slope of Mt. Vesuvius, was founded by the Chalcidians of Cumae, on the site of an ancient place called PARTHENOPE, after the Siren of that name. Hence we find the town called Parthenope by Virgil and Ovid. When the town is first mentioned in Roman history, it consisted of 2 parts, divided from each other by a wall, and called respectively Palaeopolis, or the "Old City," and Neapolis, or the "New City." This division probably arose after the capture of Cumae by the Samnites, when a large number of the Cumaeans took refuge in the city they had founded; whereupon the old quarter was called Palaeopolis, and the new quarter, built to accommodate the new inhabitants, was named Neapolis. In B.C. 327 the town was taken by the Samnites, and in 290 it passed into the hands of the Romans, but it continued to the latest times a Greek City. Under the Romans the 2 quarters of the city were united, and the name of Palaeopolis disappeared. Its beautiful scenery, and the luxurious life of its Greek population, made it a favourite residence with many of the Romans. In the neighbourhood of Neapolis there were warm baths, the celebrated villa of Lucullus, and the villa Pausïlÿpi or Pausïlÿpum, bequeathed by Vedius Pollio to Augustus, and which has given its name to the celebrated grotto of *Posilippo*, between Naples and Puzzoli, at the entrance of which the tomb of Virgil is still shown.—(2) A part of Syracuse. [SYRACUSAE.]

NEARCHUS (-i), an officer of Alexander, who conducted the Macedonian fleet from the mouth of the Indus to the Persian gulf, B.C. 326—325. He left a history of the voyage, the substance of which has been preserved to us by Arrian.

NEBO, a mountain of Palestine, on the E. side of the Jordan, and in the S. part of the range called Abarim. It was on a summit of this mountain, called Pisgah, that Moses died.

NEBRŌDĒS (-ae), the principal chain of mountains in Sicily, running through the whole of the island, and a continuation of the Apennines.

NECESSĬTĀS (-ātis), called ANANKĒ by the Greeks, the personification of Necessity, is represented as a powerful goddess, whom

Necessitas.   (Causei, Museum Romanum, vol. 1, tav. 28.)

neither gods nor men can resist. She carries in her hand brazen nails, with which she fixes the decrees of fate.

NĚCO or NECHO, King of Egypt B.C. 617—601, son and successor of Psammetichus. In his reign the Phoenicians, in his service, are said to have circumnavigated Africa. In his march against the Babylonians he defeated at Magdolus (Megiddo) Josiah, king of Judah, who was a vassal of Babylon; and he afterwards defeated the Babylonians themselves at the Euphrates, and took Carchemish or Circesium; but in 606 he was in his turn defeated by Nebuchadnezzar.

NECTANĀBIS (-is). (1) King of Egypt, B.C. 374—864, who successfully resisted the invasion of the Persian force under Pharnabazus and Iphicrates. He was succeeded by Tachos. — (2) The nephew of Tachos, deprived the latter of the sovereignty in 361, with the assistance of Agesilaus. He was defeated by the Persians in 350, and fled into Aethiopia.

NĚLEUS (-ĕŏs, ĕĭ, or eī), son of Poseidon (Neptune), and of Tyro, the daughter of Salmoneus. Together with his twin-brother Pelias, he was exposed by his mother, but the children were found and reared by some countrymen. They subsequently learnt their parentage; and after the death of Cretheus, king of Iolcos, who had married their mother, they seized the throne of Iolcos, excluding Aeson, the son of Cretheus and Tyro. But Pelias soon afterwards expelled his brother, and thus became sole king. Thereupon Neleus went with Melampus and Bias to Pylos, in Peloponnesus, of which he became king. [PYLOS.] Neleus had 12 sons, but they were all slain by Hercules, when he attacked Pylos, with the exception of Nestor.

NĚLĬDĒS or NĒLĒĬADES (-ae), patronymics of Neleus, by which either Nestor, the son of Neleus, or Antilochus, his grandson, is designated.

NĔMAUSUS (-i : *Nismes*), an important town of Gallia Narbonensis, the capital of the Arecomici and a Roman colony, was situated W. of the Rhone on the high road from Italy to Spain. The Roman remains at *Nismes* are some of the most perfect on this side of the Alps.

NĔMĔA (-ae) or NĔMĔE (-ēs), a valley in Argolis between Cleonae and Phlius, celebrated in mythical story as the place where Hercules slew the Nemaean lion. [See p. 196.] In this valley there was a splendid temple of Zeus Nemĕus (the Nemaean Jupiter) surrounded by a sacred grove, in which the Nemaean games were celebrated every other year.

NĔMĔSĬĀNUS (-i), M. AURELĬUS ŌLYMPĬUS, a Roman poet at the court of the emperor Carus (A.D. 283), the author of an extant poem on hunting, entitled *Cynegetica*.

NĔMĔSIS (-is), a Greek goddess, who measured out to mortals happiness and misery, and visited with losses and sufferings all who were blessed with too many gifts of fortune. This is the character in which she appears in the earlier Greek writers ; but subsequently she was regarded, like the Erinnyes or Furies, as the goddess who punished crimes. She is frequently mentioned under the surnames of Adrastia, and Rhamnusia or Rhamnusis, the latter from the town of Rhamnus, in Attica, where she had a celebrated sanctuary.

Nemesis and Elpis. (From the Chigi Vase.)

NEMETACUM or NEMETOCENNA. [Atrebates.]

NĔMĔTES (-um) or NĔMĔTAE (-ārum), a people in Gallia Belgica on the Rhine, whose chief town was Noviomagus, subsequently Nemetae (*Speyer* or *Spires*).

NĔMŌRENSIS LACUS. [Aricia.]

NEMOSSUS. [Arverni.]

NĔŎBŪLĔ. [Archilochus.]

NĔŎCAESARĔA (-ae), a city of Pontus, in Asia Minor, standing on the river Lycus.

NĔON, an ancient town in Phocis, at the E. foot of Mt. Tithorea, a branch of Mt. Parnassus, destroyed by the Persians under Xerxes, but rebuilt and named Tithorea, after the mountain on which it was situated.

NEONTĪCHOS (*i. e.* New Wall). (1) One of the 12 cities of Aeolis, on the coast of Mysia.—(2) A fort on the coast of Thrace, near the Chersonesus.

NĔOPTŎLĔMUS (-i), also called PYRRHUS, son of Achilles and DeidamIa, the daughter of Lycomedes. He was named Pyrrhus on account of his fair (πυῤῥὸς) hair, and Neoptolemus because he came to Troy late in the war. From his father he is sometimes called *Achillīdes*, and from his grand-father or great-grandfather, *Pelīdes* and *Aeacīdes*. Neoptolemus was brought up in Scyros, in the palace of Lycomedes, and was fetched from thence by Ulysses, because it had been prophesied that Neoptolemus and Philoctetes were necessary for the capture of Troy. At Troy Neoptolemus showed himself worthy of his great father. He was one of the heroes concealed in the wooden horse. At the capture of the city he killed Priam at the sacred hearth of Zeus (Jupiter), and sacrificed Polyxena to the spirit of his father. When the Trojan captives were distributed among the conquerors, Andromachē, the widow of Hector, was given to Neoptolemus. On his return to Greece, he abandoned his native kingdom of Phthia, in Thessaly, and settled in Epirus, where he became the ancestor of the Molossian kings. He married Hermione, the daughter of Menelaus, but was slain in consequence by Orestes, to whom Hermione had been previously promised.

NĔPĔTĔ or NĔPET (-is : *Nepi*), an ancient town of Etruria, situated near the saltus Ciminius.

NĔPHĔLĔ (-es), wife of Athamas and mother of Phrixus and Helle. Hence Helle is called *Nĕphĕlĕis*. [Athamas.]

NĔPOS (-ōtis), CORNĔLĬUS (-i), the contemporary and friend of Cicero, Atticus, and Catullus, was probably a native of Verona, and died during the reign of Augustus. Nepos wrote several historical works ; and there is still extant under his name a work entitled *Vitae Excellentium Imperatorum*, containing biographies of several distinguished commanders. But in all MSS. this work is ascribed to an unknown Aemilius Probus, living under Theodosius at the end of the 4th century of the Christian aera ; with the exception, however, of the life of Atticus, and the fragment of a life of Cato the Censor, which are expressly attributed to Cornelius Nepos. These 2 lives may safely be assigned to Cornelius Nepos ; but the Latinity of the other biographies is such that we cannot suppose them to have been written by a learned contemporary of Cicero. It is probable that Probus abridged the work of Nepos, and that the biographies, as they now exist, are in reality epitomes of lives actually written by Nepos.

NEPTŪNUS (-i), called PŎSEIDON by the Greeks. Neptunus was the chief marine divinity of the Romans ; but as the early Romans were not a maritime people, we know next to nothing of the worship of the Italian god of this name. His temple stood in the Campus Martius. At his festival the people formed tents (*umbrae*) of the branches of trees, in which they enjoyed themselves in feasting and drinking. In the Roman poets Neptune is completely identified with the Greek Poseidon, and accordingly all the attributes of the latter are transferred to them to the former. [POSEIDON.]

NĒRĔIS or NĒRĒIS (-ĭdis), daughter of Nereus and Doris, and used especially in the plural, NĒRĒIDES or NĒRĒĬDES (-um), to indicate the 50 daughters of Nereus and Doris. The *Nereïdes* were the marine nymphs of the Mediterranean, in contradistinction to the *Naïädes*, the nymphs of fresh water, and the *Ŏcĕănĭdes*, the nymphs of the great ocean. One of the most celebrated of the Nereides was Thetis, the mother of Achilles. They are described as lovely divinities, dwelling with their father at the bottom of the sea, and were believed to be propitious to sailors. They were worshipped in several parts of Greece, but more especially in seaport towns. They are frequently represented in works of art, and commonly as youthful beautiful maidens; but sometimes they appear on gems as half maidens and half fishes.

NĒRĒIUS (-i), a name given by the poets to a descendant of Nereus, such as Phocus and Achilles.

NĒREUS (-ĕŏs, -ĕĭ, or -ĕi), son of Pontus and Gaea, and husband of Doris, by whom he became the father of the 50 Nereides. He is described as the wise and unerring old man of the sea, at the bottom of which he dwelt. His empire is the Mediterranean or more particularly the Aegaean sea, whence he is sometimes called the Aegaean. He was believed, like other marine divinities, to have the power of prophesying the future, and of appearing to mortals in different shapes ; and in the story of Hercules he acts a prominent part, just as Proteus in the story of Ulysses, and Glaucus in that of the Argonauts. In works of art, Nereus, like other sea-gods, is sometimes represented with pointed sea-weeds taking the place of hair in the eyebrows, the chin, and the breast.

Nereus. (Panofka, Musée Blacas, pl. 20.)

NĒRĪCUS. [LEUCAS.]

NĒRĪNĒ (-ēs), equivalent to Nērĕis, a daughter of Nereus. [NEREIS.]

NĒRĬO, NĒRĬĒNĒ, or NĒRĬĒNIS. [MARS.]

NERITUM or -US (-i), a mountain in Ithaca, and also a small rocky island near Ithaca. The adjective *Nĕrĭtĭus* is often used by the poets as equivalent to Ithacan or Ulyssean.

NĒRO (-ōnis), the name of a celebrated family of the Claudia gens. (1) C. CLAUDIUS

NERO, consul B.C. 207, when he defeated and slew Hasdrubal, the brother of Hannibal, on the river Metaurus.—(2) TIB. CLAUDIUS NERO, husband of Livia, and father of the emperor Tiberius and of his brother Drusus. [LIVIA.] —(3) ROMAN EMPEROR, A.D. 54—68, was the son of Cn. Domitius Ahenobarbus, and of Agrippina, daughter of Germanicus. Nero's original name was *L. Domitius Ahenobarbus*, but after the marriage of his mother with her uncle, the emperor Claudius, he was adopted by Claudius (A.D. 50), and was called *Nero Claudius Caesar Drusus Germanicus.* Nero was born at Antium, A.D. 37. Shortly after his adoption by Claudius, Nero, being then 16 years of age, married Octavia, the daughter of Claudius and Messalina (53). Among his early instructors was Seneca. On the death of Claudius (54), Agrippina secured the succession for her son, to the exclusion of Britannicus, the son of Claudius. The young emperor soon distinguished himself by his licentiousness, brutality, and cruelty. He put to death Britannicus, his mother Agrippina, and finally his wife Octavia; he murdered the latter that he might marry his mistress, Poppaea Sabina, the wife of Otho. The great fire at Rome happened in Nero's reign (A.D. 64), but it is hardly credible that the city was fired by Nero's order, as some ancient writers assert. The emperor set about rebuilding the city on an improved plan, with wider streets. The odium of the conflagration, which the emperor could not remove from himself, he tried to throw on the Christians, and many of them were put to a cruel death. The tyranny of Nero at last (A.D. 65) led to the organisation of a formidable conspiracy against him, usually called Piso's conspiracy, from the name of one of the principal accomplices. The plot was discovered, and many distinguished persons were put to death, among whom was Piso himself, the poet Lucan, and the philosopher Seneca. Three years afterwards, Julius Vindex, the governor of Gaul, raised the standard of revolt. His example was followed by Galba, who was governor of Hispania Tarraconensis. Soon after this news reached Rome, Nero was deserted. He fled to a house about 4 miles from Rome, where he put an end to his life on hearing the trampling of the horses on which his pursuers were mounted, A.D. 68. The most important external events in his reign were the conquest of Armenia by Domitius Corbulo [CORBULO], and the insurrection of the Britons under Boadicea, which was quelled by Suetonius Paulinus.

NERVA (-ae), M. COCCEIUS (-i), Roman emperor, A.D. 96—98, was born at Narnia, in Umbria, A.D. 32. On the assassination of Domitian, Nerva was declared emperor, and his administration at once restored tranquillity to the state. The class of informers was suppressed by penalties, and some were put to death. At the commencement of his reign, Nerva swore that he would put no senator to death; and he kept his word, even when a conspiracy had been formed against his life by Calpurnius Crassus. Though Nerva was virtuous and humane, he did not possess much energy and vigour. He adopted as his son and successor, M. Ulpius Trajanus. [TRAJANUS.]

NERVII (-ōrum), a powerful and warlike people in Gallia Belgica, whose territory extended from the river Sabis (*Sambre*) to the ocean.

NESIS (-idis: *Nisita*), a small island off the coast of Campania between Puteoli and Neapolis, a favourite residence of the Roman nobles.

NESSONIS, a lake in Thessaly, a little S. of the river of Peneus.

NESSUS. [HERCULES, p. 200.]

NESTOR (ŏris), king of Pylos, son of Neleus and Chloris, and the only one of the 12 sons of Neleus, who was not slain by Hercules. [NELEUS.] In his early manhood, Nestor was a distinguished warrior. He defeated both the Arcadians and Eleans. He took part in the fight of the Lapithae against the Centaurs, and he is mentioned among the Calydonian hunters and the Argonauts. Although far advanced in age, he sailed with the other Greek heroes against Troy. Having ruled over three generations of men, he was renowned for his wisdom, justice, and knowledge of war. After the fall of Troy he returned home, and arrived safely in Pylos. Respecting the position of this Pylos, see PYLOS.

NESTUS, sometimes NESSUS (-i), a river in Thrace, rising in Mt. Rhodope, and falling into the Aegaean sea opposite the island of Thasos. The Nestus formed the E. boundary of Macedonia from the time of Philip and Alexander the Great.

NETUM (-i), a town in Sicily S.W. of Syracuse.

NEURI (-ōrum), a people of Sarmatia Europaea, to the N.W. of the sources of the Tyras (*Dniester*).

NICAEA (-ae). (1) A celebrated city of Asia, situated on the E. side of the lake Ascania in Bithynia, built by Antigonus, king of Asia, and originally called Antigonēa; but Lysimachus soon after changed the name into Nicaea, in honour of his wife. Under the kings of Bithynia it was often the royal residence; and under the Romans it continued to be one of the chief cities of Asia. It is famous in ecclesiastical history as the seat of the great Oecumenical Council, which Constantine convoked in A.D. 325, chiefly for the decision of the Arian controversy, and which drew up the Nicene Creed.—(2) A fortress of the Epicnemidian Locrians on the sea, near the pass of Thermopylae, which it commanded.—(3) (*Nizza,'Nice*), a city on the coast of Liguria, a little E. of the river Var; a colony of Massilia, and subject to that city.

NĬCANDER (-dri), a Greek poet, grammarian and physician, was a native of Claros near Colophon in Ionia, and flourished about B.C. 185—135. Two of his poems are extant, entitled *Theriaca* and *Alexipharmaca*.

NĪCĒ (-ēs), called VICTŌRĬA (-ae), by the Romans, the goddess of victory, is described as a daughter of Pallas and Styx, and as a sister of Zelus (zeal), Cratos (strength), and Bia (force). Nice had a celebrated temple on the acropolis of Athens, which is still extant. She is often seen represented in ancient works of art, especially with other divinities, such as Zeus (Jupiter), and Athena (Minerva), and with conquering heroes whose horses she guides. In her appearance she resembles Athena, but has wings, and carries a palm or a wreath, and is engaged in raising a trophy, or in inscribing the victory of the conqueror on a shield.

NĬCĒPHŎRĬUM (-i), a fortified town of Mesopotamia, on the Euphrates, and due S. of Edessa, built by order of Alexander, and probably completed under Seleucus.

NĬCĒPHŎRĬUS (-i), a river of Armenia Major, on which Tigranes built his residence Tigranocerta. It was a tributary of the Upper Tigris; probably identical with the Centrites, or a small tributary of it.

NĪCĬAS (-ae). (1) A celebrated Athenian general, was a man of large fortune and the leader of the aristocratical party during the Peloponnesian war. It was through his influence that peace was concluded with Sparta in B.C. 421. He used all his efforts to induce the Athenians to preserve this peace, but he was opposed by Alcibiades, who had now become the leader of the popular party. In 415, the Athenians resolved on sending their great expedition to Sicily, and appointed Nicias, Alcibiades and Lamachus to the command, although Nicias disapproved of the expedition altogether. Alcibiades was soon afterwards recalled [Alcibiades]; and the irresolution and timidity of Nicias were the chief causes of the failure of the expedition. Notwithstanding the large reinforcements, which were sent to his assistance in B.C. 413, under the command of Demosthenes, the Athenians were defeated, and obliged to

retreat.—(2) A celebrated Athenian painter, flourished about B.C. 320.

NĬCŎLĀUS DĂMASCĒNUS (-i), a Greek historian, was a native of Damascus, and an intimate friend both of Herod the Great and of Augustus. Some fragments of his works have come down to us, of which the most important is a portion of a life of Augustus.

NĬCŎMĂCHUS (-i). (1) Father of Aristotle.—(2) Son of Aristotle by the slave Herpyllis.—(3) Of Thebes, a celebrated painter, flourished B.C. 360, and onwards.

NĬCŎMĒDĒS (-is), the name of 3 kings of Bithynia.—(1) Reigned B.C. 278—250, was the eldest son and successor of Zipoetes. He founded the city of Nicomedia, which he made the capital of his kingdom.—(2) Surnamed Epiphanes, reigned B.C. 142—91, and was the son and successor of Prusias II., whom he dethroned and put to death. He was a faithful ally of the Romans.—(3) Surnamed Philopator, son and successor of the preceding, reigned B.C. 91—74. He was twice expelled by Mithridates, and twice restored by the Romans. Having no children, he bequeathed his kingdom to the Roman people.

NĬCŎMĒDĬA (-ae), a celebrated city of Bithynia, built by king Nicomedes I. (B.C. 264), at the N.E. corner of the Sinus Astacenus. Under the Romans it was a colony, and a favourite residence of several of the later emperors, especially of Diocletian and Constantine the Great. It is memorable in history as the scene of Hannibal's death. It was the birthplace of the historian Arrian.

NICŌNĬA or NICŌNĬUM, a town in Scythia on the right bank of the Tyras (*Dniester*).

NĬCŎPŎLIS (-is), a city at the S.W. extremity of Epirus, on the point of land which forms the N. entrance to the Gulf of Ambracia, opposite to Actium. It was built by Augustus in memory of the battle of Actium, and was peopled from Ambracia, Anactorium, and other neighbouring cities, and also with settlers from Aetolia.

NĪGER (-gri), a great river of Aethiopia Interior, which modern usage has identified with the river called *Joli-ba* (*i.e.* Great River) and *Quorra*, in W. Africa. Many of the ancients imagined the Niger to be a branch of the Nile.

NĪGER, C. PESCENNĬUS (-i), was saluted emperor by the legions in the East, after the death of Commodus, A.D. 193, but in the following year he was defeated and put to death by Septimius Severus.

NĪLUS (-i), one of the most important rivers of the world, flowing through Aethiopia and Egypt northwards into the Mediterranean sea. An account of its course through Egypt, and of its periodical rise, is given under AEGYPTUS.

NĪNUS, NĬNUS (-i). (1) The reputed founder of the city of Ninus, or Nineveh, and the husband of Semiramis. [SEMIRAMIS.]—(2) Or NINEVEH, the capital of the great Assyrian monarchy, stood on the E. side of the Tigris, at the upper part of its course, in the district of Aturia. The prophet Jonah (B.C. 825) describes it as "an exceeding great city, of 3 days' journey," and as containing "more than 120,000 persons that cannot discern between their right and their left hand," which, if this phrase refers to children, would represent a population of 600,000 souls. Diodorus also describes it as an oblong quadrangle of 150 stadia by 90, making the circuit of the walls 480 stadia (more than 55 statute miles) : if so, the city was twice as large as London together with its suburbs. In judging of these statements, not only must allowance be made for the immense space occupied by palaces and temples, but also for the Oriental mode of building a city, so as to include large gardens and other open spaces within the walls. The walls of Nineveh are described as 100 feet high, and thick enough to allow 3 chariots to pass each other on them; with 1500 towers, 200 feet in height. The city is said to have been entirely destroyed by fire when it was taken by the Medes and Babylonians, about B.C. 606 ; and frequent allusions occur to its desolate state. Under the Roman empire, however, we again meet with a city Nineve, in the district of Adiabene, but this must have been some later place built among or near the ruins of the ancient Nineveh. Of all the great cities of the world, none was thought to have been more utterly lost than the capital of the most ancient of the great monarchies. Tradition pointed out a few shapeless mounds opposite *Mósul* on the Upper Tigris, as all that remained of Nineveh; but within the last years, those shapeless mounds have been shown to contain the remains of great palaces. The excavations conducted by Layard and Botta have brought to light the sculptured remains of immense palaces, not only at the traditional site of Nineveh, namely *Kouyunjik* and *Nebbi-Younis*, opposite to *Mósul*, and at *Khorsábad*, about 10 miles to the N.N.E., but also in a mound, 18 miles lower down the river, in the tongue of land between the Tigris and the *Great Záb*, which still bears the name of *Nimroud*. Which of these ruins corresponds to the true site of Nineveh, or whether that vast city may have extended all the way along the Tigris from *Kouyunjik* to *Nimroud*, and to a corresponding breadth N.E. of the river, as far as *Khorsábad*, are questions still under discussion. Some splendid fragments of sculpture obtained by Layard from *Nimroud*, are now to be seen in the British Museum.

NĬŎBĒ (-ēs) or NĬŎBA (-ae), daughter of Tantalus, and wife of Amphion, king of Thebes. Proud of the number of her children, she deemed herself superior to Lēto (Latona), who had given birth to only 2 children. Apollo and Artemis (Diana), indignant at such presumption, slew all her children with their arrows. Niobe herself was metamorphosed by Zeus (Jupiter) into a stone on Mt. Sipylus in Lydia, which during the summer always shed tears. The number of her

Niobe and her Children. (Visconti, Mus. Pio. Clem., vol. 4, tav. 17.)

children is stated variously, but the usual number in later times was 7 sons and 7 daughters. The story of Niobe and her children was a favourite subject with ancient artists. There is at Florence a beautiful group consisting of Niobe, who holds her youngest daughter on her knees, and 13 statues of her sons and daughters.

NĬPHĀTĒS (-ae), a mountain chain of Armenia, forming an E. prolongation of the Taurus.

The Group of Niobe. (Zannoni, Gal. di Firenze, serie 4, vol. l.)

NĪREUS (-ĕŏs, ĕĬ, or eĬ), son of Charopus and Aglaia, and the handsomest among the Greeks at Troy.

NĬSAEA. [MEGARA.]

NĬSAEUS CAMPUS, a plain in the N. of Great Media, near Rhagae, celebrated for its breed of horses.

NĬSĬBIS (-is), also ANTIOCHIA MYGDONIAE, a celebrated city of Mesopotamia, and the capital of the district of Mygdonia, stood on the river Mygdonius in a very fertile district. It was of great importance as a military post. Its name was changed into Antiochia, but it soon resumed its original name. In the successive wars between the Romans, and the Parthians and Persians, it was several times taken and retaken, until at last it fell into the hands of the Persians in the reign of Jovian.

NĬSUS (-i). (1) King of Megara, and father of Scylla. Scylla having fallen in love with Minos when the latter was besieging Megara, pulled out the purple or golden hair which grew on the top of her father's head, and on which his life depended. Nisus thereupon died, and Minos obtained possession of the city. Minos, however, was so horrified at the conduct of the unnatural daughter, that he ordered her to be fastened to the poop of his ship, and drowned her in the Saronic gulf. According to others, Minos left Megara in disgust; Scylla leapt into the sea, and swam after his ship; but her father, who had been changed into a sea-eagle (haliaeëtus),

pounced down upon her, whereupon she was metamorphosed into either a fish or a bird called Ciris.—Scylla, the daughter of Nisus, is sometimes confounded by the poets with Scylla, the daughter of Phorcus. Hence the latter is sometimes erroneously called Nisēia Virgo, and Nisēis. [SCYLLA.]—Nisaea, the port town of Megara, is supposed to have derived its name from Nisus, and the promontory of Scyllaeum to have been named after his daughter.—(2) Son of Hyrtacus, and a friend of Euryalus. The two friends accompanied Aeneas to Italy, and perished in a night attack against the Rutulian camp.

NISȲRUS (-i), a small island in the Carpathian Sea, off Caria. Its volcanic nature gave rise to the fable respecting its origin, that Poseidon (Neptune) tore it off the neighbouring island of Cos to hurl it upon the giant Polybotes.

NITIOBRĪGES (-um), a Celtic people in Gallia Aquitanica between the Garumna and the Liger.

NĬTŌCRIS. (1) A queen of Babylon, mentioned by Herodotus, is supposed by modern writers to be the wife of Nebuchadnezzar.—(2) A queen of Egypt, elected to the sovereignty in place of her brother, whom the Egyptians had killed. After putting to death the Egyptians who had murdered her brother, she threw herself into a chamber full of ashes. She is said to have built the third pyramid.

NITRĬAE, NITRARĬAE, the celebrated

natron lakes in Lower Egypt, which lay in a valley on the S.W. margin of the Delta.

NŌBILĬOR (-ōris), the name of a distinguished family of the Fulvia gens. The most distinguished member of the family was M. FULVIUS NOBILIOR, consul B.C. 189, when he conquered the Aetolians, and took the town of Ambracia. He had a taste for literature and art, and was a patron of the poet Ennius, who accompanied him in his Aetolian campaign.

NŌLA (-ae : *Nola*), one of the most ancient towns in Campania, 21 Roman miles S.E. of Capua, celebrated as the place where the emperor Augustus died. In the neighbourhood of the town some of the most beautiful Campanian vases have been found in modern times.

NŌMENTĀNUS (-i), mentioned by Horace as proverbially noted for extravagance and a riotous mode of living.

NŌMENTUM (-i), a Latin town founded by Alba, but subsequently a Sabine town, 14 (Roman) miles from Rome. Its neighbourhood was celebrated for its wine.

NŌMĬUS (-i), the Pasturer, a surname of divinities protecting the pastures and shepherds, such as Apollo, Pan, Hermes (Mercury), and Aristaeus.

NŌNĀCRIS (-is), a town in the N. of Arcadia, surrounded by lofty mountains, in which the river Styx took its origin. From this town Evander is called *Nōnācrius*, Atalanta *Nōnācrĭa*, and Callisto *Nōnācrīna Virgo*, in the general sense of Arcadian.

NŌNĬUS MARCELLUS. [MARCELLUS.]

NŌRA (-ōrum). (1) A city of Sardinia, on the coast of the Sinus Caralitanus.—(2) A mountain fortress of Cappadocia, on the borders of Lycaonia.

NORBA (-ae). (1) A town in Latium on the slope of the Volscian mountains and near the sources of the Nymphaeus, originally belonging to the Latin, and subsequently to the Volscian league. As early as B.C. 492 the Romans founded a colony at Norba.—(2) Surnamed CAESAREA (*Alcantara*), a Roman colony in Lusitania on the left bank of the Tagus. The bridge built by order of Trajan over the Tagus at this place is still extant.

NORBĀNUS (-i), C., one of the leaders of the Marian party in the war with Sulla, was consul B.C. 83.

NORBĀNUS FLACCUS. [FLACCUS.]

NŌRĒĬA (*Neumarkt*, in Styria), the ancient capital of the Taurisci or Norici in Noricum, from which the whole country derived its name. It is celebrated as the place where Carbo was defeated by the Cimbri, B.C. 113.

NORĪCUM (-i), a Roman province S. of the Danube, bounded on the N. by the Danube,

on the W. by Rhaetia and Vindelicia, on the E. by Pannonia, and on the S. by Pannonia and Italy. It thus corresponds to the greater part of *Styria* and *Carinthia*, and to a part of *Austria, Bavaria*, and *Salzburg*. One of the main branches of the Alps, the ALPES NORICAE (in the neighbourhood of Salzburg), ran right through the province. In those mountains a large quantity of excellent iron was found; and the Noric swords were celebrated in antiquity. The inhabitants of the country were Celts, divided into several tribes, of which the Taurisci, also called Norici, after their capital Noreia, were the most important. They were conquered by the Romans towards the end of the reign oi Augustus, after the subjugation of Rhaetia by Tiberius and Drusus, and their country was formed into a Roman province.

NORTĬA or NURTĬA (-ae), an Etruscan divinity, worshipped at Volsinii.

NŌTUS (-i), called AUSTER (-tri), by the Romans, the S. wind, or strictly the S.W. wind, brought with it fogs and rain.

Notus. (From the Temple of the Winds at Athens.)

NOVĀRĬA (-ae : *Novara*), a town in Gallia Transpadana, situated on a river of the same name (*Gogna*), and on the road from Mediolanum to Vercellae.

NŌVESĬUM (-i : *Neuss*), a fortified town of the Ubii on the Rhine, and on the road leading from Colonia Agrippina (*Cologne*), to Castra Vetera (*Xanten*).

NŌVĬŎDŪNUM (-i), a name given to many Celtic places from their being situated on a hill (*dun*). (1) (*Nouan*), a town of the Bituriges Cubi in Gallia Aquitanica. — (2) (*Nevers*), a town of the Aedui in Gallia Lugdunensis, at the confluence of the Niveris and the Liger, afterwards called Nevirnum. —(3) A town of the Suessones in Gallia Belgica, probably the same as Augusta Suessonum. (*Soissons*.)—(4) (*Nion*), a town of the Helvetii in Gallia Belgica, on the N. bank of the Lacus Lemanus (*Lake of Geneva*).

NŎVĬUS (-i), Q., a celebrated writer of Atellane plays, a contemporary of the dictator Sulla.

NOX (-ctis), called NYX by the Greeks, a personification of Night. She is described as the daughter of Chaos, and the sister of Erebus, by whom she became the mother of Aether (Air) and Hemera (Day). Her residence was in the darkness of Hades.

NŬBAE (-ārum), NŬBAEI (-ōrum), an African people, S. of Egypt, in modern *Nubia*.

NŪCĔRĬA (-ae). (1) Surnamed ALFATERNA (*Nocera*), a town in Campania on the Sarnus (*Sarno*), and 9 (Roman) miles from the coast. —(2) Surnamed CAMELLARIA (*Nocera*), a town in the interior of Umbria on the Via Flaminia.—(3) (*Luzzara*), a small town in Gallia Cispadana on the Po, N.E. of Brixellum.—(4) A town in Apulia, more correctly called LUCERIA.

NUITHŌNES (-um), a people of Germany, dwelling on the right bank of the Albis (*Elbe*), in the modern *Mecklenburg*.

NŪMA (-ae), POMPĬLĬUS (-i), the 2nd king of Rome, who belongs to legend and not to history. He was a native of Cures in the Sabine country, and was elected king one year after the death of Romulus, when the people became tired of the interregnum of the senate. He was renowned for his wisdom and his piety ; and it was generally believed that he had derived his knowledge from Pythagoras. His reign was long and peaceful, and he devoted his chief care to the establishment of religion among his rude subjects. He was instructed by the Camena Egeria, who visited him in a grove near Rome, and who honoured him with her love. He was revered by the Romans as the author of their whole religious worship. It was he who first appointed the pontiffs, the augurs, the flamens, the virgins of Vesta, and the Salii. He founded the temple of Janus, which remained always shut during his reign. He died after a reign of 39 or 43 years.

NŬMANTĬA (-ae : *Guarray* Ru.), the capital of the Arevacae or Arevaci in Hispania Tarraconensis, and the most important town in all Celtiberia, was situated near the sources of the Durius, on a precipitous hill. It was taken by Scipio Africanus the younger after a long siege (B.C. 133).

NŬMĔRĬĀNUS (-i), M. AURĒLĬUS, the younger son of the emperor Carus, whom he accompanied in his expedition against the Persians, A.D. 283. After the death of his father, which happened in the same year, Numerianus was acknowledged as joint emperor with his brother Carinus. Eight months afterwards he was murdered, and suspicion having fallen upon Arrius Aper, praefect of

the praetorians, and father-in-law of the deceased, the latter was stabbed to the heart by Diocletian. [DIOCLETIANUS.]

NŪMĬCĬUS or NŪMĬCUS (-i : *Numico*), a small river in Latium flowing into the Tyrrhene sea, near Ardea, on the banks of which was the tomb of Aeneas

NŪMĬDĬA (-ae), a country of N. Africa, divided from Mauretania on the W. by the river Malva or Mulucha, and on the E. from the territory of Carthage (aft. the Roman province of Africa) by the river Tusca. The inhabitants were originally wandering tribes, hence called by the Greeks *Nomads* (Νομάδες), and this name was perpetuated in that of the country. Their 2 great tribes were the Massylians and the Massaesylians, forming 2 monarchies, which were united into one under Masinissa, B.C. 201. [MASINISSA.] On the defeat of Jugurtha, in B.C. 106, the country became virtually subject to the Romans, but they permitted the family of Masinissa to govern it, with the royal title, until B.C. 46, when Juba, who had espoused the cause of Pompey in the civil wars, was defeated and dethroned by Julius Caesar, and Numidia was made a Roman province. Part of the country was afterwards added to the province of Mauretania. [MAURETANIA.] The chief city of Numidia was CIRTA.

NŪMĬTŎR. [ROMULUS.]

NURSĬA (-ae), a town of the Sabines, situated near the sources of the Nar and amidst the Apennines, whence it is called by Virgil *frigida Nursia*. It was the birthplace of Sertorius and of the mother of Vespasian.

NYCTĒIS. [NYCTEUS.]

NYCTEUS (-ĕŏs, -ĕī or eī), son of Hyrieus and Clonia and father of Antiopē, who is hence called *Nyctēis* (-ĭdis). Antiope was carried off by Epopeus, king of Sicyon ; whereupon Nycteus, who governed Thebes, as the guardian of Labdacus, invaded Sicyon with a Theban army. Nycteus was defeated, and died of his wounds, leaving his brother Lycus guardian of Labdacus. [LYCUS.]

NYCTĬMĔNĒ (-ēs), daughter of Epopeus, king of Lesbos. Having been dishonoured by her father she concealed herself in the shade of forests, where she was metamorphosed by Athenē (Minerva) into an owl.

NYMPHAE (-ārum), female divinities of a lower rank, with whom the Greeks peopled all parts of nature, the sea, springs, rivers, grottoes, trees, and mountains. These nymphs were divided into various classes, according to the different parts of nature of which they are the representatives. (1) *The Sea-Nymphs*, consisting of the *Ŏcĕănĭdes*, or Nymphs of the Ocean, who were regarded as the daughters of Oceanus; and the *Nereïdes* or *Nērēïdes*, the nymphs of the Mediterranean, who were regarded as the daughters of Nereus.—(2) The *Năïădes* or *Năïdes*, the nymphs of fresh water, whether of rivers, lakes, brooks, or springs. Many of these nymphs presided over springs which were believed to inspire those who drank of them. The nymphs themselves were, therefore, thought to be endowed with prophetic power, and to be able to inspire men. Hence all persons in a state of rapture, such as seers, poets, madmen, &c., were said to be caught by the nymphs (*lymphati, lymphatici*).—(3) *Ŏrĕădes*, the nymphs of mountains and grottoes, also called by names derived from the particular mountains they inhabited.—(4) *Năpaeae*, the Nymphs of glens.—(5) *Dryădes* and *Hămădryădes* (from δρῦς), nymphs of trees, who were believed to die together with the trees which had oeen their abode, and with which they had come into existence. There was also another class of nymphs, connected with certain races or localities, and usually named from the places with which they are associated, as Nysiades, Dodonides, Lemniae.— The sacrifices offered to nymphs consisted of goats, lambs, milk, and oil, but never of wine. They are represented in works of art as beautiful maidens, either quite naked or only half-covered.

NYMPHAEUM (-i), a mountain, with perhaps a village, by the river Aous, near Apollonia, in Illyricum.

NYMPHAEUS (-i). (1) A small river of Latium, falling into the sea above Astura, and contributing to the formation of the Pomptine marshes.—(2) A small river of Armenia, a tributary of the upper Tigris.

NYSA or NYSSA (-ae), the legendary scene of the nurture of Dionysus (Bacchus), who was therefore called *Nysaeus, Nysius, Nysēïus, Nysius, Nysigĕna*, &c. Hence the name was applied to several places sacred to that god. (1) In India, at the N.W. corner of the *Punjab*, near the confluence of the rivers Cophen and Choaspes.—(2) A city of Caria, on the S. slope of M. Messogis.—(3) A city of Cappadocia, near the Halys, the bishopric of St. Gregory of Nyssa.

NYSEÏDES or NYSIĂDES (-um), the nymphs of Nysa, who are said to have reared Dionysus, and whose names are Cisseïs, Nysa, Erato, Eriphia, Bromia, and Polyhymno.

OĂRUS (-i), a river of Sarmatia rising in the country of the Thyssagetae, and falling into the Palus Maeotis.

OASIS (-is), the Greek form of an Egyptian word, which was used to denote *an island in the sea of sand* of the great Libyan Desert. These Oasis are preserved from the shifting sands by steep hills of limestone round them, and watered by springs, which make them fertile and habitable. The name is applied especially to 2 of these islands on the W. of Egypt, which were taken possession of by the Egyptians at an early period. (1) OASIS MAJOR, the Greater Oasis, was situated 7 days' journey W. of Abydos, and belonged to Upper Egypt. This Oasis contains considerable ruins of the ancient Egyptian and Roman periods. —(2) OASIS MINOR, the Lesser or Second Oasis, was a good day's journey from the S.W. end of the lake Moeris, and belonged to the Heptanomis, or Middle Egypt. —(3) A still more celebrated Oasis than either of these was that called AMMON, HAMMON, AMMONIUM, HAMMONIS ORACULUM, from its being a chief seat of the worship and oracle of the god Ammon. It is now called *Siwah.* Its distance from Cairo is 12 days, and from the N. coast about 160 statute miles. The Ammonians do not appear to have been subject to the old Egyptian monarchy. Cambyses, after conquering Egypt in B.C. 525, sent an army against them, which was overwhelmed by the sands of the Desert. In B.C. 331, Alexander the Great visited the oracle, which hailed him as the son of Zeus Ammon.

OAXES. [OAXUS.]

OAXUS (-i), called AXUS (-i), by Herodotus, a town in the interior of Crete on the river Oaxes.

OBSĔQUENS (-entis), JŪLIUS (-i), the author of a work, entitled *De Prodigiis* or *Prodigiorum Libellus*, of which a portion is extant. Of the writer nothing is known.

OCĂLĒA (-ae), an ancient town in Boeotia, situated on a river of the same name falling into the lake Copais.

OCĔĂNĬDES. [NYMPHAE.]

OCĔĂNUS (-i), the god of the water which was believed to surround the whole earth, is called the son of Heaven and Earth, the husband of Tethys, and the father of all the river-gods and water-nymphs of the whole earth. The early Greeks regarded the earth as a flat circle, which was encompassed by a *river* perpetually flowing round it, and this *river* was Oceanus. Out of, and into this river the sun and the stars were supposed to rise and set; and on its banks were the abodes of the dead. When geographical knowledge advanced, the name was applied to the great *outer* waters of the earth; in contradistinction to the *inner* seas, and especially to the *Atlantic*, or the sea without the Pillars of Hercules, as distinguished from the *Mediterranean*, or the Sea within that limit, and thus the Atlantic is often called simply Oceanus. The epithet Atlantic (Atlantĭcum Mare), was applied to it from the mythical position of ATLAS being on its shores.

ŌCĔLUM (-i), a town in the Cottian Alps, was the last place in Cisalpine Gaul, before entering the territories of king Cottius.

ŌCHUS (-i). (1) A surname of Artaxerxes III., king of Persia. [ARTAXERXES III.]—(2) A great river of Central Asia, supposed by some to be the same as the Oxus.

OCRICŬLUM (-i : *Otricoli*), a town in Umbria, situated on the Tiber near its confluence with the Nar.

OCTĀVĬA (-ae). (1) Sister of the emperor Augustus, married first to C. Marcellus, consul, B.C. 50, and after his death to Antony, the triumvir, in 40, but the latter soon abandoned her for Cleopatra. She died B.C. 11. She had 5 children, 3 by Marcellus, a son and 2 daughters, and 2 by Antony, both daughters. Her son, M. Marcellus, was adopted by Augustus, and was destined to be his successor, but died in 23. [MARCELLUS, No. 5.] The descendants of her 2 daughters successively ruled the Roman world. [ANTONIA.]—(2) Daughter of the emperor Claudius and Messalina, and wife of Nero. She was divorced by the latter, that he might marry his mistress Poppaea, and was shortly afterwards put to death by Nero's orders, A.D. 62.

OCTĀVĬUS, the name of a Roman gens, to which the emperor Augustus belonged, whose original name was C. Octavius. Hence, when he was adopted by his great uncle C. Julius Caesar, he bore the surname of *Octavianus*. [AUGUSTUS.]

OCTŌDŪRUS (-i : *Martigny*), a town of the Veragri in the country of the Helvetii.

OCTŌGĒSA (-ae), a town of the Ilergetes in Hispania Tarraconensis near the Iberus, probably S. of the Sicoris.

ŌCȲPĔTĒ. [HARPYIAE.]

ŌCȲRHŎĒ (-ēs), daughter of the centaur Chiron.

ODENĀTHUS, the ruler of Palmyra, who checked the victorious career of the Persians after the defeat and capture of Valerian, A.D. 260. In return for these services, Gallienus bestowed upon Odenathus the title of Augustus. He was soon afterwards murdered, and was succeeded by his wife ZENOBIA, A.D. 266.

ŌDESSUS (-i : *Varna*), a Greek town in Thracia (in the later Moesia Inferior) on the Pontus Euxinus, was founded by the Milesians, and carried on an extensive commerce.

ODOĀCER (-cri), king of the Heruli, and the leader of the barbarians who overthrew

the Western empire, A.D. 476. He took the title of king of Italy, and reigned till his power was overthrown by Theodoric, king of the Goths, A.D. 493.

ODRȲSAE (-ārum,) the most powerful people in Thrace, dwelling in the plain of the Hebrus, whose king Sitalces in the time of the Peloponnesian war exercised dominion over almost the whole of Thrace. The poets often use the adjective *Odrȳsĭus* in the general sense of Thracian.

ODYSSEUS. [ULYSSES.]

OEĀGRUS, or OEĀGER (-gri), king of Thrace, and father of Orpheus and Linus. Hence *Oeăgrĭus* is used by the poets as equivalent to Thracian.

OEBĂLUS (-i). (1) King of Sparta, and father of Tyndareus. The patronymics *Oebălĭdēs*, *Oebălis* and the adjective *Oebălĭus* are not only applied to his descendants, but to the Spartans generally. Hence Tarentum is termed *Oebalia arx*, because it was founded by the Lacedaemonians ; and since the Sabines were, according to one tradition, a Lacedaemonian colony, we find the Sabine king Titus Tatius named *Oebălĭus Tĭtus*, and the Sabine women *Oebălĭdes matres.*—(2) Son of Telon by a nymph of the stream Sebethus, near Naples, ruled in Campania.

OECHĂLĬA (-ae). (1) A town in Thessaly on the Peneus near Tricca.—(2) A town in Messenia on the frontier of Arcadia.—(3) A town of Euboea in the district Eretria.—The ancients were divided in opinion as to which of these places was the residence of Eurytus, whom Hercules defeated and slew. The original legend probably belonged to the Thessalian Oechalia, and was thence transferred to the other towns.

OEDĬPUS (-i or -ŏdis), son of Laius, king of Thebes, and of Jocasta, sister of Creon. His father having learnt from an oracle that he was doomed to perish by the hands of his own son, exposed Oedipus on Mt. Cithaeron, immediately after his birth, with his feet pierced and tied together. The child was found by a shepherd of king Polybus of Corinth, and was called from his swollen feet Oedipus. Having been carried to the palace, the king reared him as his own child; but when Oedipus had grown up, he was told by the oracle at Delphi, which he had gone to consult, that he was destined to slay his father and commit incest with his mother. Thinking that Polybus was his father, he resolved not to return to Corinth; but on the road between Delphi and Daulis he met Laius, whom he slew in a scuffle without knowing that he was his father. In the mean time the celebrated Sphinx had appeared in the neighbourhood of Thebes. Seated on a rock, she put a riddle to every Theban that passed by, and who ever was unable to solve it was killed by the monster. This calamity induced the Thebans to proclaim that whoever should deliver the country of the Sphinx, should obtain the kingdom and Jocasta as his wife. The riddle ran as follows: "A being with 4 feet has 2 feet and 3 feet, and only one voice; but its feet vary, and when it has most it is weakest." Oedipus solved the riddle by saying that it was man, who in infancy crawls upon all fours, in manhood stands erect upon 2 feet, and in old age supports his tottering legs with a staff. The Sphinx thereupon threw herself down from the rock. Oedipus now obtained the kingdom of Thebes, and married his mother, by whom he became the father of Eteocles, Polynīces, Antigŏnē, and Ismēnē. In consequence of this incestuous alliance, the country of Thebes was visited by a plague. The oracle, on being consulted, ordered that the murderer of Laïus should be expelled; and the seer Tiresias told Oedipus that he was the guilty man. Thereupon Jocasta hung herself, and Oedipus put out his own eyes, and wandered from Thebes, accompanied by his daughter Antigŏnē. In Attica he at length found a place of refuge; and at Colonus near Athens, the Eumenides removed him from the earth. The tragic fate of Oedipus and of his children formed the subject of many of the noblest of the Greek tragedies.

OENEUS (-ĕŏs, ĕĭ, or eī), king of Pleuron and Calydon in Aetolia, and husband of Althaea, father of Tydeus, Meleager, Gorgē, Deianīra, &c. He was deprived of his kingdom by the sons of his brother Agrius. He was subsequently avenged by his grandson Diomedes, who slew Agrius and his sons, and placed upon the throne Andraemon, the son-in-law of Oeneus, as the latter was too old. Diomedes took his grandfather with him to Peloponnesus, but here he was slain by two of the sons of Agrius who had escaped the slaughter of their brothers. Respecting the boar, which laid waste the lands of Calydon in his reign, see MELEAGER.

OENĬĂDAE (-ārum), a town of Acarnania, near the mouth of the Achelous, and surrounded by marshes. The fortress Nēsus or Nāsus belonging to the territory of Oeniadae was situated in a small lake near Oeniadae.

OENĪDĒS (-ae), a patronymic from Oeneus, and hence given to Meleager, son of Oeneus, and Diomedes, grandson of Oeneus.

OENŎMĂUS (-i), king of Pisa in Elis, son of Ares (Mars) and father of Hippodamīa. [PELOPS.]

OENŌNĒ (-es), daughter of the river-god Cebren, and wife of Paris, before he carried off Helen. [PARIS.]

OENŎPĬA (-ae), the ancient name of AEGINA.

OENŎPHŸTA (-ōrum), a town in Boeotia, on the left bank of the Asopus, memorable for the victory gained here by the Athenians over the Boeotians, B.C. 456.

OENŎPĬŌN (-ōnis), son of Dionysus (Bacchus) and husband of the nymph Helice, and father of Meropē, with whom the giant Orion fell in love. [ORION.]

OENŌTRI, OENŌTRĬA. [ITALIA.]

OENŌTRĬDES, 2 small islands in the Tyrrhene sea, off the coast of Lucania, and opposite the town of Elea or Velia and the mouth of the Helos.

OETA (-ae) or OETĒ (-es), a rugged pile of mountains in the S. of Thessaly, an eastern branch of Mt. Pindus, extending along the S. bank of the Sperchius to the Maliac gulf at Thermopylae, thus forming the N. barrier of Greece proper. Respecting the pass of Mt. Oeta, see THERMOPYLAE. Oeta was celebrated in mythology as the mountain on which Hercules burnt himself to death.

ŎFELLA (-ae), a man of sound sense and of a straightforward character, whom Horace contrasts with the Stoic quacks of his time. Ofella was also the name of a family in the Lucretia gens.

ŌGŸGES (-is), or OGŸGUS (-i) son of Boeotus, and the first ruler of Thebes, which was called after him OGYGIA. In his reign a great deluge is said to have occurred. The name of Ogyges is also connected with Attic story, for in Attica an Ogygian flood is likewise mentioned. From Ogyges the Thebans are called by the poets Ŏgȳgĭdae, and Ŏgȳgĭus is used in the sense of Theban.

ŎĪLEUS (-ĕŏs, ĕĭ, or eī), king of the Locrians, and father of Ajax, who is hence called Ŏīlĭdēs, Ŏīlĭădēs, and Ajax Ŏīleī. He was one of the Argonauts.

OLBĬA (-ae). (1) Narbonensis, on a hill called Olbianus, E. of Telo Martius.—(2) A city near the N. end of the E. side of the island of Sardinia, with the only good harbour on this coast; and therefore the usual landing-place for persons coming from Rome.—(3) [BORYSTHENES.]

OLCĂDES (-um), a people in Hispania Tarraconensis, near the sources of the Anas, in a part of the country afterwards inhabited by the Oretani.

OLCĬNĬUM (-i: Dulcigno), a town on the coast of Illyria.

ŌLĔĂRUS. [OLIARUS.]

ŌLĔN, a mythical personage, who is represented as the earliest Greek lyric poet. He is called both an Hyperborean, and a

Lycian, and is said to have settled at Delos. His name seems to signify simply the *flute-player*.

ŌLĔNUS (-i). (1) The husband of Lethaea, changed with her into a stone.—(2) A town in Aetolia, near New Pleuron, destroyed by the Aetolians at an early period.—(3) A town in Achaia, between Patrae and Dyme. The goat Amalthaea, which suckled the infant Zeus (Jupiter), is called *Olenia capella* by the poets, either because the goat was supposed to have been born near the town of Olenus, and to have been subsequently transferred to Crete, or because the nymph Amalthaea, to whom the goat belonged, was a daughter of Olenus.

ŌLĬĂRUS or ŌLĔĂRUS (-i), a small island in the Aegean sea, one of the Cyclades, W. of Paros.

ŌLĬSĬPO (*Lisbon*), a town in Lusitania, near the mouth of the Tagus.

ŌLYMPĬA (-ae), a small plain in Elis, bounded on the S. by the river Alphēus, and on the W. by the river Cladĕus, in which the Olympic games were celebrated. In this plain was the sacred grove of Zeus (Jupiter) called Altis. The Altis and its immediate neighbourhood were adorned with numerous temples, statues, and public buildings, to which the general appellation of Olympia was given; but there was no town of this name. Among the numerous temples in the Altis the most celebrated was the *Olympiēum*, or temple of Zeus Olympius, which contained the master-piece of Greek art, the colossal statue of Zeus by Phidias. The statue was made of ivory and gold, and the god was represented as seated on a throne of cedar wood, adorned with gold, ivory, ebony, and precious stones. The Olympic games were celebrated from the earliest times in Greece. There was an interval of 4 years between each celebration of the festival, which interval was called an Olympiad; but the Olympiads were not employed as a chronological era till the victory of Coroebus in the foot-race, B.C. 776. An account of the Olympic games and of the Olympiads is given in the *Dict. of Antiq.*

ŌLYMPĬAS (-ădis), wife of Philip II., king of Macedonia, and mother of Alexander the Great, was the daughter of Neoptolemus I., king of Epirus. She withdrew from Macedonia, when Philip married Cleopatra, the niece of Attalus (B.C. 337); and it was generally believed that she lent her support to the assassination of Philip in 336. In the troubled times which followed the death of Alexander, she played a prominent part. In 317 she seized the supreme power in Macedonia, and put to death Philip Arrhidaeus

and his wife Eurydice. But being attacked by Cassander, she took refuge in Pydna, and, on the surrender of this place after a long siege, she was put to death by Cassander (B.C. 316.)

ŌLYMPĬUS, the Olympian, a surname of Zeus (Jupiter), Hercules, the Muses (*Olympiădes*), and in general of all the gods who were believed to live in Olympus, in contradistinction from the gods of the lower world.

ŌLYMPUS (-i). (1) The range of mountains, separating Macedonia and Thessaly, but more specifically the eastern part of the chain forming at its termination the northern wall of the vale in TEMPE. Its height is about 9700 feet; and its chief summit is covered with perpetual snow. In the Greek mythology, Olympus was the residence of the dynasty of gods of which Zeus (Jupiter) was the head. The early poets believed that the gods actually lived on the top of this mountain. Even the fable of the giants scaling heaven must be understood in a literal sense; not that they placed Pelion and Ossa upon *the top of* Olympus to reach the still higher *heaven*, but that they piled Pelion on the top of Ossa, and both on the *lower slopes* of Olympus, to scale the summit of Olympus itself, the abode of the gods. Homer describes the gods as having their several palaces on the summit of Olympus; as spending the day in the palace of Zeus, round whom they sit in solemn conclave, while the younger gods dance before them, and the Muses entertain them with the lyre and song. They are shut out from the view of men upon the earth by a wall of clouds, the gates of which are kept by the Hours. In the later poets, however, the real abode of the gods is transferred from the summit of Olympus to the vault of heaven (i.e. the sky) itself.—(2) A chain of lofty mountains, in the N.W. of Asia Minor, usually called the Mysian Olympus.

ŌLYNTHUS (-i), a town of Chalcidice, at the head of the Toronaic gulf, and the most important of the Greek cities on the coast of Macedonia. It was at the head of a confederacy of all the Greek towns in its neighbourhood, and maintained its independence, except for a short interval, when it was subject to Sparta, till it was taken and destroyed by Philip, B.C. 347. The Olynthiac orations of Demosthenes were delivered by the orator to urge the Athenians to send assistance to the city when it was attacked by Philip.

OMBI (-ōrum), the last great city of Upper Egypt, except Syene, stood on the E. bank of the Nile, in the Ombites Nomos, and was celebrated as one of the chief seats of the worship of the crocodile. Juvenal's 15th satire is founded on a religious war between the people of Ombi and those of Tentyra, who hated the crocodile.

OMPHĂLĒ (-ēs), a queen of Lydia, daughter of Iardanus, and wife of Tmolus, after whose death she reigned herself. The story of Hercules serving her as a slave, and of his wearing her dress, while Omphale put on the skin and carried the club, is related elsewhere, (p. 200, a.)

Omphale and Hercules. (Farnese Group, now at Naples.)

ONCHESMUS or ONCHISMUS (-i), a seaport town of Epirus, opposite Corcyra.

ONCHESTUS (-i). (1) An ancient town of Boeotia, situated a little S. of the lake Copais near Haliartus, said to have been founded by Onchestus, son of Poseidon (Neptune).—(2) A river in Thessaly, flowing by Cynoscephalae, and falling into the lake Boebëis.

ŎNŎMACRĬTUS (-ĭ), an Athenian, who lived about B.C. 520—485, and made a collection of the ancient oracles. Being detected in interpolating an oracle of Musaeus, he was banished from Athens by Hipparchus, the son of Pisistratus.

OPHĪŌN (-ŏnis). (1) One of the Titans.—(2) One of the companions of Cadmus.—(3) Father of the centaur Amycus, who is hence called Ŏphīŏnĭdes.

ŎPHĪŪSA or ŎPHĪUSSA (-ae), a name given to many ancient places, from their abounding in snakes. It was an ancient name both of Rhodes and Cyprus, whence Ovid speaks of Ophiūsia arva, that is, Cyprian.

ŎPĪCI. [Osci.]

ŎPĪMĬUS (-i), L., consul B.C. 121, when he took the leading part in the proceedings which ended in the murder of C. Gracchus. Being afterwards convicted of receiving a bribe from Jugurtha, he went into exile to Dyrrachium, in Epirus, where he died in great poverty. The year in which he was consul was remarkable for the extraordinary heat of the autumn, and the vintage of this year long remained celebrated as the Vinum Opimianum.

ŎPITERGĬUM (-i: Oderzo), a Roman colony in Venetia, in the N. of Italy, on the river Liquentia.

OPPĬĀNUS (-i), the author of 2 Greek hexameter poems still extant, one on fishing, entitled Halieutica, and the other on hunting, entitled Cynegetica. Modern critics, however, have shown that these 2 poems were written by 2 different persons of this name. The author of the Halieutica was a native of Anazarba or Corycus, in Cilicia, and flourished about A.D. 180. The author of the Cynegetica was a native of Apamea or Pella, in Syria, and flourished about A.D. 206.

OPPĬUS, the name of a Roman gens. (1) C. Oppius, tribune of the plebs B.C. 213, carried a law to curtail the expenses and luxuries of Roman women.—(2) C. Oppius, an intimate friend of C. Julius Caesar, whose private affairs he managed, in conjunction with Cornelius Balbus.

OPS (gen. Ŏpis), the wife of Saturnus, and the Roman goddess of plenty and fertility, as is indicated by her name, which is connected with opimus, opulentus, inops, and copia. She was especially the protectress of agriculture.

ŎPŪS (-untis), a town of Locris, from which the Opuntian Locrians derived their name. It was the birthplace of Patroclus.

ORBĬLĬUS PUPILLUS (-i), a Roman grammarian and schoolmaster, best known to us from his having been the teacher of Horace, who gives him the epithet of plagosus, from the severe floggings which his pupils received from him. He was a native of Beneventum, and after serving as an apparitor of the magistrates, and also as a soldier in the army, he settled at Rome in the 50th year of his age, in the consulship of Cicero, B.C. 63. He lived nearly 100 years.

ORCĂDES (-um: Orkney and Shetland Isles), a group of several small islands off the N. coast of Britain, with which the Romans first became acquainted when Agricola sailed round the N. of Britain.

ORCHŌMĔNUS (-i). (1) An ancient, wealthy, and powerful city of Boeotia, the capital of the Minyans in the ante-historical ages of Greece, and hence called by Homer the Minyan Orchomenos. It was situated N.W. of the lake Copais, on the river Cephissus. Sixty years after the Trojan war it was taken by the Boeotians, and became a member of the Boeotian league. It continued to exist as an independent town till B.C. 367, when it was taken and destroyed by the Thebans; and though subsequently restored, it never recovered its former prosperity.— (2) An ancient town of Arcadia, situated N. W. of Mantinea.

ORCUS. [HADES.]

ORDOVĬCES (-um), a people in the W. of Britain, opposite the island Mona (*Anglesey*), occupying the N. portion of the modern *Wales*.

ORĔĂDES. [NYMPHAE.]

ŌRESTAE (-ārum), a people in the N. of Epirus, on the borders of Macedonia, originally independent, but afterwards subject to the Macedonian monarchs.

ŌRESTES (-ae and -is), son of Agamemnon and Clytaemnestra. On the murder of his father by Aegisthus and Clytaemnestra, Orestes was saved from the same fate by his sister Electra, who caused him to be secretly carried to Strophius, king in Phocis, who was married to Anaxibia, the sister of Agamemnon. There he formed a close and intimate friendship with the king's son Pylades; and when he had grown up, he repaired secretly to Argos along with his friend, and avenged his father's death by slaying Clytaemnestra and Aegisthus. After the murder of his mother he was seized with madness, and fled from land to land, pursued by the Erinnyes or Furies. At length, on the advice of Apollo, he took refuge in the temple of Athena (Minerva), at Athens, where he was acquitted by the court of the Areopagus, which the goddess had appointed to decide his fate. According to another story, Apollo told him that he could only recover from his madness by fetching the statue of Artemis (Diana) from the Tauric Chersonesus. Accordingly he went to this country along with his friend Pylades; but on their arrival they were seized by the natives, in order to be sacrificed to Artemis, according to the custom of the country. But Iphigenia, the priestess of Artemis, was the sister of Orestes, and, after recognising each other, all three escaped with the statue of the goddess. After his return to Peloponnesus, Orestes took possession of his father's kingdom at Mycenae, and married Hermione, the daughter of Menelaus,

after slaying Neoptolemus. [HERMIONE; NEOPTOLEMUS.]

ŌRESTILLA, AURĒLĬA. [AURELIA.]

ORĒTĀNI (-ōrum), a powerful people in the S.W. of Hispania Tarraconensis.

ŌRĔUS (-i), a town in the N. of Euboea, originally called Hestiaea or Histiaea. Having revolted from the Athenians, in B.C. 445, it was taken by Pericles, its inhabitants expelled, and their place supplied by 2000 Athenians.

ŌRĬCUM or ŌRĬCUS (-i), an important Greek town on the coast of Illyria, near the Ceraunian mountains and the frontiers of Epirus.

ŌRĪON and ŌRĬŌN (-ōnis and -ŏnis), son of Hyrieus, of Hyria, in Boeotia, a handsome giant and hunter. Having come to Chios, he fell in love with Merope, the daughter of Oenopion; his treatment of the maiden so exasperated her father, that, with the assistance of Dionysus (Bacchus), he deprived the giant of his sight. Being informed by an oracle that he should recover his sight if he exposed his eye-balls to the rays of the rising sun, Orion found his way to the island of Lemnos, where Hephaestus (Vulcan) gave him Cedalion as his guide, who led him to the East. After the recovery of his sight he lived as a hunter along with Artemis (Diana). The cause of his death is related variously. According to some, Orion was carried off by Eos (Aurora), who had fallen in love with him; but as this was displeasing to the gods, Artemis killed him with an arrow in Ortygia. According to others, he was beloved by Artemis; and Apollo, indignant at his sister's affection for him, asserted that she was unable to hit with her arrow a distant point which he showed her in the sea. She thereupon took aim, the arrow hit its mark, but the mark was the head of Orion, who was swimming in the sea. A third account, which Horace follows, states that he offered violence to Artemis, and was killed by the goddess with one of her arrows. A fourth account states that he was stung to death by a scorpion; and that Aesculapius was slain by Zeus (Jupiter) with a flash of lightning, when he attempted to recall the giant to life. After his death, Orion was placed among the stars, where he appears as a giant with a girdle, sword, a lion's skin and a club. The constellation of Orion set at the commencement of November, at which time storms and rain were frequent; hence he is often called *imbrifer, nimbosus,* or *aquosus.*

ŌRĪTHYĬA (-ae), daughter of Erechtheus, king of Athens, and of Praxithea, who was seized by Boreas, and carried off to Thrace, where she became the mother of Cleopatra, Chionë, Zetes, and Calais.

ORMĔNUS (-i), son of Cercaphus, and father of Amyntor. Hence Amyntor is called *Ormĕnĭdēs*, and Astydamīa, his granddaughter, *Ormĕnis*.

ORNĔAE (-ārum), an ancient town of Argolis, near the frontiers of the territory of Phlius, subdued by the Argives in the Peloponnesian war, B.C. 415.

ŎRŌDES (-ae), the names of 2 kings of Parthia. [ARSACES XIV., XVII.]

ŎRONTES (-is or -ae), the largest river of Syria, rising in the Antilibanus, flowing past Antioch, and falling into the sea at the foot of Mt. Pieria.

ŎRŌPUS (-i), a town on the eastern frontiers of Boeotia and Attica, was long an object of contention between the Boeotians and Athenians. It finally remained permanently in the hands of the Athenians.

ORPHEUS (*gen.* ĕŏs, ĕi or eī; *dat.* eī or eo; *acc.* ĕa or eum; *voc.* eu; *abl.* eo), a mythical personage, regarded by the Greeks as the most celebrated of the poets who lived before the time of Homer. The common story about him ran as follows. Orpheus, the son of Oeagrus and Calliope, lived in Thrace at the period of the Argonauts, whom he accompanied in their expedition. Presented with the lyre by Apollo, and instructed by the Muses in its use, he enchanted with its music not only the wild beasts, but the trees

Orpheus. (From a Mosaic.)

and rocks upon Olympus, so that they moved from their places to follow the sound of his golden harp. After his return from the Argonautic expedition, he took up his abode in Thrace, where he married the nymph Eurydice. His wife having died of the bite

of a serpent, he followed her into the abodes of Hades. Here the charms of his lyre suspended the torments of the damned, and won back his wife from the most inexorable of all deities. His prayer, however, was only granted upon this condition, that he should not look back upon his restored wife till they had arrived in the upper world : at the very moment when they were about to pass the fatal bounds, the anxiety of love overcame the poet; he looked round to see that Eurydice was following him; and he beheld her caught back into the infernal regions. His grief for the loss of Eurydice led him to treat with contempt the Thracian women, who in revenge tore him to pieces under the excitement of their Bacchanalian orgies. After his death, the Muses collected the fragments of his body, and buried them at Libethra, at the foot of Olympus. His head was thrown into the Hebrus, down which it rolled to the sea, and was borne across to Lesbos. His lyre was also said to have been carried to Lesbos; but both traditions are simply poetical expressions of the historical fact that Lesbos was the first great seat of the music of the lyre. The astronomers taught that the lyre of Orpheus was placed by Zeus (Jupiter) among the stars, at the intercession of Apollo and the Muses. Many poems ascribed to Orpheus were current in the flourishing period of Greek literature; but the extant poems, bearing the name of Orpheus, are the forgeries of Christian grammarians and philosophers of the Alexandrian school; though among the fragments, which form a part of the collection, are some genuine remains of the Orphic poetry, known to the earlier Greek writers.

ORTHĬA (-ae), a surname of Artemis, at Sparta, at whose altar the Spartan boys had to undergo the flogging, called *diamastigosis*.

ORTHRUS (-i), the two-headed dog of Geryones. [See p. 199.]

ORTȲGĬA (-ae) and ORTȲGĬĒ (-ēs). (1) The ancient name of Delos. Since Artemis (Diana) and Apollo were born at Delos, the poets sometimes call the goddess *Ortygia*, and give the name of *Ortygiae boves* to the oxen of Apollo. The ancients connected the name with *Ortyx*, a quail.—(2) An island near Syracuse. [SYRACUSAE.]—(3) A grove near Ephesus, in which the Ephesians pretended that Apollo and Artemis were born. Hence the Cayster, which flowed near Ephesus, is called *Ortygius Cayster*.

OSCA (-ae: *Huesca*, in Arragonia), an important town of the Ilergetes, and a Roman colony in Hispania Tarraconensis, on the road from Tarraco to Ilerda, with silver mines.

OSCI or ŎPĬCI (-ōrum), one of the most ancient tribes of Italy, inhabiting the centre of the peninsula, especially Campania and Samnium. They were subdued by the Sabines and Tyrrhenians, and disappeared from history at a comparatively early period. They are identified by many writers with the Ausones or Aurunci. The Oscan language was closely connected with the other ancient Italian dialects, out of which the Latin language was formed; and it continued to be spoken by the people of Campania long after the Oscans had disappeared as a separate people. A knowledge of it was preserved at Rome by the Fabulae Atellanae, which were a species of farce or comedy written in Oscan.

OSĪRIS (-is and -ĭdis), the great Egyptian divinity, and husband of Isis, is said to have been originally king of Egypt, and to have reclaimed his subjects from a barbarous life by teaching them agriculture, and by enacting wise laws. He afterwards travelled into foreign lands, spreading, wherever he went, the blessings of civilisation. On his return to Egypt, he was murdered by his brother Typhon, who cut his body into pieces, and threw them into the Nile. After a long search Isis discovered the mangled remains of her husband, and with the assistance of her son Horus defeated Typhon, and recovered the sovereign power, which Typhon had usurped. [ISIS.]

OSRŎĒNĒ (-ēs), a district in the N. of Mesopotamia, separated by the Chaboras from Mygdonia on the E., and from the rest of Mesopotamia on the S. Its capital was EDESSA.

OSSA (-ae), a celebrated mountain in the N. of Thessaly, connected with Pelion on the S.E., and divided from Olympus on the N.W. by the vale of TEMPE. It is mentioned in the legend of the war of the Giants, respecting which see OLYMPUS.

OSTĬA (-ae : Ostia), a town at the mouth of the river Tiber, and the harbour of Rome, from which it was distant 16 miles by land, situated on the left bank of the left arm of the river. It was founded by Ancus Martius, the 4th king of Rome, was a Roman colony, and became an important and flourishing town. The emperor Claudius constructed a new and better harbour on the right arm of the Tiber, which was enlarged and improved by Trajan. This new harbour was called simply Portus Romanus or Portus Augusti, and around it there sprang up a flourishing town, also called Portus. The old town of Ostia, whose harbour had been already partly filled up by sand, now sank into insignificance, and only continued to exist through its salt-works

(salinae), which had been established by Ancus Martius.

OSTORĬUS SCAPŬLA. [SCAPULA.]

ŌTHO (-ōnis), L. ROSCĬUS (-i), tribune of the plebs B.C. 67, when he carried the law which gave to the equites a special place at the public spectacles, in fourteen rows or seats (in quattuordecim gradibus sive ordinibus), next to the place of the senators, which was in the orchestra. This law was very unpopular; and in Cicero's consulship (63) there was such a riot occasioned by the obnoxious measure, that it required all his eloquence to allay the agitation.

ŌTHO (-ōnis), M. SALVĬUS, Roman emperor from January 15th to April 16th, A.D. 69, was born in 32. He was one of the companions of Nero in his debaucheries; but when the emperor took possession of his wife, the beautiful but profligate Poppaea Sabina, Otho was sent as governor to Lusitania, which he administered with credit during the last 10 years of Nero's life. Otho attached himself to Galba, when he revolted against Nero, in the hope of being adopted by him, and succeeding to the empire. But when Galba adopted L. Piso, on the 10th of January, 69, Otho formed a conspiracy against Galba, and was proclaimed emperor by the soldiers at Rome, who put Galba to death. Meantime Vitellius had been proclaimed emperor at Cologne by the German troops on the 3rd of January. When this news reached Otho, he marched into the N. of Italy to oppose the generals of Vitellius. His army was defeated in a decisive battle near Bedriacum, whereupon he put an end to his own life at Brixellum, in the 37th year of his age.

ŌTHRY̆ĂDĒS and ŌTHRY̆̆ĂDES (-ae). (1) A patronymic given to Panthous or Panthus, the Trojan priest of Apollo, as the son of Othrys.—(2) The survivor of the 300 Spartan champions, who fought with the 300 Argives for the possession of Thyrea. Being ashamed to return to Sparta as the only survivor, he slew himself on the field of battle.

ŌTHRYS and ŌTHRYS (-yŏs), a lofty range of mountains in the S. of Thessaly, extending from Mt. Tymphrestus, or the most S.-ly part of Pindus, to the E. coast. It shut in the great Thessalian plain on the S.

ŌTUS (-i), and his brother, ĔPHĬALTĒS, are better known by their name of the Ălōīdae. [ALOEUS.]

ŎVĬDĬUS NĀSO, P., (-ōnis), the Roman poet, was born at Sulmo, in the country of the Peligni, on the 20th March, B.C. 43. He was descended from an ancient equestrian family. He was destined to be a pleader, and studied rhetoric under Arellius Fuscus and Porcius Latro. His education was completed at Athens, and he afterwards travelled with the poet Macer, in Asia and Sicily. His love for poetry led him to desert the practice of the law; but he was made one of the *Centumviri*, or judges who tried testamentary, and even criminal causes; and in due time he was promoted to be one of the *Decemviri*, who presided over the court of the Centumviri. He married twice in early life at the desire of his parents, but he speedily divorced each of his wives in succession, and lived a life of licentious gallantry. He afterwards married a third wife, whom he appears to have sincerely loved, and by whom he had a daughter, Perilla. After living for many years at Rome, and enjoying the favour of Augustus, he was suddenly banished by the emperor to Tomi, a town on the Euxine, near the mouths of the Danube. The pretext of his banishment was his licentious poem on the Art of Love (*Ars Amatoria*), which had been published nearly 10 years previously; but the real cause of his exile is unknown. It is supposed by some that he had been guilty of an intrigue with the younger Julia, the granddaughter of the emperor Augustus, who was banished in the same year with Ovid. Ovid draws an affecting picture of the miseries to which he was exposed in his place of exile. He sought some relief in the exercise of his poetical talents. Not only did he write several of his Latin poems in his exile, but he likewise acquired the language of the Getae, in which he composed some poems in honour of Augustus. He died at Tomi, in the 60th year of his age, A.D. 18. Besides his amatory poems, the most important of his extant works are the *Metamorphoses*, consisting of such legends or fables as involved a transformation, from the Creation to the time of Julius Caesar, the last being that emperor's change into a star: the *Fasti*, which is a sort of poetical Roman calendar; and the *Tristia*, and Epistles *ex Ponto*, which are elegies written during his banishment.

OXUS or OXUS (-i: *Jihoun* or *Amou*), a great river of Central Asia, forming the boundary between Sogdiana on the N. and Bactria and Margiana on the S., and falling into the Caspian. The *Jihoun* now flows into the S.W. corner of the *Sea of Aral*; but there are still distinct traces of a channel in a S.W. direction from the *Sea of Aral* to the Caspian, by which at least a portion, and probably the whole, of the waters of the Oxus found their way into the Caspian. The Oxus occupies an important place in history, having been in nearly all ages the extreme boundary between the great monarchies of

south-western Asia and the hordes which wander over the central steppes. Herodotus does not mention the Oxus by name, but it is supposed to be the river which he calls Araxes.

PĂCHȲNUS or PĂCHȲNUM (-i), a promontory at the S.E. extremity of Sicily.

PĂCŌRUS (-i). (1) Son of Orodes I., king of Parthia. His history is given under ARSACES XIV. — (2) King of Parthia. [ARSACES XXIV.]

PACTŌLUS (-i), a small but celebrated river of Lydia, rising on Mt. Tmolus, and flowing past Sardis into the Hermus. The golden sands of Pactolus have passed into a proverb, and were one of the sources of the wealth of ancient Lydia.

PACTȲĒ (-ēs), a town in the Thracian Chersonesus, on the Propontis, to which Alcibiades retired when he was banished by the Athenians, B.C. 407.

PĂCŬVĬUS (-i) M., the greatest of the Roman tragic poets, was born about B.C. 220, at Brundisium, and was the son of the sister of Ennius. After living many years at Rome, where he acquired great reputation as a painter, as well as a poet, he returned to Brundisium, where he died in the 90th year of his age, B.C. 130. His tragedies were taken from the great Greek writers; but he did not confine himself, like his predecessors, to mere translation, but worked up his materials with more freedom and independent judgment.

PĂDUS (-i: *Po*), the chief river of Italy, identified by the Roman poets with the fabulous Eridanus, from which amber was obtained. This notion appears to have arisen from the Phoenician vessels receiving at the mouths of the Padus the amber which had been transported by land from the coasts of the Baltic to those of the Adriatic. The Padus rises on Mt. Vesula (*Monte Viso*), in the Alps, and flows in an E.-ly direction through the great plain of Cisalpine Gaul, which it divides into 2 parts, Gallia Cispadana and Gallia Transpadana. It receives numerous affluents, which drain the whole of this vast plain, descending from the Alps on the N., and the Apennines on the S. These affluents, increased in the summer by the melting of the snow on the mountains, frequently bring down such a large body of water as to cause the Padus to overflow its banks. The whole course of the river, including its windings, is about 450 miles. About 20 miles from the sea the river divides itself into 2 main branches, and falls into the Adriatic sea by several mouths, between Ravenna and Altinum.

PAEĀN (-ānis), that is, "the healing," was originally the name of the physician of the Olympian gods. Subsequently the name was used in the more general sense of deliverer from any evil or calamity, and was thus applied to Apollo. From Apollo himself the name was transferred to the song dedicated to him, and to the warlike song sung before or during a battle.

PAEŌNES (-um), a powerful Thracian people, who in histo≈ical times inhabited the whole of the N. of Macedonia, from the frontiers of Illyria to some little distance E. of the river Strymon. Their country was called PAEONIA.

PAESTĀNUS SĪNUS. [PAESTUM.]

PAESTUM (-i), called PŌSĪDŌNIA (-ae) by the Greeks, was a city in Lucania, situated 4 or 5 miles S. of the Silarus, and near the bay which derived its name from the town (Paestanus Sinus: *G. of Salerno*). It was colonised by the Sybarites about B.C. 524, and soon became a powerful and flourishing city. Under the Romans it gradually sank in importance; and in the time of Augustus it is only mentioned on account of the beautiful roses grown in its neighbourhood. The ruins of two Doric temples at Paestum are some of the most remarkable remains of antiquity.

PAETUS (-i), a cognomen in many Roman gentes, signified a person who had a slight cast in the eye.

PAETUS, AELĬUS, the name of 2 brothers, Publius, consul B.C. 201, and Sextus, consul B.C. 198, both of them, and especially the latter, jurists of eminence.

PAETUS THRĀSĔA. [THRASEA.]

PĂGĀSAE (-arum) or PĂGĂSA (-ae), a town of Thessaly, on the coast of Magnesia, and on the bay called after it SINUS PAGASAEUS or PAGASICUS. It was the port of Iolcos, and afterwards of Pherae, and is celebrated in mythology as the place where Jason built the ship Argo. Hence the adjective *Pagasaeus* is applied to Jason, and is also used in the general sense of Thessalian. Apollo is called Pagasaeus from having a temple at the place.

PĂLAEMŌN (-ŏnis), son of Athamas and Ino, originally called Melicertes, became a marine god, when his mother leapt with him into the sea. [ATHAMAS.] The Romans identified Palaemon with their own god Portunus, or Portumnus. [PORTUNUS.]

PĂLAEŎPŎLIS. [NEAPOLIS.]

PĂLAESTĒ (-ēs), a town on the coast of Epirus, and a little S. of the Acroceraunian mountains, where Caesar landed when he crossed over to Greece to carry on the war against Pompey.

PĂLAESTĪNA (-ae), the Greek and Roman form of the Hebrew word which was used to denote the country of the Philistines, and which was extended to the whole country. The Romans called it JUDAEA, extending to the whole country the name of its S. part. It was regarded by the Greeks and Romans as a part of Syria. It was bounded by the Mediterranean on the W.; by the mountains of Lebanon on the N.; by the Jordan and its lakes on the E.; and by the deserts which separated it from Egypt on the S. The Romans did not come into contact with the country till B.C. 63, when Pompey took Jerusalem. From this time the country was really subject to the Romans. At the death of Herod, his kingdom was divided between his sons as tetrarchs; but the different parts of Palestine were eventually annexed to the Roman province of Syria, and were governed by a procurator.

PĂLĂMĒDĒS (-is), son of Nauplius and Clymenē, and one of the Greek heroes, who sailed against Troy. When Ulysses feigned madness that he might not be compelled to sail with the other chiefs, Palamedes detected his stratagem by placing his infant son before him while he was ploughing. [ULYSSES.] In order to revenge himself, Ulysses bribed a servant of Palamedes to conceal under his master's bed a letter written in the name of Priam. He then accused Palamedes of treachery; upon searching his tent they found the fatal letter, and thereupon Palamedes was stoned to death by the Greeks. Later writers describe Palamedes as a sage, and attribute to him the invention of lighthouses, measures, scales, the discus, dice, &c. He is further said to have added the letters θ, ξ, χ, φ, to the original alphabet of Cadmus.

PĂLĀTĪNUS MONS. [ROMA.]

PĂLĀTĬUM. [ROMA.]

PĂLĒS (-is), a Roman divinity of flocks and shepherds, whose festival, the Palilia, was celebrated on the 21st of April, the day on which Rome was founded.

PĂLĪCI (-ōrum) were Sicilian gods, twin sons of Zeus (Jupiter) and the nymph Thalia. Their mother, from fear of Hera (Juno), prayed to be swallowed up by the earth; her prayer was granted; but in due time twin boys issued from the earth, who were worshipped in the neighbourhood of Mt. Aetna, near Palice.

PĂLĪNŪRUM (-i : *C. Palinuro*), a promontory on the W. coast of Lucania, said to have derived its name from Palinurus, pilot of the ship of Aeneas, who fell into the sea, and was murdered on the coast by the natives.

PALLĂDĬUM (-i), properly any image of Pallas Athena (Minerva), but specially applied to an ancient image of this goddess at Troy, on the preservation of which the safety of the town depended. It was stolen by Ulysses and Diomedes, and was carried by the latter to Greece. According to some accounts, Troy contained two Palladia, one of which was carried off by Ulysses and Diomedes, while the other was conveyed by Aeneas to Italy. Others relate that the Palladium taken by the Greeks was a mere imitation, while that which Aeneas brought to Italy was the genuine image. But this twofold Palladium was probably a mere invention to account for its existence at Rome.

PALLANTĬA (-ae), the chief town of the Vaccaei, in the N. of Hispania Tarraconensis, and on a tributary of the Durius.

PALLANTĬAS (-ădis) and PALLANTIS (-ĭdie), patronymics given to Aurora, the daughter of the giant Pallas.

PALLANTĬUM (-i), an ancient town of Arcadia, near Tegea, said to have been founded by Pallas, son of Lycaon. Evander is said to have come from this place, and to have called the town which he founded on the banks of the Tiber, *Pallantēum* (afterwards *Pălantĭum* and *Pălātĭum*), after the Arcadian town. Hence Evander is called *Pallantius heros*.

PALLAS (-ădis), a surname of Athēna. [ATHENA.]

PALLAS (-antis). (1) One of the giants.— (2) The father of Athēna, according to some traditions.—(3) Son of Lycaon, and grandfather of Evander. [PALLANTIUM.]—(4) Son of Evander, and an ally of Aeneas.—(5) Son of the Athenian king Pandion, from whom the celebrated family of the Pallantidae at Athens traced their origin.—(6) A favourite freedman of the emperor Claudius, who acquired enormous wealth. Hence the line in Juvenal, *ego possideo plus Pallante et Licinio*.

PALLĒNĒ (-ēs), the most W.-ly of the 3 peninsulas running out from Chalcidice in Macedonia.

PALMȲRA (-ae: *Tadmor*), a celebrated city of Syria, standing in an oasis of the great Syrian Desert, which from its position was a halting place for the caravans between Syria and Mesopotamia. Here Solomon built a city, which was called in Hebrew Tadmor, that is, *the city of palm trees ;* and of this name the Greek Palmyra is a translation. Under Hadrian and the Antonines it was highly favoured and reached its greatest splendour. The history of its temporary elevation to the rank of a capital, in the 3rd century of the Christian era, is related under ODENATHUS and ZENOBIA. Its splendid ruins, which form a most striking object in the midst of the Desert, are of the Roman period.

PAMPHȲLĬA (-ae), a narrow strip of the

S. coast of Asia Minor, extending in a sort of arch along the Sinus Pamphyllus (*G. of Adalia*), between Lycia on the W., and Cilicia on the E., and on the N. bordering on Pisidia. The inhabitants were a mixture of races, whence their name Pamphyli (Πάμφυλοι), *of all races*. There were Greek settlements in the land, the foundation of which was ascribed to MOPSUS, from whom the country was in early times called MOPSOPIA. It was successively a part of the Persian, Macedonian, Greco-Syrian, and Pergamene kingdoms, and passed by the will of Attalus III. to the Romans (B.C. 130), under whom it was made a province ; but this province of Pamphylia included also Pisidia and Isauria, and afterwards a part of Lycia. Under Constantine Pisidia was again separated from Pamphylia.

PĀN (Pānŏs), the great god of flocks and shepherds among the Greeks, usually called a son of Hermes (Mercury), was originally an Arcadian god ; and Arcadia was always the principal seat of his worship. From this country his name and worship afterwards spread over other parts of Greece ; but at Athens his worship was not introduced till the time of the battle of Marathon. He is described as wandering among the mountains and valleys of Arcadia, either amusing himself with the chase, or leading the dances of the nymphs. He loved music, and invented the syrinx or shepherd's flute. Pan, like other gods who dwelt in forests, was dreaded by travellers, to whom he sometimes appeared, and whom he startled with sudden awe or

Pan. (From a Bronze Relief found at Pompeii.)

terror. Hence sudden fright, without any visible cause, was ascribed to Pan, and was called a Panic fear. The Romans identified their god Faunus with Pan. [FAUNUS.] In works of art Pan is represented as a sensual being, with horns, puck-nose, and goat's feet, sometimes in the act of dancing, and sometimes playing on the syrinx.

PANAETIUS (-i), a native of Rhodes, and a celebrated Stoic philosopher, lived some years at Rome, where he became an intimate friend of Laelius and of Scipio Africanus the younger. He succeeded Antipater as head of the Stoic school, and died at Athens, at all events before B.C. 111. The principal work of Panaetius was his treatise on the theory of moral obligation, from which Cicero took the greater part of his work *De Officiis.*

PANDAREOS, son of Merops of Miletus, whose daughters are said to have been carried off by the Harpies.

PANDARUS (-i). (1) A Lycian, distinguished in the Trojan army as an archer. —(2) Son of Alcanor, and twin-brother of Bitias, one of the companions of Aeneas, slain by Turnus.

PANDATARIA (-ae: *Vendutene*) a small island off the coast of Campania, to which Julia, the daughter of Augustus, was banished.

PANDION (-onis). (1) King of Athens, son of Erichthonius, and father of Procne and Philomela. The tragic history of his daughters is given under TEREUS.—(2) King of Athens, son of Cecrops, was expelled from Athens by the Metionidae, and fled to Megara, of which he became king.

PANDORA (-ae), the name of the first woman on earth. When Prometheus had stolen the fire from heaven, Zeus (Jupiter) in revenge caused Hephaestus to make a woman out of earth, who by her charms and beauty should bring misery upon the human race. Aphrodite (Venus) adorned her with beauty; Hermes (Mercury) bestowed upon her boldness and cunning; and the gods called her Pandora, or *All-gifted,* as each of the gods had given her some power by which she was to work the ruin of man. Hermes took her to Epimetheus, who made her his wife, forgetting the advice of his brother Prometheus not to receive any gifts from the gods. Pandora brought with her from heaven a box containing every human ill, upon opening which they all escaped and spread over the earth, Hope alone remaining. At a still later period the box is said to have contained all the blessings of the gods, which would have been preserved for the human race, had not Pandora opened the vessel, so that the winged blessings escaped.

PANDOSIA (-ae). (1) A town of Epirus in the district Thesprotia, on the river Acheron.—(2) A town in Bruttium near the frontiers of Lucania, situated on the river Acheron. It was here that Alexander of Epirus fell, B.C. 326, in accordance with an oracle.

PANDROSOS (-i), *i.e.* "the all-bedewing," or "refreshing," was a daughter of Cecrops and a sister of Herse and Aglauros.

PANGAEUS (-i) or PANGAEA (-orum), a range of mountains in Macedonia, between the Strymon and the Nestus, and in the neighbourhood of Philippi, with gold and silver mines, and with splendid roses.

PANIONIUM (-i), a spot on the N. of the promontory of Mycale, with a temple to Poseidon (Neptune), which was the place of meeting for the cities of Ionia.

PANNONIA (-ae), a Roman province between the Danube and the Alps, separated on the W. from Noricum by the Mons Cetius, and from Upper Italy by the Alpes Juliae, on the S. from Illyria by the Savus, on the E. from Dacia by the Danube, and on the N. from Germany by the same river.—The Pannonians (Pannonii) were probably of Illyrian origin. They were a brave and warlike people, and were conquered by the Romans in the time of Augustus (about B.C. 33). In A.D. 7 the Pannonians joined the Dalmatians and the other Illyrian tribes in their revolt from Rome, but were conquered by Tiberius, after a struggle, which lasted 3 years (A.D. 7—9). Pannonia was originally only one province, but was afterwards divided into 2 provinces, called *Pannonia Superior* and *Pannonia Inferior.*

PANOMPHAEUS (-i), *i.e.* the author of all signs and omens, a surname of Zeus (Jupiter).

PANOPE (-es) or PANOPAEA (-ae), a nymph of the sea, daughter of Nereus and Doris.

PANOPEUS (-eos or -ei). (1) Son of Phocus, accompanied Amphitryon on his expedition against the Taphians or Teleboans, and was one of the Calydonian hunters. — (2) Or Panope (-es), an ancient town in Phocis on the Cephissus and near the frontiers of Boeotia.

PANOPTES. [ARGUS.]

PANORMUS (-i: *Palermo*), an important town on the N. coast of Sicily, founded by the Phoenicians, and which at a later time received its Greek name from its excellent harbour. From the Phoenicians it passed into the hands of the Carthaginians, and was taken by the Romans in the 1st Punic war, B.C. 254.

PANSA (-ae), C. VIBIUS, consul with Hirtius, B.C. 43. [HIRTIUS.]

PANTAGIAS or PANTAGIES (-ae), a small river on the E. coast of Sicily, flowing into the sea between Megara and Syracuse.

PANTHEUM (-i), a celebrated temple at

Rome in the Campus Martius, which is still extant and used as a Christian church, resembles in its general form the Colosseum in the Regent's Park, London. It was built by M. Agrippa, B.C. 27, and was dedicated to Mars and Venus.

PANTHŌUS, contr. PANTHŪS (Voc. *Panthū*), a priest of Apollo at Troy, and father of Euphorbus, who is therefore called *Panthŏïdēs*. Pythagoras is also called *Panthŏïdēs* because he maintained that his soul had in a previous state animated the body of Euphorbus. He is called by Virgil *Othrȳădēs*, or son of Othryas.

PANTICĂPAEUM, a town in the Tauric Chersonesus, situated on a hill on the Cimmerian Bosporus, was founded by the Milesians, about B.C. 541, and became the residence of the Greek kings of the Bosporus.

PĂNȲĂSIS, a native of Halicarnassus, and a relation, probably an uncle, of the historian Herodotus, flourished about B.C. 480, and was celebrated as an epic poet.

PAPHLĂGŌNĬA (-ae), a country of Asia Minor, bounded by Bithynia on the W., by Pontus on the E., by Phrygia and afterwards by Galatia on the S., and by the Euxine on the N. In the Trojan war the Paphlagonians are said to have come to the assistance of the Trojans, from the land of the Heneti, under the command of Pylaemenes. The Paphlagonians were subdued by Croesus, and afterwards formed part of the Persian empire. Under the Romans Paphlagŏnia formed part of the province of Galatia ; but it was made a separate province by Constantine.

PĂPHUS (-i). (1) Son of Pygmalion, and founder of the city of the same name.—(2) The name of 2 towns on the W. coast of Cyprus, called " Old Paphos" (Παλαίπαφος) and " New Paphos," the former near the promontory Zephyrium, 10 stadia from the coast, the latter more inland, 60 stadia from the former. Old Paphos was the chief seat of the worship of Aphrodītē (Venus), who is said to have landed at this place after her birth among the waves, and who is hence frequently called the Paphian goddess (Paphia). Here she had a celebrated temple, the high priest of which exercised a kind of religious superintendence over the whole island.

PĂPĪNĬĀNUS (-i), AEMĬLĬUS, a celebrated Roman jurist, was praefectus praetorio, under the emperor Septimius Severus, and was put to death by Caracalla, A.D. 212.

PĂPĪNĬUS STĂTĬUS. [STATIUS.]

PĂPĪRĬUS CARBO. [CARBO.]

PĂPĪRĬUS CURSOR. [CURSOR.]

PĂRAETĂCĒNĒ (-ēs), a mountainous region on the borders of Media and Persis.

PĂRAETŌNĬUM (-i) or AMMŌNĬA (-ae),

an important city on the N. coast of Africa, belonged politically to Egypt : hence this city on the W. and Pelusium on the E. are called " cornua Aegypti." The adjective *Paraetonius* is used by the poets in the general sense of Egyptian.

PARCAE. [MOIRAE.]

PĂRIS (-ĭdis). (1) Also called ALEXANDER (-dri), was the second son of Priam and Hecuba. Before his birth Hecuba dreamed that she had brought forth a firebrand, the flames of which spread over the whole city. Accordingly as soon as the child was born, he was exposed on Mt. Ida, but was brought up by a shepherd, who gave him the name of Paris. When he had grown up, he distinguished himself as a valiant defender of the flocks and shepherds, and was hence called Alexander, or the defender of men. He succeeded in discovering his real origin, and was received by Priam as his son. He married Oenōnē, the daughter of the river god Cebren, but he soon deserted her for Helen. The tale runs that when Peleus and Thetis solemnised their nuptials, all the gods were invited to the marriage with the exception of Eris (Discordia), or Strife. Enraged at her exclusion, the goddess threw a golden apple among the guests, with the inscription, " to the fairest." Thereupon Hera (Juno), Aphrodītē (Venus), and Athēna (Minerva), each claimed the apple for herself. Zeus (Jupiter) ordered Hermes (Mercury) to take the goddesses to Mt. Ida, and to intrust the decision of the dispute to the shepherd Paris.

Paris. (Aegina Marbles.)

The goddesses accordingly appeared before him. Hera promised him the sovereignty of

Asia, Athena renown in war, and Aphrodite the fairest of women for his wife. Paris decided in favour of Aphrodite, and gave her the golden apple. This judgment called forth in Hera and Athena fierce hatred against Troy. Under the protection of Aphrodite, Paris now sailed to Greece, and was hospitably received in the palace of Menelaus at Sparta. Here he succeeded in carrying off Helen, the wife of Menelaus, who was the most beautiful woman in the world. Hence arose the Trojan war. Before her marriage with Menelaus, she had been wooed by the noblest chiefs of all parts of Greece. Her former suitors now resolved to revenge her abduction, and sailed against Troy. [AGAMEMNON.] Paris fought

with Menelaus before the walls of Troy, and was defeated, but was carried off by Aphrodite. He is said to have killed Achilles, either by one of his arrows, or by treachery. [ACHILLES.] On the capture of Troy, Paris was wounded by Philoctetes with one of the arrows of Hercules, and then returned to his long abandoned wife Oenone. But as she refused to heal the wound, Paris died. Oenone quickly repented, and put an end to her own life. Paris is represented in works of art as a beautiful youth, without a beard, and with a Phrygian cap.—(2) The name of two celebrated pantomimes, of whom the elder lived in the reign of the emperor Nero, and the younger in that of Domitian.

Judgment of Paris.   (From a painted Vase.)

PĂRISĬI. [LUTETIA PARISIORUM.]

PĂRĬUM (-i), a city of Mysia, on the Propontis, founded by a colony from Miletus and Paros.

PARMA (-ae : *Parma*), a town in Gallia Cispadana, situated on a river of the same name, between Placentia and Mutina, originally a town of the Boii, but made a Roman colony B.C. 183. It was celebrated for its wool.

PARMĔNĬDĔS (-is), a distinguished Greek philosopher, was a native of Elea in Italy, and the founder of the Eleatic school of philosophy, in which he was succeeded by Zeno. He was born about B.C. 513, and visited Athens in 448, when he was 65 years of age.

PARMĔNĬŎN (-ōnis), a distinguished Macedonian general in the service of Philip and Alexander the Great. In Alexander's invasion of Asia, Parmenion was regarded as second in command, and is continually spoken of as the most attached of the king's friends.

But when Philotas, the son of Parmenion, was accused in Drangiana (B.C. 330) of being privy to a plot against the king's life, he not only confessed his own guilt, when put to the torture, but involved his father also in the plot. Whether the king really believed in the guilt of Parmenion or deemed his life a necessary sacrifice to policy after the execution of his son, he caused his aged friend to be assassinated in Media before he could receive the tidings of his son's death.

PARNASSUS (-i), a range of mountains extending S.E. through Doris and Phocis, and terminating at the Corinthian gulf between Cirrha and Anticyra. But the name was more usually restricted to the highest part of the range a few miles N. of Delphi. Its 2 highest summits were called Tithŏrĕa and Lycōrĕa ; hence Parnassus is frequently described by the poets as double-headed. The sides of Parnassus were well-wooded ; at its foot grew myrtle, laurel and olive-trees, and higher up firs; and its summit was covered with snow during the greater part of the year. It contained numerous caves, glens, and romantic ravines. It is celebrated as one of the chief seats of Apollo and the Muses, and an inspiring source of poetry and song. On Mt. Lycorea was the Corycian cave, from which the Muses are sometimes called the Corycian nymphs. Just above Delphi was the far-famed Castalian spring, which issued from between 2 cliffs, called *Nauplia* and *Hyamplia*. These cliffs are frequently called by the poets the summits of Parnassus, though they are in reality only small peaks at the base of the mountain. The mountain also was sacred to Dionysus (Bacchus), and on one of its summits the Thyades held their Bacchic revels. Between Parnassus Proper and Mt. Cirphis was the valley of the Plistus, through which the sacred road ran from Delphi to Daulis and Stiris; and at the point where the road branched off to these 2 places (called σχιστή), Oedipus slew his father Laius.

PARNES (-ēthis), a mountain in the N.E. of Attica, was a continuation of Mt. Cithaeron, and formed part of the boundary between Boeotia and Attica. It was well wooded, abounded in game, and on its lower slopes produced excellent wine.

PAROPAMISUS (-i), the part of the great chain of mountains in Central Asia, lying between the Sariphi M. (*M. of Kohistan*) on the W., and M. Imaus (*Himalaya*) on the E., or from about the sources of the river Margus on the W. to the point where the Indus breaks through the chain on the E. The Greeks sometimes called them the Indian Caucasus, a name which has come down to our times in the native form of *Hindoo-Koosh*. Its inhabitants were called Paromisadae or Paropamisii.

PAROS (-i), an island in the Aegean sea, one of the larger of the Cyclades, was situated S. of Delos, and W. of Naxos, being separated from the latter by a channel 5 or 6 miles wide. It is about 36 miles in circumference. It was inhabited by Ionians, and became so prosperous, even at an early period, as to send out colonies to Thasos and to Parium on the Propontis. In the first invasion of Greece by the generals of Darius, Paros submitted to the Persians; and after the battle of Marathon, Miltiades attempted to reduce the island, but failed in his attempt, and received a wound of which he died. [MILTIADES.] After the defeat of Xerxes, Paros came under the supremacy of Athens, and shared the fate of the other Cyclades The most celebrated production of Paros was its marble, which was extensively used by the ancient sculptors. It was chiefly obtained from a mountain

called *Marpessa*. Paros was the birthplace of the poet Archilochus.—In Paros was discovered the celebrated inscription called the *Parian Chronicle*, which is now preserved at Oxford. In its perfect state it contained a chronological account of the principal events in Greek history from Cecrops, B.C. 1582 to the archonship of Diognetus, B.C. 264.

PARRHASIA (-ae), a district in the S. of Arcadia. The adjective *Parrhasius* is frequently used by the poets as equivalent to Arcadian.

PARRHASIUS (-i), one of the most celebrated Greek painters, was a native of Ephesus, but practised his art chiefly at Athens. He flourished about B.C. 400. Respecting the story of his contest with Zeuxis, see ZEUXIS.

PARTHENI. [PARTHINI.]

PARTHENIUM (-i). (1) A town in Mysia, S. of Pergamum.—(2) A promontory in the Chersonesus Taurica, on which stood a temple of the Tauric Artemis (Diana) from whom it derived its name. It was in this temple that human sacrifices were offered to the goddess.

PARTHENIUS (-i). (1) Of Nicaea, a celebrated grammarian, who taught Virgil Greek.—(2) A mountain on the frontiers of Argolis and Arcadia. It was on this mountain that Telephus, the son of Hercules and Auge, was suckled by a hind; and here also the god Pan appeared to Phidippides, the Athenian courier, shortly before the battle of Marathon.—(3) The chief river of Paphlagonia, flowing into the Euxine, and forming in the lower part of its course the boundary between Bithynia and Paphlagonia.

PARTHENON (-ōnis: i. e. *the virgin's chamber*), the usual name of the temple of Athena (Minerva) Parthenos on the Acropolis of Athens. It was erected under the administration of Pericles, and was dedicated B.C. 438. Its architects were Ictinus and Callicrates, but all the works were under the superintendence of Phidias. It was built entirely of Pentelic marble: its dimensions were, 227 English feet long, 101 broad, and 65 high: it was 50 feet longer than the edifice which preceded it. Its architecture was of the Doric order, and of the purest kind. It consisted of an oblong central building (the *cella*), surrounded on all sides by a peristyle of pillars. The cella was divided into 2 chambers of unequal size, the *prodomus* or *pronaos* and the *opisthodomus* or *posticum;* the former, which was the larger, contained the statue of the goddess, and was the true sanctuary, the latter being probably used as a treasury and vestry. It was adorned, within and without, with colours and gilding, and with sculptures which are regarded as the master-pieces of ancient art. (1.) *The tympana of the pediments* were filled with groups of detached colossal statues, those of the E. or principal front representing the birth of Athena, and those of the W. front the contest between Athena and Poseidon (Neptune) for the land of Attica. (2.) In the *frieze of the entablature*, the *metopes* were filled with sculptures in high relief, representing subjects from the Attic mythology, among which the battle of the Athenians with the Centaurs forms the subject of the 15 metopes from the S. side, which are now in the British Museum. (3.) Along the top of the external wall of the *cella*, under the ceiling of the peristyle, ran a frieze sculptured with a representation of the Panathenaic procession, in very low relief. A large number of the slabs of this frieze were brought to England by Lord Elgin, with the 15 metopes just mentioned, and a considerable number of other fragments, including some of the most important, though mutilated, statues from the pediments; and the whole collection was purchased by the nation in 1816, and deposited in the British Museum. The worst of the injuries which the Parthenon has suffered from war and pillage was inflicted in the siege of Athens by the Venetians in 1687, when a bomb exploded in the very centre of the Parthenon, and threw down much of both the side walls. Its ruins are still, however, in sufficient preservation to give a good idea of the construction of all its principal parts.

PARTHENOPAEUS (-i), son of Meleager and Atalanta, and one of the 7 heroes who marched against Thebes. [ADRASTUS.]

PARTHENOPE. [NEAPOLIS.]

PARTHIA, PARTHYAEA (-ae), PARTHIENE (-ēs: *Khorassan*), a country of Asia, to the S.E. of the Caspian, originally bounded on the N. by Hyrcania, on the E. by Aria, on the S. by Carmania, and on the W. by Media. The Parthians were a very warlike people, and were especially celebrated as horse-archers. Their tactics became so celebrated as to pass into a proverb. Their mail-clad horsemen spread like a cloud round the hostile army, and poured in a shower of darts, and then evaded any closer conflict by a rapid flight, during which they still shot their arrows backwards upon the enemy. The Parthians were subject successively to the Persians and to the Greek kings of Syria; but about B.C. 250 they revolted from the Seleucidae, under a chieftain named Arsaces, who founded an independent monarchy. Their empire extended over Asia from the Euphrates to the Indus, and from the Indian Ocean to

the Paropamisus, or even to the Oxus. The history of their empire till its overthrow by the Persians in A.D. 226 is given under ARSACES. The Latin poets of the Augustan age use the names Parthi, Persae, and Medi indifferently.

PARTHINI or PARTHENI (-ōrum), an Illyrian people in the neighbourhood of Dyrrhachium.

PARYADRES, a mountain chain of Asia, connecting the Taurus and the mountains of Armenia, was considered as the boundary between Cappadocia and Armenia.

PARYSATIS (-ĭdis), daughter of Artaxerxes I. Longimanus, king of Persia, and wife of her own brother Darius Ochus, and mother of Artaxerxes Mnemon, and Cyrus. She supported the latter in his rebellion against his brother Artaxerxes, B.C. 401. [CYRUS.] She afterwards poisoned Statira, the wife of Artaxerxes, and induced the king to put Tissaphernes to death, whom she hated as having been the first to discover the designs of Cyrus to his brother.

PASARGADA (-ae), or -AE (-ārum), the older of the 2 capitals of Persis (the other and later being Persepolis), is said to have been founded by Cyrus the Great, on the spot where he gained his great victory over Astyages. The tomb of Cyrus stood here in the midst of a beautiful park. The exact site is doubtful. Most modern geographers identify it with *Murghab*, N.E. of Persepolis, where there are the remains of a great sepulchral monument of the ancient Persians.

PASIPHAE (-es), daughter of Helios (the Sun) and Perseis, wife of Minos, and mother of Androgeos, Ariadnē, and Phaedra. Hence Phaedra is called *Pasiphäeïa* by Ovid. Pasiphaë was also the mother of the Minotaurus, respecting whom see p. 269.

PASITHEA (-ae), or PASITHEE (-es), one of the Charites, or Graces, also called Aglaia.

PASITIGRIS (-ĭdis), a river rising on the confines of Media and Persis, and flowing through Susiana into the head of the Persian Gulf, after receiving the Eulaeus on its W. side. Some geographers make the Pasitigris a tributary of the Tigris.

PASSARON (-ōnis), a town of Epirus in Molossia, and the ancient capital of the Molossian kings.

PATALA, PATALENE. [PATTALA, PATTALENE.]

PATARA (-ae), one of the chief cities of Lycia, situated on the coast a few miles E. of the mouth of the Xanthus. It was early colonised by Dorians from Crete, and became a chief seat of the worship of Apollo, who had here a very celebrated oracle, which uttered responses in the winter only. Hence

Apollo is called by Horace " Delius et *Pata-reus* Apollo."

PĂTĂVĬUM (-i : *Padua*), an ancient town of the Veneti in the N. of Italy, on the Medoacus Minor, and on the road from Mutina to Altinum, said to have been founded by the Trojan Antenor.   Under the Romans it was the most important city in the N. of Italy, and, by its commerce and manufactures (of which its woollen stuffs were the most celebrated), it attained great opulence.   It is celebrated as the birth-place of the historian Livy.

PĂTERCŬLUS (-i), C. VELLĔIUS, a Roman historian, served under Tiberius in his campaigns in Germany in the reign of Augustus, and lived at least as late as A.D. 30, as he dedicated his history to M. Vinicius, who was consul in that year.   This work is a brief compendium of Roman history, commencing with the destruction of Troy, and ending with A.D. 30.

PATMOS (-i), one of the islands called Sporades, in the Icarian Sea, celebrated as the place to which the Apostle John was banished, and in which he wrote the Apocalypse.

PATRAE (-ārum : *Patras*), one of the 12 cities of Achaia, situated W. of Rhium, near the opening of the Corinthian gulf.   Augustus made it the chief city of Achaia.

PATROCLUS (-i), sometimes PATROCLĒS (-is), son of Menoetius of Opus and Sthenĕlē, and grandson of Actor and Aegina, whence he is called *Actorĭdes.*   Having involuntarily, committed murder while a boy, his father took him to Peleus at Phthia, where he became the intimate friend of Achilles.   He accompanied the latter to the Trojan wars, but when his friend withdrew from the scene of action, Patroclus followed his example. But he afterwards obtained permission to lead the Myrmidons to the fight, when the Greeks were hard pressed by the Trojans. Achilles equipped him with his own armour and arms ; and Patroclus succeeded in driving the Trojans back to their walls, where he was slain by Hector.   The desire of avenging the death of Patroclus led Achilles again into the field.   [ACHILLES.]

Patroclus.   (Aegina Marbles.)

PATTĂLA.   [PATTALENE.]

PATTĂLĒNĒ or PĂTĂLĒNĒ (-es), the name of the great delta formed by the 2 principal arms by which the Indus falls into the sea.   At the apex of the delta stood the city Pattăla or Pătăla, the Sanscrit *patăla*, which means *the W. country*, and is applied to the W. part of N. India about the Indus, in contradistinction to the E. part about the Ganges.

PĂTULCĬUS.   [JANUS.]

PAULĪNUS (-i), C. SUĔTŌNĬUS, governor of Britain A.D. 59—62, during which time the Britons rose in rebellion under Boadicea. [BOADICEA.]   In 66 he was consul ; and after the death of Nero in 68 he was one of Otho's generals in the war against Vitellius.

PAULUS (-i), the name of a celebrated patrician family in the Aemilia gens.   (1) L.

AEMILIUS PAULUS, consul B.C. 219, when he conquered Demetrius of the island of Pharos, in the Adriatic, and compelled him to fly for refuge to Philip, king of Macedonia.   He was consul a 2nd time in B.C. 216, with C. Terentius Varro.   This was the year of the memorable defeat at Cannae.   [HANNIBAL.]   The battle was fought against the advice of Paulus, and he was one of the many distinguished Romans who perished in the engagement, refusing to fly from the field when a tribune of the soldiers offered him his horse.   Hence we find in Horace, " animaeque magnae prodigum Paulum superante Poeno."   Paulus was a staunch adherent of the aristocracy, and was raised to the consulship by the latter party to counterbalance the influence of the plebeian Terentius Varro.—(2) L. AEMILIUS

PAULUS, surnamed MACEDONICUS, son of the preceding, consul for the first time B.C. 181, and a 2nd time in 168, when he brought the war against Perseus to a conclusion by the defeat of the Macedonian monarch near Pydna, on the 22d of June. [PERSEUS.] Before leaving Greece, Paulus marched into Epirus, where, in accordance with a cruel command of the senate, he gave to his soldiers 70 towns to be pillaged, because they had been in alliance with Perseus. He was censor with Q. Marcius Philippus, in 164, and died in 160, after a long and tedious illness. The Adelphi of Terence was brought out at the funeral games exhibited in his honour. Two of his sons were adopted into other families, and are known in history by the names of Q. Fabius Maximus and P. Scipio Africanus the younger.

PAULUS (-i), JŪLĬUS, one of the most distinguished of the Roman jurists, was praefectus praetorio under the emperor Alexander Severus.

PAUSĂNĬĂS (-ae). (1) Son of Cleombrotus and nephew of Leonidas. Several writers incorrectly call him king; but he was only agent for his cousin Plistarchus, the infant son of Leonidas. He commanded the allied forces of the Greeks at the battle of Plataea, B.C. 479, and subsequently captured Byzantium, which had been in the hands of the Persians. Dazzled by his success and reputation, he now aimed at becoming tyrant over the whole of Greece, with the assistance of the Persian king, who promised him his daughter in marriage. His conduct became so arrogant, that all the allies, except the Peloponnesians and Aeginetans, voluntarily offered to transfer to the Athenians that pre-eminence of rank which Sparta had hitherto enjoyed. In this way the Athenian confederacy first took its rise. Reports of the conduct and designs of Pausanias having reached Sparta, he was recalled; and the ephors accidentally obtained proofs of his treason. A man, who was charged with a letter to Persia, having his suspicions awakened by noticing that none of those sent on similar errands had returned, counterfeited the seal of Pausanias, and opened the letter, in which he found directions for his own death. He carried the letter to the ephors, who prepared to arrest Pausanias; but he took refuge in the temple of Athena (Minerva). The ephors stripped off the roof of the temple and built up the door; the aged mother of Pausanias is said to have been among the first who laid a stone for this purpose. When he was on the point of expiring, the ephors took him out, lest his death should pollute the sanctuary. He died as soon as he got outside, B.C. 470.—(2) Son

of Plistoanax, and grandson of the preceding, was king of Sparta from B.C. 408 to 394.—(3) A Macedonian youth of distinguished family. Having been shamefully treated by Attalus, he complained of the outrage to Philip; but as Philip took no notice of his complaints, he directed his vengeance against the king himself, whom he murdered at the festival held at Aegae, B.C. 336.—(4) The traveller and geographer, perhaps a native of Lydia, lived under Antoninus Pius and M. Aurelius. His work entitled a *Periegesis* or *Itinerary of Greece*, is in 10 books, and contains a description of Attica and Megaris (i.), Corinthia, Sicyonia, Phliasia, and Argolis (ii.), Laconica (iii.), Messenia (iv.), Elis (v. vi.), Achaea (vii.), Arcadia (viii.), Boeotia (ix.), Phocis (x.). The work shows that Pausanias visited most of the places in these divisions of Greece, a fact which is clearly demonstrated by the minuteness and particularity of his descriptions.

PAUSĬĂS (-ae), a native of Sicyon, one of the most distinguished Greek painters, was contemporary with Apelles, and flourished about B.C. 360—330.

PAUSĬLЎPUM. [NEAPOLIS.]

PĂVŎR (-ōris), *i.e.*, Fear, the attendant of Mars.

PAX (Pācis), the goddess of peace, called IRĒNE by the Greeks. (IRENE.)

PĒDĂSA (-ōrum) or PĒDĂSUM (-i), a very ancient city of Caria, originally a chief abode of the Leleges.

PĒDĂSUS (-i), a town of Mysia, on the Satnioïs, mentioned several times by Homer.

PĒDĬĀNUS, ASCŌNĬUS. (Asconius.)

PĒDĬUS (-i), Q., the great-nephew of the dictator C. Julius Caesar, being the grandson of Julia, Caesar's eldest sister. He served under Caesar in the civil war, and in Caesar's will was named one of his heirs. After the fall of the consuls, Hirtius and Pansa, at the battle of Mutina, in April, B.C. 43, Octavius marched upon Rome at the head of an army, and in the month of August he was elected consul along with Pedius, who died towards the end of the year, shortly after the news of the proscription had reached Rome.

PEDNELISSUS (-i), a city in the interior of Pisidia.

PĒDO ALBĪNŎVĀNUS. [ALBINOVANUS.]

PĒDUM (-i), an ancient town of Latium, on the Via Laviciana, which fell into decay at an early period.

PĒGAE. [PAGAE.]

PĒGĂSIS (-ĭdis), *i. e.* sprung from Pegasus, was applied to the fountain Hippocrēnē, which was called forth by the hoof of Pegasus. The Muses are also called *Pĕgăsĭdes*, because the fountain Hippocrene was sacred to them.

Oenonē is also called *Pĕgăsis*, simply as a fountain nymph (from πηγή).

PĒGĂSUS (-i), the winged horse, which sprang from the blood of Medusa, when her head was struck off by Perseus. He was called Pegasus, because he made his appearance near the sources (πήγαι) of Oceanus. While drinking at the fountain of Pirēnē, on the Acrocorinthus, he was caught by Bellerophon with a golden bridle, which Athena (Minerva) had given the hero. With the assistance of Pegasus, Bellerophon conquered the Chimaera, but endeavouring to ascend to heaven upon his winged horse, he fell down upon the earth. [BELLEROPHON.] Pegasus, however, continued his flight to heaven, where he dwelt among the stars.—Pegasus was also regarded as the horse of the Muses, and in this connexion is more celebrated in modern times than in antiquity; for with the ancients he had no connexion with the Muses, except producing with his hoof the inspiring fountain Hippocrēnē. Pegasus is often represented in ancient works of art along with Athena and Bellerophon. [See drawings on pp. 76, 110.]

Pegasus. (Coin of Corinth, in British Museum.)

PĔLĂGŌNĬA (-ae). (1) A district and city in Macedonia, inhabited by the Pelagones, and situated S. of Paeonia upon the Erigon. —(2) A district in Thessaly, situated W. of Olympus, and belonging to Perrhaebia.

PĔLASGI (-ōrum), the earliest inhabitants of Greece who established the worship of the Dodonaean Zeus (Jupiter), Hephaestus (Vulcan), the Cabiri, and other divinities belonging to the earliest inhabitants of the country. They claimed descent from a mythical hero Pelasgus, of whom we have different accounts in the different parts of Greece inhabited by Pelasgians. The nation was widely spread over Greece and the islands of the Grecian archipelago; and the name of *Pelasgia* was given at one time to Greece. One of the most ancient traditions represented Pelasgus as a descendant of Phoroneus, king of Argus; and it was generally believed by the Greeks that the Pelasgi spread from Argos to the other countries of Greece. Arcadia, Attica, Epirus, and Thessaly, were, in addition to Argos, some of the principal

seats of the Pelasgi. They were also found on the coasts of Asia Minor, and according to some writers in Italy as well. Of the language, habits, and civilisation of this people we possess no certain knowledge. Herodotus says they spoke a barbarous language, that is, a language not Greek; but from the facility with which the Greek and Pelasgic languages coalesced in all parts of Greece, and from the fact that the Athenians and Arcadians are said to have been of pure Pelasgic origin, it is probable that the 2 languages had a close affinity. The Pelasgi are further said to have been an agricultural people, and to have possessed a considerable knowledge of the useful arts. The most ancient architectural remains of Greece, such as the treasury or tomb of Athens at Mycenae, are ascribed to the Pelasgians, and are cited as specimens of Pelasgian architecture, though there is no positive authority for these statements.

PĒLASGĬŌTIS, a district in Thessaly, between Hestiaeotis and Magnesia. [THESSALIA.]

PĒLASGUS. [PELASGI.]

PĔLĒTHRŌNĬUM (-i), a mountainous district in Thessaly, part of Mt. Pelion, where the Lapithae dwelt.

PĒLEUS (*gen.* -ĕŏs or -ĕī, *acc.* Pēlĕa, *voc.* Pēleu, *abl.* Pēlĕo), son of Aeacus and Endeïs, and king of the Myrmidons at Phthia in Thessaly. Having, in conjunction with his brother Telamon, murdered his half-brother Phocus, he was expelled by Aeacus from Aegina, and went to Phthia in Thessaly. Here he was purified from the murder by Eurytion, the son of Actor, who gave Peleus his daughter Antigŏnē in marriage, and a third part of his kingdom. Peleus accompanied Eurytion to the Calydonian hunt; but having involuntarily killed his father-in-law with his spear, he became a wanderer a second time. He now took refuge at Iolcus, where he was again purified by Acastus, the king of the place. Here he was falsely accused by Astydamia, the wife of Acastus, and in consequence nearly perished on Mt. Pelion. [ACASTUS.] While on Mt. Pelion, Peleus married the Nereid Thetis. She was destined to marry a mortal; but having the power, like Proteus, of assuming any form she pleased, she endeavoured in this way to escape from Peleus. The latter, however, previously taught by Chiron, held the goddess fast till she promised to marry him. The gods took part in the marriage solemnity; and Eris or Strife was the only goddess who was not invited to the nuptials. By Thetis Peleus became the father of Achilles. Peleus was too old to accompany Achilles against Troy; he remained at home and survived the death of his son.

Peleus and Thetis. (From a painted Vase.)

PĒLĬĀDES. [PELIAS.]

PĒLĬAS (-ae), son of Poseidon (Neptune) and Tyro, a daughter of Salmoneus, and twin-brother of Neleus. The twins were exposed by their mother, but they were preserved and reared by some countrymen. They subsequently learnt their parentage; and after the death of Cretheus, king of Iolcus, who had married their mother, they seized the throne of Iolcus, to the exclusion of Aeson, the son of Cretheus and Tyro. Pelias soon afterwards expelled his own brother Neleus, and thus became sole ruler of Iolcus. After Pelias had long reigned there, Jason, the son of Aeson, came to Iolcus and claimed the kingdom as his right. In order to get rid of him, Pelias sent him to Colchis to fetch the golden fleece. Hence arose the celebrated expedition of the Argonauts. After the return of Jason, Pelias was cut to pieces and boiled by his own daughters (the *Pelīădes*), who had been told by Medēa that in this manner they might restore their father to vigour and youth. His son Acastus held funeral games in his honour at Iolcus, and expelled Jason and Medea from the country. [JASON; MEDEA; ARGONAUTAE.] Among the daughters of Pelias, was Alcestis, the wife of Admetus.

PĒLĪDES (-ae), the son of Peleus, *i.e.* Achilles.

PĒLIGNI (-ōrum), a brave and warlike people of Sabine origin in central Italy, bounded by the Marsi, the Marrucini, the Samnites, and the Frentani. They took an active part in the Social war (90—89), and their chief town Corfinium was destined by the allies to be the new capital of Italy in place of Rome.

PĒLION, more rarely PĒLĬOS (-ii), a lofty range of mountains in Thessaly in the district of Magnesia, situated between the lake Boebēis and the Pagasaean gulf. Its sides were covered with wood, and on its summit was a temple of Zeus (Jupiter) Actaeus. Mt. Pelion was celebrated in mythology. Near its summit was the cave of the Centaur Chiron. The giants in their war with the gods are said to have attempted to heap Ossa and Olympus on Pelion, or Pelion and Ossa on Olympus, in order to scale heaven. On Pelion the timber was felled with which the ship Argo was built.

PELLA (-ae). (1) An ancient town of Macedonia in the district Bottiaea, situated upon a lake formed by the river Lydias. Philip made it his residence and the capital of the Macedonian monarchy. It was the birthplace of Alexander the Great. Hence the poets give the surname of *Pellaea* to Alexandria in Egypt, because it was founded by Alexander the Great, and also use the word in a general sense as equivalent to Egyptian. —(2) A city of Palestine, E. of the Jordan, in Peraea. It was the place of refuge of the Christians who fled from Jerusalem before its capture by the Romans.

PELLĒNĒ (-ēs), the most E.-ly of the 12 cities of Achaia, near the frontiers of Sicyonia, and situated on a hill 60 stadia from the city. The inhabitants of the peninsula of Pallene in Macedonia professed to be descended from the Pellenaeans in Achaia, who were shipwrecked on the Macedonian coast on their return from Troy.

PĒLŎPĒA or PĒLŎPĬA (-ae), daughter of Thyestes, and mother of Aegisthus. [AEGISTHUS.]

PĒLŎPĬDAS (-ae), a celebrated Theban general, and an intimate friend of Epaminondas. He took a leading part in expelling the Spartans from Thebes, B.C. 379; and from this time until his death there was not a year in which he was not entrusted with some important command. He was slain in battle at Cynoscephalae in Thessaly, fighting against Alexander of Pherae, B.C. 364.

PĒLŎPONNĒSUS (-i : *Morea*), the S. part of Greece or the peninsula, which was connected with Hellas proper by the isthmus of Corinth. It is said to have derived its name Peloponnesus or the " island of Pelops," from the mythical Pelops. [PELOPS.] This name does not occur in Homer. In his time the peninsula was sometimes called *Apia*, from Apis, son of Phoroneus, king of Argos, and sometimes *Argos;* which names were given to it on account of Argos being the chief power in Peloponnesus at that period. On the E. and S. there are 3 great gulfs, the Argolic, Laconian, and Messenian. The ancients compared the shape of the country to the leaf of a plane tree; and its modern name, the *Morea*, which first occurs in the 12th century of the Christian era, was given it on account of its resemblance to a mulberry-leaf. Peloponnesus was divided into various provinces, all of which were bounded on one side by the sea, with the exception of ARCADIA, which was in the centre of the country. These provinces were ACHAIA in the N., ELIS in the W., MESSENIA in the W. and S., LACONIA in the S. and E., and CORINTHIA in the E. and N. An account of the geography of the peninsula is given under these names. The area of Peloponnesus is computed to be 7779 English miles; and it probably contained a population of upwards of a million in the flourishing period of Greek history.—Peloponnesus was originally inhabited by Pelasgians. Subsequently the Achaeans, who belonged to the Aeolic race, settled in the E. and S. parts of the peninsula, in Argolis, Laconia, and Messenia; and the Ionians in the N. part, in Achaia; while the remains of the original inhabitants of the country, the Pelasgians, collected chiefly in the central part, in Arcadia. Eighty years after the Trojan war, according to mythical chronology, the Dorians, under the conduct of the Heraclidae, invaded and conquered Peloponnesus, and established Doric states in Argolis, Laconia, and Messenia, from whence they extended their power over Corinth, Sicyon, and Megara. Part of the Achaean population remained in these provinces as tributary subjects to the Dorians under the name of Perioeci; while others of the Achaeans passed over to the N. of Peloponnesus, expelled the Ionians, and settled in this part of the country, which was called after them Achaia. The Aetolians, who had invaded Peloponnesus along with the Dorians, settled in Elis and became intermingled with the original inhabitants. The peninsula remained under Doric influence during the most important period of Greek history, and opposed to the great Ionic city of Athens. After the conquest of Messenia by the Spartans, it was under the supremacy of Sparta, till the overthrow of the power of the latter by the Thebans at the battle of Leuctra, B.C. 371.

PELOPS (-ŏpis), grandson of Zeus (Jupiter), and son of Tantalus, king of Phrygia. Being expelled from Phrygia, he came to Elis, where he married Hippŏdămĭa, daughter of Oenomaus, whom he succeeded on the throne. By means of the wealth he brought

with him, his influence became so great in the peninsula that it was called after him "the island of Pelops." The legends about Pelops consist mainly of the story of his being cut to pieces and boiled, of his contest with Oenomaus and Hippŏdămĭa, and of his relation to his sons. 1. *Pelops cut to pieces and boiled.* Tantalus, the favourite of the gods, once invited them to a repast, and on that occasion killed his own son, and having boiled him set the flesh before them that they might eat it. But the immortal gods, knowing what it was, did not touch it; Demeter (Ceres) alone, being absorbed by grief for her lost daughter, consumed the shoulder. Hereupon the gods ordered Hermes (Mercury) to put the limbs of Pelops into a cauldron, and thereby restore him to life. When the process was over, Clotho took him out of the cauldron, and as the shoulder consumed by Demeter was wanting, the goddess supplied its place by one made of ivory; his descendants (the Pelopidae), as a mark of their origin, were believed to have one shoulder as white as ivory. 2. *Contest with Oenomaus and Hippŏdămĭa.* An oracle having declared to Oenomaus, king of Pisa in Elis, that he should be killed by his son-in-law, he declared that he would bestow the hand of his daughter Hippŏdămĭa upon the man who should conquer him in the chariot-race, but that whoever was conquered should suffer death. This he did, because his horses were swifter than those of any other mortal. He had overtaken and slain many a suitor, when Pelops came to Pisa. Pelops bribed Myrtilus, the charioteer of Oenomaus, by the promise of half the kingdom if he would assist him in conquering his master. Myrtilus agreed, and took out the linch-pins of the chariot of Oenomaus. In the race the chariot of Oenomaus broke down, and he was thrown out and killed. Thus Hippŏdămĭa became the wife of Pelops. But as Pelops had now gained his object, he was unwilling to keep faith with Myrtilus; and accordingly as they were driving along a cliff he threw Myrtilus into the sea. As Myrtilus sank, he cursed Pelops and his whole race. Pelops returned with Hippŏdămĭa to Pisa in Elis, and soon made himself master of Olympia, where he restored the Olympian games with greater splendour than ever. 3. *The sons of Pelops.* Chrysippus was the favourite of his father, and was in consequence envied by his brothers. The two eldest among them, Atreus and Thyestes, with the connivance of Hippŏdămĭa, accordingly murdered Chrysippus, and threw his body into a well. Pelops, who suspected his sons of the murder, expelled them from the country. Pelops, after his death, was honoured at Olympia above all other heroes. The name of Pelops was so celebrated that it was constantly used by the poets in connexion with his descendants and the cities they inhabited. Hence we find Atreus, the son of Pelops, called *Pelopeïus Atreus,* and Agamemnon, the grandson, or great-grandson of Atreus, called *Pelopeïus Agamemnon.* In the same way Iphigenia, the daughter of Agamemnon, and Hermione, the wife of Menelaus, are each called by Ovid *Pelopeïa virgo.* Virgil uses the phrase *Pelopēa moenia* to signify the cities in Peloponnesus, which Pelops and his descendants ruled over; and in like manner Mycenae is called by Ovid *Pelopeïades Mycenae.*

PĒLŌRIS (-ĭdis), PĒLŌRĬAS (-ădis), or PĒLŌRUS (-i: *C. Faro*), the N.E. point of Sicily, and one of the 3 promontories which formed the triangular figure of the island. According to the usual story it derived its name from Pelorus, the pilot of Hannibal's ship; but the name was more ancient than Hannibal's time, being mentioned by Thucydides.

PELTAE (-ārum), an ancient and flourishing city in the N. of Phrygia.

PĒLŪSĬUM (-i; O.T. Sin.: both names are derived from nouns meaning *mud*), a celebrated city of Lower Egypt, standing on the E. side of the E.-most mouth of the Nile, which was called after it the Pelusiac mouth, 20 stadia (2 geog. miles) from the sea, in the midst of morasses, from which it obtained its name. As the key of Egypt on the N.E., and the frontier city towards Syria and Arabia, it was strongly fortified, and was the scene of many battles and sieges. It was the birthplace of the geographer Ptolemaeus.

PĒNĀTES (-um), the household gods of the Romans, both those of a private family and of the state, as the great family of citizens. Hence we have to distinguish between private and public Penates. The name is connected with *penus;* and the images of these gods were kept in the *penetralia,* or the central part of the house. The Lares were included among the Penates, and both names are often used synonymously. The Lares, however, though included in the Penates, were not the only Penates; for each family had usually no more than one Lar, whereas the Penates are always spoken of in the plural. Most ancient writers believed that the Penates of the state were brought by Aeneas from Troy into Italy, and were preserved first at Lavinium, afterwards at Alba Longa, and finally at Rome. The private Penates had their place at the hearth of every house, and the table also was sacred to them. On the hearth a perpetual fire was kept up in their honour, and the table always con-

tained the salt-cellar and the firstlings of fruit for these divinities.

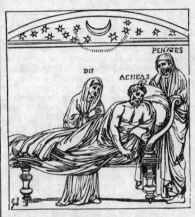

Penates. (From the Vatican Virgil.)

PĒNĒIS (-ĭdis), that is, Daphnē, daughter of the river-god Pēneus.

PĒNĒLŎPĒ (-ēs), daughter of Icarius and Periboea of Sparta, married Ulysses, king of Ithaca. [Respecting her marriage, see ICA-RIUS, No. 2.] By Ulysses she had an only child, Telemachus, who was an infant when her husband sailed against Troy. During the long absence of Ulysses she was beleaguered by numerous and importunate suitors, whom she deceived by declaring that she must finish a large robe which she was making for Laërtes, her aged father-in-law, before she could make up her mind. During the daytime she accordingly worked at the robe, and in the night she undid the work of the day. By this means she succeeded in putting off the suitors. But at length her stratagem was betrayed by her servants; and when, in consequence, the faithful Penelope was pressed more and more by the impatient suitors, Ulysses at length arrived in Ithaca, after an absence of 20 years. Having recognised her husband by several signs, she heartily welcomed him, and the days of her grief and sorrow were at an end. [ULYSSES.] While Homer describes Penelope as a chaste and faithful wife, some writers charge her with being the reverse, and relate that she became the mother of Pan by Hermes or by all the suitors. They add that Ulysses repudiated her when he returned; whereupon she went to Sparta, and thence to Mantinea. According to another tradition, she married Telegonus, after he had killed his father Ulysses.

PĒNĒUS (-i). (1) The chief river of Thessaly, rising in Mt. Pindus, and after

Penelope. (British Museum.)

receiving many affluents, forcing its way through the vale of Tempe between Mts. Ossa and Olympus into the sea. [TEMPE.] As a god Peneus was a son of Oceanus and Tethys, and father of Daphne and Cyrene.— (2) A river of Elis, rising on the frontiers of Arcadia, and flowing into the Ionian sea.

PĒNĪUS (-i), a little river of Pontus, falling into the Euxine.

PENNĪNAE ALPES. [ALPES.]

PENTĂPŎLIS (-is), the name for any association of 5 cities, was applied specifically to the 5 chief cities of Cyrenaïca, in N. Africa, Cyrenē, Berenicē, Arsinoë, Ptolemaïs, and Apollonia.

PENTĒLICUS (-i), a mountain in Attica, celebrated for its marble, is a branch of Mt. Parnes, from which it runs in a S.E.-ly direction between Athens and Marathon to the coast.

PENTHĒSĪLĒA (-ae), daughter of Ares (Mars) and Otrera, and queen of the Amazons. After the death of Hector, she came to the assistance of the Trojans, but was slain by Achilles, who mourned over the dying queen on account of her beauty, youth, and valour. Thersites ridiculed the grief of Achilles, and was in consequence killed by the hero. Thereupon Diomedes, a relative of Thersites, threw the body of Penthesilea into the river Scamander; but, according

to others, Achilles himself buried it on the banks of the Xanthus.

PENTHEUS (-ĕos or -ĕi ; acc. -ĕa or -ĕum), son of Echīon and Agāvē, the daughter of Cadmus. He succeeded Cadmus as king of Thebes ; and having resisted the introduction of the worship of Dionysus (Bacchus) into his kingdom, he was driven mad by the god, his palace was hurled to the ground, and he himself was torn to pieces by his own mother and her two sisters, Ino and Autonoë, who in their Bacchic frenzy believed him to be a wild beast. The place where Pentheus suffered death is said to have been Mt. Cithaeron or Mt. Parnassus. It is related that Pentheus got upon a tree, for the purpose of witnessing in secret the revelry of the Bacchic women, but on being discovered by them was torn to pieces.

PENTRI (-ōrum), one of the most important of the tribes in Samnium. Their chief town was BOVIANUM.

PĒPĂRĒTHUS (-i), a small island in the Aegaean sea, off the coast of Thessaly, and E. of Halonesus. It produced a considerable quantity of wine.

PĒPHRĒDŌ. [GRAEAE.]

PĒRAEA (-ae), i.e., the country on the opposite side, a general name for any district belonging to or closely connected with a country, from the main part of which it was separated by a sea or river. (1) The part of Palestine E. of the Jordan. — (2) PERAEA RHODIORUM, a district in the S. of Caria, opposite to the island of Rhodes, and subject to the Rhodians, extending from Mt. Phoenix on the W. to the frontier of Lycia on the E. —(3) A city on the W. coast of Mysia, near Adramyttium, one of the colonies of the Mytilenaeans.

PERCOTE .(-ēs), a very ancient city of Mysia, between Abydos and Lampsacus, near the Hellespont.

PERDICCAS (-ae). (1) The founder of the Macedonian monarchy, according to Herodotus, though later writers represent Caranus as the 1st king of Macedonia, and make Perdiccas only the 4th. [CARANUS.] Perdiccas and his two brothers, Gauanes and Aëropus, are said to have come from Argos, and settled near Mt. Bermius, from whence they subdued the rest of Macedonia.—(2) King of Macedonia, from about B.C. 454 to 413, son and successor of Alexander I. In the Peloponnesian war we find him at one time in alliance with the Spartans, and at another time with the Athenians; and it is evident that he joined one or other of the belligerent parties, according to the dictates of his own interest at the moment.—(3) King of Macedonia, B.C. 364—359, second son of Amyntas II., obtained the throne by the assassination of the usurper Ptolemy of Alorus. He fell in battle against the Illyrians.—(4) One of the most distinguished of the generals of Alexander the Great. The king on his death-bed is said to have taken the royal signet ring from his finger and to have given it to Perdiccas. After the death of the king (323), Perdiccas had the chief authority entrusted to him under the command of the new king Arrhidaeus. His ambitious schemes induced Antipater, Craterus, and Ptolemy, to unite in a league, and declare open war against Perdiccas. Thereupon Perdiccas marched into Egypt against Ptolemy, but having been defeated in battle, he was slain by his own troops, B.C. 321.

PERDIX (-īcis), the nephew of Daedalus, and the inventor of the saw, the chisel, the compasses, &c. His skill excited the jealousy of Daedalus, who threw him headlong from the temple of Athena (Minerva), on the Acropolis, but the goddess caught him in his fall, and changed him into the bird which was named after him, perdix, the partridge.

PERENNA, ANNA. [ANNA.]

PERGA (-ae), an ancient and important city of Pamphylia, lay a little inland, N.E. of Attalia, between the rivers Catarrhactes and Cestrus, 60 stadia (6 geog. miles) from the mouth of the former. It was a celebrated seat of the worship of Artemis (Diana). It was the first place in Asia Minor visited by the apostle Paul on his first missionary journey.

PERGAMA and PERGAMIA. [PERGAMON, No. 1.]

PERGAMUM or PERGAMUS (-i). The former by far the most usual form in the classical writers, though the latter is more common in English, probably on account of its use in our version of the Bible, *Rev.* ii. 13. The word is significant, connected with πύργος, *a tower.* (1) The citadel of Troy, and used poetically for Troy itself : the poets also use the forms PERGAMA (-ōrum) and PERGAMIA (-ae).—(2) A celebrated city of Asia Minor, the capital of the kingdom of Pergamus, and afterwards of the Roman province of Asia, was situated in the district of S. Mysia called Teuthrania, on the N. bank of the river Caïcus, about twenty miles from the sea. The kingdom of Pergamus was founded about B.C. 280 by Philetaerus, who had been entrusted by Lysimachus with the command of the city. The successive kings of Pergamus were : PHILETAERUS, B.C. 280 —263; EUMENES I., 263—241 ; ATTALUS I., 241—197 ; EUMENES II., 197—159 ; ATTALUS II. PHILADELPHUS, 159—138 ; ATTALUS III. PHILOMETOR, 138—133. The kingdom reached its greatest extent after the defeat of Antiochus the Great by the Romans, in B.C. 190, when the Romans bestowed upon Eumenes II. the whole of Mysia, Lydia, both Phrygias, Lycaonia, Pisidia and Pamphylia. It was under the same king that the celebrated library was founded at Pergamus, which for a long time rivalled that of Alexandria, and the formation of which occasioned the invention of parchment, *Charta Pergamena.* On the death of Attalus III. in B.C. 133, the kingdom, by a bequest in his will, passed to the Romans. The city was an early seat of Christianity, and is one of the Seven Churches of Asia, to which the Apocalyptic epistles are addressed. Among the celebrated natives of the city were the rhetorician Apollodorus and the physician Galen.

PERGE. [PERGA.]

PERIANDER (-dri), son of Cypselus, whom he succeeded as tyrant of Corinth, B.C. 625, and reigned 40 years, to B.C. 585. His rule was mild and beneficent at first, but afterwards became oppressive. He was a patron of literature and philosophy; and Arion and Anacharsis were in favour at his court. He was very commonly reckoned among the Seven Sages.

PERICLES (-is or -i), the greatest of Athenian statesmen, was the son of Xanthippus, and Agariste, both of whom belonged to the noblest families of Athens. The fortune of his parents procured for him a careful education, and he received instruction from Damon, Zeno of Elea, and Anaxagoras. In B.C. 469, Pericles began to take part in public affairs, 40 years before his death, and was soon regarded as the head of the more democratical part in the state, in opposition to Cimon. It was at his instigation that his friend Ephialtes proposed in 461 the measure by which the Areopagus was deprived of those functions which rendered it formidable to the democratical party. This success was followed by the ostracism of Cimon. Pericles was distinguished as a general as well as a statesman, and frequently commanded the Athenian armies in their wars with the neighbouring states. In 448 he led the army which assisted the Phocians in the Sacred War; and in 445 he rendered the most signal service to the state by recovering the island of Euboea, which had revolted from Athens. After the death of Cimon in 449, the aristocratical party was headed by Thucydides, the son of Melesias; but on the ostracism of the latter in 444, Pericles was left without a rival, and throughout the remainder of his political course no one appeared to contest his supremacy. The next important event in which Pericles was engaged was the war against Samos, which had revolted from Athens, and which he subdued after an arduous campaign, 440. The poet Sophocles was one of the generals who fought with Pericles against Samos. For the next 10 years till the outbreak of the Peloponnesian war, the Athenians were not engaged in any considerable military operations. Pericles employed this time of peace in adorning Athens with public buildings, which made this city the wonder and admiration of Greece. [PHIDIAS.] The enemies of Pericles made many attempts to ruin his reputation, but failing in these, they attacked him through his friends. His friends Phidias and Anaxagoras, and his mistress Aspasia were all accused before the people. Phidias was condemned and cast into prison [PHIDIAS]; Anaxagoras was also sentenced to pay a fine and quit Athens [ANAXAGORAS]; and Aspasia was only acquitted through the entreaties and tears of Pericles.—The Peloponnesian war has been falsely ascribed to the ambitious schemes of Pericles. It is true that he counselled the Athenians not to yield to the demands of the Lacedaemonians; but he did this because he saw that war was inevitable; and that as long as Athens retained the great power which she then possessed, Sparta would never rest contented. On the outbreak of the war in 431 a Peloponnesian army under Archidamus invaded

Attica, and upon the advice of Pericles, the Athenians conveyed their property into the city, and allowed the Peloponnesians to desolate Attica without opposition. Next year (430) when the Peloponnesians again invaded Attica, Pericles pursued the same policy as before. In this summer the plague made its appearance in Athens. It carried off his two sons Xanthippus and Paralus, and most of his intimate friends. In the autumn of 429 Pericles himself died of a lingering sickness. He left no legitimate children. His son Pericles, by Aspasia, was one of the generals at the battle of Arginusae, and was put to death by the Athenians with the other generals, B.C. 406.

PERICLYMENUS (-i), one of the Argonauts, son of Neleus, and brother of Nestor.

PERILLUS. [PHALARIS.]

PERINTHUS (-i), an important town of Thrace on the Propontis, and founded by the Samians about B.C. 559, situated 22 miles W. of Selymbria on a small peninsula. At a later time, it was called *Heraclea*, and sometimes *Heraclea Thraciae* or *Heraclea Perinthus*.

PERIPHAS (-antis). (1) A king of Attica. —(2) One of the Lapithae.—(3) A companion of Pyrrhus at the siege of Troy.

PERMESSUS (-i), a river in Boeotia, descending from Mt. Helicon, and falling into the lake Copais near Haliartus.

PERO (-ōnis), daughter of Neleus and Chloris, and wife of Bias.

PERPERENA (-ae), a small town of Mysia, S. of Adramyttium.

PERPERNA or PERPENNA (-ae: the former is the preferable form). (1) M., consul B.C. 130, when he defeated Aristonicus in Asia, and took him prisoner.—(2) M. PERPERNA VENTO, son of the last, joined the Marian party in the civil war, and was raised to the praetorship. He afterwards crossed over into Spain and fought under Sertorius for some years; but being jealous of the latter, Perperna and his friends assassinated Sertorius at a banquet in 72. His death soon brought the war to a close. Perperna was defeated by Pompey, was taken prisoner, and was put to death.

PERRHAEBI (-ōrum), a powerful and warlike Pelasgic people in the N. of Thessaly. Homer places the Perrhaebi in the neighbourhood of the Thessalian Dodona and the river Titarosius; and at a later time the name of Perrhaebia was applied to the district bounded by Macedonia and the Cambunian mountains on the N., by Pindus on the W., by the Peneus on the S. and S.E., and by the Peneus and Ossa on the E. The Perrhaebi were members of the Amphictyonic league.

PERSAE. [PERSIS.]

PERSĒ (-ēs), or PERSA (-ae), daughter of Oceanus, and wife of Helios (the Sun), by whom she became the mother of Aeëtes, Circē, Pasiphaë and Perses.

PERSĒÏS (-ĭdis), a name given to Hecate, as the daughter of Perses by Asteria.

PERSĒPHŎNE (-ēs), called PRŌSER-PĬNA (-ae) by the Romans, a goddess, daughter of Zeus (Jupiter), and Demeter (Ceres). In Attica she was worshipped under the name of Cŏrē (Κόρη), that is, the *Daughter*, namely, of Demeter; and the two were frequently called *The Mother and the Daughter*. Homer describes her as the wife of Hades (Pluto), and the formidable, vene-rable, and majestic queen of the Shades, who rules over the souls of the dead, along with her husband. Hence she is called by later writers *Juno Inferna, Averna,* and *Stygia;* and the Erinnyes (Furies), are said to have been her daughters by Pluto. The story of her being carried off by Hades, the wander-ings of her mother in search of her, and the worship of the 2 goddesses in Attica at the festival of the Eleusinia, are related under DEMETER. Persephone is usually represented in works of art with the grave and severe character of the Juno of the lower world.

PERSĒPŎLĬS (-is), the capital of Persis and of the Persian empire. It appears how-ever to have been seldom used as the royal residence. Neither Herodotus, Xenophon, Ctesias, nor the sacred writers during the Persian period, mention it at all; though they often speak of Babylon, Susa, and Ecba-tana, as the capitals of the empire. It is only from the Greek writers after the Mace-donian conquest that we learn its rank in the empire, which appears to have consisted chiefly in its being one of the 2 burial places of the kings (the other being Pasargada), and also a royal treasury; for Alexander found in the palace immense riches, which were said to have accumulated from the time of Cyrus. It preserved its splendour till after the Macedonian conquest, when it was burnt; Alexander, as the story goes, setting fire to the palace with his own hand, at the end of a revel, by the instigation of the courtesan Thaïs, B.C. 331. It was not, how-ever, so entirely destroyed as some historians represent. It appears frequently in subse-quent history, both ancient and medieval. It is now deserted, but its ruins are con-siderable. It was situated in the heart of Persis, in the part called Hollow Persis, not

Persephone (Proserpine) enthroned. (Gerhard, Archäolog. Zeit. tav. 11.)

far from the border of the Carmanian De-sert, in a valley, watered by the river Araxes, and its tributaries the Medus and the Cyrus.

PERSĒS (-ae), son of Helios (the Sun) and Persē, brother of Aeëtes and Circē, and father of Hecate.

PERSEUS (-ĕŏs or -eī). (1) The famous Argive hero, son of Zeus (Jupiter), and Danaë, and grandson of Acrisius. An oracle had told Acrisius that he was doomed to perish by the hands of Danaë's son; and he therefore shut up his daughter in an apartment made of brass or stone. But Zeus having metamorphosed himself into a shower of gold, came down through the roof of the prison, and became by her the father of Perseus. From this circumstance Perseus is sometimes called *aurigena*. As soon as Acrisius discovered that Danaë had given birth to a son, he put both mother and son into a chest, and threw them into the sea; but Zeus caused the chest to come ashore at Seriphos, one of the Cyclades, when Dictys, a fisherman, found Danaë and her son, and carried them to Polydectes, the king of the country, who treated them with kindness. In course of time Polydectes fell in love with Danaë, and wishing to get rid of Perseus, who had meantime grown up to manhood, he sent the young hero to fetch the head of Medusa, one of the Gorgons. Guided by Hermes (Mercury) and Athena (Minerva), Perseus first went to the Graeae, the sisters of the Gorgons, took from them their one tooth and their one eye, and would not restore them until they showed him the way to the nymphs, who possessed the winged sandals, the magic wallet, and the helmet of Hades (Pluto), which rendered the wearer invisible. Having received from

Perseus and Medusa. (From a terra-cotta, in the British Museum.)

the nymphs these invaluable presents, from Hermes a sickle, and from Athena a mirror, he mounted into the air, and arrived at the abode of the Gorgons, who dwelt near Tartessus, on the coast of the Ocean. He found them asleep, and cut off the head of Medusa, looking at her figure through the mirror, for a sight of the monster herself would have changed him into stone. Perseus put her head into the wallet which he carried on his back, and as he went away he was pursued by the two other Gorgons; but his helmet, which rendered him invisible, enabled him to escape in safety. Perseus then proceeded to Aethiopia, where he saved and married Andromeda. [ANDROMEDA.] Perseus is also said to have changed Atlas into the mountain of the same name by means of the Gorgon's head. On his return to Seriphos, he found that his mother had taken refuge in a temple to escape the violence of Polydectes. He then went to the palace of Polydectes, and metamorphosed him and all his guests, into stone. He then gave the head of Gorgon to Athena, who placed it in the middle of her shield or breastplate. Perseus subsequently went to Argos, accompanied by Danaë and Andromeda. Acrisius, remembering the oracle, escaped to Larissa, in the country of the Pelasgians; but Perseus followed him in disguise in order to persuade him to return. On his arrival at Larissa, he took part in the public games, and accidentally killed Acrisius with the discus. Perseus, leaving the kingdom of Argos to Megapenthes, the son of Proetus, received from him in exchange the government of Tiryns. Perseus is said to have founded Mycenae.—(2) Or PERSES (-ae), the last king of Macedonia, was the eldest son of Philip V., and reigned 11 years, from B.C. 178 to 168. His war with the Romans lasted 4 years (B.C. 171—168), and was brought to a close by his decisive defeat by L. Aemilius Paulus at the battle of Pydna in 168. Perseus adorned the triumph of his conqueror, and was permitted to end his days in an honourable captivity at Alba.

PERSIA. [PERSIS.]

PERSĬCUS SĬNUS, PERSĬCUM MĂRE, the name given by the later geographers to the great gulf of the Mare Erythraeum (*Indian Ocean*), extending between the coast of Arabia and the opposite coast of Susiana, Persis, and Carmania, now called the *Persian Gulf.*

PERSIS (-ĭdis) very rarely PERSIA (-ae), originally a small district of Asia, bounded on the S.W. by the Persian Gulf, on the N.W. and N. by Susiana, Media, and Parthia, and on the E. towards Carmania, by no definite boundaries in the Desert. The only level part of the country was the strip of sea-coast: the rest was intersected with mountains. The inhabitants were divided into 3 classes or castes : 1st, the nobles or warriors, containing the 3 tribes of the PASARGADAE, who were the most noble, and to whom the royal family of the Achaemenidae belonged. 2ndly, the agricultural and other settled tribes. 3rdly, the tribes which remained nomadic. The Persians had a close ethnical affinity to the Medes, and followed the same customs and religion [MAGI ; ZOROASTER.] On their first appearance in history they are represented as a nation of hardy shepherds, who under their leader Cyrus overthrew the empire of the Medes, and became the masters of Western Asia, B.C. 559. [CYRUS.] In the reign of Darius, the 3rd king of Persia, the empire extended from Thrace and Cyrenaïca on the W. to the Indus on the E., and from the Euxine, the Caucasus, the Caspian, and the Oxus and Jaxartes on the N. to Aethiopia, Arabia, and the Erythraean Sea on the S. It embraced, in Europe, Thrace and some of the Greek cities N. of the Euxine; in Africa, Egypt and Cyrenaïca; in Asia, on the W., Palestine, Phoenicia, Syria, the several districts of Asia Minor, Armenia, Mesopotamia, Assyria, Babylonia, Susiana, Atropatene, Great Media ; on the N., Hyrcania, Margiana, Bactriana, and Sogdiana ; on the E., the Paropamisus, Arachosia, and India (i.e. part of the Punjab and Scinde) ; on the S. Persis, Carmania, and Gedrosia ; and in the centre of the E. part, Parthia, Aria, and Drangiana. The capital cities of the empire were Babylon, Susa, Ecbatana in Media, and, though these were seldom, if ever, used as residences, Pasargada and Persepolis in Persis. (See the several articles.) Of this vast empire Darius undertook the organisation, and divided it into 20 satrapies. Of the ancient Persian history, an abstract is given under the names of the several kings; a list of whom is subjoined : (1) CYRUS, B.C. 559—529 ; (2) CAMBYSES, 529—522; (3) Usurpation of the pseudo-SMERDIS, 7 months, 522—521 ; (4) DARIUS I., son of Hystaspes, 521—485 ; (5) XERXES I. 485—465; (6) Usurpation of ARTABANUS, 7 months, 465—464 ; (7) ARTAXERXES I. LONGIMANUS, 464—425 ; (8) XERXES II., 2 months ; (9) SOGDIANUS, 7 months, 425—424 ; (10) OCHUS, or DARIUS II. NOTHUS, 424 —405 ; (11) ARTAXERXES II. MNEMON, 405 —359 ; (12) Ochus, or ARTAXERXES III., 359—338 ; (13) ARSES, 338—336 ; (14) DARIUS III. CODOMANNUS, 336—331 [ALEXANDER]. Here the ancient history of Persia ends, as a kingdom ; but, as a people, the Persians proper, under the influence especially of their religion, preserved their existence, and at length regained their independence on the downfall of the Parthian

Empire [SASSANIDAE].—In reading the Roman poets it must be remembered that they constantly use Persae, as well as Medi, as a general term for the peoples E. of the Euphrates and Tigris, and especially for the Parthians.

PERSIUS FLACCUS (-i), A., the Roman poet, was a knight connected by blood and marriage with persons of the highest rank, and was born at Volaterrae in Etruria, A.D. 34. He was the pupil of Cornutus the Stoic, and while yet a youth was on familiar terms with Lucan, with Caesius Bassus, the lyric poet, and with several other persons of literary eminence. He was tenderly beloved by the high-minded Paetus Thrasea, and seems to have been well worthy of such affection for he is described as a virtuous and pleasing youth. He died in A.D. 62, before he had completed his 28th year. The extant works of Persius consist of 6 short satires, and were left in an unfinished state. They are written in an obscure style, and are difficult to understand.

PERTINAX (-ācis), HELVIUS (-i), Roman emperor from January 1st to March 28th, A.D. 193, was reluctantly persuaded to accept the empire, on the death of Commodus. But having attempted to check the license of the praetorian troops, he was slain by the latter, who then put up the empire to sale.

PERUSIA (-ae : Perugia), an ancient city in the E. part of Etruria between the lake Trasimenus and the Tiber, and one of the 12 cities of the Etruscan confederacy. It was situated on a hill, and was strongly fortified by nature and by art. It is memorable in the civil wars as the place in which L. Antonius, the brother of the triumvir, took refuge, when he was no longer able to oppose Octavianus (Augustus) in the field, and where he was kept closely blockaded by Octavianus from the end of B.C. 41 to the spring of 40. Famine compelled it to surrender ; but one of its citizens having set fire to his own house, the flames spread, and the whole city was burnt to the ground. It was rebuilt by Augustus.

PESSINUS or PESINUS (-untis), a city in the S.W. corner of Galatia, on the S. slope of Mt. Dindymus or Agdistis, was celebrated as a chief seat of the worship of Cybělě, under the surname of Agdistis, whose temple, crowded with riches, stood on a hill outside the city. In this temple was an image of the goddess, which was removed to Rome, to satisfy an oracle in the Sibylline books.

PETELIA or PETILIA (-ae : Strongoli), an ancient Greek town on the E. coast of Bruttium, founded, according to tradition, by Philoctetes.

PĔTĪLĬUS, CĂPĬTŌLĬNUS. [Capito-
linus.]

PETRA (-ae), the name of several cities
built on rocks, or in rocky places, of which
the most celebrated was in Arabia Petraea,
the capital, first of the Idumaeans, and afterwards of the Nabathaeans. It lies in the
midst of the mountains of Seir, just half-way
between the Dead Sea and the head of the
Aelanitic Gulf of the Red Sea, in a valley, or
rather ravine, surrounded by almost inaccessible precipices, which is entered by a narrow
gorge on the E., the rocky walls of which
approach so closely as in some places hardly to
permit 2 horsemen to ride abreast. On the
banks of the river which runs through this
ravine stood the city itself, and some fine
ruins of its public buildings still remain.
These ruins are chiefly of the Roman period,
when Petra had become an important city as
a centre of the caravan traffic of the Nabathaeans. It maintained its independence
under the Romans, till the time of Trajan,
by whom it was taken. It was the chief
city of Arabia Petraea ; and under the later
empire the capital of Palaestina Tertia.

PĔTREIUS (-i), M., a man of military experience, is first mentioned in b.c. 62, when he
served as legatus to C. Antonius, and defeated
the army of Catiline. He belonged to the
aristocratical party ; and in 55 he was sent
into Spain along with L. Afranius as legatus
of Pompey. He subsequently fought against
Caesar in Africa, and after the loss of the
battle of Thapsus, he and Juba fell by each
other's hands.

PĔTRĪNUM (-i), a mountain near Sinuessa on the confines of Latium and Campania,
on which good wine was grown.

PETRŎCŎRĬI (-ōrum), a people in Gallia
Aquitanica, in the modern *Perigord*.

PĔTRŌNĬUS (-i), C., or T., one of the
chosen companions of Nero, and regarded as
director-in-chief of the imperial pleasures
(*Elegantiae arbiter*). The influence which
Petronius thus acquired excited the jealousy
of Tigellinus : and being accused of treason
he put an end to his life by opening his veins.
He is said to have despatched in his last
moments a letter to the prince, taunting him
with his brutal excesses. It is uncertain
whether he is the author of the work, which
has come down to us, bearing the title *Petronii
Arbitri Satyricon*. It is a sort of comic romance, filled with disgusting licentiousness.

PEUCĒ (-ēs), an island in Moesia Inferior
formed by the 2 southern mouths of the
Danube, inhabited by the Peucīni, who were
a tribe of the Bastarnae, and took their name
from the island.

PEUCESTAS (-ae), an officer of Alexander
the Great, on whose death (b.c. 323), he
obtained the government of Persia. He fought
on the side of Eumenes against Antigonus
(317—316), and was finally deprived of his
satrapy by Antigonus.

PEUCĒTĬA. [Apulia.]

PEUCĪNI. [Peuce.]

PHACUSSA (-ae), an island in the Aegaean
sea, one of the Sporades.

PHAEĀCES (-um), a fabulous people immortalised by the Odyssey, who inhabited the
island Scheria (Σχερία), situated at the extreme western part of the earth, and who
were governed by king Alcinous. [Alcinous.]
They are described as a people of luxurious
habits ; whence a glutton is called *Phaeax*
by Horace.—The ancients identified the Homeric Scheria with Corcyra ; but it is better
to regard Scheria as altogether fabulous.

PHAEDON (-ōnis), a native of Elis, was
taken prisoner, and sold as a slave at Athens.
He afterwards obtained his freedom, and became a follower of Socrates, at whose death
he was present. He afterwards returned to
Elis, where he became the founder of a school
of philosophy. The dialogue of Plato, containing an account of the death of Socrates,
bears the name of Phaedon.

PHAEDRA (-ae), daughter of Minos, and
wife of Theseus, who falsely accused her step-
son Hippolytus. After the death of Hippolytus, his innocence became known to his
father, and Phaedra made away with herself.

PHAEDRUS (-i), the Latin Fabulist, was
originally a slave, and was brought from
Thrace or Macedonia to Rome, where he
learned the Latin language. He received his
freedom from Augustus. His fables are 97
in number, written in iambic verse : most of
them are borrowed from Aesop.

PHAESTUS (-i), a town in the S. of Crete,
near Gortyna, the birth-place of Epimenides.

PHAĒTHON (-ŏntis), that is, " the shining," used as an epithet or surname of Helios
(the Sun), but more commonly known as the
name of a son of Helios by Clymĕnē. He received the name of Phaethon from his father,
and was afterwards so presumptuous as to
request his father to allow him to drive the
chariot of the sun across the neavens for one
day. Helios was induced by the entreaties
of his son and of Clymĕnē to yield, but the
youth being too weak to check the horses,
they rushed out of their usual track, and
came so near the earth, as almost to set it on
fire. Thereupon Zeus killed him with a flash
of lightning, and hurled him down into the
river Eridanus. His sisters, the *Helĭădae* or
Phăĕthontĭădes, who had yoked the horses
to the chariot, were metamorphosed into

poplars, and their tears into amber. [HE-
LIADAE.]

PHAËTHŪSA. (HELIADAE.)
PHĂLANTHUS (-i), the leader of the

Phaethon. (Zannoni, Gal. di Firenze, serie 4. vol. 2.)

Lacedaemonians, who founded Tarentum in
Italy, about B.C. 708.

PHĂLĂRIS (-idis), ruler of Agrigentum
in Sicily, has obtained a proverbial celebrity
as a cruel and inhuman tyrant. He reigned
from about B.C. 570 to 564. He perished by
a sudden outbreak of the popular fury. No
circumstance connected with him is more
celebrated than the brazen bull in which he
is said to have burnt alive the victims of his
cruelty, and of which we are told that he
made the first experiment upon its inventor
Perillus. The Epistles bearing the name of
Phalaris, have been proved by Bentley to be
the composition of some sophist.

PHĂLĒRUM (-i), the most E.-ly of the
harbours of Athens, and the one chiefly used
by the Athenians before the time of the
Persian wars. After the establishment by
Themistocles of the harbours in the peninsula
of Piraeus, Phalerum was not much used.

PHĂNAE (-ārum), the S. point of the
island of Chios, celebrated for its temple of
Apollo, and for its excellent wine.

PHĂNĂGŎRĬA (-ae), a Greek city on the
Asiatic coast of the Cimmerian Bosporus, was
chosen by the kings of Bosporus as their
capital in Asia.

PHĂÖN (-ōnis), a boatman at Mytilene, is
said to have been originally an ugly old man ;
but having carried Aphroditē (Venus) across
the sea without accepting payment, the goddess gave him youth and beauty. After this
Sappho is said to have fallen in love with
him, and, when he slighted her, to have
leapt from the Leucadian rock. [SAPPHO.]

PHĂRAE (-ārum). (1) A town in the W.
part of Achaia, and one of the 12 Achaean
cities, situated on the river Pierus.—(2) A

town in Messenia on the river Nedon, near
the frontiers of Laconia.

PHARMACŪSA (-ae), an island off the
coast of Miletus, where Julius Caesar was
taken prisoner by pirates.

PHARNABĀZUS (-i), satrap of the Persian
provinces near the Hellespont, towards the
end of the Peloponnesian war, and for many
years subsequently. His character is distinguished by generosity and openness. He
has been charged, it is true, with the murder
of Alcibiades ; but the latter probably fell by
the hands of others. [ALCIBIADES.]

PHARNĂCES (-is). (1) King of Pontus,
and grandfather of Mithridates the Great,
reigned from about B.C. 190 to 156.—
(2) King of Pontus, or more properly of the
Bosporus, was the son of Mithridates the
Great, whom he compelled to put an end to
his life in 63. [MITHRIDATES VI.] After the
death of his father, Pompey granted him the
kingdom of the Bosporus. In the civil war
between Caesar and Pompey, Pharnaces
seized the opportunity to reinstate himself
in his father's dominions ; but he was defeated by Caesar in a decisive action near
Zela (47). The battle was gained with such
ease by Caesar, that he informed the senate
of his victory by the words, Veni, vidi, vici.
In the course of the same year, Pharnaces
was slain by Asander, one of his generals.
[ASANDER.]

PHARNĂCĬA, a flourishing city of Asia
Minor, on the coast of Pontus, built near
(some think on) the site of Cerasus, probably
by Pharnaces, the grandfather of Mithridates
the Great.

PHARSĀLUS (-i), a town in Thessaly in
the district Thessaliotis, W. of the river

Enipeus. Near Pharsalus was fought the decisive battle between Caesar and Pompey, B.C. 48, which made Caesar master of the Roman world. It is frequently called the battle of Pharsalïa, which was the name of the territory of the town.

PHĂRUS or PHĂROS (-i). (1) A small island off the coast of Egypt. When Alexander the Great planned the city of Alexandria, on the coast opposite to Pharos, he caused the island to be united to the coast by a mole 7 stadia in length, thus forming the 2 harbours of the city. [ALEXANDRIA.] The island was chiefly famous for the lofty tower built upon it by Ptolemy II., for a light-house, whence the name of *pharus* was applied to all similar structures.—(2) An island of the Adriatic, off the coasts of Dalmatia, E. of Issa.

PHĂSĒLIS (-ĭdis), a town on the coast of Lycia, near the borders of Pamphylia, founded by Dorian colonists. It became afterwards the head-quarters of the pirates who infested the S. coasts of Asia Minor, and was therefore destroyed by P. Servilius Isauricus. Phaselis is said to have been the place at which the light quick vessels called Phaseli were first built.

PHĂSIS (-ĭs, or -ĭdis). (1) A celebrated river of Colchis, flowing into the E. end of the Pontus Euxinus (*Black Sea*). It was famous in connexion with the story of the Argonautic expedition. Hence Medea is called *Phăsĭas*, and the adjective *Phăsĭăcus* is used in the sense of Colchian. [ARGO-NAUTAE.] It has given name to the *pheasant* (phasianus), which is said to have been first brought to Greece from its banks.—(2) Near the mouth of the river, on its S. side, was a town of the same name, founded by the Milesians.

PHĒGEUS (-ĕŏs or -ĕī), king of Psophis in Arcadia, purified Alcmaeon after he had killed his mother, and gave him his daughter Alphesiboea in marriage. [ALCMAEON.]

PHĒMIUS (-i), a celebrated minstrel, who sung to the suitors in the palace of Ulysses in Ithaca.

PHĒNĒUS (-i), an ancient town in the N.E. of Arcadia, at the foot of Mt. Cyllene.

PHĒRAE (-ārum), an ancient town of Thessaly in the Pelasgian plain, 90 stadia from its port-town Pagasae on the Pagasaean gulf. It is celebrated in mythology as the residence of Admetus, and in history on account of its tyrants, who extended their power over nearly the whole of Thessaly. Of these the most powerful was Jason, who was made Tagus or generalissimo of Thessaly about B.C. 374.

PHĒRAE. [PHARAE.]

PHERĒCRĀTĒS (-is), of Athens, one of the best poets of the Old Comedy, contemporary with Aristophanes. He invented a new metre, which was named, after him, the *Pherecratean*.

PHERĒCÝDĒS (-is). (1) Of Syros, an early Greek philosopher, ficurished about B.C. 544. He is said to have been the teacher of Pythagoras, and to have taught the doctrine of the Metempsychosis.—(2) Of Athens, one of the early Greek logographers, was a contemporary of Herodotus.

PHERĒS (-ētis), son of Cretheus and Tyro, father of Admetus and Lycurgus, and founder of Pherae in Thessaly. Admetus, as the son of Pheres, is called *Phĕrētĭădēs*.

PHĪDĬĂS (-ae), the greatest sculptor and statuary of Greece, was born at Athens about B.C. 490. He was entrusted by Pericles with the superintendence of all the works of art which were erected at Athens during his administration. Of these works the chief were the Propylaea of the Acropolis, and, above all, the temple of Athena on the Acropolis, called the *Parthĕnon*, on which the highest efforts of the best artists were employed. The sculptured ornaments of this temple, the remains of which form the glory of the British Museum, were executed under the immediate superintendence of Phidias; but the colossal statue of the divinity made o. ivory and gold, which was enclosed within that magnificent shrine, was the work of the artist's own hand. The statue was dedicated in 438. Having finished his great work at Athens, he went to Elis and Olympia, where he finished his statue of the Olympian Zeus, the greatest of all his works. On his return to Athens he fell a victim to the jealousy against his great patron, Pericles. [PERICLES.] Phidias was first accused of peculation, but this charge was at once refuted, as, by the advice of Pericles, the gold had been affixed to the statue of Athena, in such a manner that it could be removed, and the weight of it examined. The accusers then charged Phidias with impiety, in having introduced into the battle of the Amazons, on the shield of the goddess, his own likeness and that of Pericles. On this latter charge Phidias was thrown into prison, where he died from disease, in 432.

PHĪDIPPĪDĒS or PHĪLIPPĪDĒS (-is), a celebrated courier, who was sent by the Athenians to Sparta in B.C. 490, to ask for aid against the Persians, and arrived there on the second day from his leaving Athens.

PHĪDŌN (-ōnis), a king of Argos, who extended his sovereignty over the greater part of Peloponnesus. In B.C. 748, he deprived the Eleans of their presidency at the

Olympic games, and celebrated them jointly with the Pisans; but the Eleans not long after defeated him, with the aid of Sparta, and recovered their privilege. The most memorable act of Phidon was his introduction of copper and silver coinage, and a new scale of weights and measures, which, through his influence, became prevalent in the Peloponnesus, and ultimately throughout the greater portion of Greece. The scale in question was known by the name of the Aeginetan, and it is usually supposed that the coinage of Phidon was struck in Aegina; but this name was perhaps given to it only in consequence of the commercial activity of the Aeginetans.

PHIGALIA (-ae), a town in the S.W. corner of Arcadia on the frontiers of Messenia and Elis, which owes its celebrity in modern times to the remains of a splendid temple in its territory, built in the time of Pericles. The sculptures in alto-relievo, which ornamented the frieze in the interior, are now preserved in the British Museum. They represent the combat of the Centaurs and the Lapithae, and of the Greeks and the Amazons.

PHILADELPHIA (-ae). (1) A city of Lydia, at the foot of Mt. Tmolus, built by Attalus Philadelphus, king of Pergamus. It was an early seat of Christianity, and its church is one of the 7 to which the Apocalypse is addressed.—(2) A city of Cilicia Aspera, on the Calycadnus, above Aphrodisias.

PHILADELPHUS (-i), a surname of Ptolemaeus II., king of Egypt [PTOLEMAEUS], and of Attalus II., king of Pergamum. [ATTALUS.]

PHILAE (-ārum), an island in the Nile, just below the first cataract, on the S. boundary of the country towards Aethiopia. It was inhabited by Egyptians and Ethiopians jointly, and was covered with magnificent temples, whose splendid ruins still remain.

PHILAENI (-ōrum), 2 brothers, citizens of Carthage, of whom the following story is told. A dispute having arisen between the Carthaginians and Cyrenaeans about their boundaries, it was agreed that deputies should start at a fixed time from each of the cities, and that the place of their meeting should thenceforth form the limit of the 2 territories. The Philaeni departed from Carthage, and advanced much farther than the Cyrenaean party. The Cyrenaeans accused them of having set forth before the time agreed upon, but at length consented to accept the spot which they had reached as a boundary-line, if the Philaeni would submit to be buried alive there in the sand. The Philaeni accordingly devoted themselves for their country in the way proposed. The Cartha-

ginians paid high honours to their memory, and erected altars to them where they had died; and from these the place was called " The Altars of the Philaeni."

PHILAMMON (-ŏnis), a mythical poet and musician, said to have been the son of Apollo, and the father of Thamyris and Eumolpus.

PHILEMON (-ŏnis). (1) An aged Phrygian, and husband of Baucis, who hospitably entertained Zeus (Jupiter) and Hermes (Mercury).—(2) A celebrated Athenian poet of the New Comedy, was a native of Soli in Cilicia, but at an early age went to Athens, and there received the citizenship. He flourished in the reign of Alexander, a little earlier than Menander, whom, however, he long survived. He began to exhibit about B.C. 330, and lived nearly 100 years. Although Philemon was inferior to Menander as a poet, yet he was a greater favourite with the Athenians, and often conquered his rival in the dramatic contests. [MENANDER.] —(3) The younger Philemon, also a poet of the New Comedy, was a son of the former.

PHILETAERUS. [PERGAMUM.]

PHILETAS (-ae), of Cos, a distinguished Alexandrian poet and grammarian, and the tutor of Ptolemy II. Philadelphus.

PHILIPPI (-ōrum), a celebrated city in Macedonia adjecta, situated on a steep height of Mt. Pangaeus, and founded by Philip of Macedon, on the site of an ancient town, CRENIDES, a colony of the Thasians. Philippi is celebrated in history in consequence of the victory gained here by Octavianus and Antony over Brutus and Cassius, B.C. 42, and as the place where the Apostle Paul first preached the gospel in Europe, A.D. 53. One of St. Paul's Epistles is addressed to the church at Philippi.

PHILIPPOPOLIS (-is, *Philippopoli*), an important town in Thrace, founded by Philip of Macedon, was situated in a large plain, S.E. of the Hebrus, on a hill with 3 summits, whence it was sometimes called Trimontium. Under the Roman empire it was the capital of the province of Thracia.

PHILIPPUS (-i).—I. *Kings of Macedonia.* (1) Son of Argaeus, was the 3rd king, according to Herodotus and Thucydides, who, not reckoning CARANUS and his two immediate successors, look upon Perdiccas I. as the founder of the monarchy.—(2) Youngest son of Amyntas II. and Eurydice, reigned B.C. 359—336. He was born in 382, and was brought up at Thebes, whither he had been carried as a hostage by Pelopidas, and where he received a most careful education. Upon the death of his brother, Perdiccas III., Philip obtained the government of Macedonia, at first merely as guardian to his infant nephew Amyntas; but at the end of a few months he set aside the claims of the young prince, and assumed for himself the title of king. As soon as he was firmly established on the throne, he introduced among the Macedonians a stricter military discipline, and organised their army on the plan of the phalanx. He then directed his views to the aggrandisement of his kingdom. He resolved first to obtain possession of the various Greek cities upon the Macedonian coast. Amphipolis, Pydna, Potidaea, Methone, and, finally, Olynthus, successively fell into his hands. Demosthenes, in his Philippic and Olynthiac orations, endeavoured to rouse the Athenians to the danger of Athens and Greece from the ambitious schemes of Philip; but the Athenians did not adopt any rigorous efforts to check the progress of the Macedonian king. On the invitation of the Amphictyons he subdued the Phocians, and was rewarded with the place of the latter in the Amphictyonic council (B.C 346). The Athenians at length became thoroughly alarmed at his aggrandisement; and accordingly, when he marched through Thermopylae, at the invitation of the Amphictyons, to punish the Locrians of Amphissa, they resolved to oppose him. Through the influence of Demosthenes, they succeeded in forming an alliance with the Thebans; but their united army was defeated by Philip in the month of August, 338, in the decisive battle of Chaeronēa, which put an end to the independence of Greece. A congress was now held at Corinth of the Grecian states, in which war with Persia was determined on, and the king of Macedonia was appointed to command the forces of the national confederacy. But in the midst of his preparations for his Asiatic expedition, he was murdered during the celebration of the nuptials of his daughter with Alexander, of Epirus, by a youth of noble blood, named Pausanias. His motive for the deed is stated by Aristotle to have been private resentment against Philip, to whom he had complained in vain of a gross outrage offered to him by Attalus. His wife, Olympias, however, was suspected of being implicated in the plot. [OLYMPIAS.] Philip died in the 47th year of his age, and the 24th of his reign, and was succeeded by Alexander the Great.—(3) The name of Philip was bestowed by the Macedonian army upon Arrhidaeus, the bastard son of Philip II., when he was raised to the throne after the death of Alexander the Great. He accordingly appears in the list of Macedonian kings as Philip III. [ARRHIDAEUS.]—(4) Eldest son of Cassander, whom he succeeded on the throne, B.C. 296,

but he reigned only a few months.—(5) Son of Demetrius II., reigned B.C. 220—178. He succeeded his uncle, Antigonus Doson, at 17 years of age. During the first 3 years of his reign he conducted the war against the Aetolians at the request of the Achaeans and Aratus. But soon after bringing this war to a conclusion, he became jealous of Aratus, whom he caused to be removed by a slow and secret poison. Philip was engaged in two wars with the Romans. The first lasted from B.C. 215, when he concluded an alliance with Hannibal, to 205. The second commenced in 200, and was brought to an end by the defeat of Philip, by the consul Flamininus, at the battle of Cynoscephalae, in 197. [FLAMININUS.] Through the false accusations of his son Perseus, he put to death his other son Demetrius; but discovering afterwards the innocence of the latter, he died (B.C. 179) a prey to remorse. He was succeeded by Perseus.—II. *Family of the Marcii Philippi.*—(1) L. MARCIUS PHILIPPUS, consul B.C. 91, opposed with vigour the measures of the tribune Drusus. He was one of the most distinguished orators of his time.—(2) L. and MARCIUS PHILIPPUS, son of the preceding, consul B.C. 56, and step-father of Augustus, having married his mother, Atia.—III. *Emperors of Rome.*—M. JULIUS PHILIPPUS, the name of two Roman emperors, father and son, of whom the former reigned A.D. 244—249. He was an Arabian by birth, and rose to high rank in the Roman army. He obtained the empire by the assassination of Gordian. He was slain near Verona, either in battle against Decius, or by his own soldiers. His son, whom he had proclaimed Augustus two years before, perished at the same time.

PHILISTUS (-i), a Syracusan, and a friend of the younger Dionysius, commanded the fleet of the latter in a battle with Dion, and being defeated put an end to his life. He was the author of a celebrated history of Sicily, in which he closely imitated Thucydides.

PHILO (-ōnis). (1) An academic philosopher, was a native of Larissa and a disciple of Clitomachus. After the conquest of Athens by Mithridates he removed to Rome, where he had Cicero as one of his hearers—(2) Of Byzantium, a celebrated mechanician, and a contemporary of Ctesibius, flourished about B.C. 146.—(3) Judaeus, or surnamed the Jew, was born at Alexandria, and was sent to Rome in A.D. 40 on an embassy to the emperor Caligula. He wrote several works which have come down to us, in which he attempts to reconcile the Sacred Scriptures with the doctrines of the Greek philosophy.

PHĪLO, Q. PUBLĪLĬUS, a distinguished general in the Samnite wars, proposed, in his dictatorship, B.C. 339, the celebrated *Publiliae Leges*, which abolished the power of the patrician assembly of the curiae, and elevated the plebeians to an equality with the patricians for all practical purposes.

PHĪLOCTĒTĒS (-is), a son of Poeas (whence he is called *Poeantĭădes*), was the most celebrated archer in the Trojan war. He was the friend and armour-bearer of Hercules, who bequeathed to him his bow and the poisoned arrows, for having set fire to the pile on Mt. Oeta, on which Hercules perished. Philoctetes was also one of the suitors of Helen, and thus took part in the Trojan war. On his voyage to Troy, while staying in the island of Chryse, he was bitten in the foot by a snake, or wounded by one of his arrows. The wound produced such an intolerable stench that the Greeks, on the advice of Ulysses, left Philoctetes on the solitary coast of Lemnos. He remained in this island till the 10th year of the Trojan war, when Ulysses and Diomedes came to fetch him to Troy, as an oracle had declared that the city could not be taken without the arrows of Hercules. He accompanied these heroes to Troy, and on his arrival Aesculapius or his sons cured his wound. He slew Paris and many other Trojans. On his return from Troy he is said to have settled in Italy.

PHĪLŎDĒMUS (-i), of Gadara, in Palestine, an Epicurean philosopher, and epigrammatic poet, contemporary with Cicero. He is also mentioned by Horace (*Sat.* i. 2. 121).

PHĪLŎLĀUS (-i), a distinguished Pythagorean philosopher, was a native of Croton or Tarentum, and a contemporary of Socrates.

PHĪLŎMĒLA (-ae), daughter of Pandion, king of Athens, and sister of Procnē, who had married Tereus, king of Thrace. Being dishonoured by the latter, Philomela was metamorphosed into a nightingale. The story is given under TEREUS.

PHĪLŎMĒLĬUM or PHĪLŎMĒLUM (-i), a city of Phrygia, on the borders of Lycaonia and Pisidia, said to have been named from the numbers of nightingales in its neighbourhood.

PHĪLŎPOEMĒN (-ĕnis), of Megalopolis in Arcadia, one of the few great men that Greece produced in the decline of her political independence. The great object of his life was to infuse into the Achaeans a military spirit, and thereby to establish their independence on a firm and lasting basis. He distinguished himself at the battle of Sellasia (B.C. 221), in which Cleomenes was defeated. Soon afterwards he sailed to Crete, and served for some years in the wars between the cities of that island. In B.C. 208 he was elected

strategus, or general of the Achaean league, and in this year slew in battle with his own hand Machanidas, tyrant of Lacedaemon. He was 8 times general of the Achaean league, and discharged the duties of his office with honour to himself and advantage to his country. In B.C. 183, when he was marching against the Messenians who had revolted from the Achaean league, he fell in with a large body of Messenian troops, by whom he was taken prisoner, and carried to Messene, where he was compelled to drink poison.

PHĪLOSTRĀTUS, FLĀVĬUS (-i). (1) A native of Lemnos, flourished in the 1st half of the 3rd century of the Christian era, and taught rhetoric first at Athens and afterwards at Rome. He wrote several works, of which the most important is the *Life of Apollonius of Tyana* in 8 books.—(2) The younger, and a grandson of the preceding. He wrote a work entitled *Imagines*.

PHĪLŌTAS (-ae), son of Parmenion, enjoyed a high place in the friendship of Alexander, but was accused in B.C. 330 of being privy to a plot against the king's life. There was no proof of his guilt; but a confession was wrung from him by torture, and he was stoned to death by the troops. [PARMENION.]

PHĪLOXĒNUS (-i), of Cythera, one of the most distinguished dithyrambic poets of Greece, was born B.C. 435 and died 380. He spent part of his life at Syracuse, where he was cast into prison by Dionysius, because he had told the tyrant, when asked to revise one of his poems, that the best way of correcting it would be to draw a black line through the whole paper. Only a few fragments of his poems have come down to us.

PHĪLUS, L. FŪRĬUS (-i), consul B.C. 136, was fond of Greek literature and refinement, and is introduced by Cicero as one of the speakers in his dialogue *De Republica*.

PHĪLŸRA (-ae), a nymph, daughter of Oceanus, and mother of the centaur Chiron, was changed into a linden-tree. Hence Chiron was called *Phĭlÿrĭdēs*, and his abode *Phĭlÿrēïa tecta*.

PHĪNEUS (-ĕŏs, -ĕī, or -eī). (1) Son of Belus and Anchinoe, and brother of Cepheus, slain by Perseus. [ANDROMEDA and PERSEUS.] —(2) Son of Agenor, and king of Salmydessus, in Thrace, and a celebrated soothsayer. He deprived his sons of sight, in consequence of a false accusation made against them by Idaea, their step-mother. The gods, in consequence, punished him with the loss of his sight, and sent the Harpies to torment him. [HARPYIAE.] When the Argonauts visited Thrace he was delivered from these monsters by Zetes and Calais, the sons of Boreas. Phineus in return explained to the Argonauts the further course they had to take. According to other accounts he was slain by Hercules.

PHINTĬAS. [DAMON.]

PHLĔGĔTHŌN (-ontis), *i. e.* the flaming, a river in the lower world, in whose channel flowed flames instead of water.

PHLEGRA. [PALLENE.]

PHLEGRAEI CAMPI (-ōrum), the name of the volcanic plain extending along the coast of Campania from Cumae to Capua, so called because it was believed to have been once on fire.

PHLĔGȲAS (-ae), son of Ares (Mars) and Chryse, and king of Orchomenos, in Boeotia. He was the father of Ixion and Coronis, the latter of whom became by Apollo the mother of Aesculapius. Enraged at this, Phlegyas set fire to the temple of the god, who killed him with his arrows, and condemned him to severe punishment in the lower world. His descendants, Phlegyae, are represented as a mythical race, who destroyed the temple at Delphi.

PHLĬŪS (-untis), the chief town of a small province in the N.E. of Peloponnesus, whose territory, PHLIASIA, was bounded by Sicyonia, Arcadia, and Argos.

PHŌCAEA (-ae), the N.-most of the Ionian cities on the W. coast of Asia Minor, celebrated as a great maritime state, and especially as the founder of the Greek colony of MASSILIA, in Gaul. The name of Phocaean is often used with reference to Massilia.

PHŌCĬŌN (-ōnis), an Athenian general and statesman, born about B.C. 402. He frequently opposed the measures of Demosthenes, and recommended peace with Philip; but he was not one of the mercenary supporters of the Macedonian monarch. On the contrary, his virtue is above suspicion, and his public conduct was always influenced by upright motives. When the Piraeus was seized by Alexander, the son of Polysperchon, in 318, Phocion was suspected of having advised Alexander to take this step; whereupon he fled to Alexander, but was basely surrendered by Polysperchon to the Athenians. He was condemned to drink the hemlock, and thus perished in 317, at the age of 85. The Athenians are said to have repented of their conduct.

PHŌCIS (-Idis), a country in Northern Greece, bounded on the N. by the Locri Epicnemidii and Opuntii, on the E. by Boeotia, on the W. by the Locri Ozolae and Doris, and on the S. by the Corinthian gulf. It was a mountainous and unproductive country, and owes its chief importance in history to the fact of its possessing the Delphic oracle. Its chief mountain was PARNASSUS, and its chief river the CEPHISSUS. The Phocians played no con-

spicuous part in Greek history till the time of Philip of Macedon ; but at this period they became involved in a war, called the Phocian or Sacred War, in which the principal states of Greece took part. At the instigation of the Thebans, the inveterate enemies of the Phocians, the Amphictyons imposed a fine upon the Phocians, and, upon their refusal to pay it, declared the Phocian land forfeited to the god at Delphi. Thereupon the Phocians seized the treasures of the temple at Delphi for the purpose of carrying on the war. This war lasted 10 years (B.C. 357—346), and was brought to a close by the conquest of the Phocians by Philip of Macedon. All their towns were razed to the ground with the exception of Abae ; and the 2 votes which they had in the Amphictyonic council were taken away and given to Philip.

PHŌCUS (-i), son of Aeacus and the Nereid Psamathe, was murdered by his half-brothers Telamon and Peleus. [PELEUS.]

PHŌCȲLĬDĒS (-is), of Miletus, a gnomic poet, contemporary with Theognes, was born B.C. 560.

PHOEBĒ (-ēs). (1) A surname of Artemis (Diana) as the goddess of the moon (Luna), the moon being regarded as the female Phoebus or sun.—(2) Daughter of Tyndareos and Leda, and a sister of Clytaemnestra.—(3) Daughter of Leucippus.

PHOEBUS (-i), the *Bright* or *Pure,* an epithet of Apollo.

PHOENĪCĒ (-ēs), a country of Asia, on the coast of Syria, extending from the river Eleutherus on the N. to below Mt. Carmel on the S., and bounded on the E. by Coele-Syria and Palestine. It was a mountainous strip of coast land, not more than 10 or 12 miles broad, hemmed in between the Mediterranean and the chain of Lebanon, whose lateral branches run out into the sea in bold promontories, upon which were situated some of the greatest maritime states of the ancient world. For the history of those great cities, see SIDON, TYRUS, &c. The people were of the Semitic race, and their language was a dialect of the Aramaic, closely related to the Hebrew and Syriac. Their written characters were the same as the Samaritan or Old Hebrew ; and from them the Greek alphabet, and through it most of the alphabets of Europe, were undoubtedly derived; hence they were regarded by the Greeks as the inventors of letters. Other inventions in the sciences and arts are ascribed to them ; such as arithmetic, astronomy, navigation, the manufacture of glass, and the coining of money. That, at a very early time, they excelled in the fine arts, is clear from the aid which Solomon received from Hiram, king of

Tyre, in the building and the sculptured decorations of the temple at Jerusalem, and from the references in Homer to Sidonian artists. In the sacred history of the Israelitish conquest of Canaan, in that of the Hebrew monarchy, and in the earliest Greek poetry, we find the Phoenicians already a great maritime people. Their voyages and their settlements extended beyond the pillars of Hercules, to the W. coasts of Africa and Spain, and even as far as our own islands. [BRITANNIA.] Within the Mediterranean they planted numerous colonies, on its islands, on the coast of Spain, and especially on the N. coast of Africa, the chief of which was CARTHAGO. They were successively subdued by the Assyrians, Babylonians, Persians, Macedonians, and Romans; but these conquests did not entirely ruin their commerce, which was still considerable at the Christian era. Under the Romans Phoenice formed a part of the province of Syria.

PHOENIX (-īcis). (1) Son of Agenor and brother of Europa. Being sent by his father in search of his sister, who was carried off by Zeus (Jupiter), he settled in the country, which was called after him Phoenicia.— (2) Son of Amyntor by Cleobule or Hippodamia. His father having neglected his wife, and attached himself to a mistress, Cleobule persuaded her son to gain the affections of the latter. Phoenix succeeded in the attempt, but was in consequence cursed by his father. Thereupon he fled to Phthia in Thessaly, where he was hospitably received by Peleus, who made him ruler of the Dolopes, and entrusted to him the education of his son Achilles. He afterwards accompanied Achilles to the Trojan war. According to another tradition, Amyntor put out the eyes of his son, who fled in this condition to Peleus; but Chiron restored his sight.

PHŎLŎE (-ēs), a mountain forming the boundary between Arcadia and Elis; mentioned as one of the seats of the Centaurs. [PHOLUS.]

PHŎLUS (-i), a Centaur, accidentally slain by one of the poisoned arrows of Hercules, and buried in the mountain called Pholoe after him. For the details of his story see p. 197.

PHORCUS (-i), PHORCYS (-ўŏs), or PHORCYN (-ỹnŏs), a sea deity, son of Pontus and Ge, and father of the Graeae and Gorgones, who are hence called Phorcĭdes, Phorcўdes, or Phorcўnĭdes (-um.)

PHORMĬŌN (-ōnis), a celebrated Athenian general in the Peloponnesian war.

PHŎRŌNEUS (-ĕŏs or -ĕĭ), son of Inachus and Melia, one of the fabulous kings of Argos, and father of Niobe, and Apis. Hence

Phŏrōnēus and Phŏrōnis are used in the general sense of Argive.

PHRĀĀTĒS (-ae), the name of 4 kings of Parthia. [ARSACES, V. VII. XII. XV.]

PHRĀORTĒS, 2nd king of Media, son and successor of Deioces, reigned B.C. 656—634. He was killed while laying siege to Ninus (Nineveh).

PHRIXUS (-i), son of Athamas and Nephele, and brother of Helle. In consequence of the intrigues of his stepmother, Ino, he was to be sacrificed to Zeus (Jupiter); but Nephele rescued her 2 children, who rode away through the air upon the ram with the golden fleece, the gift of Hermes (Mercury). Between Sigeum and the Chersonesus, Helle fell into the sea which was called after her the Hellespont; but Phrixus arrived in safety in Colchis, the kingdom of Aeetes, who gave him his daughter Chalciope in marriage. Phrixus sacrificed to Zeus the ram which had carried him, and gave its fleece to Aeetes, who fastened it to an oak tree in the grove of Ares (Mars). This fleece was afterwards carried away by Jason and the Argonauts. [JASON.]

PHRŸGIA MATER. [PHRYGIA.]

PHRŸGIA (-ae), a country of Asia Minor, which was of different extent at different periods. Under the Roman empire, Phrygia was bounded on the W. by Mysia, Lydia, and Caria, on the S. by Lycia and Pisidia, on the E. by Lycaonia (which is often reckoned as a part of Phrygia) and Galatia (which formerly belonged to Phrygia), and on the N. by Bithynia. The Phrygians are mentioned by Homer as settled on the banks of the Sangarius, where later writers tell us of the powerful Phrygian kingdom of GORDIUS and MIDAS. It would seem that they were a branch of the great Thracian family, originally settled in the N.W. of Asia Minor, as far as the shores of the Hellespont and Propontis, and that the successive migrations of other Thracian peoples, as the Thyni, Bithyni, Mysians, and Teucrians, drove them farther inland. They were not, however, entirely displaced by the Mysians and Teucrians from the country between the shores of the Hellespont and Propontis and Mts. Ida and Olympus, where they continued side by side with the Greek colonies, and where their name was preserved in that of the district under all subsequent changes, namely PHRYGIA MINOR or PHRYGIA HELLESPONTUS. The kingdom of Phrygia was conquered by Croesus, and formed part of the Persian, Macedonian, and Syro-Grecian empires; but, under the last, the N.E. part, adjacent to Paphlagonia and the Halys, was conquered by the Gauls, and formed the W. part of GALATIA; and under the Romans was included in the province of Asia. In connexion with the early intellectual culture of Greece, Phrygia is highly important. The earliest Greek music, especially that of the flute, was borrowed in part, through the Asiatic colonies, from Phrygia. With this country also were closely associated the orgies of Dionysus (Bacchus), and of Cybele, the Mother of the Gods, the Phrygia Mater of the Roman poets. After the Persian conquest, however, the Phrygians seem to have lost all intellectual activity, and they became proverbial among the Greeks and Romans for submissiveness and stupidity. The Roman poets constantly use the epithet Phrygian as equivalent to Trojan.

PHRYNĬCHUS (-i), an Athenian, and one of the early tragic poets, gained his first tragic victory in B.C. 511, 12 years before Aeschylus (499).

PHTHĬA. [PHTHIOTIS.]

PHTHĬŌTIS (-ĭdis), a district in the S.E. of Thessaly, bounded on the S. by the Maliac gulf, and on the E. by the Pagasaean gulf, and inhabited by Achaeans. [THESSALIA.] Homer calls it PHTHIA, and mentions a city of the same name, which was celebrated as the residence of Achilles. Hence the poets call Achilles *Phthius hero*, and his father Peleus *Phthius rex*.

PHŸCŬS (-untis), a promontory on the coast of Cyrenaica, a little W. of Apollonia.

PHŸLĂCĒ (-ēs), a small town of Thessaly in Phthiotis, the birthplace of Protesilaus, hence called *Phylacides:* his wife Laodamia is also called *Phylaceïs*.

PHŸLĒ (-es), a strongly fortified place in Attica, on the confines of Boeotia, and memorable as the place which Thrasybulus and the Athenian patriots seized soon after the end of the Peloponnesian war, B.C. 404, and from which they directed their operations against the 30 Tyrants at Athens.

PHYLLIS. [DEMOPHON.]

PHYLLUS (-i), a town of Thessaly in the district Thessaliotis. The poets use *Phylleïs* and *Phylleïus* in the sense of Thessalian.

PHYSCON. [PTOLEMAUS.]

PĬCĒNI. [PICENUM.]

PĬCENTĬA (-ae : *Vicenza*), a town in the S. of Campania at the head of the Sinus Paestanus. The name of Picentini was not confined to the inhabitants of Picentia, but was given to the inhabitants of the whole coast of the Sinus Paestanus, from the promontory of Minerva to the river Silarus. They were a portion of the Sabine Picentes, who were transplanted by the Romans to this part of Campania after the conquest of Picenum, B.C. 268, at which time they founded the town of Picentia.

PĬCENTĬNI. [PICENTIA.]

PĬCĒNUM (-i), a country in central Italy, was a narrow strip of land along the coast of the Adriatic, and was bounded on the N. by Umbria, on the W. by Umbria and the territory of the Sabines, and on the S. by the territory of the Marsi and Vestini. It is said to have derived its name from the bird *picus*, which directed the Sabine immigrants into the land. They were conquered by the Romans in B.C. 268, when a portion of them was transplanted to the coast of the Sinus Paestanus, where they founded the town Picentia. [PICENTIA.]

PICTI (-ōrum), a people inhabiting the northern part of Britain, appear to have been either a tribe of the Caledonians, or the same people as the Caledonians, though under another name. They were called Picti by the Romans, from their practice of painting their bodies. They are first mentioned in A.D. 296 ; and after this time their name frequently occurs in the Roman writers, and often in connexion with that of the Scoti.

PICTŌNES (-um), subsequently PICTĂVI (-orum), a powerful people on the coast of Gallia Aquitanica. Their chief town was Limonum, subsequently Pictăvi (*Poitiers*).

PĬCUMNUS and PĬLUMNUS (-i), two gods of matrimony in the rustic religion of the ancient Romans. Pilumnus was considered the ancestor of Turnus.

PĬCUS (-i), a Latin prophetic divinity, son of Saturnus, husband of Canens, and father of Faunus. The legend of Picus is founded on the notion that the woodpecker is a prophetic bird, sacred to Mars. Pomona was beloved by him ; and when Circe's love for him was not requited, she changed him into a woodpecker, who retained the prophetic powers which he had formerly possessed as a man.

PĬĒRĬA (-ae). (1) A narrow slip of country on the S.E. coast of Macedonia, extending from the mouth of the Peneus in Thessaly to the Haliacmon, and bounded on the W. by Mt. Olympus and its offshoots. A portion of these mountains was called by the ancient writers PIERUS, or the Pierian mountain. The inhabitants of this country were a Thracian people, and are celebrated in the early history of Greek poetry and music, since their country was one of the earliest seats of the worship of the Muses, who are hence called *Piĕrĭdes*. After the establishment of the Macedonian kingdom in Emathia in the 7th century, B.C., Pieria was conquered by the Macedonians, and the inhabitants were driven out of the country.—(2) A district in Macedonia, E. of the Strymon, near Mt. Pangaeum, where the Pierians settled, who had been driven out of their original abodes by the Macedonians, as already related.—(3) A district on the N. coast of Syria, so called from the mountain Pieria, a branch of the Amanus, a name given to it by the Macedonians after their conquest of the East.

PĪĔRĪDES (-um). (1) A surname of the Muses. [Pieria, No. 1.]—(2) The nine daughters of Pierus, king of Emathia (Macedonia), to whom he gave the names of the 9 Muses. They afterwards entered into a contest with the Muses, and, being conquered, were metamorphosed into birds.

PĪĔRUS. (1) Mythological. [Pierides.] —(2) A mountain. [Pieria, No. 1.]

PĪLUMNUS. [Picumnus.]

PIMPLEA (-ae), a town in the Macedonian province of Pieria, sacred to the Muses, who were hence called *Pimplēīdes*. Horace uses the form *Pimplēa* in the singular, and not *Pimplēis*.

PINĂRA (-ōrum), an inland city of Lycia.

PĪNĂRĪI and PŎTĪTĪI (-ōrum), the name of two ancient Roman families, who presided over the worship of Hercules at Rome.

PĪNĂRUS (-i), a river of Cilicia, rising in Mt. Amānus, and falling into the gulf of Issus.

PINDĂRUS (-i), the greatest lyric poet of Greece, was born at Cynoscephalae, a village in the territory of Thebes, about B.C. 522. He commenced his career as a poet at an early age, and was soon employed by different states and princes in all parts of the Hellenic world to compose for them choral songs for special occasions. He received money and presents for his works; but he never degenerated into a common mercenary poet, and he continued to preserve to his latest days the respect of all parts of Greece. The praises which he bestowed upon Alexander, king of Macedonia, are said to have been the chief reason which led Alexander the Great to spare the house of the poet, when he destroyed the rest of Thebes. He died in his 80th year, B.C. 442. Pindar wrote poems of various kinds, most of which are mentioned in the well-known lines of Horace:

"Seu per audaces nova dithyrambos
Verba devolvit, numerisque fertur
  Lege solutis:
Seu deos (*hymns and paeans*) regesve (*encomia*)
  canit, deorum
Sanguinem : . . .
Sive quos Elea domum reducit
Palma caelestes (*the Epinicia*) : . . .
Flebili sponsae juvenemve raptum
  Plorat" (*the dirges*).

But his only poems which have come down to us entire are his *Epinicia*, which were composed in commemoration of victories in the public games. They are divided into

4 books, celebrating the victories gained in the Olympian, Pythian, Nemean, and Isthmian games.

PINDĔNISSUS (-i), a fortified town of Cilicia, which was taken by Cicero when he was proconsul of Cilicia.

PINDUS (-i). (1) A lofty range of mountains in northern Greece, a portion of the great back bone, which runs through the centre of Greece from N. to S. The name of Pindus was confined to that part of the chain which separates Thessaly and Epirus; and its most N.-ly and also highest part was called LACMON.—(2) One of the 4 towns in Doris.

PINNA (-ae), the chief town of the Vestini at the foot of the Apennines.

PĪRAEEUS (-ĕŏs) or PĪRAEUS (-i : *Porto Leone* or *Porto Dracone*), the most important of the harbours of Athens, was situated in the peninsula about 5 miles S.W. of Athens. This peninsula, which is sometimes called by the general name of Piraeeus, contained 3 harbours, PIRAEEUS proper on the W. side, by far the largest of the 3; ZEA on the E. side, separated from Piraeeus by a narrow isthmus, and MUNYCHIA (*Pharnari*) still further to the E. It was through the suggestion of Themistocles that the Athenians were induced to make use of the harbour of Piraeeus. Before the Persian wars their principal harbour was Phalerum, which was not situated in the Piraean peninsula at all, but lay to the E. of Munychia. [PHALERUM.] The town or demus of Piraeeus was surrounded with strong fortifications by Themistocles, and was connected with Athens by means of the celebrated Long Walls under the administration of Pericles. (See p. 66.) The town possessed a considerable population, and many public and private buildings.

PĪRĒNĒ (-ēs), a celebrated fountain at Corinth, at which Bellerophon is said to have caught the horse Pegasus. It gushed forth from the rock in the Acrocorinthus, was conveyed down the hill by subterraneous conduits, and fell into a marble basin, from which the greater part of the town was supplied with water. The poets frequently used *Pirēnis* in the general sense of Corinthian.

PĪRĪTHŌUS (-i), son of Ixion and Dia, and king of the Lapithae in Thessaly. Pirithoüs once invaded Attica, but when Theseus came forth to oppose him, he conceived a warm admiration for the Athenian king; and from this time a most intimate friendship sprang up between the two heroes. When Pirithoüs was celebrating his marriage with Hippodamia, the intoxicated Centaur Eurytion or Eurytus carried her off, and this act occasioned the celebrated fight between the Centaurs and Lapithae, in which the Centaurs were defeated. Theseus, who was present at the wedding of Pirithoüs, assisted him in his battle against the Centaurs. Hippodamia afterwards died, and each of the two friends resolved to wed a daughter of Zeus (Jupiter). With the assistance of Pirithoüs, Theseus carried off Helen from Sparta. Pirithoüs was still more ambitious, and resolved to carry off Persephone (Proserpina), the wife of the king of the lower world. Theseus would not desert his friend in the enterprise, though he knew the risk which they ran. The two friends accordingly descended to the lower world, but they were seized by Pluto and fastened to a rock, where they both remained till Hercules visited the lower world. Hercules delivered Theseus, who had made the daring attempt only to please his friend; but Pirithoüs remained for ever in torment.

PISA (-ae), the capital of PISATIS (-idis), the middle portion of the province of Elis, in Peloponnesus. [ELIS.] Pisa itself was situated N. of the Alphaeus, at a very short distance E. of Olympia, and, in consequence of its proximity to the latter place, was frequently identified by the poets with it. The history of the Pisatae consists of their struggle with the Eleans, with whom they contended for the presidency of the Olympic games. The Pisatae obtained this honour in the 8th Olympiad (B.C. 748) with the assistance of Phidon, tyrant of Argos, and also a 2nd time in the 34th Olympiad (644) by means of their own king Pantaleon. In the 52nd Olympiad (572) the struggle between the 2 peoples was brought to a close by the conquest and destruction of Pisa by the Eleans.

PISAE (-ārum : *Pisa*), an ancient city of Etruria, and one of 12 cities of the confederation, was situated at the confluence of the Arnos and Ausar (*Serchio*), about 6 miles from the sea. According to some traditions, Pisae was founded by the companions of Nestor, the inhabitants of Pisa in Elis, who were driven upon the coast of Italy on their return from Troy; whence the Roman poets give the Etruscan town the surname of Alphea. In B.C. 180 it was made a Latin colony. Its harbour, called PORTUS PISANUS, at the mouth of the Arnus, was much used by the Romans.

PISANDER (-dri), an Athenian, the chief agent in effecting the revolution of the Four Hundred, B.C. 412.

PISATIS. [PISA.]

PISAURUM (-i : *Pesara*), an ancient town of Umbria, near the mouth of the river PISAURUS (*Foglia*), on the road to Ariminum.

PISIDIA (-ae), an inland district of Asia Minor, lying N. of Lycia and Pamphylia, was a mountainous region, inhabited by a warlike people, who maintained their indepeu-

dence against all the successive rulers of Asia Minor.

PISISTRATIDAE (-ārum), a name given to Hippias and Hipparchus, as the sons of Pisistratus.

PISISTRATUS (-i), an Athenian, son of Hippocrates, belonged to a noble family at Athens. His mother was cousin-german to the mother of Solon. When Solon had retired from Athens, after the establishment of his constitution, the old rivalry between the parties of the Plain, the Coast, and the Highlands, broke out into open feud. The first was headed by Lycurgus, the second by Megacles, the son of Alcmaeon, and the third by Pisistratus, who had formed the design of making himself tyrant or despot of Athens. Solon, on his return, quickly saw through his designs, and attempted in vain to dissuade him from overthrowing the constitution. When Pisistratus found his plans sufficiently ripe for execution, he one day made his appearance in the agora, his mules and his own person exhibiting recent wounds, and pretended that he had been nearly assassinated by his enemies as he was riding into the country. An assembly of the people was forthwith called, in which one of his partisans proposed that a body-guard of 50 citizens, armed with clubs, should be granted to him. Pisistratus took the opportunity of raising a much larger force, with which he seized the citadel, B.C. 560, thus becoming tyrant of Athens. His first usurpation lasted but a short time. Before his power was firmly rooted, the factions headed by Megacles and Lycurgus combined, and Pisistratus was compelled to evacuate Athens. But Megacles and Lycurgus soon quarrelled; whereupon the former offered to reinstate Pisistratus in the tyranny if he would marry his daughter. The proposal was accepted by Pisistratus, who thus became a second time tyrant of Athens. Pisistratus now married the daughter of Megacles; but in consequence of the insulting manner in which he treated his wife, Megacles again made common cause with Lycurgus, and Pisistratus was a second time compelled to evacuate Athens. He retired to Eretria, in Euboea; and after spending 10 years in making preparations to regain his power, he invaded Attica, and made himself master of Athens for the third time. He was not expelled again, but continued to hold his power till his death. His rule was not oppressive. He maintained the form of Solon's institutions, and not only exacted obedience to the laws from his subjects and friends, but himself set the example of submitting to them. He was a warm patron of literature; and it is to him that we owe the first written text of the whole of the poems of Homer, which, without his care, would most likely now exist only in a few disjointed fragments. [HOMERUS.] He died in B.C. 527, and was succeeded in the tyranny by his two sons Hippias and Hipparchus. They continued the government on the same principles as their father. Hipparchus inherited his father's literary tastes. Several distinguished poets lived at Athens under the patronage of Hipparchus, as, for example, Simonides of Ceos and Anacreon of Teos. After the murder of Hipparchus, in B.C. 514, an account of which is given under HARMODIUS, a great change ensued in the character of the government. Under the influence of revengeful feelings and fears for his own safety, Hippias now became a morose and suspicious tyrant. His old enemies the Alcmaeonidae, to whom Megacles belonged, availed themselves of the growing discontent of the citizens; and after one or two unsuccessful attempts they at length succeeded, supported by a large force under Cleomenes, in expelling Hippias from Attica. Hippias first retired to Sigeum, B.C. 510. He afterwards repaired to the court of Darius, and looked forward to a restoration to his country by the aid of the Persians. He accompanied the expedition sent under Datis and Artaphernes, and pointed out to the Persians the plain of Marathon as the most suitable place for their landing. He was now (490) of great age. According to some accounts he fell in the battle of Marathon; according to others he died at Lemnos, on his return.

PISO (-ōnis), the name of a distinguished family of the Calpurnia gens. The name is connected with agriculture, the most honourable pursuit of the ancient Romans: it comes from the verb *pisere* or *pinsere*, and refers to the pounding or grinding of corn. The chief members of the family are:—(1) L. CALPURNIUS PISO CAESONINUS, consul B.C. 112, served as legatus under L. Cassius Longinus, B.C. 107, and fell in battle against the Tigurini, in the territory of the Allobroges. This Piso was the grandfather of Caesar's father-in-law, a circumstance to which Caesar alludes in recording his own victory over the Tigurini at a later time.—(2) L. CALPURNIUS PISO FRUGI, consul B.C. 133, received, from his integrity and conscientiousness, the surname of Frugi, which is nearly equivalent to our "man of honour." He was a staunch supporter of the aristocratical party, and offered a strong opposition to the measures of C. Gracchus. He wrote Annals, which contained the history of Rome from the earliest period to the age in which Piso himself lived. —(3) C. CALPURNIUS PISO, consul B.C. 67,

belonged to the aristocratical party. He afterwards administered the province of Narbonese Gaul as pro-consul. In 63 he was accused of plundering the province, and was defended by Cicero. The latter charge was brought against Piso at the instigation of Caesar; and Piso, in revenge, implored Cicero, but without success, to accuse Caesar as one of the conspirators of Catiline.— (4) M. CALPURNIUS PISO, usually called M. PUPIUS PISO, because he was adopted by M. Pupius. He was elected consul B.C. 61, through the influence of Pompey.—(5) CN. CALPURNIUS PISO, a young noble who had dissipated his fortune by his extravagance and profligacy, and therefore joined Catiline in what is usually called his first conspiracy (66). The senate, anxious to get rid of Piso, sent him into Nearer Spain as quaestor, but with the rank and title of propraetor. His exactions in the province soon made him so hateful to the inhabitants, that he was murdered by them.— (6) L. CALPURNIUS PISO, consul B.C. 58, was an unprincipled debauchee and a cruel and corrupt magistrate. Piso and his colleague, Gabinius, supported Clodius in his measures against Cicero, which resulted in the banishment of the orator. Piso afterwards governed Macedonia, and plundered the province in the most shameless manner. On his return to Rome (55), Cicero attacked him in a speech which is extant (*In Pisonem*). Calpurnia, the daughter of Piso, was the last wife of the dictator Caesar.—(7) C. CALPURNIUS PISO FRUGI, the son-in-law of Cicero, married his daughter Tullia, in B.C. 63. He died in 57.— (8) CN. CALPURNIUS PISO was appointed by Tiberius to the command of Syria in A.D. 18, in order that he might thwart and oppose Germanicus, who had received from the emperor the government of all the eastern provinces. Plancina, the wife of Piso, was also urged on by Livia, the mother of the emperor, to vie with and annoy Agrippina. Germanicus and Agrippina were thus exposed to every species of insult and opposition from Piso and Plancina; and when Germanicus fell ill in the autumn of 19, he believed that he had been poisoned by them. Piso, on his return to Rome (20), was accused of murdering Germanicus; the matter was investigated by the senate; but before the investigation came to an end, Piso was found one morning in his room with his throat cut, and his sword lying by his side. The powerful influence of Livia secured the acquittal of Plancina.— (9) C. CALPURNIUS PISO, the leader of the well-known conspiracy against Nero in A.D 65. On the discovery of the plot he put an end to his life by opening his veins.

PISTOR (-ōris), the Baker, a surname of

Jupiter at Rome, because when the Gauls were besieging Rome, he suggested to the besieged the idea of throwing loaves of bread among the enemies, to make them believe that the Romans had plenty of provisions.

PISTŌRĬA (-ae), or PISTŌRĬUM (-i: *Pistoia*), a small place in Etruria, on the road from Luca to Florentia, rendered memorable by the defeat of Catiline in its neighbourhood.

PĬTĂNĒ (-ēs), a seaport town of Mysia, on the coast of the Elaitic gulf; the birthplace of the Academic philosopher Arcesilaus.

PITHĒCŪSA. [AENARIA.]

PĪTHŌ (-ūs), the Greek goddess of persuasion, called SUADA or SUADELA by the Romans. Her worship was closely connected with that of Aphroditē (Venus.)

PITTĂCUS (-i), one of " the Seven Wise Men " of Greece, was a native of Mytilene in Lesbos, and was highly celebrated as a warrior, a statesman, a philosopher, and a poet. In B.C. 606, he commanded the Mytilenaeans, in their war with the Athenians for the possession of Sigeum, and signalised himself by killing in single combat Phrynon, the commander of the Athenians. The supreme power at Mytilene was fiercely disputed between a succession of tyrants, and the aristocratic party, headed by Alcaeus, and the latter was driven into exile. As the exiles tried to effect their return by force of arms, the popular party chose Pittacus as their ruler, with absolute power, under the title of *Aesymnetes.* He held this office for 10 years (589—579) and then voluntarily resigned it, having restored order to the state. He died in 569, at an advanced age.

PITTHEUS (-ĕŏs and -ĕī), king of Troezene, was son of Pelops, father of Aethra, and grandfather and instructor of Theseus. Aethra as his daughter is called *Pittheis.*

PLĂCENTĬA (-ae : *Piacenza*), a Roman colony in Cisalpine Gaul, founded at the same time as Cremona, B.C. 219, and situated on the right bank of the Po, not far from the mouth of the Trebia. It was taken and destroyed by the Gauls in B.C. 200, but was soon rebuilt by the Romans, and became an important place.

PLANASĬA (-ae : *Pianosa*), an island between Corsica and the coast of Etruria, to which Augustus banished his grandson Agrippa Postumus.

PLANCĪNA. [PISO, No. 9.]

PLANCĬUS, CN. (-i), whom Cicero defended B.C. 54, in an oration still extant, when he was accused of having practised bribery in order to gain his election as curule aedile.

PLANCUS (-i), the name of a distinguished family of the Munatia gens. The surname Plancus signified a person having flat splay feet without any bend in them. (1) L. MUNATIUS PLANCUS, a friend of Julius Caesar, who nominated him to the government of Transalpine Gaul for B.C. 44. Here he joined Antony and Lepidus. He was consul in 42, and governed in succession the provinces of Asia and Syria. He deserted Antony and Augustus shortly before the breaking out of the civil war between the two in 31. Both the public and private life of Plancus was stained by numerous vices. One of Horace's odes (*Carm.* i. 7) is addressed to him.—(2) T. MUNATIUS PLANCUS BURSA, brother of the former, was tribune of the plebs B.C. 52, and was condemned to banishment on account of his proceedings in this year. He fought on Antony's side in the campaign of Mutina.—(3) CN. MUNATIUS PLANCUS, brother of the two preceding, was praetor in 43.—(4) L. PLAUTIUS PLANCUS, brother of the 3 preceding, was adopted by a L. Plautius. He was included in the proscription of the triumvirs, 43, with the consent of his brother Lucius, and was put to death.

PLĂTAEA (-ae), more commonly PLĂTAEAE (-ārum), an ancient city of Boeotia, on the N. slope of Mt. Cithaeron, not far from the sources of the Asopus, and on the frontiers of Attica. It was said to have derived its name from Plataea, a daughter of Asopus. At an early period the Plataeans deserted the Boeotian confederacy and placed themselves under the protection of Athens; and when the Persians invaded Attica, B.C. 490, they sent 1000 men to the assistance of the Athenians, and fought on their side at the battle of Marathon. Ten years afterwards (480) their city was destroyed by the Persian army under Xerxes at the instigation of the Thebans; and the place was still in ruins in the following year (479), when the memorable battle was fought in their territory, in which Mardonius was defeated, and the independence of Greece secured. In consequence of this victory, the territory of Plataea was declared inviolable. It now enjoyed a prosperity of 50 years; but in the 3rd year of the Peloponnesian war (429) the Thebans persuaded the Spartans to attack the town, and after a siege of 2 years at length succeeded in obtaining possession of the place (427). Plataea was now razed to the ground, but was again rebuilt after the peace of Antalcidas (387). It was destroyed the 3rd time by its inveterate enemies the Thebans in 374. It was once more restored under the Macedonian supremacy, and continued in existence till a very late period.

PLĂTO (-ōnis). (1) The Athenian comic poet, was a contemporary with Aristophanes, and flourished from B.C. 428 to 389. He ranked among the very best poets of the Old Comedy.—(2) The philosopher, was the son of Ariston and Perictione or Potone, and was born at Athens either in B.C. 429 or 428. According to others, he was born in the neighbouring island of Aegina. His paternal family boasted of being descended from Codrus; his maternal ancestors of a relationship with Solon. He was instructed in grammar, music, and gymnastics by the most distinguished teachers of that time; and in his 20th year he became a follower of Socrates, and one of his most ardent admirers. After the death of Socrates (399) he withdrew to Megara, and subsequently visited Egypt, Sicily, and the Greek cities in Lower Italy, through his eagerness for knowledge. During his residence in Sicily he became acquainted with the elder Dionysius, but soon fell out with the tyrant. According to a common story he was sold as a slave by the tyrant, but was set at liberty by Anniceris of Cyrene. After his return he began to teach in the gymnasium of the Academy and its shady avenues, whence his school was subsequently called the Academic. Over the vestibule of his house he set up the inscription, " Let no one enter who is unacquainted with geometry." Plato's occupation as an instructor was twice interrupted by his voyages to Sicily; first when Dion persuaded him to try to win the younger Dionysius to philosophy; the second time, a few years later (about 360), when the invitation of Dionysius to reconcile the disputes which had broken out between him and Dion, brought him back to Syracuse. His efforts were both times unsuccessful and he owed his own safety to nothing but the earnest intercession of Archytas. He died in the 82nd year of his age, B.C. 347. Plato wrote a great number of works on different philosophical subjects, which are still extant. They are in the form of dialogue, and are distinguished by purity of language and elegance of style.

PLAUTUS (-i), T. MACCĬUS (not ACCĬUS), the most celebrated comic poet of Rome, was a native of Sarsina, a small village in Umbria, and was born abcut B.C. 254. In early life he was in needy circumstances. He was first employed in the service of the actors, and having saved a little money, he left Rome and set up in business. But his speculations having failed, he returned to Rome, and entered the service of a baker, who employed him in turning a hand-mill. While thus engaged he wrote 3 plays, the sale of which to the managers of the public games enabled him to quit his drudgery, and begin his literary career. He was then probably about 30

years of age (224). He continued his literary occupation for about 40 years, and died in 184, when he was 70 years of age. 20 of his comedies have come down to us. They enjoyed unrivalled popularity among the Romans, and continued to be represented down to the time of Diocletian. They appear to be all founded upon Greek models; but he takes greater liberties with the originals than Terence.

PLEÏADES or PLEÏÄDES (-um), were the daughters of Atlas and Plēïŏnē, whence they bear the name of the *Atlantides*. They were called *Vergiliae* by the Romans. They were the sisters of the Hyades, and 7 in number, 6 of whom are described as visible and the 7th as invisible. Some call the 7th Sterŏpe, and relate that she became invisible from shame, because she alone had loved a mortal man. The Pleiades were virgin companions of Artemis (Diana), and, together with their mother Pleione, were pursued by the hunter Orion in Boeotia; their prayer to be rescued from him was heard by the goάs, and they were metamorphosed into doves (πιλειάδες), and placed among the stars. The rising of the Pleiades in Italy is about the beginning of May, and their setting about the beginning of November. Their names are Electra, Maia, Taygete, Alcyone, Celaeno, Sterope, and Merope.

PLEMMȲRIUM (-i), a promontory on the S. coast of Sicily, immediately S. of Syracuse.

PLEÏŎNĒ (-ēs) a daughter of Oceanus, and mother of the Pleiades by Atlas. [ATLAS; PLEIADES.]

PLEUMOXĬI (-ōrum), a small tribe in Gallia Belgica, subject to the Nervii.

PLEURŌN (-ōnis), an ancient city in Aetolia, situated at a little distance from the coast. It was abandoned by its inhabitants when Demetrius II., king of Macedonia, laid waste the surrounding country, and a new city was built under the same name near the ancient one. The 2 cities are distinguished by geographers under the names of Old Pleuron and New Pleuron respectively.

PLĪNĬUS (-i). (1) C. PLINIUS SECUNDUS, frequently called Pliny the Elder, was born A.D. 23, either at Verona or Novum Comum (*Como*) in the N. of Italy. In his youth he served in the army in Germany, and afterwards practised for a time as a pleader at Rome. But he spent the greater part of his time in study, and was one of the most laborious students that ever lived. He perished in the celebrated eruption of Vesuvius, which overwhelmed Herculaneum and Pompeii, in A.D. 79, being 56 years of age. He was at the time stationed at Misenum in the command of the Roman fleet; and it was his anxiety to examine more closely the extraordinary phenomenon, which led him to sail to Stabiae, where he landed and perished. Pliny wrote a great number of works, but the only one which has come down to us is his *Historia Naturalis*. It is divided into 37 books, and is dedicated to Titus, the son of Vespasian, with whom Pliny lived on very intimate terms.—(2) C. PLINIUS CAECILIUS SECUNDUS, frequently called Pliny the younger, was the son of C. Caecilius, and of Plinia, the sister of the elder Pliny. He was born at Comum in A.D. 61 ; and having lost his father at an early age, he was adopted by his uncle. From his youth he was devoted to letters. In his 14th year he wrote a Greek tragedy, and in his 19th year he began to speak in the forum, and became distinguished as an orator. He was a friend of the historian Tacitus. In A.D. 100 he was consul, and in 103 he was appointed propraetor of the province Pontica, where he did not stay quite 2 years. His extant works are his *Panegyricus*, which is a fulsome eulogium on Trajan, and the 10 books of his *Epistolae*.

PLISTHENES (-is), son of Atreus, and husband of Aërŏpē or Eriphȳlē, by whom he became the father of Agamemnon, Menelaus, and Anaxibia ; but Homer makes the latter the children of Atreus. [AGAMEMNON ; ATREUS.]

PLISTŎĂNAX or PLISTŎNAX (-actis), king of Sparta B.C. 458—408, was the eldest son of the Pausanias who conquered at Plataea, B.C. 479. During 19 years of his reign (445—426), he lived in exile, but was afterwards recalled, in obedience to the Delphic oracle.

PLISTUS (-i), a small river in Phocis, rising in Mt. Parnassus, and falling into the Crissaean gulf.

PLŎTINA, POMPĒIA (-ae), the wife of the emperor Trajan, who persuaded her husband to adopt Hadrian.

PLŎTINUS (-i), the founder of the Neo-Platonic system, was born in Egypt, about A.D. 203. He taught during the latter part of his life at Rome, where he had among his disciples the celebrated Porphyry. His works, which have come down to us, were put into their present form by Porphyry. Plotinus died at Puteoli, in Campania, A.D. 262.

PLŪTARCHUS (-i), the biographer and philosopher, was born at Chaeronea, in Boeotia, probably in the reign of Claudius. He lived for some time at Rome, and in other parts of Italy ; and he was lecturing at Rome during the reign of Domitian. He spent the later years of his life at Chaeronea, where he discharged various magisterial offices, and held a priesthood. The time of his death is

unknown. The work which has immortalised Plutarch's name is his *Parallel Lives* of Greeks and Romans. Perhaps no work of antiquity has been so extensively read in modern times as these Lives. The reason of their popularity is that Plutarch has rightly conceived the business of a biographer : his biography is true portraiture. His other writings, above 60 in number, are placed under the general title of *Moralia*, or Ethical works. The best of them are practical ; and their merits consist in the soundness of his views on the ordinary events of human life, and in the benevolence of his temper.

PLŪTO or PLŪTŌN (-ŏnis), the giver of wealth, at first a surname of Hades, the god of the lower world, and afterwards used as the real name of the god. An account of the god is given under HADES.

PLŪTUS (-i), the god of wealth, is described as a son of Iasion and Demeter (Ceres). [IASION.] Zeus (Jupiter) is said to have deprived him of sight, that he might distribute his gifts blindly, and without any regard to merit.

PLŪVIUS (-i), *i.e.*, "the sender of rain," a surname of Jupiter among the Romans, to whom sacrifices were offered during longprotracted droughts.

PODĀLIRIUS (-i), son of Aesculapius, and brother of Machaon, along with whom he led the Thessalians of Tricca against Troy. He was, like his brother, skilled in the medical art. On his return from Troy he was cast by a storm on the coast of Syros, in Caria, where he is said to have settled.

PŎDARCĒS (-is). (1) The original name of Priam. [PRIAMUS.]—(2) Son of Iphiclus, and grandson of Phylacus, was a younger brother of Protesilaus, and led the Thessalians of Phylace against Troy.

PODARGĒ. [HARPYIAE.]

POEAS (-antis), father of Philoctetes, who is hence called *Poeantiades*, *Poeantius heros*, *Poeantia proles*, and *Poeante satus*. Poeas is mentioned among the Argonauts. [HERCULES ; PHILOCTETES.]

POENI (-orum), a common name of the Carthaginians, because they were a colony of Phoenicians.

PŎGŌN (-ŏnis), the harbour of Troezen, in Argolis.

POLA (-ae), an ancient town in Istria, situated on the W. coast, and near the promontory POLATICUM, said to have been founded by the Colchians, who had been sent in pursuit of Medea. It was subsequently a Roman colony, and an important commercial town, being united by good roads with Aquileia and the principal towns of Illyria. Its importance is attested by its magnificent ruins, of which the principal are those of an amphitheatre, of a triumphal arch, and of several temples.

PŎLĔMŌN (-ōnis). (1) I. King of Pontus and the Bosporus, was the son of Zenon, the orator, of Laodicea. He was appointed by Antony in B.C. 39 to the government of a part of Cilicia; and he subsequently obtained in exchange the kingdom of Pontus. After the battle of Actium he was able to make his peace with Augustus, who confirmed him in his kingdom. About B.C. 16 he was intrusted by Agrippa with the charge of reducing the kingdom of Bosporus, of which he was made king after conquering the country. He afterwards fell in an expedition against the barbarian tribe of the Aspurgians. He was succeeded by his wife, Pythodoris.—(2) II. Son of the preceding and of Pythodoris, was raised to the sovereignty of Pontus and Bosporus by Caligula, in A.D. 39. He was induced by Nero to abdicate the throne in A.D. 62, and Pontus was reduced to the condition of a Roman province.—(3) Of Athens, an eminent Platonic philosopher. ∡n his youth he was extremely profligate; but one day, when he was about 30, on his bursting into the school of Xenocrates. at the head of a band of revellers, his attention was so arrested by the discourse, which chanced to be upon temperance, that hè tore off his garland, and remained an attentive listener. From that day he adopted an abstemious course of life, and continued to frequent the school, of which, on the death of Xenocrates, he became the head, B.C. 315. He died in 273, at a great age.—(4) A Stoic philosopher and an eminent geographer, surnamed *Periegetes*, lived in the time of Ptolemy Epiphanes, at the beginning of the 2nd century B.C.— (5) ANTONIUS, a celebrated sophist and rhetorician, flourished under Trajan, Hadrian, and the first Antoninus. He was born of a consular family, at Laodicea, but spent the greater part of his life at Smyrna. His most celebrated disciple was Aristides. During the latter part of his life he was so tortured by the gout, that he resolved to put an end to his existence; he caused himself to be shut up in the tomb of his ancestors at Laodicea, where he died of hunger, at the age of 65.—(6) The author of a short Greek work on Physiognomy, which is still extant. He probably lived in the 2nd or 3rd century after Christ.

PŎLĔMŌNĬUM (-i), a city on the coast of Pontus in Asia Minor, built by King POLEMON (probably the 2nd), on the site of the older city of Side, and at the bottom of a deep gulf.

PŎLĬAS (-ădis), *i.e.* "the goddess protecting the city," a surname of Athena at Athens, where she was worshipped as the protecting divinity of the acropolis.

PŎLĬORCĔTĔS, DĒMĒTRĬUS. [DEMETRIUS.]

PŎLĬTĔS (-ae), son of Priam and Hecuba and father of Priam the younger, was slain by Pyrrhus.

POLĬTŌRĬUM (-i), a town in the interior of Latium, destroyed by Ancus Martius.

POLLA, ARGENTĀRĬA (-ae), the wife of the poet Lucan.

POLLENTĬA (-ae: *Polenza*), a town of the Statielli in Liguria at the confluence of the Sturia and the Tanarus. It was celebrated for its wool. In its neighbourhood Stilicho gained a victory over the Goths under Alaric.

POLLĬO (-ōnis), ĀSĬNĬUS (-i), a distinguished orator, poet, and historian of the Augustan age. He was born at Rome in B.C. 76, and became distinguished as an orator at an early age. In the civil war he fought on Caesar's side, and at the death of the dictator held the command of the Further Spain. He subsequently united his forces to those of Octavian, Antony, and Lepidus. He was afterwards appointed by Antony to settle the veterans in the lands which had been assigned to them in the Transpadane Gaul. It was upon this occasion that he saved the property of the poet Virgil at Mantua from confiscation. In B.C. 40 Pollio took an active part in effecting the reconciliation between Octavian and Antony at Brundusium. In the same year he was consul; and it was during his consulship that Virgil addressed to him his 4th Eclogue. In B.C. 39 Antony went to Greece, and Pollio, as the legate of Antony, defeated the Parthini and took the Dalmatian town of Salonae. It was during his Illyrian campaign that Virgil addressed to him the 8th Eclogue. From this time Pollio withdrew from political life, and devoted himself to the study of literature. He died A.D. 4, in the 80th year of his age. Pollio was not only a patron of Virgil, Horace, and other great poets and writers, but he was also the first person to establish a public library at Rome. None of Pollio's own works have come down to us, but they possessed sufficient merit to lead his contemporaries to class his name with those of Cicero, Virgil, and Sallust; as an orator, a poet, and an historian. It was as an orator that he possessed the greatest reputation; and Horace speaks of him as "Insigne maestis praesidium reis et consulenti, Pollio, curiae." Pollio wrote the history of the civil wars in 17 books, commencing with the consulship of Metellus and Afranius, B.C. 60. As a poet Pollio was best known by his tragedies, which are spoken of in high terms by Virgil and Horace, but which probably did not possess any great merit, as they are hardly mentioned by subsequent writers.

POLLĬO (-ōnis), VEDĬUS, a friend of Augustus, who used to feed his lampreys with human flesh. Whenever a slave displeased him, the unfortunate wretch was forthwith thrown into the pond as food for the fish. He died B.C. 15, leaving a large part of his property to Augustus. It was this Pollio, who built the celebrated villa of Pausilypum near Naples.

POLLUX or PŎLȲDEUCĒS. [DIOSCURI.]

POLLUX (-ŭcis), JŪLĬUS (-i), of Naucratis in Egypt, a Greek sophist and grammarian, who lived in the reign of Commodus. He is the author of an extant work, entitled *Onomasticon*, in 10 books, containing explanations of the meanings of Greek words.

PŎLȲAENUS (-i). (1) Of Lampsacus, a mathematician and a friend of Epicurus.—(2) A Macedonian, the author of the work on Stratagems in war, which is still extant, lived about the middle of the 2nd century of the Christian era.

PŎLȲBĬUS (-i), the historian, the son of Lycortas, and a native of Megalopolis, in Arcadia, was born about B.C. 204. His father Lycortas was one of the most distinguished men of the Achaean league; and Polybius at an early age took part in public affairs. After the conquest of Macedonia by the Romans, in B.C. 168, Polybius was one of the 1000 distinguished Achaeans who were carried as prisoners to Rome. On his arrival in Italy he acquired the friendship of the younger Scipio Africanus. After remaining in Italy 17 years, Polybius returned to Peloponnesus in B.C. 151, with the surviving Achaean exiles, who were at length allowed by the senate to revisit their native land. Soon afterwards he joined Scipio in his campaign against Carthage, and was present at the destruction of that city in 146. Immediately afterwards he hurried to Greece, where he arrived soon after the capture of Corinth ; and he exerted all his influence to alleviate the misfortunes of his countrymen, and to procure favourable terms for them. He undertook journeys into foreign countries for the purpose of visiting the places which he had to describe in his history. He died at the age of 82, in consequence of a fall from his horse, about B.C. 122. His history consisted of 40 books. It began B.C. 220, where the history of Aratus left off, and ended at 146, in which year Corinth was destroyed. It consisted of 2 distinct parts. The first part comprised a period of 35 years, beginning with the 2nd Punic war, and the Social

war in Greece, and ending with the conquest of Perseus and the downfal of the Macedonian kingdom, in 168. This was in fact the main portion of his work, and its great object was to show how the Romans had in this brief period of 53 years conquered the greater part of the world ; but since the Greeks were ignorant, for the most part, of the early history of Rome, he gives a survey of Roman history from the taking of the city by the Gauls to the commencement of the 2nd Punic war, in the first 2 books, which thus form an introduction to the body of the work. The second part of the work, which formed a kind of supplement to the former part, comprised the period from the conquest of Perseus in 168, to the fall of Corinth in 146. This history of Polybius is one of the most valuable works that has come down to us from antiquity ; but unfortunately the greater part of it has perished. We possess the first 5 books entire, but of the rest we have only fragments and extracts.

PŎLȲBUS (-i), king of Corinth, by whom Oedipus was brought up. [OEDIPUS.]

PŎLȲCLĒTUS (-i), of Argos, probably by citizenship, and of Sicyon, probably by birth, was one of the most celebrated statuaries of the ancient world. He was also a sculptor, an architect, and an artist in toreutic. He was somewhat younger than Phidias, and flourished about B.C. 452—412. Phidias was unsurpassed in making the images of the gods, Polycletus in those of men.

PŎLȲCRĀTĒS (-is), tyrant of Samos, and one of the most powerful of all the Greek tyrants. He possessed a large navy and extended his sway over several of the neighbouring islands. The most eminent artists and poets found a welcome at his court ; and his friendship for Anacreon is particularly celebrated. But in the midst of his prosperity Oroetes, the satrap of Sardis, allured him to the mainland, where he was arrested soon after his arrival, and crucified, B.C. 522.

PŎLȲDĀMĀS (-antis), son of Panthous and Phrontis, was a Trojan hero, a friend of Hector, and brother of Euphorbus.

PŎLȲDECTĒS (-ae), king of the island of Seriphos, received kindly Danaë and Perseus. [PERSEUS.]

PŎLȲDEUCĒS, called by the Romans Pollux. [DIOSCURI.]

PŎLȲDŌRUS (-i). (1) King of Thebes, son of Cadmus and Harmonia, husband of Nycteïs, and father of Labdacus.—(2) The youngest among the sons of Priam and Laotoë, was slain by Achilles. This is the Homeric account ; but later traditions make him a son of Priam and Hecuba, and give a different account of his death. When Ilium was on the point of falling into the hands of the Greeks, Priam entrusted Polydorus and a large sum of money to Polymestor or Polymnestor, king of the Thracian Chersonesus. After the destruction of Troy, Polymestor killed Polydorus for the purpose of getting possession of his treasures, and cast his body into the sea. His body was afterwards washed upon the coast, where it was found and recognised by his mother Hecuba, who took vengeance upon Polymestor by killing his two children, and putting out his eyes. Another tradition stated that Polydorus was entrusted to his sister Iliona, who was married to Polymestor. She brought him up as her own son, while she made every one else believe that her own son Deïphilus or Deïpylus was Polydorus. Polymestor, at the instigation of the Greeks, slew his own son, supposing him to be Polydorus; whereupon the latter persuaded his sister Iliona to put Polymestor to death.

POLYGNŌTUS (-i), one of the most celebrated Greek painters, was the son of Aglaophon, and a native of the island of Thasos, but he received the citizenship of Athens, on which account he is sometimes called an Athenian. He lived on intimate terms with Cimon and his sister Elpinice; and he probably came to Athens in B.C. 463 : after the subjugation of Thasos by Cimon he continued to exercise his art almost down to the beginning of the Peloponnesian war (431).

PŌLŸHYMNĬA. [Musae.]

PŌLŸMESTOR or PŌLYMNESTOR. [Polydorus.]

PŌLYMNĬA. [Musae.]

PŌLŸNĬCĔS (-is), son of Oedipus and Jocasta, and brother of Eteocles and Antigone. [Eteocles; Adrastus.]

PŌLŸPHĒMUS (-i), son of Poseidon (Neptune), and the Nymph Thoosa, was one of the Cyclopes in Sicily. [Cyclopes.] He is represented as a gigantic monster, having only one eye in the centre of his forehead, caring nought for the gods, and devouring human flesh. He dwelt in a cave near Mt. Aetna, and fed his flocks upon the mountain. He fell in love with the nymph Galatea, but as she rejected him for Acis, he destroyed the latter by crushing him under a huge rock. When Ulysses was driven upon Sicily, Polyphemus devoured some of his companions ; and Ulysses would have shared the same fate, had he not put out the eye of the monster, while he was asleep. [Ulysses.]

The Cyclops Polyphemus.　(Zoëga, Bassirilievi, tav. 57.)

POLYSPERCHŌN (-ontis), a Macedonian, and a distinguished officer of Alexander the Great. Antipater on his death-bed (B.C. 319) appointed Polysperchon to succeed him as regent in Macedonia, while he assigned to his own son Cassander the subordinate station of Chiliarch. Polysperchon soon became involved in war with Cassander, and finally submitted to the latter.

POLŸXĒNA (-ae), daughter of Priam and

Hecuba, was beloved by Achilles. [See p. 5, b.] When the Greeks, on their voyage home, were still lingering on the coast of Thrace, the shade of Achilles appeared to them, demanding that Polyxena should be sacrificed to him. Neoptolemus accordingly slew her on the tomb of his father.

PŎLYXŎ (-ūs). (1) The nurse of queen Hypsipyle in Lemnos, celebrated as a prophetess.—(2) An Argive woman, married to Tlepolemus, son of Hercules, followed her husband to Rhodes, where, according to some traditions, she put to death the celebrated Helen. [HELENA.]

PŎMŌNA (-ae), the Roman divinity of the fruit of trees, hence called *Pomorum Patrona.* Her name is derived from *Pomum.* She is represented by the poets as beloved by several of the rustic divinities, such as Silvanus, Picus, Vertumnus, and others.

POMPĒIA (-ae). (1) Daughter of Q. Pompeius Rufus, son of the consul of B.C. 88, and of Cornelia, the daughter of the dictator Sulla. She married C. Caesar, subsequently the dictator, in B.C. 67, but was divorced by him in 61, because she was suspected of intriguing with Clodius, who stealthily introduced himself into her husband's house while she was celebrating the mysteries of the Bona Dea.—(2) Daughter of Pompey, the triumvir, by his third wife Mucia. She married Faustus Sulla, the son of the dictator, who perished in the African war, 46.—(3) Daughter of Sex. Pompey, the son of the triumvir and of Scribonia. At the peace of Misenum in 39 she was betrothed to M. Marcellus, the son of Octavia, the sister of Octavian, but was never married to him.

POMPĒII (-ōrum), a city of Campánia, was situated on the coast, at the foot of Mt. Vesuvius; but in consequence of the physical changes which the surrounding country has undergone, the ruins of Pompeii are found at present about 2 miles from the sea. It was overwhelmed in A.D. 79, along with Herculaneum and Stabiae, by the great eruption of Mt. Vesuvius. The lava did not reach Pompeii, but the town was covered with successive layers of ashes and other volcanic matter, on which a soil was gradually formed. Thus a great part of the city has been preserved; and the excavation of it in modern times has thrown great light upon many points of antiquity, such as the construction of Roman houses, and in general all subjects connected with the private life of the ancients. About half the city is now exposed to view.

POMPĒIŎPŎLIS. [SOLOE.]

POMPĒIUS (-i). (1) Q. POMPEIUS, said to have been the son of a flute-player, was the first of the family who rose to dignity in the state. He was consul in 141, when he carried on war unsuccessfully against the Numantines in Spain. — (2) Q. POMPEIUS RUFUS, a zealous supporter of the aristocratical party, was consul B.C. 88, with L. Sulla. When Sulla set out for the East to conduct the war against Mithridates, he left Italy in charge of Pompeius Rufus, and assigned to him the army of Cn. Pompeius Strabo, who was still engaged in carrying on war against the Marsi. Strabo, however, who was unwilling to be deprived of the command, caused Pompeius Rufus to be murdered by the soldiers. — (3) CN. POMPEIUS STRABO, consul B.C. 89, when he carried on war with success against the allies, subduing the greater number of the Italian people who were still in arms. He continued in the S. of Italy as proconsul in the following year (88), when he caused Pompeius Rufus to be assassinated. Shortly afterwards, he was killed by lightning. His avarice and cruelty had made him hated by the soldiers to such a degree, that they tore his corpse from the bier, and dragged it through the streets. — (4) CN. POMPEIUS MAGNUS, the TRIUMVIR, son of the last, was born on the 30th of September, B.C. 106, and was consequently a few months younger than Cicero, who was born on the 3rd of January in this year, and 6 years older than Caesar. He fought under his father in 89 against the Italians, when he was only 17 years of age. When Sulla returned to Italy (84), Pompey marched to his assistance; and in the war which followed against the Marian party, he distinguished himself as one of Sulla's most successful generals. In consequence of his victories in Africa over the Marian party, he was greeted by Sulla with the surname of MAGNUS, a name which he bore ever afterwards. He was allowed to enter Rome in triumph (81), although he was still a simple eques, and had not held any public office. Pompey continued faithful to the aristocracy after Sulla's death (78), and supported the consul Catulus in resisting the attempts of his colleague Lepidus to repeal the laws of Sulla. He was afterwards sent into Spain as proconsul, to assist Metellus against Sertorius, and remained in that country for five years (76—71). [SERTORIUS.] On his return to Rome he was consul with M. Crassus, B.C. 70. In his consulship he openly broke with the aristocracy, and became the great popular hero. He carried a law, restoring to the tribunes the power of which they had been deprived by Sulla. In 67 the tribune A. Gabinius brought forward a bill, proposing to confer upon Pompey the command of the war against the pirates with extraordinary powers. This bill was carried, and in the course of three months he cleared the Mediterranean of the pirates, who had long been the terror of the Romans. Next year (66) he was appointed to succeed Lucullus in the command of the war against Mithridates. The bill, conferring upon him this command, was proposed by the tribune C. Manilius, and was supported by Cicero in an oration which has come down to us. He easily defeated Mithridates, who fled to the Cimmerian Bosporus. He received the submission of Tigranes, king of Armenia; made Syria a Roman province; took Jerusalem; and, after settling the affairs of Asia, returned to Italy in 62. He disbanded his army after landing at Brundisium, and thus calmed the apprehensions of many, who feared that he would seize upon the supreme power. He entered Rome in triumph on the 30th of September, B.C. 60. The senate, however, refused to ratify his acts in Asia; whereupon Pompey entered into a close alliance with Caesar. To be more sure of carrying their plans into execution, they took the wealthy Crassus into their counsels. The three agreed to assist one another against their mutual enemies; and thus was formed the first triumvirate. This union of the three most powerful men at Rome crushed the aristocracy for the time. To cement their union more closely, Caesar gave to Pompey his daughter Julia in marriage. Next year (58) Caesar went to his province in Gaul, but Pompey remained in Rome. While Caesar was gaining glory and influence in Gaul, Pompey was gradually losing influence at Rome. In 55 Pompey was consul a second time with Crassus. Pompey received as his provinces the two Spains, which were governed by his legates, L. Afranius and M. Petreius, while he himself remained in the neighbourhood of the city. Caesar's increasing power and influence at length made it clear to Pompey that a struggle must take place between them, sooner or later. The death of his wife Julia, in 54, to whom he was tenderly attached, broke the last link which still connected him with Caesar. In order to obtain supreme power, Pompey secretly encouraged the civil discord with which the state was torn asunder; and such frightful scenes of anarchy followed the death of Clodius at the beginning of 52, that the senate had no alternative but calling in the assistance of Pompey, who was accordingly made sole consul in 52, and succeeded in restoring order to the state. Soon afterwards Pompey became reconciled to the

aristocracy, and was now regarded as their acknowledged head. The history of the civil war which followed is related in the life of CAESAR. After the battle of Pharsalia (48) Pompey sailed to Egypt, where he was put to death by order of the ministers of the young king Ptolemy. Pompey got into a boat, which the Egyptians sent to bring him to land; but just as the boat reached the shore, and he was stepping on land, he was stabbed in the back in sight of his wife, who was anxiously watching him from the ship. He was slain on the 29th of September, B.C. 48, and had just completed his 58th year. His head was cut off, and was brought to Caesar when he arrived in Egypt soon afterwards, but he turned away from the sight, shed tears at the melancholy death of his rival, and put his murderers to death. Pompey was married 5 times. The names of his wives were—1. Antistia. 2. Aemilia. 3. Mucia. 4. Julia. 5. Cornelia.—(5) CN. POMPEIUS MAGNUS, elder son of the triumvir, by his third wife Mucia, carried on war against Caesar in Spain, and was defeated at the battle of Munda, B.C. 45. He was shortly afterwards taken prisoner, and put to death. —(6) SEX. POMPEIUS MAGNUS, younger son of the triumvir by his third wife Mucia, fought, along with his brother, against Caesar at Munda, but escaped with his life. After Caesar's death (44) he obtained a large fleet, became master of the sea, and took possession of Sicily. He was eventually defeated by the fleet of Augustus, and fled from Sicily to Asia, where he was taken prisoner, and put to death (35).

POMPĒIUS FESTUS. [FESTUS.]

POMPĒIUS TROGUS. [JUSTINUS.]

POMPĒLŌN (-ōnis : *Pamplona*), equivalent to Pompeiopolis, so called by the sons of Pompey, was the chief town of the Vascones in Hispania Tarraconensis.

POMPILĬUS, NŬMA. [NUMA.]

POMPŌNĬA (-ae). (1) Sister of T. Pomponius Atticus, was married to Q. Cicero, the brother of the orator, B.C. 68. The marriage proved an unhappy one. Q. Cicero, after leading a miserable life with his wife for almost 24 years, at length divorced her B.C. 45 or 44.—(2) Daughter of T. Pomponius Atticus, married to M. Vipsanius Agrippa. Her daughter, Vipsania Agrippina, married Tiberius, the successor of Augustus.

POMPŌNĬUS, SEXTUS (-i), a distinguished Roman jurist, who lived under Antoninus Pius and M. Aurelius.

POMPŌNĬUS ATTĬCUS. [ATTICUS.]

POMPŌNĬUS MĒLA. [MELA.]

POMPTĪNAE or **PONTĪNAE** (-arum), **PĂLŪDES** (-um), the *Pontine Marshes*, the name of a low marshy plain on the coast of Latium, between Circeii and Terracina, said to have been so called after an ancient town Pontia, which disappeared at an early period. The marshes are formed chiefly by a number of small streams, which, instead of finding their way into the sea, spread over this plain. The miasmas arising from these marshes are exceedingly unhealthy in the summer. At an early period they either did not exist at all, or were confined to a narrow district. We are told that originally there were 23 towns in this plain ; and in B.C. 312, the greater part of it must have been free from the marshes, since the censor Appius Claudius conducted the celebrated Via Appia in that year through the plain, which must then have been sufficiently strong to bear the weight of this road. In the time of Augustus there was a navigable canal running along side of the Via Appia from Forum Appii to the grove of Feronia, which was intended to carry off a portion of the waters of the marshes. Horace embarked upon this canal on his celebrated journey from Rome to Brundisium in 37.

PONTIA (-ae : *Ponza*), a rocky island off the coast of Latium, opposite Formiae, taken by the Romans from the Volscians, and colonised B.C. 313. Under the empire it was used as a place of banishment for state criminals.

PONTIUS (-i), C., general of the Samnites in B.C. 321, defeated the Roman army in one of the mountain passes near Caudium, and compelled them to pass under the yoke. Nearly 30 years afterwards, Pontius was defeated by Q. Fabius Gurges (292), was taken prisoner, and put to death after the triumph of the consul.

PONTUS (-i), the N.E.-most district of Asia Minor, along the coast of the Euxine, E. of the river Halys, having originally no specific name, was spoken of as the country *on the Pontus* (*Euxinus*), and hence acquired the name of Pontus, which is first found in Xenophon's *Anabasis.* The name first acquired a *political* importance, through the foundation of a new kingdom in it, about the beginning of the 4th century B.C., by ARIOBARZANES I. This kingdom reached its greatest height under Mithridates VI., who for many years carried on war with the Romans. [MITHRIDATES VI.] In A.D. 62 the country was constituted by Nero a Roman province. It was divided into the 3 districts of PONTUS GALATICUS, in the W., bordering on Galatia, P. POLEMONIACUS in the centre, so called from its capital POLEMONIUM, and P. CAPPADOCIUS in the E., bordering on Cappadocia (Armenia Minor). Pontus was a mountain-

ous country ; wild and barren in the E., where the great chains approach the Euxine ; but in the W. watered by the great rivers HALYS and IRIS, and their tributaries, the valleys of which, as well as the land along the coast, are extremely fertile. The E. part was rich in minerals, and contained the celebrated iron mines of the Chalybes.

PONTUS EUXINUS, or simply PONTUS (-i : *the Black Sea*), the great inland sea enclosed by Asia Minor on the S., Colchis on the E., Sarmatia on the N., and Dacia and Thracia on the W., and having no other outlet than the narrow BOSPORUS THRACIUS in its S.W. corner. Its length is about 700 miles, and its breadth varies from 400 to 160. The Argonautic legends show that the Greeks had some acquaintance with this sea at a very early period. It is said that they at first called it Ἄξεινος (*inhospitable*), from the savage character of the peoples on its coast, and from the supposed terrors of its navigation, and that afterwards, on their favourite principle of *euphemism* (i.e. abstaining from words of evil omen), they changed its name to Εὔξεινος, Ion. Εὔξεινος, *hospitable.* The Greeks of Asia Minor, especially the people of Miletus, founded many colonies and commercial emporiums on its shores.

POPILLIUS LAENAS. [LAENAS.]

POPLICOLA. [PUBLICOLA.]

POPPAEA SABINA. [SABINA.]

POPPAEUS SABINUS. [SABINUS.]

POPULONIA (-ae), or POPULONIUM (-i), an ancient town of Etruria, situated on a lofty hill, sinking abruptly to the sea, and forming a peninsula. It was destroyed by Sulla in the civil wars.

PORCIA (-ae) (1) Sister of Cato Uticensis, married L. Domitius Ahenobarbus, consul B.C. 54, who was slain in the battle of Pharsalia.—(2) Daughter of Cato Uticensis, married first to M. Bibulus, consul B.C. 59, and afterwards to M. Brutus, the assassin of Julius Caesar. She induced her husband on the night before the 15th of March to disclose to her the conspiracy against Caesar's life, and she is reported to have wounded herself in the thigh in order to show that she had a courageous soul, and could be trusted with the secret. She put an end to her own life after the death of Brutus in 42.

PORCIUS CATO. [CATO.]

PORCIUS FESTUS. [FESTUS.]

PORCIUS LATRO. [LATRO.]

PORCIUS LICINUS. [LICINUS.]

PORPHYRION (-onis), one of the giant who fought against the gods, slain by Zeus (Jupiter) and Hercules.

PORPHYRIUS (-i), usually called POR-PHYRY, a Greek philosopher of the Neo-

Platonic school, was born A.D. 233, either in Batanea in Palestine or at Tyre. His original name was *Malchus*, the Greek form of the Syrophoenician *Melech*, a word which signified king. He studied at Athens under Longinus, who changed his name into *Porphyrius* (in allusion to the usual colour of royal robes). He settled at Rome in his 30th year, and there became a disciple of Plotinus, whose writings he corrected and arranged. [PLOTINUS.] His most celebrated work was his treatise against the Christian religion, which was publicly destroyed by order of the emperor Theodosius.

PORSĒNA, PORSĒNA, or PORSENNA (-ae), LARS (-tis), king of the Etruscan town of Clusium, marched against Rome at the head of a vast army, in order to restore Tarquinius Superbus to the throne. He took possession of the hill Janiculum, and would have entered the city by the bridge which connected Rome with the Janiculum, had it not been for the superhuman prowess of Horatius Cocles. [COCLES.] He then proceeded to lay siege to the city, which soon began to suffer from famine. Thereupon a young Roman, named C. Mucius, resolved to deliver his country by murdering the invading king. He accordingly went over to the Etruscan camp, but ignorant of the person of Porsena, killed the royal secretary instead. Seized, and threatened with torture, he thrust his right hand into the fire on the altar, and there let it burn, to show how little he heeded pain. Astonished at his courage, the king bade him depart in peace; and Scaevola, as he was henceforward called, told him, out of gratitude, to make peace with Rome, since 300 noble youths had sworn to take the life of the king, and he was the first upon whom the lot had fallen. Porsena thereupon made peace with the Romans, and withdrew his troops from the Janiculum after receiving 20 hostages from the Romans. Such was the tale by which Roman vanity concealed one of the earliest and greatest disasters of the city. The real fact is, that Rome was completely conquered by Porsena, and compelled to pay tribute.

PORTŪNUS or PORTUMNUS (-i), the protecting genius of harbours among the Romans, identified with the Greek Palaemon. [PALAEMON.]

PŌRUS (-i). (1) King of the Indian provinces E. of the river Hydaspes, offered a formidable resistance to Alexander, when the latter attempted to cross this river, B.C. 327. He was conquered by Alexander, and was afterwards received into his favour. We are told that Porus was a man of gigantic stature

—not less than five cubits in height; and that his personal strength and prowess in war were not less conspicuous than his valour.— (2) Another Indian monarch at the time of Alexander's expedition. His dominions were subdued by Hephaestion, and annexed to those of the preceding Porus, who was his kinsman.

POSEIDŌN, called NEPTŪNUS (-i) by the Romans, was the god of the Mediterranean sea. His name seems to be connected with πότος, πόντος, and ποταμός, according to which he is the god of the fluid element. He was a son of Cronos (Saturnus) and Rhea, whence he is called *Cronius*, and by Latin poets *Saturnius*. He was accordingly a brother of Zeus (Jupiter) and Hades (Pluto); and it was determined by lot that he should rule over the sea. Like his brothers and sisters, he was, after his birth, swallowed by his father Cronos, but thrown up again. In the Homeric poems Poseidon is described as equal to Zeus in dignity, but less powerful. He resents the attempts of Zeus to intimidate him; he even threatens his mightier brother, and once conspired with Hera (Juno) and Athena (Minerva) to put him in chains; but on other occasions we find him submissive to Zeus. The palace of Poseidon was in the depth of the sea near Aegae in Euboea, where he kept his horses with brazen hoofs and golden manes. With these horses he rides in a chariot over the waves of the sea, which become smooth as he approaches, while the monsters of the deep play around his chariot. Poseidon in conjunction with Apollo is said to have built the walls of Troy for Laomedon, whence Troy is called *Neptunia Pergama*. Laomedon refused to give these gods the reward which had been stipulated, and even dismissed them with threats. Poseidon in consequence sent a marine monster, which was on the point of devouring Laomedon's daughter, when it was killed by Hercules. He continued to bear an implacable hatred against the Trojans, and he sided with the Greeks in the war against their city. In the Odyssey, he appears hostile to Ulysses, whom he prevents from returning home in consequence of his having blinded Polyphemus, a son of Poseidon by the nymph Thoosa. He is said to have created the horse, when he disputed with Athena as to which of them should give name to the capital of Attica. [ATHENA.] He was accordingly believed to have taught men the art of managing horses by the bridle, and to have been the originator and protector of horse races. He even metamorphosed himself into a horse, for the purpose of deceiving Demeter (Ceres). Poseidon was married to Amphitrite, by whom he had three children, Triton, Rhode, and Benthesicyme ; but he had also a vast number of children by other divinities and mortal women. The sacrifices offered to him generally consisted of black and white bulls ; but wild boars and rams were also sacrificed to him. Horse and chariot races were held in his honour on the Corinthian isthmus. The symbol of Poseidon's power was the trident, or a spear with three points, with which he used to shatter rocks, to call forth or subdue storms, to shake the earth, and the like. In works of art, Poseidon may be easily recognised by his attributes—the dolphin, the horse, or the trident, and he is frequently represented in groups along with Amphitrite, Tritons, Nereids, dolphins, &c. The Roman god NEPTUNUS is spoken of in a separate article.

Poseidon (Neptunus).   (Coin of Hadrian.)

PŌSĪDŌNĬA. [PAESTUM.]

PŌSĪDŌNĬUS (-i), a distinguished stoic philosopher, born at Apamea in Syria, about B.C. 135. He studied at Athens under Panaetius, and taught at Rhodes with great success. He gave instruction to Cicero, and numbered Pompey among his friends. In B.C. 51 Posidonius removed to Rome, and died soon after, at the age of 84.

POSTŬMĬUS. [ALBINUS.]

POSTŬMUS (-i), assumed the title of emperor in Gaul, A.D. 258, and reigned till 267, when he was slain by his soldiers.

POSTVERTA or POSTVORTA (-ae), a Roman goddess, presiding over childbirth.

PŌTENTĬA (-ae), a town of Picenum, on the river Flosis.

PŌTĪDAEA (-ae), a town in Macedonia, on the narrow isthmus of the peninsula Pallene, was a colony of the Corinthians. It afterwards became tributary to Athens, and its revolt from the latter city, in B.C. 432, was one of the immediate causes of the Pelopon-

nesian war. It was taken by the Athenians in 429, after a siege of more than 2 years, its inhabitants expelled, and their place supplied by Athenian colonists. In 356 it was taken by Philip, who destroyed the city and gave its territory to the Olynthians. Cassander built a new city on the same site, to which he gave the name of Cassandrëa, and which soon became the most flourishing city in all Macedonia.

PŌTĪTĬI. [PINARIA GENS.]

POTNĬAE (-ārum), a small town in Boeotia, on the Asopus. The adjective Potniades (sing. Potnias) is an epithet frequently given to the mares which tore to death Glaucus of Potniae. [GLAUCUS, No. 1.]

PRAENESTE (-is: Palestrina), one of the most ancient towns of Latium, situated on a steep and lofty hill, about 20 miles S.E. of Rome. It was said to have been founded by Telegonus, the son of Ulysses. It was strongly fortified by nature and by art, and frequently resisted the attacks of the Romans. Together with the other Latin towns, it became subject to Rome, and was at a later period made a Roman colony. It was here that the younger Marius took refuge, and was besieged by Sulla's troops. Praeneste possessed a celebrated temple of Fortuna, with an oracle, which is often mentioned under the name of Praenestīnae sortes. In consequence of its lofty situation, Praeneste was a cool and healthy residence in the great heats of summer (hence frigidum Praeneste, in Horace).

PRAETŌRĬA AUGUSTA. [AUGUSTA, No.4.]

PRASĬI (-ōrum), a great and powerful people of India, on the Ganges, governed at the time of Seleucus I. by king SANDROCOTTUS. Their capital city was Palibothra (Patna).

PRATĪNAS (-ae), one of the early tragic poets at Athens, and a contemporary of Aeschylus.

PRAXĬTĔLĒS (-is), one of the most distinguished sculptors of Greece, flourished about B.C. 364 and onwards. He was a citizen, if not a native, of Athens. He stands, with Scopas, at the head of the later Attic school, so called in contradistinction to the earlier Attic school of Phidias. Without attempting those sublime impersonations of divine majesty, in which Phidias had been so inimitably successful, Praxiteles was unsurpassed in the exhibition of the softer beauties of the human form, especially in the female figure. His most celebrated work was a marble statue of Aphrodite (Venus), which was distinguished from other statues of the goddess by the name of the Cnidians, who purchased it.

PRĬĀMĬDĒS or PRĬĀMĬDĒS (-ae), that is, a son of Priam, by which name Hector, Paris,

Helenus, Deiphobus, and the other sons of Priam, are frequently called.

PRIAMUS (-i), the famous king of Troy, at the time of the Trojan war, was a son of Laomedon. His original name was Podarces, *i.e.* "the swift-footed," which was changed into Priamus, "the ransomed," (from *πρίαμαι*), because he was ransomed by his sister Hesione, after he had fallen into the hands of Hercules. He was first married to Arisba, and afterwards to Hecuba. According to Homer he was the father of 50 sons, 19 of whom were children of Hecuba. In the earlier part of his reign, Priam supported the Phrygians in their war against the Amazons. When the Greeks landed on the Trojan coast, Priam was advanced in years, and took no active part in the war. Once only did he venture upon the field of battle, to conclude the agreement respecting the single combat between Paris and Menelaus. After the death of Hector, Priam went to the tent of Achilles to ransom his son's body for burial, and obtained it. Upon the capture of Troy, he was slain by Pyrrhus, the son of Achilles.

PRIAPUS (-i). (1) Son of Dionysus (Bacchus) and Aphroditē (Venus), was born at

Priapus. (Visconti, Mus. Pio. Clem., vol. 1, pl. 50.)

Lampsacus, on the Hellespont, whence he is sometimes called *Hellespontiacus.* He was regarded as the god of fruitfulness, in gene-

ral, and was worshipped as the protector of flocks of sheep and goats, of bees, of the vine, and of all garden produce. He was represented in carved images, mostly in the form of hermae, carrying fruit in his garment, and either a sickle or cornucopia in his hand.—(2) A city of Mysia, on the Propontis, E. of Parium, a colony of the Milesians, and a seat of the worship of the god Priapus.

PRIĒNĒ (-es), one of the 12 Ionian cities on the coast of Asia Minor, stood in the N.W. corner of Caria, at the foot of Mt. Mycale. It was the birthplace of Bias, one of the Seven Sages of Greece.

PRIMUS, M. ANTŌNIUS (-i), a general of Vespasian, who gained a victory over the Vitellian army at Bedriacum, A.D. 69.

PRISCIĀNUS (-i), a Roman grammarian, flourished about A.D. 450, and taught grammar at Constantinople. Several of his grammatical works are extant.

PRISCUS, HELVIDIUS (-i), son-in-law of Thrasea Paetus, distinguished by his love of virtue, philosophy, and liberty, was put to death by Vespasian.

PRIVERNUM (-i), an ancient town of Latium, on the river Amasenus.

PRŌBUS, AEMILIUS. [NEPOS, CORNELIUS.]

PRŌBUS, M. AURĒLIUS (-i), Roman emperor A.D. 276—282, was the successor of Tacitus. During his reign he gained many brilliant victories over the barbarians on the frontiers of Gaul and Illyricum, and in other parts of the Roman empire. He was killed in a mutiny of his own soldiers.

PRŌCAS (-ae), one of the fabulous kings of Alba Longa, father of Numitor and Amulius.

PRŌCHYTA (-ae : *Procida*), an island off the coast of Campania, near the promontory Misenum.

PROCLĒS, one of the twin sons of Aristodemus. [EURYSTHENES.]

PROCLUS (-i), one of the most celebrated teachers of the Neo-Platonic school, was born at Byzantium A.D. 412, and died A.D. 485. He laid claim to the possession of miraculous power, and his philosophical system is characterised by vagueness and mysticism. Several of his works are still extant.

PROCNĒ (-es), daughter of king Pandion of Athens, and wife of Tereus. [TEREUS.]

PRŌCONNĒSUS (-i : *Marmara*), an island of the Propontis which takes from it its modern name (*Sea of Marmara*) off the N. coast of Mysia, N.W. of the peninsula of Cyzicus or Dolionis. The island was celebrated for its marble ; and hence its modern name.

PROCRIS (-is), daughter of Erechtheus and wife of Cephalus. [CEPHALUS.]

PROCRUSTĒS (-ae), that is, "the Stretcher," a surname of the famous robber l;clypemon or Damastes. He used to tie all travellers who fell into his hands upon a bed : if they were shorter than the bed, he stretched their limbs till they were of the same length ; if they were longer than the bed, he made them of the same size by cutting off some of their limbs. He was slain by Theseus.

PROCULEIUS, C., a Roman eques, one of the friends of Augustus, is said to have divided his property with his brothers (perhaps cousins) Caepio and Murena, who had lost their property in the civil wars.

PROCULUS (-i), the jurist, was the contemporary of the jurist Nerva the younger, who was probably the father of the emperor Nerva. The fact that Proculus gave his name to the school or sect (*Proculiani* or *Proculeiani*), which was opposed to that of the Sabiniani, shows that he was a jurist of note.

PROCULUS, JULIUS (-i), a Roman senator, is said to have informed the Roman people, after the death of Romulus, that their king had appeared to him, and bade him tell the people to honour him in future as a god under the name of Quirinus.

PRODICUS (-i), a celebrated sophist, was a native of Iulis in the island of Ceos, and lived in the time of the Peloponnesian war and subsequently. He frequently visited Athens.

PROETIDES. [PROETUS.]

PROETUS (-i), son of Abas and Ocalea, and twin-brother of Acrisius. In the dispute between the 2 brothers for the kingdom of Argos, Proetus was expelled, whereupon he fled to Iobates in Lycia, and married Antea or Sthenoboea, the daughter of the latter. With the assistance of Iobates, Proetus returned to his native land ; and Acrisius gave him a share of his kingdom, surrendering to him Tiryns, Midea, and the coast of Argolis. Proetus had 3 daughters, Lysippe, Iphinoë, and Iphianassa, who are often mentioned under the general name of PROETIDES. When these daughters arrived at the age of maturity, they were stricken with madness, either from despising the worship of Dionysus (Bacchus), or from presuming to compare their beauty with that of Hera (Juno). [MELAMPUS.] The frenzy spread to the other women of Argos ; till at length Proetus agreed to divide his kingdom between Melampus and his brother Bias, upon the former promising that he would cure the women of their madness. Proetus also plays a prominent part in the story of Bellerophon. [BELLEROPHON.]—According to Ovid, Acrisius was expelled from his kingdom by Proetus ; and Perseus, the grandson of Acrisius, avenged his grandfather by turning Proe-

tus into stone by means of the head of Medusa.

PROMETHEUS (-ĕŏs or -ĕī), son of the Titan Iapetus and Clymene, and brother of Atlas, Menoetius, and Epimetheus. His name signifies "forethought," as that of his brother Epimetheus denotes "afterthought." He is represented as the great benefactor of men in spite of Zeus (Jupiter). He stole fire from heaven in a hollow tube, and taught mortals

Prometheus. (Bellorii, Ant. Lucern. Sepolc. tav. 2.)

all useful arts. In order to punish men, Zeus gave Pandora as a present to Epimetheus, in consequence of which diseases and sufferings of every kind befell mortals. [PANDORA.] He also chained Prometheus to a rock on Mt. Caucasus, where in the daytime an eagle consumed his liver, which was restored in each succeeding night. Prometheus was thus exposed to perpetual torture ; but Hercules killed the eagle and delivered the sufferer, with the consent of Zeus, who in this way had an opportunity of allowing his son to gain immortal fame. There was also a legend, which related that Prometheus created man out of earth and water. He is said to have given to men a portion of all the qualities possessed by the other animals.

PRONUBA (-ae), a surname of Juno among the Romans, describing her as the deity presiding over marriage.

PROPERTIUS (-i), SEX. AURELIUS, the Roman poet, was a native of Umbria, and was born about B.C. 51. He began to write poetry at a very early age, and the merit of his productions attracted the attention and patronage of Maecenas. The year of his death is unknown. Propertius is one of the principal of the Roman elegiac poets.

PROPONTIS (-Idis : *Sea of Marmara*), so called from its position with reference to the Pontus (Euxinus), being πρὸ τοῦ Πόντου, "before the Pontus," is the small sea uniting the Euxine and the Aegaean, and dividing

Europe (Thracia) from Asia (Mysia and Bithynia).

PRŌSERPĬNA. [PERSEPHONE.]

PRŌTĀGŌRĀS (-ae), a celebrated sophist, was born at Abdēra, in Thrace, probably about B.C. 480, and died about 411, at the age of nearly 70 years. He was the first who called himself a sophist, and taught for pay ; and he practised his profession for the space of 40 years. His instructions were so highly valued that he sometimes received 100 minae from a pupil ; and Plato says that Protagoras made more money than Phidias and 10 other sculptors. In 411 he was accused of impiety by Pythodorus, one of the Four Hundred. His impeachment was founded on his book on the gods, which began with the statement : " Respecting the gods, I am unable to know whether they exist or do not exist." The impeachment was followed by his banishment, or, as others affirm, only by the burning of his book.

PROTĒSĬLĀUS (-i), son of Iphiclus and Astyoche, was a native of Phylace in Thessaly. He is called *Phylacius* and *Phylacides*, either from that circumstance or from his being a grandson of Phylacus. He led the warriors of several Thessalian places against Troy, and was the first of all the Greeks who was killed by the Trojans, being the first who leaped from the ships upon the Trojan shore. According to the common tradition he was slain by Hector.

PRŌTEUS (-ĕŏs, ĕi, or ēi), the prophetic old man of the sea, is described in the earliest legends as a subject of Poseidon (Neptune), whose flocks (the seals) he tended. According to Homer he resided in the island of Pharos, at the distance of one day's journey from the river Aegyptus (Nile) ; whereas Virgil places his residence in the island of Carpathos, between Crete and Rhodes. At mid-day Proteus rose from the sea, and slept in the shade of the rocks, with the monsters of the deep lying around him. Any one wishing to learn futurity from him was obliged to catch hold of him at that time : as soon as he was seized, he assumed every possible shape, in order to escape the necessity of prophesying, but whenever he saw that his endeavours vere of no avail, he resumed his usual form, and told the truth. After finishing his prophecy he returned into the sea. Homer ascribes to him a daughter Idothea.— Another set of traditions describes Proteus as a son of Poseidon, and as a king of Egypt, who had two sòns, Telegonus and Polygonus or Tmolus.

PRŌTŌGĒNĒS (-is), a celebrated Greek painter. He was a native of Caunus, in Caria, a city subject to the Rhodians, and flourished B.C. 332—300. He resided at Rhodes almost entirely ; the only other city of Greece which he is said to have visited is Athens, where he executed one of his great works in the Propylaea. Up to his 50th year he is said to have lived in poverty and in comparative obscurity. His fame had, however, reached the ears of Apelles, who, as the surest way of making the merits of Protogenes known to his fellow-citizens, offered him for his finished works the enormous sum of 50 talents *a piece*, and thus led the Rhodians to understand what an artist they had among them.

PROXĔNUS (-i), a Boeotian, was a disciple of Gorgias, and a friend of Xenophon.

PRŪSA or PRŪSĬAS (-ae). (1) A great city of Bithynia, on the N. side of Mt. Olympus, 15 Roman miles from Cius and 25 from Nicaea. —(2) Some writers distinguish from this a smaller city, which stood N.W. of the former, and was originally called CIERUS.

PRŪSĬAS (-ae). (1) King of Bithynia from about B.C. 228 to 180. He was the son of Zielas, whom he succeeded. He appears to have been a monarch of vigour and ability, and raised his kingdom of Bithynia to a much higher pitch of power and prosperity than it had previously attained. He basely surrendered Hannibal, who had taken refuge at his court, to the Romans ; but who escaped falling into the hands of his enemies by a voluntary death.—(2) The son and successor of the preceding, reigned from about 180 to 149. He courted assiduously the alliance of the Romans. He carried on war with Attalus, king of Pergamus, with whom, however, he was compelled by the Romans to conclude peace in 154.

PSAMMENITUS (-i), king of Egypt, succeeded his father Amasis in B.C. 526, and reigned only 6 months. He was conquered by Cambyses in 525, and his country made a province of the Persian empire.

PSAMMIS, king of Egypt, succeeded his father Necho, and reigned from B.C. 601 to 595.

PSAMMĬTĬCHUS or PSAMMĔTĬCHUS (-i), a king of Egypt, and founder of the Saitic dynasty, reigned from B.C. 671 to 617. He was originally one of the 12 kings who obtained an independent sovereignty in the confusion which followed the death of Setho. Having been driven into banishment by the other kings, he took refuge in the marshes : but shortly afterwards, with the aid of some Ionian and Carian pirates, he conquered the other kings, and became sole ruler of Egypt. The employment of foreign mercenaries by Psammitichus gave great offence to the military caste in Egypt; and being indignant at other treatment which they received from him, they emigrated in a body of 240,000 men, into Ethiopia, where settlements were assigned to them by the Ethiopian king.

PSŌPHIS (-idis: *Khan of Tripotamo*), a town in the N.W. of Arcadia, on the river Erymanthus, is said to have been originally called PHEGIA.

PSȲCHĒ (-ēs), "the soul," occurs in the later times of antiquity, as a personification of the human soul. Psyche was the youngest of the 3 daughters of a king, and excited by her beauty the jealousy and envy of Venus. In order to avenge herself, the goddess ordered Cupid or Amor to inspire Psyche with a love for the most contemptible of all men: but Cupid was so stricken with her beauty that he himself fell in love with her. He accordingly conveyed her to a charming spot, where unseen and unknown, he visited her every night, and left her as soon as the day began to dawn. But her jealous sisters made her believe that in the darkness of night she was embracing some hideous monster, and accordingly once, while Cupid was asleep, she drew near to him with a lamp, and, to her amazement, beheld the most handsome and lovely of the gods. In the excitement of joy and fear, a drop of hot oil fell from her lamp upon his shoulder. This awoke Cupid, who censured her for her mistrust, and fled. Psyche's happiness was now gone, and after attempting in vain to

Psyche. (From an ancient Gem.)

throw herself into a river, she wandered about from temple to temple, inquiring after her lover, and at length came to the palace

of Venus. There her real sufferings began, for Venus retained her, treated her as a slave, and imposed upon her the hardest and most humiliating labours. Psyche would have perished under the weight of her sufferings, had not Cupid, who still loved her in secret, invisibly comforted and assisted her in her toils. With his aid she at last succeeded in overcoming the jealousy and hatred of Venus: she became immortal, and was united to him for ever. In this pleasing story Psyche evidently represents the human soul, which is purified by passions and misfortunes, and thus prepared for the enjoyment of true and pure happiness. In works of art Psyche is represented as a maiden with the wings of a butterfly, along with Cupid in the different situations described in the allegory.

PSYLLI (-ōrum), a Libyan people, the earliest known inhabitants of the district of N. Africa called Cyrenaica.

PSYTTALĒA. [SALAMIS.]

PTELĒUM (-i). (1) (*Ptelia*), an ancient seaport town of Thessaly in the district Phthiotis, at the S.W. extremity of the Sinus Pagasaeus, was destroyed by the Romans.— (2) A town in Elis Triphylia, said to have been a colony from the preceding.—(3) A fortress of Ionia, on the coast of Asia Minor, belonging to Erythrae.

PTŎLĔMAEUS (-i), usually called PTO-LEMY, the name of several kings of Egypt. I. surnamed SOTER, the Preserver, but more commonly known as the son of Lagus, reigned B.C. 323—285. His father Lagùs was a Macedonian of ignoble birth, but his mother Arsinoë had been a concubine of Philip of Macedon, on which account it seems to have been generally believed that Ptolemy was in reality the offspring of that monarch. Ptolemy accompanied Alexander throughout his campaigns in Asia, and on the division of the empire which followed Alexander's death (323), obtained the government of Egypt. He afterwards enlarged his dominions by seizing upon the important satrapy of Phoe-nicia and Coele-Syria, and made himself master of Jerusalem, by attacking the city on the Sabbath day. These provinces he lost, but again recovered in a war with Antigonus and his son Demetrius. Ptolemy subse-quently crossed over to Greece, where he announced himself as the liberator of the Greeks, but he effected little. In 306 he was defeated by Demetrius in a great sea fight off Salamis in Cyprus, by which he lost that important island. Next year (305) Ptolemy rendered the most important assistance to the Rhodians, who were besieged by Demetrius; and when Demetrius was at length compelled to raise the siege (304), the Rhodians paid divine honours to the Egyptian monarch as their saviour and preserver (*Soter*). The latter years of Ptolemy's reign appear to have been devoted almost entirely to the arts of peace, and in 285 he abdicated in favour of his youngest son Ptolemy Philadelphus. He survived this event 2 years, and died in 283. The character of Ptolemy does not merit unqualified praise ; but he distinguished himself as a ruler, and as a patron of literature and science. He is thought to have founded the Library and the Museum of Alexandria. Many men of literary eminence were gathered around the Egyptian king : among whom may be especially noticed Demetrius of Phalerus, the great geometer Euclid, the philosophers Stilpo of Megara, Theodorus of Cyrene, and Diodorus surnamed Cronus ; as well as the elegiac poet Philetas of Cos, and the grammarian Zenodotus. Ptolemy was himself an author, and composed a history of the wars of Alexander.—II. PHILADELPHUS (B.C. 285 —247), the son of Ptolemy I. by his wife Berenice, was born in the island of Cos, 309. His long reign was marked by few events of a striking character. He was long engaged in war with his half-brother Magas, for the possession of the Cyrenaïca, which he eventually ceded to Magas. Ptolemy also concluded a treaty with the Romans. He was frequently engaged in hostilities with Syria, which were terminated towards the close of his reign by a treaty of peace, by which Ptolemy gave his daughter Berenice in marriage to Antiochus II. Ptolemy's chief care, however, was directed to the internal administration of his kingdom, and to the patronage of literature and science. Under him the Museum of Alexandria became the resort and abode of all the most distinguished men of letters of the day, and in the library attached to it were accumulated all the treasures of ancient learning. According to a well-known tradition, it was by his express command that the Holy Scriptures of the Jews were translated into Greek. The new cities or colonies founded by him in different parts of his dominions were extremely numerous. All authorities concur in attesting the great power and wealth to which the Egyptian monarchy was raised under Philadelphus ; but his private life and relations do not exhibit his character in as favourable a light as we might have inferred from the splendour of his administration.— III. EUERGETES (B.C. 247—222), eldest son and successor of Philadelphus. Shortly after his accession he invaded Syria, in order to avenge the death of his sister Berenice. He advanced as far as Babylon and Susa, and after reducing all Mesopotamia, Babylonia, and

Susiana, received the submission of all the upper provinces of Asia as far as the confines of Bactria and India. From this career of conquest he was recalled by the news of seditions in Egypt, and returned to that country, carrying with him an immense booty, comprising, among other objects, all the statues of the Egyptian deities which had been carried off by Cambyses to Babylon or Persia, and which he restored to their respective temples. Hence he obtained the title of Euergetes (the Benefactor). His fleets were equally successful ; but it appears that the greater part of the eastern provinces speedily fell again into the hands of Seleucus, while Ptolemy retained possession of the maritime regions and a great part of Syria itself. During the latter years of his reign he subdued the Ethiopian tribes on his southern frontier, and advanced as far as Adule, a port on the Red Sea. Ptolemy Euergetes is scarcely less celebrated than his father for his patronage of literature and science.—IV. PHILOPATOR (B.C. 222—205), eldest son and successor of Euergetes, was very far from inheriting the virtues or abilities of his father : and his reign was the commencement of the decline of the Egyptian kingdom. Its beginning was stained with crimes of the darkest kind. He put to death his mother Berenice, his brother Magas, and his uncle Lysimachus, and then gave himself up without restraint to a life of indolence and luxury, while he abandoned to his minister Sosibius the care of all political affairs. Antiochus the Great, king of Syria, availed himself of this state of disorder, and conquered the greater part of Coele-Syria and Palestine, but in the 3rd year of the war (217), he was completely defeated by Ptolemy in person at the decisive battle of Raphia. On his return from his Syrian expedition, Ptolemy gave himself up more and more to every species of vice and debauchery, and thus shortened his life. He died in 205. Like his predecessors, he encouraged philosophers and men of letters, and especially patronised the distinguished grammarian Aristarchus. — V. EPIPHANES (B.C. 205—181), son and successor of Ptolemy IV. He was a child of 5 years old at the death of his father, 205. Philip king of Macedonia and Antiochus III. of Syria, took advantage of the minority of Ptolemy, and entered into a league to divide his dominions between them. In pursuance of this arrangement, Antiochus conquered Coele-Syria, while Philip reduced the Cyclades and the cities in Thrace which had still remained subject to Egypt ; but the Romans commanded both monarchs to refrain from further hostilities, and restore all the conquered cities. In 196 the young king was declared of age, and the ceremony of his Anacleteria, or coronation, was solemnised with great magnificence, on which occasion the decree was issued which has been preserved to us in the celebrated inscription known as the Rosetta stone. As long as Ptolemy continued under the guidance and influence of Aristomenes, his administration was equitable and popular. Gradually, however, he became estranged from his able and virtuous minister, and at length compelled him to take poison. Towards the close of his reign Ptolemy conceived the project of recovering Coele-Syria from Seleucus, the successor of Antiochus, as the latter monarch had not restored that province, according to treaty, when Ptolemy married his daughter, Cleopatra. But having, by an unguarded expression, excited the apprehensions of some of his friends, he was cut off by poison in the 24th year of his reign and the 29th of his age, 181. His reign was marked by the rapid decline of the Egyptian monarchy, and at his death Cyprus and the Cyrenaïca were almost the only foreign possessions still attached to the crown of Egypt. —VI. PHILOMETOR (B.C. 181—146), eldest son and successor of Ptolemy V. He was a child at the death of his father in 181, and the regency was assumed during his minority by his mother Cleopatra. After her death, in 173, his ministers had the rashness to engage in war with Antiochus Epiphanes, king of Syria, in the vain hope of recovering the provinces of Coele-Syria and Phoenicia. But their army was totally defeated by Antiochus, near Pelusium, and Antiochus advanced as far as Memphis, 170. The young king himself fell into his hands, but was treated with kindness and distinction, as Antiochus hoped by his means to make himself the master of Egypt. But being unable to take Alexandria, which was defended by Ptolemy's younger brother, Antiochus withdrew into Syria, after establishing Philometor as king at Memphis, but retaining in his hands the frontier fortress of Pelusium. This last circumstance, together with the ravages committed by the Syrian troops, awakened Philometor, who had hitherto been a mere puppet in the hands of the Syrian king, to a sense of his true position, and he hastened to make overtures of peace to his brother, who during Ptolemy's captivity had assumed the title of king Euergetes II. It was agreed that the two brothers should reign together, and that Philometor should marry his sister Cleopatra. Upon this Antiochus advanced a second time to the walls of Alexandria, but withdrew to his own dominions, 168, at the command of M. Popillius Laenas, the Roman ambassador. Dissensions soon broke out between the two brothers, and Euergetes expelled Philometor from Alexandria. Hereupon Philometor repaired in person to Rome, 164, where he was received by the senate with the utmost honour, and deputies were appointed to reinstate him in the sovereign power. The remainder of his reign was chiefly occupied with Syrian affairs. In 146 he gained a decisive victory over Alexander Balas, but died a few days afterwards, in consequence of a fall from his horse during the battle. He had reigned 35 years from the period of his first accession, and 18 from his restoration by the Romans. Philometor is praised for the mildness and humanity of his disposition, and if not one of the greatest, he was at least one of the best of the race of the Ptolemies.—VII. EUERGETES II. or PHYSCON, that is *Big-Belly*, reigned B.C. 146 — 117. In order to secure undisputed possession of the throne, he married his sister Cleopatra, the widow of his brother Philometor, and put to death his nephew Ptolemy, who had been proclaimed king under the surname of Eupator. A reign thus commenced in blood was continued in a similar spirit. Many of the leading citizens of Alexandria, who had taken part against him on the death of his brother, were put to death, and the streets of the city were repeatedly deluged with blood. At the same time that he thus incurred the hatred of his subjects by his cruelties, he rendered himself an object of their aversion and contempt by abandoning himself to the most degrading vices. He became enamoured of his niece Cleopatra (the offspring of his wife by her former marriage with Philometor), and he did not hesitate to divorce the mother, and receive her daughter instead, as his wife and queen. By this proceeding he alienated still more the minds of his Greek subjects; and his vices and cruelties at length produced an insurrection at Alexandria. Thereupon he fled to Cyprus, and the Alexandrians declared his sister Cleopatra queen (130). Enraged at this, Ptolemy put to death Memphitis, his son by Cleopatra, and sent his head and hands to his unhappy mother. But Cleopatra having been shortly afterwards expelled from Alexandria in her turn, Ptolemy found himself unexpectedly reinstated on the throne (127). He died after reigning 29 years from the death of his brother Philometor. Although the character of Ptolemy Physcon was stained by the most infamous vices, and by the most sanguinary cruelty, he still retained that love of letters which appears to have been hereditary in the whole race of the Ptolemies.—VIII. Soter II., and also Philometor, but more commonly called Lathyrus or Lathurus, reigned B.C. 117—107, and also 89—81. Although he was of full age at the time of his father's death (117), he was obliged to reign jointly with his mother, Cleopatra, who had been appointed by the will of her late husband to succeed him on the throne. After reigning 10 years, he was expelled from Alexandria by an insurrection of the people, which she had excited against him (107). His brother Alexander now assumed the sovereignty of Egypt, in conjunction with his mother, and reigned for 18 years. After the death of Cleopatra and the expulsion of Alexander in 89, Ptolemy Lathyrus, who had established himself at Cyprus, was recalled by the Alexandrians, and established anew on the throne of Egypt, which he occupied thenceforth without interruption till his death in 81. The most important event of this period was the revolt of Thebes, in Upper Egypt, which was taken after a 3 years' siege, and reduced to the state of ruin in which it has ever since remained. —IX. Alexander I., youngest son of Ptolemy VII., reigned conjointly with his mother Cleopatra from the expulsion of his brother Lathyrus, B.C. 107 to 90. In this year he assassinated his mother; but he had not reigned alone a year, when he was compelled by a general sedition of the populace and military to quit Alexandria.—X. Alexander II., son of the preceding, put to death by the Alexandrians shortly after his accession.— XI. Dionysus, but more commonly known by the appellation of Auletes, the flute-player, an illegitimate son of Ptolemy Lathyrus, was on the death of Alexander II. proclaimed king by the Alexandrians, B.C. 80. To obtain the ratification of his title from the Romans, he expended immense sums, which he was compelled to raise by the imposition of fresh taxes, and the discontent thus excited combining with the contempt entertained for his character, led to his expulsion by the Alexandrians, in 58. Thereupon he proceeded in person to Rome to solicit assistance; but it was not till 55 that A. Gabinius, proconsul in Syria, was induced, by the influence of Pompey, aided by the enormous bribe of 10,000 talents from Ptolemy himself, to undertake his restoration. One of his first acts was to put to death his daughter Berenice (whom the Alexandrians had placed on the throne) and many of the leading citizens of Alexandria. He died in 51, after a reign of 29 years from the date of his first accession. —XII. Eldest son of the preceding. By his father's will the sovereign power was left to

himself and his sister Cleopatra jointly; but the latter was expelled by the minister Pothinus after she had reigned in conjunction with her brother about 3 years. Hereupon she took refuge in Syria, and assembled an army, with which she invaded Egypt. Shortly after, Caesar arrived in Egypt, and as Cleopatra's charms gained her his support, Pothinus determined to excite an insurrection against him. Hence arose what is usually called the Alexandrian war. Ptolemy, who was at first in Caesar's hands, managed to escape, and put himself at the head of the insurgents, but he was defeated by Caesar, and was drowned in an attempt to escape by the river (47).—XIII. Youngest son of Ptolemy Auletes, was declared king by Caesar in conjunction with Cleopatra, after the death of his elder brother; but in 43 Cleopatra put him to death.—*Kings of other Countries:* (1) Ptolemy, surnamed Alorites, that is, of Alorus, regent, or, according to some authors, king of Macedonia, assassinated by Perdiccas III., 364.—(2) Surnamed Apion, king of Cyrene (117—96), an illegitimate son of Ptolemy Physcon, king of Egypt.—(3) Surnamed Ceraunus, son of Ptolemy I., king of Egypt, assassinated Seleucus (280) and took possession of the Macedonian throne. After reigning a few months he was defeated in battle by the Gauls, taken prisoner, and put to death.—(4) Tetrarch of Chalcis, in Syria, reigned from about 70 to 40.—(5) King of Cyprus, the younger brother of Ptolemy Auletes, king of Egypt, put an end to his own life, 57.—(6) King of Epirus, the 2nd son of Alexander II. The date of his reign cannot be fixed with certainty, but it may be placed between 239—229.—(7) King of Mauretania, was the son and successor of Juba II. By his mother Cleopatra he was descended from the kings of Egypt, whose name he bore. He reigned from A.D. 18, or earlier, till A.D. 40, when he was summoned to Rome by Caligula, and shortly after put to death.

PTOLEMAEUS (-i), CLAUDIUS, a celebrated mathematician, astronomer, and geographer. Of Ptolemy himself we know absolutely nothing but his date. He certainly observed in A.D. 139, at Alexandria; and since he survived Antoninus he was alive A.D. 161. His *Geography*, in 8 books, is his most celebrated work.

PTOLEMAIS (-idis). (1) Also called Ace (in O. T. Acco: Arab. *Akka*, Fr. *St. Jean d'Acre*, Eng. *Acre*), a celebrated city on the coast of Phoenicia, S. of Tyre, and N. of Mt. Carmel, lies at the bottom of a bay surrounded by mountains, in a position marked out by nature as a key of the passage between Coele-Syria and Palestine. It is one of the oldest cities of Phoenicia, being mentioned in the Book of Judges (i. 31).—(2) (At or near *El-Lahum*), a small town of Middle Egypt, in the Nomos Arsinoïtes.—(3) P. HERMII (*Menshieh*, Ru.), a city of Upper Egypt, on the W. bank of the Nile, below Abydos.—(4) P. THERON, or EPITHERAS, a port on the Red Sea, on the coast of the Troglodytae.—(5) (*Tolmeïta*, or *Tolometa*, Ru.), on the N.W. coast of Cyrenaica, one of the 5 great cities of the Libyan Pentapolis.

PUBLICOLA, or POPLICULA, or POPLICOLA (-ae), a Roman cognomen, signifying "one who courts the people" (from *populus* and *colo*), and thus "a friend of the people." The form *Poplicula* or *Poplicola* was the more ancient, but *Publicola* was the one usually employed by the Romans in later times. (1) P. VALERIUS PUBLICOLA, took an active part in expelling the Tarquins from the city, and was thereupon elected consul with Brutus (B.C. 509). He secured the liberties of the people by proposing several laws, and ordered the lictors to lower the fasces before the people, as an acknowledgment that their power was superior to that of the consuls. Hence he became so great a favourite with the people, that he received the surname of *Publicola*. He was consul 3 times again, namely in 508, 507, and 504. He died in 503.—(2) L. GELLIUS PUBLICOLA, consul with Cn. Lentulus Clodianus, B.C. 72. He belonged to the aristocratical party. In 63 he warmly supported Cicero in the suppression of the Catilinarian conspiracy.—(3) L. GELLIUS PUBLICOLA, son of the preceding, espoused the republican party and went with M. Brutus to Asia, but deserted to the triumvirs, Octavian and Antony, for which treachery he obtained the consulship in 36. In the war between Octavian and Antony, he espoused the side of the latter, and commanded the right wing of Antony's fleet at the battle of Actium.

PUBLILIA (-ae), the 2nd wife of M. Tullius Cicero, whom he married B.C. 46.

PUBLILIUS PHILO. [PHILO.]

PUBLILIUS, (-i), VOLERO (-ōnis), tribune of the plebs, B.C. 472, and again 471, effected an important change in the Roman constitution. In virtue of the laws which he proposed, the tribunes of the plebs and the aediles were elected by the comitia tributa, instead of by the comitia centuriata, as had previously been the case, and the tribes obtained the power of deliberating and determining in all matters affecting the whole nation, and not such only as concerned the plebs.

PUBLIUS SYRUS. [SYRUS.]

PUDICITIA (-ae), a personification of modesty, was worshipped both in Greece and

at Rome. At Athens an altar was dedicated to her. At Rome two sanctuaries were dedicated to her, one under the name of *Pudicitia patricia*, and the other under that of *Pudicitia plebeia*.

PULCHER, CLAUDIUS. [CLAUDIUS.]

PULCHRUM PROMONTORIUM (-i), a promontory on the N. coast of the Carthaginian territory in N. Africa, probably identical with the APOLLINIS PROMONTORIUM.

PUPIENUS MAXIMUS, M. CLODIUS (i-), was elected emperor with Balbinus, in A.D. 238, when the senate received intelligence of the death of the two Gordians in Africa ; but the new emperors were slain by the soldiers at Rome in the same year.

PUPIUS (-i), a Roman dramatist.

PURPURARIAE INSULAE (-ārum), (prob. the *Madeira* group), a group of islands in the Atlantic Ocean, off the N.W. coast of Africa.

PUTEOLANUM (-i), a country-house of Cicero near Puteoli, where he wrote his *Quaestiones Academicae*, and where the emperor Hadrian was buried.

PUTEOLANUS SINUS (-i : *Bay of Naples*), a bay of the sea on the coast of Campania between the promontory Misenum and the promontory of Minerva, which was originally called Cumanus.

PUTEOLI (-ōrum : *Pozzuoli*), originally named DICAEARCHIA, a celebrated seaport town of Campania, situated on a promontory on the E. side of the Puteolanus Sinus, and a little to the E. of Cumae, was founded by the Greeks of Cumae, B.C. 521, under the name of Dicaearchia. It obtained the name of Puteoli, either from its numerous wells or from the stench arising from the mineral springs in its neighbourhood. The town was indebted for its importance to its excellent harbour, which was protected by an extensive mole to which Caligula attached a floating bridge, which extended as far as Baiae, a distance of 2 miles. Puteoli was the chief emporium for the commerce with Alexandria and with the greater part of Spain. The town was colonised by the Romans in B.C. 194, and also anew by Augustus, Nero, and Vespasian. It was destroyed by Alaric in A.D. 410, by Genseric in 455, and also by Totilas in 545, but was on each occasion speedily rebuilt. There are still many ruins of the ancient town at the modern Pozzuoli.

PYDNA (-ae : *Kitron*), a town of Macedonia in the district Pieria, was situated at a small distance W. of the Thermaic gulf, on which it had a harbour. It was originally a Greek colony, but it was subdued by the Macedonian kings, from whom, however, it frequently revolted. It was subdued by Philip, who enlarged and fortified the place. It is especially memorable on account of the victory gained under its walls by Aemilius Paulus over Perseus, the last king of Macedonia, 168. Under the Romans it was also called Citrum or Citrus.

PYGĒLA or PHYGĒLA (-ae), a small town of Ionia, on the coast of Lydia.

PYGMAEI (-ōrum), *i.e. men of the height of a πυγμή*, i.e. 13½ inches, a fabulous people first mentioned by Homer, as dwelling on the shores of Ocean, and attacked by cranes in spring-time. Some writers place them in Aethiopia, others in India, and others in the extreme N. of the earth.

PYGMĀLĬON (-ōnis). (1) King of Cyprus. He is said to have fallen in love with the ivory image of a maiden which he himself had made, and to have prayed to Aphroditē (Venus) to breathe life into it. When the request was granted, Pygmalion married the maiden, and became by her the father of Paphus.—(2) Son of Belus and brother of Dido, who murdered Sichaeus, Æido's husband. [Dido.]

PŸLĂDES (-is). (1) Son of Strophius and Anaxibia, a sister of Agamemnon. His father was king of Phocis; and after the death of Agamemnon, Orestes was secretly carried to his father's court. Here Pylades contracted that friendship with Orestes, which became proverbial. He assisted Orestes in murdering his mother Clytaemnestra, and eventually married his sister Electra. [Orestes.]— (2) A pantomime dancer in the reign of Augustus.

PŸLAE (-ārum), a general name for any narrow pass, such as Thermopylae, Pylae Albaniae, Caspiae, &c.

PYLĒNĒ (-es), an ancient town of Aetolia near the coast, mentioned by Homer. The Aeolians who took Pylene afterwards removed higher up into the country and founded Proschium.

PŸLŎS (-i), the name of 3 towns on the W. coast of Peloponnesus. (1) In Elis, at the foot of Mt. Scollis, and about 70 or 80 stadia from the city of Elis on the road to Olympia, near the confluence of the Ladon and the Peneus.—(2) In Triphylia, about 30 stadia from the coast, on the river Mamaus, W. of the mountain Minthe, and N. of Lepreum.—(3) In the S.W. of Messenia, was situated at the foot of Mt. Aegaleos on a promontory at the N. entrance of the basin, now called the *Bay of Navarino*, the largest and safest harbour in all Greece. This harbour was fronted and protected by the small island of Sphacteria (*Sphagia*), which stretched along the coast about 1¾ mile, leaving only

2 narrow entrances at each end. Pylos became memorable in the Peloponnesian war, when the Athenians under Demosthenes built a fort on the promontory Coryphasium a little S. of the ancient city, and just within the N. entrance to the harbour (B.C. 425). The attempts of the Spartans to dislodge the Athenians proved unavailing; and the capture by Cleon of the Spartans, who had landed in the island of Sphacteria was one of the most important events in the whole war.

PŸRACMŌN. [Cyclopes.]

PŸRĂMUS. [Thisbe.]

PYRĂMUS (-i : *Jihan*), one of the largest rivers of Asia Minor, rises in the Anti-Taurus range, near Arabissus, in Cataonia (the S.E. part of Cappadocia), and after running S.E., first underground, and then as a navigable river, breaks through the Taurus chain by a deep and narrow ravine, and then flows S.W. through Cilicia, in a deep and rapid stream, about 1 stadium (606 feet) in width, and falls into the sea near Mallus.

PŸRĒNE (-es) or PŸRĒNAEI (-ōrum) MONTES (*Pyrenees*), a range of mountains, extending from the Atlantic to the Mediterranean, and forming the boundary between Gaul and Spain. The length of these mountains is about 270 miles in a straight line; their breadth varies from about 40 miles to 20; their greatest height is between 11,000 and 12,000 feet. The continuation of the mountains along the Mare Cantabricum was called Saltus Vasconum, and still further W. Mons Vindius or Vinnius.

PŸRĒNĒS PRŌMONTŌRĬUM, or PROM. VĒNĒRIS (*C. Creus*), the S.E. extremity of the Pyrenees in Spain, on the frontiers of Gaul, derived its 2nd name from a temple of Venus on the promontory.

PYRGI (-ōrum). (1) The most S.-ly town of Triphylia, in Elis, near the Messenian frontier, said to have been founded by the Minyae.—(2) (*Santa Severa*), an ancient Pelasgic town on the coast of Etruria, was used as the port of Caere or Agylla, and was a place of considerable importance as a commercial emporium.

PYRGŎTĒLES (-is), one of the most celebrated gem-engravers of ancient Greece, was a contemporary of Alexander the Great, who placed him on a level with Apelles and Lysippus, by naming him as the only artist who was permitted to engrave seal-rings for the king.

PŸRIPHLĔGĔTHON (-ontis), that is, flaming with fire, the name of one of the rivers in the lower world.

PYRRHA (-ae). (1) [Deucalion.]—(2) A town on the W. coast of the island of Lesbos, on the inner part of the deep bay named after it, and consequently on the narrowest part of the island. — (3) A town and promontory of Phthiotis, in Thessaly, on the Pagasaean gulf, and near the frontiers of Magnesia. Off this promontory there were 2 small islands named Pyrrha and Deucalion.

PYRRHO (-ōnis), the founder of the Sceptical or Pyrrhonian school of philosophy, was a native of Elis, in Peloponnesus. He is said to have been poor, and to have followed, at first, the profession of a painter. He is then said to have been attracted to philosophy by the books of Democritus, to have attended the lectures of Bryson, a disciple of Stilpon, to have attached himself closely to Anaxarchus, and with him to have joined the expedition of Alexander the Great. He asserted that certain knowledge on any subject was unattainable; and that the great object of man ought to be to lead a virtuous life. Pyrrho wrote no works, except a poem addressed to Alexander, which was rewarded by the latter in a royal manner. His philosophical system was first reduced to writing by his disciple Timon. He reached the age of 90 years; but we have no mention of the year either of his birth or of his death.

PYRRHUS (-i). (1) Mythological. [NEOPTOLEMUS.]—(2) I. King of Epirus, son of Aeacides and Phthia, was born B.C. 318, Cassander having prevailed upon the Epirots to expel their young king, Pyrrhus, who was only 17 years of age, accompanied his brother-in-law Demetrius to Asia, and was present at the battle of Ipsus, 301, in which he gained great renown for his valour. Afterwards he went as a hostage for Demetrius into Egypt, where he married Antigone, the daughter of Berenice. Ptolemy now supplied him with forces, with which he regained his kingdom (295). After this he made an attempt to conquer Macedonia, and actually obtained a share of the throne with Lysimachus, but was driven out of the country after a reign of 7 months (286). For the next few years Pyrrhus reigned quietly in Epirus; but in 280 he accepted the invitation of the Tarentines to assist them in their war against the Romans. He crossed over to Italy with a large army, and in the 1st campaign defeated the Roman consul, M. Valerius Laevinus, near Heraclea. The battle was long and bravely contested; and it was not till Pyrrhus brought forward his elephants, which bore down everything before them, that the Romans took to flight. The loss of Pyrrhus, though inferior to that of the Romans, was still very considerable. Hence he advanced within 24 miles of Rome; but as he found it impossible to compel the

Romans to accept peace, he retraced his steps, and withdrew into winter-quarters to Tarentum. In the 2nd campaign (279) Pyrrhus gained another victory near Asculum over the Romans, who were commanded by the consuls P. Decius Mus and P. Sulpicius Saverrio. The battle, however, was followed by no decisive results, and his forces were so much exhausted by it, that he lent a ready ear to the invitations of the Greeks in Sicily, who begged him to come to their assistance against the Carthaginians. He accordingly crossed over into Sicily, where he remained from the middle of 278 to the end of 276. At first he met with brilliant success, but having failed in an attempt upon Lilybaeum, he lost his popularity with the Greeks, who began to form cabals and plots against him. His position in Sicily at length became so uncomfortable and dangerous, that he returned to Italy in the autumn of 276. The following year he was defeated with great loss near Beneventum by the Roman consul Curius Dentatus, and obliged to leave Italy. He brought back with him to Epirus only 8000 foot and 500 horse, and had not money to maintain even these without undertaking new wars. He therefore invaded Macedonia, of which he became king a second time, and afterwards turned his arms against Sparta and Argos. In the last city he was killed (272) by a tile hurled by a woman from the house-top, in the 46th year of his age, and 23rd of his reign. Pyrrhus was the greatest warrior, and one of the best princes of his time.—(3) II. King of Epirus, son of Alexander II. and Olympias, and grandson of Pyrrhus I.

PYTHĀGŌRAS (-ae). (1) A celebrated Greek philosopher, a native of Samos, flourished in the times of Polycrates and Tarquinius Superbus (B.C. 540—510). He studied in his own country under Creophilus, Pherecydes of Syros, and others, and is said to have visited Egypt and many countries of the East for the purpose of acquiring knowledge. He believed in the transmigration of souls; and is said to have pretended that he had been Euphorbus, the son of Panthos, in the Trojan war, as well as various other characters. He paid great attention to arithmetic, and its application to weights, measures, and the theory of music. He pretended to divination and prophecy; and he appears as the revealer of a mode of life calculated to raise his disciples above the level of mankind, and to recommend them to the favour of the gods. Having settled at Crotona, in Italy, he formed a select brotherhood or club of 300, bound by a sort of vow to Pythagoras and each other, for the purpose of cultivating the religious and ascetic observances enjoined by their master, and of studying his religious and philosophical theories. It appears that they had some secret conventional symbols, by which members of the fraternity could recognise each other, and they were bound to secresy. But the populace of Crotona rose against them; the building in which they assembled was set on fire, and only the younger and more active members escaped. Similar commotions ensued in the other cities of Magna Graecia, in which Pythagorean clubs had been formed. Respecting the fate of Pythagoras himself, the accounts varied. Some say that he perished in the temple with his disciples; others that he fled first to Tarentum, and that, being driven thence, he escaped to Metapontum, and there starved himself to death.—(2) Of Rhegium, one of the most celebrated statuaries of Greece, probably flourished B.C. 480—430.

PȲTHĔAS (-ae). (1) An Athenian orator, distinguished by his unceasing animosity against Demosthenes.—(2) Of Massilia, in Gaul, a celebrated Greek navigator, who probably lived in the time of Alexander the Great, or shortly afterwards. He appears to have undertaken voyages, one in which he visited Britain and Thule, and a second in which he coasted along the whole of Europe from Gadira (*Cadiz*) to the Tanais, and the description of which probably formed the subject of his *Periplus*. Pytheas made Thule a 6 days' sail from Britain; and said that the day and the night were each 6 months long in Thule. Hence some modern writers have supposed that he must have reached Iceland; while others have maintained that he advanced as far as the Shetland Islands. But either supposition is very improbable.

PȲTHĬUS (-i), the Pythian, a surname of the Delphian Apollo. [PYTHON.]

PȲTHŌN (-ōnis), the celebrated serpent, which was produced from the mud left on the earth after the deluge of Deucalion. He lived in the caves of Mt. Parnassus, but was slain by Apollo, who founded the Pythian games in commemoration of his victory, and received in consequence the surname *Pythius*.

PYXUS. [BUXENTUM.]

QUADI, a powerful German people of the Suevic race, dwelt in the S.E. of Germany, between Mt. Gabreta, the Hercynian forest, the Sarmatian mountains, and the Danube. They were bounded on the W. by the Marcomanni, with whom they were always closely united, on the N. by the Gothini and Osi, on the E. by the Iazyges Metanastae, from whom they were separated by the river Granuas (*Gran*), and on the S. by the Pannonians, from whom they were divided by the Danube. In the reign of Tiberius, the Quadi were taken under the protection of the Romans. In the reign of M. Aurelius, however, they joined the Marcomanni and other German tribes in the long and bloody war against the empire, which lasted during the greater part of that emperor's reign. Their name is especially memorable in the history of this war by the victory which M. Aurelius gained over them in 174. The Quadi disappear from history towards the end of the 4th century.

QUADRĬFRONS (-ontis), a surname of Janus. It is said that after the conquest of the Faliscans an image of Janus was found with 4 foreheads. Hence a temple of Janus Quadrifrons was afterwards built in the Forum transitorium, which had 4 gates. The fact of the god being represented with 4 heads is considered by the ancients to be an indication of his being the divinity presiding over the year with its 4 seasons.

QUADRĪGĀRĬUS, Q. ·CLAUDĬUS (-i), a Roman historian who flourished B.C. 100—78. His work commenced immediately after the destruction of Rome by the Gauls, and must in all probability have come down to the death of Sulla.

QUINTĬLĬUS VĀRUS. [VARUS.]

QUINTĬLĬĀNUS, M. FABĬUS (-i), the most celebrated of Roman rhetoricians, was born at Calagurris (*Calahorra*), in Spain, A.D. 40. He completed his education at Rome, and began to practise at the bar about 68. But he was chiefly distinguished as a teacher of eloquence, ·bearing away the palm in this department from all his rivals, and associating his name, even to a proverb, with pre-eminence in the art. By Domitian he was invested with the insignia and title of consul (*consularia ornamenta*), and is, moreover, celebrated as the first public instructor, who, in virtue of the endowment by Vespasian, received a regular salary from the imperial exchequer. He is supposed to have died about 118. The great work of ·Quintilian is a complete system of rhetoric, in 12 books, entitled *De Institutione Oratoria Libri XII.*, or sometimes *Institutiones Oratoriae*, dedicated to his friend Marcellus Victorius, himself a celebrated orator, and a favourite at court. This production bears throughout the impress of a clear, sound judgment, keen discrimination, and pure taste, improved by extensive reading, deep reflection, and long practice. There are also extant 164 declamations under the name of Quintilian, but no one believes these to be the genuine productions of Quintilian, and few suppose that they proceeded from any one individual.

T. QUINTIUS CĂPITŌLĪNUS BARBĀTUS (-i), a celebrated general in the early history of the republic, and equally distinguished in the internal history of the state. He was six times consul, namely, in B.C. 471, 468, 465, 446, 443, 439.—Several of his descendants held the consulship, but none of these require mention except T. QUINTIUS PENNUS CAPITOLINUS CRISPINUS, who was consul 208, and was defeated by Hannibal.

QUINTIUS CINCINNĀTUS. [CINCINNATUS.]

QUINTIUS FLAMĬNĪNUS. [FLAMININUS.]

QUINTUS CURTIUS. [CURTIUS.]

QUINTUS SMYRNAEUS (-i), commonly called QUINTUS CALABER, author of a Greek epic poem on the events of the Trojan war from the death of Hector to the return of the Greeks. Quintus closely copied Homer, but not a single poetical idea of his own seems ever to have inspired him.

QUĬRĪNĀLIS MONS. [ROMA.]

QUĬRĪNUS (-i), a Sabine word, perhaps derived from quiris, a lance or spear. It occurs first of all as the name of Romulus, after he had been raised to the rank of a divinity; and the festival celebrated in his honour bore the name of Quirinalia. It is also used as a surname of Mars, Janus, and even of Augustus.

RĂBĪRĬUS (-i). (1) C., an aged senator, was accused in B.C. 63, by T. Labienus, tribune of the plebs, of having put to death the tribune L. Appuleius Saturninus in 100, nearly 40 years before. [SATURNINUS.] The accusation was set on foot at the instigation of Caesar, who judged it necessary to deter the senate from resorting to arms against the popular party. The Duumviri Perduellionis, (an obsolete tribunal), appointed to try Rabirius were C. Caesar himself and his relative L. Caesar. Rabirius was condemned, but appealed to the people in the comitia of the centuries. The case excited the greatest interest; since it was not simply the life or death of Rabirius, but the power and authority of the senate, which were at stake. Rabirius was defended by Cicero; but the eloquence of his advocate was of no avail, and the people would have ratified the decision of the duumvirs, had not the meeting been broken up by the praetor, Q. Metellus Celer, who removed the military flag which floated on the Janiculum.—(2) C. RABIRIUS POSTUMUS was the son of the sister of the

preceding. After the restoration of Ptolemy Auletes to his kingdom by means of Gabinius, in B.C. 55, Rabirius repaired to Alexandria, and was invested by the king with the office of Dioecetes, or chief treasurer. In this office his extortions were so terrible that Ptolemy had him apprehended; but Rabirius escaped from prison, probably through the connivance of the king, and returned to Rome. Here a trial awaited him. Gabinius had been sentenced to pay a heavy fine on account of his extortions in Egypt; and as he was unable to pay this fine, a suit was instituted against Rabirius, who was liable to make up the deficiency, if it could be proved that he had received any of the money of which Gabinius had illegally become possessed. Rabirius was defended by Cicero, and was probably condemned.—(3) A Roman poet, who lived in the last years of the republic, and wrote a poem on the Civil Wars.

RAMSES, the name of many kings of Egypt of the 18th, 19th, and 20th dynasties.

RAPHĬA or RAPHĒA (-ae : Repha), a seaport town in the extreme S.W. of Palestine, beyond Gaza, on the edge of the desert.

RASĒNA. [ETRURIA.]

RATOMĀGUS or ROTOMĀGUS (-i : Rouen),the chief town of the Vellocasses in Gallia Lugdunensis.

RAUDĬI CAMPI. [CAMPI RAUDII.]

RAURĂCI (-ōrum), a people in Gallia Belgica, bounded on the S. by the Helvetii, on the W. by the Sequani, on the N. by the Tribocci, and on the E. by the Rhine. They must have been a people of considerable importance, as 23,000 of them are said to have emigrated with the Helvetii in B.C. 58, and they possessed several towns, of which the most important were Augusta (August) and Basilia (Basle or Bâle).

RĂVENNA (-ae : (Northern Italy) Ravenna), an important town in Gallia Cisalpina, on the river Bedesis and about a mile from the sea, though it is now about 5 miles in the interior, in consequence of the sea having receded all along this coast. Ravenna was situated in the midst of marshes, and was only accessible in one direction by land, probably by the road leading from Ariminum. It was said to have been founded by Thessalians (Pelasgians), and afterwards to have passed into the hands of the Umbrians, but it long remained an insignificant place, and its greatness does not begin till the time of the empire, when Augustus made it one of the 2 chief stations of the Roman fleet. Ravenna thus suddenly became one of the most important places in the N. of Italy. When the Roman empire was threatened by the barbarians, the emperors of the West took up their residences at Ravenna, which, on account of its situations and fortifications, was regarded as impregnable. After the downfall of the Western empire, Theodoric also made it the capital of his kingdom ; and after the overthrow of the Gothic dominion by Narses, it became the residence of the Exarchs or the governors of the Byzantine empire in Italy, till the Lombards took the town, A.D. 752.

RĒĀTĒ (-is : *Rieti*), an ancient town of the Sabines in Central Italy, said to have been founded by the Aborigines or Pelasgians, was situated on the Lacus Velinus and the Via Salaria. It was the chief place of assembly for the Sabines, and was subsequently a praefectura or a municipium. The valley in which Reate was situated was so beautiful that it received the name of Tempe ; and in its neighbourhood is the celebrated waterfall, which is now known under the name of the fall of *Terni* or the *Cascade delle Marmore.*

REDŌNES (-um), a people in the interior of Gallia Lugdunensis, whose chief town was Condate (*Rennes*).

REGILLUS LACUS (-i), a lake in Latium, memorable for the victory gained on its banks by the Romans over the Latins, B.C. 498. It was E. of Rome in the territory of Tusculum, and between Lavicum and Gabii ; but it cannot be identified with certainty with any modern lake.

RĒGĬUM LĒPĬDI, RĒGĬUM LĔPĬDUM, or simply REGĬUM, also FŌRUM LĒPĬDI (*Reggio*), a town of the Boii in Gallia Cisalpina.

RĒGŬLUS (-i), the name of a family of the Atilia gens. (1) M. ATILIUS REGULUS, consul B.C. 267, conquered the Sallentini, took the town of Brundusium, and obtained in consequence the honour of a triumph. In 256, he was consul a 2nd time with L. Manlius Vulso Longus. The 2 consuls defeated the Carthaginian fleet, and afterwards landed in Africa with a large force. They met with great and striking success; and after Manlius returned to Rome with half of the army, Regulus remained in Africa with the other half, and prosecuted the war with the utmost vigour. The Carthaginian generals, Hasdrubal, Bostar, and Hamilcar, withdrew into the mountains, where they were attacked by Regulus, and defeated with great loss. The Carthaginian troops retired within the walls of the city, and Regulus now overran the country without opposition. The Carthaginians in despair sent a herald to Regulus to solicit peace; but the Roman general would only grant it on such intolerable terms that the Carthaginians resolved

to continue the war, and hold out to the last. A Lacedaemonian named Xanthippus pointed out to the Carthaginians that their defeat was owing to the incompetency of their generals, and not to the superiority of the Roman arms. Being placed at the head of their forces, he totally defeated the Romans, and took Regulus himself prisoner (255). Regulus remained in captivity for the next 5 years, till 250, when the Carthaginians, after their defeat by the proconsul Metellus, sent an embassy to Rome to solicit peace, or at least an exchange of prisoners. They allowed Regulus to accompany the ambassadors on the promise that he would return to Rome if their proposals were declined. This embassy of Regulus is one of the most celebrated stories in Roman history. It is related that he dissuaded the senate from assenting to a peace, or even to an exchange of prisoners, and that resisting all the persuasions of his friends to remain in Rome, he returned to Carthage, where a martyr's death awaited him. On his arrival at Carthage he is said to have been put to death with the most excruciating tortures. When the news of the barbarous death of Regulus reached Rome, the senate is said to have given Hamilcar and Bostar, 2 of the noblest Carthaginian prisoners, to the family of Regulus, who revenged themselves by putting them to death with cruel torments. But many writers have supposed that this tale was invented in order to excuse the cruelties perpetrated by the family of Regulus on the Carthaginian prisoners committed to their custody. Regulus was one of the favourite characters of early Roman story. Not only was he celebrated on account of his heroism in giving the senate advice which secured him a martyr's death, but also on account of his frugality and simplicity of life. —(2) C., surnamed SERRANUS, consul 257, when he defeated the Carthaginian fleet off the Liparean islands, and obtained possession of the islands of Lipara and Melite. He was consul a second time in 250, with L. Manlius Vulso. This Regulus is the first Atilius who bears the surname of *Serranus*.

RĒMI or RHEMI (-ōrum), one of the most powerful people in Gallia Belgica, inhabited the country through which the Axona flowed, and were bounded on the S. by the Nervii, on the S.E. by the Veromandui, on the E. by the Suessiones and Bellovaci, and on the W. by the Nervii. They formed an alliance with Caesar, when the rest of the Belgae made war against him, B.C. 57. Their chief town was Durocortorum, afterwards called Remi (*Rheims*).

RĒMUS. [ROMULUS.]

RĒSAINA, RESAENA, RESINA (-ae

Ras-el-Ain), a city of Mesopotamia, near the sources of the Chaboras, on the road from Carrae to Nisibis. After its restoration and fortification by Theodosius, it was called THEODOSIOPOLIS.

REUDIGNI (-ōrum), a people in the N. of Germany, on the right bank of the Albis, N. of the Langobardi.

REX (Rēgis), MARCĬUS. (1) Q., praetor B.C. 144, built the aqueduct called *Aqua Marcia.*—(2) Q., consul in 118, founded in this year the colony of Narbo Martius, in Gaul.—(3) Q., consul 68, and proconsul in Cilicia in the following year. Being refused a triumph on his return to Rome, he remained outside the city till the Catilinarian conspiracy broke out in 63, when the senate sent him to Faesulae, to watch the movements of C. Mallius or Manlius, Catiline's general.

RHA (*Volga*), a great river of Asia, first mentioned by Ptolemy, who describes it as rising in the N. of Sarmatia, in 2 branches, Rha Occidentalis and Rha Orientalis (the *Volga* and the *Kama*), after the junction of which it flowed S.W., forming the boundary between Sarmatia Asiatica and Scythia, till near the Tanaïs (*Don*), where it suddenly turns to the S.E., and falls into the N.W. part of the Caspian.

RHĂDĂMANTHUS (-i), son of Zeus (Jupiter) and Europa, and brother of king Minos of Crete. From fear of his brother he fled to Ocalea in Boeotia, and there married Alcmēne. In consequence of his justice throughout life, he became after his death, one of the judges in the lower world.

RHAETĬA (-ae), a Roman province S. of the Danube, was originally distinct from Vindelicia, and was bounded on the W. by the Helvetii, on the E. by Noricum, on the N. by Vindelicia, and on the S. by Cisalpine Gaul, thus corresponding to the *Grisons* in Switzerland, and to the greater part of the Tyrol. Towards the end of the first century, however, Vindelicia was added to the province of Rhaetia, whence Tacitus speaks of Augusta Vindelicorum as situated in Rhaetia. At a later time Rhaetia was subdivided into 2 provinces, *Rhaetia Prima* and *Rhaetia Secunda*, the former of which answered to the old province of Rhaetia, and the latter to that of Vindelicia. Rhaetia was a very mountainous country, since the main chain of the Alps ran through the greater part of the province. These mountains were called Alpes Rhaeticae, and extended from the St. Gothard to the Orteler by the pass of the Stelvio; and in them rose the Oenus (*Inn*) and most of the chief rivers in the N. of Italy, such as the Athesis (*Adige*), and the Addua (*Adda*). The original inhabitants of the country, the

RHAETI, are said by most ancient writers to have been Tuscans, who were driven out of the N. of Italy by the invasion of the Celts, and who took refuge in this mountainous district under a leader called Rhaetus. They were a brave and warlike people, and caused the Romans much trouble by their marauding incursions into Gaul and the N. of Italy. They were not subdued by the Romans till the reign of Augustus, and they offered a brave and desperate resistance against both Drusus and Tiberius, who finally conquered them. Rhaetia was then formed into a Roman province, to which Vindelicia was afterwards added, as has been already stated. The only town in Rhaetia of any importance was TRIDENTINUM (*Trent*).

RHĂGAE (-ārum : *Rai*, Ru. S.E. of *Tehran*), the greatest city of Media, lay in the extreme N. of Great Media, at the S. foot of the mountains (Caspius M.), which border the S. shores of the Caspian Sea, and on the W. side of the great pass through those mountains called the Caspiae Pylae. It was therefore the key of Media towards Parthia and Hyrcania. Having been destroyed by an earthquake, it was restored by Seleucus Nicator, and named EURŌPUS. In the Parthian wars it was again destroyed, but it was rebuilt by Arsaces, and called ARSACIA. In the middle ages it was still a great city under its original name, slightly altered (*Rai*); and it was finally destroyed by the Tartars in the 12th century.

RHAMNŪS (-untis : *Obrio Kastro*), a demus in Attica, belonging to the tribe Aeantis, which derived its name from the *rhamnus*, a kind of prickly shrub. Rhamnus was situated on a small rocky peninsula on the E. coast of Attica, 60 stadia from Marathon. It possessed a celebrated temple of Nemesis, who is hence called by the Latin poets *Rhamnusia dea* or *virgo*.

RHAMPSINĬTUS (-i), one of the ancient kings of Egypt, succeeded Proteus, and was succeeded by Cheops. Rhampsinitus belongs to the 20th dynasty, and is known in inscriptions by the name of *Ramessu Neter-kek-pen*.

RHĒA (-ae), an ancient Greek goddess, appears to have been a goddess of the earth. She is represented as a daughter of Urănus and Gē, and the wife of Crŏnos (Saturn), by whom she became the mother of Hestia (Vesta), Demeter (Ceres), Hera (Juno), Hades (Pluto), Poseidon (Neptune), and Zeus (Jupiter). Crŏnos devoured all his children by Rhea, but when she was on the point of giving birth to Zeus, she went to Lyctus, in Crete, by the advice of her parents. When Zeus was born she gave to Crŏnos a stone wrapped up like an infant, which the god swallowed, supposing it to be his child.

Crete was undoubtedly the earliest seat of the worship of Rhea; though many other parts of Greece laid claim to the honour of being the birthplace of Zeus. Rhea was afterwards identified by the Greeks in Asia Minor with the great Asiatic goddess, known under the name of "the Great Mother," or "the Mother of the Gods," and also bearing other names, such as Cўbĕlē, Agdistis, Dindў̆mēnē, &c. Hence her worship became of a wild and enthusiastic character, and various Eastern rites were added to it, which soon spread through the whole of Greece. From the orgiastic nature of these rites, her worship became closely connected with that of Dionysus (Bacchus). Under the name of Cybele, her worship was universal in Phrygia. Under the name of Agdistis, she was worshipped with great solemnity at Pessinus, in Galatia, which town was regarded as the principal seat of her worship. Under different names we might trace the worship of Rhea as far as the Euphrates, and even Bactriana. She was, in fact, the great goddess of the Eastern world, and we find her worshipped there under a variety of forms and names. As regards the Romans, they had from the earliest times worshipped Jupiter and his mother Ops, the wife of Saturn, who seems to have been identical with Rhea. In all European countries Rhea was conceived to be accompanied by the Curētes, who are inseparably connected with the birth and bringing up of Zeus in Crete, and in Phrygia by the Corybantes, Atys, and Agdistis. The Corybantes were her enthusiastic priests, who,

Rhea, or Cybele.   (From a Roman Lamp.)

with drums, cymbals, horns, and in full armour, performed their orgiastic dances in the forests and on the mountains of Phrygia. In Rome the Galli were her priests. The lion was sacred to her. In works of art she is usually represented seated on a throne, adorned with a mural crown, from which a veil hangs down. Lions appear crouching on the right and left of her throne, and sometimes she is seen riding in a chariot drawn by lions.

Rhea, or Cybele.   (From a Medallion of Hadrian.)

RHĔA SILVĬA.   [ROMULUS.]
RHĔDŎNES.   [REDONES.]

RHĔGĬUM (-i: *Reggio*), a celebrated Greek town on the coast of Bruttium in the S. of Italy, was situated on the Fretum Siculum, or the Straits, which separate Italy and Sicily. Rhegium was founded about the beginning of the first Messenian war, B.C. 743, by Aeolian Chalcidians from Euboea and by Doric Messenians, who had quitted their native country on the commencement of hostilities between Sparta and Messenia. Even before the Persian wars Rhegium was sufficiently powerful to send 3000 of its citizens to the assistance of the Tarentines, and in the time of the elder Dionysius it possessed a fleet of 80 ships of war. This monarch, having been offended by the inhabitants, took the city, and treated it with the greatest severity. Rhegium never recovered its former greatness, though it still continued to be a place of considerable importance. The Rhegians having applied to Rome for assistance when Pyrrhus was in the S. of Italy, the Romans placed in the town a garrison of 4000 soldiers, who had been levied among the Latin colonies in Campania. These troops seized the town in 279, killed or expelled the male inhabitants, and took possession of their wives and children

The Romans were too much engaged at the time with their war against Pyrrhus to take notice of this outrage; but when Pyrrhus was driven out of Italy, they took signal vengeance upon these Campanians, and restored the surviving Rhegians to their city. Rhegium was the place from which persons usually crossed over to Sicily, but the spot at which they embarked was called COLUMNA RHEGINA (*Torre di Curallo*), and was 100 stadia N. of the town.

RHÊNÊA (-ae), anciently called *Ortygia* and *Celadussa*, an island in the Aegean sea and one of the Cyclades, W. of Delos, from which it was divided by a narrow strait only 4 stadia in width.

RHÊNUS (-i). (1) (*Rhein* in German, *Rhine* in English), one of the great rivers in Europe, forming in ancient times the boundary between Gaul and Germany, rises in Mt. Adûlas (*St. Gothard*) not far from the sources of the Rhone, and flows first in a W.-ly direction, passing through the Lacus Brigantinus (*Lake of Constance*), till it reaches Basilia (*Basle*), where it takes a N.-ly direction and eventually flows into the ocean by several mouths. The ancients spoke of 2 main arms, into which the Rhine was divided on entering the territory of the Batavi, of which the one on the E. continued to bear the name of Rhenus, while that on the W., into which the Mosa (*Maas* or *Meuse*) flowed, was called Vahalis (*Waal*). After Drusus in B.C. 12 had connected the Flevo Lacus (*Zuyder-Zee*) with the Rhine by means of a canal, in making which he probably made use of the bed of the Yssel, we find mention of 3 mouths of the Rhine. Of these the names, as given by Pliny, are on the W., Helium (the Vahalis of other writers), in the centre Rhenus, and on the E., Flevum; but at a later time we again find mention of only 2 mouths. The Rhine is described by the ancients as a broad, rapid, and deep river. It receives many tributaries, of which the most important are the Mosella (*Moselle*) and Mosa (*Maas* or *Meuse*) on the left, and the Nicer (*Neckar*), Moenus (*Main*) and Luppia (*Lippe*) on the right. Its whole course amounts to about 950 miles. The inundations of the Rhine near its mouth are mentioned by the ancients. Caesar was the first Roman general who crossed the Rhine. He threw a bridge of boats across the river, probably in the neighbourhood of Cologne.—(2) (*Reno*), a tributary of the Padus (*Po*) in Gallia Cisalpina near Bononia, on a small is.and of which Octavian, Antony, and Lepidus formed the celebrated triumvirate.

RHÊSUS (-i). (1) A river-god in Bithynia, one of the sons of Oceanus and Tethys.

—(2) Son of king Eïoneus in Thrace, marched to the assistance of the Trojans in their war with the Greeks. An oracle had declared that Troy would never be taken if the snow-white horses of Rhesus should once drink the water of the Xanthus, and feed upon the grass of the Trojan plain. But as soon as Rhesus had reached the Trojan territory and had pitched his tents late at night, Ulysses and Diomedes penetrated into his camp, slew Rhesus himself, and carried off his horses.

RHIÂNUS (-i), of Crete, a distinguished Alexandrian poet and grammarian, flourished B.C. 222.

RHINOCOLÛRA or RHINOCORÛRA (*Kulat-el-Arish*), the frontier town of Egypt and Palestine, lay in the midst of the desert, at the mouth of the brook (*El-Arish*), which was the boundary between the countries, and which is called in Scripture the river of Egypt.

RHÎPAEI MONTES (-ōrum), the name of a lofty range of mountains in the northern part of the earth, respecting which there are diverse statements in the ancient writers. The name seems to have been given by the Greek poets quite indefinitely to all the mountains in the northern parts of Europe and Asia. Thus the Rhipaei Montes are sometimes called the Hyperborei Montes. [HYPERBOREI.] The later geographical writers place the Rhipaean mountains N.E. of Mt. Alaunus on the frontiers of Asiatic Sarmatia, and state that the Tanais rises in these mountains. According to this account the Rhipaean mountains may be regarded as a western branch of the Ural Mountains.

RHÎUM (-i : *Castello di Morea*), a promontory in Achaia, opposite to the promontory of Antirrhium (*Castello di Romelia*), on the borders of Aetolia and Locris, with which it formed the narrow entrance to the Corinthian gulf, which Straits are now called the *Little Dardanelles*.

RHÔDA or RHÔDUS (-ae, or -i : *Rozas*), a Greek emporium on the coast of the Indigetae in Hispania Tarraconensis, founded by the Rhodians, and subsequently occupied by the inhabitants of Massilia.

RHÔDÂNUS (-i : *Rhône*), one of the chief rivers of Gaul, rises in Mt. Adûlas, on the Pennine Alps, not far from the sources of the Rhine, flows first in a westerly direction, and after passing through the Lacus Lemanus, turns to the S., passes by the towns of Lugdunum, Vienna, Avenio, and Arelate, receives several tributaries, and finally falls by several mouths into the Sinus Gallicus in the Mediterranean. The Rhone is a very rapid river, and its upward navigation is therefore difficult, though it is navigable for large vessels as high as Lugdunum (*Lyon*), and by means of the Arar still farther N.

RHŎDĔ. [RHODOS.]

RHŎDĬUS (-i : prob. *the brook of the Dardanelles*), a small river of the Troad, mentioned both by Homer and Hesiod. It rose on the lower slopes of Mt. Ida, and flowed N.W. into the Hellespont, between Abydus and Dardanus, after receiving the Selleïs from the W.

RHŎDŎPĔ (-ēs), one of the highest ranges of mountains in Thrace, extending from Mt. Scomius, E. of the river Nestus and the boundaries of Macedonia, in a S.E.-ly direction almost down to the coast. It is highest in its northern part, and is thickly covered with wood. Rhodope, like the rest of Thrace, was sacred to Dionysus (Bacchus).

RHŎDŎPIS (-ĭdis), a celebrated Greek courtesan, of Thracian origin, was a fellow-slave with the poet Aesop, both of them belonging to the Samian Iadmon. She afterwards became the property of Xanthus, another Samian, who carried her to Naucratis in Egypt, in the reign of Amasis, and at this great sea-port she carried on the trade of an hetaera for the benefit of her master. While thus employed, Charaxus, the brother of the poetess Sappho, who had come to Naucratis as a merchant, fell in love with her, and ransomed her from slavery for a large sum of money. She was in consequence attacked by Sappho in a poem. She continued to live at Naucratis, and with the tenth part of her gains she dedicated at Delphi 10 iron spits, which were seen by Herodotus. She is called Rhodopis by Herodotus, but Sappho in her poem spoke of her under the name of Doricha. It is therefore probable that Doricha was her real name, and that she received that of Rhodopis, which signifies the "rosy-cheeked," on account of her beauty.

RHŎDOS, sometimes called RHŎDĔ (-es), daughter of Poseidon (Neptune) and Helia, or of Helios (Sol) and Amphitrite, or of Poseidon and Aphrodite (Venus), or lastly of Oceanus. From her the island of Rhodes is said to have derived its name ; and in this island she bore to Helios 7 sons.

RHŎDUS (-i: *Rhodos, Rhodes*), the most easterly island of the Aegean, or more specifically, of the Carpathian Sea, lies off the S. coast of Caria, due S. of the promontory of Cynossema (*C. Aloupo*), at the distance of about 12 geog. miles. Its length, from N.E. to S.W., is about 45 miles; its greatest breadth about 20 to 25. In early times it was called Aethraea and Ophiussa, and several other names. There are various mythological stories about its origin and peopling. Its

Hellenic colonisation is ascribed to Tlepolemus, the son of Hercules, before the Trojan war, and after that war to Althaemenes. Homer mentions the 3 Dorian settlements in Rhodes, namely, Lindus, Ialysus, and Camirus; and these cities, with Cos, Cnidus, and Halicarnassus, formed the Dorian Hexapolis, which was established, from a period of unknown antiquity, in the S.W. corner of Asia Minor. Rhodes soon became a great maritime state, or rather confederacy, the island being parcelled out between the 3 cities above mentioned. The Rhodians made distant voyages, and founded numerous colonies. At the beginning of the Peloponnesian war, Rhodes was one of those Dorian maritime states which were subject to Athens ; but in the 20th year of the war, B.C. 412, it joined the Spartan alliance, and the oligarchical party, which had been depressed, and their leaders, the Eratidae, expelled, recovered their former power, under Dorieus. In 408, the new capital, called RHODUS, was built, and peopled from the 3 ancient cities of Ialysus, Lindus, and Camirus. At the Macedonian conquest the Rhodians submitted to Alexander, but upon his death expelled the Macedonian garrison. In the ensuing wars they formed an alliance with Ptolemy, the son of Lagus, and their city, Rhodes, successfully endured a most famous siege by the forces of Demetrius Poliorcetes, who at length, in admiration of the valour of the besieged, presented them with the engines he had used against the city, from the sale of which they defrayed the cost of the celebrated Colossus. At length they came into connexion with the Romans, whose alliance they joined, with Attalus, king of Pergamus, in the war against Philip III. of Macedon. In the ensuing war with Antiochus, the Rhodians gave the Romans great aid with their fleet ; and, in the subsequent partition of the Syrian possessions of Asia Minor, they were rewarded by the supremacy of S. Caria, where they had had settlements from an early period. A temporary interruption of their alliance with Rome was caused by their espousing the cause of Perseus, for which they were severely punished, 168 ; but they recovered the favour of Rome by the important naval aid they rendered in the Mithridatic war. In the civil wars they took part with Caesar, and suffered in consequence from Cassius, 42, but were afterwards compensated for their losses by the favour of Antonius. They were at length deprived of their independence by Claudius ; and their prosperity received its final blow from an earthquake, which laid the city of Rhodes in ruins, in the reign of Antoninus Pius, A.D. 155

RHOECUS (-i). (1) A Centaur, who, in conjunction with Hylaeus, pursued Atalanta in Arcadia, but was killed by her with an arrow. The Roman poets call him Rhoetus, and relate that he was wounded at the nuptials of Pirithous.—(2) Son of Phileas or Philaeus, of Samos, an architect and statuary, flourished about B.C. 640. He invented the art of casting statues in bronze and iron.

RHOETĒUM (-i : C. Intepeh or Barbieri), a promontory, or a strip of rocky coast, breaking into several promontories, in Mysia, on the Hellespont, near Aeantium, with a town of the same name (prob. Paleo Castro).

RHOETUS. (1) A Centaur. [RHOECUS.] —(2) One of the giants who was slain by Dionysus ; he is usually called Eurytus.

RHOXOLĀNI or ROXOLĀNI (-ōrum), a warlike people in European Sarmatia, on the coast of the Palus Maeotis, and between the Borysthenes and the Tanais, usually supposed to be the ancestors of the modern Russians.

RHYNDĂCUS (-i : Edrenos), or Lўcus, a considerable river of Asia Minor. Rising in Mt. Dindymene, opposite to the sources of the Hermus, it flows N. through Phrygia, then turns N.W., then W., and then N. through the lake Apolloniatis, into the Propontis. From the point where it left Phrygia, it formed the boundary of Mysia and Bithynia.

RHYPES, one of the 12 cities of Achaia, situated between Aegium and Patrae. It was destroyed by Augustus, and its inhabitants removed to Patrae.

RHYTĬUM (-i), a town in Crete, mentioned by Homer.

RĬCĬMER (-ēris), the Roman "King-Maker," was the son of a Suevian chief, and was brought up at the court of Valentinian III. In A.D. 472 he took Rome by storm, and died 40 days afterwards.

RŌBĬGUS or ROBĪGO (-i, or -ĭnis), is described by some Latin writers as a divinity worshipped for the purpose of averting blight or too great heat from the young cornfields. The festival of the Robigalia was celebrated on the 25th of April, and was said to have been instituted by Numa.

ROBUS (-i), a fortress in the territory of the Rauraci, in Gallia Belgica.

RŌMA (-ae : Rome), the capital of Italy and of the world, was situated on the left bank of the river Tiber, on the N.W. confines of Latium, about 16 miles from the sea. Rome is said to have been a colony from A.ba Longa, and to have been founded by Romulus, about B.C. 753. [ROMULUS.] All traditions agree that the original city comprised only the Mons Palatinus or Palatium, and some portion of the ground immediately below it. It was surrounded by walls, and was built in a square form, whence it was called Roma Quadrata. On the neighbouring hills there also existed from the earliest times settlements of Sabines and Etruscans. The Sabine town, probably called Quirium, and inhabited by Quirites, was situated on the hills to the N. of the Palatine, that is, the Quirinalis and Capitolinus, or Capitolium, on the latter of which hills was the Sabine Arx or citadel. According to traditions, the Sabines were united with the Romans, or Latins, in the reign of Romulus, and thus was formed one people, under the name of " Populus Romanus (et) Quirites." The Etruscans were settled on Mons Caelius, and extended over Mons Cispius and Mons Oppius, which are part of the Esquiline. These Etruscans were at an early period incorporated in the Roman state, but were compelled to abandon their seats on the hills, and to take up their abode in the plains between the Caellus and the Esquiline, whence the Vicus Tuscus derived its name. Under the kings the city rapidly grew in population and in size. Ancus Martius added the Mons Aventinus to the city. The same king also built a fortress on the Janiculus, a hill on the other side of the Tiber, as a protection against the Etruscans, and connected it with the city by means of the Pons Sublicius. Rome was still further improved and enlarged by Tarquinius Priscus and Servius Tullius. The completion of the city, however, was ascribed to Servius Tullius. This king added the Mons Viminalis and Mons Esquilinus, and surrounded the whole city with a line of fortifications, which comprised all the seven hills of Rome (Palatinus, Capitolinus, Quirinalis, Caelius, Aventinus, Viminalis, Esquilinus). Hence Rome was called Urbs Septicollis. These fortifications were about 7 miles in circumference. In B.C. 390 Rome was entirely destroyed by the Gauls, with the exception of a few houses on the Palatine. On the departure of the barbarians it was rebuilt in great haste and confusion, without any attention to regularity, and with narrow and crooked streets. After the conquest of the Carthaginians and of the monarchs of Macedonia and Syria, the city began to be adorned with many public buildings and handsome private houses ; and it was still further embellished by Augustus, who used to boast that he had found the city of brick and had left it of marble. The great fire at Rome in the reign of Nero (A.D. 64) destroyed two-thirds of the city. Nero availed himself of this opportunity to indulge his passion for building ; and the city new assumed a still more regular and stately appearance. The emperor Aurelian surrounded Rome with new walls, which embraced the city of Servius Tullius and all the suburbs which had subsequently grown up around it, such as the *M. Janiculus* on the right bank of the Tiber, and the *Collis Hortulorum* or *M. Pincianus*, on the left bank of the river, to the N. of the Quirinalis. The walls of Aurelian were about 11 miles in circumference. They were restored by Honorius, and were also partly rebuilt by Belisarius. Rome was divided by Servius Tullius into 4 *Regiones* or districts, corresponding to the 4 city tribes. Their names were: 1. *Suburana*, comprehending the space from the Subura to the Caelius, both inclusive. 2. *Esquilina*, comprehending the Esquiline hill. 3. *Collina*, extending over the Quirinal and Viminal. 4. *Palatina*, comprehending the Palatine hill. The Capitoline, as the seat of the gods, and the Aventine, were not included in these Regiones. These Regiones were again subdivided into 27 Sacella Argaeorum, which were probably erected where two streets (*compita*) crossed each other. The division of Servius Tullius into 4 Regiones remained unchanged till the time of Augustus, who made a fresh division of the city into 14 Regiones, viz.: 1. *Porta Capena.* 2. *Caelimontium.* 3. *Isis et Serapis.* 4. *Via Sacra.* 5. *Esquilina cum Colle Viminali.* 6. *Alta Semita.* 7. *Via Lata.* 8. *Forum Romanum.* 9. *Circus Fla-*minius. 10. *Palatium.* 11. *Circus Maximus.* 12. *Piscina Publica.* 13. *Aventinus;* and 14. *Trans Tiberim*, the only region on the right bank of the river. Each of these Regiones was subdivided into a certain number of *Vici*, analogous to the sacella of Servius Tullius. The houses were divided into 2 different classes, called respectively *domus* and *insulae.* The former were the dwellings of the Roman nobles, corresponding to the modern palazzi; the latter were the habitations of the middle and lower classes. Each insula contained several apartments or sets of apartments, which were let to different families; and it was frequently surrounded with shops. The number of insulae of course greatly exceeded that of the domi. It is stated that there were 46,602 insulae at Rome, but only 1790 domus. We learn from the Monumentum Ancyranum, that the plebs urbana, in the time of Augustus, was 320,000. This did not include the women, nor the senators, nor knights; so that the free population could not have been less than 650,000. To this number we must add the slaves, who must have been at least as numerous as the free population. Consequently the whole population of Rome in the time of Augustus must have been at least 1,300,000, and in all probability greatly exceeded that number. Moreover, as we know that the city continued to increase in size and population down to the time of

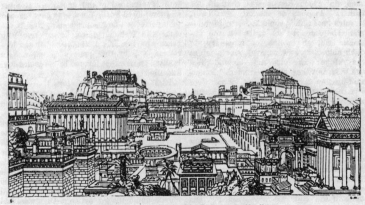

Ancient Rome.   (Restored by Professor Cockerell.)

Vespasian and Trajan, we shall not be far wrong in supposing that the city contained nearly 2 millions of inhabitants in the reigns of those emperors. The Aqueducts (*Aquaeductus*) supplied Rome with an abundance of pure water from the hills which surround the Campagna. The Romans at first had recourse to the Tiber and to wells sunk in the city. It was not till B.C. 313 that the first aqueduct was constructed, but their number was gradually increased, till they amounted to 14, in the time of Procopius, that is, the 6th century of the Christian era.

ROMULĔA (-ae), an ancient town of the Hirpini, in Samnium, on the road from Beneventum to Tarentum.

RŎMŬLUS (-i), the founder of the city of Rome, must not be regarded as a real personage. The stories about him are mythical. According to the common legend, Romulus and Remus were the sons of Rhea Silvia, by Mars. Silvia was the daughter of Numitor (a descendant of Iulus, the son of Aeneas), who had been excluded from the throne of Alba Longa, by his brother, Amulius; and as Silvia was a vestal virgin, she and her twin offspring were condemned to be drowned in the Tiber. The cradle in which the children were exposed, having stranded, they were suckled by a she-wolf, which carried them to her den, where they were discovered by Faustulus, the king's shepherd, who took the children to his own house, and gave them into the care of his wife, Acca Larentia. When they were grown up, Romulus and Remus left Alba to found a city on the banks of the Tiber. A strife arose between the brothers where the city should be built, and after whose name it should be called, in which Remus was slain by his brother. As soon as the city was built, Romulus found his people too few in numbers. He therefore set apart, on the Capitoline hill, an asylum, or sanctuary, in which homicides and runaway slaves might take refuge. The city thus became filled with men, but they wanted women. Romulus, therefore, proclaimed that games were to be celebrated in honour of the god Consus, and invited his neighbours, the Latins and Sabines, to the festival, during which the Roman youths rushed upon their guests, and carried off the virgins. This produced a war between the two nations; but during a long and desperate battle, the Sabine women rushed in between the armies, and prayed their husbands and fathers to be reconciled. Their prayer was heard; the two people not only made peace, but agreed to form only one nation. But this union did not last long. Titus Tatius, the Sabine king, who reigned conjointly with Romulus, was slain at a festival at Lavinium by some Laurentines, to whom he had refused satisfaction for outrages which had been committed by his kinsmen. Henceforward Romulus ruled

alone over both Romans and Sabines. After reigning 37 years, he was at length taken away from the world by his father, Mars, who carried him up to heaven in a fiery chariot. Shortly afterwards he appeared in more than mortal beauty to Julius Proculus, and bade him tell the Romans to worship him as their guardian god, under the name of Quirinus. Such was the glorified end of Romulus in the genuine legend; but, according to another tale, the senators, discontented with the tyrannical rule of their king, murdered him during the gloom of a tempest, cut up his body, and carried home the mangled pieces under their robes.

RŎMŬLUS AUGUSTŬLUS. [AUGUSTULUS.]

RŎMŬLUS SILVĬUS. [SILVIUS.]

ROSCIĀNUM (-i : *Rossano*), a fortress on the E. coast of Bruttium between Thurii and Paternum.

ROSCĬUS. (1) L., a Roman ambassador sent to Fidenae in B.C. 438.—(2) Sex., of Ameria, a town in Umbria, accused of the murder of his father, and defended by Cicero (B.C. 80) in an oration which is still extant. —(3) Q., the most celebrated comic actor at Rome, was a native of Solonium, a small place in the neighbourhood of Lanuvium. His histrionic powers procured him the favour of many of the Roman nobles, and, among others, of the dictator Sulla, who presented him with a gold ring, the symbol of equestrian rank. Roscius enjoyed the friendship of Cicero, who constantly speaks of him in terms both of admiration and affection. Roscius was considered by the Romans to have reached such perfection in his profession, that it became the fashion to call every one who became particularly distinguished in the histrionic art, by the name of Roscius. He realised an immense fortune by his profession, and died in 62.

ROTOMĀGUS. [RATOMAGUS.]

ROXĀNA, daughter of Oxyartes the Bactrian, fell into the hands of Alexander on his capture of the hill-fort in Sogdiana, named "the rock," B.C. 327. Alexander was so captivated by her charms, that he married her. Soon after Alexander's death (323), she gave birth to a son (Alexander Aegus), who was admitted to share the nominal sovereignty with Arrhidaeus, under the regency of Perdiccas. Roxana afterwards crossed over to Europe with her son, placed herself under the protection of Olympias, and threw herself into Pydna along with the latter. In 316 Pydna was taken by Cassander; Olympias was put to death; and Roxana and her son were placed in confinement in Amphipolis, where they were murdered by Cassander's orders in 311

ROXŌLĀNI. [RHOXOLANI.]

RŪBI (-ōrum: *Ruvo*), a town in Apulia on the road from Canusium to Brundusium.

RŪBĪCO (-ōnis), a small river in Italy, falling into the Adriatic a little N. of Ariminum, formed the boundary in the republican period between the province of Gallia Cisalpina and Italia proper. It is celebrated in history on account of Caesar's passage across it at the head of his army, by which act he declared war against the republic.

RUBRA SAXA, called Rubrae breves (-sc. petrae) by Martial, a small place in Etruria only a few miles from Rome, near the river Cremera, and on the Via Flaminia.

RUBRĒSUS LĀCUS. [NARBO.]

RŪBRUM MĀRE. [ERYTHRAEUM MARE.]

RŪDĬAE (-ārum: *Rotigliano* or *Ruge*), a town of the Peucetii in Apulia, on the road from Brundusium to Venusia, was originally a Greek colony, and afterwards a Roman municipium. Rudiae is celebrated as the birthplace of Ennius.

RŪGĬI (-ōrum), an important people in Germany, originally dwelt on the coast of the Baltic between the Viadus (*Oder*) and the Vistula. After disappearing a long time from history, they are found at a later time in Attila's army ; and after Attila's death they founded a new kingdom on the N. bank of the Danube, in Austria and Hungary, the name of which is still preserved in the modern *Rugiland*. They have left traces of their name in the country which they originally inhabited, in the modern *Rügen, Rügenwalde, Rega, Regenwalde.*

RULLUS, P. SERVĪLĬUS (-i), tribune of the plebs B.C. 63, proposed an agrarian law, which Cicero attacked in 3 orations which have come down to us.

RŪPĬLĬUS (-i), P., consul B.C. 132, prosecuted with the utmost vehemence all the adherents of Tib. Gracchus, who had been slain in the preceding year. As proconsul in Sicily in the following year he made various regulations for the government of the province, which were known by the name of Leges Rupiliae. Rupilius was condemned in the tribunate of C. Gracchus, 123, on account of his illegal and cruel acts in the prosecution of the friends of Tib. Gracchus.

RUSCĪNO (-ōnis), a town of the Sordones or Sordi, in the S.E. part of Gallia Narbonensis, at the foot of the Pyrenees.

RUSELLAE (-ārum: nr. *Grosseto*, Ru.), one of the most ancient cities of Etruria, situated on an eminence E. of the lake Prelius and on the Via Aurelia. The walls of Rusellae still remain, and are some of the most ancient in Italy.

RUSTĬCUS (-i), L. JŪNIUS ARULĒNUS, was a friend and pupil of Paetus Thrasea, and an ardent admirer of the Stoic philosophy. He was put to death by Domitian, because he had written a panegyric upon Thrasea.

RŪTĒNI (-ōrum), a people in Gallia Aquitanica, on the frontiers of Gallia Narbonensis, in the modern *Rovergne.*

RŪTĪLĬUS LŪPUS. [LUPUS.]

RŪTĪLĬUS RŪFUS (-i), P., a Roman statesman and orator. He was military tribune under Scipio in the Numantine war, praetor B.C. 111, consul 105, and legatus in 95 under Q. Mucius Scaevola, proconsul of Asia. While acting in this capacity he displayed so much honesty and firmness in repressing the extortions of the publicani, that he became an object of fear and hatred to the whole body. Accordingly, on his return to Rome, he was impeached of malversation (*de repetundis*), found guilty, and compelled to withdraw into banishment, 92.

RŪTŬBA (-ae: *Roya*), a river on the coast of Liguria, which flows into the sea near Album Intemelium.

RŪTŬLI (-orum), an ancient people in Italy, inhabiting a narrow slip of country on the coast of Latium, a little to the S. of the Tiber. Their chief town was Ardea, which was the residence of Turnus. They were subdued at an early period by the Romans, and disappear from history.

RŪTŬPAE or RŪTŬPĬAE (*Richborough*), a port of the Cantii, in the S.E. of Britain, where there are still several Roman remains.

SĂBA (-ae). (1) (O. T. Sheba), the capital of the SABAEI, in Arabia Felix, lay on a high woody mountain, and was pointed out by an Arabian tradition as the residence of the "Queen of Sheba."—(2) There was another city of the same name in the interior of Arabia Felix, where a place *Sabea* is still found, nearly in the centre of *El-Yémen.*—(3) A seaport town of Aethiopia, on the Red Sea, S. of Ptolemaïs Theron.

SABĂCON, a king of Ethiopia, who invaded Egypt in the reign of the blind king Anysis, whom he dethroned and drove into the marshes. The Ethiopian conqueror then reigned over Egypt for 50 years, but at length quitted the country in consequence of a dream, whereupon Anysis regained his kingdom. This is the account which Herodotus received from the priests (ii. 137—140) ; but it appears from Manetho, that there were 3 Ethiopian kings who reigned over Egypt, named *Sabacon, Sebichus,* and *Taracus,* whose collective reigns amount to 40 or 50 years, and who form the 25th dynasty of that writer.

The account of Manetho is to be preferred to that of Herodotus.

SĂBAEI or SĂBAE (-ōrum, or -ārum: O. T. Shebaiïm), one of the chief peoples of Arabia, dwelt in the S.W. corner of the peninsula, in the most beautiful part of Arabia Felix, the N. and centre of the province of *El-Yemen*. So at least Ptolemy places them; but the fact seems to be that they are the chief representatives of a race which, at an early period, was widely spread on both sides of the S. part of the Red Sea, where Arabia and Aethiopia all but joined at the narrow strait of *Bab-el-Mandeb;* and hence, probably, the confusion often made between the *Sheba* and *Seba* of Scripture, or between the *Shebaiim* of Arabia and the *Sebaïm* of Aethiopia. Their country produced all the most precious spices and perfumes of Arabia.

SABĂTE, a town of Etruria, on the road from Cosa to Rome, and on the N.W. corner of a lake, which was named after it LACUS SABATINUS (*Lago di Bracciano*).

SĂBĂTINI (-ōrum), a people in Campania, who derived their name from the river Sabatus (*Sabbato*), a tributary of the Calor, which flows into the Vulturnus.

SABAZĬUS (-i), a Phrygian divinity, commonly described as a son of Rhea or Cybele. In later times he was identified with the mystic Dionysus (Bacchus), who hence is sometimes called Dionysus Sabazius. For the same reason Sabazius is called a son of Zeus (Jupiter) by Persephone, and is said to have been reared by a nymph, Nysa; though others, by philosophical speculations, were led to consider him a son of Cabirus, Dionysus, or Cronos. He was torn by the Titans into 7 pieces.

SĂBELLI. [SABINI.]

SĂBĪNA (-ae), the wife of the emperor Hadrian, was the grand-niece of Trajan, being the daughter of Matidia, who was the daughter of Marciana, the sister of Trajan. Sabina was married to Hadrian about A.D. 100, but the marriage did not prove a happy one. Sabina at length put an end to her life, probably in 138, and there was a report that she had even been poisoned by her husband.

SĂBĪNA, POPPAEA (-ae), a woman of surpassing beauty, but licentious morals, was the daughter of T. Ollius, but assumed the name of her maternal grandfather Poppaeus Sabinus, who had been consul A.D. 9. She was first married to Rufius Crispinus, and afterwards to Otho, who was one of the boon companions of Nero. The latter soon became enamoured of her; and in order to get Otho out of the way, Nero sent him to govern the province of Lusitania (58). Poppaea now became the

acknowledged mistress of Nero, over whom she exercised absolute sway. Anxious to become the wife of the emperor, she persuaded Nero first to murder his mother Agrippina (59), who was opposed to such a disgraceful union, and next to divorce and shortly afterwards put to death his innocent and virtuous wife Octavia (62). She then became the wife of Nero. In 65, Poppaea being pregnant, was killed by a kick from her brutal husband.

SĂBĪNI (-ōrum), one of the most ancient and powerful of the peoples of central Italy. The ancients usually derived their name from Sabinus, a son of the native god Sancus. The different tribes of the Sabine race were widely spread over the whole of central Italy, and were connected with the Opicans, Umbrians, and those other peoples whose languages were akin to the Greek. The earliest traces of the Sabines are found in the neighbourhood of Amiternum at the foot of the main chain of the Apennines, whence they spread as far S. as the confines of Lucania and Apulia. The Sabines may be divided into 3 great classes, called by the names of Sabini, Sabelli, and Samnites respectively. The SABĪNI proper inhabited the country between the Nar, the Anio and the Tiber, between Latium, Etruria, Umbria and Picenum. The SABELLI were the smaller tribes who issued from the Sabines. To these belong the Vestini, Marsi, Marrucini, Peligni, Frentani and Hirpini. The Picentes, the Picentini, and the Lucani, were also of Sabine origin. The SAMNITES, who were by far the most powerful of all the Sabine peoples, are treated of in a separate article. [SAMNIUM.] There were certain national characteristics which distinguished the whole Sabine race. They were a people of simple and virtuous habits, faithful to their word, and imbued with deep religious feeling. Hence we find frequent mention of omens and prodigies in their country. They were a migratory race, and adopted a peculiar system of emigration. With the exception of the Sabines in Lucania and Campania, they never attained any high degree of civilisation or mental culture; but they were always distinguished by their love of freedom, which they maintained with the greatest bravery. The Sabines formed one of the elements of which the Roman people was composed. In the time of Romulus, a portion of the Sabines, after the rape of their wives and daughters, became incorporated with the Romans, and the 2 peoples were united into one under the general name of Quirites. The remainder of the Sabini proper, who were less warlike than the Samnites and Sabellians, were finally subdued by M. Curius Dentatus,

B.C. 290, and received the Roman franchise, *sine suffragio.*

SABĪNUS (-i). (1) A contemporary poet and a friend of Ovid, who informs us that Sabinus had written answers to six of his *Epistolae Heroidum.*—(2) FLAVIUS, brother of the emperor Vespasian, governed Moesia for 7 years during the reign of Claudius, and held the important office of praefectus urbis during the last 11 years of Nero's reign. He was removed from this office by Galba, but was replaced in it on the accession of Otho, who was anxious to conciliate Vespasian. He continued to retain the dignity under Vitellius. During the struggle for the empire between Vespasian and Vitellius, Sabinus took refuge in the Capitol, where he was attacked by the Vitellian troops. In the assault the Capitol was burnt to the ground, Sabinus was taken prisoner, and put to death by the soldiers in the presence of Vitellius, who endeavoured in vain to save his life. Sabinus was a man of distinguished reputation, and of unspotted character.—(3) MASSURIUS, was a distinguished jurist in the time of Tiberius. This is the Sabinus from whom the school of the Sabiniani took its name. [CAPITO.]—(4) POP-PAEUS, consul A.D. 9, was appointed in the lifetime of Augustus governor of Moesia, and was not only confirmed in this government by Tiberius, but received from the latter the provinces of Achaia and Macedonia in addition. He continued to hold these provinces till his death in 35, having ruled over Moesia for 24 years.—(5) Q. TITURIUS, one of Caesar's legates in Gaul, who perished along with L. Aurunculeius Cotta in the attack made upon them by Ambiorix in B.C. 54.

SABIS (-is : *Sambre*). (1) A broad and deep river in Gallia Belgica and in the territory of the Ambiani, falling into the river Mosa.—(2) A small river on the coast of Carmania.—(3) [SAPIS.]

SABRATA. [ABROTONUM.]

SABRĪNA (-ae), also called SABRIĀNA (*Severn*), a river in the W. of Britain, which flowed by Venta Silurum into the ocean.

SĀCAE (-ārum), one of the most numerous and most powerful of the Scythian nomad tribes, had their abodes E. and N.E. of the Massagetae, as far as Serica, in the steppes of Central Asia, which are now peopled by the *Kirghiz Khasaks,* in whose name that of their ancestors is traced by some geographers. They were very warlike, and excelled especially as cavalry, and as archers both on horse and foot. The name of the Sacae is often used loosely for other Scythian tribes, and sometimes for the Scythians in general.

SĀCER MONS. (1) An isolated hill in the country of the Sabines, on the right bank of the Anio and W. of the Via Nomentana, 3 miles from Rome, to which the plebeians repaired in their celebrated secessions.—(2) A mountain in Hispania Tarraconensis near the Minius.

SACRA VĪA, the principal street in Rome, ran from the valley between the Caelian and Esquiline hills, through the arch of Titus, and past the Forum Romanum, to the Capitol.

SACRĪPORTUS (-us), a small place in Latium, of uncertain site, memorable for the victory of Sulla over the younger Marius, B.C. 82.

SACRUM PRŌMONTŌRĪUM. (1) (*C. St. Vincent*), on the W. coast of Spain.—(2) (*C. Corsa*), the N.E. point of Corsica.—(3) (*C. Iria,* also *Makri, Efta Kavi* or *Jedi Burum,* i.e. the 7 points), the extreme point of the mountain Cragus, in Lycia, between Xanthus and Telmissus.—(4) (*C. Khelidoni*), another promontory in Lycia, near the confines of Pamphylia, and opposite the Chelidonian islands, whence it is also called, PROM. CHELIDO-NIUM.

SADYATTES (-is), a king of Lydia, succeeded his father Ardys, and reigned B.C. 629—617. He carried on war with the Milesians for 6 years, and at his death bequeathed the war to his son and successor, Alyattes. [ALYATTES.]

SAEPĪNUM or SEPĪNUM (-is : *Sepino*), a municipium in Samnium, on the road from Allifae to Beneventum.

SAETĀBIS (-is). (1) (*Alcoy ?*), a river on the S. coast of Hispania Tarraconensis, W. of the Sucro.—(2) Or SETABIS (Setabitanus : *Jativa*), an important town of the Contestani, in Hispania Tarraconensis, and a Roman municipium, was situated on a hill S. of the Sucro, and was celebrated for its manufacture of linen.

SAGALASSUS (-i : *Allahsun,* Ru.), a large fortified city of Pisidia, near the Phrygian border, a day's journey S.E. of Apamea Cibotus. It lay, as its large ruins still show, in the form of an amphitheatre on the side of a hill, and had a citadel on a rock 30 feet high.

SĀGĂRIS (-is), a river of Sarmatia Europaea, falling into a bay in the N.W. of the Euxine, which was called after it SAGARICUS SINUS, and which also received the river Axiaces.

SAGARTII (-ōrum), according to Herodotus, a nomad people of Persis. Afterwards they are found, on the authority of Ptolemy, in Media and the passes of Mt. Zagros.

SAGRA (-ae), a small river in Magna Graecia, on the S.E. coast of Bruttium, falling into the sea between Caulonia and Locri.

SĂGUNTUM, more rarely SĂGUNTUS (-i: *Murviedro*), said to have been founded by the Zacynthians, a town of the Edetani or Sedetani, in Spain, S. of the Iberus, on the river Palantias, about 3 miles from the coast. Although S. of the Iberus, it had formed an alliance with the Romans ; and its siege by Hannibal, B.C. 219, was the immediate cause of the 2nd Punic war. The ruins of a theatre and a temple of Bacchus, are extant at *Murviedro*, which is a corruption of *Muri veteres*.

SAĬS (-is : *Sa-el-Hajjar*, Ru.), a great city of Egypt, in the Delta, on the E. side of the Canopic branch of the Nile. It was the ancient capital of Lower Egypt, and contained the palace and burial-place of the Pharaohs, as well as the tomb of Osiris. The city gave its name to the Saïtes Nomos.

SAĬTIS, a surname of Athena, under which she had a sanctuary on Mt. Pontinus, near Lerna, in Argolis. The name was traced by the Greeks to the Egyptians, among whom Athena was said to have been called Saïs.

SALA (-ae : *Saale*). (1) A river of Germany, between which and the Rhine Drusus died. It was a tributary of the Albis.—(2) (*Saale*), also a river of Germany, and a tributary of the Moenus, which formed the boundary between the Hermunduri and Chatti, with great salt springs in its neighbourhood.

SĂLĂCĬA (-ae), the female divinity of the sea among the Romans, and the wife of Neptune. The name is evidently connected with *sal* (ἅλς), and accordingly denotes the wide, open sea.

SĂLĂMIS (-Inis). (1) (*Koluri*), an island off the W. coast of Attica, from which it is separated by a narrow channel. It forms the S. boundary of the bay of Eleusis. Its greatest length, from N. to S., is about 10 miles, and its width, in its broadest part, from E. to W., is a little more. It is said to have been called Salamis from a daughter of Asopus, of this name. It was colonised at an early time by the Aeacidae of Aegina. Telamon, the son of Aeacus, fled thither after the murder of his half-brother Phocus, and became sovereign of the island. His son Ajax accompanied the Greeks with 12 Salaminian ships to the Trojan war. Salamis continued an independent state till about the beginning of the 40th Olympiad (B.C. 620), when a dispute arose for its possession between the Megarians and the Athenians. After a long struggle it first fell into the hands of the Megarians, but was finally taken possession of by the Athenians through a

stratagem of Solon [SOLON], and became one of the Attic demi. It continued to belong to Athens till the time of Cassander, when its inhabitants voluntarily surrendered it to the Macedonians, 318. The Athenians recovered the island in 232 through Aratus, and punished the Salaminians for their desertion to the Macedonians with great severity. The old city of Salamis stood on the S. side of the island, opposite Aegina ; but this was afterwards deserted, and a new city of the same name built on the E. coast opposite Attica, on a small bay now called *Ambelakia*. At the extremity of the S. promontory forming this bay was the small island of PSYTTALIA (*Lypsokutali*), which is about a mile long, and from 200 to 300 yards wide. Salamis is chiefly memorable on account of the great battle fought off its coast, in which the Persian fleet of Xerxes was defeated by the Greeks B.C. 480.—(2) An ancient city of Cyprus, situated in the middle of the E. coast a little N. of the river Pediaeus. Under Constantine it suffered from an earthquake, which buried a large portion of the inhabitants beneath its ruins. It was, however, rebuilt by Constantine, who gave it the name of Constantia, and made it the capital of the island. There are still a few ruins of this town.

SĂLĂPĬA (-ae : *Salpi*), an ancient town of Apulia, in the district Daunia, was situated S. of Sipontum, on a lake named after it. It is not mentioned till the 2nd Punic war, when it revolted to Hannibal after the battle of Cannae, but it subsequently surrendered to the Romans, and delivered to the latter the Carthaginian garrison stationed in the town.

SĂLĂPĬNA PĂLUS (*Lago di Salpi*), a lake of Apulia, between the mouths of the Cerbalus and Aufidus.

SALARĬA (-ae), a town of the Bastetani in Hispania Tarraconensis, and a Roman colony.

SĂLĀRĬA VĬA, a Roman road, which ran from the Porta Salaria through Fidenae, Reate, and Asculum Picenum, to Castrum Truentinum, and thence along the coast to Ancona.

SALASSI (-ōrum), a brave and warlike people in Gallia Transpadana, in the valley of the Duria, at the foot of the Graian and Pennine Alps, whom some regarded as a branch of the Salyes or Salluvii, in Gaul. Their chief town was Augusta Praetoria (*Aosta*).

SĂLENTĪNI or SALLENTĪNI (-ōrum), a people in the S. part of Calabria, who dwelt around the promontory Iapygium, which is hence called SALENTINUM or SALENTINA.

They were subdued by the Romans at the conclusion of their war with Pyrrhus.

SALERNUM (-i : *Salerno*), an ancient town in Campania, at the innermost corner of the Sinus Paestanus, situated on a hill near the coast. It was made a Roman colony B.C. 194; but it attained its greatest prosperity in the middle ages, after it had been fortified by the Lombards.

SALGANEUS or SALGANEA (-i, or -ae), a small town of Boeotia, on the Euripus, and on the road from Anthedon to Chalcis.

SALINAE (-ārum), salt-works, the name of several towns which possessed salt-works in their vicinity. (1) A town in Britain, on the E. coast, in the S. part of Lincolnshire. —(2) A town of the Suetrii, in the Maritime Alps in Gallia Narbonensis, E. of Reii.— (3) (*Torre delle Saline*), a place on the coast of Apulia, near Salapia.—(4) A place in Picenum, on the river Sannus (*Salino*).— (5) (*Torda*), a place in Dacia.—(6) SALINAE HERCULEAE, near Herculanum, in Campania.

SALINATOR (-ōris), LIVIUS. (1) M., consul B.C. 219, with L. Aemilius Paulus, carried on war along with his colleague against the Illyrians. On their return to Rome, both consuls were brought to trial on the charge of having unfairly divided the booty among the soldiers. Livius was condemned, but the sentence seems to have been an unjust one, and Livius took his disgrace so much to heart that he retired to his estate. In 210 the consuls compelled him to return to the city, and in 207 he was elected consul a 2nd time with C. Claudius Nero. He shared with his colleague in the glory of defeating Hasdrubal on the Metaurus. [NERO, CLAUDIUS.] Next year (206) Livius was stationed in Etruria, as proconsul, with an army, and his imperium was prolonged for 2 successive years. In 204 he was censor with his former colleague in the consulship, Claudius Nero, and imposed a tax upon salt, in consequence of which he received the surname of *Salinator*, which seems to have been given him in derision, but which became, notwithstanding, hereditary in his family.—(2) C., curule aedile, 203, and praetor 202, in which year he obtained Bruttii as his province.— (3) C., praetor 191, when he had the command of the fleet in the war against Antiochus. He was consul 188, and obtained Gaul as his province.

SALLENTINI. [SALENTINI.]

SALLUSTIUS CRISPUS, C., or SALUSTIUS (-i). (1) The Roman historian, belonged to a plebeian family, and was born B.C. 86, at Amiternum, in the country of the Sabines. He was quaestor about 59, and tribune of the plebs in 52, the year in which Clodius was killed by Milo. In his tribunate he joined the popular party, and took an active part in opposing Milo. In 50 Sallust was expelled from the senate by the censors, probably because he belonged to Caesar's party, though some give as the ground of his ejection from the senate his adultery with the wife of Milo. In the civil war he followed Caesar's fortune. In 47 we find him praetor elect, by obtaining which dignity he was restored to his rank. He nearly lost his life in a mutiny of some of Caesar's troops in Campania, who had been led thither to pass over into Africa. He accompanied Caesar in his African war (46), and was left by Caesar as the governor of Numidia, in which capacity he is charged with having oppressed the people, and enriched himself by unjust means. The charge is somewhat confirmed by the fact of his becoming immensely rich, as was shown by the expensive gardens which he formed (*horti Sallustiani*) on the Quirinalis. He retired into privacy after he returned from Africa, and passed quietly through the troublesome period after Caesar's death. He died 34, about 4 years before the battle of Actium. The story of his marrying Cicero's wife, Terentia, ought to be rejected. It was probably not till after his return from Africa that Sallust wrote his historical works, namely, the *Catilina*, or *Bellum Catilinarium*, a history of the conspiracy of Catiline during the consulship of Cicero, 63 ; the *Jugurtha*, or *Bellum Jugurthinum*, the history of the war of the Romans against Jugurtha, king of Numidia ; and the *Historiarum Libri Quinque*. This last work is lost, with the exception of fragments which have been collected and arranged. Besides these there are attributed to Sallust *Duae Epistolae de Republica ordinanda*, and a *Declamatio in Ciceronem*. Some of the Roman writers considered that Sallust imitated the style of Thucydides. His language is generally concise and perspicuous : perhaps his love of brevity may have caused the ambiguity that is sometimes found in his sentences. He also affected archaic words. He has, however, probably the merit of being the first Roman who wrote what is usually called history.—(2) The grandson of the sister of the historian, was adopted by the latter, and inherited his great wealth. On the fall of Maecenas he became the principal adviser of Augustus. He died in A.D. 20, at an advanced age. One of Horace's odes (*Carm.* ii. 2) is addressed to him.

SALMANTICA (-ae : *Salamanca*), called HELMANTICA or HERMANDICA by Livy, and ELMANTICA by Polybius, an important town of the Vettones, in Lusitania, S. of the Durius, on the road from Emerita to Caesar-augusta.

SALMŌNA or SALMŌNĬA (-ae), a town of Elis, in the district Pisatis, on the river Enipeus, said to have been founded by Salmoneus.

SALMŌNEUS (-ĕŏs, -ĕī), son of Aeolus and Enarete, and brother of Sisyphus. He originally lived in Thessaly, but emigrated to Elis, where he built the town of Salmone. His presumption and arrogance were so great that he deemed himself equal to Zeus (Jupiter), and ordered sacrifices to be offered to himself; nay, he even imitated the thunder and lightning of Zeus, but the father of the gods killed him with his thunderbolt, destroyed his town, and punished him in the lower world. His daughter Tyro bears the patronymic *Salmonis.*

SALMYDESSUS (-i), called HALMYDES-SUS also in later times (*Midja* or *Midjeh*), a town of Thrace, on the coast of the Euxine, S. of the promontory Thynias. The name was originally applied to the whole coast from this promontory to the entrance of the Bosporus; and it was from this coast that the Black Sea obtained the name of Pontus *Axenos,* or inhospitable.

SĂLO (-ōnis: *Xalon*), a tributary of the Iberus, in Celtiberia, which flowed by Bil-bilis, the birth-place of Martial, who accordingly frequently mentions it in his poems.

SĂLŌNA (-ae), SĂLŌNAE (-ārum), or SALON (-ōnis : *Salona*), an important town of Illyria, and the capital of Dalmatia, was situated on a small bay of the sea. The emperor Diocletian was born at the small village Dioclea, near Salona; and after his abdication he retired to the neighbourhood of this town, and here spent the rest of his days. The remains of his magnificent palace are still to be seen at the village of *Spalatro,* the ancient SPOLATUM, 3 miles S. of Salona.

SALVĬUS OTHO. [OTHO.]

SĂLUS (-ūtis), a Roman goddess, the personification of health, prosperity, and the public welfare. In the first of these three senses she answers closely to the Greek Hygieia, and was accordingly represented in works of art with the same attributes as the Greek goddess. In the second sense she represents prosperity in general. In the third sense she is the goddess of the public welfare (*Salus publica* or *Romana*). In this capacity a temple was vowed to her in the year B.C. 307, by the censor C. Junius Bubulcus, on the Quirinal hill, which was afterwards decorated with paintings by C. Fabius Pictor. She was worshipped publicly on the 30th of

April, in conjunction with Pax, Concordia, and Janus. Salus was represented, like Fortuna, with a rudder, a globe at her feet, and sometimes in a sitting posture, pouring from a patera a libation upon an altar, round which a serpent is winding.

SĂLUSTĬUS. [SALLUSTIUS.]

SĂLȲES (-um) or SALLUVĬI (-ōrum), the most powerful and most celebrated of all the Ligurian tribes, inhabited the S. coast of Gaul from the Rhone to the Maritime Alps. They were troublesome neighbours to Massilia, with which city they frequently carried on war. They were subdued by the Romans in B.C. 123 after a long and obstinate struggle, and the colony of Aquae Sextiae was founded in their territory by the consul Sextius.

SĂMĂRA. [SAMAROBRIVA.]

SĂMĂRĬA (-ae: Heb. Shomron, Chaldee, Shamraïn: SamarĪtes, pl. SamarĪtae), aft. SEBASTE (*Sebustieh*, Ru.), one of the chief cities of Palestine, was built by Omri, king of Israel (about B.C. 922), on a hill in the midst of a plain surrounded by mountains, just in the centre of Palestine W. of the Jordan. Its name was derived from Shemer, the owner of the hill which Omri purchased for its site. It was the capital of the kingdom of Israel, and the chief seat of the idolatrous worship to which the ten tribes were addicted, until it was taken by Shalmaneser, king of Assyria (about B.C. 720), who carried away the inhabitants of the city and of the surrounding country, which is also known in history as Samaria [see below], and replaced them by heathen peoples from the E. provinces of his empire. When the Jews returned from the Babylonish captivity, those of the Samaritans who worshipped Jehovah offered to assist them in rebuilding the temple at Jerusalem; but their aid was refused, and hence arose the lasting hatred between the Jews and the Samaritans. Under the Syrian kings and the Maccabean princes, we find the name of SAMARIA used distinctly as that of a province, which consisted of the district between Galilee on the N. and Judaea on the S. Pompey assigned the district to the province of Syria, and Gabinius fortified the city anew. Augustus gave the district to Herod, who greatly renovated the city of Samaria, which he called Sebaste in honour of his patron. By the 4th century of our era it had become a place of no importance. Its beautiful site is now occupied by a poor village, which bears the Greek name of the city, slightly altered, viz. *Sebustieh.* As a district of Palestine, Samaria extended from Ginaea (*Jenin*) on the N. to Bethhoron, N.W. of Gibeon on the S.; or, along the coast, from a little S. of Caesarea on the N. to a

little N. of Joppa on the S. It was intersected by the mountains of Ephraim, running
N. and S. through its middle, and by their
lateral branches, which divide their country
into beautiful and fertile valleys. [PALAES-
TINA.]

SAMAROBRĪVA (-ae), afterwards AM-
BIĀNI (*Amiens*), the chief town of the
Ambiani in Gallia Belgica, on the river
Samara; whence its name, which signifies
Samara-Bridge.

SĀME (-ēs) or SĀMOS (-i), the ancient
name of Cephallenia. [CEPHALLENIA.] It
was also the name of one of the 4 towns of
Cephallenia. The town Same or Samos was
situated on the E. coast, opposite Ithaca, and
was taken and destroyed by the Romans,
B.C. 189.

SAMNĪUM (-i) (Samnītes, -um, more
rarely Samnītae, pl.), a country in the centre
of Italy, bounded on the N. by the Marsi,
Peligni, and Marrucini, on the W. by Latium
and Campania, on the S. by Lucania, and on
the E. by the Frentani and Apulia. The Samnites were an offshoot of the Sabines, who
emigrated from their country between the
Nar, the Tiber, and the Anio, before the
foundation of Rome, and settled in the
country afterwards called Samnium. [SABINI.]
This country was at the time of their migration inhabited by Opicans, whom the Samnites
conquered, and whose language they adopted;
for we find at a later time that the Samnites
spoke Opican or Oscan. Samnium is a country
marked by striking physical features. The
greater part of it is occupied by a huge mass
of mountains, called at the present day the
Matese, which stands out from the central
line of the Apennines. The Samnites were
distinguished for their bravery and love of
freedom. Issuing from their mountain fastnesses, they overran a great part of Campania;
and it was in consequence of Capua applying
to the Romans for assistance against the
Samnites, that war broke out between the 2
peoples in B.C. 343. The Romans found the
Samnites the most warlike and formidable enemies whom they had yet encountered in Italy;
and the war, which commenced in 343, was
continued with few interruptions for the space
of 53 years. The civil war between Marius
and Sulla gave them hopes of recovering
their independence; but they were defeated
by Sulla before the gates of Rome (82), the
greater part of their troops fell in battle, and
the remainder were put to death. Their
owns were laid waste, the inhabitants sold
as slaves, and their place supplied by Roman
colonists.

SĀMOS or SĀMUS (-i : Greek *Samo*,
Turkish *Susam Adassi*), one of the principal

islands of the Aegaean Sea, lying in that
portion of it called the Icarian Sea, off the
coast of Ionia, from which it is separated only
by a narrow strait formed by the overlapping
of its E. promontory Posidium (*C. Colonna*)
with the W.-most spur of Mt. Mycale, Pr.
Trogilium (*C. S. Maria*). This strait, which
is little more than 3-4ths of a mile wide, was
the scene of the battle of MYCALE. The
island is formed by a range of mountains
extending from E. to W., whence it derived
its name; for Σάμος was an old Greek
word signifying a mountain. The circumference of the island is about 80 miles.
According to the earliest traditions, it was a
chief seat of the Carians and Leleges, and
the residence of their first king, Ancaeus;
and was afterwards colonised by Aeolians
from Lesbos, and by Ionians from Epidaurus.
The Samians early acquired such power at
sea that, besides obtaining possession of parts
of the opposite coast of Asia, they founded
many colonies. After a transition from the
state of an heroic monarchy, through an
aristocracy, to a democracy, the island became
subject to the most distinguished of the so-
called tyrants, POLYCRATES (B.C. 532), under
whom its power and splendour reached their
highest pitch, and Samos would probably
have become the mistress of the Aegaean, but
for the murder of Polycrates. At this period
the Samians had extensive commercial relations with Egypt, and they obtained from
Amasis the privilege of a separate temple at
Naucratis. The Samians now became subject
to the Persian empire, under which they were
governed by tyrants, with a brief interval at
the time of the Ionic revolt, until the battle
of Mycale, which made them independent,
B.C. 479. They now joined the Athenian
confederacy, of which they continued independent members until B.C. 440, when an
opportunity arose for reducing them to entire
subjection and depriving them of their fleet,
which was effected by Pericles after an obstinate resistance of 9 months' duration.
In the Peloponnesian war, Samos held firm
to Athens. Transferred to Sparta after the
battle of Aegospotami, 405, it was soon
restored to Athens by that of Cnidus, 394;
but went over to Sparta again in 390. Soon
after, it fell into the hands of the Persians,
being conquered by the satrap Tigranes; but
it was recovered by Timotheus for Athens.
In the Social war, the Athenians successfully
defended it against the attacks of the confederated Chians, Rhodians, and Byzantines,
and placed in it a body of 2000 cleruchi, B.C.
352. After Alexander's death, it was taken
from the Athenians by Perdiccas, 323; but
restored to them by Polysperchon, 319. In

the Macedonian war, Samos was taken by the Rhodians, then by Philip, and lastly by the Rhodians again, B.C. 200. It took part with Mithridates in his first war against Rome, on the conclusion of which it was finally united to the province of Asia, B.C. 84. Meanwhile it had greatly declined, and during the war it had been wasted by the incursions of pirates. Its prosperity was partially restored under the propraetorship of Q. Cicero, B.C. 62, but still more by the residence in it of Antony and Cleopatra, 32, and afterwards of Octavianus, who made Samos a free state. It sank into insignificance as early as the 2nd century. Samos may be regarded as almost the chief centre of Ionian manners, energies, luxury, science, and art. In very early times, there was a native school of statuary, and Samian architects became famous beyond their own island. In painting, the island produced Calliphon, Theodorus, Agatharchus, and Timanthes. Its pottery was celebrated throughout the ancient world. In literature, Samos was made illustrious by the poets Asius, Choerilus, and Aeschrion; by the philosophers Pythagoras and Melissus; and by the historians Pagaeus and Duris.—The capital city, also called SAMOS, stood on the S.E. side of the island, opposite Pr. Trogilium, partly on the shore, and partly rising on the hills behind in the form of an amphitheatre. It had a magnificent harbour, and numerous splendid buildings, among which, besides the Heraeum and other temples, the chief were the senate-house, the theatre, and a gymnasium dedicated to Eros. In the time of Herodotus, Samos was reckoned one of the finest cities of the world. Its ruins are so considerable as to allow its plan to be traced: there are remains of its walls and towers, and of the theatre and aqueduct.

SAMOSATA (*Someisat*), the capital of the province, and afterwards kingdom, of Commagene, in the N. of Syria, stood on the right bank of the Euphrates, N.W. of Edessa. It is celebrated, in literary history, as the birthplace of Lucian, and, in church history, as that of the heretic Paul, bishop of Antioch, in the 3rd century. Nothing remains of it but a heap of ruins.

SAMOTHRACE (-ēs) and SAMOTHRACIA (-ae: *Samothraki*), a small island in the N. of the Aegaean sea, opposite the mouth of the Hebrus in Thrace, from which it was 38 miles distant. It is about 32 miles in circumference, and contains in its centre a lofty mountain, called SAOCE, from which Homer says that Troy could be seen. Samothrace was the chief seat of the worship of the Cabiri [CABIRI], and was celebrated for its religious mysteries, which were some of the most famous in the ancient world. The

political history of Samothrace is of little importance.

SAMPSICERAMUS (-i), the name of a petty prince of Emesa in Syria; a nickname given by Cicero to Cn. Pompeius.

SANCHUNIATHON (-onis), said to have been an ancient Phoenician writer, whose works were translated into Greek by Philo Byblius, who lived in the latter half of the 1st century of the Christian era. A considerable fragment of the translation of Philo is preserved by Eusebius in the first book of his *Praeparatio Evangelica;* but it is now generally agreed among modern scholars, that the work was a forgery of Philo.

SANCUS, SANGUS, or SEMO SANCUS (-i), a Roman divinity, said to have been originally a Sabine god, and identical with Hercules and Dius Fidius. The name, which is etymologically the same as *Sanctus*, and connected with *Sancire*, seems to justify this belief, and characterises Sancus as a divinity presiding over oaths. Sancus had a temple at Rome, on the Quirinal, opposite that of Quirinus, and close by the gate which derived from him the name of *Sanqualis porta.*

SANDROCOTTUS (-i), an Indian king in the time of Seleucus Nicator, ruled over the powerful nation of the Gangaridae and Prasii on the banks of the Ganges.

SANGARIUS (-i), SANGARIS, or SAGARIS (*Sakariyeh*), the largest river of Asia Minor after the Halys, had its source in a mountain called Adoreus, near the little town of Sangia, on the borders of Galatia and Phrygia, whence it flowed first N. through Galatia, then W. and N.W. through the N.E. part of Phrygia, and then N. through Bithynia, of which it originally formed the E. boundary. It fell at last into the Euxine, about half way between the Bosporus and Heraclea.

SANGIA. [SANGARIUS.]

SANNIO (-ōnis), a name of the buffoon in the mimes, derived from *sanna*, whence comes the Italian *Zanni* (hence our *Zany*).

SANNYRION (-ōnis), an Athenian comic poet, flourished B.C. 407 and onwards. His excessive leanness was ridiculed by Strattis and Aristophanes.

SANTONES (-um) or SANTONI (-ōrum), a powerful people in Gallia Aquitanica, dwelt on the coast of the ocean, N. of the Garumna. Under the Romans they were a free people. Their chief town was Mediolanum, afterwards Santones (*Saintes*).

SAPAEI (-ōrum), a people in Thrace, dwelt on Mt. Pangaeus, between the lake Bistonis and the coast.

SAPIS (-is: *Savio*), a small river in Gallia Cisalpina, rising in the Apennines, and flowing into the Adriatic S. of Ravenna, between the Po and the Aternus.

SĀPŎR. [SASSANIDAE.]

SAPPHŎ (-ūs), one of the two great leaders of the Aeolian school of lyric poetry (Alcaeus being the other), was a native of Mytilene, or, as some said, of Eresos in Lesbos. Sappho was contemporary with Alcaeus, Stesichorus, and Pittacus. That she was not only contemporary, but lived in friendly intercourse, with Alcaeus, is shown by existing fragments of the poetry of both. Of the events of her life we have no other information than an obscure allusion in the Parian Marble, and in Ovid (*Her.* xv. 51), to her flight from Mytilene to Sicily, to escape some unknown danger, between 604 and 592; and the common story that being in love with Phaon, and finding her love unrequited, she leapt down from the Leucadian rock. This story, however, seems to have been an invention of later times. At Mytilene Sappho appears to have been the centre of a female literary society, most of the members of which were her pupils in poetry, fashion, and gallantry. The ancient writers agree in expressing the most unbounded admiration for her poetry. Her lyric poems formed 9 books, but of these only fragments have come down to us. The most important is a splendid ode to Aphrodite (Venus), of which we perhaps possess the whole.

SARANCAE, SARANGAE or -ES (-ārum), a people of Sogdiana.

. SARDĀNĀPĀLUS (-i), the last king of the Assyrian empire of Ninus or Nineveh, noted for his luxury, licentiousness, and effeminacy. He passed his time in his palace unseen by any of his subjects, dressed in female apparel, and surrounded by concubines. At length Arbaces, satrap of Media, and Belesys, the noblest of the Chaldaean priests, resolved to renounce allegiance to such a worthless monarch, and advanced at the head of a formidable army against Nineveh. But all of a sudden the effeminate prince threw off his luxurious habits, and appeared an undaunted warrior. Placing himself at the head of his troops, he twice defeated the rebels, but was at length worsted and obliged to shut himself up in Nineveh. Here he sustained a siege for two years, till at length, finding it impossible to hold out any longer, he collected all his treasures, wives, and concubines, and placing them on an immense pile which he had constructed, set it on fire, and thus destroyed both himself and them, B.C. 876. This is the account of Ctesias, which has been preserved by Diodorus Siculus, and which has been followed by most subsequent writers and chronologists. Modern writers however

have shown that the whole narrative of Ctesias is mythical, and it is in direct contradiction to Herodotus and the writers of the Old Testament.

SARDI. [SARDINIA.]

SARDĪNĬA (-ae: Sardi: *Sardinia*), a large island in the Mediterranean, is in the shape of a parallelogram, upwards of 140 nautical miles in length from N. to S. with an average breadth of 60. It was regarded by the ancients as the largest of the Mediterranean islands, and this opinion, though usually considered an error, is now found to be correct; since it appears by actual admeasurement that Sardinia is a little larger than Sicily. Sardinia lies in almost a central position between Spain, Gaul, Italy, and Africa. A chain of mountains runs along the whole of the E. side of the island from N. to S. occupying about 1-3rd of its surface. These mountains were called by the ancients Insani Montes, a name which they probably derived from their wild and savage appearance, and from their being the haunt of numerous robbers. Sardinia was very fertile, but was not extensively cultivated, in consequence of the uncivilised character of its inhabitants. Still the plains in the W. and S. parts of the island produced a great quantity of corn, of which much was exported to Rome every year. Among the products of the island one of the most celebrated was the *Sardonica herba*, a poisonous plant, which was said to produce fatal convulsions in the person who ate of it. These convulsions agitated and distorted the mouth so that the person appeared to laugh, though in excruciating pain; hence the well-known *risus Sardonicus*. Sardinia contained a large quantity of the precious metals, especially silver, the mines of which were worked in antiquity to a great extent. There were likewise numerous mineral springs; and large quantities of salt were manufactured on the W. and S. coasts.—The population of Sardinia was of a very mixed kind. To what race the original inhabitants belonged we are not informed; but it appears that Phoenicians, Tyrrhenians, and Carthaginians settled in the island at different periods. The Greeks are also said to have planted colonies in the island, but this account is very suspicious. Sardinia was known to the Greeks as early as B.C. 500, since we find that Histiaeus of Miletus promised Darius that he would render the island of Sardo tributary to his power. It was conquered by the Carthaginians at an early period, and continued in their possession till the end of the first Punic war. Shortly after this event, the Romans availed themselves of the dangerous war which the Carthaginians were carrying on against their mercenaries in Africa, to take possession of Sardinia, B.C. 238. It was now formed into a Roman province under the government of a praetor; but a large portion of it was only nominally subject to the Romans; and it was not till after many years and numerous revolts, that the inhabitants submitted to the Roman dominion. Sardinia continued to belong to the Roman empire till the 5th century, when it was taken possession of by the Vandals.

SARDĪS (-is), or SARDES (-ium : Sardiāni : *Sart*, Ru.), one of the most ancient and famous cities of Asia Minor, and the capital of the great Lydian monarchy, stood on the S. edge of the rich valley of the Hermus, at the N. foot of the Mt. Tmolus, on the little river Pactolus, 30 stadia (3 geog. miles) S. of the junction of that river with the Hermus. On a lofty precipitous rock, forming an outpost of the range of Tmolus, was the almost impregnable citadel, which some suppose to be the Hyde of Homer, who, though he never mentions the Lydians or Sardis by name, speaks of Mt. Tmolus and the lake of Gyges. The erection of this citadel was ascribed to Meles, an ancient king of Lydia. It was surrounded by a triple wall, and contained the palace and treasury of the Lydian kings. At the downfall of the Lydian empire, it resisted all the attacks of Cyrus, and was only taken by surprise. Under the Persian and Greco-Syrian empires, Sardis was the residence of the satrap of Lydia. The rise of Pergamus greatly diminished its importance; but under the Romans it was still a considerable city, and the seat of a conventus juridicus. In the reign of Tiberius, it was almost entirely destroyed by an earthquake, but it was restored by the emperor's aid. It was one of the earliest seats of the Christian religion, and one of the 7 churches of the province of Asia, to which St. John addressed the Apocalypse; but the apostle's anguage implies that the church at Sardis had already sunk into almost hopeless decay (Rev. iii. 1, foll.). In the wars of the middle ages the city was entirely destroyed, and its site now presents one of the most melancholy scenes of desolation to be found among the ruins of ancient cities.

SARMĀTAE or SAURŌMĀTAE (-ārum), a people of Asia, dwelling on the N.E. of the Palus Maeotis (*Sea of Azov*), E. of the river Tanaïs (*Don*), which separated them from the Scythians of Europe. [SARMATIA.]

SARMĀTĪA (-ae), (the E. part of *Poland*, and S. part of *Russia in Europe*,) a name first used by Mela for the part of N. Europe and Asia extending from the Vistula (*Wisla*) and the SARMATICI MONTES on the W., which divided it from Germany, to the Rha (*Volga*) on the E., which divided it from Scythia; bounded on the S.W. and S. by the rivers Ister (*Danube*), Tibiscus (*Theiss*), and Tyras (*Dniester*), which divided it from Pannonia and Dacia, and, farther, by the Euxine, and beyond it by M. Caucasus, which divided it from Colchis, Iberia, and Albania; and extending on the N. as far as the *Baltic* and the unknown regions of N. Europe. The people from whom the name of Sarmatia was derived inhabited only a small portion of the country. The greater part of it was peopled by Scythian tribes; but some of the inhabitants of its W. part seem to have been of German origin, as the VENEDI on the *Baltic*, and the IAZYGES, RHOXOLANI, and HAMAXOBII in *S. Russia*: the chief of the other tribes W. of the Tanaïs were the Alauni or Alani Scythae, a Scythian people who came out of Asia and settled in the central parts of *Russia*. The whole country was divided by the river Tanaïs (*Don*) into 2 parts called respectively Sarmatia Europaea and Sarmatia Asiatica; but it should be observed that, according to the modern division of the continent, the whole of Sarmatia belongs to Europe. It should also be noticed that the Chersonesus Taurica (*Crimea*), though falling within the specified limits, was not considered as a part of Sarmatia, but as a separate country.

SARMĀTĪCAE PORTAE (-ārum), (*Pass of Dariel*), the central pass of the Caucasus, leading from Iberia to Sarmatia.

SARMĀTĪCI MONTES, (part of the *Carpathian Mountains*,) a range of mountains in central Europe, extending from the sources of the Vistula to the Danube, between Germany on the W. and Sarmatia on the E.

SARMĀTĪCUS OCEĂNUS and PONTUS, SARMĀTĪCUM MĂRE (*Baltic*), a great sea, washing the N. coast of European Sarmatia.

SARNUS (-i : *Sarno*), a river in Campania, flowing by Nuceria, and falling into the Sinus Puteolanus near Pompeii.

SĂRŌNĬCUS SĪNUS (*G. of Egina*), a bay of the Aegaean sea lying between Attica and Argolis, and commencing between the promontory of Sunium in Attica and that of Scyllaeum in Argolis.

SARPĒDON (-ŏnis). (1) Son of Zeus (Jupiter) and Europa, and brother of Minos and Rhadamanthus. Being involved in a quarrel with Minos about Miletus, he took refuge with Cilix, whom he assisted agains the Lycians. [MILETUS.] He afterwards became king of the Lycians, and Zeus granted him the privilege of living 3 generations.— (2) Son of Zeus and Laodamia, or, according to others, of Evander and Deidamia, and a brother of Clarus and Themon. He was a Lycian prince, and a grandson of No. 1. In the Trojan war he was an ally of the Trojans, and distinguished himself by his valour, but was slain by Patroclus.

SARPĒDON PRŌMONTŌRĬUM (*C. Lissan el Kapeh*), a promontory of Cilicia, in long. 34° E., 80 stadia W. of the mouth of the Calycadnus.

SARPEDŌNĬUM PROM. (-i), a promontory of Thrace betw en the mouths of the rivers Melas and Erginus, opposite the island of Imbros.

SARRASTES. [SARNUS.]

SARSĬNA (-ae : *Sarsina*), an ancient town of Umbria, on the river Sapis, S.W. of Ariminum, and subsequently a Roman municipium, celebrated as the birthplace of the comic poet Plautus.

SARUS (-i : *Scihan*), a considerable river in the S.E. of Asia Minor. Rising in the Anti-Taurus, in the centre of Cappadocia, it flows S. past Comana to the borders of Cilicia, where it receives a W. branch that has run nearly parallel to it; and thence, flowing through Cilicia Campestris in a winding course, it falls into the sea a little E. of the mouth of the Cydnus, and S.E. of Tarsus.

SĀSO or SASŌNIS INSŬLA (*Saseno, Sassono, Sassa*), a small rocky island off the coast of Illyria, N. of the Acroceraunian promontory, much frequented by pirates.

SASPĪRES (-um) or SASPIRI (-orum), a Scythian people of Asia, S. of Colchis and N. of Media, in an inland position (*i. e.* in Armenia) according to Herodotus, but, according to others, on the coast of the Euxine.

SASSANĬDAE (-ārum), the name of a dynasty which reigned in Persia from A.D. 226 to A.D. 651. (1) ARTAXERXES (the ARDISHIR or ARDSHIR of the Persians), the founder of the dynasty of the Sassanidae, reigned A.D. 226—240. He was a son of one Babek, an inferior officer. Artaxerxes had served with distinction in the army of Artabanus, the king of Parthia, was rewarded with ingratitude, and took revenge in revolt. He claimed the throne on the plea of being descended from the ancient kings of Persia, the progeny of the great Cyrus. The people warmly supported his cause, as he declared himself the champion of the ancient Persian religion. In 226 Artabanus was defeated in a decisive battle ; and Artaxerxes thereupon assumed the pompous, but national title of "King of Kings." One of his first legislative acts was the restoration of the religion of Zoroaster and the worship of fire. Having succeeded in establishing his authority at home, Artaxerxes demanded from the em-

peror Alexander Severus the immediate cession of all those portions of the Roman empire that had belonged to Persia in the time of Cyrus and Xerxes, that is, the whole of the Roman possessions in Asia, as well as Egypt. An immediate war between the two empires was the direct consequence. After a severe contest, peace was restored, shortly after the murder of Alexander in 237, each nation retaining the possessions which they held before the breaking out of the war.— (2) SAPOR I. (SHAPUR), the son and successor of Artaxerxes I., reigned 240—273. He carried on war first against Gordian, and afterwards against Valerian. The latter emperor was defeated by Sapor, taken prisoner, and kept in captivity for the remainder of his life. After the capture of Valerian, Sapor conquered Syria, destroyed Antioch, and having made himself master of the passes in the Taurus, laid Tarsus in ashes, and took Caesarea. His further progress was stopped by Odenathus and Zenobia.—(3) HORMISDAS I. (HORMUZ), son of the preceding, who reigned only one year, and died 274.—(4) VARANES or VARARANES I. (BAHRAM or BAHARAM), son of Hormisdas I., reigned 274—277. He carried on unprofitable wars against Zenobia, and after her captivity, was involved in a contest with Aurelian, which however, was not attended with any serious results, on account of the sudden death of Aurelian in 275. In his reign the celebrated Mani was put to death.—(5) VARANES II. (BAHRAM), son of Varanes I., reigned 277—294. He was defeated by Carus, who took both Seleucia and Ctesiphon, and his dominions were only saved from further conquests by the sudden death of Carus (283).—(6) VARANES III. (BAHRAM), elder son of Varanes II., died after a reign of 8 months, 294.—(7) NARSES (NARSI), younger son of Varanes II., reigned 294—303. He carried on a formidable war against the emperor Diocletian ; but in the second campaign Narses was defeated with great loss, and was obliged to conclude a disadvantageous peace with the Romans. In 303 Narses abdicated in favour of his son, and died soon afterwards.—(8) HORMISDAS II. (HORMUZ), son of Narses, reigned 303—310. During his reign nothing of importance happened regarding Rome.—(9) SAPOR II. POSTUMUS (SHAPUR), son of Hormisdas II., was born after the death of his father, and was crowned in his mother's womb, the Magi placing the diadem with great solemnity upon the body of his mother. He reigned 310 -381. His reign was signalised by a cruel persecution of the Christians. He carried on a successful war for many years against Constantius II., and his successors. Sapor has been surnamed the Great, and no Persian king had ever caused such terror to Rome as this monarch. Sapor was succeeded by 18 princes of the same dynasty ; but in 651 Yesdigerd III., the last king, was defeated and slain by Kaleb, general of the Khalif Abu-Bekr. Persia then became a Mahomedan country.

SASSŪLA (-ae), a town in Latium, belonging to the territory of Tiber.

SĂTĂLA (-ōrum), a considerable town in the N.E. of Armenia Minor, important as the key of the mountain passes into Pontus. It stood at the junction of 4 roads leading to places on the Euxine, a little N. of the Euphrates, in a valley surrounded by mountains, 325 Roman miles from Caesarea in Cappadocia, and 135 from Trapezus.

SĂTĬCŬLA (-ae), a town of Samnium, situated upon a mountain on the frontiers of Campania.

SATRĬCUM (-i : *Casale di Conca*), a town in Latium, near Antium.

SĂTŬRAE PĂLŬS (*Lago di Paola*), a lake or marsh in Latium, formed by the river Nymphaeus, and near the promontory Circeium.

SĂTŬRIUM or SĂTŬREIUM (-i : *Saturo*), a town in the S. of Italy, near Tarentum, celebrated for its horses. (Hor. *Sat.* i. 6. 59.)

SATURNĬA (-ae). (1) An ancient name of Italy [ITALIA].—(2) (*Saturnia*), formerly called AURINIA, an ancient town of Etruria, said to have been founded by the Pelasgians, was situated in the territory of Caletra, on the road from Rome to Cosa, about 20 miles from the sea.

SĂTURNĬNUS (-i). (1) One of the Thirty Tyrants, was a general of Valerian, by whom he was much beloved. Disgusted by the debauchery of Gallienus, he accepted from the soldiers the title of emperor, but was put to death by the troops, who could not endure the sternness of his discipline.—(2) A native of Gaul, and an able officer, was appointed by Aurelian commander of the Eastern frontier, and was proclaimed emperor at Alexandria during the reign of Probus, by whose soldiers he was eventually slain.

SĂTURNĬNUS (-i), L. APPULEIUS, the celebrated demagogue, was quaestor B.C. 104, and tribune of the plebs for the first time 102. He entered into a close alliance with Marius and his friends, and soon acquired great popularity. He became a candidate for the tribunate for the 2nd time, 100, and obtained it by the murder of his rival. As soon as he had entered upon office, he brought forward an agrarian law, which led to the banishment of Metellus Numidicus, as is related elsewhere. [METELLUS.] Saturninus proposed other popular measures, such as a

Lex Frumentaria, and a law for founding new colonies in Sicily, Achaia, and Macedonia. In the comitia for the election of the magistrates for the following year, Saturninus obtained the tribunate for the third time. At the same time there was a struggle for the consulship between Glaucia and Memmius, and as the latter seemed likely to carry his election, Saturninus and Glaucia hired some ruffians who murdered him openly in the comitia. This last act produced a complete reaction against Saturninus and his associates. The senate declared them public enemies, and ordered the consuls to put them down by force. Marius was unwilling to act against his friends, but he had no alternative, and his backwardness was compensated by the zeal of others. Driven out of the forum, Saturninus, Glaucia, and the quaestor Saufeius took refuge in the Capitol, but the partisans of the senate cut off the pipes which supplied the Capitol with water. Unable to hold out any longer, they surrendered to Marius. The latter did all he could to save their lives ; as soon as they descended from the Capitol, he placed them for security in the Curia Hostilia, but the mob pulled off the tiles of the senate-house, and pelted them with the tiles till they died.

SĂTURNĬUS (-i), that is, a son of Saturnus, and accordingly used as a surname of Jupiter, Neptune, and Pluto. For the same reason the name of SATURNIA is given both to Juno and Vesta.

SĂTURNUS (-i), a mythical king of Italy, whom the Romans invariably identified with the Greek Cronos, and hence made the former the father of Jupiter, Neptune, Pluto, Juno, &c. [CRONOS] ; but there is in reality no resemblance between the attributes of the two deities, except that both were regarded as the most ancient divinities in their respective countries. The resemblance is much stronger between Demeter (Ceres) and Saturn, for all that the Greeks ascribe to their Demeter is ascribed by the Italians to Saturn. Saturnus derived his name from sowing (*sero, sevi, satum*), and was reputed the introducer of civilisation and social order, which are inseparably connected with agriculture. His reign is conceived for the same reason to have been the golden age of Italy. As agricultural industry is the source of wealth, his wife was Ops, the representative of plenty. The story ran that the god came to Italy in the reign of Janus, by whom he was hospitably received, and that he formed a settlement on the Capitoline hill, which was hence called the Saturnian hill. At the foot of that hill, on the road leading up to the Capitol, there stood in after times the temple of Saturn.

Saturn then taught the people agriculture, suppressed their savage mode of life, and introduced among them civilisation and morality. The result was that the whole country was called Saturnia or the land of plenty. It is further related that Latium received its name (from *lateo*) from the disappearance of Saturn, who was suddenly removed from earth, and who for the same reason was regarded by some as a divinity of the nether world. Respecting the festival solemnised by the Romans in honour of Saturn, see *Dict. of Antiq. s. v. Saturnalia.* The statue of Saturnus was hollow and filled with oil, probably to denote the fertility of Latium in olives; in his hand he held a crooked pruning-knife, and his feet were surrounded with a woollen riband. The temple of Saturn was used as the treasury of the state, and many laws were also deposited in it.

SĂTYRI (-ōrum), the name of a class of beings in Greek mythology, who are inseparably connected with the worship of Dionysus (Bacchus), and represent the luxuriant vital powers of nature. They are commonly said to be the sons of Hermes and Iphthima, or of the Naiades. The Satyrs are represented with bristly hair, the nose round and somewhat turned upwards, the ears pointed at the top, like those of animals, with 2 small horns

Satyr. (From a Statue in the Louvre.)

growing out of the top of the forehead, and with a tail like that of a horse or goat. In works of art they are represented at different stages of life; the older ones were commonly called Sileni, and the younger ones are termed Satyrisci. The Satyrs are always described as fond of wine (whence they often appear either with a cup or a thyrsus in their hand), and of every kind of sensual pleasure, whence they are seen sleeping, playing musical instruments, or engaged in voluptuous dances with nymphs. They are dressed with the skins of animals, and wear wreaths of vine, ivy or fir. Like all the gods dwelling in forests and fields, they were greatly dreaded by mortals. Later writers, especially the Roman poets, confound the Satyrs with the Italian Fauni, and accordingly represent them with larger horns and goats' feet, although originally they were quite distinct kinds of beings.

SĂTYRUS (-i) a distinguished comic actor at Athens, is said to have given instructions to Demosthenes in the art of giving full effect to his speeches by appropriate action.

SĂVO (-ōnis: *Saone*), a river in Campania, which flows into the sea S. of Sinuessa.

SĂVUS (-i: *Save* or *Sau*), a navigable tributary of the Danube, which rises in the Carnic Alps, forms first the boundary between Noricum and Italy, and afterwards between Pannonia and Illyria, and falls into the Danube near Singidunum.

SAXA (-ae), DĒCĪDĬUS, a native of Celtiberia, and originally one of Caesar's common soldiers, eventually accompanied Antony to the East, and was made by him governor of Syria. Here he was defeated by the younger Labienus and the Parthians, and was slain in the flight after the battle (40).

SAXA (-ae), Q. VŎCŌNĬUS, tribune of the plebs, B.C. 169, proposed the Voconia lex, respecting which see *Dict. of Antiq, s. v.*

SAXA RUBRA. [RUBRA SAXA.]

SAXŌNES (-um), a powerful people in Germany, who originally dwelt in the S. part of the Cimbric Chersonesus, between the rivers Albis (*Elbe*) and Chalusus (*Trave*), consequently in the modern Holstein. The Saxones first occur in history in A.D. 286, and afterwards appear at the head of a powerful confederacy of German peoples, who became united under the general name of Saxons, and who eventually occupied the country between the Elbe, the Rhine, the Lippe, and the German ocean. A portion of the Saxons, in conjunction with the Angli, conquered Britain about the middle of the 5th century.

SCAEVA (-ae), CASSĬUS, a centurion in Caesar's army, who distinguished himself by his extraordinary feats of valour at the battle of Dyrrhachium.

SCAEVŎLA (-ae), the name of a distin-

guished family of the Mucia Gens. (1)
C. Mucius Scaevola. When King Porsenna
was blockading Rome, C. Mucius went out
of the city with the intention of killing
him, but by mistake stabbed the king's
secretary instead of Porsenna himself. The
king in his passion and alarm ordered him to
be burnt alive, upon which Mucius thrust
his right hand into a fire which was already
lighted for a sacrifice, and held it there
without flinching. The king amazed at his
firmness, ordered him to be removed from
the altar, and bade him go away free and
uninjured. To make some return for his
generous behaviour, Mucius told him that
there were 300 of the first youths of Rome
who had agreed with one another to kill the
king, that the lot fell on him to make the
first attempt, and that the rest would do the
same when their turn came. Porsenna being
alarmed for his life, which he could not
secure against so many desperate men, made
proposals of peace to the Romans, and
evacuated the territory. Mucius received
the name of Scaevola, or left-handed, from
the circumstance of the loss of his right hand.
—(2) P. Mucius Scaevola, tribune of the
plebs 141; praetor 136; and consul 133, the
year in which Tib. Gracchus lost his life.
In 131 he succeeded his brother Mucianus
as pontifex maximus. Scaevola was distinguished for his knowledge of the *Jus Ponti-
ficium*. His fame as a lawyer is recorded by
Cicero in several passages.—(3) Q. Mucius
Scaevola, the augur, married the daughter
of C. Laelius, the friend of Scipio Africanus
the younger. He was tribune of the plebs
128, plebeian aedile 125, and as praetor was
governor of the province of Asia in 121, the
year in which C. Gracchus lost his life. He
was prosecuted after his return from his
province for the offence of repetundae, in
120, by T. Albucius but was acquitted. He
was consul 117. He lived at least to the
tribunate of P. Sulpicius Rufus 88. Cicero,
who was born 106, informs us, that after he
had put on the toga virilis, his father took
him to Scaevola, who was then an old man,
and that he kept as close to him as he could,
in order to profit by his remarks. After his
death Cicero became a hearer of Q. Mucius
Scaevola, the pontifex. The augur was
distinguished for his knowledge of the law;
but none of his writings are recorded. He
is one of the speakers in the treatise *De
Oratore*, in the *Laelius*, and in the *de Republica* (i. 12).—(4) Q. Mucius Scaevola,
pontifex maximus, son of No. 2, was tribune
of the plebs in 106, curule aedile in 104, and
consul 95, with Licinius Crassus, the orator,
as his colleague. After his consulship Scae-

vola was proconsul of Asia, in which capacity
he gained the esteem of the people under his
government. Subsequently he was made
pontifex maximus. He lost his life in the
consulship of C. Marius the younger and Cn.
Papirius Carbo (82), having been proscribed
by the Marian party. The virtues of Scaevola
are recorded by Cicero, who, after the death
of the augur, became an attendant (auditor)
of the pontifex. The purity of his moral
character, his exalted notions of equity and
fair dealing, his abilities as an administrator,
an orator, and a jurist, place him among the
first of the illustrious men of all ages and
countries. He is the first Roman to whom
we can attribute a scientific and systematic
handling of the Jus Civile, which he accomplished in a work in 18 books.

SCALDIS (-is: *Scheldt*), an important
river in the N. of Gallia Belgica, flowing
into the ocean, but which Caesar erroneously
makes a tributary of the Mosa.

SCAMANDER (-dri). (1) A river in the
W. part of the N. coast of Sicily, falling into
the sea near Segesta.—(2) The celebrated
river of the Troad. [Troas.] As a mythological personage, the river-god was called
Xanthus by the gods.

SCAMANDRIUS (-i), son of Hector and
Andromache, whom the people of Troy called
Astyanax, because his father was the pro-
tector of the city of Troy.

SCANDEA. [Cythera.]

SCANDIA or SCANDINAVIA (-ae), the
name given by the ancients to Norway,
Sweden, and the surrounding islands.

SCANDILA (-ae: *Scandole*), a small
island in the N.E. of the Aegaean sea, between Peparethos and Scyros.

SCANTIA SILVA (-ae), a wood in Campania.

SCAPTE HYLE (-es), also called, but less
correctly, Scaptesyle, a small town on the
coast of Thrace, opposite the island of Thasos.
It contained celebrated gold mines, which
were originally worked by the Thasians.
Thucydides here arranged the materials for
his history.

SCAPTIA (-ae), an ancient town in Latium,
which gave its name to a Roman tribe, but
which disappeared at an early period.

SCAPULA (-ae), P. OSTORIUS, governor
of Britain about A.D. 50, defeated the powerful tribe of the Silures, took prisoner their
king Caractacus, and sent him in chains to
Rome.

SCARDUS or SCORDUS MONS (-i), a
range of lofty mountains, forming the boundary between Moesia and Macedonia.

SCARPHE (-es) SCARPHEA or SCAR-
PHIA (-ae), a town of the Epicnemidii Locri,

at which the roads leading through Thermopylae united.

SCAURUS (-i), the name of a family of the Aemilia gens. (1) M. AEMILIUS SCAURUS, raised his family from obscurity to the highest rank among the Roman nobles. He was born in B.C. 163. Notwithstanding his patrician descent, he at first thought of carrying on some mean trade, like his father, but finally resolved to devote himself to the study of eloquence, with the hope of rising to the honours of the state. He likewise served in the army, where he appears to have gained some distinction. He was curule aedile in 123. He obtained the consulship in 115, when he carried on war with success against several of the Alpine tribes. In 112 he was sent at the head of an embassy to Jugurtha; and in 111 he accompanied the consul L. Calpurnius Bestia, as one of his legates, in the war against Jugurtha. Both he and the consul took large bribes from the Numidian king-to obtain for him a favourable peace, for which offence an indictment was brought forward by C. Mamilius, the tribune of the plebs; but though Scaurus had been one of the most guilty, such was his influence in the state, that he contrived to be appointed one of the three quaesitores, who were elected under the bill, for the purpose of prosecuting the criminals. He thus secured himself, but was unable to save any of his accomplices. In 109, Scaurus was censor with M. Livius Drusus. In his consulship he restored the Milvian bridge, and constructed the Aemilian road. In 107 he was elected consul a second time, in place of L. Cassius Longinus. In the struggles between the aristocratical and popular parties, Scaurus was always a warm supporter of the former. He died about 89. —(2) M. AEMILIUS SCAURUS, eldest son of the preceding, and stepson of the dictator Sulla, served under Pompey as quaestor in the third Mithridatic war. After this he commanded an army in the East. He was curule aedile in 58, when he celebrated the public games with extraordinary splendour. In 56 he was praetor, and in the following year governed the province of Sardinia, which he plundered without mercy. On his return to Rome he was accused of the crime of repetundae. He was defended by Cicero, Hortensius, and others, and was acquitted, notwithstanding his guilt. He was accused again in 52, under Pompey's new law against ambitus, and was condemned.—(3) M. AEMILIUS SCAURUS, son of No. 2, and Mucia, the former wife of Pompey the triumvir, and consequently the half-brother of Sex. Pompey. He accompanied the latter into Asia, after the defeat of his fleet in Sicily, but betrayed

him into the hands of the generals of M. Antonius, in 35. — (4) MAMERCUS AEMILIUS SCAURUS, son of No. 3, was a distinguished orator and poet, but of a dissolute character. Being accused of majestas under Tiberius, A.D. 34, he put an end to his own life.

SCELERATUS CAMPUS (-i), a place in Rome, close to the Porta Collina, where vestals who had broken their vows were entombed alive.

SCENITAE (-ārum) (i.e. *dwellers in tents*), the general name used by the Greeks for the Bedawee (Bedouin) tribes of Arabia Deserta.

SCEPSIS (prob. *Eski-Upshi*, or *Eski-Shupshe*, Ru.), an ancient city in the interior of the Troad, S.E. of Alexandria, in the mountains of Ida.

SCHERIA. [PHAEACES.]

SCIATHUS (-i: *Skiatho*), a small island in the Aegaean sea, N. of Euboea and E. of the Magnesian coast of Thessaly, with a town of the same name upon it.

SCILLUS (-untis), a town of Elis in the district Triphylia, on the river Selinus, 20 stadia S. of Olympia.

SCIONE (-ēs), the chief town in the Macedonian peninsula of Pallene, on the W. coast.

SCIPIO (-ōnis), the name of an illustrious patrician family of the Cornelia gens, said to have been given to the founder of the family, because he served as a staff in directing his blind father. This family produced some of the greatest men in Rome, and to them she was more indebted than to any others for the empire of the world. The family tomb of the Scipios was discovered in 1780, and the inscriptions and other curiosities are now deposited in the Museo Pio-Clementino, at Rome.—(1) P. CORNELIUS SCIPIO, magister equitum, B.C. 396, and consular tribune 395, and 394.—(2) L. CORN. SCIPIO, consul 350. —(3) P. CORN. SCIPIO BARBATUS, consul 328, and dictator, 306. He was also pontifex maximus.—(4) L. CORN. SCIPIO BARBATUS, the great great-grandfather of the conqueror of Hannibal, consul 298, when he carried on war against the Etruscans, and defeated them near Volaterrae.—(5) CN. CORN. SCIPIO ASINA, son of No. 4, was consul 260, in the 1st Punic war, and a 2nd time in 254.—(6) L. CORN. SCIPIO, also son of No. 4, was consul 259. He drove the Carthaginians out of Sardinia and Corsica, defeating Hanno, the Carthaginian commander. He was censor in 258.—(7) P. CORN. SCIPIO ASINA, son of No. 5, was consul 221, and carried on war with his colleague M. Minucius Rufus, against the Istri, who were subdued by the consuls.— (8) P. CORN. SCIPIO, son of No. 6, was consul,

with Ti. Sempronius Longus, in 218, the 1st
year of the 2nd Punic war. He encountered
Hannibal, on his march into Italy, in Cisalpine Gaul ; but the Romans were defeated, the
consul himself received a severe wound, and
was only saved from death by the courage of
his young son, Publius, the future conqueror
of Hannibal. Scipio now retreated across the
Ticinus, crossed the Po also, first took up his
quarters at Placentia, and subsequently withdrew to the hills on the left· bank of the
Trebia, where he was joined by the other
consul, Sempronius Longus. The latter resolved upon a battle, in opposition to the
advice of his colleague. The result was the
complete defeat of the Roman army, which
was obliged to take refuge within the walls
of Placentia. In the following year 217,
Scipio, whose imperium had been prolonged,
crossed over into Spain ; where, with his
brother Cneius, he made head against the
Carthaginians till 211, when they were defeated and slain.—(9) Cn. Corn. Scipio
Calvus, son of No. 6, and brother of No. 8,
was consul 222, with M. Claudius Marcellus.—
(10) P. Corn. Scipio Africanus Major, son
of No. 8, was born in 234. He was unquestionably one of the greatest men of Rome,
and he acquired at an early age the confidence and admiration of his countrymen.
His enthusiastic mind led him to believe that
he was a special favourite of the gods ; and
he never engaged in any public or private
business without first going to the Capitol,
where he sat some time alone, enjoying communication from the gods. He is first mentioned in 218 at the battle of the Ticinus,
when he saved the life of his father as has
been already related. He fought at Cannae
two years afterwards (216), when he was
already a tribune of the soldiers, and was one
of the few Roman officers who survived that
fatal day. He was chosen along with Appius
Claudius to command the remains of the
army, which had taken refuge at Canusium ;
and it was owing to his youthful heroism and
presence of mind that the Roman nobles,
who had thought of leaving Italy in despair,
were prevented from carrying their rash
project into effect. He had already gained
the favour of the people to such an extent,
that he was elected aedile in 212, although
he had not yet reached the legal age. In
210, after the death of his father and uncle
in Spain, Scipio, then barely 24, was chosen
with enthusiasm to take the command in
that country. His success was striking and
rapid. In the first campaign (210) he took
the important city of Carthago Nova, and in
the course of the next 3 years he drove the
Carthaginians entirely out of Spain. He

returned to Rome in 206, and was elected
consul for the following year (205), although
he had not yet filled the office of praetor, and
was only 30 years of age. He was anxious
to cross over at once to Africa, and bring the
contest to an end at the gates of Carthage ;
and, after much opposition, obtained a fleet
and army for that purpose. After spending
the winter in Sicily, and completing all his
preparations for the invasion of Africa, he
crossed over to the latter country in the
course of the following year. Success again
attended his arms. The Carthaginians and
their ally Syphax were defeated with great
slaughter ; and the former were compelled to
recall Hannibal from Italy as the only hope of
saving their country. The long struggle
between the 2 peoples was at length brought
to a close by the battle fought near the city of
Zama on the 19th of October, 202, in which
Scipio gained a decisive and brilliant victory
over Hannibal. Carthage had no alternative
but submission ; but the final treaty was not
concluded till the following year (201).
Scipio returned to Italy in 201, and entered
Rome in triumph. He was received with
universal enthusiasm, and the surname of
Africanus was conferred upon him. He took
no prominent part in public affairs during
the next few years. He was censor in 199 with
P. Aelius Paetus, and consul a second time
in 194 with Ti. Sempronius Longus. In 193,
he was one of the 3 commissioners who were
sent to Africa to mediate between Masinissa
and the Carthaginians ; and in the same
year he was one of the ambassadors sent to
Antiochus at Ephesus, at whose court Hannibal was then residing. In 190 Africanus
served as legate under his brother Lucius in
the war against Antiochus the Great. After
their return, Lucius and subsequently Africanus himself, were accused of having
received bribes from Antiochus to let the
monarch off too leniently, and of having
appropriated to their own use part of the
money which had been paid by Antiochus to
the Roman state. The successful issue of the
prosecution of Lucius emboldened his enemies
to bring the great Africanus himself before
the people. His accuser was M. Naevius,
the tribune of the people, and the accusation
was brought in 185. When the trial came
on, and Africanus was summoned, he proudly
reminded the people that this was the anni-
versary of the day on which he had defeated
Hannibal at Zama, and called upon them to
follow him to the Capitol, in order there to
return thanks to the immortal gods, and to
pray that they would grant the Roman state
other citizens like himself. Scipio struck a
chord which vibrated on every heart, and was

followed by crowds to the Capitol. Having thus set all the laws at defiance, Scipio immediately quitted Rome, and retired to his country seat at Liturnum. The tribunes wished to renew the prosecution; but Gracchus wisely persuaded them to let it drop. Scipio never returned to Rome. The year of his death is uncertain; but he probably died in 183.— (11) L. CORN. SCIPIO ASIATICUS, also called ASIAGENES or ASIAGENUS, was the son of No. 8, and the brother of the great Africanus. He served under his brother in Spain; was praetor in 193, when he obtained the province of Sicily; and consul in 190, with C. Laelius. He defeated Antiochus at Mt. Sipylus, in 190, entered Rome in triumph in the following year, and assumed the surname of Asiaticus. His accusation and condemnation have been already related in the life of his brother.—(12) P. CORN. SCIPIO AFRICANUS, elder son of the great Africanus, was prevented by his weak health from taking any part in public affairs.—(13) L. or CN. CORN. SCIPIO AFRICANUS, younger son of the great Africanus. He accompanied his father into Asia in 190, and was taken prisoner by Antiochus. This Scipio was a degenerate son of an illustrious sire.—(14) L. CORN. SCIPIO ASIATICUS, a descendant of No. 11, belonged to the Marian party, and was consul 83 with C. Norbanus.—(15) P. CORN. SCIPIO AEMILIANUS AFRICANUS MINOR, was the younger son of L. Aemilius Paulus, the conqueror of Macedonia, and was adopted by P. Scipio [No. 12], the son of the conqueror of Hannibal. He was born about 185. In his 17th year he accompanied his father Paulus to Greece, and fought under him at the battle of Pydna, 168. Scipio devoted himself with ardour to the study of literature, and formed an intimate friendship with Polybius and Panaetius. He likewise admitted the poets Lucilius and Terence to his intimacy, and is said to have assisted the latter in the composition of his comedies. His friendship with Laelius, whose tastes and pursuits were so congenial to his own, has been immortalised by Cicero's celebrated treatise entitled "Laelius, sive de Amicitia." Although thus devoted to the study of polite literature, Scipio is said to have cultivated the virtues which distinguished the older Romans, and to have made Cato the model of his conduct. Scipio first served in Spain with great distinction as military tribune under the consul L. Lucullus in 151. On the breaking out of the 3rd Punic war in 149 he accompanied the Roman army to Africa, again with the rank of military tribune. Here he gained still more renown. By his personal bravery and military skill he repaired, to a great

extent, the mistakes of the consul Manilius, whose army on one occasion he saved from destruction. He returned to Rome in 148, and had already gained such popularity that when he became a candidate for the aedileship for the following year (147) he was elected consul, although he was only 37, and had not therefore attained the legal age. The senate assigned to him Africa as his province to which he forthwith sailed. He prosecuted the siege of Carthage with the utmost vigour; and, in spite of a desperate resistance, captured it in the spring of 146. After reducing Africa to the form of a Roman province, Scipio returned to Rome in the same year, and celebrated a splendid triumph on account of his victory. The surname of Africanus, which he had inherited by adoption from the conqueror of Hannibal, had been now acquired by him by his own exploits. In 142 Scipio was censor, and in the administration of the duties of his office he attempted to repress the growing luxury and immorality of his contemporaries. In 139 Scipio was accused by Ti. Claudius Asellus of majestas, but acquitted. The speeches which he delivered on the occasion obtained great celebrity, and were held in high esteem in a later age. It appears to have been after this event that Scipio was sent on an embassy to Egypt and Asia to attend to the Roman interests in those countries. The long continuance of the war in Spain again called Scipio to the consulship. He was appointed consul in his absence, and had the province of Spain assigned to him in 134. His operations were attended with success; and in 133 he brought the war to a conclusion by the capture of the city of Numantia after a long siege. He now received the surname of Numantinus in addition to that of Africanus. During his absence in Spain Tib. Gracchus had been put to death. Scipio was married to Sempronia, the sister of the fallen tribune, but he had no sympathy with his reforms, and no sorrow for his fate. Upon his return to Rome in 132, he took the lead in opposing the popular party, and endeavoured to prevent the agrarian law of Tib. Gracchus from being carried into effect. In the disputes that arose in consequence, he was accused by Carbo with the bitterest invectives as the enemy of the people, and upon his again expressing his approval of the death of Tib. Gracchus, the people shouted out, "Down with the tyrant." In the evening he went home with the intention of composing a speech for the following day; but next day he was found dead in his room. He is supposed to have been murdered, and Cicero mentions Carbo as his assassin. — (16) P. CORN.

Scipio Nasica, that is, "Scipio with the pointed nose," was the son of Cn. Scipio Calvus, who fell in Spain in 211. [No. 9.] He is first mentioned in 204 as a young man who was judged by the senate to be the best citizen in the state, and was therefore sent to Ostia along with the Roman matrons to receive the statue of the Idaean Mother, which had been brought from Pessinus. He was curule aedile 196 ; praetor in 194, when he fought with success in Farther Spain ; and consul 191, when he defeated the Boii, and triumphed over them on his return to Rome. Scipio Nasica was a celebrated jurist, and a house was given him by the state in the Via Sacra, in order that he might be more easily consulted.—(17) P. Corn. Scipio Nasica Corculum, son of No. 16, inherited from his father a love of jurispruence, and became so celebrated for his discernment and for his knowledge of the pontifical and civil law, that he received the surname of Corculum. He was elected pontifex maximus in 150.— (18) P. Corn. Scipio Nasica Serapio, son of No. 17, is chiefly known as the leader of the senate in the murder of Tib. Gracchus. In consequence of his conduct on this occasion Nasica became an object of such detestation to the people, that the senate found it advisable to send him on a pretended mission to Asia, although he was pontifex maximus, and ought not, therefore, to have quitted Italy. He did not venture to return to Rome, and after wandering about from place to place, died soon afterwards at Pergamum.— (19) P. Corn. Scipio Nasica, son of No. 18, was consul 111, and died during his consulship.—(20) P. Corn. Scipio Nasica, son of No. 19, praetor 94. This Scipio became the father-in-law of Cn. Pompey the triumvir, and fell in Africa in 46. His life is given under Metellus.—(21) Cn. Corn. Scipio Hispallus, son of L. Scipio who is only known as a brother of the 2 Scipios who fell in Spain. Hispallus was praetor 179, and consul 171.—(22) Cn. Corn. Scipio Hispallus, son of No. 21, was praetor 139, when he published an edict that all Chaldaeans (i. e. astrologers) should leave Rome and Italy within 10 days.

SCIRITIS, a wild and mountainous district in the N. of Laconia, on the borders of Arcadia, with a town called Scirus.

SCIRON (-ōnis), a famous robber who infested the frontier between Attica and Megaris. He not only robbed the travellers who passed through the country, but compelled them on the Scironian rock to wash his feet, and kicked them into the sea, while they were thus employed. At the foot of the rock there was a tortoise, which devoured the bodies of the robber's victims. He was slain by Theseus.

SCIRONIA SAXA (-ōrum : Derveni Bouno), large rocks on the E. coast of Megaris, between which and the sea there was only a narrow dangerous pass, called the Scironian road. The name of the rocks was derived from the celebrated robber Sciron.

SCODRA (-ae : Scodar or Scutari), one of the most important towns in Illyricum, on the left bank of the river Barbana, at the S.E. corner of the Lacus Labeatis, and about 17 miles from the coast.

SCODRUS. [Scardus.]

SCOMIUS (-i) MONS, a mountain in Macedonia, which runs E. of Mt. Scardus, in the direction of N. to S. towards Mt. Haemus.

SCOPAS (-ae). (1) An Aetolian, who held a leading position among his countrymen at the period of the outbreak of the war with Philip and the Achaeans, B.C. 220 ; in the first year of which he commanded the Aetolian army. After the close of the war with Philip, he withdrew to Alexandria. Here he was received with the utmost favour by the ministers of the young king, Ptolemy V., and was appointed to the chief command of the army against Antiochus the Great, but was ultimately unsuccessful. Notwithstanding this he continued in high favour at the Egyptian court ; but having formed a plot in 196 to obtain by force the chief administration of the kingdom, he was arrested and put to death.—(2) A distinguished sculptor and architect, was a native of Paros, and appears to have belonged to a family of artists in that island. He flourished from B.C. 395 to 350. He was the architect of the temple of Athena Alea, at Tegea, in Arcadia, which was commenced soon after B.C. 394. He was one of the artists employed in executing the bas-reliefs, which decorated the frieze of the mausoleum at Halicarnassus in Caria, a portion of which is now deposited in the British Museum. Among the single statues and groups of Scopas, the best known in modern times is his group of figures representing the destruction of the sons and daughters of Niobe. But the most esteemed of all the works of Scopas, in antiquity, was his group representing Achilles conducted to the island of Leuce by the divinities of the sea.

SCORDISCI (-ōrum), a people in Pannonia Superior, are sometimes classed among the Illyrians, but were the remains of an ancient and powerful Celtic tribe. They dwelt between the Savus and Dravus.

SCOTI (-ōrum), a people mentioned together with the Picti, by the later Roman writers as one of the chief tribes of the ancient Caledonians. They dwelt in the S.

of Scotland and in Ireland; and from them the former country has derived its name.

SCOTUSSA (-ae), a very ancient town of Thessaly, in the district Pelasgiotis, near the source of the Onchestus.

SCRĪBŌNĬA (-ae), wife of Octavianus, afterwards the emperor Augustus, had been married twice before. By one of her former husbands, P. Scipio, she had two children, P. Scipio, who was consul, B.C. 16, and a daughter, Cornelia, who was married to Paulus Aemilius Lepidus, censor B.C. 22. Scribonia was the sister of L. Scribonius Libo, who was the father-in-law of Sex. Pompey. Augustus married her in 40, on the advice of Maecenas, because he was then afraid that Sex. Pompey would form an alliance with Antony to crush him; but having renewed his alliance with Antony, Octavian divorced her in the following year (39), on the very day on which she had borne him a daughter, Julia, in order to marry Livia. Scribonia long survived her separation from Octavian. In A.D. 2 she accompanied, of her own accord, her daughter Julia into exile to the island of Pandataria.

SCRĪBŌNĬUS CŪRĬO. [CURIO.]

SCRĪBŌNĬUS LĪBO. [LIBO.]

SCRĪBŌNĬUS PRŌCŬLUS. [PROCULUS.]

SCULTENNA (-ae: Panaro), a river in Gallia Cispadana, rising in the Apennines, and flowing to the E. of Mutina into the Po.

SCȲLĀCĬUM, also SCȲLĀCĔUM, or SCYLLĒTĬUM (-i: Squillace), a Greek town on the E. coast of Bruttium, was situated on 2 adjoining hills at a short distance from the coast, between the rivers Caecinus and Carcines. From this town the SCYLACIUS or SCYLLETICUS SINUS, derived its name.

SCȲLAX (-ăcis). (1) Of Caryanda in Caria, was sent by Darius Hystaspis on a voyage of discovery down the Indus. Setting out from the city of Caspatyrus and the Pactyican district, Scylax reached the sea, and then sailed W. through the Indian Ocean to the Red Sea, performing the whole voyage in 30 months. There is still extant a Periplus bearing the name of Scylax, but which could not have been written by the subject either of this or of the following article.—(2) Of Halicarnassus, a friend of Panaetius, distinguished for his knowledge of the stars, and for his political influence in his own state.

SCYLLA (-ae) and CHĂRYBDIS (-is), the names of two rocks between Italy and Sicily. In the one nearest to Italy was a cave, in which dwelt Scylla, a daughter of Crataeis, a fearful monster, barking like a dog, with 12 feet, and six long necks and heads, each of which contained 3 rows of sharp teeth.

The opposite rock, which was much lower, contained an immense fig-tree, under which dwelt Charybdis, who thrice every day swallowed down the waters of the sea, and thrice threw them up again. This is the Homeric account; but later traditions give different accounts of Scylla's parentage. Hercules is said to have killed her, because she stole some of the oxen of Geryon; but Phorcys is said to have restored her to life. Virgil (Aen., vi. 286) speaks of several Scyllae, and places them in the lower world. Charybdis is described as a daughter of Poseidon (Neptune) and Gaea (Tellus), and as a voracious woman, who stole oxen from Hercules, and was hurled by the thunderbolt of Zeus (Jupiter) into the sea.

Scylla. (From a Coin of Agrigentum.)

SCYLLA (-ae), daughter of king Nisus of Megara, who fell in love with Minos. [NISUS, and MINOS.]

SCYLLAEUM (-i). (1) (Scigilo), a promontory on the coast of Bruttium, at the N. entrance to the Sicilian straits, where the monster Scylla was supposed to live. [SCYLLA.] —(2) (Scilla or Sciglio), a town in Bruttium, on the above-named promontory. There are still remains of the ancient citadel.—(3) A promontory in Argolis, on the coast of Troezen, forming, with the promontory of Sunium in Attica, the entrance to the Saronic gulf.

SCYLLĒTĬCUS SĬNUS. [SCYLACIUM.]

SCYLLĒTĬUM. [SCYLACIUM.]

SCYMNUS (-i), of Chios, wrote a Periegests, or description of the earth, in prose, and which is consequently different from the Periegesis in Iambic metre, which has come down to us.

SCȲROS (-i: Scyro), an island in the Aegaean sea, E. of Euboea, and one of the Sporades. Here Thetis concealed her son Achilles in woman's attire among the daughters of Lycomedes, and here also Pyrrhus, the son of Achilles by Deidamīa, was brought up. According to another tradition, the island was conquered by Achilles, in order to revenge the death of Theseus, who is said to have been treacherously destroyed in Scyros by Lycomedes. The bones of Theseus were discovered by Cimon in Scyros, after his conquest of the island in B.C. 476, and were conveyed to Athens, where they were preserved in the Theseum. From this time Scyros continued subject to Athens till the period of the Macedonian supremacy; but the Romans compelled the last Philip to restore it to Athens, B.C. 196.

SCYTHIA (-ae: Scythes, Scytha -ae, pl. Scythae -ārum; fem. Scythis -ĭdis, Scythissa), a name applied to very different countries at different times. The Scythia of Herodotus comprises, to speak generally, the S.E. parts of Europe, between the Carpathian mountains and the river Tanaïs (*Don*). The people who inhabited this region were called by the Greeks Σκύθαι, a word of doubtful origin, which first occurs in Hesiod; but, in their own language, Σκόλοτοι, i.e. *Slavonians*. They were believed by Herodotus to be of Asiatic origin; and his account of them, taken in connexion with the description given by Hippocrates of their physical peculiarities, leaves no doubt that they were a part of the great Mongol race, who have wandered, from unknown antiquity, over the steppes of Central Asia. Herodotus says further that they were driven out of their abodes in Asia, N. of the Araxes, by the Massagetae; and that, migrating into Europe, they drove out the Cimmerians. The Scythians were a nomad people, that is, shepherds or herdsmen, who had no fixed habitations, but roamed over a vast tract of country at their pleasure, and according to the wants of their cattle. They lived in a kind of covered waggons, which Aeschylus describes as "lofty houses of wicker-work, on well-wheeled chariots." They kept large troops of horses, and were most expert in cavalry exercises and archery; and hence, as the Persian king Darius found, when he invaded their country (B.C. 507), it was almost impossible for an invading army to act against them. They simply retreated, waggons and all, before the enemy, harassing him with their light cavalry, and leaving famine and exposure, in their bare steppes, to do the rest. An important modification of their habits had, however, taken place, to a certain extent, before Herodotus described them. The fertility of the plains on the N. of the Euxine, and the influence of the Greek settlements at the mouth of the Borysthenes, and along the coast, had led the inhabitants of this part of Scythia to settle down as cultivators of the soil, and had brought them

into commercial and other relations with the Greeks. Accordingly, Herodotus mentions 2 classes or hordes of Scythians who had thus abandoned their nomad life and turned husbandmen. In later times the Scythians were gradually overpowered by the neighbouring people, especially the Sarmatians, who gave their name to the whole country. [SARMATIA.] In writers of the time of the Roman empire, the name of Scythia denotes the whole of N. Asia, from the river Rha (*Volga*) on the W., which divided it from Asiatic Sarmatia, to Serica on the E., extending to India on the S. It was divided, by Mt. Imaus, into 2 parts, called respectively Scythia intra Imaum, *i.e.* on the N.W. side of the range, and Scythia extra Imaum, on its S.E. side. Of the people of this region nothing was known except some names; but the absence of knowledge was supplied by some marvellous and not uninteresting fables.

SCYTHINI (-ōrum), a people on the W. border of Armenia, through whose country the Greeks under Xenophon marched 4 days' journey.

SCYTHOPOLIS (-is: O. T. Bethshan: *Beisan*, Ru.), an important city of Palestine, in the S.E. of Galilee, according to the usual division, but sometimes also reckoned to Samaria, sometimes to Decapolis, and sometimes to Coele-Syria. It is often mentioned in O. T. history, in the time of the Maccabees, and under the Romans. It had a mixed population of Canaanites, Philistines, and Assyrian settlers. Under the late Roman empire, it became the seat of the archbishop of Palestina Secunda, and it continued a flourishing city to the time of the first Crusade.

SĒBASTĒ (-ēs := Augusta). (1) (*Ayash*, Ru.), a city on the coast of Cilicia Aspera.— (2) (*Segikler*), a city of Phrygia, N.W. of Eumenia.—(3) A city in Pontus, also called Cabira. [CABIRA.]—(4) [SAMARIA.]

SEBENNYTUS (-i: *Semennout*, Ru.), a considerable city of Lower Egypt, in the Delta, on the W. side of the branch of the Nile, called after it the Sebennytic Mouth. It was the capital of the Nomos Sebennytes or Sebennyticus.

SĒBĒTHUS (-i : *Maddalena*), a small river in Campania, flowing round Vesuvius, and falling into the Sinus Puteolanus at the E. side of Neapolis.

SĒDĒTĀNI, [EDETANI.]

SEDŪNI (-ōrum), an Alpine people in Gallia Belgica, E. of the lake of Geneva, in the valley of the Rhone, in the modern *Vallais*.

SEDUSII (-ōrum), a German people, forming part of the army of Ariovistus, when he invaded Gaul, B.C. 58. Their site cannot be determined.

SEGESTA (-ae: nr. *Alcamo,* Ru.), the later Roman form of the town called by the Greeks EGESTA or AEGESTA, in Virgil ACESTA ; situated in the N. W. of Sicily, near the coast between Panormus and Drepanum. It is said to have been founded by the Trojans on 2 small rivers, to which they gave the names of Simois and Scamander; hence the Romans made it a colony of Aeneas.

SEGESTES (-is), a Cheruscan chieftain, the opponent of Arminius.

SEGNI (-ōrum), a German people in Gallia Belgica, between the Treveri and Eburones, the name of whom is still preserved in the town of *Sinei* or *Signei.*

SEGOBRĪGA (-ae), the chief town of the Celtiberi, in Hispania Tarraconensis, S.W. of Caesaraugusta.

SEGONTĪA or SEGUNTĪA (-ae), a town of the Celtiberi, in Hispania Tarraconensis, 16 miles from Caesaraugusta.

SEGOVĪA (-ae). (1) (*Segovia*), a town of the Arevaci, on the road from Emerita to Caesaraugusta. A magnificent Roman aqueduct is still extant at Segovia.—(2) A town in Hispania Baetica on the Flumen Silicense, near Sacili.

SEGUSIĀNI (-ōrum), one of the most important peoples in Gallia Lugdunensis, bounded by the Allobroges on the S., by the Sequani on the E., by the Aedui on the N., and by the Arverni on the W. In their territory was the town of Lugdunum, the capital of the modern province.

SEGUSĪO (-ōnis: *Susa*), the capital of the Segusini and the residence of king Cottius, was situated in Gallia Transpadana, at the foot of the Cottian Alps. The triumphal arch erected at this place by Cottius in honour of Augustus is still extant.

SĒJĀNUS (-i), AELĪUS, was born at Vulsinii, in Etruria, and was the son of Seius Strabo, who was commander of the praetorian troops at the close of the reign of Augustus, A.D. 14. He succeeded his father in the command of these bands, and ultimately gained such influence over Tiberius that he made him his confidant. For many years he governed Tiberius; but not content with this high position, he formed the design of obtaining the imperial power. With this view he sought to make himself popular with the soldiers, and procured the poisoning of Drusus, the son of Tiberius by his wife Livia, whom he had seduced. After Tiberius had shut himself up in the island of Capreae, Sejanus had full scope for his machinations; and the death of Livia, the mother of Tiberius (29), was followed by the banishment of Agrippina and her sons Nero and Drusus. Tiberius at last began to suspect the designs of Sejanus, and sent Sertorius Macro to Rome, with a commission to take the command of the praetorian cohorts. Macro, after assuring himself of the troops, and depriving Sejanus of his usual guard, produced a letter from Tiberius to the senate, in which the emperor expressed his apprehensions of Sejanus. The senate decreed his death, and he was immediately executed. His body was dragged about the streets, and finally thrown into the Tiber. Many of the friends of Sejanus perished at the same time; and his son and daughter shared his fate.

SĒLEUCĪA (-ae), and rarely SĒLEUCĒA, the name of several cities in different parts of Asia, built by Seleucus I., king of Syria. (1) S. AD TIGRIN, also called S. BABYLONIA, S. ASSYRIAE, and S. PARTHORUM, a great city on the confines of Assyria and Babylonia, and for a long time the capital of W. Asia, until it was eclipsed by CTESIPHON. Its exact site has been disputed; but the most probable opinion is that it stood on the W. bank of the Tigris, N. of its junction with the Royal Canal, opposite to the mouth of the river Delas or Silla (*Diala*), and to the spot where Ctesiphon was afterwards built by the Parthians. It was a little to the S. of the modern city of *Bagdad.* It was built in the form of an eagle with expanded wings, and was peopled by settlers from Assyria, Mesopotamia, Babylonia, Syria, and Judaea. It rapidly rose, and eclipsed Babylon in wealth and splendour. Even after the Parthian kings had become masters of the banks of the Tigris, and had fixed their residence at Ctesiphon, Seleucia, though deprived of much of its importance, remained a very considerable city. In the reign of Titus, it had, according to Pliny, 600,000 inhabitants. It declined after its capture by Severus, and in Julian's expedition it was found entirely deserted.— (2) S. PIERIA (called *Seleukeh* or *Kepse,* near *Suadeiah,* Ru.), a great city and fortress of Syria, founded by Seleucus in April, B.C. 300. It stood on the site of an ancient fortress, on the rocks overhanging the sea, at the foot of Mt. Pieria, about 4 miles N. of the Orontes, and 12 miles W. of Antioch. Its natural strength was improved by every known art of fortification. In the war with Egypt, which ensued upon the murder of Antiochus II., Seleucia surrendered to Ptolemy III. Euergetes (B.C. 246). It was afterwards recovered by Antiochus the Great (219). In the war between Antiochus VIII. and IX. the people of Seleucia made themselves independent (109 or 108). The city had fallen entirely into decay by the 6th century of our era. There are considerable ruins of the harbour and mole, of the walls of the city, and of its necropolis. The surrounding district was called SELEUCIS.—(3) S. AD BELUM, a city of Syria, in the valley of the Orontes, near Apamea. Its site is doubtful.—(4) S. TRACHEOTIS (Selefkeh, Ru.), an important city of Cilicia Aspera, was built by Seleucus I. on the W. bank of the river Calycadnus, about 4 miles from its mouth, and peopled with the inhabitants of several neighbouring cities. It had an oracle of Apollo, and annual games in honour of Zeus Olympius (the Olympian Jupiter). It was the birthplace of the philosophers Athenaeus and Xenarchus, and of other learned men.—(5) S. IN MESOPOTAMIA (Bir), on the left bank of the Euphrates, opposite to the ford of Zeugma, was a fortress of considerable importance in ancient military history.—(6) A considerable city of Margiana, built by Alexander the Great, in a beautiful situation, and called Alexandria; destroyed by the barbarians, and rebuilt by Antiochus I., who named it Seleucia after his father. — (7) S. IN CARIA [TRALLES].—There were other cities of the name, of less importance, in Pisidia, Pamphylia, Palestine, and Elymaïs.

SELEUCIS, the most beautiful and fertile district of Syria, containing the N.W. part of the country, between Mt. Amanus on the N., the Mediterranean on the W., the districts of Cyrrhestice and Chalybonitis on the N.E., the desert on the E., and Coele-Syria and the mountains of Lebanon on the S.

SELEUCUS (-i), the name of several kings of Syria. I. Surnamed NICATOR, the founder of the Syrian monarchy, reigned B.C. 312—280. He was the son of Antiochus, a Macedonian of distinction among the officers of Philip II., and was born about 358. He accompanied Alexander on his expedition to Asia, and distinguished himself particularly in the Indian campaigns. After the death of Alexander (323) he espoused the side of Perdiccas, whom he accompanied on his expedition against Egypt; but he took a leading part in the mutiny of the soldiers, which ended in the death of Perdiccas (321). In the 2nd partition of the provinces which followed, Seleucus obtained the wealthy and important satrapy of Babylonia; but it is not till his recovery of Babylon from Antigonus, in 312, that the Syrian monarchy is commonly reckoned to commence. He afterwards conquered Susiana and Media, and gradually extended his power over all the eastern provinces which had formed part of the empire of Alexander, from the Euphrates to the banks of the Oxus and the Indus. In 306 Seleucus formally assumed the regal

title and diadem. Having leagued himself with Ptolemy, Lysimachus and Cassander against Antigonus, he obtained, by the defeat and death of that monarch at Ipsus (301), a great part of Asia Minor, as well as the whole of Syria, from the Euphrates to the Mediterranean. Seleucus appears to have felt the difficulty of exercising a vigilant control over so extensive an empire, and accordingly, in 293, he consigned the government of all the provinces beyond the Euphrates to his son Antiochus, upon whom he bestowed the title of king, as well as the hand of his own youthful wife, Stratonice, for whom the prince had conceived a violent attachment. In 286, with the assistance of Ptolemy and Lysimachus, he defeated and captured Demetrius, king of Macedonia, who had invaded Asia Minor. For some time jealousies had existed between Seleucus and Lysimachus; but the immediate cause of the war between the 2 monarchs, which terminated in the defeat and death of Lysimachus (281), is related in the life of the latter. Seleucus now crossed the Hellespont in order to take possession of the throne of Macedonia, which had been left vacant by the death of Lysimachus; but he had advanced no farther than Lysimachia, when he was assassinated by Ptolemy Ceraunus, to whom, as the son of his old friend and ally, he had extended a friendly protection. His death took place in the beginning of 280, only 7 months after that of Lysimachus, and in the 32nd year of his reign. He was in his 78th year. Seleucus appears to have carried out, with great energy and perseverance, the projects originally formed by Alexander himself, for the Hellenisation of his Asiatic empire; and we find him founding, in almost every province, Greek or Macedonian colonies, which became so many centres of civilisation and refinement.—II. Surnamed CALLINICUS (246—226), was the eldest son of Antiochus II. by his first wife Laodice. The first measure of his administration, or rather that of his mother, was to put to death his stepmother, Berenice, together with her infant son. To avenge his sister, Ptolemy Euergetes, king of Egypt, invaded the dominions of Seleucus, and not only made himself master of Antioch and the whole of Syria, but carried his arms unopposed beyond the Euphrates and the Tigris. During these operations Seleucus kept wholly aloof; but when Ptolemy had been recalled to his own dominions by domestic disturbances, he recovered possession of the greater part of the provinces which he had lost. Seleucus next became involved in a dangerous war with his brother, Antiochus Hierax, and after wards undertook an expedition to the East, with the view of reducing the revolted provinces of Parthia and Bactria. He was, however, defeated by Arsaces, king of Parthia, in a great battle, which was long after celebrated by the Parthians as the foundation of their independence. Seleucus appears to have been engaged in an expedition for the recovery of his provinces in Asia Minor, which had been seized by Attalus, when he was accidentally killed by a fall from his horse, in the 21st year of his reign, 226.— III. Surnamed Ceraunus (226—223), eldest son and successor of Seleucus II., was assassinated by 2 of his officers, after a reign of only 3 years, and was succeeded by his brother, Antiochus the Great. — IV. Surnamed Philopator (187—175), was the son and successor of Antiochus the Great. The reign of Seleucus was feeble and inglorious. He was assassinated in 175 by one of his own ministers.—V. Eldest son of Demetrius II., assumed the royal diadem on learning the death of his father, 125 ; but his mother, Cleopatra, who had herself put Demetrius to death, was indignant at hearing that her son had ventured to take such a step without her authority, and caused Seleucus also to be assassinated.—VI. Surnamed Epiphanes, and also Nicator (95—93), was the eldest of the 5 sons of Antiochus VIII. Grypus. On the death of his father, in 95, he ascended the throne, and defeated and slew in battle his uncle, Antiochus Cyzicenus, who had laid claim to the kingdom. But shortly after Seleucus was in his turn defeated by Antiochus Eusebes, the son of Cyzicenus, and expelled from Syria. He took refuge in the city of Mopsuestia, in Cilicia ; but in consequence of his tyranny, was burned to death by the inhabitants.

SELGE (-ēs : Sürk ? Ru.), one of the chief of the independent mountain cities of Pisidia, stood on the S. side of Mt. Taurus, on the Eurymedon, just where the river breaks through the mountain chain.

SELINUS (-untis). (1) A small river on the S.W. coast of Sicily, flowing by the town of the same name.—(2) (Crestena), a river of Elis, in the district Triphylia, near Scillus, flowing into the Alpheus W. of Olympia.— (3) (Vostitza), a river of Achaia, rising in Mt. Erymanthus. — (4) A tributary of the Caicus, in Mysia, flowing by the town of Pergamum.—(5) (Castel vetrano, Ru.), one of the most important towns in Sicily, situated upon a hill on the S.W. coast, and upon a river of the same name. It was founded by the Dorians from Megara Hyblaea, on the E. coast of Sicily, B.C. 628. It soon attained great prosperity ; but it was

taken by the Carthaginians in 409, when most of its inhabitants were slain or sold as slaves, and the greater part of the city destroyed.—(6) (Selenti), a town in Cilicia, situated on the coast.

SELLASIA (-ae), a town in Laconia, N. of Sparta, near the river Oenus.

SELLEÏS. (1) A river in Elis, on which the Homeric Ephyra stood, rising in Mt. Pholoë, and falling into the sea, S. of the Peneus.—(2) A river near Sicyon.—(3) A river in Troas, near Arisbe, and a tributary of the Rhodius.

SELLI or Helli. [Dodona.]

SELYMBRIA or SELYBRIA (-ae: Selivria), an important town in Thrace, situated on the Propontis. It was a colony of the Megarians, and was founded earlier than Byzantium.

SEMELE (-ēs), daughter of Cadmus and Harmonia, at Thebes, and accordingly sister of Ino, Agave, Autonoë, and Polydorus. She was beloved by Zeus (Jupiter). Hēra (Juno) stimulated by jealousy, appeared to her in the form of her aged nurse Beroë, and induced her to ask Zeus to visit her in the same splendour and majesty with which he appeared to Hera. Zeus warned her of the danger of her request ; but as he had sworn to grant whatever she desired, he was obliged to comply with her prayer. He accordingly appeared before her as the god of thunder, and Semele was consumed by the lightning ; but Zeus saved her child Dionysus (Bacchus), with whom she was pregnant. Her son afterwards carried her out of the lower world, and conducted her to Olympus, where she became immortal under the name of Thyone.

SEMIRAMIS (-ĭdis) and NINUS (-i), the mythical founders of the Assyrian empire of Ninus or Nineveh. Ninus was a great warrior, who built the town of Ninus or Nineveh, about B.C. 2182, and subdued the greater part of Asia. Semiramis was the daughter of the fish-goddess Dercēto of Ascalon in Syria by a Syrian youth. Derceto being ashamed of her frailty, made away with the youth, and exposed her infant daughter; but the child was miraculously preserved by doves, who fed her till she was discovered by the shepherds of the neighbourhood. She was then brought up by the chief shepherd of the royal herds, whose name was Simmas, from whom she derived the name of Semiramis. Her surpassing beauty attracted the notice of Onnes, one of the king's friends and generals, who married her. At the siege of Bactra, Semiramis planned an attack upon the citadel of the town, mounted the walls with a few brave followers and obtained possession of the place. Ninus was so charmed by her bravery and beauty, that he resolved to make her his wife, whereupon her unfortunate husband put an end to his life. By Ninus Semiramis had a son, Ninyas, and on the death of Ninus she succeeded him on the throne. Her fame threw into the shade that of Ninus; and later ages loved to tell of her marvellous deeds and her heroic achievements. She built numerous cities, and erected many wonderful buildings. In Nineveh she erected a tomb for her husband 9 stadia high, and 10 wide; she built the city of Babylon with all its wonders; and she constructed the hanging gardens in Media, of which later writers give us such strange accounts. Besides conquering many nations of Asia, she subdued Egypt and a great part of Ethiopia, but was unsuccessful in an attack which she made upon India. After a reign of 42 years she resigned the sovereignty to her son Ninyas, and disappeared from the earth, taking her flight to heaven in the form of a dove. The fabulous nature of this narrative is apparent. It is probable that Semiramis was originally a Syrian goddess, perhaps the same who was worshipped at Ascalon under the name of Astarte, or the Heavenly Aphrodite, to whom the dove was sacred. Hence the stories of her voluptuousness, which were current even in the time of Augustus.

SEMNONES, more rarely SENNONES (-um), a German people, described by Tacitus as the most powerful tribe of the Suevic race, dwelt between the rivers Viadus (*Oder*) and Albis (*Elbe*), from the Riesengebirge in the S. as far as the country around Frankfurt on the Oder and Potsdam in the N.

SEMO SANCUS. [SANCUS.]

SEMPRŌNĬA (-ae). (1) Daughter of Tib. Gracchus, censor B.C. 169, and sister of the 2 celebrated tribunes, married Scipio Africanus minor.—(2) Wife of D. Junius Brutus, consul 77, was a woman of great personal attractions and literary accomplishments, but of a profligate character. She took part in Catiline's conspiracy, though her husband was not privy to it.

SEMPRŌNĬUS GRACCHUS. [GRACCHUS.]

SĒNA (-ae). (1) (*Senigaglia*), surnamed GALLICA, and sometimes called SENOGALLIA, a town on the coast of Umbria, at the mouth of the small river Sena, founded by the Senones.—(2) (*Siena*), a town in Etruria and a Roman colony, on the road from Clusium to Florentia.

SĒNĔCA (-ae). (1) M. ANNAEUS, the rhetorician, was born at Corduba (*Cordova*) in Spain, about B.C. 61. Seneca was at Rome in the early period of the power of Augustus. He afterwards returned to Spain, and married Helvia, by whom he had 3 sons, L. Annaeus

Seneca, L. Annaeus Mela or Mella, the father of the poet Lucan, and M. Novatus. Seneca was rich, and belonged to the equestrian class. At a later period he returned to Rome, where he resided till his death, which probably occurred near the end of the reign of Tiberius. Two of Seneca's works have come down to us. 1. *Controversiarum Libri decem*, of which the 1st, 2nd, 7th, 8th, and 10th books only are extant, and these are somewhat mutilated. 2. *Suasoriarum Liber*, which is probably not complete. Seneca's works are for the most part commonplace and puerile, though now and then interspersed with some good ideas and apt expressions.—(2) L. ANNAEUS, the philosopher, the son of the preceding, was born at Corduba, probably a few years B.C., and brought to Rome by his parents when he was a child. Though he was naturally of a weak body, he was a hard student from his youth, and devoted himself with great ardour to rhetoric and philosophy. He also soon gained distinction as a pleader of causes, and excited the jealousy and hatred of Caligula by the ability with which he conducted a case in the senate before the emperor. In the first year of the reign of Claudius (A. D. 41), Seneca was banished to Corsica, on account of his intimacy with Julia, the niece of Claudius, of whom Messalina was jealous. After 8 years' residence in Corsica, Seneca was recalled (49) by the influence of Agrippina, who had just married her uncle the emperor Claudius. He now obtained a praetorship, and was made the tutor of the young Domitius, afterwards the emperor Nero, who was the son of Agrippina by a former husband. On the accession of his pupil to the imperial throne (54) after the death of Claudius, Seneca became one of the chief advisers of the young emperor. He exerted his influence to check Nero's vicious propensities, but at the same time he profited from his position to amass an immense fortune. He supported Nero in his contests with his mother Agrippina, and was not only a party to the death of the latter (60), but he wrote the letter which Nero addressed to the senate in justification of the murder. After the death of his mother, Nero abandoned himself without any restraint to his vicious propensities; and the presence of Seneca soon became irksome to him, while the wealth of the philosopher excited the emperor's cupidity. Seneca saw his danger, asked the emperor for permission to retire, and offered to surrender all that he had. Nero affected to be grateful for his past services, refused the proffered gift, and sent him away with perfidious assurances of his respect and affection. Seneca now altered his mode of life, saw little company, and seldom visited the city, on the ground of feeble health, or being occupied with his philosophical studies. But this did not save him. After the conspiracy of Piso (65) Nero sent a tribune to him with the order of death. Without showing any sign of alarm, Seneca cheered his weeping friends by reminding them of the lessons of philosophy. Embracing his wife Pompeia Paulina, he prayed her to moderate her grief, and to console herself for the loss of her husband by the reflection that he had lived an honourable life. But as Paulina protested that she would die with him, Seneca consented, and the same blow opened the veins in the arms of both. Seneca's body was attenuated by age and meagre diet; the blood would not flow easily, and he opened the veins in his legs. But even this did not suffice; and after enduring much torture he was taken into a vapour stove, where he was quickly suffocated. Seneca died, as was the fashion among the Romans, with the courage of a stoic, but with somewhat of a theatrical affectation which detracts from the dignity of the scene. Seneca's fame rests on his numerous writings, which are chiefly on moral and philosophical subjects. The most important is the *De Beneficiis*, in 7 books. He was also the author of ten tragedies; which, however, seem more adapted for recitation than for the stage. Yet they contain many striking passages, and have some merit as poems. That Seneca possessed great mental powers cannot be doubted. He had seen much of human life, and he knew well what man was. His philosophy, so far as he adopted a system, was the stoical, but it was rather an eclecticism of stoicism than pure stoicism. His style is antithetical, and apparently laboured; and where there is much labour, there is generally affectation. Yet his language is clear and forcible; it is not mere words: there is thought always.

SENONES (-um), a powerful people in Gallia Lugdunensis, dwelt along the upper course of the Sequana (*Seine*). Their chief town was Agendicum, afterwards called Senones(*Sens*). A portion of this people crossed the Alps about B.C. 400, in order to settle in Italy, and took up their abode on the Adriatic sea between the rivers Utis and Aesis (between Ravenna and Ancona), after expelling the Umbrians. In this country they founded the town of Sena. They not only extended their ravages into Etruria, but marched against Rome and took the city, B.C. 390. From this time we find them engaged in constant hostilities with the Romans, till they were at length completely subdued, and the

greater part of them destroyed by the consul Dolabella, 283.

SENTINUM (-i: nr. *Sassoferrato*, Ru.), a fortified town in Umbria, not far from the river Aesis.

SEPIAS (-ădis: *St. George*), a promontory in the S.E. of Thessaly in the district Magnesia, on which a great part of the fleet of Xerxes was wrecked.

SEPLASIA (-ōrum), one of the principal streets in Capua, where perfumes and luxuries of a similar kind were sold.

SEPPHORIS (*Sefurieh*), a city of Palestine, in the middle of Galilee, was an insignificant place, until Herod Antipas fortified it, and made it the capital of Galilee, under the name of DIOCAESAREA.

SEPTEM AQUAE, a place in the territory of the Sabini, near Reate.

SEPTEMPEDA (*San Severino*), a municipium in the interior of Picenum, on the road from Auximum to Urbs Salvia.

SEPTIMIUS GETA. [GETA.]

SEPTIMIUS SEVERUS. [SEVERUS.]

SEPTIMIUS TITIUS (-i), a Roman poet, spoken of by Horace.

SEQUANA (-ae: *Seine*), one of the principal rivers of Gaul, rising in the central parts of that country, and flowing through the province of Gallia Lugdunensis into the ocean opposite Britain. It is 346 miles in length. Its principal affluents are the Matröna (*Marne*), Esia (*Oise*) with its tributary the Axöna (*Aisne*), and Incaunus (*Yonne*). This river has a slow current, and is navigable beyond Lutetia Parisiorum (*Paris*).

SEQUANI (-ōrum), a powerful Celtic people in Gallia Belgica, inhabiting the country since called *Franche Compté* and *Burgundy*. In the later division of the provinces of the empire, the country of the Sequani formed a special province under the name of Maxima Sequanorum. They derived their name from the river Sequana, which had its source in the N.W. frontiers of their territory. Their chief town was Vesontio (*Besançon*).

SEQUESTER (-tri or -tris) VIBIUS, the name attached to a glossary which professes to give an account of the geographical names contained in the Roman poets.

SERA. [SERICA.]

SERAPION (-ōnis) a physician of Alexandria, who lived in the 3rd century, B.C.

SERAPIS or SARAPIS (-is or -ĭdĭs), an Egyptian divinity, whose worship was introduced into Greece in the time of the Ptolemies. His worship was introduced into Rome together with that of Isis. [ISIS.]

SERDICA or SARDICA (-ae), an important town in Upper Moesia, and the capital of Dacia Interior, derived its name from the Thracian people SERDI. It bore in the middle ages the name of *Triaditza*. Its extensive ruins are to be seen S. of *Sophia*.

SĒRĒNUS (-i), Q., SAMMONĪCUS (or *Samonicus*), a man of high reputation at Rome for taste and learning, murdered by command of Caracalla, A.D. 212. He left behind him many works.

SĒRES. [SERICA.]

SERGĪUS. [CATILINA.]

SĒRĪCA (-ae); (Sēres; also rarely in the sing. Sēr), a country in the extreme E. of Asia, famous as the native region of the silk-worm, which was also called σήρ; and hence the adjective 'sericus' for *silken*. The name was known to the W. nations at a very early period, through the use of silk, first in W. Asia, and afterwards in Greece. It is clear, however, that until some time after the commencement of our era, the name had no distinct geographical signification. The Serica of Ptolemy corresponds to the N. W. part of *China*, and the adjacent portions of *Thibet* and *Chinese Tartary*. The capital, SERA, is supposed by most to be *Singan*, on the *Hoang-ho*, but by some *Peking*. The Great Wall of China is mentioned by Ammianus Marcellinus under the name of Aggeres Serium.

SĒRĪPHUS (-i : *Serpho*), an island in the Aegaean sea, and one of the Cyclades. It is celebrated in mythology as the island where Danaë and Perseus landed after they had been exposed by Acrisius, where Perseus was brought up, and where he afterwards turned the inhabitants into stone with the Gorgon's head. Seriphus was colonised by Ionians from Athens, and it was one of the few islands which refused submission to Xerxes. The island was employed by the Roman emperors as a place of banishment for state criminals.

SERRĀNUS. [REGULUS.]

SERTŌRIUS (-i), Q., one of the most extraordinary men in the later times of the republic, was a native of Nursia, a Sabine village, and was born of obscure but respectable parents. He served under Marius in the war against the Teutones; and before the battle of Aquae Sextiae (*Aix*), B.C. 102, he entered the camp of the Teutones in disguise as a spy, for which hazardous undertaking his intrepid character and some knowledge of the Gallic language well qualified him. He also served as tribunus militum in Spain under T. Didius (97). He was quaestor in 91, and had before this time lost an eye in battle. On the outbreak of the civil war in 88, he declared himself against the party of the nobles, and commanded one of the 4 armies which besieged Rome under Marius and Cinna. He was however opposed to the

bloody massacre which ensued after Marius and Cinna entered Rome. In 83 Sertorius was praetor, and either in this year or the following he went into Spain; whence he crossed over to Mauretania, and gained a victory over Paccianus, one of Sulla's generals. After this, at the request of the Lusitanians, he became their leader; and for some years successfully resisted all the power of Rome. He availed himself of the superstitious character of that people to strengthen his authority over them. A fawn was brought to him by one of the natives as a present, which soon became so tame as to accompany him in his walks, and attend him on all occasions. After Sulla had become master of Italy, Sertorius was joined by many Romans, and among the rest by M. Perperna, with 53 cohorts [PERPERNA]. To give some show of form to his formidable power, Sertorius established a senate of 300, into which no provincial was admitted. The continued want of success on the part of Metellus, who had been sent against Sertorius in 79, induced the Romans to send Pompey to his assistance, but with an independent command. Pompey arrived in Spain in 76, with a large force, but was unable to gain any decisive advantages. For the next 5 years Sertorius kept both Metellus and Pompey at bay, and cut to pieces a large number of their forces. Sertorius was at length assassinated in 72 by Perperna and some other Roman officers, who had long been jealous of his authority.

SERVĪLIA (-ae). (1) Daughter of Q. Servilius Caepio and the daughter of Livia, the sister of the celebrated M. Livius Drusus, tribune of the plebs, B.C. 91. Servilia was married twice; first to M. Junius Brutus, by whom she became the mother of the murderer of Caesar, and secondly to D. Junius Silanus, consul 62.—(2) Sister of the preceding, was the 2nd wife of L. Lucullus, consul 74.

SERVĪLIUS ĀHĀLA. [AHALA.]

SERVĪLIUS CAEPĪO. [CAEPIO.]

SERVĪLIUS CASCA. [CASCA.]

SERVĪLIUS RULLUS. [RULLUS.]

SERVĪUS MAURUS HONŌRĀTUS (-i), or SERVĪUS MARIUS HONŌRĀTUS, a celebrated Latin grammarian, contemporary with Macrobius, who introduces him among the dramatis personae of the Saturnalia. His most celebrated production was an elaborate commentary upon Virgil.

SERVĪUS TULLĪUS. [TULLIUS.]

SĒSOSTRIS (-is or -ĭdis), the name given by the Greeks to the great king of Egypt, who is called in Manetho and on the monuments Ramses or Ramesses. Ramses is a name common to several kings of the 18th, 19th, and 20th dynasties; but Sesostris must be identified with Ramses, the 3rd king of the 19th dynasty, the son of Seti, and the father of Menephthah. Sesostris was a great conqueror. He is said to have subdued Ethiopia, the greater part of Asia, and the Thracians in Europe. He returned to Egypt after an absence of 9 years, and the countless captives whom he brought back with him were employed in the erection of numerous public works. Memorials of Ramses-Sesostris still exist throughout the whole of Egypt, from the mouth of the Nile to the south of Nubia.

SESTĪNUM (-i: *Sestino*), a town in Umbria on the Apennines, near the sources of the Pisaurus.

SESTĪUS. [SEXTIUS.]

SESTUS (-i: *Ialova*), a town in Thrace, situated at the narrowest part of the Hellespont, opposite Abydos in Asia, from which it was only 7 stadia distant. It was founded by the Aeolians. It was celebrated in Grecian poetry on account of the loves of Leander and Hero [LEANDER], and in history on account of the bridge of boats which Xerxes here built across the Hellespont.

SETĀBIS. [SAETABIS.]

SĒTHON, a priest of Hephaestus, made himself master of Egypt after the expulsion of Sabacon, king of the Ethiopians, and was succeeded by the Dodecarchia, or government of the 12 chiefs, which ended in the sole sovereignty of Psammitichus.

SETĪA (-ae: *Sezza* or *Sesse*), an ancient town of Latium in the E. of the Pontine Marshes. It was celebrated for the excellent wine grown in its neighbourhood, which was reckoned in the time of Augustus the finest wine in Italy.

SĒVĒRUS (-i), M. AURĒLĪUS ALEXANDER, usually called ALEXANDER SEVĒRUS, Roman emperor, A.D. 222—235, the son of Gessius Marcianus and Julia Mamaea, and first cousin of Elagabalus, was born at Arce, in Phoenicia, the 1st of October, A.D. 205. In 221 he was adopted by Elagabalus and created Caesar; and on the death of that emperor, on the 11th of March, A.D. 222, Alexander ascended the throne. After reigning in peace some years, during which he reformed many abuses in the state, he was involved in a war with Artaxerxes, king of Persia, and gained a great victory over him in 232; but was unable to prosecute his advantage in consequence of intelligence having reached him of a great movement among the German tribes. He celebrated a triumph at Rome in 233, and in the following year (234) set out for Gaul, which the Germans were devastating; but was waylaid by a small band of mutinous soldiers, instigated, it is said, by Maximinus, and slain, in the 30th year of his age, and the 14th of his reign. Alexander Severus was distinguished by justice, wisdom, and clemency in all public transactions, and by the simplicity and purity of his private life.

SĒVĒRUS, A. CAECINA. [CAECINA.]

SĒVĒRUS (-i), FLĀVĪUS VĀLĒRIUS, Roman emperor, A.D. 306—307. He was proclaimed Caesar by Galerius in 306, and was soon afterwards sent against Maxentius, who had assumed the imperial title at Rome. The expedition however was unsuccessful; and Severus having surrendered at Ravenna, was taken as a prisoner to Rome and compelled to put an end to his life.

SĒVĒRUS (-i), LIBĪUS, Roman emperor A.D. 461—465, was a Lucanian by birth, and owed his accession to Ricimer, who placed him on the throne after the assassination of Majcrian. During his reign the real government was in the hands of Ricimer. Severus died a natural death.

SĒVĒRUS (-i), L. SEPTĪMĪUS, Roman emperor A.D. 193—211, was born 146, near Leptis in Africa. After holding various important military commands under M. Aurelius and Commodus, he was at length appointed commander-in-chief of the army in Pannonia and Illyria. By this army he was proclaimed emperor after the death of Pertinax (193). He forthwith marched upon Rome, where Julianus had been made emperor by the praetorian troops. Julianus was put to death upon his arrival before the city. [JULIANUS.] Severus then turned his arms against Pescennius Niger, who had been saluted emperor by the eastern legions, defeated him in a battle near Issus, and shortly afterwards put him to death (194). Severus next laid siege to Byzantium, which refused to submit to him even after the death of Niger, and which was not taken till 196. During the continuance of this siege, Severus had crossed the Euphrates (195) and subdued the Mesopotamian Arabians. He returned to Italy in 196, and in the same year proceeded to Gaul to oppose Albinus, who had been proclaimed emperor by the troops in that country. Albinus was defeated and slain in a terrible battle fought near Lyons on the 19th of February, 197. Severus returned to Rome in the same year; but after remaining a short time in the capital, he set out for the East in order to repel the invasion of the Parthians, who were ravaging Mesopotamia. After spending 3 years in the East, where he met with the most brilliant success, Severus returned to Rome in 202. For the next 7 years he remained tranquilly at Rome; but in 208 he went to Britain with his sons Caracalla and Geta. Here he carried on war against the Caledonians, and erected the celebrated wall, which bore his name, from the Solway to the mouth of the Tyne. After remaining 2 years in Britain he died at Eboracum (York) on the 4th of February, 211, in the 65th year of his age, and the 18th of his reign.

SEXTĬAE ĀQUAE. [Aqṵ̇ ɐ SEXTIAE.]

SEXTĬUS or SESTĬUS (-i), P., quaestor B.C. 63, and tribune of the plebs 57. Like Milo, he kept a band of armed retainers to oppose P. Clodius and his partisans; and in the following year (56) he was accused of *Vis* on account of his violent acts during his tribunate. He was defended by Cicero in an oration still extant, and was acquitted on the 14th of March, chiefly in consequence of the powerful influence of Pompey. On the breaking out of the civil war in 49, Sextius first espoused Pompey's party, but he afterwards joined Caesar.

SEXTUS EMPĪRĬCUS (-i), a physician, was a contemporary of Galen, and lived in the first half of the 3rd century of the Christian era. Two of his works are extant.

SEXTUS RŪFUS (-i). (1) The name prefixed to a work entitled *De Regionibus Urbis Romae.*—(2) SEXTUS RUFUS is also the name prefixed to an abridgment of Roman History in 28 short chapters, entitled *Breviarium de Victoriis et Provinciis Populi Romani*, and executed by command of the emperor Valens, to whom it is dedicated.

SĬBYLLAE (-ārum), the name by which several prophetic women are designated. The first Sibyl, from whom all the rest are said to have derived their name, is called a daughter of Dardanus and Neso. Some authors mention only 4 Sibyls, but it was more commonly believed that there were 10. The most celebrated of them is the Cumaean, who is mentioned under the names of Herophilē, Demo, Phemonoë, Deiphobē, Demophilē, and Amalthea. She was consulted by Aeneas before he descended into the lower world. She is said to have come to Italy from the East, and she is the one who, according to tradition, appeared before king Tarquinius, offering him the Sibylline books for sale. Respecting the Sibylline books, see *Dict. of Antiq.*, art. *Sibyllini Libri*.

SĬCAMBRI. [SYGAMBRI.]

SĬCĀNI, SĬCĔLI, SICELIŌTAE. [SICILIA.]

SICCA VĔNĔRĬA (prob. *Al-Kaff*), a considerable city of N. Africa, on the frontier of Numidia and Zeugitana, built on a hill near the river Bagradas.

SICHAEUS, also called Acerbas. [ACERBAS.]

SĬCĬLĬA (-ae : *Sicily*), one of the largest islands in the Mediterranean Sea. It was supposed by the ancients to be the same as the island named *Thrinacia* by Homer, and it was therefore frequently called THRINACIA, TRINACIA, or TRINACRIS, a name which was believed to be derived from the triangular figure of the island. For the same reason the Roman poets called it TRIQUETRA. Itſ more usual name came from its later inhabitants, the Siceli, whence it was called SICELIA, which the Romans changed into SICILIA. As the Siceli also bore the name of Sicani, the island was also called SICANIA. Sicily is separated from the S. coast of Italy by a narrow channel called FRETUM SICULUM, sometimes simply FRETUM, and also SCYLLAEUM FRETUM, of which the modern name is *Faro di Messina*. The sea on the E. and S. of the island was also called MARE SICULUM. A range of mountains, which are a continuation of the Apennines, extends throughout the island from E. to W. Of these the most important were, the celebrated volcano Aetna on the E. side of the island, Eryx (*St. Giulano*), in the extreme W. near Drepaɪ um, and the Heraci Montes (*Monti Sori*) in the S., running down to the promontory Pachynus. A large number of rivers flow down from the mountains, but most of them are dry, or nearly so, in the summer. The soil of Sicily was very fertile, and produced in antiquity an immense quantity of wheat, on which the population of Rome relied to a great extent for their subsistence. So celebrated was it, even in early times, on account of its corn, that it was represented as sacred to Demeter (Ceres), and as the favourite abode of this goddess. Hence it was in this island that her daughter Persephone (Proserpina) was carried away by Pluto. Besides corn, the island produced excellent wine, saffron, honey, almonds, and the other southern fruits. The earliest inhabitants of Sicily are said to have been the savage Cyclōpes and Laestrygŏnes; but these are fabulous beings, and the first inhabitants mentioned in history are the SICANI, or SICULI, who crossed over into the island from Italy. The next immigrants into the island were Cretans; but these, if, indeed, they ever visited Sicily, soon became incorporated with the Siculi. The Phoenicians, likewise, at an early period, formed settlements, for the purposes of commerce, on all the coasts of Sicily, but more especially on the N. and N.W. parts. But the most important of all the immigrants into Sicily were the Greeks, who founded a number of very flourishing cities, such as Naxos, B.C. 735, Syracuse in 734, Leontini and Catana in 730, Megara Hyblaea in 726, Gela in 690, Selinus in 626, Agrigentum in 579, etc. The Greeks soon became the ruling race in the island, and received the name of SICELIOTAE to distinguish them from the earlier inhabitants. At a later time the Carthaginians obtained a firm footing in Sicily. After taking Agrigentum in 405, the Carthaginians became the permanent masters of the W. part of the island, and were engaged in frequent wars with Syracuse and the other Greek cities. The struggle between the Carthaginians and Greeks continued, with a few interruptions, down to the 1st Punic war; at the close of which (241) the Carthaginians were obliged to evacuate the island, the W. part of which now passed into the hands of the Romans, and was made a Roman province. The E. part still continued under the rule of Hieron of Syracuse as an ally of Rome; but after the revolt of Syracuse in the 2nd Punic war, and the conquest of that city by Marcellus, the whole island was made a Roman province, and was administered by a praetor. On the downfal of the Roman empire, Sicily formed part of the kingdom of the Ostrogoths; but it was taken from them by Belisarius in A.D. 536, and annexed to the Byzantine empire. It continued a province of this empire till 828, when it was conquered by the Saracens.

SICINĬUS (-i). (1) L. SICINIUS BELLUTUS, the leader of the plebeians in their secession to the Sacred Mount in B.C. 494. He was chosen one of the first tribunes.— (2) L. SICINIUS DENTATUS, called by some writers the Roman Achilles, from his personal prowess. He was tribune of the plebs in 454. He was put to death by the decemvirs in 450, because he endeavoured to persuade the plebeians to secede to the Sacred Mount. The persons sent to assassinate him fell upon him in a lonely spot, but he killed most of them before they succeeded in dispatching him.

SICĪNUS (-i : Sikino), a small island in the Aegaean sea, one of the Sporades, between Pholegandrus and Ios, with a town of the same name.

SĬCŎRIS (-is : Segre), a river in Hispania Tarraconensis, which had its source in the territory of the Cerretani, and fell into the Iberus, near Octogesa.

SĬCŬLI. [SICILIA.]

SĬCŬLUM FRĔTUM, SICŬLUM MĂRE. [SICILIA.]

SĬCŬLUS FLACCUS. [FLACCUS.]

SĬCȲŎNĬA (-ae), a small district in the N.E. of Peloponnesus, bounded on the E. by the territory of Corinth, on the W. by Achaia, on the S. by the territory of Phlius and Cleonae, and on the N. by the Corinthian gulf. Its area was about 100 square

miles. The land was fertile, and produced excellent oil. Its almonds and its fish were also much prized. Its chief town was SICYON, which was situated a little to the W. of the river Asopus, and at the distance of 20, or, according to others, 12 stadia from the sea. Sicyon was one of the most ancient cities of Greece. It is said to have been originally called Aegialēa or Aegiali, after an ancient king, Aegialeus; to have been subsequently named Mecōne, and finally Sicyon, from an Athenian of this name. Sicyon is represented by Homer as forming part of the empire of Agamemnon; but on the invasion of Peloponnesus it became subject to Phalces, the son of Temenus, and was henceforward a Dorian state. Sicyon, on account of the small extent of its territory, never attained much political importance, and was generally dependent either on Argos or Sparta. At the time of the 2nd Messenian war it became subject to a succession of tyrants, who administered their power with moderation and justice for 100 years. On the death of Clisthenes, the last of these, about 576, a republican form of government was established. Sicyon was for a long time the chief seat of Grecian art. It gave its name to one of the great schools of painting, which was founded by Eupompus, and which produced Pamphilus and Apelles. It is also said to have been the earliest school of statuary in Greece; but its earliest native artist of celebrity was Canachus. Lysippus was also a native of Sicyon. The town was likewise celebrated for the taste and skill displayed in the various articles of dress made by its inhabitants, among which we find mention of a particular kind of shoe, which was much prized in all parts of Greece.

SĪDA, SĪDĒ (-ae or -ēs). (1) (Eski Adalia, Ru.), a city of Pamphylia, on the coast, a little W. of the river Melas. It was an Aeolian colony from Cyme in Aeolis, and was a chief seat of the worship of Athena (Minerva), who is represented on its coins holding a pomegranate (σίδη) as the emblem of the city.—(2) The old name of POLEMONIUM.

SĪDĬCĪNI (-ōrum), an Ausonian people in the N W. of Campania and on the borders of Samnium, who, being hard pressed by the Samnites, united themselves to the Campanians. Their chief town was Teanum.

SĪDON (-ōnis and -ŏnis), (O. T. Tsidon or, in the English form, Zidon: Saida, Ru.), for a long time the most powerful, and probably the most ancient, of the cities of Phoenice. It stood in a plain about a mile wide, on the coast of the Mediterranean, 200 stadia (20 geog. miles) N. of Tyre, 400 stadia (40 geog. miles) S. of Berytus, 66 miles **W.** of Damascus, and a day's journey N.W. of the source of the Jordan at Paneas. It had a fine double harbour, now almost filled with sand ; and was strongly fortified. It was the chief seat of the maritime power of Phoenice, until eclipsed by its own colony, Tyre [TYRUS] ; and its power on the land side seems to have extended over all Phoenice, and at one period (in the time of the Judges) over at least a part of Palestine. In the time of David and Solomon, Sidon appears to have been subject to the king of Tyre. It probably regained its former rank, as the first of the Phoenician cities, by its submission to Shalmanezer at the time of the Assyrian conquest of Syria, for we find it governed by its own king under the Babylonians and the Persians. In the expedition of Xerxes against Greece, the Sidonians furnished the best ships in the whole fleet, and their king obtained the highest place, next to Xerxes, in the council, and above the king of Tyre. Sidon received the great blow to her prosperity in the reign of Artaxerxes III. Ochus, when the Sidonians, having taken part in the revolt of Phoenice and Cyprus, and being betrayed to Ochus by their own king, Tennes, burnt themselves with their city, B.C. 351. In addition to its commerce, Sidon was famed for its manufactures of glass.

SĪDŌNĬUS (-i) ĂPOLLĬNĀRĬS (-is), was born at Lugdunum (*Lyons*) about A.D. 431. He was raised to the senatorial dignity by the emperor Avitus, whose daughter he had married. After the downfal of Avitus he lived some time in retirement ; but in 467 appeared again in Rome as ambassador from the Arverni to Anthemius. He gained the favour of that prince by a panegyric ; was made a patrician, and prefect of the city ; and soon afterwards, though not a priest, bishop of Clermont in Auvergne. His extant works are some poems, and 9 books of letters.

SĪGA, a considerable sea-port town of Mauretania Caesariensis.

SĪGEUM (-i : *Yenisheri*), the N.W. promontory of the Troad, and the S. headland at the entrance of the Hellespont. It is here that Homer places the Grecian fleet and camp during the Trojan war. Near it was a seaport town of the same name.

SIGNĬA (-ae : *Segni*), a town in Latium on the E. side of the Volscian mountains, founded by Tarquinius Priscus. It was celebrated for its temple of Jupiter Urius, for its astringent wine, for its pears, and for a particular kind of pavement for the floors of houses, called *opus Signinum*.

SILA SILVA (-ae : *Sila*), a large forest in Bruttium on the Apennines, extending S. to Consentia to the Sicilian straits.

SILANĬON, an Athenian, a distinguished statuary in bronze, was a contemporary of Lysippus, and flourished B.C. 324. His statue of Sappho, which stood in the *prytaneum* at Syracuse in the time of Verres, is alluded to by Cicero in terms of the highest praise.

SĪLĀNUS (-i), JŪNĬUS. (1) M., was praetor B.C. 212. In 210 he accompanied P. Scipio to Spain, and served under him with great distinction during the whole of the war in that country. He fell in battle against the Boii in 196.—(2) M., consul 109, fought in this year against the Cimbri in Transalpine Gaul, and was defeated. He was accused in consequence, in 104, by the tribune Cn. Domitius Ahenobarbus, but acquitted.— (3) D., stepfather of M. Brutus, the murderer of Caesar, having married his mother Servilia. He was consul 62, with L. Licinius Murena, along with whom he proposed the Lex Licinia Julia.—(4) M., son of No. 3 and of Servilia, served in Gaul as Caesar's legatus in 53. After Caesar's murder in 44, he accompanied M. Lepidus over the Alps ; and in the following year Lepidus sent him with a detachment of troops into Cisalpine Gaul, where he fought on the side of Antony. He was consul in 25.

SĪLĀRUS (-i : *Silaro*), a river in lower Italy, forming the boundary between Lucania and Campania, rises in the Apennines, and falls into the Sinus Paestanus a little to the N. of Paestum.

SĪLĒNUS (-i). It is remarked in the article SATYRI that the older Satyrs were generally termed Sileni ; but one of these Sileni is commonly *the* Silenus, who always accompanies Dionysus (Bacchus), whom he is said to have brought up and instructed. Like the other Satyrs, he is called a son of Hermes (Mercury) ; but some make him a son of Pan by a nymph, or of Gaea (Tellus). Being the constant companion of Dionysus, he is said, like the god, to have been born at Nysa. Moreover, he took part in the contest with the Gigantes, and slew Enceladus. He is described as a jovial old man, with a bald head, a puck nose, fat and round like his wine-bag, which he always carried with him, and generally intoxicated. As he could not trust his own legs, he is generally represented riding on an ass, or supported by other Satyrs. In every other respect he is described as resembling his brethren in their love of sleep, wine, and music. He is mentioned along with Marsyas and Olympus as the inventor of the flute, which he is often seen playing ; and a special kind of dance was called after him, Silenus, while he himself is designated as the dancer. But it is a peculiar feature in his character that he was an inspired prophet: and when he was drunk and asleep

Silenus. (From a Bronze Statue found at Pompeii.)

he was in the power of mortals who might compel him to prophesy and sing by surrounding him with chains of flowers.

SĪLĬUS ĪTĂLĬCUS (-i), C., a Roman poet, was born about A.D. 25. He acquired great reputation as an advocate, and was afterwards one of the Centumviri. He was consul in 68, the year in which Nero perished ; he was admitted to familiar intercourse with Vitellius, and was subsequently proconsul of Asia. In his 75th year, in consequence of the pain caused by an incurable disease, he starved himself to death, in the house once occupied by Virgil. The great work of Silius Italicus was an heroic poem in 17 books, entitled *Punica*, which has descended to us entire.

SILŪRES (-um), a powerful people in Britain, inhabiting *South Wales*, long offered a formidable resistance to the Romans, and afterwards to the Saxons.

SILVĀNUS (-i), a Latin divinity of the fields and forests. He is also called the protector of the boundaries of fields. In connexion with woods (*sylvestris deus*), he especially presided over plantations, and delighted in trees growing wild ; whence he is represented as carrying the trunk of a cypress. Silvanus is further described as the divinity protecting herds of cattle, promoting their fertility, and driving away wolves. Later writers identified Silvanus with Pan, Faunus, Inuus, and Aegipan. In the Latin poets, as well as in works of art, he always appears as an old man, but cheerful

and in love with Pomona. The sacrifices offered to him consisted of grapes, ears of corn, milk, meat, wine, and pigs.

SILVĬUM (-i), a town of the Peucetii in Apulia on the borders of Lucania, 20 miles S.E. of Venusia.

SILVĬUS (-i), the son of Ascanius, is said to have been so called because he was born in a wood. All the succeeding kings of Alba bore the cognomen Silvius.

SIMMĬAS (-aē). (1) Of Thebes, first the disciple of the Pythagorean philosopher Philolaüs, and afterwards the friend and disciple of Socrates, at whose death he was present. Simmias wrote 23 dialogues on philosophical subjects, all of which are lost.

SĪMŎIS (-entis). [TROAS.] As a mythological personage, the river-god Simois is the son of Oceanus and Tethys, and the father of Astyochus and Hieromneme.

SĪMON (-ōnis), one of the disciples of Socrates, and by trade a leather-cutter.

SĬMŎNĬDĒS (-is.) (1) Of Amorgos, was the 2nd, both in time and in reputation, of the 3 principal iambic poets of the early period of Greek literature, namely, Archilochus, Simonides, and Hipponax. He was a native of Samos, whence he led a colony to the neighbouring island of Amorgos. He flourished about B.C. 664.—(2) Of Ceos, one of the most celebrated lyric poets of Greece, was born at Iulis, in Ceos, B.C. 556, and was the son of Leoprepes. He appears to have been brought up to music and poetry as a profession. From his native island he proceeded to Athens, and thence into Thessaly, where he lived under the patronage of the Aleuads and Scopads. He afterwards returned to Athens, and in 489 conquered Aeschylus in the contest for the prize which the Athenians offered for an elegy on those who fell at Marathon. He composed several other works of the same description ; and in his 80th year his long poetical career at Athens was crowned by the victory which he gained with the dithyrambic chorus (447), being the 56th prize which he had carried off. Shortly after this he was invited to Syracuse by Hiero, at whose court he lived till his death in 467. He still continued, when at Syracuse, to employ his muse occasionally in the service of other Grecian states. He made literature a profession, and is said to have been the first who took money for his poems. The chief characteristics of the poetry of Simonides were sweetness (whence his surname of *Melicertes*) and elaborate finish, combined with the truest poetic conception and perfect power of expression ; though in originality and fervour he was far inferior, not only to the early lyric poets, such as Sappho and Alcaeus, but also to his contemporary Pindar.

SIMPLĬCĬUS (-i), one of the last philosophers of the Neo-Platonic school, was a native of Cilicia and a disciple of Ammonius and Damascius. In consequence of the persecutions, to which the pagan philosophers were exposed in the reign of Justinian, Simplicius was one of the 7 philosophers who took refuge at the court of the Persian king Chosroës. He returned home about 543. Simplicius wrote commentaries on several of Aristotle's works, which are marked by sound sense and real learning. He also wrote a commentary on the Enchiridion of Epictetus, which is likewise extant.

SĪNAE (-arum), the E.-most people of Asia. Ptolemy describes their country as bounded on the N. by Serica, and on the S. and W. by India extra Gangem. It corresponded to the S. part of China and the E. part of the Burmese peninsula.

SINAĪ or SINA (Jebel-et-Tur), a cluster of dark, lofty, rocky mountains in the S. angle of the triangular peninsula enclosed between the 2 heads of the Red Sea, and bounded on the N. by the deserts on the borders of Egypt and Palestine. The name, which signifies a region of broken and cleft rocks, is used in a wider sense for the whole peninsula, which formed a part of Arabia Petraea, and was peopled, at the time of the Exodus, by the Amalekites and Midianites, and afterwards by the Nabathaean Arabs. Sinaï and Horeb in the O. T. are both general names for the whole group, the former being used in the first 4 books of Moses, and the latter in Deuteronomy. The summit on which the law was given was probably that on the N., or the one usually called Horeb.

SINDI (-ōrum). (1) A people of Asiatic Sarmatia, on the E. coast of the Euxine, and at the foot of the Caucasus. They are also mentioned by the names of SINDONES and SINDIANA.—(2) A people on the E. coast of India extra Gangem (in Cochin China), also called SINDAE, and with a capital city, SINDA.

SINDĬCE. [SINDI.]

SINGĀRA (-ōrum: Sinjar?), a strongly fortified city and Roman colony in the interior of Mesopotamia, 84 Roman miles S. of Nisibis.

SINGITĬCUS SĬNUS. [SINGUS.]

SINGUS (-i), a town in Macedonia on the E. coast of the peninsula Sithonia, which gave its name to the Sinus Singiticus.

SĬNIS or SINNIS (-is), son of Polypēmon, Pemon or Poseidon (Neptune), by Sylea, the daughter of Corinthus. He was a robber, who frequented the isthmus of Corinth, and killed the travellers whom he captured, by fastening them to the top of a fir-tree, which he bent, and then let spring up again. He himself was killed in this manner by Theseus.

SINON (-ōnis), son of Aesimus, or, according to Virgil (Aen., ii. 79), of Sisўphus, and grandson of Autŏlўcus, was a relation of Ulysses, whom he accompanied to Troy. He allowed himself to be taken prisoner by the Trojans, and then persuaded them to admit into their city a wooden horse filled with armed men, which the Greeks had constructĕd as a pretended atonement for the Palladium. The Trojans believed the deceiver, and dragged the horse into the city ; whereupon Sinon in the dead of night let the Greeks out of the horse, who thus took Troy.

SĪNŌPĒ (-es : Sinope, Sinoub, Ru.), the most important of all the Greek colonies on the shores of the Euxine, stood on the N. coast of Asia Minor, on the W. headland of the great bay of which the delta of the river Halys forms the E. headland, and a little E. of the N.-most promontory of Asia Minor. It appears in history as a very early colony of the Milesians. Having been destroyed in the invasion of Asia by the Cimmerians, it was restored by a new colony from Miletus, B.C. 632, and soon became the greatest commercial city on the Euxine. Its territory, called SINOPIS, extended to the banks of the Halys. It was the birthplace and residence of Mithridates the Great, who enlarged and beautified it. Shortly before the murder of Julius Caesar, it was colonised by the name of Julia Caesarea Felix Sinope, and remained a flourishing city, though it never recovered its former importance. At the time of Constantine it had declined so much as to be ranked second to Amasia. It was the native city of the renowned cynic philosopher Diogenes, of the comic poet Diphilus, and of the historian Baton.

SINTĬCA, a district in Macedonia, inhabited by the Thracian people SINTI, extended E. of Crestonia and N. of Bisaltia as far as the Strymon and the lake Prasias. Its chief town was Heraclea Sintica.

SĬNŪESSA (-ae : Rocca di Mandragone), the last city of Latium on the confines of Campania, to which it originally belonged, was situated on the sea-coast and on the Via Appia. It was colonised by the Romans, together with the neighbouring town of Minturnae, B.C. 296. It possessed a good harbour, and was a place of considerable commercial importance. In its neighbourhood were celebrated warm baths, called AQUAE SINUESSANAE.

SION. [JERUSALEM.]

SIPHNUS (-i : Siphno), an island in the Aegaean sea, forming one of the Cyclades.

S.E. of Seriphus. It is of an oblong form, and about 40 miles in circumference. Its original name was Merope; and it was colonised by Ionians from Athens. In consequence of their gold and silver mines, of which the remains are still visible, the Siphnians attained great prosperity, and were regarded in the time of Herodotus as the wealthiest of the islanders. Siphnus was one of the few islands which refused tribute to. Xerxes; and one of its ships fought on the side of the Greeks at Salamis. The moral character of the Siphnians stood low, and hence to act like a Siphnian (Σιφνιάζειν) became a term of reproach.

SĪPONTUM or SIPUNTUM (-i: *Siponto*), called by the Greeks Sɪᴘᴜs (-untis), an ancient town in Apulia, in the district of Daunia, on the S. slope of Mt. Garganus, and on the coast. It is said to have been founded by Diomede, and was of Greek origin. It was colonised by the Romans, under whom it became a place of some commercial importance.

SĪPĬLUS (-i: *Sipuli-Dagh*), a mountain of Lydia, in Asia Minor. It is a branch of the Tmolus, from the main chain of which it proceeds N.W. along the course of the river Hermus, as far as Magnesia and Sipylum. It is mentioned by Homer. The ancient capital of Maeonia was said to have been situated in the heart of the mountain chain, and to have been called by the same name; but it was early swallowed up by an earthquake, and its site became a little lake called Sale or Saloë, near which was a tumulus, supposed to be the grave of Tantalus. The mountain was rich in metals, and many mines were worked in it.

SIRBŌNIS LĂCUS (*Sabakat Bardowal*), a large and deep lake on the coast of Lower Egypt, E. of Mt. Casius. Its circuit was 1000 stadia. It was strongly impregnated with asphaltus.

SĪRĒNES (-um), sea-nymphs who had the power of charming by their songs all who heard them. When Ulysses came near the island, on the beach of which the Sirens were sitting, and endeavouring to allure him and his companions, he stuffed the ears of his companions with wax, and tied himself to the mast of his vessel, until he was so far off that he could no longer hear the Sirens' song. According to Homer, the island of the Sirens was situated between Aeaea and the rock of Scylla, near the S.W. coast of Italy; but the Roman poets place them on the Campanian coast. Some state that they were 2 in number, Aglaopheme and Thelxiepla; and others, that there were 3, Pisinöe, Aglaope, and Thelxiepla, or Parthenope, Ligïa, and Leucosia. They are called daughters of Phorcus, of Achelöus and Steröpe, of Terpsichöre, of Melpoměne, of Calliöpe, or of Gaea. The Sirens are also connected with the legends of the Argonauts and the rape of Persephöne. When the Argonauts sailed by the Sirens, the latter began to sing, but in vain, for Orpheus surpassed them; and as it had been decreed that they should live only till some one hearing their song should pass by unmoved, they threw themselves into the sea, and were metamorphosed into rocks.

SĪRĒNŪSAE (-ārum), called by Virgil (*Aen.* v. 864) Sɪʀᴇɴᴜᴍ Sᴄᴏᴘᴜʟɪ, 3 small uninhabited and rocky islands near the S. side of the Prom. Misenum, off the coast of Campania, which were, according to tradition, the abode of the Sirens.

SĪRĬS (-is). (1) (*Sinno*), a river in Lucania flowing into the Tarentine gulf.—(2) (*Torre di Senna*), an ancient Greek town in Lucania at the mouth of the preceding river.

SIRMĬO (-ōnis: *Sirmione*), a beautiful promontory on the S. shore of the Lacus Benācus (*Lago di Garda*), on which Catullus had an estate.

SIRMĬUM (-i: *Mitrovitz*), an important city in Pannonia Inferior, was situated on the left bank of the Savus. It was founded by the Taurisci, and under the Romans became the capital of Pannonia, and the head-quarters of all their operations in their wars against the Dacians and the neighbouring barbarians.

SĪSĂPON (-ōnis: *Almaden* in the Sierra Morena), an important town in Hispania Baetica N. of Corduba.

SISCĬA (-ae: *Sissek*), called Sᴇɢᴇsᴛᴀ by Appian, an important town in Pannonia Superior, situated upon an island formed by the rivers Savus, Colapis, and Odra, and on the road from Aemona to Sirmium.

SĪSENNA (-ae), L. CORNELĬUS, a Roman annalist, was praetor in the year when Sulla died (B.C. 78), and probably obtained Sicily for his province in 77. During the piratica war (67) he acted as the legate of Pompey, and having been despatched to Crete in command of an army, died in that island at the age of about 52. His great work was a history of his own time, but he also translated the Milesian fables of Aristides, and composed a commentary upon Plautus.

SISYGAMBIS (-is), mother of Darius Codomannus, the last king of Persia, fell into the hands of Alexander, after the battle of Issus, B.C. 333, together with the wife and daughters of Darius. Alexander treated these captives with the greatest generosity and kindness, and displayed towards Sisygambis, in particular, a reverence and delieacy of conduct, which is one of the brightest ornaments of his character. After his death she put an end to her life by voluntary starvation.

SĪSȲPHUS (-i), son of Aeŏlus and Enarĕte, whence he is called *Aeolīdes.* He was married to Merŏpe, a daughter of Atlas or a Pleiad, and became by her the father of Glaucus, Ornytion (or Porphyrion), Thersander and Halmus. In later accounts he is also called a son of Autolȳcus, and the father

of Ulysses by Anticlea [ANTICLEA]; whence we find Ulysses sometimes called *Sisyphĭdes.* He is said to have built the town of Ephyra, afterwards Corinth. As king of Corinth he promoted navigation and commerce, but he was fraudulent, avaricious, and deceitful. His wickedness during life was severely punished in the lower world, where he had to roll up hill a huge marble block, which as soon as it reached the top always rolled down again.

Sisyphus, Ixion, and Tantalus.   (Bartoli, Sepolc. Ant., tav. 56.)

SITĂCE or SITTĂCE (-ēs: *Eski-Bagdad,* Ru.), a great and populous city of Babylonia, near but not on the Tigris, and 8 parasangs within the Median wall. Its probable site is marked by a ruin called the Tower of Nimrod. It gave the name of Sittacene to the district on the lower course of the Tigris, E. of Babylonia and N.W. of Susiana.

SĪTHŌNĬA (-ae), the central one of the 3 peninsulas running out from Chalcidice in Macedonia, between the Toronaic and Singitic gulfs. The Thracians were originally spread over the greater part of Macedonia; and the ancients derived the name of Sithonia from a Thracian king, Sithon. We also find mention of a Thracian people, Sithonii, on the shores of the Pontus Euxinus; and the poets frequently use *Sithonis* and *Sithonius* in the general sense of Thracian.

SITONES (-um), a German tribe in Scandinavia, belonging to the race of the Suevi.

SITTĬUS or SITĬUS (-i), P., of Nuceria in Campania, was connected with Catiline, and went to Spain in B.C. 64, from which country he crossed over into Mauretania in the following year. He joined Caesar when the latter came to Africa, in 46, to prosecute

the war against the Pompeian party. He was of great service to Caesar, in this war, and at its conclusion was rewarded by him with the western part of Numidia, where he settled, distributing the land among his soldiers. After the death of Caesar, Arabio, the son of Masinissa, returned to Africa, and killed Sittius by stratagem.

SMĂRAGDUS MONS (*Jebel Zaburah*), a mountain of Upper Egypt, near the coast of the Red Sea, N. of Berenice. It obtained its name from its extensive emerald mines.

SMERDIS, the son of Cyrus, was murdered by order of his brother Cambȳses. A Magian, named Patizīthes, who had been left by Cambyses in charge of his palace and treasures, availed himself of the likeness of his brother to the deceased Smerdis, to proclaim this brother as king, representing him as the younger son of Cyrus. Cambyses heard of the revolt in Syria, but he died of an accidental wound in the thigh, as he was mounting his horse to march against the usurper. The false Smerdis was acknowledged as king by the Persians, and reigned for 7 months without opposition. The fraud was discovered by Phaedima, who had been one of the wives of Cambyses, and had been transferred to his successor. She communicated it to her father, Otanes, who thereupon formed a conspiracy, and in conjunction with 6 other noble Persians, succeeded in forcing his way into the palace, where they slew the false Smerdis and his brother Patizīthes in the 8th month of their reign, 521.

SMINTHEUS (-ĕŏs, ĕī, or ēi), a surname of Apollo, which is derived by some from σμίνθος, a mouse, and by others from the town of Sminthe in Troas. The mouse was regarded by the ancients as inspired by the vapours arising from the earth, and as the symbol of prophetic power.

SMYRNA, or MYRRHA. [ADONIS.]

SMYRNA and in many MSS. ZMYRNA (-ae : Smyrna, Turk. Izmir), one of the most ancient and flourishing cities of Asia Minor, and the only one of the great cities on its W. coast which has survived to this day, stood in a position alike remarkable for its beauty and for other natural advantages. Lying just about the centre of the W. coast of Asia Minor ; on the banks of the little river Meles, at the bottom of a deep bay, the Sinus Hermaeus or Smyrnaeus (G. of Smyrna), which formed a safe and immense harbour for the largest ships up to the very walls of the city ; at the foot of the rich slopes of Tmolus and at the entrance to the great and fertile valley of the Hermus, in which lay the great and wealthy city of Sardis ; and in the midst of the Greek colonies on the E. shore of the Aeagean ; it was marked out by nature as one of the greatest emporiums for the trade between Europe and Asia, and has preserved that character to the present day. There are various accounts of its origin. The most probable is that which represents it as an Aeolian colony from Cyme. At an early period it fell, by a stratagem, into the hands of the Ionians of Colophon, and remained an Ionian city from that time forth : this appears to have happened before Ol. 23. (B.C. 688). Its early history is very obscure. This much is clear, however, that, at some period the old city of Smyrna, which stood on the N.E. side of the Hermaean Gulf, was abandoned ; and that it was succeeded by a new city on the S.E. side of the same gulf (the present site), which is said to have been built by Antigonus, and which was enlarged and beautified by Lysimachus. This new city stood partly on the sea-shore and partly on a hill called Mastusia. The city soon became one of the greatest and most prosperous in the world. It was especially favoured by the Romans on account of the aid it rendered them in the

Syrian and Mithridatic wars. It was the seat of a conventus juridicus. In the Civil wars it was taken and partly destroyed by Dolabella, but it soon recovered. It occupies a distinguished place in the early history of Christianity, as one of the only two among the 7 churches of Asia which St. John addresses, in the Apocalypse, without any admixture of rebuke, and as the scene of the labours and martyrdom of Polycarp. There are but few ruins of the ancient city. In addition to all her other sources of renown, Smyrna stood at the head of the cities which claimed the birth of Homer. The poet was worshipped as a hero in a magnificent building called the Homerēum.

SMYRNAEUS SĪNUS (G. of Ismir or Smyrna), the great gulf on the W. coast of Asia Minor, at the bottom of which Smyrna stands.

SŌCRĂTES (-is). (1) The celebrated Athenian philosopher, was born in the demus Alōpĕce, in the immediate neighbourhood of Athens, B.C. 469. His father Sophroniscus was a statuary ; his mother Phaenarĕte was a midwife. In his youth Socrates followed the profession of his father, and attained sufficient proficiency to execute the group of clothed Graces which was preserved in the Acropolis, and was shown as his work down to the time of Pausanias. The personal qualities of Socrates were marked and striking. His physical constitution was healthy, robust, and enduring to an extraordinary degree. He was capable of bearing fatigue or hardship, and indifferent to heat or cold, in a measure which astonished all his companions. He went barefoot in all seasons of the year, even during the winter campaign at Potidaea, under the severe frosts of Thrace ; and the same homely clothing sufficed for him in winter as well as in summer. His ugly physiognomy excited the jests both of his friends and enemies, who inform us that he had a flat nose, thick lips, and prominent eyes, like a satyr or Silenus. Of the circumstances of his life we are almost wholly ignorant : he served as an hoplite at Potidaea, Delium, and Amphipŏlis, with great credit to himself. He seems never to have filled any political office until 406, in which year he was a member of the senate of Five Hundred, and one of the Prytănes, when on the occasion of the trial of the 6 generals, he refused, in spite of all personal hazard, to put an unconstitutional question to the vote. He displayed the same moral courage in refusing to obey the order of the Thirty Tyrants for the apprehension of Leon the Salaminian.—At what time Socrates relinquished his profession as a statuary we do not know ; but it is certain that at least all the middle and later part of his life was devoted to the self-imposed task of teaching, to the exclusion of all other business, public or private, and to the neglect of all means of fortune. But he never opened a school, nor did he, like the sophists of his time, deliver public lectures. He was persuaded that he had a special religious mission, and that he constantly heard the monitions of a divine or supernatural voice. Everywhere, in the market-place, in the gymnasia and in the workshops, he sought and found opportunities for awakening and guiding, in boys, youths, and men, moral consciousness and the impulse after knowledge respecting the end and value of our actions. His object, however, was only to aid them in developing the germs of knowledge; to practise a kind of mental midwifery, just as his mother Phaenarete exercised the corresponding corporeal art; and he therefore fought unweariedly against all false appearance and conceit of knowledge. This was probably the reason why he was selected for attack by Aristophanes and the other comic writers. Attached to none of the prevailing parties, Socrates found in each of them his friends and his enemies. Hated and persecuted by Critias, Charicles, and others among the Thirty Tyrants, who had him specially in view in the decree which they issued, forbidding the teaching of the art of oratory, he was impeached after their banishment and by their opponents. An orator named Lycon, and a poet (a friend of Thrasybulus) named Melētus, united in the impeachment with the powerful demagogue Anÿtus, an embittered antagonist of the sophists and their system, and one of the leaders of the band which, setting out from Phyle, forced their way into the Piraeus, and drove out the Thirty Tyrants. The judges also are described as persons who had been banished, and who had returned with Thrasybulus. The chief articles of impeachment were, that Socrates was guilty of corrupting the youth, and of despising the tutelary deities of the state, putting in their place other new divinities; but the accusation was doubtless also dictated by political animosity. The substance of the speech which Socrates delivered in his defence is probably preserved by Plato in the piece entitled the "Apology of Socrates." Being condemned by a majority of only 6 votes, he refused to acquiesce in any greater punishment than a fine of 60 minae, on the security of Plato, Crito, and other friends. Incensed by this speech, the judges condemned him to death by a majority of 80 votes. The sentence could not be carried into execution until after the return of the vessel which had been sent to Delos on the periodical Theoric mission. The 30 days which intervened between its return and the execution of Socrates were devoted by him to poetic attempts (the first he had made in his life), and to his usual conversation with his friends. One of these conversations, on the duty of obedience to the laws, Plato has reported in the Crito, so called after the faithful follower of Socrates, who had endeavoured without success to persuade him to make his escape. In another, imitated or worked up by Plato in the Phaedo, Socrates, immediately before he drank the cup of hemlock, developed the grounds of his immovable conviction of the immortality of the soul. He died with composure and cheerfulness in his 70th year, B.C. 399. He must be considered as having laid the foundation of formal logic. —(2) The ecclesiastical historian, was born at Constantinople about A.D. 379. He was a pupil of Ammonius and Helladius, and followed the profession of an advocate in his native city, whence he is surnamed Scholasticus. The Ecclesiastical History of Socrates extends from the reign of Constantine the Great, 306, to that of the younger Theodosius, 439.

SÒDŎMA (-ōrum and -ae; also -um, gen. -i; and -i, gen. -ōrum), a very ancient city of Canaan, in the beautiful valley of Siddim, closely connected with Gomorrha, over which and the other 3 "cities of the plain," the king of Sodom seems to have had a sort of supremacy. In the book of Genesis we find these cities as subject, in the time of Abraham, to the king of Elam and his allies (an indication of the early supremacy in W. Asia of the masters of the Tigris and Euphrates valley), and their attempt to cast off the yoke was the occasion of the first war on record. (Gen. xiv.) Soon afterwards, the abominable sins of these cities called down the divine vengeance, and they were all destroyed by fire from heaven, except Zoar, which was spared at the intercession of Lot.

SOEMIS or SOAEMĪAS, JŪLĬA, daughter of Julia Maesa, and mother of Elagabalus, became the chosen counsellor of her son and encouraged and shared his follies and enormities. She was slain by the praetorians on the 11th of March, A.D. 222.

SOGDIĀNA (-ae), (Old Persian, Sughda : parts of Turkestan and Bokhara, including the district still called Sogd), the N.E. province of the ancient Persian Empire, separated on the S. from Bactriana and Margiana by the upper course of the Oxus (Jihoun); on the E. and N. from Scythia by the Sogdii

Comedarum and Oscii M. (*Kara-Dagh*, *Alatan* and *Ak Tagh*) and by the upper course of the Jaxartes (*Sihoun*); and bounded on the N.W. by the great deserts E. of the *Sea of Aral*.

SOGDIĀNUS (-i), one of the illegitimate sons of Artaxerxes I. Longimanus, acquired the throne on the death of his father B.C. 425, by the murder of his legitimate brother Xerxes II. Sogdianus, however, was murdered in his turn, after a reign of 7 months, by his brother Ochus.

SOGDII MONTES. [SOGDIANA.]

SŌL. [HELIOS.]

SŌLI (-ōrum), or SŎLŎE. (1) *Mezetlu*, Ru.), a city on the coast of Cilicia, between the rivers Lamus and Cydnus, said to have been colonised by Argives and Lydians from Rhodes. Pompey restored the city which had been destroyed by Tigranes, and peopled it with the survivors of the defeated bands of pirates; and from this time forth it was called POMPEIOPOLIS. It was celebrated in literary history as the birthplace of the Stoic philosopher Chrysippus, of the comic poet Philemon, and of the astronomer and poet Aratus.—(2) (*Aligora*, in the valley of *Solea*, Ru.), a considerable sea-port town in the W. part of the N. coast of Cyprus.

SOLĪNUS (-i), C. JŪLIUS, the author of a geographical compendium, divided into 57 chapters, containing a brief sketch of the world as known to the ancients, diversified by historical notices, remarks on the origin, habits, religious rites and social condition of various nations enumerated. It displays but little knowledge or judgment. Solinus may perhaps be placed about A.D. 238.

SŌLIS FONS. [OASIS, No. 3.]

SŎLŎE. [SOLI.]

SŎLŎIS (*C. Cantin*, Arab. *Ras el Houdik*), a promontory running far out into the sea, in the S. part of the W. coast of Mauretania.

SŌLŌN (-ōnis), the celebrated Athenian legislator, was born about B.C. 638. His father Execestides was a descendant of Codrus, and his mother was a cousin of the mother of Pisistratus. Execestides had seriously crippled his resources by a too prodigal expenditure; and Solon consequently found it either necessary or convenient in his youth to betake himself to the life of a foreign trader. It is likely enough that while necessity compelled him to seek a livelihood in some mode or other, his active and inquiring spirit led him to select that pursuit which would furnish him the amplest means for its gratification. Solon early distinguished himself by his poetical abilities. His first effusions were in a somewhat light and amatory strain, which afterwards gave way to the more dignified and earnest purpose of inculcating profound reflections or sage advice. So widely indeed did his reputation spread, that he was ranked as one of the famous 7 sages. The occasion which first brought Solon prominently forward as an actor on the political stage, was the contest between Athens and Megara respecting the possession of Salamis. Indignant at the dishonourable renunciation of their claims by the Athenians, he feigned madness, rushed into the agora, and there recited a short elegiac poem of 100 lines, in which he called upon the Athenians to retrieve their disgrace and reconquer the *lovely island*. The pusillanimous law was rescinded; war was declared; and Solon himself appointed to conduct it. The Megarians were driven out of the island, but a tedious war ensued, which was finally settled by the arbitration of Sparta. Both parties appealed, in support of their claim, to the authority of Homer; and it was currently believed in antiquity that Solon had surreptiously inserted the line (*Il.* ii. 558) which speaks of Ajax as ranging his ships with the Athenians. The Spartans decided in favour of the Athenians, about B.C. 596. Solon himself, probably, was one of those who received grants of land in Salamis, and this may account for his being termed a Salaminian. Soon after these events (about 595) Solon took a leading part in promoting hostilities on behalf of Delphi against Cirrha, and was the mover of the decree of the Amphictyons by which war was declared. It was about the time of the outbreak of this war, that, in consequence of the distracted state of Attica, which was rent by civil commotions, Solon was called upon by all parties to mediate between them, and alleviate the miseries that prevailed. He was chosen archon 594, and under that legal title was invested with unlimited power for adopting such measures as the exigencies of the state demanded. In fulfilment of the task entrusted to him, Solon addressed himself to the relief of the existing distress; which he effected by his celebrated *disburdening ordinance* (σεισάχθεια). This measure was framed to relieve the debtors with as little infringement as possible on the claims of the wealthy creditors; and seems principally to have consisted of a depreciation of the coinage. The success of the Seisachtheia procured for Solon such confidence and popularity that he was further charged with the task of entirely remodelling the constitution. He repealed all the laws of Draco except those relating to bloodshed, and introduced a great many reforms by a new distribution of the different classes of citizens, by enlarging the functions of the *Ecclesia*, or popular assembly, and by instituting the *Boulé* or senate of 400. Besides the arrangement of the general political relations of the people, Solon was the author of a great variety of special laws, which do not seem to have been arranged in any systematic manner. The laws of Solon were inscribed on wooden rollers (ἄξονες) and triangular tablets (κύρβεις), and were set up at first in the Acropolis, afterwards in the Prytaneum. The Athenians were also indebted to Solon for some rectification of the calendar. It is said that Solon exacted from the people a solemn oath, that they would observe his laws without alteration for a certain space, and then absented himself from Athens for 10 years. He first visited Egypt; and from thence proceeded to Cyprus, where he was received with great distinction by Philocyprus, king of the little town of Aepea. Solon persuaded the king to remove from the old site, and build a new town on the plain. The new settlement was called Soli, in honour of the illustrious visitor. He is further said to have visited Lydia; and his interview with Croesus was one of the most celebrated stories in antiquity. [CROESUS.] During the absence of Solon the old dissensions were renewed, and shortly after his arrival at Athens, the supreme power was seized by Pisistratus. The tyrant, after his usurpation, is said to have paid considerable court to Solon, and on various occasions to have solicited his advice, which Solon did not withhold. Solon probably died about 558, two years after the overthrow of the constitution, at the age of 80. Of the poems of Solon several fragments remain. They do not indicate any great degree of imaginative power, but their style is vigorous and simple.

SOLYMA (-ōrum). (1) (*Taktalu-Dagh*), the mountain range which runs parallel to the E. coast of Lycia, and is a S. continuation of Mt. Climax.—(2) Another name for JERUSALEM.

SOLYMI. [LYCIA.]

SOMNUS (-i), the personification and god of sleep, is described as a brother of Death, and as a son of Night. In works of art, Sleep and Death are represented alike as two youths, sleeping or holding inverted torches in their hands. [MORS.]

SONTIUS (-i : *Isonzo*), a river in Venetia, in the N. of Italy, rising in the Carnic Alps, and falling into the Sinus Tergestinus, E. of Aquileia.

SOPHENE (-ēs), a district of Armenia Major, lying between the ranges of Antitaurus and Masius; separated from Melitene, in Armenia Minor, by the Euphrates, from Mesopotamia by the Antitaurus, and from the E. part of Armenia Major by the river Nymphius.

SOPHOCLES (-is). (1) The celebrated tragic poet, was born at Colōnus, a village little more than a mile to the N.W. of Athens, B.C. 495. He was 30 years younger than Aeschylus, and 15 years older than Euripides. His father's name was Sophilus, or Sophillus, of whose condition in life we know nothing for certain; but it is clear that Sophocles received an education not inferior to that of the sons of the most distinguished citizens of Athens. In both of the leading branches of Greek education, music and gymnastics, he was carefully trained, and in both he gained the prize of a garland. Of the skill which he had attained in music and dancing in his 16th year, and of the perfection of his bodily form, we have conclusive evidence in the fact that, when the Athenians were assembled in solemn festival around the trophy which they had set up in Salamis to celebrate their victory over the fleet of Xerxes, Sophocles was chosen to lead, naked, and with lyre in hand, the chorus which danced about the trophy, and sang the songs of triumph, 480. His first appearance as a dramatist took place in 468, under peculiarly interesting circumstances; not only from the fact that Sophocles, at the age of 27, came forward as the rival of the veteran Aeschylus, whose supremacy had been maintained during an entire generation, but also from the character of the judges. The solemnities of the Great Dionysia were rendered more imposing by the occasion of the return of Cimon from his expedition to Scyros, bringing with him the bones of Theseus. Public expectation was so excited respecting the approaching dramatic contest, and party feeling ran so high, that Apsephion, the Archon Eponymus, whose duty it was to appoint the judges, had not yet ventured to proceed to the final act of drawing the lots for their election, when Cimon, with his 9 colleagues in the command, having entered the theatre, the Archon detained them at the altar, and administered to them the oath appointed for the judges in the dramatic contests. Their decision was in favour of Sophocles, who received the first prize; the second only being awarded to Aeschylus, who was so mortified at his defeat, that he left Athens, and retired to Sicily. From this epoch Sophocles held the supremacy of the Athenian stage, until a formidable rival arose in Euripides, who gained the first prize for the first time in 441. In the spring of 440 Sophocles brought out the *Antigone*, a play which gave the Athenians such satisfaction, that they appointed him one of the ten *strategi*, of whom Pericles was the chief, in the war against Samos. In his last years his son Iophon, jealous of his father's love for his grandson Sophocles, and apprehending that he purposed to bestow upon this grandson a large proportion of his property, is said to have summoned his father before the Phratores, on the charge that his mind was affected by old age. As his only reply, Sophocles exclaimed, "If I am Sophocles, I am not beside myself; and if I am beside myself, I am not Sophocles;" and then read from his *Oedipus at Colonus*, which was lately written, but not yet brought out, the magnificent *parodos*, beginning—

Εὐίππου, ξίνε, τᾶσδε χώρας,

whereupon the judges at once dismissed the case, and rebuked Iophon for his undutiful conduct. Sophocles died soon afterwards, in 406, in his 90th year. The manner of his death is variously and fictitiously related. Less heroic than those of Aeschylus, less homely and familiar than those of Euripides, the tragedies of Sophocles are the perfection of the Greek drama. The number of plays ascribed to him was 130 ; and it is remarkable, as proving his growing activity and success, that of these 81 were brought out after his 54th year.—(2) Son of Ariston and grandson of the elder Sophocles, was also an Athenian tragic poet. In 401 he brought out the *Oedipus at Colonus* of his grandfather ; but he did not begin to exhibit his own dramas till 396.

SOPHONISBA (-ae), daughter of the Carthaginian general Hasdrubal, the son of Gisco. She had been betrothed by her father, at a very early age, to the Numidian prince Masinissa, but at a subsequent period Hasdrubal being desirous to gain over Syphax, the rival monarch of Numidia, to the Carthaginian alliance, gave her in marriage to that prince. After the defeat of Syphax, and the capture of his capital city of Cirta by Masinissa, Sophonisba fell into the hands of the conqueror, upon whom her beauty exercised so powerful an influence, that he determined to marry her himself. Their nuptials were accordingly celebrated without delay, but Scipio (who was apprehensive lest she should exercise the same influence over Masinissa which she had previously done over Syphax) refused to ratify this arrangement ; and upbraiding Masinissa with his weakness, insisted on the immediate surrender of the princess. Unable to resist this command, the Numidian king spared her the humiliation of captivity, by sending her a bowl of poison,

which she drank without hesitation, and thus put an end to her own life.

SŌPHRŌN (-ŏnis), of Syracuse, was the principal writer of that species of composition called the *Mime* (μῖμος), which was one of the numerous varieties of the Dorian Comedy. He flourished about B.C. 460—420. When Sophron is called the inventor of Mimes, the meaning is, that he reduced to the form of a literary composition a species of amusement which the Greeks of Sicily, who were preeminent for broad humour and merriment, had practised from time immemorial at their public festivals. Plato was a great admirer of Sophron ; and the philosopher is said to have been the first who made the Mimes known at Athens. The serious purpose which was aimed at in the works of Sophron was always, as in the Attic Comedy, clothed under a sportive form.

SOPHRONISCUS. [SOCRATES.]

SŌRA (-ae). (1) (*Sora*), a town in Latium, on the right bank of the river Liris and N. of Arpinum, with a strongly fortified citadel. —(2) A town in Paphlagonia.

SŌRACTĒ (-is : *Monte di S. Oreste*), a celebrated mountain in Etruria, in the territory of the Falisci, near the Tiber, about 24 miles from Rome, but the summit of which, frequently covered with snow, was clearly visible from the city. (Hor. *Carm.* i. 9.) The whole mountain was sacred to Apollo, and on its summit was a temple of this god.

SŌRANUS (-i). (1) A Sabine divinity, usually identified with Apollo, worshipped on Mt. Soracte.—(2) A physician, a native of Ephesus, practised his profession first at Alexandria, and afterwards at Rome, in the reigns of Trajan and Hadrian, A.D. 98—138. There are several medical works still extant under the name of Soranus, but whether they were written by the native of Ephesus cannot be determined.

SŌSĪGĚNĒS (-is), the peripatetic philosopher, was the astronomer employed by Julius Caesar to superintend the correction of the calendar (B.C. 46).

SŌSĬUS (-i). (1) C., quaestor B.C. 66, and praetor 49. He was afterwards one of Antony's principal lieutenants in the East, and in 37 placed Herod upon the throne of Jerusalem.—(2) The name of two brothers (Sosii), booksellers at Rome in the time of Horace.

SOSPĬTA (-ae), that is, the "saving goddess," was a surname of Juno at Lanuvium and at Rome, in both of which places she had a temple.

SOSTRĀTUS (-i), the son of Dexiphanes, of Cnidus, was one of the great architects who flourished during and after the life of Alexander the Great.

SŌTĔR (-ēris), *i. e.*, "the Saviour," (Lat. *Servator* or *Sospes*), occurs as the surname of several divinities, especially of Zeus (Jupiter). It was also a surname of Ptolemaeus I., king of Egypt, as well as of several of the other later Greek kings.

SOTTIĀTES or SOTIĀTES (-um), a powerful and warlike people in Gallia Aquitanica, on the frontiers of Gallia Narbonensis, were subdued by P. Crassus, Caesar's legate.

SPARTA (-ae : Spartiātes, Spartanus), also called LACEDAEMON (Lacedaemonius), the capital of Laconia and the chief city of Peloponnesus, was situated on the right bank of the Eurōtas (*Iri*), about 20 miles from the sea. It stood on a plain which contained within it several rising grounds and hills. It was bounded on the E. by the Eurotas, on the N.W. by the small river Oenus (*Kelesina*), and on the S.E. by the small river Tisia (*Magula*), both of which streams fell into the Eurotas. The plain in which Sparta stood was shut in on the E. by Mt. Menelaium, and on the W. by Mt. Taygĕtus ; whence the city is called by Homer " the hollow Lacedaemon." It was of a circular form, about 6 miles in circumference, and consisted of several distinct quarters, which were originally separate villages, and which were never united into one regular town. Its site is occupied by the modern villages of *Magula* and *Psykhiko ;* and the principal modern town in the neighbourhood is *Mistra*, which lies about 2 miles to the W. on the slopes of Mt. Taygĕtus. During the flourishing times of Greek independence, Sparta was never surrounded by walls, since the bravery of its citizens, and the difficulty of access to it, were supposed to render such defences needless. It was first fortified by the tyrant Nabis ; but it did not possess regular walls till the time of the Romans. Sparta, unlike most Greek cities, had no proper Acropolis, but this name was only given to one of the steepest hills of the town, on the summit of which stood the temple of Athena (Minerva) Poliūchos, or Chalcioecus. Sparta is said to have been founded by Lacedaemon, a son of Zeus (Jupiter) and Taygete, who married Sparta, the daughter of Eurotas, and called the city after the name of his wife. In the mythical period, Argos was the chief city in Peloponnesus, and Sparta is represented as subject to it. Here reigned Menelaus, the younger brother of Agamemnon ; and by the marriage of Orestes, the son of Agamemnon, with Hermione, the daughter of Menelaus, the two kingdoms of Argos and Sparta became united. The Dorian conquest of Peloponnesus, which, according to tradition, took place 80 years after the Trojan war,

made Sparta the capital of the country. Laconia fell to the share of Eurysthenes and Procles, the 2 sons of Aristodemus, who took up their residence at Sparta, and ruled over the kingdom conjointly. After the complete subjugation of the country, we find three distinct classes in the population : the Dorian conquerors, who resided in the capital, and who were called Spartiatae or Spartans ; the Perioeci or old Achaean inhabitants, who became tributary to the Spartans, and possessed no political rights ; and the Helots, who were also a portion of the old Achaean inhabitants, but were reduced to a state of slavery. From various causes the Spartans became distracted by intestine quarrels, till at length Lycurgus, who belonged to the royal family, was selected by all parties to give a new constitution to the state. The constitution of Lycurgus, which is described in a separate article [LYCURGUS], laid the foundation of Sparta's greatness. In B.C. 743 the Spartans attacked Messenia, and after two wars conquered it, and made it an integral portion of Laconia. [MESSENIA.] After the close of the 2nd Messenian war the Spartans continued their conquests in Peloponnesus. At the time of the Persian invasion, they obtained by unanimous consent the chief command in the war. But after the final defeat of the Persians the haughtiness of Pausanias disgusted most of the Greek states, particularly the Ionians, and led them to transfer the supremacy to Athens (477). The Spartans, however, regained it by the overthrow of Athens in the Peloponnesian war (404). But the Spartans did not retain this supremacy more than 30 years. Their decisive defeat by the Thebans under Epaminondas at the battle of Leuctra (371), gave the Spartan power a shock from which it never recovered ; and the restoration of the Messenians to their country 2 years afterwards completed the humiliation of Sparta. About 30 years afterwards the greater part of Greece was obliged to yield to Philip of Macedon. The Spartans, however, kept haughtily aloof from the Macedonian conqueror, and refused to take part in the Asiatic expedition of his son Alexander the Great. Under the later Macedonian monarchs the power of Sparta still further declined. Agis endeavoured to restore the ancient institutions of Lycurgus ; but he perished in the attempt (240). Cleomenes III., who began to reign 236, was more successful. His reforms infused new blood into the state ; and for a short time he carried on war with success against the Achaeans. But his defeat in 221 was followed by the capture of Sparta, which now sank into insignificance, and was at length compelled to join the Achaean league. Shortly afterwards it fell, with the rest of Greece, under the Roman power.

SPARTĂCUS (-i), by birth a Thracian, was successively a shepherd, a soldier, and a chief of banditti. On one of his predatory expeditions he was taken prisoner, and sold to a trainer of gladiators. In 73 he was a member of the company of Lentulus, and was detained in his school at Capua, in readiness for the games at Rome. He persuaded his fellow-prisoners to make an attempt to gain their freedom. About 70 of them broke out of the school of Lentulus, and took refuge in the crater of Vesuvius. Spartacus was chosen leader, and was soon joined by a number of runaway slaves. They were blockaded by C. Claudius Pulcher at the head of 3000 men, but Spartacus attacked the besiegers and put them to flight. His numbers rapidly increased, and for 2 years (B.C. 73—71) he defeated one Roman army after another, and laid waste Italy, from the foot of the Alps to the southernmost corner of the peninsula. After both the consuls of 72 had been defeated by Spartacus, M. Licinius Crassus, the praetor, was appointed to the command of the war, which he terminated by a decisive battle near the river Silarus, in which Spartacus was defeated and slain.

SPARTI (-ōrum), the Sown-Men, is the name given to the armed men who sprang from the dragon's teeth sown by Cadmus.

SPARTIĀNUS (-i), AELIUS, one of the *Scriptores Historiae Augustae*, lived in the time of Diocletian and Constantine, and wrote the biographies of several emperors.

SPERCHĔUS (-i : *Elladha*), a river in the S. of Thessaly, which rises in Mt. Tymphrestus, runs in an E.-ly direction through the territory of the Aenianes and through the district Malis, and falls into the innermost corner of the Sinus Maliacus. As a river-god Spercheus is a son of Oceanus and Ge, and the father of Menesthius by Polydora, the daughter of Peleus.

SPES (-ei), the personification of Hope, was worshipped at Rome, where she had several temples, the most ancient of which had been built in B.C. 354, by the consul Atilius Calatinus, near the Porta Carmentalis. The Greeks also worshipped the personification of Hope, *Elpis*, and they relate the beautiful allegory, that when Epimetheus opened the vessel brought to him by Pandora, from which all kinds of evils were scattered over the earth, Hope alone remained behind. Hope was represented in works of art as a youthful figure, lightly walking in full attire, holding in her right hand a flower, and with the left lifting up her garment.

SPEUSIPPUS (-i), the philosopher, was a native of Athens, and the son of Eurymĕdon and Potone, a sister of Plato. He succeeded Plato as president of the Academy, but was at the head of the school for only 8 years (B.C. 347—339).

SPHACTĒRIA. [Pylos.]

SPHAERĬA (-ae : *Poros*), an island off the coast of Troezen in Argolis, and between it and the island of Calauria.

SPHINX (-gis), a she-monster, born in the country of the Arimi, daughter of Orthus and Chimaera, or of Typhon and Echidna, or lastly of Typhon and Chimaera. She is said to have proposed a riddle to the Thebans, and to have murdered all who were unable to guess it. Oedipus solved it, whereupon the Sphinx slew herself. [Oedipus.] The legend appears to have come from Egypt, but the figure of the Sphinx is represented somewhat differently in Greek mythology and art. The Egyptian Sphinx is the figure of a lion without wings, in a lying attitude, the upper part of the body being that of a human being. The common idea of a Greek Sphinx, on the other hand, is that of a winged body of a lion, the breast and upper part being the figure of a woman.

SPĪNA (-ae). (1) (*Spinazzino*), a town in Gallia Cispadana, in the territory of the Lingones, on the most S.-ly of the mouths of the Po, which was called after it Ostium Spineticum.—(2) (*Spino*), a town in Gallia Transpadana, on the river Addua.

SPOLATUM. [Salona.]

SPŌLĒTĬUM or SPOLĒTUM (-i : *Spoleto*), a town in Umbria, on the Via Flaminia, colonised by the Romans B.C. 242. It suffered severely in the wars between Marius and Sulla.

SPŌRĂDES (-um), a group of scattered islands in the Aegaean sea, off the island of Crete and the W. coast of Asia Minor, so called in opposition to the Cyclades, which lay in a circle around Delos.

SPURINNA (-ae) VESTRITIUS, the haruspex who warned Caesar to beware of the Ides of March.

STĀBĬAE (-ārum : *Castell a Mare di Stabia*), an ancient town in Campania, between Pompeii and Surrentum, which was destroyed by Sulla in the Social war, but which continued to exist down to the great eruption of Vesuvius in A.D. 79, when it was overwhelmed along with Pompeii and Herculaneum. It was at Stabiae that the elder Pliny perished.

STAGĪRUS (-i), subsequently STAGĪRA (-ae : *Stavro*), a town of Macedonia, in Chalcidice, on the Strymonic gulf, and a little N. of the isthmus which unites the promontory of Athos to Chalcidice. It was a colony of Andros, was founded B.C. 656, and was originally called Orthagoria. It is celebrated as the birthplace of Aristotle.

STASĪNUS (-i), of Cyprus, an epic poet, to whom some of the ancient writers attributed the poem of the Epic Cycle, entitled *Cypria*, and embracing the period antecedent to the Iliad.

STĂTĬELLI (-ōrum), STĂTĬELLĀTES, or STĂTĬELLENSES (-ium), a small tribe in Liguria, S. of the Po, whose chief town was Statiellae Aquae (*Acqui*), on the road from Genoa to Placentia.

STĂTĬLĬA MESSALĪNA. [Messalina.]

STĂTĬLĬUS TAURUS. [Taurus.]

STATĪRA (-ae). (1) Wife of Artaxerxes II., king of Persia, was poisoned by Parysatis, the mother of the king.—(2) Sister and wife of Darius III., celebrated as the most beautiful woman of her time. She was taken prisoner by Alexander, together with her mother-in-law Sisygambis, and her daughters, after the battle of Issus, B.C. 333. They were all treated with the utmost respect by the conqueror ; but Statira died shortly before the battle of Arbela, 331—(3) Also called Barsine, elder daughter of Darius III. [Barsine.]

STĀTĬUS (-i), P. PAPINĬUS, was born at Neapolis, about A.D. 61, and was the son of a distinguished grammarian. He accompanied his father to Rome, where the latter acted as the preceptor of Domitian, who held him in high honour. Under the skilful tuition of his father, the young Statius speedily rose to fame, and became peculiarly renowned for the brilliancy of his extemporaneous effusions, so that he gained the prize three times in the Alban contests ; but having, after a long career of popularity, been vanquished in the quinquennial games, he retired to Neapolis, the place of his nativity, along with his wife Claudia, whose virtues he frequently commemorates. He died about A.D. 96. His chief work is the *Thebais*, an heroic poem, in 12 books, on the expedition of the Seven against Thebes. There is also extant a collection of his miscellaneous poems, in 5 books, under the title of *Silvae ;* and an unfinished poem called the *Achilleïs.* Statius may justly claim the praise of standing in the foremost rank among the heroic poets of the Silver Age.

STATŌNĬA (-ae), a town in Etruria, and a Roman Praefectura, on the river Albinia, and on the Lacus Statoniensis.

STĂTOR (-ōris), a Roman surname of Jupiter, describing him as staying the Romans in their flight from an enemy, and generally as preserving the existing order of things.

STENTOR (-ōris), a herald of the Greeks

in the Trojan war, whose voice was as loud as that of 50 other men together.

STENTŌRIS LĂCUS. [Hebrus.]

STĔNYCLĔRUS (-i), a town in the N. of Messenia, which was the residence of the Dorian kings of the country.

STĔPHĂNUS (-i), of Byzantium, the author of the geographical lexicon, entitled *Ethnica* (of which, unfortunately, we possess only an epitome. Stephanus was a grammarian at Constantinople, and lived after the time of Arcadius and Honorius, and before that of Justinian II. His work was reduced to an epitome by a certain Hermolaus, who dedicated his abridgment to the emperor Justinian II.

STĔRŎPĒ (-ēs), one of the Pleiads, wife of Oenomaus, and daughter of Hippodamĭa.

STĔRŎPES. [Cyclopes.]

STĒSĬCHŎRUS (-i), of Himĕra, in Sicily, a celebrated Greek poet, contemporary with Sappho, Alcaeus, Pittăcus, and Phalăris, is said to have been born B.C. 632, to have flourished about 608, and to have died in 552, at the age of 80. Stesichorus was one of the 9 chiefs of lyric poetry recognised by the ancients. He stands, with Alcman, at the head of one branch of the lyric art, the choral poetry of the Dorians.

STĔSIMBROTUS (-i), of Thasos, a rhapsodist and historian in the time of Cimon and Pericles, who is mentioned with praise by Plato and Xenophon.

STHĔNĔBOEA (-ae), called ANTĔA by many writers, was a daughter of the Lycian king Iobătes, and the wife of Proetus. [Bellerophontes.]

STHĔNĔLUS (-i). (1) Son of Perseus and Andromĕda, king of Mycenae, and husband of Nicippe, by whom he became the father of Alcinŏë, Medūsa, and Eurystheus. —(2) Son of Androgeos, and grandson of Minos. He accompanied Hercules from Paros on his expedition against the Amazons, and together with his brother Alcaeus, he was appointed by Hercules ruler of Thasos.— (3) Son of Actor, likewise a companion of Hercules in his expedition against the Amazons.— —(4) Son of Capaneus and Evadne, was one of the Epigŏni, by whom Thebes was taken, and commanded the Argives under Diomedes, in the Trojan war, being the faithful friend and companion of Diomedes.—(5) Father of Cycnus, who was metamorphosed into a swan. Hence we find the swan called by Ovid *Stheneleis volucris* and *Stheneleia proles.*—(6) A tragic poet, contemporary with Aristophanes, who attacked him in the *Wasps.*

STHENO. [Gorgones.]

STĬLĬCHO (-ōnis), son of a Vandal captain, became one of the most distinguished generals of Theodosius I., on whose death he became the real ruler of the West under the emperor Honorius. He was put to death at Ravenna in 408.

STILO (-ōnis), L. AELĬUS PRAECO-NĬNUS, a celebrated Roman grammarian, one of the teachers of Varro and Cicero.

STILPO (-ōnis), a celebrated philosopher, was a native of Megara, and taught philosophy in his native town. He is said to have surpassed his contemporaries in inventive power and dialectic art, and to have inspired almost all Greece with a devotion to the Megarian philosophy.

STĬMŪLA (-ae), the name of Semele, according to the pronunciation of the Romans.

STOBAEUS (-i) JOANNES, derived his surname apparently from being a native of Stobi, in Macedonia. Of his personal history we know nothing. Stobaeus was a man of extensive reading, in the course of which he noted down the most interesting passages; and to him we are indebted for a large proportion of the fragments that remain of the lost works of poets.

STŎBI (-ōrum), a town of Macedonia, and the most important place in the district Paeonia, was probably situated on the river Erigon, N. of Thessalonica, and N.E. of Heraclea. It was made a Roman colony and a municipium, and under the later emperors was the capital of the province Macedonia II. or Salutaris.

STOECHĂDES (-um) INSŬLAE (I. d'Hières), a group of 5 small islands in the Mediterranean, off the coast of Gallia Narbonensis, and E. of Massilia.

STOENI (-ōrum), a Ligurian people, in the Maritime Alps, conquered by Q. Marcius Rex B.C. 118.

STRĂBO (-ōnis), a cognomen in many Roman gentes, signified a person who squinted, and is accordingly classed with Paetus, though the latter word did not indicate such a complete distortion of vision as Strabo.

STRABO, the geographer, was a native of Amasia, in Pontus. The date of his birth is unknown, but may perhaps be placed about B.C. 54. He lived during the whole of the reign of Augustus, and during the early part, at least, of the reign of Tiberius. He is supposed to have died about A.D. 24. He lived some years at Rome, and also travelled much in various countries. We learn from his own work that he was with his friend Aelius Gallus in Egypt in B.C. 24. He wrote an historical work in 43 books, which is lost. It began where the history of Polybius ended, and was probably continued to the battle of Actium. He also wrote a work on Geography (Γεωγραφικά), in 17 books, which has come down to us entire, with the exception of the 7th, of which we have only a meagre epitome. Strabo's work, according to his own expression, was not intended for the use of all persons. It was designed for all who had had a good education, and particularly for those who were engaged in the higher departments of administration. His work forms a striking contrast with the geography of Ptolemy, and the dry list of names, occasionally relieved by something added to them, in the geographical portion of the Natural History of Pliny.

STRABO SEIUS. [SEJANUS.]

STRĂTON (-ōnis), son of Arcesilaus, of Lampsăcus, was a distinguished peripatetic philosopher, and the tutor of Ptolemy Philadelphus. He succeeded Theophrastus as head of the school in B.C. 288, and, after presiding over it 18 years, was succeeded by Lycon. He devoted himself especially to the study of natural science, whence he obtained the appellation of Physicus.

STRĂTŎNĬCĒ (-ēs), daughter of Demetrius Poliorcētes and Phila, the daughter of Antipater. In B.C. 300, at which time she could not have been more than 17 years of age, she was married to Seleucus, king of Syria. Notwithstanding the disparity of their ages, she lived in harmony with the old king for some years, when it was discovered that her step-son Antiochus was deeply enamoured of her, and Seleucus, in order to save the life of his son, which was endangered by the violence of his passion, gave up Stratonice in marriage to the young prince.

STRĂTŎNĬCĒA (-ae: Eski-Hisar, Ru.), one of the chief inland cities of Caria, built by Antiochus I. Soter, who fortified it strongly, and named it in honour of his wife Stratonice. It stood E. of Mylasa and S. of Alabanda, near the river Marsyas, a S. tributary of the Maeander. Under the Romans it was a free city.

STRATUS (-i: Nr. Lepenu or Lepanou, Ru.), the chief town in Acarnania, 10 stadia W. of the Achelous. Its territory was called STRATICE.

STRŎPHĂDES (-um) INSŬLAE, formerly called PLOTAE (Strofadia and Strivali), 2 islands in the Ionian sea, off the coast of Messenia and S. of Zacynthus. The Harpies were pursued to these islands by the sons of Boreas; and it was from the circumstance of the latter returning from these islands after the pursuit that they are supposed to have obtained the name of Strophades.

STRŎPHĬUS (-i), king of Phocis, son of Crissus and Antiphatia, and husband of

Cydragora, Anaxibia or Astyochia, by whom he became the father of Astydamia and Pylades. [ORESTES.]

STRȲMŎN (-ŏnis: *Struma*, called by the Turks *Karasu*), an important river in Macedonia, forming the boundary between that country and Thrace down to the time of Philip. It rose in Mt. Scomius, flowed first S. and then S.E., passed through the lake Prasias, and, immediately S. of Amphipolis, fell into a bay of the Aegaean Sea, called after it STRYMONICUS SINUS.

STYMPHĀLĪDES. [STYMPHALUS.]

STYMPHĀLUS (-i), a town in the N.E. of Arcadia, the territory of which was bounded on the N. by Achaia, on the E. by Sicyonia and Phliasia, on the S. by the territory of Mantinea, and on the W. by that of Orchomenus and Pheneus. The town itself was situated on a mountain of the same name, and on the N. side of the lake STYMPHALIS (*Zaraka*), on which dwelt, according to tradition, the celebrated birds, called STYMPHALIDES, destroyed by Hercules.

STYRA (-ōrum: *Stura*), a town in Euboea on the S.W. coast, not far from Carystus, and nearly opposite Marathon in Attica.

STYX (-ȳgis), connected with the verb στυγέω, to hate or abhor, is the name of the principal river in the nether world, around which it flows 7 times. Styx is described as a daughter of Oceanus and Tethys. As a nymph she dwelt at the entrance of Hades, in a lofty grotto which was supported by silver columns. As a river Styx is described as a branch of Oceanus, flowing from its 10th source; and the river Cocytus again is a branch of the Styx. By Pallas Styx became the mother of Zelus (zeal), Nice (victory), Bia (strength), and Cratos (power). She was the first of all the immortals who took her children to Zeus (Jupiter), to assist him against the Titans; and, in return for this, her children were allowed for ever to live with Zeus, and Styx herself became the divinity by whom the most solemn oaths were sworn. When one of the gods had to take an oath by Styx, Iris fetched a cup full of water from the Styx, and the god, while taking the oath, poured out the water.

STYX (*Mavra-neria*), a river in the N. of Arcadia, near Nonacris, descending from a high rock, and falling into the Crathis.

SUĀDA (-ae), the Roman personification of persuasion, the Greek *Pītho* (Πειθώ), also called by the diminutive *Suadela*.

SUBLĀQUĔUM (-i: *Subiaco*), a small town of the Aequi in Latium, on the Anio near its source.

SUBLĪCĬUS PONS, the oldest of the bridges at Rome, said to have been built by

Ancus Martius. It was of wood (*Sublĭcae*: piles); and being often carried away by the floods, was always to the latest period rebuilt of that material, from a feeling of religious respect.

SŪBŪRA or SUBURRA (-ae), a populous district of Rome, comprehending the valley between the Esquiline, Quirinal, and Viminal.

SŪCRO (-ōnis). (1) (*Xucar*), a river in Hispania Tarraconensis, rising in a S. branch of Mt. Idubeda in the territory of the Celtiberi, and falling S. of Valentia into a gulf of the Mediterranean called after it Sinus Sucronensis (*Gulf of Valencia*).—(2) (*Cullera*), a town of the Edetani in Hispania Tarraconensis, on the preceding river, and between the Iberus and Carthago Nova.

SŪESSA AURUNCA (-ae: *Sessa*), a town of the Aurunci in Latium, E. of the Via Appia, between Minturnae and Teānum, on the W. slope of Mt. Massĭcus. It was the birthplace of the poet Lucilius.

SŪESSA PŎMĒTĬA (-ae), also called PŎMĒTĬA simply, an ancient and important town of the Volsci in Latium, S. of Forum Appii, taken by Tarquinius Priscus. It was one of the 23 cities situated in the plain afterwards covered by the Pomptine Marshes, which are said indeed to have derived their name from this town.

SUESSETĀNI (-ōrum), a people in Hispania Tarraconensis, mentioned in connexion with the Edetani.

SUESSIŌNES or SUESSŌNES (-um), a powerful people in Gallia Belgica, who were reckoned the bravest of all the Belgic Gauls after the Bellovaci, and who could bring 50,000 men into the field in Caesar's time. The Suessiones dwelt in an extensive and fertile country E. of the Bellovaci, S. of the Veromandui, and W. of the Remi. They possessed 12 towns, of which the capital was Noviodunum, subsequently Augusta Suessonum or Suessones (*Soissons*.)

SUESSŬLA (-ae: *Torre di Sessola*), a town in Samnium, on the southern slope of Mt. Tifata.

SUETONĬUS PAULĪNUS. [PAULINUS.]

SUĒTŌNĬUS (-i), TRANQUILLUS, C., the Roman historian, was born about the beginning of the reign of Vespasian, and practised as an advocate at Rome in the reign of Trajan. He lived on intimate terms with the younger Pliny, many of whose letters are addressed to him. At the request of Pliny, Trajan granted to Suetonius the *jus trium liberorum*, for though he was married he had not 3 children, which number was necessary to relieve him from various legal disabilities. Suetonius was afterwards appointed private secretary (Magister Epistolarum) to Hadrian, but was deprived of this office by the emperor, along with Septicius Clarus, the Praefect of the Praetorians, on the ground of associating with Sabina, the emperor's wife, without his permission. His chief work is his Lives of the Caesars. Sue-tonius does not follow the chronological or-der in his Lives, but groups together many things of the same kind. His language is very brief and precise, sometimes obscure, without any affectation of ornament. The treatise *De illustribus Grammaticis* and that *De claris Rhetoribus* are probably only parts of a larger work. The only other productions of Suetonius still extant are a few lives of Roman authors.

SUĒVI (-ōrum), one of the greatest and most powerful peoples of Germany, or, more properly speaking, the collective name of a great number of German tribes, who were grouped together on account of their mi-gratory mode of life, and spoken of in oppo-sition to the more settled tribes, who went under the general name of Ingaevones. The Suevi are described by all the ancient writers as occupying the greater half of all Germany; but the accounts vary respecting the part of the country which they inhabited.

SUIDAS (-ae), a Greek lexicographer, of whom nothing is known. The Lexicon of Suidas, though without merit as to its execution, is valuable both for the literary history of antiquity, for the explanation of words, and for the citations from many ancient writers.

SUIŌNES (-um), the general name of all the German tribes inhabiting Scandinavia.

SULLA (-ae), the name of a patrician family of the Cornelia gens. (1) P., great grandfather of the dictator Sulla, and grand-son of P. Cornelius Rufinus, who was twice consul in the Samnite wars. [RUFINUS, CORNELIUS.] His father is not mentioned. He was flamen dialis, and likewise praetor urbanus and peregrinus in B.C. 212, when he presided over the first celebration of the Ludi Apollinares.—(2) L., surnamed FELIX, the dictator, was born in B.C. 138. Although his father left him only a small property, his means were sufficient to secure for him a good education. He studied the Greek and Roman literature with diligence and success, and appears early to have imbibed that love for literature and art by which he was dis-tinguished throughout life. At the same time he prosecuted pleasure with equal ardour, and his youth, as well as his man-hood, was disgraced by the most sensual vices. He was quaestor in 107, when he served under Marius in Africa, and displayed both zeal and ability in the discharge of

his duties. Sulla continued to serve under Marius with great distinction in the cam-paigns against the Cimbri and Teutones; but Marius becoming jealous of the rising fame of his officer, Sulla left Marius in 102, and took a command under the colleague of Marius, Q. Catulus, who entrusted the chief management of the war to Sulla. Sulla now returned to Rome, where he appears to have lived quietly for some years. He was praetor in 93, and in the following year (92) was sent as propraetor into Cilicia, with special orders from the senate to restore Ariobar-zanes to his kingdom of Cappadocia, from which he had been expelled by Mithridates. Sulla met with complete success. He defeated Gordius, the general of Mithridates, in Cap-padocia, and placed Ariobarzanes on the throne. The enmity between Marius and Sulla now assumed a more deadly form. Sulla's ability and increasing reputation had already led the aristocratical party to look up to him as one of their leaders; and thus political animosity was added to private hatred; but the breaking out of the Social War hushed all private quarrels for the time. Marius and Sulla both took an active part in the war against the common foe. But Marius was now advanced in years; and he had the deep mortification of finding that his achievements were thrown into the shade by the superior energy of his rival. Sulla gained some brilliant victories over the enemy, and took Bovianum, the chief town of the Samnites. He was elected consul for 88, and received from the senate the com-mand of the Mithridatic war. The events which followed,—his expulsion from Rome by Marius, his return to the city at the head of his legions, and the proscription of Marius and his leading adherents—are related in the life of Marius. Sulla remained at Rome till the end of the year, and set out for Greece at the beginning of 87, in order to carry on the war against Mithridates. After driving the generals of Mithridates out of Greece, Sulla crossed the Hellespont, and early in 84 con-cluded a peace with the king of Pontus. Sulla now prepared to return to Italy, where, during his absence, the Marian party had obtained the ascendancy. After leaving his legate, L. Licinius Murena, in command of the province of Asia, with two legions, he set sail with his own army to Athens. While preparing for his deadly struggle in Italy, he did not lose his interest in literature. He carried with him from Athens to Rome the valuable library of Apellicon of Teos, which contained most of the works of Aristotle and Theophrastus. [APELLICON.] He landed at Brundusium in the spring of 83. The Marian party far outnumbered him in troops, and had every prospect of victory. By bribery and promises, however, Sulla gained over a large number of the Marian soldiers, and he persuaded many of the Italian towns to espouse his cause. In the field his efforts were crowned by equal success; and he was ably supported by several of the Roman nobles. In the following year (82) the struggle was brought to a close by the decisive battle gained by Sulla over the Samnites and Lucanians under Pontius Telesinus before the Colline gate of Rome. This victory was followed by the surrender of Praeneste and the death of the younger Marius, who had taken refuge in this town. Sulla was now master of Rome and Italy; and he resolved to take the most ample vengeance upon his enemies, and to extirpate the popular party. One of his first acts was to draw up a list of his enemies who were to be put to death, called a *Proscriptio*. Terror now reigned, not only at Rome, but throughout Italy. Fresh lists of the proscribed constantly appeared. No one was safe; for Sulla gratified his friends by placing in the fatal lists their personal enemies, or persons whose property was coveted by his adherents. At the commencement of these horrors Sulla had been appointed dictator for as long a time as he judged to be necessary, during which period he endeavoured to restore the power of the aristocracy and senate, and to diminish that of the people. At the beginning of 81, he celebrated a splendid triumph on account of his victory over Mithridates. In order to strengthen his power, Sulla established military colonies throughout Italy. 23 legions, or, according to another statement, 47 legions received grants of land in various parts of Italy. Sulla likewise created at Rome a kind of body-guard for his protection, by giving the citizenship to a great number of slaves, who had belonged to persons proscribed by him. The slaves thus rewarded are said to have been as many as 10,000, and were called Cornelii after him as their patron. After holding the dictatorship till the beginning of 79, Sulla resigned this office, to the surprise of all classes. He retired to his estate at Puteoli, and there surrounded by the beauties of nature and art, he passed the remainder of his life in those literary and sensual enjoyments in which he had always taken so much pleasure. His dissolute mode of life hastened his death. The immediate cause of his death was the rupture of a blood-vessel, but some time before he had been suffering from the disgusting disease, which is known in modern times by the name of Morbus Pediculosus or Phthiriasis. He died in 78 in the 60th year of

his age.—(3) FAUSTUS, son of the dictator by his fourth wife, Caecilia Metella, and a twin brother of Fausta, was born not long before 88, the year in which his father obtained his first consulship. Faustus accompanied Pompey into Asia, and was the first who mounted the walls of the Temple of Jerusalem in 63. In 60 he exhibited the gladiatorial games which his father in his last will had enjoined upon him. In 54 he was quaestor. He married Pompey's daughter, and sided with his father-in-law in the civil war. He was present at the battle of Pharsalia, and subsequently joined the leaders of his party in Africa. After the battle of Thapsus in 46, he attempted to escape into Mauretania, but was taken prisoner by P. Sittius, and carried to Caesar. Upon his arrival in Caesar's camp he was murdered by the soldiers in a tumult. —(4) P., nephew of the dictator, was elected consul along with P. Autronius Paetus for the year 65, but neither he nor his colleague entered upon the office, as they were accused of bribery by L. Torquatus the younger, and condemned. It was currently believed that Sulla was privy to both of Catiline's conspiracies. In the civil war Sulla espoused Caesar's cause. He served under him as legate in Greece, and commanded along with Caesar himself the right wing at the battle of Pharsalia (48). He died in 45.—(5) SERV., brother of No. 4, took part in both of Catiline's conspiracies.

SULMO (-ōnis). (1) (*Sulmona*), a town of the Peligni in the country of the Sabines, celebrated as the birthplace of Ovid.—(2) (*Sermoneta*), an ancient town of the Volsci in Latium on the Ufens.

SULPĬCĬA (-ae), a Roman poetess who flourished towards the close of the 1st century, celebrated for sundry amatory effusions, addressed to her husband Calenus.

SULPĬCĬUS GALBA. [GALBA.]

SULPĬCĬUS RŬFUS (-i). (1) P., one of the most distinguished orators of his time, was born B.C. 124. In 93 he was quaestor, and in 89 he served as legate of the consul Cn. Pompeius Strabo in the Marsic war. In 88, he was elected to the tribunate; but he deserted the aristocratical party, and joined Marius. When Sulla marched upon Rome at the head of his army, Marius and Sulpicius took to flight. Marius succeeded in making his escape to Africa, but Sulpicius was discovered in a villa, and put to death.—(2) P., probably son or grandson of the last, was one of Caesar's legates in Gaul and in the civil war. He was praetor in 48.—(3) SERV., with the surname LEMONIA, indicating the tribe to which he belonged, was a contemporary and friend of Cicero, and of about the same age. He became one of the best jurists as well as most eloquent orators of his age. He was quaestor of the district of Ostia, in 74; curule aedile, 69; praetor, 65; and consul 51 with M. Claudius Marcellus. He appears to have espoused Caesar's side in the civil war, and was appointed by Caesar proconsul of Achaia (46 or 45). He died in 43 in the camp of M. Antony, having been sent by the senate on a mission to Antony, who was besieging Dec. Brutus in Mutina. Sulpicius wrote a great number of legal works.

SUMMANUS (-i), a derivative form from summus, the highest, an ancient Roman or Etruscan divinity, who was of equal or even of higher rank than Jupiter. As Jupiter was the god of heaven in the bright day, so Summanus was the god of the nocturnal heaven, and hurled his thunderbolts during the night. Summanus had a temple at Rome near the Circus Maximus.

SUNIUM (-i: C. Colonni), a celebrated promontory forming the S. extremity of Attica, with a town of the same name upon it. Here was a splendid temple of Athena, elevated 300 feet above the sea, the columns of which are still extant, and have given the modern name to the promontory.

SURENAS, the general of the Parthians, who defeated Crassus in B.C. 54. [CRASSUS.]

SUPERUM MARE. [ADRIA.]

SURRENTUM (-i: Sorrento), an ancient town of Campania opposite Capreae, and situated on the promontory (Prom. Minervae) separating the Sinus Paestanus from the Sinus Puteolanus.

SUSA (-orum: O. T. Shusan: Shus, Ru.), the winter residence of the Persian kings, stood in the district Cissia of the province Susiana, on the eastern bank of the river Choaspes.

SUSARION (-ōnis), to whom the origin of the Attic Comedy is ascribed, was a native of Megara, whence he removed into Attica, to the village of Icaria, a place celebrated as a seat of the worship of Dionysus (Bacchus). The Megaric comedy appears to have flourished, in its full development, about B.C. 500 and onwards; and it was introduced by Susarion into Attica between 580—564.

SUSIANAE (-ae, or -es) or SUSIS (-Idis: nearly corresponding to Khuzistan), one of the chief provinces of the ancient Persian empire, lay between Babylonia and Persis, and between Mt. Parachoatras and the head of the Persian Gulf. In this last direction, its coast extended from the junction of the Euphrates with the Tigris, to about the mouth of the river Oroatis (Tab). It was divided from Persis on the S.E. and E. by a mountainous tract, inhabited by independent

tribes, who made even the kings of Persia pay them for a safe passage. On the N. it was separated from Great Media by Mt. Charbanus; on the W. from Assyria by an imaginary line drawn S. from near the Median pass in Mt. Zagros to the Tigris; and from Babylonia by the Tigris itself.

SUTRIUM (-i: Sutri), an ancient town of Etruria on the E. side of the Saltus Ciminius, and on the road from Vulsinii to Rome, made a Roman colony B.C. 383.

SYBARIS (-is). (1) (Coscile or Sibari), a river in Lucania, flowing by the city of the same name, and falling into the Crathis.— (2) A celebrated Greek town in Lucania, was situated between the rivers Sybaris and Crathis at a short distance from the Tarentine gulf, and near the confines of Bruttium. It was founded B.C. 720 by Achaeans and Troezenians, and soon attained an extraordinary degree of prosperity and wealth. Its inhabitants became so notorious for their love of luxury and pleasure, that their name was employed to indicate any voluptuary.

SYBOTA (-orum: Syvota), a number of small islands off the coast of Epirus, and opposite the promontory Leucimne in Corcyra, with a harbour of the same name on the main land.

SYCHAEUS or SICHAEUS (-i), also called ACERBAS. [ACERBAS.]

SYENE (-ēs: Assouan, Ru.), a city of Upper Egypt on the E. bank of the Nile, just below the First Cataract. It was an important point in the astronomy and geography of the ancients, as it lay just under the tropic of Cancer, and was therefore chosen as the place through which they drew their chief parallel of latitude.

SYENNESIS, a common name of the kings of Cilicia. Of these the most important are: —(1) A king of Cilicia, who joined with Labynetus (Nebuchadnezzar) in mediating between Cyaxares and Alyattes, the kings respectively of Media and Lydia, probably in B.C. 610.—(2) Contemporary with Darius Hystaspis, to whom he was tributary. His daughter was married to Pixodorus.—(3) Contemporary with Artaxerxes II. (Mnemon), ruled over Cilicia when the younger Cyrus marched through his country in his expedition against his brother Artaxerxes.

SYGAMBRI, SUGAMBRI, SIGAMBRI, SYCAMBRI or SICAMBRI (-ōrum), one of the most powerful peoples of Germany at an early time, belonged to the Istaevones, and dwelt originally N. of the Ubii on the Rhine, from whence they spread towards the N. as far as the Lippe. They were conquered by Tiberius in the reign of Augustus. Shortly afterwards they disappear from history, and are not mentioned again till the time of Ptolemy, who places them much farther N., close to the Bructeri and the Langobardi, somewhere between the Vecht and the Yssel. At a still later period we find them forming an important part of the confederacy known under the name of Franci.

SYLLA. [SULLA.]

SYLVĀNUS. [SILVANUS.]

SYLVĪUS. [SILVIUS.]

SYMAETHUS (-i: *Giaretta*), a river on the E. coast of Sicily and at the foot of Mt. Aetna, forming the boundary between Leontini and Catana.

SYMĒ (-ēs), a small island off the S.W. coast of Caria, lay in the mouth of the Sinus Doridis to the W. of the promontory of Cynossema.

SYMMĀCHUS (-i), Q. AURĒLĬUS, a distinguished scholar, statesman, and orator in the latter half of the 4th century of the Christian aera, remarkable for his zeal in upholding the ancient pagan religion of Rome. He was proconsul of Africa in 373 ; and in 391 Theodosius raised him to the consulship. Of his works there are still extant 10 books of epistles and some fragments of orations.

SYNNĂDA (-ae), also SYNNAS (-ădis : prob. *Afiour-Kara-Hisar*, Ru.), a city in the N. of Phrygia Salutaris, at first inconsiderable, but afterwards a place of much importance, and from the time of Constantine, the capital of Phrygia Salutaris.

SYPHAX (-ācis), king of the Massaesylians, the W.-most tribe of the Numidians. His history is related in the life of his contemporary and rival, MASINISSA. Syphax was taken prisoner by Masinissa, B.C. 203, and was sent by Scipio, under the charge of Laelius, to Rome, where he died shortly after.

SYRĀCŪSAE (-ārum : *Siracusa* in Italian, *Syracuse* in English), the wealthiest and most populous town in Sicily, was situated on the S. part of the E. coast, 400 stadia N. of the promontory Plemmyrium, and 10 stadia N.E. of the mouth of the river Anāpus, near the lake or marsh called *Syraco*, from which it derived its name. It was founded B.C. 734, one year after the foundation of Naxos, by a colony of Corinthians and other Dorians, led by Archias the Corinthian. The town was originally confined to the island Ortygia lying immediately off the coast ; but it afterwards spread over the neighbouring mainland, and at the time of its greatest extension under the elder Dionysius it consisted of 5 distinct towns, namely ORTYGIA, often called simply the ISLAND, in which was the fountain of Are-

thusa ; ACHRADINA, TYCHE, NEAPOLIS, and EPIPOLAE. After Epipolae had been added to the city, the circumference of Syracuse was 180 stadia or upwards of 22 English miles ; and the entire population of the city is supposed to have amounted to 500,000 souls, at the time of its greatest prosperity. —Syracuse had 2 harbours. The Great Harbour, still called *Porto Maggiore*, is a splendid bay about 5 miles in circumference formed by the island Ortygia and the promontory Plemmyrium. The Small Harbour, also called *Laccius*, lying between Ortygia and Achradina, was capacious enough to receive a large fleet of ships of war.—There were several stone quarries (*lautumiae*) in Syracuse, which are frequently mentioned by ancient writers, and in which the unfortunate Athenian prisoners were confined. On one side of these quarries is the remarkable excavation, called the Ear of Dionysius, in which it is said that this tyrant confined the persons whom he suspected, and that he was able from a little apartment above to overhear the conversation of his captives. This tale however is clearly an invention.—The modern city of Syracuse is confined to the island. The remaining quarters of the ancient city are now uninhabited, and their position marked only by a few ruins. Of these the most important are the remains of the great theatre, and of an amphitheatre of the Roman period.—The government of Syracuse was originally an aristocracy, and afterwards a democracy, till Gelon made himself tyrant or sovereign of Syracuse, B.C. 485. Under his rule and that of his brother Hieron, Syracuse was raised to an unexampled degree of wealth and prosperity. Hieron died in 467, and was succeeded by his brother Thrasybulus : but the rapacity and cruelty of the latter soon provoked a revolt among his subjects, which led to his deposition and the establishment of a democratical form of government. The next most important event in the history of Syracuse was the siege of the city by the Athenians, which ended in the total destruction of the great Athenian armament in 413. The democracy continued to exist in Syracuse till 406, when the elder Dionysius made himself tyrant of the city. After a long and prosperous reign he was succeeded in 367 by his son, the younger Dionysius, who was finally expelled by Timoleon in 343. A republican form of government was again established ; but it did not last long ; and in 317 Syracuse fell under the sway of Agathocles. This tyrant died in 289 ; and the city being distracted by factions, the Syracusans voluntarily conferred the supreme power upon Hieron II., with the title of king, in

270. Hieron cultivated friendly relations with the Romans; but on his death in 216, at the advanced age of 92, his grandson Hieronymus, who succeeded him, espoused the side of the Carthaginians. A Roman army under Marcellus was sent against Syracuse; and after a siege of 2 years, during which Archimedes assisted his fellow-citizens by the construction of various engines of war [ARCHIMEDES], the city was taken by Marcellus in 212. From this time Syracuse became a town of the Roman province of Sicily.

SȲRĬA DEA (-ae), "the Syrian goddess," a name by which the Syrian Astartē or Aphroditē (Venus), is sometimes designated. There can be no doubt that the worship of Aphrodite came from the East to Cyprus, and thence was carried into the south of Greece.

SȲRĬA (-ae : in Aramaean *Surja: Soris-tan*, Arab. *Esh-Sham*, i.e. the land *on the left*, *Syria*), a country of W. Asia, lying along the E. end of the Mediterranean Sea, between Asia Minor and Egypt. In a wider sense the word was used for the whole tract of country bounded by the Tigris on the E., the mountains of Armenia and Cilicia on the N., the Mediterranean on the W., and the Arabian Desert on the S.; the whole of which was peopled by the Aramaean branch of the great Semitic (or Syro-Arabian) race, and is included in the O. T. under the name of Aram. The people were of the same races, and those of the N. of the Taurus in Cappadocia and Pontus are called White Syrians [LEUCOSYRI] in contradistinction to the people of darker complexion in Syria Proper, who are some-times even called Black Syrians (Σύροι μέλανες). Even when the name of Syria is used in its ordinary narrower sense, it is often con-founded with Assyria, which only differs from Syria by having the definite article pre-fixed. Again, in the narrower sense of the name, Syria still includes 2 districts which arc often considered as not belonging to it, namely, PHOENICE and PALESTINE, and a 3rd which is likewise often considered separate, namely, COELESYRIA; but this last is gene-rally reckoned a part of Syria. In this narrower sense, then, Syria was bounded on the W. (beginning from the S.) by Mt. Hermon, at the S. end of Anti-Libanus, which separated it from Palestine, by the range of Libanus, dividing it from Phoenice, by the Mediterranean, and by Mt. Amānus, which divided it from Cilicia; on the N. (where it bordered on Cappadocia) by the main chain of Mt. Taurus, almost exactly along the parallel of 38° N. lat., and striking the Euphrates just below Juliopolis, and con-siderably above Samosata: hence the Euphrates

forms the E. boundary, dividing Syria, first from a very small portion of Armenia, and then from Mesopotamia, to about or beyond the 36th parallel of N. lat., whence the S.E. and S. boundaries, towards Babylonia and Arabia, in the Great Desert, are exceedingly indefinite. [Comp. ARABIA.] The W. part of the S. boundary ran just below Damascus, being formed by the highlands of Trachonitis. The W. part of the country was intersected by a series of mountains, running S. from the Taurus, under the names of AMANUS, PIERIA, CASIUS, BARGYLUS, and LIBANUS, and ANTI-LIBANUS; and the N. part, between the Amanus and the Euphrates, was also moun-tainous. The chief river of Syria was the ORONTES, and the smaller rivers CHALUS and CHRYSORRHOAS were also of importance. In the earliest historical period, Syria contained a number of independent kingdoms, of which DAMASCUS was the most powerful. These were subdued by David, but became again independent at the end of Solomon's reign; till Tiglath-Pileser, king of Assyria, took Damascus and probably conquered all Syria, about B.C. 740. Having been a part suc-cessively of the Assyrian, Babylonian, Persian, and Macedonian empires, it fell, after the battle of Ipsus (B.C. 301), to the share of Seleucus Nicator, and formed a part of the great kingdom of the Seleucidae, whose history is given in the articles SELEUCUS, ANTIOCHUS, DEMETRIUS, &c. In this partition, however, Coelesyria and Palestine went, not to Syria, but to Egypt, and the possession of those provinces became the great source of contention between the Ptolemies and the Seleucids. By the irruptions of the Parthians on the E., and the unsuccessful war of Antiochus the Great with the Romans on the W., the Greek Syrian kingdom was reduced to the limits of Syria itself, and became weaker and weaker, until it was overthrown by TIGRANES, king of Armenia, B.C. 79. Soon afterwards, when the Romans had conquered Tigranes as well as Mithridates, Syria was quietly added by Pompey to the empire of the republic and was constituted a province, B.C. 64; but its N. district, COMMAGENE, was not included in this arrangement. The attempt of Zenobia to make Syria the seat of empire is noticed under PALMYRA and ZENOBIA. While the Roman emperors de-fended this precious possession against the attacks of the Persian kings with various success, a new danger arose, as early as the 4th century, from the Arabians of the Desert, who began to be known under the name of Saracens; and, when the rise of Mohammed had given to the Arabs that great religious impulse which revolutionised the E. World,

Syria was the first great conquest that they made from the E. empire, A.D. 632—638.

SȲRĬAE PORTAE (-ārum : *Pass of Beilan*), a most important pass between Cilicia and Syria, lying between the shore of the Gulf of Issus on the W., and Mt. Amānus on the E.

SȲRINX (-ingis), an Arcadian nymph, who being pursued by Pan, fled into the river Ladon, and at her own prayer was metamorphosed into a reed, of which Pan then made his flute.

SȲROS, or SȲRUS (-i : *Syra*), an island in the Aegaean sea, and one of the Cyclades, lying between Rhenea and Cythnus.

SYRTĬCA RĒGĬO (W. part of *Tripoli*), the special name of that part of the N. coast of Africa which lay between the 2 Syrtes, from the river Triton, at the bottom of the Syrtis Minor, on the W., to the Philaenorum Arae, at the bottom of the Syrtis Major, on the E. It was for the most part a very narrow strip of sand, interspersed with salt marshes, between the sea and a range of mountains forming the edge of the Great Desert (*Sahara*), with only here and there a few spots capable of cultivation, especially about the river Cinyps. It was peopled by Libyan tribes. Under the Romans it formed a part of the province of Africa. It was often called TRIPOLITANA, from its 3 chief cities, ABROTONUM, OEA, and LEPTIS MAGNA ; and this became its usual name under the later empire, and has been handed down to our own time in the modern name of the Regency of *Tripoli*.

SYRTIS (-is and Ĭdis), and SYRTES (-Ĭum), the 2 great gulfs in the E. half of the N. coast of Africa. Both were proverbially dangerous, the Greater Syrtis from its sandbanks and quicksands, and its unbroken exposure to the N. winds, the Lesser from its shelving rocky shores, its exposure to the N.E. winds, and the consequent variableness of the tides in it. (1) SYRTIS MAJOR (*Gulf of Sidra*), the E. of the 2, is a wide and deep gulf on the shores of Tripolitana and Cyrenaica, exactly opposite to the Ionic sea, or mouth of the Adriatic, between Sicily and Peloponnesus. The Great Desert comes down close to its shores, forming a sandy coast [SYRTICA REGIO]. The terror of being driven on shore in it is referred to in the narrative of St. Paul's voyage to Italy (Acts xxvii. 17).— (2) SYRTIS MINOR (*Gulf of Khabs*), lies in the S.W. angle of the great bend formed by the N. coast of Africa as it drops down to the S. from the neighbourhood of Carthage, and then bears again to the E. : in other words, in the angle between the E. coast of Zeugitana and Byzacena (*Tunis*) and the N. coast of Tripolitana (*Tripoli*).

SȲRUS (-i), PŬBLĬUS, a slave brought to Rome some years before the downfal of the republic, who soon became highly celebrated as a mimographer. He may be said to have flourished B.C. 45. A compilation containing probably many lines from his mimes is still extant under the title *Publii Syri Sententiae*.

TĂBERNAE. [TRES TABERNAE.]
TĂBURNUS (-i : *Taburno*), a mountain belonging half to Campania and half to Samnium. It shut in the Caudine pass on its S. side.

TĂCĂPĒ (-ēs : *Khabs*, large Ru.), a city of N. Africa, in the Regio Syrtica, at the innermost angle of the Syrtis Minor, to which the modern town gives its name.

TACFARINAS, a Numidian, and Roman auxiliary, who deserted, and became the leader of the Musulamii, a people bordering on Mauretania. He was at length defeated and slain in battle by Dolabella, A.D. 24.

TACHOMPSO, also TACOMPSOS, aft. CONTRAPSELCIS, a city in the Dodecaschoenus, that is, the part of Aethiopia immediately above Egypt.

TACHŌS, king of Egypt, succeeded Acoris, and maintained the independence of his country for a short time during the latter end of the reign of Artaxerxes II.

TĂCĬTUS (-i). (1) C. CORNELIUS, the historian. The time and place of his birth are unknown. He was a little older than the younger Pliny, who was born A.D. 61. Tacitus was first promoted by the emperor Vespasian, and he received other favours from his sons Titus and Domitian. In 78 he married the daughter of C. Julius Agricola, to whom he had been betrothed in the preceding year, while Agricola was consul. In the reign of Domitian, and in 88, Tacitus was praetor, and he assisted as one of the quindecemviri at the solemnity of the Ludi Seculares which were celebrated in that year. Agricola died at Rome in 93, but neither Tacitus nor the daughter of Agricola was then with him. It is not known where Tacitus was during the last illness of Agricola. In the reign of Nerva, 97, Tacitus was appointed consul suffectus, in the place of T. Virginius Rufus, who had died in that year, and whose funeral oration he delivered. Tacitus and Pliny were most intimate friends. In the collection of the letters of Pliny, there are 11 letters addressed to Tacitus. The time of the death of Tacitus is unknown, but he appears to have survived Trajan, who died 117. The extant works of Tacitus are a Life of Agricola, his father-in-law : the *Historiae*, which comprehended the period from the second consulship of Galba, 68, to the death of Domitian, 96, and the author designed to add the reigns of Nerva and Trajan;—the first 4 books alone are extant in a complete form; the 5th book is imperfect : the *Annales*, which commence with the death of Augustus, 14, and comprise the period to the death of Nero, 68, a space of 54 years ; the greater part of the 5th book is lost, and also the 7th, 8th, 9th, 10th, the beginning of the 11th, and the end of the 16th, which is the last book : the treatise *De Moribus et Populis Germaniae*, describing the Germanic nations, and lastly the *Dialogus de Oratoribus*, a work whose genuineness has been disputed, but probably without reason. The moral dignity of Tacitus is impressed upon his works ; the consciousness of a love of truth, of the integrity of his purpose. His great power is in the knowledge of the human mind, his insight into the motives of human conduct ; and he found materials for this study in the history of the emperors, and particularly Tiberius, the arch-hypocrite, and perhaps half madman. The style of Tacitus is peculiar, though it bears some resemblance to that of Sallust. In the Annals it is concise, vigorous, and pregnant with meaning ; .aboured, but elaborated with art, and stripped of every superfluity. A single word sometimes gives effect to a sentence, and if the meaning of the word is missed, the sense of the writer is not reached.—(2) M. CLAUDIUS, Roman emperor from the 25th September, A.D. 275, until April, A.D. 276. Tacitus was at the time of his election 70 years of age, and was with difficulty persuaded to accept the purple. The high character which he had borne before his elevation to the throne he amply sustained during his brief reign. He died either at Tarsus or at Tyana, about the 9th of April, 276.

TAENARUM (-i : *C. Matapan*), a promontory in Laconia, forming the S.-ly point of the Peloponnesus, on which stood a celebrated temple of Pŏseidōn (Neptune), possessing an inviolable asylum. A little to the N. of the temple and the harbour of Achilleus was a town also called TAENARUM or TAENARUS, and at a later time CAENEPOLIS. On the promontory was a cave, through which Hercules is said to have dragged Cerberus to the upper world. Here also was a statue of Arion seated on a dolphin, since he is said to have landed at this spot after his miraculous preservation by a dolphin. In the time of the Romans there were celebrated marble quarries on the promontory.

TĂGES (-ĕtis), a mysterious Etruscan being, who is described as a boy with the wisdom of an old man. Tages, the son of a Genius Jovialis, and grandson of Jupiter, rose suddenly out of the ground, and instructed Tarchon and the Etruscans in the art of the haruspices. The Etruscans afterwards wrote down all he had said, and thus arose the books of Tages, which, according to some, were 12 in number.

TĂGUS (-i : Spanish *Tajo*, Portuguese *Tego*, English *Tagus*), one of the chief rivers in Spain, rising in the land of the Celtiberians, between the mountains Orospeda and Idubeda, and, after flowing in a W.-ly direction, falling into the Atlantic.

TĂLĂUS (-i), son of Bias and Pero, and king of Argos. He was married to Lysimache (Eurynome, or Lysianassa), and was father of Adrastus, Parthenopaeus, Pronax, Mecisteus, Aristomachus, and Eriphyle. The patronymic *Tălăiŏnides* is given to his sons Adrastus and Mecisteus.

TALOS. [PERDIX.]

TALTHЎBIUS (-i), the herald of Agamemnon at Troy. He was worshipped as a hero at Sparta and Argos, where sacrifices also were offered to him.

TĂMASSUS or TĂMĂSUS (-i), probably the same as the Homeric TEMĔSĒ, a town in the middle of Cyprus, N.W. of Olympus, and 29 miles S.E. of Soloë.

TĂMĔSIS (-is) or TĂMĔSA (-ae : *Thames*), a river in Britain, on which stood Londinium, flowing into the sea on the E. coast. Caesar crossed the Thames at the distance of 80 Roman miles from the sea, probably at Cowey Stakes, near Oatlands and the confluence of the Wey.

TAMŌS, a native of Memphis in Egypt, was lieutenant-governor of Ionia under Tissaphernes, and afterwards attached himself to the service of the younger Cyrus.

TĂNĂGER (-gri : *Negro*), a river of Lucania, rising in the Apennines, which, after flowing in a N.E.-ly direction, loses itself under the earth near Polla for a space of about 2 miles, and finally falls into the Silarus near Forum Popilii.

TĂNĂGRA (-ae : *Grimadha*, or *Grimala*), a celebrated town of Boeotia, situated on a steep ascent on the left bank of the Asōpus, 13 stadia from Oropus, and 200 stadia from Plataeae, in the district Tanagraea, which was also called Poemandris. Tanagra was supposed to be the same town as the Homeric Graea. Being near the frontiers of Attica, it was frequently exposed to the attacks of the Athenians ; and near it the Athenians sustained a celebrated defeat, B.C. 457.

TĂNĂÏS (-is, or -ĭdis). (1) (*Don*, i.e. *Water*), a great river, which rises in the N.

of Sarmatia Europaea (about the centre of *Russia*), and flows to the S.E. till it comes near the *Volga*, when it turns to the S.W., and falls into the N.E. angle of the Palus Maeotis (*Sea of Azov*). It was usually considered the boundary between Europe and Asia.—(2) (Ru., near *Kassatchei*), a city of Sarmatia Asiatica, on the N. side of the S. mouth of the Tanaïs, at a little distance from the sea.

TĀNĀQUIL. [TARQUINIUS.]

TANETUM (-i: *Taneto*), a town of the Boii, in Gallia Cispadana, between Mutina and Parma.

TĀNIS (O. T. Zoan: *San*, Ru.), a very ancient city of Lower Egypt, in the E. part of the Delta, on the right bank of the arm of the Nile, which was called after it the Tanitic, and on the S.W. side of the great lake between this and the Pelusiac branch of the Nile, which was also called, after the city, Tanis (*Lake of Menzaleh*). It was one of the capitals of Lower Egypt, under the early kings, and the chief city of the Tanītes Nomos.

TANTĀLUS (-i). (1) Son of Zeus (Jupiter) and the nymph Pluto. His wife is called by some Euryanassa, by others Taygete or Dione, and by others, Clytia, or Eupryto. He was the father of Pelops, Broteas, and Niobe. All traditions agree in stating that he was a wealthy king; but while some call him king of Lydia, others describe him as king of Argos or Corinth. Tantalus is particularly celebrated in ancient story for the terrible

Tantalus. (From an ancient Gem.)

punishment inflicted upon him after his death. According to the common account, Tantalus divulged the secrets intrusted to him by Zeus, and was punished in the lower world by being afflicted with a raging thirst, and at the same time placed in the midst of a lake, the waters of which always receded from him as soon as he attempted to drink them. Over his head, moreover, hung branches of fruit, which receded in like manner when he stretched out his hand to reach them. In addition to all this there was suspended over his head a huge rock, ever threatening to crush him. Another

tradition relates that, wishing to test the gods, he cut his son Pelops in pieces, boiled them, and set them before the gods at a repast; whilst a third account states that he stole nectar and ambrosia from the table of the gods. According to a fourth story, Tantalus incurred his punishment by receiving a golden dog, which Rhea had appointed to watch Zeus and his nurse, and which was stolen by Pandareus. The punishment of Tantalus was proverbial in ancient times, and from it the English language has borrowed the verb "to tantalise," that is, to hold out hopes or prospects which cannot be realised. — (2) Son of Thyestes, who was killed by Atreus.—(3) Son of Amphion and Niobe.

TAŎCHI (-ōrum), a people of Pontus, on the borders of Armenia.

TĂPHĪAE INSŬLAE (-ārum), a number of small islands in the Ionian sea, lying between the coasts of Leucadia and Acarnania. They were also called the islands of the Teleboae, and their inhabitants were in like manner named TAPHII, or TELEBOAE. The largest of these islands is called TAPHUS by Homer, but TAPHIUS or TAPHIUSA by later writers.

TĂPHUS. [TAPHIAE.]

TAPRŎBĀNĒ (-ēs: *Ceylon*), a great island of the Indian ocean, opposite to the S. extremity of India intra Gangem.

TĂRAS. [TARENTUM.]

TARBELLI (-ōrum), one of the most important people in Gallia Aquitanica, between the ocean and the Pyrenees. Their chief town was AQUAE TARBELLICAE or AUGUSTAE, on the Aturus (*Dacqs* on the Adour).

TARCHON (-ōnis or -ŏntis), son of Tyrrhenus, who is said to have built the town of Tarquinii. [TARQUINII.] Virgil represents him as coming to the assistance of Aeneas against Turnus.

TĂRENTĪNUS SĬNUS (*G. of Tarentum*), a great gulf in the S. of Italy, between Bruttium, Lucania and Calabria, beginning W. near the Prom. Lacinium, and ending E. near the Prom. Iapygium, and named after the town of Tarentum.

TĂRENTUM (-i), called TĂRAS (-antis) by the Greeks (*Taranto*), an important Greek city in Italy, situated on the W. coast of the peninsula of Calabria, and on a bay of the sea, about 100 stadia in circuit, forming an excellent harbour, and being a portion of the great Gulf of Tarentum. The city stood in the midst of a beautiful and fertile country, S. of Mt. Aulon and W. of the mouth of the Galaesus. It was originally built by the Iapygians, who are said to have been joined by some Cretan colonists from the neighbouring town of Uria, and it derived its name from the mythical Taras, a son of Poseidon. The greatness of Tarentum, however, dates from B.C. 708, when the original inhabitants were expelled, and the town was taken possession of by a strong body of Lacedaemonian Partheniae under the guidance of Phalanthus [PHALANTHUS]. It soon became the most powerful and flourishing city in the whole of Magna Graecia, and exercised a kind of supremacy over the other Greek cities in Italy. With the increase of wealth the citizens became luxurious and effeminate, and being hard pressed by the Lucanians and other barbarians in the neighbourhood, they were obliged to apply for aid to the mother-country. Archidamus, son of Agesilaus, was the first who came to their assistance, in B.C. 338; and he fell in battle fighting on their behalf. The next prince whom they invited to succour them was Alexander, king of Epirus, and uncle to Alexander the Great. At first he met with considerable success, but was eventually defeated and slain by the Bruttii in 326, near Pandosia, on the banks of the Acheron. Shortly afterwards the Tarentines had to encounter a still more formidable enemy. Having attacked some Roman ships, and then grossly insulted the Roman ambassadors who had been sent to demand reparation, war was declared against the city by the powerful republic. The Tarentines were saved for a time by Pyrrhus, king of Epirus, who came to their help in 281; but two years after the defeat of this monarch and his withdrawal from Italy, the city was taken by the Romans (272). In the second Punic war Tarentum revolted from Rome to Hannibal (212); but it was retaken by the Romans in 207, and was treated by them with great severity. From this time Tarentum declined in prosperity and wealth. It was subsequently made a Roman colony, and it still continued to be a place of considerable importance in the time of Augustus. Its inhabitants retained their love of luxury and ease; and it is described by Horace as *molle Tarentum* and *imbelle Tarentum*.

TARICHÉA (-ae), or -ÉAE (-ārum: *El-Kereh*, Ru.), a town of Galilee, at the S. end of the lake of Tiberias.

TARNÉ (-ēs), a city of Lydia, on Mt. Tmolus, mentioned by Homer.

TARPEIA (-ae), daughter of Sp. Tarpeius, the governor of the Roman citadel on the Saturnian hill, afterwards called the Capitoline, was tempted by the gold on the Sabine bracelets and collars to open a gate of the fortress to T. Tatius and his Sabines. As they entered, they threw upon her their shields, and thus crushed her to death. The

Tarpeian rock, a part of the Capitoline, was named after her.

TARPHÉ (-ēs), a town in Locris, on Mt. Oeta, mentioned by Homer, and subsequently called Pharygae.

TARQUINIA. [TARQUINIUS.]

TARQUINII (-ōrum: *Turchina* nr. *Corneto*), a city of Etruria, situated on a hill and on the river Marta, S.E. of Cosa and on a road leading from the latter town to Rome. It was one of the 12 Etruscan cities, and was probably regarded as the metropolis of the Confederation. It is said to have been founded by Tarchon, the son or brother of Tyrrhenus, who was the leader of the Lydian colony from Asia to Italy. It was at Tarquinii that Demaratus, the father of Tarquinius Priscus, settled; and it was from this city that the Tarquinian family came to Rome. Tarquinii was subsequently made a Roman colony and a municipium; but it gradually declined in importance; and in the 8th or 9th century of the Christian aera it was deserted by its inhabitants, who founded Corneto on the opposite hill. Some of the most interesting remains of Etruscan art have been discovered at Tarquinii.

TARQUINIUS (-i), the name of a family in early Roman history, to which the 5th and 7th kings of Rome belonged. The legend of the Tarquins ran as follows. Demaratus, their ancestor, who belonged to the noble family of the Bacchiadae at Corinth, settled at Tarquinii in Etruria, where he married an Etruscan wife, by whom he had two sons, Lucumo and Aruns. Demaratus bequeathed all his property to Lucumo, and died himself shortly afterwards. But, although Lucumo was thus one of the most wealthy persons at Tarquinii, and had married Tanaquil, who belonged to a family of the highest rank, he was excluded, as a stranger, from all power and influence in the state. Discontented with this inferior position, he set out for Rome, riding in a chariot with his wife, and accompanied by a large train of followers. When they had reached the Janiculus, an eagle seized his cap, and, after carrying it away to a great height, placed it again upon his head. Tanaquil, who was skilled in the Etruscan science of augury, bade her husband hope for the highest honour from this omen. Her predictions were soon verified. The stranger was received with welcome, and he and his followers were admitted to the rights of Roman citizens. He took the name of L. TARQUINIUS, to which Livy adds PRISCUS. His wealth, his courage, and his wisdom, gained him the love both of Ancus Marcius and of the people. The former appointed him guardian of his children; and, when he died, the senate and the people unanimously elected Tarquinius to the vacant throne. The reign of Tarquinius was distinguished by great exploits in war, and by great works in peace. He defeated the Latins and Sabines; and the latter people ceded to him the town of Collatia, where he placed a garrison under the command of Egerius, the son of his deceased brother Aruns, who took the surname of Collatinus. Some traditions relate that Tarquinius defeated the Etruscans likewise. He erected many public buildings, and other works, at Rome, the most celebrated of which are the vast sewers which still remain. Tarquinius also made some important changes in the constitution of the state. He was murdered after a reign of 38 years at the instigation of the sons of Ancus Marcius. But the latter did not secure the reward of their crime, for Servius Tullius, with the assistance of Tanaquil, succeeded to the vacant throne. Servius Tullius, whose life is given under TULLIUS, was murdered after a reign of 44 years, by his son-in-law, L. Tarquinius, who ascended the vacant throne.—L. TARQUINIUS SUPERBUS, commenced his reign without any of the forms of election. One of his first acts was to abolish the rights which had been conferred upon the plebeians by Servius; and at the same time all the senators and patricians whom he mistrusted, or whose wealth he coveted, were put to death or driven into exile. He surrounded himself by a bodyguard, by means of which he was enabled to do what he liked. His cruelty and tyranny obtained for him the surname of *Superbus*. But, although a tyrant at home, he raised Rome to great influence and power among the surrounding nations. He gave his daughter in marriage to Octavius Mamilius of Tusculum, the most powerful of the Latin chiefs; and under his sway Rome became the head of the Latin confederacy. He defeated the Volscians, and took the wealthy town of Suessa Pometia, with the spoils of which he commenced the erection of the Capitol which his father had vowed. In the vaults of this temple he deposited the 3 Sibylline books, which he purchased from a Sibyl or prophetess for 300 pieces of gold; a price which he had at first scornfully refused. He next engaged in war with Gabii, one of the Latin cities, which refused to enter into the league. Unable to take the city by force of arms, Tarquinius had recourse to stratagem. His son, Sextus, pretending to be ill-treated by his father, and covered with the bloody marks of stripes, fled to Gabii. The infatuated inhabitants intrusted him with the command of their troops; whereupon, at a

hint of his father, who struck off the heads of the tallest poppies in his garden before the eyes of Sextus's messenger, he put to death or banished all the leading men of the place, and then had no difficulty in compelling it to submit to his father. In the midst of his prosperity Tarquinius fell through a shameful outrage committed by his son Sextus on Lucretia, the wife of his cousin Tarquinius Collatinus. As soon as Sextus had departed, Lucretia sent for her husband and father. Collatinus came, accompanied by L. Brutus; Lucretius, by P. Valerius, who afterwards gained the surname of Publicola. They found her in an agony of sorrow. She told them what had happened, enjoined them to avenge her dishonour, and then stabbed herself to death. They all swore to avenge her. Brutus threw off his assumed stupidity, and placed himself at their head. Brutus, who was Tribunus Celerum, summoned the people, and related the deed of shame. All classes were inflamed with the same indignation. A decree was passed deposing the king, and banishing him and his family from the city. Tarquinius, with his two sons, Titus and Aruns, took refuge at Caere in Etruria. Sextus repaired to Gabii, his own principality, where he was shortly after murdered by the friends of those whom he had put to death. Tarquinius reigned 24 years. He was banished B.C. 510. The people of Tarquinii and Veii espoused the cause of the exiled tyrant, and marched against Rome. The two consuls advanced to meet them. A bloody battle was fought, in which Brutus and Aruns, the sons of Tarquinius, slew each other. Tarquinius next repaired to Lars Porsena, the powerful king of Clusium, who marched against Rome at the head of a vast army. The history of this memorable expedition is related under PORSENA. After Porsena quitted Rome, Tarquinius took refuge with his son-in-law, Mamilius Octavius of Tusculum. Under the guidance of the latter, the Latin states espoused the cause of the exiled king, and declared war against Rome. The contest was decided by the celebrated battle of the lake Regillus, in which the Romans gained the victory by the help of Castor and Pollux. Tarquinius now fled to Aristobulus at Cumae, where he died a wretched and childless old man. Such is the story of the Tarquins according to the ancient writers; but it contains numerous inconsistencies, and must not be received as a real history.

TARRĂCĪNA (-ae : *Terracina*), more anciently called ANXUR (-ŭris), an ancient town of Latium situated 58 miles S.E. of Rome on the Via Appia and upon the coast, with a strongly fortified citadel upon a high hill, on which stood the temple of Jupiter Anxurus.

TARRĂCO (-ōnis : *Tarragona*), an ancient town on the E. coast of Spain situated on a rock 760 ft. high, between the river Iberus and the Pyrenees on the river Tulcis. It was founded by the Massilians, and was made the head quarters of the 2 brothers P. and Cn. Scipio, in their campaigns against the Carthaginians in the 2nd Punic war. It subsequently became a populous and flourishing town ; and Augustus, who wintered here (B.C. 26) after his Cantabrian campaign, made it the capital of one of the 3 Spanish provinces (*Hispania Tarraconensis*) and also a Roman colony.

TARSĬUS (-i : *Tarza* or *Balikesri*), a river of Mysia, rising in Mt. Temnus, and flowing N.E., through the Miletopolites Lacus, into the Macestus.

TARSUS, TARSOS (-i : *Tersus*, Ru.), the chief city of Cilicia, stood near the centre of Cilicia Campestris, on the river Cydnus, about 12 miles above its mouth. All that can be determined with certainty as to its origin seems to be that it was a very ancient city of the Syrians, who were the earliest known inhabitants of this part of Asia Minor, and that it received Greek settlers at an early period. At the time of the Macedonian invasion, it was held by the Persian troops, who were about to burn it, when they were prevented by Alexander's arrival. After playing an important part as a military post in the wars of the successors of Alexander, and under the Syrian kings, it became, by the peace between the Romans and Antiochus the Great, the frontier city of the Syrian kingdom on the N.W. As the power of the Seleucidae declined, it suffered much from the oppression of its governors, and from the wars between the members of the royal family. At the time of the Mithridatic War, it suffered, on the one hand, from Tigranes, who overran Cilicia, and, on the other, from the pirates, who had their strongholds in the mountains of Cilicia Aspera, and made frequent incursions into the level country. From both these enemies it was rescued by Pompey, who made it the capital of the new Roman province of Cilicia, B.C. 66. Under Augustus, the city obtained immunity from taxes, through the influence of the emperor's tutor, the Stoic Athenodorus, who was a native of the place. It enjoyed the favour, and was called by the names, of several of the later emperors. It was the scene of important events in the wars with the Persians, the Arabs, and the Turks, and also in the Crusades. Tarsus was the birth-place of many

distinguished men, and above all, of the Apostle Paul.

TARTĂRUS (-i), son of Aether and Gē, and by his mother Ge the father of the Gigantes, Typhoeus, and Echidna. In the Iliad Tartarus is a place beneath the earth, as far below Hades as Heaven is above the earth, and closed by iron gates. Later poets use the name as synonymous with Hades.

TARTESSUS (-i), an ancient town in Spain, and one of the chief settlements of the Phoenicians, probably the same as the *Tarshish* of Scripture. The whole country W. of Gibraltar was also called TARTESSIS.

TARUSCON or TARASCON (-onis : *Tarascon*), a town of the Salyes in Gaul, on the E. bank of the Rhone, N. of Arelate, and E. of Nemausus.

TARVISĬUM (-i : *Treviso*), a town of Venetia in the N. of Italy, on the river Silis, which became the seat of a bishopric, and a place of importance in the middle ages.

TĂTĬUS, T., king of the Sabines. [ROMULUS.]

TATTA (*Tuz-Göl*), a great salt lake in the centre of Asia Minor.

TAULANTĬI (-ōrum), a people of Illyria, in the neighbourhood of Epidamnus.

TAUNUS (-i : *Taunus*), a range of mountains in Germany, at no great distance from the confluence of the Moenus (*Main*) and the Rhine.

TAURASĬA. [TAURINI.]

TAURENTUM (-i) and TAURŎĬS (-entis), a fortress belonging to Massilia, and near the latter city.

TAURI (-ōrum), a wild and savage people in European Sarmatia, who sacrificed all strangers to a goddess whom the Greeks identified with Artemis (Diana). The Tauri dwelt in the peninsula which was called after them Chersonesus Taurica.

TAURĬNI (-ōrum), a people of Liguria dwelling on the upper course of the Po, at the foot of the Alps. Their chief town was Taurasia, afterwards colonised by Augustus, and called Augusta Taurinorum (*Turin*).

TAURISCI (-ōrum), a Celtic people in Noricum, and probably the old Celtic name of the entire population of the country.

TAURŎĬS. [TAURENTUM.]

TAURŎMĒNIUM (-i : *Taormina*), a city on the E. coast of Sicily, situated on Mt. Taurus, from which it derived its name, and founded B.C. 358 by Andromachus with the remains of the inhabitants of Naxos.

TAURUS (-i : from the Aramaean Tur, *a high mountain : Taurus, Ala-Dagh*, and other special names), a great mountain chain of Asia. In its widest extent, the name was applied, by the later geographers, to the whole of the great chain, which runs through

Asia from W. to E.; but in its usual signification, it denotes the mountain-chain in the
S. of Asia Minor, which begins at the Sacrum
or Chelidonium Prom. at the S.E. angle of
Lycia, surrounds the gulf of Pamphylia,
passing through the middle of Pisidia ; then
along the S. frontier of Lycaonia and Cappadocia, which it divides from Cilicia and Commagene ; thence, after being broken through
by the Euphrates, it proceeds almost due E.
through the S. of Armenia, forming the
water-shed between the sources of the Tigris
on the S., and the streams which feed the
upper Euphrates and the Araxes on the N. ;
thus it continues as far as the S. margin of
the lake Arsissa, where it ceases to bear the
name of Taurus, and is continued in the
chain which, under the names of Niphates,
Zagros, &c., forms the N.E. margin of the
Tigris and Euphrates valley.

TĀVĪUM (-i: prob. *Boghaz Kieni*, Ru.),
the capital of the Trocmi, in Galatia, stood
on the E. side of the Halys, but at some distance from the river, and formed the centre
of meeting for roads leading to all parts of
Asia Minor.

TAXĪLA or TAXĬĀLA (-ōrum), an important city of India intra Gangem, stood in
a large and fertile plain between the Indus
and the Hydaspes, and was the capital of the
Indian king Taxiles.

TAXĪLĒS. (1) An Indian prince or king,
who reigned over the tract between the Indus
and the Hydaspes, at the period of the expedition of Alexander, B.C. 327. His real name
was Mophis, or Omphis, and the Greeks
appear to have called him Taxiles or Taxilas,
from the name of his capital city of Taxila.
—(2) A general in the service of Mithridates
the Great.

TAŸGĔTĒ, (-ēs), daughter of Atlas and
Pleione, one of the Pleiades, from whom
Mt. Taygetus in Laconia is said to have
derived its name. By Zeus (Jupiter), she
became the mother of Lacedaemon and of
Eurotas.

TAŸGĔTUS or TAŸGĔTUM (-i), or
TAŸGĔTA (-ōrum), a lofty range of mountains of a wild and savage character, separating Laconia and Messenia, and extending
from the frontiers of Arcadia down to the
Prom. Taenarum.

TĔĀNUM (-i). (1) APULUM (nr. *Ponte
Rotto*), a town of Apulia on the river Frento
and the confines of the Frentani, 18 miles
from Larinum.—(2) SIDICINUM (*Teano*), an
important town of Campania, and the capital
of the Sidicini, situated on the N. slope of
Mt. Massicus and on the Via Praenestina,
6 miles W. of Cales.

TĔĀRUS (-i: *Teara, Deara* or *Dere*), a

river of Thrace, the waters of which were
useful in curing cutaneous diseases.

TĔĀTE (-is: *Chieti*), the capital of the
Marrucini, situated on a steep hill on the
river Aternus, and on the road from Aternum to Corfinium.

TECMESSA (-ae), the daughter of the
Phrygian king Teleutas, whose territory was
ravaged by the Greeks during a predatory
excursion from Troy. Tecmessa was taken
prisoner, and was given to Ajax, the son of
Telamon, by whom she had a son, Eurysaces.

TECTŌSĀGES (-um). (1) In Gallia.
[VOLCAE.]—(2) In Asia Minor. [GALATIA.]

TĔGĒA (-ae). (1) (*Piali*), an important
city of Arcadia, and the capital of the district
TEGEATIS, which was bounded on the E. by
Argolis and Laconica, on the S. by Laconia,
on the W. by Maenalia, and on the N. by
the territory of Mantinea. It was one of the
most ancient towns of Arcadia, and is said to
have been founded by Tegeates, the son of
Lycaon. The Tegeatae sent 3000 men to
the battle of Plataea, in which they were
distinguished for their bravery. They remained faithful to Sparta in the Peloponnesian
war ; but after the battle of Leuctra they
joined the rest of the Arcadians in establishing their independence. During the wars of
the Achaean league Tegea was taken both by
Cleomenes, king of Sparta, and Antigonus
Doson, king of Macedonia, and the ally of
the Achaeans.—(2) A town in Crete, said to
have been founded by Agamemnon.

TĔLĂMŌN (-ōnis), son of Aeacus and
Endeïs, and brother of Peleus. Having
assisted Peleus in slaying their half-brother
Phocus [PELEUS], Telamon was expelled from
Aegina, and came to Salamis. Here he was
first married to Glauce, daughter of Cychreus,
king of the island, on whose death Telamon
became king of Salamis. He afterwards
married Periboea or Eriboea, daughter of
Alcathous, by whom he became the father of
Ajax, who is hence frequently called *Tela-
moniǎdēs*, and *Telamonius heros*. Telamon
himself was one of the Calydonian hunters
and one of the Argonauts. He was also a
great friend of Hercules, whom he joined in
his expedition against Laomedon of Troy,
which city he was the first to enter. Hercules, in return, gave to him Theanira or
Hesione, a daughter of Laomedon, by whom
he became the father of Teucer and Trambelus.

TĔLĂMŌN (*Telamone*), a town and harbour
of Etruria, a few miles S. of the river Umbro,
said to have been founded by Telamon on his
return from the Argonautic expedition.

TELCHĪNES (-um), a family or a tribe,
said to have been descended from Thalassa or
Poseidon (Neptune). They are represented

in 3 different aspects :—(1.) *As cultivators of the soil and ministers of the gods.* As such they came from Crete to Cyprus, and from thence to Rhodes, where they founded Cami-rus, Ialysus, and Lindus. Rhodes, which was named after them *Telchinis,* was aban-doned by them, because they foresaw that the island would be inundated. Poseidon was intrusted to them by Rhea, and they brought him up in conjunction with Caphira, a daughter of Oceanus. Rhea, Apollo and Zeus (Jupiter), however, are also described as hostile to the Telchines. Apollo is said to have assumed the shape of a wolf, and to have thus destroyed the Telchines, and Zeus to have overwhelmed them by an inundation. (2.) *As sorcerers and envious daemons.* Their very eyes and aspect are said to have been destructive. They had it in their power to bring on hail, rain, and snow, and to assume any form they pleased ; they further mixed Stygian water with sulphur, in order thereby to destroy animals and plants. (3.) *As artists,* for they are said to have invented useful arts and institutions, and to have made images of the gods. They worked in brass and iron, made the sickle of Cronos and the trident of Poseidon.

TĔLĔBŎAE. [TAPHIAE.]

TELEGONUS (-i), son of Ulysses and Circe. After Ulysses had returned to Ithaca, Circe sent out Telegonus in search of his father. A storm cast his ship on the coast of Ithaca, and being pressed by hunger, he began to plunder the fields. Ulysses and Telemachus being informed of the ravages caused by the stranger, went out to fight against him ; but Telegonus ran Ulysses through with a spear which he had received from his mother. At the command of Athena (Minerva). Telegonus, accompanied by Tele-machus and Penelope, went to Circe in Aeaea, there buried the body of Ulysses, and mar-ried Penelope, by whom he became the father of Italus.

TĔLĔMĂCHUS (-i), son of Ulysses and Penelope. He was still an infant when his father went to Troy ; and when the latter had been absent from home nearly 20 years, Telemachus went to Pylos and Sparta, to gather information concerning him. He was hospitably received by Nestor, who sent his own son to conduct Telemachus to Sparta. Menelaus also received him kindly, and com-municated to him the prophecy of Proteus concerning Ulysses. From Sparta Telema-chus returned home ; and on his arrival there he found his father, whom he assisted in slaying the suitors.

TELEMUS (-i), son of Eurymus, and a celebrated soothsayer.

TĔLĔPHUS (-i), son of Hercules and Auge, the daughter of king Aleus of Tegea. On reaching manhood, he consulted the Delphic oracle to learn his parentage, and was ordered to go to king Teuthras in Mysia. He there found his mother, and succeeded Teuthras on the throne of Mysia. He married Laodice or Astyoche, a daughter of Priam ; and he attempted to prevent the Greeks from landing on the coast of Mysia. Dionysus (Bacchus), however, caused him to stumble over a vine, whereupon he was wounded by Achilles. Being informed by an oracle that the wound could only be cured by him who had inflicted it, Telephus re-paired to the Grecian camp ; and as the Greeks had likewise learnt from an oracle that without the aid of Telephus they could not reach Troy, Achilles cured Telephus by means of the rust of the spear with which he had been wounded. Telephus, in return, pointed out to the Greeks the road which they had to take.

TELESĬA (-ae : *Telese*), a town in Sam-nium, on the road from Allifae to Bene-ventum.

TĔLĔSILLA (-ae), of Argos, a celebrated lyric poetess and heroine, flourished about B.C. 510. She led a band of her country-women in the war with the Spartans.

TELESĪNUS, PONTĬUS. [PONTIUS.]

TELLENAE (-arum), a town in Latium between the later Via Ostiensis and the Via Appia.

TELLUS. [GAEA.]

TELMESSUS or TELMISSUS (-i). (1) (*Mèi*, the port of *Macri*, Ru.), a city of Lycia, near the borders of Caria, on a gulf called Telmissicus Sinus, and close to the promontory Telmissis.—(2) A town of Caria, 60 stadia (6 geog. miles) from Halicarnassus.

TĔLO (-ōnis), MARTIUS (*Toulon*), a port town of Gallia Narbonensis on the Medi-terranean.

TĔLOS (-i : *Telos* or *Piskopi*), a small island of the Carpathian sea, one of the Sporades.

TELPHUSSA. [THELPUSA.]

TĔMĔNĬDAE. [TEMENUS]

TĔMĔNUS (-i), son of Aristomachus, was one of the Heraclidae who invaded Pelopon-nesus. After the conquest of the peninsula, he received Argos as his share. His de-scendants, the Temenidae, being expelled from Argos, are said to have founded the kingdom of Macedonia, whence the kings of Macedonia called themselves Temenidae.

TĔMĔSA or TEMPSA (-ae : *Torre del Lupi*), a town in Bruttium on the Sinus Terinaeus, and one of the most ancient Auso-nian towns in the S. of Italy.

TEMPÊ (neut. pl. indcl.), a beautiful and romantic valley in the N. of Thessaly between Mts. Olympus and Ossa, through which the Peneus escapes into the sea. The lovely scenery of this glen is frequently described by the ancient poets and declaimers ; and it was also celebrated as one of the favourite haunts of Apollo, who transplanted his laurel from this spot to Delphi. So celebrated was the scenery of Tempé that its name was given to any beautiful valley. Thus we find a Tempé in the land of the Sabines, near Reate, through which the river Velinus flowed ; and also a Tempé in Sicily, through which the river Helorus flowed, hence called by Ovid *Tempe Heloria.*

TENCTĒRI or TENCHTĒRI (-ōrum), a people of Germany dwelling on the Rhine between the Ruhr and the Sieg, S. of the Usipetes, in conjunction with whom their name usually occurs.

TĒNĒDOS or TĒNĒDUS (-i), a small island of the Aegaean sea, off the coast of Troas, of an importance very disproportionate to its size, on account of its position near the mouth of the Hellespont, from which it is about 12 miles distant. It appears in the legend of the Trojan War as the station to which the Greeks withdrew their fleet, in order to induce the Trojans to think that they had departed, and to receive the wooden horse. In the Persian War it was used by Xerxes as a naval station. It afterwards became a tributary ally of Athens, and adhered to her during the whole of the Peloponnesian War, and down to the peace of Antalcidas, by which it was surrendered to the Persians. At the Macedonian conquest the Tenedians regained their liberty.

TĒNES or TENNES, son of Cycnus and Proclea, and brother of Hemithea. Cycnus was king of Colonae in Troas. His 2nd wife was Philonome, who fell in love with her step-son ; but as he repulsed her advances she accused him to his father, who put both his son and daughter into a chest, and threw them into the sea. But the chest was driven on the coast of the island of Leucophrys, of which the inhabitants elected Tenes king, and which he called Tenedos, after his own name.

TĒNOS (-i : *Tino*), a small island in the Aegaean sea, S.E. of Andros and N. of Delos.

TENTỸRA (-ōrum : *Denderah*, Ru.), a city of Upper Egypt, on the western bank of the Nile, between Abydos and Coptos, with celebrated temples of Athor (the Egyptian Venus), Isis, and Typhon. There are still magnificent remains of the temples of Athor and of Isis : in the latter was found the celebrated Zodiac, which is now preserved at Paris.

TĒŌS (-i : *Sighajik*), one of the Ionian cities on the coast of Asia Minor, renowned as the birthplace of the lyric poet Anacreon It stood at the bottom of the bay between the promontories of Coryceum and Myonnesus.

TĒRENTĪA (-ae). (1) Wife of M. Cicero, the orator, to whom she bore 2 children, a son and daughter. She was a woman of sound sense and great resolution ; and her firmness of character was of no small service to her weak and vacillating husband in some important periods of his life. During the civil war, however, Cicero was offended with her conduct, and divorced her in B.C. 46. Terentia is said to have attained the age of 103.— (2) Also called TERENTILLA, the wife of Maecenas, and also one of the favourite mistresses of Augustus.

TĒRENTIUS (-i) AFER, P., usually called TERENCE, the celebrated comic poet, was born at Carthage, B.C. 195. By birth or purchase he became the slave of P. Terentius Lucanus, a Roman senator. A handsome person and promising talents recommended Terence to his master, who afforded him the best education of the age, and finally manumitted him. On his manumission, according to the usual practice, Terence assumed his patron's name, Terentius, having been previously called Publius or Publipor. The *Andria* was the first play offered by Terence for representation. The curule aediles referred the piece to Caecilius, then one of the most popular play-writers at Rome. Unknown and meanly clad, Terence began to read from a low stool his opening scene. A few verses showed the elder poet that no ordinary writer was before him, and the young aspirant, then in his 27th year, was invited to share the couch and supper of his judge. This reading of the *Andria*, however, must have preceded its performance nearly two years, for Caecilius died in 168, and it was not acted till 166. Meanwhile, copies were in circulation, envy was awakened, and Luscius Lavinius, a veteran, and not very successful play-writer, began his unwearied attacks on the dramatic and personal character of the author. The *Andria* was successful, and, aided by the accomplishments and good address of Terence himself, was the means of introducing him to the most refined and intellectual circles of Rome. His chief patrons were Laelius and the younger Scipio, both of whom treated him as an equal, and are said even to have assisted him in the composition of his plays. After residing some years at Rome, Terence went to Greece, where he devoted himself to the study of Menander's comedies. He never returned to Italy, and we have various, but no certain, accounts of his death. He died in the 36th year of his age, in 159, or in the year following. Six comedies are all that remain to us ; and they are probably all that Terence produced. They are founded on Greek originals, but we have corresponding fragments enough of Menander to prove that Terence retouched and sometimes improved his model. In summing up his merits, we ought not to omit the praise which has been universally accorded him—that, although a foreigner and a freedman, he divides with Cicero and Caesar the palm of pure Latinity.

TĔRENTĬUS VARRŌ. [VARRO.]

TĔREUS (-ĕos, or -ei), son of Ares (Mars), king of the Thracians in Daulis, afterwards Phocis. Pandion, king of Attica, who had 2 daughters, Philomēla and Procne, called in the assistance of Tereus against some enemy, and gave him his daughter Procne in marriage. Tereus became by her the father of Itys, and then concealed her in the country, that he might thus marry her sister Philomela, whom he deceived by saying that Procne was dead. At the same time he deprived Philomela of her tongue. Ovid (Met. vi. 565) reverses the story by stating that Tereus told Procne that her sister Philomela was dead. Philomela, however, soon learned the truth, and made it known to her sister by a few words which she wove into a peplus. Procne thereupon killed her own son Itys, and served up the flesh of the child in a dish before Tereus. She then fled with her sister. Tereus pursued them with an axe, and when the sisters were overtaken they prayed to the gods to change them into birds. Procne, accordingly, became a nightingale, Philomela a swallow, and Tereus a hoopoo. According to some, Procne became a swallow, Philomela a nightingale, and Tereus a hawk.

TERGESTĔ (-is : Trieste), a town of Istria, on a bay in the N.E. of the Adriatic gulf called after it Tergestinus Sinus. It was made a Roman colony by Vespasian.

TĔRĪDĀTES. [TIRIDATES.]

TĔRĪNA (-ae : St. Eufemia), a town on the W. coast of Bruttium, from which the Sinus Terinaeus derived its name.

TERIŎLIS or TERIŎLA CASTRA, a fortress in Rhaetia, which has given its name to the country of the Tyrol.

TERMESSUS (-i : prob. Shenet, Ru.), a city of Pisidia, high up on the Taurus.

TERMĬNUS (-i), a Roman divinity, presiding over boundaries and frontiers. His worship is said to have been instituted by Numa, who ordered that every one should mark the boundaries of his landed property by stones consecrated to Jupiter, and at these boundary-stones every year sacrifices should be offered at the festival of the Terminalia. The Terminus of the Roman state originally stood between the 5th and 6th milestone on the road towards Laurentum, near a place called Festi. Another public Terminus stood in the temple of Jupiter in the Capitol.

TERPANDER (-dri), the father of Greek music, and through it of lyric poetry. He was a native of Antissa in Lesbos, and flourished between B.C. 700 and 650. He established the first musical school or system that existed in Greece, and added 3 strings to the lyre, which before his time had only 4.

TERPSĬCHŎRĔ (-ēs), one of the 9 Muses, presided over the choral song and dancing. [MUSAE.]

TERRA. [GAEA.]

TERRACĪNA. [TARRACINA.]

TESTA (-ae), C. TREBĀTĬUS, a Roman jurist, and a contemporary and friend of Cicero. Trebatius enjoyed considerable reputation under Augustus as a lawyer. Horace addressed to him the 1st Satire of the 2nd Book.

TĒTHȲS (-ȳos, acc. -ȳă, and -ȳn), daughter of Uranus and Gaea, and wife of Oceanus, by whom she became the mother of the Oceanides and or the numerous river-gods.

TĔTRĬCA (-ae), a mountain on the frontiers of Pisenum and the land of the Sabines, belonging to the great chain of the Apennines.

TĔTRĬCUS (-i), C. PESUVIUS, one of the Thirty Tyrants, and the last of the pretenders who ruled Gaul during its separation from the empire under Gallienus and his successor, A.D. 267—274.

TEUCER (-cri). (1) Son of the river-god Scamander by the nymph Idaea, was the first king of Troy, whence the Trojans are sometimes called Teucri.—(2) Son of Telamon and Hesione, was a step-brother of Ajax, and the best archer among the Greeks at Troy. He founded the town of Salamis, in Cyprus, and married Eune, the daughter of Cyprus, by whom he became the father of Asteria.

TEUCRI. [TROAS.]

TEUMESSUS (-i), a mountain in Boeotia, near Hypatus, and close to Thebes, on the road from the latter place to Chalcis.

TEUTHRĀNĪA. [MYSIA.]

TEUTHRAS (-antis), an ancient king of Mysia. He was succeeded in the kingdom of Mysia by Telephus. [TELEPHUS.] The 50 daughters of Teuthras, given as a reward to Hercules, are called by Ovid Teuthrantia turba.

TEUTHRAS (prob. Demirji-Dagh), a mountain in the Mysian district of Teuthrania, a S.W. branch of Temnus.

TEUTŎBURGIENSIS SALTUS, a range of

hills in Germany, extending from Osnabrück to Paderborn (the *Teutoburger Wald* or *Lippische Wald*). It is celebrated on account of the defeat and destruction of Varus and 3 Roman legions by the Germans under Arminius, A.D. 9.

TEUTONES (-um) or TEUTONI (-ōrum), a powerful people in Germany, who probably dwelt on the coast of the Baltic, near the Cimbri. They invaded Gaul and the Roman dominions, along with the Cimbri, at the latter end of the 2nd century B.C.

THABOR, TABOR, or ATABYRIUM (-i: *Jebel Tur*), an isolated mountain at the E. end of the plain of Esdraelon in Galilee.

THAÏS (-ĭdis), a celebrated Athenian courtesan, who accompanied Alexander the Great on his expedition into Asia. After the death of Alexander, Thaïs attached herself to Ptolemy Lagi, by whom she became the mother of two sons, Leontiscus and Lagus, and of a daughter, Irene.

THALA (-ae), a great city of Numidia, mentioned by Sallust and other writers, and probably identical with TELEPTE or THELEPTE, a city in the S. of Numidia, 71 Roman miles N.W. of Capsa.

THALASSIUS, TALASSIUS (-i), or TALASSIO (-ōnis), a Roman senator of the time of Romulus. At the time of the rape of the Sabine women, when a maiden of surpassing beauty was carried off for Thalassius, the persons conducting her, in order to protect her against any assaults from others, exclaimed "for Thalassius." Hence, it is said, arose the wedding shout with which a bride at Rome was conducted to the house of her bridegroom.

THALES (-ētis and -is), the Ionic philosopher, and one of the Seven Sages, was born at Miletus about B.C. 636, and died about 546, at the age of 90, though the exact date neither of his birth nor of his death is known. He is said to have predicted the eclipse of the sun which happened in the reign of the Lydian king Alyattes ; to have diverted the course of the Halys in the time of Croesus; and later, in order to unite the Ionians, when threatened by the Persians, to have instituted a federal council in Teos. He was one of the founders in Greece of the study of philosophy and mathematics. Thales maintained that water is the origin of things, meaning thereby, that it is water out of which every thing arises, and into which every thing resolves 'tself. Thales left no works behind him.

THALES or THALETAS (-ae), the celebrated musician and lyric poet, was a native of Gortyna, in Crete, and probably flourished shortly after Terpander.

THALIA (-ae). (1) One of the 9 Muses,

and, at least in later times, the Muse of Comedy. [MUSAE.]—(2) One of the Nereides. —(3) One of the Charites or Graces.

THALLO. [HORAE.]

THAMYRIS (-is) or THAMYRAS (-ae), an ancient Thracian bard, was a son of Philammon, and the nymph Argiope. In his presumption he challenged the Muses to a trial of skill, and being overcome in the contest, was deprived by them of his sight and of the power of singing. He was represented with a broken lyre in his hand.

THANATOS. [MORS.]

THAPSACUS (-i: O.T. Thipsach : an Aramean word, signified a *ford :* at the ford of *El-Hamman*, near *Rakkah*, Ru.), a city of Syria, in the province of Chalybonitis, on the left bank of the Euphrates, 2000 stadia S. of Zeugma, and 15 parasangs from the mouth of the river Chaboras (the Araxes of Xenophon).

THAPSUS (-i). (1) A city on the E. coast of Sicily, on a peninsula of the same name (*Isola degli Magnisi*). — (2) (*Demas*, Ru.), a city on the E. coast of Byzacena, in Africa Propria.

THASOS or THASUS (-i : *Thaso* or *Tasso*), an island in the N. of the Aegaean sea, off the coast of Thrace, and opposite the mouth of the river Nestus. It was at a very early period taken possession of by the Phoenicians, on account of its valuable gold mines. According to tradition the Phoenicians were led by Thasus, son of Poseidon (Neptune), or Agenor, who came from the East in search of Europa, and from whom the island derived its name. Thasos was afterwards colonised by the Parians, B.C. 708, and among the colonists was the poet Archilochus. The Thracians once possessed a considerable territory on the coast of Thrace, and were one of the richest and most powerful peoples in the N. of the Aegaean. They were subdued by the Persians under Mardonius, and subsequently became part of the Athenian maritime empire. They revolted, however, from Athens, in B.C. 465, and after sustaining a siege of 3 years, were subdued by Cimon in 463. They again revolted from Athens in 411, and called in the Spartans, but the island was again restored to the Athenians by Thrasybulus in 407.

THAUMAS (-antis), son of Pontus and Ge, and by the Oceanid Electra, the father of Iris and the Harpies. Hence Iris is called *Thaumantias*, *Thaumantis*, and *Thaumantēa virgo*.

THEANO (-ūs). (1) Daughter of Cisseus, wife of Antenor, and priestess of Athena (Minerva) at Ilion.—(2) A celebrated female philosopher of the Pythagorean school,

appears to have been the wife of Pythagoras, and the mother by him of Telauges,
Mnesarchus, Myia, and Arignote; but the
accounts respecting her were various.

THEBAE (-ārum), in the poets sometimes
THEBE (-ēs), aft. DIOSPŌLIS MAGNA,
i.e., *Great City of Jove*, in Scripture NO, or
NO AMMON, was the capital of Thebaïs, or
Upper Egypt, and, for a long time, of the
whole country. It was reputed the oldest
city of the world. It stood in about the
centre of the Thebaïd, on both banks of the
Nile, above Coptos, and in the Nomos Cop-
tites. It appears to have been at the height
of its splendour, as the capital of Egypt, and
as a chief seat of the worship of Ammon,
about B.C. 1600. The fame of its grandeur
had reached the Greeks as early as the time
of Homer, who describes it, with poetical
exaggeration, as having a hundred gates,
from each of which it could send out 200
war chariots, fully armed. Its real extent
was calculated by the Greek writers at 140
stadia (14 geog. miles) in circuit. That
these computations are not exaggerated, is
proved by the existing ruins, which extend
from side to side of the valley of the Nile,
here about 6 miles wide; while the rocks
which bound the valley are perforated with
tombs. These ruins, which are perhaps the
most magnificent in the world, enclose
within their site the 4 modern villages of
Carnac, Luxor, Medinet Abou, and *Gournou.*

THĒBAE (-ārum), in *Europe.* (1) (*Theba,*
Turkish *Stiva*), the chief city in Boeotia, was
situated in a plain S.E. of the lake Hylice, and
N.E. of Plataeae. Its acropolis, which was an
oval eminence, of no great height, was called
CADMEA, because it was said to have been
founded by Cadmus, the leader of a Phoenician colony. It is said that the fortifications
of the city were constructed by Amphion and
his brother Zethus; and that, when Amphion
played his lyre, the stones moved of their
own accord, and formed the wall. The territory of Thebes was called THEBAÏS, and
extended E.-wards as far as the Euboean sea.
No city is more celebrated in the mythical
ages of Greece than Thebes. It was here
that the use of letters was first introduced
from Phoenicia into W. Europe. It was the
reputed birthplace of the 2 great divinities,
Dionȳsus (Bacchus) and Hercules. It was
also the native city of the seer Tiresias, as
well as of the great musician, Amphion. It
was the scene of the tragic fate of Oedipus,
and of the war of the "Seven against
Thebes." A few years afterwards "The
Epigoni," or descendants of the seven heroes,
marched against Thebes to revenge their
fathers' death; they took the city, and razed

it to the ground. It appears at the earliest
historical period as a large and flourishing
city; and it is represented as possessing 7
gates, the number assigned to it in the
ancient legends. The Thebans were from an
early period inveterate enemies of their
neighbours, the Athenians. In the Peloponnesian war they espoused the Spartan side,
and contributed not a little to the downfall of
Athens. But, in common with the other
Greek states, they soon became disgusted
with the Spartan supremacy, and joined the
confederacy formed against Sparta in B.C.
394. The peace of Antalcidas, in 387, put
an end to hostilities in Greece; but the
treacherous seizure of the Cadmea by the
Lacedaemonian general, Phoebidas, in 382,
and its recovery by the Theban exiles in 379,
led to a war between Thebes and Sparta, in
which the former not only recovered its independence, but for ever destroyed the Lacedaemonian supremacy. This was the most
glorious period in the Theban annals; and
the decisive defeat of the Spartans at the
battle of Leuctra, in 371, made Thebes the
first power in Greece. Her greatness, however, was mainly due to the pre-eminent
abilities of her citizens, Epaminondas and
Pelopidas; and with the death of the former
at the battle of Mantinea, in 362, she lost the
supremacy which she had so recently gained.
The Thebans were induced, by the eloquence
of Demosthenes, to forget their old animosi-
ties against the Athenians, and to join the
latter in protecting the liberties of Greece
against Philip of Macedon; but their united
forces were defeated by Philip, at the battle
of Chaeronea, in 338. Soon after the death
of Philip and the accession of Alexander, the
Thebans made a last attempt to recover their
liberty, but were cruelly punished by the
young king. The city was taken by Alexander in 336, and was entirely destroyed,
with the exception of the temples, and the
house of the poet Pindar; 6000 inhabitants
were slain, and 20,000 sold as slaves. In
316 the city was rebuilt by Cassander, with
the assistance of the Athenians. In 290 it
was taken by Demetrius Poliorcetes, and
again suffered greatly. After the Macedonian
period Thebes rapidly declined in importance;
and it received its last blow from Sulla, who
gave half of its territory to the Delphians.—
(2) Surnamed PHTHIOTICAE, an important
city of Thessaly, in the district Phthiotis.

THĒBĀÏS. [AEGYPTUS.]

THĒBĒ (-ēs), a city of Mysia, on the
wooded slope of M. Placus, destroyed by
Achilles. It was said to have been the birthplace of Andromache and Chryseïs.

THEMIS (-ĭdis), daughter of Uranus and

Gĕ, was married to Zeus (Jupiter), by whom she became the mother of the Horae, Eunomia, Dice (Astraea), Irene, and of the Moerae. In the Homeric poems, Themis is the personification of the order of things established by law, custom, and equity, whence she is described as reigning in the assemblies of men, and as convening, by the command of Zeus, the assembly of the gods. She dwells in Olympus, and is on friendly terms with Hera (Juno). She is also described as a prophetic divinity, and is said to have been in possession of the Delphic oracle as the successor of Ge, and predecessor of Apollo. Nymphs, believed to be daughters of Zeus and Themis, lived in a cave on the river Eridanus, and the Hesperides also are called daughters of Zeus and Themis. On coins she often bears a resemblance to the figure of Athena (Minerva), and holds a cornucopia and a pair of scales.

THĔMISCȲRA, a plain on the coast of Pontus, extending E. of the river Iris, beyond the Thermōdon, celebrated from very ancient times as the country of the Amazons.

THĔMISTĬUS (-i), a distinguished philosopher and rhetorician, was a Paphlagonian, and flourished, first at Constantinople, and afterwards at Rome, in the reigns of Constantius, Julian, Jovian, Valens, Gratian, and Theodosius.

THĔMISTŎCLĒS (-is), the celebrated Athenian, was the son of Neocles and Abrŏtŏnon, a Thracian woman, and was born about B.C. 514. In his youth he had an impetuous character; he displayed great intellectual power, combined with a lofty ambition, and desire of political distinction. He began his career by setting himself in opposition to those who had most power, and especially to Aristides, to whose ostracism (in 483) he contributed. From this time he was the political leader in Athens. In 481 he was Archon Eponymus; about which time he persuaded the Athenians to employ the produce of the silver mines of Laurium in building ships, instead of distributing it among the Athenian citizens. Upon the invasion of Greece by Xerxes, Themistocles was appointed to the command of the Athenian fleet; and to his energy, prudence, foresight, and courage, the Greeks mainly owed their salvation from the Persian dominion. Upon the approach of Xerxes, the Athenians, on the advice of Themistocles, deserted their city, and removed their women, children, and infirm persons, to Salamis, Aegina, and Troezen. A panic having seized the Spartans and other Greeks, Themistocles sent a faithful slave to the Persian commanders, informing them that the Greeks

intended to make their escape, and that the Persians had now the opportunity of accomplishing a noble enterprise, if they would only cut off their retreat. The Persians believed what they were told, and in the night their fleet occupied the whole of the channel between Salamis and the mainland. The Greeks were thus compelled to fight; and the result was the great and glorious victory, in which the greater part of the fleet of Xerxes was destroyed. This victory, which was due to Themistocles, established his reputation among the Greeks. Yet his influence does not appear to have survived the expulsion of the Persians from Greece and the fortification of the ports of Athens, to which he had advised the Athenians. He was probably accused of peculation, and perhaps justly, for he was not very scrupulous; at all events he was ostracised in 471, and retired to Argos. After the discovery of the treasonable correspondence of Pausanias with the Persian king, the Lacedaemonians sent to Athens to accuse Themistocles of being privy to the design of Pausanias; whereupon the Athenians sent off persons with the Lacedaemonians with instructions to arrest him (466). Themistocles, hearing of what was designed against him, first fled from Argos to Corcyra; then to Epirus, where he took refuge in the house of Admetus, king of the Molossi, and finally reached the coast of Asia in safety. Xerxes was now dead (465), and Artaxerxes was on the throne. Themistocles went up to visit the king at his royal residence; and on his arrival he sent the king a letter, in which he promised to do him a good service, and prayed that he might be allowed to wait a year, and then to explain personally what brought him there. In a year he made himself master of the Persian language and the Persian usages, and, being presented to the king, obtained the greatest influence over him, and was presented with a handsome allowance, after the Persian fashion. Magnesia supplied him with bread, Lampsacus with wine, and Myus with the other provisions. But before he could accomplish anything he died, probably by poison, administered by himself, from despair of accomplishing anything against his country. Themistocles had great talents, but little morality; and thus ended his career, unhappily and ingloriously. He died in 449, at the age of 65.

THĔŎCLȲMĔNUS (-i), a soothsayer, son of Polyphides of Hyperasia, and a descendant of Melampus.

THĔOCRITUS (-i). (1) Of Chios, an orator, sophist, and perhaps an historian, in the time of Alexander the Great. None of his works are extant with the exception of 2 or 3 epigrams, among which is a very bitter one upon Aristotle.—(2) The celebrated bucolic poet, was a native of Syracuse, and the son of Praxagŏras and Philinna. He visited Alexandria during the latter end of the reign of Ptolemy Soter, where he received the instruction of Philetas and Asclepiades, and began to distinguish himself as a poet. His first efforts obtained for him the patronage of Ptolemy Philadelphus, who was associated in the kingdom with his father, Ptolemy Soter, in B.C. 285, and in whose praise the poet wrote the 14th, 15th, and 17th Idyls. Theocritus afterwards returned to Syracuse, and lived there under Hiero II. It appears from the 16th Idyl that he was dissatisfied, both with the want of liberality on the part of Hiero in rewarding him for his poems, and with the political state of his native country. It may therefore be supposed that he devoted the latter part of his life almost entirely to the contemplation of those scenes of nature and of country life, on his representations of which his fame chiefly rests. Theocritus was the creator of bucolic poetry as a branch of Greek, and through imitators, such as Virgil, of Roman literature. The bucolic idyls of Theocritus are of a dramatic and mimetic character, and are pictures of the ordinary life of the common people of Sicily.

THĒŎDECTĒS (-ae), of Phaselis, in Pamphylia, was a highly distinguished rhetorician and tragic poet in the time of Philip of Macedon. The greater part of his life was spent at Athens, where he died at the age of 41.

THĒŎDŎRĬCUS or THĒŎDĔRĬCUS. (I.) King of the Visigoths from A.D. 418 to 451, fell fighting on the side of Aëtius and the Romans at the great battle of Chalons, in which Attila was defeated, 451.— (II.) King of the Visigoths A.D. 452—466, 2nd son of Theodoric I., was assassinated in 466 by his brother Euric, who succeeded him on the throne. Theodoric II. was a patron of letters and learned men.— (III.) Surnamed the GREAT, king of the Ostrogoths, succeeded his father Theodemir, in 475. Theodoric entered Italy in 489, and after defeating Odoacer in 3 great battles, and laying siege to Ravenna, compelled Odoacer to capitulate on condition that he and Theodoric should rule jointly over Italy; but Odoacer was soon afterwards murdered by his more fortunate rival (493). Theodoric thus became master of Italy, which he ruled for 33 years, till his death in 526. His long reign was prosperous and beneficent. Theodoric was

a patron of literature; and among his ministers were Cassiodorus and Boëthius, the two last writers who can claim a place in the literature of ancient Rome.

THĒŎDŌRUS (-i). (1) Of Byzantium, a rhetorician, and a contemporary of Plato.— (2) A philosopher of the Cyrenaic school, usually designated by ancient writers " the Atheist." He resided for some time at Athens ; and being banished thence, went to Alexandria, where he entered the service o' Ptolemy son of Lagus.—(3) An eminent rhetorician of the age of Augustus, was a native of Gadara. He settled at Rhodes, where Tiberius, afterwards emperor, during his retirement (B.C. 6—A.D. 2) to that island, was one of his hearers. He also taught at Rome. Theodorus was the founder of a school of rhetoricians called " Theodorei."

THĒŎDŌSĬUS (-i). (I.) Surnamed the GREAT, Roman emperor of the East, A. D. 378—395, was the son of the general Theodosius, and was born in Spain about 346. He acquired a considerable military reputation in the lifetime of his father, under whom he served ; and after the death of Valens, was proclaimed emperor of the East by Gratian. The Roman empire in the East was then in a critical position, owing to the inroads of the Goths ; but Theodosius gained two signal victories over the barbarians, and concluded a peace with them in 382. In 387 he defeated and put to death Maximus, whom he had previously acknowledged emperor of Spain, Gaul, and Britain. In 390 Theodosius gave a signal instance of his savage temper. A serious riot having broken out at Thessalonica, in which the imperial officer and several of his troops were murdered, Theodosius resolved to take the most signal vengeance upon the whole city. The inhabitants were invited to the games of the Circus ; and as soon as the place was full, the soldiers were employed for 3 hours in slaughtering them. It was on this occasion that St. Ambrose, archbishop of Milan, after representing his crime to Theodosius, refused him admission to the church, and finally compelled him to entreat pardon before all the congregation. Theodosius died at Milan 17th January, 395.—(II.) Roman emperor of the East, A.D. 408—450, was born in 401, and was only 7 years of age at the death of his father Arcadius, whom he succeeded. Theodosius was a weak prince ; and his sister Pulcheria possessed the virtual government of the empire during his long reign. The compilation called the *Codex Theodosianus* was begun in his reign.

THĒOGNIS (-ĭdis), of Megara, an ancient elegiac and gnomic poet, is said to have

flourished B.C. 548 or 544. He was a noble by
birth ; and all his sympathies were with the
nobles. He was banished with the leaders of
the oligarchical party, having previously been
deprived of all his property ; and most of his
poems were composed while he was an exile.
The genuine fragments of Theognis contain
much that is highly poetical in thought, and
elegant as well as forcible in expression.

THEON (-ōnis). (1) The name of 2 mathematicians, namely, Theon the elder, of
Smyrna, an arithmetician, who lived in the
time of Hadrian ; and Theon the younger, of
Alexandria, the father of HYPATIA, best
known as an astronomer and geometer, who
lived in the time of Theodosius the elder.—
(2) AELIUS THEON, of Alexandria, a sophist
and rhetorician of uncertain date, wrote
several works, of which one entitled *Progymnasmata* is still extant.—(3) Of Samos, a
painter who flourished from the time of
Philip onwards to that of the successors of
Alexander.

THEŌNOĒ (-ēs), daughter of Proteus and
Psammathe, also called Idothea. [IDOTHEA.]

THEŌPHANĒS (-is), CN. POMPĒIUS, of
Mytilene in Lesbos, a learned Greek, was one
of the most intimate friends of Pompey, and
wrote the history of his campaigns.

THEŌPHRASTUS (-i), the Greek philosopher, was a native of Eresus in Lesbos,
and studied philosophy at Athens, first under
Plato, and afterwards under Aristotle. He
became the favourite pupil of Aristotle, who
named Theophrastus his successor in the
presidency of the Lyceum, and in his will
bequeathed to him his library and the originals of his own writings. Theophrastus
was a worthy successor of his great master,
and nobly sustained the character of the
school. He is said to have had 2000 disciples,
and among them such men as the comic poet
Menander. He was highly esteemed by the
kings Philippus, Cassander, and Ptolemy,
and was not the less the object of the regard
of the Athenian people, as was decisively
shown when he was impeached of impiety ;
for he was not only acquitted, but his accuser
would have fallen a victim to his calumny,
had not Theophrastus generously interfered to
save him. He died in B.C. 287, having presided over the Academy about 35 years. His
age is variously stated. According to some
accounts he lived 85 years, according to
others 107 years. He is said to have closed
his life with the complaint respecting the
short duration of human existence, that
it ended just when the insight into its pro-
blems was beginning. He wrote a great
number of works, the great object of which
was the development of the Aristotelian

philosophy ; his *Characteres* and his work
On Plants are extant.

THEŌPOMPUS (-i). (1) King of Sparta,
reigned about B.C. 770—720. He is said to
have established the ephoralty, and to have
been mainly instrumental in bringing the 1st
Messenian war to a successful issue.—(2) Of
Chios, a celebrated Greek historian, was the
son of Damasistratus and the brother of
Caucalus the rhetorician. He was born
about B.C. 378, and attended the school of
rhetoric, which Isocrates opened at Chios.
He accompanied his father into banishment,
when the latter was exiled on account of his
espousing the interests of the Lacedaemonians,
but he was restored to his native country in
the 45th year of his age (333), in consequence
of the letters of Alexander the Great, in which
he exhorted the Chians to recal their exiles.
On his return, Theopompus, who was a man
of great wealth as well as learning, naturally
took an important position in the state ; but
his vehement temper, and his support of the
aristocratical party, soon raised against him
a host of enemies. Of these one of the most
formidable was the sophist Theocritus. As
long as Alexander lived, his enemies dared
not take any open proceedings against
Theopompus ; and even after the death of the
Macedonian monarch, he appears to have
enjoyed for some years the protection of the
royal house ; but he was eventually expelled
from Chios as a disturber of the public peace,
and fled to Egypt to Ptolemy, about 305,
being at the time 75 years of age. We are
informed that Ptolemy not only refused to
receive Theopompus, but would even have
put him to death as a dangerous busybody,
had not some of his friends interceded for
his life. Of his farther fate we have no
particulars. None of the works of Theopompus have come down to us. Besides his
Histories he composed several orations. His
style resembled that of his master Isocrates,
and he is praised by the ancients for his
diligence and accuracy, but censured for the
severity and acrimony of his judgments.

THĒRA (-ae : *Santorin*), an island in the
Aegaean sea, and the chief of the Sporades,
distant from Crete 700 stadia, and 25 Roman
miles S. of the island of Ios.

THĒRAMĒNĒS (-is), an Athenian, son of
Hagnon, was a leading member of the oligarchical government of the 400 at Athens, in
B.C. 411. Subsequently, however, he not
only took a prominent part in the deposition
of the 400, but came forward as the accuser
of Antiphon and Archeptolemus, who had
been his intimate friends, but whose death he
was now the mean and cowardly instrument
in procuring. After the capture of Athens

by Lysander, Theramenes was chosen one of the Thirty Tyrants (404). But as from policy he endeavoured to check the tyrannical proceedings of his colleagues, Critias accused him before the council as a traitor, and procured his condemnation by violence. When he had drunk the hemlock, he dashed out the last drops from the cup, exclaiming, "This to the health of the lovely Critias!"

THĔRAPNAE (-ārum), a town in Laconia, on the left bank of the Eurotas, and a little above Sparta, celebrated in mythology as the birthplace of Castor and Pollux. Menelaus and Helen were said to be buried here.

THĔRAS, a Spartan, who colonised and gave name to the island of Thera.

THĔRASĬA (-ae), a small island W. of Thera.

THERMA, a town in Macedonia, afterwards called Thessalonīca [Thessalonica], situated at the N.E. extremity of a great gulf of the Aegaean sea, called Thermaicus or Thermaeus Sinus, from the town at its head. This gulf was also called Macedonicus Sinus: its modern name is *Gulf of Saloniki*.

THERMAE (-ārum), a town in Sicily, built by the inhabitants of Himera, after the destruction of the latter city by the Carthaginians. [Himera.]

THERMAICUS SINUS. [Therma.]

THERMŎDON (-ontis: *Thermeh*), a river of Pontus, in the district of Themiscyra, the reputed country of the Amazons, rises in a mountain called Amazonius M. (and still *Mason Dagh*), near Phanaroea, and falls into the sea about 30 miles E. of the mouth of the Iris. At its mouth was the city of Themiscyra; and there is still, on the W. side of the mouth of the *Thermeh*, a place of the same name, *Thermeh*.

THERMŎPЎLAE, often called simply PЎLAE (-arum), that is, the *Hot Gates* or the *Gates*, a celebrated pass leading from Thessaly into Locris. It lay between Mt. Oeta and an inaccessible morass, forming the edge of the Malic Gulf. At one end of the pass, close to Anthela, the mountain approached so close to the morass as to leave room for only a single carriage between; this narrow entrance formed the W. gate of Thermopylae. About a mile to the E. the mountain again approached close to the sea, near the Locrian town of Alpeni, thus forming the E. gate of Thermopylae. The space between these 2 gates was wider and more open, and was distinguished by its abundant flow of hot springs, which were sacred to Hercules: hence the name of the place. The pass of Thermopylae is especially celebrated on account of the heroic defence of Leonidas and the 300 Spartans against the mighty host of Xerxes.

THERMUM (-i) or THERMA (-ătis), a town of the Aetolians near Stratus, with warm mineral springs, and regarded for some time as the capital of the country.

THĔRON (-ōnis), tyrant of Agrigentum in Sicily, reigned from about B.C. 488 till his death in 472. He shared with Gelon in the great victory gained over the Carthaginians in 480.

THERSANDER (-dri), son of Polynices and Argia, and one of the Epigoni, went with Agamemnon to Troy, and was slain in that expedition by Telephus.

THERSĪTES (-ae), son of Agrius, the most deformed man and impudent talker among the Greeks at Troy. According to the later poets he was killed by Achilles, because he had ridiculed him for lamenting the death of Penthesilea, queen of the Amazons.

THĒSEUS (-ĕŏs, -ĕi, or -eī), the great legendary hero of Attica, was the son of Aegeus, king of Athens, and of Aethra, the daughter of Pittheus, king of Troezen. He was brought up at Troezen; and when he reached maturity, he took, by his mother's directions, the sword and sandals, the tokens which had been left by Aegeus, and proceeded to Athens. Eager to emulate Hercules, he went by land, displaying his prowess by destroying the robbers and monsters that infested the country. By means of the sword which he carried, Theseus was recognised by Aegeus, acknowledged as his son, and declared his successor, to the exclusion of the sons of Pallas. The capture of the Marathonian bull, which had long laid waste the surrounding country, was the next exploit of Theseus. After this he went of his own accord as one of the 7 youths, whom the Athenians were obliged to send every year, with 7 maidens, to Crete, in order to be devoured by the Minotaur. When they arrived at Crete, Ariadne, the daughter of Minos, became enamoured of Theseus, and provided him with a sword with which he slew the Minotaur, and a clue of thread by which he found his way out of the labyrinth. Having effected his object, Theseus sailed away, carrying off Ariadne. There were various accounts about Ariadne; but according to the general account Theseus abandoned her in the island of Naxos on his way home. [Ariadne.] He was generally believed to have had by her two sons, Oenonopion and Staphylus. As the vessel in which Theseus sailed approached Attica, he neglected to hoist the white sail, which was to have been the signal of the success of the expedition; whereupon Aegeus, thinking that his son had perished, threw himself into the sea. [Aegeus.] Theseus thus became king of Athens. One of the most celebrated of the adventures of

Theseus was his expedition against the Amazons. He is said to have assailed them before
they had recovered from the attack of Hercules, and to have carried off their queen,
Antiope. The Amazons in their turn invaded
Attica, and penetrated into Athens itself; and
the final battle in which Theseus overcame
them was fought in the very midst of the city.
By Antiope, Theseus was said to have had a
son named Hippolytus or Demophoon, and
after her death to have married Phaedra
[HIPPOLYTUS, PHAEDRA]. Theseus figures in
almost all the great heroic expeditions. He
was one of the Argonauts; he joined in the
Calydonian hunt, and aided Adrastus in recovering the bodies of those slain before
Thebes. He contracted a close friendship
with Pirithous, and aided him and the Lapithae against the Centaurs. With the assistance of Pirithous, he carried off Helen from
Sparta while she was quite a girl, and placed
her at Aphidnae, under the care of Aethra.
In return he assisted Pirithous in his attempt
to carry off Persephone from the lower world.
Pirithous perished in the enterprise, and
Theseus was kept in hard durance until he
was delivered by Hercules. Meantime Castor
and Pollux invaded Attica, and carried off
Helen and Aethra, Academus having informed
the brothers where they were to be found
[ACADEMUS]. Menestheus also endeavoured
to incite the people against Theseus, who on
his return found himself unable to re-establish
his authority, and retired to Scyros, where
he was treacherously slain by Lycomedes.
The departed hero was believed to have
appeared to aid the Athenians at the battle
of Marathon. There can be no doubt that
Theseus is a purely legendary hero, though
the Athenians in later times regarded him as
an historical personage, and as the author
of several of their political institutions.

THESPIAE (-arum) or THESPIA (-ae :
Eremo or *Rimokastro*), an ancient town in
Boeotia on the S.E. slope of Mt. Helicon, at
no great distance from the Crissaean Gulf.
It was burnt to the ground by the Persians,
but subsequently rebuilt. At Thespiae was
preserved the celebrated marble statue of
Eros by Praxiteles, who had given it to
Phryne, by whom it was presented to her
native town. [PRAXITELES.] From the
vicinity of Thespiae to Mt. Helicon the
Muses are called *Thespĭădes*, and Helicon
itself is named the *Thespia rupes.*

THESPIS (-is), the celebrated father of
Greek tragedy, was a contemporary of Pisistratus, and a native of Icarus, one of the
demi in Attica, where the worship of Dionysus
(Bacchus) had long prevailed. The alteration
made by Thespis, and which gave to the old

tragedy a new and dramatic character, was
very simple but very important. He introduced an actor, for the sake of giving rest
to the chorus, in which capacity he probably
appeared himself, taking various parts in the
same piece, under various disguises, which
he was enabled to assume by means of linen
masks, the invention of which is ascribed to
him. The first representation of Thespis was
in B.C. 535. For further details see *Dict. of
Antiq.* art. *Tragoedia.*

THESPIUS (-i), son of Erechtheus, who,
according to some, founded the town of
Thespiae in Boeotia. His descendants are
called *Thespiadae.*

THESPROTI (-orum), a people of Epirus,
inhabiting the district called after them
THESPROTIA or THESPROTIS, which extended
along the coast from the Ambracian gulf N.-
wards as far as the river Thyamis, and
inland as far as the territory of the Molossi.
The Thesproti were the most ancient inhabitants of Epirus, and are said to have
derived their name from Thesprotus, the son
of Lycaon. They were Pelasgians, and in
their country was the oracle of Dodona, the
great centre of the Pelasgic worship. From
Thesprotia issued the Thessalians, who took
possession of the country afterwards called
Thessaly.

THESSALIA (-ae), the largest division of
Greece, was bounded on the N. by the Cambunian mountains, which separated it from
Macedonia; on the W. by Mt. Pindus, which
separated it from Epirus; on the E. by the
Aegaean sea; and on the S. by the Maliac
gulf and Mt. Oeta, which separated it from
Locris, Phocis, and Aetolia. Thessaly Proper
is a vast plain shut in on every side by mountain barriers, broken only at the N.E. corner
by the valley and defile of Tempe, which
separates Ossa from Olympus. This plain is
drained by the river Penēus and its affluents,
and is said to have been originally a vast
lake, the waters of which were afterwards
carried off through the vale of Tempe by
some sudden convulsion, which rent the rocks
of this valley asunder. In addition to the
plain already described there were 2 other
districts included under the general name of
Thessaly : one called Magnesia, being a long
narrow strip of country, extending along the
coast of the Aegaean sea from Tempe to the
Pagasaean gulf, and bounded on the W. by
Mts. Ossa and Olympus; and the other being
a long narrow vale at the extreme S. of the
country, lying between Mts. Othrys and Oeta,
and drained by the river Sperchēus. Thessaly Proper was divided in very early times
into 4 districts or tetrarchies — a division
which we still find subsisting in the Pelo-

ponnesian war. These districts were—(1) HESTIAEOTIS, the N.W. part of Thessaly, bounded on the N. by Macedonia, on the W. by Epirus, on the E. by Pelasgiotis, and on the S. by Thessaliotis : the Peneus may be said in general to have formed its S. limit.— (2) PELASGIOTIS, the E. part of the Thessalian plain, was bounded on the N. by Macedonia, on the W. by Hestiaeotis, on the E. by Magnesia, and on the S. by the Sinus Pagasaeus and Phthiotis.—(3) THESSALIOTIS, the S.W. part of the Thessalian plain, was bounded on the N. by Hestiaeotis, on the W. by Epirus, on the E. by Pelasgiotis, and on the S. by Dolopia and Phthiotis. — (4) PHTHIOTIS, the S.E. of Thessaly, bounded on the N. by Thessaliotis, on the W. by Dolopia, on the S. by the Sinus Maliacus, and on the E. by the Pagasaean gulf. It is in this district that Homer places Phthia and Hellas Proper, and the dominions of Achilles. Besides these there were 4 other districts, viz. :—(5) MAGNESIA. [MAGNESIA.]—(6) DOLOPIA, a small district bounded on the E. by Phthiotis, on the N. by Thessaliotis, on the W. by Athamania, and on the S. by Oetaea. The Dolopes were an ancient people, for they are not only mentioned by Homer as fighting before Troy, but they also sent deputies to the Amphictyonic assembly.—(7) OETAEA, a district in the upper valley of the Spercheus, lying between Mts. Othrys and Oeta, and bounded on the N. by Dolopia, on the S. by Phocis, and on the E. by Malis.—(8) MALIS. [MALIS.]—The Thessalians were a Thesprotian tribe, and under the guidance of leaders, who are said to have been descendants of Hercules, invaded the W. part of the country, afterwards called Thessaliotis, whence they subsequently spread over the other parts of the country. For some time after the conquest, Thessaly was governed by kings of the race of Hercules ; but the kingly power seems to have been abolished in early times, and the government in the separate cities became oligarchical, the power being chiefly in the hands of a few great families descended from the ancient kings. Of these two of the most powerful were the Aleuadae and the Scopadae, the former of whom ruled at Larissa, and the latter at Crañon or Crannon. At an early period the Thessalians were united into a confederate body. Each of the 4 districts into which the country was divided probably regulated its affairs by some kind of provincial council ; and in case of war, a chief magistrate was elected under the name of *Tagus* (Ταγός), whose commands were obeyed by all the 4 districts. This confederacy, however, was not of much practical benefit to the Thessalian people, and appears

to have been only used by the Thessalian nobles as a means of cementing and maintaining their power. The Thessalians never became of much importance in Grecian history. In B.C. 344 Philip completely subjected Thessaly to Macedonia, by placing at the head of the 4 divisions of the country governors devoted to his interests. The victory of T. Flamininus at Cynoscephalae, in 197, again gave the Thessalians a semblance of independence under the protection of the Romans.

THESSALONĪCA (-ae : *Saloniki*), more anciently THERMA, an ancient city in Macedonia, situated at the N.E. extremity of the Sinus Thermaicus. Under the name of Therma it was not a place of much importance. It was taken and occupied by the Athenians a short time before the commencement of the Peloponnesian war (B.C. 432), but was soon after restored by them to Perdiccas. It was made an important city by Cassander, who collected in this place the inhabitants of several adjacent towns (about B.C. 315), and who gave it the name of Thessalonica, in honour of his wife, the daughter of Philip, and sister of Alexander the Great. From this time it became a large and flourishing city. It was visited by the Apostle Paul about A.D. 53 ; and about 2 years afterwards he addressed from Corinth 2 epistles to his converts in the city.

THESTĪUS (-i), son of Ares (Mars), and Demonice or Androdice, and, according to others, son of Agenor, and grandson of Pleuron, the king of Aetolia. Hè was the father of Iphiclus, Euippus, Plexippus, Eurypylus, Leda, Althaea, and Hypermnestra. The patronymic THESTIADES is given to his grandson Meleager, as well as to his sons, and the female patronymic THESTIAS, to his daughter Althaea, the mother of Meleager.

THESTŌR (-ŏris), son of Idmon and Laothoë, and father of Calchas, Theoclymenus, Leucippe, and Theonoë. The patronymic THESTORIDES is frequently given to his son Calchas.

THĒTIS (-ĭdis), one of the daughters of Nereus and Doris, was a marine divinity, and dwelt like her sisters, the Nereids, in the depths of the sea, with her father, Nereus. She there received Dionysus (Bacchus) in his flight from Lycurgus, and the god, in his gratitude, presented her with a golden urn. When Hephaestus (Vulcan) was thrown down from heaven, he was likewise received by Thetis. She had been brought up by Hera (Juno), and when she reached the age of maturity, Zeus (Jupiter) and Hera gave her, against her will, in marriage to. Peleus. Poseidon (Neptune) and Zeus himself are said by some to have sued for her hand ;

but when Themis declared that the son of Thetis would be more illustrious than his father, both gods desisted from their suit. Others state that Thetis rejected the offers of Zeus, because she had been brought up by Hera; and the god, to revenge himself, decreed that she should marry a mortal. Chiron then informed his friend Peleus how he might gain possession of her, even if she should metamorphose herself; for Thetis, like Proteus, had the power of assuming any form she pleased. Peleus, instructed by Chiron, held the goddess fast till she assumed her proper form, and promised to marry him. The wedding was honoured with the presence of all the gods, except Eris or Discord, who was not invited, and who avenged herself by throwing among the assembled gods the apple, which was the source of so much misery. [PARIS.] By Peleus, Thetis became the mother of Achilles, on whom she bestowed the tenderest care and love. [ACHILLES.]

THIA (-ae), daughter of Urănus and Gē, one of the female Titans, became by Hyperīon the mother of Helios (Sol), Eos (Aurora), and Selēnē (Luna), that is, she was regarded as the deity from whom all light proceeded.

THIS, a great city of Upper Egypt, capital of the Thinites Nomos, and the seat of some of the ancient dynasties.

THISBĒ (-ēs), a beautiful Babylonian maiden, beloved by Pyramus. The lovers, living in adjoining houses, often secretly conversed with each other through an opening in the wall, as their parents would not sanction their marriage. Once they agreed upon a rendezvous at the tomb of Ninus. Thisbe arrived first, and while she was waiting for Pyramus, she perceived a lioness, which had just torn to pieces an ox, and took to flight. While running she lost her garment, which the lioness soiled with blood. In the meantime Pyramus arrived, and finding her garment covered with blood, he imagined that she had been murdered, and made away with himself under a mulberry tree, the fruit of which henceforth was as red as blood. Thisbe, who afterwards found the body of her lover, likewise killed herself.

THISBĒ (-ēs), afterwards THISBAE (-arum : Kakosia), a town of Boeotia, on the borders of Phocis, and between Mt. Helicon and the Corinthian gulf.

THŌANTĒA (-ae), a surname of the Taurian Artemis (Diana), derived from Thoas, king of Tauris.

THŌAS (-antis). (1) Son of Andraemon and Gorge, was king of Calydon and Pleuron, in Aetolia, and sailed with 40 ships against Troy.—(2) Son of Dionysus (Bacchus) and Ariadne, was king of Lemnos, and married to Myrina, by whom he became the father of Hypsipyle and Sicinus. When the Lemnian women killed all the men in the island, Hypsipyle saved and concealed her father, Thoas. The patronymic THOANTIAS is given to Hypsipyle, as the daughter of Thoas.—(3) Son of Borysthenes, and king of Tauris, into whose dominions Iphigenia was carried by Artemis, when she was to have been sacrificed.

THŌRĬCUS (-i : Theriko), one of the 12 ancient towns in Attica, and subsequently a demus belonging to the tribe Acamantis, was situated on the S.E. coast, a little above Sunium.

THRĀCĬA (-ae), was in earlier times the name of the vast space of country bounded on the N. by the Danube, on the S. by the Propontis and the Aegaean, on the E. by the Pontus Euxinus, and on the W. by the river Strymon, and the eastern-most of the Illyrian tribes. It was divided into 2 parts by Mt. Haemus (the Balkan), running from W. to E., and separating the plain of the lower Danube from the rivers which fall into the Aegaean. Two extensive mountain ranges branch off from the S. side of Mt. Haemus; one running S.E. towards Constantinople; and the other called Rhodope, E. of the preceding one, and also running in a S.E.-ly direction near the river Nestus. Between these two ranges there are many plains, which are drained by the Hebrus, the largest river in Thrace. At a later time the name Thrace was applied to a more limited extent of country. Thrace, in its widest extent, was peopled in the times of Herodotus and Thucydides by a vast number of different tribes: but their customs and character were marked by great uniformity. They were savage, cruel, and rapacious, delighting in blood, but brave and warlike. In earlier times, however, some of the Thracian tribes must have been distinguished by a higher degree of civilisation than prevailed among them at a later period. The earliest Greek poets, Orpheus, Linus, Musaeus, and others, are all represented as coming from Thrace. Eumolpus, likewise, who founded the Eleusinian mysteries at Attica, is said to have been a Thracian, and to have fought against Erechtheus, king of Athens. We find mention of the Thracians in other parts of southern Greece, and also in Asia. The principal Greek colonies along the coast, beginning at the Strymon and going E.-wards, were AMPHIPOLIS, ABDERA, DICAEA or Dieaepolis, MARONEA, STRYME, MESEMBRIA, and AENOS. The Thracian Chersonesus was probably colonised by the Greeks at an early period, but it did not contain any important Greek settlement till the migration of the first Miltiades to the country, during the reign of Pisistratus at Athens. [CHERSONESUS.] On the Propontis the 2 chief Greek settlements were those of PERINTHUS and SELYMBRIA ; and on the Thracian Bosporus was the important town of BYZANTIUM. There were only a few Greek settlements on the S.W. coast of the Euxine; the most important were those of APOLLONIA, ODESSUS, CALLATIS, TOMI, renowned as the place of Ovid's banishment, and ISTRIA, near the S. mouth of the Danube. The Thracians are said to have been conquered by Sesostris, king of Egypt, and subsequently to have been subdued by the Teucrians and Mysians; but the first really historical fact respecting them is their subjugation by Megabazus, the general of Darius. After the Persians had been driven out of Europe by the Greeks, the Thracians recovered their independence ; and at the beginning of the Peloponnesian war, almost all the Thracian tribes were united under the dominion of Sitalces, king of the Odrysae, whose kingdom extended from Abdera to the Euxine and the mouth of the Danube. In the 3rd year of the Peloponnesian war (B.C. 429), Sitalces, who had entered into an alliance with the Athenians, invaded Macedonia with a vast army of 150,000 men, but was compelled by the failure of provisions to return home, after remaining in Macedonia 30 days. Sitalces fell in battle against the Triballi in 424, and was succeeded by his nephew Seuthes, who during a long reign raised his kingdom to a height of power and prosperity which it had never previously attained. After the death of Seuthes, which appears to have happened a little before the close of the Peloponnesian war, we find his powerful kingdom split up into different parts. Philip, the father of Alexander the Great, reduced the greater part of Thrace ; and after the death of Alexander the country fell to the share of Lysimachus. It subsequently formed a part of the Macedonian dominions. We do not know at what period it became a Roman province.

THRASEA (-ae), P. PAETUS, a distinguished Roman senator, and Stoic philosopher, in the reign of Nero, was a native of Patavium and was probably born soon after the death of Augustus. He made the younger Cato his model, of whose life he wrote an account. He married Arria, the daughter of the heroic Arria, who showed her husband Caecina how to die ; and his wife was worthy of her mother and her husband. At a later period he gave his own daughter in marriage

to Helvidius Priscus, who trod closely in the footsteps of his father-in-law. After incurring the hatred of Nero by the independence of his character, and the freedom with which he expressed his opinions, he was condemned to death by the senate by command of the emperor, A.D. 66.

THRASYBULUS (-i). (1) Tyrant of Miletus, was a contemporary of Periander and Alyattes, the king of Lydia.—(2) A celebrated Athenian, son of Lycus. He was zealously attached to the Athenian democracy, and took an active part in overthrowing the oligarchical government of the 400 in B.C. 411. On the establishment of the Thirty Tyrants at Athens he was banished, but, by the assistance of the Thebans, succeeded in overthrowing the Ten, who had succeeded to the government, and eventually obtained possession of Athens, and restored the democracy, 403. In 390 he commanded the Athenian fleet in the Aegaean, and was slain by the inhabitants of Aspendus.—(3) Brother of Gelon and Hieron, tyrants of Syracuse, the latter of whom he succeeded in B.C. 467, but was soon afterwards expelled by the Syracusans, whom he had provoked by his rapacity and cruelty.

THRASYMACHUS (-i), a native of Chalcedon, was a sophist, and one of the earliest cultivators of the art of rhetoric. He was a contemporary of Gorgias.

THRASYMENUS. [TRASIMENUS.]

THRONIUM (-i : Romani), the chief town of the Locri Epicnemidii, on the river Boagrius, at a short distance from the sea, with a harbour upon the coast.

THUCYDIDES (-is). (1) An Athenian statesman, and leader of the aristocratic party in opposition to Pericles. He was ostracised in B.C. 444.—(2) The great Athenian historian, of the demus Halimus, was the son of Olorus or Orolus and Hegesipyle, and was born in B.C. 471. Thucydides is said to have been instructed in oratory by Antiphon, and in philosophy by Anaxagoras. Either by inheritance or by marriage he possessed gold mines in that part of Thrace which is opposite to the island of Thasos, where he was a person of the greatest influence. He commanded an Athenian squadron of 7 ships, at Thasus, 424, when Eucles, who commanded in Amphipolis, sent for his assistance against Brasidas ; but, failing in that enterprise, he became an exile, probably to avoid a severer punishment. He himself says that he lived 20 years in exile (v. 26), and as it commenced in the beginning of 423, he may have returned to Athens in the beginning of 403, about the time when Thrasybulus liberated Athens. Thucydides is said to have been

assassinated at Athens soon after his return ;
and at all events his death cannot be placed
later than 401. With regard to his work,
we may conclude that we have a more exact
history of a long eventful period by Thucydides than we have of any period in modern
history, equally long and equally eventful.

THŪLĒ (-ēs), an island in the N. part of
the German Ocean, regarded by the ancients
as the most N.-ly point in the whole earth,
and by some supposed to have been Iceland ;
by others, one of the Shetland group.

THŪRII (-orum), more rarely THŪRIUM
(-i : *Terra Nuova*), a Greek city in Lucania,
founded B.C. 443, near the site of the ancient
Sybaris, which had been destroyed more than
60 years before. [SYBARIS.] It was built by
the remains of the population of Sybaris,
assisted by colonists from all parts of Greece,
but especially from Athens. Among these
colonists were the historian Herodotus and
the orator Lysias. The new city, from which
the remains of the Sybarites were soon expelled, rapidly attained great power and prosperity, and became one of the most important
Greek towns in the S. of Italy.

THYĀMIS (-is : *Kalama*), a river in
Epirus, forming the boundary between Thesprotia and the district of Cestryna.

THYĀDES. [THYIA.]

THYĚSTĒS (-ae), son of Pelops and
Hippodamia, was the brother of Atreus and
the father of Aegisthus. [ATREUS and
AEGISTHUS.]

THYIA (-ae), a daughter of Castalius or
Cephisseus, became by Apollo the mother of
Delphus. She is said to have been the first
to have sacrificed to Dionysus (Bacchus),
and to have celebrated orgies in his honour.
From her the Attic women, who went yearly
to Mt. Parnassus to celebrate the Dionysiac
orgies with the Delphian Thyiades, received
themselves the name of THYIADES or THYADES.
This word, however, comes from Θύω, and
properly signifies the raging or frantic
women.

THYMBRA (-ae). (1) A city of the Troad,
N. of Ilium Vetus, with a celebrated temple
of Apollo, who derived from this place the
epithet Thymbraeus.—(2) A wooded district
in Phrygia, no doubt connected with
THYMBRIUM.

THYMBRĪUM (-i), a small town of Phrygia, 10 parasangs W. of Tyriaeum, with the
so-called fountain of Midas.

THYMBRĪUS (-i : *Thimbrek*), a river
of the Troad, falling into the Scamander.

THYMĚLĒ (-ēs), a celebrated mima or
female actress in the reign of Domitian, with
whom she was a great favourite.

THYMOETĒS (-ae), one of the elders of
Troy, whose son was killed by the order of
Priam, because a soothsayer had predicted
that Troy would be destroyed by a boy, born
on the day on which this child was born.

THYNI (-orum), a Thracian people, whose
original abodes were near Salmydessus, but
who afterwards passed over into BITHYNIA.

THYNIA (-ae). (1) The land of the Thyni
in Thrace.—(2) Another name for BITHYNIA.

THYŌNĒ (-ēs), the name of Semēlē, under
which Dionysus (Bacchus), fetched her from
Hades, and introduced her among the immortals. Hence Dionysus is also called
THYONEUS.

THYRĚA (-ae), the chief town in Cynuria, the district on the borders of Laconia and
Argolis, was situated upon a height on the bay
of the sea called after it SINUS THYREATES.
The territory of Thyrea was called THYREATIS.

THYSSĀGĚTAE (-arum), a people of Sarmatia Asiatica, on the E. shores of the Palus
Maeotis.

TIBĀRĒNI or TIBĀRI (-orum), a quiet
agricultural people on the N. coast of Pontus,
E. of the river Iris.

TIBĚRIAS. (1) A city of Galilee, on the
S.W. shore of the Lake of Tiberias, built by
Herod Antipas in honour of the emperor
Tiberius.—(2) Or GENNESARET, also the SEA
OF GALILEE, in the O.T. CHINNERETH (*Bahr
Tubariyeh*), the 2nd of the 3 lakes in Pales-
tine, formed by the course of the Jordan.
[JORDANES.] Its length is 11 or 12 geogra-
phical miles, and its breadth from 5 to 6. It
lies deep among fertile hills, has very clear
and sweet water, and is full of excellent fish.

TIBĚRINUS (-i), one of the mythical
kings of Alba, son of Capetus, and father of
Agrippa, is said to have been drowned in
crossing the river Albula which was hence
called Tiberis.

TĪBĚRIS also TĪBRIS, TYBRIS, THYBRIS
(-is or -idis), AMNIS TIBĚRINUS or simply
TIBĚRINUS (-i : *Tiber* or *Tevere*), the chief
river in central Italy, on which stood the
city of Rome. It is said to have been originally called *Albula*, and to have received the
name of *Tiberis* in consequence of Tiberinus,
king of Alba, having been drowned in it.
The Tiber rises from 2 springs of limpid
water in the Apennines, near Tifernum, and
flows in a S.W.-ly direction, separating
Etruria from Umbria, the land of the Sabines,
and Latium. After flowing about 110 miles
it receives the Nar (*Nera*), and from its confluence with this river its regular navigation
begins. Three miles above Rome, at the
distance of nearly 70 miles from the Nar, it
receives the Anio (*Teverone*), and from this
point becomes a river of considerable importance. Within the walls of Rome, the Tiber

is about 300 feet wide, and from 12 to 18 feet deep. After heavy rains the river in ancient times, as at the present day, frequently overflowed its banks, and did considerable mischief to the lower parts of the city. (Hor. *Carm.* i. 2.) The waters of the river are muddy and yellowish, whence it is frequently called by the Roman poets *flavus Tiberis*. The poets also give it the epithets of *Tyrrhenus*, because it flowed past Etruria during the whole of its course, and of *Lydius*, because the Etruscans are said to have been of Lydian origin.

TIBERIUS (-i), Emperor of Rome, A.D. 14—37. His full name was TIBERIUS CLAUDIUS NERO CAESAR. He was the son of T. Claudius Nero and of Livia, and was born on the 16th of November, B.C. 42, before his mother married Augustus. He was carefully educated and became well acquainted with Greek and Latin literature. In 20 he was sent by Augustus to restore Tigranes to the throne of Armenia. In 13, Tiberius was consul with P. Quintilius Varus. In 11, while his brother Drusus was fighting against the Germans, Tiberius conducted the war against the Dalmatians and Pannonians. In 6 he obtained the tribunitia potestas for 5 years, but during this year he retired with the emperor's permission to Rhodes, where he spent the next 7 years. His chief reason for this retirement was to get away from his wife Julia, the daughter of Augustus, whom he had been compelled by the emperor to marry. He returned to Rome A.D. 2. From the year of his adoption by Augustus, A.D. 4, to the death of that emperor, Tiberius was in command of the Roman armies, though he visited Rome several times. On the death of Augustus at Nola, on the 19th of August, A.D. 14, Tiberius, who was on his way to Illyricum, was immediately summoned home by his mother Livia, and took possession of the imperial power without any opposition. He began his reign by putting to death Postumus Agrippa, the surviving grandson of Augustus. When he felt himself sure in his place, he began to exercise his craft. He took from the popular assembly the election of the magistrates, and transferred it to the senate. Notwithstanding his suspicious nature, Tiberius gave his complete confidence to Sejanus, who for many years possessed the real government of the state. In A.D. 26 Tiberius left Rome, and withdrew into Campania. He never returned to the city. He left on the pretext of dedicating temples in Campania, but his real motives were his dislike to Rome, where he heard a great deal that was disagreeable to him, and his wish to indulge his sensual propensities in private.

In order to secure still greater retirement, he took up his residence (27) in the island of Capreae, at a short distance from the Campanian coast. In 31, Sejanus who aimed at nothing less than the imperial power, was put to an ignominious death, which was followed by the execution of his friends ; and for the remainder of the reign of Tiberius, Rome continued to be the scene of tragic occurrences. Tiberius died on the 16th of March 37, at the villa of Lucullus, at Misenum ; having been smothered by the order of Macro, the prefect of the praetorians.

TIBISCUS or TIBISSUS (-i), probably the same as the PARTHISCUS or PARTHISSUS (*Theiss*), a river of Dacia, forming the W. boundary of that country.

TIBULLUS (-i), ALBIUS, the Roman poet, was of equestrian family. His birth is placed by conjecture B.C. 54, and his death B.C. 18. Of his youth and education, absolutely nothing is known. The estate belonging to the equestrian ancestors of Tibullus was at Pedum, between Tibur and Praeneste, and the poet spent there the better portion of his short, but peaceful and happy life. His great patron was Messala, whom he accompanied in 31 into Aquitania, and the following year into the East. Tibullus, however, was taken ill, and obliged to remain in Corcyra, from whence he returned to Rome. So ceased the active life of Tibullus ; his life is now the chronicle of his poetry and of those tender passions which were the inspiration of his poetry. His elegies are addressed to two mistresses, under the probably fictitious names of Delia and Nemesis ; besides whom, as we learn from Horace (Od. i. 33), he celebrated another beauty named Glycera. The poetry of his contemporaries shows Tibullus as a gentle and singularly amiable man. To Horace especially he was an object of warm attachment, and his epistle to Tibullus gives the most full and pleasing view of his poetical retreat, and of his character.

TIBUR (-ūris : *Tivoli*), one of the most ancient towns of Latium, 16 miles N.E. of Rome, situated on the slope of a hill (hence called by Horace *supinum Tibur*), on the left bank of the Anio, which here forms a magnificent waterfall. It became subject to Rome with the other Latin cities on the final subjugation of Latium, in B.C. 338. Under the Romans Tibur continued to be a large and flourishing town, since the salubrity and beautiful scenery of the place led many of the most distinguished Roman nobles to build here magnificent villas. Of these the most splendid was the villa of the emperor Hadrian, in the extensive remains of which many valuable specimens of ancient art have been discovered. Here also the celebrated Zenobia lived after adorning the triumph of her conqueror Aurelian. Horace likewise had a country house in the neighbourhood of Tibur, which he preferred to all his other residences.

TĬCĪNUM (-i: *Pavia*), a town of the Laevi, or, according to others, of the Insubres, in Gallia Cisalpina, on the left bank of the Ticinus.

TĬCĪNUS (-i: *Tessino*), an important river in Gallia Cisalpina, rises in Mons Adula, and after flowing through Lacus Verbanus (*Lago Maggiore*), falls into the Po, near Ticinum. It was upon the bank of this river that Hannibal gained his first victory over the Romans by the defeat of P. Scipio, B.C. 218.

TIFĀTA, a mountain in Campania, E. of Capua.

TIFERNUM (-i). (1) TĬBERINUM (*Citta di Castello*), a town of Umbria, near the sources of the river Tiber, whence its surname, and upon the confines of Etruria.—(2) METAURENSE (*S. Angelo in Vado*), a town in Umbria, E. of the preceding, on the river Metaurus.—(3) A town in Samnium, on the river Tifernus.

TĬFERNUS (-i: *Biferno*), a river of Samnium, rising in the Apennines, and flowing through the country of the Frentani into the Adriatic.

TĬGELLĪNUS, SOPHONĬUS (-i), son of a native of Agrigentum, the minister of Nero's worst passions, and of all his favourites the most obnoxious to the Roman people. On the accession of Otho, Tigellinus was compelled to put an end to his own life.

TĬGELLĬUS HERMŌGĔNES. [HERMOGENES.]

TĬGRĀNES (-is), kings of Armenia. (I.) Reigned B.C. 96—56 or 55. In 83 he made himself master of the whole Syrian monarchy, from the Euphrates to the sea. In 69, having refused to deliver up his son-in-law, Mithridates, to the Romans, Lucullus invaded Armenia, defeated the mighty host which Tigranes led against him, and followed up his victory by the capture of Tigranocerta. Subsequently Tigranes recovered his dominions; but on the approach of Pompey, in 66, he hastened to make overtures of submission, and laid his tiara at his feet, together with a sum of 6000 talents. Pompey left him in possession of Armenia Proper with the title of king. Tigranes died in 56 or 55.—(II.) Son of Artavasdes, and grandson of the preceding.

TĬGRĂNOCERTA (-orum, i.e., in Armenian, the City of Tigranes : *Sert*, Ru.), the

later capital of Armenia, built by Tigranes on a height by the river Nicephorius, in the valley between Mt. Masius and Niphates.

TĬGRIS (-Ĭdis and -is), a great river of W. Asia, rises from several sources on the S. side of that part of the Taurus chain called Niphates, in Armenia, and flows S.E., first through the narrow valley between Mt. Masius and the prolongation of Mt. Niphates, and then through the great plain which is bounded on the E. by the last-named chain, till it falls into the head of the Persian Gulf, after receiving the Euphrates from the W.

TĬGURĪNI (-orum), a tribe of the Helvetii, who joined the Cimbri in invading the country of the Allobroges in Gaul, where they defeated the consul L. Cassius Longinus, B.C. 107. They formed in the time of Caesar the most important of the 4 cantons (*pagi*) into which the Helvetii were divided.

TILPHŪSĬUM (-i), a town in Boeotia, situated upon a mountain of the same name, S. of lake Copais, and between Coronea and Haliartus. It derived its name from the fountain Tilphūsa, which was sacred to Apollo, and where Tiresias is said to have been buried.

TĪMAEUS (-i). (1) The historian, was the son of Andromachus, tyrant of Tauromenium in Sicily, and was born about B.C. 352. He was banished from Sicily by Agathocles, and passed his exile at Athens, where he had lived 50 years when he wrote the 34th book of his history. He probably died about 256. The great work of Timaeus was a history of Sicily from the earliest times to 264.—(2) Of Locri, in Italy, a Pythagorean philosopher, is said to have been a teacher of Plato.

TĪMĀGĔNĔS (-is), a rhetorician and an historian, was a native of Alexandria, from which place he was carried as a prisoner to Rome, where he opened a school of rhetoric, and taught with great success.

TĪMANTHĒS (-is), a celebrated Greek painter at Sicyon, contemporary with Zeuxis and Parrhasius, about B.C. 400. The masterpiece of Timanthes was his celebrated picture of the sacrifice of Iphigenia, in which Agamemnon was painted with his face hidden in his mantle.

TĪMĀVUS (-i), a small river in the N. of Italy, forming the boundary between Istria and Venetia, and falling into the Sinus Tergestinus in the Adriatic, between Tergeste and Aquileia.

TĪMOCRĔON (-ontis), of Rhodes, a lyric poet, celebrated for the bitter and pugnacious spirit of his works, and especially for his attacks on Themistocles and Simonides.

TIMŎLĔON (-ŏnis), son of Timodemus or Timaenetus and Demariste, belonged to one of the noblest families at Corinth. His early life was stained by a dreadful deed of blood. We are told that so ardent was his love of liberty, that when his brother Timophanes endeavoured to make himself tyrant of their native city, Timoleon murdered him rather than allow him to destroy the liberty of the state. At the request of the Greek cities of Sicily, the Corinthians dispatched Timoleon with a small force in B.C. 344 to repel the Carthaginians from that island. He obtained possession of Syracuse, and then proceeded to expel the tyrants from the other Greek cities, of Sicily, but was interrupted in this undertaking by a formidable invasion of the Carthaginians, who landed at Lilybaeum in 339, with an immense army, under the command of Hasdrubal and Hamilcar, consisting of 70,000 foot and 10,000 horse. Timoleon could only induce 12,000 men to march with him against the Carthaginians; but with this small force he gained a brilliant victory over the Carthaginians on the river Crimissus (339). The Carthaginians were glad to conclude a treaty with Timoleon in 338, by which the river Halycus was fixed as the boundary of the Carthaginian and Greek dominions in Sicily. Subsequently he expelled almost all the tyrants from the Greek cities in Sicily, and established democracies instead. Timoleon, however, was in reality the ruler of Sicily, for all the states consulted him on every matter of importance; and the wisdom of his rule is attested by the flourishing condition of the island for several years even after his death. He died in 337.

TIMON (-ōnis). (1) The son of Timarchus of Phlius, a philosopher of the sect of the Sceptics, flourished in the reign of Ptolemy Philadelphus, about B.C. 279, and onwards. He taught at Chalcedon as a sophist with such success that he realised a fortune. He then removed to Athens, where he passed the remainder of his life, with the exception of a short residence at Thebes. He died at the age of almost 90.—(2) The Misanthrope, an Athenian, lived in the time of the Peloponnesian war. In consequence of the ingratitude he experienced, and the disappointments he suffered, from his early friends and companions, he secluded himself entirely from the world, admitting no one to his society except Alcibiades. He is said to have died in consequence of refusing to have a broken limb set.

TIMOTHEUS (-i). (1) A celebrated musician and poet of the later Athenian dithyramb, was a native of Miletus, and the son of Thersander. He was born B.C. 446, and died in 357, in the 90th year of his age. He was at first unfortunate in his professional efforts.

Even the Athenians, fond as they were of novelty, were offended at the bold innovations of Timotheus, and hissed off his performance. On this occasion it is said that Euripides encouraged Timotheus by the prediction that he would soon have the theatres at his feet. This prediction appears to have been accomplished in the vast popularity which Timotheus afterwards enjoyed. He delighted in the most artificial and intricate forms of musical expression, and he used instrumental music, without a vocal accompaniment, to a greater extent than any previous composer. Perhaps the most important of his innovations, as the means of introducing all the others, was his addition to the number of the strings of the *cithara*, which he seems to have increased to 11.—(2) A distinguished flute-player of Thebes, flourished under Alexander the Great.

TINGIS (-is : *Tangier*), a city of Mauretania, on the S. coast of the Fretum Gaditanum (*Straits of Gibraltar*), was a place of very great antiquity. It was made by Augustus a free city, and by Claudius a colony, and the capital of Mauretania Tingitana.

TINIA (-ae), a small river in Umbria, rising near Spoletium, and falling into the Tiber.

TIRESIAS (-ae), a Theban, was one of the most renowned soothsayers in all antiquity. He was blind from his seventh year, but lived to a very old age. The occasion of his blindness and of his prophetic power is variously related. In the war of the Seven against Thebes, he declared that Thebes should be victorious, if Menoeceus would sacrifice himself; and during the war of the Epigoni, when the Thebans had been defeated, he advised them to commence negotiations of peace, and to avail themselves of the opportunity that would thus be afforded them, to take to flight. He himself fled with them (or, according to others, he was carried to Delphi as a captive), but on his way he drank from the well of Tilphossa, and died. Even in the lower world Tiresias was believed to retain the powers of perception, while the souls of other mortals were mere shades, and there also he continued to use his golden staff. The blind seer Tiresias acts so prominent a part in the mythical history of Greece, that there is scarcely any event with which he is not connected in some way or other; and this introduction of the seer in so many occurrences separated by long intervals of time, was facilitated by the belief in his long life.

TIRIDATES or TERIDATES (-is). (1) The second king of Parthia. [ARSACES II.]—(2) King of Armenia, and brother of Vologeses I. (Arsaces XXIII.), king of Parthia. He was made king of Armenia by his brother, but was driven out of the kingdom by Corduio, the Roman general, and finally received the Armenian crown from Nero at Rome in A.D. 63.

TĪRO (ōnis), M. TULLĬUS, the freedman of Cicero, to whom he was an object of tender affection. He appears to have been a man of very amiable disposition, and highly cultivated intellect. He was not only the amanuensis of the orator, and his assistant in literary labour, but was himself an author of no mean reputation, and notices of several works from his pen have been preserved by ancient writers. After the death of Cicero, Tiro purchased a farm in the neighbourhood of Puteoli, where he lived until he reached his 100th year. It is usually believed that Tiro was the inventor of the art of short-hand writing (*Notae Tironianae*).

TĪRYNS (-this), an ancient town in Argolis, S.E. of Argos, and one of the most ancient in all Greece, is said to have been founded by Proetus, the brother of Acrisius, who built the massive walls of the city with the help of the Cyclopes. Proetus was succeeded by Perseus; and it was here that Hercules was brought up. Hence we find his mother, Alcmena, called *Tirynthia*, and the hero himself, *Tirynthius*. The remains of the city are some of the most interesting in all Greece, and are, with those of Mycenae, the most ancient specimens of what is called Cyclopean architecture.

TĪSĂMĒNUS (-i). (1) Son of Orestes and Hermione, was king of Argos, but was deprived of his kingdom when the Heraclidae invaded Peloponnesus. He was slain in a battle against the Heraclidae.

TĪSĬPHŎNĒ. [EUMENIDAE.]

TISSAPHERNĒS (-is), a famous Persian, who was appointed satrap of Lower Asia in B.C. 414. He espoused the cause of the Spartans in the Peloponnesian war, but he did not give them any effectual assistance, since his policy was to exhaust the strength of both parties by the continuance of the war. His plans, however, were thwarted by the arrival of Cyrus in Asia Minor in 407, who supplied the Lacedaemonians with cordial and effectual assistance. At the battle of Cunaxa, in 401, Tissaphernes was one of the 4 generals who commanded the army of Artaxerxes, and his troops were the only portion of the left wing that was not put to flight by the Greeks. When the 10,000 had begun their retreat, Tissaphernes promised to conduct them home in safety; but in the course of the march he treacherously arrested Clearchus and 4 of the other generals. As a reward for his services, he was invested by the king, in addition to his own satrapy, with all the authority which Cyrus had

enjoyed in western Asia. This led to a war with Sparta, in which Tissaphernes was unsuccessful; on which account, as well as by the influence of Parysatis, the mother of Cyrus, he was put to death in 395 by order of the king.

TITĀNES (-um). (1) The sons and daughters of Urănus (Heaven) and Gē (Earth), originally dwelt in heaven, whence they are called Uranidae. They were 12 in number, 6 sons and 6 daughters, namely, Oceanus, Coeus, Crius, Hyperion, Iapĕtus, Cronus, Thia, Rhea, Themis, Mnemosўne, Phoebe, and Tethys; but their names are different in other accounts. It is said that Uranus, the first ruler of the world, threw his sons, the Hecatoncheires, (Hundred-Handed),—Briareus, Cottys, Gyes,—and the Cyclōpes,—Arges, Sterŏpes, and Brontes—into Tartarus. Gaea, indignant at this, persuaded the Titans to rise against their father, and gave to Cronus (Saturn) an adamantine sickle. They did as their mother bade them, with the exception of Oceanus. Cronus, with his sickle, unmanned his father, and threw the part into the sea; from the drops of his blood there arose the Erinnyes,—Alecto Tisiphone, and Megaera. The Titans then deposed Uranus, liberated their brothers who had been cast into Tartarus, and raised Cronus to the throne. But Cronus hurled the Cyclopes back into Tartarus, and married his sister Rhea. It having been foretold to him by Gaea and Uranus, that he should be dethroned by one of his own children, he swallowed successively his children Hestia (Vesta), Demeter (Ceres), Hera (Juno), Pluto, and Poseidon (Neptune). Rhea, therefore, when she was pregnant with Zeus (Jupiter) went to Crete, and gave birth to the child in the Dictaean Cave, where he was brought up by the Curetes. When Zeus had grown up he availed himself of the assistance of Thetis, the daughter of Oceanus, who gave to Cronus a potion which caused him to bring up the stone and the children he had swallowed. United with his brothers and sisters, Zeus now began the contest against Cronus and the ruling Titans. This contest (usually called the Titanomachia) was carried on in Thessaly, Cronus and the Titans occupying Mt. Othrys, and the sons of Cronus Mt. Olympus. It lasted 10 years, till at length Gaea promised victory to Zeus if he would deliver the Cyclopes and Hecatoncheires from Tartarus. Zeus accordingly slew Campe, who guarded the Cyclopes, and the latter furnished him with thunder and lightning. The Titans then were overcome, and hurled down into a cavity below Tartarus, and the Hecatoncheires were set to guard them. It must be observed that the fight of the Titans is sometimes confounded by ancient writers with the fight of the Gigantes.—(2) The name Titans is also given to those divine or semi-divine beings who were descended from the Titans, such as Prometheus, Hecate, Latona, Pyrrha, and especially Helios (the Sun) and Selēnē (the Moon), as the children of Hyperion and Thia, and even to the descendants of Helios, such as Circe.

TĪTĂRĒSĬUS (-i : *Elassonitiko* or *Xeraghi*), a river of Thessaly, also called Europus, rising in Mt. Titarus, flowing through the country of the Perrhaebi, and falling into the Peneus, S.E. of Phalanna.

TĪTHŌNUS (-i), son of Laomedon and Strymo, and brother of Priam. By the prayers of Eos (Aurora), who loved him, he obtained from the gods immortality, but not eternal youth, in consequence of which he completely shrank together in his old age; whence a decrepit old man was proverbially called Tithonus. Eos changed him into a cicada, or grasshopper.

TITHORĔA. [Neon.]

TĪTHRAUSTES, a Persian, who succeeded Tissaphernes in his satrapy, and put him to death by order of Artaxerxes Mnemon, B.C. 395.

TĬTUS FLĀVĬUS SĂBĪNUS VESPĂSĬĀNUS (-i), Roman emperor, A.D. 79—81, commonly called by his praenomen TITUS, was the son of the emperor Vespasianus and his wife Flavia Domitilla. He was born on the 30th of December, A.D. 40. When a young man he served as tribunus militum in Britain and in Germany, with great credit. After having been quaestor, he had the command of a legion, and served under his father in the Jewish wars. Vespasian returned to Italy, after he had been proclaimed emperor on the 1st of July, A.D. 69; but Titus remained in Palestine to prosecute the siege of Jerusalem, during which he showed the talents of a general with the daring of a soldier. The siege of Jerusalem was concluded by the capture of the place, on the 8th of September, 70. Titus returned to Italy in the following year (71), and triumphed at Rome with his father. He also received the title of Caesar, and became the associate of Vespasian in the government. His conduct at this time gave no good promise, and his attachment to Berenice, the sister of Agrippa II., also made him unpopular, but he sent her away from Rome after he became emperor. Titus succeeded his father in 79, and his government proved an agreeable surprise to those who had anticipated a return of the times of Nero. During his whole reign Titus displayed a sincere desire for the happiness

of the people, and he did all that he could to relieve them in times of distress. He assumed the office of Pontifex Maximus after the death of his father, and with the purpose, as he declared, of keeping his hands free from blood, a resolution which he kept. The 1st year of his reign is memorable for the great eruption of Vesuvius, which desolated a large part of the adjacent country, and buried with lava and ashes the towns of Herculaneum and Pompeii. Titus endeavoured to repair the ravages of this great eruption; and he was also at great care and expense in repairing the damage done by a great fire at Rome, which lasted 3 days and nights. He completed the Colosseum, and erected the baths which were called by his name. He died on the 13th of September, A.D. 81, after a reign of 2 years and 2 months, and 20 days. He was in the 41st year of his age; and there were suspicions that he was poisoned by his brother, Domitian.

TĪTŸUS (-i), son of Gaea, or of Zeus (Jupiter) and Elara, the daughter of Orchomenus, was a giant in Euboea. Instigated by Hera (Juno), he attempted to offer violence to Artemis (Diana), when she passed through Panopaeus to Pytho, but he was killed by the arrows either of Artemis or Apollo; according to others, Zeus destroyed him with a flash of lightning. He was then cast into Tartarus, and there he lay outstretched on the ground, covering 9 acres, whilst 2 vultures or 2 snakes devoured his liver.

TLĒPŎLĔMUS (-i), son of Hercules by Astyoche, daughter of Phylas, or by Astydamia, daughter of Amyntor. He was king of Argos, but after slaying his uncle Licymnius, he settled in Rhodes. He joined the Greeks in the Trojan war with 9 ships, and was slain by Sarpedon.

TLŌS, a considerable city, in the interior of Lycia, about 2½ miles E. of the river Xanthus.

TMŌLUS (-i). (1) God of Mt. Tmolus in Lydia, is described as the husband of Pluto (or Omphale) and father of Tantalus, and is said to have decided the musical contest between Apollo and Pan—(2) (*Dagh*), a celebrated mountain of Asia Minor, running E. and W. through the centre of Lydia, and dividing the plain of the Hermus, on the N., from that of the Caÿster, on the S.

TOLĒNUS or TĚLŌNĬUS (-i : *Turano*), a river in the land of the Sabines, rising in the country of the Marsi and Aequi, and falling into the Velinus.

TŌLĒTUM (-i : *Toledo*), the capital of the Carpetani in Hispania Tarraconensis, situated on the river Tagus, which nearly encompasses the town.

TOLISTOBOGI, TOLISTOBOII. [GALA-TIA.]

TŎLŌSA (-ae : *Toulouse*), a town of Gallia Narbonensis, and the capital of the Tectosages, was situated on the Garumna, near the frontiers of Aquitania. It was subsequently made a Roman colony, and was surnamed *Palladia.* It was a large and wealthy town, and contained a celebrated temple, in which is said to have been preserved a great part of the booty taken by Brennus from the temple of Delphi. The town and temple were plundered by the consul Q. Servilius Caepio, in B.C. 106.

TŎLUMNĬUS (-i) LĂR (-tis), king of the Veientes, to whom Fidenae revolted in B.C. 438, and at whose instigation the inhabitants of Fidenae slew the 4 Roman ambassadors who had been sent to inquire into the reasons of their recent conduct. In the war which followed, Tolumnius was slain in single combat by Cornelius Cossus.

TŎMĬ (-ōrum) or TŎMIS (-is : *Tomiswar* or *Jegni Pangola*), a town of Thrace (subsequently Moesia), situated on the W. shore of the Euxine, and at a later time the capital of Scythia Minor. It is renowned as the place of Ovid's banishment.

TOMȲRIS (-is), a queen of the Massagetae, by whom Cyrus was slain in battle, B.C. 529.

TŎRŌNĔ (-ēs), a town of Macedonia, in the district of Chalcidice, and on the S.W. side of the peninsula Sithonia, from which the gulf between the peninsulas Sithonia and Pallene was called Sinus Toronaicus.

TORQUĀTUS (-i), the name of a patrician family of the Manlia Gens. (1) T. MANLIUS IMPERIOSUS TORQUATUS, the son of L. Manlius Capitolinus Imperiosus, dictator B.C. 363, was a favourite hero of Roman story. Manlius is said to have been dull of mind in his youth, and was brought up by his father in the closest retirement in the country. In 361 he served under the dictator T. Quintius Pennus in the war against the Gauls, and in this campaign earned immortal glory by slaying in single combat a gigantic Gaul. From the dead body of the barbarian he took the chain (*torques*) which had adorned him, and placed it around his own neck ; and from this circumstance he obtained the surname of Torquatus. He was dictator in 353, and again in 349. He was also three times consul, namely in 347, 344, and in 340. In the last of these years Torquatus and his colleague, P. Decius Mus, gained the great victory over the Latins at the foot of Vesuvius, which established for ever the supremacy of Rome over Latium. Shortly before the battle, when the two armies were encamped opposite to one another, the consuls published a pro-

clamation that no Roman should engage in single combat with a Latin on pain of death. This command was violated by young Manlius, the consul's son, who was in consequence executed by the lictor in presence of the assembled army. This severe sentence rendered Torquatus an object of detestation among the Roman youths as long as he lived ; and the recollection of his severity was preserved in after ages by the expression *Manliana imperia.* —(2) T. MANLIUS TORQUATUS, consul B.C. 235, when he conquered the Sardinians ; censor 231 ; and consul a 2nd time in 224. He possessed the hereditary sternness and severity of his family ; and we accordingly find him opposing in the senate the ransom of those Romans who had been taken prisoners at the fatal battle of Cannae. He was dictator in 210.—(3) L. MANLIUS TORQUATUS, consul B.C. 65 with L. Aurelius Cotta. He took an active part in suppressing the Catilinarian conspiracy in 63 ; and he also supported Cicero when he was banished in 58.— (4) L. MANLIUS TORQUATUS, son of No. 3, belonged to the aristocratical party, and accordingly opposed Caesar on the breaking out of the civil war in 49. He was praetor in that year, and was stationed at Alba with 6 cohorts. He subsequently joined Pompey in Greece, and in the following year (48) he had the command of Oricum intrusted to him, but was obliged to surrender both himself and the town to Caesar, who, however, dismissed Torquatus uninjured. After the battle of Pharsalia Torquatus went to Africa, and upon the defeat of his party in that country in 46 he attempted to escape to Spain along with Scipio and others, but was taken prisoner by P. Sittius at Hippo Regius and slain together with his companions. Torquatus was well acquainted with Greek literature, and is praised by Cicero, with whom, in early life, he was closely connected, as a man well trained in every kind of learning.— (5) A. MANLIUS TORQUATUS, praetor in 52, when he presided at the trial of Milo for bribery. On the breaking out of the civil war he espoused the side of Pompey, and after the defeat of the latter retired to Athens, where he was living in exile in 45. He was an intimate friend of Cicero.

TRĂBĔA (-ae), Q., a Roman comic dramatist who occupies the eighth place in the canon of Volcatius Sedigitus. The period when he flourished is uncertain, but he has been placed about B.C. 130.

TRĂCHIS or TRĂCHIN (-Inis). (1) Also called HERACLEA TRACHINIAE, or HERACLEA PHTHIOTIDIS, or simply HERACLEA, a town of Thessaly in the district Malis, celebrated as the residence of Hercules for a time.—(2) A *own of Phocis, on the frontiers of Boeotia, and on the slope of Mt. Helicon in the neighbourhood of Lebadea.

TRACHONĪTIS or TRACHON, the N. district of Palestine beyond the Jordan, lay between Anti-Libanus and the mountains of Arabia, and was bounded on the N. by the territory of Damascus, on the E. by Auranitis, on the S. by Ituraea, and on the W. by Gaulanitis.

TRĀJĀNUS (-i) M. ULPĬUS, Roman emperor A.D. 98—117, was born at Italica, near Seville, the 18th of September, 52. He was trained to arms, and served with distinction in the East and in Germany. He was consul in 91, and at the close of 97 he was adopted by the emperor Nerva, upon whose death in the following year Trajan succeeded to the empire with the title of *Imperator Caesar Nerva Trajanus Augustus.* His accession was hailed with joy, and he did not disappoint the expectations of the people. At the time of Nerva's death, Trajan was at Cologne, and did not return to Rome for some months, when he entered it on foot, accompanied by his wife Pompeia Plotina. Trajan was employed for the next 2 or 3 years in a war with Decebalus, king of the Daci, whom he defeated, and compelled to sue for peace. Trajan assumed the name of Dacicus, and entered Rome in triumph (103). In the following year (104) he commenced his 2nd Dacian war against Decebalus, who, it is said, had broken the treaty. Decebalus was completely defeated, and put an end to his life (106). After the death of Decebalus, Dacia was reduced to the form of a Roman province; strong forts were built in various places, and Roman colonies were planted. On his return Trajan had a triumph, and he exhibited games to the people for 123 days. About this time Arabia Petraea was subjected to the empire by A. Cornelius Palma, the governor of Syria; and an Indian embassy came to Rome. In 114 Trajan left Rome to make war on the Armenians and the Parthians. He spent the winter of 114 at Antioch, and in the following year he invaded the Parthian dominions. The most striking and brilliant success attended his arms. In the course of 2 campaigns (115—116), he conquered the greater part of the Parthian empire, and took the Parthian capital of Ctesiphon. In 116 he descended the Tigris, and entered the Erythraean Sea (the Persian Gulf). While he was thus engaged the Parthians rose against the Romans, but were again subdued by the generals of Trajan. On his return to Ctesiphon, Trajan determined to give the Parthians a king, and placed the diadem on the head of Parthamaspates. In 117 Trajan

fell ill, and as his complaint grew worse he set out for Italy. He lived to reach Selinus in Cilicia, afterwards called Trajanopolis, where he died in August, 117, after a reign of 19 years, 6 months, and 15 days. He left no children. Trajan was strong and laborious, of majestic appearance, and simple in his mode of life. Though not a man of letters, he had a sound judgment, and felt a sincere desire for the happiness of his people. Trajan constructed several great roads in the empire; he built libraries at Rome, one of which, called the *Ulpia Bibliotheca,* is often mentioned; and a theatre in the Campus Martius. His great work was the Forum Trajanum, in the centre of which was placed the column of Trajan.

TRĀJECTUM (-i: *Utrecht*), a town of the Batavi on the Rhine, called at a later time *Trajectus Rheni* or *Ad Rhenum.*

TRALLES (-ium), or TRALLIS (-is: *Ghiuzel-Hisar*, Ru., near *Aidin*), a flourishing commercial city of Asia Minor, reckoned sometimes to Ionia, and sometimes to Caria. It stood on a quadrangular height at the S. foot of Mt. Messogis (with a citadel on a higher point), on the banks of the little river Eudon, a N. tributary of the Maeander, from which the city was distant 80 stadia (8 geog. miles). Under the Seleucidae it bore the names of Seleucia and Antiochia.

TRĀPEZŪS (-untis). (1) (Near *Mavria*), a city of Arcadia, on the Alpheus.—(2) *Tarabosan, Trabezun,* or *Trebizond*), a colony of Sinope, at almost the extreme E. of the N. shore of Asia Minor. After Sinope lost her independence, Trapezus belonged, first to Armenia Minor, and afterwards to the kingdom of Pontus. Under the Romans, it was made a free city, probably by Pompey, and, by Trajan, the capital of Pontus Cappadocius. Hadrian constructed a new harbour; and the city became a place of first-rate commercial importance. It was taken by the Goths in the reign of Valerian; but it had recovered, and was in a flourishing state in the time of Justinian, who repaired its fortifications. In the middle ages it was for some time the seat of a fragment of the Greek empire called the empire of Trebizond. It is now the second commercial port of the Black Sea, ranking next after Odessa.

TRĀSĬMĒNUS LĂCUS (i: *Lago di Perugia*), sometimes, but not correctly written, THRASYMĒNUS, a lake in Etruria, between Clusium and Perusia, memorable for the victory gained by Hannibal over the Romans under Flaminius, B.C. 217.

TREBA (-ae: *Trevi*), a town in Latium, near the sources of the Anio, N:E. of Anagnia.

TRĒBĀTĬUS TESTA. [TESTA.]

TRĔBELLĬUS (-i) POLLĬO (-ōnis), one of the 6 *Scriptores Historiae Augustae*, flourished under Constantine.

TRĔBĬA (-ae : *Trebbia*), a small river in Gallia Cisalpina, falling into the Po near Placentia. It is memorable for the victory which Hannibal gained over the Romans, B.C. 218.

TRĔBŌNĬUS (-i), C., played rather a prominent part in the last days of the republic. He commenced public life as a supporter of the aristocratical party, but changed sides soon afterwards, and in his tribunate of the plebs (55) he proposed the *Lex Trebonia*, by which Pompey obtained the 2 Spains, Crassus Syria, and Caesar the Gauls and Illyricum for another period of 5 years. For this service he was rewarded by being appointed one of Caesar's legates in Gaul. In 48, Trebonius was city-praetor, and towards the end of 47 succeeded Q. Cassius Longinus as pro-praetor in the government of Farther Spain. Caesar raised him to the consulship in October, 45, and promised him the province of Asia. In return for all these honours and favours, Trebonius was one of the prime movers in the conspiracy to assassinate Caesar, and after the murder of his patron (44) he went as proconsul to the province of Asia. In the following year (43), Dolabella surprised the town of Smyrna, where Trebonius was residing, and slew him in his bed.

TRĔBŪLA (-ae). (1) (*Tregghia*), a town in Samnium situated in the S.E. part of the mountains of *Cajazzo*.—(2) MUTUSCA, a town of the Sabines of uncertain site.—(3) SUFFENA, also a town of the Sabines, and of uncertain site.

TRĔRUS (-i : *Sacco*), a river in Latium, and a tributary of the Liris.

TRES TĂBERNAE (-ārum). (1) A station on the Via Appia in Latium, between Aricia and Forum Appii. It is mentioned in the account of St. Paul's journey to Rome.— (2) (*Borghetto*), a station in Gallia Cisalpina, on the road from Placentia to Mediolanum.

TRĔVĪRI or TRĔVĔRI (-ōrum), a powerful people in Gallia Belgica, who were faithful allies of the Romans, and whose cavalry was the best in all Gaul. The river Mosella flowed through their territory, which extended W.-ward from the Rhine as far as the Remi. Their chief town was made a Roman colony by Augustus, and was called AUGUSTA TREVIRORUM (*Trier* or *Treves*). It stood on the right bank of the Mosella, and became under the later empire one of the most flourishing Roman cities N. of the Alps. It was the capital of Belgica Prima ; and after the division of the Roman world by Diocletian (A.D. 292) into 4 districts, it became the residence of the Caesar who had the government of Britain, Gaul, and Spain. The modern city still contains many interesting Roman remains.

TRIBALLI (-ōrum), a powerful people in Thrace, a branch of the Getae dwelling along the Danube, who were defeated by Alexander the Great, B.C. 335.

TRIBOCCI (-ōrum), a German people, settled in Gallia Belgica, between Mt. Vogesus and the Rhine, in the neighbourhood of *Strasburg*.

TRICASSES, TRICASĬI, or TRICASSĪNI (-ōrum), a people in Gallia Lugdunensis, E. of the Senones, whose chief town was Augustobona, afterwards Tricassae (*Troyes*).

TRĪCASTĬNI (-ōrum), a people in Gallia Narbonensis, inhabiting a narrow slip of country between the Drome and the Isère. Their chief town was Augusta Tricastinorum, or simply Augusta (*Aouste*).

TRICCA (-ae), subsequently TRICĂLA (*Trikkala*), an ancient town of Thessaly in the district Hestiaeotis, situated on the Lethaeus, N. of the Peneus. Homer represents it as governed by the sons of Aesculapius ; and it contained in later times a celebrated temple of this god.

TRĪCŎRĬI (-ōrum), a Ligurian people in Gallia Narbonensis, a branch of the Sallyi, in the neighbourhood of Massilia and Aquae Sextiae.

TRIDENTUM (-i : *Trent*, in Italian *Trento*), the capital of the TRIDENTINI, and the chief town of Rhaetia, situated on the river Athesis (*Adige*), and on the pass of the Alps leading to Verona.

TRĪNACRĬA. [SICILIA.]

TRINOBANTES (-um), one of the most powerful people of Britain, inhabiting the modern Essex.

TRĬŎPAS (-ae), son of Poseidon (Neptune) and Canace, a daughter of Aeolus, or of Helios (the Sun) and Rhodos, and the father of Iphimedia and Erysichthon. Hence, his son Erysichthon is called *Triopēïus*, and his grand-daughter Mestra or Metra, the daughter of Erysichthon, *Triopēïs*.

TRĬŎPĬUM (-i: *C. Krio*), the promontory which terminates the peninsula of Cnidus, forming the S.W. headland of Caria and of Asia Minor.

TRĬPHŸLIA (-ae), the S. portion of Elis, lying between the Alpheus and the Neda, is said to have derived its name from the 3 different tribes by which it was peopled. Its chief town was PYLOS.

TRĬPŎLIS (-is), properly the name of a confederacy composed of 3 cities, or a district containing 3 cities, but it is also applied to single cities which had some such relation

to others as to make the name appropriate.
(1) (*Kash Yeniji*), a city on the Maeander,
12 miles W. of Hierapolis, on the borders of
Phrygia, Caria, and Lydia, to each of which
it is assigned by different authorities.—
(2) (*Tireboli*), a fortress on the coast of Pontus,
on a river of the same name (*Tireboli Su*),
90 stadia E. of the Prom. Zephyrium (*C.
Zefreh*).—(3) (*Tripoli, Tarabulus*), on the
coast of Phoenicia, consisted of 3 distinct
cities, 1 stadium (600 feet) apart, each having
its own walls, but all united in a common
constitution, having one place of assembly,
and forming in reality one city. They were
colonies of Tyre, Sidon, and Aradus respectively. It is now a city of about 15,000
inhabitants, and the capital of one of the
pachalicks of Syria, that of *Tripoli.*—(4) The
district on the N. coast of Africa, between
the 2 Syrtes, comprising the 3 cities of
Sabrata (or Abrotonum), Oea, and Leptis
Magna, and also called Tripolitana Regio.
[SYRTICA.]

TRIPTŎLĔMUS (-i), son of Celeus, king
of Eleusis, and Metanira or Polymnia.
Others describe him as son of king Eleusis
by Cothonea, or of Oceanus and Gaea, or of
Trochilus by an Eleusinian woman. Triptolemus was the favourite of Demeter (Ceres),
and the inventor of the plough and agriculture, and of civilisation, which is the result
of it. He was the great hero in the Eleusinian
mysteries. According to the common legend
he hospitably received Demeter at Eleusis,
when she was wandering in search of her
daughter. The goddess, in return, wished to
make his son Demophon immortal, and placed
him in the fire in order to destroy his mortal
parts; but Metanira screamed out at the
sight, and the child was consumed by the
flames. As a compensation for this bereave-
ment, the goddess gave to Triptolemus a
chariot with winged dragons and seeds of
wheat. In this chariot Triptolemus rode
over the earth, making man acquainted with
the blessings of agriculture. On his return
to Attica, Celeus endeavoured to kill him,
but by the command of Demeter he was
obliged to give up his country to Triptolemus,
who now established the worship of Demeter,
and instituted the Thesmophoria. Triptolemus is represented in works of art as a
youthful hero, sometimes with the petasus,
on a chariot drawn by dragons, and holding
in his hand a sceptre and corn ears.

TRITAEA (-ae). (1) A town of Phocis,
N.W. of Cleonae, on the left bank of the
Cephissus and on the frontiers of Locris.—
(2) One of the 12 cities of Achaia, 120 stadia
E. of Pharae and near the frontiers of Arcadia.

TRĪTŌ (-ūs), or TRĪTŎGĔNĬA (-ae), a

surname of Athena (Minerva), derived by
some from lake Tritonis in Libya, by others
from the stream Triton near Alalcomenae in
Boeotia; and by the grammarians from τριτώ,
which, in the dialect of the Athamanians, is
said to signify "head."

TRĪTON (-ōnis), son of Poseidon (Neptune)
and Amphitrite (or Celaeno), who dwelt
with his father and mother in a golden
palace in the bottom of the sea, or, according
to Homer, at Aegae. Later writers describe
him as riding over the sea on sea horses or

Triton. (From a Roman Lamp.)

other monsters. Sometimes we find mention of Tritons in the plural. Their appearance is variously described; though they are
always conceived as having the human figure
in the upper part of their bodies, and that of
a fish in the lower part. The chief charac-
teristic of Tritons in poetry as well as in
works of art is a trumpet made out of a shell
(*concha*), which the Tritons blow at the
command of Poseidon, to soothe the restless
waves of the sea.

TRĪTON (-ōnis) FL., TRĪTŌNIS (-is), or
TRĪTŌNĪTIS PĂLUS, a river and lake on
the Mediterranean coast of Libya, which are
mentioned in several old Greek legends, especially in the mythology of Athena (Minerva),
whom one account represented as born on the
lake Tritonis. The lake is undoubtedly the
great salt lake, in the S. of *Tunis*, called *El-
Sibkah*. Some of the ancient writers gave
altogether a different locality to the legend,
and identify the Triton with the river usually
called LATHON, in Cyrenaïca.

TRĪVĬCUM (-i : *Trivico*), a small town in
Samnium, situated among the mountains
separating Samnium from Apulia.

TRŎAS (-ădis: *Chan*), the territory of

Ilium or Troy, formed the N.W. part of Mysia. It was bounded on the W. by the Aegaean sea, from Pr. Lectum to Pr. Sigeum, at the entrance of the Hellespont; on the N.W. by the Hellespont, as far as the river Rhodius, below Abydus; on the N.E. and E. by the mountains which border the valley of the Rhodius, and on the S. by the N. coast of the Gulf of Adramyttium along the S. foot of Ida; but on the N.E. and E. the boundary is sometimes extended so far as to include the whole coast of the Hellespont and part of the Propontis, and the country as far as the river Granicus, thus embracing the district of Dardania, and somewhat more. The Troad is for the most part mountainous, being intersected by Mt. IDA and its branches : the largest plain is that in which Troy stood. The chief rivers were the SATNOIS on the S., the RHODIUS on the N., and the SCAMANDER and SIMOIS in the centre. These 2 rivers, so renowned in the legends of the Trojan War, flow from 2 different points in the chain of Mt. Ida, and unite in the plain of Troy, through which the united stream flows N.W. and falls into the Hellespont E. of the promontory of Sigeum. The precise locality of the city of Troy, or, according to its genuine Greek name, Ilium, is the subject of much dispute. The most probable opinion seems to be that which places the original city in the upper part of the plain, on a moderate elevation at the foot of Mt. Ida, and its citadel (called Pergăma, Πέργαμα), on a loftier height, almost separated from the city by a ravine, and nearly surrounded by the Scamander. This city seems never to have been restored after its destruction by the Greeks. The Aeolian colonists subsequently built a new city, on the site, as they doubtless believed, of the old one, but really much lower down the plain; and this city is the TROJA, or ILIUM VETUS, of most of the ancient writers. After the time of Alexander this city declined, and a new one was built still farther down the plain, below the confluence of the Simoïs and Scamander, and near the Hellespont, and this was called ILIUM NOVUM. The mythical account of the origin of the kingdom of Troy is briefly as follows :—Teucer, the first king in the Troad, had a daughter, who married Dardanus. [DARDANIA]. From this Teucer the people were called Teucri. Dardanus had 2 sons, Ilus and Erichthonius; and the latter was the father of Tros, from whom the country and people derived the names of Troas and Troës. Tros was the father of Ilus, who founded the city, which was called after him ILIUM, and also, after his father, TROJA. The next king was LAOMEDON, and after him Priam. [PRIAMUS.] In his reign the city

was taken and destroyed by the confederated Greeks, after a 10 years' siege. The chronologers assigned different dates for the capture of Troy; the calculation most generally accepted placed it in B.C. 1184.

TROCMI or -II. [GALATIA.]

TROËS. [TROAS.]

TROEZEN (-ēnis: *Dhamala*), the capital of TROEZENIA, a district in the S.E. of Argolis, on the Saronic gulf, and opposite the island of Aegina. The town was situated at some little distance from the coast, on which it possessed a harbour called POGON, opposite the island of Calauria. Troezen was a very ancient city, and is said to have been originally called Poseidonia, on account of its worship of Poseidon (Neptune). It received the name of Troezen from Troezen, one of the sons of Pelops; and it is celebrated in mythology as the place where Pittheus, the maternal grandfather of Theseus, lived, and where Theseus himself was born. In the historical period it was a city of some importance.

TROGILIAE (-ārum), 3 small islands, lying off the promontory of Trogilium.

TROGLODYTAE (-ārum : i. e. *dwellers in caves*), the name applied by the Greek geographers to various uncivilised people, who had no abodes but caves, especially to the inhabitants of the W. coast of the Red Sea, along the shores of Upper Egypt and Aethiopia. There were also Troglodytae in Moesia, on the banks of the Danube.

TROGUS, POMPEIUS. [JUSTINUS.]

TROILIUM. [TROSSULUM.]

TROÏLUS (-i), son of Priam and Hecuba, or according to others, son of Apollo. He fell by the hands of Achilles.

TROJA (-ae), the name of the city of Troy or Ilium, also applied to the country. [TROAS.]

TROPHONIUS (-i), son of Erginus, king of Orchomenus, and brother of Agamedes. He and his brother built the temple at Delphi, and the treasury of king Hyrieus in Boeotia. [AGAMEDES.] Trophonius after his death was worshipped as a hero, and had a celebrated oracle in a cave near Lebadea, in Boeotia. (See *Dict. of Antiq.*, art. *Oraculum.*)

TROS (-ōis), son of Erichthonius and Astyŏche, and grandson of Dardănus. He was married to Callirrhoë, by whom he became the father of Ilus, Assarăcus, and Ganymēdes, and was king of Phrygia. The country and people of Troy derived their name from him. He gave up his son Ganymedes to Zeus (Jupiter), for a present of horses. [GANYMEDES.]

TROSSULUM (-i: *Trosso*), a town in Etruria, 9 miles from Volsinii, which is said to have been taken by some Roman equites, without the aid of foot-soldiers; whence the Roman equites obtained the name of Trossuli.

TRŬENTUM (-i), a town of Picenum on the river Truentus or Truentinus (*Tronto*).

TRUTULENSIS PORTUS, a harbour on the N.E. coast of Britain, near the aestuary Taus (Tay).

TŪBĔRO (-ōnis), AELĬUS. (1) Q., son-in-law of L. Aemilius Paulus, served under the latter in his war against Perseus, king of Macedonia.—(2) Q., son of the preceding, was a pupil of Panaetius, and is called the Stoic. He had a reputation for talent and legal knowledge. He was praetor in 123, and consul suffectus in 118. He was an opponent of Tib. Gracchus, as well as of C. Gracchus, and delivered some speeches against the latter, 123. Tubero is one of the speakers in Cicero's dialogue *De Republica*.—(3) L., an intimate friend of Cicero. On the breaking out of the civil war, Tubero espoused the party of Pompey, under whom he served in Greece. He was afterwards pardoned by Caesar, and returned with his son Quintus to Rome. Tubero cultivated literature and philosophy.—(4) Q., son of the preceding, obtained considerable reputation as a jurist, and is often cited in the Digest.

TUCCA (-ae), PLŌTĬUS, a friend of Horace and Virgil, to whom and Varius the latter bequeathed his unfinished works.

TŬDER (-ĕris : *Todi*), an ancient town of Umbria, situated on a hill near the Tiber, and on the road from Mevania to Rome.

TULLĬA (-ae), the name of the 2 daughters of Servius Tullius, the 6th king of Rome.

TULLĬA (-ae), frequently called by the diminutive TULLĬŎLA, was the daughter of M. Cicero and Terentia, and was probably born B.C. 79 or 78. She was betrothed in 67 to C. Calpurnius Piso Frugi, whom she married in 63, during the consulship of her father. During Cicero's banishment Tullia lost her first husband. She was married again in 56 to Furius Crassipes, a young man of rank and large property ; but she did not live with him long, though the time and the reason of her divorce are alike unknown. In 50 she was married to her 3rd husband, P. Cornelius Dolabella, who was a thorough profligate. The marriage took place during Cicero's absence in Cilicia, and, as might have been anticipated, was not a happy one. In 46 a divorce took place by mutual consent. At the beginning of 45 Tullia was delivered of a son, her 2nd child by Dolabella. As soon as she was sufficiently recovered to bear the fatigues of a journey, she accompanied her father to Tusculum, but she died there in February.

TULLĬĀNUM (-i), a dismal subterranean dungeon, added by Servius Tullius to the Carcer Mamertinus. It now serves as a chapel to a small church built on the spot, called S. Pietro in Carcere.

TULLĬUS CĬCĔRO. [CICERO.]

TULLĬUS, SERVĬUS (-i), the 6th king of Rome. The account of the early life and death of Servius Tullius is full of marvels, and cannot be regarded as possessing any title to a real historical narrative. His mother, Ocrisia, was one of the captives taken at Corniculum, and became a female slave of Tanaquil, the wife of Tarquinius Priscus. He was born in the king's palace, and notwithstanding his servile origin was brought up as the king's son, since Tanaquil by her powers of divination had foreseen the greatness of the child ; and Tarquinius placed such confidence in him, that he gave him his daughter in marriage, and entrusted him with the exercise of the government. The sons of Ancus Marcius, fearing lest he should deprive them of the throne which they claimed as their inheritance, procured the assassination of Tarquinius [TARQUINIUS] ; but Tanaquil, by a stratagem, preserved the royal power for Servius. Three important events are assigned to his reign by universal tradition. First, he gave a new constitution to the Roman state. The two main objects of this constitution were to give the plebs political independence, and to assign to property that influence in the state which had previously belonged to birth exclusively. [For details see *Dict. of Antiq.* art. *Comitia*.] Secondly, he extended the pomoerium, or hallowed boundary of the city, and completed the city by incorporating with it the Quirinal, Viminal, and Esquiline hills. [ROMA.] Thirdly, he established an important alliance with the Latins, by which Rome and the cities of Latium became the members of one great league. By his new constitution Servius incurred the hostility of the patricians, who conspired with L. Tarquinius to deprive him of his life and of his throne. According to the legend, Tullia, one of the daughters of Servius, an ambitious woman, who had paved the way for her marriage with L. Tarquinius by the murder of her former husband, Aruns, and of her sister, the former wife of Tarquinius, was one of the prime movers in this conspiracy. At her instigation Tarquinius entered the forum arrayed in the kingly robes, seated himself in the royal chair in the senate-house, and ordered the senators to be summoned to him as their king. At the first news of the commotion, Servius hastened to the senate-house, and, standing at the doorway, ordered Tarquinius to come down from the throne. Tarquinius sprang forwards, seized the old man, and flung him down the stone steps. Covered with blood, the king was hastening home; but, before he reached it, he was overtaken by the servants of Tarquinius, and murdered. Tullia drove to the senate-house, and greeted her husband as king; but her transports of joy struck even him with horror. He bade her go home; and as she was returning, her charioteer pulled up, and pointed out the corpse of her father lying in his blood across the road. She commanded him to drive on: the blood of her father spirted over the carriage and on her dress; and from that day forward the street bore the name of the *Vicus Sceleratus*, or Wicked Street. Servius had reigned 44 years. His memory was long cherished by the plebeians.

TULLĪUS TĪRO. [TĪRO.]

TULLUS HOSTĪLĪUS (-i), 3rd king of Rome, is said to have been the grandson of Hostus Hostilius, who fell in battle against the Sabines in the reign of Romulus. His legend ran as follows: Tullus Hostilius departed from the peaceful ways of Numa, and aspired to the martial renown of Romulus. He made Alba acknowledge Rome's supremacy in the war wherein the 3 Roman brothers, the Horatii, fought with the 3 Alban brothers, the Curiatii, at the Fossa Cluilia. Next he warred with Fidenae and with Veii, and being straitly pressed by their joint hosts, he vowed temples to Pallor and Pavor—Paleness and Panic. And after the fight was won, he tore asunder with chariots Mettius Fufetius, the king or dictator of Alba, because he had desired to betray Rome; and he utterly destroyed Alba, sparing only the temples of the gods, and bringing the Alban people to Rome, where he gave them the Caelian hill to dwell on. Then he turned himself to war with the Sabines; and being again straitened in fight in a wood called the Wicked Wood, he vowed a yearly festival to Saturn and Ops, and to double the number of the Salii, or priests of Mamers. And when, by their help, he had vanquished the Sabines, he performed his vow, and its records were the feasts Saturnalia and Opalia. In his old age Tullus grew weary of warring; and when a pestilence struck him and his people, and a shower of burning stones fell from heaven on Mt. Alba, and a voice as of the Alban gods came forth from the solitary temple of Jupiter on its summit, he remembered the peaceful and happy days of Numa, and sought to win the favour of the gods, as Numa had done, by prayer and divination. But the gods heeded neither his prayers nor his charms, and when he would inquire of Jupiter Elicius, Jupiter was wroth, and smote Tullus and his whole house with fire. Perhaps the only historical fact embodied in the legend of Tullus is the ruin of Alba.

TŪNES or TŪNIS (-is: *Tunis*), a strongly fortified city of N. Africa, stood at the bottom of the Carthaginian gulf, 10 miles S.W. of Carthage, at the mouth of the little river Catada.

TUNGRI (-ōrum), a German people, who crossed the Rhine, and settled in Gaul in the country formerly occupied by the Aduatici and the Eburones. Their chief town was called TUNGRI or ADUACA TONGRORUM (*Tongern*).

TURDĒTĀNI (-ōrum), the most numerous people in Hispania Baetica, dwelt in the S. of the province, on both banks of the Baetis, as far as Lusitania.

TURDŬLI (-ōrum), a people in Hispania Baetica, situated to the E. and S. of the Turdetani, with whom they were closely connected.

TŪRĬA (-ae), or TŪRĬUM (-i: *Guadalaviar*), a river on the E. coast of Spain, flowing into the sea at Valentia, memorable for the battle fought on its banks between Pompey and Sertorius.

TURNUS (-i). (1) Son of Daunus and Venilia, and king of the Rutuli at the time of the arrival of Aeneas, in Italy. He was a brother of Juturna, and related to Amata, the wife of king Latinus; and he fought against Aeneas, because Latinus had given to the Trojan hero his daughter Lavinia, who had been previously promised to Turnus. He appears in the *Aeneid* as a brave warrior; but in the end he fell by the hand of Aeneas. —(2) A Roman satiric poet, was a native of Aurunca, and lived under Vespasian and Domitian.

TURNUS HERDŌNĬUS. [HERDONIUS.]

TŪRŌNES (-um), TŪRŌNI or TŪRŌNII (-ōrum), a people in the interior of Gallia Lugdunensis, between the Aulerci, Andes, and Pictones. Their chief town was CAESARODUNUM, subsequently TURONI (*Tours*), on the Liger (*Loire*).

TURRIS HANNĪBĂLIS (-is: *Bourj Salektah*, Ru.), a castle on the coast of Byzacena, between Thapsus and Acholla, belonging to Hannibal, who embarked here when he fled to Antiochus the Great.

TURRIS STRĂTŌNIS. [CAESAREA, No. 3.]

TUSCI, TUSCĬA. [ETRURIA.]

TUSCŬLUM (-i: nr. *Frascati*, Ru.), an ancient town of Latium, situated about 10 miles S.E. of Rome, on a lofty summit of the mountains, which are called after the town, TUSCULANI MONTES. It is said to have been founded by Telegonus, the son of Ulysses; and it was always one of the most important of the Latin towns. Cato the Censor was a native of Tusculum. Its proximity to Rome, its salubrity, and the beauty of its situation, made it a favourite residence of the Roman nobles during the summer. Cicero, among others, had a favourite villa at this place, which he frequently mentions, under the name of TUSCULANUM.

TŪTĬCĂNUS (-i), a Roman poet, and a friend of Ovid.

TŸĂNA (-ōrum: *Kiz Hisar*, Ru.), a city of Asia Minor, stood in the S. of Cappadocia, at the N. foot of Mt. Taurus. Tyana was the native place of Apollonius, the supposed worker of miracles. The S. district of Cappadocia, in which the city stood, was called Tyanītis.

TŸCHĒ. (1) FORTUNA.—(2) SYRACUSAE.

TŸDEUS (-ĕŏs, -ĕi, or -eī), son of Oeneus, king of Calydon, and Periboea. He was obliged to leave Calydon in consequence of some murder which he had committed, but which is differently described by different authors. He fled to Adrastus at Argos, who purified him from the murder, and gave him his daughter Deïpyle in marriage, by whom he became the father of Diomedes, who is hence frequently called TYDIDES. He accompanied Adrastus in the expedition against Thebes, where he was wounded by Melanippus, who, however, was slain by him. When Tydeus lay on the ground wounded, Athena (Minerva) appeared to him with a remedy which she had received from Zeus (Jupiter), and which was to make him immortal. This, however, was prevented by a stratagem of Amphiaraus, who hated Tydeus, for he cut off the head of Melanippus, and brought it to Tydeus, who divided it and ate the brain, or devoured some of the flesh. Athena, seeing this, shuddered, and left Tydeus to his fate, who consequently died, and was buried by Macon.

TYMPHAEI (-ōrum), a people of Epirus, on the borders of Thessaly, so called from MT. TYMPHE. Their country was called TYMPHAEA.

TYMPHRESTUS (-i: *Elladha*), a mountain in Thessaly, in the country of the Dryopes, in which the river Sperchēus rises.

TYNDĂRĔUS (-ĕi: not TYNDARUS), was son of Perieres and Gorgophone, or, according to others, son of Oebalus, by the nymph Batīa or by Gorgophone. Tyndareus and his brother Icarius were expelled by their step-brother Hippocoon and his sons; whereupon Tyndareus fled to Thestius, in Aetolia, and assisted him in his wars against his neighbours. In Aetolia Tyndareus married Leda, the daughter of Thestius, and was afterwards restored to Sparta by Hercules. By Leda, Tyndareus became the father of Timandra, Clytaemnestra, and Philopoë. One

night Leda was embraced both by Zeus (Jupiter) and Tyndareus, and the result was the birth of Pollux and Helena, the children of Zeus, and of Castor and Clytaemnestra, the children of Tyndareus. The patronymic TYNDARIDAE is frequently given to Castor and Pollux, and the female patronymic TYNDARIS to Helen and Clytaemnestra. When Castor and Pollux had been received among the immortals, Tyndareus invited Menelaus to come to Sparta, and surrendered his kingdom to him.

TYNDĂRIS (-ĭdis) or TYNDĂRĬUM (-i: *Tindare*), a town on the N. coast of Sicily, a little W. of Messana, founded by the elder Dionysius, B.C. 396.

TŸPHON (-ōnis) or TŸPHŌEUS (-ŏĕŏs, -ŏĕi, or -ŏeī), a monster of the primitive world, is described sometimes as a destructive hurricane, and sometimes as a fire-breathing giant. According to Homer, he was concealed in the earth in the country of the Arimi, which was lashed by Zeus (Jupiter) with flashes of lightning. In Hesiod, Typhaon and Typhoeus are 2 distinct beings. Typhaon is represented as a son of Typhoeus, and a fearful hurricane, and as having become, by Echidna, the father of the dog Orthus, Cerberus, the Lernaean hydra, Chimaera, and the Sphynx. Typhoeus, on the other hand, is called the youngest son of Tartarus and Gaea, or of Hera (Juno) alone, because she was indignant at Zeus having given birth to Athena (Minerva). He is described as a monster with 100 heads, fearful eyes, and terrible voices; he wanted to acquire the sovereignty of gods and men, but, after a fearful struggle, was subdued by Zeus with a thunderbolt. He begot the winds, whence he is also called the father of the Harpies; but the beneficent winds Notus, Boreas, Argestes, and Zephyrus, were not his sons. He was buried in Tartarus, under Mt. Aetna, the workshop of Hephaestus (Vulcan), which is hence called by the poets *Typhois Aetna*.

TŸRANNĬON (-ōnis). (1) A Greek grammarian, a native of Amisus, in Pontus, was taken captive by Lucullus, and carried to Rome, B.C. 72. He was given by Lucullus to Murena, who manumitted him. At Rome Tyrannion occupied himself in teaching. He was also employed in arranging the library of Apellicon, which Sulla brought to Rome, and which contained the writings of Aristotle. Cicero speaks in the highest terms of his learning and ability.—(2) A native of Phoenicia, the son of Artemidorus, and a disciple of the preceding.

TŸRAS (-ae: *Dniester*), subsequently called DANASTRIS, a river in European Sarmatia, forming in the lower part of its course the boundary between Dacia and Sarmatia, and falling into the Pontus Euxinus, N. of the Danube.

TYRIAEUM (-i : *Ilghun*), a city of Lycaonia, 20 parasangs W. of Iconium.

TYRŌ (-ūs), daughter of Salmoneus and Alcidice. She was wife of Cretheus, and beloved by the river-god Enipeus in Thessaly, in whose form Poseidon (Neptune) appeared to her, and became by her the father of Pelias and Neleus. By Cretheus she was the mother of Aeson, Pheres, and Amythaon.

TYRRHENI, TYRRHENIA. [ETRURIA.]

TYRRHENUM MĀRE. [ETRURIA.]

TYRRHENUS (-i), son of the Lydian king Atys and Callithea, and brother of Lydus, is said to have led a Pelasgian colony from Lydia into Italy, into the country of the Umbrians, and to have given to the colonists his name. Others call Tyrrhenus a son of Hercules by Omphale, or of Telephus and Hiera, and a brother of Tarchon. The name Tarchon seems to be only another form of Tyrrhenus.

TYRRHEUS (-ei), a shepherd of king Latinus.

TYRTAEUS (-i), son of Archembrotus, of Aphidnae in Attica. According to the older tradition, the Spartans during the 2nd Messenian war were commanded by an oracle to take a leader from among the Athenians, and thus to conquer their enemies, whereupon they chose Tyrtaeus. Later writers embellish the story, and represent Tyrtaeus as a lame schoolmaster, of low family and reputation, whom the Athenians, when applied to by the Lacedaemonians, purposely sent as the most inefficient leader they could select, being unwilling to assist the Lacedaemonians in extending their dominion in the Peloponnesus, but little thinking that the poetry of Tyrtaeus would achieve that victory which his physical constitution seemed to forbid his aspiring to. The poems of Tyrtaeus exercised an important influence upon the Spartans, composing their dissensions at home, and animating their courage in the field, in their conflict with the Messenians. He must have flourished down to B.C. 668, which was the last year of the 2nd Messenian war.

TYRUS (-i : Aram. Tura : O. T. Tsor : *Sur*, Ru.), one of the greatest and most famous cities of the ancient world, stood on the coast of Phoenice, about 20 miles S. of Sidon. It was a colony of the Sidonians, and is therefore called in Scripture " the daughter of Sidon." In the time of Solomon, we find its king, Hiram, who was also king of Sidon, in close alliance with the Hebrew monarch. The Assyrian king Shalmaneser laid siege to Tyre for 5 years, but without success. It was again besieged for 13 years by Nebuchadnezzar. At the period when the Greeks began to be well acquainted with the city, its old site had been abandoned, and a new city erected on a small island about half a mile from the shore. In B.C. 322 the Tyrians refused to open their gates to Alexander, who laid siege to the city for 7 months, and united the island on which it stood to the mainland by a mole constructed chiefly of the ruins of Old Tyre. This mole has ever since formed a permanent connexion between the island and the mainland. After its capture and sack by Alexander, Tyre never regained its former consequence, and its commerce was for the most part transferred to Alexandria. It was, however, a place of considerable importance in mediaeval history, especially as one of the last points held by the Christians on the coast of Syria.

UBĬĬ (-ōrum), a German people, who originally dwelt on the right bank of the Rhine, but were transported across the river by Agrippa in B.C. 37, at their own request, because they wished to escape the hostilities of the Suevi. They took the name of Agrippenses, from their town COLONIA AGRIPPINA.

UCĀLEGŌN (-ōntis), one of the elders at Troy, whose house was burnt at the destruction of the city.

ŪFENS (-entis: *Uffente*), a river in Latium, flowing from Setia, and falling into the Amasenus.

UFFUGUM (-i), a town in Bruttium, between Scyllacium and Rhegium.

ULPĬĀNUS (-i), DŌMĬTĬUS, a celebrated Roman jurist, derived his origin from Tyre. Under Alexander Severus, he became the emperor's chief adviser, and held the offices of Scriniorum magister, Praefectus Annonae, and Praefectus Praetorio. Ulpian perished in the reign of Alexander by the hands of the soldiers, who forced their way into the palace at night, and killed him in the presence of the emperor and his mother, A.D. 228. The great legal knowledge, the good sense, and the industry of Ulpian place him among the first of the Roman jurists.

ULTOR (-ōris), " the avenger," a surname of Mars, to whom Augustus built a temple at Rome in the Forum, after taking vengeance upon the murderers of his great-uncle, Julius Caesar.

ŬLŪBRAE (-ārum), a small town in Latium, of uncertain site, but in the neighbourhood of the Pontine Marshes.

ŬLYSSĒS, ŬLYXĒS, or ŬLIXĒS (-is or -ĕi, eī), called ŎDYSSEUS by the Greeks, one of the principal Greek heroes in the Trojan war, was a son of Laërtes and Anticlēa, or, according to a later tradition, of Sisyphus and Anticlea, and was married to Penelope, the daughter of Icarius, by whom he became the father of Telemachus. During the siege of Troy he distinguished himself by his valour, prudence, and eloquence, and after the death of Achilles contended for his armour with the Telamonian Ajax, and gained the prize. He is said by some to have devised the stratagem of the wooden horse, and he was one of the heroes concealed within it. He is also said to have taken part in carrying off the palladium. But the most celebrated part of his story consists of his adventures after the destruction of Troy, which form the subject of Homer's *Odyssey*. After visiting the Cicones and Lotophagi, he sailed to the western coast of Sicily, where with 12 companions he entered the cave of the Cyclops Polyphemus. This giant devoured 6 of the companions of Ulysses, and kept Ulysses himself and the 6 others prisoners in his cave. Ulysses, however, contrived to make the monster drunk, and having with a burning pole deprived him of his one eye, succeeded in making his escape with his friends, by concealing himself and them under the bodies of the sheep which the Cyclops let out of his cave. Ulysses next arrived at the island of Aeolus ; and the god on his departure gave him a bag of winds, which were to carry him home ; but the companions of Ulysses opened the bag, and the winds escaped, whereupon the ships were driven back to the island of Aeolus, who indignantly refused all further assistance. After a visit to Telepylos, the city of Lamus, his fate carried him to Aeaea, an island inhabited by the sorceress Circe. Ulysses sent part of his people to explore the island, but they were changed by Circe into swine. Eurylochus alone escaped, and brought the sad news to Ulysses, who, when he was hastening to the assistance of his friends, was instructed by Hermes how to resist the magic powers of Circe. He succeeded in liberating his companions, who were again changed into men, and were most hospitably treated by the sorceress. By her advice he sailed across the river Oceanus, and having landed in the country of the Cimmerians, he entered Hades, and consulted Tiresias about the manner in which he might reach his native island. Ulysses

Ulysses and Tiresias. (Winckelmann Mon. Ined., No. 157.)

then returned with his companions to Aeaea, when Circe again sent them a wind which carried them to the island of the Sirens. Ulysses, in order to escape their enticing but dangerous songs, filled the ears of his companions with wax, and fastened himself to the mast of his ship, until he was out of reach of their voices. In sailing between Scylla and Charybdis, the former monster carried off and devoured 6 of the companions of Ulysses.

Having next landed on Thrinacia, his companions, contrary to the admonitions of Tiresias, killed some of the oxen of Helios; in consequence of which, when they next put to sea, Zeus destroyed their ship by lightning, and all were drowned with the exception of

Ulysses and the Sirens.   (From a Vase in the British Museum.)

Ulysses, who saved himself by means of the mast and planks, and after 10 days reached the island of Ogygia, inhabited by the nymph Calypso. She received him with kindness, and desired him to marry her, promising immortality and eternal youth. But Ulysses, who had spent 8 years with Calypso, longed for his home; and at the intercession of Athena (Minerva), Hermes (Mercury) carried to Calypso the command of Zeus to dismiss Ulysses. The nymph obeyed, and taught him how to build a raft, on which he left the island. In 18 days he came in sight of Scheria, the island of the Phaeacians, when Poseidon (Neptune) sent a storm, which cast him off the raft; but by the assistance of Leucothea and Athena he swam ashore. The exhausted hero slept on the shore until he was awoke by the voices of maidens. . He found Nausicaa, the daughter of king Alcinous and Arete, who conducted the hero to her father's court. Here the minstrel Demodocus sang of the fall of Troy, which moved Ulysses to tears, and being questioned about the cause of his emotion, he related his whole history. A ship was provided to convey him to Ithaca, from which he had been absent 20 years. During his absence his father Laërtes, bowed down by grief and old age, had withdrawn into the country, his mother Anticlea had died of sorrow, his son Telemachus had grown up to manhood, and his wife Penelope had rejected all the offers that had been made to her by the importunate suitors from the neighbouring islands. In order that he might not be recognised, Athena metamorphosed Ulysses into an unsightly beggar. He was kindly received by Eumaeus, the swineherd, a faithful servant of his house; and while staying with Eumaeus, Telemachus returned from Sparta and Pylos, whither he had gone to obtain information concerning his father. Ulysses made himself known to him, and a plan of revenge was resolved on. Penelope, with great difficulty, was made to promise her hand to him who should conquer the others in shooting with the bow of Ulysses. As none of the suitors was able to draw this bow, Ulysses himself took it up, and, directing his arrows against the suitors, slew them all. Ulysses now made himself known to Penelope, and went to see his aged father. In the meantime the report of the death of the suitors was spread abroad, and their relatives rose in arms against Ulysses; but Athena, who assumed the appearance of Mentor, brought about a reconciliation between the people and the king.

UMBRĬA (-ae) called by the Greeks OM-BRĬCA, a district of Italy, bounded on the N. by Gallia Cisalpina, from which it was separated by the river Rubicon; on the E. by the Adriatic sea; on the S. by the rivers Aesis and Nar; and on the W. by the Tiber. Its inhabitants, the UMBRI (sing. Umber), called by the Greeks UMBRICI, were one of the most ancient and powerful peoples in central Italy, and originally extended across the peninsula from the Adriatic to the Tyrrhene seas. Thus they inhabited the country afterwards called Etruria; and we are expressly told that Crotona, Perusia, Clusium, and other Etruscan cities, were built by the Umbrians. They were afterwards deprived of their possessions W. of the Tiber by the Etruscans, and their territories were still further diminished by the Senones, a Gallic people, who took possession of the whole country on the coast, from Ariminum to the Aesis. The Umbri were subdued by the Romans, B.C. 307; and after the conquest of the Senones by the Romans in 283, they again obtained possession of the country on the coast of the Adriatic. The chief towns of Umbria were ARIMINUM, FANUM FORTUNAE, MEVANIA, TUDER, NARNIA, and SPOLETIUM.

UMBRO (-ōnis: Ombrone), one of the largest rivers in Etruria, falling into the Tyrrhene sea, near a town of the same name.

UNELLI (-orum), a people on the N. coast of Gaul, on a promontory opposite Britain (the modern Cotantin), belonging to the Armorici.

ŬPIS. (1) A surname of Artemis (Diana), as the goddess assisting women in child-birth. —(2) The name of a mythical being, who is said to have reared Artemis, and who is mentioned by Virgil as one of the nymphs in her train. The masculine Upis is mentioned by Cicero as the father of Artemis.

UR. [EDESSA.]

ŬRĀNĬA (-ae). (1) One of the Muses, a daughter of Zeus (Jupiter) by Mnemosyne. The ancient bard Linus is called her son by Apollo, and Hymenaeus also is said to have been a son of Urania. She was regarded, as her name indicates, as the Muse of Astronomy, and was represented with a celestial globe, to which she points with a small staff. —(2) Daughter of Oceanus and Tethys, who also occurs as a nymph in the train of Persephone (Proserpine).—(3) A surname of Aphroditē (Venus) describing her as "the heavenly," or spiritual, to distinguish her from Aphroditē Pandēmos. Plato represents her as a daughter of Uranus, begotten without a mother. Wine was not used in the libations offered to her.

ŬRĂNUS (-i) or HEAVEN, sometimes called a son, and sometimes the husband of Gaea (Earth). By Gaea Uranus became the father of Oceanus, Coeus, Crius, Hyperion, Iapetus, Thia, Rhea, Themis, Mnemosyne, Phoebe, Tethys, Cronos; of the Cyclopes, —Brontes, Steropes, Arges; and of the Hecatoncheires—Cottus, Briareus, and Gyes. According to Cicero, Uranus was also the father of Mercury by Dia, and of Venus by Hemera. Uranus hated his children, and immediately after their birth he confined them in Tartarus, in consequence of which he was unmanned and dethroned by Cronos at the instigation of Gaea. Out of the drops of his blood sprang the Gigantes, the Melian nymphs, and, according to some, Silenus, and from the foam gathering around his limbs in the sea sprang Aphroditē.

URBĪNUM (-i). (1) HORTENSE (Urbino), a town in Umbria and a municipium.—(2) METAURENSE (Urbania), a town in Umbria on the river Metaurus, and not far from its source.

URĬA (-ae: Oria) called HYRIA by Herodotus, a town in Calabria, on the road from Brundisium to Tarentum, was the ancient capital of Iapygia, and is said to have been founded by the Cretans under Minos.

URĬUM (-i), a small town in Apulia, from which the Sinus Urius took its name, being the bay on the N. side of Mt. Garganus opposite the Diomedean islands.

USĪPĒTES (-um) or USIPĪ (-orum) a German people who, in the time of Caesar, took up their abode on the Lippe. At a later time they become lost under the general name of Alemanni.

USTĬCA (-ae), a valley near the Sabine villa of Horace.

ŬTĬCA (-ae: Bou-Shater, Ru.), the greatest city of ancient Africa, after Carthage, was a Phoenician colony, older than Carthage, and rather her ally than subject. It stood on the shore of the N. part of the Carthaginian Gulf, a little W. of the mouth of the Bagradas, and 27 Roman miles N.W. of Carthage. In the 3rd Punic War, Utica took part with the Romans against Carthage, and was rewarded with the greatest part of the Carthaginian territory. It afterwards became renowned to all future time as the scene of the last stand made by the Pompeian party against Caesar, and of the glorious, though mistaken self-sacrifice of the younger Cato. [CATO.]

UXELLODŪNUM (-i), a town of the Cadurci in Gallia Aquitanica.

UXENTUM (-i: Ugento), a town in Calabria, N.W. of the Iapygian promontory.

UXĬI (-orum), a warlike people, of predatory habits, who had their strongholds in Mt. Parachoathras, on the N. border of Persis, in the district called Uxia, but who also extended over a considerable tract of country in Media.

VACCA, VAGA, or VABA (*Beja*), a city of Zeugitana in N. Africa, a good day's journey S. of Utica. It was destroyed by Metellus in the Jugurthine War, but was restored and colonised by the Romans. Justinian named it Theodorias in honour of his wife.

VACCAEI (-orum), a people in the interior of Hispania Tarraconensis, occupying the modern *Toro, Palencia, Burgos*, and *Valladolid*. Their chief towns were PALANTIA and INTERCATIA.

VADĪMŌNIS LĂCUS (*Lago di Bassano*), a small lake of Etruria of a circular form, with sulphureous waters, and renowned for its floating islands. It is celebrated in history for the defeat of the Etruscans in 2 great battles, first by the dictator Papirius Cursor, in B.C. 309; and again in 283, when the allied forces of the Etruscans and Gauls were routed by the consul Cornelius Dolabella.

VĂGIENNI (-orum), a small people in Liguria, whose chief town was Augusta Vagiennorum.

VĂHĂLIS. [RHENUS.]

VĂLENS (-entis), emperor of the East A.D. 364—378, was born about A.D. 328. He was defeated by the Goths, near Hadrianople, on the 9th of August, 378, and was never seen after the battle.

VĂLENTIA (-ae). (1) (*Valencia*), the chief town of the Edetani on the river Turia, 3 miles from the coast, and on the road from Carthago Nova to Castulo.—(2) (*Valence*), a town in Gallia Narbonensis on the Rhone, and a Roman colony—(3) A town of Sardinia of uncertain site.—(4) Or VALENTIUM, a town in Apulia, 10 miles from Brundusium.—(5) A province in the N. of Britain, beyond the Roman wall. It existed only for a short time. [BRITANNIA.]

VĂLENTĪNĬĀNUS (-i), (I.), Roman emperor A.D. 364—375, was the son of Gratianus, and was born A.D. 321, at Cibalis in Pannonia. He expired suddenly at Bregetio, while giving an audience to the deputies of the Quadi, on the 17th of November, 375.—(II.), Roman emperor A.D. 375—392, younger son of the preceding, was proclaimed Augustus by the army after his father's death, though he was then only 4 or 5 years of age. In 392 Valentinian was murdered by the general Arbogastes, who raised Eugenius to the throne.—(III.), Roman emperor A.D. 425

—455, was born 419, and was the son of Constantius III. He was slain in 455 by Petronius Maximus, whose wife he had violated.

VĂLĔRĬA GENS, one of the most ancient patrician houses at Rome, was of Sabine origin, and their ancestor Volesus or Volusus is said to have settled at Rome with Titus Tatius. One of the descendants of this Volesus, P. Valerius, afterwards surnamed Publicola, plays a distinguished part in the story of the expulsion of the kings, and was elected consul in the first year of the republic, B.C. 509. From this time down to the latest period of the empire, for nearly 1000 years, the name occurs more or less frequently in the Fasti, and it was borne by several of the emperors. The Valeria gens enjoyed extraordinary honours and privileges at Rome. In early times they were always foremost in advocating the rights of the plebeians, and the laws which they proposed were the great charters of the liberties of the second order. (See *Dict. of Antiq.*, *s. v. Leges Valeriae*.) The Valeria gens was divided into various families under the republic, the most important of which bore the names of CORVUS, FLACCUS, MESSALA, and PUBLICOLA.

VĂLĔRĬĀNUS (-i). (1) Roman emperor, A.D. 253—260. He was entrapped into a conference by the Persians, taken prisoner (260), and passed the remainder of his life in captivity, subjected to every insult which Oriental cruelty could devise.—(2) Son of the preceding, perished along with Gallienus at Milan in 268. [GALLIENUS.]

VĂLĔRĬUS. [VALERIA GENS.]

VĂLĔRĬUS VOLŬSUS MAXĬMUS (-i), M., was a brother of P. Valerius Publicola, and was dictator in B.C. 494, when the dissensions *de Nexis* between the burghers and commonalty of Rome were at the highest. Valerius was popular with the plebs, and induced them to enlist for the Sabine and Aequian wars, by promising that when the enemy was repulsed, the condition of the debtors (*nexi*) should be alleviated. He defeated and triumphed over the Sabines; but, unable to fulfil his promise to the commons, resigned his dictatorship.

VĂLĔRĬUS MAXĬMUS (-i) is known to us as the compiler of a large collection of historical anecdotes, entitled *De Factis Dictisque Memorabilibus Libri IX*. He lived in the reign of the emperor Tiberius, to whom he dedicated his work. In an historical point of view the work is by no means without value, since it preserves a record of many curious events not to be found elsewhere; but its statements do not always deserve implicit confidence.

VĂLĔRĬUS FLACCUS. [FLACCUS.]

VALGĬUS RŪFUS (-i), C., a Roman poet, and a contemporary of Virgil and Horace.

VANDĂLI, VANDĂLĬI, or VINDĂLĬI (-orum), a confederacy of German peoples, who dwelt originally on the N. coast of Germany, but were afterwards settled N. of the Marcomanni in the Riesengebirge, which are hence called Vandalici Montes. They subsequently appear for a short time in Dacia and Pannonia; but at the beginning of the 5th century (A.D. 409) they traversed Germany and Gaul, and invaded Spain. In this country they subjugated the Alani, and founded a powerful kingdom, the name of which is still preserved in Andalusia (Vandalusia). In A.D. 429 they crossed over into Africa, under their king Genseric, and conquered all the Roman dominions in that country. Genseric subsequently invaded Italy, and took and plundered Rome in 455. The Vandals continued masters of Africa till 535, when their kingdom was destroyed by Belisarius, and annexed to the Byzantine empire.

VANGIŌNES (-um), a German people, dwelling along the Rhine, in the neighbourhood of the modern *Worms*.

VARAGRI. [VERAGRI.]

VARGUNTEĬUS (-i), a senator, and one of Catiline's conspirators, undertook, in conjunction with C. Cornelius, to murder Cicero in B.C. 63, but their plan was frustrated by information conveyed to Cicero through Fulvia.

VĂRĬUS RŪFUS (-i), L., one of the most distinguished poets of the Augustan age, the companion and friend of Virgil and Horace. By the latter he is placed in the foremost rank among the epic bards, and Quintilian has pronounced that his tragedy of Thyestes might stand a comparison with any production of the Grecian stage.

VARRO (-ōnis), TĔRENTĬUS. (1) C., consul B.C. 216 with L. Aemilius Paulus. Of low origin and ultra-democratic opinions, Varro, notwithstanding the strong opposition of the aristocracy, was raised to the consulship by the people, to bring the war against Hannibal to a close. His colleague was L. Aemilius Paulus, one of the leaders of the aristocratical party. The 2 consuls were defeated by Hannibal at the memorable battle of Cannae [HANNIBAL], which was fought by Varro against the advice of Paulus. The Roman army was all but annihilated. Paulus and almost all the officers perished. Varro was one of the few who escaped and reached Venusia in safety, with about 70 horsemen. His conduct after the battle seems to have been deserving of high praise. He proceeded to Canusium, where the remnant of the Roman army had taken refuge, and there adopted every precaution which the exigencies of the case required. His conduct was appreciated by the senate and the people, and his defeat was forgotten in the services he had lately rendered.—(2) M., the celebrated writer, whose vast and varied erudition in almost every department of literature earned for him the title of the "most learned of the Romans," was born B.C. 116. Varro held a high naval command in the wars against the pirates and Mithridates, and afterwards served as the legatus of Pompeius in Spain in the civil war, but was compelled to surrender his forces to Caesar. He then passed over into Greece, and shared the fortunes of the Pompeian party till after the battle of Pharsalia, when he sued for and obtained the forgiveness of Caesar, who employed him in superintending the collection and arrangement of the great library designed for public use. His death took place B.C. 28, when he was in his 89th year. Varro composed no fewer than 490 books; but of these only 2 works have come down to us, and one of them in a mutilated form, viz., the treatises *De Re Rustica*, and *De Lingua Latina*.—(3) P., a Latin poet of considerable celebrity, surnamed ATACINUS, from the *Atax*, a river of Gallia Narbonensis, his native province, was born B.C. 82. Of his personal history nothing further is known.

VĀRUS, a cognomen in many Roman gentes, signified a person who had his legs bent inwards.

VĀRUS (-i) ALFĒNUS. (1) A Roman jurist, the "Alfenus vafer" of Horace, was a native of Cremona, where he carried on the trade of a barber or a cobbler. Having come to Rome, he became a pupil of Servius Sulpicius, attained the dignity of the consulship, and was honoured with a public funeral. —(2) A general of Vitellius, in the civil war in A.D. 69.

VĀRUS (-i) QUINTĬLĬUS, was consul B.C. 13, and was subsequently appointed to the government of Syria, where he acquired enormous wealth. Shortly after his return from Syria he was made governor of Germany (probably about A.D. 7), and was instructed by Augustus to introduce the Roman jurisdiction into that newly conquered country. The Germans, however, were not prepared to submit thus tamely to the Roman yoke, and found a leader in Arminius, a noble chief of the Cherusci, who organised a general revolt of all the German tribes between the Visurgis and the Weser. When he had fully matured his plans, he suddenly attacked Varus, at the head of a countless host of barbarians, as the Roman general was marching with his 3 legions through a pass of the *Saltus Teutoburgiensis*, a range of hills covered with wood, which extends N. of the

Lippe from Osnabrück to Paderborn, and is known in the present day by the name of the Teutoburgerwald or Lippische Wald. The battle lasted 3 days, and ended with the entire destruction of the Roman army. Varus put an end to his own life. His defeat was followed by the loss of all the Roman possessions between the Weser and the Rhine, and the latter river again became the boundary of the Roman dominions. When the news of this defeat reached Rome, the whole city was thrown into consternation; and Augustus, who was both weak and aged, gave way to the most violent grief, tearing his garments and calling upon Varus to give him back his legions.

VĀRUS (-i: *Var*, or *Varo*), a river in Gallia Narbonensis, forming the boundary between that province and Italy, rises in Mt. Cema in the Alps, and falls into the Mediterranean Sea, between Antipolis and Nicaea.

VASCŌNES (-um), a powerful people on the N. coast of Hispania Tarraconensis, between the Iberus and the Pyrenees, in the modern *Navarre* and *Guipuzco*. Their chief towns were POMPELON and CALAGURRIS.

VATĪNĬUS (-i). (1) P., a political adventurer in the last days of the republic, who is described by Cicero as one of the greatest scamps and villains that ever lived. Vatinius was quaestor B.C. 63, and tribune of the plebs 59, when he sold his services to Caesar, who was then consul along with Bibulus. In 56 he appeared as a witness against Milo and Sestius, two of Cicero's friends, in consequence of which the orator made a vehement attack upon the character of Vatinius, in the speech which has come down to us. Vatinius was praetor in 55, and in the following year (54) he was accused by C. Licinius Calvus of having gained the praetorship by bribery. He was defended on this occasion by Cicero, in order to please Caesar, whom Cicero had offended by his former attack upon Vatinius. During the civil war Vatinius attached himself to the fortunes of Caesar.—(2) Of Beneventum, one of the vilest and most hateful creatures of Nero's court, equally deformed in body and in mind, and who, after being a shoemaker's apprentice and a buffoon, ended by becoming a *delator*, or public informer.

VECTIS or VECTA (*Isle of Wight*), an island off the S. coast of Britain.

VĒDĬUS POLLĬO. [POLLIO.]

VĔGĒTĬUS (-i), FLĀVĬUS RĔNĀTUS, the author of a treatise, *Rei Militaris Instituta*, or *Epitome Rei Militaris*, dedicated to the emperor Valentinian II.

VĒII (-orum: *Isola Farnese*), one of the

most ancient and powerful cities of Etruria, situated on the river Cremĕra, about 12 miles from Rome. It was one of the 12 cities of the Etruscan Confederation, and apparently the largest of all. As far as we can judge from its present remains, it was about 7 miles in circumference, which agrees with the statement of Dionysius, that it was equal in size to Athens. Its territory (*Ager Veiens*) was extensive, and appears originally to have extended on the S. and E. to the Tiber; on the S.W. to the sea, embracing the salinae or salt-works, at the mouth of the river; and on the W. to the territory of Caere. The Ciminian forest appears to have been its N.W. boundary; on the E. it must have embraced all the district S. of Soracte and E.-ward to the Tiber. The cities of Capena and Fidenae were colonies of Veii. The Veientes were engaged in almost unceasing hostilities with Rome for more than 3 centuries and a half, and we have records of 14 distinct wars between the 2 peoples. Veii was at length taken by the dictator Camillus, after a siege which is said to have lasted 10 years. From this time Veii was abandoned; but after the lapse of ages it was colonised afresh by Augustus, and made a Roman municipium. The new colony, however, occupied scarcely a 3rd of the ancient city, and had again sunk into decay in the reign of Hadrian.

VĒIŌVIS (-is), a Roman deity, whose name is explained by some to mean "little Jupiter;" while others interpret it "the destructive Jupiter," and identify him with Pluto. Originally Veiovis was probably an Etruscan divinity, whose fearful lightnings produced deafness, even before they were actually hurled. His temple at Rome stood between the Capitol and the Tarpeian rock. He was represented as a youthful god armed with arrows.

VĒLĂBRUM (-i), a district in Rome, originally a morass, on the W. slope of the Palatine, between the Vicus Tuscus and the Forum Boarium.

VELAUNI, or VELLAVI (-orum), a people in Gallia Aquitanica, in the modern *Velay*, who were originally subject to the Arverni, but subsequently appear as an independent people.

VĔLĒDA (-ae), a prophetic virgin, who by birth belonged to the Bructeri, and in the reign of Vespasian was regarded as a divine being by most of the nations in central Germany.

VĔLĬA or ĔLĔA (-ae), also called HYĔLĒ (-ēs: *Castell' a Mare della Brucca*), a Greek town of Lucania, on the W. coast between Paestum and Buxentum, was founded by the Phocaeans, who had abandoned their native city to escape from the Persian sovereignty, about B.C. 543. It was situated about 3 miles E. of the river Hales, and possessed a good harbour. It is celebrated as the birthplace of the philosophers Parmenides and Zeno, who founded a school of philosophy usually known under the name of the Eleatic.

VELINUS (-i: *Velino*), a river in the territory of the Sabines, rising in the central Apennines, and falling into the Nar. This river in the neighbourhood of Reate overflowed its banks, and formed several small lakes, the largest of which was called LACUS VELINUS (*Pié di Lago*, also *Lago delle Marmore*).

VELITRAE (-orum: *Velletri*), an ancient town of the Volscians, in Latium, but subsequently belonging to the Latin League. It is chiefly celebrated as the birthplace of the emperor Augustus.

VELLAUNODUNUM (-i: *Beaune*), a town of the Senones, in Gallia Lugdunensis.

VELLAVI. [VELAUNI.]

VELLEIUS PATERCULUS. [PATERCULUS.]

VELLOCASSES, a people in Gallia Lugdunensis, N.W. of the Parisii, extending along the Sequana as far as the ocean; their chief town was RATOMAGUS.

VENAFRUM (-i: *Venafri*), a town in the N. of Samnium, near the river Vulturnus, and on the confines of Latium, celebrated for the excellence of its olives.

VENEDI (-orum) or VENEDAE (-arum), a people in European Sarmatia, dwelling on the Baltic, E. of the Vistula. The SINUS VENEDICUS (*Gulf of Riga*), and the VENEDICI MONTES, a range of mountains between Poland and East Prussia, were called after this people.

VENETIA (-ae). (1) A district in the N. of Italy, was originally included under the general name of Gallia Cisalpina, but was made by Augustus, the 10th Regio of Italy. It was bounded on the W. by the river Athesis, which separated it from Gallia Cisalpina; on the N. by the Carnic Alps; on the E. by the river Timavus, which separated it from Istria; and on the S. by the Adriatic Gulf. Its inhabitants, the VENETI, frequently called HENETI by the Greeks, were not an Italian race, but their real origin is doubtful. In consequence of their hostility to the Celtic tribes in their neighbourhood, they formed at an early period an alliance with Rome; and their country was defended by the Romans against their dangerous enemies. On the conquest of the Cisalpine Gauls, the Veneti likewise became included

under the Roman dominions. The Veneti continued to enjoy great prosperity down to the time of the Marcomannic wars, in the reign of the emperor Aurelius; but from this time their country was frequently devastated by the barbarians who invaded Italy; and at length, in the 5th century, many of its inhabitants, to escape the ravages of the Huns under Attila, took refuge in the islands off their coast, on which now stands the city of Venice. The chief towns of Venetia in ancient times were, PATAVIUM, ALTINUM, and AQUILEIA.—(2) A district in the N.W. of Gallia Lugdunensis, inhabited by the Veneti. Off their coast was a group of islands called INSULAE VENETICAE.

VENETUS LACUS. [BRIGANTINUS LACUS.]

VENILIA (-ae), a nymph, daughter of Pilumnus, sister of Amata, wife of king Latinus, and mother of Turnus and Juturna by Daunus.

VENNONES (-um), a people of Rhaetia, and according to Strabo the most savage of the Rhaetian tribes, inhabiting the Alps near the sources of the Athesis (*Adige*).

VENTA (-ae). (1) BELGARUM (*Winchester*), the chief town of the Belgae in Britain. The modern city still contains several Roman remains.—(2) ICENORUM. [ICENI.]—(3) SILURUM (*Caerwent*), a town of the Silures in Britain, in Monmouthshire.

VENTI (-orum), the winds. They appear personified, even in the Homeric poems, but at the same time they are conceived as ordinary phenomena of nature. The master and ruler of all the winds is Aeolus, who resides in the island Aeolia [AEOLUS]; but the other gods also, especially Zeus (Jupiter), exercise a power over them. Homer mentions by name Boreas (N. wind), Eurus (E. wind), Notus (S. wind), and Zephyrus (W. wind). According to Hesiod, the beneficial winds, Notus, Boreas, Argestes, and Zephyrus, were the sons of Astraeus and Eos; and the destructive ones, such as Typhon, are said to be the sons of Typhoeus. Later, especially philosophical, writers endeavoured to define the winds more accurately, according to their places on the compass. Thus Aristotle, besides the 4 principal winds (Boreas or Aparctias, Eurus, Notus, and Zephyrus), mentions 3, the Meses, Caicias, and Apeliotes, between Boreas and Eurus; between Eurus and Notus he places the Phoenicias; between Notus and Zephyrus he has only the Lips; and between Zephyrus and Boreas he places the Argestes (Olympias or Sciron) and the Thrascias. It must further be observed that, according to Aristotle, the Eurus is not due E. but S.E. In the Museum Pio-Clementinum there exists a marble monument upon which the winds are described with their Greek and Latin names, viz. Septentrio (Aparctias), Eurus (Euros or S.E.,, and between these 2 Aquilo (Boreas), Vulturnus (Caicias) and Solanus (Apeliotes). Between Eurus and Notus (Notos) there is only one, the Euro-Auster (Euro-Notus); between Notus and Favonius (Zephyrus) are marked Austro-Africus (Libonotus), and Africus (Lips); and between Favonius and Septentrio we find Chrus (Iapyx) and Circius (Thracius). The winds were represented by poets and artists in various ways; the latter usually represented them as beings with wings at their heads

Venti, the Winds.   (Bartoli, Vatican Virgil, p. 29.)

and shoulders. Black lambs were offered as sacrifices to the destructive winds, and white ones to favourable or good winds.

VENTIDIUS BASSUS (-i), P., a celebrated Roman general, at first gained a poor living by jobbing mules and carriages. Caesar, however, saw his abilities, and employed him in Gaul, and in the civil war. After Caesar's death Ventidius sided with M. Antony, and in 43 was made consul suffectus. In 39 Antony sent Ventidius into Asia, where he defeated the Parthians and Labienus; and in the 2nd campaign gained a still more brilliant victory over the Parthians, who had again invaded Syria. For these services he obtained a triumph in 38.

VENUS (-ĕris), the goddess of love among the Romans. Before she was identified with the Greek Aphroditē, she was one of the least important divinities in the religion of the Romans; but still her worship seems to have been established at Rome at an early time. Here she bore the surnames of *Murtea*, or *Murcia*, from her fondness for the myrtle tree (*myrtus*), and of *Cloacina* and *Calva*. The etymology of the last two epithets is variously given. That of *Calva* probably refers to the fact that on her wedding day the bride, either actually or symbolically, cut off a lock of hair to sacrifice it to Venus. In later times the worship of Venus became much more extended, and her identification with the Greek Aphroditē introduced various new attributes. At the beginning of the second Punic war, the worship of Venus Erycina was introduced from Sicily. In the year B.C. 114, on account of the general corruption, and especially among the Vestals, a temple was built to Venus Verticordia (the goddess who turns the human heart). After the close of the Samnite war, Fabius Gurges founded the worship of Venus Obsequens and Postvorta; Scipio Africanus the younger, that of Venus Genitrix, in which he was afterwards followed by Caesar, who added that of Venus Victrix. The worship of Venus was promoted by Caesar, who traced his descent from Aeneas, supposed to be the son of Mars and Venus. The month of April, as the beginning of spring, was thought to be peculiarly sacred to the goddess of love. Respecting the Greek goddess see APHRODITE.

VĒNŪSIA (-ae: *Venosa*), an ancient town of Apulia, S. of the river Aufidus, and near Mt. Vultur, situated in a romantic country, and memorable as the birthplace of thé poet Horace.

VERĀGRI or VARĀGRI (-ōrum), a people in Gallia Belgica, on the Pennine Alps, near the confluence of the Dranse and the Rhone.

VERBĀNUS LĀCUS (*Lago Maggiore*), a lake in Gallia Cisalpina, and the largest in all Italy, being about 40 miles in length from N. to S.: its greatest breadth is 8 miles.

. VERCELLAE (-ārum: *Vercelli*), the chief town of the Libici in Gallia Cisalpina.

VERCINGETŌRIX (-ỹgis), the celebrated chieftain of the Arverni, who carried on war with great ability against Caesar in B.C. 52. He was taken to Rome after the capture of Alesia, where he adorned the triumph of his conqueror in 45, and was afterwards put to death.

VERETUM (-i: *Alessano*), more anciently called BARIS, a town in Calabria, on the road from Leuca to Tarentum, and 600 stadia S.E. of the latter city.

VERGELLUS (-i), a rivulet in Apulia, said to have been choked by the dead bodies of the Romans slain in the battle of Cannae.

VEROLAMĪUM or VERULAMĪUM (-i: *Old Verulam*, near St. Albans), the chief town of the Catuellani in Britain, probably the residence of the king Cassivellaunus, which was conquered by Caesar.

VEROMANDUI (-ōrum), a people in Gallia Belgica, between the Nervii and Suessiones, in the modern *Vermandois*. Their chief town was AUGUSTA VEROMANDUORUM (*St. Quentin*).

VĒRŌNA (-ae: *Verona*), an important town in Gallia Cisalpina, on the river Athesis, was originally the capital of the Euganei, but subsequently belonged to the Cenomani. At a still later time it was made a Roman colony, with the surname Augusta; and under the empire it was one of the largest and most flourishing towns in the N. of Italy. It was the birthplace of Catullus; and, according to some accounts, of the elder Pliny. There are still many Roman remains at Verona, and among others an amphitheatre in a good state of preservation.

VERRĒS (-is), C., was quaestor B.C. 82, to Cn. Papirius Carbo, and therefore at that period belonged to the Marian party; but he afterwards went over to Sulla. After being legate and proquaestor of Dolabella in Cilicia,

Verres became praetor urbanus in 74, and afterwards propraetor in Sicily, where he remained nearly 3 years (73—71). The extortions and exactions of Verres in the island have become notorious through the celebrated orations of Cicero. His three years' rule desolated the island more effectually than the two recent Servile wars, or the old struggle between Carthage and Rome for the possession of the island. As soon as he left Sicily, the inhabitants resolved to bring him to trial. They committed the prosecution to Cicero, who had been Lilybaean quaestor in Sicily in 75, and had promised his good offices to the Sicilians whenever they might demand them. Cicero heartily entered into the cause of the Sicilians, and spared no pains to secure a conviction of the great criminal. Verres was defended by Hortensius, and was supported by the whole power of the aristocracy. Hortensius endeavoured to substitute Q. Caecilius Niger as prosecutor instead of Cicero; but the judges decided in favour of the latter. The oration which Cicero delivered on this occasion, was the *Divinatio in Q. Caecilium*. Cicero was allowed 110 days to collect evidence, but, assisted by his cousin Lucius, completed his researches in 50. Hortensius now grasped at his last chance of an acquittal—that of prolonging the trial till the following year, when he himself would be consul. Cicero therefore abandoned all thought of eloquence or display, and merely introducing his case in the first of the Verrine orations, rested all his hopes of success on the weight of testimony alone. Hortensius was quite unprepared with counter-evidence, and after the first day abandoned the cause of Verres. Before the nine days occupied in hearing evidence were over, Verres quitted the city in despair, and was condemned in his absence. He retired to Marseilles, retaining so many of his treasures of art as to cause eventually his proscription by M. Antony in 43.

VERTĪCORDIA. [VENUS.]

VERTUMNUS or VORTUMNUS (-i), is said to have been an Etruscan divinity, but this story seems to be refuted by his genuine Roman name; viz. from *verto*, to change. The Romans connected Vertumnus with all occurrences to which the verb *verto* applies, such as the change of seasons, purchase and sale, the return of rivers to their proper beds, &c. But in reality the god was connected only with the transformation of plants and their progress from blossom to fruit. Hence the story, that when Vertumnus was in love with Pomona, he assumed all possible forms, until at last he gained his end by metamorphosing himself into a blooming youth.

Gardeners accordingly offered to him the first produce of their gardens and garlands of budding flowers. The whole people celebrated a festival to Vertumnus on the 23rd of August, under the name of the *Vortumnalia*, denoting the transition from the beautiful season of autumn to the less agreeable one. The importance of the worship of Vertumnus at Rome is evident from the fact, that it was attended to by a special flamen (*flamen Vortumnalis*).

Vertumnus.   (Musée Bouillon, vol. 3, pl. 14.)

VERULAE (-arum : *Veroli*), a town of the Hernici in Latium, S.E. of Aletrium, and N. of Frusino, subsequently a Roman colony.

VERULAMIUM. [VEROLAMIUM.]

VĔRUS (-i), L. AURĒLĬUS, the colleague of M. Aurelius in the empire, A.D. 161—169. He was adopted by M. Antonius, and on his death succeeded to the empire along with M. Aurelius. The history of his reign is given under AURELIUS. Verus died suddenly at Altinum in the country of the Veneti, towards the close of 169.

VESCĪNUS ĀGER, a district of the Aurunci, in Latium.

VĔSĔVUS. [VESUVIUS.]

VĔSONTĬO (-ōnis : *Besançon*), the chief town of the Sequani in Gallia Belgica, situated on the river Dubis (*Doubs*), which flowed around the town, with the exception of a space of 600 feet, on which stood a mountain, forming the citadel of the town.

VESPĂSĬĀNUS (-i), T. FLĀVĬUS SABĪNUS, Roman emperor, A.D. 70—79, was born on the 17th of November, A.D. 9. His father was a man of mean condition, of Reate, in the country of the Sabini. His mother,

Vespasia Polla, was the daughter of a praefectus castrorum, and the sister of a Roman senator. Vespasian served as tribunus militum in Thrace, and was quaestor in Crete and Cyrene. He was afterwards aedile and praetor. About this time he took to wife Flavia Domitilla, the daughter of a Roman eques, by whom he had 2 sons, both of whom succeeded him. In the reign of Claudius he was sent into Germany as legatus legionis ; and in 43 he held the same command in Britain, and reduced the Isle of Wight. He was consul in 51, and proconsul of Africa under Nero. He was at this time very poor, and was accused of getting money by dishonourable means. But he had a great military reputation, and was liked by the soldiers. Nero afterwards sent him to the East (66), to conduct the war against the Jews. His conduct of this war raised his reputation, and when the war broke out between Otho and Vitellius, Vespasian was proclaimed emperor at Alexandria on the 1st of July 69, and soon after all through the East. He came to Rome in the following year (70), leaving his son Titus to continue the war against the Jews. On his arrival at Rome, he worked with great industry to restore order in the city and in the empire. The simplicity and frugality of his mode of life formed a striking contrast with the profusion and luxury of some of his predecessors, and his example is said to have done more to reform the morals of Rome than all the laws which had ever been enacted. He was never ashamed of the meanness of his origin, and ridiculed all attempts to make out for him a distinguished genealogy. He is accused of avarice, and of a taste for low humour. Yet it is admitted that he was liberal in all his expenditure for purposes of public utility. In 71 Titus returned to Rome, and both father and son triumphed together on account of the conquest of the Jews. The reign of Vespasian was marked by few striking events. The most important was the conquest of North Wales and the island of Anglesey by Agricola, who was sent into Britain in 78. In the summer of 79 Vespasian, whose health was failing, went to spend some time at his paternal house in the mountains of the Sabini, and expired on the 24th of June in that year, at the age of 69.

VESTA (-ae), one of the great Roman divinities, identical with the Greek HESTIA [HESTIA]. She was the goddess of the hearth, and therefore inseparably connected with the Penates ; for Aeneas was believed to have brought the eternal fire of Vesta from Troy, along with the images of the Penates ;

and the praetors, consuls, and dictators, before entering upon their official functions, sacrificed, not only to the Penates, but also to Vesta at Lavinium. In the ancient Roman house, the hearth was the central part, and around it all the inmates daily assembled for their common meal (*coena*); every meal thus taken was a fresh bond of union and affection among the members of a family, and at the same time an act of worship of Vesta, combined with a sacrifice to her and the Penates. Every dwelling-house therefore was, in some sense, a temple of Vesta; but a public sanctuary united all the citizens of the state into one large family. This sanctuary stood in the Forum, between the Capitoline and Palatine hills, and not far from the temple of the Penates. The goddess was not represented in her temple by a statue, but the eternal fire burning on her hearth or altar was her living symbol, and was kept up and attended to by the Vestals, her virgin priestesses, who were chaste and pure like the goddess herself. Respecting their duties and obligations, see *Dict. of Antiq.* art. *Vestales.* On the 1st of March in every year the sacred fire of Vesta, and the laurel tree which shaded her hearth, were renewed, and on the 15th of June her temple was cleaned and purified. The dirt was carried into an angiportus behind the temple, which was locked by a gate that no one might enter it. The day on which this took place was a *dies nefastus,* the first half of which was thought to be so inauspicious, that the priestess of Juno was not allowed to comb her hair or to cut her nails, while the second half was very favourable to contracting a marriage or entering upon other important undertakings. A few days before that solemnity, on the 9th of June, the Vestalia were celebrated in honour of the goddess, on which occasion none but women walked to the temple, and that with bare feet.

VESTINI (-ōrum), a Sabellian people in central Italy, lying between the Apennines and the Adriatic sea, and separated from Picenum by the river Matrinus, and from the Marrucini by the river Aternus. They were conquered by the Romans, B.C. 328, and from this time appear as the allies of Rome.

VESŬVĬUS (-i), also called VESĒVUS, VESBĬUS, or VESVĬUS, the celebrated volcanic mountain in Campania, rising out of the plain S.E. of Neapolis. There are no records of any eruption of Vesuvius before the Christian era, but the ancient writers were aware of its volcanic nature from the igneous appearance of its rocks. In A.D. 63 the volcano gave the first symptoms of agi-

tation in an earthquake, which occasioned considerable damage to several towns in its vicinity; and on the 24th of August, A.D. 79, occurred the first great eruption of Vesuvius, which overwhelmed the cities of Stabiae, Herculaneum, and Pompeii. It was in this eruption that the elder Pliny lost his life.

VETRANĬO (-ōnis) commanded the legions in Illyria and Pannonia, in A.D. 350, when Constans was treacherously destroyed, and was proclaimed emperor by his troops; but at the end of 10 months resigned in favour of Constantius.

VETTĬUS (-i), L., a Roman eques, in the pay of Cicero in B.C. 63, to whom he gave some valuable information respecting the Catilinarian conspiracy. In 59 he accused Curio, Cicero, L. Lucullus, and many other distinguished men, of having formed a conspiracy to assassinate Pompey. Cicero regarded this accusation as the work of Caesar, who used the tribune Vatinius as his instrument. On the day after he had given his evidence, Vettius was found strangled in prison.

VETTŌNES or VECTONES (-um), a people in the interior of Lusitania, E. of the Lusitani, and W. of the Carpetani, extending from the Durius to the Tagus.

VETŬLŌNĬA (-ae), VETŬLŌNĬUM (-i), or VETŬLŌNĬI (-ōrum), an ancient city of Etruria, and one of the 12 cities of the Etruscan confederation. From this city the Romans are said to have borrowed the insignia of their magistrates—the fasces, sella curulis, and toga praetexta—as well as the use of the brazen trumpet in war. Its site has been discovered within the last few years near a small village called *Magliano,* between the river Osa and the Albegna, and about 8 miles inland.

VETŬRĬUS MĀMŬRĬUS (-i), is said to have been the armourer who made the 11 ancilia exactly like the one that was sent from heaven in the reign of Numa. His praises formed one of the chief subjects of the songs of the Salii.

VĬĂDUS (-i: *Oder*), a river of Germany, falling into the Baltic.

VĬBĬUS PANSA. [Pansa.]

VĬBĬUS SĔQUESTER. [Sequester.]

VIBO (-ōnis: *Bivona*), the Roman form of the Greek town Hipponium, situated on the S.W. coast of Bruttium, and on a gulf called after it Sinus Vibonensis, or Hipponiates. It is said to have been founded by the Locri Epizephyrii; but it was destroyed by the elder Dionysius, who transplanted its inhabitants to Syracuse. It was afterwards restored; and at a later time it fell into the hands of the Bruttii, together with the other

Greek cities on this coast. It was taken from the Bruttii by the Romans, who colonised it B.C. 194, and called it VIBO VALENTIA. Cicero speaks of it as a municipium; and in the time of Augustus it was one of the most flourishing cities in the S. of Italy.

VĬCENTĬA or VĬCĔTĬA (-ae), less correctly, VINCENTĬA (*Vicenza*), a town on the river Togisonus, in Venetia, in the N. of Italy, and a Roman municipium.

VICTOR (-ōris), SEX. AURĒLĬUS, a Latin writer, was born of humble parents, but rose to distinction by his zeal in the cultivation of literature. Having attracted the attention of Julian when at Sirmium, he was appointed by that prince governor of one division of Pannonia. At a subsequent period, he was elevated by Theodosius to the high office of city praefect. He is the reputed author of a work entitled *De Caesaribus;* besides which, 2 or 3 others are ascribed to him.

VICTŌRĬA (-ae), the personification of victory among the Romans.

VICTŌRĬA or VICTŌRĪNA (-ae), the mother of Victorinus, after whose death she was hailed as the mother of camps (*Mater Castrorum*); and coins were struck, bearing her effigy. She transferred her power first to Marius, and then to Tetricus.

VICTŌRĪNUS (-i), one of the Thirty Tyrants, was the 3rd of the usurpers who in succession ruled Gaul during the reign of Gallienus. He was assassinated at Agrippina by one of his own officers in A.D. 268, after reigning somewhat more than a year.

VICTRIX. [VENUS.]

VIENNA (-ae: *Vienne*), the chief town of the Allobroges in Gallia Lugdunensis, situated on the Rhone, S. of Lugdunum.

VĪMĬNĀLIS (-is), PORTA, a gate of Rome in the Servian walls, leading to the Via Tiburtina.

VINDĒLĬCĬA (-ae), a Roman province, bounded on the N. by the Danube, which separated it from Germany, on the W. by the territory of the Helvetii in Gaul, on the S. by Rhaetia, and on the E. by the river Oenus (*Inn*), which separated it from Noricum, thus corresponding to the N.E. part of Switzerland, the S.E. of Baden, the S. of Würtemberg and Bavaria, and the N. part of the Tyrol. It was originally part of the province of Rhaetia, and was conquered by Tiberius in the reign of Augustus. At a later time Rhaetia was divided into two provinces, *Rhaetia Prima* and *Rhaetia Secunda*, the latter of which names was gradually supplanted by that of Vindelicia. It was drained by the tributaries of the Danube, of which the most important were the Licias, or Licus

(*Lech*), with its tributary the Vindo, Vinda, or Virdo (*Werlach*), the Isarus (*Isar*), and Oenus (*Inn*). The E. part of the Lacus Brigantinus (*Lake of Constance*) also belonged to Vindelicia. It derived its name from its chief inhabitants, the VINDELICI, a warlike people dwelling in the S. of the country. The other tribes in Vindelicia were the Brigantii on the Lake of Constance, the Licatii or Licates on the Lech, and the Breuni in the N. of Tyrol on the Brenner. The chief town in the province was Augusta Vindelicorum (*Augsburg*), at the confluence of the Vindo and the Licus.

VINDĬCĬUS (-i), a slave, who is said to have given information to the consuls of the conspiracy, which was formed for the restoration of the Tarquins, and who was rewarded in consequence with liberty and the Roman franchise.

VINDĬLI. [VANDILI.]

VINDOBONA (-ae: *Vienna*, Engl.; *Wien*, Germ.), a town in Pannonia, on the Danube, was originally a Celtic place, and subsequently a Roman municipium. Under the Romans it became a town of importance; it was the chief station of the Roman fleet on the Danube, and the head quarters of a Roman legion.

VINDONISSA (-ae: *Windisch*), a town in Gallia Belgica, on the triangular tongue of land between the Aar and Reuss, was an important Roman fortress in the country of the Helvetii.

VIPSĀNĬA AGRIPPĪNA (-ae). (1) Daughter of M. Vipsanius Agrippa by his first wife Pomponia. Augustus gave her in marriage to his step-son Tiberius, by whom she was much beloved; but after she had borne him a son, Drusus, Tiberius was compelled to divorce her by the command of the emperor, in order to marry Julia, the daughter of the latter. Vipsania afterwards married Asinius Gallus. She died in A.D. 20.—(2) Daughter of M. Vipsanius Agrippa by his second wife Julia, better known by the name of Agrippina. [AGRIPPINA.]

VIPSĀNĬUS AGRIPPA, M. [AGRIPPA.]

VIRBĬUS (-i), a Latin divinity worshipped along with Diana in the grove at Aricia, at the foot of the Alban Mt. He is said to have been the same as Hippolytus, who was restored to life by Aesculapius at the request of Diana.

VIRDO. [VINDELICIA.]

VIRGĬLĬUS (-i) or VERGĬLĬUS MĂRO, P., the Roman poet, was born on the 15th of October, B.C. 70, at Andes (*Pietola*), a small village near Mantua in Cisalpine Gaul. Virgil's father probably had a small estate which he cultivated: his mother's name was Maia.

He was educated at Cremona and Mediolanum (*Milan*), and he took the toga virilis at Cremona in 55, on the day on which he commenced his 16th year. It is said that he subsequently studied at Neapolis (*Naples*) under Parthenius, a native of Bithynia, from whom he learned Greek. He was also instructed by Syron an Epicurean, and probably at Rome. Virgil's writings prove that he received a learned education, and traces of Epicurean opinions are apparent in them. After completing his education, Virgil appears to have retired to his paternal farm, and here he may have written some of the small pieces which are attributed to him. In the division of land among the soldiers after the battle of Philippi (42), Virgil was deprived of his property; but it was afterwards restored at the command of Octavian. It is supposed that Virgil wrote the Eclogue which stands first in our editions, to commemorate his gratitude to Octavian. Virgil probably became acquainted with Maecenas soon after writing his Eclogues, in which Maecenas is not mentioned. His most finished work, the *Georgica*, was undertaken at the suggestion of Maecenas (*Georg.* iii. 41); and was completed after the battle of Actium, B.C. 31, while Octavian was in the East. The *Aeneid* was probably long contemplated by the poet. While Augustus was in Spain (27), he wrote to Virgil expressing a wish to have some monument of his poetical talent. Virgil appears to have commenced the Aeneid about this time. In 23 died Marcellus, the son of Octavia, Caesar's sister, by her first husband; and as Virgil lost no opportunity of gratifying his patron, he introduced into his 6th book of the Aeneid (883) the well-known allusion to the virtues of this youth, who was cut off by a premature death. Octavia is said to have been present when the poet was reciting this allusion to her son, and to have fainted from her emotions. She rewarded the poet munificently for his excusable flattery. As Marcellus did not die till 23, these lines were of course written after his death, but that does not prove that the whole of the 6th book was written so late. A passage in the 7th book (606) appears to allude to Augustus receiving back the Parthian standards, which event belongs to 20.· When Augustus was returning from Samos, where he had spent the winter of 20, he met Virgil at Athens. The poet, it is said, had intended to make a tour of Greece, but he accompanied the emperor to Megara, and thence to Italy. His health, which had been long declining, was now completely broken, and he died soon after his arrival at Brundusium on the 22nd of September, 19, not having quite completed his 51st year. His remains were transferred to Naples, which had been his favourite residence, and interred near the road from Naples to Puteoli (*Pozzuoli*), where a monument is still shown, supposed to be the tomb of the poet. Virgil had been enriched by the liberality of his patrons, and he left behind him a considerable property and a house on the Esquiline Hill, near the gardens of Maecenas. In his fortunes and his friends Virgil was a happy man. Munificent patronage gave him ample means of enjoyment and of leisure, and he had the friendship of all the most accomplished men of the day, among whom Horace entertained a strong affection for him. He was an amiable, good-tempered man, free from the mean passions of envy and jealousy; and in all but health he was prosperous. Besides the *Bucolica*, *Georgica*, and *Aeneid*, several shorter pieces are attributed to Virgil, which may possibly have been the productions of his youth. Such are the *Culex*, *Ciris*, *Copa*, &c. Of all his works the *Georgica* are both the most finished and the most original. The *Aeneid* leaves on the whole a feeble impression, notwithstanding the exquisite beauty of some passages, and the good taste which reigns throughout. Nevertheless, Virgil must be considered as by far the first of all the Roman epic poets.

VIRGINIA (-ae), daughter of L. Virginius, a brave centurion, was a beautiful and innocent girl, betrothed to L. Icilius. Her beauty excited the lust of the decemvir Appius Claudius, who instigated one of his clients to seize the damsel and claim her as his slave. Her father, who had come from the camp the morning on which Claudius gave judgment assigning Virginia to his client, seeing that all hope was gone, prayed the decemvir to be allowed to speak one word to the nurse in his daughter's hearing, in order to ascertain whether she was really his daughter. The request was granted; Virginius drew them both aside, and snatching up a butcher's knife from one of the stalls, plunged it in his daughter's breast, exclaiming, "There is no way but this to keep thee free:" then holding his bloody knife on high, he rushed to the gate of the city, and hastened to the Roman camp. The result is known. Both camp and city rose against the decemvirs, who were deprived of their power, and the old form of government was restored. L. Virginius was the first who was elected tribune, and by his orders Appius was dragged to prison, where he put an end to his own life.

VIRGINIA or VERGINIA GENS, patrician and plebeian. The patrician Virginii frequently filled the highest honours of the state during the early years of the republic.

VIRGĬNĬUS (-i), L., father of Virginia, whose tragic fate occasioned the downfal of the decemvirs, B.C. 449. [VIRGINIA.]

VĬRĬĀTHUS (-i), a celebrated Lusitanian, is described by the Romans as originally a shepherd or huntsman, and afterwards a robber, or, as he would be called in Spain in the present day, a guerilla chief. He was one of the Lusitanians who escaped the treacherous and savage massacre of the people by the proconsul Galba in B.C. 150. [GALBA, No. 2.] He collected a formidable force, and for several successive years defeated one Roman army after another. In 140, the proconsul Fabius Servilianus concluded a peace with Viriathus, in order to save his army, which had been enclosed by the Lusitanians in a mountain pass. But Servilius Caepio, who succeeded to the command of Farther Spain in 140, renewed the war, and shortly afterwards procured the assassination of Viriathus by bribing 3 of his friends.

VIRIDOMARUS (-i). (1) Or BRITOMARTUS, the leader of the Gauls, slain by Marcellus. [MARCELLUS, No. 1.]—(2) Or VIRDUMARUS, a chieftain of the Aedui, whom Caesar had raised from a low rank to the highest honour, but who afterwards joined the Gauls in their great revolt in B.C. 52.

VIRTUS (-ūtis), the Roman personification of manly valour. She was represented with a short tunic, her right breast uncovered, a helmet on her head, a spear in her left hand, a sword in the right, and standing with her right foot on a helmet. A temple of Virtus was built by Marcellus close to one of Honor. [HONOR.]

VISTŬLA (ae: *Vistula*, Engl.; *Weichsel*, Germ.), an important river of Germany, forming the boundary between Germany and Sarmatia, rising in the Hercynia Silva and falling into the Mare Suevicum or the Baltic.

VĬSURGIS (-is: *Weser*), an important river of Germany, falling into the German Ocean.

VĬTELLĬUS (-i), Ă., Roman emperor from January 2nd to December 22nd, A.D. 69, was the son of L. Vitellius, consul in A.D. 34. He had some knowledge of letters and some eloquence. His vices made him a favourite of Tiberius, Caius Caligula, Claudius, and Nero, who loaded him with favours. People were much surprised when Galba chose such a man to command the legions in Lower Germany, for he had no military talent. The soldiers of Vitellius proclaimed him emperor at Colonia Agrippinensis (*Cologne*) on the 2nd of January, 69. His generals Fabius Valens and Caecina marched into Italy, defeated Otho's troops at the decisive battle of Bedriacum, and thus secured for Vitellius the undisputed command of Italy. He displayed some moderation after his accession; but he was a glutton and an epicure, and his chief amusement was the table, on which he spent enormous sums of money. Meantime Vespasian was proclaimed emperor at Alexandria on the 1st of July; and the legions of Illyricum, under Antonius Primus, entered the N. of Italy and declared for him. Vitellius despatched Caecina with a powerful force to oppose Primus; but Caecina was not faithful to the emperor. Primus defeated the Vitellians in two battles; then marched upon Rome, and forced his way into the city, after much fighting. Vitellius was seized in the palace, led through the streets with every circumstance of ignominy, and dragged to the Gemoniae Scalae, where he was killed with repeated blows.

VITRUVĬUS POLLĬO (-ōnis), M., the author of the celebrated treatise on Architecture, appears to have served as a military engineer under Julius Caesar, in the African war, B.C. 46, and he was broken down with age when he composed his work, which is dedicated to the emperor Augustus. Comparatively unsuccessful as an architect, for we have no building of his mentioned except the basilica at Fanum, he attempted to establish his reputation as a writer upon the theory of his art. His style is so obscure as to be often unintelligible.

VŎCONTĬI (-ōrum), a powerful and important people in Gallia Narbonensis, inhabiting the S.E. part of Dauphiné and a part of Provence between the Drac and the Durance, bounded on the N. by the Allobroges, and on the S. by the Salyes and Albioeci. They were allowed by the Romans to live under their own laws.

VŎGĒSUS or VOSGĒSUS (-i: *Vosges*), a range of mountains in Gaul, in the territory of the Lingones, running parallel to the Rhine, and separating its basin from that of the Mosella. The rivers Sequana (*Seine*), Arar (*Saône*), and Mosella (*Moselle*), rise in these mountains.

VŎLĂTERRAE (-ārum: *Volaterra*), called by the Etruscans VELATHRI, one of the 12 cities of the Etruscan Confederation, was built on a lofty and precipitous hill, about 1800 English feet above the level of the sea. It was the most N.-ly city of the Confederation, and its dominions extended E.-ward as far as the territory of Arretium, which was 50 miles distant; W.-ward as far as the Mediterranean, which was more than 20 miles off; and S.-ward at least as far as Populonia, which was either a colony or an acquisition of Volaterrae. In consequence of possessing the 2 great ports of Luna and Populonia,

Volaterrae, though so far inland, was reckoned as one of the powerful maritime cities of Etruria. We have no record of its conquest by the Romans. Like most of the Etruscan cities it espoused the Marian party against Sulla; and it was not till after a siege of two years that the city fell into Sulla's hands. After the fall of the Western Empire it was for a time the residence of the Lombard kings. The modern town contains several interesting Etruscan remains.

VŎLĂTERRĀNA VĀDA, a small town in the territory of Volaterrae.

VOLCAE (-ārum), a powerful Celtic people in Gallia Narbonensis, divided into the 2 tribes of the Volcae Tectosages and Volcae Arecomici, extending from the Pyrenees and the frontiers of Aquitania along the coast as far as the Rhone. They lived under their own laws, without being subject to the Roman governor of the province, and they also possessed the Jus Latii. The chief town of the Tectosages was ToLOSA. A portion of the Tectosages left their native country under Brennus, and were one of the 3 great tribes into which the Galatians in Asia Minor were divided. [GALATIA.]

VOLCI or VULCI. (1) (Vulci), an inland city of Etruria, about 18 miles N.W. of Tarquinii. Of the history of this city we know nothing, but its extensive sepulchres, and the vast trܢ sures of ancient art which they contain, prove that Vulci must at one time have been a powerful and flourishing city.—(2) (Vallo), a town in Lucania, 36 miles S.E. of Paestum on the road to Buxentum.

VOLĒRO PUBLĪLĬUS. [PUBLILIUS.]

VOLOGESES, the name of 5 kings of Parthia. [ARSACES XXIII., XXVII., XXVIII., XXIX., XXX.]

VOLSCI (-ōrum), an ancient people in Latium, but originally distinct from the Latins, dwelt on both sides of the river Liris, and extended down to the Tyrrhene sea. They were not completely subdued by the Romans till B.C. 338.

VOLSĬNĬI, or VULSĬNĬI (-ōrum: Bolsena), called VELSINA or VELSUNA by the Etruscans, one of the most ancient and most powerful of the 12 cities of the Etruscan Confederation, was situated on a lofty hill on the N.E. extremity of the lake called after it, LACUS VOLSINIENSIS and VULSINIENSIS (Lago di Bolsena). The Volsinienses carried on war with the Romans in B.C. 392, 311, 294, and 280, but were on each occasion defeated, and in the last of these years appear to have been finally subdued. Their city was then razed to the ground by the Romans, and its inhabitants were compelled to settle on a less defensible site in the plain, that of the modern Bolsena.

VOLTURCĬUS, or VULTURCĬUS (-i), T., of Crotona, one of Catiline's conspirators, who turned informer upon obtaining the promise of pardon.

VŎLUMNĬA (-ae), wife of Coriolanus. [CORIOLANUS.]

VŎLŬPĬA (-ae), or VOLUPTAS (-ātis), the personification of sensual pleasure among the Romans, who was honoured with a temple near the porta Romanula.

VŎMĀNUS (-i: Vomano), a small river in Picenum.

VŎNŌNES (-is), the name of two kings of Parthia. [ARSACES XVIII., XXII.]

VŎPISCUS (-i), a Roman praenomen, signified a twin-child, who was born safe, while the other twin died before birth. Like many other ancient Roman praenomens, it was afterwards used as a cognomen.

VŎPISCUS (-i), FLĀVĬUS, a native of Syracuse, and one of the 6 Scriptores Historiae Augustae, flourished about A.D. 300.

VOSGĒSUS. [VOGESUS.]

VULCĀNĬAE INSŬLAE. [AEOLIAE INSULAE.]

VULCĀNUS (-i), the Roman god of fire, whose name seems to be connected with fulgere, fulgur, and fulmen. Tatius is reported to have established the worship of Vulcan along with that of Vesta, and Romulus to have dedicated to him a quadriga after his victory over the Fidenatans, and to have set up a statue of himself near the temple of the god. According to others the temple was also built by Romulus, who planted near it the sacred lotus-tree which still existed in the days of Pliny. These circumstances, and what is related of the lotus-tree, show that the temple of Vulcan, like that of Vesta, was regarded as a central point of the whole state, and hence it was perhaps not without a meaning that the temple of Concord was subsequently built within the same district. The most ancient festival in honour of Vulcan seems to have been the Fornacalia or Furnalia, Vulcan being the god of furnaces; but his great festival was called Vulcanalia, and was celebrated on the 23rd of August. The Roman poets transfer all the stories which are related of the Greek Hephaestus to their own Vulcan. [HEPHAESTUS.]

VULCI. [VOLCI.]

VULGIENTES, an Alpine people in Gallia Narbonensis, whose chief town was Apta Julia (Apt).

VULSĬNĬI. [VOLSINII.]

VULTUR (-ŭris), a mountain dividing Apulia and Lucania near Venusia, is a branch of the Apennines. It is celebrated by Horace as one of the haunts of his youth. From it the S.E. wind was called VULTURNUS by the Romans.

VULTURNUM (-i : *Castel di Volturno*), a town in Campania, at the mouth of the river Vulturnus.

VULTURNUS (-i : *Volturno*), the chief river in Campania, rising in the Apennines in Samnium, and falling into the Tyrrhene sea. Its principal affluents are the Calor (*Calore*), Tamarus (*Tamaro*), and Sabatus (*Sabato*).

XANTHIPPE (-ēs), wife of Socrates, said to have been of a peevish and quarrelsome disposition.

XANTHIPPUS (-i). (1) Son of Ariphron and father of Pericles. He succeeded Themistocles as commander of the Athenian fleet in B.C. 479, and commanded the Athenians at the decisive battle of Mycale.—(2) The Lacedaemonian, who commanded the Carthaginians against Regulus. [REGULUS.]

XANTHUS (-i), rivers. (1) [SCAMANDER.] —(2) (*Echen Chai*), the chief river of Lycia, rises in Mt. Taurus, and flows S. through Lycia, between Mt. Cragus and Mt. Massicytus, falling at last into the Mediterranean Sea, a little W. of Patara. It is navigable for a considerable part of its course.

XANTHUS (-i : *Gunik*, Ru.), the most famous city of Lycia, stood on the W. bank of the river of the same name, 60 stadia from its mouth. Twice in the course of its history it sustained sieges, which terminated in the self-destruction of the inhabitants with their property, first against the Persians under Harpagus, and long afterwards against the Romans under Brutus. The city was never restored after its destruction on the latter occasion. Xanthus was rich in temples and tombs, and other monuments of a most interesting character, and several important remains of its works of art are now exhibited in the British Museum.

XENOCRATES (-is), the philosopher, was a native of Chalcedon. He was born B.C. 396, and died 314 at the age of 82. He attached himself first to Aeschines the Socratic, and afterwards, while still a youth, to Plato, whom he accompanied to Syracuse. After the death of Plato he betook himself, with Aristotle, to Hermias, tyrant of Atarneus ; and, after his return to Athens, he was repeatedly sent on embassies to Philip of Macedonia, and at a later time to Antipater during the Lamian war. He became president of the Academy even before the death of Speusippus, and occupied that post for 25 years.—The importance of Xenocrates is

shown by the fact that Aristotle and Theophrastus wrote upon his doctrines, and that Panaetius and Cicero entertained a high regard for him. Only the titles of his works have come down to us.

XENOPHANES (-is), a celebrated philosopher, was a native of Colophon, and flourished between B.C. 540 and 500. He was also a poet, and considerable fragments have come down to us of his elegies, and of a didactic poem " On Nature." According to the fragments of one of his elegies, he left his native land at the age of 25, and had already lived 67 years in Hellas, when, at the age of 92, he composed that elegy. He quitted Colophon as a fugitive or exile, and must have lived some time at Elea (Velia) in Italy, as he is mentioned as the founder of the Eleatic school of philosophy. Xenophanes was usually regarded in antiquity as the originator of the Eleatic doctrine of the oneness of the universe.

XENOPHON (-ŏntis). (1) The Athenian, was the son of Gryllus, and a native of the demus Erchīa. The time of his birth is not known, but it may probably be placed in about B.C. 444, and he appears to have lived above 90 years. Xenophon is said to have been a pupil of Socrates at an early age, and the latter saved his life at the battle of Delium in 424. The most memorable event in Xenophon's life is his connexion with the Greek army, which marched under Cyrus against Artaxerxes in 401. He accompanied Cyrus into Upper Asia. In the battle of Cunaxa, Cyrus lost his life, his barbarian troops were dispersed, and the Greeks were left alone on the wide plains between the Tigris and the Euphrates. It was after the treacherous massacre of Clearchus and others of the Greek commanders by the Persian satrap Tissaphernes, that Xenophon came forwards. He had held no command in the army of Cyrus, nor had he in fact served as a soldier. He was now elected one of the generals, and took the principal part in conducting the Greeks in their memorable retreat along the Tigris over the high table lands of Armenia to Trapezus (*Trebizond*), on the Black Sea. From Trapezus the troops were conducted to Chrysopolis, which is opposite to Byzantium. The Greeks were in great distress, and some of them under Xenophon entered the service of Seuthes, king of Thrace. As the Lacedaemonians under Thimbron were now at war with Tissaphernes and Pharnabazus, Xenophon and his troops were invited to join the army of Thimbron, and Xenophon led them back out of Asia to join Thimbron, 399. Socrates was put to death in 399, and it seems probable that Xenophon was banished from Athens either shortly before or shortly after that event. In 396 he was with Agesilaus, the Spartan king, who was commanding the Lacedaemonian forces in Asia against the Persians. When Agesilaus was recalled (394), Xenophon accompanied him; and he was on the side of the Lacedaemonians in the battle which they fought at Coronea (394) against the Athenians. It seems that he went to Sparta with Agesilaus after the battle of Coronea, and soon after he settled at Scillus in Elis not far from Olympia, where he was joined by his wife Philesia and his children. Xenophon was at last expelled from his quiet retreat at Scillus by the Eleans after remaining there about 20 years. The sentence of banishment from Athens was repealed on the motion of Eubulus but it is uncertain in what year. There is no evidence that Xenophon ever returned to Athens. He is said to have retired to Corinth after his expulsion from Scillus, and as we know nothing more, we assume that he died there. The two principal works of Xenophon are the *Anabasis* and the *Cyropaedia*. In the former he describes the expedition of Cyrus and the retreat of the Greeks; the latter is a kind of political romance, the basis of which is the history of Cyrus, the founder of the Persian monarchy. His *Hellenica*, a continuation of the history of Thucydides, is a dry narrative of events. The *Memorabilia* of Socrates, in 4 books, was written by Xenophon to defend the memory of his master against the charge of irreligion and of corrupting the Athenian youth. That it is a genuine picture of the man is indisputable, and it is the most valuable memorial that we have of the practical philosophy of Socrates. Besides these Xenophon was the author of several minor works. All antiquity and all modern writers agree in allowing Xenophon great merit as a writer of a plain, simple, perspicuous, and unaffected style; but his mind was essentially practical, and not adapted for pure philosophical speculation.—(2) The Ephesian, the author of a romance, still extant, entitled *Ephesiaca*, or the Loves of Anthia and Abrocomas. The age of Xenophon is uncertain; but he is probably the oldest of the Greek romance writers.

XERXĒS (-is). (I.) King of Persia B.C. 485 —465, was the son of Darius and Atossa. After reducing the revolted Egyptians to subjection, Xerxes, in the spring of 480, set out from Sardis on his memorable expedition against Greece. He crossed the Hellespont by a bridge of boats, and continued his march through the Thracian Chersonese till he reached the plain of Doriscus. Here he resolved to number both his land and naval forces, which are said by Herodotus to have amounted to 2,641,610 fighting men. This statement is incredible, yet we may well believe that the numbers of Xerxes were greater than were ever assembled in ancient times, or perhaps at any known epoch of history. Xerxes, continuing his march, ordered his fleet to sail through the canal that had been previously dug across the isthmus of Athos—of which the remains are still visible [ATHOS]—and await his arrival at Therme. Hence he marched through Macedonia and Thessaly, and arrived in safety with his land forces before Thermopylae. Here the Greeks had resolved to make a stand, and when Xerxes attempted to force his way through the pass, his troops were repulsed again and again by Leonidas the Spartan king; till a Malian, of the name of Ephialtes, showed the Persians a pass over the mountains of Oeta, and thus enabled them to fall on the rear of the Greeks. Leonidas and his Spartans disdained to fly, and were all slain. [LEONIDAS.] Hence Xerxes marched through Phocis and Boeotia, and at length reached Athens. About the same time as Xerxes entered Athens, his fleet, which had been crippled by storms and engagements, arrived in the bay of Phalerum. He now resolved upon an engagement with the Greek fleet. The history of the memorable battle of Salamis is related elsewhere. [THEMISTOCLES.] Xerxes witnessed, from a lofty seat on one of the declivities of Mount Aegaleos, the defeat and dispersion of his mighty armament. Xerxes now became alarmed for his own safety, and leaving Mardonius with 300,000 troops to complete the conquest of Greece, with the remainder set out on his march homewards. He entered Sardis towards the end of the year 480. In the following year, 479, the war was continued in Greece; but Mardonius was defeated at Plataea by the combined forces of the Greeks, and on the same day another victory was gained over the Persians at Mycale in Ionia. We know little more of the personal history of Xerxes. He was murdered by Artabanus in 465, after a reign of 20 years.—(II.) The son of Artaxerxes I., succeeded his father as king of Persia in 425, but was murdered after a reign of only 2 months by his half-brother Sogdianus.

XŌÏS, or CHŌÏS, an ancient city of Lower Egypt, N. of Leontopolis, on an island of the Nile, in the Nomos Sebennyticus, the seat, at one time, of a dynasty of Egyptian kings. Its site is very doubtful.

XŪTHUS (-i), son of Hellen, by the nymph Orseis, and a brother of Dorus and Aeolus. He was king of Peloponnesus, and the husband of Creusa, the daughter of Erechtheus, by whom he became the father of 'Achaeus and Ion. Others state that after the death of his father, Hellen, Xuthus was expelled from Thessaly by his brothers, and went to Athens, where he married the daughter of Erechtheus. After the death of Erechtheus, Xuthus being chosen arbitrator, adjudged the kingdom to his eldest brother-in-law, Cecrops, in consequence of which he was expelled by the other sons of Erechtheus, and settled in Aegialus, in Peloponnesus.

ZAB TUS. [LYCUS, No. 5.]

ZĂCYNTHUS (-i : *Zante*), an island in the Ionian sea, off the coast of Elis, about 40 miles in circumference. It contained a large and flourishing town of the same name upon the E. coast, the citadel of which was called Psophis. Zacynthus was inhabited by a Greek population at an early period. It is said to have derived its name from Zacynthus, a son of Dardanus, who colonised the island from Psophis, in Arcadia. It was afterwards colonised by Achaeans, from Peloponnesus. It formed part of the maritime empire of Athens, and continued faithful to the Athenians during the Peloponnesian war. At a later time it was subject to the Macedonian monarchs, and on the conquest of Macedonia by the Romans, passed into the hands of the latter. It is now one of the Ionian islands, under the protection of Great Britain.

ZAGREUS, a surname of the mystic Dionysus (Bacchus), whom Zeus (Jupiter), in the form of a dragon, is said to have begotten by Persephone (Proserpina), before she was carried off by Pluto. He was torn to pieces by the Titans ; and Athena (Minerva) carried his heart to Zeus.

ZĂLEUCUS (-i), the celebrated lawgiver of the Epizephyrian Locrians, is said by some to have been originally a slave, but is described by others as a man of good family. He could not, however, have been a disciple of Pythagoras, as some writers state, since he lived upwards of 100 years before Pythagoras. The date of the legislation of Zaleucus is assigned to B.C. 660. His code, which was severe, is stated to have been the first collection of written laws that the Greeks possessed.

ZALMOXIS, or ZĂMOLXIS (-is), said to have been so called from the bear's skin (Ζάλμοξις), in which he was clothed as soon as

he was born. He was, according to the story current among the Greeks on the Hellespont, a Getan, who had been a slave to Pythagoras in Samos, but was manumitted, and acquired not only great wealth, but large stores of knowledge from Pythagoras, and from the Egyptians, whom he visited in the course of his travels. He returned among the Getae, introducing the civilisation and the religious ideas which he had gained, especially regarding the immortality of the soul. Herodotus, however, suspects that he was an indigenous Getan divinity.

ZĂMA RĔGĬA (-ae : *Zowareen*, S.E. of *Kaff*), a strongly fortified city in the interior of Numidia, on the borders of the Carthaginian territory. It was the scene of one of the most important battles in the history of the world, that in which Hannibal was defeated by Scipio, and the 2nd Punic War was ended, B.C. 202.

ZANCLĔ. [MESSANA.]

ZĒLA or ZIELA, a city in the S. of Pontus, not far S. of Amasia. The surrounding district was called Zelētis or Zelītis. At Zela the Roman general Valerius Triarius was defeated by Mithridates ; but the city is more celebrated for another great battle, that in which Julius Caesar defeated Pharnaces, and of which he wrote this despatch to Rome :— VENI : VIDI : VICI.

ZELĬA (-ae), an ancient city of Mysia, at the foot of Mt. Ida, and on the river Aesepus, 80 stadia from its mouth, belonging to the territory of Cyzicus.

ZĒLUS (-i), the personification of zeal or strife, is described as a son of Pallas and Styx, and a brother of Nice.

ZĒNO or ZĒNON (-ōnis). (1) The founder of the Stoic philosophy, was a native of Citium, in Cyprus, and the son of Mnaseas. He began at an early age to study the writings of the Socratic philosophers. At the age of 22, or, according to others, of 30 years, Zeno was shipwrecked in the neighbourhood of Piraeus ; whereupon he was led to settle in Athens, and to devote himself entirely to the study of philosophy. The weakness of his health is said to have first determined him to live rigorously and simply ; but his desire to make himself independent of all external circumstances seems to have been an additional motive, and to have led him to attach himself to the Cynic Crates. He is said to have studied under various Megaric and Academic philosophers, for a period of 20 years. At its close, and after he had developed his peculiar philosophical system, he opened his school in the porch adorned with the paintings of Polygnotus (*Stoa Poecile*), which, at an earlier time, had been a place in which poets met. From this place his disciples were called *Stoics*. Among the warm admirers of Zeno was Antigonus Gonatas, king of Macedonia. The Athenians likewise placed the greatest confidence in him, and by a decree of the people, a golden crown and a public burial in the Ceramicus were awarded to him. We do not know the year either of Zeno's birth or death. He is said to have presided over his school for 58 years, and to have died at the age of 98. He is said to have been still alive in the 130th Olympiad (B.C. 260).—(2) The Eleatic philosopher, was a native of Elea (Velia), in Italy, son of Teleutagoras, and the favourite disciple of Parmenides. He was born about B.C. 488, and at the age of 40 accompanied Parmenides to Athens, where he resided some time. His love of freedom is shown by the courage with which he exposed his life in order to deliver his native country from a tyrant. Zeno devoted all his energies to explain and develope the philosophical system of Parmenides. [PARMENIDES.] — (3) An Epicurean philosopher, a native of Sidon, was a contemporary of Cicero, who heard him when at Athens.

ZĒNŌBĬA (-ae), queen of Palmyra. After the death of her husband, Odenathus, whom, according to some accounts, she assassinated (A.D. 266), she assumed the imperial diadem, as regent for her sons. But not content with enjoying the independence conceded by Gallienus, and tolerated by Claudius, she sought to include all Syria, Asia, and Egypt within the limits of her sway, and to make good the title which she claimed of Queen of the East. By this rash ambition she lost both her kingdom and her liberty. She was defeated by Aurelian, taken prisoner on the capture of Palmyra (273), and carried to Rome, where she adorned the triumph of her conqueror (274). Her life was spared by Aurelian, and she passed the remainder of her years with her sons in the vicinity of Tibur (*Tivoli*). Longinus lived at her court, and was put to death on the capture of Palmyra. [LONGINUS.]

ZĒNŌDŌTUS (-i), of Ephesus, a celebrated grammarian, superintendent of the great library at Alexandria, flourished under Ptolemy Philadelphus, about B.C. 208. Zenodotus was employed by Philadelphus, together with his 2 contemporaries, Alexander the Aetolian and Lycophron the Chalcidian, to collect and revise all the Greek poets.

ZĒPHȲRĬUM (-i), i.e., *the western promontory*, the name of several promontories of the ancient world, not all of which, however, faced the west. The chief of them were: (1) (*C. di Brussano*), a promontory

in Bruttium, forming the S.E. extremity of the country, from which the Locri, who settled in the neighbourhood, are said to have obtained the name of *Epizephyrii*. [LOCRI.] —(2) A promontory on the W. coast of Cyprus.—(3) In Cilicia (prob. *C. Cavalière*), a far-projecting promontory, W. of Prom. Sarpedon.

ZĒPHȲRUS (-i), the personification of the W. wind, is described by Hesiod as a son of Astraeus and Eos. Zephyrus and Boreas are frequently mentioned together by Homer, and both dwelt together in a palace in Thrace. By the Harpy Podarge, Zephyrus became the father of the horses Xanthus and Balius, which belonged to Achilles; but he was married to Chloris, whom he had carried off by force, and by whom he had a son Carpus.

Zephyrus. (From the Temple of the Winds at Athens.)

ZĒYRNTHUS (-i), a town of Thrace, in the territory of Aenos, with a temple of Apollo, and a cave of Hecate, who are hence called *Zerynthius* and *Zerynthia* respectively.

ZĒTES (-ae) and CĂLĂIS (-is), sons of Boreas and Orithyia, frequently called the BOREADAE, are mentioned among the Argonauts, and are described as winged beings. Their sister, Cleopatra, who was married to Phineus, king of Salmydessus, had been thrown with her sons into prison by Phineus, at the instigation of his second wife. Here she was found by Zetes and Calaïs, when they arrived at Salmydessus, in the Argonautic expedition. They liberated their sister and her children, gave the kingdom to the latter, and sent the second wife of Phineus to her own country, Scythia. Others relate that the Boreadae delivered Phineus from the Harpies; for it had been foretold that the Harpies might be killed by the sons of Boreas, but that the sons of Boreas must die, if they should not be able to overtake the Harpies. Others again state that the Boreadae perished in their pursuit of the

Harpies, or that Hercules killed them with his arrows near the island of Tenos.

ZETHUS (-i), brother of Amphion. [AMPHION.]

ZEUGIS, ZEUGITĀNA RĔGIO, (N. part of *Tunis*), the N. district of Africa Propria. [AFRICA.]

ZEUGMA (ătis: prob. *Rumkaleh*), a city of Syria, on the borders of Commagene and Cyrrhestice, built by Seleucus Nicator, on the W. bank of the Euphrates, at a point where the river was crossed by a bridge of boats, which had been constructed by Alexander the Great.

ZEUS (Dios), called JŪPĪTER by the Romans, the greatest of the Olympian gods, was a son of Cronus (Saturnus) and Rhea, a

according to his own choice he assigns good or evil to mortals ; and fate itself was subordinate to him. He is armed with thunder and lightning, and the shaking of his aegis produces storm and tempest : a number of epithets of Zeus, in the Homeric poems, describe him as the thunderer, the gatherer of clouds, and the like. By Hera he had two sons, Ares (Mars) and Hephaestus (Vulcanus), and one daughter, Hebe. Hera sometimes acts as an independent divinity ; she is ambitious, and rebels against her lord, but she is nevertheless inferior to him, and is punished for her opposition ; his amours with other goddesses or mortal women are not concealed from her, though they generally rouse her jealousy and revenge. Zeus,

Head of Olympian Zeus (Jupiter). (Visconti, Mus. Pio Clem., vol. 6. tav. 1.)

Zeus (Jupiter) (A Medal of M. Aurelius, in British Museum.)

brother of Poseidon (Neptunus), Hades (Pluto), Hestia (Vesta), Demeter (Ceres), Hera (Juno), and was also married to his sister, Hera. When Zeus and his brothers distributed among themselves the government of the world by lot, Poseidon obtained the sea, Hades the lower world, and Zeus the heavens and the upper regions, but the earth became common to all. According to the Homeric account Zeus dwelt on Mt. Olympus, in Thessaly, which was believed to penetrate with its lofty summit into heaven itself. He is called the father of gods and men, the most high and powerful among the immortals, whom all others obey. He is the supreme ruler, who with his counsel manages everything ; the founder of kingly power, and of law and order, whence Dice, Themis, and Nemesis, are his assistants. Every thing good, as well as bad, comes from Zeus ;

no doubt, was originally a god of a portion of nature. Hence the oak, with its eatable fruit and the prolific doves, were sacred to him at Dodona and in Arcadia. Hence, also, rain, storms, and the seasons, were regarded as his work. Hesiod also calls Zeus the son of Cronus and Rhea, and the brother of Hestia, Demeter, Hera, Hades, and Poseidon. Cronus swallowed his children immediately after their birth ; but when Rhea was pregnant with Zeus, she applied to Uranus and Ge to save the life of the child. Uranus and Ge therefore sent Rhea to Lyctos, in Crete, requesting her to bring up her child there. Rhea accordingly concealed Zeus in a cave of Mt. Aegaeon, and gave to Cronos a stone wrapped up in cloth, which he swallowed in the belief that it was his son. Other traditions state that Zeus was born and brought up on Mt. Dicte or Ida (also the Trojan Ida), Ithome in Messenia, Thebes in Boeotia,

Aegion in Achaia, or Olenos in Aetolia. According to the common account, however, Zeus grew up in Crete. In the meantime Cronus, by a cunning device of Ge or Metis, was made to bring up the children he had swallowed, and first of all the stone, which was afterwards set up by Zeus at Delphi. The young god now delivered the Cyclopes from the bonds with which they had been fettered by Cronus, and they, in their gratitude, provided him with thunder and lightning. On the advice of Ge, Zeus also liberated the hundred-armed Gigantes, Briareos, Cottus, and Gyes, that they might assist him in his fight against the Titans. The Titans were conquered and shut up in Tartarus, where they were henceforth guarded by the Hecatoncheires. Thereupon Tartarus and Ge begot Typhoeus, who began a fearful struggle with Zeus, but was conquered. Zeus now obtained the dominion of the world, and chose Metis for his wife. When she was pregnant with Athena (Minerva), he took the child out of her body and concealed it in his head, on the advice of Uranus and Ge, who told him that thereby he would retain the supremacy of the world. For if Metis had given birth to a son, this son (so fate had ordained it) would have acquired the sovereignty. After this Zeus became the father of the Horae and Moerae, by his second wife Themis; of the Charites or Graces, by Eurynome; of

Zeus (Jupiter) and the Giants. (Neapolitan Gem.)

Persephone (Proserpine) by Demeter; of the Muses, by Mnemosyne; of Apollo and Artemis (Diana) by Leto; and of Hebe, Ares, and Ilithyia by Hera. Athena was born out of the head of Zeus; while Hera, on the other hand, gave birth to Hephaestus without the co-operation of Zeus. The family of the Cronidae accordingly embraces the 12 great gods of Olympus, Zeus (the head of them all), Poseidon, Apollo, Ares, Hermes (Mercury), Hephaestus, Hestia, Demeter, Hera, Athena, Aphrodite (Venus), and Artemis. These 12 Olympian gods, who in some places were worshipped as a body, were recognised not only by the Greeks, but were adopted also by the Romans, who, in particular, identified their Jupiter with the Greek Zeus. The Greek and Latin poets give to Zeus or Jupiter an immense number of epithets and surnames, which are derived partly from the places where he was wor-shipped, and partly from his powers and functions. The eagle, the oak, and the summits of mountains were sacred to him, and his sacrifices generally consisted of goats, bulls and cows. His usual attributes are, the sceptre, eagle, thunderbolt, and a figure of Victory in his hand, and sometimes also a cornucopia. The Olympian Zeus sometimes wears a wreath of olive, and the Dodonaean Zeus a wreath of oak leaves. In works of art Zeus is generally represented as the omnipotent father and king of gods and men, according to the idea which had been embodied in the statue of the Olympian Zeus by Phidias. Respecting the Roman god see JUPITER.

ZEUXIS (-ĭdis), the celebrated Greek painter, was a native of Heraclea, and flourished B.C. 424—400. He came to Athens soon after the beginning of the Peloponnesian War, when he had already achieved a great reputation, although a young man. He lived some years in Macedonia, at the court of Archelaüs, and must have spent some time in Magna Graecia, as we learn from the story respecting the picture of Helen, his masterpiece, which he painted for the city of Croton. Zeuxis acquired a great fortune by his art. The time of his death is unknown. The accurate imitation of inanimate objects was a department of the art which Zeuxis and his younger rival Parrhasius appear to have carried almost to perfection.

ZŌÏLUS (-i), a grammarian, was a native of Amphipolis, and flourished in the time of Philip of Macedon. He was celebrated for the asperity with which he assailed Homer, and his name became proverbial for a captious and malignant critic.

ZŌPȲRUS (-i). (1) A distinguished Persian, son of Megabyzus. After Darius Hystaspis had besieged Babylon for 20 months in vain, Zopyrus resolved to gain the place for his master by the most extraordinary self-sacrifice. Accordingly, one day he appeared before Darius, with his body mutilated in the most horrible manner; both his ears and nose were cut off, and his person otherwise disfigured. After explaining to Darius his intentions, he fled to Babylon as a victim of the cruelty of the Persian king. The Babylonians gave him their confidence, and placed him at the head of their troops. He soon found means to betray the city to Darius, who severely punished the inhabitants for their revolt. Darius appointed Zopyrus satrap of Babylon for life, with the enjoyment of its entire revenues.—(2) The Physiognomist, who attributed many vices to Socrates, which the latter admitted were his natural propensities, but said that they had been overcome by philosophy.—(3) A surgeon at Alexandria, the tutor of Apollonius Citiensis and Posidonius, about the beginning of the 1st century, B.C.

ZOROASTER, or ZOROASTRES (-tri), the ZARATHUSTRA of the Zendavesta, and the ZERDUSHT of the Persians, was the founder of the Magian religion. The most opposite opinions have been held by both ancient and modern writers respecting the time in which he lived; but it is quite impossible to come to any conclusion on the subject. As the founder of the Magian religion he must be placed in remote antiquity, and it may even be questioned whether such a person ever existed.

ZŌSĬMUS (-i), a Greek historian who lived in the time of the younger Theodosius. He wrote a history of the Roman empire in 6 books, which is still extant. Zosimus was a pagan, and comments severely upon the faults and crimes of the Christian emperors. Hence his credibility has been assailed by several Christian writers.

ZOSTER (-ĕris: *C. of Vari*), a promontory on the W. of Attica, between Phalerum and Sunium.

THE END.